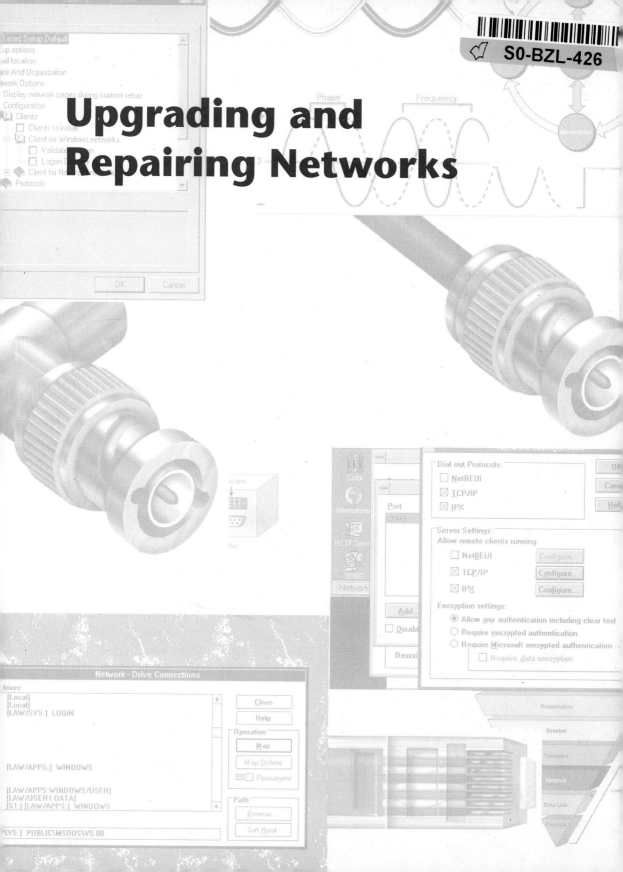

Upgrading and
Repairing Networks

Upgrading and Repairing Networks

Craig Zacker and Paul Doyle

with

Christa Anderson

Darren Mar-Elia

Alexia Prendergast

Robert Thompson

Kevin Makela

Michele Petrovsky

Paul Robichaux

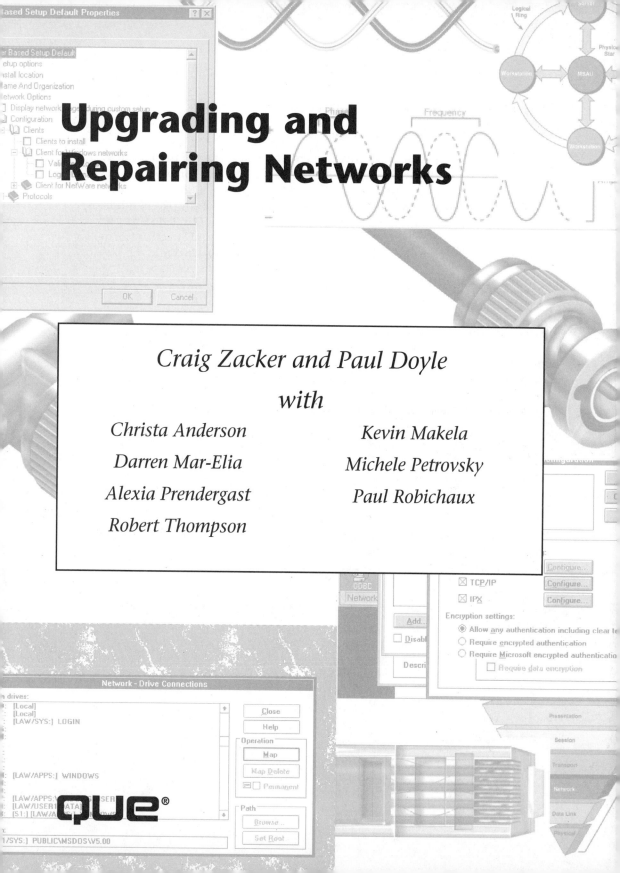

Upgrading and Repairing Networks

Copyright© 1996 by Que®Corporation.

Library of Congress Catalog No.: 95-71740

ISBN: 0-7897-0181-2

98 97   6 5 4 3

Interpretation of the printing code: the rightmost double-digit number is the year of the book's printing; the rightmost single-digit number, the number of the book's printing. For example, a printing code of 96-1 shows that the first printing of the book occurred in 1996.

Screen reproductions in this book were created using Collage Plus from Inner Media, Inc., Hollis, NH.

Credits

President
Roland Elgey

Publisher
Joseph B. Wikert

Editorial Services Director
Elizabeth Keaffaber

Managing Editor
Sandy Doell

Director of Marketing
Lynn E. Zingraf

Senior Series Editor
Chris Nelson

Title Manager
Bryan Gambrel

Acquisitions Editor
Fred Slone

Product Directors
Kevin Kloss
Chuck Martini
Stephen Miller

Production Editor
Patrick Kanouse

Editors
Kelli Brooks, Elizabeth Bruns
Mark Enochs, Audra Gable
Noelle Gasco, C. Kazim Haidri
Mike La Bonne, Susan Ross Moore
Katie Purdum, Caroline Roop
Linda Seifert

Assistant Product Marketing Manager
Kim Margolius

Technical Editors
Michele Petrovsky
Ablaze

Technical Support Specialist
Nadeem Muhammed

Acquisitions Coordinator
Angela Kozlowski

Operations Coordinator
Patty Brooks

Editorial Assistant
Andrea Duvall

Book Designer
Kim Scott

Cover Designer
Dan Armstrong

Production Team
Steve Adams, Brian Buschkill, Jason Carr,
Anne Dickerson, Jenny Earhart, Joan Evan,
Judy Everly, Bryan Flores, DiMonique Ford,
Trey Frank, Amy Gornik, George Hanlin,
Damon Jordan, Daryl Kessler, Bob LaRoche,
Glenn Larsen, Stephanie Layton, Michelle Lee,
Beth Lewis, Julie Quinn, Kaylene Riemen,
Mike Thomas, Karen Walsh, Kelly Warner,
Suzanne Whitmer, Paul Wilson, Jody York

Indexer
Craig A. Small

Composed in *Stone Serif* and *MCPdigital* by Que Corporation

To Ann, Heather and Eimear.—P.D.

About the Authors

Craig Zacker got his first experience with computers in high school on a minicomputer "with less memory than I now have in my wristwatch." His first networking responsibility was a NetWare 2.15 server and six 286 workstations which eventually evolved into NetWare 4 and over 100 plus WAN connections to remote offices. He's done PC and network support onsite, in the field, and over the phone for more than five years, and now works for a large manufacturer of networking software on the east coast, as a technical editor and online services engineer.

Paul Doyle has several years of experience in the planning, implementation, and management of networks in multi-protocol, multi-vendor environments. His specialist areas include client configuration and server management.

Christa Anderson started working with computers in the 1980s, long before anyone let it slip to her that you could make a living with them. Since 1992, she has written on such subjects as PC troubleshooting, data communications, and PC security, with her current interests centered on local and wide-area networking issues. Previously a member of a cutting-edge consulting team in the Washington, DC area, since her move to a city with better parking, she is now an independent technical writer and researcher.

Darren Mar-Elia graduated from the University of California, Berkeley in 1986. He has been a network and systems administrator for the last 10 years. He is a Novell CNE, and has been involved in design and installation of heterogeneous LAN/WAN environments for large and small companies alike. Most recently, he was part of the design team for a nationwide deployment of Windows NT at a large financial services firm and is currently part of that firm's network engineering group.

Alexia Prendergast is an information developer who has been writing and designing user manuals, system administration guides, and courseware for five years. Her experience includes documenting client/server business applications in the healthcare industry, application development software systems in the banking industry, and three-tiered automated manufacturing systems in the steel and metals industry. Alexia has worked with a variety of platforms, including UNIX client/server networks, corporate mainframes, and PC and Macintosh desktops. When not working, she can be found designing Web pages and surfing the Net, doing genealogical research, and spending quality time with her partner and their four animals.

With a Bachelor's Degree in Spanish and Russian, and a Master's Degree in Information Science, both from the University of Pittsburgh, **Michele Petrovsky** has over 15 years experience in data processing. In 1990, she moved from programming and system administration to freelance technical editing and writing in a number of environments and teaching at the community college level. Michele lives on a farm near Wilmington, Delaware. Her outside interests include *Star Trek* and science fiction in general, cats, gardening, and linguistics. She dedicates her work on this book to her parents Mike and Betty and welcomes reader comments and inquiries at **mpetrovsky@aol.com**.

Paul Robichaux, who has been an Internet user since 1986 and a software developer since 1983, is currently a software consultant for Intergraph Corporation, where he writes Windows NT and Windows 95 applications. In his spare time, he writes books and Macintosh applications but still manages to spend plenty of time with his wife and young son. He can be reached via e-mail at **perobich@ingr.com**.

Robert Bruce Thompson is the president of Triad Technology Group Inc., a Winston-Salem, NC networking and internetworking consulting firm. He is certified by Novell as a CNE, ECNE, and MCNE; by AT&T in Network Systems Design, and by IBM in Advanced Connectivity. He is currently working on his Microsoft CSE. Mr. Thompson holds an MBA from Wake Forest University. You can reach him via Internet mail at **thompson@ttgnet.com**.

Acknowledgments

I wish to record my gratitude to my family for their patience and indulgence while I worked on this book. Without their support, I would have been unable to undertake a project of this scale.

Thanks, also, to Fred Slone for the opportunity to work on this project and for an impressive display of patience and encouragement.

My thanks to my colleagues in UCG for their words of wisdom and unstintingly high standard of comradeship. Thanks, also, to those less proximate colleagues who share their ideas, questions, and other work on the Internet.

Oh, and I promised Pat Rooney a mention.

—Paul Doyle

Without the help of some terrific people my contribution to this book would never have happened. Nancy Stevenson put me in touch with Fred Slone at Que, Fred gave me lots of support and encouragement, Scott Anderson provided moral support and shoulder rubs, and Mark Minasi showed me that you really can make a living at this stuff. My special thanks to all those who helped me research my contributions, particularly Geoff Milner, Curtis Taylor, Glenn Stern, and Michael Willett. Finally, I really appreciate the efforts of the editorial and production staff at Que, who've worked to make this book such a good one.

—Christa Anderson

We'd Like To Hear from You!

As part of our continuing effort to produce books of the highest possible quality, Que would like to hear your comments. To stay competitive, we *really* want you, as a computer book reader and user, to let us know what you like or dislike most about this book or other Que products.

You can mail comments, ideas, or suggestions for improving future editions to the address below, or send us a fax at (317) 581-4663. For the online inclined, Macmillan Computer Publishing has a forum on CompuServe (type **GO QUEBOOKS** at any prompt) through which our staff and authors are available for questions and comments. The address of our Internet site is **http://www.mcp.com** (World Wide Web).

In addition to exploring our forum, please feel free to contact me personally to discuss your opinions of this book: I'm **74201,1064** on CompuServe and **kloss@que.mcp.com** on the Internet.

Thanks in advance—your comments will help us to continue publishing the best books available on computer topics in today's market.

Kevin Kloss
Product Development Specialist
Que Corporation
201 W. 103rd Street
Indianapolis, Indiana 46290
USA

Contents at a Glance

Contents

II Hardware Platforms: Servers and Workstations

133

5 The Server Platform

135

6 The Workstation Platform

197

9 Microsoft Windows NT   371

10 UNIX Operating Systems   409

18 Backup Technology: Uninterruptible Power Supplies   651

19 Antivirus Technology

20 Tools for Restricting Access

21 Disaster Planning for Networks   739

VI Adding Network Services   779

23 Adding Network Printing   781

24 Adding Network CD-ROMs   823

VII Troubleshooting Hardware and Software Problems 967

30 Network Management and SNMP 969

Introduction

Who Should Read This Book?

To the computer semi-literate, the administrator is "the source." He is the person who knows everything that there is to know about computers and networking. LAN administrators like this reputation and, where novice users are concerned, it is not difficult to maintain. As more and more people begin to see computing as a way of life, however, the knowledge required for the administrator to maintain her reputation for omnipotence is increasing at a rapid rate. That's where this book comes in.

It may just be a casual question from a user, regarding something that he saw on his monitor, like "What does IPX stand for, anyway?" It may be a practical complaint, like "Why can't I print from my Macintosh to the laser printer near my desk, rather than walking all the way over to Marketing, where the Apple printers are?" Given the way in which computing and the Internet has invaded the mainstream media, it may be a guy from Sales, who has a computer at home, stopping by your office, sticking his head in the door and saying, "Hey, what's the difference between a SLIP and a PPP connection?" Or, worst of all, it may be your boss, telling you that "I want us to be on the Internet by the end of the month."

Whatever the case, there is going to be, at some point, something that you don't know or that you can't handle, and when it comes to networking, this book is designed to be the first place for the LAN administrator to go for information. Product manuals give you the "How?" This book is about the "What?" and the "Why?" For instructions on how to install a stand-alone printer on your network, you go to a product manual. You have already made the decisions as to what kind of printer to buy and what kind of network connection you are going to use. This book is designed to help you in making those decisions. Its value comes earlier in the process, when you are asking the most basic questions, like "How can I provide printing services to the greatest number of different clients, with the fewest administration headaches, for the least amount of money?"

What Are the Main Objectives of This Book?

You may be the new LAN Administrator at a company, faced with a lot of equipment with which you are unfamiliar. This book can help you get up to speed. You may be working for a growing company that wants to expand its computing services around the office, around the building, the country, or the world. This book is the first step, telling you what is involved in a certain procedure, providing you with information that will be useful in talking to salespeople and evaluating products and pointing you in the right direction for the next step in the process.

This is the age of the heterogeneous network. Computers and LANs that may have been installed as separate systems are now being interconnected to provide uniform access to hardware and information resources and to simplify administration and maintenance. A company may be in the process of phasing out their mainframe systems and replacing them with LANs. In the interim, however, the two will have to be connected. The benefits of connecting a company's remote offices and traveling personnel to a central information source are now widely recognized, and the technology has been developed to make this practice logistically and economically feasible. The vast resources of the Internet are rapidly becoming a fixture, not only in offices but in private homes as well. It is very likely that, within five to ten years, Internet connections will be as common as telephones and televisions.

To the non-technical corporate management, a LAN administrator is expected to know something about all of these things. Telecommunications, cable installation, electrical engineering, systems analysis, project management, and technical training are just some of the disciplines involved. We've come a long way from the time when a person could learn how to use DOS, take a few NetWare courses, and hang out her shingle as a network administrator. Unfortunately, in most companies, management has little conception of the true breadth of knowledge required to cover all of these divergent needs. A typical network administrator may know a great deal about some of these disciplines, a little about all of them, or even nothing about any of them, in some cases.

For every practitioner, in every profession, there are elements of his field about which he is expected to know but doesn't. Most are aware of it, and some are even smug about it (I once met a Professor of English Literature who admitted to having never read *Hamlet!*). The LAN administrator is no different, and the savvy ones are those who have arrived at the point when faced with a subject that they have heard of and should be familiar with, but aren't, will nod their heads knowingly, promise to look into the situation, and then read up on it at the next opportunity.

This is the book that they should turn to first.

Will it tell them absolutely everything that they need to know? Of course not. A single work that covered every aspect of modern computer networking would be the size of the *Encyclopedia Britannica* and would have to be revised at least once a week. The field is growing and developing at an incredibly rapid rate, and a network administrator must continuously expand and update his knowledge in order to remain current. That is why great pains have been taken in this book to cover the latest developments in the networking industry. You will find information on a great many of the new technologies that are just entering into general use or are soon to be so. We are not talking about speculative possibilities, though, but concrete products and services that exist in the real world and not just on a drawing board.

No one can predict whether or not an emerging technology will become a networking standard. That is as much a question about marketing as it is about the technology itself. Keeping current in today's networking industry consists largely of anticipating new trends and making sensible judgments as to when (or if) it would be safe, practical, and economical to adopt them for use at your network installation. Those who judge wisely, remain employed. Those who don't, usually end up making a big mess that must be cleaned up by the next administrator. Unfortunately, a good portion of the effort devoted to the development of an emerging technology is expended on devising ways to convince you that this product or service is the one that you need and that, until you have it, you will never be up to speed with the industry. We hope, in this book, to separate the publicity from the facts and provide you with more of the latter than the former.

What Should You Get Out of This Book?

Computer networking, and indeed computing in general, is about communications. To accomplish even the simplest task using a computer, literally dozens of different forms of electronic signaling and communications are used by the various components involved. People speak of this as the digital age and of binary code as the fundamental communications medium for all computers, everywhere. But how do the zeroes and ones get from one place to another? Just as you can telescope in on a video, audio, or textual format to see its binary code, you can zoom in even farther and look at how electrical currents or light pulses are used to make up the binary format.

Many people know a lot about computers, but no one person knows everything about them. From the microscopic inner workings of a microprocessor to the sealed environment where magnetic particles store data on the platters of a hard disk drive all the way up to the microwave and satellite technologies used to transmit data between computers located thousands or even millions of miles apart, the variety and complexity of the signaling and communications techniques involved in networking is colossal in scope.

You don't need to know how to design a microprocessor to purchase a computer. You don't need to know how to build a space shuttle to bounce a signal off of a satellite. Indeed, you probably do both more frequently than you think, without even knowing it. But there may well be times when you want to know something about what goes on within these "transparent" systems. When you are charged with making a decision as to which processor to have in the thousand computers that your company may be purchasing this year, it is good to know something more about the subject than you would normally get in a magazine ad or a TV commercial.

That's what this book is for. The more that you know about the inner workings of a computer or a network, the more sense can be made from its outside manifestations, and your troubleshooting skills become that much more acute as a result.

No one is expected to sit down and read a book like this, from cover to cover. It is more likely to be used as a point of reference, a background source that examines most of the tasks that are likely to be asked of a network administrator as well as most of the technology with which he comes into daily contact. Keeping it handy will help you to field a lot of the user questions that you normally would not be able to answer. And it will let you keep your rep as the "all-knowing network guru" for a little while longer.

Part I

Understanding Networks

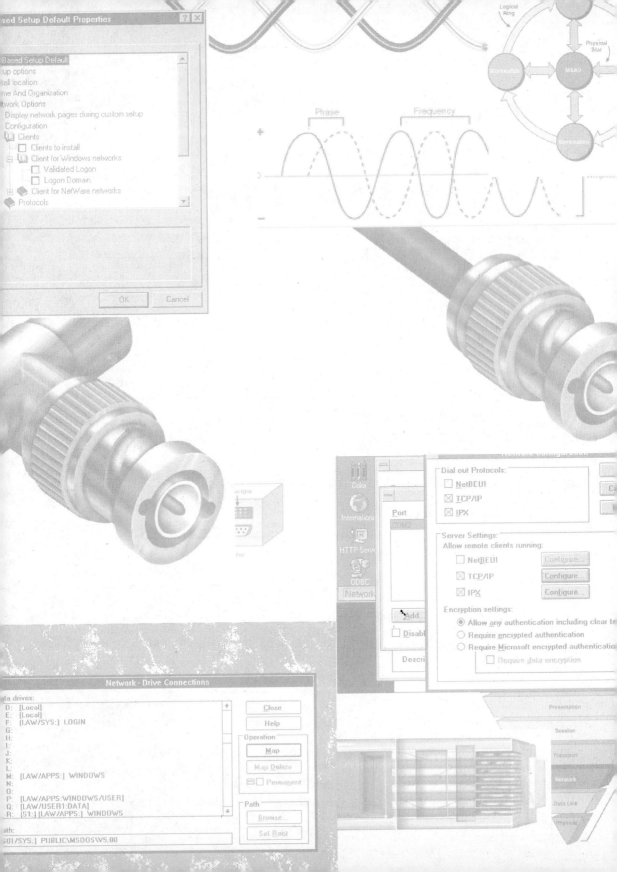

Chapter 1

Network Background

Computer networks have grown dramatically in complexity, geographical range and ubiquity over the last few years. This introductory chapter looks at the current state of networking and provides a brief conceptual context for the mass of technical information contained in the remainder of this book.

The Nature of the Network

Data traversing the modern global network must run the gauntlet of a wide range of modern communications technology. Each packet is transmitted, bounced, copied, and mangled so often during its brief life that, at times, it seems remarkable that it is delivered at all. Yet, despite its complexity, the modern network is robust and reliable. This is testimony to the rapid pace of developments in communications hardware but perhaps equally as much to the adoption of a consensus approach to design issues by developers.

Heterogeneity

Modern networks are remarkably heterogeneous. IBM compatibles and Macintoshes rub shoulders with workstations and mainframes; DOS and Windows platforms share data with UNIX and every other operating system; Ethernet and token ring converse with FDDI and ATM; and all of this takes place over a chaotic mixture of physical media. A single network packet might pass through thinnet, twisted-pair, and fiber-optic cables and laser line-of-sight links before being bounced off a satellite to pass through a similar mix of media at the receiving end.

Modularity

Heterogeneity is made possible by the growing emphasis on modularity in the design of network hardware and software. There was a time when many developers produced network environments that used proprietary network software running over proprietary hardware, using a single type of cable. These simple networks were attractive to many consumers who required a simple, out-of-the-box network solution. Inevitably, however, requirements arose that could not be met by a purely proprietary system. For example, the consumers decided to link their network to another different type of network, or they discovered that they needed to share a resource over the network only to find that it was incompatible with their network product.

The modular approach overcame these difficulties to a large extent. Network products began to focus on a small area of the network landscape. By the late 1980s, instead of having to decide which network to purchase, consumers found themselves making separate choices for network adapters, cabling systems, interconnection devices, network operating systems (NOSs), and network applications.

Increasing modularity in network software has had an especially profound impact. This is particularly apparent on the desktop, where network protocols can be mixed and matched to suit the user's needs. Modularity's effects are becoming increasingly marked on a more macroscopic level, as network administrators combine NOSs to provide the required combination of services rather than rely on a single product.

Standards

The modular approach is possible only when adequate standards are agreed upon. Nobody can predict exactly what a user is going to want to send over the network, nor can anyone know with certainty what the next stage of development in network technology will bring. The only way a developer can be sure that its product will work with the rest of the network is by adhering rigorously to the recognized standards. Each hardware manufacturer must know exactly what it can expect as input to its part of system and what its system must generate as output. Software developers work to similar specifications.

The OSI network model discussed in chapter 3, "The OSI Model: Bringing Order to Chaos," has been extremely influential in this regard, allowing for a clear, logical delineation of responsibilities between the many components of a network. At the desktop level, Novell's ODI specification has allowed what would previously have been unimaginable—several different network protocols running simultaneously and smoothly on the same hardware. In both cases, the adoption of a standard has made development possible.

The Scope of Networking

The rapid growth in the number of networked computers over the last decade or so has been dramatic. One index of this growth is the number of Internet host computers, which is now in excess of six million. Figure 1.1 depicts the increase over several years to mid-1995, using data produced by Network Wizards and available on **http://www.nw.com/**. The number of people with Internet access is extremely difficult to quantify but is currently in excess of twenty million worldwide.

Estimates in the growth of Internet connections, while difficult, are at least possible because of the integrated nature of the Internet. The growth in enterprise-level computing is similarly dramatic but impossible to measure in the same way, as many LANs are isolated from the world beyond the enterprise.

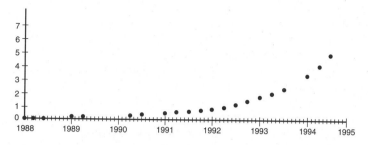

Figure 1.1

This is the growth of Internet hosts from 1988 to 1995.

Growth Rate

A remarkable feature of this expansion is that the rate of growth has continued to increase over a period of years, which has led to predictions of one Internet node for every human being in the planet by the early years of the next century. This acceleration in growth rate is because when two networks are connected, both are expanded and enhanced. Connecting thousands of LANs made the combined resources of the Internet so vast that it eventually became unrealistic for network planners to attempt to rival it; better to connect to it, take advantage of it, and at the same time, contribute to it.

This exponential growth cannot continue indefinitely but by the time it begins to slow, it is likely that Internet access will be as commonplace as cable television. Networks in the home may have seemed unlikely a few years ago, yet some homes have already been fitted with network cabling. The emergence of cost-effective broadband technologies such as ISDN suggests that domestic network access at speeds is not far away.

Network Awareness

In tandem with this rapid growth in the extent of networks in general and the Internet in particular, there has been a significant change in the general level of awareness of networks. Most computer literate people have by now at least heard of the Internet; many who are not otherwise familiar with computers have also heard of it. In fact, a substantial number of people are now buying their first computer for the purpose of accessing the Internet. Access to the network has become an end in itself.

This heightened awareness of networking has been fueled by the rapid expansion of networks into everyday life, which has in turn fueled the heightened awareness of networking. Networking the office is no longer a matter of office equipment, the impact of which can be compared with the arrival of a new fax machine. Instead, it brings a fundamental change in the way the enterprise functions internally—in the relationship between the enterprise and the world outside and in the staff's perception of their relationship to the world beyond the office. There is now an increasing awareness within organizations that networking can make this type of change.

Network Readiness

Application software has been tracking this shift in awareness for some time. Not so many years ago, many applications would balk at working in a networked environment; how many packages refused to use drive letters beyond E? Yet today, more and more packages are claiming to be "network ready" or "network aware" as software developers increasingly recognize networked computers as the norm rather than the exception. Recent developments in software monitoring and license enforcement as described in appendix D, "Software License Metering," reflect this change.

Technology

The technological innovations that have driven these changes are not as extensive as may be imagined. Most of the building blocks of the modern network—data packets, protocols, cabling systems—were invented by Rank Xerox in the 1970s. While the speed and capacity of network hardware have developed enormously in recent years, and while today's networks are built with increasingly sophisticated components, there has been nothing like the paradigm shift introduced by the invention of, say, the transistor.

Today's Networks

The rapid pace of change in network hardware and software is reflected in the range of systems in use across the world at the present time. Most network installations, particularly those in the medium and large categories, consist of a mixture of old and new hardware and software.

Legacy Systems

Some of the most out-of-date network equipment is found at some of the most progressive institutions. These were the pioneers, the ones who invested in early systems at a time when networking was still experimental. They had to struggle with relatively primitive equipment and endure frequent crashes and network hiccups, only to find that their system was obsolete almost as soon as it was stable.

They then faced a dilemma. Should they write off the old equipment to experience and graduate to a better system, incurring high capital and manpower costs? Or did it make more sense to stick with the old system, enhancing it where possible and hoping to switch at some point in the future? In many cases, the scale of investment required to change was too high. As a result, the existing systems were retained after they had ceased to be worth the maintenance effort. New equipment was brought in on a piecemeal basis to shore up the creaking system until, finally, something gave and the required investment was made.

This reluctance or inability to move on to more modern systems has left a considerable amount of old equipment in use. The new products are faster, more modular, and more robust, but most network administrators have to support at least some software and hardware that they would rather see scrapped.

The Modern Network

The modular nature of modern network products and the lessons learned about investment and obsolescence have helped to make recent networks more manageable. They are designed with a view to the finite life span of the components. Obsolescence is planned rather than being allowed to creep up, and the initial investment is made with the understanding that substantial ongoing resources, both monetary and human, will be required to maintain the network as a functioning entity. There is a realization that no matter what capacity is provided, the users will almost certainly exhaust it within a matter of months.

Hardware. Computers bought for network access are most likely to be IBM-compatible PCs, Macintoshes, and UNIX systems, in that order. Apple in the past relied on superior technical innovation, particularly in the network arena; this having failed, Apple has now staked a good deal on its PowerPC. As yet, this has not made a significant impact.

Many of the computers connected to networks around the world were of course bought before any network was available. These legacy systems will be around for the foreseeable future, and they form a significant part of most network communities. They make their presence felt by being less powerful and less well integrated into the network than their more modern cousins.

Software. The software products of the past are much less likely to feature on today's networks. LocalTalk, LAN Manager, and many others have faded from prominence over a short period of time. Once such products began to be seen as having lost the battle for market preeminence, their demise accelerated as consumers began to back the winners with a vengeance.

Those leaders in the desktop market are Novell NetWare for client-server systems and Microsoft Windows (Windows for Workgroups and Windows 95) for peer-to-peer systems. Both are primarily PC-based, reflecting Apple's slip from the top of the desktop machine market. Larger systems are almost universally TCP/IP based, as in fact are a significant number of smaller systems.

Networking. The bulk of new LANs are Ethernet based. Fiber-optic links between buildings are now the norm, with leased telecommunications lines taking the place of the public data network for wide area links.

LANs that are strictly local make less and less sense. Electronic mail has become the *sine qua non* of network access; this requires a gateway machine of some description and a connection to the world outside. Internet access may have already replaced e-mail in this regard, despite the higher demands it places on bandwidth and other expensive resources.

The Future

In such a rapidly changing field as computer networking, trying to predict the future is almost certainly an act of folly. If the author could be certain that his predictions were accurate, he would be implementing them rather than merely speculating about them! However, a number of trends appear to be clear.

Desktop hardware and software products are increasingly being seen as consumer goods. They have left the realm of specialist retailers and entered the mainstream of office equipment and home appliances. This shift, partly driven by the growth in networking, will itself continue to fuel the demand for network access and for better and faster network services.

This shift will also accelerate the change in the typical profile of a network user. Academic institutions will soon cease to be the core of the international network community, and office workers will no longer represent the bulk of LAN users. Instead, domestic network access will rank with professional use in terms of numbers and traffic. The network may not become as ubiquitous as the telephone, but it will become much more commonplace than at present.

Just as with telephones, the continuing advances in telecommunications will help to make networking more mobile. Laptop and pocket PCs will claim their stake in the cellular communications world and, through sheer weight of traffic, will play a significant part in shaping the successor to the current cellular technology.

The trend away from public data networks may well reverse as network providers produce more secure and cost-effective solutions. Utility companies would like to see a move toward complete network packages, where the provider bundles a physical link with gateway and domain management services. Whether they can persuade the network management to go for this depends on design issues on which the jury is still most definitely out.

Summary

Technological advances in networking hardware and software have led to greater throughput on all scales and to increasingly tighter integration of networking with all aspects of computing. In tandem with these advances, the idea of networking has entered the common consciousness to an extent that would have been unimaginable a few short years ago. This shift in perception has led to an expansion of networking beyond the workplace, which is already beginning to shape developments in networking technology.

Chapter 2

Overview of Network Systems and Services

A network is an interconnected system of computing devices that provide shared, economical access to computer services. The task of managing the access to shared services is given to a specialized type of software known as a *network operating system (NOS)*. There are many NOSs available in the marketplace today—the major players are covered in detail in part III, "Software Platforms: NOSs and Clients." This chapter provides a high-level view of the two main types of local area networks (LAN): client/server and peer-to-peer. It also examines the basic hardware structure that comprises the modern LAN, and looks at some of the features and services furnished by this combination of networking hardware and software. In the process, a good many of the basic networking terms and concepts used throughout this book will also be introduced.

The Client/Server Network

Client/server computing is a buzzword that has been bandied about a great deal in the computer press, often without being specifically defined. Basically, the client/server concept describes a computing system in which the actual processing needed to complete a particular task is divided between a centralized host computer, the *server*, and a user's individual workstation, the *client*. The two are connected by cables (or infrared, radio, or microwaves) for communication (see fig. 2.1). (Note that the connecting lines in the figure represent the network's pattern of data traffic and not the physical cabling system).

Although they are both PCs with the same basic architecture, the client and server computers usually have very different hardware and software configurations. The primary function of each in relation to the other can be stated in simple terms: the client requests services from the server, and the server responds by providing those services. A few examples of client/server operations might make this distinction clear:

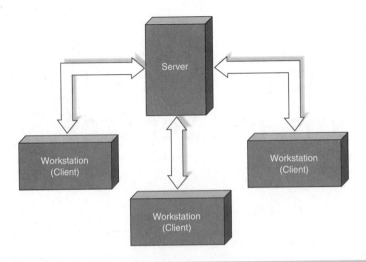

Figure 2.1

This is the logical architecture of a typical client/server network.

- A computer running DOS, requesting a file that is stored on a NetWare file server

- A PC running Windows 95, dialing out to a bulletin board using a modem connected to a RISC-based computer running Windows NT Advanced Server

- A Windows application on a user's PC, requesting data from a computer running Lotus Notes

- A PC running DOS and Sun's PC-NFS product, printing a large report using a high-speed printer attached to a SparcServer

- A computer running OS/2, connected to a mainframe, receiving up-to-the-minute data about commodity prices, and displaying a constantly updated chart reflecting the price changes

- An Apple Macintosh Performa being used for photo-retouching of a high-resolution scanned image from a Scitex publishing system

- A PC, connected to the Internet, running Netscape Navigator and viewing multi-media documents stored on a UNIX host on another continent

In each case, it is clear which system is the client and which is the server. It is also clear that the computer operating as the server is providing a service to the client that is essential to complete the task at hand. Indeed, the server could be providing these services to dozens or even hundreds of clients simultaneously. It is not surprising, therefore, that a server is generally a more powerful, complex, and expensive machine—running more powerful, complex, and expensive software—than the clients with which it interacts.

The differences in function and ability between the server and the client are in accordance with the reasons that PC networks were originally developed and have been so successful: to provide shared, economical access to services such as large disk drives, high-quality printers, high-speed modems, and other expensive items. Concentrating the most expensive and important pieces of the network at a server allows those items to be protected and maintained by trained professionals, while allowing many more people to use them.

This centralized location of shared equipment is, of course, nothing new to computing. It is the essence of the host-based system, in which a mainframe holds all of the data and runs all of the applications, and users interact with the host using terminals to input data and view results. Clearly, another aspect is necessary for a system to be considered a client/server network, and that is the distributed processing previously mentioned. In a host-based system, all the important processing happens on the mainframe. The application running on the mainframe even controls most of the functions of the users' terminals, telling them where to display certain characters, when to beep and for how long, and when to accept user input.

In a client/server relationship, the server does some of the necessary data processing, and the client does some. The degree to which the processing tasks are separated between the two machines can vary greatly, and this is the source of confusion to many. When a user launches an application at his workstation, it may be a spreadsheet whose software is stored and operated solely within the workstation computer, or it may be a database client that interacts with a server to bring information to that workstation. If the data file being opened by the spreadsheet is stored on a network file server, both of these instances can, by strict definition, be called client/server applications. Server processes are needed to provide both the spreadsheet and the database with the data files that they need to operate.

However, there is a question of degree here that cannot be overlooked. Once the file server has delivered the spreadsheet's data file to the workstation, its participation in the process is ended, until it is time to write the modified file back to the server. The database application, on the other hand, requires the continuous participation of both sides of the client/server paradigm to function. The database client is useless (and sometimes cannot even be launched) unless the server process is active.

This is what is really meant by client/server computing. Instead of the entire functionality for multiple users being carried out by a single computer, as in the mini/mainframe situation, the processing capabilities of the server and all of the client machines are combined into a whole that is inherently more efficient. This is because of reductions in the amount of data being transmitted over the network, as well as the combined increase in pure computing power.

There are several types of systems that can be considered servers in a client/server environment. At the most basic level is a *file server* that performs high-performance data storage duty for multiple clients, and perhaps provides shared print services as well. There can also be large *application servers*, running high volume applications—such as database access, updating, indexing, selection, and retrieval—on behalf of less powerful clients. Smaller, *special-purpose servers* may provide fax services, electronic mail pickup and delivery, or modem sharing.

Even though many servers have very powerful, expensive hardware, it is the software differences between clients and servers that really distinguish them. In some client/server networks, the server hardware may not be all that different from that of the client. Most of these servers are ordinary IBM-compatible PCs, as are most of the clients. The server may have 16M, 32M, or more of RAM, 1G or more of disk space, and perhaps a tape backup system, but it is not unusual today to find PCs with similar hardware resources being used as clients or stand-alone systems.

The server, though, is running a NOS, such as Novell NetWare, Microsoft's Windows NT Advanced Server, or Banyan VINES, or it is running a server application on top of a high-performance general purpose operating system (OS), like IBM LAN Server or Microsoft LAN Manager running on OS/2. In any case, the software has special features: extensive security measures designed to protect the system and the data it contains from unauthorized access, enhanced file system software with features to protect files from damage or loss while handling simultaneous requests from multiple users, and a communications system capable of receiving, sorting out, and responding correctly to hundreds or thousands of varied requests each second from different clients.

To support the demands placed on a server in a client/server environment, the server software usually runs on a computer dedicated solely to the purpose of hosting that software and supporting its services. It might be possible to use the server computer to run a regular software application or to support a client session at the same time as the server software is functioning, but server processes and functions have priority access to the system's resources.

The Peer-To-Peer Network

While client/server networks are distinguished by how different the clients and servers are, each with a clearly defined role, *peer-to-peer networks* are just the opposite. There are still clients and servers in a peer-to-peer system, but generally, any fully functioning client may simultaneously act as a server. The resources of any computer on the network—disk drives, files, applications, printers, modems, and so on—can be shared with any other computer, as shown in figure 2.2 (again displaying the pattern of data communications between the nodes and not the physical cabling diagram).

Peer-to-peer networking software might be included in the base client OS, or it might be purchased separately as an add-on feature. Until recently, it was common for all of the nodes in a peer-to-peer network to be running the same client OS—DOS, Windows for Workgroups, OS/2 Warp Connect, Windows NT, or Macintosh System 7. Some exceptions to this rule have always existed. A PC running DOS can be a client in a Windows for Workgroups network, but it cannot be a server. With TOPS, both PCs and Macintoshes can share resources as clients and servers. Artisoft's LANtastic peer-to-peer systems can accommodate Macintoshes as clients, but servers must be DOS-based. A PC running OS/2 usually can be configured to be either a client or server in a DOS-based peer-to-peer network by running the DOS software in one or more *DOS virtual machines*, although the network resources may not be available to OS/2 applications.

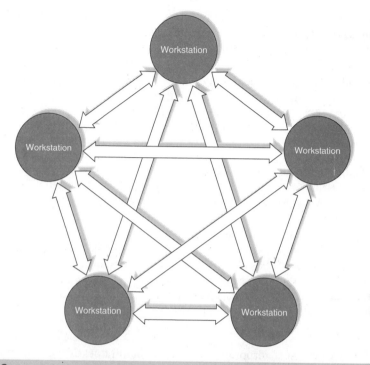

Figure 2.2

This is the logical architecture of a typical peer-to-peer network.

The release of Windows 95, however, signals the achievement of Microsoft's goal of providing peer-to-peer interoperability between all of its Windows OSs. Windows for Workgroups, Windows 95, and Windows NT all ship with a fully integrated peer-to-peer networking functionality that allows all three OSs to share resources with any of the others. The ease and simplicity with which basic networking functions can be configured and enabled in these OSs, not to mention the economy of their inclusion in the standard OS package, bodes ill for add-on products like LANtastic and Personal NetWare, which offer little in the way of additional features or performance.

Peer-to-peer networks are often comprised of only a few workstations, perhaps sharing a printer or two and the data files on each other's hard drives. The upper limit on the number of nodes that can function as both clients and servers on a peer-to-peer network with performance levels that remain reasonable is usually somewhere between 10 and 25. Beyond this number, a peer-to-peer machine can be used as a dedicated server with additional high-performance hardware. It then can handle as many as 50 or 100 clients that aren't too demanding. When networks grow beyond this point, though, it is time to migrate to a full client/server architecture.

The distinctions between client/server and peer-to-peer NOSs can get blurry at times. It is very common for a computer to be more or less dedicated to the role of a server in a peer-to-peer network to provide good performance and responsiveness to clients' requests. Conversely, the server OS in most client/server networks allows one or more client sessions to be run on the same computer as the server. In NetWare 2.x, the server can be set up in *non-dedicated server mode*, which allows a single DOS client session on the server. NetWare 4.x is usually thought of as a stand-alone client/server NOS, but it can be run as an application atop OS/2, allowing multiple OS/2, Windows, and DOS applications to be run on the same computer. LAN Manager, LAN Server, and Windows NT Advanced Server all allow one or more client sessions to be active on the server. Older computers such as IBM XTs and ATs can live on in a client/server environment as specialized print, mail, and fax servers, long after their usefulness as client workstations has ended.

Further confusing the picture is the fact that the client software in a peer-to-peer system is often nearly the same as the client software in a client/server system. Computers running Windows for Workgroups, Windows 95, or Windows NT in a peer-to-peer system can be configured to simultaneously access resources on many client/server systems, such as NetWare, Windows NT Advanced Server, or LAN Manager. LANtastic clients can also use the file and print services of NetWare. In fact, Artisoft resells a modified version of NetWare 4.x as the basis of its CorStream Server client/server product. Novell's Personal NetWare uses the same basic client software as the latest versions of its client/server packages, NetWare 3.12 and NetWare 4.1. Using this software, a DOS or Windows PC can easily access resources on both a Personal NetWare server and a dedicated NetWare 3.x or 4.x server.

Back in the days when most corporations regarded mainframes and minicomputers to be their only strategic computing platforms, individual branches and departments put in PC networks to quickly and economically share information and servers. As these networks have grown and become connected with each other, and now function as the strategic computing platform in many corporations, peer-to-peer networking software is being used within larger networks to continue sharing resources and information on a local level.

Client/Server versus Peer-To-Peer

Without question, the primary advantage of the peer-to-peer network is its low cost. For little more than the price of network interface cards and cabling, a handful of stand-alone PCs can be assembled into a basic functional small business network, often without the need for high-priced consultants or administrative talent.

This last point should not be taken lightly. A small business that chooses to install a client/server network (perhaps anticipating their future growth) is often placed into the difficult position of being incapable of running the network themselves, while at the same time being unable to justify employing a full-time network administrator. They are usually forced, as a result, to engage consultants for a high hourly fee.

The administrative factor, along with the high cost of the NOS software itself (while the peer-to-peer NOS is, in many cases, free with the client OS), presents a good reason for the small business to stick with peer-to-peer. This is fine, as long as the requirements of the business remain within the scope of the functionality that peer-to-peer systems provide. File and print services are sufficient for many types of operations, but if the business has the potential for generating truly large amounts of data that will have to be organized and retrieved on a regular basis, then the judicious course might be to run a client/server network from the very beginning.

Fortunately, the task of migrating from a peer-to-peer system to a client/server one has become much simpler over the years. Indeed, in the case of a Microsoft Windows network, simply adding a machine running Windows NT Advanced Server to an existing network of Windows for Workgroups or Windows 95 machines all but accomplished the task. Adding a NetWare server to such a peer-to-peer network is not terribly difficult either, although it will be necessary to reconfigure all of the workstations to accommodate both network types.

Deciding whether to go with a peer-to-peer or client/server network is an important decision. The pros and cons of both are presented in table 2.1. It is, however, not nearly as crucial as some of the others presented in this chapter, and throughout this book. If the selection of the networking hardware and infrastructure is made well, then a low-cost peer-to-peer network can be upgraded to a client/server system with virtually no expenditures wasted.

Table 2.1   Advantages and Disadvantages of Peer-To-Peer and Client/Server Networks

Advantages	Disadvantages
Peer-To-Peer	
Inexpensive or free NOS	Limited size
Low maintenance cost	File and print services only
Easy installation	Limited connectivity
Client/Server	
Extremely expandable	Expensive NOS
Unlimited connectivity	High maintenance cost
Wide range of services	Difficult to install

Fundamental Networking Concepts

Having defined the roles of clients and servers in a LAN, we shall now consider the network itself—that is, the medium that links all of the component computers and the data communications conducted through it. Computer networking is a highly complex and technical subject. What appears to be a simple network transaction, such as the transfer of a file from server to workstation, is actually an extraordinarily complicated procedure, encompassing many different forms of communication on many levels.

Fortunately, the average LAN administrator does not usually need to be an expert on all facets of the communication that occurs between computers. This section is designed to serve as an introduction to some of the more in-depth discussions occurring later in this book. The basic vocabulary of networking will be introduced, and we will take a brief look at the hardware and network types covered elsewhere in greater depth.

Protocols

In any discussion of the technologies and methods underlying network communications, the term *network protocol* will be used often (perhaps too often). A protocol is nothing more than a set of rules and specifications governing how two entities communicate. Human societies develop protocols at many levels. Languages are protocols that are formulated to allow people to understand each other. Improper use of language results in misunderstanding or prevents any communication at all. Later more advanced protocols specify what is considered proper and polite behavior for the use of language evolve. When someone violates these rules, they are often considered rude or disruptive and may be ignored or perhaps even punished.

Computers also have certain defined protocols specifying proper behavior for communication between them. When any hardware or software violates these rules, proper communications may not be able to take place over the network, even between other systems that are following the rules. Messages generated by a machine not conforming to accepted protocols probably won't be acknowledged by other computers. As with humans, such messages will be considered to be disruptive noise and will be ignored.

All of the rules and standards that make computer-to-computer communication possible are properly called protocols. Because, as with humans, communication occurs at many levels, however, it is helpful to distinguish some different types of protocols. Understanding these different types is where a construction such as the OSI network model comes in handy. The OSI model is a construction that is designed to illustrate the seven basic levels of network communication, ranging from the physical medium of the network all the way up to the application interface appearing on the workstation. It is covered in much greater depth in chapter 3, "The OSI Model: Bringing Order to Chaos."

NCP (NetWare Core Protocol), TCP/IP, Ethernet, and UTP are all technically considered protocols, even though they refer to very different communication levels that have little in common beyond being components of a network transmission. A quick look at each protocol, in reference to the OSI network model, will help make the distinctions clear.

In accordance with the OSI network model, *unshielded twisted pair* (*UTP*) is a protocol that refers to the physical layer, specifying a type of cable that can be used to connect computers, how the connectors need to be wired together, and the electrical characteristics of the signals on the wire. To avoid confusion when talking about this and other physical layer protocols, people usually refer to *cabling systems*, *cabling types*, or other terms clearly identifying that they mean the physical link between systems. Since the physical layer need not take the form of an actual cable and may use infrared or radio transmissions, for example, a general term that covers all possibilities is *transmission medium*.

Ethernet is a protocol that functions at the data link layer, providing the basic rules for how the signals transmitted over the network medium must be formatted to contain data, how physical stations on the network are uniquely identified, and how access to the physical medium is governed so as to allow all of the stations on the network an equal opportunity to transmit. Ethernet is one of several data link layer protocols in use today and will function properly with UTP, or one of several other physical layer protocols. The protocols operating at physical and data link layers of the OSI model are often considered together because they are dependent on each other. As explained fully in the chapter on the OSI model, the use of a particular protocol at the data link layer imposes certain limitations on the physical layer and vice versa.

Transport Control Protocol/Internet Protocol (TCP/IP) is a broad set of rules and standards, sometimes called a *protocol suite*, that works at the network, transport, and session layers of the OSI model. These rules control how data on the network is sent on the correct path to reach its intended destination, how some communication errors are handled, and how logical connections between nodes on the network are established, maintained, and ended. There are several other protocols of this type in use today. Partially because these protocols cover several adjacent layers of the OSI model, they are sometimes referred to as *protocol stacks*.

The *NetWare Core Protocol (NCP)* is a set of rules that govern how applications and computer systems communicate at the presentation and application layers to carry out common data processing functions such as creating, reading, writing, and erasing files, sending and accepting print jobs, and logging on and off of a server. Other common protocols of this type are Server Message Blocks (SMB), Network Filing System (NFS), and AppleShare/AppleTalk.

As you can see from figure 2.3, these four examples encompass all of the layers of the OSI model, moving from bottom to top. The four protocols discussed above need not be and usually are not used together. They are provided merely as common examples what comprises the nature of the protocols running at the different networking communication levels. The rest of this chapter covers some basic concepts concerning these different levels, ranging from hardware to software as we progress again from the physical to the application layer.

Cable Types

The first computer networks were constructed on a foundation of serial ports and cables, like those used to connect a modem or serial printer to a PC. Serial networks are hampered by severe speed and distance limitations but are still used today. In fact, DOS 6.2 comes with Interlink, a simple peer-to-peer network application that allows two PCs to be connected with serial or parallel cables and redirects drives or printers to the other PC.

Coaxial Cable. The first big advance in networking was when *coaxial cable*, similar to the cable that carries radio and TV signals over long distances in cable TV systems, was adapted for data communications. Coaxial contains a single conducting wire, surrounded by an insulating material, which in turn is surrounded by a metal sheath or braid that can be grounded to help shield the signal on the conductor from interference, and then still more insulation. All of these components share a single axis at the center of the cable—hence the term coaxial.

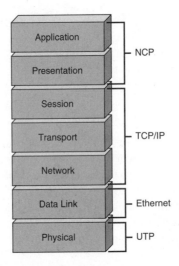

Figure 2.3

These are four examples of networking protocols.

The first systems to use coaxial used the same signaling techniques as cable TV systems. The stream of data bits being transmitted was converted into a radio wave signal of a specific frequency, and broadcast on the wire. This system, called *broadband signaling*, has the advantage of allowing multiple signals or channels to be carried on a single cable at the same time, using a technique called *frequency-division multiplexing* (FDM), that assigned different base frequencies to different channels. The ability of a single cable to carry as many as 12 simultaneous TV channels must have seemed at the time like an unlimited amount of bandwidth that could never be used up, especially when compared to the slow teletype speeds achieved with serial connections that were the current standard.

Although analog TV signals can be carried for several miles on coaxial cable before acceptable signal quality is compromised, such distances could not be achieved with digital data. Any electrical signal carrying information can be thought of as a series of waves. The distance between the waves is the *frequency* of the signal, and the height of the waves is the strength, or *amplitude*, of the signal. The information in a signal, whatever the data type, is carried in small variations of either the frequency or amplitude. While a signal might start out well-defined, as it travels over the wire the variations that carry the information become blurred and distorted. The effect is similar to looking at an object through multiples panes of window glass. The image that passes through one pane is almost indistinguishable from looking directly at the actual object. As more panes are added, the object becomes blurry and indistinct, until finally it is unrecognizable. This distortion is called *attenuation*.

Digital data is much more susceptible than analog to the noise and signal distortions that are introduced as signals travel greater distances. The amount of distortion that would cause an annoying but acceptable amount of "snow" in a TV signal will utterly destroy the information carried in a digital data stream. Because of this, network systems using broadband coaxial cable are limited to reaching only a few dozen (or maybe hundreds) of feet, unless *signal repeaters* are used to regenerate the signal periodically. Simple amplifiers would not suffice, as they would only amplify the noise and distortion that the signal picks up as it travels down the wire.

The next advance in networking used similar coaxial cable, but instead of encoding the stream of digital data bits into a radio signal, the bits were directly transmitted on the cable with different voltage levels corresponding to different values, each level being maintained for a small but consistent time period. This is known as *baseband signaling*, the method still used in the vast majority of LANs today. Rather than decoding small variations in amplitude or frequency from a larger signal to decipher information, a receiving station now simply measures the voltage level on the wire at specific intervals.

This method of signaling allows much cheaper transmitting and receiving apparatus to be used on a network. It does raise a problem of *signal collisions*, though—only one station is able to successfully transmit at a time. If two or more nodes transmit at the same time, neither signal will be intelligible, but this problem is dealt with by the next level in the OSI model. With the development and use of baseband signaling, the limiting factor in network distance has become not how *far* a clean signal of a certain frequency can be transmitted, but how *fast* the signal can get from one end of the cable to the other. Signal quality considerations still come into play, of course, particularly in limiting the data speed, or *signaling rate*, of the network, which decreases as distance goes up for any particular type of cable.

Coaxial with a single conductor is an unbalanced transmission medium, as opposed to *balanced media* that use two similar wires carrying signals of opposite polarity or voltage. Balanced media are more resistant to noise and interference. Some IBM systems uses a balanced cable type, similar to coaxial, that has two conductors inside the shielding braid—this is called *twinax*.

Most baseband coaxial network systems have a maximum signaling rate of 10 megabits per second (Mbps) or less. Depending on the specific type of cabling used, they work at this speed over distances of more than a mile when simple repeaters are used to regenerate the signal. For a long time, coaxial was the only economical choice for use in high-speed LANs. The drawbacks to setting up and maintaining a coaxial cable system include the fact that the cable is difficult and expensive to manufacture, is difficult to work with in confined spaces, can't be bent too sharply around tight corners, and is subject to frequent mechanical failure at the connectors. Because a failure at any point usually renders the entire cable system unusable, the overall reliability of coaxial systems has always been less than stellar.

Twisted-Pair Cable. The biggest network in the world, the telephone network, originally used only *twisted-pair cabling* and still does for most local connections. The name comes from the fact that each individually insulated conductor is part of a pair, making this a balanced medium, and that each pair is twisted together along its length, which helps further protect it from interference. Twisted-pair cabling comes shielded, with a metal sheath or braid around it, similar to coaxial, or unshielded. The two are commonly known as STP (shielded twisted pair) and UTP (unshielded twisted pair). All signaling over twisted pair is of the baseband type. STP is commonly used in token-ring networks, but UTP is by far the most popular LAN cabling protocol today, used in the majority of Ethernet networks and in many token-ring networks as well.

Fiber-Optic Cable. A relatively new technology, *fiber-optic cable*, uses light signals transmitted over thin, glass fiber to carry data. Fiber-optic cable offers higher speed, greater reliability, and spans longer distances than other methods. It is more expensive to install than coaxial or twisted pair but is usually cheaper to maintain. It often is used at larger companies to interconnect servers or departmental networks at high speed, over a long distance, or where high security is desired.

A high-speed link dedicated to the connection of servers and other selected network components (as opposed to workstations) is called a *backbone*. Fiber-optic cable is completely resistant to electromagnetic interference and signals cannot be intercepted without breaking the cable. It is also far less susceptible to attentuation than copper cable. Ethernet over fiber-optic cable transmits at 10 Mbps at distances of over two miles, much farther than over any other media. FDDI is a standard network topology that allows 100 Mbps communications between nodes up to a mile or more apart.

Network Topologies

A *topology* is the pattern by which the cabling medium is used to interconnect the various computers that form the network. Like the cable types discussed above, the topology used is intimately connected with the data link layer protocol. Once cannot simply choose a cable type and wire to according to any topology desired. The mechanism by which the data link layer protocol passes the data from the computer onto the network imposes definite restrictions on the way that the cable is wired. The amount of attentuation inherent to the medium, the speed of the signal, and the length of the cable segments are all factors that must be accounted for by the data link protocol. A topology is therefore selected in most cases as the result of a data link protocol decision.

The Bus Topology. There are several general categories of LAN physical topologies, which really are just different ways of stringing cable from station to station. The simplest, and the first true LAN topology, is the *bus topology* (see fig. 2.4), which is a single long cable with unconnected ends, to which all of the networked computers (sometimes called *nodes*) are attached along its length. The bus topology is most often used with coaxial cable, although other computing interfaces that utilize components wired in series (such as SCSI) are sometimes called a bus.

Depending on the width (and subsequent unwieldiness) of the cable, the bus may extend directly from computer to computer, as in thin Ethernet, or it may be wired to the vicinity of the computer and a short cable used to attach it to the bus cable, as in thick Ethernet. Both ends of a bus must always be terminated; otherwise, signals reaching the end of the cable may echo back along its length, corrupting transmissions.

Like any circuit wired in series, the bus topology is inherently unreliable in that a break anywhere in the cable disrupts service to all of the stations on the far side of the break. Like old-fashioned Christmas tree lights, a single blown bulb can affect the entire string—or network.

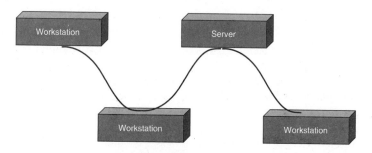

Figure 2.4

This is a representation of the bus topology.

The Star Topology. Although developed later, the *star topology* has become the most popular topology in networking, due in no small part to its overcoming the Christmas-tree light effect. In a star topology, each machine on the network has its own dedicated connection to a *hub* or concentrator. A hub is a device, installed in a central location, that functions as a wiring nexus for the network. Servers and workstations alike are attached to the hub, as shown in figure 2.5, and if any particular cable segment fails, only the computer attached with that segment is affected. All of the others continue to operate normally. The star topology is used mostly with twisted pair cabling, usually in an Ethernet or token-ring network environment.

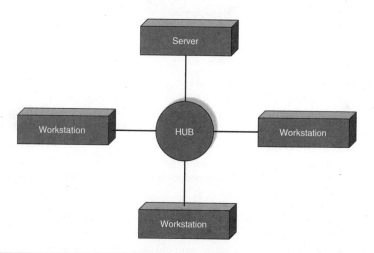

Figure 2.5

This is a representation of the star topology.

If there is a drawback to the star topology, it is the additional cost imposed for the purchase of one or more hubs. Usually, though, this expense is offset by twisted-pair cable's easier installation and cheaper cost than coaxial.

The Ring Topology. Essentially, a bus topology where the two ends are connected forms a *ring topology* (see fig. 2.6). This is primarily a theoretical construct, though, for very few networks today are actually wired in a ring. The popular token-ring network type is actually wired using a star topology, but there can be *a logical topology* that differs from the physical topology. The logical topology describes how the network signaling works, rather than how the cable looks. In the case of a token-ring network, special hubs are used to create a data path that passes signals from one workstation to the next in a procession that concludes at the station where the transmission originated. Thus, the topology of this network is that of a physical star but a logical ring.

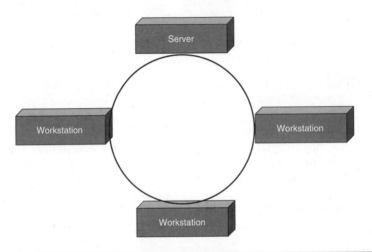

Figure 2.6

This is a representation of the ring topology.

The Mesh Topology. The mesh topology is another example of a cabling system that is almost never used. Describing a network in which every computer contains a dedicated connection to every other computer, it is another theoretical construction that overcomes one networking problem while creating another. One of the fundamental problems of networking at the data link layer of the OSI model is the method by which signals from many different workstations are to be transmitted over a shared network medium without interference. The mesh network eliminates this problem by not sharing the medium.

As shown in figure 2.7, each workstation has its own link to every other workstation, allowing it to transmit freely to any destination, at any time when it is not actually receiving a transmission. Of course, problems quickly arise as the number of workstations grows. Even a modest 10-node network would require 100 NICs and 100 cable runs, making it by far the most expensive network ever created, both in terms of hardware costs and in maintenance. We won't even speak about finding computers that can run 10 NICs each.

Hybrid Topologies. In many cases, the network topologies described above are combined to form hybrids. For example, multiple hubs, each the center of a star, are often connected using a bus segment. In other cases, hubs are added to the ends of segments extending out from another hub, forming what is sometimes called a *tree topology*.

As always, care must be taken when using these techniques to ensure that the requirements set down by the data link layer protocol are not violated too severely. There is a certain amount of leeway to many of the specifications, but wanton disregard of the network's signaling requirements can be severely detrimental to the performance of the network.

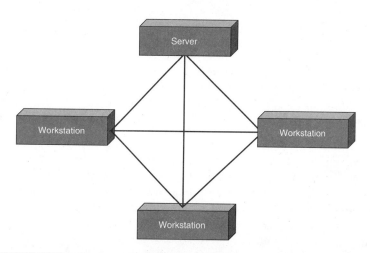

| **Figure 2.7** |

This is a representation of the mesh topology.

Data Link Standards

Several data link standards which are in common use today are briefly introduced in the following sections. This list is by no means exhaustive; there are other possible topologies that have been used on LANs in the past, are still being used today, and will continue to be used in the future. However, the vast majority of new networks installed today utilize one or more of these protocols. The following sections are brief introductions to the data link protocols and some of the concepts that they introduce. They are all covered in greater detail in chapter 7, "Major Network Types."

In any data link protocol, a quantity of data is packaged into a *frame*, or *packet*, which has addressing, routing, control, and other information added to it so that other stations on the network can recognize the data that is meant for them and know what to do with data meant to go elsewhere.

Ethernet. Originally developed by the Digital Equipment, Intel, and Xerox corporations in the late 1970s, Ethernet has since been adopted as an international standard and has become the predominant LAN-data link protocol in use today.

Ethernet was originally specified with a 10 Mbps signaling rate and uses a method of network access control known as *Carrier Sense Multiple Access/Collision Detection (CSMA/CD)*. Instead of passing a token from station to station to allow access to the network for transmissions, any Ethernet workstation is allowed to transmit a frame at any time, as long as the network is not occupied by transmissions from other stations.

When two or more stations do begin transmitting at the same time, a collision occurs. The stations involved usually detect the collision and stop transmitting. After a randomly chosen period of time (only a few milliseconds at most) each of the stations attempts to transmit again, after first listening to make sure that the line is clear. Small numbers of collisions and other errors are normal on an Ethernet network.

Because it is impossible to determine with precision which node will be the next one to transmit and equally impossible to guarantee that the transmission will be successful, Ethernet is called a *probabilistic network*. There is a small, but very real, chance that a particular frame will not be able to be transmitted successfully within the time required because of the possibility of collisions happening at every try. As the amount of traffic increases on an Ethernet network, the number of collisions and errors increases, and the chance of a particular frame being communicated successfully decreases.

The bottom line is that as an Ethernet network grows, it reaches a point where adding active stations causes the maximum data throughput on the network to decrease. When a particular network will reach this saturation point is hard to predict with certainty. The mix of traffic, applications, and activity varies greatly from one network to another and also changes on a network over time. To avoid saturation problems, strict limits on cable segment lengths and the allowed number of nodes are specified for each of the cable types that can be used for Ethernet.

Due to continued development of the standard during its long history, Ethernet has evolved into a very flexible communications protocol that can be used with a wide range of transmission media. When referring to the various Ethernet cabling standards, abbreviations like 10Base2 are used. As shown in figure 2.8, the first number, 10, refers to the signaling rate for the medium in megabits per second (Mbps). The word after the first number is either "Base" or "Broad," indicating a baseband or broadband transmission. The last number refers to the length, in units of 100 meters, to which a single cable segment is limited. Later additions to the Ethernet standards began using letters in this position (like "T" for twisted pair) to indicate cable type.

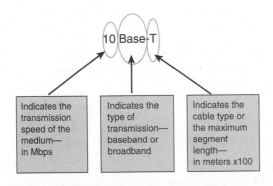

Figure 2.8

Here's the explanations for the 10BaseX cable naming standard.

The most common forms of Ethernet are *10Base5*, *10Base2*, and *10BaseT*, which are often known colloqially as thick Ethernet, thin Ethernet, and UTP, respectively. The latter type uses telephone cabling, as discussed earlier, while the others both use forms of coaxial cable. Several less common Ethernet topologies are also available, as well as some new varieties running at 100 Mbps that are rapidly gaining in popularity. Many Ethernet networks use a combination of two or more topologies. For example, a thick Ethernet cable may be used as a backbone running throughout a large facility. Or multiport thin Ethernet repeaters may be used to branch off segments connected to 10BaseT hubs, which are used for the final connection to the workstations. These mixed-media networks are allowed as long as each segment type adheres to the Ethernet standards for that medium.

Ethernet NICs, hubs, and cabling equipment are readily available for all media types and all PC buses. There are even pocket-sized external adapters that attach to a laptop's parallel port or to a Macintosh's SCSI port to enable network access for computers without expansion slots. Universally recognized as an economical data link protocol offering good performance for traditional network applications, Ethernet can be used for networks running virtually any of the NOSs and transport protocols available today, including NetWare, Windows NT, LAN Server, VINES, and many UNIX variants.

Token Ring. Token Ring was developed in the mid-1980s by IBM and accepted as an industry standard shortly thereafter. Stations on a token-ring network are allowed access to the network medium only when they are in possession of a *token*, a special frame that is passed from one station to the next. Token ring is physically wired in a star configuration, with cables running from each station to a central access point called the *multistation access unit* (*MSAU*). The MSAU attaches each station only to the one preceding it in the ring (the *upstream neighbor*), from which it receives transmissions, and the one after it in the ring (the *downstream neighbor*), to which all its transmissions are sent. MSAUs are interconnected by a cable running from the Ring In port of one MSAU to the Ring Out port of another. The last MSAU's Ring Out is connected to the first MSAU's Ring In. This forms a logical ring topology because a frame originating at a particular workstation is passed to every other station in turn, finally returning to its origin, where it is removed from the network.

The original Token Ring signaling rate was 4 Mbps. Today, many token-ring networks run at 16 Mbps. Most token-ring equipment such as NICs and MSAUs can be configured to operate at either rate, although all stations on a ring must be set to the same speed. In a token-ring network, it can always be precisely determined who will next be able to transmit, and their transmission is practically guaranteed to be successful as long as there are no hardware errors on the network. This certainty leads to token ring being called a *deterministic network*, unlike Ethernet. Also unlike Ethernet, collisions are not an expected occurrence. Consistently occurring collisions on a token-ring network are a matter of concern to the network administrator.

Because a token-ring station needs to be able to discover who its upstream and downstream neighbors are, each station needs to be able to determine and modify the overall configuration of the ring. The ring needs to be able to cope if the station with the token gets turned off or otherwise removed from the ring before passing the token on. There are many more kinds of errors that can disrupt the normal functioning of the ring, and each station must be able to detect and recover from these errors. This requires token-ring NICs to have a lot of error detection and correction circuitry that is not needed or present on Ethernet or ARCnet adapters.

The rules governing the design of a token-ring network are much more complex than those for an Ethernet network. Early token-ring networks used proprietary cables sold only by IBM, but these were thick and unwieldy and had to be purchased in predetermined lengths and strung together to span long distances. Modem token-ring networks all use either STP or UTP cable. The type of cable used determines the segment length and number of node limitations that are imposed on the network, with STP providing the greater flexibility in both areas.

For a long time, IBM only supported use of STP cable on token-ring networks. This, along with a smaller number of token-ring equipment suppliers when compared to Ethernet, and the additional "intelligence" required of token-ring NICs, made token-ring equipment much more expensive than Ethernet or ARCnet. In spite of the higher costs, however, its reliability and IBM's reputation and support have helped make token ring the second most popular network topology in use today. UTP cable is now allowed if a *media filter* is used at the workstation, at either speed, reducing the cost of a token-ring installation. In addition, token-ring NICs and MSAUs today are available from many vendors, and the increasing competition has helped lower equipment costs dramatically.

FDDI/CDDI. *Fiber Distributed Data Interface* (*FDDI*) is a high-speed, fault-tolerant topology that supports transmission speeds of 100 Mbps over a network size of up to 100 kilometers (60 miles). The maximum distance between nodes is two kilometers. It uses dual strands of fiber-optic cable to attach stations together, with the overall topology being a counter-rotating dual ring—that is, two separate rings with traffic moving in opposite directions. Nodes can be attached to one fiber-optic cable (a single-attached station) or both (a dual-attached station). A failure of any one station or a break in one or both cables will still allow communication to continue among most of the remaining stations. The dual-attached stations closest to the break will detect the break and shunt signals from one ring to the other, maintaining the overall ring topology. Two or more simultaneous cable breaks result in two or more isolated but still functioning networks.

FDDI uses a token-passing method of network access. Its high speed, reliability, and fault-tolerance have made it a popular choice for large *backbone networks* (internetworks providing connections between multiple LANs in an enterprise). Its complete resistance to electromagnetic interference also makes it a popular choice for connections between buildings. Routers then provide connections between the FDDI backbone and local Ethernet or token-ring networks. FDDI equipment and administration is very expensive when compared to the other technologies, which limits its acceptance for other uses such as direct workstation connections.

A somewhat cheaper alternative to FDDI that retains its reliability is *Copper Distributed Data Interface* (*CDDI*), which uses the FDDI communication standards over UTP or STP cable. The distance between nodes is reduced from 2,000 meters to 100 meters with UTP.

Comparable performance, although at shorter distances and with less reliability, can be achieved relatively cheaply using TCNS (a 100 Mbps version of ARCnet from Thomas Conrad), 100BaseT, or 100VG AnyLan.

LocalTalk. LocalTalk is used almost exclusively with Macintoshes. Every Mac has an integrated LocalTalk network interface and comes with AppleTalk networking software included in the OS. Apple's LocalTalk specification calls for nodes to be connected in a daisy-chain or bus configuration, using STP cabling. A company named Farallon has also developed a connector that enables LocalTalk to work over UTP cabling. This enables a Macintosh network to be wired together using a single extra pair in existing telephone wiring—this technique is called PhoneNet.

LocalTalk was originally developed to enable easy sharing of peripherals such as printers. Most Macintosh-compatible printers use a LocalTalk connection to one or more Macintoshes on a simple network. The signaling rate of LocalTalk is a relatively slow 230.4 Kbps. This is faster than the printer ports on an IBM-compatible PC, however, making LocalTalk a good choice for printer sharing. It is quite slow when used for file sharing, running at about the same speed that floppy disk drives read and write.

No more than 32 nodes can be connected to a LocalTalk network, which can be a maximum of 1,000 feet long. Repeaters, bridges, or routers can be used to connect LocalTalk networks, enabling communications over a much wider area. Using LocalTalk for file sharing once required purchasing additional software, such as AppleShare software from Apple or TOPS from Sun Microsystems. Recent versions of the Macintosh OS, System 7.x, include peer-to-peer networking capabilities.

ARCnet. One of the first network communication topologies to be developed, ARCnet (Attached Resource Computing Network), was commercially released in 1977 and is still occasionally used today. Originally, it used a star topology constructed out of the same type of coaxial cabling used to connect IBM 3270 terminals to mainframes. ARCnet is limited to a signalling rate of 2.5 Mbps. There can be no more than 255 active nodes on an ARCnet network, and node addresses are a single byte in length. Unlike the other network types considered here, node addresses are manually set with jumpers or switches on the NIC, while those for Ethernet and token-ring NICs are assigned at the factory. Care must be taken in an ARCnet network to make sure that no two nodes are given the same address.

ARCnet also uses a *token-passing* method of network access control; only the station possessing the *token* is allowed to transmit a data packet onto the network. The token is passed along the network as in a logical bus, from the first station to the last.

ARCnet has always had some advantages: the components were quite inexpensive when compared to other networking systems; signals could travel over relatively long distances of up to 2,000 feet; and ARCnet provides a high level of resistance to external electrical interference and noise, which makes it popular in manufacturing environments. The relatively slow signaling rate of the original ARCnet specification has been viewed as a disadvantage by some, but the actual performance of ARCnet in real-world networks is often surprisingly high. Because of its token-passing architecture, ARCnet handles traffic levels close to its theoretical maximum very efficiently. ARCnet is also a much simpler protocol than IBM's Token Ring, so less of the available bandwidth is taken up with managerial communications, leaving more for actual data throughput.

ARCnet today can use a star, a bus, or a combination of topologies, over coaxial, STP, UTP, or fiber-optic cabling. Signaling rates today can be a mix of the original 2.5 Mbps and a newer 20 Mbps. A variation of ARCnet known as TCNS (Thomas Conrad Network System) is available that can go as high as 100 Mbps on STP, coaxial, or fiber-optic.

Inexpensive ARCnet network adapters and hubs are available from many sources. All manufacturers of ARCnet equipment are required by licensing agreements to adhere to the standards set by DataPoint, the original developer of ARCnet, so usually there are no problems with mixing equipment from different sources. Still the user base for ARCnet equipment has dwindled considerably, to the point at which it can no longer be considered a major competitor in the network marketplace.

Repeaters, Bridges, Routers, and Switches

The individual data link segments that we have considered thus far are, as we have seen, limited in the distance they can cover and the number of workstations they can support. This section, then will deal with the ways in which these segments can be connected together to form the large *internetworks* that are commonplace today.

Repeaters

Repeaters are used to interconnect network segments into larger LANs. These devices do just what the name implies—they repeat every signal received on one port out to all its other ports. Because of this, repeaters spread not only good data across networks but also collisions and other errors. Repeaters operate at the physical layer of the OSI model, as shown in figure 2.9, and have no traffic filtering or packet translation ability. They can be used only to connect similar or identical network segments within a relatively small area. For example, a repeater can be used to connect a 10BaseT Ethernet segment using UTP to a 10BaseF Ethernet segment using fiber-optic cable. A repeater cannot be used to connect an Ethernet 10BaseT segment to a 100BaseX segment or a token-ring segment to any kind of Ethernet. To extend a network's reach beyond the strict limits of repeaters requires a different type of device to interconnect two or more networks; one that operated at a higher OSI layer.

Bridges

The simplest of these is called a *bridge*. A bridge operates at the data link layer of the OSI model (see fig. 2.10). Early bridges required address tables to be hand-entered, but most bridges today are *learning bridges*. The technique used most often with Ethernet is known as *transparent bridging*. As a transparent bridge operates, it monitors traffic on all of its ports and stores the node addresses of the sending stations connected to each port in a table in memory. When it receives a packet on one port that is destined for a node address on a different port, it forwards the packet to that port so that it can reach its destination. If it receives a packet destined for an unknown node, it broadcasts the packet on all ports and listens for a response. When it receives a response on one port, it adds that node address to the table for that port, and also passes the response back to the original sender. In this way, each bridge eventually learns through which of its ports each node on the network can be reached. Special procedures are used to deal with unusual situations like multiple paths to a destination.

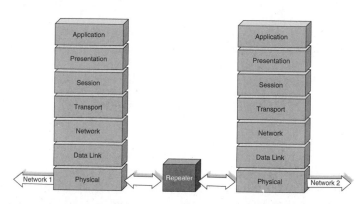

Figure 2.9

Repeaters are used to connect network segments at the physical layer.

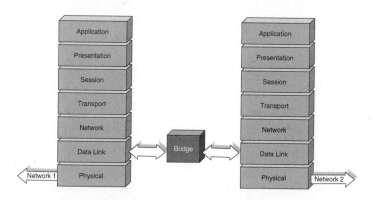

Figure 2.10

Bridges are used to connect network segments at the data link layer.

The bridging technique used most often on token-ring networks is called *source-route bridging*. In this method, a bridge is not required to learn where every node resides on the network in relation to itself. However, a station that wants to send a packet to a station on another network must know the path to that station, including all intervening bridges that the data must cross. This information is included in the packet. Each intermediate bridge looks at a received packet to see where it has to go next, modifies the addressing information in the packet accordingly, and sends it on its way to the next bridge or to its final destination.

Stations learn the path to another node by sending out discovery packets to the destination address. Bridges add their own address to these packets and forward them out of one or all bridge ports. When a discovery packet reaches its destination, it contains the addresses of all of the bridges that it has passed through. This allows the destination node to send a packet back to the originating station containing the route of the shortest or fastest path between that origin and destination.

Almost any network protocol can pass over a bridge because the only requirements are node addresses for the destination and source. Bridges can even be used to connect dissimilar networks, such as ARCnet and Ethernet, or to provide LAN connections to a WAN, provided that the traffic on each side of the bridge uses the same higher-level protocols such as IPX, NetBEUI, or TCP/IP.

Routers

Routers operate at the network layer of the OSI model (see fig. 2.11). Each individual network in a routed environment is identified with a unique network address. A router initially needs to be given the addresses of the networks that it is directly connected to. Routers then learn about which distant networks exist and the best path to them from other routers. When a router receives a packet on one port that has a destination network address different than the source network address and reachable through a different port, it retransmits the packet out of that port. A router does not modify the addressing information in the packet; each router on an interconnected network only has to know the destination network address to correctly forward the packet.

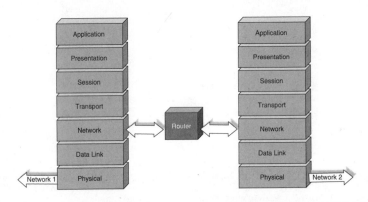

Figure 2.11

Routers are used to connect network segments at the network layer.

Once the packet reaches its destination network, the station with the destination node address specified in the packet processes the packet and responds appropriately. Instead of needing to know the node addresses of all the intermediate stations, and including this information in the packet as in source routing, a station communicating with another distant node merely needs to know the network address and node address of the ultimate destination. It includes this information in the packet and relies on the network routers to see that it reaches its destination.

Routers are able to handle multiple paths between a source and destination easily. When a router learns of a distant network from another router, it also learns how many "hops" away that network is—that is, how many routers a packet must pass through to reach its destination network. If a destination network is reachable through more than one port, then the one with the least number of hops is used to forward packets. This is known as a *distant-vector routing* algorithm. Routers broadcast information about all known networks periodically using *router information protocol* (*RIP*) packets, usually every 30 seconds. AppleTalk has a similar method known as *router table maintenance protocol* (*RTMP*), except that each AppleTalk router broadcasts its entire routing table every 10 seconds.

Under RIP, each hop initially is considered to be the same length and speed as any other hop. Because this is not always true (compare a high-speed FDDI link to a low-speed dialup line), different "costs" can be associated with each route. Routers can determine costs themselves by measuring the amount of time it takes to receive a response from a distant router, or a cost "metric" can be manually assigned to different ports. Routers add up the total costs associated with each route. In this way, a router can choose "least-cost routing" to a distant network. If one link becomes unavailable, eventually all the routers that know about that link learn about it and can use alternative, higher-cost routes. The RIP method of determining routes can be used with XNS (Xerox Network Services, the original Ethernet network protocol), IPX, and TCP/IP.

Routers can continuously measure traffic delays and monitor the status of attached links. Routers that communicate routing information among themselves only when there is a significant change to report are said to be using a *link-state protocol*. This is more efficient than using RIP. Under RIP, a large internetwork with many routers can be flooded with router information every 30 seconds, impeding other traffic. More importantly, a link-state protocol almost instantly relays the status of a failed router or communication line to other routers, enabling them to pick alternative routes right away, rather than waiting for the changes to be passed from one router to another once every 30 seconds, as with RIP. These features make link-state protocols desirable on extremely large networks. TCP/IP traffic on the Internet is routed using a link-state protocol called *open shortest path first* (*OSPF*). OSI networks use a similar protocol called *intermediate system to intermediate system* (*IS–IS*). NetWare uses *NetWare link-state protocol* (*NLSP*) to make it easier to manage worldwide NetWare networks. Apple has developed a new routing protocol as part of AppleTalk Phase 2, *AppleTalk update-based routing protocol*, which is similar to a link-state protocol.

Not every network protocol can be routed, because many of them do not include the necessary network addressing information. XNS, TCP/IP, OSI, and IPX have already been mentioned as routable protocols. IBM's mainframe SNA and the NetBEUI protocol used by Microsoft and IBM in their PC networking systems cannot be routed and must be bridged. Routers capable of handling more than one protocol sometimes have the ability to bridge protocols that don't have network addressing information and are sometimes called *brouters* (for bridge/routers).

Another way of handling non-routable protocols is to use *tunneling*. Tunneling encapsulates an entire packet of one protocol as the data portion inside an envelope of another protocol that contains network addressing information. When the envelope reaches its destination network, it is stripped off and the original packet's protocol is restored.

Switches

A recently developed technology designed to meet the demand for more bandwidth in Ethernet networks is *switching*. Ethernet switches are really nothing more than extremely fast bridges with many ports. Only one or a few workstations are connected to each port, and the connection to the server usually is with a higher-speed link, such as full-duplex 10BaseT (a non-standard way of doubling throughput), FDDI, CDDI, or 100BaseT. This way, the full 10 Mbps bandwidth of Ethernet can be dedicated to one or a few workstations in a single collision domain, and high bandwidth connectivity to a server can be provided without changing any of the hardware or software at the workstation. Switching is rapidly gaining in popularity as the equipment drops in price. Many people believe that it will eventually overtake the traditional router in sales.

Network Services

As you may have noticed, the discussion of networking systems thus far in this chapter has generally progressed from the bottom, or physical, layer of the OSI model upwards. As we pass beyond the more concrete mechanisms that concern the actual transmission of data from one network location to another, we come to the intermediate layer network services that take the lower level protocols for granted. The remainder of this chapter will cover some of the basic networking features that both rely on the lower layers to function and provide their own services to the layers above.

We are no longer directly concerned here with protocols per se. Networking features like file systems and print services utilize protocols to function but operate on a higher level. In a like manner, applications running at the top of the OSI model rely on the services of file and print systems, without concerning themselves with the details of their operation. This functionary isolation is what allows networking products by different vendors to interact successfully.

If the developers of an application know exactly what capabilities to expect from a network file system, then the means by which that system operates is irrelevant to them. In the same manner, if a file system can rely on a network protocol to efficiently move data between a server and a workstation, then it doesn't matter exactly what protocol is being used. The file system can be said to have transcended the particulars of the protocol, just as the application has transcended the particulars of the file system.

File Serving and Sharing

The first resource that networks were designed to share was disk space. In fact, the large computers at the heart of most networks are still commonly called file servers even though they may provide a great many other services to network users.

Every computer OS has its own method of storing, retrieving, and keeping track of files on a disk, with different rules, restrictions, and requirements. These methods comprise the *file system* of the OS. File serving to a network requires a high level of compatibility between file systems because the client should be able to view, store, and retrieve files from the server no differently than if it was accessing a local disk. Yet in many cases, the file server uses completely different operating and file systems than the client, and there may be different clients using different file systems trying to access the same data on the server. To accomplish this, the NOS has to be able to closely emulate the native file systems of whatever clients it supports. Let's look at the file systems of several common client and server OSs to understand how this is done.

If all the clients on your network use the same file system, the differences are probably not a big concern, as long as your file server can store and retrieve files using that same format. If you have clients that use more than one type of file system and wish to share files between them, this becomes more of a problem because the NOS now must present information to client applications about the same files in two different—often incompatible—formats, including the file name, size, date, time, and any other information associated with the file.

The FAT File System. The basis of the file system used by all versions of DOS is called the *file allocation table* (*FAT*). The FAT file system can also be used by OS/2, Windows 95, and Windows NT. Under the FAT file system, the disk is divided into *allocation units*, or *clusters*, of uniform size. The FAT that keeps track of these clusters is limited in size to about 65,000 entries. Because of this, larger disks require larger clusters to keep the number of clusters below the limit. A file that contains even a single byte requires the space of an entire cluster to be stored on the disk; whatever space isn't actually used by the file is wasted. On average, each file wastes about half a cluster—therefore, the larger cluster sizes used on bigger hard disks waste more space.

A FAT is stored at a specific location of the disk. Two copies of the FAT are kept on disk as a safety measure; if one of the copies is damaged, the information can be recovered from the other copy. The FAT keeps track of which clusters on the disk are already in use by files and which are free to be used. Each entry in the FAT corresponds directly to a cluster on the disk. If an entry has the value 0, the corresponding cluster is unused and available. Values from 0xFFF0 to 0xFFF7 indicate that the cluster is reserved by the OS. Values from 0xFFF8 to 0xFFFF mean that this is the last cluster in a file. If any other value is stored in a cluster, it is the number of the next cluster in that file. In this way, the FAT is made up of chained entries that contain the locations of all parts of the files on the disk, allowing the OS to retrieve files from the disk in the correct order.

Another area of the disk is set aside for the *root directory*, another table of structured entries that are each 32 bytes long. The directory contains the file name and other information about the file, such as the date and time it was created or last modified, size of the file in bytes, file attributes, and FAT number of the first cluster used by this file. An entry can refer to a file or to another directory called a *subdirectory*. File and directory names can be up to eight characters long, with a three-character extension following a period separator. All alphabetic characters in a DOS file name are stored in uppercase, and only certain non-alphanumeric characters are allowed. Characters explicitly not allowed in file names and extensions include:

. " / \ [ ] : ; | = , ? * < >

Entries in a subdirectory can point to files—which are then considered to be stored in that directory, regardless of where they are actually stored on the disk itself—or they can point to still more subdirectories. This allows more files to be stored on a disk and allows files to be organized and grouped in a hierarchical tree structure, branching out from the root.

File attributes are single-bit flags that are interpreted by the OS to indicate the type of file or other information. Under the FAT file system, the attributes can indicate that the entry is a file, directory, or volume label, is read-only or can be written to, is visible or hidden in a normal directory listing, or is a special system file or regular file. Another bit can indicate if the file has been changed since the last backup.

Of course, it is not necessary for the average user to know the intimate details of how the FAT file system works to use it. Whenever a user interacts with the file system (by issuing a DOS command, for example), all that they have to know is that certain commands generate certain actions and responses. The same is true for an application that makes use of a file system. This is why a NOS can emulate the performance of the FAT file system through a completely different means. As long as the same commands generate the same responses, the two are compatible.

The FAT file system is the simplest and most common file system used in PCs today. It has very little operational overhead and only a small portion of the disk space is needed for system tables and other uses. This leaves almost the entire disk space for file storage. Because of the low overhead and small amount of information maintained about files on the system, FAT performs extremely well on small- to medium-sized hard disks up to several hundred megabytes. As hard disks become larger, FAT performance begins to suffer. The more the disk fills up, the farther the heads on the drive have to travel between reading the FAT, which is located at the beginning of the disk, and reading the files, which may be scattered in fragments all over the disk.

There are many NOSs on the market that run on DOS and use the FAT file system as their native file system, including most peer-to-peer systems such as LANtastic, Personal NetWare, and Windows for Workgroups. These NOSs usually do not support clients other than those running DOS.

The Macintosh File System. The Macintosh file system is significantly more flexible than the FAT system that DOS users have to contend with. The Macintosh file system allows file names to be up to 31 characters long and include any character except the colon, even spaces, periods, and other characters not allowed in DOS. It is case-sensitive: ThIsFiLe is different than tHiSfIlE to a Macintosh. In addition, the Macintosh file system stores information about the type of file, the application that created it, and a pointer to the file's *resource fork*. The resource fork contains additional information about the file, including how it should look when viewed as an icon on the Mac's graphical desktop and special fonts, drivers, or other executable code that might be needed to use the file.

Because the file system data stored by the Macintosh can easily accommodate FAT-style file names and attributes, there have been several NOSs developed that run on the

Macintosh and support DOS, as well as other Macintosh machines as clients. However, problems with file names can arise when files created by a Macintosh client have to be shared with DOS clients because file names under FAT are much more restricted than under the Macintosh OS. Sometimes, DOS clients are prohibited from accessing files that don't adhere to the FAT file name rules. More often, the NOS performs some type of file name translation whenever a directory is read or a file is accessed by a DOS client.

The High Performance File System. The *High Performance File System (HPFS)*, first introduced with OS/2 version 1.2 and now also available in Windows NT, has extended the FAT file system's capabilities by allowing long file names up to 255 characters and additional information in the root directory, such as file creation, modification, and access dates and times. Also added in HPFS are *access control lists*, which control who can access certain files and directories when used in a multi-user system like a network file server. HPFS allocates disk space in units of one sector (512 bytes). This wastes less disk space.

Compared to FAT, HPFS has several other characteristics that earn it the "High Performance" moniker. First, HPFS tries to store files in one contiguous piece whenever possible. This reduces the fragmentation of files that occurs under FAT and speeds the process of reading files from disk. HPFS also has a distributed sector allocation table instead of one large file allocation table. This allows information about available sectors to be stored near those sectors, reducing disk head travel when the OS is looking for free space. HPFS also offers automatic recovery from some disk errors. When a bad sector is found on the disk, its data is stored in a good sector and a hot-fix table is updated to redirect disk access requests to the new location.

The higher performance and safety of HPFS has made OS/2 a good platform on which to build critical file server applications. Microsoft, IBM, 3Com, and others have all sold NOSs that ran on top of OS/2 and took advantage of the HPFS. As 32-bit CPUs became more widespread, Microsoft LAN Manager and IBM LAN Server began using a 32-bit version of HPFS called HPFS/386, which offered even higher performance and greater safety in a shared file server environment.

Because all the data needed by the FAT file system is also kept by HPFS, it is relatively easy for a NOS running on OS/2 and using HPFS to provide file services to DOS or other clients that expect files to be stored in the FAT file system. Some of the additional attributes and other information that HPFS keeps track of is used by the NOS to control access to files.

Some OS/2-based NOSs support Macintosh clients. The 31-character length of Macintosh file names is easily handled by HPFS, but the Macintosh system is capable of utilizing many non-ASCII characters in its file names that HPFS cannot handle. Macintosh clients, therefore, usually have to restrict their file names to the character set allowed by HPFS.

The Windows NT File System. The hot-fix feature and access control lists of OS/2 are not available in HPFS under Windows NT. However, Microsoft introduced a new file system, *NTFS*, that incorporates these features of HPFS and adds several new features. One major improvement is giving each file both an HPFS-compatible long name and a FAT-compatible short name. This allows DOS applications to see and access files stored on an NTFS volume without translation.

Long file names under NTFS are not case-sensitive, meaning that `This_Long_Filename` is treated the same as `this_long_filename`. However, NTFS does store whatever mixture of uppercase and lowercase characters the file is named with. NTFS long names cannot use the following characters:

> ? " / \ < > * | :

NTFS returns to the cluster allocation scheme of FAT, allowing allocation units of 512, 1024, 2048, or 4096 bytes.

In designing NTFS, Microsoft included fault-tolerant features beyond those in FAT and HPFS. NTFS has a hot-fix feature like HPFS does but goes further in that it doesn't require any specific locations on the disk for any special system files or tables—under FAT and HPFS, if the disk has or develops a bad sector in one of the reserved locations, then the entire disk probably is unusable. NTFS also maintains a record of transactions against the file system and can roll back any changes that were not completed because a client lost its connection to the server or because a server disk crashed. One feature that NTFS does not have, unfortunately, is the ability to undelete files that are normally, but mistakenly, deleted.

The NetWare File System. Novell has continuously enhanced the NetWare file system, adding important new features to each of the various incarnations of the NOS. Because NetWare is a special-purpose OS designed to function as a server in a client/server environment, its file system has features specifically designed to support a variety of clients. In this section, we'll examine the NetWare 3.x file system in some detail and then briefly describe some of the new features in the NetWare 4.x file system.

The basic file system in NetWare 3.x shares many features with the FAT file system used in DOS. There is a file allocation table, although it can now have as many as entries as needed, rather than be limited to 64K, as under the FAT system. To avoid the performance penalty experienced with FAT due to excessive head travel on large volumes, NetWare reads the entire FAT into memory when the volume is mounted. NetWare has selectable cluster sizes (called *blocks*) ranging from 4K up to 64K. Larger block sizes allow for faster performance with lower memory requirements but increase the amount of wasted space left over in blocks containing small files.

A NetWare volume has a *directory entry table* (*DET*) that stores information about all of the files and directories on the volume. The DET is divided into 4K blocks, each with 32 128-byte entries called *nodes*. DET blocks are cached in memory as they are accessed. NetWare 3.x supports volume sizes of up to 32 terabytes (1 terabyte = 1,000 gigabytes), and each volume can have as many as two million nodes in the DET. On a newly created volume, the DET is small, but it grows on demand as files and directories are created on the volume.

There are three types of nodes in the DET: directory nodes, file nodes, and trustee nodes. Every directory on the volume has at least one *directory node*, which includes such information as the directory name, creation date and time, owner ID, a link to the parent directory, a link to the beginning of the associated FAT chain, directory attributes, and security information such as the *inherited rights filter* and *trustee assignments*.

Similarly, every file on the volume has at least one *file node*, which records the following: file name, owner ID; creation, access, and modification dates and times; a link to the parent directory; file attributes; and similar security information.

The third type of node, the *trustee node*, is used as an extension to store additional security information that doesn't fit in the primary file and directory nodes.

The FAT and DET structures contain enough information for NetWare to manage disk space; provide a high level of fault tolerance, error detection, and correction through hot-fix and *transaction tracking* (covered in greater detail in chapter 8, on "Novell NetWare"); and also serve files to DOS clients and others using the FAT file system. Novell describes this by saying that the *DOS name space* is native to NetWare. This does not mean that NetWare uses the same FAT file system as DOS and that all of the features of the FAT file system are supported as a subset of NetWare's native file system. To a DOS client, as long as the same ends are accomplished, the means to those ends are irrelevant. In fact, the NetWare 3.x file system goes well beyond DOS's FAT file system in the types of attributes that files and directories can have, in maintaining access control and security information as part of the file system, and in allowing deleted files to be salvaged long after they were deleted.

A unique feature of the NetWare file system is that additional name space support modules are included and can be used as options on any NetWare volume. Perhaps the most commonly used name space module is the one for the Macintosh file system. When this is loaded, it adds all the features of the Macintosh file system to the NetWare file system, and makes these features available to Macintosh clients. The Macintosh name space, along with other included software, enables a NetWare file server to appear to Macintosh clients as a native Macintosh (also known as an AppleShare) server.

When the Macintosh name space is added to a NetWare volume, all files and directories on that volume are given a second entry, or node, in the DET. This node contains some of the same data as the original DOS name space node—dates, times, and trustees. It also contains data specific to the Mac name space, such as a 31-character file name or folder name, and a pointer to the FAT chain containing the file's resource fork if it has one. The two nodes for a particular file are linked so that if either type of client accesses the file, the common information in both nodes is updated. This allows a Mac client, for example, to modify a document originally created on a DOS machine and still preserve all the DOS-specific information that NetWare stores about that file.

The other name space module that is supplied with NetWare 3.x is that for HPFS. This allows OS/2 clients to transparently access files either locally or on a NetWare file server and share data with DOS and Macintosh clients on the same server. The HPFS name space is also used to support the long file names that are a feature of Windows 95. While not as innovative as NTFS, Windows 95's file system simultaneously maintains an 8.3 DOS-style file name in addition to long file names with the same restrictions as in Windows NT. Both file names are retained on a NetWare volume with HPFS name space support added.

Novell also offers two additional name space modules as parts of other add-on products. These are for NFS, the UNIX standard file system, and FTAM, used in OSI-based networks. NetWare supplies support for these various name spaces as optional modules because the addition of each name space substantially increases the amount of memory required to maintain the file system. Name spaces should only be added to volumes on which those particular file types are to be stored. Although any or all of the supplied name space modules can be added to the same volume, this practice is not recommended for this reason.

The NetWare file system has other features that are useful in a file-serving environment. NetWare uses all available RAM not taken up by other processes to cache recently accessed data. It also uses an *elevator seeking algorithm* to organize and prioritize disk read and write requests to minimize head movement. NetWare tries to read ahead on large sequential files when client activity indicates that this data will be requested soon. This allows these requests to be served out of memory instead of requiring additional disk accesses. NetWare can evenly distribute read requests across mirrored or duplexed disk pairs, potentially doubling the overall file system throughput.

When Novell introduced NetWare 4.0, it also introduced an improved file system that includes all the features of NetWare 3.x, plus several important new ones:

- Larger default block sizes
- Block suballocation
- File compression
- Data migration

A larger block size allows more of a file to be read in a single disk read request and reduces the amount of memory required to manage a given volume size. Instead of wasting the entire unused portion of a partially used disk block, NetWare 4.x divides these blocks into 512-byte suballocation blocks. These suballocation blocks are used to share the block with the "leftover" ends of other files.

NetWare 4.x introduces an integrated file compression system that can increase available disk space by as much as 63%, according to Novell. Individual files and directories can be included or excluded from the compression, and the length of time that a file remains unused before being eligible for compression can be varied. With the proper hardware, NetWare 4.x can also automatically migrate seldom-used files to less expensive mass storage media, such as optical disks or tape.

Thus, you can see that a NOS's file system must be considerably more versatile than that of a workstation's OS. In addition to supporting different types of clients, it must also be able to maintain performance levels for far greater amounts of storage space. To the client, however, what is important is not how these tasks are accomplished but simply that they are.

File Sharing. When developing a multi-user file system, a lot of attention must be given to either preventing concurrent access to a particular file or allowing concurrent access while protecting the file from multiple attempts to change it. Otherwise, many situations will arise in which files are damaged or data is lost.

As an example, suppose that client A's PC reads a file from the server into an editing program. While client A is working on the data in the PC's memory, client B's PC reads the same file into an editing program and makes some changes. Client B saves the edited file back to the server, overwriting the original contents of the file. Later, client A saves his version of the changed file back to server, believing that he also is overwriting the original contents of the file. In fact, client A has overwritten the edited file saved by client B, thereby wiping out client B's changes.

Network-aware versions of programs such as word-processors and spreadsheets can detect situations such as these and prevent data from being lost. Because file serving systems in use today allow a client to treat files on a remote, shared disk just like files on a local disk, programs that are designed for use on stand-alone systems usually do not change their behavior on a network client, sometimes damaging files and losing data.

Multitasking, single-user OSs such as Microsoft Windows and OS/2 allow multiple applications to be run simultaneously on a single PC, potentially leading to several applications accessing the same file on a local disk. This can be just as dangerous as multiple users accessing the same file on a remote server's disk.

A variety of methods are used by both client and NOSs to prevent multiple clients or applications from simultaneously accessing files in ways likely to result in lost data. To illustrate how those methods are used, we will look at several examples. Most of the examples use DOS as a client and NetWare as a file server because these are by far the most commonly used client and server. Other client and server OSs have similar capabilities.

Single- and Multi-User File Access Methods. PC OSs have well-defined file access methods for use by applications and utility programs. DOS versions since 3.1, for example, use both access codes and sharing modes, along with file attributes, to control file access by multiple applications or users. Every time an application opens a file through DOS, it must explicitly set both an access code and a sharing mode.

Access codes allow an application to open a file for read access, write access, or both, depending on the application's needs. If an application attempts to open a file for write access or read/write access and the file has the read-only attribute bit set to 1 (True), the attempt fails. This should result in a helpful error message displayed to the user.

Sharing modes control access from other applications by allowing the opening application to deny write access, read access, or both kinds of access to other applications. An application can open a file with a deny read/write mode that prevents any other application from opening the file until the first application closes it. If an application uses the deny write mode, other applications or users can read or view the file, but are not allowed to change it in any way. This has practically the same effect as setting the read-only attribute on the file and often generates the same error message in an application that attempts to write to the file when not allowed to do so.

DOS-based NOSs, such as peer-to-peer networks, have to rely on the DOS file access control methods and good programming practices to develop the applications used on them. There is no explicit security at the file system level. When files are stored on a file server with a more sophisticated file system like HPFS, NTFS, or NetWare, however, security features such as access control lists are included as an integral part of the file system. As long as a file server is physically secure, the file system security on the server usually cannot be compromised by a client unless that client knows the logon name and password of a privileged user.

In HPFS, each file is represented in the directory structure by an entry 512 bytes long that contains the file name, location on the disk of the first sector of the file, and a list of permissions associated with the file. More extensive access control can be accomplished with the use of *extended attributes*. Each file can have up to 64K of extended attributes, and NOSs running on OS/2 can define their own uses for them.

The file systems in NetWare versions 3.x and 4.x provide extensive and flexible security features. Novell's terminology differs from that of other NOSs, though the same basic concepts apply. Instead of granting various permissions over files and directories to users and groups, users and groups are made *trustees* of directories and files with associated *trustee rights*.

Trustee rights flow downward from parent directories to subdirectories and files through a process called *inheritance*. For example, if a user is granted certain rights to a directory, then that user also has those same rights to any files and subdirectories below that directory. The inheritance of these rights can be blocked, however, through the use of an *inherited rights filter* (*IRF*). The IRF blocks specific rights from being passed down to subdirectories. Only by explicitly granting the user rights to those subdirectories can the filter be bypassed.

A NetWare user's *effective rights* to a file or directory are therefore dependent on a combination of several factors, including the user's individual trustee assignments to the object and its parents minus any rights blocked by an IRF.

File attributes are used often as additional protection against mistakes. Executable files, including overlays, dynamic link libraries (DLLs), fonts, and drivers on a NetWare file server may often be flagged with the Read-Only and Sharable attributes. This prevents any accidental change or deletion of the file but allows multiple users simultaneous read access.

Automatic and Manual File Locking. The default settings that DOS uses in creating, opening, and modifying files allow for certain automatic protections against lost data. Files usually are created as read/write instead of read-only. Other default attributes are non-system and non-hidden. When such a file is created by a DOS client on a NetWare file server, it is flagged non-sharable by default. When a DOS application or utility opens such a file for write or read/write access, any other application using default settings is unable to open the file except for read-only access for as long as the first application has the file open.

This level of automatic *file locking* usually prevents lost data even from programs that are not network-aware and from common user and programmer errors. For example, another user is prevented from erasing, copying over, or renaming a file you have opened in this default mode because any of those actions would require the file to be opened with write or read/write access.

To allow the maximum sharing of data while protecting it from loss and damage, many applications initially open a file such as a word processing document or spreadsheet in read-only mode. Often the file is closed once the data is read into memory. Only when the application is about to save changes to disk is the mode changed to allow writing. At an even greater level of sophistication, some applications see if another user has modified the file since it was first opened, by checking the date and time stamp on the file, and will not allow another user's changes to be overwritten. Protection at this level relies heavily on the intentions and achievements of the programmers who created your applications.

Rather than relying on the default protection of automatic file locking, many applications take a more aggressive approach to protecting data. For example, a word processing program might initially open a file containing a document for read/write access, with the sharing mode set to deny write access to other users, and keep the file open as long as the user is editing it. If other users attempt to open the same file using this application, they get a message telling them that someone else already has the file open and offering to either create a copy of the file or open the file in read-only mode—either of these actions requires only read access. Just as with automatic file locking, it is up to the programmers of an application to ensure that the correct modes are used to achieve the desired results.

Sharable Files and Transactions. Sometimes an application requires multiple users to have simultaneous read and write access to a particular file—this is common for database and accounting applications. In this case, the application must open its data files with a read/write access code and a deny sharing mode. These files must be flagged sharable in NetWare. Usually, such an application has some internal method of keeping track of who is allowed to change each record or part of the file.

Even when this is not the case, NetWare can provide some protection using a method known as *transaction tracking*. Files stored on a NetWare file server can have a special *Transactional* (*T*) attribute set. When this is set, the NetWare NOS keeps track of all changes a particular client makes to the file. Only changes made between valid file open events and file close events by that client are permanently saved to the file.

If a client opens a file, makes some changes to it, and then crashes or otherwise ends abnormally without closing the file, NetWare's transaction tracking system detects the abnormal end and undoes all the changes made by the client in that session since the last time the client opened the file.

Transaction tracking also comes into play when problems occur on the server. If a volume is dismounted for any reason, unfinished transactions on any files flagged T are backed out (that is, returned to their original state) by NetWare the next time the volume is mounted.

Page, Block, or Record Locking. When several clients might be updating data in a file at the same time, some means of locking portions of the file for the brief time those portions are being updated is required. Safe multi-user file access in a database or accounting application relies even more on correct programming than full file locking does. PC OSs allow any part of a file to be locked by specifying the beginning and length of a byte range. When an application is finished updating the file it should unlock the same range. While the range is locked, other users and applications can neither read nor write data in that area of the file. A database application programming language usually has functions that automatically calculate the values needed by the OS to lock particular records, freeing the programmer from having to develop routines to calculate these values.

Programmers do, however, still have to avoid the situation of *deadlocks*. Suppose that client A locks record 101 in a certain file for the purpose of updating the record. Client B locks record 201 in a different file for the purpose of updating that record. If client A needs to read some information from the record that client B has locked to complete its update of record 101, and client B needs to read some information from the record that client A has locked to complete its update, then both clients will be denied the read access they need to finish their transaction. If both clients keep retrying the read, waiting for the other to finish and release its lock, they will be stuck forever in a classic deadlock. This is a very simple example of a deadlock; the situation can become much more complicated with numerous clients at different times starting and stopping transactions that affect a large number of files. To prevent such problems, one of the clients has to detect a deadlock and respond to the situation in some other way, perhaps by aborting its entire transaction and releasing all of its locks.

To enable DOS support for application *range locking* within files on a local disk, the DOS command SHARE.EXE, included with DOS versions since 3.1, must be executed before the application is launched. If the programs that will be doing the sharing and locking are Windows programs, then a Windows device driver, VSHARE.386, can be used instead of the DOS TSR SHARE.EXE. The VSHARE.386 driver has been available from Microsoft since late 1992, when it was released as part of Windows for Workgroups 3.11.

When loaded, SHARE.EXE or VSHARE.386 maintains a table in memory recording which areas of the file have been locked and by which applications and users. The OS refers to this table before executing any file read or write requests and causes such requests to fail if the relevant region of the file is already locked. This usually is sufficient for running multiple applications on a stand-alone DOS or Windows machine or a DOS machine that is sharing its disk with other PCs in a peer-to-peer network.

Because SHARE.EXE keeps its table of locks in conventional memory, which is always a scarce resource, only enough memory to track 20 locks is reserved by default. Many applications that require SHARE.EXE to be loaded do not work with such a small number of available locks; Microsoft recommends increasing this number to 500 or more (using the /L:500 parameter) if sufficient memory is available. VSHARE.386 runs in the Enhanced Mode of Windows, and therefore has much greater memory resources available to it, including virtual memory. Because of this, VSHARE.386 does not have any arbitrary limit on the number of locks it can handle at once; it merely allocates memory as needed for the number of locks required.

Some Windows programs such as Microsoft Access are designed to work with VSHARE.386, and therefore expect to be able to utilize many more record locks at once than would be feasible with SHARE.EXE. This can present some problems with NOSs that only try to emulate the older, more limited behavior of SHARE.EXE for DOS clients, such as NetWare versions 2.2 and 3.11. Microsoft Access is known to cause NetWare 3.11 server crashes under certain circumstances when accessing files on the server. The currently shipping versions of NetWare do not have these problems, and older versions can be patched to avoid them.

When the file in question is stored on a remote file server, the DOS mechanism for range locking must still function correctly. This requires the NOS to keep track of all lock and unlock requests from every client and allow file reads and writes of a locked portion of the file only by the client that requested the lock. In addition, the NOS should detect when a client workstation crashes or stops processing without properly clearing its locks and should clear the locked regions of the file that were reserved by that workstation without manual intervention by the system administrator.

The concerns of network file systems clearly involve a good deal more than just transporting files from one place to another and servicing the applications running at the top of the OSI model. They must also be concerned with the way in which services are provided to individual workstation clients at the session and presentation layers to ensure that the needs of the different users do not cause conflicts that can corrupt important data.

Printer Sharing

Providing every computer user in an office with a separate printer is an expensive proposition, and yet almost every user needs access to one. The sharing of printers has been one of the most rudimentary services expected from a LAN ever since its inception. In fact, even before business networks became commonplace, there were many fairly sophisticated *printer sharing* devices on the market that allowed printers to be accessed by multiple computers using standard serial or parallel ports.

Some of these devices polled each computer in rapid succession to see if it had data to be printed and then sent PRINTER BUSY signals to the other computers while one was printing. A better design incorporated a large memory buffer, allowing the device to accept print data from more than one computer at a time and then feed it to the printer in proper order.

The process of printing to a network printer, as shown in figure 2.12, is in most cases very much like using a printer sharing device that incorporates a large memory buffer. Instead of being directly connected to a printer with a cable, the client computer sends its printer output to another device—a print queue directory or print spooler file on a file server—in a process called *print spooling*. The print queue or print spooler collects the data until the client is finished printing, then feeds it out to the printer in a steady stream in a process called *despooling*. This all is done under the control of a *print server*, which can take the form of a software program running on the file server, on another PC, or within the printer itself. The print server manages the print output from many different clients, ensures that each individual print job is handled correctly and separately, and provides administrative services to printer users and managers.

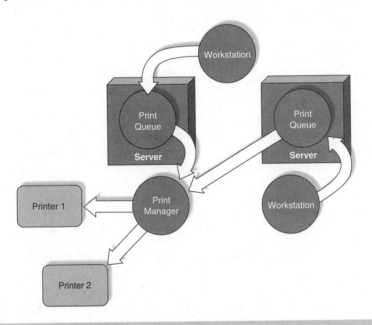

Figure 2.12

This is a simple network printing model.

While the whole process sounds simple enough, network printing is at least as complicated as the interaction of file systems. As with network data storage, a workstation must very often be fooled into thinking that it is interacting with a locally attached printer. In addition to this, however, the printer itself must also be fooled into thinking that it is dealing with a single attached workstation. Given that, even on a small network, several different types of printers may be connected to a single print server, with a multitude of different workstation types attempting to use them, the task of managing all of this activity can be very problematic indeed.

Network printing differs from network file storage in another significant way, as well. Because network users usually can't access their local hard drives and the files themselves are invisible in any case, it doesn't look or feel very different to access a file on drive Z, which may be miles away, than it does to access a file on drive C, which resides in the user's own computer.

Network and local printers are very different, though. If users have a local printer, they know it. It's usually big, ugly, too noisy, and users can reach out and touch it. It probably has a label on the front that says what type of printer it is, helping users to pick the correct print drivers in their applications. A local printer provides immediate feedback as to whether the job was successful or not, and an unsuccessful printing attempt often has a very visible cause—the printer is out of paper, offline, not turned on, and so on—that can be remedied by the average user.

A network printer also is probably big, ugly, and noisy—usually even more so—but users often can't reach right out and touch it. Because clients don't print directly to the printer but instead print to a queue or spooler file, there may be little or no indication of what type of printer the job will end up on, and there might be no feedback to the user indicating when the job is complete or whether it was successful.

Confusing the issue even more is that different NOS vendors use different terms to refer to the same things, and sometimes use the same term to refer to different things. For example, what is called a *print queue* in NetWare, LAN Manager, LAN Server, and Windows 95 is called a *printer* in Windows NT Advanced Server and is called a *spool directory* in Windows for Workgroups. A *print server* in NetWare is a *printer share* in Windows NT, a *print subsystem* in Windows 95, and a *print manager* or *print spool* in LAN Manager, LAN Server, and Windows for Workgroups. Almost every vendor calls an actual physical printer a *printer*, except for Windows NT Advanced Server, which calls it a *printing device*. Of course, there are several different naming conventions and styles for all these objects and devices, but there is no requirement that these names be in any way meaningful to users. It is usually left up to the LAN administrator to devise a means that can be used to identify the various printers to the unsophisticated network user.

NetWare Print Queues. In discussing network print services we will use Novell's terminology as defined in NetWare 2.2 and 3.x, not because it is any more correct than the terms used by other NOSs, but because it is consistent and familiar to more people. Equivalent concepts and terms used by other networking systems will be defined when appropriate.

Network printing begins at the client workstation. Most DOS and Windows applications don't understand network print queues and printer redirection any more than they do network server and volume names. They know only about LPT1, LPT2, and LPT3, the common physical printing ports on PCs. Therefore, the first step is to use some method to ensure that printer output from an application will actually go to a network printer instead of a local one. This is the same sort of resource redirection that occurs when files are accessed from network drives. In NetWare, the MAP command is used to assign a local workstation drive letter to a network volume for the duration of a session, and the CAPTURE command likewise redirects printer output to the network interface until the command is countermanded or the network connection closed. A typical usage is

```
CAPTURE LPT1 /S=SERVER1 /Q=PRINTQ_0
```

This redirects any output intended for LPT1 to the print queue directory named PRINTQ_0 on the NetWare server named SERVER1. The CAPTURE command has several other parameters that can be used to modify the look of the printed output and provide administrative services, such as banner pages identifying the originator of the print job.

Under NetWare versions 2.2 and 3.x, network printing is redirected explicitly to a print queue, which is nothing other than a subdirectory on a file server. Because the print output of a client is simply stored in a file, users are able to print from their applications even when the physical printer they intend to use might not be available because it is out of paper, offline, or malfunctioning. Several clients can print to the same print queue at the same time; each client's print job is stored in a uniquely named file in the queue directory. The job is not sent to the printer until the client application is finished printing and the file is closed. The print queues on a particular server need to have been defined ahead of time by the system administrator.

This first step is where a lot of network printing problems arise. Many circumstances can prevent a print job from immediately reaching the printer. Users might not realize what the problem is, so they might reprint jobs many times in the hope that one of them will actually print. Once the printing problem is resolved by the system administrator or help desk, all the copies of the print job that the user generated might print.

Another common problem occurs when a user chooses the wrong printer driver, or an application is configured to expect a certain type of printer but the client's printer port is redirected to a queue serviced by a different type of printer. Sending a print job with a graphic intended for a LaserJet to a dot matrix printer, or vice versa, often results in many pages of useless random characters. When this happens at a local printer, it is usually noticed right away and the print job aborted. A network printer often is in a different room or location than the client PC, however, and often is in a room with no people around. In addition, the user often will not hold a sufficient security clearance to directly manipulate a network print queue. Hundreds of pages of garbage might print out before an administrator notices the existence of a problem.

NetWare Print Servers. The next step in the printing process is that a print server assigned to service this particular print queue notices the new file in the queue directory, and begins reading the file from disk. The print server is a software application that can be running in one of several places. Novell supplies print server software that can run on the NetWare server, a dedicated PC, or a NetWare bridge/router. Several companies also manufacture dedicated print servers—these may take the form of a small cabinet that has a network interface and one or more printer connections or an expansion card that installs into a slot within the printer itself. In either case, the print server is actually a small computer running NetWare-compatible print server software.

The convenience of this latter solution has made print server cards, especially the JetDirect line made by Hewlett Packard, a very popular means of networking printers. Once the card has been configured, one simply plugs a network connection directly into the printer and turns it on. The printer is then automatically logged on to the appropriate server, and the hardware is ready to go.

Whatever form it takes, the print server software is configured by the system administrator when it is installed. This involves defining one or more printers to be handled by the print server, and assigning print queues to printers. The dedicated print servers previously mentioned usually can only service printers connected directly to them. In the case of a card installed directly in a printer, only that printer can be managed by the server. External print servers have from one to three printer ports where you can attach printers to be managed by the server.

The print server software included with NetWare versions 2.x and 3.x can manage up to 16 printers. This software may be running on the NetWare server itself as an NLM, which does not take up a licensed connection. It may also be running on a PC dedicated to this job, which must be logged on to all file servers that contain print queue directories to be serviced.

Network Printers under NetWare. Network printers either can be directly attached to the computer running the print server software or can be remote printers. Remote printers can be attached to DOS, Windows, or OS/2 workstations that run RPRINTER.EXE, a small DOS TSR program. RPRINTER runs in the background on the workstation, and moves print jobs from the print server to the printer port. It can notify the print server if the printer has an error condition such as being out of paper or offline. The print server in turn can be configured to notify one or more users or groups that there is a printer problem.

To further confuse the issue, many of the dedicated print servers mentioned earlier can be configured to operate in Remote Printer mode. This allows them to be managed by a different print server without needing to take up one of the concurrent logons allowed by your NetWare license. A single print server can service queues on up to eight different file servers at once. This allows users on different file servers to share a printer without needing to be logged on to the file server where the print server is located. All they need to do is redirect their printer output to a queue located on their default file server.

Printing Security. In most NOSs, printing services have several security features. When a print queue is created in NetWare, the group EVERYONE is automatically assigned rights as a queue user and is allowed to place print jobs in a queue. The group EVERYONE can be removed as a queue user, and other groups or individual users can be added. This feature comes in handy when there are special-purpose printers to which only a few people should have access, such as a printer in Accounting used to print checks.

Other network systems have access control lists containing the users and groups allowed to use certain printers and might allow a password to be assigned to a shared printer. When users try to use such a printer, they are prompted for the password and must enter it correctly.

Similarly, the user Supervisor is made the default *queue operator*. Queue operators can open and close the queue, rearrange the order in which queued jobs will print, delete jobs before or while they are printing, and add or remove queue users.

There can be many print queues on several file servers, used by different users running different applications using various printer drivers and special print job configurations, served by multiple print servers, each of which can have many printers. The configuration of print queues, file servers, print servers, and local and remote printers can get quite complex in larger networks. It's no wonder that users often don't know where their print job has gone, or why it comes out looking the way it does.

Of course, as difficult as all this may seem to the user, the many levels of communication needed between the various components of the network printing system are assuredly more complex than she would ever imagine. In the case of NetWare, a special network level protocol called SPX (Sequenced Packet Exchange) is devoted almost entirely to printing-related communications. This is because a high level of reliability is required to deliver data to a printer. A single incorrect character can turn a 50-page report into 150 wasted pages.

Once again, we see the way in which intermediate level network mechanisms service the higher layer processes (such as the applications and printer drivers that generate the printer file) and at the same time are serviced by the lower layer protocols, which deliver the files to the appropriate destination, as ignorant of their contents as postal workers are of the letters they carry.

Network Accounting and Auditing

In addition to services that directly benefit the end user, such as file and print systems, all modern NOSs have built-in accounting services to track network usage. These can be combined with account restrictions to control access to network resources. These systems function at the intermediate levels of the OSI model as well. A user can instruct an application to overwrite a particular file on a network drive, and the Network protocol can deliver the file to the destination, but it is the NOS's accounting and security measures that will intervene between the two and prevent any proscribed activity from being completed.

In addition to those built in to the NOS, there also are add-on network management packages that can supplement or replace these services. A network administrator can measure, record, and control such events as

- User logons and logoffs
- Disk space used by specific users and groups
- Network traffic generated (in packets, bytes, or both)
- Print jobs sent to network printers
- Number of pages printed
- Applications used, including when and for how long

NetWare has a great many options available for network accounting and auditing, although other NOSs are catching up fast. Fueling the push to further develop these network features is the growing realization that installing and maintaining network services has many hidden costs. The majority of the expenses associated with a network occur after it has been installed.

No matter how much future growth is assumed when a network is designed, users always seem to deplete resources faster than anticipated, creating chronic shortages of disk space and bandwidth. Constant and rapid expansion of the network's capacity in response to the ever-growing demand is not economically feasible for most organizations, yet controlling network usage requires knowing who is using what resources and how much. Many organizations require detailed justifications for capital expenditures for new equipment; also, some organizations need to charge back to individual departments a proportionate amount of the expense of shared resources such as the phone system and computer network. Network accounting and auditing services make the processes easier and more accurate.

Some of the auditing and control features of NetWare are built into NetWare's security system. For example, logon times can be restricted to normal working hours, and particular users can be restricted to certain workstations. By using NetWare accounting services, complete records can be maintained of when and where users log on and off. Similarly, disk space usage can be limited for individual users and in specific directories. This can help postpone the nearly inevitable need to expand disk storage on a server. The number of blocks of data written to and read from network disks by each user over a period of time can be recorded, and network traffic statistics can be broken down by user.

New in NetWare 4.x is a type of user called an *auditor*. The auditor can monitor almost any kind of event or resource usage on a network, including such events as file and directory creations or deletions, trustee rights modifications, or any change to a user account, without needing the kind of rights usually reserved for a system administrator or supervisor. Indeed, the feature is specifically designed to be independent from the role of the administrators so that they too can be supervised when necessary.

Local Area Network Communications Applications

File and printer sharing were the basis for the conception and acceptance of the LAN in the business world. However, the ubiquitous presence of the enterprise network and the communications capabilities that are inherent in a LAN have, in recent years, given rise to a class of network applications and services that are rapidly becoming indispensable in the business world.

E-Mail. The first specifically LAN-oriented application to be developed, and the most common one today, is electronic mail (e-mail). All e-mail programs allow a user to type a message at a workstation, designate one or more recipients, and send the message on its way. The message is delivered to each recipient's mailbox, where it can be viewed, filed, forwarded, replied to, or simply discarded.

If the sender and recipient both have access to the same file server or *electronic post office*, the message may be delivered by the sender's e-mail application itself by writing to a file on the server where the receiver's e-mail application will look for new messages. This is similar to one person putting a note in a neighbor's mailbox, instead of sending it through the postal service. When the sender and receiver don't share access to the same post office, however, a different service must be used to deliver the mail. Depending on the vendor, this service may be called a *mail hub, messaging server, message handling service, message transfer agent, mail router*, or some other name.

Communication between users of different, incompatible mail systems is made possible by the use of *gateways* that translate messages from one format to another. Messages can be delivered to distant recipients over a WAN or with the use of mail hubs or routers using modems to communicate over dialup lines. E-mail is the primary reason for the establishment of a WAN in many organizations.

Many PC e-mail applications allow word processing documents and other files to be sent along with a message as an *attachment*. Many programs include several viewers so that commonly used document types can be read without running the program used to create the attachment. Messages can also have *return receipts* requested so that the sender is notified when a recipient reads the message.

One of the common administrative problems with e-mail systems is the task of address book or directory maintenance and synchronization. As new users are added to a LAN, and other users are removed, many e-mail systems require the same changes to be made manually to the e-mail address book. Some e-mail programs have utilities that attempt to periodically update their address book with changes in the network's user database. These have varying degrees of success. Synchronizing changes between post offices to maintain an up-to-date corporate-wide address book is another area where a lot of administrative work is usually involved, although some e-mail vendors are attempting to address this problem. The biggest nightmare in corporate-wide e-mail systems is that different programs might be in use in different locations. Gateways are available to successfully deliver mail to another system, but very little has been done by anyone to enable automatic synchronization of address books or user directories between systems from different vendors.

The recent growth of Internet services opens the bounds of e-mail beyond the enterprise. Many corporate users are now accustomed to corresponding with clients and associates around the globe on a regular basis. Many even require the same file attachment services over Internet e-mail links, which compounds the administrator's headaches enormously.

Group Scheduling. E-mail can be used to eliminate some of the phone tag and multiple back-and-forth calls often necessary to schedule a meeting with several people. The person organizing the meeting simply sends a message to all participants, giving the meeting topics, date, time, and place. The participants respond whether they are available for the meeting or rearrange their schedules if the person requesting the meeting has sufficient authority.

Even with e-mail, finding a time when every member of a large group of people is available can be a hit-or-miss proposition and can end up taking more time than the meeting itself. *Group scheduling* software has been developed to address this problem. Several packages are on the market; some e-mail programs include a group scheduling module, but with others it must be purchased separately. In many cases, the group scheduling program can be made to work through an existing e-mail system for meeting notifications, requests, and confirmations.

A typical group scheduling application works like this: the person trying to organize a meeting creates an event. They may specify the participants, date, time, location, purpose, and duration of the meeting, or only a few of these items. The application examines the schedules of all the participants to see if they are available at the time specified, or might suggest a date and time when all the participants have a free time period long enough to accommodate the desired meeting duration. The program also might be able to check for conference room availability, as well as reserve other resources (overhead projector, screen, coffee pot, and so on) for the meeting.

In order for the application to be most beneficial, all users must keep their appointments detailed in the program's database, including events that are not scheduled through the program. This allows other users to see what free time they actually have available for meetings. Usually, security features can prevent other users from seeing what actual appointments a particular person may schedule, allowing them only to see what blocks of time are reserved or free. Busy executives often want their assistants to manage their group scheduling just as they manage other appointments, and most group scheduling software allows for this.

Forms-Based Workflow. A large part of the work of any organization is taken up by filling out forms with information, then forwarding them to someone else for reading, consolidation, reporting, or filing. These forms usually are paper-based, costly to design and print, and expensive to store or dispose of after they are used. Putting any information that you consider confidential in a paper form also increases the risk that it might fall into the wrong hands.

If the organization has a network infrastructure that can reach everyone, this paper trail can be reduced. Software programs exist that allow a form to be designed on a computer, and distributed over a network. The forms then can be filled out on-screen by users, and the data in various fields automatically stored in a database for later retrieval and analysis. The forms can have calculated fields—that is, fields that fill themselves in with certain information based on data entered elsewhere on the form. Individual fields may be made read-only or not viewable at all by certain users. Sophisticated forms software includes security features such as digital signatures that can be used to verify the identity of the person entering data, and forms can be sent to designated recipients via e-mail whenever desired.

Summary

As you can see, these communications-related applications are, in most cases, quintessential examples of the client/server paradigm. Users access server-based resources that are modified by workstation processes and delivered back to the server for storage or dissemination to other users. With services like these, we approach the top of the OSI networking model. A front end, or client application, running at the workstation, makes use of a server application that may provide it with database management or message handling services. These server applications then may make use of the security, auditing, and file systems operating at the intermediate levels of the model, which in turn utilize the network, data link, and physical layer protocols to send data to other locations on the network. Each of these systems operates independently, cooperating perfectly, and yet deliberately ignorant of the other's purpose.

This chapter was not intended to present a detailed representation of the OSI reference model. That may be found in chapter 3, "The OSI Model: Bringing Order to Chaos." Nor was it intended to provide complete coverage of network cabling types and data link layer protocols (see chapter 7, "Major Network Types"), specific NOS features (see part III, "Software Platforms: NOSs and Clients"), or printing services (see chapter 23, "Adding

Network Printing"). The intention was to present some of the features and services any or all of which may be operating on a network at any one time. It is sometimes easy to forget that even the simplest tasks are complicated immensely by the need to reduce all communication to a single signal traveling over a copper wire (or some other medium). As you read through the sections of this book that zoom in on particular networking topics to show great detail, never forget the whole picture and the myriad other operations that all contribute the successful operation of the network.

Chapter 3

The OSI Model: Bringing Order to Chaos

The OSI reference model is the product of two independent development projects undertaken by the International Standards Organization (ISO) and the CCITT (which translates from the French as the International Telegraph and Telephone Consultative Committee), beginning in the late 1970s. Two separate documents were produced, each defining a seven-layer model for network communications, but in 1983 the two were combined and eventually published as the ISO 7498 standard. The same document is also available from the Telecommunications Standardization Sector of the International Telecommunications Union (ITU-T0), which is the new name given to the CCITT in 1992. Documents published by this body are known as *recommendations*, and the OSI model recommendation, officially known as The Basic Reference Model for Open Systems Interconnection, is called X.200.

The OSI reference model is a structure that was designed as a general guideline to the various levels of communication that take place in a data network. The model's origins stem from a desire to move away from proprietary implementations of network architectures and develop a set of openly defined protocols that could be used as the components of actual network products. The idea was that by defining in detail the requirements for networked data communications, stratifying those requirements, and then specifically delineating the services provided by each of the strata to the others, a development environment could be realized in which independent teams would work on individual layers, all of which would function properly as a whole when assembled. Thus, in theory, the development time required for such a protocol suite should be far shorter than that of a single, unified effort, providing at the same time a fully documented product. This part of the effort, however, has not materialized exactly as planned. The OSI protocols themselves are still under development, which will very likely continue for many years to come, and products utilizing them are few. The reference model, however, has come to be a widely known learning tool for the basic building blocks of computer networking.

The OSI model is not intended to be a generalization of any particular network type or product, nor are many specific network structures or products designed to conform precisely to the model. Comparisons of the model with the actual network implementations in popular use today are rife with exceptions, discrepancies, and caveats. Its primary value is as a template of the relationships between the various elements needed to transmit data from one computer to another. Systems designed with this template as a general guide are more likely to be able to communicate with each other than if each was created from an entirely independent architecture. The existence of the OSI model thus promotes interoperability between network systems.

At the top of the model, as shown in figure 3.1, is the user interface, that is, the *application* or process that initiates a request for access to a resource located somewhere else on the network. At the bottom of the model is the actual *physical* medium that serves to connect the various entities that comprise the network. A request, generated at the top, or *application layer*, travels down seven layers to the bottom, or *physical layer*. During this process, it is ultimately converted from an API call within the originating application to a series of impulses encoded in such a manner so as to transmit binary information over the network medium to another machine.

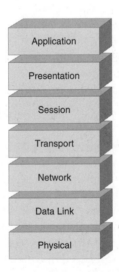

Figure 3.1

The OSI networking reference model splits the communications processes of computer networks into seven distinct layers.

The impulses transmitted over the physical layer can be electrical, optical, magnetic, microwave, or radio carrier frequencies. In traveling downward through the layers of the OSI model, the application request undergoes a number of different encoding processes that are designed to allow specific layers of the model to communicate with their counterpart layers in the destination machine. These processes are called *protocols*. Once having arrived at the destination machine, the impulses undergo the exact same process in reverse, traveling upwards through the model and being decoded until they arrive at the functional equivalent of the topmost layer at the other machine. In this manner, the top operational layers of both computers can interact transparently, functioning as though the networked resources that they are accessing are no different from those available within the local machine. This is the basis for networking compatibility. An application running on a network workstation need not be aware that the files it is accessing are located elsewhere on the network. The functionality of the OSI model is thus completely invisible to the user interface.

The different protocols used by a single computer network may be proprietary products of a single manufacturer, or they may be open standards, developed and governed by committees composed of employees of many different companies, or they could be a mixture of the two. Such committees, like the *Institute of Electrical and Electronics Engineers (IEEE)*, the American National Standards Institute (ANSI), and even ISO exist for no other purpose than to define and publish standards by which competing manufacturers can develop products that are capable of operating with each other.

In the early days of computer networking proprietary systems were recognized as inherently counter-productive. The computer industry is a highly volatile one, and for a consumer to invest large sums of money on networking equipment that is the product of a single corporation, which cannot be used with the products of any other corporation, is very risky. There are relatively few firms that have the resources to manufacture all of the hardware and software components that comprise a computer network. Interoperability fosters healthy competition and encourages users to purchase equipment that they know will continue to be viable, even if the original manufacturer does not remain so.

The OSI reference model makes no distinctions concerning the actual protocols used to transmit data over the network medium or the equipment used to do it. It is intended to be an illustration of computer networking in its most abstract form, and networks composed of computers using radically different microprocessors, operating systems, and communications protocols can all conform to the model to some degree. Therefore, the purpose of this chapter is not to define the protocols or the hardware used in any great detail beyond identifying the layers at which they operate, although it would be quite possible to use the OSI model as the basic outline for this entire book. Many of the components and protocols mentioned here are examined more thoroughly elsewhere, in other chapters, and references will be provided directing the reader to the appropriate locations for further reading.

This chapter is designed to provide an overview of the way in which the often disparate elements of this book can be linked together to provide a functional model for today's business-oriented LAN. We will cover each layer of the OSI reference model, discuss its function in general, and illustrate how it is realized in the actual networking products in use today.

Terminology

One of the greatest problems in discussing the layers of the OSI model and the role that each one plays in network communications is in the nomenclature used to describe the elements formed by each layer. It is often said, for example, that *frames* are generated by the data link layer, *datagrams* by the network layer, *messages* by the application layer, and so on with the term *packet* being used for the communications at almost any layer. These terms often end up being confused and interchanged at will, so I will attempt to set a precedent and define the terms that will be used throughout this book in the hope that others will follow.

In its most basic, overly simplified form, network communications can be broken down into *requests* and *replies*. Most of the traffic found on a typical network will consist of requests generated by users at workstations, and the replies from the resources to whom the requests were directed. The fundamental unit of data that is transmitted over the network is a *packet*. Packets can be of different sizes, depending on their function and on the network type, but it is essential that data be transmitted in some form of discrete unit so that there is a measure of empty space on the network medium between transmissions. This is necessary because, by definition, any station on the network must be allowed to transmit its own data at some time. If communications took the form of an uninterrupted stream of data, there could be no opportunity for multiple stations to utilize the same bandwidth. The only way that this would be possible would be if every station on the network had a dedicated link to every other station. This is called a mesh network, and it is virtually never used, due to its obvious impracticality. (Imagine 50 workstations, each with 49 network interface cards installed in it and 49 wires extending out to each of the other stations).

Therefore, every request and reply generated by a station on the network will be composed of one or more packets. Within each packet, at its core, is a request or the reply to a request. For example, an application at a workstation generates a request to open a file that is stored on a server volume. The server, receiving the request, honors it and replies by sending the file to the workstation. The packets sent by both the server and the workstation contain the actual request for the file and the file itself, sent in reply, but there is also a great deal more data included within those packets. The network must have some means of addressing the packet so that it arrives at the proper destination. There is also usually a means by which the packet can be acknowledged as having been received at its destination, a method for checking that the packet has arrived in the same condition in which it was sent, and a mechanism to ensure that packets are not sent to the destination too quickly. These last three features are known as *guaranteed delivery*, *error checking*, and *flow control*, respectively.

These additional functions are provided by information contained within *frames*, generated by the various layers of the OSI model, which surround the actual request or reply. For our purposes, the term *frame* does not refer to any specific layer of the model. Frame is used in its most literal sense, as a structure that surrounds and contains the original data being transmitted. As we examine the various frames required to get a simple file request from one place to another, you may be surprised to find out that this network overhead, or *control information*, often comprises more actual bytes of data than the request itself. One of the marks of a particular network's efficiency is the amount of communications overhead that is necessary for the transmission of normal network traffic.

As a request travels down the layers of the OSI model, several different frames are added, with each one applied to the outside of the existing structure. In other words, the original request is at the heart of the packet. A succeeding layer then applies its frame, and the request is included as the data field of that frame. A *field* is a discrete group of contiguous bytes within a packet that is used to perform a particular function. For example, the address of the destination node on the network will be in its own field, and each of the network control functions described earlier may also be realized by the inclusion of information in separate fields.

Each one of the frames within a packet, therefore, consists of a header, which is a series of fields added to the front of the packet, followed by the data field which, in this case, consists of the original request generated by the top layer. Depending on the layer and the network type involved, there may or may not be a footer, which is another series of fields appended to the end of the packet. The packet is then sent down to the next layer of the model, which may apply its own frame to the structure, including the existing packet with the previous frame already applied, as its data field.

Once a frame is applied to a packet, nothing disturbs the arrangement of the bytes inside that frame, until the packet reaches its destination. Later manipulations may add additional fields to the outside of the existing structure only. Thus, by the time the packet arrives at the bottom of the model, it consists of the original request, surrounded by a frame, which is surrounded by another frame, and another, and so on, as shown in figure 3.2. Therefore, when discussing the data link layer, at which the last possible frame is applied, what is referred to as its data field actually contains the original request, plus several other upper-layer frames arrayed around it. This framing data, exclusive of the actual request data being carried by the packet, is called the *protocol control information.*

Another way of looking at this process is to approach the construction from the bottom. Picture the lowest data-oriented layer of the model, the data link layer, as producing a data header and a footer, with an empty hole in between, which is its data field. The next layer up, the network layer, provides its own frame that fills the hole, but which contains its own hole within it. Each successive layer fills the hole left by the previous layer until, at the top of the model, the original request generated by the application plugs the final hole, thus creating a single uninterrupted stream of data, which is a packet.

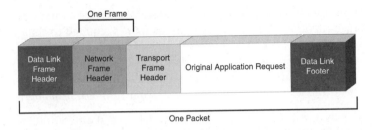

Figure 3.2

A typical network packet consists of an original request, surrounded by several frames, which are applied by successive OSI layers; each frame is composed of several distinct fields.

This concept of applying multiple frames to a single packet leads to further naming problems. Packets are sometimes referred to by the name of the data link frame, such as an Ethernet packet or an 802.5 packet. This is the one frame that is absolutely required for every packet transmitted over a network, and a reference such as this is usually made when an internetwork combines multiple data link types that must be distinguished. However, packets are more often referred to by the frame that defines their primary function, as in an IP, a SAP, or an SPX packet. In nearly all cases, a reference such as this refers to a particular frame that is carried within one or more other frames, including one of the data link frame types mentioned above. Thus, a NetWare SAP packet, for example, may also be called an IPX packet, an 802.2 packet, or an Ethernet packet, with equal validity.

Nowhere is this type of confusion more evident than in the case of NetWare frame types, one of which must be selected when configuring a server for network access. Two of the possible choices, 802.3 and Ethernet II, describe data link frame formats. The two others, 802.2 and Ethernet SNAP, actually refer to higher-level frame types, both of which are carried within an 802.3 frame. Thus, three of the four possible NetWare frame types can actually be correctly referred to as 802.3 frames. This matter is dealt with in greater detail in chapter 8, "Novell NetWare."

The point being made here is that references to specific protocols being used in a particular packet are not necessarily exclusive of all other protocols. Indeed, this is nearly never the case. Virtually every packet being transmitted over the network utilizes at least two different communications protocols, and many use four or five. One of the main purposes of the OSI reference model, and of this chapter, is to identify the layers at which the most commonly used protocols operate and define the ways in which they interact with the other protocols that may be in use at the same time. This knowledge brings the administrator a greater awareness of the nature of the traffic on his network. With the addition of a protocol analysis tool such as LANalyzer or Sniffer, adjustments can be made to the network operating system (NOS) and router parameters that will maximize the efficiency of the network in precisely the areas that need to be addressed.

The Physical Layer

The physical layer of the model, as shown in figure 3.3, consists of the actual medium through which bits are transmitted from one location to another, in other words, the fabric of the network itself. The connection between two network stations may be in the form of copper or some other electrically conductive cable, fiber optic, radio signals, microwaves, lasers, infrared, or any other medium practically suited to the environment. The OSI model makes no distinctions concerning the actual hardware involved, but the physical layer comprises every component that is needed to realize the connection. This includes any and all connectors, hubs, transceivers, network interfaces, and ancillary hardware, as well as the physical medium or cable itself, if any. This layer also includes the environmental specifications necessary to maintain the validity of the medium, as well as the method of signaling used to transmit bits to a remote location.

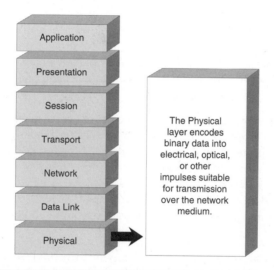

Figure 3.3

The physical layer of the OSI model is usually realized in the form of a cable network connecting separate computers.

Therefore, what we have at the physical layer is the most fundamental element of the communications process. The upper layers of the model reduce the data to be transmitted down to binary code, and it is the sole function of the physical layer to see that those ones and zeroes are transmitted from one location on the network to the next. The physical layer is completely oblivious of the nature of the data that it is transmitting. It is not concerned with packets, frames, addressing, or the ultimate destination of the data. It cannot read the binary code that it is transmitting, beyond a basic awareness of the difference between a zero and a one, which it converts into suitable impulses of electricity or light that can be sent over the network medium. Each transmitting device on the physical layer is aware of nothing but its adjacent neighbors on the network, from whom it receives and to whom it is responsible for sending these impulses, in whatever form they may take.

Each station on the network contains the functional equivalent of a *transceiver* as part of the network interface. As the name implies, a transceiver both receives signals from its nearest upstream neighbor and transmits them to its nearest downstream neighbor. Depending on the nature of the network, these neighbors may be one and the same, but the function is identical.

Physical Layer Media Specifications

As with all of the protocols used in networking, the standard by which the physical layer of the network is constructed can be an open or a proprietary one. The physical layer is more likely to utilize open standards as a guideline for its fabrication, however, for several reasons. The first and most practical, is that the physical realization of a network is usually installed at a site by a contractor who will have little or no involvement with the assembly or maintenance of the rest of the LAN. Even large organizations with extensive in-house network support resources will often outsource large cabling tasks. It is therefore necessary to have an agreed set of standards by which such work is to be done.

The second and more obvious reason is that the utilization of an open standard for the physical layer is more likely to provide alternative uses for the same medium, should substantial changes to the network have to be made. Many office data networks have been constructed using existing telephone cabling, and most new office construction today consolidates the telephone and data networks into a single cable installation. The use of a cabling standard like 10BaseT (detailed in the IEEE 802.3 specification), which is designed to take advantage of the existing skills of telephone cable installation personnel, is clearly a practical and economical advantage.

Because of the wide array of media that can be used at the physical layer, there are a great many published standards used as guidelines for the design and construction of network systems. These may be the product of bipartisan committees like the ISO, or they may be published by individual corporations that advocate the use of particular media. Many of the most common media types used in PC networking today are covered in this book, particularly in chapter 7, "Major Network Types," but this coverage is not meant to be a guide by which a network medium is to be installed.

It is extremely important that the people installing a cabling or transmission system for a data network be fully acquainted with the exact specifications by which that medium should be installed. Aside from the familiar limitations such as segment length and distance between nodes, factors such as proximity to lighting fixtures, electrical, and other services; compliance with local building and safety codes; and licensing with federal agencies must be taken into account.

There are a great many factors involved in a proper physical layer installation, no matter what the medium type. Failure to comply with the appropriate specifications can cause, at the very least, poor network performance, and at most, an extreme safety hazard. Both of these can be very costly to correct after the installation is completed. This is why such installations are frequently outsourced.

If you are attempting to perform such an installation yourself, you should be familiar both with the documents defining the limitations of the data link layer that will be running over the physical medium, such as IEEE 802.3 or 802.5, and with the ANSI/EIA/TIA-568-1991 document, also known as the American National Standards Institute/Electronic Industry Association/Telecommunications Industry Association "Commercial Building Telecommunications Wiring Standard." There are also two technical bulletins with which familiarity may be advised, called "Additional Cable Specifications for Unshielded Twisted Pair Cables," (EIA/TIA Tech Sys Bulletin TSB-36, November 1991), and "Additional Transmission Specifications for UTP Connecting Hardware," (EIA/TIA Tech Sys Bulletin TSB-40A, December 1993). Other standards may apply, depending on the physical medium being installed, and familiarity with local building codes is also advised. These standards documents can be obtained by contacting your local ANSI branch.

Perhaps now the reasons are more obvious for outsourcing physical layer installation work. However, even if you are contracting someone else to do the job for you, you should be sure that they are familiar with the requirements documented in these standards. Compliance with the appropriate specifications should be agreed upon by both parties and included in any contractual agreement. Choosing a subcontractor with adequate insurance is also a good idea.

Signaling Types

Amidst the discussion of all of the other complex protocols used in computer networking, the one that is most often neglected is the most fundamental—that is, the signaling method by which binary code is transmitted over the physical layer. The basic concept is simple: variations in electrical voltage, radio carrier attributes, microwaves, or pulses of light indicate the transition between a zero and a one. The actual construction of such a system presents a number of problems, however, that must be resolved before the communication can be considered reliable.

The first factor to be considered is whether network communications are conducted over an analog or a digital medium. Unbounded (that is, wireless) analog media, such as radio waves, are occasionally used for data networks in cases where physical access between two sites is limited and economic factors make unbounded and bounded digital links impractical. Analog signals can take any value within a specified range. Transition between two values is gradual, and cycles through the entire range, illustrated by the familiar sine wave signal pattern. The encoding of binary data into an analog signal involves the fluctuation of the signal's amplitude, frequency, or phase or a combination of these attributes, shown in figure 3.4. The distance (in signal strength) between the highest and lowest values of the sine curve is the *amplitude*. The distance (in time) between successive occurrences of the signal's highest value is its *frequency*, and two concurrent signals in which the highest values occur at different times are said to differ in *phase*. Regular variations in one or more of these attributes are used to signal the transition between values of zero and one, thus allowing binary data to be encoded. This is called *modulation*, and quite often, more than one of the three attributes is modulated to provide an additional measure of reliability.

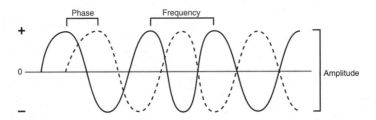

Figure 3.4

Analog signals are used to transmit binary data by modulating one or more of their three primary attributes.

Most computer networks use digital signaling, however, including the coaxial, twisted-pair, and fiber-optic media that comprise the vast majority of business LANs. Digital signals have discrete values (that is, voltages or light pulses) with transitions occurring almost instantaneously. Digital signaling systems can utilize multiple values, but most represent binary code through transitions between a positive and a negative value. A zero value is sometimes used as well.

The primary concern in the accuracy of digital signaling is timing. For the transitions between values sent from a transmitting station to a receiving station to have any significance, both stations must have some means of clocking the frequency of the transitions. Remember, most LAN communications are *asynchronous*—that is, they take the form of bursts of data separated by spaces when no activity occurs. This is done to allow multiple stations equal access to the same network medium. Some signaling types are self-clocking, in that the encoding method includes station synchronizing information as part of the signal, while others require an external timing signal.

For example, the simple signaling scheme illustrated in figure 3.5 utilizes two values, a positive and a negative, which could take the form of positive or negative voltages or the presence or absence of a beam of light. A positive value represents a zero, and a negative represents a one. Thus, binary code can be transmitted using this system, which is called *polar signaling*.

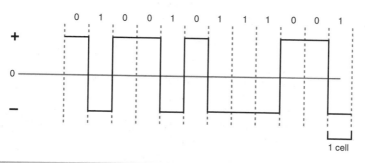

Figure 3.5

Polar coding is the simplest form of binary transmission, but it lacks a timing signal.

The problem with this system becomes evident, though, when two or more consecutive zeroes or ones must be sent. The bit stream is divided into *cells*, which are virtual divisions, each of which contains a single bit of data. When values alternate between zeroes and ones, the transitions delineate the boundaries of the cells. However, two or more cells in a row containing zero bits require no value transitions, and the receiving station has no precise method of tracking exactly how many zero bits are represented by a continuous value during a certain elapsed time.

These value transitions, of course, may be occurring hundreds or thousands of times per second, and the slightest speed fluctuation can turn a binary data stream of this type into mere noise. If an external clocking signal is supplied, indicating to both sender and receiver that bit transitions are to occur once every microsecond, for example, the signaling system is reliable. The cells are clearly delineated, and the recipient simply has to register the value of the signal each microsecond to be sure that the proper bit values are being transmitted.

Supplying an external clocking signal, however, is not a practical alternative for a baseband network (a *baseband* network is one in which a single signal occupies the entire bandwidth of the network medium). Other signaling systems, though, are able to supply a timing signal while they are transmitting data. In figure 3.6, the voltages themselves have no bearing on the values of the data being transmitted. This signaling system, called *Manchester encoding*, has a value transition in the middle of every cell. A transition from low to high indicates a binary value of one, and a high to low transition is equivalent to a zero. The other transitions made at the beginning of the cells exist only to adjust the voltage to the proper position to facilitate the correct mid-bit transition. Some Manchester systems may reverse these values, but this is the signaling scheme used by all Ethernet LANs. Even when several consecutive bits all contain the same binary value, a transition occurs at the midpoint of every cell. This regular and invariable occurrence of a transition is what supplies the timing signal to the receiving node. This type of signaling is also known as *biphase signaling*.

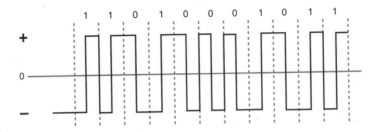

Figure 3.6

Manchester coding is the system used by all Ethernet networks.

Another variation on biphase coding is called *Differential Manchester* (see fig. 3.7). In this system, the voltage of the signal is even more remote from the actual bit value being represented. In this scheme, there is also a midpoint transition in every cell, but it is used only for timing purposes. The bit value of the cell is determined solely by the presence or absence of a transition at the beginning of the cell. The direction of the transition, up or down, is irrelevant. Its existence only denotes a bit value of zero. Its absence indicates a value of one. Differential Manchester encoding is used by token-ring LANs.

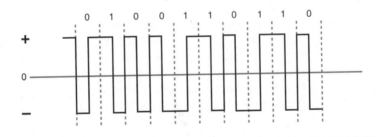

Figure 3.7

Differential Manchester encoding is used primarily by token-ring networks.

The physical layer is clearly the basis upon which the entire OSI reference model rests. It is treated differently from the other layers, in that it concerns matters concrete and visible. As a result, it is fairly common to see a distinct separation between people with extensive expertise in the physical layer, and those who have mastered the intricacies of the upper layer protocols.

The Data Link Layer

As the interface between the network medium and the higher protocols, the data link layer is responsible for the final packaging of the upper-level binary data into discrete packets before it goes to the physical layer. Its frame is outermost on the packet and contains the basic addressing information that allows it to be transmitted to its destination. The data link layer also controls access to the network medium (see fig. 3.8). This is a crucial element of local area networking because dozens of workstations may be vying for use of the same medium at any one time. Were all of these stations to transmit their packets simultaneously, the result would be chaos. Protocols operating at this layer may also provide other services, such as error checking and correction and flow control.

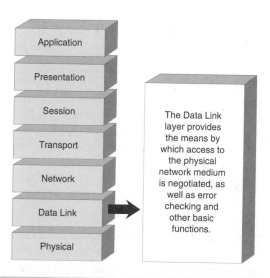

Figure 3.8

The data link layer of the OSI model applies the outermost frame to every packet transmitted.

The protocols used at the data link layer are sometimes incorrectly referred to as topologies. In actuality, a *topology* refers to the way that each station on the network is connected to the other stations. A single cable, stretched from one station to the next and terminated at each end is called a *bus topology*. Joining these two ends forms a *ring topology*. Connections extending from each workstation to a single access point, or *hub*, is known as a *star topology*. The *mesh* system described early in this chapter is another example of a topology. The actual protocols used at this layer of the model are frequently associated with specific topologies, hence the terminology confusion. Various combinations and hybrids of these topologies are also frequently used.

The most popular data link layer protocols in use today for local area networking are Ethernet and token ring. These are sometimes referred to (again, incorrectly) as *media types*. ARCnet and FDDI are also data link protocols, as are obsolete architectures like StarLAN and LattisNet. As is often the case, these protocols are available in various flavors that have different origins. Ethernet has always been based on open standard, the product of bipartisan committees, while Token Ring was originally developed by IBM, who continues to be its greatest champion.

The documents defining these protocols consist primarily of one or more physical layer specifications, a media access control mechanism, and a definition of the fields that comprise the protocol frame. This is just the first of many instances in which the functions of the various OSI model layers overlap. Cabling specifications seem to clearly belong to the physical layer, but in fact, the way that the cable is installed is a direct result of the limitations imposed by the data link protocol's media access control function and the nature (and particularly the length) of the frame being transmitted. These matters are more easily understood when a specific protocol is being discussed. The architecture and functionality of these protocols is dealt with specifically and at length in chapter 7, "Major Network Types." Here, it will suffice to explain only what is being done and not the precise manner it which it is accomplished.

Media Access Control

Media access control (MAC) is the final task of the data link layer before passing the complete packet onto the physical medium of the network. As mentioned earlier, it is essential that every station on a LAN be given the opportunity to transmit its data in a timely manner. Otherwise, one station's request to open a file may be delayed extensively if other stations are monopolizing the network medium. Therefore, it is essential that a mechanism be realized to facilitate this sharing of a common resource. This is, of course, why data being sent over the network is divided into discrete packets instead of a continuous stream. The problem remains, however, as to when a station is to know at what time it is safe to transmit its packets.

This is most often done by one of two basic methods. Either a "token" packet is passed from station to station in turn and only the station possessing the token is permitted to transmit, or stations are allowed to transmit whenever they detect no other activity on the network and a mechanism is supplied to deal with the inevitable occasions when two stations transmit at the exact same moment. The first method is called *token passing* and is used by the token-ring, FDDI, and ARCnet protocols. The second is known as a *contention* method or, more specifically, *Carrier Sense Multiple Access with Collision Detection (CSMA/CD)*. This is the MAC method used by Ethernet networks.

In both cases, the length of the packet being transmitted and the specifications by which the physical network medium is constructed are vital to the proper functioning of the MAC method. This is why these three functions are grouped into a single protocol standard document. They are functionally inseparable, and the neat dividing lines provided by the OSI model must be abandoned in the interests of logistical practicality.

It must, therefore, be understood that the functionality of the data link layer may theoretically end when it passes a packet to the physical layer, where it is encoded and transmitted to its destination, but a single protocol (such as Ethernet or token ring) defines the specifications for both layers.

Addressing

The frame definition is also a vital aspect of the data link layer. It contains, among other things, the network and node addresses of the source and destination nodes on the network—that is, the most basic information needed to move the packet from one station to another. It should be noted that the data included in the frame supplied by one layer is available to all of the layers at another node. Just because a field in the data link frame supplies the network address of the packet's destination doesn't mean that only another data link layer can read that information. By the time the packet is transmitted over the network medium, it is a contiguous series of fields, and any destination process can utilize the data in any of those fields, without limitation.

Like the physical layer, the data link protocol is not responsible for the ultimate delivery of the packet to its destination. It is only concerned with moving the packet to the next consecutive station on the network. Each station checks to see if it is the intended recipient of the packet and passes it along to the next station. The packet is thus passed hand to hand until it reaches its destination. The more complicated elements of this travel are handled by the layers higher up in the OSI model.

Error Checking

Another field that is nearly always included in the data link frame is one that provides a means for error checking, which is a method of verifying that the packet arrives at its destination in the same condition as when it was transmitted. This is usually realized in the form of a *cyclic redundancy check* (*CRC*). A mathematical algorithm is applied to the contents of a packet, and the result of that algorithm is included within the packet, usually near the end. Once having been received at the destination, the same algorithm is again applied to the packet by the recipient, and the results compared with those enclosed within. Matching results indicate a proper transmission. Discrepancies cause a packet to be discarded.

In some cases, a mechanism is included to signal to the sender that the packet must be retransmitted, while in others, this function is left to the higher layers. The formation of a standardized unit length for error checking is another reason for imposing strict limitations on packet size. Larger packets are more difficult to verify and require a greater amount of data to be retransmitted for every error, lowering overall efficiency. The average number of transmission failures over a link is thus affected both by the underlying error rate of the signaling performed at the physical layer and the packet size imposed at the data link layer. For any given physical layer error rate, there exists a theoretical packet length that will cause all individual packet transmissions to fail. The maximum packet length for a data link protocol must, therefore, be one that accommodates both the needs of the MAC mechanism and the error checking algorithm.

The other fields of a data link frame generally contain information that is needed to facilitate the functionality of the MAC mechanism. These fields are highly specific to the mechanism being employed. For example, the overall packet length is included in an Ethernet frame, while control bits used for various housekeeping functions are part of a token-ring frame. The leading and trailing bytes of the packet usually contain some means of indicating to the rest of the network that a packet transmission is arriving and that it has ended. These are frequently realized as a series of bits that deliberately violate the physical layer's binary encoding scheme. This is treated as an unmistakable signal that a new transmission is beginning.

The Logical Link Control Frame

The data link layer also defies the organization of the OSI model in another significant way. The most commonly used family of data link protocols in network computing today are the specifications first published by the 802 committees of the IEEE in 1985.

What has thus far in this chapter been referred to as Ethernet (a similar protocol that has existed since the late 1970s and thus predates the OSI model by several years) is actually the IEEE standard 802.3. The token-ring protocol has been published as document 802.5. The entire story about the development of these competing specifications is told in chapter 7, "Major Network Types." Other, lesser used, protocols were also defined by this organization, such as the 802.4 Token Bus network and the 802.6 Metropolitan Area Network standard.

Another, very crucial, document was produced by the IEEE's 802.2 committee. This specification defines a second frame that is still considered to be part of the data link layer. Also known as the *logical link control (LLC) sublayer*, this frame is a common construction utilized without modification by each of the other 802.x standards previously mentioned. Carried within the frame provided by the MAC sublayer, which varies for the different network types, it provides various services to the network layer protocol above it, including flow control and error recovery (as opposed to the error checking provided at the MAC sublayer). It is also used to establish connections at various levels (or *classes*) of reliability between sending and receiving stations, depending on the nature of the protocols used at the higher layers. The frame and the functions of this protocol are also examined in greater depth in chapter 7, in the discussion of Ethernet. It is mentioned here to illustrate the fluid dynamic between the theoretical constructions of the OSI reference model and practical networking considerations. As shown in figure 3.9, the MAC sublayer of the IEEE data link protocols can actually be thought of as extending from the middle of the data link layer down into the physical layer, to a certain degree. The LLC sublayer then comprises the upper half of the data link layer, providing services to and an interface with the network layer protocol, to be discussed next.

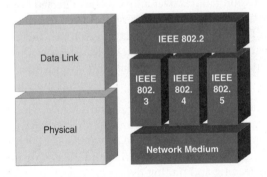

Figure 3.9

The IEEE 802 Standards cross the boundaries between layers of the OSI reference model.

The Network Layer

The network layer is where the most crucial dividing line in network communications occurs (see fig. 3.10), for this is the only layer that is actually concerned with the complete transmission of packets, or *protocol data units (PDUs)*, from source to destination.

The functions provided by the physical and data link layers are local. They are designed only to move the packets to the next station on the network medium. The primary task of the network layer is to provide the routing functionality by which packets can be sent across the boundaries of the local network segment to a destination that may be located on an adjacent network or on one thousands of miles away. What's more, the route actually taken by the packet must often be selected from many possible options, based on the relative efficiency of each.

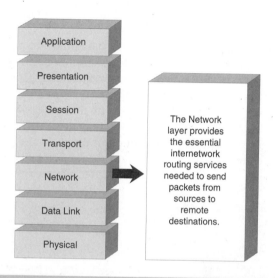

Figure 3.10

The network layer of the OSI model is concerned with the overall station to station journey of the packet.

To the entire protocol stack above this level, the functionality of the network, data link, and physical layers must be totally transparent. The source and destination systems for a particular data transaction must be allowed to interact in an identical fashion, whether they are sitting next to each other or in different countries. As long as the proper lower-level protocols are in place and a uniform system for network addressing exists, the source may be the Ethernet node on my desk, running on 10BaseT, connected via satellite link to a Macintosh workstation on an FDDI network in Beijing; but to the applications on each of the machines, these technologies are completely irrelevant.

In addition to this service, several additional functions may take place at the network layer, including

- The division of the binary data stream into discrete packets of a specified length

- Error detection

- Error correction through the retransmission of bad packets

- Flow control

These functions may look suspiciously like those frequently provided by data link layer protocols; in fact, they are. The difference is that these functions must now be provided for the entire end-to-end transmission from the source to the destination and not simply to the next adjacent node. This factor greatly complicates the performance of these functions, and indeed, in many systems, some or all of them are deferred to other layers of the model for that reason.

This complication is because an internetwork transmission involves not only the two *end systems*, which contain all seven layers of the OSI model and represent the sender and the recipient of the packet, but also one or more *intermediate systems*, or routers, whose functionality reaches no higher than the network, data link, and physical layers and through which the packets must pass in order to reach their destination (see fig. 3.11). Intermediate systems may also be known by many other names, such as *packet switch nodes*, *data switching exchanges*, or *interface message processors* (IMPs). The properties of the intermediate systems and the limitations imposed by them may vary widely, depending on the nature of the link that they provide. WANs may use links between remote locations that are far slower and place greater limitations on packet length than local area systems. In addition, complex networks may provide a multiplicity of possible paths to the destination, through various combinations of intermediate systems.

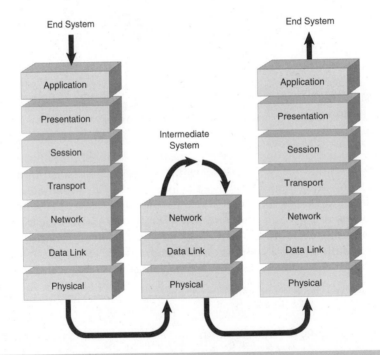

Figure 3.11

Network layer routing between networks forces packets to traverse the lower layers of intermediate systems.

Also understand that packets from different sources and intended for different destinations will be passing through the same intermediate systems on a regular basis. This is the basic method of multiplexing used by data networks. Like a single-lane highway with many on- and off-ramps, packets are placed onto the network by individual workstations, through their appropriate MAC methods. Depending on the traffic patterns at any one moment and the type of protocol being used, the flow of packets may be redirected to take advantage of a lesser populated avenue. Thus, packets may arrive at their destination in a different order from that in which they were transmitted and by several different routes.

Connection-Oriented Protocols

In light of these factors, the task of providing the functions discussed in the previous section is complicated enormously. For example, to provide flow control at this level— that is, some means of informing a sending system that it must temporarily cease its transmissions because the receiving station is being overwhelmed or suffering data loss— each possible path that might be taken from end system to end system must be treated as a separate entity. This is called a *connection*, which is established before the transmission and broken down afterwards.

This is because the station that is receiving too much data may be an end system or one of many intermediate systems. The request to cease transmitting must be directed only at the stations transmitting packets to that system or traffic may be halted at other locations unnecessarily. The flow control message must also be directed at all of the systems transmitting to the overwhelmed station or packets may be lost unnecessarily. The reaction of a sending station will be to cease transmitting for a time, until traffic conditions ease, after which it will resume. To provide this kind of functionality, *logical channel identifiers* are created for each connection before data is transmitted and destroyed when the connection is broken. These identifiers are used in flow control messages to indicate the exact process in need of attention.

What has just been described is known as a *connection-oriented protocol (CO protocol)*. This is a protocol where a logical connection from source to destination is established before every transaction and an acknowledgment of successful transmission returned afterwards. A *transaction* may be defined as an exchange of binary messages, intended to accomplish a single purpose (such as a request that a file be sent from a server to a workstation and the subsequent return of the file), which has been split into a series of discrete packets to facilitate transmission over the network. Some protocols operating at the network layer, such as X.25 (created by the CCITT and the most widely implemented of the native OSI protocols), are connection-oriented, providing the full range of services listed earlier for the entire end-to-end transmission, as illustrated in the following steps:

1. A connection is established from the source end system, through any intermediate systems, to the destination end system, taking the most efficient possible route.

2. The actual data packets of the transaction are transmitted by the source.

   3. If traffic conditions affect the successful flow of data between any two systems on the path of the connection, a flow control message is transmitted in the opposite direction to the next upstream system on the connection, indicating that transmission must cease, at least temporarily. Further exchanges, all using the previously established logical channel identifier to identify the offending packet, will then be necessary to resume transmission.

   4. Once having arrived at its final destination, the packets are checked for integrity. Depending on the outcome, either an acknowledgment of a successful transmission or a request that the packet be retransmitted is sent back over the same connection to the source.

   5. The connection is then broken, and the logical channel identifier erased.

In such transmissions, the accurate and timely transmission of data is absolutely guaranteed by the individual acknowledgment of every packet and the retransmission of any missing packets. The establishment of the logical connection also guarantees that the packets will arrive at the destination in the same order that they were sent. The classic simile likens a connection-oriented protocol to a telephone call, exchanging enough information between end systems to establish a connection before any information (that is, speech) is transmitted. Creating a protocol to enact such a transmission on a data network is an extraordinarily complex undertaking, and the amount of control data needed to perform all of the tasks necessary for every transaction adds significantly to the overall network traffic.

Connectionless Protocols

Because of this overhead, there are occasions when the flow control and error correction functions need not be performed by the network protocol. They may be undertaken by another layer in the OSI model (usually the transport layer), thus rendering them redundant here, or depending on the function of the packets being transmitted, they may not be needed at all. For example, a particular transaction may call for the regular transmission of only one packet every few minutes. Establishing a logical connection and leaving it open for occasional use such as this would be a waste of usable bandwidth.

The network layer protocol may then, at times, perform only the routing and framing functions needed for end-to-end transmission, as well as error detection (but not correction). When this is the case, the establishment of the logical end-to-end connection is unnecessary, as are the extra signals used to create it, break it down, and send flow control and retransmission instructions back to the source. In fact, the only packets that need be transmitted for this type of protocol are those containing the data itself.

This is called a *connectionless protocol* (*CL protocol*), and the price of its economy is a lesser degree of reliability. Packets, also called *datagrams* in a connectionless service, may be lost during transmission, due to corruption or traffic congestion, and the network layer will have no means of compensating for the loss or even, in some cases, of being aware of it. This means that incomplete transactions must be dealt with by the higher layers, thus introducing a greater penalty in time and traffic overhead, as a result, but only when packets are actually lost. In many of the cases where connectionless protocols are employed, this penalty amounts to less delay than would be entailed by the use of a CO protocol. If a CO protocol is akin to a telephone call, then a connectionless one is usually compared to a postal service. Packets are sent on their way with what is hoped to be a valid address, and the system takes over from there, providing the source with no indication of the packet's successful delivery, other than a possible complaint by the recipient at a later time. The *Connectionless Network Protocol* (*CLNP*) is the name of the OSI implementation of an unacknowledged network layer service.

The absence of a logical connection also means that individual packets belonging to a single transaction may take different routes to their destination, arriving at different times, and in a different order from that in which they were transmitted. In some cases, this can be an advantage, as datagrams can be dynamically rerouted to avoid network traffic delays in situations where a CO protocol would have to halt transmission entirely. The upper layers of the OSI model, however, will be required to have a mechanism that can compensate for this, reordering the packets at the end system and verifying that all of the required datagrams for a particular transaction have arrived, before that transaction is processed. Every datagram transmitted must also contain a complete address to the destination node, while CO packets need only contain a logical channel identifier, thus lowering the amount of overhead data carried by the individual packets. Still, however, a CO transaction will contain far more control overhead than a CL one.

Within the committees that were tasked to create the OSI model, the question of whether a connection-oriented or connectionless protocol should be used at the network layer was a heated one, that was never fully resolved. Facilities for both types of protocols are therefore included in the specifications. For the purposes of the LAN communications that are our primary concern, however, the most commonly implemented networks in use today utilize a connectionless protocol at the network layer. Novell's IPX (Internetwork Packet Exchange), IP (Internet Protocol), and AppleTalk's Datagram Delivery Protocol (DDP) are all connectionless protocols, but each is part of a suite that also includes higher-layer connection-oriented protocols of various types. Although the connection-oriented protocol itself may be very complex, it is a rather simple matter to implement one using the connectionless service at the network layer as a carrier. This allows the network operating system to select the appropriate level of reliability to suit the task at hand.

WAN links, on the other hand, are more likely to utilize a connection-oriented protocol. As a service usually provided to a privately owned network by an outside agency, WAN links trade on their reliability, and it is more practical for them to provide that reliability themselves, than to be dependent upon the higher-level equipment at each end of the link, over which they have no control. The conflict within the standards committees over the CO versus CL issue ended up primarily being a dispute between digital communications service providers, such as public telephone and telegraph companies (PTTs), and the manufacturers of the networking equipment linked by such services. Each preferred to rely on its own products for the higher-level functions like flow control and error correction. The outcome of this conflict was a very advantageous one, however.

The two opposing camps essentially compromised, agreeing to include both CO and CL protocols into the specifications and continuing to develop and maintain their respective mechanisms for providing reliable service. There are now, therefore, mature and well-developed systems of both types available for use by the designers of networks.

The Transport Layer

The transport layer (see fig. 3.12), as its primary function, provides the balance of the essential services not provided by the network layer protocol. A full-featured CO protocol at the network layer results in a relatively simple transport layer protocol, but as the functionality at the network layer diminishes, the complexity of the transport layer increases. The transport layer's task, therefore, is to provide whatever functions are necessary to elevate the network's *quality of service* (QOS) to a level suitable for the communications required of it.

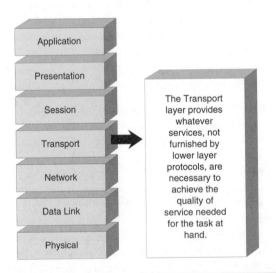

Figure 3.12

The transport layer of the OSI model, together with the network layer, provide the functionality for a complete end-to-end transmission.

To perform this service, the transport layer, like the network layer, has the flexibility to utilize CO or CL protocols. The selection of the appropriate protocol to the task is referred to as *mapping* a transport service onto the network service, and any combination of service types is available. A CO transport protocol can be mapped onto a CO or a CL network protocol, and the same is true for a CL transport protocol (see fig. 3.13).

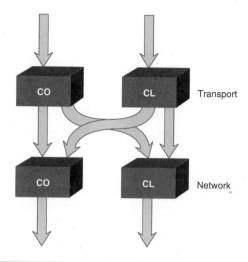

Figure 3.13

Protocol mapping in the network and transport layers allows for any combination of CO and CL protocols to be used in combination.

However, whatever protocol the transport layer uses, it relies completely on the network and lower-layer protocols to carry the data to its destination. In fact, the transport layer, along with the session and presentation layers above it, are both literally and figuratively the center of the OSI model. They operate solely within the two end systems involved in any network transaction, independently from the communications techniques below and the application above. They service the latter and are serviced by the former but remain isolated in their functionality.

Quality of Service Criteria

When defining the quality of service mentioned in the previous section, we are referring to a series of criteria that, when applied to the transport layer, comprise both the requirements of the application at the top of the OSI model and the features furnished by the layers below. The transport layer attempts to bring as many of these criteria, which are the same as those used by the network layer, up to the level of quality requested by the application as it can. QOS criteria do exist, however, over which the transport layer has no control. Inherent limitations of the network itself cannot be affected by the end systems which utilize it. No attempt is made by the transport layer, therefore, to address these deficiencies.

In the majority of transactions, the level of quality requested by the application amounts to the capabilities of what we have defined as a CO service. Applications do exist that require only the services of a CL protocol, and the OSI model does contain specifications for CL service all the way up to the top layer. However, these are comparatively rare, and the following material is concerned with the varying degrees of CO service that are more frequently requested. The main criteria used to evaluate a network's quality of service, which can be addressed by the transport layer, are as follows:

- Cost of communication

- Bandwidth available for communication

- Recovery from errors signaled by the network layer

- Recovery from unsignaled packet loss

- Reordering of packets arriving out of sequence

- Detection of errors not found by lower-layer processes

To address as many of these issues as possible, the transport layer, as defined in the OSI model, selects one protocol out of five *classes* of CO functionality for use with each transaction. Based upon a single generalized implementation, varying levels of service are provided by each class, thus avoiding the need for the development of five completely separate protocols while providing only the services needed for any particular transaction. The five classes of transport protocol are numbered from TP0 to TP4 and provide CO functions as follows:

- TP0   No additional functionality at all. By its selection, it is assumed that the lower layers already provide all of the transport services required by the application.

- TP1   Signaled error recovery. Provides the capability to correct errors that have already been detected by lower-layer protocols.

- TP2   Multiplexing (both upwards and downwards).

- TP3   Signaled error recovery and multiplexing (that is, TP1's and TP2's functions combined).

- TP4   Complete CO services including error detection (suitable for use with a connectionless network protocol).

The following sections clarify the functions and techniques used in these transport layer protocols, illustrating the ways in which they serve to address the QOS criteria.

Multiplexing
Multiplexing—that is, a process by which several discrete signals can be combined for transmission over a single communications channel—is used to address both the cost of network communications and the amount of bandwidth available to the communicating entities.

Reducing the cost of communications is, logically, dependent on the way in which the network medium is tariffed. For a privately owned LAN, this is clearly a physical layer issue, but wide area links between remote sites can incur usage charges according to a number of different models. One of the most common ways of charging for such a link is to combine a fee for the actual amount of data transmitted with a charge for the amount of time that the connection remains open. The only way of affecting the amount of data transmitted is through compression, but this, strangely enough, is not considered to be a part of the transport layer, according to the OSI model. It is, instead, included with encryption as part of the presentation layer, dealt with later in this chapter, in the section "The Presentation Layer."

If the amount of data is to remain constant, then the only way of lowering communications costs is by reducing the time that the connection remains active. This is done so routinely on WANs that its advantages are often taken for granted. If multiple workstations at one location require access to resources at a remote site, a non-multiplexing system requires that a dedicated link be established for each and every workstation during the entire time that access is required. Multiplexing the data from all of the workstations into one link effectively lowers the connect time charges enormously, as long as all of the workstations require access at the same time.

This is a function of the logical channel identifiers introduced earlier in this chapter, in the section on the network layer. Each packet being sent over a single connection includes fields within its frame that identify the workstation and application processes from which it originates and to which it is destined. While on a LAN, individual connections are used for each workstation's transactions, a single wide area connection can be used to service dozens or even hundreds of workstations at each side of the link. This type of multiplexing, in which a single link is used to service several transactions simultaneously, is called *upwards multiplexing* (see fig. 3.14).

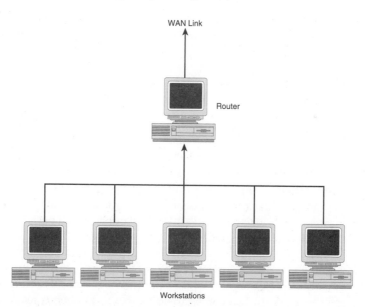

WAN Link

Router

Workstations

Figure 3.14

Upwards multiplexing combines several signals for transmission over a single connection.

Were you to look at figure 3.14 upside down, it would give you some idea of the opposite procedure used by the transport layer, called *downwards multiplexing*. This is a technique that can be used to maximize the bandwidth available to a particular process, thus addressing one of the other quality of service criteria. When the entire bandwidth of a link between two end systems is completely occupied by the transmission of a single transaction, the only way that an improvement can be realized (disregarding the use of compression, once again) is to utilize additional links. Downwards multiplexing is actually a process where a single signal is, in effect, de-multiplexed into several discrete data streams and then transmitted over multiple links to the destination end system, where it is re-multiplexed into a single transaction again.

The problem inherent in this technique is that packets arriving at the destination are almost sure to be in an order different from that in which they were transmitted. It is therefore necessary for each packet in a single transaction to be numbered so that it can be reassembled into the proper order at the destination. Fortunately, this process is completely identical to the packet sequencing that is needed when a CL network protocol is used for transmission. Therefore, no additional protocol development need be performed or control overhead added to take advantage of this technique.

Obviously, these two multiplexing techniques are mutually exclusive, with each one aiding in the increase of service quality in one criterion, while being directly detrimental to another. A selection must be made as to which is preferable, reduced operational cost or increased bandwidth, but with the proper facilities, this decision can conceivably be made dynamically in accordance with the needs of the individual data transaction.

Error Detection and Recovery

Recovery from communications errors, in the form of retransmitted packets, is performed under several possible conditions at the transport layer. For CO protocols, the simplest of these procedures is the recovery from *signaled errors*. Signaled errors are dropped or corrupted packets whose absence or damage has already been detected by a lower-level protocol and relayed to the transport layer. To facilitate these recoveries, every packet must be numbered and stored at the source, only being discarded when a positive acknowledgment has been received from the destination end system.

Since the packets have already been identified by earlier processes, the transport layer must do nothing more than send a message back to the source listing the packets required and requesting their retransmission. When the X.25 protocol is used at the network layer, the process is even easier. A special delivery bit can be included in its frame that returns a receipt acknowledgment only if the packet has been checked and accepted by the transport layer of the destination end system. This allows successfully received packets to be erased from the source buffers without explicit messages from the destination instructing them to do so. The use of this bit, however, is optional, and provisions must always be made for the generation of the appropriate retransmission requests. The TP1 and TP3 protocols are both capable of providing this form of error recovery.

The recovery of unsignaled errors presents an entirely different and far more complex problem. Since the lost packets have not been detected by any previous process, their numbering and storage, as well as the generation of acknowledgment messages and retransmission requests and the reordering of out-of-sequence packets must all be performed by the transport layer protocol. In short, the entire complement of CO services must be provided by this one protocol, thus making it the only choice suitable for use with a connectionless network layer protocol when CO services to the application layer are required. Of the OSI transport protocols, only TP4 is capable of this service.

TP4 also contains an additional error checking capability. The standard CRC error checking calculation performed by the data link layer can only detect errors occurring during the transmission over an individual link. When a packet is received at its destination, and the CRC recalculated, a certain degree of discrepancy is expected, due to elements in the header that are routinely modified during transmission. IP, the connectionless Internet protocol, made some attempt to overcome this by altering the CRC value according to changes made to the packet frame, but the TP4 protocol goes a step farther by calculating the CRC value only on the packet contents that are supposed to remain consistent throughout the transmission, and then checking it upon receipt at the transport layer of the end system. This provides a level of end-to-end CRC checking above and beyond any that is provided at the lower layers.

Transport Protocols

It should be reiterated here that the OSI model only defines a framework for the development of a networking system. Many NOSs do not implement all of the layers and classes of protocols defined in the OSI specifications, providing instead only those needed for their own purposes. Indeed, a simplistic, monolithic NOS could be developed utilizing only a single protocol, although its usefulness would likely be quite limited. Many implementations of the actual OSI protocols themselves do not supply all of the classes of transport protocols previously outlined. Most include only TP0 and TP4, with the latter running over the CL network service, although it is capable of being used with a CO network layer as well.

In the same way, few other networking systems provide the assortment of transport layer options defined in the OSI specifications. The predominant transport layer service in the NetWare native protocol suite is Sequenced Packet Exchange (SPX) and the Transmission Control Protocol (TCP) is its counterpart in the Internet protocol suite. These are both CO protocols that generate quite large amounts of control traffic to guarantee the reliability of their transmissions. As a result, they are used only when the quality of service required by a particular application demands it.

The Session Layer

We now arrive at the session layer and pass beyond all concerns for transmission reliability, error checking, flow control, and the like. All that can be done in these areas has been done by the time that the transport layer functions have been completed. The session layer is the most misunderstood service in the OSI model (see fig. 3.15), and a great deal of discussion has gone into the question of whether its functions even warrant a layer of their own. Because of its name, it is often thought (mistakenly) to be concerned with the network logon procedure and related matters of security. The other common description is that it is concerned with matters of "dialogue control and dialogue separation." This is actually true, but more often than not, these expressions are left undefined in such treatments.

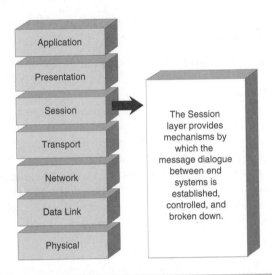

The Session layer provides mechanisms by which the message dialogue between end systems is established, controlled, and broken down.

Figure 3.15

The session layer of the OSI model is responsible for a multitude of frequently misunderstood functions.

The session layer specification cannot be thought of as having a primary function or a single reason for its presence, as the lower layers do. It functions more as a "tool kit" for the upper layers, providing 22 different services, many of them quite obscure to anyone but application developers. In fact, due to a compromise between two committees creating rival session standards, there are in many cases two tools in the kit for each task that it can perform. Clever application developers have sometimes taken this opportunity to create different uses within their applications for the same tool.

We must, at this point, digress for a moment to discuss in more detail the way that the functions for each layer of the OSI model are actually documented in the specifications. Each layer in the model provides services to the layer immediately above it—services which are requested by the issuance of commands called *service request primitives*. Therefore, a request by a workstation's application layer for access to a particular network resource originates with the passing of the appropriate service primitive (plus any additional parameters required) to the presentation layer below it. The request is then relayed down the layers of the model, in each case utilizing the appropriate primitive for that layer, thus causing the appropriate frame to be added to the packet. After transmission to the destination, the packet is decoded into *indication primitives* that are passed up the model to the receiving application.

These primitives are the tools of the toolkit, which in the session layer are broken down into a number of subsets containing primitives associated in their functionality, the use of which are negotiated during the establishment of the session connection. Apart from the Kernel Function Unit (KFU), containing basic primitives that are always available for use, there are 12 other functional units, among them the Basic Activity Subset (BAS), the Basic Combined Subset (BCS), and the Basic Synchronization Subset (BSS). When matters of compatibility with other systems caused a conflict between two proposed session layer standards, the primitives from both were, in many cases, adopted into the one final standard. This causes no inherent harm, except for a bit of confusion and the occasional argument between developers as to which set of primitives should be used.

But to return to the actual functions of the session layer, it is true, as mentioned earlier, that of its many functions, the most important are dialogue control and dialogue separation. "Dialogue," in these instances, refers to the exchange of data between two end systems linked by a logical connection. The session layer controls the way in which this dialogue is conducted during the connection. This is not to say, however, that it is concerned with the nature of the data being transmitted. Instead, its province is the flow of messages back and forth between the two end systems, and the impact that the functions requested by the application may have on that flow.

In other words, when one end system receives a message from the other end system to which it is connected, it has no way of knowing whether or not that message is based on the data that it has most recently transmitted. The message being received could have been transmitted by the other station while a packet was still in transit in the other direction. *Collision cases* such as this can present numerous problems, particularly when one end system requests that the connection between the two systems be broken, or when one of the two end systems attempts to perform a checkpoint operation. *Checkpointing* is a process in which an application writes the entire state of its current status to disk, as a safety measure. For an application running on a single, isolated PC, this is a simple affair, but for a distributed network application, a reliable checkpoint must reflect the states of two or more machines at the same exact moment and account for any data in transit as well.

The process by which the session layer provides an orderly means of initiating the contact between end systems, exchanging messages between the two, and ultimately releasing the connection, all the while ensuring that both systems have received all of the data intended for them, is known as *dialogue control*. The method by which it can insert a reference point into the data stream that serves as a division marker at which the state of both end systems can be assessed (or other functions performed) is called *data separation*.

Dialogue Control

The basic alternatives that the session layer makes available to two end systems when initiating a dialogue are called *two-way alternate mode* (*TWA*) and *two-way simultaneous mode* (*TWS*). The mode selection made at the establishment of the session connection is an irrevocable one. The mode cannot be changed without terminating the connection and reestablishing it (and this is considered by some to be a considerable drawback to the session layer model). Two-way alternate mode allows only one of the two end systems to transmit data at any one time. At the conclusion of its transmission it sends a *data token* to the other system using the S-TOKEN-GIVE primitive, upon receipt of which, permission to transmit is transferred to the other system. Another primitive, called S-TOKEN-PLEASE, also exists, with which one system can request the token from another.

Two points must be made concerning these exchanges. First, it must always be remembered that we are now in the session layer. When we speak of connections, tokens, and dialogue, we are most definitely not referring to the similar concepts that exist at the lower layers. Permission to transmit at the session layer is in no way involved with MAC, nor is the token used here related to that of the IEEE 802.5 Token Ring specification. These lower layer processes are services that the session layer may make use of. Their operational efficiency is assumed by the session layer to be completely reliable. They are a fact and not a factor of the session service.

The second point is that the actions of mode selection and passing and requesting the data token are not to be seen as an automatic, transparent process, in the way that many of the lower-level functions are. It is not a matter of a higher-level process turning a figurative ignition key and setting an elaborate hidden machine into operation without knowing how it actually works. These functions are rather to be thought of as explicit processes that must be specifically requested by the application layer (and relayed through the presentation layer). A particular application may utilize the S-TOKEN-PLEASE primitive, for example, or it may rely solely on S-TOKEN GIVE, depending on the whim of the developer. This is why the concept of service primitives has been introduced here, and these services referred to as tools.

The token-passing method adequately resolves the problem of messages being left in transit while action is already being taken by its intended recipient. It also provides a means for breaking down the session connection, through a process called *orderly termination*. To avoid any confusion between systems, each session connection is assigned a unique identifier composed of the following four parts:

- Initiator SS-USER Reference (64 bytes)

- Responder SS-USER Reference (64 bytes)

- Common Reference (64 bytes)

- Additional Reference (4 bytes)

When one end system of a particular connection signals its desire to terminate its communications session, it passes the data token and stops transmitting data but remains open to incoming messages. The other end system then receives the token, transmits any outstanding data it may still have in its buffers, and acknowledges the request to terminate by sending the S-RELEASE primitive. The original end system then confirms the release and is free to issue the S-DISCONNECT command, secure in the knowledge that there is no data currently in transmission or waiting to be transmitted. There are two special situations worth noting in which problems arise with this method. One is when both end systems request a release at once, causing a collision (once again, not to be confused with a MAC collision). To prevent this instance, the session layer specification also provides a *negotiated release* feature, by which an end system can refuse the other system's request, and the capability to utilize a special *release token*, which prevents both systems from issuing the S-RELEASE command simultaneously. The other is when a session layer option is used that results in the orderly termination of the session layer connection (through the normal method shown previously), while leaving the transport layer connection open for use by another application.

A problem can arise if the second application chooses to make use of a service primitive called S-EXPEDITED, which is designed to deliver data to its destination faster than a normal transmission would. In some cases, this could result in the expedited data arriving at the other end system before the release negotiation has been completed and therefore being delivered to the wrong application. To prevent this, the transport connection cannot be left open during a release negotiation when data is being expedited. This instance is indicative of the way that the designers of standards and protocols must attempt to anticipate the actions taken by application developers. Situations such as these often arise after a standard has been completed, forcing the creation of an amendment to the existing document. The task of standard development is one that is never truly completed.

With all of these mechanisms in place, the whole release negotiation process functions very nicely and is not terribly difficult to implement, from a protocol designer's perspective. The problem is that neither is it terribly efficient. If the round trip transmission time between the two end systems is of any significant length, such as when connected by a WAN link, two-way alternate mode communications can be very tedious and unsuitable for some applications. This is why the capability for the selection of two-way simultaneous mode communications is provided by the session layer, although it provides no mechanism facilitating the actual performance of these communications, as it does with TWA mode. In fact, from the session layer perspective, TWS is a "do nothing" protocol. Like TP0 at the transport layer, it indicates that the specifics of the process are being handled elsewhere.

Dialogue Separation

We have seen that dialogue control is enacted by allowing the application layer a choice of communications modes upon establishing a session connection. (As an aside, it should be mentioned the repeated references to the application layer requesting services of the session layer actually include the intervention of the presentation layer in between. A process can only make requests to the layer immediately beneath it, and the presentation layer contains duplicate primitives that serve to relay the requests down to the session layer.) To approach the matter of dialogue separation, we will again see a difference in functionality provided by the selection of TWA or TWS mode. The dialogue separation mechanisms for both modes, however, are conducted here, at the session layer, and the way in which they differ is sufficiently illustrative of the way that two-way simultaneous transmission complicates these processes enormously.

We have previously defined dialogue separation as a mechanism by which an application can be checkpointed—that is, its current status at any one time saved to disk in case of systems failure. At the time when the session layer was being developed, such failures were far more common than they are today and checkpointing was a crucial aspect of any distributed application. It must be emphasized, however, that the checkpointing operation is most definitely part of the application. The session layer knows nothing about it, *per se*. It simply provides, in dialogue separation, a service to the application developer, another tool that she can use.

Performing any activity on two different systems at precisely the same moment is a virtually impossible task, especially in computing, where thousands of activities can be performed every second. Even the prospect of transmitting a signal meaning "NOW" would entail a certain amount of transmission delay before it reached its destination. Synchronization between two end systems cannot, therefore, be achieved by any method that relies on one system for control or individual clocking by each of a previously scheduled event, and even if it could, the problem still remains of how to account for any packets that may be in transit between the two machines when the event occurs.

Some means must then be provided by which the two machines can mark a particular unified point, not in time, but in the exchange of data between the two. For end systems between which data is flowing in only one direction at any particular time, such as in TWA mode, the process is quite simple. A particular service primitive, called S-SYNC-MINOR, is transmitted by one system, essentially placing a point of separation into the data stream. When used for checkpointing, the sending system saves its status upon transmitting this primitive and the receiving system performs its own checkpoint upon receiving it. Thus, it can be certain that no unprocessed data is left in the channel at the synchronization point. This is called a *minor synchronization* because it only involves one exchange of control information and accounts for data flowing in only one direction at a time.

This technique is not limited to use in TWA connections, however, and accommodations have been made for the possibility of a collision between two S-SYNC-MINOR commands sent at the same time by the two end systems. A special token, distinct from the data token mentioned earlier, and called the *minor synchronization token*, is used to control which of the two end systems has permission to transmit the S-SYNC-MINOR request at any one time. The need for this additional token could be eliminated if the session layer allowed a connection to switch between two-way alternate and two-way simultaneous modes. In that case, the TWA data token could be used, but since this doesn't exist in TWS mode, an additional token is needed.

The use of two-way simultaneous communications, of course, complicates matters. Not only must transmissions from both end systems reach their respective destinations before a separation point can be determined, but the potential for expedited data from both sides must also be taken into account. Data that is transmitted using the S-EXPEDITED primitive can be thought of as having a separate high-speed pipeline to its destination, independent of the channel used by normal communications. Both of these must be flushed in sequence for a proper dialogue separation to occur.

This is called a *major synchronization*, and it begins with the transmission of the S-SYNC-MAJOR command by one end system. Clearly, the application cannot perform a checkpointing operation at the time of the primitive's transmission, as data may still be on its way to the system originating the request. In this case, it is the recipient of the primitive that first establishes a separation point, at the moment when S-SYNC-MAJOR is received. Meanwhile, the sender has stopped transmitting but continues to listen, awaiting a response to its request. The receiver of the primitive, therefore, establishes its own separation point, confident that all traffic from the sender has been received (including expedited traffic, which would have arrived before the SYNC primitive). At the same time, it transmits its confirmation of the SYNC primitive through the normal data channel, as well as a special PREPARE message back to the sender, through the expedited data pipe. The function of the PREPARE message, which will arrive before the SYNC confirmation, is to instruct the sender to buffer any expedited traffic arriving after the PREPARE for use by the second dialogue, which begins after the separation point is established at the sender's end system by the arrival of the SYNC confirmation. There is also, not surprisingly, yet another token, called the *major/activity token* (so-called because it has another use as well), which prevents collisions of two S-SYNC-MAJOR primitives from occurring.

In light of such affairs, it is perhaps no longer much of a secret why the session layer is so misunderstood. This seems like a terribly elaborate procedure to perform what should be a fairly innocuous task, but it is only one of many. For example, the handshake for the resynchronization that must be performed to restart the session connection using saved checkpoints is even more complex, requiring two PREPARE messages. This is what networking is all about, though. Simple-sounding problems often require enormously complex solutions that must remain totally transparent to other processes. At the beginning of this book, it was observed that the best running networks are those on which the users are unaware that they are even accessing a network resource. This same philosophy also holds true at every layer of the OSI model. Each layer is a "user" of the layer below, requesting services of it with little or no knowledge of how those services are performed.

Real world protocols that function at the session layer frequently overlap into areas that more strictly belong in the other information handling layers, presentation and application, as well as into the realm of the transport layer. Strict delineation of functions according to the OSI model is not a priority for most developers, as we have seen, but some of the protocols that can be said to provide session layer services are as follows:

- NetBIOS   A session interface and protocol, developed by IBM, that also provides services that span the transport, presentation, and application layers.

- NetBEUI (NetBIOS Extended User Interface)   An extension of NetBIOS used in Microsoft networking products, such as Windows NT and LAN Manager.

- ADSP (AppleTalk Data Stream Protocol)   The part of the AppleTalk protocol suite responsible for establishing reliable connections between nodes.

- PAP (Printer Access Protocol)   Provides Postscript printer access to AppleTalk networks.

The Presentation Layer

As a contrast to the numerous and varying functions of the session layer, the presentation layer provides only one additional service (see fig. 3.16), embodied in the P-ALTER CONTEXT primitives. Aside from this one, the only other primitives that it contains are exact correlatives of the session layer primitives, used to pass requests for services from the application layer to the session layer, via the Presentation Service Access Point (PSAP) and the Session Service Access Point (SSAP).

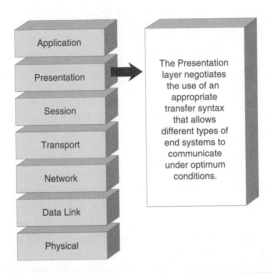

Figure 3.16

The presentation layer of the OSI model performs only a single function: the translation of different types of system syntax.

The PSAP and SSAP functions are not necessarily "do nothing" functions, however. While they do not affect the nature of the application requests or the services being requested, some of them do perform a vital translation function. A request from the application layer necessarily utilizes the native syntax of the application to generate that request. The application for which it is destined, at the other end system, may utilize a completely different syntax or bit-coding format. For example, a connection between a PC and a mainframe may require a conversion from the EBCDIC character encoding format to ASCII and many other factors may have to be considered as well. For this translation to occur, the presentation layer on both end systems is responsible for converting the system's native application layer syntax, also known as the *abstract syntax*, to a common *transfer syntax*, suitable for transmission to the other end system through the network medium.

Other factors are also considered when a transfer syntax is chosen, based on the nature of the individual presentation layer connection. Functions like data compression and encryption can be chosen, based upon the limitations of the link between the two end systems. For example, a high-speed secure FDDI link between two buildings requires little in the way of compression or encryption. These features only require additional processing time and clock cycles by both end systems, providing little real value as a result. A dialup connection using modems and public phone lines, on the other hand, is a situation in which the additional processing overhead more than offsets the savings in transmission time and additional security, should compression and encryption be used to their fullest. The negotiation by which the appropriate transfer syntax is selected for a particular connection is where the P-ALTER-CONTEXT primitives enter the picture.

For the presentation layers of the two end systems to negotiate the proper syntaxes to be used in their communications, a series of presentation contexts are sent, along with the P-CONNECT primitive, by the system initiating the connection. A *presentation context* is an association, identified with a unique odd-numbered integer called the *presentation context identifier*, between an abstract syntax and a particular transfer syntax. The sending machine is essentially informing the intended recipient of its translating capabilities. Several transfer syntaxes may be specified for any single abstract syntax. The receiving system passes the list of contexts up to the application layer, which decides on the use of a particular transfer syntax for every abstract syntax on the list (assuming that both systems can support at least one of the transfer syntaxes listed).

This list, now containing either a single transfer syntax or an error message for each abstract syntax, is passed down again to the presentation layer of the receiving system for transmission back to the sender. Once returned, this list becomes the *defined context set* for that connection. If any of the abstract syntaxes cannot be supported by a common transfer syntax, an error message is supplied containing the reason for the failure. Additional presentation contexts can then be proposed for addition to the defined context list, using the P-ALTER-CONTEXT primitive.

This primitive can also be used to remove contexts from the defined set, leaving the presentation protocol open to the same collision problems that afflicted the dialogue separation procedures at the session layer. That is, the possibility exists for a message requiring a particular presentation context to arrive at a system where that context has already been removed from the defined context set. It took over a year for the standards committees to agree on an implementation that resolved most (but not quite all) of these problems. The solution is based on a *context restoration* procedure (from a pre-existing checkpoint) that is similar to the resynchronization mechanisms of the session layer. After all of this work, however, virtually no application designers have made use of the context restoration mechanism supplied by the standard.

A similar situation exists as far as the notation schemes and encoding rules for the abstract and transfer syntaxes are concerned. Great pains were taken to create a standard that allows the use of different types of encoding, but years later, there still remains only one object naming standard that is used for abstract syntaxes, ASN.1 (Abstract Syntax Notation One, also known as ISO 8824), and one encoding scheme for transfer syntaxes, the Basic Encoding Rules (ISO 8825). This has actually caused a certain amount of consternation to some because minor attributes of these standards are particularly suitable for use with the OSI presentation layer (such as the restriction of their field lengths to multiples of eight bits), and yet these attributes are not included as part of the 7498 or X.200 standards. Issues like these are rapidly progressing to the point at which they are of interest to the standards committees and to virtually no one else. As we have seen, the realities of practical business networking often have only a limited relationship to the theories of the OSI model. We may well have arrived at the time when it is best to abandon hope of creating a practical networking system that is completely compliant with the OSI model and leave these minor points until an actual need to resolve them arises.

The Application Layer

Finally, we arrive at the top of the OSI model, and the reason for its existence in the first place. The application layer, as shown in figure 3.17, is of course, the actual interface used by every application that requires network access for any reason. The application may be a word processor attempting to open a file that just happens to be stored on a file server volume. This involves a basic local function that is being redirected to the application layer and the rest of the OSI stack to access remote resources. The application may also be one that exists solely for the purpose of providing an interface to a network resource, functioning like an executable protocol, such as Telnet or FTP. In either case and many others in between, including e-mail, database access, and file and network management, the application layer of the model provides the tools needed to access those network resources. It is, essentially, a window between application functions located on remote systems.

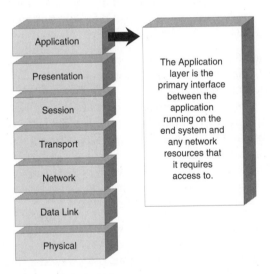

Figure 3.17

The application layer of the OSI model provides the actual interface between the workstation application and the network.

Because of the immense array of applications requiring network access, the application layer is, necessarily, the most diverse in its capabilities. Protocols running at this level can be extremely complex, requiring entire chapters or even books of their own for a full exploration, or relatively simple, performing a small set of tasks for a highly specific purpose. Many of the protocols also tend to span the boundaries of the top three layers in the OSI model in their capabilities. Once the communications issues of the lower subnet are dealt with, the barriers between layers become more fluid, and entities like Novell's NetWare Core Protocols, which account for the bulk of the communications on a NetWare network, tend to span all of the information handling layers.

For a well-defined OSI-based protocol stack, the application layer should account for up to 90% of the bits actually transmitted over the network. The efficiency of the overall network is therefore more dependent on the application layer than on any other. Application layer function protocols may request services provided by the presentation layer, below, or they may access libraries of commonly used functions that are codifed into what are known as *application service elements* (*ASEs*), which group together related functions or tools. Either of these resources may be called upon by the application programmer at will. Originally, the ASEs were divided into *common application service elements* (*CASEs*), which contained more generic sets of services, usable by many different applications, and *specific application service elements* (*SASEs*), which are more likely to apply to a single application or type of application and which make use of the infrastructure created with the CASEs. The distinction between these two has become somewhat indistinct over the years, however, and the use of these terms was officially abandoned in the late 1980s, although they still remain useful for tutorial purposes.

All of the basic standards of the application layer are now referred to simply as ASEs, which have no component parts and which do not make use of other ASEs. Instead, the concept of the *application service object* (*ASO*) was introduced by the *Extended Application Layer Structure* (*XALS*) document, which was published as an amendment to ISO standard 9545 in 1992. An ASO is a collection of (other) ASOs or ASEs, bound together by a *control function*, which determines how the different elements interact. This was done to reconcile the possibility for conflicts that could arise between the properties of different ASEs in use at the same time, such as the use by one of the session layer TWA mode, while another uses the TWS mode. Access to these is still provided by *application program interface calls* (*APIs*), however, which are the tools used by application developers to call upon specific functions from within their programs.

It must be noted that there is some trepidation on the part of the OSI standards committees as to whether the changes in the preceding paragraph should be formally integrated into their standard as well. Once again, from a practical level, it probably doesn't matter. We are dealing with questions of architecture here; more in terms of how processes are documented than of how they are constructed. These changes will not have a profound effect on actual network communications. They are merely an attempt to recognize a problem with the existing standard and provide as cogent a remedy as possible.

Some of the more important ASEs are discussed in the following sections.

ACSE (Association Control Service Element)
This is an ASE that is used by all applications requiring network access. It allows an association to be made between two application processes (APs) located on different end systems. At the application layer, we speak of *associations* between applications and not connections. Technically, a *connection* is defined as an interface between corresponding layers of the OSI model on two end systems, which provides an association between the next higher layers on both systems. Since the application layer is at the top of the model, the term connection is inappropriate, but an association may be said to exist, as a result of the efforts of the presentation layer. In other words, an application developer may choose to employ the A-ASSOCIATE primitive defined in the ACSE standard to make

contact with an application running on a remote end system. As a result, a P-CONNECT command is issued at the presentation layer, and an association between the two applications ensues. Once the association is established, the ACSE is not used until termination of the association is requested or occurs for another reason. Loss of the presentation connection also entails the loss of the association, and the ACSE contains primitives to compensate for the abnormal termination.

ROSE (Remote Operations Service Element) and RTSE (Reliable Transfer Service Element)

Originally created for use by the X.400 e-mail application protocol (an enormous subject worthy of a book in itself), ROSE and RTSE are exceptional in that they are simple, basic, and functional, with no major developmental problems that protocol developers need to address. ROSE is an ASE that is designed to facilitate the sending of messages that invoke a specified function on a remote system and is often used in *remote procedure calls* (*RPCs*). The function itself is not a part of the ASE. ROSE is simply a support service for the delivery of the request or reply. It can function in synchronous or asynchronous mode, with the reply, when in synchronous mode, to a request being sent as part of a single association. Asynchronous mode is analogous to connectionless communications, in which a reply may or may not be returned and no guarantee of reliability is given. ROSE is commonly used by LAN operating systems for brief transactions that do not require the retention of large amounts of state information.

RTSE is guaranteed delivery service utilized by ROSE, as well as by other application processes. It is the mechanism by which the application layer retries a communication process that has failed irrevocably at the lower layers, either through resending of messages or through the reestablishment of lost connections. It also provides transparent access to the full functionality of the presentation and session layers to an application without exposing it to their underlying complexities. Checkpointing, connection recovery, and like services can be provided without the need for the application to address specific primitives to the PSAP directly. RTSE (through ROSE) is the delivery mechanism used at the application layer for the MHS message handling system.

CCRSE (Commitment, Concurrency, and Recovery Service Element)

The CCRSE is used to coordinate multiple application processes that are intended to be performed as a single transaction. For example, database updates that require writes to multiple records can use CCRSE to ensure that either all or none of the individual updates are performed during the transaction. This is done through a *two phase commitment* in which each application entity must signal its ability to complete the required task before any of the updates are applied and the transaction deemed successful.

SASEs

All of the preceding ASEs are examples of what would, in the past, have been correctly called CASEs. The following are examples of the more application-specific ASEs, formerly known as SASEs:

- DS (Directory Services)   Facilitates the use of a global naming system or enterprise directory services database (such as Novell's NDS or Banyan's Street Talk) by an application.

- MHS (Message Handling System)   Provides an interface with the basic mail delivery engine used by many e-mail and messaging applications.

- VT (Virtual Terminal)   Allows an application to emulate the behavior of a terminal used to access a remote system, irrespective of the actual hardware being used.

- FTAM (File Transfer Access and Management)   Used to provide file management capabilities on a remote system.

- JTM (Job Transfer and Manipulation)   Allows an application to perform batch-style data processing on a remote system, in which multiple predetermined tasks are executed before the results are returned to the sender.

These examples attempt to portray the wide range of services that are demanded of the application layer (and by proxy, of the entire OSI model), but the full listing would be as long as a list of all of the features in all of the network applications now in use. Although the technicalities of the physical layer may seem complex, the scope and the functionality of the application layer dwarfs these concerns.

Summary

The OSI model is a construction that attempts to make an incredibly complicated system understandable to a greater audience. It can be approached even by the novice networker, to gain the most basic idea of what goes on between networked computers, or it can be used by the most advanced engineer, as an organizing tool for studies of extraordinary detail and complexity.

The OSI reference model is often illustrated in the form of a pyramid, with the application layer at the tip. This may be considered a valid metaphor, in light of the way in which each layer, from the top down, is packaged within the functionality of the next layer. But I think that a truer representation would be to show the pyramid upside-down, with the wide base of the application layer at the top, distilling its essence down to the trickle of pulses being emitted from a single pinhole at the bottom. This, to me, is a truer picture of the OSI model, and if you were to collect the printed documents detailing all of the standards involved in this immense undertaking, I daresay that such a model could be proportionately constructed out of them which would closely resemble figure 3.18.

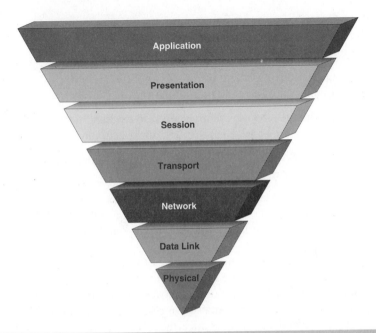

Figure 3.18

In the true OSI pyramid, enormously complex tasks are boiled down to a thin stream of impulses.

Chapter 4

Upgrading to a WAN

WAN stands for wide area network. Although the definition of how big an area has to be before it gets to be wide varies, the most common definition is that a WAN is one that extends beyond the boundaries of a single building.

Why extend a local area network (LAN) to a WAN? If it seems unnecessary to extend a network beyond the bounds of a building, think of only a few years ago when it seemed unnecessary to extend computing ability beyond a single machine. After the mainframe dependency of the sixties, stand-alone machines finally became powerful enough to hold their own data and processing power. After a time, however, the people using these powerful stand-alone computers realized that there had been some advantages to computing's physical structure in the sixties, and networking began to experience a re-naissance—first to peer-to-peer networking and then, more and more, back to some form of client/server networking.

The natural outgrowth of this new interest in networking computing resources is the WAN, as companies outgrow their original sites and move part of the operation to another office. Rather than lose the resources moved to the new building, many companies have begun exploring the possibilities of wide area networking.

Wide area networking offers a lot of advantages to companies in a position to take advantage of it:

- Flexibility of location: not all of the people using the same data have to work at the same site

- Communication between branch offices can be improved via e-mail and file sharing

- A centralized company-wide backup system

- Companies located in a number of small interrelated offices can store files centrally and access each other's information

Differentiating a WAN from a LAN

This distinction isn't as easy to make as it once was. If you're on a LAN, you work in the same office as your data and the network is generally faster than any WAN connection. Today, the distinctions between LANs and WANs have blurred.

- New technology can make some WANs as fast as LANs

- Telecommuting has led to increased use of remote access and remote control software

Speed
Until fairly recently, speed was one of the most obvious things that distinguished most WANs from most LANs; all other things being equal, the WAN was generally slower than the LAN.

Today, new technology has made native LAN speeds a reality in some parts of the United States—that is, in some areas, you can get a wide area connection that can keep up with your LAN. (You'll learn about this technology and its limitations in the "Fiber Distributed Data Interface (FDDI) across a WAN" section later in this chapter.)

Accessibility
Although a full discussion of remote control and remote node access is reserved for chapter 27, "Adding Remote Network Access (Telecommuting)," you're probably well aware that you can buy software—or some network operating systems, like Microsoft's Windows NT Server—that allow clients to dial into your network and use it from another location. Remote control access allows the client to control a physical computer attached to the network, while remote node access allows the client to dial in and become a member of the LAN, albeit a much slower one.

Telecommuting is becoming a reality for more and more companies. The numbers will only increase, what with the environmental regulations requiring companies of more than 100 employees to take steps toward instituting telecommuting where practical. Even some employers who don't have to follow the EPA line are beginning to see the advantages that telecommuting can offer and more will follow. Are these remote users connecting to a LAN, or does their presence make it a WAN?

I'd argue that telecommuters do not make a LAN if they're working from a single PC at home and using a modem to dial in. Once you start adding more PCs on the home side, a faster connection, or office users accessing the home PC, then it makes more sense to talk of a telecommuting connection as a WAN. For the present, however, most remote connections are more LAN-like than WAN-like.

What's a MAN?
MAN, which stands for metropolitan area network, is a WAN confined to a single metro area or city. Although you'll see this term in networking literature often enough that you should know what it means, it's generally not a very useful term. First of all, the definition of a metropolitan area is pretty flexible. In the Washington, DC area, for example,

the metro area covers parts of three states. Richmond, on the other hand, has a metro area that pretty much involves Richmond and a few suburbs. Applying the same term to Richmond's metro area and that of Washington, DC doesn't make much sense.

Even though the definition of a MAN is a bit ambiguous, it more or less defines the area of a *local access telephone area* (*LATA*). A LATA is a logical (as opposed to physical) grouping of telephonic points of presence (POP). As it's more or less confined to a LATA, one WAN technology is MAN-based by definition. *Switched Multimegabit Data System*, which is discussed in more detail in the section "Switched Multimegabit Data Service (SMDS)" later in this chapter, in its basic form is confined to a local telephone area.

Understanding WAN Terminology

Much of the terminology associated with WANs is similar to the jargon that you know from working with LANs. However, since the jargon used isn't always identical, you'll learn some of the WAN-specific terminology that is used to talk about the various wide area technologies.

Packets

Most newer WAN technologies transmit data in the form of *packets*, which contain both the data and the means to get that data to its destination. Packets are easiest to understand if you think of them as regular postal mail (or just *snail mail*). Packets are like mail in that

- An "envelope" identifies the packet as a unit in the flow of correspondence

- The addressing information on the envelope notes the recipient and usually the sender

- The envelope contains the actual data, which makes the bulk of the packet

The Envelope. The envelope, or the structure of the packet, puts the data into a form that the connection can understand. Just as the postal system wouldn't be able to mail your letter if you wrapped it in a lettuce leaf instead of an envelope, most connections require some kind of standard container; that's where the basic form of a packet comes from.

The Addressing. For the data to get to its destination, at the very least it requires the address of its intended recipient. For any kind of acknowledgment that the data was received, it also needs the sender's address. There is, however, a special name for packets that don't require any kind of acknowledgment—they're called *datagrams*. When you send a datagram, the only way you know that it didn't reach its destination is if the recipient tells you that he or she never got the message.

The Data. The amount of data that is included in each packet depends on the type of packet. Frames, used in frame relay (discussed in the later section "Frame Relay" contain more data than cells (discussed in the later section "Switched Multimegabit Data Services (SMDS)." For the moment, just remember that the size of the packet will always be greater than the amount of data in it, just as a letter includes more paper and writing than the paper and writing used for the letter.

You can see the basic information contained in a packet in figure 4.1.

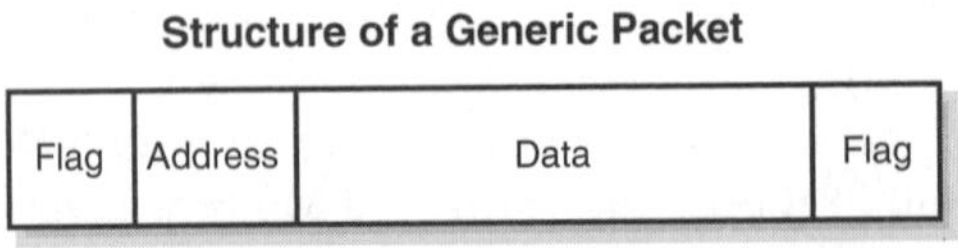

Structure of a Generic Packet

Flag	Address	Data	Flag

Figure 4.1

Generally speaking, a packet will contain the information shown here.

Different WAN technologies use different packets. For example, some older WAN technologies incorporate error-correcting information into the packet so that if some data in the packet gets lost or corrupted in transmission, the missing data can be reconstructed on the other end. Because the fiber-optic cables used in modern telephonics and WAN connections are less vulnerable to the kinds of electronic noise that can corrupt data, error-control capabilities are less necessary for the WAN technologies designed to use these digital lines. Error-control is discussed later in this section, but that's one example of how not all packets are identical.

Packets can vary not only in content but in size. For example, some WAN technologies enclose their data for transmittal in a kind of packet called a *frame*. Frames can vary in size and don't even all have to be the same size within the same kind of WAN. WAN access protocols using frames are collectively called *frame relay technologies*. Other WAN types, on the other hand, package data in small packets of fixed size (53 bytes) called *cells*. Access protocols using cells are collectively called *cell relay technologies*. If your WAN involves more than one technology and those technologies use mutually unintelligible packet types, you'll need to come up with some method of converting one packet type into the other. Generally speaking, the quoted speeds of cell relay technologies will be higher than the quoted speeds of frame relay technologies.

Frame Relay versus Cell Relay: Which Is Better?

Why is cell relay faster than frame relay if cells are smaller than frames? After all, the top speed of frame relay "in the wild" is about 2 Mbps, while SMDS starts at 1.544 Mbps and goes up from there. Asynchronous Transfer Mode (ATM), another cell relay technology, starts at around 155 Mbps and goes up to 2 Gbps. (We'll talk more about the details of particular frame relay and cell relay technologies in the course of this chapter.)

The answer to this puzzler is that cell relay isn't exactly faster, it just works differently and is meant to do different things from frame relay technologies.

Framing technologies are designed to squeeze more throughput from bandwidth than is technically possible. The idea is that you can connect a number of different sites with a relatively skinny pipe by exploiting the fact that all of those sites are probably not going to transmit at the same time. It's much the same idea as a bank that loans out its deposits—the bank depends on not every depositor demanding its money back at the same time. If there's a run on the bank, the bank can't pay everyone back; if there's a run on bandwidth (that is, more sites need it than there's room for), then frames get dropped. Because frame relay technologies interleave frames from a number of different sources at once, the frames in a single source's transmission won't necessarily arrive at their destination in a smooth stream, so frame relay WAN access works best for "bursty" data like text and static pictures where it doesn't matter which order the frames arrive in so long as they get there.

Cell relay technologies have a different function: rather than trying to squeeze more throughput out of existing bandwidth, cell relay is designed to make it possible to transmit a variety of data types (real-time voice and video and static data like text and pictures) over the same pipe. The packets used in cell relay are a uniform size (53 bytes) and travel in a steady stream to their destination. The throughput of cell relay depends on both the exact technology used and the size of the pipe through which the cells travel.

Packet Switching versus Circuit Switching

If you're wondering why you should care what a packet is, it's because packets use a different method of getting from point A to point B than some other data forms do. This method is known as *packet switching*, to distinguish it from *circuit switching*.

First of all, what is switching? Simply put, it describes how data finds a path from its source to its destination. A circuit-switching network defines a static path from one point to another; so long as the two points are connected, all data traveling between those two points will take the same path. Thus, it's unnecessary to include adddressing information in the packet with the data. Because there's only one path, the data can't get lost.

In a packet-switching network, on the other hand, there is no direct connection from point A to point B. Rather than a direct connection, the packet-switching network has a mesh of paths between the two points (see fig. 4.2).

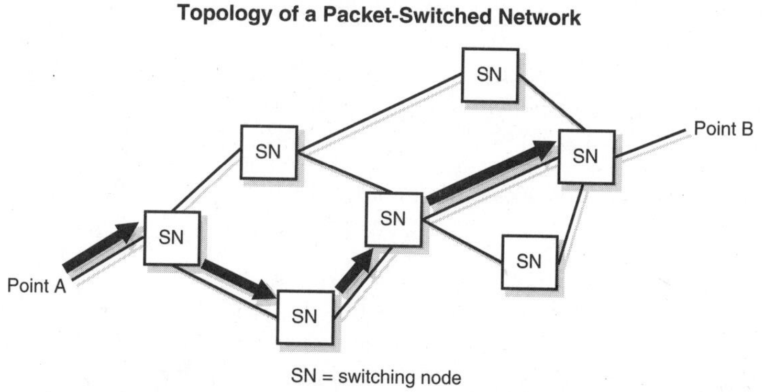

Topology of a Packet-Switched Network

SN = switching node

Figure 4.2

A packet-switching network has no set paths for data to travel.

A packet-switching network has no permanent physical path determining how data moves from point to point. Instead, the addressing information in the packet helps route the data its destination. You could think of a circuit-switching network as a complex of moving pipes, each disconnected from the others and a packet-switching network as a complex of connected pipes, through which data travels, choosing its path based on variables like traffic conditions.

> **Note**
>
> Circuit switching is faster because there's less overhead required, but packet switching is more flexible and so less vulnerable to "traffic jams."

Establishing Virtual Connections. When a connection is established between point A and point B on a packet-switching network, the network evaluates itself and sees how busy each of the paths are. Generally speaking, it will send the packets along the most direct route, but if that route is congested (that is, if another connection is already using it) it will choose a perhaps longer but less congested route. Think of it like this: you probably know the most direct route between your home and your workplace. If, however, you leave the building one day and hear that a five-car pileup has backed up traffic on your regular route, it's clear that the most direct route is not a good idea that day. Instead, you'll try your alternate route, the one that goes through three residential neighborhoods because even though the alternate is longer it'll be faster at that point.

Once a path between the two ends of the connections is established, that path won't change for the duration of the connection, even if a shorter path becomes available. Similarly, every time the connection is reestablished, the network evaluates the traffic conditions and finds the best route at that time. Packet-switching networks are not creatures of habit.

Practical Differences. The way that packet-switching networks send information affects both the kinds of data that they can transmit and the amount of overhead involved. A circuit-switching network establishes a physical connection between two points, whereas a packet-switching network establishes only a virtual connection for the duration of the session. That means that the following things are true:

- A packet-switching network requires some additional information to get the data to its destination
- There may be a slight delay as the packets get to their destination as the network figures out where they're going and how to get them there

The "additional information" noted here is the addressing information discussed in the previous section. A circuit-switching network, because it's a straight shot from one end of the network to the other, doesn't require that information any more than you have to provide directions to someone taking a subway from one stop to the end of the line: if they get on the train, they'll get to their destination. Packet switching is more like city traffic, as the network looks at the addressing information on the packets and figures out how best to get them where they need to be.

The delay in transmission is not long by human standards as such, but it's enough of a problem that until very recently packet-switching networks did not allow for transmission of time-sensitive information such as real-time video or voice. Recently, voice over packet-switching networks has been offered, but it's such a new technology that the jury's still out on how well it works.

Speed, Bandwidth, and Throughput

Although WANs don't necessarily have to be slower than LANs, they usually are. The difference does not have to be incapacitating by any means, but it's a fact of life that you've got to recognize. In fact, if you transmit much data across your WAN, you'll recognize this fact early and often.

A really good wide area connection has a practical speed of 1–2 Mbps (megabits per second). Although this doesn't sound like much when compared to the 10 Mbps of ordinary Ethernet or the 16 Mbps of fast token ring, it's not bad at all for the proper applications. Even slower WAN technologies, like ISDN, work fine with fairly large files so long as you've got your system configured properly. For example, keep as many applications on the LAN as possible and make sure that applications don't automatically search wide area connections first.

Speed, however, is not necessarily an accurate measure of a WAN pipeline's effectiveness. *Throughput*, or the measure of how much data actually gets from point A to point B in a given period, is more accurate. You can think of throughput as a function of the speed of data transmission combined with the size of the pipe—known as the *bandwidth*. Bandwidth describes the amount of data that can be squeezed into the physical medium of the cable at one time. For example, all other things being equal, a fiber-optic cable with two fibers has a higher bandwidth than a fiber-optic cable with only one fiber.

Before we continue, let me note that the number of channels—that is, the number of physical wires in the cable through which data travels—is related to bandwidth but is not necessarily the only thing determining it.

As you can see in figure 4.3, if you've got a skinny pipe (that is, low bandwidth), it doesn't matter how fast you shove data down it—only as much data as will fit in the pipe at a time will transmit. Likewise, if you've got a really wide pipe but low transmittal speed, the connection's throughput will be low because you're not pushing much down the pipe at one time. Speed is easier (and cheaper) to get than bandwidth, so you're more likely to run into the first scenario than the second.

The concepts shown in figure 4.3 may seem obvious, but keep it in mind as you continue through this chapter. Effective use of bandwidth to increase throughput is the key to making many WAN technologies work for you. Speed, bandwidth and throughput are *not* synonomous, as shown in table 4.1.

**High Bandwidth and Low Speed
versus
Low Bandwidth and High Speed**

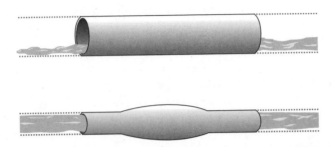

Figure 4.3

High bandwidth and low speed can contribute to the same throughput as low bandwidth and high speed.

Table 4.1 The Speed of Transmisssion Combined with the Available Bandwidth Determines Throughput	
Factor	**Explanation**
Speed	Indicates how fast data travels
Bandwidth	Indicates the width of the "pipe" through which the data travels
Throughput	The amount of data transmitted during a given interval

In other words:

Speed×Bandwidth=Throughput

Error Control

If the channels through which the data travels are prone to errors (perhaps caused by interference from other electronic signals), then some sort of error control needs to take place to ensure that the data that arrives at point B is the same data that left point A. The easiest way to do error control is to send duplicates of each packet, but this generates a lot of overhead and isn't a perfect solution anyway—if one packet gets corrupted, can you be sure that the other one isn't? How do you tell which one is right?

More elaborate forms of error control involve methods collectively known as *Cyclic Redundancy Checking* (*CDC*) using exclusive-or operations. Essentially, before the sender transmits a data packet it runs a particular algorithm using the data in the packet as the variables in the algorithm. This algorithm and the expected result is included in the packet along with the addressing information and the data. If the algorithm generates an unexpected result when the receiving node performs it, then the recipient assumes that the data was corrupted in transmission and sends a message to the sender to ask it to retransmit that packet.

For example, if the data in a particular packet consisted of the numbers 6 and 2, a potential error-checking algorithm might specify that the data should be added together, with a result of 8. If the recipient adds the data and gets 9, it knows that something went wrong in the transmission and asks the sender to resend the packet. The recipient can't correct the error as it has no way of determining what the original data was—it can only tell that the data was corrupted in transit.

CRCs are highly reliable. They add a little extra overhead to data transmission, but if there's a chance of the data being corrupted in transit, the overhead cost is lower than always sending duplicates or getting scrambled information.

Data Flow

When discussing WAN technologies, you'll encounter a couple of terms pertaining to the flow of data across the network that you may not be familiar with: *half duplex* and *full duplex*. Essentially, these terms describe the flow of packets through a connection. A half duplex connection means that data can only travel in one direction at once, while a full duplex connection means that it's possible to have data traveling in both directions at once (see fig. 4.4).

Half Duplex
versus
Full Duplex

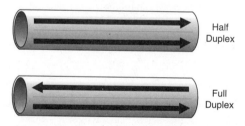

Figure 4.4

Half duplex transmissions can only send data in one direction at a time; full duplex can send in both directions simultaneously.

As you'll learn in the "Integrated Services Digital Network (ISDN)" section later in this chapter, some WAN technologies can be flexible about whether they're configured for full duplex communications or half duplex. Half duplex gives you greater throughput for one-way communications, but full duplex, if an option, means that both sides of the connection can "talk" at once, without waiting for the other side to finish.

Access Areas and WANs

The way that the telephone system is structured in the United States drives both the way that data services are structured and how you're billed for them. The FCC mapped the United States into LATAs.

LATAs do not necessarily correspond to local calling areas versus long-distance calls—you can be in the same LATA as the target of your call, but the call may be long distance. The boundaries of the LATAs only govern who can handle the call. If it's intra-LATA (within the boundaries of one LATA), either the local telephone company or a long-distance carrier can handle the call. If it's inter-LATA, on the other hand, a long-distance carrier must handle the part of the call that extends across the border. Refer to figure 4.5 to see how this works.

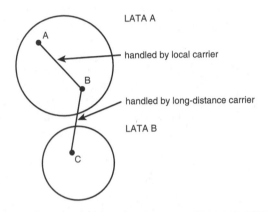

Figure 4.5

How the boundaries of LATAs govern who handles the connection.

Based on population and some other factors, the FCC may change the boundaries of a LATA. Essentially, LATAs are like the logical workgroups of the large network of the United States.

Why do you care where the LATAs are? Because the boundaries affect the data services that are available to you or (more accurately) how much those services will cost. If you need the service to span LATA boundaries, you can get it—but it will cost you.

Data services are generally offered on an intra-LATA basis. (If you buy the services from a third-party vendor, this is transparent to you.) If you want to cross a LATA boundary for your data connection, you'll need to buy space on a high-speed line (such as a T1 or T3) that connects two points within the LATAs. For example, say that your organization maintains three offices, in Greensboro, Springfield, and Hilltown. You can buy a data connection from the local carrier that will connect the sites in Greensboro and Spring-field, but a long-distance carrier will need to handle the connection between those sites and Hilltown because it is in a different LATA. To make the inter-LATA connection, you'll need to buy space on a high-speed line connecting a POP in each of the LATAs. From the POPs, the data connection works as it normally does in the LATA. Like a router, the POP bothers itself only with what it must transmit.

The lines that you use to connect your sites may vary considerably in speed. On the low end, you've got the DS0 lines that run at 64 Kbps (kilobits per second). One step up from there is a T1 connection (the physical cable used in a T1 connection is known as a DS1), which contains bandwidth equivalent to 28 DS0s or 1.544 Mbps. From there, you can get a T3 connection with bandwidth equivalent to 28 T1s or 45 Mbps. There are cables with even higher bandwidth than the T3, but that's the most that you'll probably have to worry about.

The price of these connections depends on the speed of the connection and how far you want it to stretch. As you'd expect, you'll pay more for a T3 line that extends across 200 miles than you will for a DS0 line that extends the same distance. Although there is an installation charge to connect a T1 (or whatever) line to your site, many vendors, such as AT&T, will waive the installation charges as part of a promotional deal.

Types of WANs

That should be enough background to enable you to discuss WAN types and understand their characteristics. Over the next few pages, you will learn about some of the more popular WAN types.

Integrated Services Digital Network (ISDN)

Although one of the slower wide area technologies, ISDN definitely has its uses for connecting LANs, especially LANs not too far from each other. First of all, it's relatively cheap—the slowest speed (64 Kbps or 128 Kbps depending on how you set it up) is available in most urban areas for around $40 per month plus about two cents per connected minute for each data channel. The hardware is equally reasonable because you need only two pieces of hardware on each end of the connection.

Where ISDN is available (unfortunately, it isn't everywhere) the telephone company makes a dial-up connection between two sites. Each site gets an ISDN number, which looks like a telephone number. The connection between the two sites consists of three channels. The bearer, or "B," channel carries connection information between the two sites at a rate of 16 Kbps. The data, or "D," channel transmits the actual data and runs at 64 Kbps each. Refer to figure 4.6 for an illustration of how an ISDN connection is set up.

Parts of an ISDN Connection

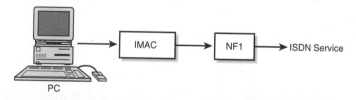

Figure 4.6

An ISDN connection consists of two data channels and one channel for transmitting connection information.

If you need data to be able to run in both directions at once (or need to use one of the data channels for voice), you can get 64 Kbps throughput from a regular ISDN connection. If a more unidirectional approach will work for you, you can double the effective speed of the connection by logically combining the channels to make the connection 128 Kbps. Combining the channels and making the ISDN connection effectively half duplex isn't as bad an idea as it may sound. First, a half duplex connection doesn't mean that data can only travel in one direction, it means that data can travel only in one direction at a time over the connection, like a travel lane that changes directions depending on the time of day. Second, in many wide area applications the flow of data is tilted to one side more than another: I need more data from you than you need data from me. Third, 128 Kbps isn't a bad speed at all, and you may well be able to clear the connection before data needs to travel the other way (or at least before there's a discernible wait). Figure 4.7 shows how you can combine ISDN channels.

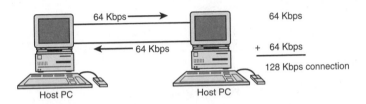

Figure 4.7

Combine ISDN channels to increase throughput.

Over time, new breeds of ISDN have evolved as everything does to become both faster and more expensive. Some areas now offer ISDN with more data channels—and thus greater throughput—that can increase the speed of the connection to 256 Kbps or even 512 Kbps. Of course, with increased speed comes more expensive hardware and more expensive connections. In addition to the installation charges, a 256 Kbps connection, where available, costs around $150 per month and the hardware runs about $1,500 per site. To have a 512 Kbps connection means a monthly charge of about $300 and hardware costs of around $5,000 per site. (Exact costs and availability for all of these will depend heavily on where you are and what's available.) If you're not sure that you'll need the 512 Kbps connection, you can get the 256 Kbps connection and upgrade the hardware later. The hardware required is a device called an IMAC, which can be either a stand-alone black box or a card that plugs into a slot on the motherboard of your NetWare or NT server. The card is easily upgradeable; modules plug into the card and then are connected to a device called an NT1 that is your site's liason to the telephone company. Each module carries 128 Kbps, so you can add more modules (up to a total of four) to get more speed.

Note

IMAC, pronounced "Eye-Mack," stands for *ISDN MAC-layer (bridge)*, meaning that it's a bridge that operates at the MAC layer of the OSI model. (You know it's a networking acronymn when it nests not one but two other acronyms.) Turn to chapters 3, "The OSI Model: Bringing Order to Chaos," for more information about the media access control layer and 14, "Repeaters and Bridges," to learn about the exact function of a bridge.

Distance. If those are the speeds available, how much does distance affect those speeds? Not at all, actually. Whether you're five blocks away or fifty miles, a 128 Kbps connection pushes data along at the same rate. This is because even fiber-optic cable can only transmit data so long without needing to bump up the signal (about three miles), so the telephone companies maintain repeaters to increase the signal volume when necessary. The signal starts afresh each time it hits a repeater, and fiber-optic signals travel so fast that the time for the signal to travel from point to point along the connection is determined by the size of the path (the bandwidth), rather than the distance that the signal has to travel.

However, distance does affect your ISDN connection in terms of cost. If you've got two ISDN sites in two different area codes, every second of connect time is billed as a long distance call. The amount of traffic sent over the line doesn't matter, any more than the cost of a half-hour long-distance telephone call depends on whether you talk a lot or sit in silence for most of the call. It's the time that the connection is maintained that determines the cost.

Connection Charges. In most cases (there are a few exceptions, but you can't count on being one of them) you'll be charged a few cents per minute for the connection. This fee is not dependent on whether you're actually sending anything during that time; if the connection is active, you'll be charged for it.

The way that ISDN connection costs are determined makes a difference in how best to set up your WAN if you're connecting two sites in the same local telephone area. If it's a flat connect fee, you can have one site call the other and never hang up. At any time, the connection between the two sites is maintained. This is much more convenient, as you don't have to redial whenever someone needs to connect to the other site.

If, however, you're charged for connect time, as most sites will be, then keeping the connection open could be very expensive. Check your tariff system before deciding whether to maintain the connection or only dial up when someone needs to transmit data.

Preparing for ISDN. So far you've read a lot about what ISDN is, how it works, and some of the options that you can set on your ISDN connection, but there's one question left unanswered: if you want an ISDN connection, how do you get it?

The local telephone company (or a local vendor working with the telephone company) offers the service. Call them and ask to talk to someone about data services—if you just tell the operator that you're interested in an ISDN connection, you may not get very far. When you call, be prepared with the telephone numbers of the sites that you want to connect.

You'll need answers to the following questions, which the vendor can help you answer:

- What's the installation fee?

- What are the flat connect charges? Are there use-based charges? What are they?

- What hardware do I need? Where do I get it, and what will it cost?

- Who's responsible for making sure that the connection is set up properly?

Using ISDN. Using ISDN isn't difficult. Your ISDN number will be programmed by the vendor) into an IMAC that connects your network to the outside world via a gateway machine. This IMAC can be either a stand-alone device or a card that plugs into a server running Netware 4.x or NT Server 3.5x or later. (The card is called a PC-IMAC, and it's available for ISA, EISA, and MCA slots.) The vendor will provide a management application to program the IMAC. Using the software on the gateway machine, you'll call the other ISDN number whenever you want to connect to another site. If you've wrangled a deal in which you don't get charged per minute of connect time, then you can call once and never hang up, leaving your WAN perpetually available. More likely, however, you'll set up the session each time you need it, perhaps every morning. The exact times that you call and hang up will of course depend on what you need from the office you connect to and whether you're connecting to more than one ISDN site.

Special Considerations about ISDN. When considering ISDN for your organization, there are a few things peculiar to ISDN that you should know about.

First, ISDN supports both voice and data. This means that, should you need more available bandwidth for your voice applications, you have a 64 Kbps channel available. You will need a special digital ISDN telephone for the connection, however, as analog telephones can't deal with the digital signals.

Second, although you can use a modem on an ISDN line, you'll need a translator to convert the digital signals to analog signals for the modem because modems can't receive digital signals. This seems like a lot of trouble and expense to go through to have a slower connection, unless you're using a special modem to get that ISDN Internet connection and download DOOM scenarios at 128 Kbps.

> **Note**
>
> Modems aren't accustomed to receiving digital signals? If this sounds odd, remember that modems modulate digital signals into analog signals that can travel along normal (analog) telephone lines. ("Modem" stands for modulator/demodulator.) The modem at the other end demodulates the signal into the digital form that the PC can understand.

Switched Multimegabit Data Service (SMDS)

ISDN is good for point-to-point connections, but what if your enterprise includes a number of points within a metro area that need to be connected? Technically, you could connect them all by ISDN (see fig. 4.8), but this situation is less than ideal for a few reasons:

- You have to make and break connections to talk to all sites—you can't switch dynamically

- Maintaining a large number of connections is expensive

- Slower than some other options

Connecting Multiple Sites with ISDN

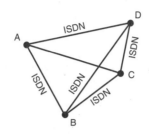

Figure 4.8

You can connect multiple sites with ISDN, but it's not an ideal solution.

SMDS is one solution to the problem of how to connect multiple sites in a relatively small area. Rather than being a point-to-point protocol, it connects each site to a WAN "cloud" that allows any SMDS client to connect to any other. You can see how SMDS can connect a number of sites in figure 4.9.

Sites Connecting to an SMDS Cloud

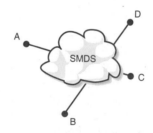

Figure 4.9

Individual sites connect to an SMDS cloud.

Note

A WAN "cloud" is the space between the sites served by the public company, in which you don't know the exact mesh pattern. The exact contents and appearance of the cloud are usually not important to the operation of your WAN.

Although it's still a mesh configuration (in that you need one connection for each site that you're connected to), SMDS has other features that render it closer to the cloud configuration illustrated in figure 4.9 than to the ISDN spiderweb. It differs from that spiderweb in that

- It's faster—at a minimum, a 1.17 Mbps connection instead of at ISDN's fastest 512 Kbps

- You pay a flat monthly rate (around $600 for each site) for the connection, so you can dial in and not hang up, meaning that your network is always operational

- Instead of dialing a number to make the connection, you order your router to do it

- You can add more addresses to your possible connections—you just can't connect to more addresses at one time than you have connections

Pricing SMDS

If the $600 monthly cost of SMDS for each site connected seems expensive, consider this: to connect a four-site WAN with SMDS, you need four router WAN ports and four SMDS CSU/DSUs for a total equipment cost of around $35,000. Getting a T1 connection (which provides the same throughput) between each site requires eight router WAN ports and eight CSU/DSUs (for a total of around $40,000), plus four T1 channels and eight T1 terminations, and however many miles of DS1 cable required to connect the sites, at around $23 per mile, for a total of around $3,000 per month. The SMDS-compatible equipment is more expensive than the T1-compatible equipment, but you need less of it.

How SMDS Works. SMDS is a *cell relay* WAN technology, meaning that the packets in which it encloses data are the 53-byte cells discussed earlier in this chapter. Using the fixed-size cells means that the connection can be faster as it takes more overhead for a connection to cope with packets of varying size. Although the Institute of Electrical and Electronics Engineers (IEEE) specification around which it was designed describes how to handle data, voice, and video, SMDS only supports data transfer. However, if you're contemplating moving to ATM, which does support all three, SMDS could be a good idea for you. (Right now, some telephone companies are offering ATM on a beta basis to a few customers, but that's about it.) The 53-byte cells that SMDS uses are completely compatible with those used by ATM, so according to theory, the upgrade will be pretty easy.

At each point on an SMDS network, the site contains a piece of hardware called an SMDSU (a CSU/DSU configured for SMDS) and a router that's been configured for SMDS. These units are connected to a high-speed line that plugs the site into the SMDS cloud illustrated in the previous figure. In other words, to connect your LAN to a SMDS network, you'll need the following:

- A router that supports SMDS, running SMDS software

- A CSU/DSU that supports SMDS

- A service agreement with the local telephone company or other provider

The router and CSU/DSU work together to get the data from the LAN to the WAN. First, the router encapsulates the LAN frame into an SMDS frame (called a L3PDU, for *level 3 protocol data unit*). Then the router encapsulates the L3PDU into a high-level data-link control (HDLC) frame that the CSU/DSU can receive. The CSU/DSU then removes the HDLC envelope and converts the L3PDU to the 53-byte cells transmitted across the network. Thus, the equipment on your site, in combination with the telephone company's hardware, links your site to the SMDS cloud and to other linked sites with addresses listed in your router (see fig. 4.10)

Equipment Chain that Links Your LAN to SMDS Cloud

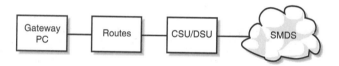

Figure 4.10

An equipment chain links your LAN to the SMDS cloud.

You can either ask the SMDS vendor to get the equipment for you or purchase your own from another source. If you purchase your own equipment, make sure that it corresponds to any hardware compatibility lists that the vendor has issued.

Tip

Interoperability can be a bit of a problem when it comes to getting routers and CSU/DSU to work together. You will probably have to purchase both devices from the same vendor—another reason to let the SMDS vendor help you find equipment.

Like most other WAN technologies, SMDS is available in a variety of speeds. The baseline version connects your sites at a little more than 1 Mbps (1.17 to be exact). You can also purchase faster connections, which can bump the connection's throughput up to 34 Mbps—more than three times an LAN Ethernet connection. For most purposes, the 1 Mbps connection is adequate.

Security: Creating Virtual Private Networks. If your SMDS connection plugs you into the main SMDS network in the area, how do you keep outsiders from calling into your system? The answer is an address-screening system. Although an SMDS network is in some ways similar to a peer-to-peer network (in that it connects several sites on an equal basis), it differs from a peer-to-peer network in that no browsing is allowed. You can only connect to those addresses listed in your router.

This sounds complicated, but it's pretty straightforward. Imagine that the four of your company's sites have just joined the network, called A, B, C, and D. However, another company's sites, E and F, are already plugged into the network. They can't see you, however. Your router only accepts calls from A–D (and, for that matter, E and F wouldn't have any idea how to find you). Part of the setup of your SMDS installation is programming the routers with the addresses of any of the sites that you'll ever need to connect to. Add a site, add an address. Think of it as telling the receptionist at your company, "I'll take any calls from Joe, Susan, or Betty, but if anyone else calls I'm not here." You don't have to deliberately exclude anyone, but if you don't include a site in your "accept calls" list, they won't be able to talk to you.

SMDS sites can have more than one address per access line (up to 16), so you can even direct connections within the site. Thus, another SMDS site could call not just a physical site, but subsets within that site. If your site A should only be connecting to a subset of site B, you can set up more than one address at site B and only permit site A to transmit data to a particular address.

SMDS Considerations. Before subscribing to SMDS, the following are a few items to keep in mind:

- The number of sites that you'll need to connect to at one time

- The kinds of networks running at each site

- The speed of connection that you need

Number of Sites. When subscribing, you'll need to buy as many connections as you intend to be connected to at one time. For example, if your company has four sites, but you know that you'll never connect to more than two of the others at a time, you can get away with two connections. Be conservative and assume that you'll need full connectibility when you're figuring what you can afford. In addition, make sure that you've got a couple of extra WAN ports on your router so that you can add more connections if you have to.

To connect to more sites, you don't necessarily need more connections. It's the number of concurrent connections that you need to plan for.

Kind of LAN at Each Site. The LANs connected via SMDS can be a little different, but you need the same logical topology on both ends (and, obviously, a mutually compatible file format) to make the connection work. You can't connect an Ethernet network to a token-ring network and expect the thing to work without the extra bells and whistles that you'd expect to connect an Ethernet and token-ring network locally. The cabling that you use matters less, however, as the two networks never touch except via the router and the WAN.

> **Tip**
>
> A logical topology describes the form in which data is packaged and passed around a network. An Ethernet network uses a different logical topology than a token-ring network (the frames and method of data transmission are different) even if the Ethernet and token-ring networks are physically arranged in the same way.

Speed Required. You can get an SMDS connection up to 34 Mbps quite easily, but you need to consider the ramifications of the speeds. First and foremost, higher-speed connections cost more. Second, the hardware may not be upgradeable, so if you know that you'll need the faster connection next year and plan to get it, look for a router that can make the connection.

The Future of SMDS. Although SMDS is an intra-LATA data service because of those FCC regulations discussed earlier in this chapter, you can buy a T1 connection to connect the POPs in the LATAs that you want to connect, thereby extending your WAN across the country. The price of these connections isn't dropping as fast as other computing hardware (in fact, the cost of a DS0 connection just went up in 1995), but it's possible to maintain the connection at local speeds. Presumably, as bandwidth technology progresses, the cost of the inter-LATA connections will drop and connecting distant sites will become more cost-effective.

In addition to widening its scope, SMDS will become faster. Already, it's available at speeds up to 34 Mbps with a high-speed line (although quite expensive). Its use of cell relay technology, with consistently-sized packets, means that it should be upgradeable to ATM, so long as you're using a line that can handle the high speeds that ATM technology requires. For now, however, high-speed WANs may take a different form, using fiber distributed data interface.

Using Fiber Distributed Data Interface (FDDI) across a WAN

The best trick in the book is a WAN that's as fast as your LAN. Sound impossible? Not any more. In some locations (not many right now, but it should be more soon) you can get native speed from your WAN by connecting to a fiber-optic ring that's using FDDI. This is called the FDDI Network Services (FNS).

What Is FNS? FNS is a public network that uses a 100 Mbps FDDI backbone to provide a connection for LANs within its geographical reach. The telephone company runs two concentric fiber rings (two so that the redundant ring can take over if the first breaks or fails) that subscribers can tap into throughout the service area. The entire setup looks like figure 4.11.

Although this technology was first described to me as a wide area Ethernet (Ethernet being the LAN type), that's not really accurate. FNS could just as easily be described as a wide area token-ring network. Because it follows both the IEEE 802.3 standards, which describe Ethernet communications, and the 802.5, which describe how token-ring networks transmit data, the fiber backbone rings can work with either. When subscribing, you tell the telephone company what kind of network you've got and they'll provide you with the proper interface.

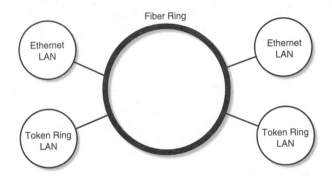

Figure 4.11

FNS can connect sites in a metropolitan area so that the WAN connection is as fast as the LAN speeds.

Of course, the LANs at the sites that you're connecting must be of the same type or else they won't recognize each other any more than an Ethernet LAN recognizes a PC bearing only a token-ring network interface card (NIC), assuming you rigged some way to connect the token-ring NIC to the rest of the LAN.

Note

Recall the discussion earlier in this chapter of packet switching versus circuit switching. Because it's using FDDI, FNS is an example of a WAN technology that isn't really either one. The ring connects the taps, and the packets on the ring get routed to the appropriate tap depending on the address in the packet header—just like those on a WAN. There are no alternate routes to switch.

Applications. The high speeds of the fiber backbone make it possible for you to do almost anything over your WAN that you can do locally.

- Share drive space
- Share peripheral devices, such as CD-ROM drives
- Back up networked drives
- Send e-mail that will arrive as fast as e-mail sent intra-office and without requiring an online service

With native LAN speeds between local sites, the only restriction that you're likely to run into is one of convenience. For example, printing to a printer three blocks away is inconvenient, at best. Even if the output is for the people in the office where the printer is located, you'd need someone to play printer administrator to make sure that the printer has paper and toner and isn't jammed. (Admittedly, some printers and operating systems provide error messages to the machine where the print job originated if something goes wrong, but most printer error messages reduce problems to the printer being out of paper, even if it isn't.)

Printing may not be a good wide area application, but backups certainly could be. If you've got one backup administrator in the main office, they can be responsible for backing up the servers at the branch offices as well—the 10 Mbps of an Ethernet connection is certainly fast enough to back up a drive. Having a centralized backup system makes it easier to collect and keep all the backup archives off-site. (See chapter 17, "Backup Technology: Programs and Data," for more about backup strategies.)

Another application in which FNS can really shine is client/server software, such as databases. One of the biggest concerns of running any kind of software over a network is response time. The longer you have to wait to make the application work, the less useful it is, and the less likely that it will get used. Even client/server software, which should be optimized so that only the processing best done at the server end is done there and the rest is done by the client machine, is vulnerable to slow connections (although less so than older applications that put all the processing at one end of the connection). So client/server applications will benefit from the higher WAN speeds available with FNS.

The usefulness of FNS to client/server goes even farther, however. One of the emerging trends in client/server processing is peer-to-peer information accessing. Rather than having a central repository of data at the server, the database is distributed among the clients. If one client updates the information in its database (perhaps a stock inventory) then all the other clients need to know about this change immediately so that their records are accurate. So long as the updates are handled well (that is, if the database writers don't try to replicate the entire database to the other clients when one entry changes), this doesn't present too much of a traffic problem for a high-speed LAN. Over a slower WAN, however, the updates take more time, especially if other traffic needs the bandwidth as well. If the clients using and updating a peer-to-peer database were connected by a WAN technology as fast as a LAN, then peer-to-peer databases over a WAN become much more possible.

In any case, if you sign your offices up for this service, think about what you'll be using it for and make sure to use the high-speed WAN for the things it's best at. If you want to use the WAN connection for something, make sure that it's something that no one needs to be on the spot for.

Hardware Requirements. One of the best things about making the fiber ring the backbone of your WAN is that the hardware requirements are almost nil. To connect a token-ring network to the ring, you need no additional hardware—the telephone company provides a multistation access unit (MAU, a term already familiar to token-ring users) and a repeater to boost the signal as required. An Ethernet network requires only a transceiver. You literally plug the network in as though you were connecting two segments of your network. In a sense, you are.

You can see how you'd connect your Ethernet or token-ring network to the fiber line in figures 4.12 and 4.13:

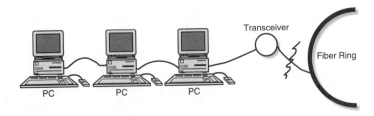

Figure 4.12

Connecting an Ethernet network to the fiber ring.

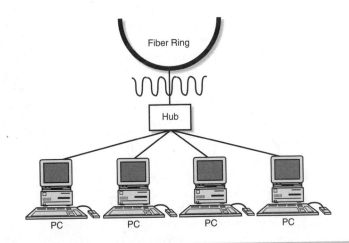

Figure 4.13

Connecting a token-ring network to the fiber ring.

Security. If anyone in a metro area with an Ethernet or token-ring network can tap into FNS, how do you keep other FNS subscribers from accessing your network? Actually, the security built into FNS is much like that built into SMDS. In each case, the routers maintain a list of the valid addresses that may connect to a given site. The only difference is who does the maintaining: if it's SMDS, you (the customer) updates the router; if it's FNS, the vendor does it. But the bottom line is that other FNS subscribers can't see into your network. So far as each subscriber's concerned, they're the only ones on the fiber ring.

Price and Availability. If FNS is so wonderful, why isn't everyone using it already? Two reasons. First, it's not available everywhere. Installing a fiber backbone like the one illustrated at the beginning of this section is an expensive enterprise, and locations without a large number of potential subscribers are not likely candidates for fiber WAN backbones.

Second, where it is available there is sometimes surprisingly little information about it. Your best bet for getting information specific to your area is probably the marketing manager for data services at your local telephone company. Outside vendors, even if they contract with the telephone company, may not know much about it (as I discovered when shopping for WAN technologies at one point).

Third, and this is really the big one keeping people from lining up in droves to sign up, a fiber connection is expensive. Even without any hardware at your site, the installation costs run about $1,300 per site, and then you've got monthly charges ranging from around $850–$1,200 per month, depending on whether you're connecting 4 Mbps token ring, 10 Mbps Ethernet, or 16 Mbps token ring. That's a lot of money to spend on networking, even if your additional hardware costs are low or nonexistent. Before purchasing a WAN that is this expensive, some serious cost-accounting is in order.

> ### Note
>
> To learn more about the mechanics of how the fiber ring transmits data, turn to chapter 7, "Major Network Types," to learn more about the FDDI logical topology.

The Future of FNS. FNS is a relatively new technology, only offered since the early to mid nineties. What's going to happen to it over the next few years?

Replacing Dark Fiber. Dark fiber, as you may know, used to be the private answer to FNS. Dark fiber is a point-to-point fiber line that the telephone company runs for you (only those with right-of-way can run cable, such as the telephone company or the television cable providers) that you maintain. With a router on each end to connect the fiber to the LAN, you could have a privately maintained, high-speed WAN, like the FNS described over the past few pages but for the fault-tolerance provided by the second ring.

Note the use of past tense here. Most telephone companies won't be offering dark fiber by the time you read this. As one telephone data services representative explained it, it's not cost-effective for them to run the fiber and have the customer maintain it. Under previous legislation, the FCC made the telephone companies offer the service, but the new rules mean that they don't have to offer it, so they don't. The bottom line is that, if you want a new fiber backbone for your WAN, you'll have to get FNS unless you own the land under which you propose to run the fiber.

More Rings. If FNS spreads across the country, it's going to do it by means of interconnected rings following population growth. Currently, four rings are deployed in the Washington, DC metro area, meaning that intra-LATA areas in Virginia, DC, and Maryland can be connected without having to have one huge fiber ring. Given that even fiber has its distance limits (about three miles before the signal needs boosting with a repeater), this means that FNS can extend farther with less hardware involved. Costs for everything in the computing industry fall eventually—look at how the price of a hard disk has fallen over just the past five years. Barring legislation that makes it more expensive for the telephone companies to run the fiber, expect the service to spread and costs to drop. Who knows? Individual taps may become reasonably priced. The path to the full-blown information highway may yet be via your computer, rather than your television.

Wide Area ATM? ATM is one of the great buzzwords of the age, but at this point not much more than that due to its extremely high costs and limited availability. ATM is a networking technology that can transmit data, real-time video, and voice. Its extremely high speeds avoid the lag time that kills voice and video (if you remember calling long distance when delay was a fact of life, you know how frustrating that can be), and its use of cell relay technology, like SMDS, means that it can split various kinds of data into a steady stream of 53-byte cells and route them smoothly to their destinations.

If FNS becomes more affordable and widespread, it's possible that it could be the physical medium that gets ATM to the desktop, not just in LANs but across the country. Although the hardware costs would still have to come down (the equipment that reverts the 53-byte cells to their original data, voice, or video form costs a lot), FNS could at least get the data to its destination. The only catch is that for inter-LATA communications, the data has to travel across a T line supplied by a long distance company. That's a lot of bandwidth to maintain the high speeds: seven T1 lines to maintain a 10 Mbps connection across a LATA.

Frame Relay

Thus far, we've talked about ISDN, a relatively cheap way of extending your LAN (apart from using modems, anyway), SMDS, a flexible way, and FNS, a super-fast way. *Frame relay* fills a different role for WANs, that of the efficient way. Operating on the principle that not every site with access to bandwidth will need all of that bandwidth at once, it interleaves data from a number of different sources, squeezing more use out of the bandwidth than it's technically capable of. Essentially, frame relay is a way of paying for less bandwidth and getting more, with one catch: sometimes you may not get anything at all.

What is frame relay? It's a wide area connection protocol (there is no such thing as a frame relay network, as such—it's only a way of accessing a network) that transmits variably sized packets called *frames*. The real trick to a frame relay connection is that it's designed to transmit more data than the bandwidth of the connection can actually accommodate. You can see a frame relay network in figure 4.14.

It does this by making use of a basic fact of networking: most of the time, if you're on a network, you're not transmitting data. You open files, you send e-mail, you access databases, but you don't do any of these things constantly. Now, if you're the only one accessing the network this doesn't matter. As this isn't the case, that means that while you're not transmitting data, your neighbors can. As you remember from earlier in this chapter, WANs divide bandwidth into channels, and in older technologies, each sender got one channel all the time, whether they were transmitting data or not. Thus, most of the time, the allocated bandwidth goes to waste. Given the high cost of WAN channels, this gets either very expensive or very slow. Frame relay, in contrast, gives the sender all the channels for the space of the transmission. Conceptually, the difference in transmission looks like figure 4.15.

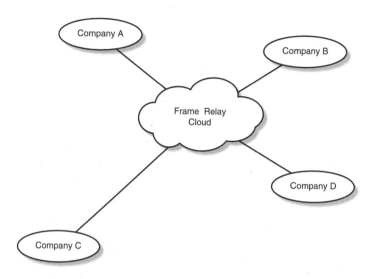

Figure 4.14

A frame relay network lets the subscribers in the area share bandwidth so that all of them get more throughput from the bandwidth than it could accommodate if each subscriber had a dedicated channel for their exclusive use.

Allocating Channels versus Allocating by Need

Virtual channels do not use bandwidth efficiently, as transmitters get channel space even when not sending.

Combining the bandwidth allows all senders to use all available bandwidth, with no wasted space.

Figure 4.15

You can allocate channels either by time or by need.

The allocation method frame relay uses is called *statistical multiplexing* (often just *stat muxing*). Stat muxing sounds obscure, but it's only allocating bandwidth as needed, on a packet-by-packet basis. Using it, frame relay networks normally give you WAN speeds of about 2 Mbps; the exact speed depends on the vendor and the speed you buy. Technically, frame relay can achieve speeds of up to 50 Mbps, but as of mid-1995, I've never heard of this speed being offered outside the lab.

Frame relay is designed to be a fast and inexpensive method of accessing a WAN. To that end, it's got the following characteristics:

- One physical link can provide access to many locations

- No error-correcting checksums (unnecessary on reliable fiber lines) mean less over-head and a faster connection

- Optionally, has flow control or error checking at end units to increase reliability on more crowded connections

All of these characteristics mean that frame relay is good for applications that sporadically transmit smallish chunks of data and have access to reliable physical connections that don't need error-correcting capabilities like those of X.25 (described later in this chapter).

How Frame Relay Works. Highway traffic provides a useful analogy for describing the elements of frame relay:

- No dedicated channels

- A guaranteed rate of throughput

- Error-managing

Let's look at each of these elements in turn, using a highway analogy in which the available bandwidth is the highway, channels are lanes, and packets are cars.

Shared Bandwidth. First, there's the matter of lanes. Older WAN technologies divided the highway into static "lanes" (the channels) that belonged to a particular sender whether that sender was using them or not. This would be like saying that, in a highway that provides access from Springfield to Richmond, Fredericksburg, and Norfolk that traffic to each of those cities was restricted to its own lane—even if no one's going to Fredericksburg or Norfolk on a given morning, and the lane for Richmond is jammed, the Richmond traffic can't use the other lanes.

Clearly, this method of managing a highway doesn't get best use out of the available highway space. To enable more traffic to get to Richmond on Monday mornings, you'd have to build another road or widen the lane, either of which would be an expensive proposition. If few people travel to Fredericksburg or Norfolk, why not remove the barriers between the lanes and let all traffic, no matter what its destination, use the same lanes? This might not remove traffic problems, but it should alleviate them.

If the frames going to their various destinations are all jumbled up during transmission, how do they get sorted out for delivery? Each frame is identified by a part called the *data link connection identifier* (*DLCI*). These DLCIs work like unloading areas—a frame is sent to a location identified in the DLCI rather than to an address. When the loading area at the network node receives the frame, it looks at the DLCI and sees if it corresponds to an address accessible from that location. If so, the data gets routed to its final destination. If the frame was routed to that location in error because a bit got scrambled on the way, the frame is dropped and the recipient (not the frame relay access) must tell the sender to resend the data.

Guaranteed Throughput. Because frame relay thus utilizes all available space on the bandwidth, getting more throughput that you'd get from dividing the channels, some mechanism for making sure that at least *some* of the traffic gets to its destination is in order. For example, the highway department might say that cars going to Richmond are guaranteed to travel 60 miles in an hour. This guarantee, the *committed information rate* (*CIR*), doesn't mean that the cars will travel at 60 Mph—the CIR guarantees a distance to travel in a certain period, not a speed. Thus, the traffic might go 0 Mph at one time and 100 Mph at other times, but the highway department guarantees that it will travel 60 miles in one hour, even if that means forcing other cars off the road.

Should a car exceed 60 Mph, the highway department tickets it. If traffic gets too heavy, ticketed cars are the first ones forced off the road into the ditch. If traffic remains manageable, however, the ticketed cars reach their destination with no penalty. The tickets are only a way of marking who's expendable. It is the same with frames. If they exceed their CIR, they can be dropped if traffic gets too heavy. If there's enough bandwidth for them, they get through. (In addition, the network can optionally ticket lower-priority frames ahead of time so that if traffic's too heavy those frames will be dropped first.)

When you buy frame relay services, the CIR you get depends on what you pay for and what the vendor offers. The minimum CIR that you need is still a matter of debate. The cheapest CIR is 0, meaning that the vendor doesn't guarantee that *any* of your data will reach its destination. Not all vendors will sell you a CIR of 0, and you'll have to decide what your lowest acceptable rate is. It's not a hard-and-fast answer, as some people find that a low CIR gets them the throughput they need at a lower cost, while others demand more ensured reliability.

> **Note**
>
> So long as usage of frame relay remains relatively low, a CIR of 0 may be acceptable because there's less competition for bandwidth among customers. As more subscribers begin jostling for space, however, you may want to increase your CIR to make sure that your data gets through.

Congestion Handling. What about those cars getting forced off the road? What happens to them? In frame relay, there's a couple of different ways of handling packets that are lost due to heavy traffic (forced off the road). These methods are not part of frame relay as such but are part of the end-user equipment that sends and receives the frames and the protocols on the connected LANs.

One type of congestion handling lets the destination handle traffic control. Part of a frame relay frame is a congestion information field. The sender can flip a bit (called the *forward explicit congestion bit* (*FECN*), if you're interested) in this field, and the recipient will monitor the number of bits it sees. If the number exceeds a certain density, the recipient will refuse to accept more frames until it has caught up. You can see how this works in figure 4.16.

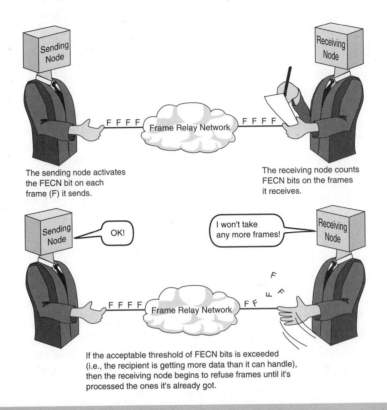

The sending node activates the FECN bit on each frame (F) it sends.

The receiving node counts FECN bits on the frames it receives.

OK!

I won't take any more frames!

If the acceptable threshold of FECN bits is exceeded (i.e., the recipient is getting more data than it can handle), then the receiving node begins to refuse frames until it's processed the ones it's already got.

Figure 4.16

How FECN congestion handling works.

Another method works in a similar manner, except that the bit to be flipped is called the *backward explicit congestion bit* (*BECN*). If the number of BECN bits exceeds a certain threshold, the recipient tells the sender to stop sending frames so quickly. Once the recipient has caught up, it notifies the sender that it can begin sending again (see fig. 4.17).

Both of these methods are called explicit, meaning that they take proactive measures to ensure that traffic never gets too bad. These methods, once again, are not part of frame relay—they're part of the protocols on either end of the connection, and the one used depends on the protocols you run, and not all protocols provide for either one.

There's one method of congestion handling that any frame relay connection can provide, however. If the user equipment is capable of measuring the number of dropped frames, it can determine when that number has exceeded a certain threshold and then tell the sender to slow down transmittal. This method isn't as good at congestion handling as the other two, as it only alleviates traffic problems after they've become *big* problems, but sometimes it's your only option. TCP/IP, for example, can only work with implicit congestion handling. Figure 4.18 shows how implicit congestion handling works.

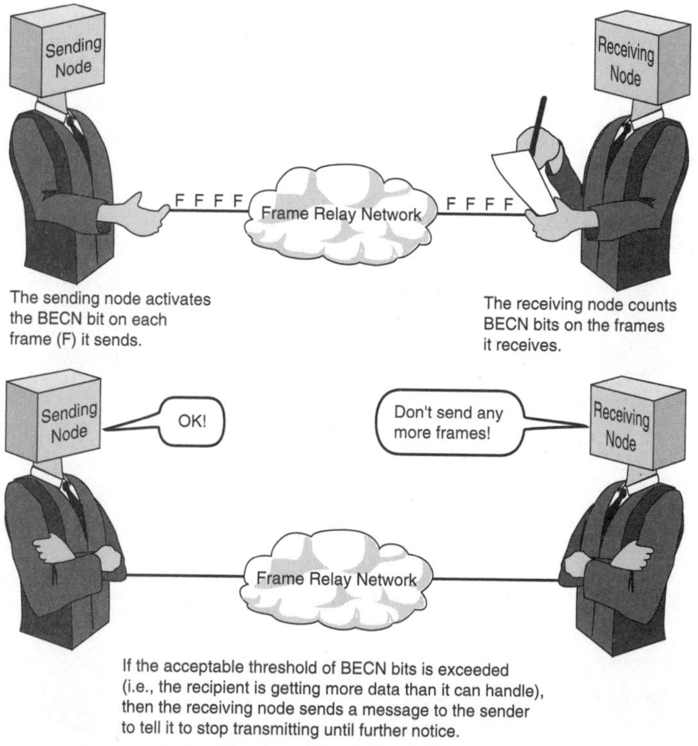
Sending Node
Receiving Node
F F F F
Frame Relay Network
F F F F
The sending node activates the BECN bit on each frame (F) it sends.
The receiving node counts BECN bits on the frames it receives.
Sending Node
OK!
Don't send any more frames!
Receiving Node
Frame Relay Network
If the acceptable threshold of BECN bits is exceeded (i.e., the recipient is getting more data than it can handle), then the receiving node sends a message to the sender to tell it to stop transmitting until further notice.

Figure 4.17

How BECN congestion handling works.

If frames are dropped, it's the job of the end protocols to notice and request that they be resent. If you find that you're having to do a lot of congestion handling or are losing a lot of frames, it might be time to consider purchasing a higher CIR.

X.25

Frame relay can do a wonderful job of connecting sites within the United States, where lines are essentially error-free. What about connecting sites in places with less reliable wide area connections? If you want to connect sites in areas where copper lines are still used, you'll need some extra protection to make sure that the data gets to its destination in one piece. That protection could come in the form of X.25.

Who's Using X.25? X.25 is not as popular in the United States as frame relay because it's not as fast (normally limited to a 64–256 Kbps connection, although some X.25 services can use T1 lines), but outside of the United States (including Europe), it's a very popular WAN type. It's available almost anywhere and its error-correcting capabilities make it very reliable.

Like frame relay, X.25 is good for applications that send a little bit of data in short bursts—what's known as "bursty" transmissions. Database entries, e-mail, and inventory systems are all good examples of this kind of transaction. X.25 is not suitable for long, continuous streams of data, like those used by video—its speed is too slow, so it's apt to make real-time data jerky.

The network can determine that frames are getting dropped because more frames are going to the recipient than it can handle. Everything looks fine to the sender, however.

The network tells the sender that it must stop transmitting for the moment, and the recipient has a chance to catch up.

Figure 4.18

How implicit congestion handling works.

What Is X.25? X.25 is not terribly complex. Like frame relay, X.25 is not a networking protocol per se; it's an access protocol, like an on-ramp that defines how data gets onto a packet-switched network and what information needs to accompany that data. It functions on three levels:

- The physical layer specifies the physical characteristics of the on-ramp

- The link layer packages the user data into the appropriate kind of frame and supervises the connection

- The network layer handles the task of transmitting the data and making sure that it reaches its destination

This sounds a little complex, but it's important for understanding how X.25 works and thus what you need to make it work.

The Physical Layer. To get the bits and bytes being transmitted on their way, X.25 uses an RS-232 serial connection, the same physical specifications that your modem uses. You don't have to worry about the specifics of RS-232 except that if you buy a router with the intention of plugging an X.25 connection into it, the router needs to have an RS-232 port.

This layer is responsible for making the sender and recipient able to talk to each other.

The Link Layer. The link layer's job is more complex than that of the physical layer. First, it defines how the sender's data gets put into a particular a frame to be sent on its way. Not all frames are alike because the requirements for user data and management data vary, but the basic elements are shown in figure 4.19.

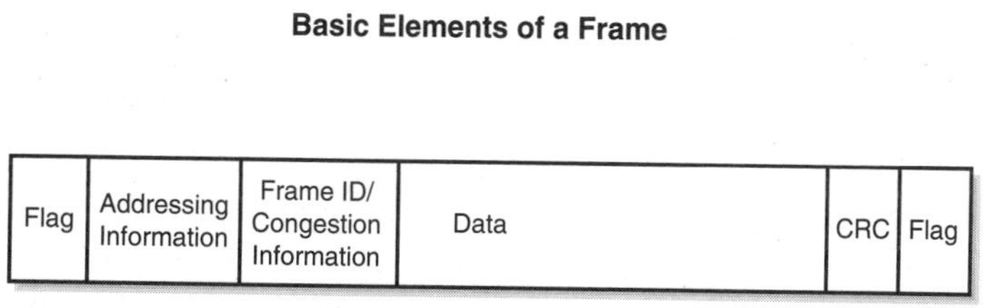

Basic Elements of a Frame

Flag	Addressing Information	Frame ID/ Congestion Information	Data	CRC	Flag

Figure 4.19

An X.25 data frame contains addressing information and error-checking, in addition to the data itself.

Each part of the frame (apart from the data) has a role to play. The flags mark the beginning and end of the frame. The addressing information provides the destination of the frame. Error-control information is stored in two places in the frame: one field contains a function for the recipient to perform and the other the solution to the function.

The error control inherent in X.25 depends on those two fields. If the recipient gets an answer to match the one in the error-control field, then it sends a message (called an ACK, for acknowledge) to the sender confirming that the data got there in one piece. If, however, the function doesn't come out right, it's assumed that the data didn't either, and the recipient asks the sender to send the data again with another message, called a NAK. The sender doesn't dispose of its data until it received an ACK from the recipient, so if it gets a NAK back, the sender just resends the data.

The link layer is also responsible for making sure that the recipient never gets more data that it can handle at any given time, using a technique known as *flow control*. An ACK signals to the sender that the data arrived in one piece and that the recipient is ready for more, so if the recipient doesn't send back an ACK the sender holds off until it receives the okay message. In some systems, the recipient can actually automatically send the sender a message telling it to stop transmitting until the recipient clears its buffers.

Finally, the link layer is responsible for keeping track of the connection. If something should sever the connection at the physical layer, the link layer is responsible for remembering the status of the connection and sending the remainder of the data when the connection is restored. Remember, not all the data in any network transmission works in one chunk, so if the transmission gets interrupted it's important for it to be able to restore where it left off.

Overall, this layer is responsible for the link between the sender and the recipient.

The Network Layer. This level of X.25 is responsible for the fine details of how the data gets from its source to its destination. To this end, it must perform the following tasks:

- Establishes a connection between the sender and recipient

- Addresses and routes the packets

- Controls flow so that no data gets lost

- Recovers from any failure of the link layer

- Provides diagnostic information about the connection's status

Once the connection's up and running and the sender and recipient are linked, this layer gets to perform the task of getting the data to its destination. It establishes the virtual connection between the two points and lists the addresses of the sending and receiving nodes. From there, it can choose the best route for the data to travel, and instead of sending the address information, it includes a sort of "map" with the data, so as to reduce data overhead. During the flow of data, this layer makes sure that the recipient never gets more data than it can handle at once. When the transmission is complete, it sends an all-done message to the sender and closes the connection.

That's the normal procedure. Should something happen to the link before the recipient gets the all-done message, this layer is responsible for remembering the status of the transmission and continuing where it left off.

Using X.25 with Frame Relay. X.25 is essentially frame relay with error-correcting ability. It's possible, if you've got sites in Europe and sites in the United States, that you might want to use the best technology for each location and somehow blend X.25 and frame relay. Well, you can. The same body that defined how X.25 and frame relay work also defined a method to hook them together. At a very simple level, it works like this: An *internetworking function* (IWF) is positioned at the junction of the two networks. Frame relay and X.25 use slightly different forms of addressing information and overhead, so when either kind of packet comes to this junction, the IWF takes the packet, removes the extraneous information apart from the data, and then adds the information needed to transmit the data onto its new network. The IWF can connect to more than one virtual connection on each side, so you can have multiple X.25 connections and multiple frame relay connections. You can see how this works in figure 4.20.

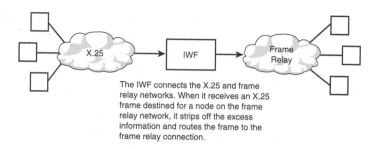

The IWF connects the X.25 and frame relay networks. When it receives an X.25 frame destined for a node on the frame relay network, it strips off the excess information and routes the frame to the frame relay connection.

Figure 4.20

Connecting frame relay and X.25.

Summary: Choosing a WAN Type

In this chapter, you learned about what a WAN is, reviewed some concepts intrinsic to wide area technologies, and read about some of the WAN technologies that you're likely to consider. At this point, you don't know everything (entire books have been written about all of the WAN technologies discussed here), but you know enough to make a beginning. Just to refresh your memory, the data in this chapter is summarized in the following lists:

ISDN

- Provides a reliable low-speed (64–512 Kbps) connection most suited to LANs in close proximity to each other

- Is not available universally—even in all regions of the United States

- Is connection-oriented, meaning that a connection must be made before data can be transmitted

- Requires an IMAC, NT1, and a gateway machine

SMDS

- Provides a medium-to-high-speed (1.17–45 Mbps) connection between LANs in a LATA

- Is available, in 1996, in most major metropolitan areas of the United States

- Is not connection-oriented—that is, no connection between sites must be established before transmittal begins

- Requires a CSU/DSU and a SMDS-compatible router with one port for each connected site

FNS

- Provides a link between sites that is as fast as the LANs that you're connecting

- Is not currently widely available, even in the United States

- Requires almost no additional equipment—the connection looks like connecting one more node to your LAN

- Transmits LAN packets

Frame Relay

- Uses statistical multiplexing to allocate bandwidth to sites based on traffic; therefore, it is able to use bandwidth very efficiently (most commonly transmits around 2 Mbps)

- Transmits frames of varying sizes

- Most suitable for "bursty" traffic that is not time-sensitive

- Designed for reliable cabling, so it includes no error-checking information

- Widely available in the United States

X.25

- Uses statistical multiplexing to allocate bandwidth to sites based on traffic; therefore, it is able to use bandwidth very efficiently, although its additional overhead makes it slower than frame relay (64–256 Kbps)

- Incorporates error-control information into its frames so that it can transmit successfully over less-reliable cabling

- Most suitable for "bursty" traffic that is not time-sensitive

- Widely available globally (if there's any cabling in place at all)

After reading this chapter, you may have an idea of what WAN technology would suit the needs of your company best. Just to review, however, you need to consider the following questions when choosing a WAN type and vendor:

- The area that the WAN needs to cover

- The amount of data that will be transmitted at one time

- The type of data that the WAN will carry

- The lowest acceptable transmittal rate

- How much money is available for the project

Area To Be Covered

WAN technologies are offered on an intra-LATA basis in the United States. If you plan to extend the WAN beyond the borders of the LATA, you'll have to purchase (or your vendor will) at least part of the service from one of the long-distance companies.

For some technologies, the smaller an area, the cheaper high speeds will be. For example, if you want the native LAN speeds of FNS, you'll have to lease multiple T1 circuits to maintain the high-speed connection over the border of a LATA (about seven T1s to keep up with 10 Mbps Ethernet). FNS within a LATA isn't cheap, but it's less expensive if you only need it locally.

And, once again, if your WAN will extend outside the United States you'll probably want to use X.25 for at least part of it. Outside the United States, many of these technologies aren't even offered, and when they are, they're not always reliable.

Amount of Data

The more data to be transmitted at one time, the more bandwidth you'll need. Frame relay, as we've discussed, is designed to get more out of existing bandwidth than older technologies can, but this has its limitations. Keep in mind that people using networks aren't using the network part most of the time—they're working with data locally. Thus, you can get away with less bandwidth than you might think based on the speeds of your LAN.

Type of Data

The technologies described in this chapter are, at this point, pretty much data-specific, although SMDS is technically capable of transmitting voice and data and frame relay product and service vendors are beginning to offer support for time-sensitive data. Even for static data, however, the type of data will affect the throughput you'll need. Complex graphics require more bandwidth than e-mail messages, for example.

If at all possible, don't run applications across a WAN (or use true client/server applications that make use of distributed processing). Use the WAN to access data, not the functionality of your software. Faster WANs have fewer problems in this regard, but keeping applications locally where feasible will make them easier to administer (and keep your users from screaming in frustration at their slow applications).

How Much Money Is Available?

To a large extent, the more money you spend on networking, the better product you have. Bandwidth is expensive and so are some of the additional services you can buy from your vendor to help you manage your WAN. Before talking your boss into a blank check, however, think about what you're going to be doing with the WAN. More features or higher speed don't always translate into a better product, if it's more than you need right now. Just make sure that you buy a product that you can upgrade, if necessary.

Before choosing a WAN technology, draw up a list of what you need from the WAN (speed, error recovery, cost, and so forth) and keep it on hand when talking to vendors. Ask lots of questions, and don't be afraid to ask the vendors to clarify something if you don't understand. You might use a form like the one in figure 4.21 to help you prepare your questions before you call.

This checklist may not cover all the eventualities that apply to your particular situation, but it's a good start.

Never forget that you're the one buying the service and keeping them in business, so there's no such thing as a stupid question.

WAN CHECKLIST

Before calling the vendor, you need to know the following:

✓ How many users will access the WAN at one time?

✓ How big of an area will the WAN cover?

✓ What cities are the other WAN sites in?

✓ What are the telephone numbers of the other sites?

✓ Do you already have an established vendor for network hardware? Who is it?

✓ What kind of data will be transmitted between WAN sites? How will this change in years to come?

✓ Does the WAN need to be integrated with the telephone service? Will it in the future?

✓ What kind of budget is available?

✓ How soon do you want to have the WAN operational?

✓ Will more WAN sites be added in the future? If so, where are they located?

✓ Who will be in charge of the WAN at each site?

When talking to prospective vendors, make sure that you get answers to these questions:

✓ What are the setup costs for the WAN?

✓ What are the estimated hardware costs for the WAN?

✓ How is the monthly cost computed and what is it estimated to be?

✓ Will the vendor supply hardware guaranteed to work together? If not, where do you get the hardware?

✓ What kind of transmission rates are guaranteed for the WAN type?

✓ What kind of technical support contract comes with the product?

✓ How would the vendor expand the scope of the WAN?

✓ How soon would the WAN be operational?

✓ Is there any time commitment for purchasing this WAN service?

✓ How will users access the WAN?

Figure 4.21

A WAN checklist like this one can help you organize your thinking and get the WAN type that best suits your company.

Part II

Hardware Platforms: Servers and Workstations

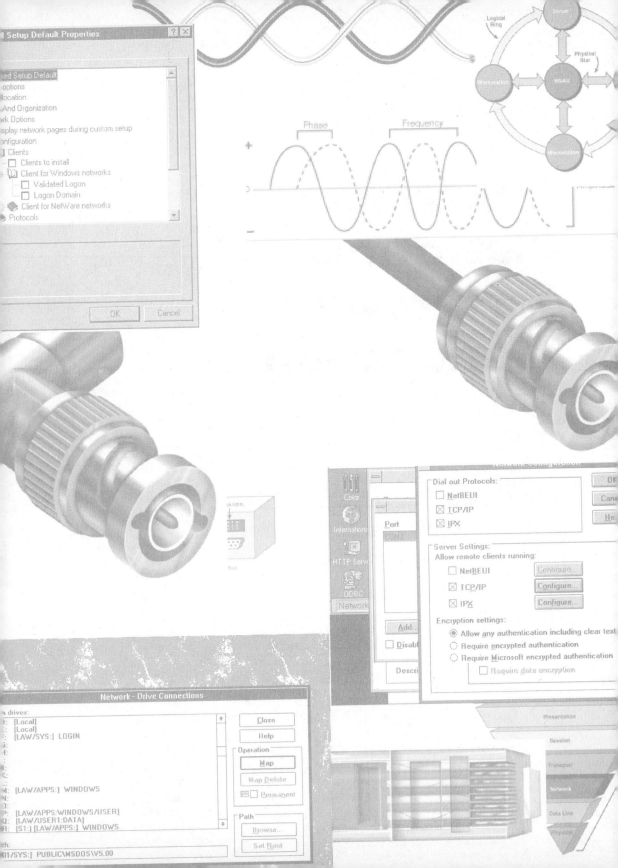

Chapter 5

The Server Platform

The *file server* is the focal point of the client/server network model. It is the means by which users on the network gain access to the resources that they need to accomplish their daily tasks. The operative concept behind the local area network is to spread a company's computing resources around the network, instead of having everything centralized as in a mainframe system. The file server functions as a gateway to all these resources, whether they've been located in the server computer or not. The server also functions as a security device, allowing users access only to the resources that they need and protecting the core operating system from intervention that could interrupt the operations of other users.

Once access is granted to the necessary network resources, users are actually performing their computing tasks using the hardware within their workstations. This is the basis of the client/server model. Processing tasks are performed by every computer on the network, decreasing the load on the central systems. Unlike a mainframe system in which all processing takes place within one computer, file servers allow individual computers to perform the same functions without the need for redundant resources at every workstation. Thus, one centrally located copy of a particular software application can be accessed by dozens of users, each using the processor and memory of their individual machines to run it and outputting their final results to a single, centrally located printer without placing an excessive burden on the server. The file server can be substantially smaller than a mainframe in size, processing capability, and most importantly cost. For a far smaller price than the "big iron," a local area network can be assembled that will provide users the same (or greater) functionality, along with far greater flexibility and fault tolerance.

Many people who are new to networking believe that there is an inherent difference between a file server and a normal workstation PC. From a pure hardware standpoint, this is nearly always not the case. The primary difference between a file server and a workstation computer is the software that is running on it. As far as the hardware is concerned, the differences are mostly a matter of degree and marketing. A file server is simply a PC with the same resources as a workstation but in greater abundance. It usually has a faster processor, more memory, a greater amount of disk space, and a wider array of peripherals—but this need not be so. The primary difference is that this machine runs a network operating system (NOS) such as Novell NetWare, as opposed to a client operating system (OS) such as DOS. See part III, "Software Platforms: NOSs and Clients," for an in-depth examination of the differences between NOSs and other OSs.

How Many Servers?

As stated earlier, the basic concept of the LAN is to spread resources around the network. In many cases, this results in the use of multiple file servers that provide network access to different areas of the enterprise. Depending on the size and needs of the company, the use of multiple servers can provide several advantages as well as disadvantages. The primary alternative to this is a server configuration that has gained increasing popularity in recent years, colloquially called the *super-server*. This consists of a single file server that takes the place of several smaller servers. This machine has a far greater amount of hardware resources than a normal server does. It ends up functioning in almost the same way as a mainframe, in that it is the single contact point of the entire network.

The primary disadvantage of the super-server is the same as that of the mainframe—fault tolerance. When operating in a *distributed network environment* (that is, one utilizing multiple servers spread around the network) users can, in the case of a server failure, log on to another server and continue working, as long as the network has been designed and configured to accommodate this sort of redundancy. In a super-server environment, users tend to be completely dependent on a single machine. Should it fail for any reason, productivity often comes to a halt until repairs are made.

One of the primary advantages of the super-server, though, is the fact that administrative tasks are centralized. Only one set of user accounts needs to be maintained, and the server hardware is all located in one place, rather than having multiple file servers located in different areas of the office, building, or campus.

One of the first questions to be considered when planning an upgrade or expansion of an existing network is whether to augment the capabilities of existing file servers or to add additional servers to the network. Hardware costs are certainly a major factor in this decision, but there are other criteria to be taken into account as well. One of these is the skill level of your user base. When administering a large network, having knowledgeable users or workgroup administrators spread throughout the enterprise can be a tremendous aid to the MIS department. If these people can be counted upon to responsibly administer the small parts of the network local to their department, then a distributed network might be more desirable. If the user base is familiar only with the operations of a workstation and has little knowledge of networking, then having fewer file servers of greater capacity allows for simpler administration and less traveling time between servers or departments.

Other criteria include the working habits and the geographical organization of the enterprise. Discrete departmental workgroups in remote locations, with little interaction and different computing requirements, would be better candidates for multiple servers than a large group of identically tasked workers in one location. Of course, circumstances are rarely this clear-cut, and the decision as to the number of servers needed is likely to be a compromise between several of these factors.

As we examine the various components of the network server, we will cover the ways in which the hardware can be assembled to provide a smooth passage of data from source to destination that is free of bottlenecks. Other sections of this book examine the ways in which a suitable level of fault tolerance can be provided for a selected hardware configuration and also accommodate the needs of the organization that use it. We will also attempt to identify the components that are the most critical to particular types of network use. This way, you should be able to find information that allows you to create a network or upgrade into something that suits the way your business works—instead of the other way around—and provide additional performance or fault tolerance in the most critical areas and in the most economical manner.

About the Motherboard

Although the microprocessor or CPU is often thought of as defining the capabilities of a computer, it is useless without an architecture designed to support it properly. At the most basic level, a computer operates on data by performing three fundamental operations: storage, transfer, and calculations. Data may be stored in memory or on a hard or floppy disk drive, and calculations are performed within the microprocessor. The task of providing the means by which the data is transferred from the storage medium to the processor and back again is accomplished by the *motherboard*.

In years past, several different means were used to connect the disparate parts of a computer. Minicomputers and mainframe systems used *backplanes* or wiring systems of a modular design that allowed for the simple replacement of individual parts. The space considerations of the modern PC, however, have led to the use of a single board onto which the processor, system memory, I/O bus, and other vital circuitry are all integrated. This is referred to as the system board, main board, or motherboard (see fig. 5.1).

Figure 5.1

This is a typical PC motherboard.

In this chapter, we examine this crucial component to a well-designed file server, as well as all the basic components that are mounted on a motherboard. We look at the means by which the different parts of the computer communicate and at the little-known ancillary components that can be crucial to the assembly of a system with true compatibility. A time will come when it seems as though technology has passed your servers by, and the only alternatives will be to upgrade or replace them. It is important to know what you have before you improve it, however, and with this book, you should be able to judge whether or not you need "the latest thing" in the networking industry and whether or not you can easily adapt your existing system to it.

Documentation

If there is one piece of advice that you retain from this entire book, it should be this one:

Document Your File Server's Motherboard!

Do not buy a PC for use as a file server (or even as a workstation, for that matter) without finding out specific information about the motherboard. If the vendor cannot tell you who makes their motherboards, hang up the phone! If they cannot tell you what chipset or BIOS is on their motherboards, hang up the phone! If they cannot furnish detailed documentation for their motherboards (by this I mean more than an 8-page pamphlet), do not buy from them! Hardware incompatibilities are a major cause of file server outages, and if you do not know what you have inside the box, then no one can help you.

When purchasing PCs as a unit, as opposed to assembling them yourself, you must be aware of the places in which unscrupulous vendors are most liable to cut corners. They realize that potential customers are likely to ask what make of hard drive is in the machine, or how much memory it has in it, but they are far less likely to ask about the speed of the memory, or the chipset on the motherboard. Any reputable vendor should be able to supply you with a *spec sheet* containing all the technical details concerning a particular system. If they can't, look for a different vendor!

If you are dealing with legacy equipment for which you have no documentation, then use a notebook, spreadsheet, or text file to keep your own documentation. As you identify aspects of the hardware in a machine, write them down in a safe place. This will save you from repeatedly having to open the system to see what's inside and will help prevent you from sounding like a fool when you're on the phone with vendors, salespeople, and consultants.

Many simple upgrades can end up being a nightmare. Always budget what you believe to be a sufficient amount of downtime when upgrading a server, and then double it. Murphy's Law always seems to be in force when you've got the case open, and the guts of your file server are all over the floor. A properly documented system often means the difference between a successful upgrade and having to put the server back the way it was because you ordered the wrong parts.

Microprocessors

The *microprocessor*, sometimes known (rather inaccurately) as the *central processing unit* or *CPU*, is the place where all the actual calculations within a computer take place. Hard drive space, memory, and even caching RAM are all merely storage media of different types and speeds that facilitate the delivery of data to the CPU, where the actual processing takes place. A microprocessor is built around thin silicon wafers that have been grown like crystals and subsequently exposed to intense heat. During the heating process, the wafers are exposed to gases containing particles that are impregnated into the silicon, thus creating different degrees of conductivity in precisely specified areas of the chip. Since the late 1950s, when the first techniques for clustering multiple transistors on a single chip were patented, these *integrated circuits* have evolved in complexity and capability at a phenomenal rate, resulting in today's microprocessors, each of which represents the equivalent computing power of a football stadium full of 1950s vacuum tubes.

On the simplest level, a microprocessor is a component that, when furnished with a particular set of electrical signals input at specified points, will always return exactly the same response. The phenomenal achievement of these devices is the speed at which millions of these responses can be generated and the way in which sequential responses can be made to interact, based on previous responses. These input signals correspond to the actions that a program requests from a processor and the data that the actions are performed upon. Every microprocessor has a vocabulary of these actions, called its *instruction set* or *command set,* which is used to form the language by which programmers create their *code*. The code, which is stored on the computer's memory chips, on a hard drive, or on some other storage device, is then reduced to binary electrical signals that are the only means of communication with the microprocessor and are fed to its *input/output (I/O) unit.*

The I/O unit of the microprocessor is essentially the staging area for the electrical input, precisely controlling the rate and timing by which signals are fed to the other two parts of the chip, the *control unit* and *arithmetic-logic unit (ALU)*. In strict technical terms, it is these two units, exclusive of the input/output unit, that compose the CPU. The I/O unit consists of two kinds of connections to the motherboard of the computer: the *address bus*, which furnishes the processor with information about the memory location of the commands and data to be processed, and the *data bus*, through which the information itself travels. Once the signals are fed to the control unit, this part of the chip's architecture then relays the data and command instructions to the ALU, where the actual calculations are performed at the proper time. The control unit contains its own internal clock which is used to control the rate at which all the units function, but the entire processor is also highly reliant on the motherboard's system clock, which is used to ensure that the vast number of electrical signals entering and exiting the microprocessor are not garbled or confused.

All three of these basic units, however, have an influence on the overall speed of the processor. The width and speed of the I/O unit's bus control the rate at which data enters and exits the processor, and the ALU controls the amount of data that can be operated on at any one time by the size and number of its *registers*. Registers are holding areas where data is temporarily stored while calculations are being performed by the ALU (see fig. 5.2). Because even simple arithmetic calculations require multiple steps when they are reduced to binary electrical signals, the registers are an integral part of the decision-making process, retaining the interim results of calculations within the processor itself, instead of having to offload this information through the I/O bus to the computer's memory chips.

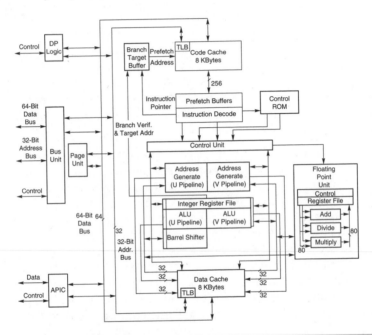

Figure 5.2

Microprocessors store interim calculation results in their internal buffers to avoid delays caused by repeated memory writes.

CISC and RISC Processors

Although different microprocessor platforms, on a high level, may be performing what are fundamentally the same operations, they often go about them in very different ways. Even a simple arithmetic calculation, when it is reduced to binary electrical signals, is performed in a series of steps, the number and complexity of which may vary greatly in different types of processors. This is due primarily to differences in the various processors' instruction sets. This can be compared to two sentences with the exact same meaning, expressed in two different languages, using two different alphabets. The meaning transmitted is the same, but the intermediate steps can be utterly unlike each other.

The first microprocessors executed many of the instructions in their command sets through the use of numerous intermediate steps. The various combinations of these intermediate steps allowed a large number of highly complex instructions to be added to the command set. These intermediate steps, by which instructions were carried out, came to be known as *microcode*. The processor's microcode is essentially the alphabet upon which its command set (or language) is based. It runs on a separate operational level within the microprocessor, called a *nanoprocessor*.

This technique allows the processor a rich and varied instruction set but also introduces an added layer of processing overhead that can lessen the overall speed at which instructions are executed. This has become known as *complex instruction set computing* or *CISC*, and is the operational model for the entire Intel PC microprocessor family. In the 1970s, it was discovered during studies of the actual usage of CISC microprocessors of the day, that roughly 20% of the instructions in the command set were being used to perform 80% of the work. In other words, only a small subset of the existing vocabulary was being used, most of the time. This discovery led to the development of microprocessors that were designed to optimize the performance of the most frequently used commands, at the expense of the seldom used ones. This resulted in what became known as *reduced instruction set computing (RISC)*. RISC processors eliminate the microcode layer that slows down the CISC processing method, substituting a relatively small vocabulary of simpler commands that can be combined to adequately emulate the seldom-used, more complex commands that comprise the other 80% of the typical CISC processor instruction set.

At the time of their introduction, RISC processors, by streamlining the command set and reducing processor overhead in other ways, significantly reduced the number of clock cycles required to execute a specific instruction and were clearly faster than their CISC counterparts in many operations. However, the continued refinement of both techniques has resulted today in microprocessors of both types that are far more comparable than their predecessors were. CISC command sets have also been streamlined to some extent, and RISC command sets have been enlarged to accommodate today's needs. Comparing the state-of-the-art in both schools of microprocessor design today demonstrates that, while the fastest processors available today still use the RISC model, both processor types offer the speed and the flexibility required by contemporary operating systems.

In addition, the ever-expanding market for these processors has resulted in development cycles that are significantly shorter than they were only a few years ago. Faster and more powerful processors are continually being introduced, and the benchmark ratings of the RISC processors used in many UNIX and Windows NT machines can now be all but matched by the Intel platform, with its Pentium and Pentium Pro processors. When considering an operating system that can run on machines using either CISC and RISC processors, such as Windows NT or SunSoft's Solaris, the RISC solution is likely to provide more pure speed, but this should not necessrily be the deciding factor in the purchase. Costs between the two processor types can vary widely, and care should be taken to decide whether the additional performance gained is worth the additional expenditure. The availability and cost of application software should also be a part of the equation.

File Server Processing

In a network file server, due to the nature of the client/server model, the speed and effectiveness of the microprocessor often do not have a major impact on the overall performance of the network, beyond a minimum required level of adequacy. On most networks, the majority of application processing is carried out by the workstation's processor. While it is obviously an essential part of the system, the microprocessor in the average file server should not be overtaxed by the administrative functions (such as network communications, file sharing, and printer sharing) that are its primary everyday tasks, unless the processor is grossly underpowered or the server is heavily overloaded. In these cases, upgrading the processor can provide little return for what might be a large expenditure in time, money, and effort.

However, in the case of servers that run database applications or other processor-intensive tasks, it is important to ensure that the processor is not overburdened because delays or even stoppages in logons and network file access can result. Machines such as these can more accurately be called *application servers,* rather than file servers. If your business requires the use of processor-intensive server modules such as these, then this is a good reason to consider using multiple servers to separate these functions from the traditional network tasks, rather than overburdening a single machine's microprocessor.

As the networking industry progresses, we should begin to see a clearer division between application and file servers. This will result naturally from the trend toward heterogeneous networks composed of mixed platforms, and the continued development of network operating systems and hardware configurations that are clearly better suited for one or another of these tasks. In the next few sections, we examine some non-Intel processors available for network use today (see chapter 6, "The Workstation Platform," for a detailed discussion of the Intel family of microprocessors). We also discuss the future in which the use of multiple processors in a single server will allow for even more powerful applications to be run across a network, using the client/server model to spread the resource load more efficiently between server and workstation.

Novell NetWare

While different NOSs are designed for use on machines running different types of microprocessors, and while some NOSs—such as Microsoft Windows NT and Sunsoft Solaris—are available in versions compiled for various different processors, the most commonly used NOS, Novell NetWare, is currently limited to operating solely on the Intel processor platform. NetWare is used on such a vast majority of network file servers primarily because of the ease and flexibility with which it provides resource sharing and security features, two basic requirements of a network. Although it is likely that the future will see something of a reduction in the overall market share that NetWare currently enjoys, it is equally likely that many networks will continue to run NetWare servers for basic networking tasks.

While the NetWare versions currently shipping can run on any PC with an Intel 80386 microprocessor or better, it is economically and technologically impractical, given the state of today's market, to consider running a NetWare file server on anything less than an Intel 80486 processor. Most of the 386 file servers constructed during the time when that was the cutting edge of processor technology have long since been relegated to the status of workstation.

I have no doubt that there are still many sites running 386 servers, and as long as the services required from the network remain unchanged, this is fine, but attempts to upgrade these machines are probably not worth the effort. Technology has advanced considerably in the past few years, not only in processors, but in memory, storage systems, and expansion buses as well. To get one of these machines up-to-speed for today's definition of a file server, you probably would be left with nothing from the original machine but the case, and even this might be inadequate.

486 and Pentium machines do, however, have processor upgrade paths, but due to the many different chips on the market, these paths may be somewhat convoluted, to say the least. The process of upgrading a NetWare server's microprocessor is no different from that of a workstation. For this reason, details of the upgrade process, as well as material on the history and architecture of the Intel microprocessor line, may be found in chapter 6, "The Workstation Platform."

Buying New Processors

Although processor upgrades may be complex, if there is one component in a new NetWare file server whose purchase can be considered a no-brainer, it is that of the microprocessor. Buy a Pentium. While I would not have said this during the initial release period of the 60MHz and 66MHz models, the technology is now more than stable enough to warrant reliance on the currently available family of chips, ranging in speed from 75MHz to 133MHz. Sufficient care is now being taken to ensure that the chips are properly cooled. At this point in time, however, I recommend a certain amount of caution concerning the new Pentium Pro units, based solely on the fact that they are the result of a new manufacturing process and have not yet been fully proven in the marketplace. Remember that your file servers are not a place to experiment. Buy the fastest, most reliable products that you can afford—and since you probably will end up paying less for a processor than for nearly any other major component of a server, why not get the best available?

Other Microprocessors

While the Intel platform dominates the file server microprocessor market by a tremendous margin—due primarily to the enduring popularity of Novell NetWare—it is by no means the only game in town. The growing popularity of Windows NT and the explosive growth of the Internet have boosted sales of several alternative processor platforms. The cross-platform support provided by Windows NT is a clear indication of the direction in which the networking industry is progressing. SunSoft Corporation also supports several different processors with its Solaris operating system, and rumors and announcements have been circulating for years concerning a processor-independent version of NetWare. While nothing is likely to disturb Intel's reign in the desktop and home PC markets, several of the cross-platform NOSs now available might be better served by non-Intel processors.

While many of the UNIX platforms available are more mature, they have also become more specialized. Our focus in this section is on platforms supporting the newer NOSs that have attracted the attention of many exclusive NetWare shops, due to the growing number of powerful client/server applications now available and in development, which run on them. The future of networking will be in open, mixed environments in which compatibility is a given and platforms can be chosen for their suitability to the task at hand, rather than their ability to conform to the needs of a restricting, proprietary architecture. This philosophy has given a new lease on life to many processor manufacturers who at one time faced a limited future in the commercial networking industry.

MIPS Technologies. Like the other major processor manufacturers who rival Intel, MIPS Technologies markets a line of RISC-based microprocessors that are used for a wide range of applications, from embedded electronics and desktop workstations to high-end graphics terminals and supercomputers. Their R4x00 line of processors is used in workstations that can run Windows NT 3.5 or UNIX V.4 as well as specialized online transaction processing systems (OLTP). Windows NT support allows for compatibility with the entire line of x86-based 16-bit DOS and Windows software, as well as the newer 32-bit applications being designed for the NT platform, thus opening the door to a whole new world of users.

The MIPS R4x00 microprocessors are based on a true 64-bit architecture, with full 64-bit registers, virtual address space, and integer and floating-point operations. An extended 36-bit address bus gives them a 64G physical address space. The capability for a 64-bit-wide virtual address space is what makes them true 64-bit processors with a virtual address space of 1 terabyte. Able to execute one instruction per clock cycle, the R4400 has separate 16K level 1 write-back caches for instructions and data. The caches are virtually indexed, to allow for simultaneous data accesses and the data cache has a two-entry store buffer so that two store operations per cycle can be executed without latency penalties or the need for instruction pairing, as in the Pentium. There is also a one-line write buffer that allows processing to continue while output is waiting to be written to memory. Support is also provided for communication with a level 2 cache up to 4M in size over a 128-bit data bus. Using standard static RAM chips, the level 2 cache can be configured as a unified cache or split into instruction and data caches.

Other processors in the MIPS line are designed for more specialized applications. For example, the R8000 utilizes a separate FPU that, in combination with its integer unit, can execute up to four instructions per clock cycle. It is now being used in 3D and graphics workstations manufactured by firms like Silicon Graphics.

DEC Alpha AXP. Digital Equipment Corporation, in designing its Alpha AXP architecture, set about plotting the growth of microprocessor technology for the next 25 years. By quantifying the advancements made since the introduction of the first microprocessors, DEC has predicted that the processors available 25 years from now will have to be 1,000 times faster than current technology to keep pace with other developments. They have, therefore, eliminated anything from their designs that they felt would become a bottleneck at any time during that period. For example, since they saw the possibility for an ultimate limit in clock speed, they concentrated on executing more instructions per clock cycle. Indeed, this has become a primary design restriction for the Alpha processors. Everything that could have a negative effect on their multiple-instruction-issue technology has been eliminated from their designs, resulting in an architecture intended to eventually sustain the execution of up to ten instructions per clock cycle.

DEC has made significant inroads toward this goal. The Alpha AXP 21164 microprocessor, available in speeds of 266MHz and 300MHz, is the first processor able to execute over 1 billion instructions per second (bips). It is listed in the *Guinness Book of World Records* as the world's fastest microprocessor. Manufactured using DEC's own fourth-generation CMOS technology, the Alpha AXP processors, like the MIPS, are also of 64-bit

RISC architecture, and are designed for the pipelining of instructions, in which execution of subsequent instructions is begun before the first is completed.

As with MIPS, DEC's processor platform is supported by Windows NT, as well as DEC's own OSF/1 and OpenVMS operating systems. Prior to the release of Windows NT, DEC's networking solutions were all highly proprietary and not at all designed for compatibility with other systems. They have recently expanded their presence in the conventional LAN world, though, by introducing lines of PCs based on both Intel and Alpha AXP processors. All processor manufacturers have vast amounts of benchmark data readily available to prove that their processors are the fastest, and DEC is no exception. I have deliberately avoided using this information because benchmarks rarely have any significance in the real world of computing, but I think it is safe to say that DEC has the fastest processors on the market. This performance comes at a heavy cost, though, as their top-of-the-line processors are priced well above the $2,000 mark, while the fastest Pentium is available for under $1,000. For a heavy-duty application server managing multiple databases or other processor intensive tasks, however, a single Alpha AXP processor might be able to replace a significantly more complex, and more costly, multiprocessor system.

PowerPC. Unlike the other processors discussed in this section, the PowerPC is not the product of a single company. It is a microprocessor designed in accordance with a standard developed jointly by IBM, Motorola, and Apple Computer. Although based on the POWER processor architecture used in IBM RS/6000 workstations, the standard calls for a *common instruction set architecture* that allows any manufacturer to design and build chips running the same code.

PowerPC microprocessors currently are available only in 32-bit implementations, but the standard is scaleable up to a full 64-bit data path. Motorola's chips range in clock speed from 50MHz to 100MHz, with all but the lowest-end processors being manufactured using a 0.5 micron CMOS technology and running separate instruction and data caches up to 16K. A prototype processor called the MPC620, manufactured by the same process but not yet in production, has 64-bit data and bus widths and runs at a 133MHz clock speed. Incorporating seven million transistors and including 32K data and instruction caches, this is the first in what is intended to be a line of high-performance processors that will rival the Alpha and MIPS chips for the workstation and application server market.

Many hardware and software companies have expressed interest in the PowerPC, due in part to the fact that an open standard will eliminate the possibility of a single chip manufacturer dominating the industry with a technological monopoly, as Intel currently does with the x86 platform. PowerPC processors are currently being manufactured by both IBM and Motorola for use in IBM RS/6000 servers and workstations and in Apple Power Macintosh computers. Power Macs use a software emulation routine that allow them to run the standard Apple System 7.x operating system, and the RS/6000s run IBM's AIX flavor of UNIX without alteration, as the processor is completely binary-compatible with the POWER-based RS/6000s.

The RS/6000 systems are also PReP compliant. The *PowerPC Reference Platform* (*PReP*) is a standard created by IBM that allows systems built by different manufacturers to be compatible with each other. All PReP-compliant machines should be able to run AIX, as well as the PowerPC versions of OS/2, Solaris, and Windows NT. Another open platform standard, called the *Common Hardware Reference Platform* (*CHRP*), has been developed by Apple, IBM, and Motorola and is designed to be compatible with both PReP and Power Mac machines. Thus, CHRP systems (which are not yet available) should be able to run the Mac OS, AIX, and the PowerPC versions of OS/2 and Windows NT. A version of NetWare for the PowerPC is in development, and plans are also in the works for the use of PowerPC processors in future generations of video game systems as well as automobiles.

The PowerPC microprocessors themselves have been available for some time, and desktop systems based on the PowerPC are available from a handful of manufacturers, including IBM. However, attempts to gain a foothold into the Intel market have been hampered by the platform's failure to deliver a persuasive reason to switch. Windows NT for the PowerPC is available, but existing NT applications must be recompiled to run on the processor. In addition, the performance improvements that were touted as being provided by the new processor turn out to hover somewhere around 15% over an Intel processor of the same clock speed, as opposed to the 30% originally estimated. And finally, the price advantage that was also supposed to facilitate the acceptance of the platform is virtually non-existent. Entry level IBM PowerPC systems are priced at $3,700 and up, hardly an incentive to experiment on a new processor with limited OS and application support.

Up to this point, the PowerPC platform has been blessed with a surfeit of good intentions and exciting speculation, but outside of the Power Macintosh, there is as yet no good reason to believe that they will have a major impact on the computing industry anytime soon.

While its potential has only been realized in a limited fashion so far, the PowerPC has garnered tremendous interest from both hardware and software manufacturers. Open systems are the way of the future in the networking industry, fostering increased competition and the technological advances that always accompany such competition.

Multiple Processors

After examining the way in which manufacturers have incorporated such remarkable technology into today's microprocessors, the prospects seem almost unlimited. The fact is, however, that software designers keep adding additional power and capabilities to their programs, and it is up to hardware designers to continue making machines that can run them faster and better. The next step in increasing the speed and capability of client/server computing in the LAN environment, as previously demonstrated in the mainframe world, is to use multiple processors in a single machine, accessing a single memory array to share an application's processing tasks evenly among them. This is known as *symmetric multiprocessing* (*SMP*), and hardware features facilitating SMP have been designed into all the contemporary microprocessor designs discussed in this section.

The use of multiple processors requires significant alterations in both the hardware of the computer and the software running on it. Among LANs, it is primarily on various flavors of UNIX that multiprocessing has been realized effectively. High-performance workstations used for graphics, CAD, and financial work, as well as large database and OLTP servers, have long made use of multiple microprocessors manufactured by IBM, DEC, and MIPS. It was only with the multiprocessor support built into Windows NT, however, that the possibilities of multiprocessor systems were made available to the primarily Intel-based commercial desktop LAN environment. In addition to this, Novell has recently released an SMP add-on package for NetWare 4.1 that will further assert the viability of this technology in the marketplace.

The existing multiprocessor LAN technologies are mostly the products of individual UNIX development companies, utilizing proprietary hardware with operating systems written specifically for that hardware. Systems range from dual processor UNIX graphics workstations to the *Massively Parallel Processing* (*MPP*) supercomputers recently marketed by Cray Research, which can utilize up to 2,048 Alpha AXP multiprocessors (this top-of-the-line model can be had for a mere $31 million—call Cray at (612)452-6650 for more information). With the introduction of multiprocessing on the Intel platform by Windows NT, however, and the subsequent NetWare release, it has been quickly realized that there will be a commercial market for this technology in the near future. Intel has therefore set about creating a hardware standard for Intel-based multiprocessor systems that will make it financially feasible for the developers of operating systems (the traditional laggards in the realization of new technologies) to modify their environments to accommodate the special needs of multiprocessing systems. Without a standard such as this, it would be necessary to customize operating systems and applications to specific hardware designs, all but relegating this technology to a niche market that would never gain widespread acceptance.

The Intel multiprocessing hardware standard is based on SMP. An SMP system is one in which all the processors are functionally identical. Each processor is capable of communicating with every other processor and with shared memory and I/O systems. Note that some multiprocessing systems are not symmetric. These asymmetric multiprocessing systems usually function by assigning specific tasks to individual processors. For example, the three-stage multiprocessor development effort undertaken by Novell for its NetWare product eventually will allow individual domains created by the NetWare 4.x NOS to be assigned to specific processors, thus allowing for an added measure of fault tolerance. The Intel standard, however (which may or may not be utilized by Novell), is designed to allow an operating system to distribute tasks dynamically among processors for increased speed. This is not to say, however, that two processors deliver twice the speed of a uniprocessor system. In fact, this is almost never the case, and if the jury remains out on this technology, it is because overall speed in some systems increases at a diminishing rate with the addition of each extra processor.

The goal of the Intel standard is to allow SMP systems to run all existing shrink-wrapped uniprocessor software as well as multiprocessor-enabled applications with a minimal amount of modification to the hardware of the system. The essential difference in hardware will be the inclusion of an *advanced programmable interrupt controller* (*APIC*) that allows communications between individual processors as well as between processors and the I/O system over a separate bus called the *interrupt controller communications* (*ICC*) *bus*. It is through this conduit that interrupts are delivered from source to destination anywhere in the SMP system. In this way, no additional interrupt traffic is created on the system's memory bus, and the processors have a dedicated communications conduit to facilitate the sharing of tasks among themselves.

Although it functions as a single unit, the APIC uses a distributed architecture and can actually be divided among several chips. The *local APIC* is the module associated with the microprocessor itself. All Pentiums of the second generation or later (that is, 75MHz or above) have a local APIC integrated into the chip; other processors require the use of the Intel 82489DX interrupt controller, which contains the local APIC as well as the I/O APIC. The I/O APIC is available also as part of an I/O chipset, such as Intel's 82430 PCI-EISA bridge chipset. Each local and I/O APIC has a unit ID register that functions as the physical name of the unit for purposes of internal communications over the ICC bus, as well as for identification of specific I/O and interprocessor interrupts by software.

Intel has also incorporated a cache consistency protocol, named MESI, into the second-generation Pentium's internal data cache design. This protocol assigns one of four states to each line in the data cache, which allow determinations to be made regarding the read/write status of each line. This is done to ensure that data in the cache remains consistent with data in memory, despite access to the same memory addresses by multiple processors.

Apart from the APIC, the primary specific hardware modifications that have to be made are in the system BIOS. It is necessary to have a BIOS that can identify and initialize all the microprocessors and other MP-related hardware in the system. Specifications other than these are more general and fall easily under the realm of common sense. Obviously, a system with more processing power creates a larger burden on other subsystems, particularly on memory. Intel recommends the use of a level 2 cache with high-performance features such as write-back technology and error correction but does not include any specifications other than that it be completely software-transparent. The Intel specification also does not recommend a specific system bus type, but the company clearly has plans to make PCI the bus of choice for these implementations, either in place of or in addition to one of the other AT standard buses.

Other standards are in development that rival Intel's standard, including one by their traditional competitor Cyrix. It is too early to tell how popular the multiple processor concept will become in the corporate network, but it is a technology that certainly merits watching. Digital's 25-year plan that predicts microprocessors becoming 1,000 times faster than those available today, specifies higher instruction-per-clock-cycle ratios as the source of the first tenfold speed increase. The second tenfold speed increase is allocated to the use of multiple processors. As our technologies approach the ultimate physical limits of their component parts, it will be replication that provides the next step in efficiency. Whether this concept is marketable on a large scale remains to be seen, but multiple processor systems are one of the most viable methods of pushing the performance envelope that forms the core of networking technology today.

Of course, for any appreciable gain in speed to be realized, application software must also be altered to accommodate SMP. NetWare 4.1 SMP, which is an add-on to the standard NetWare 4.1 product, allows for backwards compatibility with all existing NetWare

NLMs but provides only a marginal performance improvement in their operation, as well as in the standard OS file and print services. For significant gains to be realized, server-based applications will have to be modified to utilize the functionality provided by the new OS. NetWare has also released an API to facilitate this process, but the extent to which application developers will commit their efforts to the new environment remains to be seen.

At this time, I would say that if you are already using a Windows NT or NetWare application (such as a database engine) that has become available in an SMP-enabled version, and you are having problems achieving the level of performance that you require, an SMP server may be worth looking into. Otherwise, until the technology is ratified by a greater level of acceptance and commitment in the Intel community, it remains experimental, and therefore risky.

Memory

During our examination of the microprocessors used in today's network file servers, we have seen the current state of an evolutionary developmental process that began with the first PC and has progressed rapidly ever since. This section is concerned with memory, one of the other primary components of a file server, and one that has always lagged behind the rest of the computer in technological development. Intel microprocessors have advanced in speed from 4.77MHz to 133MHz, with more speed to come, and potential I/O bus throughput has increased equally dramatically, but the standard *dynamic random access memory* (*DRAM*) chips that populate the average PC have all but topped out, technologically, at a maximum refresh rate of 54 nanoseconds (ns=one billionth of a second), which works out to an approximate peak transfer speed of 18.5MHz on a bus that can run at speeds of up to 66MHz.

Additional speed can be added, though, through a layer of *static RAM* (*SRAM*) cache between the main memory banks and the microprocessor. SRAM is available with refresh rate speeds as fast as 10ns, more than enough for today's high speed buses, but it is still just a cache of 512K at most. While a system that uses SRAM as its primary memory array is possible, SRAM chips are not only much faster, but unfortunately are also much larger, run much hotter, and are ten times more expensive than normal DRAM.

Fortunately, there may be a solution in sight for this memory bottleneck. There are several new RAM technologies entering the market that promise a performance rate similar to that of SRAM, but at only a fraction of the size, heat, and cost. While it is too early to say which, if any, of these new memory types will revolutionize the industry, be assured that the players who have the most interest in the new microprocessor and I/O bus technologies (in particular, Intel) are very interested in supporting these new memory types as they become available. In this section, we examine the types of memory used in today's file servers, cover the essential aspects of memory upgrades, and then take a look at the new technologies that hopefully will bring RAM technology up to speed with the rest of the motherboard.

The Primary Memory Array (DRAM)

The basic hardware component of the *dynamic RAM* chip has changed little since the first PCs hit the market. They are essentially composed of capacitors that hold a charge, and transistors that read the state of the capacitors' charges and report them in binary format (1=charge, 0=no charge). The chips themselves have gotten faster and contain more memory in a single package thanks to the use of semiconductor equivalents on an integrated circuit instead of actual capacitors, but the inherent problems of the design remain unchanged.

Capacitors have a natural tendency to leak off their charge over time, causing a 1 to become a 0, and data corruption occurs. To prevent this, a transistor must be dedicated to each capacitor for the purpose of checking the state of the charge and refreshing it before it can decay. This refresh overhead is what imposes a speed limitation on this technology.

What has changed over the years is the hardware used to mount the chips in a computer system. In the earliest PCs, individual DRAM chips of far smaller capacity than today's models were mounted by hand onto a board. If you wanted to add more memory to your system, you bought more chips and popped them into any free sockets available on the memory board. This became increasingly impractical, due to both the increase in the average system's memory requirements and the larger amount of space that was required to make the chips accessible to human fingers or tools.

PCs today all use memory chips that have been premounted on small circuit boards called SIMMs, or *single inline memory modules* (see fig. 5.3). SIMMs make it much easier to handle large amounts of memory because several chips can be mounted on one board, and since they are permanently soldered in place, they can be placed much closer together. The primary drawback to this concept is that if one chip on a SIMM goes bad, the entire unit must be replaced (unless you are very good with a soldering iron). Older PCs may use SIPPs, or *single inline pin package modules*, which substitute pins for the SIMM's edge connectors, or even the individual chips previously mentioned, called dual inline pin chips (DIPs). Since we are concerned only with file servers in this chapter, we continue to assume that a minimum of an 80486-based PC is being used.

Adding and Replacing Memory. SIMMs are mounted roughly perpendicular to a PC's motherboard in slots specifically designed to hold them. The process of adding or removing SIMMs is quite easy, but knowing which ones to buy as well as how many and where to put them is highly dependent on the rest of the system and can be rather confusing.

The main concerns when purchasing SIMMs are

- The total amount of memory on each SIMM
- The speed of the memory chips
- The use of a parity bit
- The number of connector pins on the SIMM board itself
- The number of chips on the SIMM

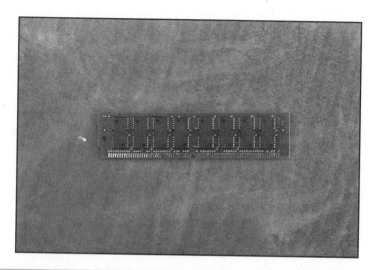

Figure 5.3

This is a typical SIMM.

If, as recommended earlier, you have obtained the documentation for your motherboard, the upgrade process should be easy. The manual should tell you what type of SIMMs to buy, and how you can safely array them in the slots provided. If you don't have the documentation, the best thing to do is to examine the SIMMs already in the machine and duplicate them as closely as possible.

Memory is arrayed on the motherboard in banks that correspond to the width of the microprocessor's data bus. A single bank may consist of up to four individual SIMM slots. Thus, a motherboard designed for a 486 is likely to have 36-bit banks (with a parity-checking mechanism accounting for the extra 4 bits above 32). A Pentium motherboard therefore has 72-bit banks (64 bits plus 8 for parity). Since SIMMs are available either as 30-pin (9-bit) or 72-pin (36-bit) modules, the 486 motherboard has either four 30-pin slots per bank (9 bits times 4 slots for a 36-bit bank) or one 72-pin slot. Most newer 486 systems use 72-pin slots and virtually all Pentium motherboards use two 72-pin slots per bank.

It is important to identify how many slots per bank your system has because all the SIMMs in any one bank must be identical. Depending on the configuration of the motherboard, this in itself can impose severe limitations on the amount of memory that you may add. If, for example, you have a 486 PC with two banks of four 30-bit slots each, you are limited to a relatively small number of memory configurations because SIMMs are only available in 1M, 4M, 16M, and 64M sizes. Since each bank must consist of four identical SIMMs, you must have either 4M, 16M, 64M, or 256M of memory in any one bank. If your system has more than one bank, then you can safely put 1M SIMMs in one bank and 4M SIMMs in the other or even leave one bank completely empty. This leaves you a limited growth path. In addition to this, you must take the possibility of future upgrades into account. If all your slots are full, and you wish to add more memory, then some of the old SIMMs must be replaced with higher capacity models. The SIMMs that are removed can be used in another machine or else go to waste. This is one of several good reasons to maintain a measure of uniformity in your PC purchases. Virtually every network has servers or workstations that could use a few more megabytes of memory; as long as other machines use the same type, SIMMs can easily be transferred.

For reasons of flexibility, then, it is preferable that you purchase a motherboard that uses the 72-pin SIMMs. In a 486 machine, this means one slot per bank, and many more possible ways to configure the server's memory to your needs, rather than the other way around.

Identifying SIMMs. SIMMs generally are looked at in one of two ways, both of which can be confusing: on paper or in your hand. That is, looking at one of the SIMMs currently installed in your PC and at the listings of available SIMM types in catalogs or advertisements and correlating the two to figure out what you already have and what you need can be difficult.

Catalogs usually do not provide illustrations of individual SIMM types since they're not much to look at, and you probably wouldn't be able to read the printing on the chips in a photograph, anyway. This section provides the means for identifying the specifications of the memory in a PC in order to purchase additional chips that are compatible. When you lack a definitive source for documentation of your motherboard, however, it is impossible to be absolutely sure that a SIMM will be compatible, unless you are able to purchase exact duplicates of those already in the machine—and this is unlikely. Therefore, be sure you know your selected chip vendor's return policies in case you have problems. Most memory vendors allow SIMMs to be returned, primarily because inserting them into an incompatible motherboard rarely results in damage. They simply do not work. Also, there is little or no packaging overhead in the sale of SIMMs. Usually, they arrive loose, in a small anti-static bag, so there are no concerns about shrink-wrapping or resale of returned modules.

Removing SIMMs from the Motherboard. It can be difficult to identify SIMMs while they are mounted on the motherboard, so the best way to know what type of SIMMs are in the machine is to remove one of them. In many cases, SIMM sockets hold the SIMMs at an angle slightly less than perpendicular to the motherboard. This is because when they are installed, they are inserted straight in and then tilted a few degrees to engage two small clips that secure the SIMM at either end (see fig. 5.4). Some SIMMs, however, are inserted at the angle and drawn perpendicular to lock in place. The locking clips are made of metal or plastic. Be particularly careful with plastic clips—if you break one, you have to choose from unattractive alternatives: replacing the motherboard (very expensive and a lot of work), or holding the SIMM in place with a rubber band or a piece of tape (unreliable at best).

Before touching the motherboard or SIMMs at all, unplug the PC from its power source, and then ground yourself to prevent a static discharge while you're working. Many components of a PC are sensitive to static, but none are more sensitive than DRAM chips, so it is advisable to wear a grounding strap or work in an environment not prone to static buildup. Avoid carpeting and wool sweaters, and be sure to touch metal before actually handling SIMMs. Also, be sure to store any loose SIMMs in an anti-static bag, even if they will be needed in just a few minutes.

Figure 5.4

Closeup view of a SIMM installed on a motherboard and the clips holding it in place.

Since SIMMs usually have to be installed in order, with each one overlapping the previous one, only the first one is immediately accessible. To remove it, release the clips at either side of the first module so that you can freely move the entire chip into an upright position, perpendicular to the motherboard. Once it is free of the clips, you should be able to lift the entire SIMM out of the socket and remove it from the system.

Number of Pins. When you look closely at a SIMM, you will see that it looks like a very small expansion card. A row of 30 or 72 gold connectors runs across the bottom of a printed circuit board that has a number of chips soldered onto one or both sides. There might be a small "30" or "72" printed on the circuit board itself, to identify the number of pins. The number of pins obviously is an indication of the type of sockets that are installed on your motherboard, but also indicate the width of the chips. 72-pin SIMMs are 32 bits wide (or 36 bits with parity checking), while 30-pin SIMMs are 8 bits wide (or 9 with parity checking).

Chip Speed. Looking at the memory chips that are mounted on the SIMM you have removed, you might see the manufacturer's name, identified by word or symbol, and a part number. A relatively small number of manufacturers make memory chips. Many more companies, however, buy the chips and mount them on SIMMs. If you see a manufacturer's name on the SIMM board, do not confuse it with the maker of the chips.

The last digit in a chip's part number usually is a 6, 7, or 8, and often has a dash in front of it. This, with a zero appended to it, indicates the speed of the chip. This is measured in nanoseconds and is a measurement of the refresh rate of the chips; the smaller the number, the faster the refresh rate, and the faster the memory performance. 60ns DRAM chips are the fastest that are commercially available. It usually is not a problem to install faster memory into a PC than the motherboard specifications require. It is not recommended, though, that different speeds be used in the same bank, and you should never use slower memory than a system specifies.

Parity. In their first PCs, IBM introduced a basic error checking concept called the *parity bit*; it has remained in popular use ever since. The system works by including one extra bit for every 8 bits (1 byte) of memory. Most SIMMs do this by including an extra memory chip on the board. Non-parity SIMMs have two or eight chips installed on them, while parity SIMMs have three or nine. As data is written to each byte of memory, this extra bit is set to a 0 or 1 by a dedicated circuit on the motherboard, depending on the state of the other eight bits. If the total value of the other eight bits is an even number, then the parity bit is turned on to make the number odd. If the eight bits add up to an odd number, then the parity bit is left off, keeping the number odd. As each byte is read from memory, the same mechanism checks to see if the total value of the byte is an odd number. If it is not, then the data on that chip is considered corrupted. Most systems generate a *non-maskable interrupt* (*NMI*) when a parity error is detected and immediately halt the system to prevent the tainted data from propagating itself into any other media. An error message usually is displayed, supplying the location of the error in memory and giving the option of continuing to work or rebooting the system. It should be emphasized that a single parity error does not necessarily indicate the failure of a memory chip. Environmental conditions can cause isolated errors that seldom or never reoccur. Repeated parity errors, however, usually indicate that a SIMM needs to be replaced.

Obviously, the parity bit is a very limited mechanism for error checking. While it should not be able to cause a false positive result, it obviously could fail 50% of the time to detect cases of data corruption in more than one bit (when the data is corrupted but the total remains odd). It is, nevertheless, an added measure of security that creates little overhead for the system. SIMMs containing the parity bit, however, cost more than those that do not, and some vendors have been known to disable parity checking on a motherboard to save a few dollars by populating the machine with cheaper SIMMs. If you wish to use parity checking, make sure that the system's motherboard is capable of supporting it (usually through DIP switch or jumper settings) and that all SIMMs installed in the system have a parity bit.

> **Note**
>
> Bear in mind that the relatively infrequent occurrences of corruption errors in today's DRAM chips makes parity checking something of a moot point in most new purchasing decisions. Do not pass up an otherwise well-equipped system merely because it lacks memory parity checking—many vendors and motherboard manufacturers are beginning to leave this feature out of their newest products.

Error Checking and Correcting Memory. While parity checking has been available for a long time, a newer technique takes the same concept further by being able to actually correct memory errors as well as check for them. On servers in which system halts due to non-maskable interrupts are unacceptable or intolerable, *error checking and correcting (ECC)* memory systems utilize a checksum technique to effectively detect errors when they occur in any two bits of a data word and then correct one of the two.

To perform these functions, a coprocessor or *application-specific integrated circuit (ASIC)* is used to compute a checksum on a data block of designated size. The checksum is appended to the block and sent to its destination. There, the checksum is computed again and compared with the original results. The nature of the algorithm is such that, should an error in a single bit be detected, the exact location of the bit can be derived from the checksum and corrected. Remember that since we are dealing with binary data at this point, simply locating the exact bit in which the error occurs is all that is needed to correct it. Errors in two bits generate an NMI and halt the system. Compared to parity checking, this technique requires much more overhead in both data storage and processing cycles. The amount of overhead is dependent on the size of the block used and the location of the ECC mechanism in the system. ECC features have been incorporated into devices ranging from tape backup drives to processor caches and everywhere in-between.

For example, in a 32-bit 486-based system, ECC increases the data path from 32 to 39 bits wide, as compared to parity, which needs a 36-bit width. This requires a significant change in the memory architecture that might not be worth the effort and expense. In 64-bit Pentium systems, however, as well as in other systems using 64-bit processors, the data overhead is only one bit, the same as for parity checking. For little more than the price of a processor, occasional memory errors that previously would have halted the system can be corrected on the fly.

There is a certain amount of disagreement in the industry regarding the real benefits of ECC memory, beyond peace of mind. System outages due to transient memory corruption are far less common than hard drive or power regulation problems, and many people feel that they occur so seldom as to be a negligible risk. If you want to have every measure of protection that you can get for your server's data, however, ECC is a giant step beyond parity checking.

Purchasing Memory. When shopping for memory, you will see SIMMs listed in ads and catalogs using an $X \times Y$ format—for example, 1×9—along with a speed listing. The first numeral identifies the amount of memory on the SIMM, and the second indicates the width of the chips, the presence of parity, and the number of pins on the SIMM. In the example above, the 1 indicates that it is a 1M SIMM, and the 9 indicates that it uses 8-bit-wide chips and therefore has a 30-pin connector, plus one bit for parity.

Since 72-pin SIMMs have four times the density of their 30-pin counterparts, the second numeral is always a 32 or a 36 (with parity). For the same reason, the first numeral is one-fourth of what normally would be shown for an 8-bit-wide SIMM. Thus, a 1×36 SIMM consists of 4M of parity memory on a 72-pin board. The same SIMM without parity would be a 1×32. If the width aspect confuses you, it is always possible to tell by the price whether you are getting 4M or just 1M.

You might also see memory described using three numerals, such as 1×9×3. This indicates that the manufacturer has utilized higher-width DRAM chips to make a lower-width SIMM. Though statistically identical to a 1×9 SIMM, this configuration has only three chips mounted on the board instead of nine; two 4 bit chips plus one 1 bit chip for parity. This same configuration has also been expressed as 1×3 by some vendors. While these are functionally equivalent to normal 1×9 SIMMs, some motherboards are intolerant of this configuration. Do not attempt to use such SIMMs if your motherboard manufacturer recommends against it.

Installing Memory. Installing new SIMMs into the motherboard is simply the opposite of the removal procedure outlined above. Follow the same precautions regarding static, and note also the way that the SIMMs should lean when fully installed. Very often, you have to insert SIMMs in order, or else previously installed SIMMs block access to other sockets. Insert a SIMM into its slot in the proper manner, either perpendicular or at an angle to the motherboard. One side of the module has a notched corner to prevent you from inserting it the wrong way. Once the SIMM is seated firmly in the slot, tilt it gently until the clips fasten themselves around the board (see fig. 5.5). You might have to open the clips by hand to accomplish this, rather than force the SIMM into place. Unlike some expansion boards and processor chips, a great amount of force is not required here, so remain gentle.

Figure 5.5

This is a correctly installed SIMM.

Once all your new memory is installed, double-check that all the banks being used are completely filled with identical SIMMs, connect the power cord, and boot the machine. If the memory check display of the BIOS (*basic input/output system*) is enabled, you should immediately see the results of your efforts as the system counts up to the total amount of memory installed in the machine. If the total does not reflect the additional memory you have installed, reflects only part of it, or the machine fails to boot at all, then one or more of the SIMMs is defective or is not fully seated in its slot, or you have not properly filled a memory bank.

If, however, the memory check displays the proper amount, yet you receive an error message from the BIOS indicating a "memory error" or "memory size mismatch," then everything is all right. What has happened is that the computer's BIOS has detected a different amount of memory in the system than is specified in its configuration ROM. Simply run the BIOS setup program (usually by holding down a certain key combination during the boot process) and save the BIOS configuration as though you had altered some of its settings. After you reboot the machine again, you should have no further problems.

Adding additional memory is one of the simplest and most effective upgrades that can be performed on a server. NetWare, as well as other NOSs, always runs better when it has enough memory to utilize because many of its processes are flexible enough to take advantage of additional memory as soon as it is supplied. For example, with more memory, greater amounts of file system information can be cached, resulting in faster file access. Therefore, while NOSs often have precise formulas to determine the amount of memory required in a server that depend on the amount of disk space in the machine and other variables, it is always recommended that some extra DRAM be added. Even as much as 25% or 50% more will not go to waste. It is not expensive, and it often makes a noticeable difference in performance.

RAM Caches (SRAM)

The word "cache" is one that is much overused in the computer industry today. Modern computers can have several different caches operating at the same time in different places. Simply put, a cache is an area of memory that is used to buffer input or output between two resources of different speeds. Your system might be running a software-based cache, like the MS-DOS Smartdrive program, that utilizes part of your computer's memory to buffer I/O from the hard drive. Hard drives or I/O controllers might have memory chips integrated into their construction to provide for onboard caching. Multiprocessors like the Intel 80486 and Pentium chips have small internal caches where data moving to or from memory can be temporarily stored. This section, though, concerns separate RAM caches that function much the same as those within the processors previously listed.

As stated earlier, the DRAM technology that is used for the primary memory arrays in modern PCs is far slower than today's processors and I/O buses. This means that the faster components often sit idle as they wait for data to be transferred to or from memory. Caching is an attempt to minimize these memory latency periods by storing a small subset of the data residing in DRAM memory in a separate, smaller, but much faster memory array. Thus, a RAM cache is a completely separate memory bank with its own controller that is located between the microprocessor and the primary DRAM array. The memory chips comprising this cache are called *static random access memory* (SRAM). While DRAM has a refresh rate of no less than 54ns, SRAM technology can provide refresh rates of as little as 10ns.

How Caches Work. When a call is made by the microprocessor for data that is present in memory, the microprocessor first checks its own internal cache arrangement (designated the *level 1 cache* or *primary cache*); if the data is not found, the request leaves the processor chip on its way to the memory array. When an SRAM cache (called a *level 2 cache* or *secondary cache*) is present, however, the data request is intercepted by the cache's controller chip. This controller's function is to maintain a continuously updated listing of the data that is currently in the cache, indexed by the data's memory address in the primary array. If the data is not found in the cache, then a *cache miss* is declared, and the request is passed on to DRAM, where it is processed in the usual manner. If the data is found in the cache, however, this is called a *cache hit*, and the data is immediately sent to the processor at its much higher speed, eliminating the delay caused by access to the slower DRAM.

While DRAM chips use equal numbers of capacitors (to hold a charge) and transistors (to read and relay the status of the charge for each capacitor), SRAM chips utilize a pair of transistors for each memory bit. There is no leak-off of the charge in a transistor as there is in a capacitor, so there is no refresh overhead. This is why such dramatically faster speeds are possible. As a tradeoff to the greater speeds, however, SRAM chips are larger than DRAM chips, they run hotter, consume more power, and are far more expensive to manufacture. This is why SRAM is used only in small amounts, for caching, rather than as a primary memory resource.

> **Note**
>
> Because of the extra heat and power consumption, SRAM caches are rarely found in laptops or portables.

Cache Designs. Different cache controller designs utilize different methods of data storage and indexing within the cache, providing various levels of performance. A *direct mapped cache* splits the main memory array into virtual blocks the same size as the cache itself, and then splits each block into lines. Data from any particular line in any DRAM block can be stored only in its corresponding line in the cache. This method allows for a very small index, but severely limits the possible locations in which a datum from DRAM can be stored in the cache, resulting in many more cache misses.

A *full associative cache* can store data from any location in the primary memory array into any location on the cache. This causes an improved cache hit ratio, but also creates a much larger index that has to be checked by the cache controller for every request, increasing overhead and decreasing overall performance levels. A *set associative cache* is something of a compromise between the previous two methods. This design calls for the splitting of the cache into a number of discrete direct mapped areas. A two-way set associative cache is thus split into two areas, a four-way into four, and so on. In this way, there is greater flexibility regarding where a particular piece of data can be stored, without creating an index as large as that of the full associative cache. Difficulties implementing this design have made it more expensive to manufacture than the other two methods, but this nevertheless is the most popular design today.

Another factor to take into account in cache design is the two-directional nature of memory access. The microprocessor is continually sending data to the main memory array and reading data from it. Wait states can be caused by memory latency in either direction, and caches can operate on data being read only from memory or bidirectionally. A *write-through cache* is one that operates only in a single direction. Data being written to memory by the processor is saved in the cache and immediately passed to main memory. If main memory signals its inability to write at that exact moment, a wait state occurs until main memory signals its readiness. A *write-back cache* operates in both directions. Data written to the cache is held there until main memory signals its readiness to receive it. This allows other operations to continue in the interim, increasing overall performance. As you can imagine, a write-back cache design essentially doubles the complexity of the caching operation, adding additional overhead to the controller and additional expense to the unit. For maximum performance, though, most PC manufacturers have accepted that a four-way set-associative write-back cache is the best possible design.

Static RAM caches range in size from 64K to 512K. They sometimes are integrated into motherboard designs, but more often are packaged as small *daughterboards* that plug into a socket on the motherboard. This allows for varying amounts of cache to be provided in a server. The general rule of thumb in caching is "more is better." While some other types of caches might run into the law of diminishing returns, in which the addition of more memory beyond a certain point leads to a disproportionate return in performance, SRAM caches utilize small enough amounts of memory for them not to be affected by this. The only drawback is system design and cost. As with most things, it is not wise to use more cache than your motherboard manufacturer indicates as a maximum. It is important also to check the width of the bus between the microprocessor and the RAM cache. Some motherboards include a dedicated 128-bit bus for this purpose, which can provide an extra measure of added performance.

The SRAM cache is the most common technique in use today for overcoming the speed limitations of DRAM memory arrays. A well-designed cache can provide a tremendous increase in a file server's performance. Care should be taken, however, to utilize only the cache design recommended by the manufacturer of the server's motherboard. There are far fewer manufacturing "standards" in place for SRAM cache design than there are for most other PC components, so the odds of buying the SRAM cache unit that you want and having it work in a particular motherboard are slim. When not purchased with the motherboard itself, cache upgrades are best purchased directly from the motherboard vendor or manufacturer. When purchasing a new file server or motherboard, however, a measure of care taken in selecting a model that provides a fast, efficient SRAM cache can provide a great deal of extra performance for the cost.

Memory Interleaving

Another technique for speeding up memory access times is *interleaving*. This is a technique in which two or more memory banks of equal capacity are used in parallel. Data bits are written alternately to the two banks, so that sequential memory reads alternate their access between the two.

While one bank is being accessed, the other is being refreshed, effectively reducing wait states. When non-sequential accesses are required, the overall efficiency diminishes, as the laws of probability determine whether or not the next bit required is located on another bank or not. This can be mitigated, however, by the use of more banks, and there is no performance penalty (beyond traditional DRAM access times) for sequential reads from the same bank. Requiring no alterations to the DRAM chips, this is probably the most inexpensive means of reducing memory access delays and can be used in conjunction with a cache for additional performance gains. This technique, however, is a property of the motherboard, not the DRAM chips themselves. Check the motherboard documentation to find out if memory interleaving is possible on your server.

New Memory Technologies

While SRAM caching provides a measure of relief for the slow performance of standard DRAM chips, it is no more than a stopgap measure. Processor and bus speeds continue to rise, and the added cost of additional SRAM chips and more powerful caching controllers will become increasingly unmanageable.

An alternative is clearly required that will provide performance near that of SRAM for the entire main memory array at a manageable cost, preferably without a major change in motherboard architecture. This sounds like a tall order, but there are several new technologies in the works that may provide just that.

As is usually the case in the computer industry, however, one problem generates several possible solutions, and the requisite period of corporate bickering over standards will no doubt ensue before any technology emerges as the dominant solution.

Nevertheless, steps are being taken in the right direction, and the first systems utilizing some of these technologies are already on the market. Never a trailblazer as far as my file servers are concerned, I do not recommend the use of any of these technologies until they have been adequately tested under real world conditions, but I certainly will be keeping a watchful eye on their progress.

EDO DRAM. *Enhanced data output* (*EDO*) *DRAM* is the first of these new memory technologies to be available on the open market today. Several giant semiconductor corporations, including Samsung, Mitsubishi, Hyundai, and particularly Micron Technologies, have announced that they will manufacture the chips, and systems and chipset manufacturers are also beginning to endorse this new technology, which is said to deliver zero wait states at bus speeds of up to 66MHz. Pentium systems using EDO DRAM are already available from Micron Computer and Toshiba. These systems contain motherboards that utilize the new Intel Triton core-logic chipset, the only chipset on the market at this time to support EDO DRAM (and synchronous DRAM as well).

EDO DRAM is based on traditional fast page mode DRAM, is pin-compatible to the old RAM chips, and does not require any substantial alterations to the system board architecture. A small modification to the DRAM chips themselves allows for data to be passed through them at increased rates, and a subsequent level of this technology, called *burst EDO*, uses a pipelining technique that allows an operation to begin before the previous one has been completed, adding additional speed.

Synchronous DRAM. Another new technology that could end up rivaling EDO for the first solid niche in the marketplace is *synchronous DRAM (SDRAM)*. Current DRAM technology uses asynchronous row and column addressing, and the SDRAM concept simply alters this arrangement so that inputs and outputs can both be conducted with each clock cycle. Column access is also pipelined, allowing a second request to begin execution before the first has finished. The result is performance equivalent to 10ns SRAM, at prices comparable to traditional DRAM.

The Triton Pentium chipset from Intel contains built-in support for both SDRAM and EDO DRAM. With this level playing field on which to compete, it remains to be seen which technology takes hold in the marketplace.

Cached DRAM. Two other manufacturers have taken separate approaches toward essentially the same end. Mitsubishi's *cached DRAM (CDRAM)* and Ramtron's *enhanced DRAM (EDRAM)* each include a small amount of SRAM cache memory along with DRAM on each chip. They differ in that CDRAM uses a set-associative cache design, while EDRAM uses a direct-mapped cache design. The SRAM portions of both chips have a refresh rate of approximately 15ns, and the apparent advantage held by CDRAM due to its superior cache design is effectively nullified by the faster refresh rate of the EDRAM chip (35ns versus 70ns). Both designs are estimated to cost $50 per megabyte.

RDRAM. While all the technologies previously listed have attempted to retain the basic memory architecture of the PC, a company named Rambus has designed a completely revolutionary scheme that uses the system's processor or a custom-designed ASIC to control the transfer of data over a proprietary Rambus channel in packets of up to 256 bytes. Twin 250MHz clocks and the ability to transfer data on both clock edges yields a maximum transfer rate of 500 M/sec, equivalent to a 2ns refresh rate. This fantastic performance is strongly mitigated, however, by the need for major hardware design changes, which motherboard manufacturers will be very reluctant to adopt. This is likely to end up as a proprietary design which, if adopted by system manufacturers with sufficient clout in the industry, could be successful, but unless the innovations described earlier prove to be unusable, the performance improvement of RDRAM over EDO DRAM will not justify the investment of millions of dollars for new motherboard designs and manufacturing techniques.

I/O Bus Types

It is fairly easy to predict the trials and tribulations that the new memory technologies will go through before a definitive standard is realized. This is because the personal computer industry has seen the same process occur several times, most notably in designs for the I/O bus that were developed as a means of improving the performance standard set by the archaic ISA bus from the original IBM PC designs. It's difficult to believe that so many systems still are being sold today with high-powered processors like the 486 and the Pentium that still rely so heavily on this antiquated architecture.

The fundamental reason that these persistent difficulties plague the PC industry is not technological but economic. The original PC was more of a marketing coup than a technological one. Many other computer designs existed that were as good or better than the PC, and in the same way, many bus designs have come and gone over the years, but they didn't last because they were proprietary systems. At one time, a giant conglomerate like IBM could create a standard just by making a decision, and this was how the ISA bus came about. When IBM said, "This is how we are going to build our machines," many other companies were more than willing to design, manufacture, and market expansion boards that would work in those machines. Unfortunately, this eventually became the problem rather than the solution. As technology moved forward, the old standards became inadequate, and new ones had to be developed that were compatible with the old so that the investments made by other companies would not be lost. This is where IBM found out that they were no longer the sole trendsetter in the PC industry. This led to a battle of competing I/O bus standards that is being waged to this day, and although the players have changed, the game remains the same.

ISA

The *Industry Standard Architecture* (*ISA*) I/O bus was developed for the original IBM PCs. Using early Intel 8088 microprocessors that ran at 4.77MHz, this 8-bit-wide bus was designed to run at the same speed. Indeed, it functioned more as an extension to the processor itself than as a separate subsystem. The processor's clock was the centralized timing source for the whole system, forcing even simple data transfers that required no calculation to be routed through the processor. In essence, this was a true local bus, with the expansion slots hardwired directly to the microprocessor's I/O pins.

It became apparent quickly that this would not do. Within months, processors were being manufactured that ran at unheard of speeds, like 6MHz or even 8MHz. The expansion cards designed by other manufacturers for the original PC bus would not run at these increased speeds, so it became necessary to unlink the bus from its direct connection to the processor clock. In order to relieve the processor of some of its routine tasks, a separate controller was added, called a *direct memory access* (*DMA*) controller. The original DMA controller in IBM machines ran at 5MHz and could access only 1M of memory, which was the addressable limit of an 8-bit architecture. These early systems still had a bus speed roughly equivalent to the processor's clock speed, but they were two separate clocks, and the bus was no longer dependent on the processor for timing information.

By the time IBM released the PC-AT in 1984, the company also had chosen to expand the existing bus design to accommodate the new Intel 80286 processors. They added an additional connector to the original 8-bit slot (see fig. 5.6) that allowed for a 16-bit data width while retaining compatibility with earlier designs. Still running at 8MHz despite processor speeds of 10MHz or 12MHz, the AT bus could now address up to 16M of memory, the limit for a 16-bit system, and had a theoretical maximum data transfer rate of 8 M/sec. This figure, of course, represents at least double the actual transfer rate that would be achieved under normal conditions. Factor in the need to accomodate the 32-bit-wide data path of today's microprocessors, and the result is a bus that is generally inadequate for many of today's computing needs. Nevertheless, this is the same ISA bus that is still used today in the vast majority of the world's PCs.

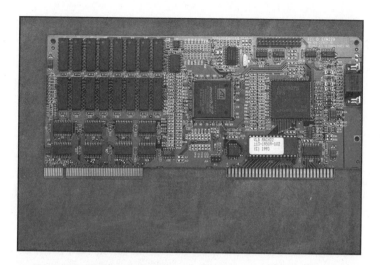

Figure 5.6

This is an adapter card's 16-bit ISA bus connector.

For use in a network file server, the ISA bus should not even be considered, except as a secondary bus type used for non-networked resources such as video adapters. ISA expansion boards still use DMA transfers and still cannot address memory above 16M. Furthermore, they force the processor to spend part of its time operating at the bus's top speed of 8MHz and still use a 16-bit data path, so that the performance capabilities of the high-speed 32- or 64-bit processor are largely going to waste.

As we consider alternatives throughout the rest of this section, bear in mind that any of them is preferable to the ISA bus for use in a file server. I don't mean to condemn it out of hand, for the ISA bus is still a valid choice for workstation use and has led a surprisingly long and useful life in a highly volatile industry. The primary function of a file server, however, is data transfer—when I see someone spend a great deal of money on a server with the latest processor and fastest drives and then run them through a 16-bit SCSI card and wonder why it's no faster than the old machine, I have only one answer.

MCA

When IBM realized the ultimate inadequacy of even their expanded AT bus, they set about creating a new bus standard that would be able to accommodate the continual improvements being made in other components of the PC. Still the dominant player in the desktop PC market, they proved their skills by developing a bus type using what they called *Micro Channel architecture* (MCA) for the PS/2 systems that went to market in 1987.

MCA was remarkably visionary in its design, capabilities, and expandability, but IBM proceeded to let the euphoria over this accomplishment go to their heads and made two drastic mistakes that forever prevented the MCA bus from becoming an industry standard. First, they decided that their requirements for the new bus overshadowed the need for backward compatibility with existing expansion cards—ISA cards cannot run in MCA slots. Second, they implemented a licensing scheme that attempted to force other manufacturers to pay retroactive royalty fees on the ISA bus technology to market systems using the MCA bus.

This caused enough of an uproar within the industry that a "gang of nine"—other PC manufacturers, usually cutthroat competitors with each other—got together to develop their own standard, which resulted in the EISA bus. As a result, the MCA bus never enjoyed the popularity that it deserved outside of IBM shops, and far fewer MCA expansion cards were made by third-party manufacturers than EISA and ISA cards. IBM continued to market and maintain MCA as a proprietary standard for nearly a decade, and only recently announced that they would discontinue further development of MCA and gradually phase out its use in favor of PCI (see the "PCI" section below). This is not due to unviability of the standard or low quality of resulting products but solely to antiquated business practices of a former industry leader now relegated to a position farther back in the crowd.

The most obvious improvement of the MCA bus was its 32-bit data path. Designed to accommodate the new 80386 processors that were just being released, the address path was also widened to 32 bits, allowing a full 4G of memory to be addressed. However, 32 bits are not required. The bus reads a signal from an expansion card that informs it of the card's capabilities. Thus, while MCA cards can be 32-bit, they do not have to be. This should be considered whenever purchasing Micro Channel adapters. The Adaptec AHA-1640 Micro Channel SCSI host adapter, for example, is a 16-bit MCA card that suffers from the same 16M memory limitation as an ISA adapter using DMA does.

From an installation standpoint, MCA expansion cards are well ahead ahead of ISA, although they do not approach the Plug and Play standards that we are striving for today. A reference disk containing the configuration program is needed, but gone are the jumpers and DIP switches that plagued the older technology. Just plug an MCA card into the slot, and the hardware aspect of the installation is finished.

The MCA bus runs at 10MHz, not blazingly fast by today's standards, but with a slight edge over ISA and even EISA systems. The primary innovation of the bus that made it incompatible with previous designs, however, was hardware-mediated bus arbitration. In a remarkably foresighted move, IBM created a bus that would be quite capable of supporting today's multiprocessor systems. The MCA bus can arbitrate between eight microprocessors and up to eight other devices, such as DMA controllers or graphics coprocessors directly at the hardware level. This is done through the inclusion of a controller on the bus called the *central arbitration point* (*CAP*) that determines which device in the system gets control of the bus at any given time. By utilizing a hierarchy that gives added weight to more critical processes (such as memory refreshes or NMIs, for example), the CAP is able to satisfy the needs of all its "customers" without monopolizing the system's microprocessor. For this to function properly, however, it is necessary for all devices involved to have comparable arbitration circuitry.

The bus also utilizes level-sensitive interrupts, which are incompatible with the edge-triggered interrupts of the ISA bus. Level-sensitive interrupts can be shared, while edge-triggered interrupts cannot, and level-sensitive ones can be sensed during the actual interrupt, while the AT bus interrupts can be sensed only at the moment that the interrupt request changes state.

Also included in the original MCA bus design was a *burst mode* that was a direct response to the extensive microprocessor overhead that is required for data transfers in the AT bus. Instead of the two step "addressing and mailing" process of the older technology, which required the processor to be involved in the transfer of every byte, MCA is able to transfer larger blocks of data, or bursts, without processor intervention by utilizing its own hardware to detect the status of the transfer.

Two years after the release of the initial PS/2 machines with the Micro Channel bus, IBM enhanced its specification to allow better performance. The original MCA design, running at 10MHz and using 32-bit words, had a maximum theoretical transfer rate of 20 M/sec. Compared to the 8 M/sec of the ISA bus, this is a vast improvement, but the Micro Channel 2 specification goes even further. While the original burst mode design was created to facilitate the transfer of random data bytes that required individual addresses, the enhanced MCA bus incorporates a process called *streaming data mode* that greatly enhances the transfer of sequential blocks of data.

It was recognized by studying the data access patterns of normal system use that larger, contiguous blocks of data are often transferred. Executables and large data files, for example, might reside in one large block on a drive and have to be read into memory by the methodical access of each subsequent byte. In this situation, it is not necessary to transfer an address location for each byte because the source and the destination are both a series of contiguous addresses. *Streaming data mode* eliminates the clock cycles devoted to the individual addressing of data bytes. Since a normal transfer utilizes one cycle for addressing and one for the actual transfer, the elimination of the former effectively doubles the maximum transfer rate, to 40 M/sec. However, since the bus design allots 32 bus lines for addressing as well as 32 for the transfer, streaming data mode leaves address lines idle after the original address for the entire block is sent. MCA multiplexes the data transfer, using the 32 idle lines to double the throughput again to a 64-bit transfer, running at 80 M/sec. Designed for use with bus masters and slaves, the best part of this extension to the MCA specification is that it is completely optional. Hardware that cannot support these techniques simply performs data transfers using the original method.

As you can see, when combined with hardware that can support its extended features, the Micro Channel architecture makes quite a robust bus that can more than adequately service the needs of the average server. Since IBM is now combining this technology in machines with the PCI bus—and eventually phasing it out altogether—it would be unwise to purchase a server that relies on MCA at this time. In addition, there never developed as wide a range of third-party hardware that supported MCA as there did for EISA and other bus types. If you already possess servers that use this bus, though, you can be sure that they will perform at least as well as EISA and far better than ISA.

EISA

As stated earlier, the EISA bus was a direct reaction to the incompatibility and licensing practices of IBM's MCA bus. Therefore, the EISA design holds compatibility with existing

Hardware Platforms

ISA adapters as its highest priority. Beyond that, the standard amounts to a collection of most of the desirable attributes of the Micro Channel bus and other proprietary standards. Perhaps due in part to the fact that they had the MCA bus as a model to work from, the committee successfully created a standard that has endured for many years. Although not as fast and capable as some newer emerging standards, such as VLB and PCI, EISA definitely is thoroughly tested, completely reliable, and well-suited for use in the average server. I do not hesitate to recommend purchasing an EISA-based server, as EISA promises to remain a viable standard for some time to come.

One of the cleverest aspects of the EISA bus design is that of the connector itself. Unlike an MCA slot, into which an ISA card could not hope to be inserted, an EISA slot has connectors of two lengths. The upper level of a connector corresponds exactly to the edge connector of a standard ISA adapter. This allows all existing ISA cards to be plugged into an EISA slot just as though it were an AT bus. Adapter cards designed to the EISA standard, however, have shorter connectors that plug into the same ISA-compatible slot, as well as longer connectors that plug into a series of contacts located deeper in the EISA slot. Special cutouts on EISA cards allow them to be fully inserted into the slot at both levels, while ISA cards are blocked from extending down to the EISA connectors and possibly causing a short circuit. Thus, the additional advantages of the EISA bus are made available without utilizing any more motherboard real estate than that taken by an ISA card.

Of course, as with MCA, EISA has taken care of the primary requirement of expanding the bus to use a 32-bit data path. 32 address lines are used, allowing the bus to address the full 4G of memory that 32-bit processors like the 386 and 486 can support. The EISA specification also takes great pains to accommodate the varying power needs of the large array of ISA and EISA adapters that are to be supported. The design calls for 45 watts at four possible voltages per EISA slot. This is far more than most ISA or EISA cards will ever need, which is lucky, because a fully populated EISA bus containing eight adapters, each using the maximum amount of power available, would require a power supply of over 300 watts for the I/O bus alone, discounting the needs of the motherboard, processor, and other devices in the machine. Obviously, this is more than the average PC power supply can furnish, but it is another indication of the designers' forward-looking intentions for the EISA bus.

In the interest of backward compatibility, though, it was necessary to keep the speed of the EISA bus the same as that of the AT bus: 8.33MHz. This speed amounts to one-fourth of 33MHz, the highest processor speed available at the time. This is because, when running in its basic mode, EISA is essentially a synchronous bus, coordinating its speed with that of the system processor. EISA, however, like MCA, has special bus mastering capabilities that greatly enhance the speed of data transfers under certain conditions. *Bus mastering* is a system in which an adapter contains its own processor for managing data transfers, thus reducing overhead and improving performance. This prevents the adapter from having to add to the burden of the system CPU or rely on the motherboard's DMA controller for processing. The EISA counterpart of Micro Channel's CAP is called the *Integrated System Peripheral (ISP) chip.*

Aside from managing the transfer of bus control between the various devices in the computer, the ISP chip allows for a compressed transfer mode that uses a special timing signal that runs at double the normal bus speed, as well as a burst mode. Unlike the burst mode of the MCA bus, though, EISA's furnishes an address with each byte, allowing for transfers of non-sequential data in a single burst. Overhead is reduced by transferring only the 10 lowest bits of each address. This limits the contents of a single burst to bytes that reside with a block of 1,024 32-bit double words. Each burst is also limited to either read or write data—the two cannot be mixed. Using burst mode, a theoretical transfer rate of 33 M/sec can be achieved (although, to swipe a disclaimer from the automobile ads, your mileage may vary).

Some EISA adapters utilize bus mastering and others do not. Those that do, usually offer increased performance and, not surprisingly, carry a higher price. Also, not every EISA slot is capable of supporting a bus mastering card. As always, consult your motherboard documentation before making a purchase decision.

EISA also expands considerably on the capabilities of DMA transfers. In addition to supporting the capabilities of the standard DMA transfer from the AT bus, EISA's DMA controller allows access to the full 4G of memory supported by the specification, instead of just 16M. Three additional DMA transfer modes are also added in the EISA specification, reducing the number of clock cycles needed to perform a transfer. The original ISA bus required eight bus clock cycles for each 8- or 16-bit transfer, most of this being superfluous. EISA type A transfers eliminate two of the eight bus cycles and type B transfers eliminate four. These modes are designated for use by legacy ISA adapters, many of which have the capability to run at one or another of these accelerated speeds. Type C transfers, synonymous with the burst mode described above, are designed solely for use by EISA adapters, and eliminate all but a single bus cycle from the sequence, with the same 1,024 double word address limitation.

The ability to recognize and translate between different bus widths is also built into the EISA specification. An *EISA bus controller* is responsible for breaking down 32-bit transfers into two or four sequential streams, 16- or 8-bits wide respectively, so that no data is lost when transferred between devices of different bus widths.

One of the design decisions that made the Micro Channel architecture incompatible with the AT bus was the use of level-sensitive interrupts that could be shared by several devices. The 15 edge-triggered interrupts of the ISA specification (which already had been raised from eight on the original PC) were clearly insufficient, and the prospect of adding more became overly complex and did not seem to be a good overall solution. The quandary was resolved by making each interrupt in an EISA machine individually configurable to edge- or level-triggered operation. The same limitations of the ISA design still apply. Edge-triggered interrupts cannot be shared with other edge- or level-triggered interrupts. However, EISA cards effectively can share level-sensitive interrupts with other EISA cards.

Installing EISA expansion cards into a PC is not quite as simple as installing MCA cards but is still a great improvement over installing ISA cards. Rather than having a number of possible memory addresses that can be used by any adapter in the system, the EISA specification calls for each slot to have an assigned range of addresses that can only be used by that slot. In addition, all EISA cards are assigned a *product identifier* that makes them uniquely recognizable to the system. Configuration is performed through the use of software (although DIP switches or jumpers are still present on many EISA cards as a backup), with settings saved in the CMOS system ROM, which has been enlarged for this purpose. Usually, it is necessary only to identify the slot into which a particular card has been inserted, and the software is able to manage the selection of all other necessary parameters.

It took several years for EISA to become as stable a standard as it is today. Software support for its full capabilities was slow in coming, and the extra circuitry involved in building an EISA machine raised the price of a PC by as much as $1,000. Both of these problems have long since been overcome, though. An EISA bus adds approximately $300 to the price of a PC today and full software support, as well as a wide range of expansion cards, has been available for some time.

The next sections examine two newer bus types that significantly expand on the capabilities of those already considered. These up-and-coming bus types are very new technology, however, so while they hold great promise, there are definite indications that all the kinks are not yet worked out. As stated earlier, your file servers are not a place to experiment. For this reason, you should make a detailed study of every aspect of the new local bus types before purchasing a server that relies exclusively upon them.

VESA Local Bus

While the Micro Channel and EISA designs both made significant increases in the overall speed of the PC's I/O expansion bus, there were aspects unrelated to their fundamental design that prevented them from being the complete solution that users were looking for. Aside from the licensing and marketing problems of the MCA bus, it was quite some time before software drivers were released that allowed the full capabilities of the EISA and MCA technologies to be exercised. Particularly in the case of the EISA bus—which without its bus mastering and burst mode was only slightly faster than ISA—the average user was not able to see an appreciable difference in transfer speed.

So, as the 1990s began, work continued on the creation of faster buses, and developers hit upon a solution that amounted more to a step backward than forward. Since microprocessors were being produced by then in speeds as fast as 33MHz, while the EISA and MCA buses were still hampered by their 8MHz and 10MHz speeds, someone hit upon the idea of relinking the I/O bus to the processor clock, as in the original IBM PC. By having both subsystems run at speeds up to 33MHz on a 32-bit-wide data path, surely this was a way to realize a noticeable increase in speed. This was also the time at which Windows 3.0 was released, and the PC computing world began to participate in the GUI revolution.

The primary bottleneck in running the new generation of graphical applications and operating systems was the video subsystem, and the newly revived concept of the *local bus* was put to work in speeding up graphics performance. Utilized at first in proprietary designs that linked video circuitry to the processor clock right on the motherboard, the concept got off to a shaky start, as no design proved dominant enough to claim a market share worthy of third-party hardware development. The speed enhancement was there, but the integration of the video circuitry onto the motherboard prevented systems from being upgraded to the latest graphic accelerator designs that were just coming into play. There was enough interest in the concept, however, that in 1992, the *Video Electronics Standards Association* (*VESA*) began work on a draft standard for a local I/O expansion bus that was ratified in August of that year.

Called the *VESA local bus*, *VL-bus*, or simply *VLB*, this standard—unlike those that had come before it—was designed to augment an existing bus design, not replace it. Using a standard 112-pin MCA connector, the bus interface was located as an extension to an existing ISA, EISA, or MCA slot. For example, an ISA-based VLB slot would consist of the original 8-bit connector, then the 16-bit extension, and the VLB connector immediately beyond. Local bus expansion cards could be designed with pins for all three connections, or just one set for the VLB connection. Likewise, a VLB slot could be utilized for a normal ISA, EISA, or MCA card, with the added connector simply left vacant, if desired. This was an ingenious piece of design work, sacrificing nothing in backward compatibility while contributing the potential for tremendous improvement. Because the specification calls for an expansion bus linked to the processor's clock as well as motherboard integration of local bus circuitry, the design became a viable one for more than just video acceleration. NICs and SCSI controllers also could be adapted for use on the VLB, and this piqued the interest of network administrators who were always looking for ways to improve hard drive and network throughput in their file servers.

Unlike the MCA and EISA standards, which set out to be revolutionary designs, the beauty and effectiveness of the VLB standard is in its simplicity. In its most basic form, it is little more than a series of address, data, and control signals extended from the Intel 80486 microprocessor to an expansion device. Using a single hardware interrupt control line to interface with the system's existing ISA, EISA, or MCA bus, VLB peripherals can take advantage of attributes provided by the other designs, such as DMA control and level-sensitive interrupts. In addition, the VESA local bus is entirely software transparent. Most of its speed is an inherent property of the basic design, which adopts the electrical and timing specifications directly from the 486 processor bus, and not the result of sophisticated bus mastering techniques that require customized software support to be effective, as with EISA.

However, the fact that the VLB was designed around the Intel 80486 microprocessor has become its primary weakness as well as its primary strength. The first VESA local bus standard called for a system bus running at a speed no greater than 40MHz and had 32 data lines and 30 address lines, enabling it to address up to 4G of memory. At this speed, the VLB could perform a write operation with no wait states and a read with one wait state. At speeds over 40MHz, penalties accrue in the form of two wait states for both reads and writes. Like the standards discussed earlier, VLB also has a burst mode that can provide a maximum theoretical throughput of 132 M/sec.

Another problem that arose due to the speed at which the bus functioned was the amount of electrical interference generated by the signal. An increase in the number of connectors causes an increase in electrical capacitance, and raising the bus frequency by almost 400% exacerbates this considerably. For this reason, the first version of the standard called for no more than three local bus devices on a 33MHz system. As clock speed increased, the number of devices was reduced. A 50MHz 486 could run only one local bus device, and it had to be integrated into the motherboard to support the specification. The version 2.0 specification allows for three devices in a 40MHz machine and two in a 50MHz machine, provided that the systems utilize a low-capacitance design. This in itself was not unduly limiting, however, as nearly all PCs could effectively utilize the increased speed only in three functions: video, disk access, and network access. For use in an average server, video is inconsequential, leaving enough bandwidth for network and disk storage connections.

Overall processor speed is also a consideration. Although the 2.0 standard allows for bus speeds of up to 66MHz, the electrical capacitance problems effectively limit bus speeds to an absolute maximum of no more than 50MHz. For use in most 486 systems, this is acceptable, as the clock-doubled and -tripled processors all interface with the system bus at speeds of no more than 33MHz. For Pentium systems, despite the fact that the system bus runs at no more than 33MHz, the VLB is not a recommended solution. Various workarounds have been proposed as a means of adapting the bus design to the new breed of processors, but a definitive solution has not yet been accepted by the industry.

The second version of the VLB standard, which was created to accommodate the release of the Pentium, calls for a 64-bit-wide path, while retaining backward compatibility with the earlier standard. When used in a Pentium system, however, or with any of the other 64-bit processors listed in the specification (such as MIPS and the Power PC), the VLB standard requires the inclusion of a bridge between the bus and the processor that technically prevents it from being a true local bus. Obviously, the revised standard is a calculated response to the double punch of Intel's Pentium processor and its PCI specification. It adds support for write-back caching and introduces an additional signal that can be used to automatically identify the 486 systems that are capable of supporting VLB's advanced burst mode features. It remains to be seen whether the VLB design can be successfully adapted to 64-bit systems and remain competitive to PCI, which was designed from the ground up as a Pentium-based specification.

When implemented in the environment for which it was intended, the VESA local bus standard provides a performance increase that is easily perceptible and undeniable. Although the gain is more obvious when it is used for video, rather than for disk or network interfaces, the gains over EISA and MCA systems are significant enough to warrant advocacy. Therefore, in any 486 file server—except one based on the 80486DX-50 processor (which runs the system bus at 50MHz)—I do not hesitate to recommend the VLB, preferably in combination with EISA, thus allowing the new standard to take advantage of the shared interrupts and advanced DMA transfers of the older one. Its simplicity and directness results in little added cost to the price of the system board, and its integration with the 486 architecture provides excellent performance. I am just as quick, however, to recommend against utilizing the VLB in a Pentium system. The expansions to the specification seem to be too much of a retrofitted solution for some fundamental inadequacies of the design, when it is run in a Pentium. This has, in recent months, become virtually a non-issue, though, as few Pentium machines are even being offered with VLB as an option anymore.

As far as configuration of the actual hardware is concerned, the VESA local bus specification makes no attempt to govern the manner in which expansion cards are configured. The decision whether to use traditional jumpers or DIP switches, a software-based configuration program, or an auto-detecting Plug and Play design is left solely up to the board manufacturers. In addition, care must be taken in the treatment of the VLB expansion cards themselves. Criticism has been leveled at several manufacturers of VLB cards regarding difficulties when inserting the card into the VLB slot. ISA and EISA cards typically are beveled and rounded at the corners of the edge connectors. VLB cards often are not, and the connectors themselves are thinner and more fragile than those on older adapters (see fig. 5.7). When adding a VLB card to a PC, make sure that the path of the card into the bus slot is unobstructed, so that it can be inserted straight down from directly above the motherboard.

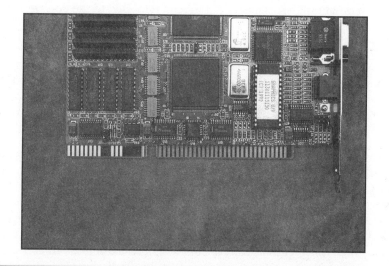

Figure 5.7

These are bus connectors of a VLB adapter. To the right are the standard 16-bit connectors and to the left are the smaller, local bus connectors.

PCI

The VESA local bus standard was conceived and ratified in less than eight months. Clearly, it was an attempt to get products using this technology to market as quickly as possible. The further development of the standard was undertaken much more slowly. This was because the VESA 2 specification was not only a response to the introduction of the Pentium but was also a direct response to the release of the Intel PCI local bus specification, a far more detailed and comprehensive specification for a different bus design, built around the Pentium processor. In fact, the PCI bus cannot truly be called a local bus at all.

Since it is a self-contained system, utilizing a bridge to establish a 33MHz synchronous connection to the microprocessor bus—rather than connecting directly to it—the *peripheral component interconnect (PCI) bus* is technically referred to as a *mezzanine bus*. A buffered PCI controller examines all signals being delivered from the processor and passes them along, as needed, to the appropriate slot—this might be PCI, or one of the slots used by the existing system bus design. This is because, like VLB, PCI is designed to augment an existing bus, not replace it. The two are dissimilar, however, in that the PCI design is not tethered to the clock speed of the microprocessor. The bus can be slowed to accommodate legacy devices or even stopped completely to save power. This is all performed completely independently from the operation of the system processor, which makes the design ideal for the new generation of bus mastering controllers that can operate with the PCI buffer as an isolated subsystem. Data transfers can be sent from the CPU to the buffer, from which they can be transferred to the destination device without any further intervention from the CPU. If the target signals a not-ready state, then the data waits in the PCI buffer until it is free to accept data—all the while, the processor continues working on other tasks. This makes PCI inherently suited to the burst mode capabilities of the Pentium processor.

The PCI connector itself, like that of the VLB, is a 124-pin MCA-type slot that is offset from the other bus slots on the motherboard. Unlike VLB, there is no aspect of the design that can accommodate the connection of one adapter to both expansion buses. Indeed, as we shall see, this is a technique that is expressly to be avoided. Some systems are available in which PCI slots share a backplane with slots for other bus types, but these are for use by one type of adapter or the other, not both.

In a manner similar to that of the MCA bus design, the pinout of the PCI connector is expressly designed to offset the same high electrical capacitance problems that have plagued VLB systems when running the bus at high speeds. Every live signal line on the connector is either next to or opposite a redundant power supply or ground line, and the specification even specifies standards for the location of the PCI chips on the motherboard, to minimize the overall length of the bus. Despite this, however, PCI systems—like those using VLB—usually are limited to a maximum of three bus mastering PCI devices (whether they are slotted or located on the motherboard), although additional slave slots up to a total of 10 can be supplied.

Some high-end servers have begun to appear with motherboards containing dual, bridged PCI subsystems that increase the number of available slots, but this should not be necessary for anything other than a "super-server" configuration, as multiport PCI NICs and SCSI adapters are currently available. Accommodations have also been made for the two different voltages currently used by Intel processors. Separate connector types are specified for 3.3v or 5v operation that prevent a card from being inserted into a slot of the wrong voltage, and an additional design is included for expansion boards that are individually keyed to fit either slot when they are capable of operating at both voltage levels.

PCI is a more forward-thinking specification than VLB. It anticipates the increasing use of high-end multimedia hardware (such as that for videoconferencing, which Intel coincidentally has a hand in developing) and multiple processors in desktop computers, and is expressly designed to be adaptable to many current and future systems. Indeed, the bus is almost completely self-contained. Protocols for arbitrated bus mastering are furnished using a dedicated 4-bit command code that makes it completely processor-independent. Although it has not yet been fully realized, PCI is very likely to set a standard for motherboard design that will accommodate all new microprocessor designs for some time to come, including the Intel Pentium Pro, and even high-performance 64-bit RISC processors designed by other manufacturers including MIPS, Alpha AXP, and the PowerPC.

PCI is also designed to be a major step toward the long-awaited but never realized Plug and Play specification. Like EISA and Micro Channel, PCI adapters utilize no jumper or DIP switches. They are required by the specification to contain 256 registers for the storage of configuration data, which is relayed to and from the bus via a signal dedicated to that purpose. Once the new breed of operating systems has fulfilled the promise of an operational Plug and Play design, then PCI, along with the use of an expanded system BIOS, will be able to meet them halfway in their goal of completely eliminating the need for manual configuration by either hardware or software means.

Despite the differences in their intents and designs, VESA local bus and PCI systems deliver performance levels that are remarkably similar. Both have a theoretical maximum throughput of around 130 M/sec, although these figures represent peak burst mode rates; neither will provide anything even close to this speed in normal use. Both technologies are perceptibly faster than either MCA or EISA, though, and each seems particularly well-suited to a specific platform. I would even go so far as to say, without hesitation, that when buying a 486-based file server, use VLB, and when buying a Pentium, include some PCI slots. In both cases, however, I would strongly recommend the inclusion of EISA slots as a subsidiary bus. In the case of the 486, the VESA local bus will be able to take advantage of EISA's attributes, and in both cases, the EISA slots provide an effective fallback. Should any problems or incompatibilities arise with these new technologies, it would be possible to revert to EISA performance levels for no more than the price of an additional adapter card.

It is unfortunate to see, though, that as 486 machines become increasingly rare in the file-server market, support for the VESA local bus is waning with them. I maintain that VLB has always had as much potential as the PCI bus but was lacking primarily in a powerful corporate advocate, such as PCI has in Intel. Now that IBM and Apple are planning to phase out their long standing MCA and NuBus designs in favor of PCI, and even non-Intel platforms such as Digital's Alpha AXP are using it, PCI's future seems assured, despite continuing compatibility problems.

Combining VLB and PCI. One innovation that is being marketed by some vendors is a line of motherboards containing both VLB and PCI slots. This is an abortive design that should be recognized immediately by anyone familiar with both technologies as a blatant attempt to appease both camps that ends up satisfying neither. PCI is, by definition, a buffered architecture that is designed to remain separate from the processor bus. When VLB is present in the same system, you essentially are attaching the PCI bus directly to the processor. This creates an additional load for the system processor that PCI was specifically designed to eliminate and degrades the performance of the PCI bus at the same time. In other words, each of the two architectures detracts from the performance of the other. They are fundamentally incompatible and should not be present in the same system.

Motherboards and Chipsets. The proliferation of PCI and other standards has caused users to take a greater interest in what is perhaps the most crucial single component in the PC, the motherboard. Many savvy users are able to quote disk drive specifications from memory and elaborate the advantages of this or that new processor but still will purchase a computer without any investigation into the manufacturer and capabilities of the motherboard. PCI, in a rather backhanded way, has changed this.

As with any new technology, the benefits tend to look far more attractive on paper than when they are realized in silicon. The first PCI adapters that went to market were fraught with a large number of incompatibility problems that still are being resolved. In fact, the problems seldom were due solely to the design of the expansion card but more often were attributable to driver software and especially to the core-logic chipset designs used on PCI motherboards. Even the early Pentium motherboard designs by Intel, using their 3.3v Neptune chipset, have been known to cause compatibility problems with certain adapters.

Intel recently has released the Triton chipset, which is reported to offer better PCI support (including an enhanced burst mode) and cache management than Neptune—it's cheaper as well. It is aimed at laying the groundwork for the introduction of the Pentium Pro processor. Other chipset designs being used by higher-end motherboard manufacturers are made by SIS and Opti, but Intel is clearly the dominant player in the field. At this time, the only way to avoid known compatibility problems is to gather as much information as possible before making any purchases. Ask motherboard vendors what chipsets they are using, and try to find out from manufacturers of expansion cards about any hardware incompatibilities they might be experiencing.

> **Note**
>
> Finding out about hardware incompatibilities is usually better accomplished by contacting the manufacturer's technical support department rather than salespeople, and it usually is best to have specific information at hand, rather than asking general questions. For example, "I'm setting up a new server and I want to use your PCI SCSI adapter. Have you encountered any problems with chipsets made by Brand X?" is more likely to get you an honest, detailed answer than "Are there any problems with your PCI SCSI card?"

Disk Subsystems

Despite the tremendous advances in microprocessors and memory discussed thus far, no component of the PC has advanced as far and as quickly as hard drive technology has.

In the space of 12 years, the maximum capacity of hard disk drives has increased over 400 times and access speeds more than 10 times. Some of the same users who wondered if they would ever fill a 10M or 20M drive now look casually at a 4G model and wonder if it will be enough. These improvements, of course, are a direct response to the needs of users and the feats of programmers, who always manage to keep the hardware industry on its toes by continually devising applications that are larger and more capable than their predecessors.

Network file servers, of course, are where this technology is most desperately needed. A substantial portion of NetWare's resources is devoted to the management of the file system, and when dozens or hundreds of users are all accessing files on one server's drives at the same time, the throughput required of the hardware can overwhelm the capabilities of even the cutting edge in storage technology. It is not just a question of drive capacity or even of raw throughput. Network environments can generate hundreds of file requests at the same time, far more than any stand-alone operating system, even those of the multithreaded, multitasking variety such as OS/2 and Windows 95.

What is required is a network storage subsystem that can support multiple devices, and manage these requests without placing an undue burden on the server's processor. The system also should be able to multitask the requests to different devices so that files can be accessed from different drives simultaneously. As a result, the system should have sufficient bandwidth to accommodate not just the maximum throughput of each individual drive but the combined transfer rates of all the devices in case they are all accessed at once.

It should not surprise you to find out that these ideals often are not fully realized in the average network file server. The purpose of this section is to identify the various components of such a subsystem, locate the areas in which bottlenecks typically occur, describe ways in which these bottlenecks can be reduced or eliminated, and finally, to describe the process of installing and configuring the hardware of such a subsystem. It should be noted that this chapter deals primarily with a basic server storage system and concentrates on throughput. Many new technologies are being used in the networking industry to provide for data redundancy on the hardware level. RAID arrays are covered in appendix C, "RAID," but these function essentially as extensions of the basic system defined here.

Storage Technologies

Advances in hard drive technology are some of the primary stepping stones that have made networking possible. When the first IBM PC arrived in the early 1980s, with its Seagate ST-506 hard drive, 10M of storage and a 120ms access time seemed like a lot, but it really didn't give the average businessperson any ideas about accessing it from across the room, let alone from across the country. By the late 1980s, however, drive technology had progressed through several incarnations (see chapter 6, "The Workstation Platform," for the whole story), resulting in two basic drive types that provided the relative speed and capacity needed for use in file servers. These were ESDI and SCSI.

The MFM and RLL drives—which ultimately developed into the IDE standard that is the most common hard drive type found in workstation and stand-alone PCs today—could not provide sufficient capacity, either in single drives or by combining multiple units. The common PC BIOS configuration—still used to this day—can support no more than two of these drives, and its addressing scheme limits them to no more than 528M each, making them unsuitable for use in file servers.

ESDI. The *enhanced small device interface (ESDI)* was developed in the early 1980s, primarily by Maxtor Corporation. It offered several advantages over the ST-506 standard that it sought to replace, among them a maximum theoretical transfer rate of 24 megabits per second. By the late 1980s, ESDI had become the dominant standard for network file servers. This did not last long, however. Forced out of the workstation market by the overwhelming popularity of IDE drives, ESDI's advocates found the network server market dwindling as well, due mostly to the increased popularity of SCSI, which offered greater expandability, support for more device types, and better performance. There also were compatibility problems that often made combining ESDI drives from different makers problematic.

ESDI drives are virtually obsolete today. They can be found in some older file servers, and are easily identifiable by the fact that they utilize two connections to the bus: a 34-pin control connector and a 20-pin data connector. These probably would be 386-based servers, as the drives had all but disappeared from mainstream use by the time the 80486 processor came into popular use. If you have a server that is utilizing ESDI drives and the performance is satisfactory for your needs, the best advice that I can give is to use them until they drop.

Most 386s have long since been reduced from servers to workstations, where they can continue to be useful for some time. It would be difficult to locate sources for new ESDI drives and controllers today, making their continued use unreliable at best. If an ESDI drive in such a machine dies, and the rest of the machine is worth saving, an IDE drive can be added for workstation use—but for a server, the smart move is to get rid of ESDI drives, as the potential for extended downtime when they fail is very high.

SCSI

The *small computer systems interface (SCSI,* pronounced "scuzzy") is far and away the predominant file server storage interface in use today. The new Enhanced IDE interfaces may prove to be suitable for smaller file servers as well as workstations (see the next chapter), but for large installations, SCSI has no rival and is not likely to have any in the near future. The standard SCSI-2 interface provides for throughput rates of up to 10 M/sec and supports up to seven devices on a single host adapter.

The devices can be hard disk, tape, optical, or CD-ROM drives, as well as autochangers and jukeboxes, providing almost unlimited storage capacity. Devices are assigned unique SCSI IDs at the physical level which are utilized for the logical addressing through which each device can be accessed using an arbitration protocol controlled by the host adapter. This makes it an ideal interface for the demands of network use, as users' requests for files on different drives can be queued and executed by the host adapter without draining the resources of the system's microprocessor. SCSI devices are in use today on a great number of different computing platforms. Apple Macintosh systems provide native SCSI access and many mini-computer and microcomputer platforms use SCSI host adapter expansion boards to take advantage of the interface.

SCSI also has a reputation for being difficult to install and configure, on both the hardware and software sides. At one time, this reputation was well-earned, but the standards by which SCSI devices are manufactured have matured considerably, and with the knowledge of some basic operational principles and a few hardware rules to live by, installing or expanding a SCSI subsystem can be a fairly easy procedure.

The SCSI Standards. SCSI is not just a controller that provides access to devices but is actually a completely self-contained system bus that is accessed through the computer's expansion bus. It has its own hardware standards, signaling protocol, and command language. It has its origins in an interface called *Shugart Associates Systems Interface* (*SASI*) that was developed by Shugart Associates and the NCR Corporation in 1981. SASI's basic goal was to develop a standardized peripheral interface that would provide high performance while remaining independent from the host system's processor. This would allow the manufacturers of peripheral devices to have a set of guidelines for the design of new products, ensuring that there would be an interface that could support them and that users would not have to re-engineer their systems to take advantage of every new hardware development.

The original standard called for up to eight devices connected by an 8-bit-wide bus and a maximum transfer rate of 5 M/sec. Each device must contain a *SCSI bus controller* that facilitates the communications between the hardware device itself and the bus. At least one of the eight devices must be a *SCSI host adapter*. The job of the host adapter (also referred to as an *initiator*) is to arbitrate all the communications taking place on the SCSI bus, as well as to provide the interface to the system bus, through which the data going to and from the SCSI devices (or *targets*) reaches the rest of the computer. The standard calls for the capability to include multiple initiators on a single bus, either in the form of multiple host adapters or by the use of target devices that can themselves function as initiators at specified times. In this manner, data transfers can take place between separate devices wholly within the confines of the SCSI bus, requiring no intervention from the system processor. This proposed standard was submitted to the American National Standards Institute (ANSI) for ratification, where it underwent extensive revisions before it finally was approved in 1986.

By the time approval took place, certain shortcomings in the original standard had already been identified and work had already begun on the SCSI-2 standard, which originated from the development of a core group of 18 basic SCSI commands that became known as the *common command set* (*CCS*). A number of other optional components were added to the specification that contributed to the overall speed and efficiency of the interface. In fact, now that SCSI-2 has been ratified, work has already begun on SCSI-3. (There is an entire subculture within the computer industry that revolves around the continuous development and ratification of standards such as this).

SCSI-2. The most important thing to know about the differences between the original SCSI and the SCSI-2 standard is that the latter is a superset of the former. In other words, every SCSI-1 device is also a SCSI-2 device and is completely supported by the newer standard. SCSI-2 peripherals can be connected safely to a SCSI-1 host adapter, but they will be unable to take advantage of any SCSI-2 features that they contain. Do not be fooled into judging the performance levels of a SCSI device merely by the SCSI-2 appellation. If there is a problem inherent in both SCSI standards, it is that too many of the features they contain are listed as optional. A vendor is perfectly within his rights to take a carload of hard drives made in 1987, slap SCSI-2 labeling on them, and sell them as such, although they contain none of the features that make SCSI-2 an improvement over the original standard.

As stated earlier, a SCSI host adapter communicates with the peripherals on its bus by means of its own proprietary command language. Unlike most communications protocols used by the average computer network today, the SCSI language is composed primarily of English words, most of which are easily comprehensible. There are many software packages that provide user access to the basic command language (usually for debugging purposes), and it is relatively easy to identify when a drive is being sent, for example, a READ or a WRITE command. The original SCSI standard contained commands sufficient primarily for the operation of hard drives. The CCS that was included as part of the SCSI-2 standard, however, was primarily designed to furnish standardized support for other types of devices that required commands not available in the original command set.

> **Note**
>
> The original standard allowed for vendor-specific additions to its command set, but this practice was likely to result in incompatibilities between devices made by different manufacturers, thwarting the very reason for the standard.
>
> For example, a tape or CD-ROM drive might be able to utilize a software function to eject the media from the drive. If two manufacturers of tape drives utilize two different commands to perform this same task, then the manufacturer of host adapters is forced to choose between them, or try to support both. This would quickly get out of hand. Customers would have to buy drives not knowing if their host adapters supported them, or be locked into purchasing products from only one manufacturer. This is the way that standards fail, and the committee that controlled the SCSI standard was quick to recognize this and take action.

Incidentally, manufacturers generally do not wait for a standard to be ratified before they start producing equipment that conforms to it. The standards are made available to the public while they are in development and a great many SCSI-2 devices were on the market long before the standard was officially ratified. This is to be expected when it takes eight years for a standard to be approved. In the case of SCSI-2, there were very few differences between the document proposed in 1986 and the final approved version in 1994, so these premature devices are not likely to cause any serious incompatibility problems (at least, not due to the standard).

SCSI-2 Options. SCSI-2 also outlines a number of distinct enhancements to the interface, nearly all of which were specified as optional. Some of them have come into common usage, while others are almost never seen in the PC world. These options provide for a large array of products on today's market, with varying capabilities. Many of these variants will function on a basic level even when incorrectly combined with mismatched equipment. As stated earlier, a Fast SCSI drive will function when attached to a host adapter that doesn't support Fast mode. That is, you are able to access the data on the drive, but the device does not function in its Fast mode unless the host adapter is compliant, so the extra money spent on the more capable drive is wasted. When purchasing a new storage subsystem or even augmenting an existing one, it is important to know the capabilities of all your equipment before making any purchasing decisions. This way you can get the performance that you expect from a product, and the most for your company's money.

Differential SCSI. One of the most fundamental options for the SCSI interface is known as *differential SCSI*. Almost never utilized in the PC networking industry, differential SCSI is opposed to *single-ended SCSI*, which is the normal implementation of the interface used by PCs. The essential difference between the two is the length of the SCSI bus. Normal single-ended SCSI is limited to an overall bus length of six meters. This includes the entire aggregate length of the bus connectors, both inside and outside the computer case. Differential SCSI utilizes two wires for each signal on the bus, while normal SCSI uses one. The use of inverted signals on a differential bus reduces the amount of noise during communications and allows for a bus length of up to 25 meters.

Differential SCSI devices are identified by a standard symbol that appears somewhere on the device (see fig. 5.8). Even though differential SCSI is very rarely seen in the PC world, I mention it because it is one of the few cases in which SCSI devices of different types cannot be intermixed. The two device types utilize the same connectors and cabling, but connecting a differential device to a single-ended SCSI bus, or vice versa, will cause a smell you've probably never encountered before and probably will smoke the entire bus.

Tagged I/O Process Queuing. The SCSI-1 standard included a specification for the transfer of individual commands from an initiator to a specified target device. This was known as *untagged queuing* because only a single process request could be sent to a device. The next request could not be sent until the process had been completed. SCSI-2 allows for optional *tagged queuing*, in which up to 256 individual process requests can be sent by one or more initiators to a single target. The processes are held in the target's buffers until executed. In addition, the processes, referred to by their queue tags, can be executed by the target in a sequence differing from that in which they were received to achieve maximum efficiency in accordance with the native logic of the target device.

Fast SCSI. *Fast SCSI* is another optional feature of the SCSI-2 standard. The term is used to refer to the synchronous transfer mode that doubles the overall transfer rate of the interface from 5 M/sec to 10 M/sec. The basic difference between synchronous transfer mode and its asynchronous equivalent is that an asynchronous transfer requires a acknowledgment (or ACK signal) for every byte transferred, while a synchronous transfer can send a series of bytes for every ACK. Again, both the SCSI host adapter and the target device must support this feature for the increase in throughput to be realized.

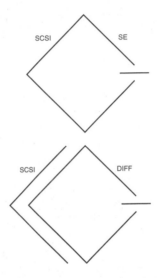

Note

Bear in mind that transfer rates cited throughout this section define a theoretical maximum burst mode rate and are furnished primarily for comparison purposes. Actual throughput under normal conditions will be considerably less.

Wide SCSI. *Wide SCSI*, as the name implies, is the optional practice of increasing the throughput of the interface by widening the bus. A Wide SCSI bus can also accommodate up to 15 Wide SCSI devices instead of the usual seven devices. Specifications have been made in the standard for 16-bit-wide as well as 32-bit-wide SCSI buses. A 16-bit bus, logically, doubles the throughput of the basic SCSI protocol from 5 M/sec to 10 M/sec. When used in combination with Fast SCSI, the overall transfer rate reaches 20 M/sec. This, quite logically, is referred to in the marketplace as *Fast & Wide SCSI*. The 32-bit implementation of the bus can double this again to a 40 M/sec transfer rate. The implementation of the Wide SCSI standard has led to the different types of SCSI cable connectors that are used to create the bus. In practice, however, while Fast & Wide SCSI has found some acceptance in the marketplace, Wide SCSI by itself is not often seen, and the 32-bit variant is virtually non-existent.

The use of Wide SCSI requires that both the host adapter and the target device be capable of utilizing the increased bandwidth. Normal 8-bit SCSI devices can be attached to a Wide SCSI host adapter, however, with an appropriate cable. The Wide SCSI functionality is implemented during the handshake between the initiator (usually the host adapter) and each target device. If either of the two is configured to utilize Wide SCSI, and both are capable of it, then the additional bandwidth is utilized. This is different behavior from that of Fast SCSI, in which both devices must be configured to use synchronous transfers.

Table 5.1 provides a brief comparison between the various SCSI busses.

Table 5.1 SCSI Variants and Specifications				
SCSI Variant	**Bus Width**	**Bus Speed**	**Cable**	**Max. Bus Length**
SCSI-1	8 bit	5 M/sec	A-cable	6 meters
Fast SCSI	8 bit	10 M/sec	A-cable+	3 meters
Wide SCSI	16 bit	10 M/sec	P-cable+	6 meters
Fast/Wide SCSI	16 bit	20 M/sec	P-cable+	3 meters
Fast/Wide SCSI	32 bit	40 M/sec	P-cable+ Q-cable	3 meters

SCSI Cables. The basic SCSI interface calls for the use of a 50-connector Centronics-type cable that is referred to in the standard as the *A-cable*. The original 16-bit-wide SCSI specification calls for a 68-connector *B-cable* that must be used in addition to the A-cable. This was not greeted with much enthusiasm by users, and one of the first acts of the SCSI-3 committee was to drop the B-cable concept in favor of a single 68-connector *P-cable* of D-shell design that replaces both the A-cable and B-cable.

The 32-bit-wide SCSI bus, which has never caught on in the marketplace, requires a P-cable and an additional 68-conductor *Q-cable*. The initial failure of 32-bit-wide SCSI to gain market acceptance was due in part to the fact that drives were not yet available to take full advantage of this much throughput. The need for a second cable, though, was definitely a contributing factor to the unpopularity of 32-bit-wide SCSI and probably will continue to be in the future.

Other cable designs are used in some SCSI implementations. Both Apple and IBM utilize proprietary cables for their SCSI connections (what a surprise!). IBM utilizes a 60-pin mini-Centronics connector. To attach a non-IBM external SCSI device to an IBM server, you must obtain a special cable from (you guessed it!) IBM. Leave it to Big Blue to de-standardize the standards. Apple's 25-pin D-shell connector also differs from the norm, looking more like a serial cable than a SCSI cable.

Caution

Even when connectors differ, a SCSI device is a SCSI device, no matter what platform or operating system it is used with. Don't be fooled by unscrupulous vendors into thinking that you need to buy particular drive because "it's a Macintosh SCSI drive" or "it's an IBM SCSI drive." This probably only means that the package includes a different cable.

While we are on the subject, it should be mentioned that buying off-brand or generic SCSI cables should be avoided. After spending thousands of dollars on SCSI drives, don't ruin your bus (and your day) with cheap cables. I have known people to spend hours trying to troubleshoot a SCSI installation—or worse yet, pay someone a hefty hourly fee to do it for them, only to find that a $20 cable was the cause of their aggravation. Remember that a SCSI bus functions as a unit. If you leave a gap anywhere in your defenses, data is sure to find a way to leak out of it.

Termination. As with other bus types, the SCSI bus must be electrically terminated at both ends of its length. This is to ensure that signals that have been propagated throughout the bus are promptly and completely removed from it. Otherwise, they can be reflected back, causing increased noise and possible data corruption. This is particularly crucial when there are two or more target devices on the bus, as signals destined for a particular target can be mixed with other signals, affecting the performance of all the targets. I have seen cases in which the terminators were removed from a bus containing one host adapter and one device, with no ill effect, but this is not recommended.

Termination of the bus can be achieved in several ways. The simplest and most common form is called *passive termination* and calls for the placement of resistor packs at both ends of the bus. The resistors negate the electrical charges that reach them, effectively removing signals from the bus. These resistors can be supplied in many different ways. External SCSI devices are either internally terminated or utilize an external *resistor pack* in the form of a plug. Internally terminated devices always should have some means to disable the termination, when desired. This can be through the use of DIP switches, jumpers, or a user interface to the device, such as an LED display. Devices using an external resistor pack usually have two SCSI connectors on them to allow for daisy chaining of devices. In this case, your SCSI cable plugs into one of the connectors, and the resistor pack plugs into the other. It makes no difference which goes into which connector. Some devices have only a single connector, and utilize a *pass-through terminator plug*. This is a resistor pack containing both male and female connectors that plugs into the SCSI device's single socket and contains an additional connector for the SCSI cable.

Internal SCSI devices, including host adapters, usually have terminating resistors integrated into their circuitry and utilize DIP switches or jumpers to enable and disable termination. The host adapter is a SCSI device just like any other and must be considered when terminating the bus. Most host adapters ship with termination enabled, but if you have both internal and external devices connected to the adapter, then it is not at the end of the bus, and termination must be disabled. Remember that termination must be provided at the physical ends of the SCSI bus. SCSI ID numbers have no bearing on this whatsoever. Some people make the mistake of assuming that the devices using SCSI IDs 0 and 7 are the ends of the bus, but this is not the case. It is also important that termination be furnished only at the ends of the bus. Other devices may ship with termination enabled and must be adjusted if they are going to be located in the middle of the bus.

Another form of termination can be used in place of the passive resistor type usually furnished with SCSI target devices. *Active termination* is a means by which an inverse voltage of the signal, instead of resistors, is used to negate the transmissions on the SCSI bus. For example, when a 5v signal is traveling along the bus and reaches a resistor pack, it is dissipated by the added resistance over the course of a period of time that, in electronic terms, would be considered quite slow, and signal fluctuations may occur. An active terminator instead supplies a signal of -5v that negates the original 5v signal far more quickly and efficiently than resistance dissipates it. The SCSI-2 specification calls for active termination whenever Fast SCSI or Wide SCSI is used. It should also be considered when the overall length of the SCSI bus is more than one or two meters. Active termination is used already on some SCSI devices available today, particularly host adapters. In other cases, active terminators must be purchased separately, but for a high-performance system they definitely are recommended.

One of the remarkable aspects of troubleshooting SCSI installations is that the root causes of problems often are found to be the simplest components of the system, and improper termination ranks very high on the list. Many of the most common symptoms of SCSI problems, such as data corruption, dismounting of drives, and excessive read or write errors can be caused by missing or improperly installed terminators. A SCSI subsystem in a file server is likely to be worked harder than one located in any workstation. It must be as bulletproof as possible, and the attention you pay to small items like terminators and cables will pay off in the long run. Additional SCSI troubleshooting checklists can be found in chapter 17, "Backup Technology: Programs and Data."

SCSI-3. No sooner had the SCSI-2 standard been ratified in 1994 than work began on the SCSI-3 specification. Judging by this standards committee's track record, the new standard should be entered into the books sometime in the year 2002. You can open a magazine today, however, and see advertisements offering SCSI-3 hard drives and controllers. Although the proposed SCSI-3 standard contains support for up to 32 devices, and work is being done on a proposed "serial SCSI" implementation, none of this is supported by these devices. SCSI-3 has come to be used solely as a reference to a Fast & Wide SCSI-2 device that utilizes a single P-cable instead of the two cables called for in the SCSI-2 specification (see the preceding section, "SCSI Cables," for more information on Fast & Wide).

SCSI Hardware. When purchasing SCSI hardware for use in a file server, the requirements are quite different from those of a workstation. The object, obviously, is to provide the greatest possible performance for the least amount of money, but it is important to account for the unique requirements of file server access when planning for an upgraded or new server. The first decision to be made is what kind of SCSI you intend to run on the machine, because all your devices must support the type of bus you choose to assemble.

When we discussed the differences between regular, Fast, and Wide SCSI earlier, throughput rates of 5 M/sec, 10 M/sec, and as much as 20 M/sec were bandied about, but remember that this is only an estimate of the best possible throughput that the bus can achieve in its fastest burst mode. If you purchase a single 4G hard drive that can transfer data at 8 M/sec and put it on a Fast & Wide SCSI bus that is capable of 20 M/sec transfers, you will get no more than 8 M/sec of throughput. If you purchase four 1G drives of the same speed, however, and install them on the same bus, their combined maximum throughput is 32 M/sec, which can more than fill the capacity of the SCSI bus. Remember that a NOS like NetWare must be treated like any other multitasking OS. If you can picture a

Windows (or maybe an OS/2) machine running dozens or even hundreds of applications at the same time, you get an idea of what the file system of a NetWare server must contend with every minute of every working day. SCSI is particularly well suited to this kind of environment because each drive on the bus contains its own controller. The computer can send multiple file requests through the host adapter to each of the individual drives, which can queue them, execute them, and furnish the required data as each drive gains control of the bus.

This is not to say, however, that every hard drive will be continuously running at its peak transfer rate. That is why the second configuration described earlier is more than sufficient for general use. There is no need to furnish sufficient bandwidth on the bus to accommodate the maximum transfer rates of all the target devices at once. What is important is to make sure to avoid bottlenecks that ultimately will waste the investment you've made in high-performance peripherals.

SCSI Hard Disk Drives. A SCSI hard disk drive is basically a normal disk drive assembly with an integrated controller, to which circuitry has been added that allows it to communicate over the SCSI bus. If you compare product lists or advertisements, you will find that most hard drive manufacturers have SCSI drive lines that are identical to their IDE drive lines in speed and capacity. This is because they are fundamentally the same drive, with a few extra chips added to the SCSI model. Like an IDE drive, the controller is wholly dedicated to communicating with this one device, so the manufacturers can make any proprietary adjustments that they wish. The only requirement is that the controller be able to communicate with the other devices on the SCSI bus using the common SCSI command language.

You might wonder what performance advantage SCSI provides over IDE, since they are fundamentally the same drive. For a stand-alone, single-user workstation, the qualified answer is: none. SCSI provides greater expandability, but essentially adds an extra amount of communications overhead to the device that can actually lessen the overall efficiency of the unit. In a file server environment, however, SCSI provides a definite advantage because of its command queuing and multitasking capabilities—IDE can only process one request at a time, and must finish that processing before executing the next one. SCSI also provides the expandability and large drive capacity needed for a network server, as well as the ability to support many different types of devices.

Most of the major SCSI hard drive manufacturers today market Fast SCSI-2 drives as their base product line, and the same is true for the manufacturers of host bus adapters. Wide SCSI-2 drives are also available from some manufacturers. I advise against purchasing new drives that do not support Fast synchronous transfers, even if you can find such drives. A Fast SCSI drive functions quite well on a 5 M/sec bus using a vintage SCSI -1 host adapter, if necessary, and this leaves you an open path for future upgrades. If you happen to come upon a source of dirt-cheap SCSI-1 hard drives, buy them, but use them in workstations instead of servers. If you are running a Wide SCSI host adapter, remember that you must buy Wide SCSI hard drives to take advantage of the extra bandwidth. In addition, Wide components have the 68-pin connectors that the feature requires— adapters or custom cables are needed to connect 8-bit SCSI peripherals to the bus.

As far as configuration is concerned, hard drives have come a long way from the early days when you had to be concerned with low-level formatting, interleave, and head skew. As with IDE, SCSI hard disk drives are low-level formatted at the factory, and since the controller is integrated and dedicated solely to the support of that one device, communications between the two have also been optimized by the manufacturer. There are a few SCSI-related settings, however, that must be considered. The following sections discuss these settings.

SCSI ID and Termination. As with any SCSI device, a hard drive must be assigned a SCSI ID different from all other devices on the bus. While different hard drives may use DIP switches or housing switches to set the ID, this is frequently accomplished by setting a combination of three jumpers on the drive according to the binary values of the numbers 0 through 7. (These are the same switch combinations that I used to input the octal code needed to boot the first computer I ever worked with, a Data General Nova 1200 mini, circa 1976. Some skills never die.) Table 5.2 displays the values of the possible jumper combinations, but be sure to consult the documentation for the unit to determine "which way is up."

Table 5.2 Jumper Settings for Specifying SCSI IDs on Hard Drives			
SCSI ID	J1	J2	J3
0	0	0	0
1	0	0	1
2	0	1	0
3	0	1	1
4	1	0	0
5	1	0	1
6	1	1	0
7	1	1	1

If, however, you purchase a drive array housing that holds several hard disk drives, the housing itself may provide selector mechanisms for the individual drives in the form of a button or rotary knob that is used to set the ID.

There are some special concerns to be noted with hard drives in respect to SCSI IDs. Some older implementations of the SCSI interface required hard drives to be assigned SCSI IDs 0 and 1. This was true particularly when the hard drive was being used as a boot device. This limitation has supposedly been eliminated, but I have run into many situations in which reassigning the SCSI IDs of the various devices to make the hard drives 0 and 1 has resolved problems that could not be remedied any other way. On the other hand, the bus arbitration protocol of the SCSI interface assigns task priorities based on SCSI IDs, with 7 having the highest priority and 0 the lowest. This is why host adapters are almost always assigned SCSI ID 7, so that they will win in any arbitration. Therefore, if you want your hard drives to receive the highest priority attention from the host adapter (and in a file server, who doesn't?), I recommend assigning them the highest possible IDs below 7, and lowering them only if absolutely necessary.

Termination, as well, is usually activated and deactivated through the use of jumper settings. Be aware that some drives ship with no terminating resistors at all—in this case, resistors must be purchased separately and mounted on the drive.

Other SCSI Hard Drive Settings. Most of the other SCSI-related settings on hard disk drives are used to enable or disable certain aspects of the communication protocol between the target device and the host adapter. In these cases, the most important thing to remember is that these features must be enabled on both devices for them to function properly.

SCSI parity is a rudimentary error checking protocol similar to the parity checking done at the memory level by many computers. Virtually all drives and host adapters on the market today support it. The ability to disable the function is usually present simply for reasons of backward compatibility with older host adapters that do not have the feature. Unlike the parity checking done by memory chips, which many people consider unnecessary due to the comparative rarity of memory corruption errors today, parity checking on the disk level is definitely recommended, as disk errors are far more prevalent.

Synchronous negotiation is the process by which a host adapter and a device perform a handshake to determine how a data transfer is going to be performed. Each device is essentially informing the other of its capabilities so that the speediest possible transfer rate can be achieved. As stated earlier, nearly all SCSI devices on the market today support Fast SCSI-2 and are capable of running in the faster synchronous mode. This feature should be enabled on all SCSI devices, except in certain cases when older drives not supporting it are negatively affected by the host adapter's attempts to negotiate. I have also seen cases in which this feature is disabled on the entire SCSI bus to accommodate certain software packages (most notably backup software) that became overwhelmed by the faster transfers provided. This, however, results in a slowdown of all devices on the bus to accommodate one device, and should be avoided if possible.

Terminator power is a setting that controls whether or not a particular device furnishes the power needed by the bus terminators. This power is required whether the termination is active or passive, and is nearly always furnished by the host adapter. No harm can be done, however, by having multiple devices furnish terminator power, so many users simply enable this feature on all devices as a fail-safe mechanism.

Delayed start is a means by which the power-up cycle of a disk drive can be delayed for a short period after the computer is powered on. Hard disk drives require far more power to start up than to actually run. Spinning the platters up to the high speeds at which they run is functionally similar to pressing the accelerator on a car. More gasoline is needed to accelerate from 0 to 60 mph than is needed to cruise at 60. When several disk drives are present in a single computer, their combined power needs can overtax an otherwise adequate power supply, should they all spin up at once. The delayed start mechanism forces the drive to wait until a signal is provided by the host adapter before it powers up. The host adapter sends the signal to each drive on the bus in turn, thus preventing multiple drives from spinning up at once. If your drives are located in an external housing, then this feature is unnecessary, but if you have several drives within the main case of the computer, this feature is recommended.

Other SCSI Devices. One of the main advantages of using the SCSI interface in a network server is the wide array of devices that are supported. SCSI tape and CD-ROM drives have become commonplace features of the corporate network, providing the means for backing up the system and furnishing the wealth of data available on CD-ROM to users all over the network. Magneto-optical drives and other technologies provide mid-range storage options that allow for faster access times than tape, and lower costs per megabyte than hard drives. Jukeboxes and autochangers provide automated switching of tape and optical cartridges, yielding a potential for enormous amounts of data storage.

Hierarchical storage management systems are available to manage these multiple devices and automatically migrate network files to less expensive media based on their usage patterns. Writeable CD-ROM "burners" have dropped dramatically in price to the point where they have become a viable, albeit permanent, storage medium, and even printers are available that can use the SCSI interface. Detailed descriptions of some of these devices and the procedures for installing them on the network are covered in part VI, "Adding Network Services," of this book.

All these devices are SCSI and can communicate with the same host adapter that controls hard drives. One of the primary improvements of the SCSI-2 specification over the earlier revision was the inclusion of standardized commands for the control of devices such as these. The rules for connecting these devices to the SCSI bus are virtually identical to those for hard disk drives. Unique SCSI IDs must be assigned to each device, and termination provided where necessary. External devices usually have some sort of selector mechanism, either mechanical or electronic, for setting the ID, and have a separate resistor pack for termination. Internal devices use the same sort of DIP switches or jumpers as hard drive units. If anything, the hardware installation of these devices is simpler than that of a hard drive. Most other SCSI devices do not have the additional configuration settings that hard drives have. Once the ID and termination are considered, it is just a matter of connecting the data and power cables, and then turning on the unit. The area in which difficulty might arise is when you try to address the device with software. This is covered later, in the "SCSI Host Adapters" section.

One of the more prevalent tendencies in these products, now that the technology has matured and confidence in the interface is high, is the combination of multiple devices in a single unit. CD-ROM changers and multiple drives are available that can hold up to 7 or 10 CD-ROMs or more, providing either simultaneous access or automatic media switching. Tape autochangers and optical jukeboxes typically consist of one or more drives for actually reading the media, and a robotic mechanism that is responsible for shuttling the cartridges in and out of the drives. Some of these units are truly gigantic. Exabyte markets several autochangers that could easily be mistaken for refrigerators. One model has four 8mm drives and holds 120 tapes, for a total capacity of up to 1,200G. That's 1.2 terabytes of storage without changing media!

Logical Unit Numbers. When more than one SCSI device is found in a single unit, each one must be assigned its own ID. For example, a tape autochanger (one more modest than the Exabyte unit described in the preceding section) might contain a single 4mm DAT drive and slots for 12 tapes. The drive itself requires a SCSI ID, of course, but the mechanism that changes the tapes requires an ID, also. This may be accomplished in one of two ways. Normal SCSI IDs may be assigned to the two devices, utilizing separate selector switches of the usual types. Some units might preassign a specific SCSI ID to one of the devices and so have only one selector. Other units might utilize a technique by which a single SCSI ID is shared by both devices. In these cases, a single selector allows for ID selection, and the chosen ID is then broken into two or more *logical unit numbers* (*LUNs*). LUNs are simply a second level of unit addressing within the SCSI architecture. Every command sequence sent to a specific SCSI ID also contains an LUN specification. Up to eight LUNs, numbered 0 through 7, can be defined for each SCSI ID on the bus. A unit that contains a single device uses LUN 0, while units with multiple devices have LUNs preassigned to each device in the unit, ensuring that the correct commands always reach the proper device.

The use of LUNs, however, does not necessarily expand the overall device capacity of the SCSI bus. Depending on the drivers and other software used to address the devices, at-tachment of a device using multiple LUNs may limit the number of other devices that can be addressed. For example, a backup software package might be able to address a tape autochanger device that uses two LUNs, but it very likely will not be able to support seven such devices on the same SCSI bus. A maximum of seven total devices usually is imposed whether or not LUNs are used. In this case, up to three autochangers using two LUNs each, plus one other single device, are all that are addressable by the particular software package. This is a limitation imposed solely by the software. The SCSI standard calls for the inclusion of LUNs in all command language addressing, even when each device on the bus uses only a single LUN.

Compatibility. SCSI device compatibility has been a sore point ever since the early days of the SCSI interface. There was a time when many administrators routinely in-stalled separate SCSI adapters for each of their devices, rather than even attempt to get all of them to function on one bus. Fortunately, this situation has changed considerably, but there are still circumstances when it is not advisable to mix devices of different types on the same SCSI bus.

If, for example, I was administering a network in a 24-hour shop and had to back up my servers while a full complement of users were logged on, I would avoid having the tape backup drive on the same bus as my hard drives. The data stream to the tape drive would undoubtedly flood the bus and slow down hard drive access significantly. In a case like this, a separate host adapter (or better yet, a dedicated backup server) is recommended. The same is true when running SCSI hard drives in a duplexed configuration. Attaching other devices to one of the host adapters could lessen the efficiency of the drive mirror-ing process. When backups are performed during off-hours, however, there should be no problem running a tape drive on the same bus as hard drives. Indeed, the data trans-fers from hard disk to tape on the same SCSI bus would be performed wholly within the confines of the bus, yielding the highest possible throughput that the devices are capable of.

SCSI Host Adapters. We finally come to the "brains" of the outfit, the SCSI host adapter. The host adapter is the communications nexus for the entire SCSI bus and provides the gateway to the rest of the computer through the expansion bus. Requests for access to a particular SCSI resource are sent to the host adapter, which prioritizes them, sends them off to the appropriate device, and then manages the responses, sending them back out through the expansion bus. Intelligent host adapters are able to manage incoming requests to maximize efficiency. While older SCSI-1 designs could only process one request at a time, remaining idle until the target device returned a result, today's adapters can send a command to a particular device, and then go about other business until the device signals its completion of the command. This is called *SCSI disconnection* and is especially useful when devices other than hard drives are on the bus.

As an example, consider that an adapter may send a command to a tape drive instructing it to rewind the tape. Depending on the type of drive, the rewind process could take from several seconds to several minutes. Rather than sit and wait for the acknowledgment from the tape drive that rewinding has been completed, the adapter disconnects from that device and is free to process other tasks. The tape drive later signals its desire to reestablish communications with the host adapter, at which time it reports its successful completion of the rewind command, and receives its next instruction. A host adapter can keep track of these communications for all the devices on the bus at once, allowing for concurrent I/O operations to occur. This is the primary advantage of SCSI in the server environment.

SCSI host adapters are available for all the bus types discussed earlier in this chapter. They range from simple ISA cards running with 5 M/sec transfer rates all the way to high-end Fast & Wide, bus mastering DMA controllers with on-board RISC processors supporting synchronous burst transfer rates of up to 20 M/sec. Most contain a built-in BIOS that allows the computer to be booted from a SCSI hard drive, and some also have optional floppy drive support, making them fully functional I/O cards. Twin channel controllers are also available; these provide host adapter functions for two completely separate SCSI buses on a single expansion card.

Many computers, such as servers available from Compaq and Hewlett Packard, have the SCSI host adapter integrated into the motherboard design. This can be very beneficial, as any components built into the motherboard cut down on signal noise and communications overhead, but be sure to determine the exact capabilities of these integrated adapters before purchasing them. Hewlett Packard, for example, uses Adaptec chipsets in most HP servers, utilizing drivers originally written by Adaptec for their AHA-2740 EISA adapter, which is very good indeed. Compaq utilizes its own proprietary drivers, but their embedded 710 EISA adapter (which is also available as a separate card) is another very good choice. Other vendors providing integrated SCSI on their motherboards, however, may opt for a less expensive, less intelligent adapter circuitry that would be better off in a workstation than a file server, so be sure to ask what chipset and system bus width is used in their designs, as well as whose drivers they use. As always, if they don't know, hang up!

When purchasing a SCSI host adapter on an expansion card, be sure that you purchase a card that can be fully supported by the expansion bus of your motherboard. For example, high-performance bus mastering cards are available for EISA, VLB, and PCI systems, but for all three of these bus types, a particular slot may or may not be capable of bus mastering. Be sure to purchase a card that will function properly in the slot you have available. If you are building a monstrous, high-performance server with multiple SCSI buses, make sure that you know how many bus mastering slots there are on your motherboard.

Host Adapter Configuration. SCSI host adapters can have a great number of configurable attributes, and several different ways of setting them. Older or lower-end cards might still use DIP switches or jumper blocks, but most of the better cards on the market have some sort of software configuration utility. This might be provided on a floppy disk or located in the adapter's ROM along with the BIOS. In any case, though, termination, SCSI ID selection, and the ability to enable or disable the card's BIOS are often provided through DIP switches as well, and these might need to be set before the card is actually installed. In some cases—as with most Adaptec cards—the BIOS needs to be enabled to access the software configuration program. Once the card has been configured, the BIOS can be disabled again if you will not be booting from a SCSI hard drive.

The added convenience of these software-configured cards should not be underestimated, especially when used with file servers. The ability to make adjustments on the fly to the basic expansion hardware configuration items—such as IRQ, memory address, and DMA channel—can save a great deal of work when you are trying to put together a heavily-loaded server with several such devices. Of course, the more advanced self-configuring bus types, such as EISA, MCA, and PCI eliminate the need for such adjustments, and their growing popularity has simplified this task considerably.

Most of the configuration options discussed earlier in the section on SCSI hard drives are also present on the host adapter. As explained earlier, it is necessary for these options to be configured in the same way on both devices for them to function properly. Settings for parity, delayed start, synchronous negotiation, and terminator power should all be present on most adapters. As is the case with hard drives, nearly all the host adapters on the market today support Fast SCSI, and most allow you to disable the synchronous transfers if you desire (usually as a troubleshooting measure). Most of the time, however, a well designed host adapter is configured to function to the fullest of its capabilities right out of the box. Default configurations almost always include SCSI ID 7, termination enabled, and the other parameters set for the best possible transfer speed. Changes need to be made only to disable termination when both internal and external SCSI devices are being used or to troubleshoot problems that occur with specific devices on the bus.

SCSI Drivers. It becomes necessary here to deviate from the hardware concentration of this chapter to discuss the software that a SCSI host adapter uses to communicate with the operating system of the computer in which it resides. While the SCSI bus is a self-contained unit completely capable of communicating among its own devices without software support, it is useless unless it is able to communicate with the rest of the computer. The host adapter is essentially a bilingual component of the system that "translates" the requests made by the operating system into its native command language and relays them to the integrated controller of the target device. (This controller then communicates with the device itself using still another language, but that doesn't concern us here.)

The NOS can receive requests for access to a SCSI device from three sources: applications running on client workstations throughout the network, applications running on the file server itself, or another server on the network. When a SCSI bus is populated only with hard drives, these procedures are relatively simple, as all the requests are fundamentally of the same format. A single driver, running on the file server, can control all the hard drives on the bus. When different types of devices are used on a single SCSI bus, however, things become more complicated, as each device type must have its own driver to facilitate the unique requests being furnished to that device.

Therefore, a backup software application may generate requests that are intended for execution by a tape drive, but the driver furnished by the backup software manufacturer communicates with the host adapter, not with the tape drive directly. Thus, the host adapter may have to contend with separate drivers for hard drives, CD-ROM drives, tape drives, and other devices all at once. Based upon the underlying technology for which the SCSI standard was designed, this is virtually impossible. A SCSI host adapter occupies one IRQ, one memory address, and perhaps one DMA channel. Once a single driver has established communications with the adapter, then subsequent drivers, attempting to address the same adapter, will find those resources already occupied and will fail to load.

ASPI. It was necessary, therefore, to create a software-based interface that could accommodate these multiple drivers and allow them unified access to a single SCSI host adapter. Actually, several such interfaces exist, but the *de facto* standard among them is known as the *Advanced SCSI Programming Interface (ASPI)*. The "A" in ASPI at one time stood for Adaptec, the company that developed it, but Adaptec has since acknowledged this standard's role as an industry standard by opening the specification to outside developers and changing the name.

Most SCSI host adapters today are *ASPI-compatible*, meaning that they ship with basic board drivers that provide hard drive access and establish an ASPI layer in memory. This layer consists of API calls, public symbols, or hooks to which other drivers can attach themselves. ASPI is a protocol that is independent of the computer's host operating system. Host adapters nearly always ship with ASPI drivers for DOS and NetWare, and might support many other operating systems as well. Some of the more advanced operating systems such as OS/2 include native ASPI support and require no additional drivers. While many host adapters are capable of running hard drives by using only the card's BIOS, it is necessary to load the software drivers to provide ASPI support.

When an ASPI layer is established in a NOS's memory, this usually is done by spawning an additional process. On a NetWare file server, loading the disk driver for an Adaptec host adapter causes an additional NLM named ASPITRAN.NLM to be loaded. At this point, public symbols—API calls or "hooks"—are made available for the use of other drivers.

Caution

It's important to note that the file name ASPITRAN.NLM is also used by some other host adapter manufacturers. Care should be taken to use the module furnished with the disk driver that you will be running, as they are not interchangeable.

The developer of a software package that requires access to a SCSI device (other than a hard drive) then furnishes a driver that addresses neither the SCSI device nor even the host adapter hardware but the ASPI layer hooks that have been provided. In this manner, all the different devices on the bus can be serviced by their respective software packages without conflict.

One of the important factors that must be considered when running multiple SCSI buses on a single NetWare file server is that there can be no more than one ASPI layer in memory on a single machine, and that the single ASPI layer can only address the devices of one SCSI bus. It might be necessary, then, to adjust the distribution of your SCSI devices between the buses to account for this limitation. Most software packages designed for use with SCSI devices have options that allow for a choice between ASPI operation or the use of a dedicated driver that addresses a host adapter directly and exclusively. Depending on the needs of your network, it might be necessary to group all hard drives onto one SCSI bus and reserve the use of ASPI for a second bus containing all the other device types. Or, to present another scenario, if you need several devices of the same type, such as multiple tape drives for a dedicated backup server, it might be better to group all those on a single bus, and use the dedicated board driver included with the backup software package—ASPI could then be used for the hard drives and other devices on a second host adapter.

Other multiple device driver interfaces do exist, but none has the wide-ranging hardware and software support that ASPI does. It is strongly recommended that any software you purchase for use with a SCSI device contains ASPI driver support, and that the SCSI host adapter you select includes drivers that can establish and support an ASPI layer in your NOS.

One Final Note. As a final aside on the subject of SCSI board drivers, be aware of the fact that hardware innovations very often outpace the progress of the driver support furnished with them. Particularly in the case of adapters for high-performance system buses such as EISA, VLB, and especially PCI, I have found that nearly all manufacturers go through several revisions of their drivers before they are adequately debugged. A great many SCSI performance and installation problems are ultimately attributable to drivers. It is strongly recommended that you obtain the latest drivers for a new model host adapter before even attempting to install it. Nearly all manufacturers are aware of these problems and offer frequent driver revisions over a variety of online services. BBSs, CompuServe forums, and the World Wide Web can be invaluable resources in this respect, offering not only software updates but also extensive troubleshooting, background, and pre-sales information.

Network Interface Cards

Despite the presence of a NOS and the enormous resources that may be present in a PC, it is still an isolated machine with one or more NICs to connect it to the rest of the network. While we considered, in previous sections, the relative transfer rates of system buses, SCSI buses, and hard drives, the speed of the network itself must also be factored into the equation. The NIC provides the link with the network medium and can be another possible location of a bottleneck in the data path from server to workstation. It is important that the NIC provide sufficient bandwidth for data to be fed to the network at the highest speed it can accommodate. This usually means that a server's NICs should utilize at the very least an EISA bus connection, but it is also possible to purchase too much of a card—that is, one whose capabilities will be underused due to limitations of the network medium or the storage subsystem feeding it.

As with SCSI adapters, NICs are available now for all the latest bus types; for file server use, these should definitely be considered. However, any NIC that is suitable for workstation use can also be installed into a file server, and likewise, there are situations, such as high-color graphics and CAD work, in which even the highest-performance PCI network card may be used in a workstation. The sole exception to this is in the case of multichanneled NICs that are specifically designed for use in a file server that also functions as a router connecting two network segments. These cards, essentially two adapters in one, allow a file server access to multiple network segments without the difficulties of configuring server resources individually for each adapter.

Otherwise, the hardware for the two platforms is interchangeable, with software drivers providing support for the different operating systems. For this reason, NICs are considered in detail in chapter 6, "The Workstation Platform." Any observations made there are equally viable when considering devices for use in a file server, except where expressly noted. The selection of NICs for use in a file server is also a matter that must be considered in coordination with the overall design of the network. For this reason, chapter 7, "Major Network Types," should also be consulted before purchasing decisions are made.

The Case and the Power Supply

This chapter has covered all the primary components of a basic file server configuration. All that is left is the power supply that feeds it all and a box to put it in. Many components of today's file servers utilize far more power than older technologies. Many large capacity hard drives designed for server use now have platters that rotate at speeds well in excess of the traditional 3,500rpm. The newer processors and expansion buses also require more power than their predecessors and generate more heat. The primary concerns in this respect—when building a computer to be used as a file server or adding additional components to an existing PC—are whether there is an adequate supply of power for all the contents and whether the system is being sufficiently cooled.

Most servers today use large tower cases because they have ample room for numerous expansion slots and drive bays. The temptation with these cases is to fill all those slots and bays with internally mounted devices—this can be done, as long as a little thought is put into the process. If the computer has been purchased in a server configuration, then the manufacturer should have anticipated this heavy usage and installed a power supply providing at least 250–300 watts or more. When purchasing a tower case for the construction of a server, you should check on the capabilities of the power supply if it is furnished as part of the package. Some power supplies also include surge protection and other power management features, which are an added plus.

Adequate cooling of the system is essential, and a well-designed PC is organized so that its fans draw air through the system in a manner intended to cool the components that generate the most heat. Many of today's better systems use two or more fans to ensure that this is done properly. This is why computers should always be run with their cases on. An open computer case dissipates the airflow provided by the fans, cooling only the area around the power supply, and leaving other vital components to be cooled by room air. This can shorten the life of the system and even cause complete failures! When adding components to an existing machine, it is wise to space them out as much as possible to allow space for air to circulate around them. For the same reason, it is advisable to stagger your populated expansion slots, if possible, leaving empty slots between filled ones.

486 and Pentium processors are well-known sources of additional heat. Most systems ship with a heat sink or fan (or both) already attached to the top of the processor chip. If you are assembling the machine yourself, aftermarket kits are available that allow the addition of either. A heat sink, to be effectively installed, requires the use of a special thermal conductive adhesive to attach it to the processor.

As an alternative to placing all the computer's components into one case, external housings for drive arrays are becoming increasingly popular, and since they contain their own dedicated power and cooling systems, both of the above problems are significantly reduced. If you plan on using four or more hard drives in a single server, for example, an arrangement such as this is preferable to cramming all those drives into even the largest tower case. Additional functionality can also be provided by these housings. Storage Dimensions makes drive arrays with a built-in SCSI backplane and power supply, allowing drives to be "hot-plugged" in and out of the system while it is running. When used in a RAID configuration, this could mean that a hard drive that has failed can be replaced with no downtime and no loss of data. In addition, these arrays can support tape drive and CD-ROM modules in the same housing, in any combination desired. This is a high-end solution, adding significant additional expense to your system, but simple external cases for the mounting of SCSI devices are also readily available.

Pre-Built or "Roll-Your-Own"

When considering all the detailed characteristics of the various components in a PC being used as a file server, the question of whether it is preferable to purchase a server intact or assemble one yourself, or "roll-your-own," naturally arises. As I've said throughout this chapter, the file server is not a good place to experiment, and my general advice is not to do anything you haven't done before. The actual assembly of the machine's components is not the difficult part—virtually anyone could take an existing PC as a model and, given all the basic units, assemble a working computer. The difficulty is in selecting components that will all work together. This applies not just to cutting edge technology but also to mundane considerations like "Does the motherboard fit in the case?" and "Do the screw holes line up?" Trivial items like these often stand in the way of a successful job.

Assembling a server yourself can ensure that you have exactly the features you desire and can save you a great deal of money, but you essentially are left without a safety net. If you have a substantial MIS infrastructure to rely on, including uses for non-returnable parts that don't fit and in-house expert help, this can be the way to go, but large corporations are likely to already have a mechanism in place for supplying new servers, making this procedure either extremely easy or out of the question (except perhaps as a training exercise).

There are still several alternatives, however, when you decide to purchase a pre-built server, depending on what technical support will be needed after the purchase, and the extent of your budget. The cheapest way to go this route is direct purchase, through mail order. There are several gigantic, direct market PC vendors that can provide pre-configured systems at very good prices and customized ones for a little more. With these vendors, "customized" generally means that you select from a fairly limited range of components, unless you are planning a very large order (500 systems or more). If you are looking for a specific make of motherboard, for example, you are probably out of luck. Smaller firms might be more willing to work with you in putting together a server to your exact specifications, but their prices will generally be higher, and you risk the company dissolving before your warranty expires.

Another alternative is to find a consulting firm in your area that will build custom servers for you. This will cost more (perhaps a lot more), but you will be able to specify exactly what you want and will have someone nearby to provide support whenever it's needed. The trick when dealing with consultants is the same as when dealing with any salesman, which is to do your homework beforehand. If you approach them with a sheepish smile and say, "I'm not a technical guy, but..." then you're essentially hanging a sign around your neck that says "SUCKER" in blinking neon letters. If you go in with a list of exactly what you want, and can talk intelligently about alternatives, then you can probably wheedle a consultant down to a reasonably fair price. As with any major purchase, you generally get what you pay for, and you might end up having to pay a good deal more to have things exactly the way that you want them. If, however, you have ever been in the position where a primary server goes down and workers are sitting around drinking coffee while you wait for a $150/hour technician to arrive, you probably will consider some added upfront expense to be worthwhile.

Summary

We have, in this chapter, examined many of the hardware components that are found in a typical network server. We have discussed the ways that a server differs from and is similar to an ordinary PC. It is due to these similarities that not all of the major server components are dealt with in this chapter. The line of Intel microprocessors used in the vast majority of network servers are the same as those used in most network workstations. To avoid repetition, these processors are examined in chapter 6, "The Workstation Platform."

For the same reason, the sections in this chapter on the various types of server memory and the procedures for upgrading them are equally applicable to workstations. It remains to be seen whether or not any of the new memory technologies discussed here will fall into common use in servers or workstations, but they serve to illustrate some of the ways that the industry is trying to overcome the limitations of current memory chip designs.

SCSI is still the dominant mass storage subsystem in the server world, but it too is frequently being used in workstations. As covered in chapter 6, new enhanced IDE technologies have taken a firm hold on the workstation platform, but these may also come to be popular in the lower-end servers of the near future.

Server technology is moving forward at an amazing pace, as is the rest of the computer industry, and the growing popularity of advanced concepts like symmetric multiprocessing all but ensures that servers will continue to increase in speed and capability. One of the most difficult aspects of network administration is achieving an appropriate medium between tried and true technology and the cutting edge. The only way to do this is to remain informed of new developments and yet to remain skeptical of them until they are definitely proven.

Chapter 6
The Workstation Platform

In the last chapter, when examining the hardware involved in assembling a network server, we narrowed our vision to the high end of the current PC market. In this chapter, we discuss the network workstation, and our survey is necessarily much wider in scope. For the purposes of this chapter, the term *workstation* refers to a PC based on one of the Intel x86 microprocessors. Other types of desktop computers, such as UNIX and Macintosh machines, may also be referred to as workstations at times. The networking aspects of Macintoshes are covered in appendix C, "Adding Macintosh Access." As to UNIX, the subject is sufficiently enormous to preclude its inclusion in a book of this type.

As we have discussed, a file server and a workstation are, from the hardware perspective, more alike than they are different. Both contain the essential elements of a network PC: a microprocessor, memory chips, usually some form of storage medium, and, of course, the network interface that links the computer to all the other resources scattered around the enterprise. However, network workstations encompass a far greater range of assets and capabilities than servers do. While it is safe for me to say that a file server should be a 486-based machine or better, workstations can range from the original IBM PCs and XTs all the way to top-of-the-line Pentiums that could adequately function as servers themselves, given the proper software.

Obviously, the tasks that can be accomplished with a networked XT are substantially different from those that can be performed on a Pentium. Both have retained their usefulness in the workplace, however, and this chapter surveys the wide range of hardware that might be found in PCs that have been adapted for network use. Since most of the information already presented in the discussion of network servers is equally valid when examining a network workstation, it will not be repeated here. We will, however, cover the hardware that was glossed over in the last chapter, discussing in detail some of the technology that is more obviously suited to workstation use.

The lines between server and workstation hardware configurations often blur, so we will cover some material that could easily be germane in a further discussion of server configurations, including a detailed examination of the entire Intel microprocessor line. Some of the newer technologies on the market, such as Enhanced IDE hard drives and other peripherals, could well become standard equipment in smaller servers, and we will also discuss network interface cards (NICs) in greater depth. The topic of NICs was deferred from the last chapter because similar or even identical cards can be used in both the server and workstation platforms. Unless stated otherwise, any discussion of network interface hardware in this chapter is equally applicable to a server.

We also will discuss the viability of hardware upgrades on the workstation platform. In many cases, the most important information is to know which machines are worth upgrading at all and which components can be replaced or augmented without investing money in an obsolete technology that is destined for the high-tech junkyard.

Workstation Types and Specifications

Although faster and more capable computers are available every year, many networks in the corporate world continue to operate productively despite a reliance on technology that dates back to the early 1980s. When a tool is created to accomplish a particular task, and the task does not change over the years, many LAN administrators see no reason to change the tool. Some companies that rely heavily on particular DOS-based programs—either commercial applications or custom-designed ones—are still running workstations as old as the original IBM XTs. This is not to say that their tasks couldn't be accomplished more quickly and efficiently with a faster machine, for they unquestionably could, but the economic factor often mitigates the drive for new technology. A shop that has hundreds of users running a simple application on a fleet of XTs may not realize a great enough gain in production to warrant replacing so many machines with newer models.

On the other hand, the problem with this philosophy is that very often the services required of the network do change and existing hardware might not be up to the task. A mass replacement of an entire fleet of machines not only incurs a large financial expense at one time, but also requires significant amounts of system downtime as well as retraining of personnel to use the new equipment. The alternative to this sort of procedure is the gradual upgrade or replacement of workstations as new technologies become available. Many shops have replaced all their workstation computers several times in the past decade. This certainly provides users with better tools to perform their tasks more efficiently, but it can be extremely expensive to regularly replace older equipment with newer equipment when the marketing pattern of the computer industry places such a high premium on the latest technology and relegates the old to the scrap heap. If you were to replace a fleet of XTs today with new machines, you very likely would have to pay someone to haul away the old hardware. Warehouses across the country have old computers stored away gathering dust because they have been replaced with newer machines and there is no market for the old ones. Occasionally, a company may engage in a project or division that requires only limited workstation capabilities, which may allow this old equipment to be put to further use. Some organizations also participate in programs that coordinate the donation of older computers to educational or charitable institutions, but this is usually the exception, not the rule.

In the following sections, we will take a walk through the Museum of Workstation Technology and examine some of the old machines that you may still find in use in network shops today. Obviously, as each day passes, fewer and fewer of the old computers remain usable, but you may someday find yourself tasked with maintaining machines such as these. We will also try to determine the exact point at which the upgrading of legacy machines such as these becomes economically and technologically impractical. In most cases, workstations based on the 80386 or earlier processors are nearing the end of their usefulness, and upgrading them is like living in a rented apartment—you don't want to make any changes that you can't take with you when you leave for use elsewhere. Indeed, the very oldest machines are nearly always not worth the effort. It usually becomes a matter of cannibalizing some of those old XTs for parts to keep others running. The intention here is to demonstrate that it is not always practical or even necessary to equip every user with a 486 or a Pentium (as much as the industry spin doctors would have you believe otherwise). A great many companies continue to use older technology to great effect, and having the knowledge and ability to maintain it demonstrates a sense of economic practicality that is lacking in many network administrators today.

The IBM PC

In 1981, when IBM released the original PC, what had been a hobbyist's toy was transformed overnight into a practical business tool. Technologically, it was not the best PC available at the time, but it was a marketing coup that set the standard for the way the PC business is conducted to this day. Built using readily available and easily upgradable components, the PC design allowed for maximum marketability and minimal financial risk on IBM's part. No one, however—IBM included—had any clue that the concept would be as successful as it was. Suddenly, the PC was a business tool, and the basic designs created by IBM for their original machines became industry standards that persist to this day.

The original IBM PCs and XTs were based on the Intel 8088 microprocessor. Throughout the 1970s, Intel had steadily built increasingly more powerful processors that were designed more for general-purpose use than for installation in specific computers. The 8086 chip, released in 1978, was an expansion of their 8080 design and was the first Intel microprocessor to have a full 16-bit design. The processor had 16-bit registers, a 16-bit-wide data bus, and a 20-bit-wide address bus, allowing it to control a full megabyte (M) of memory (a huge amount at the time, considering that the original PC shipped with only 16K). That 1M was effectively divided into sixteen 64K segments, however, making it operate like 16 of the earlier Intel 8080 chips for compatibility purposes.

Although our history begins with the PC, this was not the first personal computer on the market by any means. IBM's design was mitigated by the need for backward compatibility, even at that early date. A significant number of applications already existed for the eight-bit computers of the time, such as the Apple II, the Radio Shack TRS-80, and other machines that used a CP/M operating system (OS). By today's standards, the applications were few and very rudimentary, but IBM was attempting to protect its investment in every possible way in this venture, and it ultimately decided not to alienate the earlier accomplishments by releasing a fully 16-bit computer.

The 8088 processor was released by Intel after the 8086. The two were nearly identical, except for the fact that the 8088 had a data bus that was only eight bits wide. Use of this processor allowed the PC to be built using eight-bit components (much more readily available) and allowed for the possibility of software conversion from the CP/M OS to the BASIC that was included in the PC's system ROM. The 16-bit internal registers of the 8088 processor allowed IBM to market the PC as a "16-bit computer" without alienating the existing user base. Later IBM PS/2 models utilized the 8086 processor.

The original 8088 processor ran at 4.77MHz and took approximately 12 clock cycles to execute a typical instruction. This is glacial performance by today's standards, but speed was not a major issue at that time. Desktop computers were utterly new to the business world, and the issue was having one or not having one, as opposed to how capable a machine was. Later models of the 8088 ran at 8MHz, providing some increased performance, but that was the limit for this microprocessor design.

The original PC was marketed for $1,355 at a base configuration including 16K of memory and no storage medium other than its built-in ROM. An interface port for a typical audio cassette drive was included, but a floppy disk drive would cost you an extra $500. It's astonishing to think that all those obsolete computers now taking up warehouse space were just as expensive when they were new as today's far more capable machines. It was also the original PC that saddled us with the 640K conventional memory limitation that remains an albatross around our necks to this day. At the time, 640K was considered to be far more than any program would ever need. In fact, the PC could only support up to 256K on its system board; additional memory had to be added through the use of an expansion card. This amount was therefore arbitrarily decided upon by IBM as the place where OS-usable memory would end, and system resources such as video memory and BIOS would begin. In fact, these early machines used only a small fraction of the 384K allotted for these purposes, but the standard was set, and we are still living with it.

The XT

We have examined the original IBM PC because of its place in the history of desktop computing, but the first IBM model that can still be considered even a remotely usable network workstation today is the XT, which was first released in 1983. Still based on the Intel 8088 microprocessor, the XT is more recognizable as the prototypical business computer in many ways. From a hardware design standpoint, the placement of the XT's components and the layout of its motherboard are more akin to today's computers than the PC was. A 360K floppy drive and a whopping 10M (or later, 20M) hard disk drive were standard equipment, and the venerable ISA bus was already in place. A full 640K of memory could be mounted directly on the motherboard in later models, and serial and parallel connectors were available for connection to modems, printers, and other peripherals.

Although its original hard drive has barely the capacity to store today's entire DOS, the XT can easily be outfitted with a NIC and attached to a LAN. Obviously, its performance seems extremely slow to a sophisticated user, as its memory has a 200 nanosecond (ns) refresh rate, and its hard drive has a transfer rate of only 85K per second, but for use with small, simple applications it can be a viable workstation. Even a reasonably sophisticated program such as WordPerfect 5.1 for DOS (still a highly useful application, despite having been overshadowed by its bloated successors) runs on an XT.

This is not to say, however, that the XT is a suitable general-use computer by today's standards. It most definitely is not. I have worked in shops, though, where a company's old XTs have been put to profitable use. One such case involved the introduction of a proprietary software package that ran on an OS/2 application server and was designed for use with dumb terminals connected to the server by a "roll-your-own" network of serial connections and multiport serial concentrators. Rather than spend money on new terminals for what amounted to an experimental business venture, the company used its fleet of obsolete XTs to run a terminal emulation program over the existing LAN. This arrangement worked out very nicely—the company was able to outfit an entire department with workstations at virtually no cost, they managed to clear out some valuable storage space where the old XTs were kept, and they had a number of extra machines left over that could be used for parts to repair the operational ones. Most of the repairs needed, by the way, were minor, involving worn-out keyboards, blown monitors, and the like. The XTs had held up remarkably well, despite years of previous use, plus several more years collecting dust.

That was, of course, an isolated case where older machines were put to good use in a modern workplace. For today's LANs, the XT is rarely worth using as a workstation, for almost any worker becomes more productive on a faster machine. These old warhorses can be put to productive use as dedicated network print or fax servers, though, or even as routers, on less demanding networks. However, if asked whether someone should purchase old XT machines that they might find, I unhesitatingly answer no, unless that person has a specific purpose that the machines are suited to and the price is extremely low. If asked, however, whether a company's fleet of XTs should be stored or discarded, I almost always say to hang onto them. Donating them or even distributing them to employees for home use would be preferable to throwing them away, especially with today's environmental concerns, for it might be more expensive to dispose of them properly than it would be to keep them.

As to the prospect of upgrading XTs, don't even think about it. Like most older computing technologies, the XT is a unified whole whose parts have been selected to work together. The ST-506 hard drive that was standard equipment at the time (discussed later in this chapter) is incredibly slow by today's standards, for example, but moves data faster than the XT can operate on it. There is virtually no single component in the machine that could be upgraded to increase the overall performance of the system once it is fully populated with memory. Parts can be replaced easily from other machines (providing at least one good reason to buy any old units you come across), but the XT is essentially a dead end that is not worth an extensive amount of time, effort, or expense.

The AT

In 1984, IBM released the AT computer. Based on the Intel 80286 processor, the AT was a great step forward from a hardware standpoint but was not utilized by software developers to anything approaching its capabilities. On the whole, the AT was treated like a better, faster XT, and on this basis, it became the prototype for a huge number of imitators to emulate, giving rise to the vast IBM clone market that has since overtaken the originator in sales by a huge margin.

While the 8088 mixed an eight-bit data bus with 16-bit registers, the 80286 was a 16-bit processor in every way. By that time, the 16-bit components that were used to build the ancillary circuitry of a PC were readily available, and IBM did not fail to realize that their fears concerning the compatibility of the 16-bit data bus were unfounded. The PC was now a growing concern for all involved, and even Intel began to design its microprocessors more specifically for use in computers. Components that had previously remained on separate chips were beginning to be incorporated into the microprocessor itself. Intel's earlier chips had deliberately avoided doing this to facilitate their use in devices other than computers. Other customers would not want to pay extra for circuitry that would go unused in another application, but now that there was a practically guaranteed market for the 80286 chip, microprocessors for use in PCs rapidly became the focus of Intel's development efforts.

The explosive growth of the PC industry was evident even in the various versions of the 80286 chip that were released. Originally designed to run at 6MHz, faster and faster versions of the chip were made available, up to 20MHz. This, combined with the doubled width of the data bus, yielded a machine that was already far faster than the XT. The 286 also increased the address lines from 20 to 24, allowing up to 16M of physical memory to be addressed, as opposed to the 1M of the 8088.

The 286 was also the first processor that could utilize *virtual memory*. Virtual memory is hard disk storage space that could be utilized by the processor as a substitute for actual memory chips. Data had to be swapped from the hard drive to RAM before it could be operated upon, but this technique allowed a 286-based machine to address up to 1G of total memory (16M of actual RAM chips and 1,008M of virtual memory). This was, of course, a far greater capacity than other hardware could accommodate at the time. The original AT could only mount 512K worth of DRAM chips on the motherboard, and the idea of a 1G-capacity hard drive for a desktop computer was completely absurd. The most obvious limitation, though, was that there was no OS available that could adequately make use of these capabilities. Once again, the specter of backward compatibility had risen, forcing the industry to try to accomplish the all but impossible task of satisfying the needs of an existing user base that demanded greater performance without sacrificing its existing investment.

Real Mode versus Protected Mode. In order to make it compatible with earlier software, the 80286 microprocessor was designed to run in two different modes: real mode and protected mode. *Real mode* exactly emulates the functionality of the 8086 processor (not the 8088, as the chip still uses a 16-bit data bus) including the ability to address only the first megabyte of memory. When the computer is powered up, it initially boots into real mode and is completely capable of running any software that was written for earlier IBM PCs. The processor's *protected mode* is where the real advances in its architecture are evident. Once switched into this mode by a software command, the processor can access all the memory capabilities, both physical and virtual, that are present in the machine. Protected mode also provides the processor with the ability to *multitask*, the now commonplace practice of running multiple virtual machines where separate programs can run without affecting each other's performance.

Several problems impacted the use of this protected mode, however. The first was that despite the increased amount of memory that could be addressed, that memory was still broken up into 64K blocks, just as it had been with the 8086 and 8088 processors. This left programmers with the same memory segmentation difficulties that they had always had to work around. The only difference was that they now had more segments to work with. The other major problem was that the 286 processor, once it had been switched from real mode into protected mode, could not be switched back again except by resetting the processor—in effect, restarting the computer.

It was here that a familiar pattern in the development of the microcomputer industry first emerged. Despite the extended capabilities of the 80286 chip, it was a full three years before an OS was developed that could take advantage of the chip's protected mode. This OS was OS/2, which in its early versions was a collaborative effort between IBM and Microsoft. OS/2 could effectively multitask programs written to take advantage of this feature and could access the entire range of the computer's memory, but then, as now, few applications were written specifically for it, and the OS never achieved a significant market share.

It was not until some time later, when Windows 3.0 was released by Microsoft, that a commercially successful OS could make use of the 80286's protected mode. Windows' Standard mode was specifically designed to take advantage of existing 286 systems, and while it could address all the memory in the machine, it could not multitask DOS programs. Only native Windows applications could run simultaneously. Besides, the Intel 80386 processor was already available by that time, and this new processor could make far better use of the Windows environment. Due to the lack of software support, the 286-based computer was essentially relegated to the role of a somewhat faster version of the XT.

The Clone Wars. While the XT remained primarily an IBM platform, the AT was the first microcomputer to be duplicated (or "cloned") in large numbers by other manufacturers. Hundreds of thousands of 80286-based computers were sold during the mid to late 1980s, and new systems were still widely available as late as 1992. The original IBM models ran at 6MHz, introduced the high-density 1.2M 5 1/4-inch floppy disk drive, and were equipped with 20M or 30M hard disk drives of the same ST-506 variety as in the XT.

By the time that their popularity began to wane, however, due to the arrival of the 80386 processors, many manufacturers had substantially improved on the capabilities of the basic AT. Most shipped with a full 640K on the motherboard (while IBM's could only fit 512K; an expansion board was needed for more), ran the processor at faster speeds (up to 20MHz), and included larger and faster hard disks, including some of the first IDE drives. The 1.44M, high-density 3 1/2-inch floppy drive was also a popular addition. Video options ranged from the monochrome display adapter (MDA) of the original PC, to the Hercules monochrome graphics adapter, to the later color graphics adapter (CGA) and enhanced graphics adapter (EGA) color standards.

As a result, the 286 machines still found in network use can have a wide range of capabilities. Some are little more than slightly accelerated XTs, while others might have color graphics and enough hard drive space to actually be functional in a modern environment.

Networking ATs. Like the XT, AT-compatible computers are easily adaptable to network use. An ISA bus NIC can be easily inserted and configured to connect the system to a network. The primary drawback with the networking of 286-based and earlier computers is their general inability to load drivers into the upper memory blocks above 640K. Certain chipsets (such as those manufactured by Chips & Technologies) do allow for this possibility, but for most ATs and AT clones, all network drivers have to be loaded into conventional memory. Given the size of most network requesters, which can run up to 100K or more, this can seriously diminish the capability of the workstation to run programs. As with the XT, only simpler programs can be considered for regular use on an AT. Despite the capability of Windows 3.x to run on a 286 machine (in Standard mode only), the AT most definitely is not a suitable Windows platform for everyday use.

Upgrading ATs. Given the wide range of possible hardware configurations available on 80286-based PCs, upgrades of certain components certainly are a possibility, but the question remains whether the process is worth the effort and expense. Intel, for example, marketed a replacement chip for the 80286 called the "snap-in 386" that was the only way in which a 286 microprocessor could be upgraded because of socket and signaling differences. This upgrade could easily be applied if you could locate this chip (which I doubt), but the performance gain would probably not be worth the effort.

On the other hand, certain upgrades are worth the effort if you are committed to using machines such as these in a production environment. For example, if you value the eyesight of your users, any machine utilizing a CGA display system should be upgraded. A video graphics array (VGA) card and monitor, or even an EGA package, would be a vast improvement, applied with very little effort. Even a monochrome solution is an improvement over CGA, but it has been some time since I have seen new monochrome monitors and display adapters available through a conventional source (a fact that I find infuriating when I end up installing 1M VGA cards and monitors on file servers).

Hard drives can be added or replaced in AT machines, although I would say that locating the hardware for anything other than an IDE or SCSI installation would not be worth the effort. See the "IDE" section, later in this chapter, for more information on this process.

I spent many years working primarily with 286-based machines, and while they can be sorely lacking in many of the advanced features that are taken for granted today, they are quite capable of running many DOS applications with satisfactory performance. WordPerfect and Lotus 1-2-3 were the mainstays of the shrink-wrapped software industry at the time of the AT's heyday, and both performed adequately on these machines. The current versions of these products contain capabilities that were unheard of in DOS applications of the late 1980s, but they pride themselves on retaining backward compatibility with their vast installed user base. This is not to say that the average secretary or bookkeeper should have to make do with a 286—anyone would be more productive with a newer, faster machine—but, as with the XT, there are places in the corporate world where this antiquated technology can be put to productive use.

The Intel 80386

By the beginning of 1987, systems built around the next generation of Intel microprocessors had begun to appear on the market. The advent of the 386 was a watershed in personal computing in many ways. First of all, you may notice that this section is not named for a particular IBM computer. By this time, "clone" manufacturers were selling millions of systems around the world, and IBM had stopped being the trendsetter it had always imagined itself to be. In fact, the term "clone" could no longer be considered pejorative. Rival system manufacturers such as Compaq had long since proven themselves to be much more than makers of cheap knockoff versions of IBM machines. Compaq was, in fact, the first systems manufacturer to release an 80386-based PC.

People realized that the IBM systems, while still technologically competitive, added an extra premium to their prices for a sense of brand recognition that was of diminishing value in the real world. Therefore, while IBM's PS/2 systems did utilize the 80386 processor to great effect, and while a great many companies remained IBM-only shops for many years afterward, this was the real beginning of the commercial home computer market, and hundreds of manufacturers began turning out 386-based systems at a phenomenal rate, and selling them by means other than through franchised dealerships and traditional corporate sales calls.

The 80386 processor was a technological breakthrough as well as a marketing one. It was not simply a case of Intel creating a faster chip with a wider bus, although they did do this. The 386 increased the power of personal computers through some fundamental architectural changes that might not be immediately apparent to some users. Indeed, the 386 operates at about the same efficiency level as the 80286, taking approximately 4.5 clock cycles to execute a single instruction. An 80386-based system running a DOS program at the same clock speed as a 286 system will not be tremendously faster. The real innovation behind the 386 was the capability to move personal computing into the age of multitasking.

The 80386 processor was made available by Intel in two basic flavors: the 80386DX and the 80386SX, the latter designed more as an entry-level processor aimed at the home user or less-demanding business user. The DX chip was, first of all, a full 32-bit processor in every way. The internal registers, data bus, and memory address lines were all 32-bit. This doubled the width of the pathway in and out of the processor when compared to the 286. In addition, this meant that a 386-based system could address up to 4G of actual, physical memory chips, and up to 64 terabytes (1 terabyte=1,000G) of total (that is, physical and virtual) memory. Obviously, this is a great deal more RAM than any desktop computer can hold, even today.

Although originally offered at speeds of 12.5MHz and 16MHz, Intel quickly acceded to the demands of users and began producing chips that ran at speeds up to 25MHz and 33MHz. These two became the flagship processors of the Intel line, although other chip manufacturers such as Advanced Micro Devices (AMD) later manufactured 386-compatible chips that ran at speeds up to 40MHz.

The 80386SX chip ran at speeds of 16MHz and 20MHz and was identical to the DX version of the processor in every other way except that its external data bus was only 16 bits wide and that it had only 24 address lines, giving it the same memory-handling capacities as the 286: 16M of physical memory and up to 1G of total physical and virtual memory.

Operational Modes. The real innovation behind the 386, though, can be found in the modes that it can operate in. Like the 286, the 386 has a real mode and a protected mode similar in functionality to those of the earlier chip. The system always boots into real mode, which still emulates the 8086 processor exactly, for compatibility with existing DOS programs. The system can then be shifted into protected mode by the OS, just as the 286 can. However, unlike the 286, the 386 chips can be switched back from protected mode to real mode without resetting (that is, power cycling) the microprocessor. In addition, another operating mode was added, called *virtual real mode*. This mode allowed existing DOS programs to be multitasked without any alteration whatsoever to their code.

Virtual real mode allows individual virtual machines to be created on a single system, each of which functions like a completely independent DOS session. Attributes such as environment variables can be individually modified without affecting the rest of the system, and, should a program in one virtual machine crash, the others can continue running normally (in theory). This is done by distributing the processor's clock cycles evenly among the virtual machines in a rotational manner. This is the basis of multitasking and the fundamental innovation of Microsoft Windows.

Obviously, this function is as dependent on the OS as it is on the hardware. In this respect, the 80386 microprocessor must be considered alongside of Windows because together they completely changed the face of personal and business computing on the desktop. Within months of their release, 386-based systems had almost completely replaced 286s as the workstation of choice. With SX computers at very attractive entry-level prices and DXs positioned as the power user's platform, nearly every PC vendor on the planet signed an OEM agreement with Microsoft to bundle Windows with their computers. Other OSs also supported the multitasking capabilities of the 386, such as Quarterdeck's DESQview, IBM's OS/2, and various UNIX types, but none of these had the marketing push that Windows did, and they never caught on as suitable for everyday business use. Although the transition to Windows as the primary business platform of choice took a few years, this was the beginning of the revolution.

Networking 386s. As you can well imagine, the 386 machine became the preeminent business PC quite quickly and was just as rapidly introduced into network use. What Windows helped the 386 do to the desktop was equaled by what NetWare 386 did to the file server and the network. NOSs were able to take advantage of the chip's multitasking capabilities just as desktop OSs could, and the vastly improved memory handling of the processor allowed workstation network drivers to be loaded into the upper memory blocks between 640K and 1M, with the proper software support. This meant that most of the 640K of conventional memory could be used for running applications, instead of devoting a substantial part of it to network overhead.

The later microprocessor improvements that resulted in the 80486 chip were more of an incremental improvement than a revolutionary one. It was the 386 that set the foundation upon which today's most popular workstation processors are built. This leaves network administrators in a difficult situation, however. Millions of 386 computers were sold around the world, but now that 486s and Pentiums have garnered nearly the entire new computer market, everyone wonders what to do with the old machines.

The real problem is that these 386 workstations are not relics of another age, suitable only for use with archaic programs. 286 and earlier machines simply are incapable of running today's applications and OSs satisfactorily. This is not the case with 386s. Although somewhat slower (or even a great deal slower), a well-equipped 386-based PC can run any of the current productivity applications in use today. Their marketing cache is totally gone, however, and many computer users today express indignation at the prospect of being asked to use a 386 for general business use.

This is an unfortunate byproduct of the tremendous marketing efforts undertaken by Intel and other corporations to promote the latest PC technologies, especially the 486 and Pentium processors. Reaching out of the computer trade press and into the mainstream media, including high-tech television commercials, they have effectively convinced computer users and nonusers alike that nothing less than a 486-based machine is acceptable. Now, the message is changing to emphasize the Pentium. With the release of the Pentium Pro, even the 486 is suddenly a generation older. By the end of 1995, Intel all but ceased production of 486 processors, and now, nothing less than a Pentium is available in a new model computer. For the corporate LAN administrator, though, this should not be the case. Vendors that cater to corporate clients can still supply 486 machines in quantity and are likely to continue doing so for as long as the demand persists.

Clearly, a pattern is beginning to emerge here. Every so often, a new level of PC technology is introduced and, once the kinks are worked out, the industry tries to persuade the public that their older products must be abandoned or upgraded if they are to remain productive or competitive. Add to this the fact that product cycle times have been diminishing steadily for several years. Software upgrades are delivered every twelve or eighteen months, and Intel's primary defense against competitive processor manufacturers is no longer litigation, but simply an accelerated development cycle for its next wave of technology.

Notice also that the well-trumpeted upgradability of Intel processors has turned out to be far more limited than we were originally led to believe. The P24T Pentium Overdrive has only recently made it to market after many months of empty promises, and even this is not a true 64-bit Pentium. In fact, while some non-Intel products do exist that can effectively upgrade 386 systems to 486 performance levels, a 486 cannot be upgraded to a full Pentium, and due to architectural changes, there will be no upgrade platform at all from the Pentium to the Pentium Pro.

For the network administrator in a corporate environment, it is obviously not practical to junk an entire fleet of PCs every time a new processor is released. The 386 is really the first case in which truly usable technology is in danger of being discarded due to sales pressure applied by the computer industry. The fact remains that, for a great many PC users in the business world today, a 386-based PC with sufficient memory and hard drive space is a completely satisfactory production machine. For Windows-based e-mail, standard word processing and spreadsheet use, and even Internet access, this is quite sufficient. This is not to say that I recommend purchasing 386 machines today (even if you could find them), but to warehouse or give away existing units because they are not 486s is lunacy.

I consider 386s to be the most upgradable of PCs. Most of the system hardware packages sold when the 386 was most popular are deficient in the memory and storage capacities that are recognized as essential for business use today. Fortunately, RAM upgrades and hard drives are two components that can be added easily to an underpowered system to make it into a practical workstation. Moreover, both can be removed easily from the 386 when it is finally time to retire the machine from duty. The installation of additional system memory is covered in chapter 5, "The Server Platform," while hard drive upgrades are discussed later in this chapter.

The Intel 80486

Intel marketed its first microprocessor, the 4004, in 1971. Designed for use in the first hand-held calculators, it had a 4-bit bus that made it capable of handling numerical input but very little else. During the next two decades, Intel continued to develop and refine its line of microprocessors, and in 1989, the company released its first model in the 80486 line.

Improvements of the 80486 Processor. The 486 has a full 32-bit bus, meaning that both the data and address buses of the I/O (input/output) unit are 32 bits wide. This allows up to 4G of physical memory to be addressed by the processor and up to 64 terabytes (1 terabyte=1,000G) of virtual memory. *Virtual memory* is a technique in which storage space on a disk drive can be utilized like actual memory through the swapping of data to and from the computer's memory chips.

When compared to the innovations of the 80386 processor, the 486 is more of an evolutionary step forward than a radical new design. The silicon of the chip is etched with finer details, as small as .8 microns (1 micron=1/1,000,000 of a meter), and faster clock speeds of up to 100Mhz are supported. The capabilities of the 486's I/O unit are also significantly enhanced over the earlier processor models, allowing for off-chip memory accesses in burst modes that can deliver data to the processor at a rate of up to 32 bits per single clock cycle.

A *clock cycle* is the smallest unit of time recognized by the processor. Electrical current is applied to a quartz crystal within the processor, causing it to vibrate at a predetermined frequency that is used as a baseline for the timing of all processor operations. Therefore, a chip running at a clock speed of 100MHz is actually operating at 100 million clock cycles per second. Improvements in the architecture of the 486 allow it to execute a single instruction in two clock cycles, while the 386 needed four.

These are the two fundamental ways in which processor design can be improved—increase the speed of the clock, or execute more instructions per clock cycle.

The architectural improvements of the 486, made possible in part by the increased number of transistors that can be packaged on a single chip, allow for several important resources to be built into the processor itself, as opposed to being located in separate units connected by the computer's system bus. Any operation that can be performed without accessing off-chip resources greatly enhances the overall speed and efficiency of the system.

Always remember that, although we are dealing with minute amounts of time and fantastic speeds, computing is all relative. Data that is moved about within the processor travels at a far greater speed (and over a much shorter distance) than that which must travel to the system's memory chips. Similarly, the memory is much faster than a hard drive, a hard drive is faster than a tape drive, a tape drive is faster than a floppy drive, and a floppy drive is faster than a pad and pencil.

The *math coprocessor* (sometimes called the *floating point unit* or *FPU*), for example, is now an integrated part of the microprocessor, as opposed to the separate chip that was required in the 80386 and earlier models. There is also now an 8K on-board cache that significantly increases the efficiency of the processor's I/O unit. This is a *write-through cache* of *four-way set-associative* design. This means that the cache is broken up into four 2K pieces, each of which can be utilized by a different process at the same time, making it particularly effective for multitasking OSs like NetWare and Windows.

A write-through cache means that when the processor receives a command to read from the computer's memory, it first consults the cache to see if the desired data is present there. If it is, then I/O from the memory chips is not necessary, and processing can begin immediately using the cached data. When the processor writes to memory, however, it immediately sends its data to both the cache and the memory chips. By caching in only one direction, a processor sacrifices a measure of additional speed for the sake of data integrity. Additional off-processor RAM caching, called Level 2 or L2 cache, can also be used to great effect with the 486 chip, without interfering with the on-board cache. This sort of static RAM cache is discussed in chapter 5, "The Server Platform."

The 80486 Processor Line. The 80486DX processor is available in speeds ranging from 25MHz to 50MHz. Intel also markets an 80486SX line of processors that differ primarily by lacking an integrated math coprocessor. The intention behind this effort was to emphasize the upgradability of the 486 chip. Users were able to purchase a system with a relatively inexpensive 80486SX chip and later upgrade to the full DX version. The strategy was primarily aimed at the home computer and workstation market and is discussed in greater detail in the "Processor Upgrades" section, later in this chapter. For use in a server, you should consider nothing less than a 33MHz 80486DX processor.

Another innovation of the 486 design over the 386 was the capability for clock-doubling or clock-tripling processors. These processors, called the DX2 and DX4 versions of the 80486, are basically 25MHz or 33MHz chips that have been altered to operate at double or triple their rated speed. Thus, the maximum speed rating achieved by the Intel 80486 family is the DX4 version of the 33MHz processor, which is tripled to run at 100MHz (the native speed of the chip is actually 33.3MHz). The silicon chip itself is quite capable of performing at these high speeds, but there are two important considerations when evaluating these processors.

The first is the fact that these clock-doubled processors only run at double-speed within the processor itself. Thus, when a 33MHz chip is doubled to operate at 66MHz, the internal math coprocessor and on-board cache are effectively doubled, but the communication between the I/O unit of the chip and the rest of the computer is still conducted at only 33MHz. It is the I/O unit itself that has been given the extra capability to translate between the two clock speeds, and that is therefore the buffer between the processor and the motherboard. Actually, this arrangement works out quite well because it is unnecessary to alter the motherboard or any of the computer's other hardware to accommodate the increased speed of the processor. This is, again, part of Intel's "upgradable processor" marketing strategy. DX2 and DX4 processor chips are also available on the retail market as Intel Overdrive processors. Identical in pinout configuration to the DX chips, which means that they can be installed into the same type of socket as the DX, these are designed to be installed in systems as a replacement for—or an addition to—an existing DX processor.

It should be noted, however, that older system boards containing an extra processor socket for the installation of the upgraded chip completely disable the old processor once the new one has been installed. While this is one of the few "chip-only" processor upgrades that I ever recommend be performed in a file server or workstation, I also recommend against the use of the second overdrive socket so that the original processor chip can be removed and used elsewhere or kept as a spare.

The second area of concern with clock-doubled chips is heat. The faster a microprocessor runs, the more heat it generates, and excessive heat can turn this exquisitely etched piece of silicon technology into a high-priced guitar pick with amazing rapidity. For this reason, most 486DX2 and 486DX4 chips, as well as all Pentium processors, come with a *heat sink* attached to the top of the chip. A heat sink is simply a piece of metal or plastic with protruding fins or fingers that increases the chip's surface area through which heat can be dissipated. Many computer manufacturers are now using specially designed fans, about an inch in diameter, that are mounted directly atop the processor chip to provide additional cooling. These fans are also available as add-on kits that can be easily installed on existing machines; the kits attach to the power supply, as opposed to factory-installed models which draw power directly from the processor socket. The use of one or both of these methods for cooling down processors is recommended, particularly in a file server that might contain a greater number of heat-generating components than the average PC.

Intel Pentium

Intel released the first generation of its next processor line, the Pentium, in early 1993. The Pentium represents a major step forward in microprocessing, while retaining full backward compatibility with all previous Intel designs. This step forward is not completely without repercussions to the rest of the industry. While the chip indeed runs existing software faster and more efficiently than the 486, its most revolutionary innovations will require some effort from software developers to be fully utilized.

What's in a Name?

Intel chose not to continue using the x86 naming scheme for its microprocessors after extended litigation failed to prevent rival chip manufacturers from using the term "486" to describe their own products. A number cannot be copyrighted, so a suitable name was chosen for Intel's next generation microprocessor and duly protected by copyright. Pentium-compatible chips by Cyrix and AMD are now appearing on the market, but they cannot use the Pentium name, and Intel has remained a jump ahead by bringing their newest processor, dubbed the Pentium Pro, to market with unprecedented speed.

The primary improvement of the Pentium is that it utilizes *superscalar* technology. Unlike the 486 and all previous Intel processors, which could only execute one instruction at a time, the Pentium has dual instruction pipelines, a feature that previously has been available only in high-speed RISC microprocessors. This gives the Pentium the capability to execute two simple integer instructions simultaneously, within a single clock cycle, under certain conditions.

The primary data path, called the *u-pipe*, can execute the full range of instructions in the processor's command set. A secondary path, called the *v-pipe*, has been added. The v-pipe is not as fully functional as the u-pipe. It can only execute a limited number of instructions in the processor's command set under particular conditions, but it can do so at the same time that the u-pipe is functioning.

Because each pipe has its own ALU, the result of this is that certain combinations of instructions can be "paired" to execute simultaneously, with the results appearing exactly the same as if the instructions were performed sequentially. Other commonly used instructions have been hardwired into the processor for enhanced performance.

To take full advantage of these innovations, however, software developers have had to recompile their programs to ensure that this parallel processing capability is utilized to its fullest. By organizing software to make instructional calls using pairs that the Pentium can run utilizing both pipelines, developers ensure that a greater number of instructions are executed in the same number of clock cycles. This results in tremendous speed benefits.

Some NOSs that run on the Intel processor, such as NetWare 4.x and Windows NT, have already been recompiled to take advantage of the Pentium's capabilities. Many desktop applications will also be recompiled as they are ported to 32-bit versions designed to take advantage of newer 32-bit desktop OSs such as Windows 95 and OS/2.

Another improvement found in the Pentium is the presence of two separate 8K memory caches within the processor. Each of the two caches is of *two-way set-associative* design, split into two 4K sections using 32-bit lines (the 486 used 16-bit lines for its cache). One cache is utilized strictly for code, and therefore deals only with data traveling into the processor from the system bus. This prevents any delay of instructions arriving at the processor because of conflicts with the data traveling to and from the twin instructional pipelines.

The other cache is a data-only cache that has been improved over its 486 counterpart by being *write-back capable* (the older model was strictly a write-through cache). A write-back cache stores data on its way to and from the processor. Thus, output data remains in the cache and is not written to memory until subsequent usage forces a portion of the cache to be flushed. The write-through cache of the 486 stores data only on its way to the processor; all output is immediately written to memory, a process that can cause delays while the processor waits for memory chips to signal their readiness to accept data. The Pentium data cache can also be configured by software commands to switch from write-through to write-back mode as needed, holding its output in on-board memory buffers when the programmer deems it necessary. This helps to eliminate any possible delays caused by multiple calls to system memory. The data cache also has two separate interfaces to the system board to accommodate the two instruction pipelines of the processor, thus enabling it to deliver data to both pipes simultaneously.

Like the 486, the Pentium has a 32-bit address bus, giving it the same memory addressing capabilities as the earlier chip. However, the data bus has been increased to 64-bit, doubling the bandwidth for data transfers to memory chips on the system board. Some of the on-chip data paths have even been widened to be 256-bit to accommodate the Pentium's burst-mode capabilities, which can send 256 bits into the cache in one clock cycle. These attributes combined allow the chip to transfer data to and from memory at up to 528 Mbps, while the maximum transfer rate of a 50MHz 486 is only 160 Mbps.

Improvements have also been made in the FPU, the processor's error detection protocols, and the processor's power-management features. The FPU of the Pentium has been completely redesigned. It now utilizes an eight-stage pipeline and can consistently perform floating-point calculations in one clock cycle. Error detection is performed by two separate mechanisms: one using parity checking at the interface with the system board and an internal procedure that checks the caches, buffers, and microcode on the chip itself.

As mentioned earlier, Intel in 1993 released the first generation of Pentium microprocessors. Running at 60MHz and 66MHz, these chips possessed all the capabilities previously described but were hampered by some aspects of their design that caused a number of problems.

First, the large number of transistors on the chip (3.1 million, up from 1.2 million on the 486), combined with Intel's continued use of the three-layer 0.8 micron complimentary metal oxide semiconductor (CMOS) manufacturing technology from the 80486DX-50, required a very large die—this caused complications in the manufacturing process that severely hampered Intel's ability to deliver the chips in the quantities needed. In addition, this design caused the resulting chips to use a large amount of power, thereby generating tremendous heat. Moreover, the 60MHz version of the processor was nothing more than a 66MHz chip that had exhibited instability problems during the quality-control process when run at 66MHz. Reports like these were not received well by the consumer, and this, in combination with the initial high prices of the chips, caused informed buyers to be very cautious when considering the use of the new processor.

By March 1994, though, when the second generation of Pentiums came to market, the manufacturing techniques had been modified extensively. The chips were then made using a four-layer 0.6 micron bipolar complementary metal oxide semiconductor (BiCMOS) technology that had already been adopted by other chip manufacturers, and they required significantly less power than their earlier counterparts (3.3v, as compared to 5v for the earlier Pentium models, despite an increase in the number of transistors from 3.1 to 3.3 million).

90MHz and 100MHz versions of the chip were released, along with a 75MHz version designed for use in lower-end machines and portables. Unlike the first-generation chips, in which the processor ran at the same speed as the bus, the second-generation chips run at 150% of the bus rate. Thus, if a chip runs at 100MHz internally, communication with the system bus is actually conducted at 66MHz. At this time, 66MHz is still the fastest possible communication rate with the system bus.

Extensive power-management capabilities were also added to the second-generation Pentium processor. The chip is capable of placing itself into one of several low-power consumption modes, depending on the activities being conducted, and can even be used to control the suspension of power to other devices in the computer when they are not in use. While features of this sort are of more concern to laptop configurations than to those of file servers, bear in mind that reduced power also means reduced heat, which is beneficial to any system.

In March 1995, Intel introduced the first chips in its next generation of Pentium microprocessors. Running at 120 and 133MHz, the newest Pentiums are manufactured using a 0.35 micron process that allows for a manufacturing die one-half the size of the previous generation's die, and one-fourth the size of the original Pentium's die. Still operating at 3.3 volts and utilizing four layers of metal between silicon BiCMOS wafers, these chips not only increase Pentium performance levels still further but also allow for more efficient manufacturing processes, which means lower costs and ready availability. These are now the processors of choice in high-end Pentium machines, and prices have dropped considerably with the advent of the Pentium Pro, which now occupies the position as the premium (read: most expensive) Intel processor on the market. Indeed, there are even rumors to the effect that the 150 and 160MHz Pentiums are ready for market, waiting only for an opportune release time that will not jeopardize Pentium Pro sales.

Rival Pentiums. After extended legal battles with AMD and other rival microprocessor manufacturers, Intel has been forced to allow other companies to manufacture processors that are Intel-compatible but don't infringe upon Intel's designs.

Creating a Clean Copy

Rival manufacturers usually design their chips using a *clean room* technique. First, a team of technicians examines the target technology (in this case, an Intel chip) and documents its capabilities in great detail. Then a second team that has never examined the original technology is given the materials generated by the first team and tasked with the creation of a component that can do everything specified. This way, a product is created with the same capabilities as the original but realized in a completely independent way.

Several companies have created processors that rival the 486, some of which exceed the capabilities of Intel's 80486 line, and now the Pentium clones have begun to hit the market. NextGen's Nx586 is currently available, as are Cyrix' 6x86 and the Am5x86 by AMD. All of these manufacturers claim performance levels comparable to a 133 MHz Pentium, but offer few real advantages over a true Pentium at this time. The NextGen chip has so far failed, in the first systems using it, to provide a pervasive reason not to use Intel. Several of the larger systems manufacturers, among them Compaq, have expressed great interest in using these new processors, but their motivations are certainly more economic than technological. Until these chips are thoroughly tested in real-world situations, I would not recommend their use, especially in servers, and even if they are found to be stable, performance or price would have to be substantially better than their Intel counterparts.

Intel Pentium Pro

While the BiCMOS manufacturing method has yielded a Pentium of even greater speed than its predecessors, it has also set the stage for the next level in the Intel microprocessor family. Code-named *P6* during development, and finally named the Pentium Pro for its release, this processor was developed with one primary goal in mind, according to an Intel press release: "To achieve twice the performance of [the] Pentium processor while being manufactured on the same semiconductor process." In order to do this, a new method of executing instructions had to be developed.

All microprocessors, up to and including the Pentium, are dependent on the system bus and memory chips of the computer to deliver instructions and data to the processor for calculation. Because these components operate at slower speeds than the internal workings of the processor, there have always been times when processing halts for short periods while data is being fetched from memory chips. These *memory latency delays* result in underutilization of the processor, and because the speed of memory devices has increased over the years at a rate far less than that of processors, simply requiring faster memory is not an adequate solution.

Intel's initial attempt to address this problem came in the form of a component that was introduced in the Pentium processor called the *branch target buffer* (*BTB*), which attempted to intelligently anticipate the next instruction that would be required in a string of commands and to execute that instruction before it was actually received. When an instruction called for a branch (that is, a direction to access a command from a particular memory address), this address—along with the command—was stored in the Pentium's 256-entry BTB. The next time the same branch was called, this memory address would be located in the buffer, and its corresponding command executed before the instruction could actually be accessed from system memory. If the BTB had correctly anticipated the desired command, then the processor delay time caused by memory latency was partially offset by the immediate availability of the command's result; in other words, the command was executed while it was being accessed. If the BTB's guess was wrong, then a process called *branch recovery* was initiated, in which the results of the buffered command were discarded. The correct instruction was then executed with no significant loss of processor time.

The design of the Pentium Pro processor leaps ahead of this technique by means of *dynamic execution*. Dynamic execution is a method in which chains of commands are stored on the processor in an instruction pool and executed out of order during lag periods.

For example, the *fetch/decode unit* of the processor accesses a series of instructions from the system bus using a multiple branch prediction algorithm and a 512-entry BTB, and places them in the pool. The *dispatch/execute unit* then begins to perform the calculations of instruction #1, but the data required by the instruction cannot be found in the processor's cache and therefore cannot be completed until the required data arrives via the system bus. The processor then begins a *dataflow analysis procedure* that looks ahead to the next command in line for execution, instruction #2, but finds that it cannot be executed yet at all because it relies heavily on the results of the uncompleted instruction #1. Analyzing the next waiting instructions, the processor finds that instructions #3 and #4 do not rely on earlier results, and that all data required for their completion is already present in the cache. Therefore, they can be executed during the idle time while the processor is waiting for the data needed by instruction #1.

The results of instructions #3 and #4 cannot yet be returned to the permanent machine state, as they are still the result of a speculative procedure, so they are stored in the *retire unit*, where they wait until the results of instructions #1 and #2 are available. The retire unit then is responsible for reordering the results of all four instructions into the correct sequence, and sending them back to the programmer-visible registers where normal operations can continue, oblivious to the machinations performed within the processor. Thus, instructions enter and exit the processor in the correct order, but are actually executed in whatever order serves to most efficiently minimize idle time at the processor core.

The Intel developers predict that with their new 0.35 micron manufacturing technology they will be able to realize Pentium Pro processors running at speeds of 200MHz or more with far greater efficiency than that of any microprocessor available today. The first Pentium Pro, though, will run at 133MHz and utilize the 0.6 micron BiCMOS technology of the second-generation Pentiums. The chip will integrate 5.5 million transistors into its design, require a reduced power supply of 2.9v, and include as part of the unit an off-chip Level 2 system cache connected to the processor by a dedicated high-speed bus. Intel is relying heavily on PCI bus mastering controllers to provide the system bus speeds necessary to accommodate the faster chip, which will, at its peak, execute three instructions per clock cycle. These fundamental architectural changes mean that, while the Pentium Pro will be 100% software compatible with all previous Intel processors, there will be absolutely no upgrade path from earlier processor families without motherboard replacement.

The first systems utilizing the Pentium Pro hit the market near the end of 1995, and unfortunately, these systems do not yet demonstrate a marked improvement in processing speed over the Pentium. It is even being opined that Intel is holding up the release of its 150 and 166MHz Pentiums for fear of eclipsing the performance of its own "next generation." Particularly in light of the relative inadequacy of the first 60/66MHz

Pentiums that were released, it is safe to say that it's early days yet for the Pentium Pro. It offers little substantial improvement over the Pentium while carrying the high-ticket prices that are natural for a newly released technology. Too expensive for a workstation and too untried for a server, we can only hope that the next "next generation" will show the same refinement that was achieved in the Pentium line.

It is also important to note that the primary competition to the Intel processor type in the desktop market comes from companies that produce chips that are primarily used in high-end workstations costing anywhere from 10 to 50 times as much as the average PC. Their processors also are much more expensive, and because the market is much smaller, they tend to be manufactured in numbers counted by the thousands, while Intel manufactured more than 30 million 486 processors in 1994, and claims to be on track to surpass this number of Pentiums in 1995! The efficiency and reliability of the manufacturing process is therefore a crucial element of any Intel processor design. The industry has now progressed to the point where Intel is marketing products comparable to the high-end RISC processors for a much lower price and in quantities that probably make their competitors salivate.

With these considerations in mind, it is no wonder that Intel holds a lock on the world microprocessor market that extends far beyond PC use and into devices found in nearly every American home. It is very likely that this hold on the market will continue for some time to come.

Pentium FPU Flaws

In late 1994, the detection of a flaw in the FPU of the Pentium processor was publicized to a previously unheard-of degree, not only in trade publications, but in the mainstream press as well. The existence of the flaw, in itself, is not a terribly unusual occurrence. Indeed, many experts were quick to comment that it would be virtually impossible to produce a microprocessor of such complexity that didn't contain a flaw at some level. The problem was caused by an error in a script that was created to download a software lookup table into a hardware programmable lookup array (PLA). Five entries were omitted from the table, with the result that division operations performed on certain combinations of numbers by the Pentium's FPU return results with what Intel refers to as "reduced precision." (That means the answer is wrong.)

Determining whether or not your Pentium contains the flaw is a simple procedure. Use a spreadsheet to perform the following calculation:

$$(4195835/3145727) \times 3145727$$

Obviously, the result should be the original number: 4195835. A flawed Pentium chip, though, generates a result that is off by 256. Incidentally, while many sources have introduced software "fixes" for the problem, most of these do nothing more than disable the floating-point logic in the processor, slowing down all FP calculations considerably, including those unaffected by the flaw. Some software vendors also have made patches or switches available that disable floating-point calculations for their individual applications, allowing for mission-critical data to be protected and for the FPU to function normally elsewhere. Intel has made public a patch that intercepts only the offending floating-point calculations and executes them in a different manner, to assure correct results. This patch is in the form of code that is intended to be incorporated into application software by compilers and developers. It is not available as an executable program for use with software that has already been compiled.

No one with any experience in the computer industry can deny that products sometimes ship with flaws. It might even be safe to say that all products do, to some degree. The tremendous backlash of publicity regarding the Pentium flaw was due not so much to the problem itself but to Intel's response to industry criticism. The mathematician who discovered the problem attempted to ascertain just how serious the situation was by computing the probability of the error's reoccurrence during normal processor use. Intel immediately responded with its own figures and estimates that appeared to demonstrate that the occurrence of errors should be far less frequent than the mathematician's figures seemed to indicate. This argument continued in the press with increasing amounts of anger and statistics bandied about by all interested parties. It was also revealed that Intel had been aware of the problem for some time but had been very careful not to publicize it.

To clarify a few points, it should be noted that the problem occurs only in the FPU of the processor and that only a relatively small number of applications utilize the FPU. In the commercial desktop software field, it is primarily in spreadsheets, CAD, and similar financial and graphic-design applications that the FPU is used. Network OSs are not affected, although some server-based financial and database engines might be. In addition, many of the processor calculations performed by these applications are dedicated to file management, screen display, and other "overhead" tasks that use only integer calculations and have nothing to do with the floating-point calculations that potentially yield incorrect results. In other words, Intel was correct in its steadfast declaration that the vast majority of Pentium users will never be in a situation in which it is possible for the flaw to manifest itself. Where Intel began to go astray, however, was in the company's dealings with those users who do, in fact, utilize the FPU.

All the elaborate mathematical arguments presented by various parties were based on attempts to predict the number of divide calculations performed by particular applications under normal conditions. This was then used to calculate a probability of the flaw being manifested within a certain period of time. Intel attested, for example, that the average spreadsheet user was likely to encounter one divide error for every 27,000 years of normal spreadsheet use. This may be comforting to some, but in fact, there is no less chance that the payroll figures you calculate tomorrow will be wrong than there is that your income tax figures in the year 2296 will be wrong. There is no reason why the one time in 27,000 couldn't occur right now, no matter how many charts, graphs, and white papers attempt to prove otherwise. The bottom line is that there is a flaw, and your calculation results could be wrong.

On the basis of its probability arguments, Intel refused to implement a blanket exchange policy for purchasers of the flawed chips. They proposed instead a program in which users were to be made to prove that they had a need for a processor that functioned properly before they were given one. After massive marketing campaigns in which Intel earnestly tried to get a Pentium into every home in America, this announcement denigrating the vast majority of its users as unworthy of a product that performs as advertised was an act of staggering gall, and industry commentators proceeded to tell them so.

The final result of the conflagration was that Intel suffered a tremendous amount of bad publicity and ultimately instituted a program that provides free replacements of the flawed chips to any user requesting one. The general consensus of the press was that people in the industry did not fault Intel so much for the flawed product as they did for the way they attempted to cover up the problem, and the way they reacted once it was exposed. Indeed, as of this writing, only about 10 percent of the flawed Pentium processors have been returned to Intel. There are, however, a great many users of the Pentium upon whose calculations rest the stability of bridges, the safety of automobiles, the lives of medical patients, and so on.

We can only hope that, as a result of the incident, a lesson was learned by some vendors in this industry. Consumers finally are becoming more conscious of the games that have been run on them successfully for many years. Consumers are becoming harder for the vendors to fool, and if consumers stay the course, we can hope that it will be cheaper and easier for vendors to become forthright in all their shortcomings than to become clever enough to fool us again.

To obtain a replacement Pentium chip, call Intel at (800) 628-8686. You will be required to furnish a credit card number so that, if you fail to return the flawed processor chip within 30 days, you can be charged for the replacement. Intel representatives say that the company is doing this so that there is no way for flawed chips to remain in use or to be submitted for repeated replacements.

486 and Pentium Workstations

In chapter 5, "The Server Platform," we examined in depth the architecture and capabilities of the Intel 80486 and Pentium microprocessors. Of course, these processors that are acceptable for use in file servers also offer superb performance in a workstation. At this point in time, the standard network workstation PC configuration offered by most corporate-oriented vendors is a 80486DX2 processor running at 50 or 66MHz, 16M of memory, and approximately 300M of hard drive space. Pentiums at the workstation level are more often reserved for users with special needs, such as desktop publishing and other graphics work, CAD, and the like.

However, by the time that the Pentium Pro comes into general release, prices will certainly plummet on Pentium processors, and this eventually will become the standard desktop platform of choice. Of course, it will then be time to throw away all your company's 486s, right?

Upgrading Workstations

One of the secrets to administering a large fleet of PCs (or even one PC, actually) is to know that the processor is not the be-all and end-all of a workstation's existence. A well-designed PC can run better and more efficiently than a badly-designed one with a faster processor. To be economically realistic in today's business world, it is more important to purchase machines that can easily be upgraded in other ways to accommodate the needs of the ever-expanding software packages that will have to run on them.

Windows is the business environment of choice today, and is likely to remain so for the next few years. However, Windows applications are becoming more and more demanding of workstation resources such as memory and hard disk space. 16M of RAM is now a standard, whereas it was quite a luxury only a year or two ago. Power users and advocates of other OSs such as OS/2, Windows NT, or Windows 95 feel that 32M is now preferable. The office software suites that have sold so well recently require anywhere from 75M to 100M of storage for a full installation. (Wouldn't you love to go back in time and say this to that guy who was so proud of his new 10M hard drive in 1983?) Networking a PC, of course, can eliminate the need to have all resources present on the workstation's local drives, but there should be enough room for the OS and the user's most frequently used applications.

The key, then, to practical workstation administration is to categorize users on the basis of their computing needs and allot microprocessors accordingly. After that, make sure that all your computers have memory and disk storage sufficient for today's applications. This probably means adding additional RAM and hard drive space to virtually every 386 that you still own and assigning them to the users with the most basic needs.

The only real problem with this philosophy is that the pecking order in the corporate world sometimes does not allow for this sort of resource distribution. By purely practical standards, assistants who deal with extensive amounts of correspondence, mail-merges, and so on, should get the 486s or Pentiums, while executives who only use the computer to check their e-mail should get the older machines. I leave to the individual network administrator the task of explaining this to the executives.

For the remainder of this chapter, therefore, we examine the hardware and procedures necessary to attach a PC to the network and to keep it there as a usable resource for as long a period as possible. This means we must look at the memory and processor upgrades that are practical on the workstation platform, the addition or replacement of the hard drive types most commonly found in workstations, and the purchase and installation of NICs. The ability to perform procedures like these allows you to preserve the hardware investment your company has already made, while keeping your users productive and, if not happy, at least satisfied.

Processor Upgrades

As stated earlier, the Intel 80486 processors were more of an incremental development than a revolutionary one. It is primarily for this reason that processor upgrades from a 386 to a 486 are even remotely possible. Intel, however, would rather see you purchase an entire new 486-based computer, so it was left to their competitors to realize such products.

80386 Upgrades. Cyrix markets a line of microprocessor upgrade kits for 386s that offer 486 performance levels for nearly any 386 machine. It should be noted at the outset, however, that this is not a true 486 upgrade, but rather a means of accelerating the performance of a 386 machine to levels approaching that of a 486. Cyrix is the first to admit that an upgraded 386 machine does not equal the capabilities of a true 486, whether a genuine Intel or one of Cyrix's own, but they do promise an overall performance increase of approximately 100% for less than $300, which may be helpful in keeping those 386 machines useful in the business network environment.

Two different upgrade kits are available from Cyrix, depending on the existing processor in the 386 machine. 80386DX-based machines running at 16MHz, 20MHz, 25MHz, and 33MHz require a complete processor replacement, and Cyrix includes a chip-pulling tool for removing the old processor. The microprocessors in 80386SX-based machines are soldered to the motherboard, and the Cyrix kit for these includes a specially designed chip that snaps in place over the existing one. Both kits are designed for installation by the average user, making the process a rather simple one.

It should be noted that there are certain 80386 microprocessors that cannot be upgraded with these products. 16MHz 386SX machines manufactured before 1991 lack a float pin that is required for the new chip to function; 33MHz 386SX and 40MHz 386DX machines also cannot be upgraded. Older 387 math coprocessor chips might be incompatible with the upgrades, requiring replacement with a newer model. Cyrix has made available a listing of specific manufacturers and models that can be upgraded, as well as a free software utility that can be used to determine whether a specific machine is a viable candidate for an upgrade.

As far as software compatibility is concerned, Cyrix has certified their processor upgrades for use with all the major desktop OSs, including DOS, Windows, Windows NT, OS/2, and several varieties of UNIX. They have also certified their upgrades for use in NetWare, Banyan, and LAN Manager client workstations. Software is required to initialize the onboard 1K cache of the processor, and this is included in the kit.

Although clearly not a replacement for a true 486 workstation, an upgrade such as this provides a simple and economical way to preserve the extensive investments many companies have made in 80386 technology.

80486 Upgrades. It is only with 486 and higher-level machines that actual processor chip replacement becomes a practical upgrade alternative. The practice of upgrading the microprocessor on a PC's motherboard is one that should be approached with a good deal of caution. Basically, there are two fundamental problems involved in the process: the actual chip replacement and hardware compatibility.

Replacing the Chip. The physical act of replacing the microprocessor chip on a motherboard can be very difficult or ridiculously simple, depending on the hardware. Changing the processor in a machine with a traditional socket can be a miserable experience. First of all, because inserting the new chip into the socket requires a force of 100 pounds (or 60 pounds for the "low insertion force" socket), it will likely be necessary to remove the motherboard from the case. Most computers utilize plastic spacers at the corners to hold the motherboard away from the computer's case. Pressing down hard on the center of the board could easily crack it, so depending on the design of your PC, you might have to disassemble virtually your entire computer to get the motherboard out, unless you can manage to provide support for the board from beneath. Once you have done this, you will need a chip puller (or a small screwdriver and a lot of courage) to pry the old processor out of the socket with even pressure from all sides so that it is lifted vertically away from the motherboard. Next, you must line up the new processor over the socket so that all 273 or 296 pins are precisely lined up with their respective pin-holes, then place the heel of your hand atop this expensive piece of silicon, metal, and plastic, and gingerly press down with all your weight until the chip is well seated. There should be approximately 1/16 inch of space between the chip and the socket. If you bend one of the pins, you might be able to bend it back with a fine-nosed plier. If you break off even one pin, however, the chip is ruined.

As noted earlier, you might find that your motherboard already has a second, vacant Overdrive processor socket on it. In cases like this, you need to perform only the latter half of the above procedure, but the machine's original processor will be disabled once the new chip is in place. Worse yet, damaging the original socket in an attempt to re-move the old processor could render both sockets unusable.

You probably have gathered that I generally do not recommend replacing microproces-sor chips on this type of motherboard. This is true, but not only for the reasons outlined above. The process can be difficult and is not recommended for the uninitiated, but it can be done with the right tools and a lot of confidence. The primary reason I hesitate to recommend upgrading processors is that there generally is more risk in the process than gain in the result.

On the other hand, most new motherboards utilize a *zero insertion force (ZIF) socket* for the processor. This is a plastic construction with a lever on the side that, when engaged, locks the processor chip into place in the socket (see fig. 6.1). In these machines, replac-ing a microprocessor chip is simply a matter of flipping open the lever, taking out the old chip (no tools needed), inserting a new one, and closing the lever again. It fits so loosely into the pinholes that you would worry about it falling out if the lever wasn't there. The replacement procedure is so simple that most motherboard manufacturers have opted to include a single ZIF socket, rather than two of the conventional type, for overdrive capability. The only things you can possibly do wrong are to insert the proces-sor the wrong way, or insert the wrong processor into the socket. The first problem has been eliminated by the pin distribution in Intel's socket designs—there is only one pos-sible way to insert the chip. The second, more complicated problem is explained in the following section.

Microprocessor Interchangeability. By far, the more pervasive problem in upgrad-ing processors is knowing which models can be safely upgraded to which other models in what has become an increasingly bewildering array of chips in the Intel processor line.

If your file server is running any chip from the 80386 family, you can forget about up-grading. 386 motherboards simply cannot handle the increased requirements of the more advanced processors.

If your file server is running any chip from the 80486SX or DX family, then you defi-nitely can upgrade to a comparable DX2 Overdrive processor. If your computer's motherboard contains the original 169-pin Overdrive socket (Socket 1), then you can install the appropriate Overdrive chip for your original processor. For example, if your original CPU was a 486DX-25, you can install the 486DX2-50 Overdrive processor. Do not try to install a DX2-66, as your motherboard is configured only to run with a processor that communicates with the system bus at 25MHz.

Figure 6.1

This is an empty ZIF socket for a microprocessor.

Newer motherboards may contain the 238-pin socket, designated Socket 2 by Intel, which provides some added processor upgrade flexibility. Still running at 5v, like Socket 1, the second socket can also support the addition of the P24T, the Pentium Overdrive processor, in addition to those mentioned above. Be aware, however, that this processor is not a full 64-bit Pentium. It is a 32-bit knockdown version that might provide some additional speed but will not result in the dramatic improvement that you would expect given the earlier description of the Pentium chip's capabilities. Depending on the price and availability of the Pentium Overdrive, which is now on the market after repeated delays, you might find it more economical to upgrade to the fastest possible 486 and save your money for a true Pentium system later.

Another alternative is the clock-tripled version of the 486, called the 80486DX4. Although not originally available on retail market, an overdrive version of the DX4 can now be purchased that triples the internal speed of the processor, just as the DX2 doubles it. ("Overdrive" is simply a marketing term for these processors when they are released into the retail market. Except for the P24T, they are indistinguishable from the chips found as original equipment in preassembled systems.) The primary architectural difference is that the DX4 runs at 3.3v, while all the other 486s run at 5v. For this reason, you can only install a DX4 chip into a Socket 1 or Socket 2 motherboard with the use of a voltage-regulating adapter. If you plug a DX4 directly into a 5v socket, you will ruin the chip and probably produce a very unpleasant smell.

The Intel Socket 3 designation is the one most conducive to successful upgrades. With 237 pinholes and designed to operate at either 3.3v or 5v, Socket 3 accommodates the entire 486 family as well as all the Pentium Overdrive chips. It is extremely important to determine which socket is installed on the motherboard that you wish to upgrade (see table 6.1). Some motherboard manufacturers also incorporate DIP switches into their upgradable processor designs. It is always safest to check the documentation of the motherboard or to call the manufacturer to determine whether or not a particular upgrade is advisable, and what additional adjustments to the motherboard might be necessary.

| Table 6.1 | Intel 486/Pentium CPU Socket Types and Specifications | | | |
Socket Number	Number of Pins	Pin Layout	Voltage	Supported Processors
Socket 1	169	17×17 PGA	5v	SX/SX2, DX/DX2*
Socket 2	238	19×19 PGA	5v	SX/SX2, DX/DX2*, Pentium Overdrive
Socket 3	237	19×19 PGA	5v/3.3v	SX/SX2, DX/DX2, DX4, Pentium Overdrive, DX4 Pentium Overdrive
Socket 4	273	21×21 PGA	5v	Pentium 60/66, Pentium 60/66 Overdrive
Socket 5	320	37×37 SPGA	3.3v	Pentium 75/90/100/120/133, Pentium 90/100 Overdrive
Socket 6	235	19×19	3.3v	DX4, DX4 Pentium Overdrive

PGA=Pin Grid Array
SPGA=Staggered Pin Grid Array
*DX4 can also be supported with the addition of a 3.3v voltage regulator adapter.

An upgrade from a 486 to a full Pentium chip is not possible without replacement of the motherboard, due to the differences in their pinouts and voltage requirements. This is just as well, in a way, because a good Pentium machine requires a motherboard that has been built to accommodate the needs of the faster processor. For the same reasons, the first-generation Pentiums running at 60MHz and 66MHz and requiring the 273-pin, 5v Socket 4, cannot be upgraded to the second-generation chips running at 90MHz, 100MHz or faster, which use the 320-pin, 3.3v Socket 5.

The currently available family of Pentium processors, running at 75, 90, 100, 120, and 133MHz, all utilize this same socket, allowing them to be interchangeable on many motherboards, as long as the heat considerations of the faster chips are accounted for, which should not be a problem in most of today's Pentium systems. The Pentium Pro, however, as stated earlier, does not present a practical upgrade path from lesser processors, due to its fundamental architectural differences, particularly the integrated L2 cache.

Memory Upgrades

When considering a business-oriented workstation running Windows 3.1 or one of the newer 32-bit OSs, no other upgrade yields as immediate an increase in productivity as an installation of additional memory. A faster processor can speed up individual tasks, but memory is the lifeblood of a multitasking environment. The more RAM that is available, the greater the number of applications that can be opened and used simultaneously. For the business user, this can be critical, as the workflow of a typical day at the office often consists of numerous interruptions and digressions that require access to various resources and documents. The ability to open an additional program without having to close others can add up to tremendous time savings over long periods.

The capability of the microprocessor to utilize disk drive space as virtual memory is useful as a safety buffer. When all the system's RAM is being utilized, further operations are carried out by swapping memory blocks to and from the hard drive. Once a system is loaded to the point at which virtual memory is used, however, performance levels drop precipitously, as hard drives are far slower than RAM chips are; hard drive speeds are measured in milliseconds (thousandths of a second), while RAM speeds are measured in nanoseconds (billionths of a second). It is best, therefore, to try to avoid the use of virtual memory whenever possible, and the only way to do this without limiting the capabilities of the machine is to install more RAM.

In chapter 5, "The Server Platform," we examined the way that system memory is organized into banks that determine the possible ways in which RAM can be upgraded. To reiterate the basic rule: a bank must be completely filled with identical RAM chips or must be left completely empty. You can consult table 6.2 to learn how most workstation computers have their memory organized, but the best way to find out what type and capacity of memory modules may be safely added to a particular PC is to check the documentation for the motherboard.

Table 6.2   Memory Bank Widths on Different Systems

Processor	Data Bus	Bank Size (w/Parity)	30-Pin SIMMs per Bank	72-Pin SIMMS per Banks
8088	8 bit	9 bits	1	1 (4 banks)
8086	16 bit	18 bits	2	1 (2 banks)
286	16 bit	18 bits	2	1 (2 banks)
386SX, SL, SLC	16 bit	18 bits	2	1 (2 banks)
386DX	32 bit	36 bits	4	1
486SLC, SLC2	16 bit	18 bits	2	1 (2 banks)
486SX, DX, DX2, DX4	32 bit	36 bits	4	1
Pentium	64 bit	72 bits	8	2

The primary problem with upgrading memory in 386-based machines is that many vendors, at the time of the 386's popularity, utilized 1M SIMMs in their computers. These machines usually shipped in 4M or 8M memory configurations, and the existing SIMMs might have to be removed from the system to make room for larger-capacity modules in order to bring the system up to the 16M that is currently the typical amount of RAM for a networked Windows workstation. For example, a typical 386DX system might have eight memory slots broken into two banks of four each. The only way for the manufacturer to populate the machine with 8M of RAM would be to use 1M SIMMs in all eight slots. To perform a memory upgrade, at least one bank has to be cleared in order to install 4M SIMMs. The problem might be that you have no ready use for the 1M modules in this day and age, but letting those SIMMs go to waste is better than saddling a user with an underpowered machine.

Consult chapter 5, "The Server Platform," for more information on the actual installation of additional memory modules. The procedures are the same for a workstation as they are for a server. With memory prices hovering in the range $30 to $40 per megabyte, it might cost $500 or more to bring a machine up to 16M of RAM, but this will make the difference between a barely usable relic and a viable productivity platform. Also, remember that the SIMMs can be removed when it is finally time to retire the machine.

Workstation Storage Subsystems

Like every other component in the personal computer, the minimum requirement for hard disk drive storage has greatly increased over the past several years. While the average 386-based machine sold in the early 1990s may have had a 120M drive as a standard component, a typical workstation configuration today may have 300M, 500M, or even more storage. Even more astonishing is the way that hard drive prices have dropped. Just five years ago, it was common to pay $2 or more per megabyte of storage (we won't even discuss the $1,500 10M drives of the early 1980s). Prices today are now often less than fifty cents per megabyte, and some hard drives have capacities of several gigabytes in the same form factor that could not hold one tenth of that amount in the past.

This is, of course, a direct reaction to the needs of computer users. The average Windows application today requires from 5M to 20M of drive space just for installation, and the advent of multimedia and true-color graphics has made multimegabyte data files commonplace. In addition, the increasing use of full-motion video on the desktop promises to expand these requirements to an even greater degree.

Attaching computers to a network, however, mitigates these requirements to some degree. It can often be difficult to decide how much disk space is truly necessary for a networked workstation. Some administrators swear by the use of a server for virtually all of a workstation's storage needs, including the OS. It is quite possible to run an entire Windows workstation without any local hard drive at all, but the burden that this places on the network, along with the decrease in performance that will be seen at the workstation, hardly compensates for the small savings on the price of even a modest workstation hard drive. Even a 100M drive allows for the installation of DOS, Windows, a good-sized permanent Windows swap file, and some basic applications. In today's market, though, a 100M drive costs more per megabyte than a larger unit.

Other factors also affect your decision of which hard drive size is ideal for a networked workstation. The type of work being done, the applications used, backup procedures, and the security of the data files all must be considered. Once the decision is made, however, it may be necessary to augment or replace the hard disk drives in some older or under-powered workstations, for reasons of increased capacity, increased speed, or even drive failure. The following sections examine some of the hard drive technologies that might be found in various workstations, paying particular attention to the ATA interface (also known as IDE), which is unquestionably the most popular workstation hard disk drive interface in use today. We also explore the latest enhancements to this interface that are contributing greatly to its speed and versatility. Unlike some older technologies, ATA hard drive upgrades are easy to perform, and the units can readily be moved to other machines when necessary. With this knowledge, a LAN administrator should be able to configure workstations to the needs of their users in a simple and economical manner.

Older Technologies: ST-506/ST-412. The original IBM PC had no hard drive storage capabilities built into the machine. BASIC was loaded from ROM and the typical program of the time could be stored on a small part of a low-density floppy disk, an audio cassette tape, or even typed in via the keyboard whenever it was needed. Even the XT had no inherent hard disk drive support, but the Seagate ST-506 and ST-412 hard drives began to be included in machines soon after this model's introduction.

The ST-506 was a 5M drive and the ST-412 held 10M, formatted. The interface used a separate controller on an expansion card that also contained its own BIOS, for the original XT BIOS had no support for hard disk drives. Later models such as the first AT machines did support hard drives on the system BIOS, in which case the controller's BIOS could be disabled or used in tandem with that of the system board. The controller was connected to the hard disk drive itself by two cables, a 20-pin data cable and a 34-pin control cable. In cases where two disk drives were installed into one machine, the control cable was daisy-chained from one drive to the other, but two separate data cables were used, one connecting each drive directly to the controller.

Other drives with greater capacities and using different encoding schemes were made available by Seagate and other, now defunct, drive manufacturers, but the interface became a *de facto* industry standard and was usually referred to by the name of its original progenitors. The capacity of drives using this technology is extremely limited. Drives using *modified frequency modulation* (MFM) *encoding* held up to 152M, and those using *run length limited* (RLL) *encoding* could store up to 233M. Although drives like these are sometimes referred to by the abbreviations MFM and RLL, these are only the methods by which binary data is encoded on the magnetic medium. The names have no connection to any particular drive interface. Indeed, most drives today still use RLL encoding, regardless of their interface type.

In today's workplace, the ST-506/ST-412 interface is completely obsolete. There is no market for new equipment using this interface, due to its slow performance (by today's standards), limited capacity, and the possibility of data corruption during communications between the controller and the hard disk drive. Although it was utilized by the first AT machines, many later 286-based clones had progressed to the point where they contained drives using the ATA interface that is prevalent today. If you are running machines that use ST-506 type drives, and they are functioning satisfactorily, they can be used as is until they fail. It is recommended that they not be touched except to completely remove them from the system and discard them. In cases of network workstations like XTs and ATs that use this technology, you will probably achieve greater performance levels by relying on the network for hard drive storage, and abandoning the local drive for everything except use as a boot device and for the OS.

ESDI. The *enhanced small device interface* (*ESDI*) was developed by Maxtor Corporation as a successor to the ST-506 standard. Utilizing the same cabling system as the earlier standard, as well as the concept of separating the controller from the drive, ESDI offered greater speeds and larger capacities, leading it to be a popular drive type for network servers in the late 1980s (see chapter 5, "The Server Platform," for more information on ESDI drives). As with the ST-506 interface, though, it is not used at all today in new installations, having been eclipsed by the low prices and increased efficiency of the ATA interface in the workstation market and by the greater capacity and versatility of SCSI in servers.

SCSI. The history and architecture of the *small computer systems interface* is covered in depth in chapter 5, "The Server Platform." The exact same hardware used in a server can also be installed in a workstation, usually with considerably more ease, as special server software drivers are not necessary. A SCSI subsystem running only hard disk drives can operate on a workstation using no software support beyond the BIOS on the SCSI host adapter. The use of other devices will require additional drivers, however.

Usually, cost prevents the use of SCSI in a workstation. A SCSI host adapter costs considerably more than an IDE interface because it is a considerably more complex mechanism. The growing popularity of Enhanced IDE (covered later in this chapter) and its ability to support virtually all of the features that have made SCSI the choice for high-end workstations in the past, is also making SCSI a less popular workstation alternative. In fact, the virtually identical construction of IDE and SCSI hard drives (except for SCSI's more complicated controller apparatus) often leads to the selection of IDE as the solution with less processing overhead.

The sole exception to this preference may be in the case of a workstation containing multiple devices that will be heavily used in a preemptive multitasking environment, such as Windows NT, Windows 95, or OS/2. SCSI's ability to simultaneously process multiple requests to different devices may make it the interface of choice in this case. For a networked workstation, though, this is likely to be a comparatively rare case, as it is usually more efficient to place such extensive resources on the network, rather than on a workstation. For this reason, the bulk of this section will be devoted to the IDE interface, which is most prevalent today.

IDE. By a substantial margin, the most popular hard disk drive interface in use today in the PC world is known as *integrated drive electronics* (*IDE*). This term, however, does not define a specific interface standard. It is used to refer to any hard drive whose controller has been integrated into the drive mechanism itself, forming a single unit. By combining the two, compatibility is guaranteed because they are manufactured by the same company. An IDE drive unit can also utilize any innovative communications techniques that the manufacturer cares to develop as a protected and proprietary standard because the two units operate as a closed system. Many of the more advanced features found in hard disk drives today, such as defect handling, error recovery, cache management, and power management require full integration of the controller with the various components of the disk drive itself. In the absence of a highly detailed standard outlining the implementation of such features, it would be virtually impossible to achieve any measure of compatibility between controllers and hard drives made by different manufacturers. In addition, communications between the controller and the hard drive are far more efficient with IDE because the distance that the signals must travel is greatly reduced, and the potential for cable interference between the two is eliminated.

The most common implementation of the IDE drive type is defined by the *AT attachment* (*ATA*) standard. Work began on the ATA standard in 1988, although some IDE drives had already been in use for several years. The standard defined the configuration of the 40-pin connector cable still used today, the 16-bit connection to the AT ISA bus as well as the BIOS support by which these drives are recognized by the host computer. Other IDE bus types exist, among them an 8-bit XT IDE and a 16-bit MCA IDE. The MCA type uses a 72-pin connector, and the XT uses a 40-pin connector, but the pinouts for both types are not compatible with the ATA standard. Although useful as replacements for the specific machines that utilized them, both of these interfaces are obsolete today, having been overshadowed by the ATA standard.

The AT Attachment Standard. As with the SCSI bus standards covered in chapter 5, "The Server Platform," the ATA standard defines a great number of drive capabilities, many of which are optional. The earliest model IDE drives were, in fact, existing hard drive units with a controller bolted to them that was little different from the standard ST-506 type. They used a simple command set comprised of eight different instructions and addressed specific locations on the drive through the use of direct references to the cylinders, heads, and sectors on the drive that was being referenced. This became known as *CHS addressing*. The concept is still in use today and has given rise to some significant problems in the development of IDE technology, as we will see later. Drives such as these are known as *nonintelligent IDE drives* because they lack support for the optional features defined in the ATA standard.

The standard also defines the cable that is used to connect the IDE drive to the host adapter, which may exist on an ISA expansion card or be integrated onto the motherboard. The cable uses 40-pin connectors and is keyed by the removal of pin 20 and the plugging of the corresponding pinhole to prevent the cable from being attached in an upside-down position. In most cases, dual drive installations are daisy-chained using a single cable that runs from the host adapter to each drive in turn. Of the 40 connections, seven are designated as grounds, which are interspersed among the other signals to provide some isolation. Of the other connections, 16 are devoted to data and another 16 to control functions. The *key pin*, number 20, makes up the remainder of the connection (the key pin is actually a nonconnection).

One of the other basic requirements of the ATA standard defines a maximum of two drives on a single host adapter. Unlike a SCSI configuration, in which an intelligent host adapter sends instructions to a specified device on the bus, both devices on an ATA hard drive installation receive all commands from the system BIOS or OS. It is up to the drives themselves to know whether a specific command is intended for their own execution. To make this possible, the two drives are differentiated by one being designated as drive 0 and the other as drive 1. These two addresses are often referred to as *master* and *slave,* respectively, but this terminology has been officially supplanted by the authors of the ATA spec—the two are also referred to as *primary* and *secondary* drives. Although it has become customary to run the cable from the host adapter to the secondary drive first, and then to the primary drive, this is not required (see fig. 6.2).

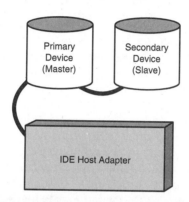

This is the IDE master-slave relationship.

The configuration of each drive is accomplished most often through the use of DIP switches on the hard drive assembly; the switches represent settings for single drive operation, drive 0 or drive 1. These settings are followed irrespective of the drive's location on the cable in relation to the host adapter. In some cases, a special cable in a Y-configuration is used in combination with a signal on pin 28 of the connector named *CSEL* (*cable select*). This cable allows this signal to pass through one branch of the Y, designating this drive as the primary, while suppressing it on the other, indicating that drive as the secondary. In either case, both hard drives receive all commands from the host adapter indiscriminately, and based upon their configuration, either act upon or ignore each command as it arrives.

In the early days of IDE drives, this addressing technique caused some compatibility problems, especially when two drives made by different manufacturers were installed in the same system. This was because no standard for the configuration of IDE drives existed. Once the ATA specification began to be followed, however, this problem was virtually eliminated. Drives manufactured today should be able to coexist with any other modern IDE drive conforming to the ATA specification. In fact, the installation of a second IDE drive in a PC today should consist of nothing more than setting the primary and secondary attributes, physically mounting the drive unit in the computer case, connecting the power and data cables, and entering the proper values into the system BIOS.

As the technology of IDE drives matured, they began to use more and more of the optional features defined in the specification. The most useful options that were added by most manufacturers were support for enhanced commands beyond the basic set of eight and sector translation. Drives that could make use of these features became known as *intelligent IDE drives.*

Enhancements to the IDE Command Set. Once IDE hard drives were marketed that supported the enhanced commands outlined in the ATA specification, the interface reached new heights of performance and convenience. These commands are present in the original ATA specification and are not to be confused with the Enhanced IDE standard now promulgated by Western Digital as a further development of ATA technology. (See the "Enhanced IDE" section, later in this chapter, for more details.)

Possibly the most useful of the new commands adopted by most manufacturers is the Identify Drive command. Sending this command to the drive causes the drive to return the contents of a 512-byte block containing extensive information about its capabilities, including the number of cylinders, heads, and sectors it uses, the drive manufacturer and model, the buffer scheme, the firmware revision, and even the serial number of the drive. While many utilities are available that can send this command to a hard drive and display the results, its most conspicuous use is in the system BIOS, which can use the information to automatically configure the computer's CMOS settings for that hard drive. This can be a lifesaver should a CMOS or battery failure lose existing settings. In a network environment with dozens (or hundreds) of computers, this is certainly handier than having to maintain records of configuration data for each machine, particularly when most hard drives on the market today do not conform to one of the 46 standard BIOS configurations.

From a pure performance standpoint, the Read Multiple and Write Multiple commands are the most valuable additions to the IDE instruction set. These commands allow for transfers of data that span across multiple sectors utilizing only a single interrupt. In combination with the system's block mode *programmed input/output (PIO)* capabilities, this essentially amounts to the equivalent of a burst mode that provides much faster data transfers than were possible using older drive technologies. PIO can be defined as any data transfer that is accomplished with the use and cooperation of the system's micro-processor. It is basically the antithesis to DMA (direct memory access) mode, which performs the same functions using a separate controller, located on a host adapter or on the motherboard, rather than the main system processor. These terms will come into play again when we discuss the new Enhanced IDE specifications that extend the capabilities of these transfer modes.

Sector Translation. As stated earlier, IDE drives use a CHS addressing scheme that is able to pinpoint any location on a hard drive by numbering the cylinders, heads, and sectors present in the drive. The original IDE drives were configured by simply entering the actual number of cylinders, heads, and sectors into the CMOS registers of the system BIOS. Thus, the same addressing scheme was used by the BIOS interface, located at software interrupt 13 (INT 13h), as was used at the device interface. This became known as operating the drive in *raw physical mode,* or sometimes as *physical CHS (P-CHS) addressing.*

In today's ATA drives, however, all sector addresses used by the host adapter are based on *logical CHS (L-CHS) addressing.* They have no relationship to the actual physical position of the sector on the drive's platters or to the position of the heads! This is because today's drives operate in *translation mode,* which causes the CHS address used at the INT 13h interface (the L-CHS) to be different from that used at the device interface (the P-CHS). This mode was realized primarily to protect the vital sectors of the drive from being overwritten during a low-level format. It is implemented simply by altering the numbers that are entered into the system BIOS so that the resulting product remains the same.

Cylinders×Heads×Sectors=Total Drive Sectors

For example, halving the number of cylinders while doubling the number of heads results in a product that is equal to that computed from the original physical CHS settings—the total number of sectors is the same. As long as the hard drive unit can translate between two address schemes in both directions, the system will function. Thus, with today's IDE drives, the figures specified by the drive manufacturer for entry into the system BIOS table as well as the figures furnished by the Identify Drive command have absolutely nothing to do with the physical geometry of the drive. Every time an address location is sent through the host adapter to the hard drive, a translation occurs. The actual physical properties of the drive are completely isolated from every other part of the computer.

IDE drives are *low-level formatted* at the factory. This process outlines the tracks and sectors of the drive by writing over the entire surface of the disk. It also incorporates the configuration settings of several important drive features into data that are meant to be permanently stored on the drive. With earlier drive types, features such as *head interleave* and *head and cylinder skew* had to be manually configured by the user in order to optimize the performance of the drive. In addition, the inevitable defective blocks found on the platters during configuration at the factory would be manually noted on a sticker attached to the unit. These bad blocks had to be manually entered into a defect table before the drive would be completely reliable. With IDE drives, however, all these elements are preset at the factory during the low-level formatting process, and their configuration parameters are stored on the drive in protected areas. When a system BIOS is configured to address the drive in raw physical mode, the performance of a low-level format by the user erases the interleave and skew settings as well as the defect table from the drive. These items can be re-created, most often through the use of specialized utilities available from the drive manufacturer, but considerable effort is required, with virtually no benefit gained in the process. When running in translation mode, a low-level format cannot overwrite these elements.

This has led to the mistaken belief by many users that performing a low-level format on an IDE drive will result in irreparable damage to the unit, and that it must be returned to the factory to be properly reformatted. This is not true, but there is no real reason to have to perform a low-level format on an IDE drive. It should be noted that a low-level format does not refer to the functions performed by the DOS FORMAT and FDISK utilities—these are high-level operations. Low-level formats are only performed by other disk utilities, some commercially available (such as Microscope or Spinrite) and others distributed by drive manufacturers specifically for use with their drives.

Sector translation, therefore, is a means of protecting the vital configuration settings of an IDE drive from accidental erasure, and insulating the end user from the need to worry about minutiae involved in the mechanical operation of hard disk drives. It has, however, led to some compatibility problems that were not even remotely anticipated by the original developers of system BIOSs, hard drives, and the ATA specification.

IDE Drive Limitations. The ATA standard allows for an IDE hard drive unit to have up to 65,535 cylinders, 16 heads, and 63 sectors. What this all means is that up to 2^{28} total sectors or 137G of storage can be addressed. The logical CHS addressing used by the system BIOS at the INT 13h interface uses two 16-bit registers, referred to as DX and CX, for each address. These are broken down as follows:

- The DX register uses eight bits to specify the head number and eight bits for the drive number.

- The CX register uses 10 bits to specify the cylinder number and six bits for the sector number.

The largest possible eight-bit number is 255, the largest 10-bit number is 1,023, and the largest six-bit number is 63. Therefore, the BIOS is limited in its addressing to 1,024 cylinders (0–1,023), 256 heads (0–255), and 63 sectors (1–63), thus supporting drives of up to 8G in capacity.

Unfortunately, the ATA specification's maximum of 16 heads, in combination with the 1,024 cylinder maximum of the INT 13h interface, results in a maximum capacity for a single IDE hard disk drive of

1,024 cylinders×16 heads×63 sectors=1,032,192
1,032,192 sectors×512 bytes/sector=528,482,304 bytes=504M

Please note that this is not in any way a hardware limitation but is simply an unfortunate clash of two software specifications. Note also that the INT 13h interface uses an eight-bit value for the head number, resulting in a maximum value of 255. This excess (since no drive has 255 physical heads) has been used to implement different translation schemes for other drive types, like ESDI and SCSI, that allow drives up to 8G in size to be addressed. Meanwhile, the 504M IDE drive size limitation, while considered to be an astronomical amount of storage to the original developers of these specifications, has become a real disadvantage in the modern computing world. This and the limitation of the interface to only two hard disk devices, as well as the inability to support other types of peripherals such as tape and CD-ROM drives, has led to the formation of several different committees attempting to expand the capabilities of the ATA interface. The following sections examine some of the ways in which these limitations are being addressed by products already on the market today, and take a look at the standardization efforts currently under way to expand the capabilities of the ATA interface even further.

Enhanced IDE. Enhanced IDE is actually no more than a marketing campaign by the Western Digital Corporation for a line of products that expand the capabilities of the ATA interface. Seagate Technologies has a similar program in place, which it refers to as Fast ATA, and as both are quite new, it remains to be seen which of the two (if either) will ultimately take control of the market. Enhanced IDE, however, is more expressive of the industry's attempts to improve more than just the speed of the interface.

The question at this point isn't whether or not to embrace this technology; it's here. If you purchase a new system today, it almost certainly includes some kind of enhancements to the ATA interface. If you buy a Seagate or a Western Digital IDE drive, it is a Fast ATA or Enhanced IDE drive. Attaching it to an existing system without any other modifications allows the device to function according to the existing ATA standard because all the hardware is fully backward compatible.

The problem is that because no specific standards have been ratified yet, a product can be called Enhanced IDE, EIDE, or Fast ATA if it possesses just one of the several features that are generally accepted to define the technology. Also needing to be considered is the matter of which of these features can be supported by an existing PC. Enhanced IDE is both a hardware and a software solution. Nearly all machines can take advantage of at least one of the improvements provided by Enhanced IDE, but for the upgrade to be economically worthwhile, a greater degree of compatibility should be desired. The following sections examine the features that are provided by the various standards, and then discuss how to implement them in existing machines.

ATA Enhancements. Enhanced IDE can be defined as a system providing any combination of the following features:

- Support for hard disk drives larger than 504M

- Support for twin connectors allowing the attachment of up to four devices

- Support for non-hard disk drive peripherals, such as CD-ROM and tape drives

- Support for the high-speed PIO mode 3 or DMA mode 1 data transfers specified by the ATA-2 standard

These features require varying degrees of support from the host adapter, BIOS, OS, and peripheral devices to function properly. Table 6.3 illustrates which of the components of a PC require modification to accommodate each of these features. We then examine each one in turn, discussing how each is accomplished and what hardware or software changes are required to implement it.

Table 6.3   Hardware and Software Support Required for IDE Enhancements

Features	Peripherals	Host Adapter	BIOS	Operating System
>504M	Yes	No	Yes	Yes, except DOS
Fast Data Transfers	Yes	Yes	Yes	Yes
Dual Host Adapters	No	Yes	Yes	Yes
Non-HDD Devices	Yes	Yes	Yes	Yes

Host Adapter and BIOS support are considered separately, though both may be supplied by the same expansion card.

Breaking the 504M Barrier. Having examined the cause for the 504M IDE drive capacity limitation, we now will cover the various means by which it can be transcended. Given the sector translation that already takes place inside modern hard drives, increasing the maximum capacity allowed is basically a matter of altering the translation algorithm so that one of the limiting factors is modified. This can be done in several ways.

The most immediately obvious solution is one that has already been exploited by SCSI host adapters for some time. Although an ATA-compatible disk drive has only four bits dedicated to the head address, for a maximum value of 16, the INT 13h interface has six or eight bits that can be devoted to this purpose. Because a sector translation is already taking place, and the values entered into the BIOS do not reflect the physical geometry of the drive, it is a fairly simple matter to alter the BIOS settings in order to increase the possible value of the head address. Of course, one of the other parameters must be decreased by the same factor so that the total number of sectors (that is, the product of cylinders×heads×sectors) remains the same. When a call is then made to the hard drive, the translation algorithm that is executed within the unit has to be changed to accommodate the altered addresses furnished by the BIOS.

For the hard drive, this is simply a modification of a translation procedure that is taking place already in another form. At the other end, however, things become a bit more difficult. Support for the modified addressing scheme must be provided by the system BIOS and, in some cases, the OS. While BIOS manufacturers have, over the years, added greater functionality in the form of features such as automatic hard drive detection and other utilities of various types, the basic functionality of the BIOS has changed little since the introduction of the AT in the 1980s. Support for drives larger than 504M must be added eventually to the system BIOS of the average PC, but it will be difficult to overcome the complacency of this particular branch of the industry and persuade them to agree on a standard implementation to be followed by all.

In the interim, support for these devices can be provided by the use of either software drivers or an additional BIOS that replaces the functionality of the original system BIOS. As an alternative, a software solution might occur in the form of a driver that resides in one of the disk boot sectors, overriding the INT 13h BIOS with one that supports the modified translation. This usually is accomplished by having the driver utilize two of the unused bits from the head address for addition to the cylinder address, thus increasing the maximum value of this setting. At the peripheral side, the same basic process is used to "borrow" two bits from the cylinder address and "lend" them to the head address. The result is support for drives up to 8.4G in size.

Other drivers may accomplish the same end in a different manner, for there is as yet no standardized protocol for the design of these drivers. Such drivers may be supplied by the disk drive manufacturer or may be a third-party product such as OnTrack's Disk Manager. The other problem is that, while this procedure may be satisfactory for DOS-based systems, protected-mode OSs often overwrite the memory resident driver when loading their kernel. This is because these drivers are loaded very near the beginning of the boot process, modifying the *master boot record* (MBR) of the hard drive and storing a dynamic drive overlay on the first disk track in order to allow the system to be booted from a supported device. If an OS, in loading itself and shifting from real to protected mode, overwrites the modified MBR, then access to the drive's partitions is lost unless another driver is provided specifically for the use of that OS.

Even the Windows 32-bit Disk Access feature will not function with this sort of driver, requiring a replacement for the standard *WDCTRL driver. This can become quite a complex array of drivers, especially for systems that are used in a multiple-boot configuration to accommodate various OSs. Also, this kind of driver has no function other than to provide access to drives larger than 504M in size. It does not support any of the other IDE enhancements.

The BIOS-based solution to breaking the 504M barrier is no more standardized than the software solution but is usually more effective. Several manufacturers have developed different solutions to the same problem. The closest thing to a standard is found in the Microsoft/IBM *INT 13 Extensions* document, but Phoenix has created what is essentially a superset of this specification that has been adopted for use by several of the best-known BIOS vendors, including Phoenix, AMI, and Award. Another implementation developed by Western Digital seems to be trailing behind these other specifications in popularity— it is reputed to be flawed and lacking in features found in the other BIOSs mentioned.

A standard system BIOS maintains a *fixed disk parameter table (FDPT)* that contains a single set of CHS addressing information. An enhanced BIOS functions by constructing, when necessary, an *enhanced disk parameter table (EDPT)* that contains two sets of CHS addressing information. This is the reference point through which the address translation takes place. Another type of translation may also be supported by an enhanced BIOS, named *logical block addressing (LBA)*. This is a completely different form of sector addressing that abandons the traditional cylinder/head/sector divisions in favor of a single address that is used to number each sector of the hard drive consecutively. Support for this type of addressing was first introduced to the IDE world as part of the ATA-2 standard, but it has always been utilized by SCSI. In order to be utilized, both the BIOS and the disk drive must support it.

Since most OSs generate their disk access requests using LBA addressing, it would be logical to assume that this is the preferred mode of operation. It is likely that within a few years, this will be the case. Because a layer of conversion overhead is being removed, it should follow that performance levels will be slightly increased. This is not always true, however. First of all, DOS, its FDISK utility, and the master boot record are all CHS-based, so support for some type of CHS-to-LBA translation will have to be provided, and because this conversion is generally slower and more complex than an L-CHS–to–P-CHS translation, additional overhead actually may be added. Second, the developers of ATA-compatible hard disk drive designs have spent many years optimizing their CHS translation procedures. LBA is relatively new to them, and drive performance levels might be reduced as a result, at least until drive designs using the technology have had some time to mature.

Determining whether or not the system BIOS of a particular machine supports the extended translation capabilities can sometimes be difficult. A BIOS that allows the specification of more than 1,024 cylinders in the CMOS table is not conclusive. Any BIOS with a copyright date prior to 1994 almost certainly does not include these capabilities, which eliminates a great many of even the newer machines on the market. In my experience, a surprisingly large number of computer manufacturers rely on BIOSs that are several years old, even in their higher-end machines.

Extended translation capabilities are most likely to be found in the products of the more popular BIOS manufacturers. An AMI BIOS dated April 24, 1995, or later and Phoenix BIOSs with version numbers of 4.03 or later should support IDE drives larger than 504M, although exceptions may be found. Disk drive settings such as "LBA," "ECHS," or even "Large" are also indications that a BIOS supports these drives. Some drive manufacturers have made utilities available that query a BIOS for the existence of an EDPT.

While support for these various types of sector translation will eventually be included in the system BIOS of every PC, they are available today primarily as BIOS implementations on the Enhanced IDE adapter cards that are designed to support some or all of the features discussed in this section. The BIOSs on these cards function much in the same way as those on SCSI host adapters, replacing or augmenting only the hard disk functionality of the system BIOS.

In the case of products that support several different types of extended translation, it is important first to be sure that your ATA peripherals all support the type of addressing that you select in the BIOS. It is important second to remember that once you have selected a particular translation mode, partitioned the drive, and installed your software, this setting should not be changed. Your existing data will not only be inaccessible but may also be corrupted beyond any hope of recovery. The same warning holds true with drives that have been partitioned and formatted using a BIOS that does not support extended translation. Although such drives have been transferred successfully to a machine with an EIDE-equipped BIOS, it is usually necessary to completely repartition and reformat the drive and then restore its files from a backup. Always make backups before attempting a transfer of this type. This technology is too new to guarantee this kind of compatibility.

In addition to BIOS support, it also is necessary to install additional drivers for most protected-mode OSs. For instance, Windows' 32-bit Disk Access feature (also known as FastDisk) will not function with BIOSs of this type without modification. This feature is named somewhat inaccurately, as it does not have anything to do with 32-bit transfers. This driver essentially replaces the disk access routines of the BIOS with Windows' own routines that operate in protected mode. DOS sessions within Windows cannot utilize virtual memory without this driver, requiring 640K of actual RAM for each one, and its presence also reduces the number of switches that have to be made between real and protected mode, offering a modest performance improvement.

Most manufacturers of Enhanced IDE host adapters have begun to include with their products a replacement for the *WDCTRL driver that provides this feature in the basic Windows environment. This driver is usually a file with a 386 extension that is loaded from the Windows SYSTEM.INI file. Incidentally, the *WDCTRL driver that ships with

Windows is also incapable of functioning with SCSI drives, more than two hard drives, 32-bit host bus transfers, block transfers, or non-hard disk IDE peripherals—several reasons why you may want to replace this driver with an enhanced version.

Fast Data Transfers. The ATA specifications define several different data transfer modes for both PIO and DMA modes. As stated earlier, the difference between these two is that the PIO modes utilize the system's microprocessor as an intermediary between the disk drive and system memory, while the DMA modes utilize a separate controller for arbitration and data transfers. PIO modes 0 through 2, as outlined in table 6.4, are defined in the original ATA specification. Modes 3 and 4 were added in the ATA-2 standard, utilizing the IORDY signal for hardware flow control to slow down the interface when necessary.

Table 6.4   PIO Data Transfer Modes Defined in the ATA and ATA-2 Specifications

PIO Mode	Data Cycle Time (ns)	Transfer Rate (M/sec)	Bus Type
0	600	3.3	ISA
1	383	5.2	ISA
2	240	8.3	ISA
3	180	11.1	VLB or PCI
4	120	16.6	VLB or PCI

The transfer rates are arrived at by multiplying the data cycle time (the time it takes to transfer one word, or 16 bits, of data) by the number of words per sector (256) by the number of sectors per megabyte (2,048).

DMA transfers can be separated into two distinct types: bus mastering and non-bus mastering. Both require more hardware than the PIO modes: a DMA arbitration unit, a DMA transfer unit, and signals from the system bus that allow the DMA controller to assume command of the bus. The difference between the two types is primarily in the location of the DMA controller. A non-bus mastering system utilizes the DMA controller located on the motherboard of the computer. The efficiency of the system is therefore dependent on the bus type used in the machine. The DMA controller on ISA systems is far too outdated and slow to achieve any of the faster transfer rates, and VLB systems are incapable of acting as DMA targets. The EISA and PCI buses, however, both have their own higher-speed DMA transfer modes defined in their specifications, providing transfer speeds of up to 4M/sec for EISA and 6 to 8M/sec for PCI.

For any bus type, though, better performance can be realized through a bus mastering host adapter, in which the DMA controller resides on the expansion card itself, resulting in less communications overhead and better integration with the rest of the system. This, of course, adds to the complexity and cost of the host adapter. As with PIO, the initial DMA modes—single-word modes 0 and 1, and multiword mode 0—were defined in the original ATA specification, while single-word mode 2 and multiword modes 1 and 2 were added in the ATA-2 document. Table 6.5 identifies the various modes available and their transfer rates.

Table 6.5 DMA Data Transfer Modes Defined in the ATA and ATA-2 Specifications

DMA Mode	Cycle Time (ns)	Transfer Rate (M/sec)	Bus Type Required
Single Word			
0	960	2.1	ISA
1	480	4.2	ISA
2	240	8.3	PCI
Multiword			
0	480	4.2	ISA
1	150	13.3	PCI
2	120	16.6	PCI

Enhanced IDE products usually provide support for PIO modes 3 or 4 and DMA modes 1 or 2, in addition to the slower modes for backward compatibility. Unfortunately, the exact modes supported by individual products vary. This is one of the differences between the Seagate Fast ATA specification and the Western Digital Enhanced IDE specification, for example. Enhanced IDE calls for support of all four of the higher-speed modes added in the ATA-2 standard, while Fast ATA only defines support for PIO mode 3 and DMA mode 1. In case you aren't confused enough, Seagate also has defined a *Fast ATA-2* standard, which incorporates PIO mode 4 and multiword DMA mode 2 into its specification (again, nomenclature here is not as accurate as it might be: this standard must accurately be thought of as [Fast ATA]-2, rather than Fast [ATA-2]).

Currently, the higher-speed PIO modes are more widely supported by available hardware than the DMA modes, although this situation will change, as advanced DMA support surely will become more prevalent. Notice, however, that the fastest modes of both types run at the same speed, 16.6M/sec, and although this is nowhere near the actual throughput that you will receive, either one is far faster than the 3.3M/sec of traditional IDE. For use with DOS and Windows 3.1, DMA transfers offer little real advantage over PIO, as the system processor has to wait for the transfer to be completed anyway before proceeding to the next task. When running a preemptive multitasking OS, however—such as OS/2, Windows 95, or Windows NT—the processor can execute other tasks while transfers are occurring, giving DMA a definite advantage over PIO. Whatever the mode used by an Enhanced IDE system, however, it must be supported by both the drive and the host adapter. The failure of one of the devices to support a given mode causes the transfer rate to drop to the fastest mode supported by both devices.

The question of whether or not a particular computer can support the higher-speed transfer modes is, for once, a simple one. In short, any computer with a PCI or VLB slot for the installation of an ATA-2 host adapter (or a motherboard with the components integrated) can support the higher speeds, and other machines cannot. These host adapters may provide other advantages as well, including 32-bit transfers on the system bus, which require FIFO logic and data buffers on the host adapter. As with the higher-capacity drives previously discussed, additional drivers for particular OSs may be needed to take advantage of the increased transfer speeds in certain environments. A FastDisk replacement for Windows 3.1 definitely is needed.

It is also necessary for an ATA-2 host adapter to have access to IRQ 14 to function properly. Some early PCI systems did not include IRQ 14 on the local bus slots, and most today only provide it on one of the PCI slots. If you are forced to use a slot that does not have access to IRQ 14, it is necessary to use a paddle card in an ISA slot to provide it. A *paddle card* is a separate expansion card—attached to the host adapter by a ribbon cable—that plugs into another slot to take advantage of attributes not provided by the slot in which the host adapter is installed. This problem does not exist in VLB machines.

One of the common misbeliefs regarding Enhanced IDE is that two devices installed on a single connector can run only as fast as the speed of the slower device—for example, that a drive capable of running in PIO mode 4 is slowed down to PIO mode 0 when a second drive is installed that supports only the latter mode. This is not the case, as long as the interface provides the proper support. The Identify Drive command defined in the ATA-2 specification can provide the host adapter with the maximum transfer rates supported by each device, and as long as the interface supports independent timing for the two devices, such a slowdown does not occur.

As with any consideration of an interface between a hard disk drive and the rest of the computer, the transfer speeds specified by manufacturers rarely provide any indication of real-life performance. Remember that no matter how fast an interface is, it cannot improve the capabilities of the drive itself. A local bus IDE interface might already provide sufficient bandwidth to accommodate the capabilities of the installed hard drives, without the need for the enhanced transfer modes. In a case like this, the installation of a new host adapter yields little or no perceivable improvement in disk performance. An IDE interface running over the ISA bus, however, rarely exceeds 2.5M/sec, in which case a bottleneck probably exists that will be eliminated by the use of an enhanced host adapter running over the local bus.

With any IDE hard drive upgrade or addition performed today, the primary concern is to try to pay only for the features that the host system can take advantage of or to try to take advantage of all of the features provided. Most of the hard drives on the market today provide support for one or more of the high-speed DMA or PIO transfer modes. A computer with only an ISA bus will not be able to operate the drive in any of these modes but will have no difficulty running at the best possible ISA speed.

Non-Hard Disk Device Support. The ever-increasing storage needs of the average PC user and the rising popularity of the CD-ROM as a data delivery medium have made it necessary for the industry to provide an interface that can support devices such as tape and CD-ROM drives, as well as hard disk drives, without resorting to the higher costs of a SCSI installation. For a networked workstation, these capabilities might not be as essential as they would be for a stand-alone PC because backups and CD-ROM access can be provided by a server, but most implementations of the various Enhanced IDE specifications include support for such alternative devices, and they are rapidly becoming standard equipment in new computers marketed for stand-alone use.

This support is provided through a specification called the *ATA Packet Interface* (*ATAPI*). A separate specification is needed because the eight-bit task file used by hard disk drives is not large enough to support some of the required CD-ROM command structures. ATAPI devices use the ATA hardware interface at the physical level, but utilize a subset of the SCSI command set at the logical level. To prevent their being mistaken by non-ATAPI-aware software as a hard disk drive, the devices remain dormant until awakened by a special command sequence, at which point they begin to operate using a command protocol that is radically different from that used by hard drives.

While ATAPI remains compatible with and utilizes the existing eight-bit ATA task file, commands may also be sent to the target device by means of the ATAPI transport protocol in packets of at least 12 bytes, as data, through the data register. For compatibility reasons, certain ATA instructions, such as the Identify Drive and Read commands, are not executed and instead are aborted immediately, generating an interrupt to signal the completion of the command with an error status of "aborted." This is done deliberately, to prevent the BIOS and older drivers from mistaking the ATAPI device for a standard ATA hard disk drive. The standard also provides support for command overlapping, which is similar in basic functionality to SCSI disconnection, in that it allows a peripheral device to release its hold on the controller so that other tasks may be performed while a command is executed by the ATAPI device. This is necessary because of the nature of CD-ROM and tape drive commands such as REWIND, which take far longer to execute than do hard drive commands.

Due in part to this use of the data register for purposes other than those for which it was originally designed, support for ATAPI devices must be provided by every component of the Enhanced IDE system. A controller that is not ATAPI-aware will not know how to handle a 12-byte packet arriving over a register that is expected to transport only 512-byte sectors. BIOSs and OSs must also be aware of the difference and not attempt to utilize the device as if it were a hard disk drive. Finally, the peripheral itself must be modified to be used with an IDE interface, although since the command set used is essentially a subset of the SCSI command set, radical redesigns are not necessary in most cases. ATAPI support is nearly always provided in IDE host adapters that provide access to more than two devices, as covered in the next section.

Dual Host Adapters. In order to be competitive with the versatility and storage capacities offered by SCSI, it is necessary for Enhanced IDE to overcome the two-device limitation to which it has always been subjected. The ability to attach non-hard disk drives to the interface makes this feature all the more essential.

Actually, the basic capability to run dual IDE host adapters has been present in PCs for a long time. The PC I/O map reserves a port for a secondary IDE adapter at IRQ 15 and base address 170, and IDE host adapters have long been available that could be configured to use it. BIOS support has not been widely available, however. The innovation of Enhanced IDE, in this respect, is to provide this BIOS support and place dual host adapter connectors on a single expansion card (see fig. 6.3). Separate cables are used to connect two separate chains of two devices each. Separating the two chains in this manner can be particularly useful when troubleshooting problems that occur through the combination of different device types. Although the ATAPI specification specifically intends for non-HDD devices to be able to exist on the same cable as a hard drive, some of the more advanced hard disk interfaces have features that can confuse device drivers that are not ATAPI-aware. The ability to segregate a tape or CD-ROM drive on its own cable may be a more acceptable solution than waiting for a new driver to be written.

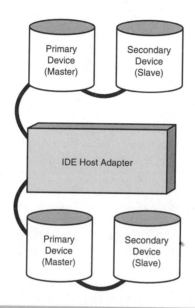

Figure 6.3

This is how an IDE dual host adapter installation looks.

Even on systems that lack a local bus interface, ISA expansion cards are available that provide support for up to four IDE devices, including non-hard disk drives. BIOS support for drives larger than 504M can also be provided. The faster PIO and DMA transfers specified in the ATA-2 specification are not available, but the availability of these products means that the storage capacity and versatility of almost any PC can be enhanced for a very modest cost (beyond the prices of the peripherals themselves).

The Future of Enhanced IDE. As you might readily imagine, after reading about the dearth of standards and specifications that make up Enhanced IDE technology, a great deal of work needs to be done to consolidate the many options available into a more coherent market structure. The physical installation of an Enhanced IDE subsystem is usually quite simple. The difficult part is the purchasing of products that will work together to provide all of the different features and enhancements that are expected of them. In nearly every problematic installation, however, access to the data on the drive will be provided. Troubleshooting Enhanced IDE usually amounts to answering questions like "Why am I not getting the 16M/sec transfers that I was promised?" or "Why does one particular method of sector addressing fail to work when the others do?"

The answer, in most cases, is that one of the vital components lacks the support for that particular feature, be it BIOS, host adapter, OS, or the peripheral itself. As the standards mature, support for all of the enhancements to the interface will become far more commonplace in most devices, and the need to investigate the capabilities of each component will diminish.

At the workstation level, a simple matter of adding an additional IDE hard disk drive should be just that: simple. It will only be the newer systems that require the fast transfer modes, and few networked PCs require more than two devices. Future plans for the ATA specification, however, include the possibility for command overlapping and other features that may allow Enhanced IDE to become a competitor in the server market as well. As it stands today, a small network could be adequately serviced by a file server using Enhanced IDE drives. A loss in performance will definitely be realized, though, in larger machines with multiple drives, as the ATA specs do not yet support the multitasking capabilities of SCSI. At the workstation, though, an important bottleneck is eliminated by the ATA-2 transfer modes when used in combination with a PCI or VLB interface. It is now up to the hard drive manufacturers to provide devices that can fill the bandwidth now made available by a fully featured Enhanced IDE storage system.

Network Interface Cards

The *network interface card* (*NIC*), also called a *LAN adapter*, is the gateway through which a stand-alone PC communicates with a LAN. Requests for access to network resources that are generated by the workstation's OS are fed to the NIC by the LAN drivers resident in the computer's memory. It is the NIC that converts these signals into packets of the proper format to be sent over the network. The packets are then sent to a transceiver, usually located on the NIC itself, which converts them from a digital format to an analog one that can be sent over the network medium. The NIC also monitors the transmissions traveling over the network medium, allowing the translated packets to pass from the workstation onto the LAN only when traffic conditions allow it. At the same time, it checks each transmission that passes by on the network to see whether it is destined for that workstation. If it is, the NIC intercepts the transmission and routes it to the OS, where it is processed as though the signal had originated within the workstation.

As with nearly every other component in a PC, NICs range from simple, inexpensive devices offering basic functionality for well under $100, to complex, high-performance units that can cost up to $1,000. Very often, a relatively low-priced NIC is perfectly adequate for the average network workstation.

The basis of computer networking is the communication that takes place between hardware devices on a great many levels. When a user at a workstation requests a file that is located on a server in the next room—or even the next state—the goal of the network administrator is to see that that file is delivered in the most efficient manner possible.

Bottlenecks rob the network of efficiency, and the NIC is one more location where bottlenecks can conceivably occur. As we have discussed in many other contexts, an improvement in the efficiency of a particular component is only needed when that component is the location of a bottleneck. A faster NIC will not provide any improvement if the desired file is stored on a slow hard drive, if the network itself is saturated with traffic, or if the workstation's bus is slow in delivering the data to the processor.

A selection of the correct NIC for a particular workstation must take into account not only the capabilities of the workstation itself but also the capabilities of the network. If you, as the administrator, have assigned available workstations to your users on the basis of their computing needs, then NIC selection should simply be an extension of those decisions. The biggest variable in the equation, however, as with all computing technology, is the question of what the needs of users will be in the future, and what solutions will be made available by the industry to satisfy them. The same advances that have led to the need for larger hard drives and more workstation memory have also placed a burden on networks, which may soon result in the need for a reassessment of the fundamental networking standards that have been sufficient for many years.

Upgrading or installing an entire network is, after all, a very different matter from adding a hard drive or even replacing an entire PC. You must consider whether or not the equipment that your network communications take place on are adequate for your company's needs, both now and several years from now. Chapter 7, "Major Network Types," examines the different network types in use today, as well as the new innovations that will most likely comprise the networks of tomorrow. The following sections do the same for NICs because NIC type and network type must be considered together if the administrator is to be forward thinking in his plans.

Two Interfaces. Since the basic function of a NIC is to be a gateway between the LAN and the workstation, the NIC must, by definition, interface with both of those resources. Therefore, there must be a connection to the workstation, usually in the form of a bus connector, as well as an interface with the LAN medium, usually in the form of a socket for a particular type of cable connector (see fig. 6.4).

Although NICs are available that interface with the workstation by plugging into a system's parallel or serial port, these are used mostly for portable computers that cannot easily support the insertion of any other kind of adapter. In virtually all other cases, a NIC is an expansion card that is connected to the computer by means of the system bus. In chapter 5, "The Server Platform," we discussed the various bus types available in PCs today—NICs are available for all those bus types, each card taking advantage of particular attributes that a certain bus provides. EISA and PCI adapters, for example, in most cases utilize the automatic configuration capabilities native to those buses, eliminating the need for manually specifying hardware parameters. ISA and VLB cards, on the other hand, might still have to be configured by the installer before they can be used.

System Bus Parameters. As with any expansion card plugged into the system bus, the computer must have some way of identifying and addressing the device. This usually is done by specifying unique interrupts and memory locations that will be used by both the card and its accompanying driver software. Early NICs used jumpers or DIP switches for this purpose. The manufacturer designed the card with a number of different IRQs and memory addresses hardwired into the device. Before the card was installed, jumpers had to be set to select particular parameters. Then the card was inserted into the slot, the computer was booted, and the driver software was configured to utilize the same settings. That way, when the OS generated network requests, they were intercepted by the driver, which routed them to the NIC according to the specified settings, and thereby to the network.

Figure 6.4

This is a typical network interface card.

Of course, if another device in the system happened to be using any of the same hardware settings, the NIC failed to function, and the other device likely failed as well. In this case, the entire process had to start over. The card had to be removed from the slot, different settings had to be chosen, and the installation had to be performed again. It might even happen that all the possible settings provided by the manufacturer resulted in some sort of conflict. In such cases, it was necessary to reconfigure another device to free up a resource that the NIC could utilize.

This process could easily end up with most of a PC disassembled, many different manuals consulted, and a great deal of time wasted. For the network administrator, this was unacceptable, primarily because there could be fifty other machines that needed to be taken through the same process. For this reason, most NICs manufactured today—indeed, most expansion cards in general—provide some means by which this process can be more efficiently completed.

As stated earlier, for EISA, PCI, and MCA cards, installation usually is a matter of simply plugging the card in the slot and then installing the drivers. At the workstation level, however, it usually is not practical, or even beneficial, to install higher-end NICs of these types. The demands of the average network user today do not warrant the performance levels they provide, and the average network does not supply the bandwidth needed for them to be fully utilized on every machine. Certainly, they are not worth purchasing simply for their ease of installation.

Most network workstations today can be adequately serviced by a NIC that uses the ISA bus. This bus, however, has no native features that support automatic configuration, so it has become necessary for individual manufacturers to develop ways to simplify the installation procedure for their products. Most ISA NICs today can configure both hardware and software through the use of a program that is supplied with the card. The program might be included on floppy disk or might be permanently installed in flash memory on the card itself. In either case, it is only necessary to insert the card into the slot once, after which all the parameters can be adjusted by the software. Different levels of interaction exist, as far as this software is concerned. Some cards can query the system themselves and determine the optimum settings without operator intervention, while others merely provide a menu-driven interface through which selections can be made. The difference, not surprisingly, is reflected in the price of the card.

One thing to remember when considering options like these is the number of systems that will have to be configured to utilize the cards that you purchase. If you have dozens of different machines that must be retrofitted for network use, highly-automated installation options are preferable. If you are installing NICs into a large number of identical new machines, however, the settings will be the same in every case, allowing you to resolve any hardware conflicts only once and simply duplicate the correct settings for all the other cards.

Another method of connecting a NIC to a workstation that has been considered by many PC manufacturers lately is the integration of the adapter circuitry onto the computer's motherboard itself. Advanced Micro Devices, for example, manufactures a single-chip, full-duplex Ethernet controller designed for integration onto motherboards. Several system vendors already offer this as an option, and although the basic philosophy is sound, I advise against purchasing systems of this type. Integrating any adapter onto the motherboard does reduce the distance that signals have to travel to reach the device and eliminates a good deal of the signal interference that may occur during a bus transfer. These advantages, though, are virtually imperceptible, and the other side of the coin is that you are locked into utilizing an adapter with features chosen by the system manufacturer. If the network is ever upgraded or modified to utilize a different medium, a new adapter must be installed into the machine, forcing the integrated unit to go to waste. The question also arises as to what different cable connectors will be made available (and how) by the manufacturer. A traditional expansion card can be relocated to a different machine or even purchased with future network upgrades in mind.

Another item to be considered is whether or not a particular NIC requires an area of memory to be reserved for its use. For some cards, it is necessary to exclude an area of upper memory from use by the workstation's memory manager or OS. This is memory that could otherwise be used to load device drivers or other TSRs high, freeing up more conventional memory for use by applications. This can be a significant factor for workstations that already will utilize an extensive amount of memory for network client software, and this should be considered when making purchasing decisions.

Network Connections. The other side of the gateway is, of course, the network connection. NICs can be purchased in models that provide sockets for all the network media currently in use. The most widely used network medium, by a substantial margin, is 10BaseT, which runs over UTP cable and utilizes standard RJ-45 connectors. Token-ring networks can also use this type of connector. Adapters are also available with BNC connectors for thinnet networks running over coaxial cable, 15-pin connectors for thicknet, and standard sockets for use with FDDI and other media.

Some NICs are sold with multiple connectors on a single expansion card. There is usually some means in the configuration software of selecting which connection is to be used, and this setting might have other effects on the card besides simply choosing a socket. The classic NE2000 card, for example, a very popular adapter manufactured by various companies for Novell, comes with a BNC connector for thinnet, as well as a 15-pin connector for thicknet. Selecting the 15-pin connector, however, not only causes that socket to be activated, but also deactivates the transceiver on the card because thicknet traditionally utilizes an external transceiver, while thinnet uses a transceiver on the NIC. This is one possible explanation for the virtual disappearance of thicknet in local area networking today.

There is very little to be gained by the user from the purchase of NICs with multiple connector types, unless a definite plan for a change in medium already exists. For example, if a network is located in a temporary space, it may be preferable to utilize thinnet, switching later to 10BaseT after a move to a more permanent location. In a case like this, NICs with a BNC and an RJ-45 connector may be worth purchasing. In any case, these NICs are usually manufactured that way as a cost-saving measure because it's cheaper in some cases to design, manufacture, and market a single card with two connectors, rather than two different cards.

Another type of dual-purpose network adapter that is becoming increasingly prevalent in today's market is the type that supports traditional 10 Mbps Ethernet as well as one of the new 100 Mbps Fast Ethernet standards. These new technologies are discussed in greater depth in chapter 7, "Major Network Types," but realize for now that NICs are available today that can automatically shift to a higher-speed mode when a concentrator supporting this mode is installed on the network, and the cable to the NIC is switched to an alternative socket. Other models do not even require the cable switch but instead auto-sense the different speeds. The workstation only has to be rebooted for the change from 10 Mbps to 100 Mbps to take effect. This allows for a gradual introduction of the new technology, thus providing sufficient time for testing and preventing downtime, while allowing the economic burden of such a project to be spread out over a longer period. Token-ring NICs have long been available that can shift between speeds of 4 Mbps and 16 Mbps, but this is the first time that a radically new network transport technology has been made available in such an efficient manner. Most other high-bandwidth alternatives now coming to market require a complete replacement of the network adapter, along with a lot of other hardware, such as hubs, switches, concentrators, and sometimes even the network cabling. For this reason alone, Fast Ethernet has a distinct edge on the competition.

Full Duplex Ethernet is another technology designed to speed up existing LAN connections. This concept essentially eliminates the need for the standard Ethernet CSMA/CD collision detection method, as two dedicated connections are provided for each adapter. Thus, workstations can send and receive data simultaneously, doubling the theoretical throughput of the LAN to 20 Mbps. Full Duplex Ethernet does not seem to be catching on with the rapidity of Fast Ethernet, but it remains to be seen which of these technologies will become the next dominant desktop standard. Indeed, the answer to this may even be both, as Full Duplex can be combined with Fast Ethernet to provide up to 200 Mbps speeds.

Also at the cutting edge of networking technology today are NICs that provide a wireless connection to the network. Utilized most often in laptops and other portables, NICs such as these utilize infrared or radio frequencies to establish a connection with the network. Drivers usually are provided that remain resident in memory, but lie dormant until the computer is carried within the network transceiver's effective range. At that time, the drivers become active, automatically attach the workstation to the network, and sometimes are even able to execute predefined tasks, such as downloading e-mail or updating databases. Technology of this type is still in its infancy, however, and well-defined standards do not yet exist. The wireless NICs on the market today function effectively with their network-based counterparts from the same manufacturer, but the universal connectability that has been realized by the more conventional NIC types is not yet available for wireless NICs. In addition, the performance levels of wireless NICs do not yet rival that of traditional wired LANs. The average wireless model generally performs data transfers at slightly more than half the speed of a 10BaseT connection, with rates diminishing dramatically as the host machine is moved farther away from the transmitting station.

Performance Features. When evaluating the various basic 10 Mbps Ethernet NICs on the market today, there is actually little difference between the various models, except for price. Most of the NICs utilize some form of the *parallel tasking* architecture pioneered by 3Com, a company that holds about 30 percent of the market share. Different manufacturers have different names for the process (SMC calls it *simultasking*), but the techniques are basically the same, allowing the NIC to transmit data onto the network before the entire packet has been received. Early NICs imposed delays by needing to wait until the entire packet had been transferred from the system bus to the NIC's buffers before transmission could begin.

Another technique that adds to the overall performance of a NIC is the presence of RAM on the card that can be used as a buffer when network traffic is high or when delays are imposed while the NIC waits for the proper time to transmit its data. 16K worth of SRAM is a fairly common configuration, but additional amounts of RAM (at an additional cost, of course) will contribute to better performance if your network is already heavily trafficked.

Bus mastering is also available on NICs that utilize the higher-speed system buses such as EISA, MCA, VLB, or PCI. This gives the NIC the ability to take control of the system bus to conduct data transfers without intervention from the computer's CPU. As with other bus mastering devices, however, you must be sure that the NIC is plugged into a slot that supports this feature. Very often a PC has several slots of a particular bus type, but not all of them are capable of bus mastering. You might also have difficulty purchasing machines that are capable of supporting several different bus mastering devices on the same bus, so a decision may have to be made as to whether the advantages of bus mastering are better devoted to a NIC or to another interface card, such as a SCSI or Enhanced IDE adapter.

In the same manner as the purveyors of SCSI and Enhanced IDE peripheral interfaces, NIC manufacturers are exploring the prospect of utilizing the PCI bus to improve the overall performance of their products. As with other interfaces, however, many of the products now available show signs of their relative newness, particularly in their drivers. There is a great amount of OEM activity in the NIC market. Cards based on the same chipsets are sold under many different names, offering varying price levels dependent on the presence of additional features such as drivers, technical support, and warranties.

Many different manufacturers even utilize the same drivers, and this has led to a recent situation in which several different PCI NICs all shipped with a driver that had been written in accordance with the wrong specification. PCI bus slots are designed to share interrupts, supposedly eliminating the need to perform any sort of manual hardware configuration. These drivers did not allow interrupts to be shared and did not function properly even when specific interrupts were assigned to specific slots. It was not until a new driver was written that conformed to the proper standard that the NICs could be made to function properly. Once this was accomplished, the NICs all performed admirably, but the fact that several different products actually shipped in this haphazard manner seems to indicate that the manufacturers are overly desperate to get their products to market to remain competitive, and quality-assurance standards are therefore given low priority. For the busy LAN administrator, it is usually preferable to wait until situations of this type are resolved by others before making any kind of serious commitment to a new technology. I do not doubt that PCI eventually will be the high-performance bus of preference—in NICs as well as other technologies—but I will wait until the products have made it through their initial growing pains before using them.

Another thing to be aware of is the tendency for some manufacturers to implement proprietary features that do not conform to accepted industry standards in their NICs. It can sometimes be difficult to determine when this is the case. You might have to wade through a great deal of "marketspeak" to find out what a flashy term really does, but it is important to find out. Some of the techniques that are touted as providing greater speed and enhanced performance might do just that, but they also might require that the same manufacturer's NICs be installed at both ends of the connection. Unless you are building a network from scratch, you want to avoid "features" such as these like the plague. Even if you are building a new network, the dangers of proprietary systems are the same as for any technology: if that manufacturer disappears, you might be stuck with unsupported hardware and no means of acquiring additional equipment.

Finally, you need to check on the driver support provided with the NICs that you decide to purchase. If you are running different OSs on your network, or if, like many users today, you are experimenting with the many new OSs coming to market in a multiple-boot environment, you want to make sure that drivers are readily available for all the OSs that you might ever use. Driver size is another consideration. As mentioned earlier in this section, equipping a PC with a network connection can require large amounts of system memory from either the conventional or upper memory areas. A well-written driver that requires only a small amount of RAM helps to optimize the performance of any network workstation.

Workstation NIC Selection. Obviously, the requirements of the individual user must determine the appropriate NIC for her workstation. Basic network services such as file access and printer sharing are adequately served by an ISA NIC connected to a standard Ethernet or token-ring network. People doing CAD, graphics, desktop publishing, or other network-intensive occupations will likely require better performance and can benefit from an EISA, VLB, or PCI NIC. Once you go beyond this into the realm of multimedia and videoconferencing, you rapidly approach the line at which the traditional network types are themselves insufficient, and a high-performance NIC alone will provide little improvement. At this time, it would be necessary to consider a more comprehensive upgrade program that will incorporate better NICs with an improved network infrastructure.

NICs are readily available that can easily accommodate all of these requirements. At this point, though, purchasing decisions begin to stretch beyond the world of the individual workstation. Quantity pricing, hardware standardization, and future network development strategies should all be taken into account before making a large investment in NICs. In the next chapter, we will examine the network types and new innovations that may have an effect on your NIC purchases. In most situations, having a good idea of where your network will be five years from now may help to avoid purchasing products that will need to be replaced later.

NIC Configuration Settings. Having discussed in general terms the functions and various types of NICs available, the following sections will examine in detail the actual process of configuring a NIC for use in a client workstation or file server. While servers and workstations use different software drivers for NICs, their hardware requirements are identical. Any hardware considerations discussed in these sections are equally applicable to both types of machines.

Each NIC model will have its own installation and configuration procedure. Many NICs can be configured using special software supplied with the NIC, while others—particularly older models—use physical jumpers that must be moved manually to change settings. In either case, the essential configurable elements are as follows:

Hardware Platforms

- Hardware Interrupt (IRQ)

- I/O Port Address

- Shared RAM

- DMA Channel

- Optional ROM

- Connector Type

These parameters allow the NIC to communicate with the workstation's CPU and bus. They are described in turn in the following sections.

Hardware Interrupt (IRQ). An IRQ line or *interrupt channel* allows the NIC to grab the CPU's attention whenever it requires it, using the following procedure:

- The NIC needs the CPU to perform some processing, perhaps because it has received data from the network.

- It uses a connector in the adapter slot to signal to the motherboard that it needs attention.

- The system interrupts whatever it was doing and saves the CPU register contents to a stack.

- The system looks in its interrupt vector table for the memory address corresponding to the interrupt that was received. In the NIC's case, this is the address in memory of the NIC's software driver.

- The system jumps to that memory address and executes the code it finds there. This performs the processing required by the NIC.

- When the software driver finishes processing, the original CPU register contents are returned from the stack to the CPU.

- The CPU resumes whatever task it was carrying out before it was interrupted.

This system allows the NIC to interrupt the current CPU process whenever it wants to, ensuring that network traffic is handled promptly.

Interrupts can interrupt each other, too. Each interrupt channel has a priority level, with the lowest IRQ numbers having the highest priority. If an interrupt is being processed when another interrupt occurs with a lower number than the first interrupt, the CPU registers are pushed onto the stack, processing of the first interrupt is suspended and the second interrupt is processed. When it finishes, the register stack is accessed, the CPU returns to its original (first interrupt) state, and processing of the first interrupt continues as described.

Traditionally, interrupt channels cannot usually be shared. There are exceptions to this, and newer bus types such as Microchannel, EISA, and PCI theoretically allow for interrupt sharing, but hardware incompatibilities are not infrequent, requiring the use of individual interrupts for each adapter. Even where it is possible, it is not desirable to share interrupts if it can be avoided, as it is less efficient than assigning one interrupt per adapter.

In brief, IRQ configuration for a NIC consists of identifying an unused interrupt channel and assigning it to the NIC.

I/O Port Address. The workstation reserves a range of low memory addresses for communication between I/O devices and the CPU. The first serial port, for example, usually uses uses memory starting at 03F8h.

Configuring an I/O port for a NIC means identifying the start address of an unused range of memory.

Shared RAM. The simplest way for a NIC to get data into the workstation's memory is for the NIC to pass the data on to the CPU and to let the CPU store the data in memory. Similarly, the CPU can read data from memory and transmit it to the NIC when asked to do so.

The problem with this approach is that it is quite inefficient. Data must be stored twice, once in the workstation's RAM and once on the NIC. The CPU must also spend valuable cycles passing the data from one storage area to the other.

Many NICs use a shared area of RAM for greater efficiency. The NIC stores its data directly in RAM, from where the workstation can read it. Likewise, the workstation needs only to store data in the right location for the NIC to be able to access it.

Not all NICs use shared RAM. If your NIC uses it, you will need to configure it when setting up the NIC. This involves identifying an available area of RAM, setting the NIC to use it, and making sure that no other software tries to use the designated shared area.

DMA Channel. Some NICs use DMA (Direct Memory Access) channels to communicate with the bus. This allows the NIC to bypass the CPU and access the workstation's memory directly. DMA transfers, however, are not as efficient as transfers using shared RAM.

A NIC will use shared RAM or DMA but not both. If your NIC uses DMA, configuration will involve locating a free DMA channel and adjusting the NIC settings to use it.

Optional ROM. If your NIC uses an optional ROM chip, such as a remote boot ROM, you need to enable it at setup time. How this is done varies from one NIC to the next. In general, there will either be a jumper on the NIC that can be set or a software setup menu option that you can choose to enable or disable the ROM. If you enable a ROM, you may also need to specify the RAM area where the ROM code is to be stored. Consult the documentation for your NIC and ROM option for detailed instructions.

Connector Type. The NIC may have more than one type of network connector, RJ-45 and AUI, for example. You should set the NIC to use the correct connector type, but when you're deep in the details of IRQs and I/O ports, it can easily be forgotten.

Configuring the Adapter. The following sections describe how to select and change settings, how to test that the NIC works with these settings, and how to set about resolving conflicts between the NIC and other system components. The configuration procedure is different for every NIC model, so the documentation for the particular NIC model being installed should always be consulted for detailed instructions.

Choosing NIC Settings. Choosing settings is easy if your workstation has a PCI, EISA, or MCA bus. The system configuration utility will generally not allow you to choose values that are already in use and will usually perform a quick check for resource conflicts before exiting.

ISA bus machines require that you do the checking yourself. Before you start, try to find out what resources are already in use on the workstation. Check interrupt channels, I/O port addresses, RAM areas, and DMA channels as necessary. One way to do this is using Microsoft's MSD utility, which has been shipped with Windows since version 3.1 and DOS since version 6.

In practice, most NICs are restricted to a small range of port addresses choices. NICs that use hardware jumpers typically offer a choice of one or two jumper combinations to select a port address. Some may only let you choose predetermined IRQ/port address combinations. NICs that come with a software setup utility tend to be more flexible but usually offer a choice of only seven or eight port addresses.

In either case, the narrow range of choices makes it possible to check all possible settings, should it be necessary in the case of a particularly recalcitrant NIC. This is rarely necessary though. The default setting is quite often acceptable and if not, one of its neighbors in the region of 280h or 300h generally does the trick.

MSD can also help when choosing a shared RAM area. Figure 6.5 shows a typical MSD memory map.

In this case, any RAM area from C800 to EFFF inclusive may be chosen. Make sure to exclude the NIC's RAM area on the EMM386 load line in CONFIG.SYS, though.

Setting the NIC. Now that appropriate settings for the NIC have been identified, it is time to implement them. Refer to the NIC's documentation for detailed instructions on how to do this for your particular NIC model.

Caution

Write down the settings in use on the NIC before you start to change them. You may want to restore the NIC to its original state if your choice of settings turns out to be inappropriate.

```
Legend:   Available "  "  RAM "##"  ROM "RR"  Possibly Available ".."
          EMS Page Frame "PP"  Used UMBs "UU"  Free UMBs "FF"
  1024K FC00 RRRRRRRRRRRRRRRR FFFF  Conventional Memory
        F800 RRRRRRRRRRRRRRRR FBFF                  Total: 639K
        F400 RRRRRRRRRRRRRRRR F7FF              Available: 572K
   960K F000 RRRRRRRRRRRRRRRR F3FF                      586064 bytes
        EC00                 EFFF
        E800                 EBFF  Extended Memory
        E400                 E7FF                  Total: 7424K
   896K E000                 E3FF
        DC00                 DFFF  XMS Information
        D800                 DBFF        XMS Version: 3.00
        D400                 D7FF     Driver Version: 3.10
   832K D000                 D3FF     A20 Address Line: Not Enabled
        CC00                 CFFF     High Memory Area: Available
        C800                 CBFF            Available: 7360K
        C400 RRRRRRRRRRRRRRRR C7FF   Largest Free Block: 7360K
   768K C000 RRRRRRRRRRRRRRRR C3FF        Available SXMS: 7360K
        BC00 ################ BFFF     Largest Free SXMS: 7360K
        B800 ################ BBFF
        B400                 B7FF
   704K B000                 B3FF
        AC00                 AFFF
        A800                 ABFF
        A400                 A7FF
   640K A000                 A3FF
```

Figure 6.5

Use MSD to obtain a memory map.

There are a few catches to watch out for. Some NICs (the SMC Elite 16, for example) are completely software configurable but have a jumper which, when set, prevents any configuration changes being saved on the card. This is a useful security feature, but it can cause confusion when settings changes are required. If your NIC has such a jumper, check if it is in the enabled position. If so,

1. Turn off the workstation.

2. Disable the jumper.

3. Run the NIC's setup utility.

4. Make the necessary settings changes.

5. Save the new settings.

6. Test the new settings.

7. Turn the workstation off again.

8. Enable the jumper again.

Some NICs (the DEC Etherworks III NIC is one example) don't register all settings changes without a cold reset of the workstation. If this is the case for your NIC, make the necessary changes using the setup utility, save the changes, and exit the utility. Then cold boot the machine and test the new settings.

Finally, don't forget to select the right connector type! This may be done using a jumper or a software utility depending on your NIC model.

Testing. If at all possible, test the settings before moving on to the next stage. You may be able to detect a settings conflict in a few seconds at this stage, which could cause a much longer delay later on.

> **Tip**
>
> If the workstation has any other installed adapters, such as a sound card or a SCSI controller, make sure the device is active and its drivers are loaded when you test the NIC. You may find that the NIC works fine on its own but not when the other adapter is in use, indicating a settings conflict.

Nearly all NICs come with a diagnostic utility that verifies that the NIC is functioning normally. These utilities generally have "internal" tests that verify that the NIC can communicate properly with the system and "external" or network tests which verify that packets can be sent and received using the designated network connector.

If your NIC came without a diagnostic utility, you may still be able to perform some simple diagnostics: Many NICs have link pulse LEDs beside the connector that flash to indicate network traffic, valid/invalid network connection, and so on. Check the LED activity against the NIC's documentation to determine if a fault is indicated.

There isn't much you can do by way of testing at this stage if you have no diagnostic utility and the NIC has no LEDs. Conflicts may manifest themselves by failure of another piece of equipment besides the NIC—for example, the video display or another adapter if one is installed. If the machine fails to boot, locks up when in use, displays garbage characters, or acts in any way unusual, a conflict of settings is most likely the cause.

A settings conflict is more likely to occur with another adapter such as the video subsystem than with the main system components. This is because adapter manufacturers generally avoid default settings that may clash with common workstation components. Instead, they tend to choose from the range of commonly available settings: IRQ 5, I/O port 280, and a RAM address starting at D000h are common defaults for many adapter types. With all manufacturers choosing from the same restricted range of settings, it's quite possible that the default settings for your NIC will clash with the settings in use for another adapter.

So if another adapter was already installed, run its diagnostic utility to verify that it hasn't stopped working. This is far from a comprehensive test, but in the absence of proper diagnostics for your NIC, it may help to catch some of the more common conflicts.

Otherwise, you will have to wait until the network software is installed and then debug your software and hardware setup at the same time. Avoid this if at all possible. It can be difficult enough trying to sort out software settings for an adapter that definitely works; trying to debug software problems on an adapter that may or may not work properly is a frustrating exercise.

> **Note**
>
> All that has been tested at this point is the availability of any resources that the card has been set to use—IRQ, I/O address, etc.—and the connection to the network. More testing remains to be done at the software configuration stage later on.

Resolving Conflicts. If your NIC doesn't pass its diagnostics after you implement your choice of settings, you may have a resource conflict of some sort.

Some diagnostic utilities (SMC Elite for example) will tell you where the conflict occurred. If the diagnostics report, for example, that the RAM area you selected is already in use, you can try another setting and test again. In many cases the diagnostic and software setup utilities are one and the same, so you can easily change settings and run diagnostics again.

Other diagnostic utilities will simply tell you that the NIC failed to pass its internal tests. In that case, you're only slightly better off than you would be if you had no diagnostic utility at all but suspected a settings conflict anyway.

Identifying the source of a settings conflict may require a certain amount of trial and error. If the system has completely locked up and will not boot, you will need to remove the NIC and restart the computer before trying a different combination of settings.

If there is a second adapter in the system, run its diagnostic software to see if there is a conflict between its settings and those of the NIC. If you don't have diagnostic software for the other adapter, temporarily disable or remove it and see if you can get the NIC to work on its own. If you can, there is clearly a resource conflict between the two adapters. If you can't get the NIC to work on its own, it may be faulty.

Once you identify the source of the conflict, you can change the relevant settings values and test the NIC again. Take note of each combination of settings you try so that time isn't wasted trying them again.

If you have tried all possible combinations of settings without success, you will have to consider the possibility of faulty hardware. The adapter slot may be faulty: move the NIC to a different slot in the workstation and try again. The NIC itself may be faulty: borrow a working NIC from another workstation and see if it works in this workstation.

> **Caution**
>
> Remember, if EMM386 or another memory manager is active on the workstation, make sure it is not trying to manage any shared RAM area used by the NIC. If in doubt, disable the memory manager temporarily until you have resolved all conflicts.

At this point, all that can be accomplished to configure a NIC from the hardware perspective should have been done. The next task is to proceed to the installation and configuration of software. How this is done will, of course, depend on the OS used on the machine. File server network software configuration is covered in chapters 8, "Novell NetWare," and 9, " Microsoft Windows NT." Workstations running DOS or Windows 3.1 are covered in chapter 11, "Network Client Software," and the 32-bit Windows OSs (Windows NT and Windows 95) are discussed in chapter 12, "Network Client Software for 32-Bit Windows."

Cases

This chapter has so far looked at virtually all the components of a PC that may have an effect on performance when connected to a network. This final section is devoted to the ways in which the entire computer can be packaged. Although it might seem a trivial matter when compared with some of the subjects covered earlier, the case that a workstation is housed in can be an important factor in the completion of the network administrator's daily tasks.

The first consideration for the case of a networked PC is, of course, its size. Cases of many different form factors have gone in and out of popularity over the years. Very early desktop models gave little thought to this subject. The idea of having a computer on your desk was so new, that users did not quibble about the "footprint" or the desk space required for the unit. Besides, there were very few choices at the time. Today, though, you must face the key decisions of where the computer's case will be located, and how much can fit within it.

Many PCs that are sold today as prepackaged network workstations offer little room for expansion within the case. Once manufacturers realized that many users balk at the idea of a large AT-style case occupying half the desktop, smaller boxes were developed, many of them packing their components inside in rather ingenious ways. Many machines using the "slimline" case have a card containing the system bus slots mounted on the motherboard, so that expansion cards can be installed into it, parallel to the motherboard. This conserves space on the main system board, often providing room for additional components to be integrated onto it. This arrangement, however, usually limits the number of expansion cards that can be installed into the machine and can make many other components difficult to access. If machines such as these are going to be used as is, with no modifications other than the insertion of a NIC, this is acceptable. If it ever becomes necessary to install an additional hard drive into the case, however, you might have difficulty squeezing even today's smallest drives in there.

Another alternative is the minitower, which can reside on a remote corner of the user's desk and generally provides more space for expansion and maintenance access. Don't, however, let your users use the case as a convenient location for refrigerator magnets to hold their notes.

Another possibility—one that I prefer to avoid—is locating the main unit of the computer under the user's desk. Mini-towers as well as traditional AT-style cases (resting on their sides) can be used this way, but maintenance access is tough on the administrator's back and knees and is rather undignified if you're in a "suit-and-tie" office. (Pardon me, would you mind sliding back a few feet so that I can crawl under your desk? Thank you very much.)

Note

I have heard from various sources over the years that a computer containing hard disk drives that rests on its side should have the disks reformatted in that position. This supposedly would accommodate the different direction in which gravity pulls the platters. I have run dozens of machines on their sides without reformatting the drives, however, and have never experienced a drive failure that could be attributed to this cause.

Summary

As we have seen, there is a tremendous amount of variance in the networked PCs currently being used in the corporate world today. Networked resources can give a new lease on life to older machines that would be all but useless on their own and can provide to even the most advanced PCs some benefits that were unheard of only a few years ago. To accommodate the needs of various types of users in as economical a manner as possible, the network administrator has to be familiar with a wide range of different machines and their capabilities. In this chapter, we have covered virtually the entire history of the personal computer, from the original IBM PC to today's cutting-edge Pentiums. This hopefully provides a means by which you can assess the continued viability of your existing equipment and realistically plan based on the future of networking in the industry in general and your organization in particular.

Chapter 7

Major Network Types

Now that you have examined the components of the average network server and several different types of workstations, you have come to the fabric that incorporates them all into what is known as a local area network (LAN).

A network may, at first glance, appear to be deceptively simple. A series of computers are wired together so that they can communicate with each other. However, each device on the network must be able to communicate with any other device at many different levels, even to perform the simplest tasks. Further, this must all be accomplished using a single transmission channel for all of the devices. Multiply these myriad levels of communication by dozens, hundreds, or even thousands of devices on a network, and the logistics become staggeringly complex.

In this chapter, you will concentrate on an examination of the basic network types in use today. You will learn about the actual physical medium that connects networked devices, but you will also learn about the basic communications methods used by each network type at the bottom two levels of the OSI reference model. These methods are integrally related with the physical medium, as they impose numerous restrictions on the way that you can construct the network fabric. You will also read about some of the new network technologies that are just coming into general acceptance in the marketplace. These offer increased network throughput to accommodate the greater demands of today's application software and data types in a variety of ways. Even if your network has no need for these technologies today, it is important to keep a finger on the pulse of the industry in order to facilitate the performance of network upgrades at a later time.

The selection of a network type is one of the first major decisions to be made in setting up a network. Once constructed, a network type can be very difficult and expensive to change later, so it is a decision that should be made correctly the first time. Consideration must be paid to the needs of your organization right now, as well as the future of the network. Knowing more about the basic communications methods utilized by a network gives you a greater understanding of the hardware involved and the problems that it may be subject to. Network communications problems can be very difficult to troubleshoot—even more so when you are unaware of what is actually going on inside the network medium.

Understanding Terminology

As you have seen in chapter 3, "The OSI Model: Bringing Order to Chaos," the basic OSI model for network communications consists of seven layers, each of which has its own set of terms, definitions, and industry jargon. It can be very difficult to keep track of all of the terminology used in networking at the various levels, and this chapter will hopefully help you understand many of the terms that are constantly used.

First of all, keep in mind that this chapter is concerned primarily with the lowest levels of the OSI reference model: the *physical* and *data link layers*. Everything discussed here is completely independent of any concerns imposed by applications and operating systems (OS) either at the server or workstation level. An Ethernet LAN, for example, can be used to connect computers running NetWare, Windows NT, numerous flavors of UNIX, or even minicomputer OSs. Each of these has its own communications protocols at higher levels in the OSI model, but Ethernet is completely unconcerned with them. They are merely the "baggage" that is carried in the data section of an Ethernet packet. Network types such as Ethernet, token ring, and FDDI are simply transport mechanisms—postal systems, if you will—that carry envelopes to specific destinations irrespective of the envelopes' contents.

Fundamentals of Network Communications

The *packet* is the basic unit used to send data over a network connection. At this level, it is also referred to as a *frame*. The *network medium* is essentially a single electrical or optical connection between a series of devices. Data must ultimately be broken down into binary bits that are transmitted over the medium using one of many possible encoding schemes designed to use fluctuations in electrical current or pulses of light to represent 1s and 0s. Since any device on the network may initiate communications with any other device at any time, it is not practical for a single device to be able to send out a continuous stream of bits whenever it wants to. This would monopolize the medium, preventing other devices from communicating until that one device is finished or, alternatively, corrupting the data stream if multiple devices were trying to communicate simultaneously.

Instead, each networked device assembles the data that it wants to transmit into packets of a specific size and configuration. Each packet contains not only the data that is to be transmitted but also the information that is needed to get the packet to its destination and reconstitute it with other packets into the original data. Thus, a network type must have some form of *addressing*—that is, a means by which every device on the network can be uniquely identified. This addressing is performed by the network interface located in each device, usually in the form of an expansion card known as a network adapter or a network interface card (NIC). Every network interface has a unique address (assigned by either the manufacturer or the network administrator) that is used as part of the "envelope" it creates around every packet. Other mechanisms are also included as part of the packet configuration, including error-checking information and the data necessary to assemble multiple packets back into their original form once they arrive at their destination.

The other responsibility of the network, at this level, is to introduce the packets onto the network medium in such a way that no two network devices are transmitting onto the same medium at precisely the same time. If two devices should transmit at the same time, a *collision* occurs, usually damaging or destroying both packets. The mechanism used to avoid collisions while transmitting packets is called *media access control (MAC)*. This is represented in the lower half of the data link layer of the OSI reference model, also known as the MAC sublayer. A MAC mechanism allows each of the devices on a network an equal opportunity to transmit its data, as well as providing a means of detecting collisions and resending the damaged packets that result.

Thus, the network types covered in this chapter each consist of the following attributes:

- A physical medium used to carry signals between networked devices

- A packet or frame configuration that consists of a standardized set of bits used to carry data over the network medium

- A set of media access control rules that allow multiple networked devices to arbitrate access to the shared network medium

Many of the following network types utilize widely different means of realizing these three attributes. Although they are all quite capable of supporting general network use, each is particularly suited to a different set of network requirements. It is also possible to connect networks of differing types into what is technically known as an *internetwork*— that is, a network of networks. You may find, therefore, that while Ethernet is completely suitable for all of the networked workstations within a particular building, an FDDI link (which actually comprises a network in itself) would be a better choice for use as a network backbone for connecting all of the servers that use higher speeds.

The growing trend today is towards *heterogeneous networks*, an amalgam of varying network types interconnected into a single entity. This and the increasing popularity of wide area network (WAN) links between remote sites has made it necessary for the LAN administrator to have knowledge of all of these network types. It is only in this way that the proper ones can be chosen to satisfy the particular needs of an installation.

Ethernet and Its Variants

With over 40 million nodes installed around the world, Ethernet is, by far, the most commonly found network type in use today. As an open standard from the very outset, its huge popularity has led to a gigantic market for Ethernet hardware, thus keeping the quality up and the prices down. The Ethernet standards are mature enough for them to be very stable, and compatibility problems between Ethernet devices produced by different manufacturers are comparatively rare.

Originally conceived in the 1970s by Dr. Robert M. Metcalfe, Ethernet has had a long history and has been implemented using a number of different media types and topologies over the years, which makes it an excellent platform with which to learn about low-level networking processes. One of the keys to its longevity was a number of remarkably foresighted decisions on the parts of its creators. Unlike other early network types that ran at what are today perceived to be excessively slow speeds, such as StarLAN's 1 Mbps and ARCnet's 2.5 Mbps, Ethernet was conceived from the outset to run at 10 Mbps.

It is only now, 20 years later, that a real need for greater speed than this has been realized, and the Ethernet specifications are currently being revised to allow network speeds of 100 Mbps as well. A number of competing standards are vying for the approval of the marketplace in this respect, but it is very likely that "Fast Ethernet," in some form or other, will be a major force in the industry for many years to come.

Ethernet Standards

Of course, as so often seems to be the case in the computing industry, nomenclature is never easy, and what is generally referred to as Ethernet actually bears a different and more technically correct name. The original Ethernet standard was developed by a committee composed of representatives from three large corporations: Digital Equipment Corporation, Intel, and Xerox. Published in 1980, this standard has come to be known as the *DIX Ethernet* standard (after the initials of the three companies). A revision of the standard was later published in 1985, which is known as Ethernet II. This document was then passed to the Institute of Electrical and Electronics Engineers (IEEE) for industry-wide standardization. The IEEE is a huge organization of technical professionals that, among other things, sponsors a group devoted to the development and maintenance of electronic and computing standards. The resulting document, ratified in 1985, was officially titled the "IEEE 802.3 Carrier Sense Multiple Access with Collision Detection (CSMA/CD) Access Method and Physical Layer Specifications." This should make it clear why most people in the industry retained the name Ethernet despite the fact that nearly all of the hardware sold today is actually 802.3 compliant.

In most ways, the 802.3 standard is a superset of the DIX Ethernet standard. While the original standard specifies only the use of thick Ethernet coaxial cabling and Ethernet II adds the thin coaxial variant, 802.3 adds the capability of using other cable types, such as unshielded twisted pair (UTP) and fiber optic, which have all but eclipsed thick Ethernet, or *thicknet*, in common network use. Other aspects of the physical layer remain the same in both standards, however. The data rate of 10 Mbps and the Baseband Manchester signaling type (the way 1s and 0s are conveyed over the medium) remain unchanged, and the physical layer configuration specs for thicknet and thinnet are identical in both standards.

One source of confusion, however, is the existence of the *SQE Test* feature in the 802.3 standard, which is often mistakenly thought to be identical to the *heartbeat* feature defined in the Ethernet II document. Both of these mechanisms are used to verify that the *medium access unit* (*MAU*) or transceiver of a particular Ethernet interface is capable of detecting collisions, or *signal quality errors* (*SQE*). A test signal is sent on the line where the collision occurred from the MAU or transceiver to the Ethernet interface following every packet transmission. The presence of this signal verifies the functionality of the collision detection mechanism, and its absence can be logged for review by the administrator. No signal is sent out over the common, or network, medium. Use of SQE Test and heartbeat are optional settings for every device on the network, and problems have often been caused by their use, particularly when combined. The essential difficulty is that the heartbeat function was only defined in the Ethernet II standard. It does not exist in Ethernet I and equipment of that type may not function properly when transceivers using heartbeat are located on the same network. In addition, the 802.3 standard specifically states that the heartbeat signal should not be used by transceivers connected to 802.3-compliant repeaters. In other words, an Ethernet II NIC connected to an 802.3 repeater must not utilize the heartbeat feature or a conflict with the repeater's jam signal may occur.

There are other differences between the two standards, but they are, for the most part, not consequential in the actual construction and configuration of a network. The original DIX Ethernet standards cover the entire functionality of the physical and data link layers, while the IEEE standard splits the data link layer into two distinct sublayers: *logical link control (LLC)* and *media access control* (see fig. 7.1).

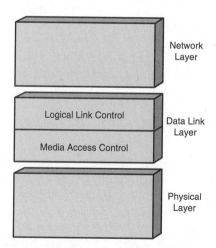

Figure 7.1

The OSI data link layer has two sublayers.

The Logical Link Control Sublayer

The top half of the OSI model's data link layer, according to the IEEE specifications, is the LLC sublayer. The function of the LLC is to effectively isolate all of the functions that occur below this layer from all of the functions occurring above it. The network layer (that is, the layer just above the data link layer in the OSI model) must be sent what appear to be error-free transmissions from the layer below. The protocol used to implement this process is not part of the 802.3 standard. In the IEEE implementation of the OSI model, the LLC is defined by the 802.2 standard, which is also utilized by other network types defined in IEEE standards, as well as by the 802.3 standard. Utilizing a separate frame within the data field of the 802.3 frame, the LLC defines error-recovery mechanisms other than those specified in the MAC sublayer, provides flow control that prevents a destination node from being overwhelmed with delivered packets, and establishes logical connections between the sending and receiving nodes.

The Media Access Control Sublayer

The other half of the data link layer, the MAC sublayer, as mentioned earlier, arbitrates access to the network medium by the individual network devices. For both of the standards, this method is called *Carrier Sense Multiple Access with Collision Detection* (CSMA/CD). This protocol has remained unchanged ever since the original DIX standard and is equally applicable to all media types and topologies used in Ethernet installations. The way this protocol works is discussed in the following section.

CSMA/CD: The Ethernet MAC Mechanism. When a networked device, also referred to as a *station*, a *node*, or a *DTE* (data terminal equipment), wants to send a packet (or series of packets), it first listens to the network to see if it is currently being utilized by signals from another node. If the network is busy, the device continues to wait until it is clear. When the network is found to be clear, the device then transmits its packet.

The possibility exists, however, for another node on the network to have been listening at the same time. When both nodes detect a clear network, they may both transmit at precisely the same time, resulting in a *collision* (also known in IEEE-speak as an *SQE*, or *signal quality error*). In this instance, the transceiver at each node is capable of detecting the collision and both begin to transmit a *jam pattern*. This can be formed by any sequence of 32–48 bits other than the correct *CRC value* (*cyclical redundancy check*, an error-checking protocol) for that particular packet. This is done so that notification of the collision can be propagated to all stations on the network. Both nodes will then begin the process of retransmitting their packets.

To attempt to avoid repeated collisions, however, each node selects a randomized delay interval, calculated using the individual station's network address (which is certain to be unique), before retransmitting. If further collisions occur, the competing nodes will then begin to back off, that is, increase the range of delay intervals from which one is randomly chosen. This process is called *truncated binary exponential backoff*. As a result of its use, repeated collisions between the same two packets become increasingly unlikely. The greater the number of values from which each node may select, the lesser the likelihood that they will choose the same value.

It should be noted that collisions are a normal occurrence on a network of this type, and while they do result in slight delays, they should not be cause for alarm unless their number is excessive. Perceptible delays should not occur on an Ethernet network until the utilization of the medium approaches 80%. This figure means that a transmission is occurring somewhere on the network 80% of the time. A typical Ethernet network should have an average utilization rate of 30–40%, meaning that the cable is idle 60–70% of the time, allowing stations to initiate transmissions with relative ease.

A collision can only occur during the brief period after a given station has begun to transmit and before the first 64 bytes of data are sent. This is known as the *slot time*, and it represents the amount of time that it takes for the transmission to be completely propagated around the network segment. 64 bytes will completely fill the wire, end-to-end, ensuring that all other stations are aware of the transmission in progress and preventing them from initiating a transmission themselves. This is why all Ethernet packets must be at least 64 bytes in length. A transmitted packet smaller than 64 bytes is called a *runt* and may cause a collision after the packet has completely left the host adapter, which is known as a *late collision*. The packets involved in a late collision cannot be retransmitted by the normal backoff procedures. It is left to the protocols operating at the higher levels of the OSI model to detect the lost packets and request their retransmission, which they often do not do as quickly or as well, possibly resulting in a fatal network error.

Late collisions do not always involve runts. They can also be caused by cable segments that are too long, faulty Ethernet interface equipment, or too many repeaters between the transmitting and receiving stations. When a segment displays an inordinately large number of collisions for the traffic that it is carrying, it is likely that late collisions are a cause of the excess. While a certain number of transmissions are expected on an Ethernet network, as we have discussed, late collisions indicate the existence of a serious problem that should be addressed immediately.

A packet can be retransmitted up to 16 times before it is discarded and actual data loss occurs. Obviously, the more highly trafficked the network, the more collisions there will be, with network performance degrading accordingly. This is why the Ethernet standards all impose restrictions on the number of nodes that can be installed on a particular network segment, as well as on the overall length and configuration of the medium connecting them. A segment that is too long can cause a packet's transmission to its destination to take longer than the 600 nanoseconds prescribed in the specifications, thus causing the collision detection mechanisms to react when, in fact, no collision has occurred. Too many nodes will naturally result in an increased number of collisions, and in either case, network performance will degrade considerably.

The Capture Effect. Although large numbers of collisions can be dealt with by an Ethernet network with no loss of data, performance can be hampered in ways beyond the simple need to repeatedly transfer the same packets. One phenomenon is known as the *capture effect*. This can occur when two nodes both have a long stream of packets to be sent over the network. When an initial collision occurs, both nodes will initiate the backoff process and, eventually, one of them will randomly select a lower backoff value than the other and win the contention. Therefore, let's say that Node A has done this, and has successfully retransmitted its packet, while Node B has not. Now, Node A attempts to transmit its second packet while Node B is still trying to retransmit its first. A collision occurs again, but for Node A, it is the first collision occurring for this packet, while for Node B, it is the second. Node A will randomly select from the numbers 0 and 1 when calculating its backoff delay. Node B, however, will be selecting from the numbers 0, 1, 2, and 3 because it is the second collision for this packet, and the number of possible values increases with each successive backoff.

Already, the odds of winning the contention are in Node A's favor. Each iteration of the backoff algorithm causes longer delay times to be added to the set of possible values. Therefore, probability dictates that Node B is likely to select a longer delay period than Node A, causing A to transmit first. Once again, therefore, Node A successfully transmits and proceeds to attempt to send its third packet, while Node B is still trying to send its first packet for the third time, increasing its backoff delay factor each time. With each repeated iteration, Node B's chances of winning the contention with Node A are reduced, as its delay time is statistically increasing, while that of Node A remains the same. It becomes increasingly likely, therefore, that Node B will continue to lose its contentions with Node A until either Node A runs out of packets to send, or Node B reaches 16 transmission attempts, after which its packet is discarded and the data lost.

Thus, in effect, Node A has captured the network for sixteen successive transmissions, due to its having won the first few contentions. Various proposals for a means to counteract this effect are currently being considered by the IEEE 802 committee, among them a different backoff algorithm called the *binary logarithmic access method* (*BLAM*). While the capture effect is not a major problem on most Ethernet networks, it is discussed here to illustrate that complex ways that heavy traffic patterns can affect the performance of an Ethernet network. Other MAC protocols, such as that used by token-ring networks, are not subject to this type of problem, as collisions are not a part of their normal operational specifications. This is another reason why it is important for the proper network type to be selected for the needs of a particular organization.

The Ethernet/802.3 Frame Specification. The process of sending data from one device on a network to another is, as stated earlier, a very complex affair. A request will originate at the highest level of the OSI model and, as it travels down through the layers to the physical medium itself, be subject to various levels of encoding, each of which adds a certain amount of overhead to the original request. Each layer accepts input from the layer above and encases it within a frame designed to its own specifications. This entire construction is then passed on to the next layer, which includes it, frame and all, in the payload area of its own specialized frame. When the packet reaches the physical layer, it consists of frames within frames within frames and has grown significantly in size. An average packet may ultimately contain more bits devoted to networking overhead than to the actual information being transmitted.

By the time that a request has worked its way down to the data link layer, additional data from every layer of the network model has been added. The upper layers add information regarding the application generating the request. Moving farther down, information concerning the transport protocol being utilized by the network operating system (NOS) is added. The request is also broken down into packets of appropriate size for transport over the network, with another frame added containing the information needed to reassemble the packets into the proper order at their destination. The LLC sublayer adds its own frame to provide error and flow control. Several other processes are interspersed throughout, all adding data that will be needed to process the packet at its destination. Once it has reached the MAC sublayer, all that remains to be done is to see that the packet is addressed to the proper destination, the physical medium is accessed properly, and the packet arrives at its destination undamaged.

The composition of the frame specified by the IEEE 802.3 standard is illustrated in figure 7.2. The frame defined by the original Ethernet specification is slightly different but only in the arrangement of the specified bits. The functions provided are identical to those of the 802.2 and 802.3 specifications in combination. The functions of each part of the frame are explicated in the following list.

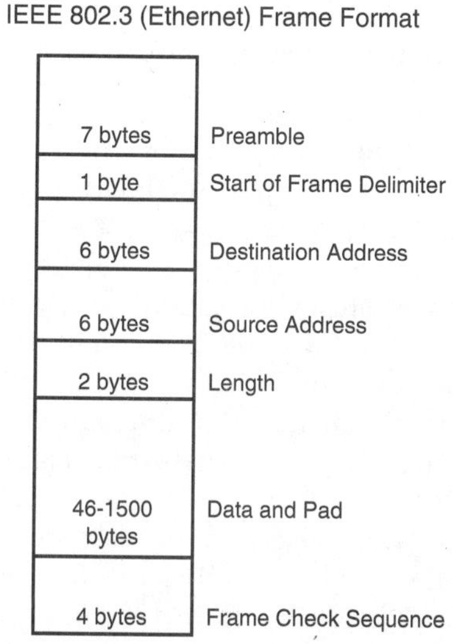

IEEE 802.3 (Ethernet) Frame Format

7 bytes	Preamble
1 byte	Start of Frame Delimiter
6 bytes	Destination Address
6 bytes	Source Address
2 bytes	Length
46-1500 bytes	Data and Pad
4 bytes	Frame Check Sequence

Figure 7.2

The fields that comprise the IEEE 802.3 Frame Format.

- *Preamble and Start of Frame Delimiter (SFD)*   These two fields, normally generated by the chipset of the Ethernet adapter and comprising a total of 8 bytes, are designed to be an indication to the rest of the network that the transmission of a packet is about to begin. The receiving station uses the Preamble to synchronize bits and the Start of Frame Delimiter for bit alignment. They are composed entirely of alternating 1s and 0s, except for the last two bits, which are two consecutive 1s. This is the indication to the receiving station(s) that "The frame information begins now."

- *Destination Address*   The full Ethernet address of a node is a hexadecimal sequence composed of a network address that is assigned by the administrator to a particular network segment plus a unique node address that is hardcoded in the network interface card (NIC) by the manufacturer. In addition to specifying a single node as the destination, a frame may be addressed to multiple nodes or broadcast, which is sending to all nodes on the network. The Source and Destination Addresses are both generated by the driver software at the transmitting node.

- *Source Address*   Following the same format as the destination address, this part of the frame defines the full Ethernet address of the sending node.

- *Length*   This two-byte field, also provided by the driver software, reports the length of the data field that follows. The number cited does not include any bytes that may have been added to the data field in order to "pad" it out to its minimum length. Thus, this field denotes only the actual amount of data in the following field. Note that these bits are only used to provide the data field length in 802.3 packets. Ethernet II packets place a frame type field in this space, information normally provided by the 802.2 LLC sublayer frame in an IEEE Ethernet installation. The frame type codes are all numbers greater than 1500 (the maximum length of the data field) so that no confusion can be made as to which type of frame is being used. Frames of both types can therefore coexist on the same network.

- *Data and Pad*   This field contains the "payload" of the packet, which is, in fact, the original data generated at the top layer of the OSI model plus all of the framing bytes added by subsequent layers up to and including the frame added by the LLC sublayer. If the total size of the data field is less than 64 bytes, it is "padded" out to that length by the addition of an appropriate number of meaningless bytes. This is necessary because, for the collision detection mechanisms of the MAC sublayer to function properly, the beginning of the packet must be propagated throughout the network and a collision detection signal sent back to the source (if necessary) before the packet has been completely transmitted by the sending node. Once the entire packet has been placed onto the network medium by the source MAU (medium attachment unit) without an indication that a collision or packet damage has occurred, the packet is then erased from the buffers and cannot be retransmitted by the MAC sublayer. In the event of a collision at this point, it would be up to the higher layers of the model to detect the missing information and begin their own process of regenerating and retransmitting the packet. This is another reason for the strict limitations on the physical medium imposed by the Ethernet specifications.

- *Frame Check Sequence (FCS)*   This is a four-byte field that comprises the MAC sublayer's primary error-checking mechanism. The chipset of the Ethernet adapter at the source node computes a CRC on all of the previous fields that comprise the packet (except for the Preamble and SFD fields). This is done using an algorithm called the *AUTODIN II polynomial* that derives a unique number based upon the data fed into it. This number is stored in the FCS field, and the packet is then transmitted to its destination. The receiving node then recomputes the CRC on the received packet using the same algorithm, and compares the result to that stored in the FCS field. If the numbers match, then the packet is assumed to have been transmitted without error. If they do not match, or if the number of bits received is not an integer multiple of 8, an *alignment error* is declared, the frame discarded, and procedures for retransmittal initiated.

Ethernet Physical Layer Types and Specification

The 802.3 standard has been revised over the years to add several different media types as they have come into popularity. Only thick Ethernet is part of the original DIX Ethernet specification. The IEEE standard defines not only the types of cabling and connectors to be used, but also imposes limitations on the length of the cables in an individual network segment, the number of nodes that can be installed on any one segment, and the number of segments that can be joined together to form a network.

For these purposes, a *network* is defined as a series of computers connected so that collisions generated by any single node are seen on the network medium by every other node. In other words, when Node A attempts to transmit a packet to Node Z and a collision occurs, the jam pattern is completely propagated around the network and may be seen by all of the nodes connected to it. A *segment* is defined as a length of network cable bounded by any combination of terminators, repeaters, bridges, or routers. Thus, two segments of Ethernet cabling may be joined by a *repeater* (which is a signal amplifying and retiming device, operating purely on an electrical level, that is used to connect network segments), but as long as collisions are seen by all of the connected nodes, there is only one network involved. This sort of arrangement may also be described as forming a single *collision domain*—that is, a single CSMA/CD network where a collision occurs if two nodes transmit at the same time.

Conversely, a packet-switching device such as a *bridge* or a *router* may be used to connect two disparate network segments. These devices, while they allow the segments to appear as one entity at the network layer of the OSI model and above, isolate the segments at the data link layer, preventing the propagation of collisions between the two segments. This is more accurately described as an *internetwork*, or a network of networks. Two collision domains exist because two nodes on opposite sides of the router can conceivably transmit at the same moment without incurring a collision.

Thick Ethernet. The original form in which Ethernet networks were realized, thick Ethernet, is also known colloquially as thicknet, "frozen yellow garden hose," or by its IEEE designation: *10Base5*. This latter is a shorthand expression that has been adapted to all of the media types supported by the Ethernet specification. The "10" refers to the 10 Mbps transfer rate of the network, "Base" refers to Ethernet's *baseband transmitting system* (meaning that a single signal occupies the entire bandwidth of the medium), and the "5" refers to the 500 meter segment length limitation.

Thicknet is used in a bus topology. The *topology* of a network refers to the way in which the various nodes are interconnected. A *bus topology* means that each node is connected in series to the next node (see fig. 7.3). At both ends of the bus there must be a 50-ohm terminating resistor, so that signals reaching the end of the medium are not reflected back.

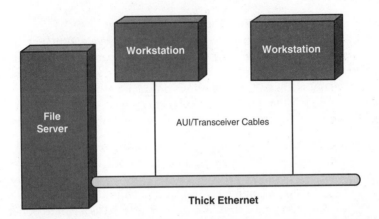

Figure 7.3

This is a basic 10Base5 thicknet network.

The actual network medium of a thicknet network is 50-ohm coaxial cable. *Coaxial cable* is so named because it contains two electrically separated connectors within one sheath (see fig. 7.4). A central core consisting of one connector is wrapped with a stiff insulating material and then surrounded by a woven mesh tube that is the second connector. The entire assembly is then encased in a tough PVC or Teflon insulating sheath that is yellow or brownish-orange in color. The Teflon variant is used for *plenum-rated* cable, which may be required by fire regulations for use in ventilation ducts, also known as plenums. The overall package is approximately 0.4 inches in diameter and more inflexible than the garden hose it is often likened to.

Figure 7.4

Here is a cutaway view of a coaxial cable.

As a network medium, coaxial cable is heavy and difficult to install properly. Installing the male N-type coaxial connectors at each end of the cable can be a difficult job, requiring the proper stripping and crimping tools and a reasonable amount of experience. With all coaxial cables, the installation is only as good as the weakest connection, and problems may occur as the result of bad connections that can be extremely subtle and difficult to troubleshoot. Indeed, with thicknet, it is usually recommended that the cable be broken in as few places as possible and that all of the segments used on a single network come from the same *cable lot* (that is, from a single spool or from spools produced in the same batch by a single manufacturer). When forced to use segments of cable from different lots, the 802.3 specification recommends that the segments used should be either 23.4, 70.2, or 117 meters long, to minimize the signal reflections that may occur due to variations in the cable itself. The specification also calls for the network to be grounded at only one end. This causes additional installation difficulties, as care must be taken to prevent any of the other cable connectors from coming in contact with a ground.

The sheer size of the thicknet cable makes it an excellent conducting medium. The maximum length for a thicknet segment is 500 meters, much longer than any other copper medium. It also provides excellent insulation against electromagnetic interference and attenuation, making it ideal for industrial applications where other machinery may inhibit the functionality of thinner network media. Thicknet has also been used to construct backbones connecting servers at distant locations within the same building. Electrical considerations, however, preclude its use for connections between buildings, as is the case with any copper-based medium.

Media Access Components. All Ethernet types utilize the same basic components to attach the network medium to the Ethernet interface within the computer. This is another area in which the 802.3 standard differs from the DIX Ethernet standard, but the differences are only in name. The components are identical, but they are referred to by different designations in the two documents. Both are provided here, as the older Ethernet terminology is often used, even when referring to an 802.3 installation.

Thicknet is an exemplary model for demonstrating the different components of the interface between the network cable and the computer. The relative inflexibility of the cable prevents it from being installed so that it directly connects to the Ethernet interface, as most of the other medium types do. Components that are integrated into the network adapter in thinnet or UTP installations are separate units in a thicknet installation.

The actual coaxial cable-to-Ethernet interface connection is through a *medium dependent interface (MDI)*. Two basic forms of MDI exist for thicknet. One is known as an *intrusive tap* because its installation involves cutting the network cable (thereby interrupting network service), installing standard N connectors on the two new ends, and then linking the two with a barrel connector that also provides the connection that leads to the computer. This method is far less popular than the *non-intrusive tap*, which is installed by drilling a hole into the coaxial cable and attaching a metal and plastic clamp that provides an electrical connection to the medium. This type of MDI can be installed without interrupting the use of the network, and without incurring any of the signal degeneration dangers that highly segmented thicknet cables are subject to.

The MDI is, in turn, directly connected to an MAU. This is referred to as a *transceiver* in the DIX Ethernet standard, as it is the unit that actually transmits data to and receives it from the network. In addition to the digital components that perform the signaling operations, the MAU also has analog circuitry that is used for collision detection. In most thicknet installations, the MAU and the MDI are integrated into a single unit that clamps onto the coaxial cable.

The 802.3 specification allows for up to 100 MAUs on a single network segment, each of which must be separated from the next by at least 2.5 meters of coaxial cable. The cabling often has black stripes on it to designate this distance. These limitations are intended to curtail the amount of signal attenuation and interference that can occur on any particular area of the network cable.

The thicknet MAU has a male 15-pin connector that is used to connect to an *attachment unit interface (AUI)* cable, also known as a *transceiver cable*. This cable, which can be no more than 50 meters long, is then attached, with a similar connector, to the Ethernet interface on the computer, from which it receives both signals and power for the operation of the MAU. Other AUI cables are available that are thinner and more manageable than the standard 0.4 inch diameter ones, but they are limited to a shorter distance between the MAU and the Ethernet interface, often 5 meters or less.

While thicknet does offer some advantages in signal strength and segment length, its higher cost, difficulty of installation and maintenance, and limited upgrade capabilities have all but eliminated it from use except in situations where its capabilities are expressly required. As with thinnet, the other coaxial network type in use today, thicknet is and always will be limited to 10 Mbps. The new high-speed standards being developed today are designed solely for use with twisted-pair or fiber-optic cabling. Despite the obsolescence of the medium itself, however, it is a tribute to the designers of the original Ethernet standard that the underlying concepts of the system have long outlived the original physical medium on which it was based.

Thin Ethernet. Thin Ethernet, also known as *thinnet*, *cheapernet*, or *10Base2* (despite the fact that its maximum segment length is 185 and not 200 meters), was standardized in 1985 and quickly became a popular alternative to thicknet. Although still based on a 50-ohm coaxial cable, thinnet, as the name implies, uses RG-58 cabling, which is much narrower (about 3/16 of an inch) and more flexible (see fig. 7.5), allowing the cable to be run to the back of the computer where it is directly attached to the Ethernet interface. The cable itself is composed of a metallic core (either solid or stranded), surrounded by an insulating, or dielectric layer, then a second conducting layer made of aluminum foil or braided strands, which functions both as a ground and as insulation for the central conductor. The entire construction is then sheathed with a tough insulating material for protection. Several different types of RG-58 cable exist, and care should be taken to purchase one with the appropriate impedance (approximately 50 ohms) and velocity of propagation rating (approximately 0.66). A network adapter for a thinnet network has the AUI, MAU, and MDI integrated into the expansion card, so there are no separate components to be purchased and accounted for.

Figure 7.5

This is a thinnet cable with a BNC connector attached.

Unlike thicknet, which may be tapped for attachment to a computer without breaking the cable, individual lengths of thinnet cabling are used to run from one computer to the next in order to form the bus topology (see fig. 7.6). At each Ethernet interface, a "T" connector is installed. This is a metal device with three *Bayonet-Neill-Concelman-type connectors* (BNC): one female for attachment to the NIC in the computer, and two males for the attachment of two coaxial cable connectors (see fig. 7.7). The cable at each machine must have a female BNC connector installed onto it, which is attached to the "T." Then a second length of cable, similarly equipped, is attached to the third connector on the "T" and used to run to the next machine. There are no guidelines in the standard concerning cable lots or the number of breaks that may be present in thinnet cabling. The only rule, in this respect, is that no cable segment may be less than 0.5 meters long.

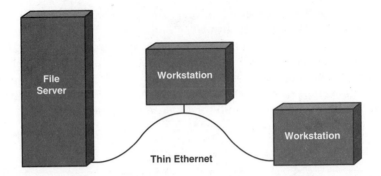

Figure 7.6

This is a basic 10Base2 thinnet network.

Figure 7.7

This is a thinnet BNC "T" connector.

Thinnet cables of varying lengths can be purchased with connectors already attached to them, but it is far more economical to buy bulk cable on a spool and attach the connectors yourself. Some special tools are needed, such as a stripper that exposes the bare copper of the cabling in the proper way and a crimper that squeezes the connectors onto the ends of the cable, but these can be purchased for $50–75 or less. Attaching the connectors to the cable is a skill that should be learned by watching the procedure done. It requires a certain amount of practice, but it is worth learning if you are going to be maintaining a thinnet network. This is because the single largest maintenance problem with this type of network is faulty cable connections.

Since thinnet requires no hub or other central connection point, it has the advantage of being a rather portable network. The simplest and most inexpensive Ethernet network possible can be created by installing NICs into two computers, attaching them with a length of thinnet cable, and installing a peer-to-peer operating system such as Windows for Workgroups. This sort of arrangement can be expanded, contracted, assembled, and disassembled at will, allowing a network to be moved to a new location with little difficulty or expense.

Thinnet cabling can be installed within the walls of an office, but remember that there always must be two wires extending to the T connector at the back of each computer. This often results in installations that are not as inconspicuous as might be desired in a corporate location. Thinnet cabling can also be left loose to run along the floor of a site, allowing for easy modification of the cabling layout, but this exposes the connectors to greater abuse from everyday foot traffic. Loose connectors are a very common cause of quirky behavior on thinnet networks, and it can often be extremely difficult to track down the connection that is causing the problem. The purchase of a good quality cable tester is highly recommended.

It is also important to note that, unlike thicknet, the thinnet cabling must extend directly to the NIC on the computer. A length of cabling running from the T connector to the NIC, also known as a *stub cable*, is not acceptable in this network type, although it may seem to function properly at first. The 802.3 specification calls for a distance of no more than 4 centimeters between the MDI on the NIC and the coaxial cable itself. The use of stub cables causes signal reflections on the network medium, resulting in increased numbers of packet retransmissions, thus slowing down the performance of the network. On highly trafficked segments, this can even lead to frame loss if the interference becomes too great.

Like thicknet, thinnet must be terminated at both ends of the bus that comprises each segment. 50-ohm terminating resistors built into a BNC connector are used for this purpose. The final length of cable is attached to the last machine's T connector along with the resistor plug, effectively terminating the bus. Although it is not specified in the standard, a thinnet network can also be grounded, but as with thicknet, it should only be grounded in one place. All other connectors should be insulated from contact with an electrical ground.

Due to the increased levels of signal attenuation and interference caused by the narrower gauge cabling, thinnet is limited to a maximum network segment length of 185 meters, with no more than 30 MAUs installed on that segment. As with thicknet, repeaters can be used to combine multiple segments into a single collision domain, but it should be noted that the MAUs within the repeater count towards the maximum of 30.

Unshielded Twisted Pair. In the same way that thinnet overtook thicknet in popularity in the late 1980s, so the use of *unshielded twisted-pair cabling* (UTP) has come to be the dominant Ethernet medium since its addition to the 802.3 standard in 1989. This revision of the standard is known as the *802.3i 10BaseT* specification. Other UTP-based solutions did, however, exist prior to the ratification of the standard—most notably LattisNet, a system developed by Synoptics that at one time was on its way toward becoming an industry standard itself. LattisNet is not compatible with 10BaseT, though, as the latter synchronizes signals at the sending end and the former at the receiving end.

A UTP or 10BaseT Ethernet network is an adaptation of the cabling commonly used for telephone systems to LAN use. The T in 10BaseT refers to the way in which the two or more pairs of wires within an insulated sheath are twisted together throughout the entire length of the cable. This is a standard technique used to improve the signal transmission capabilities of the medium.

The greatest advantages to 10BaseT are its flexibility and ease of installation. Thinner than even thinnet cable, UTP cabling is easily installed within the walls of an existing site, providing a neat, professional-looking installation in which a single length of cable attaches each DTE device to a jack within a wall plate, just as a telephone is connected. Some sites have even adapted existing telephone installations for the use of their computer networks.

Many different opinions exist concerning the guidelines by which 10BaseT cabling should be installed. For example, the EIA/TIA-569 standard for data cable installation states that data cable should not be run next to power cables, but in most cases, this practice does not show any adverse effect on a 10BaseT network. This is because any electrical interference will affect all of the pairs within the cable equally. Most of the interference should be negated by the twists in the cable, but any interference that is not should be ignored by the receiving interface because of the differential signaling method used by 10BaseT.

Another common question is whether or not the two pairs of wires in a standard four-pair UTP cable run that are unused by Ethernet communications may be used for another purpose. The general consensus is that these may be used for digital telephone connections but not for standard analog telephone because of the high ring voltage. Connections to other resources (such as minicomputers or mainframes) are also possible, but using the cable for other connections may limit the overall length of the segment. The only way to know this for sure is to try using the extra pairs under maximum load conditions, and then test to see if problems occur.

Unlike both thicknet and thinnet, 10BaseT in not installed in a bus topology. Instead, it uses a *distributed star topology*, in which each device on the network has a dedicated connection to a centralized multiport repeater known as a *concentrator* or *hub* (see fig. 7.8). The primary advantage to this topology is that a disturbance in one cable affects only the single machine connected by that cable. Bus topologies, on the other hand, are subject to the "Christmas light effect," in which one bad connection will interrupt network communications not only to one machine but to every machine down the line from that one. The greater amount of cabling needed for a 10BaseT installation is offset by the relatively low price of the cable itself, but the need for hubs containing a port for every node on the network adds significantly to the overall price of this type of network.

Two devices can be directly connected with a 10BaseT cable that provides signal crossover, without an intervening hub, but only two, resulting in an effective, if minimal, network.

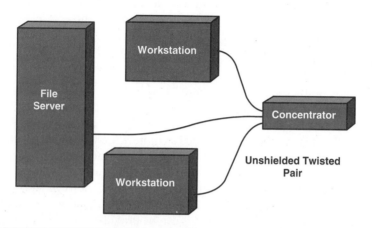

Figure 7.8

This is a basic 10BaseT UTP network.

While the coaxial cable used for the other Ethernet types is relatively consistent in its transmission capabilities, allowing for specific guidelines as to segment length and other attributes, the UTP cable used for 10BaseT networks is available in several grades that determine its transmission capabilities. Table 7.1 lists the various data grades and their properties. IBM (of course) has its own cable designations. These are listed in the section on Token Ring networks later in this chapter. The 802.3i standard specifies the maximum length of a 10BaseT segment to be 100 meters from the hub to the DTE, using Category 3 UTP cable, also known as *voice grade UTP*. This is the standard medium used for traditional telephone installations, and the 802.3i document was written on the assumption that many sites would be adapting existing cable for network use. This cable typically is 24 AWG (American Wire Gauge, a standard for measuring the diameter of a wire), copper tinned, with solid conductors, 100–105-ohm characteristic impedance, and a minimum of two twists per foot.

Table 7.1 UTP Cable Types and Their Speed Ratings		
Category	**Speed**	**Used For**
2	Up to 1 Mbps	Telephone Wiring
3	Up to 16 Mbps	Ethernet 10BaseT
4	Up to 20 Mbps	Token Ring, 10BaseT
5	Up to 100 Mbps	10BaseT, 100BaseT

In new installations today, however, the use of Category 5 cabling and attachment hardware is becoming much more prevalent. A Category 5 installation will be much less liable to *signal crosstalk* (the bleeding of signals between the transmit and receive wire pairs within the cable) and *attenuation* (the signal lost over the length of the cable) than Category 3, allowing for greater segment lengths and, more importantly, future upgrades to the 100 Mbps Fast Ethernet standards now under development. The 100-meter segment length is an estimate provided by the specification, but the actual limiting factor involved is the signal loss from source to destination, measured in decibels (dB). The maximum allowable signal loss for a 10BaseT segment is 11.5 dB, and the quality of the cable used will have a significant effect on its signal carrying capabilities.

10BaseT segments utilize standard 8-pin RJ-45 (RJ stands for *registered jack*) telephone type connectors (see fig. 7.9) both at the hub and at the MDI. Usually the cabling will be pulled within the walls or ceiling of the site from the hub to a plate in the wall near the computer or DTE. A patch cable is then used to connect the wall socket to the NIC itself. This provides a connection between the two MAUs on the circuit, one integrated into the hub and the other integrated into the network interface of the DTE. Since UTP cable utilizes separate pairs of wires for transmitting and receiving, however, it is crucial that the transmit pair from one MAU be connected to the receive pair on the other, and vice versa. This is known as *signal crossover*, and it can be provided either by a special crossover cable or it can be integrated into the design of the hub. The latter solution is preferable because it allows the entire wiring installation to be performed "straight through," without concern for the crossover. The 802.3i specification requires that each hub port containing a crossover circuit be marked with an "X" to signify this.

Figure 7.9

An RJ-45 connector looks like a telephone cable connector.

While existing Category 3 cable can be used for 10BaseT, for new cable installations, the use of Category 5 cable is strongly recommended. Future developments in networking will never give cause to regret this decision, and the savings on future upgrades will almost certainly outweigh the initial expense. In addition, if cost is a factor, considerable savings can be realized by pulling Category 5 cable and utilizing Category 3 hardware for the connectors. These can later be upgraded without the need for invasive work.

The hubs used for a 10BaseT network may contain up to 132 ports, enabling the connection of that many devices, but multiple hubs can be connected to each other using a 10Base2 or other type of segment, or the 10BaseT ports themselves (as long as signal crossover is somehow provided). Up to three mixing segments connecting multiple hubs can be created, supporting up to 30 hubs each. Thus, as with the 10BaseF variants to be examined later, it is possible to install the Ethernet maximum of 1024 nodes on a single network, without violating any of the other 802.3 configuration specifications. Hubs that conform to the standard will also contain a *link integrity circuit* that is designed to ensure that the connection between the hub port and the DTE at the other end of the cable remains intact.

Every 1/60th of a second, a pulse is sent out of each active port on a hub. If the appropriate response is not received from the connected device, then most hubs will be able to automatically disable the functionality of that port. Green LEDs on both the hub port and the NIC in the DTE will also be extinguished. This sort of link integrity checking is important for 10BaseT networks because, unlike the coaxial Ethernets, separate transmit and receive wire pairs are used. If a DTE was to have a non-functioning receive wire, for example, due to a faulty interface, it may interpret this as a quiet channel when network traffic is, in fact, occurring. This may cause it to transmit at the wrong times, perhaps even continuously, a condition known as *jabber*, resulting in many more collisions than the system is intended to cope with.

One of the frequent causes of problems on 10BaseT networks stems from the use of improper patch cables to connect computers to the wall socket. The standard satin cables used to connect telephones will appear to function properly when used to connect a DTE to a UTP network. However, these cables lack the twisting that is a crucial factor in suppressing the signal crosstalk that this medium is subject to. On a twisted-pair Ethernet network, collisions are detected by comparing the signals on the transmit and receive pairs within the UTP cable. When signals are detected at the same time on both pairs, the collision mechanism is triggered.

Excessive amounts of crosstalk can cause *phantom collisions*, which occur too late to be retransmitted by the MAC mechanisms within the Ethernet interface. These packets are therefore discarded and must later be detected and retransmitted by the upper layers of the OSI model. This process can reduce network performance considerably, especially when multiplied by a large number of computers.

Fiber-Optic Ethernet. The use of fiber-optic cable to network computers has found, with good reason, great favor in the industry. Most of the common drawbacks of copper media are virtually eliminated in this new technology. Since pulses of light are used instead of electrical current, there is no possibility of signal crosstalk and attenuation levels are far lower, resulting in much greater possible segment lengths. Devices connected by fiber-optic cable are also electrically isolated, allowing links between remote buildings to be safely created. Conducting links between buildings can be very dangerous, due to electrical disturbances caused by differences in ground potential, lightning, and other natural phenomena.

This sort of link between buildings is also facilitated by the fiber-optic cable's narrow gauge and high flexibility. Other means of establishing Ethernet connections between buildings are available, many of them utilizing *unbounded*, or wireless, media such as lasers, microwaves, or radio, but these are generally far more expensive and much less reliable. Fiber-optic cable is also capable of carrying far more data than the 10 Mbps defined by the Ethernet standards. Its primary drawback is its continued high installation and hardware costs, even after years on the market. For this reason, fiber-optic technology is used primarily as a backbone medium, to link servers or repeaters over long distances rather than for connections to the desktop, except in environments where electromagnetic interference (EMI) levels are high enough to prevent the use of other media.

FDDI is a fiber-optic-based network standard that supports speeds of 100 Mbps, and this will be examined later in this chapter, but there is also an Ethernet alternative known as *10BaseF* that utilizes the same medium. Cabling can be installed to run at the 10 Mbps provided by the Ethernet standard and later upgraded to higher speeds by the replacement of hubs and adapters. Like 10BaseT, fiber optic uses separate cables for transmitting and receiving data, but the two are not combined in one sheath, as UTP is, nor is there any reason for them to be twisted. The Ethernet fiber standards allow the use of an MAU that is external to the NIC, such as is used by thicknet networks. The fiber-optic MAU (FOMAU) is connected to the MDI using the same type of AUI cable used by thicknet MAUs. Other 10BaseF interfaces may integrate the MAU onto the expansion card, as with the other Ethernet variants.

The first fiber-optic standard for Ethernet was part of the original DIX standard of the early 1980s. Known as *the Fiber Optic Inter-Repeater Link* segment (*FOIRL*), its purpose, as the name implies, was to link repeaters at locations up to 1,000 meters away, too distant for the other Ethernet media types to span. This also provided a convenient method for linking different network types, once the thinnet and 10BaseT media standards came into use. As prices for the fiber-optic hardware came down, however (from outlandish to merely unreasonable), some users expressed a desire to use fiber links directly to the desktop. Some equipment allowing this was marketed before there was a standard supporting such practices, but the 10BaseF additions to the 802.3 specification provide a number of fiber-based alternatives to a simple repeater link segment.

When discussing the configuration of multiple Ethernet segments, the terms link segment and mixing segment are used to describe the two fundamental types of connections between repeaters. A *link segment* is one that has only two connections on it—that is, a link between two DTEs only, most often used to span the distance between two remotely located networks. A *mixing segment* is one that contains more than two connections, usually for the purpose of attaching nodes to the network. Thus, a standard thick or thin Ethernet bus connecting any number of computers would be a mixing segment. Technically, each connection on a 10BaseT network is a link segment because there are no intervening connections between the MAU in the hub and MAU on the NIC.

Several sub-designations are specified by the 10BaseF standard, and the primary difference between them is the type of segment for which they are intended to be used.

- *10BaseFL*   A replacement for the older FOIRL standard. It is designed for use as a full duplex link segment between two devices up to 2,000 meters apart, and it is backwards-compatible with existing FOIRL equipment, although use of the older repeaters limits the overall length of the segment to 1,000 meters.

- *10BaseFB*   Designed for use as a synchronous signaling backbone between repeaters. It allows the normal Ethernet 5-4-3 rule (covered later in this chapter) to be exceeded, due to its greater efficiency. Segments of this type may also be up to 2,000 meters long.

- *10BaseFP*   Defines a fiber system utilizing a *passive star* hub to connect with nodes up to 500 meters away without using repeaters. Unlike 10BaseT hubs, which electronically modify the signal to extend its range, this type of hub is purely mechanical in nature, using mirrors to split the beam of light among the outgoing ports.

Broadband Ethernet. Although it is not often used, there is a broadband standard for Ethernet networks. A *broadband* network is one in which the network bandwidth is divided or split to allow multiple signals to be sent simultaneously. This is called *multiplexing*, and the Ethernet variant uses a method of multiplexing called *frequency division multiplexing*. The concept and the cable itself are similar to those used for a cable television network. Multiple signals are all transmitted at the same time, and the receiving station chooses the appropriate one by selecting a certain frequency to monitor. This form of Ethernet is known as *10Broad36* because the maximum segment length allowed by the standard is 3,600 meters. This is far longer than any other allowable segment in the entire specification, obviously providing the capability to make connections over extremely long distances. Fiber-optic cable has become much more popular for this purpose, however, and 10Broad36 installations are few and far between.

Configuration Guidelines for Multiple Ethernet Segments

As touched upon earlier, the key to the successful operation of an Ethernet network is the proper functioning of the media access control and collision detection mechanisms. Signals must be completely propagated around a collision domain according to specific timing specifications for the system to work reliably. The two primary factors controlled by these specifications are the round-trip signal propagation delay and the inter-packet gap.

The larger an Ethernet network is and the more segments that comprise a specific collision domain, the greater the amount of signal delay incurred as each packet wends its way to the far ends of the network medium. It is crucial to the efficient operation of the system that this *round-trip signal propagation delay* not exceed the limits imposed by the 802.3 specification.

When consecutive packets are transmitted over an Ethernet network, the specification calls for a specific *inter-packet gap*—that is, a required minimum amount of space (amounting to 9.6 microseconds) between packet transmissions. The normal operations of a repeater, when combined with the standard amount of signal disturbance that occurs as a packet travels over the network medium, can lead to a reduction in the length of this gap, causing possible packet loss. This is known as *tailgating*. A typical Ethernet interface is usually configured to pause for a brief period of time after reading the end of a packet. This *blind time* prevents the normal noise at the end of a packet from being treated as the beginning of a subsequent packet. Obviously, the blind time must be less than the inter-packet gap; it usually ranges from 1 to 4 microseconds. Should the inter-packet gap time be reduced to a value smaller than the blind time, an incoming packet may not be properly recognized as such and therefore discarded.

The 802.3 specification provides two possible means of determining the limitations that must be imposed on a particular network to maintain the proper values for these two attributes. One is a complex mathematical method by which the individual components of a specific network can be enumerated and values assigned based on segment lengths, number of connections, and number and placement of repeaters to perform calculations resulting in the precise signal propagation delay and inter-packet gap figures for that installation. It is then easy to determine just what can be done to that network, while still remaining within acceptable range of values provided by the specification.

This procedure is usually only performed on networks that are a great deal more complex than the models provided as the other method for configuring a multi-segment network. This is sometimes known as the 5-4-3 rule, and it provides a series of simple guidelines to follow in order to prevent an Ethernet network from becoming too large to manage its own functions.

The basic 5-4-3 rule states that a transmission between any two devices within a single collision domain can pass through no more than five network segments, connected by four repeaters, of which no more than three of the segments are mixing segments. The transmission can also pass through no more than two MAUs and two AUIs, excluding those within the repeaters themselves. The repeaters used must also be compliant with the specifications in the 802.3 standard for their functions. When a network consists of only four segments, connected by three repeaters, then all of the segments may be mixing segments, if desired.

On a 10BaseT network, two segments are always utilized to connect the communicating machines to their respective hubs. Since these two segments are both link segments because there are no connections other than those to the MAUs in the hub and the host adapter, this leaves up to three mixing segments for use in interconnecting multiple hubs.

A number of exceptions to this basic rule are defined as part of the 10BaseF standards, and these are among the primary advantages of these standards on an Ethernet. On a network composed of five segments with four repeaters, fiber-optic link segments (whether FOIRL, 10BaseFB, or 10BaseFL) can be up to 500 meters long, while fiber-optic mixing segments (10BaseFP) can be no longer than 300 meters. On a network with only four segments and three repeaters, fiber-optic links between repeaters can be up to 1,000 meters long for FOIRL, 10BaseFB, and 10BaseFL segments and 700 meters long for 10BaseFP segments. Links between a repeater and a DTE can be no longer than 400 meters for 10BaseFL segments and 300 meters for 10BaseFP segments.

Obviously, these specifications provide only the broadest estimation of the actual values that may be found on a particular network. These rules define the maximum allowable limits for a single collision domain, and Ethernet is a network type that functions best when it is not pushed to its limits. This is not to say, however, that exceeding these limitations in any way will cause immediate problems. A segment that is longer than the recommended limit, or a segment with a few more DTEs than specified in the standard will probably not cause your network to grind to a screeching halt. It can, however, cause a slight degradation of performance that will only be exacerbated by further expansion.

Fast Ethernet

As applications and data types become larger and more demanding, a need for greater network throughput to the desktop has become apparent, and several new networking standards have risen out of that need. Although network speeds of up to 100 Mbps have been achievable for some time through the use of FDDI fiber-optic links, this technology remains too complex and expensive for use in connections to individual workstations, in most cases. However, FDDI continues to be a popular choice for network backbone links, particularly when large distances must be spanned or remote buildings on a campus network linked together.

Another technology that promises to deliver increased throughput to the desktop is asynchronous transfer mode (ATM). This new communications standard is commonly recognized as being a dominant player in the future of networking, but the absence of ratified standards has made it far too tenuous a technology to draw major commitments from network administrators at this time. The first ATM products have hit the market, but chances of interoperability between manufacturers are slim right now.

The other great drawback of these alternative high-speed networking solutions is that they both require a complete replacement of virtually every network-related component in the system, from host adapter to hub and everything in between. What was needed for the average corporate network was a system that could allow for the use of cabling already installed at the site, when necessary, and provide a gradual upgrade path for the other networking hardware so that the entire network would not have to be rebuilt in order to perform the upgrade.

To satisfy this need, several competing standards have arisen that utilize existing 10BaseT cable networks to provide 100 Mbps to the desktop. Of these competing standards, only the IEEE 802.3u document, also known as the *100BaseT* standard, can truly be called an Ethernet network. Other standards, such as the 100VG (voice grade) AnyLAN network being promulgated by Hewlett Packard and other vendors may run over the same cable types, but they use different methods of media access control, making them incompatible with existing Ethernet networks. 100BaseT utilizes the exact same frame format and CSMA/CD media access and collision detection techniques as existing 802.3 networks. This means that all existing protocol analysis and network management tools, as well as the investments made in staff training on Ethernet networks, can still be used. In addition, backwards-compatibility with standard 10BaseT traffic and a feature providing auto-negotiation of transmission speed allow for the gradual introduction of 100BaseT hardware onto an existing 10BaseT network.

Ethernet host adapters that support both 10 Mbps and 100 Mbps speeds are becoming commonplace on the market. This market is a highly competitive one, and the additional circuitry required for the adapters is minimal, causing prices to drop quickly as this technology rapidly gains in popularity. Computers with such adapters installed can be operated at standard 10 Mbps speed until a hub supporting the new standard is installed. The auto-negotiation feature will then cause the workstation to shift to the higher transmission rate. In this way, workstations can be shifted to 100 Mbps as the users' needs dictate. This is a rare instance when the network can be made to conform to the user, instead of the other way around.

Indeed, virtually every part of the 100BaseT standard is designed around compatibility issues with existing hardware. Three different cabling standards are provided to accommodate existing networks, and even new installations can benefit from the fact that the fiber-optic wiring standard, for example, is adopted wholesale from the document specifying the wiring guidelines for fiber-optic cable used in FDDI networks. This prevents cable installers from having to learn new guidelines to perform an installation and also keeps prices down. This can be an important factor when you are contracting to have wire pulled for a new site.

Remember that people may have been pulling twisted-pair cable for business office phone systems for decades but still know little or nothing about the requirements for a data-grade installation. Be sure that your contractors are familiar with the standards for the type of cabling that you choose to install and that specific details about the way in which the installation is to be performed are included in the contract. This may include specifications regarding proximity to other service connections, signal crossover, and use of other wire pairs within the same cable, as well as the type and grade of materials employed.

Another factor of a cabling installation that may be of prime importance is when the work is actually done. Unless you are installing a network into brand-new space that is not yet occupied, you will be faced with the dilemma of whether or not you should attempt to have the installation performed while business is being conducted. Standards such as 100BaseT have made it possible for network upgrades to be performed without interruption of business. The question of whether to pay overtime rates in order to have cabling installed at night or on weekends or whether to have the contractors attempt to work around your employees is one that must be individually made for every type of business. A good cabling contractor, though, should be able to work nights and still leave an unfinished job site in a state that is suitable for corporate business each day. This is often the mark of a true professional.

100BaseT Cabling Standards. The three cabling standards provided in the 100BaseT specification are designed to accommodate virtually all of the extant cabling installed for use in 10BaseT networks. Obviously, the primary goal is to allow 100BaseT speeds to be introduced onto an existing network without the need for pulling all new cable. Table 7.2 lists the three standards and type of cabling that is called for in each.

Table 7.2 100BaseT Cabling Standards		
Standard	**Cable Type**	**Segment Length**
100BaseTX	Category 5 (two pairs)	100 meters
100BaseT4	Category 3, 4, or 5 (four pairs)	100 meters
100BaseFX	62.5 micrometer Multimode Fiber (2 strands)	400 meters

All of the standards listed above utilize a similar interface between the actual network medium and the Ethernet port provided by the NIC in the DTE. A medium dependent interface, or MDI, the same as one that can be used for a 10BaseT network, connects to the network cable and is linked to the Ethernet adapter with a *physical layer device* (*PHY*) and a *media independent interface* (*MII*). These two components may take several forms.

Many 100BaseT host adapter cards are now available that integrate all of these components as circuitry on the expansion card, allowing a standard RJ-45 connection from the network medium to the adapter itself. Other realizations of the technology may take the form of a daughter card that provides switchable 10/100 Mbps capability to an existing 10BaseT adapter. This connects to the network medium utilizing an RJ-45 jack and plug directly into the Ethernet adapter in the host machine. The third possible configuration is through the use of an external physical layer device, much like the separate MAUs or transceivers used by thicknet systems. The MII of this device then connects to the Ethernet adapter using a short (no more than 0.5 meter) 40-pin cable.

In this way, a number of options are provided to accommodate the networking equipment already installed. Any one of these arrangements can be attached to any one of the designated cable types, providing enough flexibility to allow 100BaseT to be used as a high-speed networking solution. As we examine the three cabling standards in the following sections, notice the way in which they encompass virtually every twisted-pair cabling installation in place today, providing almost universal upgradeability.

100BaseTX. Generally speaking, UTP cabling that conforms to the EIA/TIA Category 5 specification is recommended for use by data transmission systems running at high speeds. The 100BaseTX standard is provided for use by installations that have already had the foresight to install Category 5 cable. Using two pairs of wires, the pinouts for a 100BaseTX connection are identical to those of a standard 10BaseT network.

Although the cabling standard for 100BaseTX is based almost entirely on the ANSI TP-PMD wiring standard, the pinouts from the ANSI standard have been changed to allow 100BaseTX segments to be connected directly to existing Category 5 networks without modification. This ANSI standard also allows for the use of 150-ohm shielded twisted-pair (STP) cable, such as that used for token-ring networks. Thus, network types other than Ethernet can also be adapted to the 100BaseT standard, although without the interoperability and auto-negotiation provided to existing 10BaseT Ethernets. Cable of this type, using 9-pin D connectors, is wired according to the ANSI TP-PMD specifications.

As with 10BaseT, the maximum segment length called for by the 100BaseTX standard is 100 meters but for a different reason. Segment length on a 10BaseT network is determined by loss of signal strength as a pulse travels over the network medium. Although 100 meters is used as a rule of thumb, a Category 5 10BaseT installation can often include segments of up to 150 meters, as long as the signal strength is maintained. Cable testers of various types can be used to determine whether the installed network maintains the signal strength necessary to extend the segment beyond 100 meters.

For a 100BaseTX segment, however, the 100-meter limitation is imposed to make sure that the round trip timing specifications of the standard are followed. Thus, it is not the strength of the signal, but the amount of time that it takes for the signal to be propagated over the segment that determines the maximum segment length. In other words, 100 meters is a strict guideline that should not be exceeded, even to the point at which the maximum 0.5 meter length of an MII cable (at each end) must be subtracted from the overall segment length.

As with 10BaseT networks, 100BaseTX segments must provide signal crossover at some location on the network. The connections for the transmit pair of wires at one end of the segment, must be attached to the receive connections at the other end, so that proper bi-directional communications can be provided. This crossover can be provided within the hub (in which case a port must be marked with an "X") or within the cable itself.

100BaseT4. In order not to alienate the administrators of the large number of installed 10BaseT networks that utilize voice grade Category 3 cabling, a cabling standard was provided to accommodate 100BaseT on networks of this type. To compensate for the decreased signal strength provided by the lesser quality cable, however, the standard requires the use of four wire pairs, instead of the two used by both 10BaseT and 100BaseTX.

Of the four pairs, the transmit (TX) and receive (RX) wires utilize the same pinouts as 100BaseTX (and 10BaseT). The two additional pairs are configured for use as bi-directional connections, labeled BI_D3 and BI_D4, using the remaining four connectors in the standard RJ-45 jack. Signal crossover for the transmit and receive pairs is identical to that of a 100BaseTX segment, but the two bi-directional pairs must be crossed over as well, with the D3 pair connected to the D4 pair and vice versa. Again, this crossover can be provided by the cable itself or within the hub.

In every other way, a 100BaseT4 segment is configured identically to a 100BaseTX segment. For installations that are limited by the quality of the cable that they are utilizing but which have the extra wire pairs available, creating 100BaseT4 segments can be more economically feasible than pulling new cable for an entire network. Transitional technology such as this allows a network to be gradually upgraded as time and finances permit. As we shall see, different 100BaseT segment types, along with 10BaseT segments, can be easily combined in a single network, allowing additional throughput to be allocated to users as needed.

100BaseFX. The 100BaseFX specification provides for the establishment of fiber-optic link segments that can take advantage of the greater distances and electrical isolation provided by fiber-optic cabling. The medium used is two separate strands of multimode fiber-optic (MMF) cable with an inner core diameter of 62.5 micrometers and an outer cladding diameter of 125 micrometers. Since the crosstalk and signal attenuation problems common to copper cabling are much less of an issue with fiber optic, separate strands of cable are used with no need for twisting, and the crossover connection can be provided by the link connections themselves, rather than inside the hub. A maximum signal loss of 11 dB over the length of the segment is specified by the standard, but the 400-meter maximum segment length is specified, again, by the need for a highly specific maximum round trip signal propagation delay, rather than concern for signal loss.

Several different connector types may be used for the 100BaseFX MDI, again to accommodate the different legacy networks that may be adapted to this technology. The connector type most highly recommended by the specification is the *duplex SC connector*, although a standard M type FDDI media interface connector (MIC), or a *spring loaded bayonet* (*ST*) connector may be used as well. Since they utilize the exact same signaling scheme, the 100BaseFX and the 100BaseTX specifications are known collectively as the *100BaseX* specifications.

100BaseT Network Configuration Guidelines. The 100BaseT specification defines two classes of multiport repeaters or hubs for use with all of the various media types. As with the 10BaseT standard, these devices are defined as concentrators that connect disparate network segments to form a single collision domain, or network. A Class I hub can be used to connect segments of different media types while a Class II hub can only connect segments of the same media type. The standard dictates that the different hub types must be labeled with the appropriate Roman numeral within a circle, for easy identification.

The fundamental 100BaseT rules for connecting segments within a single collision domain are as follows:

- Two segments of the maximum length called for by the individual media types can be connected via a Class I or Class II repeater (subject to some further limitations for certain media types).

- No more than one Class I or two Class II repeaters may lie in the path between any two networked DTEs.

Table 7.3 lists the maximum segment lengths allowed according to media type and repeater type.

Table 7.3 Maximum Collision Domain Diameters for 100BaseT

Repeater Type	100BaseTX/T4	100BaseFX	Mixed Fiber/Copper
Direct DTE-DTE	100 meters	N/A	400 meters
1 Class I Repeater	200 meters	230 meters	240 meters
1 Class II Repeater	200 meters	285 meters	318 meters
2 Class II Repeaters	205 meters	212 meters	226 meters

As you can see, the copper media types provide for fairly consistent limits throughout the various configurations, but the introduction of fiber-optic cable extends the length limitations. The one exception to this is the 205 meter limit when connecting copper segments with two Class II repeaters. This figure is valid for Category 5 cabling only. Voice grade Category 3 cable is limited to an overall length of 200 meters.

Class I repeaters generally provide greater amounts of delay overhead when translating signals for use with the various media types, so they impose greater segment length limitations than repeaters of the Class II variety. When mixed networks using both copper and fiber segments are defined, the figures provided in the table assume a 100 meter copper segment as contributing towards the total listed. It should also be noted that, for all of the network types, the maximum total one-meter length of any MII cables used (0.5 meters at each end) must be counted towards the total length of the segment.

These quibbles over what seem to be inconsequential variances in segment length should indicate how tightly these estimates are integrated into the 100BaseT specifications. 10Mbps networks do not tax the medium to the degree at which 100 Mbps ones do, and so a certain unofficial "fudge factor" can be assumed to exist on the slower systems. Long experience has determined that many standard Ethernet networks continue to function acceptably, despite physical layer installations that exceed the recommended specifications. 100BaseT is far newer technology, however, and a far narrower margin for variation is provided. It is recommended that these limitations be adhered to quite stringently, at least until experience has determined where variations can safely be made.

As with traditional Ethernet, the 100BaseT standard provides the means by which individual network segment limitations may be calculated mathematically. The primary limiting factor for 100BaseT, however, is the *Path Delay Value*, which is a measurement of the round trip signal propagation delay of the *worst case path*—that is, the two stations on the network that are the greatest distance apart, with the greatest number of repeaters between them. Cable delay values for the specific types of media used to form the network, along with the distances spanned, and the number of repeaters, are plugged into a formula, an extra margin is added for additional safety, and a specific value is derived that indicates whether or not the network meets the requirements of the 100BaseT standard. As with 10BaseT, exceeding the recommended values can result in late collisions and packet CRC errors that severely affect the efficiency and reliability of the network.

Obviously, the limitation in the number of repeaters allowed in a 100BaseT collision domain over that of 10BaseT will require a certain amount of redesign in some networks being retrofitted to the faster system. An existing network that is stretched to the limit of the 5-4-3 10BaseT guideline may have to have its repeaters relocated to conform to the new restrictions, but the increased segment lengths allowed for most of the cabling types should make the task a possible one for most existing installations. In any case, it should be clear that migrating to 100BaseT is more than just a matter of replacing NICs and hubs.

Ethernet Switching. Note also that the limitations detailed earlier apply only to segments within a single collision domain. Hubs that provide packet-switching services between the segments are becoming increasingly popular, and have come to make up a large portion of the market. A packet-switching hub essentially provides the same services as a repeater, but at a higher level. Packets received on one segment are regenerated for transmission via another. All of the OSI model from the network layer up is shared by the two segments, but the data link and the physical layer are isolated, establishing separate collision domains for the two and providing what is essentially a dedicated network for each port on the device.

In this way, a centrally located switch can be used to provide links to multiport repeaters at remote locations throughout the enterprise. These repeaters are then linked to individual workstations in the immediate area. The network, in its most strictly defined sense, extends from the switch port to the DTE, with only one intervening repeater. More demanding installations may even go so far as to use switched ports for the individual desktop connections themselves, thus providing the greatest possible amount of throughput to each workstation. As you may expect, a packet switching hub will be more expensive than a simpler repeating device, but they may be the most economical means of adapting an existing network to today's requirements. Just the time and expense saved by not having to replace dozens of LAN adapters in workstations all over the network may be enough to lure administrators towards this technology.

Bear in mind that this switching technique is by no means limited to networks using 100BaseT. Switches are becoming a popular solution for 10BaseT and even token-ring networks. In fact, adding switches to a 10BaseT network may provide enough additional performance to obviate the immediate need for a large-scale network upgrade program.

Full Duplex Ethernet. Another technique that is being used to increase the efficiency of both 10BaseT and 100BaseT links is the establishment of *full duplex Ethernet* connections. Ethernet networks normally communicate using a *half duplex* protocol. This means that only one station at a time can be transmitting over the network link. Like a two-way radio, a single station on the network may transmit and then must switch into a listen mode to receive a response. Managing this communications traffic without the loss of any data is the basic function of a media access control mechanism like CSMA/CD.

Full duplex Ethernet, on the other hand, functions more in the way that a telephone does, allowing both ends of a link segment to transmit and receive simultaneously, theoretically doubling the overall throughput of the link. For this reason, the entire Ethernet media access control system can be dispensed with when a full duplex link is established. In order to establish such a link, only two stations can be present in the collision domain. Like a party line telephone system, chaos would ensue if more than two parties were all speaking at the same time. Therefore, full duplex Ethernet is usually used to connect two packet-switched ports on remote hubs. The elimination of the media access protocol also removes the need for any concerns about signal propagation across the link, so very long distances may be spanned by 10BaseF or 100BaseFX links. The only limitation would be imposed by signal loss due to attenuation which, in fiber-optic connections, is minimal. Links of this type can span up to two kilometers or more and form an excellent means of connecting remote buildings on a campus network.

It must be noted that the full duplex Ethernet has not been standardized by the IEEE or by any other standards body. Individual hardware vendors are responsible for creating and marketing the concept. There may, therefore, be significant variations among different vendors in the rules for establishing such links. Compatibility of hardware made by different manufacturers is also not guaranteed. In addition, you will find that a full duplex link will generally not deliver the doubled throughput that theory dictates should result. This is because some of the higher layer network protocols in the OSI model also rely on what are essentially half duplex communication techniques. They cannot, therefore, make full use of the capabilities furnished by the data link layer, and the overall increase in throughput may be limited to somewhere between 25% and 50% over that of half duplex Ethernet. The cost of implementing full duplex into existing adapter and hub designs, however, is minimal, adding no more than 5% to the cost of the hardware. Therefore, even the moderate gain in throughput provided may be well worth the cost involved.

Auto-Negotiation. As on 10BaseT networks, 100BaseT utilizes a link pulse to continually test the efficacy of each network connection, but the *fast link pulse* (*FLP*) signals generated by 100BaseT adapters are utilized for another function as well. Unlike the *normal link pulse* (*NLP*) signals generated by 10BaseT, which simply signal that a proper connection exists, FLP signals are used by 100BaseT stations to advertise their communications abilites.

At the very least, an indication of the greatest possible communications speed is furnished by the FLP, but additional information may be provided as well, such as the ability of the station to establish a full duplex Ethernet connection and other data useful for network management. This information can be used by the two stations at either end of a link segment to *auto-negotiate* the fastest possible link supported by both stations. Although an optional feature, according to the 100BaseT standard, auto-negotiation is a popular option, considering the large number of hubs and adapters coming to market that can support both 10 and 100 Mbps speeds. Several different approaches to the inclusion of additional functionality into the FLP exist, however. One of these that has received a good deal of attention is called *NWay*. Developed by National Semiconductor,

NWay must reside in both the adapter and the hub for the full auto-negotiation capabilities to be utilized. Many vendors are considering it for inclusion in their products, but until a standard for this technology is realized, either by an official governing body or simply by *vox populi*, these must be considered to be proprietary techniques and evaluated as such.

Since auto-negotiation is optional, there is more control provided over the generation of the link pulse signals than with 10BaseT. Settings are usually made available at each device to allow the pulses to be generated automatically when the device is powered up, or it may be implemented manually. Fast link pulses are designed to coexist with the normal link pulses so that negotiation may take place with existing 10BaseT hardware as well. A traditional 10BaseT hub with no knowledge of auto-negotiation, when connected to an Ethernet adapter capable of operation at both 10 and 100 Mbps, will cause a link to be established at the slower speed and normal 10BaseT operations to continue without incompatibilities. This allows network managers to implement an upgrade program in any manner they choose. At this point in time, anyone with intentions of upgrading to 100BaseT should begin purchasing dual-speed Ethernet adapters for any new systems being installed. This way the replacement of a 10BaseT hub with a 100BaseT model can be performed at any future time desired, and the appropriately equipped workstations will shift to the higher-speed connection as soon as the new equipment is detected. As with 10BaseT systems, the pulses are only generated during network idle periods and have no effect on overall network traffic.

The auto-negotiation feature, when it is enabled, determines the highest common set of capabilities provided by both stations on a link segment, according to the following list of priorities, and then creates a connection using the highest priority protocol of which both sides are capable:

1. 100BaseTX Full Duplex

2. 100BaseT4

3. 100BaseTX

4. 10BaseT Full Duplex

5. 10BaseT

Notice that although 100BaseT4 and 100BaseTX are both capable of the same transmission speed, 100BaseT4 is given the higher priority. This is because it is capable of supporting a wider array of media types than 100BaseTX. A segment with hardware at both ends that supports both transmission types will default to 100BaseT4, rather than 100BaseTX, unless explicitly instructed otherwise.

When auto-negotiating hubs are used that are of the multiport repeater type, it must be noted, however, that since only a single signal is generated for use on all of the device's ports, the highest common speed of all of the devices connected to the hub will be used. In other words, a hub with ports connected to eleven DTEs with 100 Mbps network adapters and one DTE with a standard 10BaseT adapter will run all of the stations at

10 Mbps. A packet-switching hub is, of course, not subject to this limitation. Since each of its ports amounts to what is essentially a separate network, individual speed negotiations will take place for every port.

100VG AnyLAN. The primary source of competition to the 802.3u Fast Ethernet standard in the battle of the 100 Mbps networking specifications is known as *100 Voice Grade AnyLAN*, as defined in the 801.12 IEEE standard. Championed by Hewlett Packard and AT&T, as well as several other companies, it is, as the name implies, a networking standard that, like 100BaseT, provides 100 Mbps throughput but is specifically designed to take advantage of the existing voice grade Category 3 wiring that is already installed at so many network sites. Like 100BaseT4, the lower grade of cabling requires the use of four wire pairs instead of two, but beyond this, 100VG AnyLAN is radically different from 100BaseT.

First of all, 100VG AnyLAN cannot, by any means, be called an Ethernet network. In fact, it is a new protocol that is unique to the networking world and this, if anything, is its greatest drawback. All of the investments in time and money made on Ethernet or token-ring training along with management and troubleshooting tools for these environments are lost when you convert to 100VG AnyLAN. In addition, the standard is based on the assumption that the greatest single investment made in a network is in the cable installation. The basic philosophy of 100VG AnyLAN is to use a network's existing cable plant, including the existing RJ-45 jacks and cross connectors, but all other components, including hubs and adapters, must be replaced.

The cutthroat competition over these competing 100 Mbps standards is the result of users' clamor for a convenient and economical upgrade strategy for their networks. After all, FDDI and CDDI networks providing the same throughput have been available for years, but the expense and labor involved in converting to a network that runs such technology to the desktop has remained the prohibitive factor preventing its widespread acceptance. Both 100BaseT and 100VG AnyLAN provide more reasonable upgrade capabilities than FDDI and CDDI, providing the means for a gradual conversion spread out over as long a period of time as desired. Individual workstations can be upgraded to 100VG AnyLAN as the user's need arises because, as with 100BaseT, there are combination adapters available that provide plugs for both 10BaseT and AnyLAN.

In addition, the same Ethernet packet format as 10BaseT is used by 100VG AnyLAN, allowing hubs for the two network types to coexist on the same network. Although the Ethernet frame type is being supported first, there are also plans for 100VG AnyLAN hubs supporting the 802.5 frame type used by token-ring networks to be made available, as well as units supporting both packet types. The signaling scheme and the media access control protocol used by 100VG AnyLAN, however, are different from those used by any other network.

As a general rule, the overall similarity of the 100BaseT hardware to its 10BaseT counterparts will allow compatible equipment to be developed and produced more quickly and less expensively than that for 100VG AnyLAN. A combination 10BaseT/100VG AnyLAN NIC, for example, actually amounts to the components of two separate adapters on one card, while a 10/100BaseT NIC can utilize some of the same components for both functions to keep costs down. The same holds true for 100BaseT hubs and bridges, which are little more complex than 10BaseT models with the same capabilities. Also, a great many more vendors are currently producing 100BaseT hardware than 100VG AnyLAN, and many more systems manufacturers have declared their preference for its use than have advocated the other standard, giving it an immediate price advantage in the marketplace and a superior collection of testimonials.

These are all very young products, however, and it is difficult to predict the direction the pendulum will swing. Some hardware manufacturers are planning to produce equipment for both network types, refusing to take a definitive stand for one over the other. Others are attempting to combine the functionality for both networks in single devices, allowing the administrator to choose one of the two network types depending on the needs of the individual user. I dare say, though, that one of these network types will prove to be the dominant interim solution, as network administrators everywhere lick their chops in anticipation of ATM, which nearly everyone agrees will eventually come to dominate the networking industry, at some point one, two, five, or ten years down the road, depending on whose opinion you believe.

On the other side of the argument, however, is the fact that, despite the unavailability of long-term, real-world performance data, early reports indicate that 100VG AnyLAN generally provides a greater increase in network throughput than 100BaseT does. This is primarily because 100BaseT is subject to the same latency problems and tendency towards diminished performance under high-traffic conditions that normal Ethernet is. The technology that 100VG AnyLAN is based on provides nearly the entire potential throughput of the segment to each transmission.

Obviously, choosing one of the two standards is a complex decision, which must balance the need for maximum throughput versus a more solid, competitive, and economical market for the required hardware and factor in the need for staff training in order to support this new protocol. The following section examines how 100VG AnyLAN provides this allegedly superior level of performance, and provides background information to aid in the decision-making process between the two competing standards.

Quartet Signaling. A 10BaseT network utilizes two wire pairs for its communications. One is used to transmit, and the other for collision detection. The 100BaseT4 standard uses four pairs of wires, with the extra two pairs usable for communications in either direction. 100VG AnyLAN also uses four wire pairs, but it utilizes a technique called *quartet signaling* that allows it to transmit over all four wire pairs simultaneously. The encoding scheme used, called *5B/6B NRZ*, allows the number of bits transmitted per cycle to be two-and-a-half-times greater than that of 10BaseT networks. Multipled by the four pairs of wires used to transmit, this results in a tenfold overall increase in transmission speed, using only a slightly higher frequency than 10BaseT, thus allowing the use of voice grade cabling.

Demand Priority. The basic reason why all four wire pairs can be used to transmit simultaneously is that 100VG AnyLAN eliminates the need for a collision detection mechanism such as that found on Ethernet networks. The media access control method utilized by 100VG AnyLAN is called *demand priority*, and while it is radically different from the CSMA/CD method used by Ethernet, it makes a good deal of sense for the environment that it's used in.

As we have seen, the 10BaseT network standard is an adaptation of a protocol that was originally designed for a bus topology composed primarily of mixing segments, on which multiple nodes must contend for the same bandwidth. Networks wired in a star topology, however, are composed primarily of link segments. While the 802.3 standard was ingeniously adapted to the star configuration by designating the link segments for connection of the hub to the node and the mixing segments for the interconnection of the hubs, the primary sources of possible media contention are the network workstations. When the workstations are connected to a hub using link segments, negotiation for media access need only be conducted between two different entities (while on a mixing segment, up to 30 entities can be contending for the same bandwidth). 100VG AnyLAN takes advantage of the star topology by having intelligence within the hub control access to the network medium.

Demand priority calls for individual network nodes to request permission from the hub to transmit a packet. If the network is not being used, the hub permits the transmission, receives the packet, and directs it to the proper outgoing destination port. Unlike Ethernet, where every packet is seen by all of the nodes within a given collision domain, only the transmitting and receiving stations, along with the intervening hubs, ever see a particular AnyLAN packet, thus providing an added measure of security unavailable from traditional Ethernet, token-ring, or FDDI networks.

Since arbitration is provided by the hub, priorities for certain data types can also be established, allowing particular applications to be allotted an uninterrupted flow of bandwidth, if desired. For real-time multimedia applications such as videoconferencing, where careful flow control is required, this can be a crucial factor to good performance. As with token ring, there are no collisions on a 100VG AnyLAN network that is running properly. There are no delays, therefore, caused by packet retransmissions and no cause for network performance to decrease as traffic increases.

Integration with 10BaseT. 100VG AnyLAN can also be integrated into a 10BaseT segment through the use of bridges that buffer the higher speed transmissions, feeding them to the slower medium at the proper rate. This technique can also be used to attach 100VG networks to an existing backbone. No packet translation of any kind is necessary, which avoids any delays that would normally be incurred by this process and allows the necessary bridging circuitry to be easily incorporated within the hub if desired.

Overall, 100VG AnyLAN requires a higher degree of commitment from the network administrator than 100BaseT does. The hardware is much less reliant on tried-and-true technology and the innovative nature of the standard implies a greater risk as the marketplace determines whether the concept will continue to be a viable one. For the many administrators who are considering these 100 Mbps technologies as interim solutions for their networks, it would be understandable for them to be reticent to expend the time, effort, and expense to adapt to a new network type that would only be phased out within a few years. Current indications point to 100BaseT as being far more widely accepted by the industry than 100VG AnyLAN, but there are major industry players advocating both systems, and both or neither could come to dominate the high-speed networking world over the next few years.

The Workstation Bus. It should be noted that, for any network offering 100 Mbps performance levels, the ISA bus will generally be insufficient to support the needs of the network interface. 100BaseT network adapters are currently available only for EISA and PCI buses, and testing of various cards for both bus types made by the same manufacturers yields very little performance difference between the two. It should therefore not be necessary to upgrade from an EISA to a PCI machine simply to take full advantage of 100BaseT.

Adapters for the VESA Local Bus are not being produced, primarily because vendors have achieved the best performance levels from adapter designs using the bus mastering capabilities supported by the EISA and PCI buses that prevent network data from having to be moved on and off of the card to be manipulated by the system processor. Avoiding any additional burden on the processor also helps to increase overall system performance. High performance 100BaseT cards may also offer SRAM FIFO (high-speed static RAM, first in, first out) caching, coprocessors, and dedicated chips providing increased performance for the adapter's media access control functions.

While ISA cards for 100VG AnyLAN do exist, their generally poor performance levels seem to indicate that the system bus is probably the location of a greater bottleneck than any caused by the network. Obviously, the benefits and drawbacks of all of the available buses are as applicable to LAN adapters as they are to SCSI or video cards. Consult chapter 5, "The Server Platform," for in-depth coverage of the attributes of the different bus types.

Assessing User Need

Of course, as with any network-related upgrade, the question arises as to the real need for 100 Mbps to the desktop. Depending on the other hardware involved, the operating systems used by the servers and workstations, and the size and quantity of the files transmitted over the net, the overall increase in productivity provided by this type of network upgrade may prove to be negligible. This technology excels primarily in the sustained transfer of large files over the network medium. For applications that generate large amounts of network traffic, such as scientific, engineering, prepress, and software development environments, this may be a boon, and for networks that have been continually expanded in size and traffic levels without an increase in throughput, a significant performance bottleneck may be removed.

Most general-use business networks, however, are relatively empty, and the thoughtful LAN administrator faced with a slow network must be careful to determine exactly what is causing the slowdown before committing to a costly upgrade program. From a practical standpoint, Ethernet traffic problems can probably be more efficiently and economically addressed with the addition of Ethernet switches and a proper evaluation and reorganization of the network plan. A wholesale replacement of all hubs and adapters is probably not necessary just to have a properly functioning business network environment.

As to the new multimedia data types that are threatening to overwhelm traditional networks, if an administrator were to honestly ask whether her users really had a productive need for full motion video to the desktop, the answer would probably be no. Just because a new technology becomes available, doesn't mean that we should all go out and search for some way to put it to use. In fact, even full motion video can be adequately delivered to the desktop over the network, when 10 Mbps of dedicated bandwidth is supplied. When the networking industry marketing machine goes into a feeding frenzy over a new technology like Fast Ethernet, it can be difficult to find a clear path through the carnage in order to see whether the new product actually makes things better than they were before. This is a question that every LAN adminstrator must answer individually for every network that she is responsible for.

Token Ring

Barring the new networking technologies now gaining widespread attention in the marketplace, the traditional alternative to Ethernet has been the token-ring network. Originally developed by IBM, which still remains its primary champion, token-ring networks can deliver data at 16 Mbps using a media access control mechanism that is radically different from the CSMA/CD scheme used by Ethernet.

The IEEE 802.5 standard defines a token-ring network. The standard was deliberately developed to be an alternative to other 802.x media access control specifications, all of which utilize the same logical link control protocol defined in the 802.2 standard. Unlike the bus and star topologies utilized by Ethernet networks, token ring, as the name implies, organizes its connections in a *logical ring topology* so that packets can be passed from node to node in an endless rotation.

It is called a logical ring topology because the network is actually wired according to the same sort of star arrangement as a 10BaseT network. The ring exists only within the hubs to which all of the nodes are attached (see fig. 7.10). Usually known as *multistation attachment units*, MSAUs (sometimes improperly called MAUs), or simply *wiring centers* in the 802.5 document, token-ring concentrators provide more functionality than the multiport repeaters used for Ethernets. A token-ring MSAU monitors the existence of each node attached to its ports. A packet originating at any station is passed to the MSAU, which passes it in turn to the next station in the ring. That station returns it to the MSAU, which continues passing the packet around the ring until each attached node has received it. The packet is then removed from the ring by the node where it originated from.

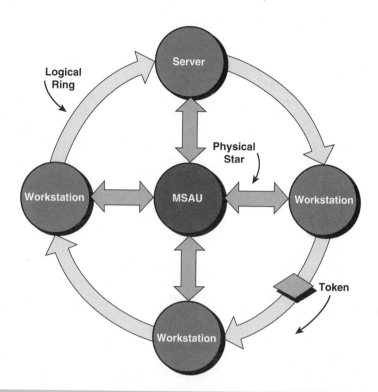

Figure 7.10

This is a basic token-ring network, showing both the physical star topology and the logical ring topology.

For this system to work, the MSAU must be constantly aware of the operation of each attached node. Should a packet be sent to a non-functioning workstation, it will not be returned to the MSAU and cannot be sent along on its way. Therefore, MSAUs continuously monitor the activity of all of the attached workstations. A node that is switched off or malfunctions is immediately removed from the ring by the bypass relays in the MSAU, and no further packets are sent to it until it signals its readiness to continue.

The original token-ring MSAUs developed by IBM actually used a mechanical device to control access to each port. Before attaching the cable that was connected to a workstation, the network administrator had to initialize the port to be used with a keying device that entered that port into the ring. In addition, the actual network medium and the connectors used were all of proprietary IBM design. The cabling was quite thick (a good deal thicker than the 50-ohm coaxial used for thin Ethernet) and the connectors large and unwieldy. Cables were also sold only in prepackaged form and available in a limited assortment of lengths. Since there was no competition at the time, the prices of all of the hardware components were gratuitously inflated. The original token-ring networks were also designed to run at a maximum speed of 4 Mbps.

It should be clear that, if these conditions had not changed considerably, token ring would have gone the way of StarLAN and ARCnet on the slow road to oblivion. However, the modern token-ring network is considerably more advanced than this, and now can provide 16 Mbps of throughput in what is, arguably, a manner that is better suited to high traffic networks than Ethernet. First of all, the preferred network medium for token ring is now type 1 *shielded twisted-pair cabling* (*STP*) that is similar to the UTP used in 10BaseT networks, except for additional insulation surrounding the twisted strands, thus providing increased resistance to EMI as well as a higher cost for the medium and its installation. The connectors used may be of the familiar RJ-45 telephone type, but DB-9 connectors (such as are used for the serial ports on PCs) can also be used. At the MSAU, self-shorting IBM data connectors are usually used.

The 802.5 document states that up to 250 stations can operate on the same ring, but it defines no specifics for the type of cable to be used, and real-world performance figures depend highly on the type of cable and the round-trip lengths of the segments extending from the MSAU to the connected node (called the *lobe length*). Token ring can even be run over conventional UTP cable, although the number of attached nodes and the lobe lengths will be further limited by the lesser capabilities of the medium. The IBM Token Ring specifications allow up to 260 lobes on an STP segment and up to 72 on a UTP segment. The following list describes the cable types, as defined by IBM, which have come into general use in the network industry.

- Type 1 Two pairs of 22 AWG cable with foil wrapped around each pair and a second foil sheath around both pairs, along with a ground. The most commonly used STP cable for token-ring networks.

- Type 2 Same as type 1 with an additional four pairs of voice grade cable attached to the outer sheath. Designed for single cable delivery of both telephone and data services.

- Type 3 Four pairs of unshielded 22 or 24 AWG cable, twisted at least twice per foot. The IBM classification for the UTP cabling used in many 10BaseT networks.

- Type 4 There is no Type 4.

- Type 5 Fiber-optic cable.

- Type 6 Two pairs of stranded, shielded 26 AWG cable used for patch or jumper cables.

- Type 7 One pair of stranded, 26 AWG cable.

- Type 8 Two pairs of 26 AWG cable run in parallel (that is, with no twisting). Used for under-carpet installations.

- Type 9 Two pairs of shielded, 26 AWG cable. Used for data, despite decreased transmission capabilities due to narrower gauge.

Generally speaking, the maximum allowable lobe length for cable types 1 and 2 is 200 meters, for type 3: 120 meters, for type 6: 45 meters, and type 5 can be up to 1,000 meters in length. The term *lobe length* is defined as the round-trip signaling distance between a workstation and an MSAU. A 100-meter cable connection therefore yields a lobe length of 200 meters. No more than three segments (joined by repeaters) can be connected in series, and there can be up to 33 MSAUs on a single network. If these last two statements seem contradictory, it is because when multiple token-ring MSAUs are interconnected to form a single ring, they do not comprise separate segments, as would the use of multiple hubs in an Ethernet network. Also, all of the nodes on a particular network must run at the same speed. Dual-speed token-ring NICs and MSAUs, which run at either 4 or 16 Mbps, are common. However, all of the ports on a single MSAU must run at the same speed and can be connected to another MSAU running at a different speed only by a bridge or a router so that two separate network domains are established.

MSAUs are also considerably more advanced than they were in the early days of token ring, with models available that provide similar features to the higher-end Ethernet concentrators. In addition, the current move of the industry towards switching over bridging or repeating also applies to token ring. Complex switches are even available that allow the connection and routing of data over multiple network types from the same device. Token ring, Ethernet, Fast Ethernet, FDDI, and even ATM networks can all be connected to the same device, and a packet entering through any port is routed directly out the port where the destination address is located, after being translated to the proper signalling type for the destination network.

Multiple MSAUs can also be interconnected to form a single ring. In a token-ring environment, a ring is the equivalent of a single collision domain or network in Ethernet parlance. Since collisions are not a normal occurrence on token-ring networks, the term collision domain is not valid, but a ring consists of a group of DTEs interconnected so that the same network segment is shared by all. Every MSAU has special ports, labeled Ring In (RI) and Ring Out (RO), which are designated for connection to other MSAUs, allowing you to create large rings of up to 250 nodes.

Media Access Control in Token-Ring Networks

As we have seen, the real key to the functionality of any network is how multiple stations can communicate using a shared network medium. Unlike Ethernet, in which each DTE essentially executes an independent instance of the accepted MAC protocol for its own use, the MSAU arbitrates token ring's media access.

Essentially, media access in a token-ring network is controlled by the passing of a specialized packet, or *token*, from one node to the next around the ring. Only one token can be present on the ring at any one time and that token contains a *monitor setting bit* that designates it as a "busy" or "free" token. Only a node in possession of a free token may transmit a frame.

When a workstation is ready to transmit a packet, it waits until a free token is sent to it by the preceding node in the ring. Once it has been received, the transmitting node appends its packet to the token, changes the monitor setting to busy, and sends it on its way to the next node in the ring. Each node in turn then receives the packet and passes it along, thus functioning in *normal repeat mode*, the functional equivalent to a unidirectional repeater.

Whether the packet is destined for use by that workstation or not, the packet is passed to the next node. Having traversed the entire ring, the packet then arrives back at the node that originated it. This node then reads the packet and compares it with what it had previously transmitted, as a check for data corruption. After passing this test, the originating workstation then removes the packet from the ring, generates a new free token and sends it to the next node, where the process begins again.

Some token-ring networks also support a feature called *early token release* (*ETR*), in which the sending node generates a free token immediately after it finishes transmitting its packet. Thus, the packet is sent without a busy token included, but with a free token following immediately after. The next station in the ring receives the data packet and the token and may then pass on the first data packet, transmit a data packet of its own, and then transmit another free token. In this manner, more than one packet may be traveling around the ring at any one time, but there will still be only one token. This eliminates the waiting periods incurred as tokens and packets are passed from station to station.

Thus, in theory, a collision should never occur on a token-ring network. Packets may be transmitted at the maximum rate allowed by the MAC protocol with no degradation of network performance. This is why many people consider token ring to be a superior type of network for heavy traffic environments. As an Ethernet network becomes busier, a larger number of collisions occur, forcing a greater number of retransmissions, and therefore, delays. On a token-ring network, although there is a greater amount of overhead traffic generated by maintenance functions, the maximum possible delay incurred before a given station can transmit is the period that the node must wait for a free token to be passed to it. The greater the traffic on the network, the longer this delay will be, but there is no additional traffic generated by the retransmission of packets damaged by collision, allowing the network to utilize virtually its entire bandwidth for authentic non-redundant traffic.

Token-ring stations are also capable of utilizing different access priority levels so that specific stations can be configured to be more likely to receive a free token that it can transmit with. The later discussion of the 802.5 frame types in this chapter covers how these priorities are exercised. There are also automatic mechanisms in a token-ring network that provide the means for recognizing and localizing error conditions on the network.

When any station on a ring detects a problem, such as a break in the ring, it begins a process called *beaconing* that helps isolate the exact location of the problem. Beacon frames are sent out over the network, which define a *failure domain*. The failure domain consists of the station detecting the failure and its *nearest active upstream neighbor* (*NAUN*). If there are any stations located between these two, they must, by definition, be inactive and are designated as the locations of the failure. An auto-reconfiguration process then begins; active stations within the failure domain activate diagnostic routines in the hope of bypassing the offending nodes, allowing communications to continue. Depending on the cause of the problem, the network may ultimately be halted, or it may continue to operate by removing problem stations from the ring.

As a means of monitoring and maintaining the network, one node on the ring acts as an *active monitor*. This station functions as the instigator for most of the ring control and maintenance procedures conducted by the network. Since all stations are capable of generating a token, for example, there must be one station that generates the first token, in order to start the process. This is one of the functions of the active monitor. It also initiates the *neighbor notification* process—each node on the network learns the identity of it nearest active upstream and downstream neighbors, provides timing services for the network, checks for the existence of packets circulating continuously around the ring, as well as performing other maintenance functions.

Any station may become the active monitor through a process called *token claiming* that is initiated whenever any station (or *standby monitor*, or *SM*) on the network fails to detect the existence of a frame or an active monitor (through the receipt of an *active monitor present*, or AMP MAC frame) within a designated amount of time. Token claiming consists of each SM sending out specialized frames based on address values. The first SM to receive three of its own frames back is designated the active monitor (AM). In this manner, the active monitor constantly checks the network, and the other nodes constantly check the active monitor to ensure that the network access mechanisms are always functioning properly.

There are many other functions defined in the *network management protocol* (*NMP*) defined in the 802.5 standard document, some of which may be performed by the active monitor or by other stations on the network, which may or may not be wholly dedicated to such a purpose. These include the *Ring Parameter Server* (*RPS*), which monitors the addresses of all nodes entering and leaving the ring; the *Ring Error Monitor* (*REM*), which tracks the occurrence and frequency of errors occurring on the ring; the *LAN Bridge Server* (*LBS*), which monitors the activities of all bridges connected to the network; and the *Configuration Report Server* (*CRS*), which gathers performance and configuration from other nodes on the network. All of the information generated by these functions can be sent to a node that has been specifically designated as the *network management node* by the running of software designed to compile, track, and analyze all of this data and adjust the network's performance characteristics accordingly.

The 802.5 Frame Format. Unlike Ethernet, which uses one basic frame type for all of its functions, the IEEE Token Ring standard defines several basic frame formats (see fig. 7.11), which are used for many different functions: a data/command frame, a token frame, and an abort sequence frame. The data/command frame is a single frame type that can be used both for transfer of LLC data to upper level protocols and for MAC information used to implement one of dozens of ring maintenance control procedures. Only the data frame contains information that is destined for use by protocols higher up in the OSI model. All of the other frame configurations are used solely for maintaining and controlling the ring.

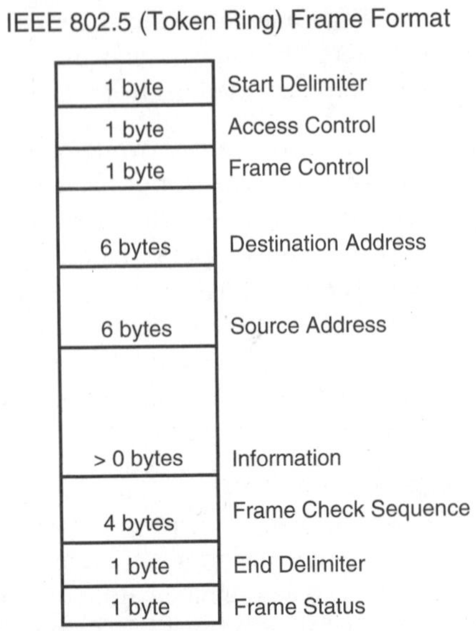

IEEE 802.5 (Token Ring) Frame Format

1 byte	Start Delimiter
1 byte	Access Control
1 byte	Frame Control
6 bytes	Destination Address
6 bytes	Source Address
> 0 bytes	Information
4 bytes	Frame Check Sequence
1 byte	End Delimiter
1 byte	Frame Status

Figure 7.11

The fields that comprise the IEEE 802.5 data/command frame.

- *Start Delimiter (SD)*   A one-byte field that indicates the beginning of a token or data/control frame by deliberately violating the Differential Manchester encoding scheme used by the 802.5 protocol. See chapter 3, "The OSI Model: Bringing Order to Chaos," for more on encoding systems.

- *Access Control (AC)*   A one-byte field containing three priority bits and three reservation bits used to implement the token-ring priority mechanism. As it receives a transmitted frame and passes it on to the next station on the ring, a workstation may alter these bits to define a priority equal to itself. Different stations can be assigned different priorities (from 0–7) based on need. When a packet arrives back at the station from which it was sent, that station generates a new free token in which the access control bits reflect the priority level of the highest priority station that received the previous frame. Only stations with that priority level can seize that token and use it to transmit data. Thus, the access control mechanism is a means by which a given station of high priority can reserve the next free token generated, for its own use. When a high priority station has finished transmitting, it is responsible for resetting the access control bits to the original (low) priority, thus allowing all stations on the network to transmit, eventually.

The other two bits of the eight designated as the access control field are used for a *token bit* and a *monitor bit*. The token bit indicates whether a given frame is a data/command frame (a value of 1) or a token frame (a value of 0). The monitor bit is utilized solely by the active monitor station on the ring. Set to 0 by the station generating the packet, the active monitor, on receiving the packet, changes the monitor bit from a 0 to a 1. Therefore, if the active monitor ever receives a packet containing a monitor bit with a value of 1, it knows that it has already processed this packet and assumes that the sending station has failed to remove the packet from the ring, as it was supposed to. The active monitor then removes the packet itself, discards it, and generates a new token. This is known as a *ring purge*.

- *Frame Control (FC)* The frame control byte declares whether the packet contains data or control information. If it is the latter, then the field is also used to define the type of control information contained within. Control frames can be used to initialize the ring, declare a station as the active monitor, check for duplicate node addresses on the ring, as well as perform other ring maintenance operations.

- *Destination Address (DA)* A six-byte field containing a unicast, multicast, or broadcast address, depending on whether the frame is to be sent to one, several, or all other stations. Each node reads this address from every passing packet and stores packets addressed to itself in memory before passing them on to the next station.

- *Source address (SA)* A six-byte field containing the complete address of the sending station.

- *Information (INFO)* In a data (or LLC) frame, a field of variable length (usually no more than 4,500 bytes, governed by the limited amount of time that a node can hold on to a token before retransmitting it) containing LLC data to be passed up to higher level protocols. Also known as the *protocol data unit* (PDU), it includes a one-byte *Destination Service Access Point* (DSAP) address that supplies information concerning the process and layer that will ultimately be receiving the packet, a one-byte *Source Service Access Point* (SSAP) address providing the same information about the process and the layer that is sending the packet, and one or two bytes worth of *control components* that indicate the type of data included in the rest of the field.

  In a MAC frame, this field contains two bytes denoting the *Length* of the MAC control information included in the field, a two-byte *Major Vector ID* (MVID) that indicates function of the frame and the ensuing control data, plus a variable number of bytes containing the control information data itself.

- *Frame Check Sequence (FCS)* A four-byte field containing the results of a CRC computation on the Frame Control, Destination Address, Source Address, and Information fields, used to check the packet for corruption when it is received back by the station that it was sent from. The four fields used in the CRC computation are the only ones in the packet that cannot have their values change as they traverse the ring.

- *End Delimiter (ED)* A one-byte field used to indicate the end of the frame by once again violating the signaling scheme used by the protocol. This field also contains bits that may be used by a destination station to indicate the presence of an FCS mismatch (denoting that packet corruption has occurred) or to indicate that the frame is the last of a sequence.

■ *Frame Status (FS)*   A one-byte field used to inform the sending station as to the success or failure of its transmission. Two A bits and two C bits are assigned a 0 value by the sending station. When the packet is successfully received at its destination, all four of these bits are changed to a value of 1. If the destination receives the frame and determines the existence of an FCS mismatch or if it cannot process the packet for any other reason, only the A bits are set to 1. The C bits are left at 0 and the sending station, upon receiving the packet back and recognizing this, retransmits the frame.

A token frame, three bytes long, consists of only the Start Delimiter, Access Control, and End Delimiter fields, just as previously defined. The *abort sequence frame*, used to clear the ring when a premature end to the transmission of a packet is detected, consists only of the Start and End Delimiters, as previously defined. These two frames are used only for control and maintenance of the 802.5 protocol.

The Downside to Token Ring. The primary drawback to a token-ring network is the additional expense incurred by the higher prices for virtually every hardware component required for its construction. Throughout its history, token ring has been dominated by IBM, which has functioned as the trendsetter for the technology far more than standards bodies like the IEEE have. Throughout its history, it has usually been IBM that was first to release innovations in token-ring technology, such as the increased 16 Mbps transmission rate, only to have them assimilated into the published standards at a later time. Indeed, the 802.5 document is very brief (less than 100 pages) when compared with the 802.3 standard. There are also fewer vendors and therefore less competition in the token-ring hardware market than there are in that of Ethernet.

Token-ring adapters can cost two or three times more than Ethernet adapters, with similar markups applied to MSAUs and other ancillary hardware. Token ring also offers fewer convenient throughput upgrade paths than Ethernet does. Migration to a 100 Mbps technology will require the wholesale replacement of virtually the entire network, except for the cabling itself. For these reasons, token ring has remained second to Ethernet in popularity, with approximately 10 million nodes installed worldwide, but its proponents are earnest and quite vocal, and its capabilities as an efficient system for business networking are incontestable.

ARCnet

Although it is hardly ever used in new installations these days, the *Attached Resource Computer Network* (*ARCnet*) is another networking standard for the physical and data link layers of the OSI model. Introduced by the Datapoint Corporation in 1977, SMC has been the primary ARCnet vendor since 1983. Running at 2.5 Mbps, ARCnet is the slowest network of those considered in this chapter. This is one of the primary causes of its unpopularity because, otherwise, ARCnet is capable of providing the same basic network services as Ethernet and token ring at far lower costs and with a great deal of physical layer flexibility.

ARCnet can be wired in a bus topology, using RG-62/U coaxial cable and BNC connectors (also known as *high impedance ARCnet*), or in a star topology, using UTP or IBM Type 1 cabling with RJ-45 or D-shell connectors (also known as *low impedance ARCnet*). Hybrid networks of mixed bus and star topologies (also known as a *tree topology*) can also be assembled, consisting of nodes daisy-chained with twisted-pair cable connected to a hub that connects to other hubs using coaxial cable. ARCnet is very forgiving in this respect. As with the other network types, care must be taken to properly terminate all segments, using a 93-ohm resistor pack for coaxial buses and a 105-ohm resistor for twisted pair. (Note that the 93-ohm resistor pack differs from the 50-ohm terminators used by thinnet, although they may be virtually identical in appearance). Even fiber-optic cable can be used with ARCnet.

The connectors used for ARCnet are standard BNC connectors for coaxial cable. Twisted pair can utilize RJ-45 connectors or the standard D-shell connectors used by the serial ports on PCs. Connection boxes called *active links* are used to connect high-impedance cable segments, and *baluns* are available for providing an interface between coaxial and twisted-pair cable types.

Three types of ARCnet hubs are available. Active hubs, containing anywhere from 8 to 64 ports, have a power supply and function as a repeater as well as a wiring nexus. Passive hubs, which have only four ports, use no power and function simply as signal splitters. Intelligent hubs are also available, which are capable of monitoring the status of their links.

High-impedance (coaxial) ARCnet must use only active hubs. Segments connecting two stations can span up to 305 meters, while segments connecting hubs can extend 610 meters. Up to eight nodes can be connected in series without an intervening hub, and there must be at least one meter of cable between nodes. Low-impedance ARCnet can use both active and passive hubs. A segment connecting an active hub and a node or two active hubs can span up to 610 meters, while a segment connecting a node or an active hub to a passive hub can be no more than 30 meters. Passive hubs can only be located between active hubs and nodes. Two passive hubs can never be directly connected to each other. High and low impedance network segments can also be mixed on the same network, provided that the limitations for each are observed. Up to 10 nodes can be connected in series when UTP cable is used.

The maximum limitations for any ARCnet network are 255 nodes (active hubs count as nodes) and a total cable length of 6,000 meters. Maximum segment lengths may vary depending on the type of cable used, but a maximum of 11 dB of signal attentuation over the entire segment at 5 MHz is all that is allowable. Two connected nodes must also have a signal propagation delay of no more than 31 microseconds.

Unlike most network types, the node addresses of ARCnet networks must be manually set (from 1 to 255) on the NICs through the use of jumper switches. Address conflicts are, therefore, a distinct possibility, resolvable only by manual examination of all of the NICs. The adapter with the lowest numerical node address automatically becomes the network's controller, similar in basic function to the active monitor on a token-ring network.

Like token ring, ARCnet uses a token-based media access mechanism. A token is generated by the controller and sent to each station in turn, giving them the opportunity to grab the token and transmit. ARCnet, however, uses a far less efficient signaling scheme to arbitrate the token passing. Once a token is grabbed, a query and an acknowledgment must be exchanged by the sending and receiving stations before the actual data frame can be transmitted. It is not until the transmitted frame is received and acknowledged by the destination that the token can be released by the sender to the next station.

This is another major drawback that has contributed to the virtual disappearance of ARCnet in the business networking world. Its 2.5 Mbps transmission rate, which is slow enough already, is further reduced by the large amount of signaling overhead required for normal communications (three bits of overhead per byte transmitted). Other exchanges of control information between sources and destinations are also required that contain no data and provide additional overhead.

There have also been known to be compatibility problems with some upper layer protocols, such as NetWare's IPX, due to the small frame size used by ARCnet. No more than 508 bytes of data can be included in an ARCnet frame, and the standard datagram size used by IPX is 576 bytes. An extra layer of translation, called the fragmentation layer, had to be devised to allow NetWare traffic to run on ARCnet. This extra layer breaks IPX packets into two smaller packets that are capable of being sent within the ARCnet frame's data field, and then reassembles them at the destination, adding still another level of overhead.

For a network that is used for absolutely nothing more than file and printer sharing, and a minimal amount of these, ARCnet may be marginally suitable and would certainly be far less expensive than any of the other major network types. For use in any business that plans on being in operation more than two years down the road, however, ARCnet is a shortsighted solution that will probably disappear from use completely within a few years and is not recommended under any conditions.

FDDI

Since its introduction in 1986, the Fiber Distributed Data Interface (FDDI) has come to be the accepted standard for high-speed network backbones and connections to high performance workstations. Running at 100 Mbps, it remains to be seen how the new high-speed technologies will affect the use of FDDI for these purposes. Both Fast Ethernet and 100VG AnyLAN offer the same speed with considerably lower upgrade and installation costs, even providing fiber-optic standards for connections over long distances and between buildings. If, once ATM becomes standardized, it proves to be half as popular as it seems that it will be, then FDDI's days could well be numbered.

The FDDI standard was created by the ANSI X3T9.5 committee. The document describes a network laid out in a dual ring topology, using the same token passing media access control mechanism that token ring uses, except that early token release is always used, instead of being optional. The dual ring provides two independent loops with traffic traveling in opposite directions to provide fault tolerance for the network (see fig. 7.12).

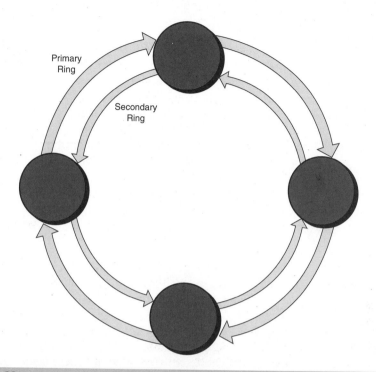

Primary
Ring

Secondary
Ring

Figure 7.12

This is a basic FDDI double-ring network

Under normal conditions, only one of the two rings actively carries traffic. When a break or other disturbance in the *primary ring* is detected, relay stations on either side of the break begin to redirect traffic onto the *secondary ring*. Stations connected to both rings have two transceivers and are designated as *dual-attachment* (*DAS*) or *Class A* stations; *single-attachment* (*SAS*) or *Class B* stations are connected to only one ring, have only one transceiver, and therefore cannot benefit from this fault tolerance.

An FDDI ring can contain up to 1,000 stations, with a cable length of no more than 200 kilometers. The use of Class A stations, however, effectively halves these limitations, as they count for two connections each and the dual rings double the length of the cable. No more than two kilometers of cable can be laid without an intervening station or repeater. Obviously, these so-called limitations provide for a larger and longer network than any of the other protocols considered thus far.

The rings by which an FDDI network is organized may be actual ones, in that the stations are wired directly to one another or a concentrator may be used, as in a token-ring network, to provide a virtual ring to what is physically a star topology physical installation. A concentrator provides an easier mechanism for automatically removing a malfunctioning station from the ring but also provides a single point of failure for the entire network. The cable called for by the standard is *graded index multimode fiber* with a core diameter of 62.5 micrometers. Other types of single mode and multimode cable have been used successfully, however, as well as standard Type 1 STP and Category 5 UTP, although these are limited to a distance of 100 meters or less between connections.

The Physical Layer

In an FDDI network, the physical layer is divided into two sublayers, the *physical medium dependent layer* (PMD) and the *physical layer* (PHY). The PMD defines the optical characteristics of the physical layer, including photodetectors and optical power sources, as well as the transceivers, medium interface connectors (MICs) and cabling, as with other network types. The power source must be able to send a signal of 25 microwatts, and the detector must be able to read a signal of as little as two microwatts. The MIC, or *FDDI connector*, was designed by ANSI especially for this standard, and it has come to be used for other fiber-optic media standards as well. It is designed to provide the best possible connection to avoid signal loss and is keyed to prevent incorrect component combinations from being connected together. Other, less expensive, connector types have also been used for some FDDI networks, although their use has not been standardized. Be sure to check on the type of connectors used by all FDDI hardware that you intend to purchase, as interoperability may be a problem with anything other than official FDDI connectors.

The PHY layer functions as the medium-independent intermediary between the PMD layer and the MAC layer above. As the first electronic layer, it is implemented (along with the MAC layer) by the chipset in the FDDI network adapter and is responsible for the encoding and decoding of data into the light pulses transmitted over the medium. The signaling scheme used by FDDI networks is quite different and more efficient than the Manchester and Differential Manchester schemes used by Ethernet and token ring. Called *NRZI 4B/5B* encoding, this method provides a signaling efficiency rate of 80%, as opposed to the 50% rate of the other network types. This means that an Ethernet network pushed from 10 to 100 Mbps would have to utilize a 200 MHz signal, while only 125 MHz is needed by FDDI, to provide the same throughput.

FDDI-I and FDDI-II

FDDI also supports a more flexible system of assigning bandwidth according to priorities than token ring does. Available bandwidth can be split into synchronous and asynchronous traffic. *Synchronous bandwidth* is a section of the 100 Mbps that is designated for use by traffic that requires a continuous data stream, such as real-time voice or video. The remaining bandwidth is devoted to *asynchronous traffic*, which can be dynamically assigned, according to an eight-level system of priorities administered by the station management (SMT) protocol that is part of the FDDI specification.

The original FDDI standard supported asynchronous communications and, while it did have a synchronous mode definition, it did not provide the degree of flow control that was needed for applications such as real-time video. Thus, the FDDI-II standard was created to define what is officially known as *hybrid ring control* (HRC) FDDI. The basic difference in the standards was the addition of a mechanism, called a *hybrid multiplexer* (HMUX) that allowed both packet-switched (from the original MAC layer) and circuit-switched data to be processed by the same PHY layer. The *circuit-switched data*, which can be defined as a real-time data stream such as voice or video is provided by an *isochronous media access control* (IMAC) mechanism called a *circuit switching multiplexer* (CMUX).

It is essentially the IMAC and the HMUX that make up the hybrid ring control element of the FDDI-II standard. Other changes made to the document at this time included the addition of alternative fiber media types, including single mode fiber-optic cabling. The *hybrid mode* capabilities of an FDDI-II are optional. The network can be run in *basic mode* that differs little from the original standard.

The FDDI Frame Type

FDDI utilizes a token passing MAC mechanism that is very similar to that used by standard token-ring networks. Two basic frame types, a token frame and a data/command frame, are defined, with the fields and their functions basically similar to those defined in the 802.5 standard. FDDI even has a Station Management (SMT) protocol that is very similar in function to Token Ring's NMT, providing ring management and frame control to the network.

The Downside to FDDI

Fiber-optic cable is very difficult and expensive to install, and while users may be tempted to try to perform a coaxial or twisted-pair physical layer installation themselves, they should not even consider doing fiber without expert help. These factors are major contributors to the limited but stable market that FDDI seems to have established for itself. It has found its niche in the networking world and it fulfills it admirably, but the fast-rising young newcomers, like Fast Ethernet and 100 VG AnyLAN are a distinct threat to its continued use. When the same speed and segment lengths can be realized with less expense, retraining, and maintenance costs, no persuasive reason can be found for installing new FDDI backbones. Unless these newer network types fail utterly, and this is doubtful, the FDDI standard may lapse from general use entirely before the end of the decade.

Cable Installation

Installing network cabling of any type is not something that can be properly learned from a book. While it may be relatively easy and inexpensive to connect a handful of PCs into a workgroup network using prepackaged cables, creating the physical fabric of a large network with results that are both functional and businesslike in appearance is a task better left to professionals. Unfortunately, it can sometimes be difficult to discern the professionals from the hacks with no training that simply hang out a consultant's shingle and purport to be networking experts.

The physical layer is often treated separately from other types of network training. CNE certification may include some basic training concerning the different types of cabling and the guidelines for the various network types, but it does not in any way cover such tasks as the crimping of connectors onto bulk cable, which are the most crucial parts of a physical layer installation. For 10BaseT installations, companies that install telephone systems certainly have the knowledge to properly pull and connect the cabling, but you should be certain that they are familiar with the special requirements for a data grade installation.

It should be quite simple to find a contractor who is capable of installing the cable properly. The problem usually lies in finding one who will do it for a good price. In any case, you should require a contractor to furnish a complete diagram of the proposed cable layout, including the locations of all connectors involved, making sure that the distances are within the specifications for the network type. Depending on your estimate of the contractor's expertise, you may or may not have to inspect the work closely to be sure that it's done properly. Since most cabling jobs will be hidden within the walls and ceilings of the site, the time to find problems is while the work is being done and not afterwards.

Summary

The physical and data link layers are the fundamental building blocks of a modern LAN. None of the higher level functions will be able to proceed normally if the foundation that they are built on is unstable. An informed and intelligent decision as to the proper network type to use for the needs of a particular organization can set the standard for the way that the network is to be built and the way that it will be run. Technology and purchasing decisions made well at the outset can ensure that a network installed today can later be adapted to whatever needs may arise.

In coordination with the material covered in chapters 5, "The Server Platform," and 6, "The Workstation Platform," nearly all of the essential hardware needed to construct a basic LAN is discussed. Other sections of this book will cover the many different products and services that can be used on the network, but all of them are dependent on this basic infrastructure. If the foundation is not solid, then the tower cannot stand for long; time and effort expended on network fundamentals will never be wasted.

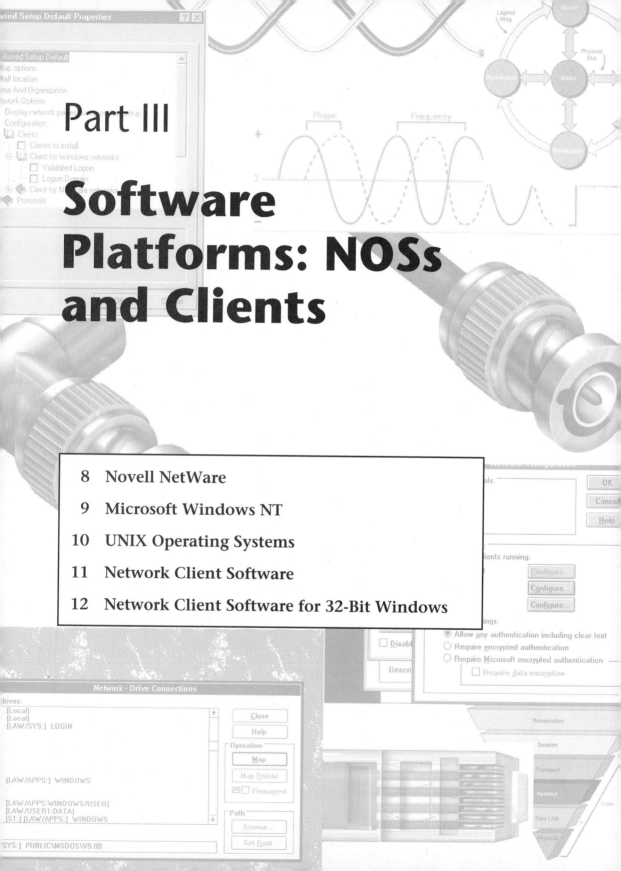

Part III

Software Platforms: NOSs and Clients

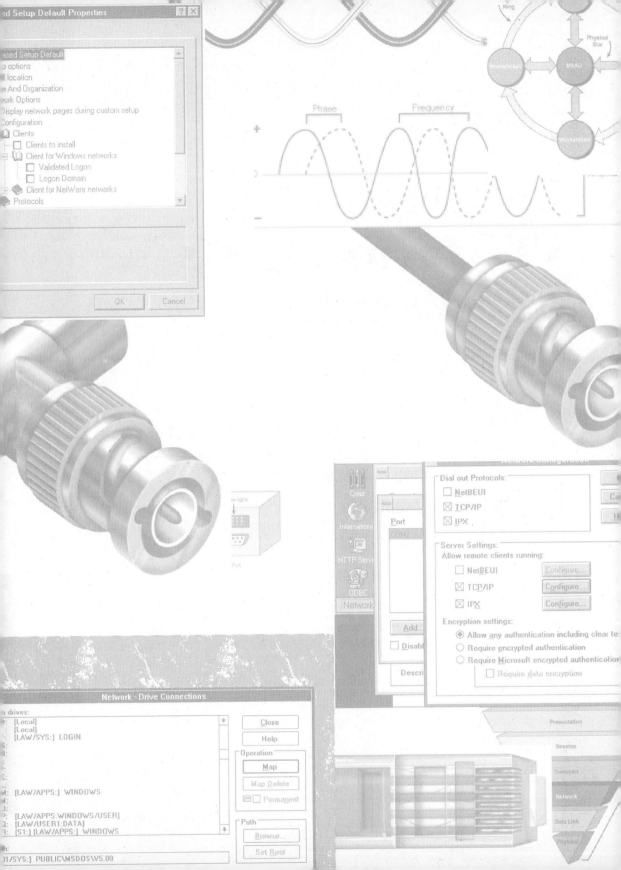

Chapter 8

Novell NetWare

The user needs that gave rise to the original conception of the local area network (LAN) were far more modest than the user needs of today. The mainstay of business networking still involves activities such as sharing printers, sharing disks, and accessing common databases, but the scale at which these activities are conducted in the modern office dwarfs the simple needs of the early 1980s. Surprisingly, though, as demands for speed and bandwidth have doubled and redoubled, a single network operating system, Novell NetWare, has been able to fulfill these evolving needs in only three major architectural forms. The course of NetWare's development through its 2.x, 3.x, and 4.x releases serves as a benchmark for the development of network computing in our time.

This chapter covers the following topics:

- The NetWare operating system architecture
- Configuring a NetWare 3.x Server for operation
- The NetWare File System
- The NetWare memory architecture
- The NetWare IPX/SPX protocol suite
- NetWare 4.x innovations

NetWare 2.x

As anachronistic as a NetWare 2.x network might seem now, do not forget that it once was on the cutting edge, providing more capability than the users of its time knew what to do with.

As with stand-alone PCs, network file servers have advanced steadily and rapidly in their voracious appetites for memory and hard drive space. This is where NetWare 2.x really shows its age. By today's standards, a NOS that can support no more than 12M of RAM and 2G of disk space that must be split into volumes no larger than 256M is suitable for only the smallest and most basic of networks. True client/server functionality was only a gleam in Novell's eye when NetWare 2.x was released, and the server applications that were available as *value-added processes* (*VAPs*) were modest little applications that provided a simple, basic function—such as a backup interface—without monopolizing the server's limited resources.

Despite the fact that they no longer are sold or supported by Novell, a significant number of NetWare 2.x servers are still running out there, and many administrators are satisfied with these servers' continued performance. Advocates of the "if it ain't broke, don't fix it" school may well save their employers some money in the short run, but they will, of course, run into problems when their storage or processing needs outgrow these systems—or when they wish to run a service that simply cannot be supported by this archaic architecture.

> **Caution**
>
> There no longer is an upgrade path from NetWare 2.x to the later versions. After a generous upgrade offer and repeated announcements, NetWare 2.x has been officially withdrawn from the market. If you're a remaining NetWare 2.x user and ever decide to upgrade, you'll have to buy a NetWare 3.x or 4.x package at full price.

NetWare 3.x

With the introduction of the 80386 microprocessor by Intel, the potential for the improvement of NOSs grew immeasurably. By definition, a NOS is intended to service the simultaneous requests of many users, and the multitasking capabilities of the new 32-bit processors seemed destined to be used for this purpose. The introduction of NetWare 386 in 1989 seemed to open up vast new horizons for networking. The new NetWare's open-ended architecture allowed for the use of enormous amounts of RAM (up to 4G) and hard disk space (up to 32 terabytes) and the introduction of *virtual loadable modules* (*VLMs*) presented third-party software companies with a robust set of development tools that challenged them to exercise their imaginations regarding uses that could be made of the tools.

Although originally dubbed NetWare 386 by its creators, this version of the NOS underwent a period of growing pains typical of any newly developed program, particularly an operating system. The first version, NetWare 3.0, supported only the native NetWare IPX protocol suite. Connectivity with Macintosh machines using AppleTalk and UNIX machines using TCP/IP was not possible. Maintenance upgrades, versions 3.10 and 3.11, were soon released, resolving these shortcomings. The 3.10 release was extremely short-lived, with 3.11 soon provided as a free upgrade. With version 3.11, the 386 was dropped and the product was known simply as NetWare 3.11. Some time later, version 3.12 was released, adding additional functionality such as networked CD-ROM access, support for

Packet Burst transmissions and Large Internet Packets, NCP Packet Signatures, as well as consolidating a number of patches into the shipping release, but this was a paid upgrade, and there are a great many sites still running 3.11 that have found no persuasive reason to upgrade. 3.12 is the only 3.x release that is currently being sold, however.

The original NetWare 386 release shipped as a large set of disks, but when version 3.12 hit the market, it was one of the first products to be shipped on CD-ROM by default. The product's online documentation was also on the disc, and Novell took a good amount of criticism for their decision to abandon the inclusion of paper manuals with their NetWare product. Manuals were available, but at a prohibitively high price. In truth, Novell's online manuals—which used a viewer named Electro-Text in the 3.x releases— were easily used, printed excellent hard copy when needed, and made searching for particular subjects far easier than poring over the numerous red books in the paper manual set.

Unlike the bootable partition created by the NetWare 2.x install program, the core of NetWare 3.x is a single DOS executable named SERVER.EXE. This file, when executed from a small DOS partition or a floppy disk, completely takes over all the resources of the computer. Indeed, even the memory used by DOS to boot the machine and run COMMAND.COM can be returned to the NOS, once SERVER.EXE has been loaded.

Running SERVER.EXE technically turns the PC on which it is executed into a self-contained Novell network. Before any of the attributes have been configured to provide the server with access to the network or to its own storage devices, the program prompts the user for a name for the server and a hexadecimal value for the server's internal IPX address. Like each of the network segments to which the server will ultimately be attached, this address is the identity by which this "one-node network" is known to the rest of the enterprise.

The SERVER.EXE file also contains the NetWare license information. The restriction in the number of users allowed by the particular license purchased is enforced by the NetWare kernel. The serial number of the product is also embedded in the file and is automatically broadcast over the network once LAN access is enabled. If any other server utilizing the same copy of SERVER.EXE is detected on the same network, repeated beeps and license violation messages are generated at the consoles of both servers every few seconds until one of them is brought down. It is a good idea in a multi-server environment, therefore, to keep track of which copy of SERVER.EXE is being used on each server, so that conflicts can be avoided.

The NetWare Command Processor

The file server is, at this point, useless for any sort of task traditionally associated with computing or networking, but already, we can observe the basic functionality of the kernel. Having supplied a server name and an IPX address, the console of the PC presents a command prompt in the form of a colon. Subsequent versions of NetWare may present the server name prior to the colon, but NetWare 3.11 or 3.12, out of the box, presents only the colon.

As with DOS, the presence of the command prompt indicates that the NetWare command processor has been loaded and is functioning. The similarity with DOS continues in that numerous commands internal to the operating system can be executed from the command prompt. For example, entering **MEMORY** at the colon displays the amount of RAM that is currently usable by NetWare in this PC.

This demonstrates another basic functionality of the NetWare kernel: memory management. Before running SERVER.EXE, the computer has to have been booted to a DOS prompt from a floppy or a DOS partition on the server's primary hard drive. Unless a DOS-based memory manager, such as HIMEM.SYS, has been loaded by mistake, all the memory on the computer above the 1,088K mark is not being addressed in any way until SERVER.EXE loads.

To demonstrate the way in which the NetWare kernel has completely taken over the functionality of the computer, you can execute another internal command from the colon prompt: REMOVE DOS totally unloads the DOS operating system and releases to NetWare the memory DOS had utilized. Enter **MEMORY** again, and a modest increase in the amount of NetWare-addressable memory should be evident. Once the file server has been completely configured and is up and running, some administrators always execute the REMOVE DOS command to gain every bit of available memory for use by NetWare.

The disadvantages of this practice, however, are made apparent even by our little demonstration. Having removed DOS from memory, you no longer have access to the DOS hard drive partition or the floppy disk drive. Since no disk or LAN drivers have been loaded into the NOS yet, you suddenly find yourself sitting alone in front of a one-node network, with no resources other than those currently in memory.

Obviously, this is not a real-world situation, but the same theory holds true for a fully configured file server. If, for example, there was a disk problem that caused the server's volumes to dismount, removing DOS would prevent you from loading VREPAIR, the NetWare volume repair utility, from a floppy disk or from the DOS partition of the server's hard drive (where you should have cleverly stored a copy, in case of such an emergency).

In that case, as in our demonstration case now, there is no alternative except to execute DOWN at the colon prompt, shutting down SERVER.EXE. On a fully functional server, this causes all server processes to cease, unloads all modules from memory, and then presents a message stating Type EXIT to return to DOS. You may do so, but you will find that there is no DOS in memory to return to. The system has halted for want of a valid COMMAND.COM file, and there is no choice but to reboot the computer and start over.

On a single-server network, the loss of disk access for any reason would be likely to bring all network users to a halt anyway, but there are many networking situations in which it is preferable to troubleshoot the server while it is still up and running. For example, on a network with several servers, the one with the problem may be functioning as a router (through the installation of multiple network adapters). Loss of disk access is an inconvenience, but bringing the server down completely could cause the users on one or more network segments to lose access to vital network resources.

There are many other internal NetWare commands that can be executed from the colon prompt, and we will use some of them while walking through the process of configuring the server for productive use. Apart from these, however, the NetWare OS can also execute external commands in the form of executable files called *NetWare command files* (*NCF files*). These are the only executables recognized by NetWare (unlike DOS, which recognizes three: EXE, COM, and BAT). In fact, NCFs are little different from DOS batch files—they are composed solely of ASCII text, are uncompiled, and consist primarily of commands that could also be executed from the command prompt.

A NetWare server nearly always has STARTUP.NCF and AUTOEXEC.NCF files resembling the CONFIG.SYS and AUTOEXEC.BAT files of a PC running DOS. These NCF files are automatically executed by the operating system as it loads, just as their DOS counterparts are.

STARTUP.NCF

The primary purpose of the STARTUP.NCF file is to load drivers that provide access to the hard disk drive that will contain the files constituting the majority of the NOS. For this reason, STARTUP.NCF is always located on and loaded from the DOS disk (either hard or floppy) where SERVER.EXE is located. Aside from COMMAND.COM and the DOS boot files, SERVER.EXE, STARTUP.NCF and the appropriate disk drivers are the only files that must be on the DOS disk; however, the disk often is also used for other purposes.

As demonstrated earlier, it can be a very good idea to store copies of emergency utilities like VREPAIR on this disk. Some systems even include enough room on a DOS hard drive partition to store a replica of the server's memory. In the case of a server *abend* (an *ab*normal *end*ing to server processing), the NetWare system is halted, but a powerful utility named NetWare Debugger is left in memory. One of the functions of the debugger is the ability to perform a *core dump*, that is, to export an exact image of the server's memory at the moment of the abend to floppy disks or a hard drive partition, for later examination by technical support personnel. Given the large amounts of memory often found in today's NetWare servers, outputting a core dump to floppy disks can be impractical; hence, you may use the DOS partition for this purpose.

NetWare Disk Drivers. A STARTUP.NCF file often contains no more than the commands necessary to provide basic hard drive access to the NOS. This is done using the internal NetWare LOAD command followed by the file name of the appropriate disk driver, as well as any parameters that are needed for the driver to locate the hard drive interface adapter. Once the operating system is loaded, however, the LOAD command can be used to execute other types of modules, most notably *NetWare loadable modules* (*NLMs*), the executable form taken by most programs that run on a NetWare server. VREPAIR, for example, is an NLM.

NetWare disk drivers are always named using a DSK extension. They may be supplied with the NetWare operating system but more often are provided by the manufacturer of the hard drive interface that they must address. It is a good idea, before you begin the installation process for any particular drive interface, to acquire the latest available version of the disk drivers. Virtually all adapter manufacturers maintain one or more online services from which current drivers can be downloaded.

Several other points should be made concerning hard disk drivers. First, even if you have booted the PC from a particular hard drive via the BIOS on the computer's motherboard or a SCSI host adapter, it is necessary to load a NetWare disk driver to provide access to the drive by the NOS. Any disk space used for a DOS partition cannot be utilized by NetWare, so at times there will be two different drivers in the computer's memory, addressing the same device.

Another thing to be concerned about is that some NetWare disk drivers *spawn* other drivers during their loading process, meaning that one driver automatically loads another without the need for explicit commands to do so.

The most common instance of such spawning occurs when you load a SCSI driver that supports the *advanced SCSI programming interface* (*ASPI*), which allows different types of peripherals to coexist on the same SCSI bus. (See chapter 5, "The Server Platform," for more information on SCSI and SCSI drivers.) Explicitly loading a driver such as AHA1540.DSK (used to support the Adaptec AHA-1540 family of SCSI host adapters) causes another driver, ASPITRAN.DSK, to be loaded, providing the ASPI functionality that allows later access of a CD-ROM drive, tape drive, or other peripheral attached to the same adapter. Of course, ASPITRAN.DSK is not loaded if it cannot be found. Be sure that all the drivers needed to support the interfaces in the server are located in the same directory as the SERVER.EXE file.

Note

The drivers can be located in another directory if fully qualified pathnames are provided in STARTUP.NCF, but the drivers should be located on the same device.

Name Space Drivers. The other drivers that usually are loaded from the STARTUP.NCF file are *name space modules*. These modules, which have the extension NAM, are supplied with all versions of NetWare. They allow NetWare volumes to support file naming and storage conventions other than the standard DOS 8.3 format that is the NetWare default, including those for Macintosh; HPFS (the native OS/2 file format); the File Transfer, Access, and Management protocol (FTAM); or NFS (used by many UNIX systems). Name space support is provided by these modules once the NetWare ADD NAME SPACE server console command has been used to modify specific volumes so that space for additional naming information is provided by the NetWare file system. ADD NAME SPACE only has to be executed once for each name space on each volume, but the appropriate NAM drivers must be loaded every time disk drivers are loaded. Multiple name spaces can be added to any volume, at the cost of additional memory and disk space required to support them. Name space support can only be removed non-destructively from a volume by using the NetWare VREPAIR utility.

Creating a STARTUP.NCF File. Since it is composed only of ASCII text, a STARTUP.NCF file can be created and revised by any DOS text editor. There is a module named EDIT.NLM included with NetWare that can be loaded from the colon prompt, which allows a text file located on a DOS partition or a NetWare volume to be edited directly from the file server console. This is a very convenient utility which many NetWare users don't know about. It can be very handy when you need to troubleshoot NCF files in a server room without a workstation nearby.

Another, more convenient method to create the STARTUP.NCF file is available. The INSTALL.NLM module, which NetWare uses to create and maintain hard disk volumes as well as to copy its system files from floppy disk or CD-ROM, has a feature by which STARTUP.NCF can be created automatically, based on the disk driver modules that have been loaded from the NetWare command prompt. After bringing up SERVER.EXE as described earlier in this chapter, use LOAD at the colon prompt to load the DSK files necessary to provide disk access. Most drivers then prompt the user for the hardware parameters needed to locate the host adapter. Once the drivers have been successfully loaded and configured, choose Create STARTUP.NCF File from the System Options menu of INSTALL.NLM; this retrieves the commands just entered at the colon prompt, and inserts them into a new STARTUP.NCF file (at the location of your choice), using the proper command-line syntax. Choose Edit STARTUP.NCF File if you want to modify a file that already exists. Since there is not yet any NetWare storage available on this server, INSTALL.NLM must be run from a DOS device—often, the original NetWare installation medium.

Other STARTUP.NCF Commands. One of the most powerful—and certainly the most versatile—of the internal NetWare system console commands is SET. Issuing this command at the colon prompt displays a series of submenus providing access to dozens of NetWare configuration parameters that can be used to fine-tune the server. Some of the SET parameters themselves will be examined later in this chapter and elsewhere in this book, but their existence is mentioned here because several of them, mostly concerned with memory or the file system, cannot be issued directly from the colon prompt or from the AUTOEXEC.NCF file. This usually is because they affect the way certain parts of the operating system are initially loaded into memory. SET commands of this type, which are clearly designated as such in the NetWare manuals, must therefore be made available as the operating system loads—this is done by placing them in STARTUP.NCF. Any of these commands added to the NCF file while the server is running do not take effect until the server is shut down (using DOWN) and restarted.

AUTOEXEC.NCF

On a fully configured NetWare server, the successful loading of the disk drivers from STARTUP.NCF causes the server's SYS: volume to be mounted automatically. The NOS then searches the SYS: volume for a \SYSTEM directory and, within that directory, looks for an AUTOEXEC.NCF file, which is executed if it's found. Like STARTUP.NCF, AUTOEXEC.NCF can be manufactured automatically by the INSTALL.NLM utility. Once the remaining tasks of configuring the file server for disk and LAN access are complete (as detailed in the following sections) and Create AUTOEXEC.NCF File is selected from the System Options menu, the file is created and placed in the SYS:\SYSTEM directory. Before this can be done, however, the INSTALL utility must be used to create the NetWare volume where this file is to be stored on a hard drive (as well as any other volumes you desire).

Creating NetWare Volumes. In NetWare parlance, a *volume* refers to the top level data storage container on a particular file server. It is similar to the DOS term *partition*, in that a single hard disk drive can be split into many volumes, up to 64 on a single server. Unlike a DOS partition, however, a NetWare volume can span multiple disk drives (up to 32). While the use of multiple drives increases the number of reads and writes that can be performed simultaneously, this practice usually is not recommended, as the failure of any one of the drives comprising a single volume renders the entire volume inaccessible.

When creating a volume with INSTALL.NLM, the user is presented with a table listing all the hard drive space that has been made available by the disk drivers. Before volumes can be created, the hard drives must be formatted. Many new drives are formatted at the factory and can be used immediately. Otherwise, they can be formatted using a program recommended by the manufacturer, the DOS FORMAT utility, or a function included as part of the INSTALL.NLM program.

Once the drives are formatted, you create each desired volume, one at a time, by specifying the desired size of the volume (in megabytes), a name for the volume, and the size of the blocks that will comprise the volume. The first volume must be named SYS:. This is where the NetWare operating system files will be stored. You may give other volumes any name as you create them; traditionally, subsequent volumes are named VOL1:, VOL2:, and so on. It is important to note that although you can make volumes larger later through the addition of more disk space, you cannot decrease their size unless you destroy and re-create them.

Block Sizes and File System Organization. As mentioned in the last section, one of the basic parameters you select when you create a volume is *block size*. This is a value (in bytes) that defines the smallest possible storage unit that can be allocated on that particular volume. No file stored on the volume will consume less than one block's worth of disk space, with additional blocks allocated as needed, in whole blocks only. The block size of a volume can be 4K, 8K, 16K, 32K, or 64K, with the default set at 4K (4,096 bytes). In other words, a 200-byte file, when copied to a NetWare volume configured to use a 4K block size, gets an entire 4K block allocated to it. Only 200 bytes of that block are filled with data, and the rest remains as empty space, sometimes referred to as *slack*, which is unusable by any other process.

The ability to select a block size allows the administrator the flexibility to organize his data storage to take as much advantage of his available disk space as possible. An organization that deals with vast numbers of very small files, for example, would be better off with a small block size, so that less disk space is wasted by slack. A volume that is used for the storage of large databases or multimedia files, however, would benefit from a larger block size because the less blocks the operating system needs to cache in memory, the more efficient it is. Different block sizes can be assigned to each volume on a server, so data can be effectively organized by the administrator and allocated to an appropriate volume, if desired. Once a volume is created, the only way to change the block size is to delete the volume entirely and then re-create it, destroying all data stored there.

NetWare has a number of features, like configurable block sizes, that subtly urge the user towards a more organized network configuration. Inexperienced administrators are often haphazard about the way in which they assign the available storage space on their network file system. Some tend to place too many files into single directories, while others go the opposite route and create too many directories, nesting them many layers deep unnecessarily. Either extreme can cause inconvenience and delays and waste system resources.

The NetWare operating system caches both file and directory information into memory. While it is not intended to cache the entire file system—networks have grown far too large for this to be practical—the NOS has been designed to keep the most frequently used file and directory entries available in areas of cache memory, to speed up disk access. Having thousands of files in a single directory or having many sparsely populated directories can cause the caches to be flooded with unneeded files, leading to the exclusion of more worthy data.

Even if you do not change the volume block size from the default, it is a good idea to have a plan delineating where specific kinds of data are to be stored before creating the volumes on your server. Most of the time, an average volume holds files of greatly varying sizes. A typical Windows application, for example, may consist of dozens—even hundreds—of tiny files, as well as some very large ones. The concept of block sizes should by no means lead you to split up a cohesive group of files, such as those devoted to a single application, across volumes according to their size. This would cause more problems than it would resolve. For general use, the default 4K block size is a good median figure.

File system organization is a subject that is usually understated in most networking manuals. When told not to put too many files in one directory, some people veer wildly in the opposite direction, creating hundreds of directories that contain only a handful of files in each. There is no need to be compulsive or neurotic about maintenance of the server file system. The idea is to provide a gentle nudge to users, urging them to be aware of what they intend to store on server drives and allowing them to make common-sense adjustments accordingly.

II

Software Platforms

Sometimes, the addition of name spaces for other file system types determines where particular types of data should be stored. Remember that name spaces require additional memory to cache their file information. It would be wasteful to create a name space on a huge volume based on the slim chance that you might someday store a Macintosh file there. If you plan to store files of different types, requiring the support of several different name spaces, it is a good idea to create the different name spaces on separate volumes, rather than creating all the name spaces on one volume.

Another factor to consider when creating volumes is the use of NetWare's Hot Fix disk capabilities. This is a system that reserves a small percentage of the blocks allocated for a particular volume as an area where data can be placed after an attempt is made to write to a bad block on the hard drive. This is done in conjunction with NetWare's *read-after-write verification*. Each time a file is written to a volume, the NOS attempts to read the just-written file. If a problem is encountered, that block is flagged as defective, and its contents redirected to the Hot Fix area. A small number of bad blocks on a hard drive is no cause for alarm, and the two percent of the volume that is assigned as the Hot Fix area is usually more than sufficient.

> **Tip**
>
> The percentage of a volume that serves as the Hot Fix area can be increased through INSTALL.NLM, but if you actually need more than two percent, you might be better off servicing or replacing your hard drive.

There may be circumstances when it is preferable to disable the read-after-write verification and Hot Fix capabilities. Some of the newer hard drive interfaces perform functions equivalent to these at the hardware level, thus rendering NetWare's software implementations redundant. Disabling the features allows a two-percent increase in available volume storage space and enhances the overall efficiency of the NetWare file system by removing the need to read every file after writing it. SET ENABLE DISK READ AFTER WRITE VERIFY = OFF disables the file verification; although this command can be issued at any time, it is recommended that you do it in STARTUP.NCF, before the disk driver is loaded. The Hot Fix area can be eliminated from the Disk Options menu in INSTALL.

Mounting Volumes. Once the volumes have been created on the server drives, all that remains to make them accessible to the NOS is to mount them. The internal server console command MOUNT is used for this purpose, with either ALL or the name of a particular volume specified on the command line. This command ultimately is included in the AUTOEXEC.NCF file so that disk access is granted automatically whenever the server is started. The mounting of the drives begins the process by which some of their contents are cached in the server's memory pools. Directory entry tables are created at this time, and files, as they are accessed, are saved in the server's file cache buffers for quick recall by later processes.

Because of this activity, the amount of server memory required to run the NOS properly is highly dependent on the amount of disk space that has been mounted on that server. One of the prime symptoms of a RAM shortage in a NetWare file server is for volumes to spontaneously dismount themselves when other processes utilize too much of the available memory. While this occurrence might also indicate the existence of a problem with a disk driver, a hard drive itself, or the other process that caused the dismount, RAM shortage is the easiest thing to check. Temporarily unload some unnecessary NLMs or other modules to free up additional memory, and then repeat the process that caused the original dismount to see if it occurs again. This kind of basic, common-sense troubleshooting is a fundamental skill of LAN administration.

The Transaction Tracking System

One of the most advanced fault tolerance mechanisms in the NetWare file system is the *transaction tracking system (TTS)*. This feature, integrated into the operating system, helps to prevent the corruption of data when a server process is interrupted. When a server crashes or abends, it is very common to see messages upon restarting the machine, indicating that a specified number of transactions have been trapped by TTS. The system asks if you want the transactions to be backed out, and processing stops until a response is entered.

TTS is implemented (in NetWare 3.12 and higher) as an integrated feature, closely associated with the file-caching system. The purpose of TTS is to protect database files that are stored on server volumes from corruption when a write to those files is interrupted for any reason. It protects the NetWare Bindery, the file system tables, and queue database files but can be equally useful for transactional database files used by other applications, such as Btrieve or other database engines.

As transactions (such as file writes) are sent to database files on the server, they are cached in memory and written to a separate NetWare system file for safekeeping until the transaction is fully completed, at which time the record of that transaction is marked as closed. If the transaction is interrupted before completion, by a hardware or power failure or by any other software or memory problem, the transaction remains marked open in TTS. Whenever the server is restarted, TTS records are examined for open entries. If any are found, then the aforementioned dialog box is displayed. If you choose, the data associated with the open transactions is *backed out* from the original database file. This means that any partial transactions applied before the interruption are undone, and the database file is restored to the condition it was in before the transactions occurred. In many cases, this process removes any database corruption that the partial transactions caused.

It is possible to suppress the dialog box when incomplete transactions are found and instead have them automatically backed out. Do so by including SET AUTO TTS BACKOUT FLAG = ON in the STARTUP.NCF file.

TTS is initialized when the SYS: volume is mounted as the server boots, as long as there is enough memory and disk space for the process to occur. If TTS does not initialize for some reason, then issuing the ENABLE TTS command at the server console can begin the process, as long as the condition that prevented the initialization in the first place has been addressed. TTS can be disabled by issuing the DISABLE TTS command at the server console or by dismounting the SYS: volume. TTS can also be toggled on and off using the FCONSOLE utility.

TTS can only protect files that are composed of discrete records that can be individually locked for access by multiple users. This includes most database files and some e-mail applications. To be protected by TTS, the files must be flagged with the Transactional attribute, using the workstation FLAG utility. TTS can protect up to 10,000 transactions at the same time on a single server. The number of transactions is controlled by the SET MAXIMUM TRANSACTIONS = *MAX* command; the default of 10,000 is the highest value allowed. This should be more than you will ever need, but since no resources are allocated unless the transactions are performed, there is no harm in leaving this parameter set to the maximum.

All TTS activities are logged into a file named TTS$LOG.ERR, which is stored at the root of the SYS: volume. No provision is made in the operating system for the purging of this file, so it is possible for it to become quite large eventually. Since it is an ASCII text file, it can be edited to remove older information or can be deleted entirely. NetWare creates a new one as needed.

The design of TTS makes it completely transparent to the applications controlling the databases. A database file and the temporary file created by TTS utilize one file handle and are therefore seen as a unified entity by the application. Although many database engines have built-in transaction rollback capabilities, utilizing the protection provided by NetWare's TTS might be preferable for several reasons. First, since the system is located within the server operating system, it is less likely to crash during an operation, and even if it did, the TTS is capable of backing out its own back-outs should the process be interrupted. Second, network traffic is reduced because the transaction tracking is performed at the same location where the files are stored. Third, the delayed write can be performed as a background process, giving greater priority to new file read requests. Fourth, TTS can provide protection for database systems that have no such capabilities of their own. Overall, TTS is one of the most stable and transparent forms of file protection in the NetWare operating system. It rarely is the source of any type of maintenance problem, and it provides excellent protection of both NetWare and third-party database files.

Server RAM Calculations

The discussion of the mounting of NetWare volumes brings us to one of the more hotly contested issues surrounding the configuration of a new file server: How much memory should be installed in the machine for proper performance? While we will examine some of the formulas provided by Novell to help answer this question, the final answer is that you always should err on the side of caution and install more memory than you think you need.

This is because nothing degrades a file server's performance more profoundly than having insufficient RAM. Memory shortage is the most common problem negatively affecting the performance of NetWare file servers, and conversely, the most significant upgrade that can be made to the server is to add RAM. NetWare uses all available memory—above the amount needed for core OS requirements and other loaded modules—as *file cache buffers*. These are areas of memory in which recently accessed files are cached, using a write-back method so that they can be more quickly accessed if requested again. (A *write-back cache* is one that caches files on their way both to and from the storage medium.) As memory is needed for other processes, it is taken from the file cache buffer pool. Depending on the process, this memory might or might not be returned to the pool when it is no longer needed.

The default size of a server's file cache buffers is 4K (4,096 bytes). This is a deliberate correlation with the default volume block size. File cache buffer size can be changed from the default by including SET CACHE BUFFER SIZE = *SIZE* in the STARTUP.NCF file. (This can only be specified in STARTUP.NCF.) The acceptable values are 4,096; 8,192; and 16,384. The buffer size specified should always be the same as the smallest block size used on any of that server's storage volumes.

The current amount and percentage of memory allocated to the file cache buffer pool can be viewed in the Resource Utilization window of MONITOR.NLM. (This server utility provides the most comprehensive look at the current state of the NetWare file server, and you learn about some of its capabilities, as well as the configuration of different file server memory pools, later in this chapter.) No memory in a NetWare file server ever goes to waste. The only potential drawback to installing too much memory is the cost incurred.

The NetWare manuals dictate that the file cache buffer pool should not be allowed to drop below 20 percent of the available server memory. This should be considered the "red line," the point at which danger lights start flashing. Many NetWare administrators begin their nervousness, however, when the file cache buffer pool drops below 50 percent. Servers perform best when this number is at 60 percent or higher. Although this statistic is unavailable until the server is actually installed, configured, and running, it's the only sure way to determine whether or not a server has enough memory installed in it.

One of the most important factors to consider when examining the figures shown in MONITOR.NLM is the current operational state of the server in relation to the various modules that you may have loaded onto it. Many of the server-based software products used today involve processes that are either launched by user demand or designed to be performed automatically at scheduled times, usually during non-production hours. Backup and communications software (such as network faxing systems) are particularly prone to this practice. A backup software package, for example, may use only a minimal amount of memory when it is idle but may spawn numerous additional processes, consuming additional memory, in the middle of the night when the backup is performed.

In a case like this, a file cache buffer percentage that looks acceptable during the day could be taken below the minimum requirement during the night, causing all sorts of problems, possibly including a server abend.

The difficulty surrounding the question of estimating the amount of memory needed by NetWare is primarily the result of contradictions emanating from Novell. The original NetWare 3.12 manual set, released in July 1993, provides two different formulas. The *Installation and Upgrade* manual gives what is intended to be a rough approximation—a simple calculation of 0.008 multiplied by the volume size, with constant values added for various amounts of system overhead. The *System Administration* manual contains the more familiar and detailed formula of 0.023 multiplied by the volume size, divided by the block size. This calculation takes the block size into account, which is quite significant in light of the fact that a volume with 4K blocks needs 16 times the amount of memory of a volume the same size with 64K blocks.

Either formula provides reasonably safe results when a server contains a relatively small amount of storage space and is not heavily loaded with other modules or applications. The limited number of possible memory configurations for the average motherboard nearly always ensures that RAM calculation is rounded off to the next highest multiple of 4M or 16M. Unfortunately, the large amount of storage now being used in many servers and the wide array of server-based applications and services now available were not fully anticipated by Novell, even as recently as 1993. Hard drive arrays with capacities of 5G, 10G, or more have become fairly commonplace, and CD-ROMs are well on their way to ubiquity. In addition, many servers are now being used to run multiple directory name spaces, database servers, multi-protocol routers, host connectivity gateways, modem-pooling and remote-access products, or e-mail routers and gateways. Each of these types of products has additional resource requirements above the basic needs of the NOS.

For a complex server configuration like this, combining all the various memory requirements for disk space and file management—as well as file and directory caching—into a single factor to multiply against the server's disk space is inappropriate. While it is true that every megabyte of disk space requires a certain amount of RAM for storing the FAT and other media management needs, estimations of memory requirements for file caching purposes is more accurate if based on the number of users rather than the total amount of disk space. When the above formulas are used on heavily loaded server configurations, the results can yield great discrepancies, often as much as 20M or more.

For this reason, Novell has officially discredited both formulas, and in December 1994, published a supplement to its *Application Notes* publication that provides a far more detailed worksheet for server memory calculation. Now, separate calculations are required for many of the factors that were grouped together in the earlier formulas. Consideration is also paid to the factors affecting memory usage by NetWare 4.x servers—these factors are covered later in this chapter.

NetWare 3 and 4 Server Memory Worksheet

from *Novell Application Notes*, December 1994

STEP 1: Calculate the following seven variables.

V1. Enter the total number of megabytes of disk connected to the server: _____ M
(Enter 1 for each M, and 1024 for each G)

V2. Calculate the number of megabytes of *usable* disk space connected to the server: _____ M
(If you are mirroring or duplexing, multiply V1×0.5; otherwise, copy V1)

V3. Enter the server's volume block size (4, 8, 16, 32, or 64): _____ K

V4. Calculate the number of disk blocks per M (Divide 1024 / V3): _____ blocks per M

V5. Calculate the total number of disk blocks (Multiply V2 × V4): _____ blocks

V6. Enter the maximum number of clients (end-users) attached to the server: _____ clients
(For example, enter 24 for 24 end-users)

V7. If suballocation is enabled, enter the maximum number of files that will reside on the server:
_____ files

STEP 2: Calculate your individual memory requirements.

Line 1.   Enter the base memory requirement for the core OS: _____ K
(Enter 2048 for NetWare 3 or 5120 for NetWare 4)

Line 2.   Calculate the memory requirements for Media Manager: _____ K
(V1 × 0.1)

Line 3.   If file compression is enabled, enter 250; otherwise enter 0: _____ K

Line 4.   If suballocation is enabled, calculate the required memory; otherwise, enter 0: _____ K
(V7 × 0.005)

Line 5.   Calculate the memory required to cache the FAT: _____ K
(V5 × 0.008)

Line 6.   Calculate the memory requirement for file cache using the following table: _____ K
This calculation uses a memory requirement of 0.4M file cache per client. The decrease as
the user community size increases is based on assumptions regarding increased repetitive
use of shared data (temporal and spatial locality) within the cache.

Less than 100 clients	V6 × 400
Between 100 and 250 clients	40,000 + ((V6 − 100) × 200)
Between 250 and 500 clients	70,000 + ((V6 − 250) × 100)
Between 500 and 1000 clients	95,000 + ((V6 − 500) × 50)

Line 7.   Enter the total memory (in kilobytes) required for support NLMs: _____ K
2000K is recommended for BTRIEVE (700), CLIB (500), INSTALL (600), and PSERVER (200)

Line 8.   Enter the total memory (in kilobytes) required for other services: _____ K
(Other services include NetWare for Macintosh, NetWare for SAA, OracleWare, NetWare
Management System, and so on.)

STEP 3: Calculate your total memory requirement.

Line 9:   Total Lines 1–8 for your total memory requirement (in kilobytes): _____ K

Line 10: Divide Line 9 by 1024 for a result in megabytes: _____ M

Using this result, round up to the server's nearest memory configuration. NetWare will enhance
server performance by using all leftover memory for additional file cache.

Name Space Memory Requirements. The preceding worksheet does not take into account the addition of name spaces to individual volumes. The addition of the NAM name space modules to the server's memory configuration produces virtually no additional memory overhead. The primary impact of name spaces is in the allocation of memory for the caching of the volumes' *directory entry tables* (*DETs*). This memory is allocated from the Permanent Memory pool in the form of *directory cache buffers* (memory pools are examined in more detail later in this chapter). The DET normally lists one entry for each file on a volume. The addition of each name space causes every file to require one additional entry in the table. Thus, while a single 4K directory cache buffer can manage 32 files with only the default DOS name space loaded, this number is reduced to 16 files with one extra name space, 10 files with two extra name spaces, and 8 files with three extra name spaces.

To compute the additional RAM required to compensate for the additional directory cache buffers needed, Novell provides the following formula:

$$0.032 \times volumesize \text{ (in M)} \div blocksize \text{ (in K)}$$

Round the result to the next highest megabyte and add to the total RAM requirement previously calculated.

It is important to understand, though, that memory allocation for additional name spaces is solely a matter of server performance, which can be tuned by the user. No additional memory (beyond the small amount needed to load the NAM module) is actually used by the name spaces, but clients' disk access speed decrease, noticeably as additional name spaces are loaded if the same amount of memory is allocated to caching directory entries. While NetWare 2.x cached the entire directory entry table into memory, this was found to be impractical on servers with large amounts of storage space, so in NetWare 3.x and 4.x only portions of the table are cached, according to a *most-recently-used* (*MRU*) algorithm. When one additional name space is added to a server's volumes, the number of directory cache buffers allocated must be doubled to achieve the same level of efficiency those volumes would have had without the added name space.

The number of directory cache buffers that can be allocated is bound by two SET commands that typically are included in the server's AUTOEXEC.NCF file when the defaults are to be changed:

Parameter	Default	Minimum	Maximum
SET MINIMUM DIRECTORY CACHE BUFFERS	20	10	2000
SET MAXIMUM DIRECTORY CACHE BUFFERS	500	20	4000

The MINIMUM setting represents the directory cache buffers that are allocated immediately when the operating system is booted. This is done because the addition of each additional buffer (beyond the minimum) incurs a 1.1 second delay. Pre-allocating a specified number of buffers that are sure to be needed helps to minimize these delays. If file access seems slow immediately after booting the server and then increases later, this parameter should be increased. Care should be taken, however, not to set this parameter too high. Memory that is allocated for use as directory cache buffers cannot be returned to the file cache buffer pool. Allocated buffers that are not actually used by the file system are wasting server memory.

The MAXIMUM setting prevents the file system from causing too much memory to be allocated to directory cache buffers. Without this setting, the operating system would eventually attempt to cache the entire directory entry table; in most cases, this would monopolize all the memory in the server.

NetWare dynamically allocates additional directory cache buffers from the Permanent Memory pool as needed. The number of buffers currently in use can be viewed in the Resource Utilization screen of the MONITOR.NLM utility. The best way to determine the optimal settings for these two parameters is to observe the increase in the number of buffers allocated over several days of typical server use. Running the server without additional name spaces loaded on the volumes allows a baseline to be established with which the additional requirements for the name spaces can be computed. For one additional name space, double the number of buffers actually allocated and use this as the MINIMUM. For two name spaces, triple it; for three, quadruple it. For the MAXIMUM, add at least 100 to MINIMUM to allow for growth during peak usage.

If a situation arises in which a production server is low on memory, these two parameters should be among the first to be lowered as a temporary stopgap measure until more memory can be installed. Performance might suffer, but this may allow important processes to continue that otherwise would be halted for want of additional RAM.

The use of name spaces on server volumes might be necessary to the operation of the network, but as we've seen, it can require significant amounts of additional memory. It therefore is recommended that, whenever possible, separate volumes be created for the files that require name space support, to prevent simple DOS files from affecting the performance of the server too greatly. It is preferable also for name space support to be added when the volumes are created, rather than after DOS files have already been written to the disk.

Adding a name space to a newly created volume ensures that the additional entry in the DET for each file is nearly always within the same directory entry block as the original entry. Name spaces added later cause the directory entries to be located in different blocks most of the time, requiring that both blocks be cached by the file system to access that file, thus decreasing the system's efficiency. When a file with multiple name spaces is accessed from a client, however, only the directory entry corresponding to that particular client is cached. In other words, a file accessed from a Macintosh workstation caches the original DOS entry in the DET as well as the Macintosh entry, but any other entries, such as HPFS or NFS, if they exist for that file, are not cached.

NetWare Server Memory Pools

The previous section exemplified one of the ways in which the NetWare operating system allocates available server memory to its many processes. We also have discussed the way in which file cache buffers comprise the primary memory pool from which all of NetWare's other pools access the memory they need. It is important to understand the interaction between the various memory pools, because while some can utilize memory as needed and then return it to the source from which it came, others allocate memory on a permanent basis, releasing it only when the operating system is shut down. Although NetWare contains some very advanced auto-tuning features that allow it to run quite efficiently—in most cases, without modification of the default settings—optimizing the way in which memory is managed by the operating system can provide a noticeable increase in server performance and efficiency.

As can be seen from the operating system's original name, NetWare 386 is based on the Intel 80386 microprocessor. The advanced memory handling capabilities of that processor were utilized by NetWare to a greater degree than any other operating system of its time. This is due primarily to the fact that backward compatibility was not considered to be an issue by the developers. NetWare 3.x was a completely new networking environment and, at the time, there were relatively few third-party products that were actually loaded directly into the server's memory structure. The VAPs of NetWare 2.x were eliminated entirely, allowing a totally new memory allocation scheme to be created.

The File Cache Buffer Pool. The 32-bit registers of the 386 processor allow NetWare to address the memory installed in the file server as a single contiguous segment, up to 4G in size (2^{32} bytes = 4,294,967,296 bytes = 4G). Rather than pre-allocate areas of memory for the operating system's various needs, as NetWare 2.x does, NetWare 3.x dynamically allocates memory from this pool, only as needed. This largest, primary pool, from which all other processes derive memory, is known as the *File Cache Buffer pool* because all memory that is not needed for other processes is used for caching file reads and writes. The primary function of the NetWare memory management system is to provide memory to any other process that requests it, while maximizing the amount of RAM available for caching. There is a minimum requirement of 20 cache buffers for the server's operation, but the more File Cache Buffer space available, the better the server will run—for this reason, installing additional RAM in a NetWare server is never a wasted action. There is no simpler or better way to enhance server performance than to add additional memory to this pool.

Figure 8.1 shows the File Cache Buffer pool and the other NetWare memory pools. The following sections describe each of the other pools, their uses, and the ways they interact with the File Cache Buffer pool, NetWare's ultimate memory source.

The Permanent Memory Pool. The *Permanent Memory pool*, as the name indicates, is used for the maintenance of permanent tables and other long-term memory needs. It is also the area in which directory and communications data is cached, in the form of directory cache buffers and packet receive buffers. It is permanent also in the sense that any memory allocated to this pool from the File Cache Buffer pool cannot be returned to the File Cache Buffer pool, except when you restart the server. On the Resource Utilization screen of MONITOR.NLM, the amount of server RAM allocated to the Permanent Memory pool appears, along with the amount that is currently in use. Amounts of memory in this pool that are not being used are going to waste, and steps should be taken to determine what processes are causing this memory to be allocated. One possible cause is that the values of either the MINIMUM DIRECTORY CACHE BUFFERS or MINIMUM PACKET RECEIVE BUFFERS parameter are set too high.

These are the NetWare 3.x file server memory pools.

The Semi-Permanent Memory Pool. The *Semi-Permanent Memory pool* is utilized primarily for LAN and disk drivers—small amounts of memory that are needed for extended lengths of time. This memory can be thought of as a nested pool or "sub-pool." Memory is allocated to this pool dynamically from the Permanent Memory pool as needed, and it can be returned to the Permanent Memory pool when no longer needed. Such returned memory can be accessed directly from the Permanent Memory pool or can be allocated to another sub-pool but cannot be returned to use as file cache buffers.

Alloc Short-Term Memory Pool. The *Alloc Short-Term Memory pool* also uses the Permanent Memory pool as its source, but unlike the Semi-Permanent Memory pool, the Alloc Short-Term Memory pool cannot return its memory to the Permanent Memory pool. When the memory is released from use, it remains in the Alloc Short-Term Memory pool, where it can be used by other processes but only within that pool. This type of memory is used for many tasks requiring small (below 4K) allocations over short periods of time, including the following:

- Drive mappings

- SAP (service advertising protocol) tables

- RIP (routing information protocol) tables

- Queue manager tables

- User connection information

- Loadable module tables

- Service requests

- Open and locked files

- Pop-up windows on the server console

Because of the one-way nature of its memory allocation, some care must be taken to not allow too much RAM to be allocated to the Alloc Short-Term Memory pool. As with the Permanent Memory pool, the size of the Alloc Short-Term Memory pool and the amount that is actually in use can be viewed in the Resource Utilization screen of MONITOR.NLM.

Practices like opening too many windows in several different menu-driven server modules at the same time (ironically, this includes MONITOR.NLM) can cause too much memory to be allocated to this pool, and this memory goes to waste once the windows are closed. Sometimes, improperly coded NLMs can cause a consistent increase in the Alloc Short-Term Memory pool. This can be checked by examining the resource tags (using MONITOR.NLM) for the various NLMs loaded on the server over a period of time, to see which one is regularly requesting more memory from the Alloc Short-Term Memory pool.

> **Note**
>
> Although "alloc" sounds like a truncated version of "allocated," I have never seen this pool referred to by any name that didn't involve "Alloc Memory."

The total amount of memory available for this pool can be controlled through the use of SET MAXIMUM ALLOC SHORT TERM MEMORY, which establishes a ceiling beyond which no more RAM can be used for the Alloc Short-Term Memory pool. The default setting for this parameter was 2M in NetWare versions 3.11 and earlier, but changes to the operating system's memory architecture in version 3.12 caused a greater amount of memory to be needed, as a rule, in the Alloc Short-Term Memory pool. The default setting for version 3.12 was raised to 8M, and the maximum setting to 32M, from 16M in earlier versions:

Parameter	Version	Default	Maximum
SET MAXIMUM ALLOC SHORT TERM MEMORY	3.11	2M	16M
	3.12	8M	32M

The Cache Movable Memory Pool. The *Cache Movable Memory pool* is one of two pools that are derived directly from the File Cache Buffer pool and that can return their memory for use as file cache buffers after being released. It is used for the maintenance of NetWare's own file allocation, directory entry, and hashing tables, which require widely fluctuating amounts of memory depending on the degree and type of server use. Because this pool is used solely for NetWare's own native processes, it is movable. That is, the operating system dynamically can adjust the location of the memory used for this pool so that, when it is released, no memory fragmentation occurs in the File Cache Buffer pool.

The Cache Non-Movable Memory Pool. The *Cache Non-Movable Memory pool* also draws memory directly from the File Cache Buffer pool and is able to return the memory when it is no longer needed. This pool is used primarily for the loading of NLMs, and as a result, it often is one of the largest allocations on the server. Memory is allocated to this pool in static amounts; that is, it is *non-expandable*. A particular NLM needs a certain amount of memory to load, and exactly that amount of memory is drawn from the File Cache Buffer pool and allocated to the Cache Non-Movable Memory pool for use by that NLM. No further memory is drawn from this pool by the NLM as it is functioning, although the NLM may draw memory from other pools for different purposes.

Memory Fragmentation. When an NLM is unloaded, memory taken from the Cache Non-Movable Memory pool is released and returned to the File Cache Buffer pool. However, as the name implies, the memory is not moved. The actual range of memory addresses used to load the NLM is released, creating the possibility for the File Cache Buffer pool to become fragmented. If you were to cite the most noticeable flaw in the NetWare memory management model, this would be it. Fragmented memory in the File Cache Buffer pool can result in a module failing to load, even though there is sufficient memory in the pool for its requirements. The problem is that a module will require that its memory be furnished in a single contiguous segment, which fragmentation prevents. The only way to eliminate memory fragmentation is to shut down and restart the server.

When NetWare 3.x was first released, this was not thought by the developers to be much of an issue for the average network server. Memory fragmentation is caused by the repeated loading and unloading of NLMs, and most third-party server applications at the time consisted of modules that were designed to be loaded once and left running continuously; however, this no longer is the case. Server applications have experienced the same rapid growth in size and capabilities as desktop software packages, and it now is common for them to consist of many different NLMs that are frequently loaded and unloaded as the program operates. For this reason, the era when NetWare 3.x servers could be left running for months or even years without interruption is all but over. It is highly recommended that servers on which this type of new software is installed be shut down regularly to defragment the File Cache Buffer pool. Once a month might be sufficient, but more frequent reboots might be necessary if file system performance becomes sluggish or if modules fail to load for want of memory when sufficient memory seems to be available.

Frequent memory fragmentation in NetWare servers can also be caused by hardware limitations. The use of the ISA bus for hard drive and network interface cards that use bus mastering or direct memory access (DMA) in file servers with more than 16M of installed memory is a practice that has been officially proscribed by Novell for many years, yet it continues unabated, even in servers with 32-bit bus slots available for use. Many 16-bit NICs use DMA to transfer packets to and from memory, and nearly all 16-bit SCSI host adapters use bus mastering, DMA, or both. The fundamental problem is that these adapters are incapable architecturally of addressing memory above 16M.

The problem arises because the 16-bit ISA expansion bus has only 24 address lines, and therefore can only directly address 16M of memory. The ISA bus was designed for the IBM AT using the Intel 80286 microprocessor, which also had only 24 address lines and could utilize a maximum of 16M of RAM. Because of this limitation, these adapters are unable to properly process a memory address above 16M or, in hexadecimal notation, 0x00FFFFFF. Instead of proceeding from this point to the next address, 0x01000000, such adapters roll over to the bottom of their memory address range, to 0x00000001. The memory address at 17M, for example, appears no differently to these adapters than the memory address at 1M. In fact, such a device may attempt to write to both locations at once, affecting whatever code happens to be resident in the memory area below 16M.

Obviously, this can cause severe problems such as memory conflicts, corruption, and fragmentation. This sort of fragmentation is not a gradual inconvenience, however, like the sort caused by the loading and unloading of NLMs. Symptoms of these problems can include not being able to mount large volumes, server errors saying `Cache memory allocator out of available memory`, and even server abends citing messages such as `Invalid Request Returned NPutIOCTL`.

Such problems occur because when the driver for a 16-bit SCSI adapter is loaded from the STARTUP.NCF file, memory is allocated from the top down, as is always the case with NetWare. The top, for this driver, is 16M. Once the driver is loaded, the SYS: volume is automatically mounted, and NetWare loads the volume's FAT and other media management information at the 16M mark, working its way down. Therefore, all the volume information for SYS:, and any other volume mounted afterward, must fit into the first 16M of RAM, along with DOS, the core NetWare OS code, the disk controller driver, and the driver buffers. As a result, NetWare might not be able to mount all the volumes installed in the server—and even if all the volumes can be mounted, the `Cache memory allocator out of available memory` message may appear later because of this.

If, however, you must use a 16-bit adapter in a server with more than 16M of RAM, be sure to strictly follow the recommendations of the card's manufacturer. They might call for the inclusion of certain switches when loading the driver for the adapter (such as Adaptec's ABOVE16=Y parameter), but usually they involve preventing NetWare from automatically recognizing memory above the 16M mark with the following commands at the beginning of the server's STARTUP.NCF:

SET AUTO REGISTER MEMORY ABOVE 16M = OFF

SET RESERVED BUFFERS BELOW 16M = 32

The first command prevents the adapter and its drivers from inadvertently writing to the memory above 16M as it is loading, by forcing the server to ignore the existence of any memory above 16M. After the drivers for the 16-bit adapter have been loaded, the REGISTER MEMORY command is used in the AUTOEXEC.NCF file to provide access to all the other memory installed in the server.

The second command reserves an area of RAM below 16M for the use of the adapter that cannot address higher memory. This prevents processes that can utilize any memory in the server from monopolizing the area below 16M. Access to the reserved memory is provided through the use of a special API call designed for this purpose. Other server modules that address the 16-bit adapter, such as tape backup software, may also make use of the reserved buffers, and their number may have to be increased as high as the maximum allowed, which is 200 for NetWare 3.11 and 300 for NetWare 3.12 or later. Both of these SET commands can only be issued from the STARTUP.NCF file.

This procedure might help to prevent memory corruption in some cases, but it does nothing to address the fragmentation that still can be caused by the initial loading of the driver at the 16M mark. One way to minimize this fragmentation is to load the driver without immediately mounting the SYS: volume. This is done by loading the driver from AUTOEXEC.NCF, rather than STARTUP.NCF. Since there is no disk access yet, however, an AUTOEXEC.NCF file must reside on the DOS device on which SERVER.EXE is loaded, and this AUTOEXEC.NCF must contain the commands naming the server and assigning its internal IPX number. Then the disk driver can be loaded. When a NetWare disk driver is loaded from the AUTOEXEC.NCF file, the SYS: volume is not automatically mounted. The server's extra memory then can be registered, after which SYS: and any other volumes can be mounted. This procedure makes all the installed memory available to NetWare for storing the volumes' file allocation tables.

When using this technique, you might find it preferable to include only the commands necessary to the procedure in the AUTOEXEC.NCF file on the DOS drive. If the last line in this file is SYS:SYSTEM\AUTOEXEC, then NetWare proceeds to run the regular AUTOEXEC.NCF file on the SYS: volume, which can contain the rest of the commands necessary to make the server fully operational.

Tip

Include some commentary in these files to document what's being done. If the technique is successful, it might be a long time before you have reason to look at these files again!

Of course, this entire procedure can be circumvented if you simply use hardware that is intended for high-performance servers. Most host adapters that use EISA, MicroChannel, or PCI buses can address the memory above 16M without any of these machinations.

It consistently amazes me that some people will spend many thousands of dollars on a server, but then skimp on a SCSI adapter to save $100.

> **Caution**
>
> Not all host adapters that use EISA, MicroChannel, or PCI buses can address memory above 16M. For example, the Adaptec AHA-1640 MCA SCSI card, despite using the MicroChannel bus, is a 16-bit adapter.

LAN Drivers

Although they obviously are important, none of the elements of the NetWare operating system discussed so far have the slightest value if there is no communication occurring with the network. For communication to occur, drivers for the LAN adapters installed in the server must be loaded and bound to a network protocol. Loading such drivers enables communication between the hardware and the data link layer interface, and binding the driver initiates communication with a suite of protocols, like IPX/SPX, AppleTalk, or TCP/IP. NetWare 3.x ships with LAN drivers for a number of popular NICs, but any card you buy these days is likely to ship with a more current version, which usually is preferable.

You can load the LAN drivers for the adapters installed in the server and create AUTOEXEC.NCF entries to automate the process on subsequent server reboots, using the same process you used for loading disk drivers (refer to the "Creating a STARTUP.NCF File" section earlier in this chapter). The server console command LOAD followed by the driver name—which always has a LAN extension—causes the user to be prompted for the parameters needed for the driver to properly address the card. After the entire LAN configuration process is complete, choose Create AUTOEXEC.NCF File from the System Options menu of INSTALL.NLM to cause all data entered at the console to be recalled and saved to an AUTOEXEC.NCF file in the SYS:SYSTEM directory.

The hardware parameters required when loading the driver (using LOAD) depend on the bus type of the hardware being used. The console prompts list all possible values for each parameter, and obviously the values entered must correspond to the hardware settings of the adapter card itself. Aside from the hardware-related settings, other parameters must be specified to allow proper communications with the network.

Board Name. When multiple LAN adapters of the same type are installed in a single server, they must utilize different hardware parameters so that they can be distinguished by the operating system. NetWare allows each board to be given an identifying name, so subsequent references to that board in the AUTOEXEC.NCF need not duplicate all the hardware parameters specified on the original LOAD line. This is done by including the NAME=*board_name* switch on the LAN driver LOAD line, where *board_name* is a unique identifying name of no more than 17 characters. This parameter is optional.

Frame Type. A frame type must be specified on the LOAD line for the LAN driver, to designate the precise configuration of the packet frames that are to be used when communicating over the network. The same frame type also must be specified at all workstations for proper communications to occur.

NetWare's *open datalink interface (ODI)*, allows a tremendous amount of flexibility in the loading and configuration of network drivers, frame types, and protocols. Multiple frame types and multiple protocols can be configured for use on the same LAN adapter, or multiple adapters can be configured to each utilize a different frame type and protocol. The *link support layer (LSL)* handles this multiplexing of frames and protocols at the workstation, recognizing the nature of each packet received and directing it to the appropriate protocol stack. To exemplify the different capabilities of this interface, a single workstation can be allowed access to both IPX and TCP/IP services with one network connection; alternatively, two separate network segments, one devoted to TCP/IP and the other to IPX workstations, can access the same server simultaneously, through separate network adapters.

To load multiple frame types on a single LAN card, a second LOAD line is entered at the server console, with the same LAN driver specified. A Do you want to load another frame type for a previously loaded board? prompt appears. Responding Yes causes the user to be prompted for the additional frame type. Responding No causes prompts to appear that allow an additional adapter board of the same model to be configured.

While this parameter on ARCnet or Token Ring networks is easily configured, selecting the frame type (or types) to be used by a LAN adapter often causes a certain amount of confusion for Ethernet administrators, and rightly so. When studying the nature of the OSI model's data link layer on an Ethernet network (see chapter 7, "Major Network Types"), the IEEE 802.3 specification document is cited as the source of the frame type used by this layer. An 802.3 packet is shown as including the 802.2 frame—that is, the *Logical Link Control (LLC)* frame—within it when necessary. Then why are you being asked to choose between an 802.3 and an 802.2 frame type when loading a LAN driver? And what are Ethernet II and Ethernet SNAP?

You have every right to be confused because the names specified as frame types here are not truly indicative of the structures they represent. In most cases—especially on networks running no other protocol besides IPX—the frame type selected is unimportant, as long as the same frame type is specified at the workstation and the server. The following sections, however, describe each of the possible Ethernet frame types, the ways in which they differ, and their various possible uses. The section headings display the frame types exactly as they should be entered on the LOAD line for the LAN driver.

ETHERNET_802.3. The 802.3 frame type is the exact model of the packet defined in the IEEE 802.3 specification. For NetWare 3.x (up to version 3.11), this was the default. This frame type can be used on networks utilizing only NetWare's native IPX protocol suite. This is because the third field in the 802.3 packet, coming just after the source and destination addresses, contains only information defining the overall length of the packet. Other frame types utilize this field to indicate the network protocol for which the frame is intended. When delivered to the LSL at the workstation, there is no way to determine the protocol stack to which it should be delivered. There can, therefore, be only a single protocol used at the workstation when the 802.3 frame is used.

ETHERNET_802.2. The 802.2 frame type, which is the default for NetWare versions 3.12 and 4.x, is the source of all the confusion previously described. The IEEE 802.2 specification defines a frame that is used in the upper half of the data link layer of the OSI model. This frame encloses the data generated by the upper layers of the model and in turn is enclosed by the IEEE 802.3 frame, operating at the lower half of the data link layer. The 802.2 frame type specified here, however, refers not to the IEEE 802.2 frame alone but to the entire 802.3 packet, including the 802.2 frame within it. This frame type, therefore, is identical to the 802.3 frame type, except for the inclusion of an IEEE 802.2 frame within its data field, which immediately follows the packet length field. The IEEE 802.2 portion of the packet provides LLC information as well as indications of the network protocol for which the packet is intended, thus rendering it usable on multi-protocol networks. This frame type is also required to use the NCP Packet Signature feature introduced in NetWare 3.12.

ETHERNET_II. The Ethernet II frame type is defined in the second revision of the original DIX Ethernet specification, which was developed in parallel to the IEEE documents. Most of the time, what is referred to as Ethernet is actually the IEEE 802.3 specification. This frame is identical to the 802.3 frame, except that the third field, which is used to specify the length of the packet in 802.3, contains a frame type specifier in Ethernet II, indicating the protocol for which the packet is intended. This frame type is required for networks that will utilize the TCP/IP protocol suite.

ETHERNET_SNAP. *Sub-Network Address Protocol* (*SNAP*) is another means of providing protocol identification data with an IEEE 802.3 frame. Like IEEE 802.2, SNAP takes the form of an additional frame that is carried in the data field of an 802.3 packet. Originally conceived to transport IP datagrams within an 802.2 or 802.3 frame, the first three fields of a SNAP frame—providing source and destination addresses, as well as control information—are identical to those of an 802.2 frame, ensuring compatibility. The rest of the frame includes network protocol information, as well as a frame type indicator, like that of an Ethernet II frame. SNAP frames are now used, however, for purposes other than IP over Ethernet. The AppleTalk protocol is supported now, and a variation called TOKEN-RING_SNAP is provided for use on multi-protocol Token Ring networks.

Binding LAN Drivers. Once the LAN driver for a network adapter has been loaded, the link between the physical layer and the data link layer is in place. What remains is for the data link layer to be connected to the network layer protocol which will be used to communicate with other stations on the network. This is called *binding* the driver to the protocol and is done with the BIND internal server command. Each frame type specified for each LAN driver must be individually bound to a protocol for communications to begin.

At its simplest, this process consists of issuing a command at the server console prompt that says: BIND *driver_name* TO IPX NET=*x*, where *driver_name* is the name of the driver that has just been loaded (using LOAD), and *x* is the network address of the segment to which the adapter is connected. When multiple LAN adapters, frame types, or protocols are being used, however, parameters are included with the BIND command to specify the adapter, frame type, or protocol that is to be addressed. This is where the board name parameter (discussed earlier in the "Board Name" section) can be extremely helpful. Alternatively, the same LAN driver parameters used to identify these variables on the LOAD LAN driver line can be specified with the BIND command.

The default network layer protocol for NetWare is its own native IPX, and nearly all NetWare servers bind this protocol to at least one driver. NET=x is the only protocol parameter that can be applied to IPX; this parameter indicates the address of the network segment that is being used for IPX communications. An existing segment already has a number assigned to it, and this number must match the number specified on the BIND line. A new segment takes as its network address whatever hexadecimal string is specified here. Each station attached to this segment must then be configured to use that address.

The IPX protocol is internal to the NetWare operating system and therefore requires no other modules for its implementation. Other protocols such as TCP/IP and AppleTalk, however, are made available by the loading of other support NLMs on the server, after which they also can be bound to a LAN driver. Other protocols require different parameters to be specified for communications to be established—these vary according to the protocol used.

The NetWare IPX/SPX Protocol Suite

What has been discussed so far as the simple act of binding a LAN driver to the IPX protocol is actually the initialization of access to the services of a suite of protocols operating at several different layers of the OSI model. All are carried within the data link layer frame type selected for use when loading the LAN driver, giving rise to some problems with terminology that require clarification at the outset.

As with the frame types outlined above, the structures used by the IPX protocol suite are sometimes referred to as "packets," in the sense that one might refer to an "IPX packet" or an "NCP packet." What is actually being discussed here is a frame of that particular type, carried within a packet. The *packet* itself, the basic unit of data that is transmitted over the network, is sometimes also called a *datagram*. The outermost frame of a packet may be based on the IEEE 802.3, 802.5, or Ethernet II specification (among others), and several different types may be used on the same network, but all the frames referred to with terms like 802.2 and SNAP—as well as IPX, SPX, and NetWare Core Protocol (NCP)—refer to additional frames carried within this outer frame.

For example, when a client workstation receives a requested file from a NetWare server over a network using a frame type of Ethernet 802.2, what really is being transmitted is the actual file data within an NCP frame, which is within an IPX frame, which is within an 802.2 frame, which is within an 802.3 frame. Each of these successive layers is needed to ensure that the data file is delivered to its destination process in a timely and error-free manner.

The file being transferred undergoes a series of different packaging and encoding processes for this purpose. First of all, unless it is a very small file, it is split into fragments that fit within the required packet size. These fragments may take different routes to their destination and may arrive at different times or out of their original order. Information within the various frames provides the destination of the packets involved, not only in the form of a node address but mentioning the specific process for which the included data is to be used. It provides a means for ensuring that the packet is delivered at the correct rate of speed, to avoid packet loss due to a destination interface that is overwhelmed with too much data. It provides a means by which receipt of the intact packets can be acknowledged to the sender. Finally, it provides the receiving station with information necessary to reassemble the pieces to form a coherent whole and deliver this whole to the appropriate workstation process.

Note

This description does not even take into account the entire process by which the binary data used by the computers at each end is encoded and decoded into electrical signals, pulses of light, or radio carrier waves for the actual transmission.

As you can see, this is a highly complex procedure, but I hope the entire concept has become more comprehensible thanks to splitting up the various levels of packaging. The form of the outer frame (the datagram), has been covered in chapter 7, "Major Network Types," and the basic conceptual organization of the OSI reference model has been examined in chapter 3, "The OSI Model: Bringing Order to Chaos." This section primarily covers the protocol frames that are used at the network and transport layers of the OSI model on a standard Novell network; we examine the structure as well as various uses of these protocols, which are usually referred to as the *IPX/SPX protocol suite*.

Although this protocol suite is the default in NetWare networks, and as a result is very widely used, by no means is it the only game in town. The *TCP/IP protocol suite*, the dominant protocol for UNIX systems and the Internet, is a correlative to IPX/SPX and is used more and more widely as an additional protocol over NetWare networks. There is a product named NetWare/IP that allows TCP/IP to be used as the primary NetWare protocol, replacing IPX/SPX entirely. *AppleTalk* is another protocol, used to provide connectivity for Macintosh machines. These alternative protocols are covered elsewhere in this book. The purpose of this section is to illustrate the functions for which the IPX/SPX protocol suite is used and the basic manner in which IPX/SPX performs those functions. Once you understood these basics, other protocols are basically variations on a theme. They may have radically different names and definitions, but their functions are the same.

The Internetwork Packet Exchange (IPX) Protocol. Based on the XNS (Xerox Network Services) Internetwork Datagram Packet (IDP) protocol, the *Internetwork Packet Exchange (IPX) protocol* is the basic, connectionless network layer protocol used by NetWare. A *connectionless protocol* is one in which receipt of the packet by the destination is not guaranteed by any mechanism within the frame. Addressed packets are sent off without any knowledge of the current status of the recipient system, in much the same way that letters are sent in a postal system. A *connection-oriented* protocol, on the other hand, sends a series of control packets to the destination to establish a logical connection before any live data is actually sent, in much the same way that a telephone call occurs.

IPX is primarily used as a carrier for other, higher-layer protocols in the suite, some of which have their own means of guaranteeing receipt of a packet, so do not assume that a packet with an IPX frame is any less reliable because of its connectionless nature. It may simply mean that the mechanics for ensuring reliable delivery, if needed, are provided elsewhere. Although it sometimes is referred to in general terms as a "transport protocol," it should be noted that IPX, being routable, is definitely a network layer protocol, and in this book is referred to as such.

Most of the other protocols examined in this section are carried within the IPX frame, such as SPX, RIP, SAP, and NCP. The primary function of IPX is to deliver its contents to the proper destination address, whether that is located on the local network segment or requires routing to another segment a great distance away on an internetwork. IPX also has broadcast capabilities for the transmission of packets to all the stations on an internetwork.

Figure 8.2 shows the layout of the IPX frame, with its parts labeled. The following list explains the function of each field. Remember, however, that this is only the IPX portion of the packet. The IPX frame encases a higher-level frame within its data field and is itself encased by a lower-level frame.

- **Checksum (2 bytes)**   Designated for the inclusion of a CRC value, this field always carries the value FFFFh, as the function is disabled. It is still included to maintain consistency with the original IDP packet from which it was derived, but CRC checking is performed at the data link layer and therefore is not needed here.

- **Length (2 bytes)**   Specifies the length of the IPX frame, including its header and data but exclusive of any outer (that is, lower-level) frames. Specified in octets (8-bit groups, or bytes); possible values range from 30 to 576.

- **Transport Control (1 byte)**   Set to zero when the frame is created, this field is incremented by one each time the packet passes through a router on its way to its destination. This usually is referred to as *hop count*, the number of hops between the source and destination. This field is particularly important when performing a protocol analysis of an internetwork, as it can help to determine if the network is routing packets in the most efficient manner possible.

- **Packet Type (1 byte)**   Indicates the service or upper-layer protocol carried within the IPX frame, according to the following values:

0	Unknown Packet Type
1	Routing Information Packet (RIP)
4	Packet Exchange Packet (PEP)
5	Sequenced Packet Exchange (SPX)
17	NetWare Core Protocol

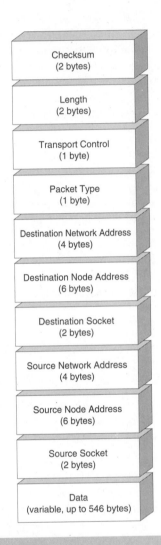

Figure 8.2

This is the IPX protocol frame.

■ **Destination Network Address (4 bytes)** Contains the network address, as assigned by the network administrator, of the segment on which the destination is located. A value of zero indicates that the destination is located on the same segment as the source, so no routing between networks is needed. In this case, the packet is sent directly to the destination node. If the destination resides on a different network, then the packet is sent to the router through which the destination node may be reached. If an IPX packet is being sent to a remote network for the first time (since the network has been initialized), then a *RIP packet* is generated and transmitted, to determine the most efficient route to the destination. Once determined, this information is then maintained in the static tables at the router for use when later packets are sent to that same remote network.

- **Destination Node Address (6 bytes)**   Specifies the unique station address assigned to the network interface within the destination. Depending on the network type, this may be permanently assigned by the NIC manufacturer (Ethernet or Token Ring) or by the network administrator (ARCnet). Unused bits are filled with zeroes, and broadcast packets are completely filled with ones.

- **Destination Socket (2 bytes)**   Indicates the process within the destination where the packet is to be used. A *socket* is a general purpose logical mechanism through which a program or process at one location communicates with a network—or with a program or process—at another location. It is used, in this case, to further define the ultimate destination of the packet within the active memory of the destination. The following values may be used:

0451h	NetWare Core Protocol
0452h	Service Advertising Protocol
0453h	Routing Information Protocol
0455h	NetBIOS
0456h	Diagnostic Packet
0457h	Serialization Packet
4000h–6000h	Custom sockets for file server processes

- **Source Network Address (4 bytes)**   The network address of the node originating the packet, specified using the same format as the Destination Network Address.

- **Source Node Address (6 bytes)**   The node address of the sending station, specified using the same format as the Destination Node Address.

- **Source Socket (2 bytes)**   The socket from which the packet originates, specified using the same parameters as the Destination Socket.

- **Data (variable, up to 546 bytes)**   Contains data destined for higher-level protocols.

The Sequenced Packet Exchange (SPX) Protocol. The *Sequenced Packet Exchange* (SPX) *protocol* is a connection-oriented protocol that guarantees delivery of packets to the destination and that provides error correction, flow control, and packet sequencing services. A connection-oriented protocol ensures the proper delivery of packets by establishing a virtual connection between the source and destination before any live data is sent. Once the connection is established, packets containing data are individually sent and acknowledged, and after the entire transmission, another control packet is sent to break down the connection.

To aid in verifying the validity of the SPX virtual connection, probe packets are sent out at periodic intervals when no other activity is occurring. SPX also uses a dynamically adjusted *timeout value* to decide at what time the retransmission of any particular packet is necessary. The frequency at which connection verification packets are sent, as well as other SPX control variables, can be altered through settings in a workstation's NET.CFG file. Timeout values also can be adjusted using the SPXCONFG.NLM utility at the server console.

These features add a great deal of overhead to an SPX transmission, and as a result, this protocol is not often used in normal network activities, despite the fact that it is frequently mentioned together with IPX as the dominant NetWare protocol (IPX/SPX). Only services that require absolute reliability in transmission make use of SPX—primarily the NetWare printing services, which use it for communications between print servers, print queues, and remote printers, and the NetWare remote console (RCONSOLE). Third-party products such as gateways, database engines, and backup software also sometimes make use of SPX connections.

The SPX protocol was derived from the Xerox Sequenced Packet Protocol and is implemented within the data field of an IPX packet. Figure 8.3 shows the layout of the SPX frame header, and the following list explains the function of each of the fields.

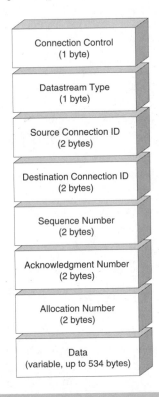

Figure 8.3

This is the SPX protocol frame.

- **Connection Control (1 byte)** Contains a code that regulates flow control during the entire connection. Through the values entered in this field, the connection is established, maintained, and broken. Possible values are as follows:

10h	End of message
20h	Attention
40h	Acknowledgment required
80h	System packet

■ **Datastream Type (1 byte)**   Indicates the nature of the data included in the packet, and identifies the higher-layer process for which it is destined. This field may also contain information concerning the cause of a connection loss.

■ **Source Connection ID (2 bytes)**   Contains an identifying code that is generated when the virtual connection is established between the source and the destination. Every packet sent during the connection contains this and the Destination Connection ID.

■ **Destination Connection ID (2 bytes)**   Code used to identify the destination node for a given virtual connection. It also is used to demultiplex multiple virtual connections that all may be accessing one IPX socket, as in a file server.

■ **Sequence Number (2 bytes)**   Contains a number with which the correct order for the packets of a given virtual connection is established. It is used to detect packets missing from a transmission and also to reassemble packets into the proper order if they arrive at the destination out of sequence.

■ **Acknowledgment Number (2 bytes)**   Contains the mechanism by which an SPX connection guarantees packet delivery. By indicating in this field the next packet expected by the destination, the proper receipt of all previous packets is acknowledged.

■ **Allocation Number (2 bytes)**   Indicates the number of available packet receive buffers at the destination node. It is used to control the flow of data from the source to the destination, so that packets are not lost due to excessively high delivery rates. This is the means, for example, by which a print server knows when to stop sending data to a printer because the printer's memory buffers are full.

■ **Data (variable, up to 534 bytes)**   Contains the data destined for higher-level processes. The maximum size of the data field is the result of subtracting 30 bytes for the IPX header and 12 bytes for the SPX header from the maximum overall length of an IPX packet (576 bytes).

The Packet Exchange Protocol (PXP). Not quite as reliable as SPX, yet more reliable than IPX, the *Packet Exchange protocol* is a connection-oriented transport layer protocol that is functionally different from SPX primarily in that it does not have a mechanism to prevent the transmission of duplicate requests. It therefore is suitable only for single transactions (that is, the exchange of one request and one reply) in which the receipt of duplicate requests by the destination can have no deleterious effect. These are known as *idempotent transactions*. For example, a request to read a block from a file is an idempotent transaction, but the transmission of data for output to a printer is not.

Carried within an IPX frame, the PXP header consists solely of a four-byte field that contains a Transaction ID used to associate a request with its reply.

The NetWare Core Protocol (NCP). The *NetWare Core Protocol* (*NCP*) is the packet type responsible for the vast majority of the traffic on a typical NetWare network, as it is responsible for all the file system traffic between servers and workstations. It also is used for numerous other functions that span the session, presentation, and application layers of the OSI model, such as file locking and synchronization, bindery lookups, and name management.

At the transport layer, NCP provides connection-oriented packet transfers between a server and a workstation. Due to NCP's many functions, different types of NCP packets have different requirements. Some, such as a workstation's request to write a file to a server volume, require that each transmitted packet be received and acknowledged before transmission of the next packet can begin, thus providing guaranteed delivery on a par with the SPX protocol. Others do not require such extensive verification procedures. This flexibility is one of NCP's greatest advantages. The failure of a workstation to receive the required acknowledgment for one of its packets after several attempts are made results in the familiar Network Error: Abort, Retry? message at the workstation.

NCP functions at the session layer by being responsible for initiating and breaking down a workstation's connection with the server. The GET NEAREST SERVER command generated by a workstation shell or requester as it is loaded is sent out over the network using NCP. The server responds with a similar packet, containing the GIVE NEAREST SERVER command and the server's name. After an exchange of routing information, and the negotiation of a common packet size (also performed using NCP packets), a connection between the server and workstation is granted, and a You are attached to server XXXXX message appears at the workstation. This is one occasion where a connection-oriented protocol can actually result in connection information being visible on the server's screen. This is not the case with an SPX connection, which represents only a virtual connection established to facilitate an exchange of data. A single NCP connection remains open for the entire time that the workstation is attached to its primary server, thus reducing the amount of control traffic needed to establish and break down connections (recall that SPX required quite a bit of control traffic).

To provide service at the presentation and application layers, an NCP packet contains codes that define the packet's exact purpose. For example, when a workstation shell or requester intercepts a DOS File Read request that specifies a network drive as the file's source, an NCP packet is created with the corresponding NCP code for File Read in the header. NCP packets are also used for print services (print jobs redirected by the CAPTURE command), as well as other higher-layer functions that are redirected to network resources.

To accommodate these diverse uses, the NetWare Core Protocol has separate frame headers for requests and replies, which are carried within the data field of the standard IPX frame. Figure 8.4 shows the header fields for the NCP request frame, and the following list explains the function of each field.

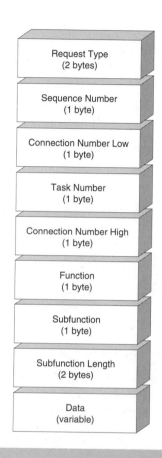

Figure 8.4

This is the NetWare Core Protocol request frame.

- **Request Type (2 bytes)** Contains a code indicating the primary purpose of the packet, according to the following values:

1111	Create a Service Connection Used to begin the process of establishing a connection with a NetWare server.
2222	File Server Request Used to request that a File Read be performed or other information be supplied from a NetWare server. This is the request type that is most often found in NCP packets.
5555	Connection Destroy Used to terminate an NCP connection with a server.
7777	Burst Mode Protocol Packet Used to request the initiation of a Burst Mode transfer (covered in the next section).

- **Sequence Number (1 byte)** Indicates the order in which NCP packets are transmitted. Used to ensure that packets at the destination are processed in the proper order.

- **Connection Number Low (1 byte)** Indicates the NCP connection number between the workstation and the server. This value is the same as the connection number displayed on the Connection Information screen of the MONITOR.NLM utility.

- **Task Number (1 byte)** Contains a code indicating the task that is being requested of the server by the workstation. Used to associate requests with replies.

- **Connection Number High (1 byte)** Currently unused.

- **Function (1 byte)** Contains codes that provide the precise function that is being requested.

- **Subfunction (1 byte)** Contains information used to further define the function being requested.

- **Subfunction Length (2 bytes)** Indicates the length of the additional data related to the function fields.

- **Data (variable)** Contains additional information to aid in the processing of the function being requested. For example, this field may contain file offsets that indicate the precise location of a file being requested.

Figure 8.5 shows the header fields for the NCP reply frame, and the following list explains the function of each field.

- **Reply/Response Type (2 bytes)** Contains a code that indicates the nature of the reply to a previously transmitted request, according to the following values:

3333	File Server Reply Used to indicate that the packet contains a reply to a previously transmitted request containing the 2222 Request Type code.
7777	Burst Mode Protocol Packet Used to indicate that the initialization of a Burst Mode transfer has been successfully completed (covered later in this chapter).
9999	Positive Acknowledge Used to indicate that a previously transmitted request is currently being processed, thus preventing the connection from timing out due to a late response. This reply also might indicate a problem in satisfying the request.

- **Sequence Number (1 byte)** As in the request frame header, indicates the order in which NCP packets are transmitted. Used to ensure that packets at the destination are processed in the proper order.

- **Connection Number Low (1 byte)** As in the request frame header, indicates the NCP connection number between the workstation and the server. This value is the same as the connection number displayed on the Connection Information screen of the MONITOR.NLM utility.

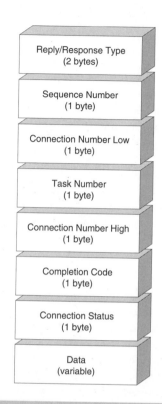

Reply/Response Type
(2 bytes)

Sequence Number
(1 byte)

Connection Number Low
(1 byte)

Task Number
(1 byte)

Connection Number High
(1 byte)

Completion Code
(1 byte)

Connection Status
(1 byte)

Data
(variable)

Figure 8.5

This is the NetWare Core Protocol reply frame.

- **Task Number (1 byte)**   Contains the code indicating the task number that has been assigned to the request transmitted by the workstation. Used to associate requests with replies.

- **Connection Number High (1 byte)**   Currently unused.

- **Completion Code (1 byte)**   Indicates the status of the server's response to the workstation's request, such as whether or not the request has been completed.

- **Connection Status (1 byte)**   Indicates whether or not the connection between the server and the workstation is still open and valid.

- **Data (variable)**   Contains any data pursuant to the reply sent by the server. In the case of a File Read request, for example, this field contains the actual file requested.

Although NCP utilizes far less overhead than an SPX transmission, its dominance as the primary component of NetWare network traffic has led many to criticize the need for an acknowledgment to every packet transmitted over the network. As a result, Novell has implemented a variation on the NCP transmission, called the *NetWare Core Packet Burst protocol*, or *Burst Mode transmission* (see the next section). The currently shipping versions of NetWare now utilize Burst Mode by default, as there is no drawback to the process.

The following section explains how this enhancement to NCP has been realized, and identifies the changes that have been made in the frame header to accommodate this new type of transmission.

The NetWare Core Packet Burst (NCPB) Protocol. *NetWare Core Packet Burst (NCPB) protocol* is a transmission technique through which multiple NCP packets can be sent from workstation to client without requiring a separate request and acknowledgment for each packet. (The previous section explained that NCP is an IPX implementation specifically tailored for all the communications that take place between a workstation and server.) One of the most misunderstood aspects of this type of communication is that transmission techniques like NCPB, despite being connection-oriented, are definitely IPX-based and do not use SPX, which though it is similar and also connection-oriented, is not used by NCPB in any way. In fact, SPX requires individual requests and acknowledgments for each packet, rendering it unsuitable for use in packet burst transmissions.

NCPB was implemented because it was realized that when transmitting large files from servers to clients, particularly over WAN links, a good deal of time and bandwidth was wasted in the transmission of control traffic; these resources could better be devoted to the transmission of actual user data. When connected through a standard NetWare router, which is limited to a maximum packet size of 512 bytes, transferring a 64K file with original NCP required 128 separate packet transactions, each of which had to be requested and acknowledged by the client, resulting in what became known as the *ping-pong effect*. A packet burst transmission, under optimal conditions, can send all 128 packets consecutively, without requiring an acknowledgment until after the last packet has been sent.

NCPB is included with the NetWare 3.12 and 4.x operating systems and operates by default when the VLM client is being used at the workstation. The technology actually was introduced before the release of version 3.12, in the form of an NLM named PBURST.NLM and a replacement client shell named BNETX.EXE. There were significant drawbacks to the use of the BNETX shell, however, and with the advent of VLMs, Novell withdrew BNETX from release in 1993. At the time, it became recommended that a network run no less than NetWare 3.12 on its servers and version 1.03 of the VLMs, if the network was to be reliant on packet burst for a significant number of its transmissions. The fully integrated version of the technology is surely more reliable than the add-on version.

NCPB uses two primary flow-control mechanisms to ensure the continued viability of its transmissions. Using a modified *sliding window* technique, a client can request the transmission of a file in the form of a burst, or window, that can consist of many packets, but only requires one acknowledgment for the entire transmission. The BNETX shell could accommodate windows up to 64K in size, while the window size when using the VLM requester is theoretically unlimited. The defaults when using VLMs, however, are set to 16 packets during a read request and 10 packets during a write request. These defaults can be overridden with the following entries in the workstation's NET.CFG file:

Parameter	Default	Min	Max
PBURST READ WINDOW SIZE =	16	3	255
PBURST WRITE WINDOW SIZE =	10	3	255

The size of the window is dynamically adjusted by the client, based on the occurrence of bad or missed packets in previous transmissions. If too many packets are lost in a particular exchange, then the *transmission rate control algorithm* causes the window size to be reduced exponentially. The client also is capable of informing the server exactly which packets in a transmission have been lost or corrupted, so that only those packets are retransmitted. Traditional windowing protocols, when an error occurs, must resend the entire window from the point of the first bad packet until the end of the transaction.

Adjustment of the window size is the sole flow-control mechanism when the BNETX shell was used. Use of this shell also required an entry in the workstation's NET.CFG file (PB BUFFERS=*x*) that specified the number of buffers (each the size of the frame type being used) that were to be created in workstation memory. Burst packets received were transferred first to these buffers and then into workstation memory for processing. There were several drawbacks to this technique. Since there was a 64K segment limit imposed on the network shell, it was possible to specify a number of buffers that was too large to be stored in memory. Also, the interim step of transferring packets to the buffers before main memory slowed down the process significantly.

When VLMs were designed, packet burst was fully integrated into their functionality. As part of the FIO.VLM module, the 64K window size limit and the use of interim packet buffers in memory were gone. A second flow-control mechanism was added, in the form of a dynamically adjustable *interpacket gap* (IPG). This process is also known as *packet metering*. For the VLM requester, prior to version 1.03, this was the only flow-control algorithm used. Versions 1.03 and later utilize packet metering as the primary method but are capable also of adjusting the window size when the maximum IPG has been reached.

When packets are being sent to a client at a rate that is too fast for the client, some packets are lost, creating the need for *resends*. Resends lessen the overall efficiency of the transmission in two ways: first, by the redundant transmission of specific packets, and second, by the increased control overhead that is necessary for the receiver to inform the sender which packets are missing and to acknowledge their eventual receipt. By dynamically increasing the interpacket gap—the amount of time elapsed between the transmission of each packet—the flow can be lessened to the point at which the client can comfortably cope with the input.

The algorithm by which the interpacket gap is adjusted was also changed during the upgrade from VLM version 1.02 to 1.03. Both begin the process by sending a number of *pings* to the destination—these are signals that are returned immediately to the source upon receipt at the destination, so that the round-trip time can be measured. The fastest round-trip time is halved, and this becomes the maximum interpacket gap. VLM version 1.02 and earlier started transmission with an interpacket gap of zero, monitored the number of packet failures that occurred, and increased the gap until the failures ceased. Later VLM versions began transmitting with the IPG set at half the maximum value and used a binary algorithm to adjust the gap to the optimal value. This usually incurred fewer overall failures during the adjustment process and was a faster method of arriving at the gap best suited to a particular environment.

Both of these flow-control methods can effectively reduce the number of packets lost or corrupted during transmission, but packet metering is the more efficient of the two, because it achieves the same end with far less control overhead. Reduced window size means that a greater number of requests and acknowledgments must be sent, while packet metering can allow for the largest possible window size, and the fewest number of control packets. Therefore, packet metering is the primary flow-control method now used by the NetWare VLMs, with adjustment of the window size remaining as a secondary method, once the maximum IPG value has been achieved. For this reason, the latest implementations of the packet burst technique should always be used, especially when connecting through a wide-area link of limited bandwidth. Also, while default values have been chosen that provide excellent performance in a wide range of environments, significant performance increases sometimes can be realized over local-area links by adjusting the default window sizes.

A related feature that also enhances communication of this type is the *large Internet packet* (*LIP*). Previously, a NetWare router could transfer packets no longer than 576 bytes. Any longer packets transmitted from a workstation were broken down into smaller ones at the first router encountered, and then sent along for reassembly at the destination. This was a limitation imposed by NetWare. The Ethernet and Token Ring specifications have always allowed longer packets than this, and much of the router hardware on the market also could support longer packets. The LIP now allows the router itself to determine the maximum length of an individual packet. Like a packet burst transmission, this lowers the overall amount of transmitted data that is devoted to control information, further increasing the overall efficiency of network communications. When used in conjunction, LIPs and packet bursts are a major improvement over the old protocols.

Implementation of the packet burst technique required substantial changes to the NCP frame header format. When Burst Mode is used, this modified header is used in place of the NCP headers, not in addition to them. Figure 8.6 shows the header designed specifically for Burst Mode transmissions, and the following list explains the function of each standard field.

- **Request Type (2 bytes)** As in the original NCP request frame headers, this code indicates the nature of the function being requested. For packet burst requests, the value in this field is always 7777.

- **Flags (1 byte)** Contains information pertaining to the flow-control status of this packet. It defines whether or not the destination node should be waiting for subsequent packet transfers from the source. Possible values are as follows:

SYS	System packet
SAK	Transmit missing fragment list

EOB   Last portion of burst data

BSY   Server busy

ABT   Abort—session not valid

- **Stream Type (1 byte)**   Used by the server to determine whether or not its reply should be in the form of a Packet Burst transfer.

- **Source ID (4 bytes)**   Contains a randomly generated number, usually derived from the current time of day, that is used to identify the sender for this particular packet burst connection. (This is not the Connection ID of the NCP session described in the traditional NCP frame header).

- **Destination ID (4 bytes)**   Contains the unique, random ID for the intended recipient of this packet burst connection.

- **Packet Sequence (4 bytes)**   Indicates the sequence number of this packet within the particular burst or window. Don't confuse this with the Burst Sequence Number described later.

- **Send Delay Time (4 bytes)**   Contains the period of delay (the interpacket gap) between individual packet transmissions, specified in units of approximately 100 microseconds.

- **Burst Sequence Number (2 bytes)**   Indicates the sequence number of this burst within the overall Burst Mode connection. The transfer of a single file, for example, might consist of enough data to warrant the transmission of numerous bursts, each containing numerous packets. The entire sequence of bursts comprises the overall *connection* or *transaction*.

- **Acknowledgment Sequence Number (2 bytes)**   Contains the burst sequence number of the window expected next at the destination. The incrementing of this value with each burst transmission serves to verify the successful receipt of the previous burst.

- **Total Burst Length (4 bytes)**   Indicates the aggregate length of the entire burst being transmitted currently; this is also known as the window size. This value can be dynamically adjusted by the protocol for each burst, depending on the successful completion of previous transmissions. This number is also used in the process of formulating a missing fragment list at the destination node.

- **Burst Packet Offset (4 bytes)**   Indicates where, in the context of the burst, the data carried within this packet is supposed to go.

- **Burst Packet Length (2 bytes)**   Indicates the overall length of the packet burst transaction (comprising multiple bursts or windows).

- **Fragment List (2 bytes)**   Defines the fragments still to be received by the destination node to complete the burst transfer. When packet transfers occur without error, this field contains one fragment, initially comprising the entire burst and decremented sequentially as successive packets are successfully transmitted. When packets are lost due to transmission problems, this field contains multiple fragments, each of which defines a range of contiguous packets still needing to be transmitted.

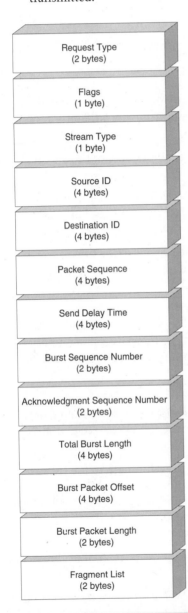

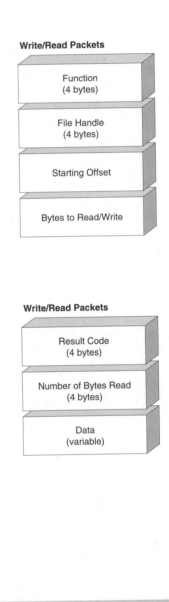

Figure 8.6

This is the NCPB frame.

The following four fields are included only in Burst Mode packets requesting that a read or write operation be performed:

- **Function (4 bytes)**   Indicates whether the transaction currently in progress is a read or write transaction.

- **File Handle (4 bytes)**   Identifies the file to be read or written

- **Starting Offset (4 bytes)**   Indicates where, in the file being read or written, the portion to be included in this packet is located.

- **Bytes to Read/Write (4 bytes)**   Indicates the number of bytes, beginning at Starting Offset, that are to be included in this particular packet.

The following fields are included in Burst Mode packets that are replying to a previously transmitted read request:

- **Result Code (4 bytes)**   Contains a code indicating the success or failure of the destination in fulfilling the request. Replies to read request packets can contain the following values:

0	No error
1	Initial error
2	I/O error
3	No data read

- **Number of Bytes Read (4 bytes)**   Indicates the number of bytes read successfully.

- **Data (variable)**   Contains a portion of the actual data requested by a previously transmitted read request packet.

Note

If an error occurred during the read transmission, only Result Code is included in the reply packet.

The reply packet to a previously transmitted write request consists only of the following field:

- **Result Code (4 bytes)**   Contains a code indicating the success or failure of the destination in fulfilling the request. Replies to write request packets can contain the following values:

0	No error
4	Write error

The write reply error codes are so limited because the only possible cause for such an error is that the destination device did not contain sufficient storage space for the operation to be completed. A write to a bad volume segment would be compensated for by NetWare's Hot Fix feature, eliminating segment problems as a possible source of error.

The Service Advertising Protocol (SAP). *Service Advertising Protocol* (*SAP*) is the means by which a NetWare server maintains its internal database of other servers and routers on the internetwork and informs other servers and routers of its own presence. This normally is done by the transmission of a SAP broadcast packet every 60 seconds. Each server, upon receipt of these packets, creates a temporary bindery or NDS entry for every server, including its location and routing information that can be used to address future transmissions to that server. Each NetWare server can communicate with up to seven other servers using SAP packets, and fields within the packet allow data concerning other servers to be relayed, thus providing each recipient with a complete picture of the location of all servers on the internetwork.

Although these broadcasts are their primary function, SAP packets also can be used by one server to explicitly request specific information from other servers on the network, which can be furnished in a SAP reply packet. This technique is often used to implement copy protection mechanisms for server-based software packages. Indeed, this is the method by which NetWare itself prevents the use of the same NOS license on multiple servers on the same network.

It is sometimes found that SAP packets are the source of excessive amounts of traffic on the network. Particularly where WAN links are concerned, they can consume too much bandwidth or force the continued operation of bandwidth-on-demand links such as ISDN unnecessarily. A module for regulating the amount of SAP traffic on a network, SAFILTER.NLM, was developed by Novell for use on NetWare 3.x servers. The frequency of SAP packet generation on NetWare 4.x servers can be directly manipulated with the SERVMAN utility. When you make adjustments to these parameters, all servers on the network should be modified in the same manner.

The SAP frame is carried within an IPX frame and has different forms for requests and replies. Figure 8.7 shows the request and reply frame header layouts, and the following two lists explain the function of each field.

■ **Packet Type (2 bytes)** Indicates the packet function according to the following values:

3h	Nearest Server Request
4h	Nearest Server Reply
1h	Standard Server Request
2h	Standard Server Reply

Standard Server Request and Standard Server Reply are the Packet Type values used for the regular broadcast of SAP identification packets. Nearest Server Request and Nearest Server Reply are used to ascertain the identity of the specific server closest to the transmitting server.

- **Server Type (2 bytes)**   Indicates whether the server is a file server, print server, backup server, or is devoted to another specific job.

Request Frame

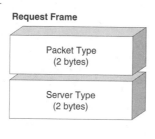

Reply Frame

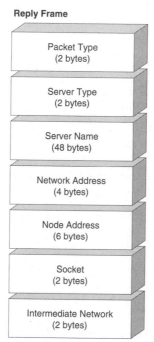

These are the Service Advertising Protocol frames.

The reply frame contains the same two fields as the request frame, plus the following two fields:

- **Server Name (48 bytes)**   Contains the full name of the server transmitting the packet.

- **Network Address (4 bytes)**   Contains the address of the network segment on which the transmitting server is located.

- **Node Address (6 bytes)**   Contains the specific node address of the transmitting server.

■ **Socket (2 bytes)**   Indicates the process associated with this SAP transmission.

■ **Intermediate Network (2 bytes)**   Indicates the number of network addresses (that is, hops) between the transmitting server and the recipient.

The Routing Information Protocol (RIP). *Routing Information Protocol* (*RIP*) performs an information gathering process much like that of SAP, except that the data gathered is used to keep every router on an internetwork updated regarding the presence and location of all other routers. Note that the term *router* includes any server that has more than one network interface installed within it, for these servers perform routing functions between two connected segments exactly as a dedicated router does.

Every router on an internetwork maintains its own tables that contain the locations of all other routers on the network, as well as the distance and amount of time that a packet must travel to reach that location. With this information, the most efficient path to any destination on the internetwork can be selected as a packet travels from router to router.

RIP packets, which can contain up to 50 sets of routing data (a set consists of the last three fields listed below), are transmitted by every router when it is initialized, and every 45 to 60 seconds thereafter. Packets also can be generated spontaneously whenever a router needs information that it doesn't have, such as when configuration information changes on any of the network's routers or when a router goes down and an alternate route to a destination must be plotted. As with SAP packets, the rate at which RIP packets are transmitted can be modified on NetWare 4.x servers with the SERVMAN utility.

Like the other protocols covered in this section, RIP frames are carried within an IPX frame. Like IPX, RIP is adapted from XNS but has been altered to improve the route selection algorithm, to the extent that it no longer is compatible with pure XNS installations. Figure 8.8 shows the RIP frame header layout, and the following list explains the function of each field.

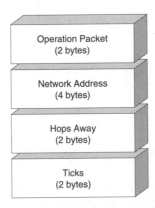

Figure 8.8

This is the Routing Information Protocol frame.

- **Operation Packet Type (2 bytes)**   Indicates whether the packet is a request (01h) or a reply (02h).

- **Network Address (4 bytes)**   Contains the address of the network segment on which the router resides. The IPX header also contains information about the router that is used for the maintenance of the router tables.

- **Hops Away (2 bytes)**   Indicates the number of routers that the RIP packet must pass through on its way to the destination router.

- **Ticks (2 bytes)**   Indicates the amount of time that it will take a packet to travel from the source to the destination. This is measured in ticks (one second = 18.21 ticks).

NetWare 4.x

The chapter so far has examined the basic components of the NetWare 3.x operating system needed to attach a server to a network and initiate the communication process. As we have seen, and as becomes more evident in everyday practice, there are several fundamental drawbacks to NetWare 3.x. Four years is a long stretch of time in the computing industry, and by 1993, Novell had examined the shortcomings of its products and developed what the company hoped was a solution to many of those shortcomings. The result was NetWare 4.0, released in April 1993. It was the intention of the developers of NetWare 4.0 to create a NOS that could accommodate the needs of larger organizations that were turning to client/server networks for their computing needs. Two free maintenance releases, 4.01 and 4.02, came in rapid succession, and NetWare 4.1 was released in late 1994.

The high maintenance costs of mainframe systems overwhelmed their functionality in many cases, but NetWare 3.x was too restrictive in its "server-centric" design. This means that the true distribution of network services among many different servers gave rise to a great deal of administrative inconvenience when NetWare 3.x was used. The individual Bindery databases that had to be maintained for each server required that users must have an individual account on each server to which they required access. Each new hire at a large company thus may have required as many as ten or more server accounts to gain access to all the resources that he or she needed.

In addition, the inherent limitations of the NetWare 3.x memory pool arrangement and the problems inherent in file storage on NetWare volumes added to the burden on administrative personnel who were already (by long tradition) severely overworked. NetWare 4.x is meant to change this by introducing several new features designed to address these problems—in particular, the NetWare Directory Services database. Despite this, however, much of the core functionality of NetWare remains unchanged. It is primarily the means of accessing that functionality that has been altered. The following sections examine the similarities and differences between the last two generations of NetWare, in hopes of guiding the user familiar with NetWare 3.x into the territory of NetWare 4.x as smoothly as possible.

Many of the improvements made in NetWare 4.x amount to little more than the elimination of difficulties from NetWare 3.x. Like driving a car with an automatic transmission for the first time, after being long accustomed to a standard shift, you suddenly will not need certain well-developed skills anymore. For example, the elaborate system of memory pools from NetWare 3.x is gone. There is one File Cache Buffer pool from which all other memory needs are allocated and to which all memory can be returned after use.

Also, the installation procedure for NetWare 4.x is far simpler than that for NetWare 3.x. Running a single installation program guides the user through every step of configuring LAN and disk drivers, leaving a fully configured server at the end of the process. Determining the correct responses to some of the prompts is another story, as a NetWare 4.x installation requires a good deal more prior planning than a NetWare 3.x installation does, but as far as usability of the process is concerned, the improvement is enormous. A simple default NetWare 4.x server installation can be performed very easily.

Storage Issues

Arguably the single biggest difference in the average NetWare server over the last five years is in the amount of hard drive storage that it is likely to contain. Even though standard workstation configurations are shipping with ever larger hard drives and the diskless workstation is all but a thing of the past, the amount of network storage space required by users has grown enormously and continues to grow further with the continuing development of larger applications, the permanent commitment of more information to online databases, increasing dependency on e-mail for both file and message transfer, and the expansion of multimedia.

NetWare has taken several major steps to facilitate more efficient management of disk storage. First, and most satisfying, is the *block suballocation* feature, which overcomes the wasteful practice of allocating an entire block of storage space on a NetWare volume, even if only a fraction of that block is required for use. On a NetWare 3.x server using a 4K block size for its volumes, every file or fragment of a file under 4K in size occupies an entire block, even if only a single byte is needed. The rest of that block goes to waste, and on a server volume containing many small files, the use of a utility that can display the actual bytes stored versus the number of bytes allocated can be a disturbing experience. NetWare 4.x, however, is capable of suballocating blocks in 512-byte segments, cutting down on this wasted space significantly. Small files or fragments left over from the storage of larger multi-block files can therefore share a single block. Since the default block size is still selected during the creation of a volume, this feature also can allow for the use of a larger block size than normally would be selected for a NetWare 3.x volume. This saves memory as well, since fewer blocks have to be cached.

More profound savings can be derived from NetWare 4.x's compression feature; resembling workstation utilities such as Stacker and DriveSpace, this feature compresses and decompresses files on the fly, as they are written to and read from server volumes. This can cause available disk space to be effectively doubled, with even greater savings available from certain other data file types, such as uncompressed graphics and database formats. Individual files and directories can be flagged to control if and when compression is performed on them. Compression is enabled by default during the installation of a new NetWare 4.x server. It is not enabled, however, during an upgrade from a NetWare 3.x server, which can be cause for concern.

Mixing compressed and uncompressed volumes on a network can lead to restrictions in the operation of network backup products. Use of the *Target Service Agent* (*TSA*) for the NetWare file system allows compressed files to be backed up in their compressed state. This allows for faster backups, as the decompression procedure and any hardware compression performed at the tape drive gets avoided. Files backed up in this manner, however, can only be restored to a volume with compression enabled. They cannot be restored to an uncompressed volume or to a workstation hard drive. Depending on the level of knowledge of the personnel responsible for performing restore operations on the network, this feature may not be as transparent as an administrator might like it to be. File compression, as well as block suballocation, can therefore be disabled if the administrator desires. NetWare recommends that both be enabled, except when NetWare's *High Capacity Storage System* (*HCSS*) is in use.

The HCSS is another new innovation in NetWare; it's designed to be used along with the NOS's *data migration* feature. For many purposes, hard disk drive storage is not the most efficient medium possible. Its relatively high price per megabyte can make it impractical for storing files that need to be accessed only on an irregular basis. Archiving files to tape or another medium, however, imposes additional difficulties in the cataloging and retrieval of files. Data migration is a system by which files are automatically moved from NetWare volumes to a secondary medium, the HCSS, which is usually an *optical jukebox*. As the name implies, this is a device containing one or more optical disk drives and a robotic mechanism that can load and unload optical platters on demand. A jukebox has significantly slower access times than a hard disk drive, but the cost of storage per megabyte is significantly lower.

Based on parameters set by the network administrator, files that have not been accessed for a particular length of time are moved to the optical disks in the jukebox whenever the capacity of the NetWare volumes reaches a certain level. In place of the original files on the volumes, small *migration key* files are left behind. These keys indicate the actual locations of the files on the optical disks, and allow users to "see" the files when performing a directory listing of a NetWare volume.

When any operation attempts to access such a file—whether the operation is an application call, a DOS command, or a native NetWare process—the file is demigrated automatically from the optical disk to its original location, where it can be accessed normally. The only indication to the user that demigration has taken place is the additional time it takes to load the proper optical disk, access the file, and copy it to the volume. This time lag can vary, depending on the size of the file and the hardware being used, but usually amounts to no more than 10 or 15 seconds. Obviously, this much of a delay would be impractical for applications consisting of many files, but for data files, it can be a practical solution in many cases. As with compression, migration can be controlled on an individual file or directory basis through NetWare attributes by using the FLAG command at the workstation. As with all these new storage system features, data migration can be disabled for individual volumes from the INSTALL.NLM server console utility.

Communications Issues

Compared with the storage subsystem, communications with the LAN did not see significant change in NetWare 4.x. The primary innovations in this area—NCP Packet Burst mode, Large Internet Packets, and the VLM Requester—were all released some time before NetWare 4.x and are discussed elsewhere in this and other chapters. These features all have been fully integrated into NetWare 4.x, however, and are enabled by default during a server installation. The rest of the IPX/SPX protocol suite has not been changed, allowing complete backward compatibility with existing network communications hardware.

The implementation of the server's LAN communications, however, has been simplified. Support for the TCP/IP and AppleTalk protocol suites can now be installed through the INSTALL.NLM utility, instead of being provided as a separate process.

Memory Issues

Due to its additional features, the base memory requirements for the NetWare operating system have more than doubled. In addition, as mentioned earlier, memory allocation has been greatly streamlined in NetWare 4.x. Memory is still allocated for the same processes, but instead of coming from one of several different pools, each with different capabilities to return that memory for use by other processes, it all is taken from a single File Cache Buffer pool, to which it can later be returned. This makes the process of configuring a server for optimal performance a much simpler one.

Another memory-related innovation is clearly a reaction to the greatly increased market for server-based applications and utilities. NetWare 4.x allows an administrator to establish a separate memory area called the *OS_PROTECTED domain*, where untested third-party NLMs can be run without endangering the stability of the operating system. This is done by loading the new DOMAIN.NLM file from the server's STARTUP.NCF file. This creates two domains on the server, OS and OS_PROTECTED. Once the server is fully operational, the current domain can be changed by issuing the DOMAIN=OS_PROTECTED command at the server console. Any NLMs loaded after this point cannot cause the operating system to crash, as they are running in a domain that utilizes the outer rings (rings 1 through 3) of the Intel processor's memory architecture.

These rings provide greater memory protection and less privileges as one moves outward. The OS domain of the NetWare NOS runs in ring 0, providing the greatest amount of privileges and performance, at the cost of having virtually no protection. Novell's own NLMs, though, have been extensively tested and can safely be run in this unprotected domain. Depending on the architecture of the NLMs being run in a protected domain, it might be necessary to load certain Novell support NLMs—such as CLIB or STREAMS—there as well. This only needs to be done if the NLM being tested does not have the capability to communicate with these Novell NLMs across the domain barrier.

Certain Novell modules—such as IPXS, SPXS, and TLI—cannot be run in the protected domain at all, which might lead to problems when you want to test certain third-party NLMs in this manner. Of course, the surest protection for experimentation of this kind is to set up a separate test server on the network, but when this is impractical, these domain separation procedures can allow an untried NLM to be tested in a live production environment without endangering the productivity of the network's users.

Novell is continuing to explore the concept of separated memory domains. There is a long-range plan for the implementation of a NetWare version that will support multiple Intel microprocessors in a single server. Initial stages of the plan call for symmetric multiprocessing, where all tasks are equally shared by all the processors—much like Windows NT—but later versions may dedicate each processor to a separate memory domain, allowing even greater isolation between applications running on the same server.

NetWare Utilities

Many of the familiar menu-driven and command-line utilities from NetWare 3.x have been eliminated in NetWare 4.x. Their functionality remains but has been assimilated into other existing utilities or into new utilities created specifically for NetWare 4.x. The \PUBLIC directory of a NetWare 4.x server, however, contains batch files with the same names as the obsolete programs, informing the user what the correct utility is in NetWare 4.x. People who are very set in their ways might find it useful to actually add the new command to these batch files, so that after the warning is presented, the utility is loaded, avoiding the need for additional typing. Table 8.1 lists the utilities that no longer exist in NetWare 4.x, along with the names of their replacements.

Table 8.1 NetWare 3.x Utilities Replaced in NetWare 4.x	
3.x Utility	**4.x Replacement**
ALLOW, GRANT, REMOVE, REVOKE, TLIST	RIGHTS
ACONSOLE	RCONSOLE
ATTACH	LOGIN
BINDFIX, BINDREST	DSREPAIR
CASTON, CASTOFF	SEND
FCONSOLE	MONITOR
FLAGDIR, SMODE	FLAG
LISTDIR, CHKDIR, CHKVOL	NDIR
MAKEUSER	UIMPORT
NBACKUP	SBACKUP
SALVAGE, PURGE, VOLINFO	FILER
SESSION	NETUSER
SYSCON, SECURITY, DSPACE, USERDEF	NWADMIN, NETADMIN
USERLIST, SLIST	NLIST

Many new utilities have been added to NetWare 4.x. Table 8.2 lists the most important ones and gives a brief description of each one's function.

Table 8.2   New Utilities in NetWare 4.x

Utility	Type	Function
ATCON	NLM	Monitors AppleTalk network activity
AUDITCON	EXE	Audits a wide array of network transactions
CONLOG	NLM	Captures all server console messages to the SYS:/ETC/CONSOLE.LOG file
CX	EXE	Changes the user's context in the NDS tree
DOMAIN	NLM/EXE	Creates the OS_PROTECTED memory domain for the testing of new NLMs
DSMERGE	NLM	Merges and renames NDS trees
DSREPAIR	EXE	Examines and repairs damage to the NDS database
FILTCFG	NLM	Creates filters for network routing protocols (IPX, TCP/IP, and AppleTalk)
INETCFG	NLM	Configures network drivers and binds protocols for server NICs
IPXCON	NLM	Monitors IPX routers and network segments
IPXPING	NLM	Sends packets to a particular IPX node address to determine if it can be contacted over the network
KEYB	NLM	Configures the server to utilize a particular language
NETADMIN	EXE	Creates NDS objects and modifies rights and properties of objects in a character-based environment
NLIST	EXE	Displays information about files, directories, users, groups, volumes, servers, and queues
NWADMIN	EXE	Creates NDS objects and modifies rights and properties of objects in a GUI environment
PARTMGR	EXE	Creates and manages partitions of the NDS database
PING	NLM	Sends packets to a particular IP node address to determine if it can be contacted over the network
SCHDELAY	NLM	Prioritizes, schedules, and slows down server processes to minimize processor use at specific times
SERVMAN	NLM	Adjusts SET parameters in server NCF files for system tuning purposes
TIMESYNC	NLM	Controls time synchronization on servers to facilitate NDS functions
UIMPORT	EXE	Imports database information into NDS

NetWare Directory Services

Of course, the single greatest innovation of NetWare 4.x, one that goes beyond the boundaries of the individual server and proposes to deal with the entire enterprise network, is *NetWare Directory Services* (*NDS*). NDS is a global, replicated database of networked objects and their properties, offering a single point of entry to all of an enterprise's network resources. In English this means that the NDS database is an attempt to overcome the administration problems in a multi-server environment that were inherent in the NetWare 3.x architecture.

When a user that is logged on to a 3.x server requires access to a resource controlled by another server, he must first attach to that server (assuming that he has been given an account and the appropriate access rights), and then configure his application to access the new resources (for example, by mapping a drive or by connecting to a print server). Extra steps are also required of the network administrator, who must see to it that all of the network's users have individual accounts on the servers to which they need access. For a network with 100 users, this is a chore but a manageable one. For a large corporation with thousands of users, this is a full-time occupation.

NDS, also known as the *Directory* (with a capital "D"), is an object-oriented database of all the resources on a network, including all servers, printers, modems, and users. A user object in the Directory can be given access rights to any resource, anywhere on the network, greatly simplifying the administrator's maintenance tasks. When that user logs on from a workstation, he is not logging on to a preferred server, as with NetWare 3.x, but instead is logging on to the Directory and is immediately granted rights to all the resources to which he requires access. Moreover, because the Directory is partitioned and replicated among various servers throughout the network, the user is able to access his account, even if his home server is not functioning.

This provides a built-in administrative fault tolerance for both users and administrators. Even in a disaster recovery situation, it should never be necessary for the network administrator to restore the NDS from backups, unless several servers in the enterprise have been damaged. From a user's perspective, if the network has been designed with sufficient resource redundancy, he should never be rendered incapable of performing his required functions, unless a widespread disaster occurs. When the enterprise is composed of remote offices connected by WAN links, the NDS can be replicated at different sites, providing protection for the database under virtually all conditions except perhaps a global disaster.

Directory Design. As you might imagine, all this functionality is not without cost. Use of the Directory introduces a number of problems that only careful attention can overcome. The first and foremost of these is the planning of the Directory itself. Using the familiar inverted tree metaphor that is common to portrayals of file systems, the NDS consists basically of container objects and leaf objects. Simply put, a *container object* is one that holds one or more other objects—much like a group in the NetWare 3.x bindery but much more versatile. A *leaf object* is the exact opposite of this—an object that is incapable of containing another object; for example, a user, a printer, or a modem.

Moving down from the origin or [root] of the NDS tree, container objects can be created, beginning with *Organizations (Os)* and then *Organizational Units (OUs)*. Servers, users, printers, and other objects can be contained in any O or OU and are identified by a fully qualified name consisting of the object's name, followed by all the container object names in which it resides, in order, all the way back to the root of the tree. In other words, a user named JOHNDOE may be a leaf object within an OU named ACCOUNTING, which in turn is part of an O named NEWYORK. The full name of the user is JOHNDOE.ACCOUNTING.NEWYORK. Names of Os and OUs are assigned by the designer of the Directory, according to whatever organizational method is preferred. There can be as many levels of organization as are desired, although Novell recommends no more than four levels, to prevent having gratuitously long object names.

Directory trees often are organized according to either the departmental or geographic boundaries of an enterprise, but these divisions might not always provide an efficient access design. Consideration must be made of the proximity of users requiring access to similar equipment, as well as other factors. To group a number of users with widely different resource needs together, simply because they happen to work in the same building or answer to the same supervisor, might be an efficient corporate organizational design but isn't necessarily an efficient network design.

Every object in an NDS tree also contains a number of *properties* that define its nature and its capabilities. Among these properties are the trustee rights that allow users to gain access to that object. One of the primary functions of container objects is to provide groups of leaf objects access to specific resources without the need to modify individual accounts. If, for example, the users in five different OUs, all stemming from a single O, require access to one printer, then the easiest way to do this is to locate the printer object directly off of the O and assign each of the OUs in the O object properties list rights to that printer. That way, any user objects added later to any of the five OUs automatically is given access to that printer, as well. This is because, as with the NetWare file system, all rights granted to a container object are *inherited* by the objects it contains.

> **Tip**
>
> Rights also can be *masked* using an *Inherited Rights Filter*, which prevents certain rights from being passed downward to the next level of the tree.

It must also be understood that the NDS tree, as well as the system of object and property rights, is completely separate from the NetWare file system. In the NWADMIN graphical utility, which replaces SYSCON and provides the Windows interface where an administrator can create and manage objects and their properties, a server object can be expanded to display its volumes and files, but those rights are granted separately from the rights to the server object itself. The entire issue of effective rights is at least doubled in complexity from the days of NetWare 3.x.

Moreover, the NDS is designed to make use of a distributed management philosophy. There need not be a single SUPERVISOR account that retains full rights to all the objects and properties of an enterprise's directory. Indeed, providing one person with complete control of a giant corporation's entire network is a security risk which many organizations are not willing to take. Therefore, although an ADMIN user with full rights is created during a NetWare server installation, this account has no unique properties, as the NetWare 3.x SUPERVISOR did. Rights can be removed from the ADMIN account, or the account can be deleted entirely; deleting ADMIN, however, makes it possible for network administrators to lose control over parts of the NDS tree. It is all too easy, using the NWADMIN and NETADMIN tools, to delete rights held by no other user in the Directory—in other words, to saw off the branch of the tree upon which one is standing.

As you can see, concerns such as these make the overall design of the NDS tree absolutely crucial to its functionality. In a small enterprise, with fewer than five servers, the NetWare 4.x installation routine is quite capable of creating an adequate, if rudimentary, NDS tree. A company of this size, however, really does not require the level of sophistication that the NDS database provides, as much as Novell would like that company to think it does. Medium and large enterprises are the ones that stand to gain considerably from use of the Directory, and it is virtually impossible to automate the process of designing an NDS tree that can adequately serve such a large entity. This is the primary drawback of NDS.

The administrative staff of a large organization is faced suddenly with an entirely new way of thinking about its network. A new mindset is required, and new experiences must be assimilated before true understanding of the way in which the Directory works can be achieved. Unfortunately, this experience cannot be gained until a tree is actually created and used over a period of time. Companies cannot stand still while their MIS staff experiments with new organizational flowcharting methods. They require network upgrades to be performed in short order, and this is the basic Catch-22 of NetWare 4.x networking. For a large enterprise to be successfully upgraded to NetWare 4.x, it is strongly recommended that personnel familiar with both the workings of NDS and the organization of the enterprise be engaged to design the tree. In many cases, it is judicious to run NetWare 4.x users solely in bindery emulation mode, until sufficient time has been allowed for design of the database.

Bindery emulation is the mode in which NetWare 4.x operates to retain backward compatibility with NetWare 3.x. The container object in which a server resides becomes, by default, the *bindery context* for a user logging on under bindery emulation mode (which is done by using the /B switch with the LOGIN command, as in LOGIN /B *username*). The user has access only to those resources within the context of the server he logs on to. The bindery context for a particular server can be altered through the use of the SET BINDERY CONTEXT= command at the server console prompt or through the server's AUTOEXEC.NCF file.

Directory Partitions and Replication. Another important aspect of NDS management is the partitioning and replication of the Directory among the various servers on the network. A Directory tree can be split into discrete segments, called *partitions*, usually composed of single Os or OUs, and all the objects contained within them. This is done with the NetWare PARTMGR utility. Partitions are stored on different servers throughout the network, corresponding with the location of the resources they contain. Each partition also has several replicas of itself, stored on different servers. These replicas provide fault tolerance for the system and also lessen the overall volume of network traffic for NDS maintenance.

A single unified Directory at one central site would force users at remote locations to log on by accessing the central tree. The entire NDS concept, however, is based on support for large networks, especially those with distant locations connected by WAN links. The amount of traffic generated by such remote users logging on to a Directory over a low-bandwidth link would slow performance to a crawl. By instead having regional partitions located at various sites on the network, users can log on to a local partition with expectations of reasonable speed.

Unfortunately, this arrangement still generates a large amount of background traffic. To maintain the integrity of the Directory, all changes made to the individual partitions must be propagated all over the network to update the various replicas. Despite substantial improvements to the efficiency of this process over the course of NetWare's 4.01, 4.02, and 4.10 releases, it still can be a source of considerable delays, particularly when low-bandwidth WAN links are involved.

Further complications arise due to timing considerations. For partitions and replicas to be updated properly, there must be a mechanism in place to ensure that revisions are processed in the proper order. As we have seen, communications across network segments can fall victim to many types of disturbances, and if a transaction changing the properties of an NDS object arrives at a particular location before the transaction that creates the object, problems are bound to ensue. Multiply this simple scenario by many locations with dozens or even hundreds of servers at each one, and the organizational difficulties soon seem enormous. This is why the Directory relies heavily on a mechanism whereby the time kept by all servers on the network is regularly synchronized. All NDS updates, therefore, are provided with a time stamp that ensures their processing in the proper order.

Maintaining a synchronized time signal across a widely dispersed network can be an extremely difficult task, and in cases of large networks, many different servers may be responsible for keeping and propagating the correct time signal. Again, this is for reasons of fault tolerance and traffic control. Of course, this generates still more traffic, in the form of SAP packets continuously transmitted between all servers on the network.

Thus, as we have seen, the NDS database is responsible for performing a number of very difficult tasks, and as a working tool, it still shows a good deal of immaturity. Even though more than two years have elapsed since its initial release, a surprisingly small number of third-party applications and utilities are fully compliant with NDS. Client/server applications fully supporting NDS are just beginning to hit the market, and tools for managing the Directory are desperately needed by administrators to perform tasks that are simply impossible with the tools provided with the operating system. Even Novell itself has experienced considerable delays in developing NDS clients for other operating systems. Windows NT and Windows 95 clients that fully support the Directory have just recently become available (these are examined in chapter 12, "Network Client Software for 32-Bit Windows").

It is not my intention here to present more than a cursory overview of NDS. The issues involved in designing, constructing, and maintaining a large Directory tree are so numerous and complex that they easily warrant a book of their own. As is the case throughout this book, the intention is to provide an overview; once you're introduced to the new concepts and improvements provided in NetWare 4.x, you can consider an upgrade or the construction of a new network fully aware of some issues that you might face.

NetWare 4.x is a product for which an extensive period of testing and exploration is advised before you fully commit a large network to its use.

If you're an administrator, the best way to approach NetWare 4.x is to familiarize yourself with the operating system by setting up one or more test servers in a non-production environment. These can be safely attached to the regular network, so that real-life data and traffic conditions can be provided, but users should not be permitted to rely on NDS until a Directory tree has been developed that is sufficient for permanent use. You might have to do several dry runs—which means partially or completely unsuccessful attempts at tree design—before a usable Directory is realized. Training is an integral part of mastering the NetWare 4.x environment. Even more than with earlier versions of NetWare, the new version is not something that can be learned adequately in a static laboratory environment (or by reading a book, for that matter). NDS is designed to be a solution for the real world, and it must be tested as such to determine whether or not it is sufficient for the needs of your network, and how it can best be used.

Summary

As stated at the beginning of this chapter, Novell's NetWare spans virtually the entire lifetime of the PC LAN. Over, the years, it has grown in its capabilities along the same lines as the hardware and applications that it supports. Only recently have other NOSs begun to make serious inroads into Novell's overwhelming market share. The rising popularity of Windows NT and the more common integration of UNIX and PC networks have made the simple sharing of resources (such as printers and hard drives) no longer the sole reason for a network's existence. Access to communications media, such as e-mail, the Internet, and networked modems, is now taken for granted as a network service in modern offices, and other NOSs are showing themselves to be capable application servers to whichever new uses are being applied. Of course, as with any market, a little competition is always beneficial to the consumer.

The next chapter considers some of the other NOSs on the market; you learn the ways in which the other NOSs are similar to and different from NetWare, as well as factors you should consider when interconnecting multiple NOSs on the same network. It is impossible to say what the dominant networking platform will be in years to come or even if one platform will be dominant. Many people see the industry tending towards a greater amount of NOS specialization, with one server NOS providing file and print services, another communications services, and still another specialized application services. This might allow each of the NOSs discussed in this book to attempt to locate its own niche in the networking industry, achieving greater efficiency in its chosen task.

Chapter 9

Microsoft Windows NT

Windows NT Server, a new breed of network operating system, made its appearance in 1994. From its first incarnation as Windows NT Advanced Server 3.1, Microsoft's new NOS had an easy-to-use user interface, high security, and was straightforward enough that you could begin to use it almost immediately. Since that time, it has only improved. NT Server (currently on version 3.51) is an excellent choice for many networking environments. Not only is it a good product in its own right, but it can connect smoothly to other NOSs (such as Novell NetWare) without difficulty—a real advantage because many of us don't have the luxury of dealing with only one operating system.

You've seen rows of fat books about NT Server, so you know that we can't possibly cover all of its ins and outs in one chapter of one book. In this chapter, we'll discuss the basic architecture of NT Server and talk about the basics of how you can use it on your network. After completing this chapter, you should have a pretty good idea whether or not NT Server is the right network operating system for you.

Our space is limited, so let's jump right in.

> **Note**
>
> If you've inherited NT Server 3.5 and don't plan to upgrade to 3.51 (although you should—it's only $40 for the upgrade) this chapter still can help you get acquainted with your operating system, as version 3.51 is quite similar to version 3.5. The newer version has some added features, such as built-in software metering ability, but overall the two are fairly similar.

Why Use NT Server in Your Network?

Although NT Server's cooperation with other NOSs means that you don't necessarily have to make it the sole NOS for your organization, you might wonder why you would even make it one of them. NetWare has been the market leader in network software for quite some time. Is NT Server giving NetWare a run for its money? The answer is yes, and the following sections explore a few of NT Server's key strengths.

Easy To Use

One of the main reasons for NT Server's success is that it's really easy to use (I've heard one person describe it as the "Mr. Rogers" NOS). Rather than a command-line interface that requires you to remember obscure syntax and hot-key combinations if you want to do anything, NT Server is designed on the same point-and-click idea as other Windows products. For that matter, if you can't recall the exact point-and-click procedures that you need to do something, the online help system is pretty good.

Designed for High-Powered Systems

Although NT Server works just fine on a 486 with 16M of RAM (with caveats as noted in the "Check Your Hardware!" section later in this chapter), it is designed to work with bigger and badder machines. Out of the box, it can support up to four CPUs in the system, and you can get *hardware abstraction layers* (*HALs*) from Microsoft that let it support up to 32 CPUs. On the RAM front, it can support up to 4G of memory. Of course, we'll have to wait for 1G SIMMs to come out before this is physically practical, but the support is there. NT Server's NTFS file system also means that it can support hard disks larger than 2G, the limit for the FAT file system that DOS and Windows use. (If you're shaky on what multiprocessor support and lots of memory are good for, turn to chapter 5, "The Server Platform.")

Not only does NT Server support multiple processors, but it also supports *multi-threaded applications*. Multi-threaded applications are those designed as much as possible in a series of discrete steps so that a processor can perform more than one operation at once (people are fond of saying that multi-threaded applications let the processor walk and chew gum at the same time). This only works with operations that are not dependent on each other (in other words, if the third step in a program is dependent on the outcome of the second, then the second and third steps cannot be performed simultaneously), but when it does work, it speeds things up tremendously.

Security

NT Server is designed for security—although it took until 1995 to receive its C-2 certification (see the sidebar), it was designed toward that aim from the beginning. Part of the security strength lies in its file system, which cannot be accessed by booting from a DOS floppy. Part of it lies in the key sequence (Ctrl+Alt+Del) used to log on, which removes any password-grabbing viruses that cannot survive a reboot. Also in the security plan are user rights that can be specified down to individual file access for an individual user, and logging that can track the activities of each logged-on user.

What Is C-2 Certification?

"C-2 certification" is one of those terms that gets tossed around frequently but perhaps is not understood fully by everyone using it. The United States government has a security manual named *Trusted Computer System Evaluation*, but more commonly known as the *Orange Book*. It's essentially a manual for determining how secure a computer system is and describing the testing required to prove that level of security. The levels of security that it identifies range from D (none) to A1 (highest, held by very few systems). A "C-2" rating means that NT Server has been certified to be a system with controlled access protection and with the ability to track user activity, assign individual rights to individual users, and overwrite the information attached to objects such as reassigned user IDs so that the information cannot be gleaned from the hard disk.

Other certified C-2 systems include DEC's VAX 4.3 and Hewlett Packard's MPE V/E. As of the time this book went to print, NetWare 4.1 was not yet C-2 certified, although it is C-2 compliant and is expected to be certified in the first half of 1996.

Interoperability

As noted earlier, getting NT Server doesn't mean that you must scrap your other NOSs. NT Server has built-in connectivity to NetWare, so you can set up your NetWare and NT Server servers to be accessible to anyone on your network, no matter how they log on. Additionally, NT Server supports several different transport protocols, including TCP/IP, used for connecting to UNIX machines and the Internet, and IPX/SPX, which NetWare uses. NT Server even has an easy way of connecting to Macintosh computers (see chapter 8, "Novell NetWare," for a discussion of transport protocols).

Centralized Control

An NT Server network is organized into groups of machines called *domains*. Rather than logging on to a single machine, you log on to a domain and through that connection have access to all the servers in the domain to which you're permitted access. This centralized control makes things easier on users (who only have to log on once to access multiple servers) and network administrators (who only have to create one user account for a domain, rather than one for each server). As we'll discuss later in this chapter, you can even create relationships between domains to permit users to log on to another domain using their account on their home domain.

NT Server also allows you to set very specific file permissions on shared drives, directories, and individual files, so that you can precisely control user access.

Long File Name Support

NT Server's native file system, *NT File System* (*NTFS*), supports case-sensitive long file names and provides added security to your server. NTFS volumes are not accessible if you boot from a DOS floppy, which, although it keeps you from accessing volumes if you must boot to DOS, also keeps crackers from doing the same thing.

Caution

Unfortunately, NT Server's long file names are not compatible with those used in OS/2's HPFS file system or in Windows 95's version of FAT with long file name support.

Logging Capabilities

NT Server includes three kinds of logging that you can activate for use in trouble-shooting your system and metering activity on it. The Security log shows logon attempts (including failed ones, if you want, which can be useful for catching attempted break-ins); the Application log monitors who's accessing what on the server; and the System log shows system events such as network services starting (or failing to start) so that it's easier to track down a problem such as why your graphics division can't log on to the server with their Macs.

UPS Service

If your server is important enough for you to spend $700 on good networking software for it, it's important enough to power-protect. NT Server, recognizing that power quality is getting worse instead of better, includes an *uninterruptible power supply* (*UPS*) service that Microsoft co-developed with American Power Conversion (APC), one of the major suppliers of power protection. UPSs and other forms of power protection are discussed in detail in chapter 18, "Backup Technology: Uninterruptible Power Supplies."

Software Metering

If you're concerned about keeping up with your licensing requirements, NT Server 3.51 comes with a software metering capability that keeps track of your client licenses. When installing NT Server, you'll have a choice of "per server" or "per seat" licensing. The first option sets the number of concurrent connections permitted to a single server on the domain; the second sets a limit on the number of workstations that can log on to the domain through all servers.

Built-In Remote Access Services (RAS) Capability

If your network includes telecommuters who need access to a server, then you can set up a dialup account to permit them to do so. As NT Server is extremely security-conscious, this dialup capability has not only password protection but also call-back capability—you can set it up so that users can dial in from only one telephone number. *Remote Access Services* (*RAS*) can connect to a modem line, ISDN, or X.25, providing extreme flexibility to meet your needs. (ISDN and X.25 are discussed in chapter 4, "Upgrading to a WAN," and other remote access products are discussed in chapter 27, "Adding Remote Network Access (Telecommuting).")

That's a quick run-through of NT Server's features. Now, let's talk about the basic concepts behind its design.

The NT Server Universe

Before you figure out what you can do with NT Server, it's useful to understand where it's coming from, how it's designed, how it organizes the members of the network, and how to navigate it.

Important NT Server Terms

Although most of the vocabulary and concepts we'll use in our discussions of NT Server are well-known to networkers, there are a few you'll need to know that are specific to the product. The following sections explain these terms.

The Registry. The core of NT Server is the *Registry*. Although you may never have to alter it directly, every system configuration you make is stored in this central database. From auditing setup to establishing user accounts to setting new system colors, it's all stored here.

You can view the contents of the Registry by running REGEDT32.EXE (not REGEDIT.EXE—that only shows the file types stored on your system).

Using the Registry is complicated and, frankly, not often very useful. Almost every system setting can be more easily edited elsewhere (the few exceptions are not settings you're likely to run across unless you're having a very serious problem), and when working with the Registry it's very easy to do major damage to your system without meaning to. If you need to adjust your system settings, use the Control Panel or the User Manager for Domains—don't try to make a change in the Registry unless you're willing to flirt with the possibility of reinstalling the operating system. (Admittedly, as NOS installations go, NT Server's installation process isn't bad, but I'm sure that you can think of a better way to spend two hours.)

The real reason you need to know about the Registry is to make sure that you back it up. If you include the Registry every time you do a backup, then if you ever have to reinstall you won't need to set up the entire system again—just restore the Registry you've backed up, and most of your system settings (including user accounts) are the way they were when you last saved them.

Domains. A *domain* is a rather nebulous concept, like a workgroup, but essentially it's a logical group of servers (notice that that's *machines*, not users) organized by some user-defined criteria. You can have a Personnel domain that encompasses all the servers dealing with personnel files, or you can have a Main domain that encompasses all the servers at the main office of your corporation. The grouping depends on your preferences. The crucial point concerning a domain is that the logical grouping means users don't have to log on to individual servers—each user logs on to a domain and therefore has access to all the servers in that domain (to the extent of that user's permitted access, of course).

> **Note**
>
> You don't log on to individual servers on an NT Server network; you log on to a domain to access the servers that are part of that domain. In other words, to access multiple servers, you need to log on only once.

You're not limited to accessing NT Server machines when you log on to a domain; any machine capable of sharing resources, such as an NT Workstation (the client version of NT Server) or a Windows 95 machine, can make its resources available to those who log on to the domain. NT Server machines can do certain special things in a domain (such as remote administration) as we'll discuss shortly, but in terms of sharing files and resources, domain membership is pretty flexible.

If you've got a large network—or are spread out over more than one physical site—chances are good that you have more than one domain. If so, you can create a *trust relationship* between domains that permits your users to access the resources of another domain without requiring an account in that domain. We'll talk later in this chapter about the mechanics of how to set up a trust relationship.

Groups. Domains are arbitrary collections of servers; *groups* are arbitrary collections of users. In the User Manager for Domains, located in the Administrative Tools window, you can see the wide variety of preset groups to which you can assign users. The basic function of a group is to provide a handy way of assigning certain network rights to a bunch of users, without having to set up each user account individually. One right you can assign, for example, is the ability to perform backups. Rather than forcing you to manually set the account of each potential backup administrator, you can add all the users who need to be able to run the backup program to a group named Backup Administrators. Similarly, if someone who was a backup administrator changes job duties, you can remove their ability to run backups by removing them from the group—no other action is required.

> **Note**
>
> NT Server comes with a wide variety of user groups, but you also can build your own groups with a particular set of privileges if none of the built-in groups have the configuration you need.

Multiple Group Membership. A user can belong to more than one group at a time. For example, by default all users are members of the Domain Users group (a basic group that permits its members to do the things most users need to do, like accessing files, but does not allow its members to do things most users don't need to do, like logging on to the NT Server machine itself). Every user must be a member of one of the Domain groups, and whenever the need arises, you can make any given user a member of more than one group.

Rights are cumulative; that is, if you belong to more than one group, the group with the most rights controls what you can do. The only exception to this is the No Access right, which forbids access to a particular drive or directory and overrides any rights that other group memberships give you.

Not only can you add users to groups, but it's also possible to put one group inside another group, so that the members of the interior group have the same rights as those of the exterior group without having to actually join it. The simple restriction is that only local groups can contain other groups and only global groups can be contained.

Local groups? Global groups? Read on...

Local Groups versus Global Groups. NT Server recognizes two kinds of groups: local and global. As neither the documentation nor the online help really explains the difference between the two, it's worth exploring here. Both kinds of groups can perform the same functions (there are local and global users, local and global administrators, local and global print operators, and so on). The important difference between local and global groups relates to membership. Local groups can contain both users and global groups, while global groups can contain only users.

Local groups are the important ones for local administration. Backup Operators, Account Operators, and so on (any group that doesn't have "Domain" at the beginning of its name) are all local groups. Local groups can contain both users and global groups, but cannot contain other local groups.

Global groups are generic in function. NT Server only includes three (Domain Users, Domain Administrators, and Domain Guests). Although all users by default are members of the Domain Users group, if you only have one domain—or have no trust relationship—then the global groups don't matter much.

Global groups really begin to matter when you've set up a trust relationship between domains and want to give users of one domain access to another domain without creating new user accounts on the second domain. The idea is this: if you've gotten domains VERDE and ROJA to trust each other so that the users on VERDE can access the resources on ROJA, then you've got three options for how to set this up:

- Add each VERDE user to ROJA's user list. This works, but it's time-consuming and silly. Why should you have to duplicate all the work you did when you set up these users on VERDE?

- Add each VERDE user to ROJA's Users group. This is a better idea, but it's still a slow process.

- Add VERDE's Domain Users group to ROJA's Users group. Bingo! In one step, you've made every VERDE user a ROJA user.

If you have trouble remembering whether global groups go into local groups or the other way around, try thinking of global groups as ships, and local groups as ports. Ships—which travel the globe—can sail into ports, but certainly cannot sail into other ships. Ports—where all the local activity takes place—can contain ships, but cannot contain other ports. (Thanks to David Sheridan for this excellent analogy.)

Users. The smallest unit in the NT Server universe is the *user*. Like groups, users are people, rather than machines. The concept of a user is a simple one: it's your key to the domain. If you don't have an account on the domain—even one without a password—you can't log on to the domain and access its resources. (Depending on how your network is set up, you may still be able to log on to individual servers, but you won't be able to access the domain members as a group.)

You can assign rights to users in addition to the rights they have as group members.

Rights versus Permissions. We've been talking about the rights that users and user groups can have, but what are those rights? How are they different from permissions, another NT Server security concept?

In a nutshell, *rights* are things that people can do; *permissions* are access privileges attached to files and directories. Rights consist of such events as logging on to the server directly at the server, activating a backup program, or creating a printer. Permissions include things like read access, change access, or full control. You assign rights to people and permissions to data.

That's about it for describing the way NT Server sees the world: it identifies domains, which are collections of machines; groups, which are collections of users; and individual users. Hanging onto this mental map, let's see what the operating system looks like.

Where the Toys Are: Tool Locations

NT Server is designed to be simple to use. To that end, it uses a *graphical user interface* (*GUI*) that is very similar to the one in Windows 3.x. As in any GUI, the idea is to free the user from having to remember command syntax or hot-key combinations. When you're in a hurry, you don't have to remember if you should type **net use** or **net view** to connect to network resources like disk drives and printers: you just have to pick a command from a menu.

> **Note**
>
> All 3.x versions of NT Server use the Program Manager and window design features that are familiar to Windows 3.x users. NT Server 4.0, however, is expected to have an interface closer to that of Windows 95—a taskbar across the bottom and a Start menu with program groups branching from it.

As in Windows 3.x, the starting point for just about everything you do in NT Server 3.5x is the Program Manager (see fig. 9.1). It works just like the Windows 3.x Program Manager—point to the icon representing the tool you want to activate and double-click.

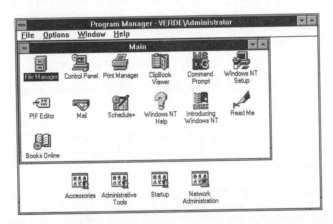

Figure 9.1

The Program Manager is the starting point for everything you do in NT Server 3.5x.

In the Main program group, the tool you'll probably use most often is File Manager. As you can see in figure 9.2, the NT Server File Manager has a few options that Windows 3.x users won't recognize. The Security menu is the starting point for setting permissions for shared files, taking ownership of files, or auditing file access.

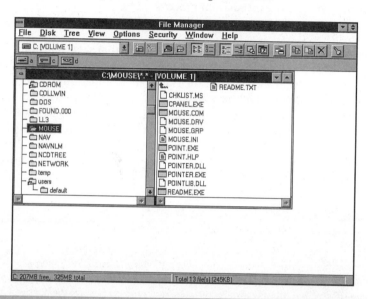

Figure 9.2

The NT Server File Manager is good for more than just file sharing—it's also where you set file and directory permissions.

As you saw in figure 9.1, there are a few program groups in Program Manager. The one where you'll do most of your work is the Administrative Tools program group (see fig. 9.3).

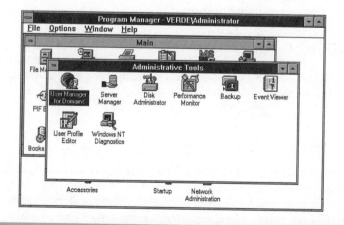

Figure 9.3

The Administrative Tools program group contains the icons for basic network administration.

Installation

By this point, you should have a pretty good idea what to expect from NT Server and what to do with it. But if you're going to use it, you have to install it first. The following sections walk you through the installation process.

Check Your Hardware!

Before you start the installation, you've got to make sure that your hardware is up to snuff. First, it needs to be compatible with the operating system. The best way to ensure compatibility is to get hardware that's on the Hardware Compatibility List included in the NT Server package. If you don't have that option, then think generic and standardized. Generally speaking, SCSI-II devices like hard drives, tape drives, and CD-ROM drives are a good bet if you go with a reliable vendor, like Adaptec, which doesn't stop supporting a product as soon as the next model comes out. Some IDE devices are okay, too, but stay away from anything that uses a proprietary interface (like a CD-ROM drive that plugs into a sound card).

Make Sure That the BIOS Is Compatible!

Even if all the other hardware in your machine meets the system requirements, you still can run into problems with one small but crucial component: the BIOS. I had a frustrating experience once with a rental system that I'd handpicked to be NT-compatible from a reliable rental company. All the hardware checked out, but the installation would not proceed beyond the floppy portion (as you'll see shortly, installation has a floppy section and a CD-ROM section)—when the machine was supposed to reboot during installation, it locked up. Occasionally, I got obscure messages indicating that crucial parts of NT were not loading, but the files were where they were supposed to be. Neither reformatting nor repartitioning the hard disk had any effect.

Finally, I called in the Marines by paying $150 to talk to Microsoft. After a little discussion, we established that the BIOS of the AST machine I was using was too old—the version I had was 1.0, and NT Server would only work with version 2.1 or later. I switched to an identical machine with a newer BIOS, and the installation went seamlessly.

Oddly enough, a BIOS that's too *new* can also be a potential problem. I've heard of a situation in which a Compaq BIOS had to be "downdated" to an older version so that it would work with NT Server. The fact that Compaq machines aren't quite as generic as many other IBM-compatible types might have had something to do with it, but it's worth noting that the newest BIOS might not always be the one that works in a particular situation.

NT Server is very picky about hardware performance. The fact that the hardware worked under DOS does not, unfortunately, mean that it will work under NT Server—this is because DOS is not exactly an operating system. When it comes down to it, the DOS applications run the show more than DOS itself does—they're permitted to control hardware, so theoretically, if something goes wrong with some of that hardware (like parity errors in your memory chips), the application is supposed to take care of it. As you might know from bitter experience, what happens more often than not in practice is that the application crashes, perhaps taking your entire system with it. It's not really the application's fault because that should be the job of the operating system. Letting a spreadsheet program control hardware is like disbanding the fire department and giving everyone in town a bucket: as long as nothing happens, it's fine, but when there really is a fire the townspeople are neither trained nor equipped to deal with the problem.

The point is that you really need to test your hardware exhaustively before attempting to install an operating system like NT Server that insists on everything working right. Do a slow disk test (not the fast one—you want the slow one that can take all night or even a couple of days) and a complete memory test.

Back Up Existing Data

Most people install NT Server on a machine that already has data on it, rather than a brand-new one. This is fine, but don't forget that you need some way of getting that data *back*. (Don't even think about installing a new operating system on your server without backing it up first.) "Not a problem," I hear you say. "I've backed up the drive and have the tape right here." The only difficulty with this is that NT Server's proprietary tape backup system will not be able to read the tapes, and the DOS backup program will not run on NT Server because applications cannot manipulate hardware. In fact, that's worth repeating for those who are skimming.

> **Caution**
>
> Do not back up your disk with a DOS backup system, and assume that the tapes will work after you've installed NT Server. The DOS backup program won't work under NT Server, and NT's proprietary backup system will not be able to read the tapes.

Well, what's to be done about this? If you've got a networked machine with enough unused space on its hard disk, you can XCOPY everything to that machine, and then just XCOPY it back after NT Server is installed. (Don't forget the /s or /e switch to copy subdirectories, or you'll only copy the contents of your root directory.)

Another option is to install NT Server onto a FAT volume (you get to choose the file system during installation). After you've finished installing, you can boot from a DOS floppy, run the DOS-based backup program to restore the files to the FAT volume, and then, if you're using NTFS, run the conversion routine to convert the FAT volume to NTFS. If you've got the space required for the conversion routine, this beats the third alternative of installing a tape drive on a networked machine and restoring across the network, as you won't have to crack the case if it's an internal drive. Make sure, however, that you back up immediately after you've restored so that you've then got a backup of your system that you can access without all the rigmarole.

Installing NT Server

In addition to the manuals and registration information, your NT Server package should contain three floppy disks and a CD-ROM.

> **Note**
>
> Although you can order NT Server on floppy disk, the CD-ROM contains some features of NT that the floppies do not. It's also much easier to install the NOS from CD-ROM since you don't have to constantly swap disks.

Once you've tested your hardware, boot from the first floppy to begin the installation.

The first thing that the installation routine does is to run a routine named NTDETECT.COM to make sure that it can work with all your hardware.

> **Tip**
>
> If NT won't start and you think that it's due to a hardware failure, you can use a debug version of NTDETECT, named NTDETECT.CHK. It's on the CD-ROM in \SUPPORT\DEBUG\I386. To use it, diskcopy the boot disk onto a blank, formatted floppy; then copy NTDETECT.CHK onto the floppy. Delete NTDETECT.COM from the new floppy, then rename NTDETECT.CHK to NTDETECT.COM. Restart the installation, booting from the new floppy. NT shows the progress of the hardware check as it looks at each component. If it hangs when you see "Detecting Floppy Component," for example, then you know that it doesn't like something about the floppy system.

The installation process is pretty straightforward. There are a few potential pitfalls, which can be avoided if you do the following:

- Choose Custom Setup rather than pressing Enter for Express Setup. You're only going to install this server a few times, so you might as well look at what you're doing and make sure that it's correct, instead of trusting the defaults.

- Don't force the issue. When NT Server attempts to identify your mass storage devices, if it doesn't find one of yours that you think should be compatible, don't try to force NT Server to accept the device. Press F3 to halt the installation, check the device to make sure that it's installed properly—and, if a SCSI device, terminated properly—and then start over. NT Server is very good at identifying hardware, so if it doesn't see a device, there probably is a hardware problem.

- Keep it simple. When choosing a network protocol, don't bother installing TCP/IP (the default) at this point if you don't have to. You can set up TCP/IP at a later date because it's complicated enough to slow down your installation (and increase the amount of time before you get the server to work).

- Pay attention. You'll have a choice of making this machine a domain controller or a server. The first NT Server machine on your network must be a *domain controller* (that's the machine that verifies all security information like logons). It's a good idea to have two domain controllers per domain, one to be the primary domain controller and one to be the backup in case you need to take down the primary domain controller, but you must have one for the network to work properly—the domain controller handles all security settings, such as user passwords. If you make it a server by mistake, you'll have to reinstall.

■ Choose a domain name carefully. If creating a domain, don't assign it a "throw-away" name and assume that you can change it later. You cannot change a domain's name without reinstalling.

■ Choose a server name carefully. Give your server a name that neither corresponds to a person's name on your network nor has spaces in it. Using people's names as machine names can be confusing, and makes for extra housekeeping if machine assignments change. Spaces in a name complicate matters if you ever have to use the command line to connect to that machine (as you do, for example, if you connect a DOS client).

■ Choose a password carefully. During the installation process, you'll set up the administrator's account. If you assign a password at this point, do not forget it. You won't be able to do anything else on the system, including log on, without that password. If you ever forget the administrator's password, you'll have to reinstall the operating system.

There are many issues to think about when installing NT Server, but those are the big ones. Generally speaking, installing NT Server is a trouble-free experience—if the hardware works.

Using NT: Basic System Setup

There are two aspects to setting up an operating system: what you need to do to get the network running and keep it that way, and the extras that might not need to be done right away. This chapter, therefore, first covers the basics of using NT Server and then covers advanced topics separately.

The first thing you need to do is to set up some user accounts and share drives and directories as appropriate, so that your users can work while you tweak the system. Let's start by setting up a user account.

Creating and Tuning User Accounts

Activate the Administrative Tools program group, and open the User Manager for Domains. You'll see a window that resembles figure 9.4.

Let's begin by creating an account like the ones that most of your users will require. Choose User, New User to open the dialog box shown in figure 9.5.

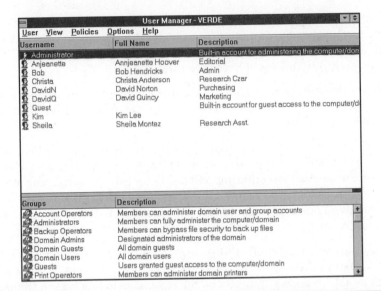

Figure 9.4

In the User Manager window, you'll create and fine-tune user accounts and establish cross-domain relationships.

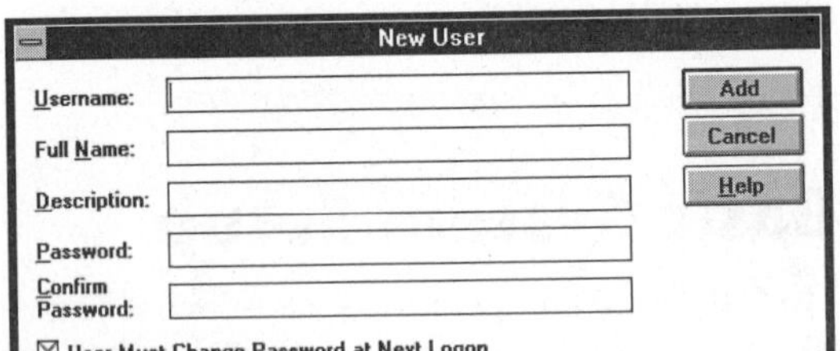

Figure 9.5

Create a user account by filling in the New User dialog box.

Fill in the user's logon name, full name (the two may not be identical; for example, if you've got a Bob Jones in your office, you would set something like BobJ as his user name) and password. Using the buttons at the bottom of the dialog box, you can also set the following for this user:

- Group memberships

- User profile (establishing the location of a short logon script to execute whenever this user logs on to the system)

- Logon hours

- Locations from which they may log on

- Password characteristics

We won't discuss all these in detail. Some, like logon hours, are quite straightforward; others, like user profiles, are not required for all installations. Password characteristics and user groups are the ones most likely to require tweaking, so the next two sections discuss these settings.

User Password. The password that you fill in can be up to 15 characters long. If the user will be logging on from an NT Workstation, you can make the password case-sensitive to make it more difficult to guess (for example, passWord), but if the user will be logging on from a Windows 95 or DOS/Windows workstation, case doesn't matter when a password is typed. Notice the User Must Change Password at Next Logon check box; to keep yourself from knowing the user's password (thereby increasing network security), you can mark this box to force users to make up a new password the first time they use the account.

> **Note**
>
> Unfortunately, you cannot automatically set password restrictions for your users with NT Server; that is, you cannot invalidate certain words (such as user names) as passwords. You can, however, tweak the available password settings. In the User Manager window, choose Policies, Account to set the minimum and maximum length and age for a password and determine how often passwords can be reused.

Click the Account button in the lower-right of the User Properties dialog box to change the account policies. You see a dialog box like the one shown in figure 9.6.

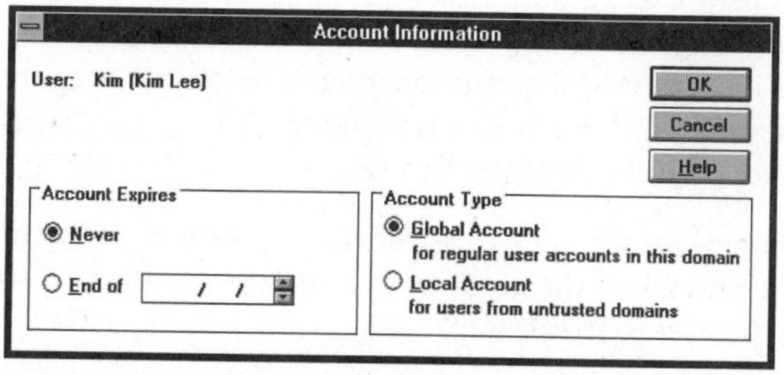

Figure 9.6

In the Account Information dialog box, you can determine whether the account is a global one that can be extended to another domain or a local one for use only in the local domain.

Unless you're setting up an account for a member of another, untrusted domain, you probably should select Global Account. This makes the account usable on any trusted domains as well as on the user's home domain. Also, you can determine here any expiration date for the account—after the date you type, the account will be disabled until you enable it again.

User Group Membership. The other setting that you're likely to adjust is the user group membership. When you create an entirely new account—that is, when it's not created using another account as a template, which you can do to save time—then by default the user is a member of the Domain Users group with all the rights that most network users require. For those who need additional rights (such as a person who'll be doing backups), there are additional groups that you can add them to. To do so, in the New User dialog box, click the Groups button. You'll reach the Group Memberships dialog box (see fig. 9.7).

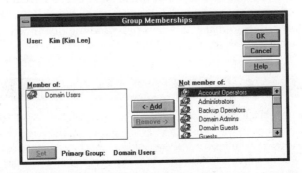

Figure 9.7

You can change group memberships in this dialog box.

A user must be a member of a global group. Because the only built-in global groups are Domain Administrators and Domain Users, this generally means that all your users are members of the Domain Users group. However, you can choose as many other groups as you want. Just don't forget that the user account you're setting up will have all the rights associated with the most powerful group to which it belongs. For example, you should never casually assign someone to the Administrators or Domain Administrators account because administrators can do anything to a server.

To add the user to a new group, click to select the appropriate group in the column on the right. Click Add, and when the group appears in the Member Of column, you've successfully added the user to that group.

How do you make sure that you're selecting the correct group for a particular user? To see which rights are associated with each group, you need to return to the main screen of the User Manager window and choose Policies, User Rights. As shown in figure 9.8, you can click to select the name of a group and then open the Right drop-down list to see all the rights granted to that group.

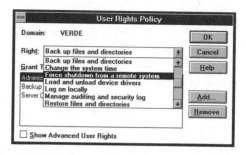

Figure 9.8

In the User Rights Policy dialog box, you can see which rights are associated with which groups.

Once you've set the group memberships, password, and other information for the new account, click Add in the New User dialog box to add the new account to the security database. Click Close (the button that was labeled Cancel until you clicked Add) to exit and return to the User Manager window.

Tip

If you're setting up a bunch of user accounts that are pretty much alike, you can use an existing account as a template for new ones. At the User Manager window, click the user account to be used as a template, and choose User, Copy. All you need to do for each new user is fill in a new username and password and then click Add; the existing settings (including group memberships) are copied to the new user account.

Tip

To change the settings for an account, double-click it to open the User Properties dialog box.

To review, the steps for creating a new user account are as follows:

1. Open the User Manager window.

2. Choose User, New User.

3. In the New User dialog box, type in the user's account name, real name, and password. Adjust their logon times, group memberships, and logon locations as necessary.

4. Click Add to add the new account to the security database.

5. Repeat steps 1–4 to add another user, or click Close to return to the User Manager window.

Setting Up Cross-Domain Access. If you've only got one domain on your network, you don't need to worry about how to make multiple domains talk to each other. It's the nature of networks to grow, however, so the possibility of establishing cross-domain access is worth considering. Permitting domains to trust each other is not difficult, and it can make network administration easier. A trust relationship between domains means that you can log on to one domain's domain controller and administer another domain or that users of one domain can access files and peripherals associated with another domain without logging on to the second domain.

Trust relationships don't have to be mutual. Just because you give your house key to your neighbor when you go on vacation doesn't necessarily mean that he'll give his house key to you when he goes away. Likewise, one domain can trust another without the second domain trusting the first. If you want a two-way trust relationship, then you have to establish two trust relationships: one going in one direction, and the second going in the opposite direction.

Not only are trust relationships essentially one-way, but they also are intransitive—the fact that domain A trusts domain B, and domain B trusts domain C, does *not* mean that domain A trusts domain C. To make A trust C, you need to set up a separate trust relationship between them.

Setting up a trust relationship requires action on both domain controllers. In the User Manager window, choose Policies, Trust Relationships. You'll see a dialog box like the one shown in figure 9.9.

Figure 9.9
You can set up cross-domain relationships in the Trust Relationships dialog box of the User Manager for Domains.

Tip

The order of these steps is important—you cannot trust a domain until you're permitted to trust it and the permission is recorded in that domain's security database.

First, you need to permit each domain to trust the other, just as you'd ask your neighbor if he would mind watching your house before you hand him a house key. In the Trust Relationships dialog box, click the lower Add button and type the name of the domain that wants to trust yours in the space provided. If you like, you can password-protect this trust in the same dialog box in which you identify the trusted domain, so that only those domains with the password can trust yours. When you click OK, the domain's name appears in the Permitted To Trust This Domain list.

> **Note**
>
> There is no browse list available when setting up a trust relationship. You must know the exact name of the domain that you want to set up.

To trust a domain that you've been permitted to trust, click the upper Add button and type in the name of the domain and any passwords required. When you click OK, that domain's name appears in the Trusted Domains list.

You need to perform both operations at the other domain to complete the trust relationship. To review, the process of building a two-way trust relationship goes like this:

1. Open the User Manager window. Choose Policies, Trust Relationships.

2. Permit the other domain to trust your domain.

3. On the primary domain controller of the other domain, permit your domain to be trusted.

4. At each domain's primary domain controller, trust the other domain.

This sounds cumbersome, and to some extent it is, but it's worth it. Once the trust relationship is built, you can add domain groups of one domain to the local groups of the other domain, thereby letting the other domain's members access shared resources on the trusting domain. You also can log on to a trusting domain from the trusted one, from either a workstation or a server.

Sharing Directories and Setting Permissions

The users you have set up need something to do after they log on to the server. To provide some productive activity for them, let's use File Manager to share files as required.

As mentioned earlier, NT Server's File Manager (see fig. 9.10) looks very much like the Windows 3.x File Manager, with a few extra menu options.

Because Windows is so common, we'll assume that most people are familiar with the basics of sharing files and directories (you do so by choosing Disk, Share As), and skip to the issues unique to NT Server.

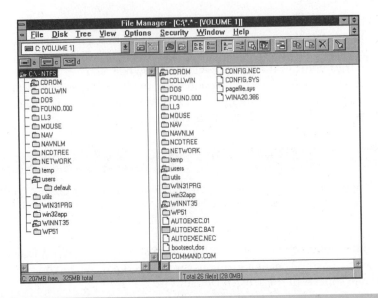

Although the NT Server File Manager looks similar to the one used by Windows 3.x, it has a much broader function. Not only can you share drives and directories here, but you can set security options and audit file access.

Basic File and Directory Permissions. You learned earlier in this chapter that permissions are different from user rights. Rights give a user the ability to *do* something, such as log on to the server or run a backup program. Permissions, on the other hand, determine the level of access a user or group has to particular files and directories. For example, you could permit the administrative staff "read-only" access to the directory in which memos were stored, so that they could look up memos but not edit them. To do this, you would either create a group for the administrative staff and assign read-only permission to the pertinent directory to the group or set permissions for that directory on an individual basis.

File Permissions and the NTFS File System

Although NT Server supports FAT and HPFS file systems, many of the advanced security features of NT Server are available only if you're using NTFS. Individual file permissions are such a feature. You cannot use the permissions, file ownership, or access auditing features from the Security menu in File Manager on a partition formatted for anything other than NTFS.

To convert the file system to NTFS, open the MS-DOS prompt (really a misnamed NT Server text interface) and type **convert** *driveletter***: /fs:ntfs** (where *driveletter* is the letter assigned to the partition you want to convert). If your drive has a single partition, you get a message telling you that the conversion cannot take place until the system restarts (because it needs the system files to keep NT working) and asking if you want that to happen. Type **Y**, and the conversion routine will run the next time you reboot.

You cannot convert from NTFS to either FAT or HPFS—the conversion routine works in only one direction.

You can set a directory's permissions while setting up the initial share. Highlight the directory you want to share and then choose Disk, Share As. You reach the New Share dialog box (see fig. 9.11).

In this dialog box, you can share the directory under a certain name and indicate the number of people who can access the directory at one time.

Most of the options here are fairly self-explanatory. The User Limit section determines whether you want only a certain number of people accessing the share at one time or want to allow as many people as there are client licenses to access it simultaneously. To adjust the permissions attached to this share, click Permissions. You reach the Access Through Share Permissions dialog box (see fig. 9.12).

By default, everyone has full control (read/write, change, and delete abilities) over shared directories.

Notice two things here: First, everyone on the domain has full control over the share, meaning that they can do anything to it (including delete it). Second, because everyone has full control, only one group is represented here. (If everyone can do anything to a share, then there's little use in specifying any other permissions.) At this point, you have two options. You can change the permissions that everyone has to the share (by selecting a different option from the Type of Access drop-down list) or you can click Add and then set permissions based on user accounts and groups.

> ### Caution
>
> For your permission assignments to do any good, you need to put an end to everyone having full control. In the Directory Permissions or File Permissions dialog box (depending on which kind of share you're configuring), either click Remove to eliminate that permission set entirely, or change the permissions for Everyone. Otherwise, setting specific permissions for other groups won't make any difference, as Everyone's full control overrides anything else you set.

If you click Add in the Directory Permissions or File Permissions dialog box, you reach the Add Users and Groups dialog box (see fig. 9.13).

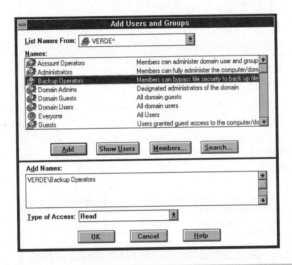

Figure 9.13

In this dialog box, you select groups or users to set permissions for.

To set directory permissions for the Backup Operators group, for example, you have to highlight it in the Names list and then click Add to add it to the Add Names box at the bottom. To set permissions for the Backup Operators, select the desired permission (Read, Change, Full Control, or No Access) from the Type of Access drop-down list. Click OK to return to the previous dialog box, where the group for which you just specified permissions has been added to the list.

Advanced File Security. As stated earlier, you need NTFS for real file security (the file security you paid $700 for). If you're using NTFS, you can

- Set file permissions on individual files
- Audit file access
- Take ownership of files

Permissions. Setting permissions using the Security menu is similar to the process of setting permissions for shares that was described earlier; however, there are two big differences. First, the New Share permissions settings only permit you to set permissions to the directory level. Even if you select an individual file and attempt to share it, you'll share the entire directory in which that file is located. With the Advanced Permissions tool on the Security menu, you can set discrete file permissions on individual files and subdirectories. Second, when you set permissions on individual files, you are not limited to the Read, Change, Full Control, and No Access permissions. The Special File Access option leads to more choices that let you narrowly define the permissions attached to the file.

To understand this better, let's look at how you can set permissions for a shared file. Click on a file to share and then choose Security, Permissions. The File Permissions dialog box appears (see fig. 9.14).

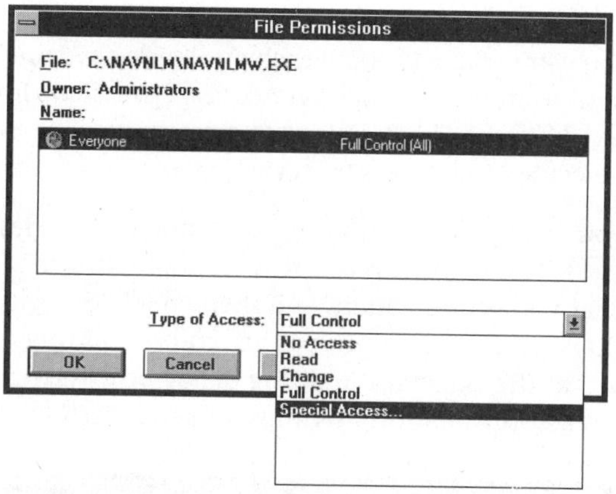

Figure 9.14

This dialog box allows you to fine-tune the permissions assigned to shared files.

When setting the permissions on an individual file, you'll notice a new entry, Special Access, on the drop-down list of file permissions. Click this entry to reach the Special Access dialog box shown in figure 9.15.

Note

When setting permissions on a directory, the initial dialog box looks much like the one shown in figure 9.14, except that you'll also have the option of choosing to replace permissions in subdirectories and existing files with the ones you choose there.

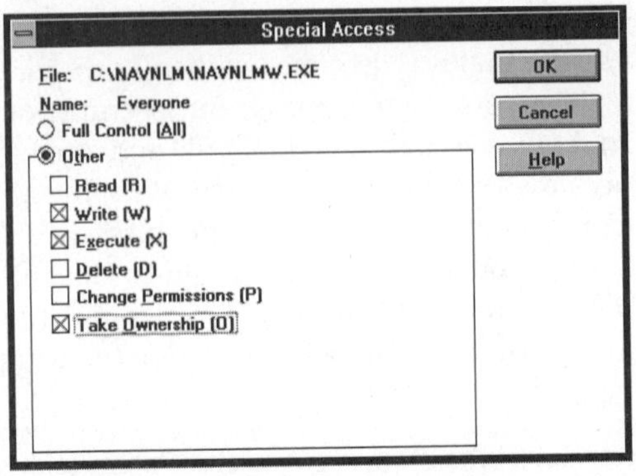

Figure 9.15

When setting the Special Access permissions, you can select as many or as few of the options as you like.

Check each option you want; these become the permissions assigned to this file for Everyone. If you ever want to modify the Special Access permissions for a different group, you just have to click Add in the File Permissions dialog box, click to select the group you want, and then select Special Access from the Type of Access drop-down list.

Auditing Files. If you want to see who's been accessing which files and directories, you need to set up *auditing*. If you're using NTFS, this is simple. In File Manager, highlight the file or directory that you want to audit, and then choose Security, Auditing. The resulting dialog box looks much the same whether you're auditing a file or a directory; the only difference is that the Directory Auditing dialog box (see fig. 9.16) includes settings for overriding the existing auditing settings for subdirectories and files.

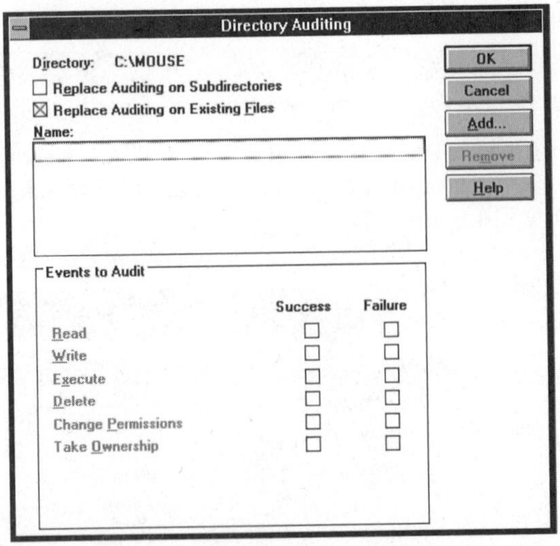

Figure 9.16

With the auditing settings, you can monitor both successful and failed attempts to access files and directories.

Most people are more interested in monitoring failures than successes. Failures might indicate that someone has been attempting to access information to which they do not have permission; successes often do little more than fatten your auditing files.

For auditing to work, you must first enable it in the User Manager for Domains (located in the Administrative Tools program group). Choose <u>P</u>olicies, <u>A</u>udit and set up the options that you need.

Take Ownership. You've seen the Take Ownership option in several dialog boxes. What is *ownership* and why is it important? Essentially, the *owner* of a file can grant permissions to it—setting the way in which any member of the network, including the administrator, can access the file. When you choose <u>S</u>ecurity, <u>O</u>wner, the Owner dialog box appears (see fig. 9.17).

Figure 9.17

Only the administrator can take ownership of a file which she does not own or have full control over, but once owned, a file cannot be returned to its original owner.

By default, the person who creates a file is the owner. Although the administrator can take ownership of a file which she does not own or have full control over, it's impossible to relinquish ownership of a file once you've got it, so the original owner will be able to tell if you've taken a file.

Protect Your System Files. When sharing drives and directories, it's wise to create a *user data directory* and share it to look like drive C. Why? You really don't want people messing around in the system files or saving files in the root directory. (Your life is complicated enough without cleaning DOOM scenarios out of the /I386 directory.) When you've identified a good user data directory, share it as C—it will look to your users as though they're connecting to the entire hard drive.

If you want to share a directory but keep it off the browse list, put a dollar sign after its share name. Users who know the directory's name (and that it's shared) can connect to it, but this keeps "casual connectors" from attaching to shared directories just because they can. In addition, you can assign passwords to shared directories to limit access to those directories.

Setting Up Printers

Printer administration under NT Server is not difficult—you create, share, and set the properties for a printer within a single dialog box.

Open the Control Panel (in the Main program group) and choose Printers; alternatively, double-click the Print Manager icon in the Main program group. Either action starts Print Manager (see fig. 9.18).

Note

Although you had the option of installing a printer while installing the operating system, for the moment we'll assume that you didn't.

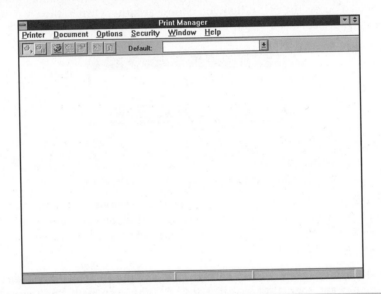

Figure 9.18

All printer administration takes place in one window—you needn't share printers in one place and install them in another.

Creating a Printer. To create a printer, choose Printer, Create Printer. This brings up the Create Printer dialog box (see fig. 9.19).

Most of the settings in this dialog box are self-explanatory—the printer needs a name, the appropriate drivers (NT Server supports a wide variety of printers, so your printer should show up on the list), and a port.

Tip

To hide your shared printer (so that only those who know its name can connect to it) put a dollar sign after its name; for example, **PRINTER$**.

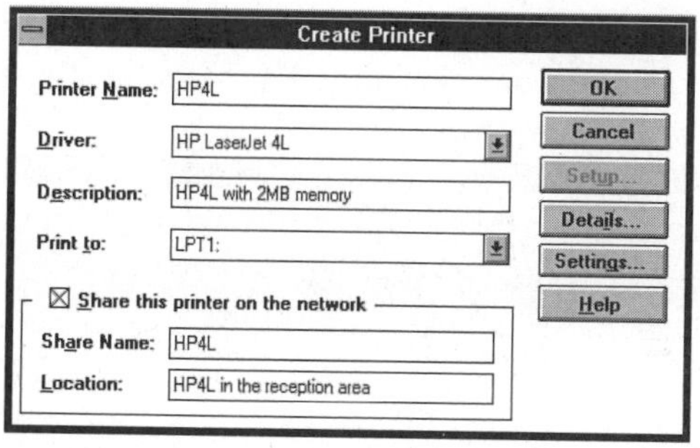

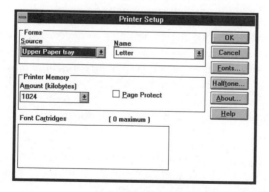

Figure 9.19

Before you can share a printer, you must create it.

To make it useful to the rest of the network, the printer needs to be shared. (For some reason, sharing the printer is not the default option. That seems odd in a network server product, but that's the way NT Server is.)

Tip

To keep it simple, make the printer's share name the same as the printer name. Also, describe the printer's location to reduce the number of people who connect to it by mistake and then complain that their documents aren't printing. (Such documents usually *are* printing—they're just printing somewhere other than where the user expected.)

Click OK to install the printer. NT Server pulls the drivers from the /I386 directory, then opens the Printer Setup dialog box (see fig. 9.20).

Figure 9.20

When you first create a printer, NT Server automatically opens the Printer Setup dialog box, where you can set the paper source or specify the installed font cartridges and printer memory.

Select the options appropriate to your printer, and click OK. You return to the main screen of Print Manager, where your new printer appears (see fig. 9.21).

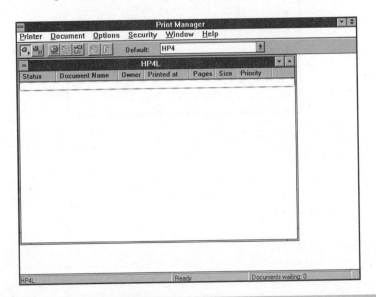

Figure 9.21

The new printer appears in the Print Manager as soon as you've set it up.

If you have shared the printer, it's now available to the rest of the network.

To change the properties of a printer (for example, if you have installed the wrong driver), choose Printer, Properties. You'll be back in the Create Printer dialog box where you named the printer and chose its driver. Notice that the Setup button is now available (it was unavailable before you finished installing the printer).

Setting Printer Security. It's not always desirable to have everyone on the network have access to a printer or have access at all times. The reasons don't have to be sinister: a color printer on the network is an expensive liability if people play with it, so you might want to secure it from anyone on the network who's not in the graphics department. Similarly, if someone whose job doesn't generally require him to send many print jobs suddenly produces a number of one-page documents, it might be worth investigating.

The first line of defense in printer security is putting a dollar sign ($) at the end of each printer's share name, so that the printer does not show up on a browse list. If that isn't sufficient, NT Server provides other security options:

- Setting printer permissions
- Conducting printer auditing
- Taking ownership of a printer

These security settings work just as they did in File Manager: setting permissions determines how extensive each person's access to the printer is; auditing keeps track of print jobs and their originators; and whoever has ownership of a printer can set the permissions on it. The permissions to be granted are slightly different, and the permission level only goes to the printer itself (you can't, for instance, give someone permission to delete only print jobs belonging to a particular person), but the basic idea is much the same.

Backing Up and Restoring Files

The final task we'll cover in this section is backing up and restoring files. NT Server is essentially a file server (as opposed to a print server or application server), and as such, it contains files that must be backed up regularly. Exactly how regularly depends upon your organization's needs, but if you generate data of any importance at all, then daily backups are advisable. Re-creating a day's worth of work is bad enough, but re-creating a week's worth could be nearly impossible.

Before you can use the backup utility, you need to install a tape drive. (Oddly enough, you can't install it while you install the operating system.) To do so, double-click the Windows NT Setup icon in the Main program group and then choose Options, Add/Remove Tape Devices to open the Tape Device Setup dialog box. No devices are in the list of installed tape drives, but don't worry—just click Add and then choose your tape drive from the list in the next dialog box that appears. (If you don't see the exact model that you have, try selecting another model by the same manufacturer.) NT Server loads the drivers from the /I386 directory on the CD-ROM and then returns to the Tape Device Setup dialog box, where your tape drive now appears in the list of installed devices. Click Close to exit Tape Device Setup, and then choose Options, Exit to exit NT Setup. You need to restart the server before the tape drive is fully installed.

> **Note**
>
> If you start NT Backup before installing the tape drive, you get an error message reminding you that no tape drive is installed yet.

Like many of the other tools discussed in this chapter, NT Server's backup utility is in the Administrative Tools program group. Double-click the Backup icon to start the utility (see fig. 9.22).

Performing a Backup. Backing up isn't difficult. To back up an entire drive, select its check box in the Drives window (notice that you can back up a CD-ROM drive as well as a hard disk drive). To back up only certain directories, double-click the drive's icon to display its directories (the tree structure works like File Manager), and then select each directory or file you want to back up. Click Backup (or choose Operations, Backup), and you'll see a dialog box in which you can place the following information:

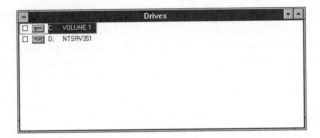

Figure 9.22

NT Server's backup and restore utility has an easy-to-use graphical interface for backing up and restoring data.

■ The type of backup:

  Normal   Backs up all files, and resets the archive bit.

  Differential   Backs up all files changed since the last normal backup.

  Incremental   Backs up all files changed since the last backup of any kind.

  Copy   Backs up all files, but does not reset the archive bit.

■ This backup's name and description (for tracking purposes, it helps to name the backup according to its type and date)

■ Whether you want to append this backup to any data already on the tape or over-write any existing data

■ Whether or not you want to log the backup process (a good idea)

■ Whether or not you want to back up the Registry (a *very* good idea)

Caution

If you select Restrict Access to Owner or Administrator in the Backup Information dialog box, then no one except the administrator will be able to restore the backups.

Click OK, and the backup begins.

Restoring Backups. The process of restoring backups is very similar to the process of backing up. Open the Backup utility again, but this time activate the Tapes window. Select the check box of the tape if you want to restore the entire backup (the name of the tape in the drive appears next to the drive's icon), or double-click the tape icon to catalog it and reveal its directory structure, allowing you to select individual files or directories. When you've selected what is to be restored, click Restore to set the Restore options (such as logging, restoring file permissions, and restoring the Registry), click OK, and the process begins.

> **Note**
>
> If any file being restored has a name that matches a file on the drive, you get an error message asking if you want to replace the existing file.

> **Caution**
>
> Don't restore the Registry unless you want to restore all the security information to the way it was when you performed that backup. For example, if you restore a two-week old Registry, all the user accounts you've created since then will be gone the next time you restart the computer. However, you should always back up the Registry, whether you plan to restore it or not. If you must reinstall NT Server for any reason, and if you can restore the Registry, you won't have to set up most of your security options (such as user accounts) again.

Advanced NT Options

So far in this chapter, we've discussed NT Server's design and how it works and have looked briefly at the processes for some of the most common administrative tasks that you'll perform with NT Server. By now, you should have a pretty good idea how this NOS operates.

There is much more to this operating system than just user groups and file sharing, however, and that's what we'll cover next. Remember that this chapter is not designed to do what other books have used a thousand pages to cover, so we'll stick with just three advanced topics: disk administration for RAID, keeping and reviewing logs to help with monitoring and troubleshooting the system, and connecting to NetWare and Macintosh networks.

Data Protection and Disk Management

NT Server's Disk Administrator, shown in figure 9.23, includes tools for both disk management and software RAID protection against data loss.

You can better understand how the Disk Administrator works if you are familiar with the following terms:

- *Free Space* Unpartitioned, unformatted space on a drive.

- *Primary Partition* A bootable partition of a disk, containing the system files for an operating system. Primary partitions cannot be subdivided.

- *Extended Partition* A non-bootable partition created from free (unpartitioned) space on a disk. Extended partitions can be broken into logical drives.

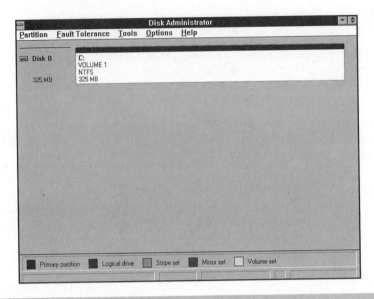

Figure 9.23

The Disk Administrator provides a handy arena for setting up software RAID protection of your data, and organizing your disk space.

■ *Logical Drive* A partition (or part of one) formatted for a particular file system. A logical drive does not have to be as large as a physical drive, but at most it can span one physical drive.

■ *Volume Set* A logical drive that spans more than one disk. You can add free space to a volume set to increase the volume's size, but you cannot decrease its size without deleting the volume (and destroying the data in it). Although volume sets permit you to store data on scraps of free space, they are prone to data loss since every physical disk in a volume set must be operational for the volume set to be accessible.

■ *Mirror Set* A data-protection setup in which one drive is dynamically copied to space on another physical disk. A mirror set requires twice as much room as the amount of data you want to mirror.

■ *Stripe Set* With parity, a stripe set is a data-protection setup in which data is written to at least three physical disks, along with parity information to re-create the data in case a disk fails. Without parity, striping is a mechanism to increase data retrieval speed by permitting the data to be read from two or more locations at once; this is dangerous because if one disk fails, all the data is destroyed.

Note

The characteristics of the various RAID types are covered in detail in appendix C, "RAID."

Setting Up RAID. Creating RAID protection for your data is not difficult. To set up mirroring, you have to Ctrl-click two partitions on different disks to select them both (the selected partitions have heavy black lines around them); then choose Fault Tolerance, Establish Mirror. Both sides of the mirror set will be the same size.

> **Note**
>
> You can break apart a mirror set (to reclaim the disk space it uses) without damaging the data in it. Select the mirror set, then choose Fault Tolerance, Break Mirror. The two halves of the mirror set will be independent of each other.

To set up a stripe set with parity, select at least three areas of free space on three different physical disks, and choose Fault Tolerance, Create Stripe Set with Parity. The stripe set does not have to be as big as the combined areas of free space you have chosen; you have the option of reducing its size in the Create Stripe Set dialog box that appears. Click OK, and the stripe set is created.

To set up a stripe set without parity, select free space on at least two physical disks, and choose Partition, Create Stripe Set. (Notice that this option is available from the Partition menu, not Fault Tolerance.) Once again, you have the option of setting the size of the stripe set.

> **Note**
>
> Stripe sets without parity are grouped with mirror sets and stripe sets with parity because they're a RAID type (level 4) like the other two, but remember that striping without parity offers you no data protection.

Arranging Data Space. As noted earlier, you can use the Disk Administrator not only to protect your data, but to arrange it on your physical disks in the way that's best for you.

To create a primary partition, select an area of free space on a drive, and choose Partition, Create. You can make the partition any size you want, as long as it fits on the physical drive.

> **Tip**
>
> Only make a primary partition as large as you need it to be for the system files (for example, about 100M for NT Server). That way, you're able to allocate the other space on the disk as you like—primary partitions can't be subdivided, so any space that goes unused in one is wasted.

To create an extended partition, click an area of free space, and choose Partition, Create Extended. (You do not need to have a primary partition on the drive to create an extended one.) Select the size for the extended partition, and click OK.

To create a logical drive, select an extended partition, and choose Partition, Create. (Notice that this is the same command used to create a primary partition—the difference is that here you're selecting unused space in an extended partition, while there you were selecting free (unpartitioned) space.) Select the size of the logical drive, assign it a drive letter, and click OK.

To create a volume set, select all the areas of free space on all disks that you want to make part of the volume, and choose Partition, Create Volume Set. Select the size of the set, and click OK.

Formatting New Disk Divisions. No matter how you're slicing up your disk, you need to partition the divisions before you can use them. In earlier versions of NT, this required using the command-line FORMAT command, but NT Server 3.51 lets you format drives and sets within the Disk Administrator. Select the unformatted section (it should be highlighted with a heavy black border), and then choose Tools, Format. Select the file system you want (remembering that only NTFS lets you fully exploit NT Server's security features) and click OK. When you leave the Disk Administrator, you get a message advising you that the changes you have made will not take place until you restart the system and asking if you want to restart it. If you do not restart now—perhaps to avoid disrupting users who are accessing the server—don't forget to do so at the earliest possible chance.

Keeping Tabs on the System

In the Administrative Tools program group, there are two tools you can use to monitor the system: Performance Monitor, which tracks what your server is doing, and Event Viewer, which tracks security, system, and application events.

Performance Monitor. By default, Performance Monitor is turned off, as you can see in figure 9.24. To turn it on, you need to create or open a new chart, log, alert system, or report.

For example, let's set up a chart to track CPU activity. Click the Chart button (the icon at the far left that looks like a chart) and then choose Edit, Add to Chart. The Add to Chart dialog box appears (see fig. 9.25), displaying options for what gets monitored (you can chart more than one parameter at a time—color-coded lines help you distinguish between them), and how data gets displayed. Clicking Explain displays information about the option highlighted in the Counter list to appear in the Counter Definition area at the bottom of the screen. In figure 9.25, we've selected the Processor Time counter, which displays the amount of time that the CPU is actually doing anything.

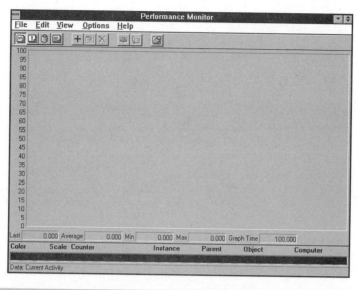

You can use Performance Monitor to maintain charts or logs of system activity, to alert you when pre-set thresholds have been exceeded, or to create reports about system activity.

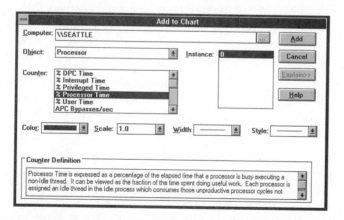

In the Add to Chart dialog box, you choose the items to be charted and specify how data should be displayed.

When you click Add, the Cancel button is relabeled Done. Clicking Done allows you to view the chart displaying CPU activity (see fig. 9.26).

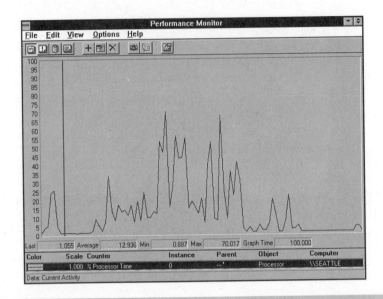

Figure 9.26

Performance Monitor displays graphical information about particular aspects of your server's performance.

Although the ins and outs of Performance Monitor are too complex to describe in this short section, you can trust the online help system to explain how to use it. The information you view in Performance Monitor can tell you exactly what demands are being placed on your hardware and can help you determine when you need to upgrade.

Event Viewer. Event Viewer, also found in the Administrative Tools program group, is a helpful tool for finding out what's going on in your system. If you want to know why a certain NIC won't work, what time Cindy logged off last night, or why the Macintosh clients cannot connect to the server, Event Viewer is a good place to look.

Unlike Performance Monitor, Event Viewer is turned on by default. It contains three types of logs: System, which records system events such as the failure of a device driver to load; Security, which records security-related events such as logon attempts and any changes to the security database; and Application, which records events noted by applications, such as the data noted by the conversion utility that switches FAT volumes to NTFS.

To view a log, choose Log, and then choose the type of log that you want to view. The log appears on-screen, looking something like the one shown in figure 9.27.

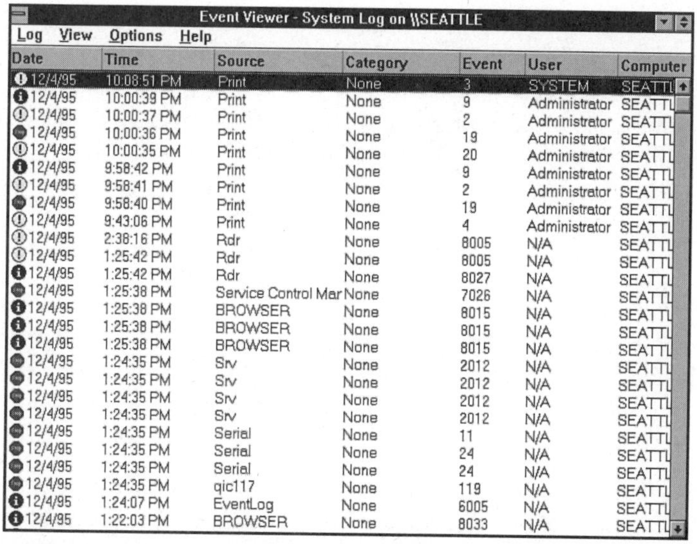

```
┌─────────────────────────────────────────────────────────────────┐
│ ▄             Event Viewer - System Log on \\SEATTLE        ▼ ▲│▼│
│ Log   View   Options   Help                                      │
├────────┬───────────┬───────────────┬──────────┬───────┬──────────┬──────────┤
│Date    │Time       │Source         │Category  │Event  │User      │Computer  │
├────────┼───────────┼───────────────┼──────────┼───────┼──────────┼──────────┤
│❶12/4/95│10:08:51 PM│Print          │None      │3      │SYSTEM    │SEATTL ▲  │
│❶12/4/95│10:00:39 PM│Print          │None      │9      │Administrator│SEATTL │
│①12/4/95│10:00:37 PM│Print          │None      │2      │Administrator│SEATTL │
│●12/4/95│10:00:36 PM│Print          │None      │19     │Administrator│SEATTL │
│①12/4/95│10:00:35 PM│Print          │None      │20     │Administrator│SEATTL │
│❶12/4/95│9:58:42 PM │Print          │None      │9      │Administrator│SEATTL │
│①12/4/95│9:58:41 PM │Print          │None      │2      │Administrator│SEATTL │
│●12/4/95│9:58:40 PM │Print          │None      │19     │Administrator│SEATTL │
│①12/4/95│9:43:06 PM │Print          │None      │4      │Administrator│SEATTL │
│①12/4/95│2:38:16 PM │Rdr            │None      │8005   │N/A       │SEATTL    │
│①12/4/95│1:25:42 PM │Rdr            │None      │8005   │N/A       │SEATTL    │
│❶12/4/95│1:25:42 PM │Rdr            │None      │8027   │N/A       │SEATTL    │
│●12/4/95│1:25:38 PM │Service Control Mar│None  │7026   │N/A       │SEATTL    │
│❶12/4/95│1:25:38 PM │BROWSER        │None      │8015   │N/A       │SEATTL    │
│❶12/4/95│1:25:38 PM │BROWSER        │None      │8015   │N/A       │SEATTL    │
│❶12/4/95│1:25:38 PM │BROWSER        │None      │8015   │N/A       │SEATTL    │
│●12/4/95│1:24:35 PM │Srv            │None      │2012   │N/A       │SEATTL    │
│●12/4/95│1:24:35 PM │Srv            │None      │2012   │N/A       │SEATTL    │
│●12/4/95│1:24:35 PM │Srv            │None      │2012   │N/A       │SEATTL    │
│●12/4/95│1:24:35 PM │Srv            │None      │2012   │N/A       │SEATTL    │
│●12/4/95│1:24:35 PM │Serial         │None      │11     │N/A       │SEATTL    │
│●12/4/95│1:24:35 PM │Serial         │None      │24     │N/A       │SEATTL    │
│●12/4/95│1:24:35 PM │Serial         │None      │24     │N/A       │SEATTL    │
│●12/4/95│1:24:35 PM │qic117         │None      │119    │N/A       │SEATTL    │
│❶12/4/95│1:24:07 PM │EventLog       │None      │6005   │N/A       │SEATTL    │
│❶12/4/95│1:22:03 PM │BROWSER        │None      │8033   │N/A       │SEATTL ▼  │
└────────┴───────────┴───────────────┴──────────┴───────┴──────────┴──────────┘
```

Figure 9.27

The System Log shows system events and errors that occur on your system.

In figure 9.27, a Stop icon indicates an error, a blue icon indicates a successful action, and a yellow icon indicates an action that represents a change but usually does not present any problems. You can export the contents of a log to an ASCII file for use as a report. To do so, choose Log, Save As, and then in the Save File as Type drop-down list, choose *.TXT as the file type. (Saving it as a LOG file takes a snapshot of the log that you can load in Event Viewer but does not put the log on to text form.)

Connecting to Other Network Types

NT Server comes equipped to connect to two distinctly different network types: NetWare and Macintosh networks. When NT Server is connected to a NetWare server, the NT Server machine effectively becomes a gateway to the NetWare machine, permitting anyone who logs on to the NT Server to access the NetWare server. The Macintosh connection is more limited—it's really a way of permitting Mac clients to access the NT Server and store data on it, rather than being a full gateway service permitting NT users to talk to the Macintosh machines.

Each of the connection services is initially installed through the Networks icon in the Control Panel. Click the Network icon to open the Network Settings dialog box, click Add Software, and select either Gateway Services for NetWare or Services for Macintosh to be added to your system. After you restart the machine, you'll be able to connect to your preferred server on the NetWare network or set up Mac-accessible volumes in File Manager.

> **Note**
>
> Gateway Services for NetWare is mentioned here only to alert you to its existence. For the nuts and bolts of how it works and how to set it up, see chapter 12, "Network Client Software for 32-Bit Windows," which offers a detailed discussion of this connection service.

Summary

That's the flying tour of Windows NT Server 3.51. This chapter has explained what NT Server is designed to do and has shown you how to perform some basic network tasks. By now, you should have a pretty good idea how NT Server would fit into your network—at least enough to compare it with the descriptions in this book of other server products.

NT Server is the first major server-oriented graphical network operating system. It contains both the features that you'll need every day, such as simple user administration tools and backup utilities, and more advanced features that let you configure software redundant disk systems, connect to other network operating systems, and monitor your network's and server's activity. Not only is it easy to use and comprehensive in scope, it's quite security-conscious, being one of the few network operating systems with C-2 certification.

Chapter 10

UNIX Operating Systems

Developments in networking connectivity and compatibility have been phenomenal in the past twenty years, and the biggest contributor has been the UNIX operating system. UNIX was developed with networking capabilities built in—as opposed to other operating systems that rely on external network operating systems. Since UNIX is a very sophisticated system, I can't delve into every detail in this chapter. However, I will give you enough of an overview that you will understand how the UNIX network system as a whole operates, along with some of its most prominent features.

In this chapter, you learn the following:

- How UNIX came to be
- What the UNIX philosophy is
- What the different flavors of UNIX are
- What UNIX has to do with networking
- What each UNIX network layer consists of
- What tasks make up UNIX network administration
- How to choose the UNIX that's best for you

The History of UNIX

UNIX (originally known as *Unics*) was developed by Ken Thompson and Dennis Ritchie in the Bell Telephone Labs at AT&T in 1969 on a DEC PDP-7. In 1970 it was moved to a PDP-11/20. In 1973, Thompson and Ritchie rewrote the kernel in C. Developed in a research environment, the original UNIX was free from commercial constraints and was a hacker's dream. Its kernel was tightly coded and portable, freely distributed, and almost completely modifiable. Most other operating systems of the time were clunky, machine-dependent, expensive, and not changeable.

> **Note**
>
> The kernel is the innermost part of the UNIX operating system.

So if UNIX was so great, why didn't it become another high-priced operating system on the market? Because AT&T was constrained by anti-trust laws from competing in the computer industry. So the company distributed the code to research and educational establishments, who quickly ported and modified UNIX. The first release of UNIX to be distributed for educational purposes was the Fifth Edition (also known as V5). The Sixth and Seventh Editions followed (not surprisingly) in the mid-to-late 1970s. Finally, System V, which was released in 1983, was accepted as the industry standard. Through the 1980s, several releases of System V (SVR2, SVR3, and SVR4) appeared. The latest is System V Release 4.2—also known as *Destiny*. In 1990, AT&T created a subsidiary called UNIX System Laboratories (USL), which joined forces with Novell to create UnixWare—a compliment to Novell's NetWare.

While AT&T was developing these improved releases of UNIX, the Santa Cruz Operation (SCO), along with Microsoft, developed XENIX, a fully licensed version of UNIX designed to run on the IBM PC. The success of the PC rocketed XENIX into success along with it, and SCO reported the distribution of more than 100,000 licenses by 1987.

The Computer Science Department at the University of California at Berkeley made tremendous contributions to the ongoing development of UNIX. The Berkeley version of UNIX was called BSD, and included features such as the C shell, a text editor called *vi*, and support for TCP/IP communications protocols. However, Berkeley was not a commercial institution and did not provide reliable support for its versions of UNIX. In June of 1993, Berkeley stopped further UNIX development. (The timeline in figure 10.1 summarizes how UNIX developed.)

> **Note**
>
> *Shells* are programs that let you communicate with the operating system. The shell's job is to intercept your commands and protect you from the kernel—and believe me, you want that protection.

With the growth of workstations, as opposed to PCs, UNIX became the operating system of choice among Sun Microsystems, IBM, Hewlett Packard, and countless others because of its innate portability and flexibility. Because of all the separate modifications to the original UNIX, there were some compatibility problems between different versions of UNIX. However, many UNIX vendors are working to unify UNIX through the Common Open Software Environment (COSE).

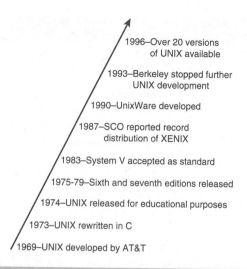

1996–Over 20 versions
of UNIX available

1993–Berkeley stopped further
UNIX development

1990–UnixWare developed

1987–SCO reported record
distribution of XENIX

1983–System V accepted as standard

1975-79–Sixth and seventh editions released

1974–UNIX released for educational purposes

1973–UNIX rewritten in C

1969–UNIX developed by AT&T

Figure 10.1

This timeline illustrates the development of UNIX.

The UNIX Philosophy

In three words, the UNIX philosophy is compatibility, portability, and interoperability. These three words are a theme throughout this chapter and throughout any discussion of UNIX.

- *Compatibility*   Compatibility means that various platforms and applications can work together, enabled by conformance to protocols and standards.

- *Portability*   Portable computer code, whether an operating system like UNIX or an application, can run on multiple platforms like IBM PCs or Sun workstations. Since 100 percent platform independence is rare, code is called portable if it can be *ported* to a different computer processor with little effort.

- *Interoperability*   A system is said to have interoperability if the devices and links on the network, supplied by different vendors, can transfer data reliably and efficiently.

The Different Flavors of UNIX

As you saw in our history lesson, many people got involved in "improving" UNIX. Table 10.1 shows many of the varieties of UNIX and each one's vendor.

II

Software Platforms

Table 10.1   Today's Various UNIX Flavors

Type of UNIX	Vendor
A/UX	Apple Computer
AIX	IBM
BRL UNIX	Ballistic Research Labs
Cromix	Cromenco
Genix	National Semiconductor
HP/UX	Hewlett Packard
IDRIS	Whitesmith
IN/ix	Interactive Systems
IRIX	Silicon Graphics
Mach	Carnegie Mellon
Minix	Prentice-Hall
MMOS	FCC
more/BSD	Mt Xinu
Opus 5	Opus Systems
QNX	QNX Software Systems
SunOS/Solaris	Sun Microsystems
System V	AT&T
System V/AT	Microport Systems
Thoroughbred	Omega
Ultrix	DEC
Unimos	Alphamicro
UTS	Amdahl
Venix	VentureCom

The biggies are Hewlett Packard's HP/UX, Sun Microsystems SunOS/Solaris, IBM's AIX, and DEC's Ultrix.

UNIX and Networking

A UNIX network can consist of two UNIX machines connected via modem, or it can be a collection of many networks that lets you connect to hundreds of thousands of other machines. The Internet is the perfect example of the latter. Figure 10.2 shows a representative sample of a UNIX network.

Connecting machines to form a network gives you many more resources than you would have from just one machine. You can share files, send electronic mail, access USENET news articles, perform searches for information, and much more. By connecting your users to each other and even to the world, you can increase their productivity and efficiency.

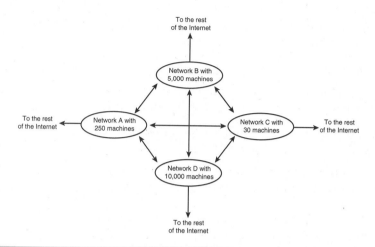

Figure 10.2

A UNIX network can consist of a few machines or tens of thousands of machines.

Networking is inherent in the UNIX operating system. UNIX was built with networking and connectivity in mind from the beginning. The first UNIX connectivity protocol was the UNIX-to-UNIX Copy Program (UUCP), which let you connect two machines via serial line. The original service provided by UUCP was simply to copy files between the two machines, but the developers quickly added additional services on top of UUCP that let you execute certain commands (like sending mail). The most common version of UUCP today is Basic Networking Utilities (BNU). Now that most networks are larger than two computers linked together, TCP/IP has overtaken UUCP. TCP/IP is discussed in detail in "The Layers of a UNIX Network" further on in this chapter.

A UNIX network is based on the client/server model, in which a client requests services of a server and the server responds, and the Open Systems Interface Reference Model. By conforming to standards like the client/server model and the Open Systems Interface Reference Model, networks can communicate and work together much more easily. For a good understanding of networks and their components, read chapter 1, "Network Background."

The Client/Server Model

Everywhere you turn, people are talking about client/server, but what exactly is it? In the most general sense, *client/server* refers to a basic change in computing style—the shift from machine-centered systems to user-centered systems.

More specifically, a client/server system is one in which a network ties various computing resources together so clients (the front end) can request services from a server (the back end) that can supply information or additional computer power as needed.

Why is client/server such a hot topic? It is mainly because some of the expected goals of client/server computing include the following:

- Use computing power more effectively and efficiently by conserving resources.

- Decrease maintenance costs by creating client/server systems that require less maintenance and cost less to upgrade than the old mainframe systems.

- Increase productivity by providing users with transparent access to needed data through standard, easy-to-use interfaces.

- Increase flexibility, interoperability, and portability by using standards to create open systems—systems that support varied hardware and software platforms.

As you can see from these goals, organizations that move forward to client/server technology greatly increase their competitive edge.

Let's look at the client/server process a bit more closely. The client process first sends a message to "wake up" the server. Once the client and server have established communication, the client can submit the request. Figure 10.3 shows how clients and servers interact.

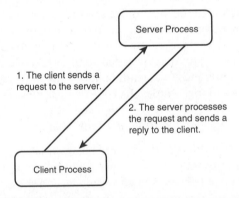

Figure 10.3

Exchanges between clients and servers basically consist of a request and a response to that request.

The client is the requester of services. Even though most illustrations show the client as being a workstation, the client is really no more than a process. Services requested by a client may exist on the same workstations or on remote workstations and hosts connected via a network. The client always initiates the communication. Read chapter 6, "The Workstation Platform," for a complete discussion of the network client.

Servers respond to requests made by clients. Just as clients are processes, so are servers. Servers are the process that responds to client requests by performing the desired actions. A client can act as a server if it is receiving and processing requests as well as sending them (for example, a workstation also used as a printer server for others). Servers do not initiate communication—they listen for client requests. Read chapter 5, "The Server Platform," for a complete discussion of the network server.

Let's use a simple example of a network printer server: the client asks the server to print a document on a specific printer, the server adds the print job to the queue and then notifies the client when the document has been successfully printed. The client process may physically reside on the same workstation as the server process. In this example, a print command could be issued on the network server workstation, making use of the print server process on that workstation.

The OSI Model

Open systems follow standards that allow different machines and platforms to communicate with each other as if they were the same. The standards define the format in which data is exchanged, how remote systems are accessed, and how systems are invoked.

The Open Systems Interface (OSI) reference model is a set of seven functional layers that define how information is exchanged over a network. As data is passed from machine A to machine B, it passes down through each layer on machine A and then up through each layer on machine B. Each layer is self-contained, which means that one protocol can be replaced with another at a particular layer without affecting the layers above or below it.

The seven layers are application, presentation, session, transport, network, data link, and physical. As figure 10.4 shows, the layers are categorized into *upper* and *lower*. Each layer requests services or data from the layer above it and satisfies requests from the layer below it. Read chapter 3, "The OSI Model: Bringing Order to Chaos," for a complete explanation of the OSI model.

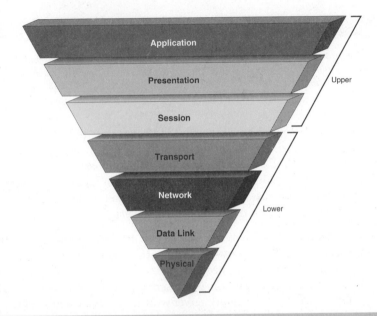

Figure 10.4
The seven layers of the OSI model provide a way to standardize network creation.

Table 10.2 describes the function of each layer of the OSI model.

Table 10.2 The Seven-Layer OSI Model		
Layer Number	**Layer Function**	**Description**
7	Application	Supports applications. This level is primarily where a NOS and its utilities are defined.
6	Presentation	Codes and formats translation.
5	Session	Manages dialogue between client and server.
4	Transport	Defines more specific network addressing and controls quality of packet transmission.
3	Network	Routes data through and switches data between networks.
2	Data Link	Defines the types of access control and message units used in a network.
1	Physical	Defines the physical connection between a station and the network.

Now let's look at each layer in more detail and see what protocols are used for UNIX networks.

The Layers of a UNIX Network

Networks are the cloudiest component of the client/server equation—and that means that client/server computing is doing its job. People generally don't know much about how networks really work with client/server systems because client/server systems are designed to make the network transparent to the user. In addition to being transparent to users, networks must be reliable. Without the network, the client/server system does not exist. Therefore, the network must be able to maintain connections, detect errors, and recover immediately from failures.

The networking side of UNIX is designed to control the server's communication services and to protect client and server programs from having direct contact with each other. The system focuses on providing reliable service, minimizing traffic across the network, and minimizing downtime.

Let me give you an example of how information is transferred over a network. Let's say you want to mail a letter to a friend. You would perform the following steps:

1. Place the letter in the envelope.

2. Address the envelope with your friend's address and your return address, along with any special instructions (for example, first class or air mail).

3. Drop the letter off at the post office.

4. The post office delivers the letter.

5. Your friend gets the letter out of the mailbox, opens the envelope, and reads the letter.

Transferring data over the network is similar to mailing a letter. The data is packaged, addressed, and sent to its destination, where it is unpacked and read. Each of these steps is controlled by a layer in the OSI reference model.

The Physical Layer

The physical layer is, quite simply, the actual hardware (cables, hubs, and so on) required to create a connection between two devices. When you mail a letter to your friend, the mail delivery truck and the roads traveled make up the physical layer. Ethernet media— thin, thick, and twisted-pair cables and various connectors and converters—are common to UNIX networks.

The Data Link Layer

The data link layer moves the transmitted signal from the hardware to the software by creating *frames* addressed to a unique network address—the *media access control (MAC)* address. Frames are series of data bits with a beginning (the header) and an end (the trailer). For example, you begin your letter with "Dear Ingrid" and end it with "Sincerely, Kay." You put that letter in an envelope, or a *packet*, and then write the address on the envelope. The Ethernet interface makes sure packets are sent and arrive correctly.

> **Note**
>
> MAC addresses are also known as physical addresses or hardware addresses.

MAC addresses are 48 bits long. The first 24 bits are assigned to network equipment manufacturers to ensure that each manufacturer has a unique prefix, and the manufacturer is responsible for assigning each machine a unique 24-bit suffix. The addresses are represented as pairs of hex digits separated by colons like the following:

9:1:17:fh:7:5a

The data link layer uses the source and destination MAC addresses to send the packet to the correct machine on the network.

The Network Layer

The network layer determines the actual physical routing of the packet (also called a *datagram* at this layer) from node to node, taking into consideration network conditions and priorities. For example, if you send a letter via overnight express mail, the post office will send your letter by plane. However, if you send your letter third class, the post office may send your letter by truck. The protocol used by UNIX networks for the network layer is the *Internet Protocol* (*IP*).

In the 1970s, the United States Department of Defense created the Defense Advanced Research Projects Administration (DARPA). DARPA was given the task of creating the *Internet*, the network of networks. Originally, the network was called the ARPAnet, and it used IP to control the connections.

One of the primary functions of IP is *routing*, which is the process of directing datagrams over a network. IP only keeps track of the first *hop*, or jump to another network. For example, if you send an e-mail message to someone, your message *hops* from network to network until it reaches its destination. Each node in the path only knows two things: the node the packet just came from and the next node in the path. This procedure is called *store and forward routing* and is controlled by IP (see fig. 10.5).

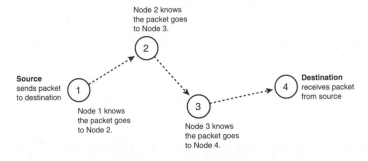

Figure 10.5

Store and forward routing means a node only has to know the packet's immediate destination, not its final destination.

Tip

Routing is automatic; however, you can turn off the automatic forwarding by modifying some TCP parameters. This modification is called a *firewall* and is used to prevent breaches of security.

IP identifies the recipients by a unique 32-bit IP address, also called a *dotted quad*. The IP address is written as a set of four 8-bit octets separated by decimals, like the following:

152.52.2.2

Note

The IP address refers to a machine's connection to the network, not to the actual machine itself. Therefore, if you move the location of a machine on the network, you must change the IP address.

IP addresses are assigned by the Network Information Center (NIC) at the Stanford Research Institute. (However, if your network is not connected to the Internet, you can determine your own numbering.) Each IP address falls into one of four categories: Class A through Class D. Table 10.3 shows the format of each class.

Table 10.3   The Four Classes of IP Addresses

Class	Network Address Size (bits)	Local Address Size (bits)	Value of First Octet
A	8	24	1 to 126
B	16	16	128 to 191
C	24	8	192 to 223
D	32	0	0, 255

Class A IP addresses are for very large networks with up to about sixteen and a half million machines. These addresses begin with a number from 1 to 126. Very few Class A numbers are assigned because very few organizations or countries have enough machines to justify a Class A address. Class B addresses are for intermediate networks with up to about sixty-five thousand machines. These addresses begin with a number from 128 to 191. Class C addresses are for smaller networks with about two hundred and fifty machines. These addresses begin with a number from 192 to 223. Class D addresses are used for broadcast messages, which are messages sent to all nodes on a network or a subnet. Class D addresses begin with either 0 or 255.

Netmasks are bit masks that distinguish between packets that are local (addressed to your network) and are not routed or packets that are addressed to other networks and need to be routed. Most versions of IP use the following default netmasks:

- Class A: 255.0.0.0
- Class B: 255.225.0.0
- Class C: 255.255.255.0

As you can see, broadcast messages and netmasks both can start with 255. That's because you rarely will broadcast beyond your own network.

> ### Tip
>
> IP addresses have to be unique on a network. MAC addresses, on the other hand, have to be unique in the world.

The Address Resolution Protocol. Since the network and data link layers are using different addressing schemes, you need a way for the network to identify physical addresses from IP addresses. The Address Resolution Protocol (ARP) does this for you by matching IP addresses with physical addresses. For example, if a request comes in for a machine with a particular IP address, ARP looks up the corresponding physical address in a cache address translation table. The Reverse Address Resolution Protocol (RARP) does the opposite—RARP works in the background to transparently convert physical addresses to IP addresses.

Domain Name System. Dotted quad IP addresses are not the most intuitive to remember. You wouldn't normally say to yourself, "Oh, I think I'll get that file off of 152.53.52.12 now." The Internet Domain Name System (DNS) supplies unique addresses that consist of easier-to-remember labels instead of numbers (although, to be quite honest, some of the labels can be quite cryptic). What this allows you to do is specify the *domain name* in a command instead of the IP address. A domain name server then maps the name to the correct IP address.

For example, you can type **telnet serenity.kayos.org**. Behind the scenes, the DNS client (also called a *resolver*) sends a query to the domain name server for the IP address that matches the domain name you specified. The domain name server looks up the IP address for serenity.kayos.org (which is 152.53.52.12). If the domain name server doesn't have the IP address for a particular domain name, it may have to send requests to other domain name servers to find it. The server then sends the IP address to the DNS client. Your system then says to itself, "Oh, telnet serenity.kayos.org really means telnet 152.52.52.12," and proceeds with the command.

The domain names themselves are a series of text labels and, like the IP addresses, are separated by periods and are hierarchical in nature. At the end of the series of labels (all the way to the right) is the most general label—a label that usually identifies the kind of network to which a machine is connected. Each successive label to the left is more specific, until you reach the label all the way on the left, which usually refers to a specific machine. Each domain name must be unique. See figure 10.6 for an illustration of how domain names work. You would read the domain name of the machine called "mystery" as

mystery.cloake_and_dagger.com.

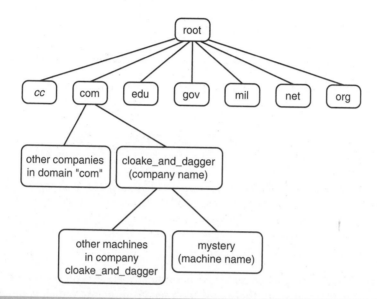

Figure 10.6

The hierarchical nature of the domain name system provides a logical way to assign unique domain names.

Note

The last label can also be a two-letter country code, like *au* for Australia or *uk* for United Kingdom. The country codes are specified in the International Standards Organization's document 3166.

The high-level (or *root*) domain—the label all the way on the right—separates networks into administrative domains. Within each domain, the administrator of that domain is responsible for making sure all domain names are unique. Table 10.4 describes the high-level domains in use today and what they mean.

Table 10.4   High-Level Domains and Their Meanings

Domain	Used by
com	Businesses
edu	Educational institutions

(continues)

Table 10.4 Continued	
Domain	**Used by**
gov	United States government organizations
mil	United States military organizations
net	Networking service providers
org	Nonprofit organizations
cc	Countries (for example, *us* for United States)

The root domain is a direct descendant of the ARPAnet, which created the com, edu, gov, mil, net, and org domains.

Tip

The country code is a bit tricky at first because it seems to not be consistently used. The logic behind it is this: normally, only countries other than the United States use the country code at the end of the domain name. United States organizations' domain names end in com, edu, gov, mil, net, or org. However, there is one exception (you knew that was coming, didn't you?). Primary and secondary schools, local organizations, and governments end in the country code *us*.

Some domain names actually just refer to other domain names—these domain names are called *aliases*. An alias is just another name for a server, similar to a nickname. Aliases often have functional significance. For example, many aliases begin with ftp because those aliases refer to the servers being used for FTP by particular organizations.

The Transport Layer

The transport layer is responsible for making sure the packet is transferred transparently and without errors. The transport layer is also the interface between the upper, application-oriented layers and the lower, network-related layers. For example, the quality assurance department at the post office makes sure your letter is delivered to the right place and in one piece. UNIX networks are built on two transport protocols: the Transmission Control Protocol (TCP) and the User Datagram Protocol (UDP). TCP links two computer programs, much like UUCP links two computers. UDP lets two programs send short messages to each other.

TCP is very reliable: it keeps track of the order in which to deliver packets and which packets need to be re-sent because of problems. TCP can do this by maintaining *state* information for each transmission. State information describes the state of the connection and the transmission (for example, *successful* or *failed*). TCP is usually used when datagrams must be delivered in a particular order and when long-term network connections must be maintained—which is one reason TCP is used for the Internet.

UDP is less reliable than TCP. Where TCP delivers packets in order, UDP does not. Where TCP resends packets that arrive with errors (or don't arrive at all), UDP does not.

However, UDP is a simpler and much faster protocol than TCP, which makes it an attractive choice when you are using applications that can perform TCP's functions themselves.

Both TCP and UDP use *port numbers*, which are another set of addresses. Where the MAC and IP addresses are equivalent to street addresses, the port number is equivalent to an apartment number. A single machine (which therefore has a single IP and MAC address) can have many processes using TCP and UDP at the same time. Each of these processes uses a port number to send and receive packets of data from other processes, local or remote. The packet header, which includes the source IP address, source port number, destination IP address, and destination port uniquely identifies every connection between two processes on the network. Port numbers from 1 to 1024 are reserved for processes run by superusers (anyone privileged to log on as *root* on a UNIX system). Port numbers above 1024 can be used by anyone.

Look in the file /etc/services to see the list of services and their assigned port numbers. Here's a sample of a partial /etc/services file. The first column lists the service, and the second column lists the port number and protocol being used.

hostnames	101/tcp
link	87/tcp
http	80/tcp
telnet	23/tcp
ftp	21/tcp
echo	7/udp
radius	1645/udp

And so on...

> **Note**
>
> Whenever a new protocol is adopted as a standard, a port number is assigned to it. That port number will always be used for that protocol.

The Session Layer

The session layer establishes, synchronizes, and controls a *communication session* between two processes. The communication session is simply a group of transactions. Once the exchange finishes, the session layer terminates the communication. The most common session protocol is the *remote procedure call* (RPC). RPCs are essentially client and server processes. As figure 10.7 shows, the client process on the originating machine sends a request to the server process on another machine. The session is equivalent to the delivery of your letter—from when you dropped it off at the post office to when your friend receives it. Once your friend receives the letter, the post office's job is done.

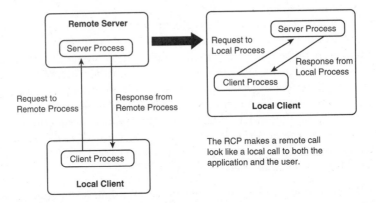

Figure 10.7

A remote procedure call "hides" the remote part of the call from you.

Note

When a request is *transparent*, the request looks like it is part of the local process; however, it is really coming from another machine on the network.

The Presentation Layer

The presentation layer provides the interface between the application and the services it requires. In other words, the presentation layer formats the data that is being sent or received. This layer can also compress or encrypt the data. The presentation layer corresponds to the process of putting your thoughts into words on the paper and your friend reading the words on the paper and understanding what you wrote. You could also have folded the letter up to fit into a very small envelope (compression) or written it in code so no one else could read it (encryption).

The presentation layer is critical in a heterogeneous network, where data is exchanged across multiple platforms. An example of a presentation layer protocol is the External Data Representation (XDR) protocol developed by Sun Microsystems. XDR lets different machines on the same network exchange data regardless of the type of machine that is sending or receiving the data. The way it works is by converting data into a common format called *canonical representation*. XDR takes machine-dependent data from the application layer and converts it into machine-independent data for the session and lower layers.

The Application Layer

The application layer includes services like electronic mail and network management applications that support users and other applications. In our example, you and your friend are the equivalents of the application layer.

The Network File System. The network file system (NFS) was developed by Sun Micro-systems in the mid-eighties and has revolutionized networking. NFS lets you share files and peripheral devices on different machines transparently, as if all the files or devices were on one machine—even if those different machines operate on different platforms like mainframes, workstations, and personal computers.

How does NFS work? Well, when you set up the file system, you assign permissions that allow certain files and directories to be shared. The NFS server exports those directories, and the clients (the workstations or PCs on which your users are working) *mount* the directories they need. Mounting a directory just means accessing a directory remotely (on another machine), but having the directory appear to be local (on your machine).

Let's look at a quick example: Say you set up a small network for three users: Karen, Patty, and Tim. Karen is working on a top-secret project, so no one is allowed to access her files. Karen, however, needs to access Patty and Tim's files because they are produc-ing supporting data for her project. As the system administrator, you set up Patty's and Tim's directories so that NFS exports them. Karen can mount them anytime she needs them and can use the remote files along with her local files. Patty and Tim, on the other hand, cannot mount Karen's directory (see fig. 10.8).

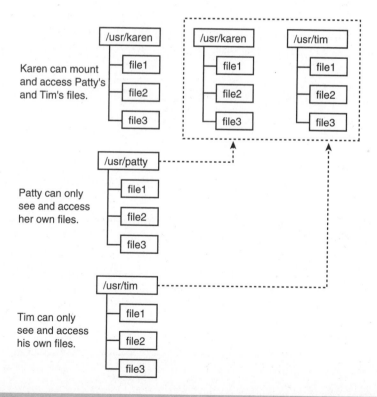

Figure 10.8

The network file system means you don't have to keep multiple copies of files and applications on your users' workstations.

> **Note**
>
> Note that your users only mount the files and directories they need—NFS does not automatically make things globally available to all users.

Not only does NFS let users access files more conveniently, but NFS also makes your job as administrator much easier. NFS is a distributed system, which means that you can centralize file system administration. Instead of having multiple copies of files and applications on many machines, you can keep them all on one or more NFS servers and let your users access them remotely.

NFS is based on the client/server model and uses remote procedure calls to make file systems available. In the client/server model, a client issues a request and the server returns a response or takes a series of actions. The server can act on the request immediately or add the request to a queue. Acting on a request immediately might mean the server calculates a number and returns it right away to the client. Adding the request to a queue might mean the request has to "wait in line" to be served. A good example of this is when you print a document to a network printer. The server puts your request in a queue along with print requests from other clients. It then processes the request according to priority, which, in this case, is determined by the order in which the server received the request. NFS makes directories or peripheral devices available in the same way.

> **Tip**
>
> Servers can be considered to be event-driven because, essentially, the server is in a waiting state until it gets a request from the client.

In addition to being able to mount file systems on demand, NFS has a feature that lets UNIX auto-mount and dismount file systems as needed.

The Network Information System. The network information system (NIS) was developed by Sun Microsystems to provide information. In fact, NIS used to be called the Yellow Pages, but for legal reasons it changed its name. NIS manages password and group files, and other information needed for administrative reasons. Essentially, NIS takes all the user and group information for all or most servers in a system, and creates a common list. That way, you only have to update the common list instead of the information on each machine.

> **Tip**
>
> NIS commands begin with *yp*, a holdover from the days when NIS was known as the Yellow Pages.

One example of the convenience NIS provides is passwords. Instead of having a different logon and password for every machine and device on the network, NIS allows you to have one logon and one password for any machine on the network (that runs NIS). In a word, NIS is a collection of *maps*. NIS not only lets you easily administer passwords but also the following services:

- Account information
- Aliases
- Automounter configurations and maps
- IP addresses
- Netmasks
- Network names
- NIS map versions
- Physical addresses
- Port names
- Protocol names
- Some security
- Time conversions
- UNIX groups
- User names

Daemons. In UNIX networks, much of the work is done by *daemons*, which are processes that run in the background. Some of the daemons working for you on a UNIX network are described in table 10.5.

> **Note**
>
> Daemon names end in *d*, so they are easy to recognize.

Table 10.5 Some UNIX Networking Daemons

Daemon	Description
inetd	inetd works for TCP to listen for connection requests. inetd works for UDP to listen for packets being received.
rpcbind	rpcbind is used by NFS, NIS, and many application programs. rpcbind forwards requests to the appropriate server process.

(continues)

Table 10.5 Continued	
Daemon	**Description**
routed	routed listens for Router Interchange Protocol (RIP) packets. When it hears them, it adds their routing information to the routing tables.
gated	gated is used on very large networks to listen for RIP, External Gateway Protocol (EGP), Boundary Gateway Protocol (BGP), and HELLO packets. When it hears them, it adds their routing information to the routing tables.
syslogd	syslogd logs messages generated by various processes, what process generated them, and what severity they are.

The daemons listed in table 10.5 are just a sampling—UNIX has more, as do NFS, NIS, and many other applications. In fact, even some of the daemons have daemons.

Remote Services. The main remote services are the ones which allow you to log on remotely, and transfer files. As you will see in the following sections, *rlogin, telnet, rcp,* and *ftp* are very versatile services.

Logging on Remotely. Two services, *rlogin* and *telnet*, let you connect to a remote computer over the network. For example, say you're in California for business. You have a laptop computer with you, but you need a file that is stored on your workstation in New York. You can use rlogin or telnet to log in to your workstation and retrieve the file.

Both services use the TCP/IP protocol over the network to make the connection. rlogin *hostname* (where *hostname* is the actual name of the machine you want to log into) simply logs you on to your remote machine and lets you issue commands and manipulate files as though you were actually sitting in New York using your machine. telnet *hostname* does the same thing. However, the telnet command offers more. If you use telnet by itself, you start up the telnet service in command mode. At the telnet prompt (telnet>), you can issue various commands, like *send*, which lets you send commands to remote hosts; *open*, which lets you connect to a particular host; and *quit*, which closes any existing connection and exits telnet.

> **Note**
>
> Telnet has many commands you can use. Refer to your system documentation for a complete list with explanations of each command. Or access telnet and type a question mark (?) at the prompt for just the list of commands.

Transferring Files. Files and file systems are the heart of the UNIX system and, therefore, of the UNIX network. Several services let you get the files you need. If you are using NFS, you can mount remote directories on your machine and use them as if they were local. You can use rlogin and telnet to access the files remotely. But what if you want a copy of the file on your own machine? How do you get it? You can use *rcp* or *ftp*.

rcp is the remote version of the UNIX copy command, *cp*. This command lets you copy one or more files from one location to another.

> **Note**
>
> You can also use rcp to copy entire directories from a remote host!

The file transfer protocol, ftp for short, connects to a remote host and lets you manipulate files. The two main differences between ftp and rcp are the following:

- ftp supports user authentication. rcp does not.

  When you initiate a connection with ftp, you must enter a valid name and password to log on to the remote system.

- ftp lets you perform commands. rcp merely lets you copy files.

  ftp has many commands similar to telnet, as well as many standard UNIX commands (like *cd*, *pwd*, *mkdir*, and *rmdir*).

> **Note**
>
> ftp has many commands you can use. Refer to your system documentation for a complete list with explanations of each command. Or access ftp and type a question mark (?) at the prompt for help.

Anonymous ftp is a way to get around the need for user authentication. For example, say a university has an ftp server on which it stores shareware that anyone can copy. Now, obviously it isn't going to be very convenient, or even possible, for the university to set up a logon and password for everyone who wants to download a file. Instead, users can use the logon *anonymous* and their e-mail address as their password. (Some systems require the logon *ftp* and some other string as the password.) Once you log on as anonymous, you have limited access to an anonymous ftp directory and files and subdirectories contained within.

> **Note**
>
> *Anonymous* really isn't anonymous—most ftp servers will log the connection, password, and actions taken.

Understanding UNIX Network Management Tasks

The purpose of network management is to build and maintain a network in such a way that you maximize productivity and efficiency. The primary network management tasks, each of which can be broken down into subtasks, are the following:

- Planning

- Installing

- Setting up

- Securing

- Managing

- Backing up and restoring

- Tuning

- Troubleshooting

Now, each of these tasks apply to any network—not just UNIX networks. However, UNIX provides built-in ways for you to complete each task easily and efficiently.

Planning the Network

Good planning is a must. Without good planning, I can guarantee you will lose time and money—which you probably have limited amounts to play with—during both the creation and implementation stages. Consider the following basic goals of network design:

- Interoperability   Rarely do you have a situation where you will only be using one type of machine on a network. One of the most important features of UNIX networks is the fact that you can use multiple hardware and software platforms together.

- Transparency   The functioning of the network should not be noticeable to your users. In fact, the better you design your network, the less your users will be aware of the network. Remote processes seem like local processes.

- Security   Remember to secure your system from physical and logical intruders, whether the "intruder" is a naive user who makes a mistake or a skilled hacker who wants sensitive information.

- Efficiency   Design your network so that you can maintain it easily and efficiently and so that it runs easily and efficiently. If you make your network too simple or too complex, performance may suffer or you may need a larger staff to troubleshoot and maintain the system.

- Reliability   Unscheduled downtime on a network is not just frustrating to your users. Unscheduled downtime costs time and money (you'll notice that *saving time and money* is a repetitive theme in network administration).

- Accessibility   Accessibility is not at odds with security; accessibility means that you must be able to reach every node on the network from every other node.

- Cost   Cost, again in terms of *time* and *money*, is a major consideration. The network, by increasing efficiency and productivity, should save you time and money.

- Scalability   Don't ever assume you won't need to expand your network. Odds are you will, and if you don't make your network scalable, or expandable, you may end up paying much more to expand than you would have if you had considered the issue in the first place.

UNIX is your best choice for every one of these design considerations, especially if you are running a medium-to-large, heterogeneous network. See chapter 2, "Overview of Network Systems and Services," for a complete discussion of networks and their associated systems and services.

Setting Up the Network

Setting up machines on a UNIX network involves several tasks—mainly editing some configuration files. As with installing, every flavor has different requirements. However, I can list some of the basic tasks. Then you can refer to your UNIX vendor documentation for more information.

> **Note**
>
> Every flavor of UNIX has different installation requirements and different delivery mechanisms. Refer to the installation documentation for the particular UNIX you are interested in.

The following tasks are examples of setup tasks:

- Map domain names to IP addresses
- Map network names to network numbers
- Set up netmasks
- Map physical names and IP addresses
- Map domain names to interfaces
- Configure the interfaces
- Set static and default routes
- Synchronize time and date among machines
- Start TCP/IP

Securing the Network

Securing the network is also called *security management*. Security management is the process of identifying and authenticating users and controlling and auditing logical access to network resources.

Not only can you control who can use what data, you can also monitor who attempts to access that data and when. For example, if you find that during certain periods there are many unsuccessful remote logon attempts to a database that contains top secret information, you have a security concern. You would check to make sure the database is secure and try to track down the user who is attempting to log on. Several tools automate these security management tasks for UNIX networks.

One of the caveats of a UNIX system is that UNIX was designed for maximum interoperability, which means that potential unauthorized remote logons are a real threat. However, much research has been done in this area over the years. Kerberos, from MIT, is a network security tool that is included in some versions of UNIX. NFS has improved security control, and UNIX itself has improved through the use of shadow files and encryption techniques.

> **Note**
>
> A *shadow file* is a file that hides the password encryption in the passwd file from the user.

The bottom line in security for UNIX is that you *must* understand the UNIX system well to be able to set up and enforce a viable security net. Read chapter 20, "Tools for Restricting Access," for more information about security.

Managing the Network

Managing the network (called *configuration management*) is a very broad category that involves several tasks. Configuration management is the art of managing the setup of all network devices. Why is configuration management important? Because, as network administrator or system administrator, you need to be aware at all times of what devices make up your network, what versions of software you are running, and so on. Configuration management is a must before you modify, secure, or tune your system. Also, if you are audited, you must be prepared to produce reports. For example, you can count on being audited to find out whether or not you have only legal software on all the devices on your network. If you maintain an inventory and regularly review this inventory, you will be aware of illegal software and will be able to remove it from your network promptly.

> **Note**
>
> Configuration management may not seem very glamorous but is essential to running any system.

We can break configuration management down further into these three steps:

- Getting current network configuration data.
- Analyzing that data and modifying the network configuration to create a more reliable, efficient network.
- Maintaining a current inventory of the network configuration.

Getting current network configuration data can be done manually or automatically. To get the data manually, you have to remotely log on to every device on your network to record the serial number and addresses. However, you need to be able to find every device to do this. Also, if you have several thousand devices on your network, getting the data manually may just not be practical. In this case, you can gather the data automatically, using a network management protocol to regularly record the data or by using an auto-discovery tool to list all devices on a network. Auto-discovery tools can also create a modifiable geographic or functional map of the network.

Analyzing the data and modifying the configuration can be done manually or automatically, depending on whether or not the data was gathered manually or automatically. Automatically is the better way to do it since the changes made are recorded so others can see what you changed and how. Also, some tools can even confirm whether or not your proposed changes are appropriate and what effect they will have on the network.

Maintaining the configuration information can be done by using a simple ASCII file. The benefit of the ASCII file is that most applications can read ASCII files, and you can use any available text editor to produce them. However, ASCII files consume a great deal of space, and large files are difficult to search. More importantly, an ASCII file is a glob of information that can't create relationships between data. A better way to store the information is in a relational database. Relational databases store, sort, and restore data efficiently and let you search for data quickly and easily. They also let you create relationships between various types of data. However, relational databases require more expertise because they are more complex to administer and often they have their own language (usually a flavor of SQL). Relational databases are also less portable than the simple ASCII file.

> **Note**
>
> Relational databases introduced the Structured Query Language (SQL). SQL lets you perform searches without having to know anything about the structure of the data—data access is transparent. SQL has been accepted by the computer industry as the standard data access language because of its ability to make databases transparent.

Backing Up and Restoring the Network

Since the UNIX network provides you with a network that is centrally administered, backing up and restoring the network is much easier than it might be on other systems.

The following three basic utilities let you back up the network:

- dump/restore

- tar

- cpio

Each command basically works by copying the contents of the source host to the target device. Of course, there are any number of commercial products with graphical user interfaces (GUIs) that are on the market.

A disaster recovery plan is a critical part of any network. See chapter 21, "Disaster Planning for Networks," for more information.

Tuning the Network

Tuning the network is also known as *performance management*. Performance management is critical to any organization because it is what increases network efficiency and productivity. Performance management involves three subtasks: monitoring performance, analyzing data, and optimizing the system.

Let's look at an example of performance management. If your users start complaining that the system is responding slowly to their requests, you need to do several things. First, determine whether there is a fault. If you determine there is no fault, then you need to examine the performance of each device and connection between the user and the network. When you find a performance problem (such as a device that is at maximum capacity), you decide what action to take. Now, as you can imagine, this process could be like searching for a needle in a haystack, even if your network isn't very large.

Performance management tools are designed to monitor and analyze data to detect problems for you, so you can concentrate on optimizing the performance of the network. See the following section, "Troubleshooting the Network," for some of the utilities that you can use for tuning. And, of course, there are plenty of commercial GUI products available.

Troubleshooting the Network

Troubleshooting the network is more formally referred to as *fault management*. All that means is that you find, identify, and fix problems (faults) in the network.

For example, if a user calls you and says she can no longer access the network, you need to determine what the problem is and fix it. First, you would try to figure out if there really is a network problem (as opposed to a user problem). Once you determine there is a problem, you would have to check each device and connection between the user's machine and the network. Then you would have to figure out how to fix the problem. (See chapter 31, "Locating the Problem: Server versus Workstation versus Links," for more information.)

Now, this process could be very tedious and time-consuming, and let's face it: time is a luxury you don't have. Therefore, instead of trying to troubleshoot manually, you would probably turn to one of several fault management tools available for UNIX systems.

UNIX has standard troubleshooting utilities that are available with all versions, and each vendor has its own tools to add to the list. Some of the standard UNIX utilities are described in table 10.6.

Table 10.6   Some Standard UNIX Troubleshooting Utilities

Utility	Description
arp	Displays the current address resolution protocol cache table. Useful to find incorrect MAC addresses.
ifconfig	Reports the current configuration of the interface. Useful for a quick picture of the status of the host.
netstat	Reports what processes are using the network, along with vital statistics. Useful to see if there are too many network collisions.
nfsstat	Checks the overall performance of the NFS system. Useful to see if there are performance bottlenecks.
nslookup	Queries the DNS for the address of a specified host name. Useful encountering errors or delays in name service.
ping	Asks the remote computer to echo a sent message. Useful to find out if host is unreachable or down.
snoop	Listens, records, and analyzes all network traffic. Useful to determine whether packets were sent or not.
traceroute	Determines where in the network a packet was lost. Useful to narrow down where you need to start looking for problems.

Comparing UNIX to Other Network Operating Systems

As you have seen thus far, UNIX has utilities to deal with just about every situation you could run into on a network. But how does it stack up against third-party network operating systems? Table 10.7 summarizes some of the main features of the "big three": UNIX, NetWare, and Windows NT.

Table 10.7   Comparing UNIX, NetWare, and Windows NT

Network Goals	UNIX	NetWare	Windows NT
Interoperability	Excellent	Good	Fair
Transparency	Good	Good	Fair
Security	Good	Good	Good
Efficiency	Excellent	Good	Fair
Reliability	Excellent	Good	Good
Accessibility	Good	Excellent	Fair
Cost	Depends	Fair	Fair
Scalability	Excellent	Good	Fair

(continues)

II

Software Platforms

Table 10.7 Continued

Network Goals	UNIX	NetWare	Windows NT
Third-party utilities available	Excellent	Good	Fair
Directory services	Excellent	Good	Fair
Flexibility	Excellent	Good	Fair
Performance	Excellent	Good	Fair
Print support	Good	Good	Fair
Years of experience	>25	>10	<10

If you are running a small network, the differences between these three operating systems might not be very obvious. However, I guarantee that the larger you go and the more diverse platforms you run, the more you need an operating system with the features UNIX offers. To make your comparison between the three operating systems, read chapter 8, "Novell NetWare," and chapter 9, "Microsoft Windows NT."

Summary

As I have said, this is only the tip of the iceberg. UNIX is a very mature, developed system with many features and even more tools available either commercially or as shareware on the Internet. Don't be intimidated by the seeming complexity, though. Ease-of-use has been one of the major improvements over the years, and your users can use the UNIX GUI system instead of working by command line. However, a complete understanding of the system and its philosophy is necessary to efficiently and wisely administer the system.

Chapter 11

Network Client Software

The goal of network client configuration is to enable the client to use the network with the optimal balance of high performance and low memory use. When you factor in your time constraints, finding that balance can be something of an art form.

This chapter looks at network software configuration for clients. It examines the software components and how to install them, and it covers network and memory configuration issues. It gives you the information you need to get a reasonably well-configured client up and running in a reasonably short time and to fine-tune that client to meet your particular requirements.

Workstation Software Configuration

This part of the chapter deals with the nuts and bolts of client configuration. It describes how to install and configure the various software components, and it takes a detailed look at the numerous configuration parameters.

The broad idea behind client configuration is to allow your client workstation to transmit and receive packets of a particular type (or types) on your network. Before you begin, you need to know which Ethernet frame type the server uses and which protocol or protocols your client is going to use.

Client Network Software Components

There are two major elements to network client software. First, there is the *network driver*, the software that controls the network adapter. Then there is either a *shell* or *redirector* to translate all the network traffic into something meaningful to the OS.

The form taken by both of these components has changed considerably over the last few years. Broadly speaking, DOS workstations have seen three types of configurations:

- Monolithic IPX driver and NetWare shell (IPX.COM and NETX)

- ODI driver and NetWare shell (MLID and NETX)

- ODI driver and NetWare requester (MLID and VLM)

The next few sections look at the various components.

Monolithic IPX Driver: IPX.COM. The original NetWare network drivers were monolithic, dedicated IPX drivers. A single executable file contained all the software needed to control the network adapter, along with the hardware configuration information for the adapter.

Adapter manufacturers distributed their NetWare drivers as an object file, which then was linked to NetWare code to produce an executable file with the adapter configuration embedded in it. If one of the adapter parameters was changed, the driver had to be rebuilt. These drivers supported IPX only—no other protocol could be used while they were loaded and in control of the network adapter.

Such drivers are obsolete and therefore are discussed no further in this chapter.

> ### Caution
>
> Dedicated IPX drivers are obsolete! If your workstation currently uses such a driver, refer to "Upgrading Client Software" later in this chapter, for more information.

How do you tell if the network driver on a workstation is a dedicated IPX driver or not? Dedicated IPX drivers generally are named IPX.COM; however, the name may have been changed to indicate the type of adapter the driver supports. You may not be able to tell from the time stamp on the file, either. Although Novell has not certified monolithic drivers for network adapters since 1990, the COM file might have been linked since then. The best way to tell if a network driver is a dedicated IPX driver or not is by trying to load it without the Link Support Layer (see the following section)—if it complains about the LSL not being loaded, then it is an ODI driver rather than an IPX driver.

ODI Driver: MLID. Novell developed the *Open Datalink Interface* (*ODI*) specification with Apple in 1989. A network driver that complies with this specification is known as a *Multiple Link Interface Driver* (*MLID*).

The strength of the ODI concept lies in its modularization of network functions. There are at least three components in the adapter driver software end of an ODI client:

- ODI Driver (MLID)
- Link Support Layer (LSL)
- One or more protocol-specific drivers (for example, IPXODI)

These work together according to the instructions in the configuration file NET.CFG to provide network connectivity to the OS. The following sections look at each component in turn.

Multiple Link Interface Driver (MLID). The MLID handles all communications between the physical network adapter and the other network components. Each adapter model needs its own MLID; these are written and distributed by the adapter manufacturers.

The MLID is the only software component that deals directly with the adapter. If you replace an adapter with a different model, just swap in the MLID for the new adapter and update the NET.CFG file.

Link Support Layer (LSL). The *Link Support Layer (LSL)* communicates between the MLID and the various protocol drivers (such as IPXODI) as described later.

The LSL may seem like an extraneous layer. Why not have the protocol drivers talk directly to the MLID? The answer lies in the benefits of modularizing the network functions. Consider the complexity of an ODI workstation. It may have several network adapters, each using multiple protocols. Network traffic must be routed between each adapter and the protocol-specific software that uses it. It would be quite difficult for a number of MLIDs in memory to coordinate their traffic-passing with each other. Even a single MLID for a single adapter would have difficulty keeping the various protocols separate, passing each type of traffic on to the correct driver.

The LSL lies between the MLID and the protocol drivers in logical—or even purely chronological—terms. It passes data from the MLID to the protocol drivers, and vice versa. It must, however, be loaded before the MLID. This is because the MLID needs to have the LSL to communicate with as soon as the MLID loads and also because there might be many MLIDs but only one LSL. It is easier to get each MLID to register with the LSL as it loads than to try to get the LSL to figure out which MLIDs are present when the LSL loads.

IPXODI and Others. MLID and LSL can look after the delivery of data from the adapter to the protocol drivers and vice versa. The purpose of the drivers is to interpret incoming data and to package outgoing data, according to the protocol that they support.

IPXODI, for example, looks after incoming IPX packets, unpacks them and passes them on to the shell or redirector. Likewise, it accepts data from the shell or redirector for packaging as IPX packets and then passes them on through the LSL to the MLID for processing by the adapter.

This is where the versatility of the ODI scheme is most apparent. If your workstation needs only IPX support, just load IPXODI. If you want to add TCP/IP support, load TCPIP.EXE or some similar driver. Provided you keep the NET.CFG file in order, the workstation then handles both protocols.

NetWare Shell: NETX. The *NetWare shell*, NETX.EXE, adds network functionality to the workstation environment by intercepting calls made to DOS and handling some of them itself.

> **Note**
>
> Early versions of the NetWare shell were DOS version-specific. NET3.COM worked with DOS 3, NET4.COM worked with DOS 4, and so on. More recent versions work with any DOS version and are named NETX.EXE. Notice that it has become an EXE file rather than a COM file—if you have NETX.COM, it's obsolete.

NETX is loaded into the workstation's memory when the workstation makes its initial connection to a file server. From then on, it watches a number of DOS interrupts. If an interrupt request can be handled by the OS, NETX simply passes it on to DOS.

If an interrupt call was made that requires action by NetWare rather than by the OS—for example, a reference to a network drive—NETX handles the interrupt itself. It puts together an IPX request and passes it on to the network via the network adapter and its associated software. Figure 11.1 illustrates the relationship between DOS, NETX, and the other network components.

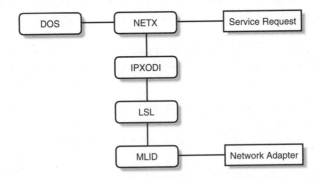

Figure 11.1

NETX intercepts DOS calls and redirects them to network resources.

NetWare Requester: VLM. The *NetWare requester*, VLM.EXE, also adds network functionality to the workstation environment; however, it does so quite differently than the NetWare shell does.

The requester incorporates a redirector that relies on DOS's redirection capabilities. If DOS receives an interrupt request relating to a network service, such as access to a network drive, it passes the request on to the requester. The redirector then handles the request in much the same way as the shell would—it makes an IPX request and transmits it to the network. Figure 11.2 illustrates the relationship between DOS, VLM, and the other network components.

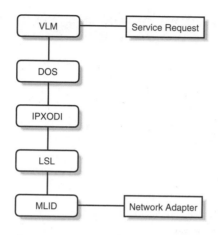

Figure 11.2

The VLM requester takes advantage of DOS's ability to redirect interrupt requests.

The requester has a modular architecture. *Virtual Loadable Modules* (*VLMs*) are loaded by the VLM.EXE as required. Modules that are not needed do not need to be loaded. Individual modules may be replaced or reconfigured without affecting other modules. The requester uses advanced memory management techniques to make optimal use of client memory.

Table 11.1 lists the available VLMs. Notice that some VLMs are required and others are optional. If you are unsure whether a VLM is required, you can load it anyway—it won't clash with another VLM. Be aware, though, that there is a memory cost for each VLM loaded. A better approach is to omit the VLM and see if you can get by without it. If you get error messages, you can always include the required VLM later.

Table 11.1   Virtual Loadable Modules

File	Manages	Required
AUTO.VLM	Auto reconnection and auto retry	No
BIND.VLM	NetWare protocol (Bindery)	Bindery mode only
CONN.VLM	Connection table	Yes
FIO.NLM	File input/output	Yes
GENERAL.VLM	Support functions for NETX and REDIR	Yes
IPXNCP.VLM	IPX communications	Yes
MIB2IF.VLM	MIB-II interface	No
MIB2PROT.VLM	MIB-II TCP/IP support	No
NDS.VLM	NetWare protocol (NDS)	NDS mode only
NETX.VLM	NetWare shell emulation	No
NMR.VLM	NetWare management responder	No
NWP.VLM	Multiplexor for NetWare protocols	Yes

(continues)

Table 11.1 Continued		
File	**Manages**	**Required**
PNW.VLM	NetWare protocol (Personal NetWare)	PNW mode only
PRINT.VLM	Printer redirection	No
REDIR.VLM	DOS redirector	Yes
RSA.VLM	Encryption for Directory Services	No
SECURITY.VLM	NetWare security	No
TRAN.VLM	Multiplexor for transport protocols	Yes
WSASN1.VLM	SNMP ASN translation	No
WSREG.VLM	MIB network management	No
WSSNMP.VLM	SNMP network management	No
WSTRAP.VLM	SNMP traps	No

Shell versus Requester. There are a number of differences between the shell and the requester, in terms of both architecture and the user's point-of-view:

■ Modularity

■ Memory management

■ Relationship with DOS

■ Last DOS drive

■ First network drive

■ Global mappings

■ File handles

The next few sections explore these differences.

Modularity. The requester consists of a number of VLMs and the VLM manager, VLM.EXE. VLM.EXE takes care of loading the VLMs into the workstation's memory, as well as managing memory allocation from various sources to the VLMs.

This modular approach differs from the monolithic NETX.EXE, which consists of a single file with a single memory allocation. NETX takes up one large chunk of memory rather than several small chunks. NETX also encapsulates all network functionality in a single file. The VLMs, in contrast, modularize network functionality so that unneeded components need not be loaded.

Memory Management. VLM.EXE looks after memory allocation for the VLMs. It is capable of using conventional, extended (XMS), and expanded (EMS) memory. Unless instructed otherwise, it loads individual VLMs into memory in the following order of preference:

1. XMS memory if available

2. EMS memory if available

3. Conventional memory

Therefore, the first few VLMs can be loaded into XMS while others are loaded into EMS or conventional memory. Using XMS rather than conventional memory has a performance cost, however—XMS is slower to access than conventional memory.

Relationship with DOS. When the shell is in use, it gets first call on requests. It decides which requests are network-related and which are not; any non-network requests are passed to DOS. When the requester is in use, though, DOS gets first call. DOS decides which requests are network-related and which are not; network requests are passed to the VLMs.

This architectural difference has several implications, as explained in the following sections.

Last DOS Drive. The NetWare shell creates drive mappings using only drive letters that are not in use by DOS. If DOS uses drives A through E (the default), then the first network drive is drive F, and drives F through Z are available for mapping by the shell. If a DOS request comes through for drive M, it is handled by the shell. If a request comes along for drive C, the shell passes it along for DOS to deal with.

The requester doesn't work that way—remember that it only has to handle requests that DOS decides are network requests. If DOS is using drives A through E, and a request comes along that refers to drive M, DOS returns an `Invalid drive` error, and the requester never sees the request.

It is necessary when using the requester to tell DOS to use more drive letters than the default five (A–E). It usually is best to make all drive letters available by setting the last DOS drive to Z. This is done by using the command

```
LASTDRIVE=Z
```

in the workstation's CONFIG.SYS file.

Once this has been done, requests involving network drives are handled differently. If a DOS request comes through for drive M, DOS recognizes the drive letter as valid but also recognizes that VLM.EXE has taken over the operation of drive M. It therefore passes the request on to the requester for handling. Requests for local drives such as drive C are handled in the normal way, without the involvement of the requester: DOS recognizes the drive, knows that the drive is DOS's responsibility, and therefore handles the request itself.

First Network Drive: Specifying. The shell and requester both map the first network drive to the server's logon area when the initial connection is established.

Using NETX, the first network drive is the next drive after the *local drives* or *DOS drives*. Assuming that the workstation uses the DOS default of five available drives (A–E), the first network drive is drive F. This is true even if some of the DOS drive letters are unused. If there is no hard disk, for example, and only drives A and B are in use, the first network drive still is drive F.

As explained in the preceding section, DOS and the requester share a range of drive letters. DOS examines each request and either deals with the request itself (if for a local drive) or passes the request on to the requester (if for a network drive). The mechanism used by NETX to decide on the first network drive—the first one after the DOS range—therefore does not work. Instead, VLM uses the first available DOS drive letter for the first network drive. If a workstation has no hard disk, for example, and uses only drives A and B, the first network drive is drive C; if the workstation has a hard disk drive (C) and a CD-ROM drive (D), the first network drive is drive E.

You can force VLM to use a particular letter as its first network drive by using the First Network Drive parameter in NET.CFG. See the "NET.CFG Parameters" section, later in this chapter, for details.

First Network Drive: Root Mapping or Not. The DOS prompt looks different when you switch to the first network drive, depending on whether you use NETX or VLM. Suppose that the first network drive in each case is drive F.

Under NETX, the mapping is not a fake root—the DOS prompt reads F:\LOGIN>. You cannot switch to the root directory, F:\, until you log on. That does not matter to NETX—it happily intercepts all requests that refer to drive F and makes sure that you do not get to F:\.

This is not true of DOS because DOS cannot maintain a subdirectory when the parent directory is inaccessible. As soon as VLM attaches to the file server, it creates a root mapping to the logon area; therefore, the DOS prompt reads F:\>.

Global Mappings. Drive mappings in Windows DOS sessions using NETX are private by default. Under VLM, such mappings are global. This means that if you have multiple DOS sessions running, and you change a drive mapping in one session, the drive is also remapped in the other sessions.

File Handles. NETX regards network files as its own. It allocates handles for these files when it loads, either using the default value of 40 or a different number if there is a File Handles= entry in NET.CFG. Local files are DOS's business and have nothing to do with NETX, so DOS maintains file handles for local files. The number of file handles used by DOS can be set in CONFIG.SYS using the FILES= statement.

Using VLMs, all file handles are managed by DOS. The total number of network and local file handles is set in the CONFIG.SYS file using the FILES= statement. You might need a larger FILES= setting in CONFIG.SYS when using VLMs.

Installing NetWare Clients. The installation procedure for the NetWare clients for DOS and Windows has been greatly simplified over the years. The original monolithic adapter driver had to be generated from its component parts into an executable file (IPX.COM) with the adapter's hardware settings hard-coded into the driver. To change a setting, the entire driver had to be recompiled. Once this was done, however, the simple loading of two TSRs from the workstation's AUTOEXEC.BAT was the only remaining procedure.

The advent of the ODI architecture eliminated the need for driver generation and eased the process of configuring the adapter's hardware settings. It also simplified the procedure for using multiple network protocols on a workstation. However, as a result, the number of executables required increased from two to four.

The VLM client plus the adoption of Microsoft Windows as the standard business workstation environment increased the complexity of the NetWare client beyond the point at which it could be conveniently installed manually. Finally, an installation program was created for the VLM client that automates the procedure. If you are installing network support to a workstation for the first time, the use of the automated installation program is highly recommended.

Installing the VLM Client. The NetWare VLM client installation files ship with the NetWare 4.x operating system. It is installed by default to the \PUBLIC\CLIENT\ DOSWIN directory during the normal NetWare server installation process. The kit is also available for download from Novell's NetWire service on CompuServe.

> **Note**
>
> The NetWare VLM Client Installation Kit is available from CompuServe (**GO NWCLIENT**) as six files called VLMKT1.EXE through VLMKT6.EXE. VLMKT6, however, contains only support for TCP/IP. If you will not be running Novell's TCP/IP, you do not need to download this file. Note that the full VLM kit contains all of the modules needed to support NetWare in all its available languages. The client upgrade archives mentioned elsewhere in this chapter, such as WINDR3.EXE, support U.S. English only.

You don't need a complete client installation to establish basic network connectivity. In the case of most corporate networks, an administrator uses a boot disk containing the basic files needed: LSL.COM, and MLID, IPXODI.COM, and NETX.EXE to connect to the network, from which she runs the full client installation.

If you have downloaded the Client Installation Kit from an online service, copy all the self-extracting files to a single empty directory and execute each one in turn. After you agree to the Novell terms and conditions, the files are decompressed and a directory structure is created. Certain files, such as NWUNPACK.EXE and LICENSE.TXT, exist in all of the archives. You can safely overwrite these files, as they are not required for the client installation.

Once you have extracted the archives, run the INSTALL.EXE program from the directory you have created. The VLM client installation program then performs the following tasks:

- Copies all necessary files to the workstation.

- Optionally installs Windows support.

- Optionally installs NetWare SBACKUP agent.

- Installs an MLID of the user's selection.

- Inserts user-specified adapter hardware settings into a NET.CFG file.

- Creates a STARTNET.BAT file that loads the client software.

- Modifies CONFIG.SYS, AUTOEXEC.BAT, WIN.INI, and SYSTEM.INI files.

After you have completed the installation process, you may want to make additional adjustments to the NET.CFG file using the settings explained in "NET.CFG Parameters," later in this chapter. You should, however, be able to reboot your system and connect to the network.

Installing the NETX Client. There is no dedicated installation program for the NETX client. If you have reason to perform an installation of the NETX client on a new computer with no networking support, you should still utilize the VLM Installation Kit to install the client, and then substitute NETX.EXE (or XMSNETX.EXE or EMSNETX.EXE) for VLM.EXE in the STARTNET.BAT file. This way, you have a complete set of client files that have been tested and are known to work together.

If you are familiar with the structure of the NET.CFG file and you will not be running Windows on the computer, then you may find it simpler just to copy LSL.COM, and MLID, IPXODI.COM and NETX.EXE to a workstation drive and load them from the AUTOEXEC.BAT file—once you have created a NET.CFG containing the appropriate hardware settings. Most NetWare client workstations today are used to run Windows, however, and while you can install the client's Windows support manually (see "Manually Upgrading Windows Network Components," later in this chapter), it is far simpler to use the installation program.

Upgrading Client Software

Every network client machine requires a software upgrade sooner or later. The upgrade may be prompted by a hardware or operating system change, the need to replace buggy or inefficient software, or the desire to take advantage of the enhanced functionality of newer software.

This section describes why, when, and how to upgrade the client network software components. It tells you which files you should have and what you are missing in each case by not upgrading. It also explains how to replace existing software as smoothly as possible. It points out the changes you can expect and shows how to avoid losing functionality—including the ability to use the network—by taking appropriate precautionary steps.

> **Note**
>
> This chapter is focused on the upgrade procedures *per se* rather than on the particular software components. It may tell you, for example, that you should upgrade from IPX.COM to an ODI driver without giving a full explanation of what an ODI driver is.

Upgrading Guidelines. You want client upgrades to be successful and worth the effort. An upgrade that adds nothing to the client is a waste of time; if the client loses functionality as a result of your efforts, you will have to restore it to its previous state. The following precautionary steps can help you to ensure a successful upgrade and to backtrack gracefully in the event of a disaster.

Backups. Few experiences in network configuration can match the feeling you get when an upgrade kills the client so that it can no longer connect to the network. This is especially true if you skipped the step of backing up all network related files before carrying out the upgrade.

> **Caution**
>
> It is generally advisable to have a full backup of all hard disks in the system before carrying out any software upgrades—network or otherwise. Before you dismiss this as excessively cautious, consider the implications for yourself and for the users of the workstation if data is lost on the hard disk. If you are about to upgrade a workstation that is maintained by someone else, ask him first if the backups for the machine are in a satisfactory state. If not, you should warn him that there is a risk of data loss during the upgrade.

Make a backup copy of all network files on floppy disk or copy them to another directory or extension (such as *.OLD) before carrying out an upgrade that might replace any of them. Use the following checklist as a guideline:

- AUTOEXEC.BAT
- CONFIG.SYS
- IPX.COM or MLID
- LSL.COM and IPXODI.COM (if ODI is in use)
- SHELL.CFG or NET.CFG (if present)
- NETX.EXE or NETX.COM (if shell is in use)

- VLM.EXE (if requester is in use)

- WIN.INI (\WINDOWS directory)

- SYSTEM.INI (\WINDOWS directory)

- NETWARE.DRV (\WINDOWS directory)

- NWUSER.EXE (\WINDOWS directory)

- NETAPI.DLL (\WINDOWS directory)

- NWCALLS.DLL (\WINDOWS directory)

- NWIPXSPX.DLL (\WINDOWS\SYSTEM directory)

- NWLOCALE.DLL (\WINDOWS\SYSTEM directory)

- NWNET.DLL (\WINDOWS\SYSTEM directory)

- NWNETAPI.DLL (\WINDOWS\SYSTEM directory)

- NWPOPUP.EXE (\WINDOWS\SYSTEM directory)

- NWPSERV.DLL (\WINDOWS\SYSTEM directory)

- NWPSRV.DLL (\WINDOWS\SYSTEM directory)

- VIPX.386 (\WINDOWS\SYSTEM directory)

- VNETWARE.386 (\WINDOWS\SYSTEM directory)

- VPICDA.DLL (\WINDOWS\SYSTEM directory)

- NWGDI.DLL (\WINDOWS\SYSTEM directory, if requester is in use)

Remember to check in subdirectories for these files. There may be older versions of the files in one directory and more recent versions in another. This is bad practice but it does happen, and it can mean that you accidentally back up the wrong files. Check AUTOEXEC.BAT to see where the files are loaded from.

Look for different versions of the Windows network files in both the \WINDOWS and \WINDOWS\SYSTEM subdirectories. If you find any, make backups of both for simplicity. Copy them to separate subdirectories on the backup floppy. You can experiment with deleting older versions and moving newer versions to the correct location *after* the successful completion of the upgrade.

Bootable Disk. Make sure you have a bootable floppy disk before starting the upgrade process. Check that it works on the specific client machine that you are configuring and that the hard disk is accessible after booting from it.

Ideally, use a floppy boot disk formatted using the same DOS version as the one installed on the PC. Using a floppy boot disk with the same DOS version means you can use the external DOS commands stored in the PC's DOS directory after booting from the floppy.

Copy your favorite utilities to the floppy boot disk so they will be ready when you need them. Include a text editor for working on the PC's configuration files.

Remove Stray Copies of Files. There may be old versions of the network files lying around in directories other than the one from which the current files are loaded. Search for any such files and remove them from the hard disk before starting the upgrade. This helps to avoid confusion at a later stage, when it might not be clear which copy of a particular program should be loaded. It is best to keep copies of these files on a special backup floppy disk for reference purposes and as a safety precaution.

Checking Current File Versions. You may need to establish the current version number and revision level of a particular file before you can decide whether to replace it with another. There are a number of ways to do this.

A simple comparison of file dates is often sufficient. If one copy of LSL.COM is from 1992 and another from 1994, install the 1994 version. Sometimes the date stamp is misleading though; for example, it may be the date on which the file was downloaded from an online service.

In many cases, running the program with the /? command line option gives quite detailed version information. Compare the first line in the /? output from two copies of LSL.COM:

```
NetWare Link Support Layer v2.05 (930910)
NetWare Link Support Layer v2.14 (941011)
```

The version numbers tell you that the second file is the more recent. The date stamp in parentheses at the end of the line tells you how much more recent: the first was released on September 10, 1993, and the second on October 11, 1994.

In some cases, you can't trust even this information. MLIDs are particularly prone to mislabeling, as hardware manufacturers can be sloppy about software version numbering. For example, two early versions of ODIDEPCA.COM reported the same version number:

```
Digital Equipment Corp DEPCA DOSODI driver V1.0 (920515)
Digital Equipment Corp DEPCA MLID  V1.00 (930122)
```

Yet the second is eight months more recent than the first and is considerably more reliable.

In summary, compare file date stamps and the version numbers reported by the programs themselves, but don't rely completely on this information. The only way you can be certain you have the most recent version of a file is to contact the supplier, as explained in the next section.

Sourcing the New Files. The most recent versions of the NetWare files—LSL.COM, IPXODI.COM, NETX.EXE, VLM.EXE, and the Windows files—can be found in Novell's NETWIRE forum on CompuServe and in various Internet mirrors. If you don't have access to the Internet or to CompuServe, your NetWare dealer should be able to provide these files to you.

Note

All the NetWare client update archives can be downloaded from the **NWOSFILES** forum on CompuServe.

Novell packages the files into a number of self-extracting archives, each of which contains a set of related files. The latest VLM files at the time of writing, for example, are distributed in a file called VLMUP4.EXE. Unpack the archive into a new, empty directory to avoid mixing up its contents with any older files. Use the following commands to do so:

```
C:\> cd tmp
C:\TMP> md vlmup4
C:\TMP> cd vlmup4
C:\TMP\VLMUP4> c:\imports\vlmup4
```

The contents are unpacked from the archive file into the current directory. Any subdirectories contained in the archive file are automatically re-created in this directory.

The *easiest* place to find an MLID for your network adapter is on the adapter configuration disk supplied with the adapter. The place to find the *most recent* one is usually on the adapter manufacturer's World Wide Web or FTP server or in their CompuServe forum.

Upgrading Specific Files

The following pages look at the various client network software components in turn. Topics covered include reasons for upgrading, upgrade instructions, and the benefits of particular upgrades.

Obsolete Files. IPX.COM and NETX.COM should simply not be used anymore.

IPX.COM. Novell stopped certifying dedicated IPX drivers years ago. If any of your workstations still use one, it's time to get rid of it.

Replace IPX.COM (or whatever the dedicated IPX driver is called on your workstation) with a recent version of the Multiple Link Interface Driver (MLID) for your network adapter. Refer to the following "ODI Files" section for details.

Upgrading from a dedicated IPX driver to an MLID provides the client with a more robust and flexible interface. Above all, it gives the client the ability to run multiple network protocols simultaneously.

NETX.COM. The NetWare shell was originally DOS version specific, with NET3.COM written for DOS 3 and NET4.COM written for DOS 4. These were replaced with a single shell that worked on all DOS versions: NETX.COM. This was replaced in turn by NETX.EXE.

If NET3.COM, NET4.COM, or NETX.COM is in use on the workstation, replace it with the most recent version of NETX.EXE (see the "NETX.EXE" section later in this chapter). Alternatively, migrate to the NetWare DOS requester, as discussed in the "Migrating from NETX to VLM" section later in this chapter.

ODI Files. The modular architecture of ODI means there are at least three network programs to upgrade on a NetWare client. These are the Link Support Layer driver (LSL), the IPX driver (IPXODI), and the MLID for the workstation's network adapter.

LSL.COM. The functionality of LSL is clearly defined in the ODI specification. Newer versions offer bug fixes or efficiency improvement over older versions without any change in core functionality. In other words, upgrading LSL.COM won't break anything but it may fix a problem or avoid a potential problem, so always use the most recent version!

At time of writing, the most recent LSL.COM available on NetWire is v2.14, released on April 17, 1995. Check the current revision of your copy of LSL.COM by using LSL's /? switch:

```
C:\> LSL /?
NetWare Link Support Layer v2.16 (950417)
(C) Copyright 1990-1995 Novell, Inc. All Rights Reserved.
```

Upgrading from an old version is a snap—just replace the old version with the new one. Installing ODI drivers from scratch—for example, when upgrading from IPX.COM to ODI—is more complex.

IPXODI.COM. Like LSL, IPXODI has a clearly defined role in the ODI scheme and is a stable entity as a result. It cannot change dramatically between releases; to do so would disrupt a huge number of client machines around the world. New releases generally offer bug fixes.

Check the version of your current copy of IPXODI.COM using IPXODI's /? switch:

```
C:\> IPXODI /?
NetWare IPX/SPX Protocol with Mobile Support v3.02 (950808)
(C) Copyright 1990-1995 Novell, Inc.  All Rights Reserved.
```

The current version of IPXODI.COM at time of writing is v3.02, released on August 8, 1995.

Just as for LSL.COM, you can replace an old version of IPXODI.COM with a newer version by simply replacing it. Always use the most recent version you can find—as a minimum, you will avoid potential problems that may be inherent in the older version.

MLID. LSL.COM and IPXODI.COM are universal in application, in the sense that they are designed to run on any PC with any network adapter. They are tested exhaustively before being released, and the introduction of new problems in an upgrade of either file is very unlikely.

This is not the case with the ODI driver or MLID for a given network adapter. These programs are written by the adapter manufacturer, working to the ODI specification. MLIDs are occasionally released with serious bugs that have escaped the manufacturer's testing procedures. This is particularly true of initial releases of drivers; if you are having strange network problems while using version 1.00 of the ODI driver for a particular adapter, an upgrade is a good idea.

You can generally establish the current revision number and release date of an MLID using the /? command-line option. Here's an example from the 3Com Etherlink II MLID:

```
3Com 3C503 EtherLink II MLID  v1.30 (930203)
(C) Copyright 1992 3Com Corporation.  All Rights Reserved.
(C) Copyright 1991 Novell, Inc.  All Rights Reserved.
```

Upgrading an MLID is the first step to take if you are experiencing unusual, client-specific network problems that you cannot reliably attribute to any other source. Keep a copy of the old version in case the new one is faulty.

A little more care is necessary when upgrading the MLID than when upgrading LSL. This is because the MLID works in close cooperation with the workstation's hardware, particularly the network adapter and system RAM. It is not a simple "plug-in" component like LSL. In particular, default settings may change from one version of an MLID to the next; values that you did not need to specify in NET.CFG may need to be explicitly stated when using the new version.

The following procedure explains how to upgrade a given MLID. It is assumed that you have located a new version of the MLID and verified that it is designed for use with your particular adapter model. It is also assumed that you have taken all the precautions listed in the "Backups" section earlier in this chapter.

1. Read any documentation that came with the new MLID. This may consist of a README.TXT file on the disk or in the archive file in which you obtained the new MLID or a sample NET.CFG file. Pay particular attention to any references to changes in default settings. The old MLID may have used a 32K RAM area while the new one uses 64K, for example.

2. Determine the hardware interrupt (IRQ), I/O port address, and shared RAM address used by the adapter. These are best established using the adapter's diagnostic/setup utility. If you don't have a copy, run a system diagnostic utility (such as Microsoft's MSD) with the old MLID running. Note the hardware settings that are actually in use by the card. As a last resort, check the INT, PORT, and MEM values previously entered under the adapter's Link Driver section in the workstation's NET.CFG file. Remember not to take these values too seriously, though.

3. Examine the NET.CFG file. It should explicitly state the hardware settings used by the adapter. Don't rely on default values—they may have worked in the past but the new MLID may use different defaults. If any of the hardware settings (INT, PORT, MEM, or DMA, if applicable) are not explicitly stated, add an entry with the correct value.

4. If you made any changes to the NET.CFG file, reboot the workstation to check that the old MLID still works. This is a quick check that the settings you entered are in fact correct.

5. If you haven't already done so, make a copy of the old MLID. If the new one doesn't work for some reason, you will need to revert to the old.

6. For the same reason, make a copy of the old NET.CFG file.

7. If the network files were in the root directory or in an inappropriate location, this is a good time to move them. Copy LSL.COM, IPXODI.COM, and so on, into a suitable directory (C:\NWCLIENT, for example) and edit the batch file that loaded the drivers in the past to reflect the change of path.

8. Copy the new MLID into place.

9. Search for and remove any old versions of the MLID on the hard disk. These can cause confusion—you may upgrade the workstation only to have someone else change your configuration at a later stage so that the older driver is loaded.

10. Restart the machine and test the new MLID.

On those rare occasions when an MLID upgrade results in a deterioration in client performance, be ready to switch back to the previous MLID while you source a newer driver from the adapter manufacturer.

Shell and Requester. The user interface to the network, shell or requester, can be upgraded independently of the other components. The next two sections describe how to do this.

> **Note**
>
> These sections cover only the upgrading of existing drivers—migrating from shell to requester is covered in the "Migrating from NETX to VLM" section later in this chapter.

NETX.EXE. The latest version of the NetWare shell—NETX.EXE—at the time of writing is v3.32, released on November 22, 1994. Novell has ceased development of NETX, and future releases are likely to be limited to bug fixes. You can check your current NETX version using NETx's /? command-line option:

```
NetWare Workstation Shell  v3.32 (941122) PTF
(C) Copyright 1994 Novell, Inc.  All Rights Reserved.
Note: For use with DOS v3.X through v7.X.
```

As you can see from the last line here, NETX.EXE retained some of the version-specific nature of its NET3.COM and NET4.COM predecessors. It was manifested in a slightly different way; Novell couldn't guarantee that NETX.EXE would work on all possible future versions of DOS, so they made NETX check the DOS version at load time. If the DOS version was not within the range they had tested, NETX would refuse to load. So, for example, version 3.32 of NETX.EXE only loads if the DOS major version is between 3 and 7 inclusive—i.e., from DOS version 3.00 to 7.99.

It is possible to force NETX to load on later versions of DOS using the SETVER utility, as explained in the "NETX and DOS" section later in this chapter. However, it is better to upgrade to a version of NETX that has been tested on the version of DOS that is installed on the workstation.

Upgrade an existing version of NETX.EXE by simply replacing the old version with the new one. To protect against mistakes or the possibility of a corrupt executable file, make sure you back up the old one first. Search for and remove old versions of NETX from the hard disk to avoid confusion.

VLM.EXE. The DOS requester is a relatively recent appearance in the network client software world, and updates to VLM.EXE and the various VLM files are still likely to appear at regular intervals. Check the version of VLM.EXE currently installed on a workstation using the /? command line option:

```
VLM.EXE NetWare virtual loadable module manager  v1.20 REV B (951002)
(C) Copyright 1993, 1994, 1995 Novell, Inc.  All Rights Reserved.
```

Whenever you replace the VLM.EXE executable, be sure to include any new *.VLM modules in the upgrade archive, as well. These are located in a directory called \VLMS that is created when you extract the files from the archive.

Aside from replacing the old VLM files with the new versions, upgrading should involve a review of the entries in the NetWare DOS requester section of the workstation's NET.CFG. The parameters in table 11.2 are new in version 1.20.

Table 11.2   New NET.CFG Parameters, VLM v1.20

Parameter	Default
CONFIRM CRITICAL ERROR ACTION	ON
EOJ	ON
FORCE FIRST NETWORK DRIVE	OFF
LIP START SIZE	0
LOAD LOW FIO	OFF
LOAD LOW NETX	OFF
LOAD LOW REDIR	OFF
LOCK DELAY	1
LOCK RETRIES	3

In addition, the default value for the READ ONLY COMPATIBILITY parameter changed from ON to OFF with the release of version 1.20.

The new parameters listed in table 11.2 represent a major improvement in the DOS requester. In particular, the ability to control whether the FIO, NETX, and REDIR VLMs load into upper or conventional memory gives you significantly more control over that all-important balance between performance and memory use.

Remember, these changes arose in a particular minor upgrade of VLM.EXE. The scope and extent of changes illustrates the importance of reading all relevant documentation that accompanies such releases.

Windows Components

It is not absolutely necessary to install the Windows network components. Windows can use network drive and printer services that were set up under DOS before Windows was loaded. If you map drive X under DOS and then load Windows, for example, drive X is accessible to Windows applications.

Leaving all the network management to DOS is fine as far as DOS activity goes, but it makes for a very restricted network environment under Windows. To change a drive mapping, for example, you have to exit Windows, issue a MAP command, and then restart Windows.

When the Windows network components are installed, errors have been relatively common in the past. The infamous Black Screen of Death (BSOD) syndrome in particular has caused much frustration for users and network administrators alike, with PCs dropping out of Windows to DOS or hanging intermittently, leaving a blank screen with just a cursor in the top left-hand corner. Fortunately, most of the bugs that caused these errors have now been tracked down. Applying the latest Windows NetWare patches should leave you with a fairly stable system.

There are a number of interrelated files that allow Windows to use NetWare services. These files are listed in table 11.3. Because of the way these files interact, it is advisable that you upgrade all files in a set together, rather than mixing and matching from different Novell distribution sets. Everything may seem to work well enough initially, but some functions may not work. For example, mismatched copies of NETWARE.DRV and NWPOPUP.EXE can prevent network broadcast messages from appearing on-screen. No error or warning messages appear about the mismatch but neither does the broadcast pop-up window.

Table 11.3 lists the files that must be installed to allow Windows to manage the NetWare environment. The second column lists the most recent file versions at the time of this book's publication. The third column indicates whether the files are for use with NETX or VLM.

Table 11.3 Windows NetWare Files

File	Version	VLM/NETX	Purpose
*NETAPI.DLL	1.30	Both	SQL Server support
NETWARE.DRV	3.03	VLM	Client Windows driver for NetWare
NETWARE.DRV	2.02	NETX	Client Windows driver for NetWare
NETWARE.HLP		Both	Windows Help file for NETWARE.DRV
NWCALLS.DLL	4.10	Both	NCP communications
NWGDI.DLL	1.01	VLM	Graphical display interface for NETWARE.DRV, version 3 or later
NWIPXSPX.DLL	4.10	Both	IPX/SPX communications
NWLOCALE.DLL	4.10	Both	Localization/Internationalization

(continues)

Table 11.3 Continued			
File	**Version**	**VLM/NETX**	**Purpose**
NWNET.DLL	4.10	Both	Support for NDS
*NWNETAPI.DLL	1.30	Both	NCP communications
NWPOPUP.EXE	3.01	Both	Displays a broadcast message in a dialog box under Windows
*NWPSERV.DLL	1.30	Both	Print server support
NWPSRV.DLL	4.10	Both	Print server support
NWUSER.EXE	1.02	VLM	Utility for managing a workstation's network environment under Windows
VIPX.386	1.19	Both	Virtual IPX/SPX driver
VNETWARE.386	2.04	Both	Virtual NetWare driver
**VPICDA.386		Both	Virtual interrupt driver

* Outdated files that are no longer maintained by Novell—some older applications may still require them.
** VPICDA.386 is for Windows 3.0 only. It fixes a problem with network adapters using IRQ 2 or an IRQ of 9 or higher.

Manually Upgrading Windows Network Components

For a workstation that has no Windows network support (or for a workstation that has become hopelessly muddled), the NetWare Client Installation program is the best way to ensure that all the correct files are copied to the appropriate directories on the workstation. There are times, however, when it may benefit you to know exactly what the benefits of the Windows components are, as well as what files should go where.

This section describes how to manually install or upgrade the Windows network software components. When installed, they enable you to do the following:

- Manage network connections
- Manage drive mappings
- Manage printer mappings
- Receive broadcast messages

Network connections and mappings can be managed using File Manager or from within applications that use the standard Windows file selection dialog boxes. If the Windows network software components are installed, Windows presents a Network button in these dialog boxes. Clicking the Network button displays a dialog box like the one shown in figure 11.3.

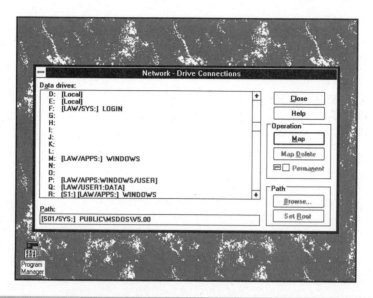

Figure 11.3

The Windows Network-Drive Connections dialog box is used to associate network drives with workstation drive letters.

Caution

The following instructions apply to the latest available Novell file distributions at the time of writing, contained in WINDR3.EXE, NWDLL2.EXE, NET33X.EXE (NETX workstations only), and VLMUP4.EXE (VLM workstations only). If you are using a more recent release of any of these files, check the accompanying documentation carefully before installing any files. Also, check before installing any files that the versions you are installing are in fact more recent than the versions you are replacing! Although many of the same files are included in the NetWare Client Installation Kit, they are packaged for use with the installation program included. The release files listed previously are more easily manageable when you are performing a manual installation.

Windows Network Files.

1. Get a copy of the latest update distribution sets.

2. For VLM workstations, apply the patches in VLMUP4.EXE. The version of VIPX.386 (v1.19) in WINDR3.EXE requires version 2.12 or higher of LSL.COM and version 3.01 or higher of IPXODI.COM.

3. For NETX workstations, apply the patches in NET33X.EXE. The version of NETWARE.DRV in NET33X.EXE is 2.02 and is for use with NETX. WINDR3.EXE contains version 3.03 of NETWARE.DRV, which is for use with VLM.

4. Create an expanded distribution set from WINDR3.EXE. Create a new directory for the purpose, change to the new directory, and run the self-extracting archive from there. WINDR3 expands its files into the following directories:

   (top level)
   VLMDRVS
   NTSWD
   READMES
   STANDARD
   VXDS

   The following instructions refer to these subdirectories by name. For example, the instruction "Copy WINDR3\VXDS\VIPX.386 to the Windows SYSTEM directory" means "Copy the file VIPX.386 from the VXDS subdirectory of the expanded WINDR3 distribution set to the workstation's Windows SYSTEM directory."

5. Create an expanded distribution set from NWDLL2.EXE. Create a new directory for the purpose, change to the new directory, and run the self-extracting archive from there. NWDLL2 expands its files into the following directories:

   (top level)
   NWDLL
   OLDDLLS

   The following instructions refer to these subdirectories by name. For example, the instruction "Copy NWDLL2\NWDLL\NWCALLS.DLL to the Windows SYSTEM directory" means "Copy the file NWCALLS.DLL from the NWDLL subdirectory of the expanded NWDLL2 distribution set to the workstation's Windows SYSTEM directory."

6. Identify the Windows and the Windows System directories. These are usually \WINDOWS and \WINDOWS\SYSTEM, respectively, on the PC's boot disk, but they could also appear under a different directory name.

7. Check for stray copies of the NetWare files in the wrong directories. You may install the latest version of a file in the \WINDOWS\SYSTEM directory only to have an overlooked older version in the \WINDOWS directory load instead of the new one.

8. Edit the SYSTEM.INI file (located in the \WINDOWS directory) using a text editor. Add the following entries or, if entries already exist for these parameters, make sure that the values match those given here:

```
[boot]
network.drv=netware.drv
[386Enh]
network=*vnetbios,vnetware.386,vipx.386
TimerCriticalSection=10000
```

9. Edit the `load=` line under the `[windows]` section of WIN.INI (in the \WINDOWS directory) to include NWPOPUP.EXE. If no other programs are listed for loading, you end up with the following:

```
load=NWPOPUP.EXE
```

If other programs are listed for loading by Windows, leave them there; add NWPOPUP.EXE at the end, resulting in something like the following:

```
load=SCHED.EXE,NWPOPUP.EXE
```

10. If you are upgrading a shared network installation of Windows, make sure that no users are running Windows before you start the upgrade and that none can start Windows while you perform the upgrade. If they do, their workstation may open VIPX.386, for example, and you can't overwrite it with the new version. This could result in a partial upgrade in which some files are updated and others are not—a situation that could leave you worse off than when you started.

11. Refer to the "Backups" section earlier in this chapter and make sure you have taken all necessary precautions before proceeding.

What you do next depends on the version of Windows you are running, the mode in which it runs, and whether you are using the NetWare shell or the DOS requester. The following sections explain what to do in each case.

All Windows Installations. In all cases, copy the following files to the Windows SYSTEM directory:

WINDR3\NWPOPUP.EXE

WINDR3\VXDS\VIPX.386

WINDR3\VXDS\VNETWARE.386

NWDLL2\NWDLL\NWCALLS.DLL

NWDLL2\NWDLL\NWIPXSPX.DLL

NWDLL2\NWDLL\NWLOCALE.DLL

NWDLL2\NWDLL\NWNET.DLL

NWDLL2\NWDLL\NWPSRV.DLL

On Personal NetWare systems, also copy NWDLL2\NWDLL\PNW.DLL to the Windows System directory.

If any of the files NETAPI.DLL, NWNETAPI.DLL, or NWPSERV.DLL exist in the workstation's Windows or Windows System directory, copy the corresponding files from the OLDDLLS directory of the NWDLL2 distribution set.

NetWare Shell. If the workstation uses the NetWare shell (NETX.EXE), make sure you have copied NETWARE.DRV and its accompanying Help file NETWARE.HLP, from the NET33X distribution set to the Windows System directory.

NetWare DOS Requester.

> ### Caution
>
> Version 1.19 of VIPX.386, as distributed in WINDR3.EXE, requires version 2.12 or higher of LSL.COM and version 3.01 or higher of IPXODI.COM. These are distributed in VLMUP4.EXE. Refer to the previous VLM upgrade instructions, and make sure that these files are at the appropriate revision level before carrying out the Windows upgrade.

If the workstation uses the NetWare DOS requester (VLM.EXE), copy the following files to the Windows SYSTEM directory:

NWDLL2\NWDLL\NWGDI.DLL

WINDR3\VLMDRVS\NETWARE.DRV

WINDR3\VLMDRVS\NETWARE.HLP

WINDR3\VLMDRVS\NWUSER.EXE

Create a program icon for NWUSER.EXE if one does not already exist. If an icon already exists, check that it points to the new NWUSER.EXE that you have just installed.

Create a subdirectory called NLS of the WINDOWS directory if it doesn't already exist. Copy the following files into it:

WINDR3\VLMDRVS\1252_UNI.001

WINDR3\VLMDRVS\437_UNI.001

WINDR3\VLMDRVS\850_UNI.001

WINDR3\VLMDRVS\UNI_1252.001

WINDR3\VLMDRVS\UNI_437.001

WINDR3\VLMDRVS\UNI_850.001

WINDR3\VLMDRVS\UNI_COL.001

WINDR3\VLMDRVS\UNI_MON.001

The DOS requester allows drive mappings in DOS sessions under Windows to be either global or private. If mappings are global, a change in drive mappings in one DOS session affects all other DOS Windows, too. Private mappings allow each DOS session to maintain separate mappings. Mappings are private by default; to change them to global, add the following line to the [NetWare] section of SYSTEM.INI:

```
NWShareHandles=TRUE
```

Migrating from NETX to VLM

The NetWare DOS requester offers many advantages over the NetWare shell. The modular architecture allows you to load only those components that you need; the intelligent, automatic memory optimization features can be overridden using NET.CFG entries; and the switch from a shell to a redirector gives you a networking environment that interacts more smoothly with the operating system. The features of the NetWare DOS requester are covered in more detail in chapter 8, "Novell NetWare."

The fundamental architectural and conceptual differences between the shell and requester mean that migrating from NETX to VLM is not seamless. This part of the chapter deals with the issues you have to confront when migrating.

Installing the VLM Upgrade. The installation itself is quite straightforward:

> **Note**
>
> The following upgrade procedure assumes that the workstation is working correctly using the NetWare shell, NETX.EXE. If not, refer to "Installing the VLM Client" earlier in this chapter and perform a full installation from scratch.

1. Get a copy of the latest client distribution kit. At the time of writing, this is VLMUP4.EXE.

2. Create an expanded distribution set from VLMUP4.EXE. Create a new directory for the purpose, change to the new directory, and run the self-extracting archive from there. VLMUP4 expands its files into the following directories:

   (top level)
   ODIDRV
   VLMS

3. Create a new network client software directory (for example, \NWCLIENT) on the workstation. It is best to leave the NETX setup in place until you are satisfied that the VLM setup is working properly.

4. Copy the MLID for your adapter and your NET.CFG file from the old (NETX) client directory to your new (VLM) directory.

5. Make sure you have the most recent LSL and IPXODI programs by copying the following files to the new directory. Copy the version in the VLMS directory of the expanded distribution set, unless the version in the old NETX directory happens to be more recent:

   LSL.COM
   LSL.MSG
   IPXODI.COM
   IPXODI.MSG

6. Copy VLM.EXE and *.VLM from the VLMS directory of the expanded distribution set to the new client directory.

7. Edit AUTOEXEC.BAT (or whatever batch file loads the network drivers) to load LSL, IPXODI, and so on, from the new client directory, and to load VLM instead of NETX.

8. Reboot the workstation and test the connection!

Note that this is a minimal DOS upgrade. Refer to the other sections in this chapter on Windows, user environment, and tuning to complete the upgrade.

Windows Changes. Refer to the "Windows Network Files" section earlier in this chapter. Upgrade the workstation according to those instructions, making sure in particular that:

■ NETWARE.DRV is version 3.03 or later—the old version that worked with NETX does not suffice with VLM.

■ NWGDI.EXE has been copied to the Windows SYSTEM directory.

■ Any stray older network files in the WINDOWS directory have been removed.

User Environment Changes. The architectural differences between NETX and VLM result in a number of changes from the user's point of view, as discussed in detail in chapter 8, "Novell NetWare." Follow these steps to make the transition from shell to requester as smooth as possible:

1. Add the line

   ```
   LASTDRIVE = Z
   ```

   to the workstation's CONFIG.SYS. The NetWare shell uses drive letters beginning after the last DOS drive; the requester uses driver letters up to and including the last DOS drive. Adding this line allows the requester to use the same range of drive letters as the shell used.

2. The FILES parameter in the workstation's CONFIG.SYS limits the number of files that DOS can have open at one time. NETX handles network file requests without involving DOS' file handling mechanism, so the FILES parameter applies only to local files. The requester is different—it allows DOS to handle all files, local and network. This means that the FILES parameter must be increased to account for network files as well as local files.

   Increase the number of DOS file handles by editing the FILES line in CONFIG.SYS. If there is no such line there, add one:

   ```
   FILES = 100
   ```

How big a value should you use? You can easily duplicate the NETX limit under VLM by adding together the DOS and network file handle limits. Suppose for example that CONFIG.SYS specified FILES=30 and the NET.CFG or SHELL.CFG had no File Handles line. This means that NETX was maintaining the default of 40 file handles, giving a total of 70 file handles in all. Changing the FILES value in CONFIG.SYS from 30 to 70 gives the same maximum file limit as before.

This may be a good time to review the file limit. In most cases, a value of 100 or so is appropriate, particularly if the workstation runs Windows. The amount of memory required per file handle is about 60 bytes, so increasing the FILES value from 30 to 100 uses an additional 4K of RAM. Bear in mind that this memory cost will be more than compensated for by the substantial improvements in memory you get by switching from NETX to VLM.

3. Create a NetWare DOS Requester section in the workstation's NET.CFG file.

4. Force the first network drive to be the same as it was under NETX by adding the following line to NET.CFG's NetWare DOS Requester section:

```
First Network Drive = F
```

If the first network drive letter under NETX was not F, substitute the appropriate letter here.

This change is required because NETX uses the first drive letter after the last DOS drive as the first network drive; VLM uses the first available DOS drive letter. Users accustomed to using F: as the logon drive may be confused if it suddenly appears as drive D:.

5. The first network drive is mapped to a server's logon area when the workstation establishes a connection. VLM performs a root mapping, while NETX does not. This difference is due to the fact that DOS cannot cope with a subdirectory (\LOGIN) of a drive when the root is not accessible. The result is that the prompt at the first network drive changes from something like

```
F:\LOGIN>
```

to

```
F:\>
```

Alert users to this change. Also, check any batch files that may have referred explicitly to F:\LOGIN and use F:\ instead. If that is not possible—if both NETX and VLM workstations will use these batch files—try using F: without a path. This should work whether the drive is root mapped or not.

Note that these steps are designed to make the transition from NETX to VLM as smooth as possible for the user. It may be more appropriate to use the default VLM configuration, particularly in the case of experienced users. The "NET.CFG" section later in this chapter describes how to take full advantage of the flexibility of the DOS requester by using appropriate entries in the `NetWare DOS Requester` section of NET.CFG.

Migrating from SHELL.CFG to NET.CFG. The NET.CFG file stores configuration information for a number of network components, including LSL, IPX, and other protocol-specific drivers and either the NetWare shell or DOS requester. Entries in the various sections (called "options") of NET.CFG override the default behavior of the relevant program.

Before the introduction of ODI, the configuration information for the NetWare shell was stored in a file called SHELL.CFG in the root directory of the workstation's boot disk. This section explains how to migrate the entries in an existing SHELL.CFG file to NET.CFG, retaining the configuration settings in the SHELL.CFG.

> **Note**
>
> If there is no SHELL.CFG file on the workstation that you are upgrading, this section does not apply.

If the workstation has a SHELL.CFG file, review the entries in it and decide which, if any, are still necessary. For each entry that you decide to keep, copy the relevant line in SHELL.CFG to the appropriate section of NET.CFG. Table 11.4 lists the possible SHELL.CFG entries and the corresponding NET.CFG options.

Table 11.4   SHELL.CFG Parameters and NET.CFG

SHELL.CFG Parameter	NET.CFG Option
ALL SERVERS	(Obsolete)
CACHE BUFFERS	NetWare DOS requester
CONFIG OPTION	(Obsolete)
ENTRY STACK SIZE	(Obsolete)
EOJ	NetWare DOS requester
FILE HANDLES	(Obsolete)
HOLD	(Obsolete)
INT64	Protocol IPX
INT7A	Protocol IPX
IPATCH	Protocol IPX
IPX PACKET SIZE LIMIT	Protocol IPX
IPX RETRY COUNT	Protocol IPX
IPX SOCKETS	Protocol IPX
LOCAL PRINTERS	NetWare DOS requester
LOCK DELAY	NetWare DOS requester
LOCK RETRIES	NetWare DOS requester

SHELL.CFG Parameter	**NET.CFG Option**
LONG MACHINE TYPE	NetWare DOS requester
MAX CUR DIR LENGTH	(Obsolete)
MAX PATH LENGTH	(Obsolete)
MAX TASKS	NetWare DOS requester
NETBIOS ABORT TIMEOUT	NetBIOS
NETBIOS BROADCAST COUNT	NetBIOS
NETBIOS BROADCAST DELAY	NetBIOS
NETBIOS COMMANDS	NetBIOS
NETBIOS INTERNET	NetBIOS
NETBIOS LISTEN TIMEOUT	NetBIOS
NETBIOS RECEIVE BUFFERS	NetBIOS
NETBIOS RETRY COUNT	NetBIOS
NETBIOS RETRY DELAY	NetBIOS
NETBIOS SEND BUFFERS	NetBIOS
NETBIOS SESSIONS	NetBIOS
NETBIOS VERIFY TIMEOUT	NetBIOS
NPATCH	NetBIOS
PATCH	(Obsolete)
PREFERRED SERVER	NetWare DOS requester
PRINT HEADER	NetWare DOS requester
PRINT TAIL	NetWare DOS requester
READ ONLY COMPATIBILITY	NetWare DOS requester
SEARCH MODE	NetWare DOS requester
SET STATION TIME	NetWare DOS requester
SHARE	(Obsolete)
SHORT MACHINE TYPE	NetWare DOS requester
SHOW DOTS	NetWare DOS requester
SPECIAL UPPERCASE	(Obsolete)
SPX ABORT TIMEOUT	Protocol SPX
SPX CONNECTIONS	Protocol SPX
SPX LISTEN TIMEOUT	Protocol SPX
SPX VERIFY TIMEOUT	Protocol SPX
TASK MODE	(Obsolete)

So for example, to migrate a SHELL.CFG consisting of just two lines:

```
LOCAL PRINTERS = 0
FILE HANDLES = 30
```

Add the LOCAL PRINTERS = 0 line to the NetWare DOS Requester section of NET.CFG, and then delete the SHELL.CFG file.

Additional Protocols

One of the greatest strengths of the ODI system is the ease with which a workstation can be configured to handle new protocols. A NetWare client that uses only IPX may have a `Link Driver` section something like this:

```
Link driver NE2000
      Int   3
      Mem   C8000
      Port 300
      Frame Ethernet_II
      Protocol IPX     8137 Ethernet_II
```

The MLID can be instructed to handle IP packets too, by adding a line here that tells the MLID which protocol ID is used by IP when using Ethernet II frames. This example is for Beame & Whiteside's TCP/IP package—note that their ETHDEV.SYS driver program requires a protocol of its own:

```
Link driver NE2000
      Int   3
      Mem   C8000
      Port 300
      Frame Ethernet_II
      Protocol IPX     8137 Ethernet_II
      Protocol ETHDEV 0    Ethernet_II
      Protocol IP      0800 Ethernet_II
      Protocol ARP     0806 Ethernet_II
```

Refer to table 11.6 for a list of some of the more common protocol ID values.

Of course, this by itself just tells the MLID how to handle IP packets, not how to send them or what to do with them if any should arrive! To make use of IP, the workstation also needs to load an IP protocol driver such as Novell's TCPIP.EXE.

DOS Upgrades

Workstations may require a few changes in the network software configuration after a DOS upgrade. Other adjustments, while not absolutely necessary, may allow you to take advantage of the new DOS version. This section describes what to look out for after a DOS upgrade.

NETX and DOS Versions. Upgrading DOS used to mean upgrading to a new NET*.COM. NET3.COM was designed to work with DOS 3.x, so if a workstation was upgraded to version 4 of DOS, it needed a copy of NET4.COM. This is no longer the case, but a certain degree of sensitivity to DOS versions remains on workstations that are using the NetWare shell.

When NETX starts to load, it asks DOS for its version number. If the number returned by DOS is outside the range that NETX considers acceptable, NETX refuses to load, reporting an error:

```
SHELL-332-29: Shell requires DOS v3.X through v6.X.
The NetWare shell is not loaded
```

So, a version of NETX that has been running without difficulty on a workstation may suddenly refuse to load after a DOS upgrade.

You can persuade NETX to load in such circumstances by using the DOS SETVER utility. First, make sure SETVER is loaded in the workstation's CONFIG.SYS. Look for a line like this on the form:

```
DEVICEHIGH=C:\DOS\SETVER.EXE
```

If no such line is present, add one (substituting the appropriate DOS path). Then tell SETVER to lie to NETX.EXE about the DOS version:

```
C:\> SETVER NETX.EXE 6.0
```

and reboot the machine for this change to take effect. From now on, when DOS receives a query from NETX.EXE to return its version number, it returns 6.0, regardless of the DOS version that is really running. NETX should then load without complaint.

NET.CFG Parameters

The NET.CFG file can hold entries to control almost every aspect of networking on a workstation. This section looks at the possible entries, their parameters, and the reasons why you might use each of them.

NET.CFG Location and Layout

By default, LSL.COM looks for NET.CFG in the directory from which LSL.COM was loaded. If NET.CFG is not found there, then LSL.COM looks in the current working directory. You can override this search mechanism by specifying a path for NET.CFG using LSL's /C parameter, as in the following example:

```
LSL /C=C:\NWCLIENT\NET.CFG
```

The NET.CFG file has a simple structure. Edit it using a text editor, in accordance with the following guidelines:

- NET.CFG is laid out in sections known as *options*.

- Each option has a heading that is flush with the left margin.

- The individual parameters that apply to the option are listed, one per line, under the option heading.

- Parameter lines must be indented at least one space from the left margin—indent one tab space for clarity.

- Comment lines begin with a semicolon. A semicolon at the start of a parameter line disables that parameter line; a semicolon at the start of an option heading line disables the entire section.

- Include as many blank lines and comment lines as you want—these make the file easier to read. It's a good idea to insert comments to remind yourself later why you chose a particular parameter value.

NET.CFG entries fall into a number of categories:

- Link Driver

- Link Support

- Protocol IPX

- NetWare DOS requester

The following sections look at these categories in detail.

Link Driver

Entries in the Link Driver section of NET.CFG specify parameters related to the MLID. If your workstation has more than one network adapter, you can enter more than one Link Driver section. The section heading is of the form

```
Link Driver <MLID>
```

where <MLID> is the name of the adapter's ODI driver.

> **Note**
>
> The driver name required on the heading line is the internal name of the MLID. This usually, but not always, is the name of the executable file. If you're using an MLID named EWRK3.COM, the name to use in the section heading is probably EWRK3.
>
> Run the MLID with the /? command-line option to see the internal MLID name.

The Link Driver section can contain both hardware and software settings. Strictly speaking, you only need to enter a hardware setting if the setting on the workstation's adapter is different from the default value assumed by the MLID. The defaults, however, might change between versions of the MLID. In practice, it makes sense to enter all the settings here rather than rely on the MLID to provide the default values you want.

You can specify more than one value for some of the hardware options (MEM, PORT, INT, and DMA). For example, a board might use two I/O port address ranges. If so, specify the second value using the #2 qualifier, as in the following example:

```
PORT #2 300
```

You can specify the first value with or without using the #1 qualifier. Any value given is assumed to be the first value unless you stipulate otherwise.

Table 11.5 lists the available Link Driver entries.

Entry	Parameters	Purpose
DMA	Channel	Specify DMA channel used by adapter
FRAME	Type	Enable a frame type on the adapter
INT	IRQ	Specify interrupt used by adapter
MEM	Start [Length]	Specify adapter's shared RAM area
PORT	Start [Number]	Specify adapter's I/O port
PROTOCOL	Name ID Frame	Define a protocol to the adapter
SLOT	Number	Specify adapter slot

Table 11.5 NET.CFG: Link Driver Entries

The Link Driver entries are explained in turn below.

DMA. If the adapter uses a DMA channel, specify the channel number here, as in the following example:

```
Link Driver WLAN40
    DMA 2
```

FRAME. An ODI driver can handle several frame types at once. To do this, the MLID sets up a logical board for each frame type on each adapter. Frames of one type on a particular adapter are treated as if they come from a specific logical board; frames of another type on the same adapter are treated as if they come from a different logical board.

In the Link Driver section, insert one FRAME entry for each frame type that will be handled by the adapter. The following are valid Ethernet frame types:

- Ethernet_802.2 (Default)

- Ethernet_802.3

- Ethernet_II

- Ethernet_SNAP

Here's an example of how to specify the frame type:

```
Link Driver WLAN40
    FRAME Ethernet_802.3
    FRAME Ethernet_II
```

INT. With INT you specify the interrupt channel used by the adapter. You must get this right or your client is unable to use the network!

Here's an example of a valid INT entry:

```
Link Driver WLAN40
    INT 5
```

MEM. If the adapter uses a shared RAM area, enter the start address in hexadecimal following MEM. You also can specify the length (again, in hexadecimal), but this usually is unnecessary—the adapter just uses what it needs. Use the X= parameter on the EMM386 line in CONFIG.SYS to reserve the necessary memory for the adapter.

Here's an example of a valid MEM entry:

```
Link Driver WLAN40
    MEM D0000
```

PORT. With PORT, you specify (in hexadecimal) the I/O port used by the adapter. You also can specify the number of ports to reserve, but that usually is unnecessary.

Here's an example of a valid PORT entry:

```
Link Driver WLAN40
    PORT 280
```

PROTOCOL. You must specify each protocol that is to be handled by the adapter. This means adding a PROTOCOL entry for each protocol to the adapter's Link Driver section of NET.CFG. Each PROTOCOL entry must specify the following:

- Protocol name
- Protocol ID
- Frame type

The protocol ID is a hexadecimal number that has been assigned to identify a protocol and frame type combination. For example, IPX using Ethernet_802.3 frames has ID 0, and IPX using Ethernet_II frames has ID 8137.

Table 11.6 lists some common frame types and the corresponding protocol IDs.

Table 11.6   Protocol IDs

Protocol	Frame Type	Protocol ID
IPX	Ethernet_802.2	E0
IPX	Ethernet_802.3	00
IPX	Ethernet_II	8137
IPX	Ethernet_SNAP	8137
IPX	Token-Ring	E0
IP	Ethernet_II	800
IP	Ethernet_SNAP	800
AppleTalk	Ethernet_II	809B

Here's an example that contains two valid PROTOCOL entries:

```
Link Driver WLAN40
    PROTOCOL IP 800 Ethernet_II
    PROTOCOL IPX E0 Ethernet_802.2
```

SLOT. EISA and MicroChannel bus machines generally can locate the slot holding the adapter card by scanning all slots. Use this option to force the machine to use a given slot.

The use of SLOT is very straightforward, as shown in the following example:

```
SLOT 5
```

Link Support

The Link Support section of NET.CFG contains settings related to buffers and stacks used by the network software. Table 11.7 lists the valid Link Support entries.

Entry	Parameters	Purpose
Table 11.7 NET.CFG: Link Support Entries		
BUFFERS	Number [Size]	Specify LSL receive buffers
MAX BOARDS	Number	Specify maximum logical boards
MAX STACKS	Number	Specify maximum logical protocol stack IDs
MEMPOOL	Number	Specify size of LSL memory pool buffers

The Link Support entries are explained in turn.

BUFFERS. Use the BUFFERS setting to override the default of zero buffers maintained by the LSL. Some protocol stacks require the LSL to maintain *receive buffers*. IPX does not—it maintains its own buffers. The default size is 1,130 bytes; you can override this by specifying the size as a second parameter on the BUFFERS line, as in the following example:

```
Link Support
    BUFFERS 8 1564
```

This instructs the LSL to maintain eight buffers of 1,564 bytes each. The memory hit is easily calculated—in this case, it is 8×1,564 bytes, or just over 12K.

Increasing the number of buffers might help to improve performance on workstations that make many connections. The optimal buffer size is close to the largest packet size that will be received by the workstation.

Do not allow the total buffer space to exceed 59K. The buffers are allocated from the same 64K segment as the MEMPOOL and some of the LSL program code.

MAX BOARDS. The LSL can handle up to 16 logical adapters. The default number of logical adapters is four, which means that the number of adapter/frame type combinations cannot exceed four unless this value is increased. A single adapter using four frame types, therefore, works with the default setting, but adding a second adapter with four frame types means having to increase this value to eight, as in the following example:

```
Link Support
    MAX BOARDS 8
```

The memory hit for allowing the LSL to handle extra logical boards is fairly low, about 200 bytes per logical board. Similarly, the memory saved by reducing the maximum logical boards is roughly 200 bytes per board.

MAX STACKS. The LSL can maintain up to 16 logical protocol stack IDs. The default is four. If you need to define more than four protocol IDs (using PROTOCOL lines in the Link Driver sections), use a value greater than four, as in the following example:

```
Link Support
     MAX STACKS 8
```

You can save a tiny amount of memory by limiting the maximum number of stacks to the number actually in use.

MEMPOOL. Some protocols require that the LSL maintain memory buffers of a particular size. Use the MEMPOOL option to set this value:

```
Link Support
     MEMPOOL 2K
```

IPXODI does not use MEMPOOL.

Protocol IPX

Some of the IPX protocol's default parameter values can be changed, although this rarely is necessary. Table 11.8 lists the valid Protocol IPX entries.

Table 11.8   NET.CFG: Protocol IPX Entries

Entry	Parameters	Purpose
BIND	Board	Force bind to specific board
INT64	on/off	Stop IPX using Int 64
INT7A	on/off	Stop IPX using Int 7A
IPX PACKET SIZE LIMIT	Number	Set maximum packet size used
IPX RETRY COUNT	Number	Tell SPX how often to resend
IPX SOCKETS	Number	Set maximum IPX sockets maintained

The Protocol IPX entries are explained in turn.

BIND. Protocols usually bind to the first MLID they find. The BIND option can be used to force a protocol to bind to a specific MLID. For example, to force IP to bind to the EWRK3 driver, use the following:

```
Protocol IPX
     BIND EWRK3
```

If you have loaded multiple drivers, differentiate between them by specifying the driver number, as well:

```
Protocol IPX
     BIND EWRK3 #2
```

INT64. Some applications may need to use interrupt 64h, which ordinarily is used by NetWare. Set the INT64 parameter to off to avoid such clashes:

```
Protocol IPX
        INT64 off
```

INT7A. Some applications might need to use interrupt 7Ah, which ordinarily is used by NetWare. Set the INT7A parameter to off to avoid such clashes:

```
Protocol IPX
        INT7A off
```

IPX PACKET SIZE LIMIT. IPX packets can vary in size, up to 6,500 bytes. Some MLIDs insist on a smaller limit; in fact, you may want to set the limit lower if the client workstation is running into memory allocation trouble. The default limit is 4,160 bytes unless the MLID specifies a smaller value. The minimum size limit is 576 bytes.

To set a value of 1,500 bytes, for example, use the following:

```
Protocol IPX
        IPX PACKET SIZE LIMIT 1500
```

IPX RETRY COUNT. IPX does not resend packets, but SPX does if it gets no response. The IPX RETRY COUNT option is used to tell SPX how many times it should try sending a packet.

The default value is 20 times. Increasing this to 40 might be necessary on a network that drops a lot of packets. You can cause such an increase with the following entry:

```
Protocol IPX
        IPX RETRY COUNT 40
```

IPX SOCKETS. IPX normally maintains 20 sockets on the workstation. Some programs that use IPX directly might require more sockets than this. You can increase the value by using the IPX SOCKETS option as follows:

```
Protocol IPX
        IPX SOCKETS 50
```

NetWare DOS Requester

VLM.EXE uses the same NET.CFG file as LSL.COM. The NetWare DOS Requester section of NET.CFG controls many aspects of the operation of VLM.EXE and the individual VLMs (see table 11.9). Careful attention to this section can help to tune workstation performance, memory use, and the user environment.

> **Note**
>
> NetWare DOS Requester entries in NET.CFG use an equal sign (=) between the name of the option and the value that it takes. This differs from the entries in the NET.CFG sections described earlier.

Table 11.9 NET.CFG: NetWare DOS Requester Entries

Entry	Default	Parameters	VLMs Affected
AUTO LARGE TABLE =	ON	ON/OFF	AUTO
AUTO RECONNECT =	OFF	ON/OFF	AUTO, NDS
AUTO RETRY =	0	Number	AUTO
AVERAGE NAME LENGTH =	48	Number	CONN
BIND RECONNECT =	OFF	ON/OFF	AUTO, BIND
CACHE BUFFER SIZE =	—	Number	FIO
CACHE BUFFERS =	5	Number	FIO
CACHE WRITES =	ON	ON/OFF	FIO
CHECKSUM =	1	Number	IPXNCP, NWP
CONFIRM CRITICAL ERROR ACTION =	ON	ON/OFF	—
CONNECTIONS =	8	Number	AUTO, CONN, FIO, NDS, SECURITY
DOS NAME =	MSDOS	Name	GENERAL, NETX
EOJ =	ON	ON/OFF	NETX, REDIR
EXCLUDE VLM =	—	VLMs	—
FIRST NETWORK DRIVE =	—	Letter	GENERAL, NETX
FORCE FIRST NETWORK DRIVE =	OFF	ON/OFF	GENERAL
LARGE INTERNET PACKETS =	ON	ON/OFF	IPXNCP, NWP
LIP START SIZE =	0	Number	IPXNCP, NWP
LOAD CONN TABLE LOW =	OFF	ON/OFF	CONN
LOAD LOW CONN =	ON	ON/OFF	CONN
LOAD LOW FIO =	OFF	ON/OFF	FIO
LOAD LOW IPXNCP =	ON	ON/OFF	IPXNCP
LOAD LOW NETX =	OFF	ON/OFF	NETX
LOAD LOW REDIR =	OFF	ON/OFF	REDIR
LOCAL PRINTERS =	3	Number	PRINT
LONG MACHINE TYPE =	IBM_PC	Name	GENERAL, NETX
MAX TASKS =	31	Number	CONN
MESSAGE LEVEL =	1	Number	—
MESSAGE TIMEOUT =	0	Number	NWP
MINIMUM TIME TO NET =	—	Number	—
NAME CONTEXT =	—	Name	NDS
NETWARE PROTOCOL =	—	List	—
NETWORK PRINTERS =	3	Number	PRINT
PB BUFFERS =	1	Number	FIO, IPXNCP
PREFERRED SERVER =	—	Name	BIND
PREFERRED TREE =	—	Name	NDS
PRINT BUFFER SIZE =	64	Number	PRINT
PRINT HEADER =	64	Number	PRINT

Entry	Default	Parameters	VLMs Affected
PRINT TAIL =	16	Number	PRINT
READ ONLY COMPATIBILITY =	OFF	ON/OFF	REDIR
SET STATION TIME =	ON	ON/OFF	—
SHORT MACHINE TYPE =	IBM	Name	GENERAL, NETX
SHOW DOTS =	OFF	ON/OFF	REDIR
SIGNATURE LEVEL =	1	Number	NWP, SECURITY
USE DEFAULTS =	ON	ON/OFF	—
VLM =	—	Path	—

The NetWare DOS Requester entries are explained in the following sections.

AUTO LARGE TABLE. AUTO.VLM tries to restore network connections that have been lost. To do this, it must store username and password information for each connection established. It normally uses just 34 bytes to store this information. If the length of the username and password combined is likely to be greater than 32 characters (that's 34 characters, including the terminators), then you need to tell AUTO.VLM to reserve more space for the reconnection information.

For example, the entry

```
AUTO LARGE TABLE = ON
```

tells AUTO.VLM to use 178 bytes per connection rather than the default 34 bytes per connection.

For this parameter to have any effect, AUTO.VLM must be loaded and BIND RECONNECT must be set to ON. For NDS reconnections, RSA.VLM also must be loaded.

AUTO RECONNECT. As explained in the preceding section, AUTO.VLM attempts to re-establish network connections in the event of a lost connection. You can turn off this behavior if you want to:

```
AUTO RECONNECT = OFF
```

If this option is used, AUTO.VLM fails to load. Removing AUTO.VLM from the list of VLMs to be loaded has the same effect as setting AUTO RECONNECT = OFF.

AUTO RETRY. As explained earlier, AUTO.VLM attempts to reestablish network connections in the event of a lost connection. The AUTO RETRY option tells AUTO.VLM how many seconds to wait before attempting to reestablish a connection. The default behavior is for AUTO.VLM to try to reconnect as soon as a critical network error message occurs. You can tell it to wait a longer time before retrying; to do so, use a line such as the following:

```
AUTO RETRY = 10
```

This tells AUTO.VLM to wait 10 seconds before retrying the connection.

For this parameter to have any effect, AUTO.VLM must be loaded. For NDS reconnections, RSA.VLM also must be loaded.

> **Caution**
>
> The entry AUTO RETRY = 0 is regarded by AUTO.VLM as an instruction to not reconnect at all. This obviously is not the same as AUTO.VLM waiting the default of 0 seconds before retrying.

AVERAGE NAME LENGTH. CONN.VLM stores server names in a table that has a fixed size when VLM.EXE loads. It allows a default of 48 characters per server name, for the number of servers specified using the CONNECTIONS setting. You can tell CONN.VLM to use less memory for its connection table by setting AVERAGE NAME LENGTH to a value smaller than the default. For example,

    AVERAGE NAME LENGTH = 8

saves 40 characters per allowed connection. If the maximum number of connections is the default (eight), then a total of 320 bytes of memory are saved by making this change.

> **Note**
>
> The name lengths referred to here include a terminating character. Thus, specifying an AVERAGE NAME LENGTH of 8 only allows for an average of seven characters per file server name.

BIND RECONNECT. AUTO.VLM normally tries to reestablish lost network connections without restoring any drive mappings and printer connections that were lost when the connection was broken.

    BIND RECONNECT = ON

tells AUTO.VLM to attempt to restore the drive mappings and printer connections that were in effect before the connection was dropped. This makes for a more stable environment.

For this parameter to have any effect, AUTO.VLM must be loaded and AUTO RECONNECT must be set to ON.

CACHE BUFFER SIZE. FIO.VLM uses memory buffers to cache data being read from or written to network files. This can significantly increase I/O performance. Files that are flagged Shareable or Transactional are not included; the file may be in use on the server while the workstation is still using its cached copy.

The default buffer size is 64 bytes less than the maximum packet size for the network media—if your network uses Ethernet, then the buffer size defaults to 1,436 bytes. Increasing this value uses more memory but can enhance workstation performance.

Valid buffer sizes are from 64 bytes to 4,096 bytes. For example, the line

```
CACHE BUFFER SIZE = 4096
```

should increase performance, but at a cost of 2,660 bytes.

Caution

Don't set CACHE BUFFER SIZE to be greater than the maximum packet size that can be handled by the workstation's adapter. Check your adapter documentation before deciding on a setting.

CACHE BUFFERS. As explained above concerning CACHE BUFFER SIZE, FIO.VLM uses memory buffers to cache network file reads and writes. It uses one buffer per cached file. The number of buffers created at VLM load time defaults to five, and can be set to any number between zero and 64.

Remember that the maximum number of files that the workstation can have open is set using the FILES= statement in CONFIG.SYS. Large numbers of cache buffers might not make sense if they approach the FILES setting: There is no point in setting aside 40 cache buffers if the workstation can only have 30 files open at a time. Keep the number of cache buffers at least five below the FILES= setting in CONFIG.SYS.

Consider the following example:

```
CACHE BUFFERS = 20
```

This allows 15 files more than the default to be cached. Assuming the default cache buffer size for Ethernet of 1,436 bytes, this enhanced caching uses an additional 21,540 bytes (roughly 21K) of memory. The increase in performance should be significant, especially if the workstation is doing a lot of sequential reading from or writing to files on the network.

Tip

If you carry out workstation-based backups of your server, increase the number and size of cache buffers on the backup workstation.

CACHE WRITES. *Write caching*—storing data in a local cache before sending it over the network—is a useful trick for increasing efficiency and boosting performance. So is *read caching*, where data is read from the server and transmitted over the network in one big chunk before being stored in the workstation's cache. There is, however, a major difference between the two in terms of robustness.

If read caching is in operation and the server goes down, there is no data loss. Whatever was in the workstation's cache is still there; assuming the server is unharmed, the data is still stored on its disk. The same cannot be said of write caching. If an application on a workstation writes data to a cache, there is an assumption that the cache will be written to disk at some stage in the near future. If the server goes down before the contents of the cache are written to disk, then the data probably is irretrievably lost.

This is similar to having SmartDrive perform write caching on a local hard disk. If you save data from an application to a cached file, and then power off the machine before SmartDrive has a chance to commit the data to disk, the data is lost.

FIO.VLM implements write caching as well as read caching by default. You can turn write caching off by using the following line:

```
CACHE WRITES = OFF
```

This way, you lack the performance benefits of buffered writes to the server but also reduce the risk of losing data between the cache and the server. Unless you absolutely need the higher write speed, protect your data by turning cache writes off.

CHECKSUM. IPX packets can carry a checksum that allows the recipient to verify that they were received as they were transmitted. This feature improves data integrity but adds some performance overhead because the checksums must be calculated by both sender and recipient.

By default, IPXNCP.VLM only uses checksums when the recipient insists on them. You can alter this behavior by changing the CHECKSUM setting, using the following possible values:

0	Don't do checksums
1	Do checksums if the recipient insists
2	Do checksums if the recipient can do them
3	Insist on checksums

For example, the line

```
CHECKSUM = 2
```

gets the workstation to use IPX checksums as much as possible without actually refusing to talk to stations that do not support it.

CONFIRM CRITICAL ERROR ACTION. Windows responds to many critical network errors either quietly or by displaying a dialog box with the message Cannot read from device network. The user then selects Cancel or Retry. If the user selects Cancel, VLM attempts to rebuild the lost connection.

By default, VLM displays a dialog box before it tries to recover lost connections. This dialog box shows the name of the server affected and asks the user to confirm that she wants to reconnect. The line

```
CONFIRM CRITICAL ERROR ACTION = OFF
```

turns off these dialog boxes. Windows then responds to critical errors itself, without awaiting confirmation from the user.

CONNECTIONS. CONN.VLM maintains just eight connections by default. You can change that to as few as two or as many as 50. Increasing the value costs memory, as explained in the earlier discussion of AVERAGE NAME LENGTH. Here's an example of a valid CONNECTIONS entry:

```
CONNECTIONS = 10
```

This allows two connections more than the default.

DOS NAME. Workstations that run DOS from the server need a search mapping to the DOS drive. This can be set up in the logon script using the %OS variable. VLM automatically detects MS DOS and DR DOS; if you want to override its automatic detection, or if you're using another OS, use DOS NAME. For example, the line

```
DOS NAME = MSDOS
```

forces the replacement of %OS with MSDOS in the logon script.

EOJ. Some applications close all files and locks that they have used, by issuing a special DOS interrupt that issues *End of Job (EOJ)* commands. An EOJ command sent to the server closes any files that the application has had open. The simple line

```
EOJ = OFF
```

tells the workstation not to send EOJ commands to the file server.

EXCLUDE VLM. VLM.EXE loads the VLMs listed later (see the "USE DEFAULTS" section) unless they are not in the VLM directory or are explicitly excluded using EXCLUDE VLM. For example, the line

```
EXCLUDE VLM PRINT.VLM
```

tells VLM.EXE not to load support for printer redirection.

FIRST NETWORK DRIVE. When the workstation establishes its initial connection to a file server, it maps the first available drive letter to the logon area on the server, unless told otherwise. A workstation with a hard disk (drive C) and no drive letters in use after that gets drive D as its first network drive.

You can override this by using FIRST NETWORK DRIVE.

```
FIRST NETWORK DRIVE = F
```

forces VLM to map F to the logon area rather than D. Drive D is still available for mapping.

FORCE FIRST NETWORK DRIVE. If your default drive when you log off from a server is a network drive, then the drive letter it uses is remapped to SYS:LOGIN. Thus, if your current directory is R:DATA when you issue the LOGOUT command, it changes to R:\, which then is mapped to SYS:LOGIN.

More consistent behavior is produced by using the following setting:

```
FORCE FIRST NETWORK DRIVE = ON
```

This way, when you log off from a network drive, that drive mapping is lost, the first network drive used when the initial connection was made is remapped to SYS:LOGIN, and that drive becomes your default drive. For example, if your current directory is R:DATA when you issue the LOGOUT command, and F was your first network drive, then your current directory changes to F:\, which is mapped to SYS:LOGIN.

LARGE INTERNET PACKETS. NetWare packets crossing bridges or routers used to be limited to 576 bytes. Ethernet and Token Ring both can handle much larger packets than this, so in most cases you can allow a workstation and server to communicate across bridges and routers using the maximum packet size negotiated by them for local area communications.

If you experience difficulty passing larger packets across a bridge or router, you can restrict the internetwork packet size to 576 bytes by using the following line:

```
LARGE INTERNET PACKETS = OFF
```

LIP START SIZE. The client and server negotiate a maximum packet size when they first make contact. The size they finally agree on depends upon a number of factors, including network topology. The negotiation process can take a noticeable amount of time if the link is very slow.

If you know in advance what the size is likely to be, then you can speed up the negotiations a bit by using a line like the following:

```
LIP START SIZE = 12000
```

This example tells the workstation to begin internetwork packet size negotiations at 12,000 characters. Novell reports that, in some cases, specifying a suitable LIP START SIZE parameter can reduce the amount of negotiation traffic from 60K to approximately 3K. This can mean a significant speedup in establishing a connection over a slow link.

LOAD CONN TABLE LOW. The connection table usually is loaded into an upper memory block, if one is available. You can force VLM.EXE to load the connection table in conventional memory by using the following option:

```
LOAD CONN TABLE LOW = ON
```

LOAD LOW CONN/FIO/IPXNCP/NETX/REDIR. VLM.EXE normally loads CONN.VLM and IPXNCP.VLM into conventional memory and FIO.VLM, NETX.VLM, and REDIR.VLM into upper memory, if suitable upper memory blocks are available at VLM load time. You can override this behavior in all cases by using the following option:

```
LOAD LOW CONN = OFF
```

This forces VLM.EXE to attempt to load CONN.VLM into upper memory.

You need to do a certain amount of experimentation with these VLMs to see which combination of low and high loading gives the best combination of performance and memory use for your needs. The optimum depends on your requirements as well as on the workstation hardware and memory configuration.

> **Tip**
>
> Load REDIR.VLM into conventional memory unless you absolutely cannot spare the conventional memory. The performance gain from loading REDIR low is significant.

LOCAL PRINTERS. The BIOS assumes that there is a printer attached to each parallel port, unless told otherwise. You can use LOCAL PRINTERS to tell it otherwise:

```
LOCAL PRINTERS = 0
```

This really doesn't have much to do with NetWare. It was introduced to SHELL.CFG—a precursor of NET.CFG that was used by older versions of NETX—as a convenient way to stop workstations from hanging if the Shift+PrintScreen key combination was pressed when no printer was attached.

LONG MACHINE TYPE. You might need to refer to the machine type in the system logon script using the %MACHINE variable. Use this option to force the VLM to give a particular response when the machine type is queried. For example, the line

```
LONG MACHINE TYPE = COMPAQ
```

forces the replacement of %MACHINE with COMPAQ in the logon script.

MAX TASKS. CONN.VLM needs to keep track of each task running in a multitasking or task-switching environment such as Windows. CONN.VLM allocates space for a fixed number of tasks at VLM load time (the default is 31). Increase or decrease this number to any value from 5 through 254 by using MAX TASKS. For example, the line

```
MAX TASKS = 100
```

forces CONN.VLM to allocate enough memory and handles to keep track of as many as 100 tasks.

MESSAGE LEVEL. In keeping with the general emphasis on customizability, VLM.EXE can be either very verbose or very quiet about what it is doing when it loads VLMs. The levels of verbosity are selected through MESSAGE LEVEL as follows:

0	Display copyright information and report critical errors
1	Level 0 and display warning messages (this is the default)
2	Level 1 and display VLM program load information
3	Level 2 and display configuration information
4	Level 3 and display diagnostic information

You might want to turn up the level while debugging the VLMs by using a line such as the following:

```
MESSAGE LEVEL = 4
```

MESSAGE TIMEOUT. Messages displayed on-screen usually stay there until the user presses Ctrl+Enter (DOS) or clicks OK (Windows). You can specify a time interval after which messages are automatically cleared from the screen. The time is expressed in CPU ticks, up to a maximum of 10,000 ticks. For example, the line

```
MESSAGE TIMEOUT = 1000
```

establishes that any messages still on-screen a minute or so after they first appeared will be cleared.

MINIMUM TIME TO NET. A router may decide on a timeout value for connections on the basis of local area conditions. This value might be inappropriate for wide area connections where the connection would take considerably longer. If, for example, a user is dialing in to a network using a slow modem and then traversing a bridge or router to get to a server, you might need to specify a relatively large time to allow them to establish their connection. For example, the line

```
MINIMUM TIME TO NET = 3000
```

gives the user three seconds (3,000 milliseconds) to establish the connection.

NAME CONTEXT. You can specify your starting point in the directory tree when connecting to a NetWare 4 network. Here's an example:

```
NAME CONTEXT = "OU=home.O=groceries"
```

The quotation marks are required to facilitate parsing the name.

NETWARE PROTOCOL. VLM.EXE by default loads NDS.VLM, BIND.VLM, and PNW.VLM—in that order. If any of these files are absent from the VLM directory, or if they explicitly have been excluded from loading using the EXCLUDE VLM option, then the others are loaded.

You can change the combination of NetWare protocols used by VLM or the sequence in which they are loaded, using NETWARE PROTOCOL. For example, the line

```
NETWARE PROTOCOL Bind, NDS
```

tells VLM.EXE to load the Bindery mode protocol first and then the NDS protocol. Personal NetWare is not loaded.

> **Note**
>
> If NETWARE PROTOCOL is used, it must appear as the first line in the NetWare DOS Requester section of NET.CFG.

NETWORK PRINTERS. NetWare by default allows you to capture three printer ports. You can capture as many as nine by using a line such as the following:

```
NETWORK PRINTERS = 9
```

There is, however, a slight increase in memory use if you do so.

You can also turn off printer redirection, with the following line:

```
NETWORK PRINTERS = 0
```

This prevents PRINT.VLM from loading.

PB BUFFERS. The DOS requester uses packet burst to transmit data on the network in efficient, large chunks. You can turn off this behavior, with the following line:

```
PB BUFFERS = 0
```

This might result, however, in a significant decrease in workstation performance.

All non-zero values on this line have the same effect—packet burst is enabled. The number of buffers and their size are set using CACHE BUFFERS and CACHE BUFFER SIZE as described earlier.

PREFERRED SERVER. VLM using the NetWare Bindery protocol attaches to the first server to respond to a GET NEAREST SERVER request, unless it is told to attach to a specific server. For example, the line

```
PREFERRED SERVER = INDIE
```

tells BIND.VLM to try to attach to INDIE when it loads. If INDIE has a free connection slot, then the workstation attaches to it; if not, the workstation attaches to the first server to respond to a GET NEAREST SERVER request.

> **Note**
>
> PREFERRED SERVER has no effect if PREFERRED TREE is also specified *and* NDS establishes its connection first.

PREFERRED TREE. VLM using the NetWare Directory Services protocol attaches to the nearest tree that contains a user object for the user who is attaching. For example, the line

```
PREFERRED TREE = DISTRIB
```

tells NDS.VLM to try to attach to DISTRIB when it loads. If DISTRIB has a server with a free connection slot, then the workstation attaches to it; if not, the workstation attaches to the nearest tree that contains a user object for the user who is attaching.

> **Note**
>
> PREFERRED TREE has no effect if PREFERRED SERVER is also specified *and* BIND establishes its connection first.

PRINT BUFFER SIZE. Some applications print one byte at a time, leading to slow print throughput. VLM maintains a print buffer to improve the efficiency of such printing. The default buffer size is 64 bytes, but you can set this to any size from 0 through 255 bytes. A line such as

```
PRINT BUFFER SIZE = 100
```

provides only a tiny amount of extra memory, but this can give a noticeable improvement in printing speed.

PRINT HEADER/TAIL. Print header information is stored in a buffer that has a default size of 64 bytes. If you generate printouts with large headers—due to specifying a lot of print options, font changes, or the like—then 64 bytes might not be enough, and the printer might not initialize as you instruct it to. In such cases, you should increase the print buffer size, using a line like the following:

```
PRINT HEADER 512
```

The maximum size for the print header is 1,024 bytes.

The same theory applies to the print tail, which can contain instructions for the printer to reinitialize or eject a page after the job has been printed. If the behavior is not what you instructed, try increasing the print tail buffer size from its default of 16 bytes:

```
PRINT TAIL 256
```

The maximum print tail size is also 1,024 bytes.

READ ONLY COMPATIBILITY. When an application opens a file, it signals to DOS whether it is opening the file for reading, writing, or both. Some applications insist on opening files for writing when they do not actually need to write to them. This is not a problem on a stand-alone machine where the user generally has write access to all files but can cause problems with applications run from a server. On a server, the user probably doesn't have write access to application files and doesn't really need to write anything to the files, but an application might still try to open them for writing.

Whether the application succeeds in opening the files in write mode (without write access) depends on the network client software on the workstation. Older versions of the NetWare shell allowed the application to open the files for writing. Attempting to actually write to the files caused an error. More recent versions of NETX are compatible with DOS in that they do not allow a read-only file to be opened for writing.

You can tell the requester to use either approach with such applications. The default behavior is to be strict and disallow opening read-only files with write access. The following line causes the requester to allow such unorthodox accesses:

```
READ ONLY COMPATIBILITY = ON
```

SET STATION TIME. The workstation sets its time to the server's time when it makes its initial attachment. That's all very well if your server has a radio clock and is accurate to a fraction of a second; if it isn't, your users might complain about the time on their workstations being incorrect. The following line tells VLM.EXE not to synchronize the workstation time with the server:

```
SET STATION TIME = OFF
```

SHORT MACHINE TYPE. Novell uses a series of machine type-specific overlay files for its standard menu-based utilities. It loads IBM$RUN.OVL for certain purposes on IBM machines and CPQ$RUN.OVL for the same purposes on Compaq machines.

Even if VLM cannot identify your machine type, you can force the issue. For example, the following line identifies your workstation as being an IBM PC or compatible:

```
SHORT MACHINE TYPE = IBM
```

SHOW DOTS. DOS has directory entries for the current and parent directories (. and .. respectively). NetWare does not have these entries by default but can display them in directory listings if you use the following line:

```
SHOW DOTS = ON
```

> **Tip**
>
> Turning the dots on makes it much easier to use Windows file and directory dialog boxes.

SIGNATURE LEVEL. You can trade performance for security by using *packet signatures*. The packet signature options are

0	Don't sign packets
1	Sign packets if the server insists
2	Sign packets if the server can deal with signed packets
3	Sign all packets and insist on signed packets

Depending on the level of security selected, workstations and servers can be limited to reading only the packets that are addressed to them. The following line configures your workstation for the highest level of security:

```
SIGNATURE LEVEL = 3
```

> **Note**
>
> To use packet signatures, network servers must also be configured for an appropriate level of security. This is done using SET commands from the file server console.

USE DEFAULTS. If you want to override the default VLM load order (see the following section), you can do so using the VLM= option. If you do so, and if you specify the names of any of the standard VLMs listed in the following section, use the following command to avoid error messages about attempting to load VLMs twice:

```
USE DEFAULTS = NO
```

VLM. The default load order for VLMs is as follows:

1. CONN.VLM

2. IPXNCP.VLM

3. TRAN.VLM

4. SECURITY.VLM

5. NDS.VLM

6. BIND.VLM

7. NWP.VLM

8. FIO.VLM

9. GENERAL.VLM

10. REDIR.VLM

11. PRINT.VLM

12. NETX.VLM

If you want to load a VLM that is not in this list, you must force VLM.EXE to load it. Here's an example of the VLM= line that does this:

```
VLM=C:\NWCLIENT\AUTO.VLM
```

You can specify as many as 50 VLMs to load here, but each must be specified on a separate line, with its own VLM= statement. All VLMs listed in this manner are loaded after the defaults. If you want to modify the load order of the default VLMs, you must disable the default load and specify each VLM individually—in the order that you want them to load.

Summary

As the years have passed, the NetWare clients have become increasingly complex, but they are also far more flexible now—and more easily configured, as well. Their primary burden on the workstation, which is their use of conventional memory, has been eased by the improved memory handling capabilities of the VLM requester and by the modularization of the client into several pieces, which can be more easily shoehorned into small upper memory areas.

Performance has improved, as well. You can configure the client to suit the needs of your network by trading off speed for security, if necessary, or by eliminating unneeded VLM modules from the requester. Novell has a version of its Client32 currently in development for the DOS/Windows workstation, which will probably replace the VLM client before long; however, considering the age of the NetWare operating system, the number of revisions undergone by the client seems, in hindsight, to be remarkably few.

Chapter 12

Network Client Software for 32-Bit Windows

At its outset, the Microsoft Windows NT product was positioned as a client/server platform to challenge the overwhelming market share held by Novell NetWare. As NT matured through several revisions, however, Microsoft's viewpoint evolved, and it was recognized that the trend in networking was toward the mixing of different NOS and client platforms into unified networks. The current stance taken by Microsoft is that its intention is to produce a server NOS that can be addressed by any type of client platform, and to produce clients that can attach to any type of server.

With a few notable exceptions, Microsoft has come very close to achieving this goal. Support for networking has been assimilated into the Windows NT workstation and Windows 95 operating systems to a greater degree than it has been in DOS, OS/2, Banyan, or most other major network client OSs. The actual task of installing and configuring the network client support in the 32-bit Windows OSs is so simple that it barely needs to be mentioned. Clients, protocols, and services are selected from pick lists, and all the adjustable parameters are presented in a simple, unified interface that is light-years beyond the multiple TSRs and ASCII configuration files used for traditional OS client installations.

The area in which difficulties arise is the abundance of client choices that are available to the network administrator for each OS. There are several different methods, provided by different vendors, through which Windows 95 and NT workstations can access the services provided by each NOS on the network, and assessments of the users' needs and the resources available must be made to determine the best possible configuration. This chapter will cover the various alternative client services available for Windows NT and Windows 95 workstations. In the process, there will be discussion concerning some of the NOS features that are designed to facilitate various client services, as well as the different methods by which these client OSs can be installed using the network as a source medium.

At the bottom line, therefore, this chapter is more about arriving at an ideal client configuration than it is a guide through the process of connecting a single workstation to multiple NOSs. That task has, happily, become a rather simple one. To use the most common configuration as an example, a Windows 95 workstation can be made to access an NT server and a NetWare server simultaneously, with very little intervention from the installer of the OS. Most common NICs are auto-detected, along with their hardware settings. Protocols can be selected with a few mouse clicks and maybe the specification of a frame type. Even the installation of TCP/IP support can be quick and automatic.

The selection of which client to use, however, must be based on the overall design of the network and the services required by individual users. In many cases, you find that a single client operating system and network interface selection is not suitable for every user in a given enterprise. The combination of different network types in today's hetero-geneous environments is, by definition, intended to accommodate the needs of a widely divergent pool of users, and the versatility provided by the various network client soft-ware interfaces for these operating systems allows network administrators to cater the workstation to their, and the users', individual needs.

Windows NT

Like all of the Microsoft OSs designed with integrated networking, Windows NT can function as either a peer-to-peer or a client/server network. Indeed, in earlier releases, the differences between the NT Advanced Server and Workstation products were few, and the OSs were almost indistinguishable. This situation has changed with the release of NT Server, version 3.5—and more so with version 3.51—but the non-dedicated functionality of the server product still remains. This means that resources can be located all over the LAN. A printer need not be associated with a machine dedicated as a server; it can be attached to any NT machine and access granted to all users by making it a shared re-source. The same holds true for hard disk storage. Remote access to any Windows NT drive on the LAN can be granted to users by using passwords for each drive or assigning rights to user accounts.

The native network requester that provides a Windows NT machine access to other NT (or Windows for Workgroups or Windows 95) machines is fully integrated in the NT operating system for both servers and clients. As noted above, the installation process is simple, routinely accomplishing many of the tasks that must be performed manually during a NetWare 3.1x server or client installation. For its own networking, Windows uses a set of protocols based on several accepted industry standards. Figure 12.1 illus-trates the correlation of the protocols to the standard OSI reference model.

For the physical layer, Windows networks utilize the standard Ethernet and token-ring cabling systems documented in the IEEE 802 committee family of standards; however, the similarity to NetWare networks ends there. At the data link layer, NIC drivers written to the NDIS 3.0 or 3.1 standards must be used. The *Network Device Interface Specification* is a standard developed jointly by Novell and 3Com beginning in 1989. It defines a layer linking the functionality of the adapter driver in the media access control (MAC) sublayer and the transport protocols operating at the network and transport layers. (See chapter 3, "The OSI Model: Bringing Order to Chaos," for more on these concepts.) Much like the logical link control (LLC) sublayer defined in the IEEE 802.2 standard,

NDIS can provide unified access to several different protocol stacks at one time. Most NICs in production today include an NDIS driver along with the MLID driver needed for NetWare and whatever other drivers might be needed for other network types.

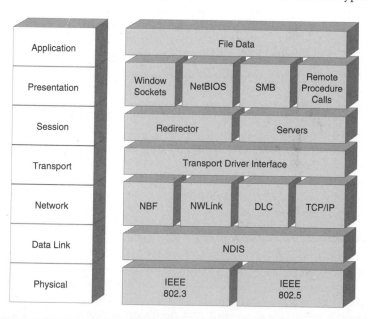

Figure 12.1

The networking protocols used by Windows NT in relation to the OSI reference model.

Atop the NDIS interface, Windows NT provides support for several different protocol stacks, any or all of which can be running at the same time:

- *NetBEUI Frame (NBF)* Derived from the NetBEUI protocol, NBF provides access to other Windows NT, Windows for Workgroups, and Windows 95 workstations, as well as to LAN Manager, LAN Server, and MS Net installations. This is the default protocol for Windows networks, just as IPX/SPX is in NetWare.

- *NWLink* An NDIS-compliant version of the NetWare IPX/SPX protocol, NWLink can be used to connect to other Windows Network clients, as well as to any other NetWare client via upper-level protocols such as NetBIOS, Windows Sockets, or Remote Procedure Calls (RPCs). Not capable of providing file system access to NetWare clients, this protocol is used primarily for connections to Windows NT server-based applications, such as Microsoft SQL Server.

- *Microsoft Data Link Control (DLC)* DLC provides access to mainframes and networked printers.

- *TCP/IP* The standard routable WAN protocol, TCP/IP is also used to provide UNIX and Internet connectivity.

Knowledge of these protocols is useful to the personnel responsible for installing and configuring these network clients. On a Windows NT workstation, installing an additional protocol is as simple as picking one from a list and then providing the OS with access to the appropriate NT installation files. Many administrators who are unfamiliar with the usefulness of the protocols that ship with Windows NT tend to install more of them than are necessary—sometimes even all of them—since the process is so easy. Doing this can slow down the operation of the workstation and the network significantly and should be avoided. Learn what the function of each installed protocol is, and only install those that are actually needed. Others can always be added later.

Above the transport protocol stacks is another buffering layer called the *Transport Device Interface* (*TDI*). This functions much like the NDIS layer, providing unified transport protocol access to the protocols functioning at the session layer and above. Just above the TDI will be any requesters installed on the system (in NT parlance, these often are referred to as *redirectors*), as well as various server application processes. It is the TDI that receives the network access requests from the redirectors and channels them to the appropriate transport protocol stack.

The server processes are the means by which distributed applications (that is, applications that split their processing functionality between client and server computers) enable communications between the client and the server. Among these can be NetBIOS, Windows Sockets, and the System Message Block (SMB) protocols. The latter, designed jointly by Microsoft, IBM, and Intel, is the protocol most commonly used by Windows NT at this layer. It is used for requesting files from servers and delivering them to clients, filling much the same role that the NetWare Core Protocol (NCP) does in NetWare networks.

Thus, a basic file access request using the standard Windows NT protocols (see fig. 12.2) begins as an SMB message, generated by the originating workstation application's API call, which is channeled through the redirector (that is, the native Microsoft client) to the TDI, which sends it as an NBF down to the NDIS interface, which directs it to the NIC driver, and then to the network interface itself, and onto the network medium. Arriving at the server, of course, the process is essentially reversed, with the data traveling up the stack to the server NOS application, which then responds in much the same way.

Client Services for Microsoft Networks

The native client services for Windows NT provide access to a network of other systems running Windows NT Workstation or Advanced Server, Windows for Workgroups, or Windows 95. They can also connect to LAN Manager servers and remain compatible with the original MSNet OS. The functionality of a Microsoft network connection is essentially the same, whether it is achieved using peer-to-peer or client/server access. The original Windows NT releases contained few differences between server and workstation, and although their feature sets have since been modified to accentuate the differences between the two, any Windows NT machine can share drives and resources with any other. Even a machine configured as a server can be used to access drives on other Windows machines in the same way that a workstation does.

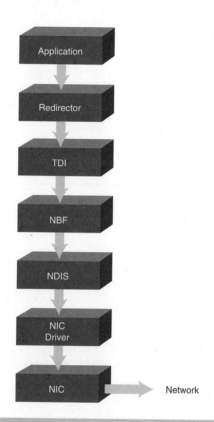

Figure 12.2

The path of communications through the Windows NT protocol stack.

Installing the Microsoft client services on Windows NT consists of procedures that are fundamentally the same as those performed on the configuration of a NetWare server: A LAN adapter driver is installed to directly address the network hardware, then one or more protocols are specified. Driver and protocols are then bound together. A link is thereby established between the physical and data link layers of the OSI model to the session layer and above, by means of the protocol, which occupies the network and transport layers. The theory is the same as in a NetWare network, but where NT excels is in simplifying these tasks so that they can all be accomplished at the same time, using a familiar Windows graphical interface (see fig. 12.3). The Windows NT installation procedure can auto-detect most LAN cards, and even if an older or unsupported card is used, the process is an easy one. Any card for which there is an NDIS driver is usable with Windows NT, and the hardware variables to be configured are, of course, the same as with any NIC installation. The proper settings simply need to be selected from a dialog box, and that part of the procedure is completed.

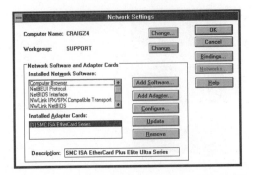

The Network Settings dialog box is where all configuration of the Windows NT networking components takes place.

The default transport protocol for the Windows network, as you learned earlier, is the *NetBEUI Frame* (*NBF*). Selecting any other protocols to be used requires some knowledge of what applications and services are going to be running over the network; bear in mind that additional protocols can be bound to the adapter at a later time by returning to the Network applet in the Control Panel application and modifying the existing configuration. The Bindings button in the Network Settings dialog box provides a visual display of the way in which the various networking components are interconnected (see fig. 12.4). This is particularly useful when multiple LAN adapters and protocols are in use. Up to ten protocols can be bound to any one adapter (though I don't think you can find uses for ten), and multiple adapters, each utilizing multiple protocols if you desire, can be installed onto one machine. Individual bindings can also be enabled and disabled at will, without uninstalling the support files associated with the protocols and adapters, providing a convenient troubleshooting tool for networking problems.

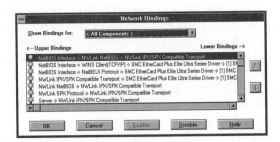

In the Windows NT Network Bindings dialog box, clients can be associated with specific protocols.

In many cases, this is the end of the procedure. Restart the machine, and as long as no error messages appear, support for the Windows network is loaded and operational. Access to specific network resources can then be provided in several different ways, some of which are utterly transparent to the user and others of which require additional configuration. Client/server applications usually operate using one or more of the additional upper-layer protocols mentioned in earlier sections, like Windows Sockets, SMBs, or NetBIOS. In these instances, access to the server portion of the application is automatically provided when the client is installed and executed. For file and printer access, Windows NT can map drive letters to specific network resources, just as in NetWare. This procedure, too, has been greatly simplified by the use of the Windows GUI, in the form of a Map Network Drives window that is functionally similar to the one in Windows for Workgroups or Windows 95.

For a drive or printer on any Windows network computer to be accessible to other users, it must first be *shared* by the user on the host machine. (These resources often are referred to simply as *shares*.) Sharing a drive or printer is the process of selecting an object, giving it a name by which it will be known to the network, and establishing security to control access to it from the network. Again, this process can be performed on every networked machine, forming a peer-to-peer network, or only on the drives of certain machines designated as servers, for a client/server network. Whether a particular machine is running the Windows NT workstation or server product is irrelevant, in this respect. Both OSs can share drives and printers and attach to other shares on the network.

Opening the Share As dialog box in File Manager after selecting a drive or directory on a local machine provides the means by which shares are configured for network access. This dialog box prompts the user for a name to identify the share, which may or may not reflect the name of the actual drive or directory. A field for descriptive comments is also provided to help to identify the contents or usefulness of the shared drive. Network users thus can be given access to specific machine resources without them being able to ascertain the actual volume or directory where the files reside.

The Permissions dialog box, accessible from the File Manager's Security menu, allows the owner of the machine to specify which users have access to the resource and the level of access that they are to be granted. The security provisions available in Windows NT are extensive and can be made to function in a manner similar to those of NetWare. User accounts must be created on the host machine, and rights to the shared resources can be controlled if you want to limit users to read-only or another specific type of access. The number of users able to access any particular drive can also be controlled here, protecting performance from degradation based on too many simultaneous accesses.

One of the most immediately perceptible differences between Microsoft and Novell networking is the syntax by which network resources are identified. To those familiar with the traditional NetWare canonical notation, which uses the *SERVER/ VOLUME:DIRECTORY/FILE* syntax, the Uniform Naming Convention (UNC) used by Microsoft networks is basically a different means of expressing the same networking hierarchy. Volume names are replaced by share names, which need not represent an entire subdivision of a server. Let's consider the UNC name:

`\\SERVER\SHARE\SUBDIRECTORY\FILENAME`

SHARE can represent the root of an entire drive or partition or a single directory on a particular drive, providing access to all the files and subdirectories contained within it.

Any other directories on the drive that are not included as part of the share are completely invisible to network users, unless they are shared in a similar manner. It should be noted that *SERVER* here refers to any machine on the Windows network that has been configured to share any of its resources with other machines. A computer running any network-capable Windows OS can be considered a server, in this respect.

To gain access to a shared drive, directory, or printer, the Connect Network Drive dialog box (see fig. 12.5) is accessed through Windows NT's File Manager. Here, a drive letter is chosen for the mapping, and a browser allows the user to select from all the shares visible on the network. The browser presents an inverted tree-style display, with a root object labeled `Microsoft Windows Network`. Stemming from the root are all the workgroups and domains containing Windows machines that have been recognized by the network, whether they have been configured to share resources or not.

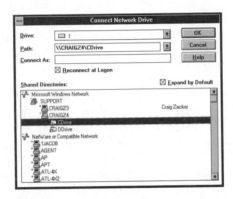

Figure 12.5

In the Windows NT Connect Network Drive dialog box, you can assign drive letters to network shares.

Every computer on a Microsoft Windows network belongs either to a workgroup or a domain (even if it is a workgroup consisting only of one machine). Both are logical groupings of computers that allow administrators to organize the computers on the network according to department, location, or any other criteria desired and to provide for the security measures that safeguard the network's resources. Workgroup and domain names, as well as the names of the machines themselves, are created by the user or administrator when the OS is installed or when a domain or workgroup is created. A *workgroup* is a collection of computers, each of which maintains its own security system. A machine running Windows for Workgroups, for example, can password-protect its shares, allowing network users either read-only or read/write access, depending on the password provided. The Windows NT Workstation OS, however, contains considerably more elaborate security features. User accounts and groups can be created and configured to provide a much greater degree of access control to its shares. Even so, every machine must be individually configured with appropriate accounts for all the users on the network.

This is the inherent drawback of a peer-to-peer network when it grows beyond a handful of computers. Imagine an administrator of a large network having to sit down at every machine on the LAN to create an account every time a new employee joins the company. It is for this reason that the Windows NT Advanced Server (NTAS) product was given the capability to establish *domains*—that is, groups of computers for which the user account information is stored on one machine, known as the *primary domain controller* (*PDC*). Replicas of the user account databases can be stored on other NTAS machines, for fault tolerance purposes. A network user logs on to a domain and immediately receives access to all the network resources allotted to him that are contained within it. This obviously is more in keeping with the client/server networking model.

Despite their differences, however, workgroups and domains behave identically within the tree display of the Map Network Drives browser. Each can be expanded to show all the machines within that workgroup or domain, and each machine can be expanded to show all the shares that it makes available to other users. Differences in functionality between workgroups and domains might arise when actually attempting to map a drive to a shared resource. A domain user that has already been granted access to the share will see the drive mapping take effect immediately, but in a workgroup, users might have to supply passwords before each individual share is mapped. Once a share is mapped to a specific drive letter, that drive appears in File Manager and in every Windows drive letter pick list. It can be accessed, and its contents manipulated, just as if it were a local resource (assuming sufficient access rights are provided). If the Reconnect at Logon option is enabled, then the access passwords provided are saved to an encrypted file on the local machine, and this drive mapping will be restored each time that computer is started. Unless access is interrupted at the source, this is a permanently available resource for that user.

Printers are shared and mapped in much the same way, except that you use the Print Manager application. The same naming convention shown above can apply to a printer as well as a drive or directory. There are no subdirectory or file specifiers needed, so the syntax is as follows (*SHARE* is the name given to the printer when the local user shares it):

```
\\SERVER\SHARE
```

As a result of these features, Microsoft networks contain a great degree of flexibility in terms of user interaction with the network. Domain user accounts and logon scripts can virtually duplicate the functionality of NetWare, if desired, mapping all of a user's network drives and printers and providing a ready-to-work environment. A greater capacity for self-configuration of network access is also available, however, within the Windows GUI environment. Unlike NetWare networks, in which users are restricted to accessing dedicated file servers over the network, users of a Windows network can quickly and easily share files on their local drives with other users. This is where the term *workgroup computing* really makes sense. Network users in an organization frequently work closely together in teams, sharing and developing the same resources, and the mixture of peer-to-peer and client/server functionality provided by Windows NT and the other Windows NOSs is ideal for this sort of interaction.

Connecting to Novell NetWare Networks

As we have seen, creating a Microsoft-only network is a relatively simple matter. The vast majority of networks containing Windows NT workstations, however, also have one or more NetWare servers on them, and the NT users nearly always require access to some of the resources provided by NetWare. Many installations position Windows NT Advanced Server as an application server platform, leaving the basic file and print services to NetWare. This means that NetWare resources may be accessed by the NT server, as well. Therefore, for Windows NT to be fully assimilated into a heterogeneous network, both as a server and as a workstation OS, support in two directions must be provided: NetWare server access to Windows NT clients, and NT server access to NetWare clients. This can be accomplished in different ways, based on several important factors, the most significant of which is the state of the professional relationship between Microsoft and Novell.

These two software giants, while clearly competitors in the networking field, are forced by reasons of practicality to work together to some degree. After all, the vast majority of NetWare clients are running a Microsoft OS on their workstations, and Microsoft cannot expect to effectively assault NetWare's overwhelming market share by denying that other NOSs exist. The number of Microsoft-only networks that have not been migrated from NetWare is very small indeed. It therefore is agreed by both companies that interoperability between their products must be achieved, but the logistical details, such as who is going to write the client software and when, have been a source of long-standing disagreement.

Microsoft Client Services for NetWare

It originally was assumed that Novell would create the requester for the Windows NT operating system, but when delays, as well as some highly problematic beta versions, appeared, Microsoft undertook the task of designing a NetWare client itself. Windows NT 3.1, therefore, shipped without integrated NetWare support, but one of the most important pieces toward that end, the *NWLink protocol*, was already in place. Providing full 32-bit IPX functionality in the network and transport layers, NWLink was a vital tool needed to provide NetWare connectivity, but by itself, it could not handle the NCP packets that are the primary component of NetWare's client/server traffic. For this, a requester was needed, operating at the session layer and above, which could access NWLink through the TDI.

Microsoft released such a requester as a free, downloadable add-on to the Windows NT 3.1 OS, and beginning with version 3.5, it was included as part of the shipping product. This requester, originally called *NetWare Workstation Compatible Service* (*NWCS*), was very efficient at providing basic functional access to NetWare resources. It operated alongside the native NT client, allowing NetWare drives to be assigned to drive letters just as NT drives could be and providing full access to NetWare-based printers and other resources at performance levels that were virtually indistinguishable from those of the Microsoft network resources.

There were some drawbacks, however. First, it was required that NWCS be run along with the native Microsoft client services, even if both were utilizing the same transport protocol. (Remember that the TDI effectively isolates the requester from the protocol stack.) NWCS could not be used in place of it, thus raising the minimum memory requirement for Windows NT to 16M. This, however, is not nearly as great an issue as it is in the DOS or Windows 3.1 world, in which running additional client software for several networks can mean utilizing large amounts of precious conventional memory for TSR drivers. Windows NT's 32-bit flat memory model allows sufficient memory to be allocated for the additional drivers, as needed. More memory might be required in the machine, but there are no complex memory optimization chores to be performed by the user.

Despite lower official recommendations, 16M should be considered the absolute practical minimum for a Windows NT workstation today. Moreover, the benefits in speed that are realized when memory is increased beyond this point are significant enough to make it well worth the investment. With the release of Windows 95, Windows NT Workstation is coming to be used more often as a workstation OS for power users, due in part to these greater hardware requirements. As with many OSs, greater performance levels can be more readily achieved through the installation of additional RAM than through any other upgrade.

The second major problem with the NWCS requester is that no support is provided for the execution of NetWare logon scripts. This is unfortunate, as it means that any mass migration of workstations to Windows NT requires the individual reconfiguration of drive mappings and other environmental settings into NT logon scripts for each node. Virtually the same functionality can be provided by the NT equivalent script, but the conversion process can be lengthy and problematic. In addition, no support is provided for logging on to the NetWare Directory Services database. This means that not only are the resources provided to a Windows NT user by the NDS limited to those available under bindery emulation, but the NDS configuration utilities, such as CX, NWADMIN, and NETADMIN, cannot run on Windows NT using its native NetWare client. These are serious drawbacks for the network administrator that can (and have) prevented wholesale conversion to Windows NT in many cases. Both are currently being addressed by Novell and Microsoft; this is discussed later in the chapter.

Remote Access Service. Another popular feature built into Windows NT from its inception was the ability to provide remote or mobile users with access to the network through *Remote Access Service (RAS)*. RAS consists of a service that runs on an NT Server (with the appropriate communications hardware) and an RAS graphical phone book that runs on any Windows for Workgroups, Windows 95, or Windows NT workstation. The connection to the remote machine can be made using asynchronous modems, ISDN, or X.25 wide-area links. RAS provides the remote user with complete (albeit slower, in most cases) access to all the same network resources available to a LAN-connected client. It should be understood that RAS provides a true network connection to the remote user. It is not a remote control solution, such as PC/Anywhere or Carbon Copy, in which keyboard, mouse, and display signals are redirected to a remotely located machine. The RAS server's processor is devoted to communications tasks, and any applications accessing network resources from the remote workstation are actually running on the remote workstation's processor.

Users of Windows NT 3.1 were very enthusiastic about the RAS feature, but when the NetWare client became available, they were troubled to discover that the RAS connection could support only SMB traffic. NCP packets could not be relayed in this manner, preventing remote users from accessing NetWare resources. This was considered another major shortcoming of Microsoft's NetWare requester, and the problem was subsequently addressed by the addition of a gateway feature to beta versions of the client that could translate between the SMB and NCP protocols. This allowed the RAS host server to literally become a client of a NetWare server and reshare the NetWare drives and other resources to its own remote clients. Obviously, the translation mechanism entailed some further performance degradation, but access was successfully granted to resources that previously were unavailable.

This feature was subsequently removed from the NWCS client software package and included as part of the Windows NT Advanced Server 3.5 product as the *NetWare Gateway Service*. By doing this, Microsoft took a significant step toward differentiating the NT server and workstation products, but more importantly, it provided this gateway service to all the clients on the network, even those not running a NetWare requester themselves. This can be seen as extremely advantageous, in several different ways. For clients running only Windows network drivers, access to NetWare resources can be provided without the need for reconfiguring the client workstation—allocating more of its memory for the additional client software—or utilizing an additional NetWare server connection. For example, in the case of a standard Windows for Workgroups workstation, only the protected-mode Windows network drivers have to be loaded or configured. There is no need for the NetWare real-mode ODI client software, resulting in significant savings of both conventional memory and the time that would have to be spent configuring the machine for the use of both clients. As far as the NetWare server is concerned, there is only one connection being utilized—that of the NT server, which logs on using a normal account and the regular NWCS client. Dozens or hundreds of NT client users, however, can access the NetWare server through that one NT gateway.

Again, there is a performance hit involved, and it certainly increases as more clients utilize the gateway. Moreover, there is little reason for Windows NT or Windows 95 workstations to use the gateway, when they can so easily install the full client services themselves. For workstations that require only occasional access to NetWare resources, however, this solution is ideal and very economical. NetWare drives and printers appear just as though they were normal shared resources on the NT server, leaving end users unaware that they are even accessing NetWare devices. This can save the cost of additional training for end users and can also be a powerful tool, enabling network administrators to perform a gradual migration from NetWare to Windows NT. The client software on a company's workstations can be converted from NetWare to NT, with both server types remaining active until the process is completed. This is preferable to a mass migration in which all the workstations would have to be reconfigured at once.

Thus, Windows NT's NetWare Gateway and RAS are two elements that help to provide network administrators with a great deal of flexibility in their selection of network client software for their workstations. As with most software products that are in the relatively early stages of development, the aim of the manufacturer is to provide a set of tools to users and then observe how those tools are best utilized in real-world situations. The continued development of tools like these depends on their popularity with users and the additional functionality requested by those users.

Novell NetWare Client for Windows NT. Due in no small part to user requests and despite its late appearance, there is now a 32-bit NetWare client for Windows NT that has been produced by Novell. It is free for downloading from any of Novell's online services and consists of the client software itself, as well as 32-bit versions of RCONSOLE and NWADMIN, the GUI version of the NetWare Directory Services administration program. As the inclusion of NWADMIN implies, this Novell client is now capable of logging users on to the NetWare Directory and providing them with access to all their defined NDS resources, something the Microsoft Client Services for NetWare is not yet capable of doing. Apart from this feature, however (which is surely one of major importance to many users), there are very few persuasive reasons to utilize Novell's client instead of Microsoft's, and there are several good reasons not to.

First, the selection of a NetWare client is very much an either/or situation. If the Microsoft Client Service for NetWare has been previously installed, all vestiges of it must be removed from the system configuration before you install the Novell client, including all NetWare printers, drive mappings, and the Gateway Services for NetWare. The files need not be deleted, but the client service must be removed in the Network dialog box of the Control Panel. Severe problems can result if this is not done, in some cases requiring a complete reinstallation of the OS. There are no such vital concerns, however, when switching from the Novell client to the Microsoft client for NetWare.

Second, Novell has packaged the client files in a manner that provides for a needlessly annoying installation procedure. Considering that the vast majority of the software's users are obtaining it through a download from an online service, it is odd for Novell to require that installation floppies be made. The two self-extracting archive files that are downloaded expand into other archives of the installation files, along with instructions in the form of a Windows HLP file and a utility to make disks, which is the only ready method of extracting the actual installation files from the archives. Network administrators, most of whom are about to install this client on multiple machines, are forced to make a floppy disk set to copy the actual installable software back to their network drives. This is the equivalent of insisting that, if I decide to buy a new Chevrolet, I must walk to the dealership to pick it up, rather than driving my old Ford.

The 32-bit version of the NWADMIN program, which also must be extracted onto floppies, can be installed only through the INSTALL.NLM utility on the NetWare server, which is another odd requirement since the installation procedure does nothing more than copy files to the server drive. Once the files are extracted, the installation of the client proceeds easily enough. Added as a service through the Control Panel in the same manner as the Microsoft client, the Novell software does not call for any unusual configuration procedures. Novell's client can utilize an NDIS driver for the NIC or one of the 32-bit ODI drivers included with the client software. If the Microsoft Windows network client is active, then an NDIS driver has already been installed, which can be used to drive both services simultaneously. Novell recommends the use of an ODI driver, citing increased levels of performance, but admits to including 32-bit ODI support for only a very limited number of network adapters in the current release of its NT client (and many of these are several years outdated). Use of an ODI driver instead of an NDIS one also prevents users from logging on to their Windows NT domains. In addition to this, there was a well-publicized bug in the initial release of the NDS client involving the use of NDIS drivers when attaching to NetWare 3.11 servers. Attempts to access the directory structure on these servers were producing errors in the NT File Manager. A patch was released to address the problem—it, along with other patches, is in an archive named NTC3.EXE, available from the various Novell online services.

After the installation process, the Novell NetWare banner appears whenever the Windows NT system boots, and then a Logon dialog box appears in which the user enters an NDS tree name, a preferred server, and the server context. This is in addition to the standard Windows NT client logon; both must be completed whenever the system is started. No browsing ability is provided for the context, which, unlike Novell's real-mode clients, must be entered in full to log on to the directory. The Novell client adds a NetWare applet to the Control Panel, which displays the server drives to which the workstation is currently attached and allows for the configuration of the standard NetWare printing options, such as the inclusion of a banner page at the beginning and a form feed at the end of each print job.

Once the NWADMIN program has been installed on a NetWare server, a program icon to run it must be manually created on the Windows NT desktop. Once launched, NWADMIN is identical in features and operation to the 16-bit version included with NetWare 4.x, right down to its somewhat sluggish performance. The administration capabilities of NWADMIN, and the access to network resources provided by the Directory logon, comprise the entire NDS functionality of the Novell client. In fact, no support at all for the NetWare API is provided in the Windows NT MS-DOS session. A separate DOS Support program icon is created by the client installation that must be used to open a DOS session that is capable of running NetWare command-line and menu-based utilities such as MAP and PCONSOLE.

What's more, the DOS Support program provides a window that operates as a completely separate network environment from the Windows NT GUI. After launching the program, the user must manually change to the default network drive and log on again. Unlike the main NDS logon, there is support for logon scripts here, but the DOS Support program, oddly enough, is limited to Bindery Emulation mode, and therefore only bindery logon scripts are supported. NDS utilities, such as CX and NETADMIN, cannot run within this interface, and the user is limited to accessing only the resources in the current server context. In addition, no drive mappings or other network settings are carried over from the main NT session, nor are any settings that are modified while in the DOS Support program propagated back to the rest of the OS. Overall, this seems like a thrown-together system, more of a stopgap workaround than a full release. The client does not provide a convenient environment for NetWare administration tasks, which is the main reason why anyone would choose it over the Microsoft Client for NetWare.

One interesting benefit in the DOS Support program is that, due to its complete isolation from the rest of the NT environment, it is possible to log on to two different servers and execute different logon scripts by opening two separate DOS Support windows. On a network such as mine, which is divided into separate Production and R&D domains, with a single server providing routing between the two, it is possible to log on to a gateway server for each domain, providing access to both at the same time, a trick that could not be accomplished with any other client, on any OS. This is not a typical working situation, though, and it certainly was not enough of a benefit to persuade me to leave the Novell client on a production NT machine. Perhaps the most telling assessment of the client is that I could not get it off my systems soon enough for my taste—a process which, incidentally, led me eventually to reinstall the OS, rather than troubleshoot a series of system peculiarities that might or might not have been directly related to the Novell client.

As far as access to NetWare resources through the standard Windows NT interface is concerned, the Novell client behaves in much the same way as the Microsoft version. Drives are mapped within File Manager through the regular Map Network Drives dialog box, and printers can be attached either through Print Manager or from the NetWare applet in the Control Panel (which provides for capturing LPT ports). An expandable NetWare Directory Services tree entry is provided in the Print and File Manager browsers, along with a NetWare Servers listing, from which objects can be selected for access. Printers outside of the current context, however, cannot be seen. The context must be changed through File Manager or the Network applet to provide access to outside printers.

The Network applet is also the place where many of the client settings that normally would be included in a DOS/Windows workstation's NET.CFG file can be adjusted. This is done by selecting the various components of the NetWare client and clicking the Configure button. For example, under Novell NetWare IPX/SPX Transport, the Frame Type, SPX connections, retries, and Watchdog settings can be modified. The Preferred Tree, context, and burst mode settings can be altered by configuring the NetWare Client Services entry.

Although NetWare drive mappings made with File Manager are retained across Windows NT sessions, just as those of the Microsoft client are, there is no provision for the processing of NetWare logon scripts during the main NDS logon. NT's user profile scripts can emulate some of the NetWare logon script functions, including the mapping of drives (with the NET USE command) and network search drives can be permanently established by adding them to the system environment path in the System applet of the Control Panel, but this does not avoid the fact that individual environments must be configured at each workstation, just as though a network is being built from scratch. Any large-scale migration to Windows NT workstations on a NetWare network would, therefore, not be facilitated in any way by the use of this client. Also, no support is presently included for the Windows NT RAS feature, although this is promised for a later release. Remote network users are limited to accessing only Windows resources when they attach to a Windows NT server running this NetWare client.

Thus, in general, the Novell NetWare Client for Windows NT offers little to recommend it to the average user. Its overall performance is perceptibly slower than that of the Microsoft Client for NetWare, and several significant bugs have been registered by users and addressed by Novell in various patch releases. Even the NetWare administration capabilities that one would expect to see, due to the inclusion of NWADMIN, are severely limited. Until these issues are addressed and complete support for the entire collection of NetWare utilities is provided, there still will be a need for a Windows 3.1 workstation on a NetWare administrator's desk. In that case, it probably is preferable to enjoy the increased performance and unified NetWare API support that the Microsoft NetWare Client provides to the Windows NT environment.

Appearing more than a year later than the Microsoft version, this initial release of the Novell client was a major disappointment to a great many Windows NT and NetWare Directory Services users. Hopefully, improvements in both stability and capabilities will be realized in the near future. Novell promises to include global NDS support in future releases, as well as support for NetWare Connect and the Packet Signature security options. In the meantime, however, Microsoft has announced its intention to develop its own NDS-compatible NetWare Client for Windows NT. Few companies outside of Novell have yet proven themselves capable of writing software that fully supports the NetWare Directory. Indeed, even Novell appears to be having trouble in this respect. But if, as we shall see later in this chapter, Microsoft is capable of writing Windows client software that can execute NetWare logon scripts, while Novell seemingly cannot, then perhaps Microsoft is up to the task.

File and Print Services for NetWare. In the same way that Microsoft's Gateway Services for NetWare provides Windows network users with access to NetWare resources, a product named *File and Print Services for NetWare (FPSN)*, soon to be released by Microsoft as an add-on, allows NetWare workstations to gain transparent access to Windows NT resources. FPSN accomplishes this by making a Windows NT server appear to NetWare workstations just as though it is a NetWare 3.12 server on the network. NetWare users can see the server with the SLIST command and log on to it just as though it were a NetWare server, gaining access to its shared drives and printers within the native context of their workstation environment. Like the Gateway Services, this is an extremely valuable tool for a network that is undergoing a gradual migration between NOSs. NT servers can be added to an existing NetWare network and accessed without the need to reconfigure all the workstations to use two different clients.

It must be stressed, however, that as the name implies, this product only provides users with access to Windows NT file systems and print queues in the context of a NetWare server. It is not a means to run NLMs or other NetWare services on a Windows NT machine. FPSN does, however, allow NetWare client workstations access to any other Windows NT application services that may be running on the server. In addition, they can be given access either to NetWare-compatible printers on the network or to printers connected locally to the Windows NT machine.

For a network site that is switching from NetWare to Windows NT as its primary NOS, the combination of FPSN and the Migration Tool for NetWare, which ships as part of the NT Advanced Server product, allows for a simplified migration of NetWare file systems, user and group accounts, security, and permissions to a Windows NT machine. The Migration Tool can replicate NetWare files, directories, binderies, and logon scripts to a Windows NT server with complete safety. A "pre-flight" feature allows for the creation of a log that details the exact changes that will be made by the process before it is actually performed. Of course, this is not possible when a single computer is going to be migrated from NetWare to Windows NT. The process must be performed on two separate machines, the original NetWare server and a Windows NT machine with enough disk space to hold the entire contents of the NetWare server volumes to be migrated.

Once the migration has been performed, the installation of FPSN creates a directory named \SYSVOL on the Windows NT server that simulates the actual directory structure of a NetWare SYS: volume. This directory, therefore, contains \PUBLIC, \SYSTEM, \LOGIN, and \MAIL directories, and utilities are furnished with the product that precisely simulate the performance of their familiar NetWare counterparts—ATTACH, LOGIN, LOGOUT, MAP, SLIST, CAPTURE, and so on.

FPNW also adds extensions to the Windows NT User, Server, and File Manager applications to allow for the administration of NetWare users in a manner similar to that of an actual NetWare server. An Enable NetWare Access right is added to the User Manager, and standard NetWare account management attributes, like grace logons, station and time restrictions, and intruder lockout policies, are all present. Also, by deploying the Windows NT Directory, users (even NetWare users running the NETX shell) can access all the resources in the enterprise with a single logon, and the account can be replicated among Windows NT machines for fault tolerance.

Thus, with a combination of the tools described above, even large networks can be migrated to, or integrated with, Windows NT servers and workstations in a planned and methodical manner. One server at a time can be moved to Windows NT, if desired, or NT servers added, and NetWare user accounts replicated until administrative personnel have been trained, native NT account policies have been created, and workstation client upgrades have been performed. Microsoft has come to realize the gravity of the decision to change NOSs, and it has made a great effort to facilitate the process, by providing administrators with client and server tools that can be adapted to almost any existing network environment.

Windows 95

Windows 95 was planned, from the outset, to be the ultimate network client. Microsoft has made it compatible with virtually every NOS in use today and has simplified the configuration of network services even more than in Windows NT. The simplest way to achieve network connectivity on a Windows 95 machine is to install it on a machine that is already a functioning network client. The setup routine autodetects a wide range of NICs and their hardware settings, acknowledges the existing network client software, and upgrades it accordingly. For NetWare, Windows, and TCP/IP network users, the 32-bit protected-mode clients that ship with Windows 95 are, quite simply, the fastest and most easily manageable network clients available today. Network services have been fully integrated into the OS, avoiding the performance delays and conventional memory requirements of the TSR network drivers that were needed in the past.

An upgrade to Windows 95 migrates any non-standard settings and parameters found specified in Windows INI or NetWare NET.CFG files to the Windows Registry; these are accessible through the Registry Editor or through the Network tabbed dialog box in Control Panel, which provides a far more elegant and functional window into the workings of the network software. Like the Windows NT applet, the Windows 95 version lists each network client, adapter, protocol, and service that has been installed (see fig. 12.6).

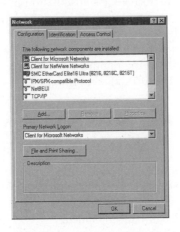

Figure 12.6

The Network tabbed dialog box, accessed through Control Panel, is the central interface for all of the operating system's networking components.

Unlike NT, however, which provides a single unified (and sometimes confusing) Bindings dialog box for all the network components, Windows 95 has a Properties sheet for each component that contains not only all the adjustable parameters for that module but an individual Bindings tab that displays, for example, all the clients that are utilizing a particular protocol or all the protocols that are bound to a particular adapter. This allows for simplified troubleshooting of network communications problems. For example, examining the bindings for the IPX/SPX protocol (see fig. 12.7) shows whether or not it is being used by the Microsoft network client, perhaps explaining why only workgroups on the local network segment are visible in the browser (since NetBEUI is not routable).

Network-related *services* also are visible through the Network tabbed dialog box. Services are software modules that are functionally equivalent to TSRs, in that they are always available for use by any part of the OS but without the drawbacks in conventional memory usage to which TSRs usually are subject. For example, Windows 95 (on CD-ROM) ships with services that function as client agents for network backup packages by Cheyenne Software and Arcada Software, as well as printer control software by Hewlett-Packard. A service can be made permanently available (allowing system backups or printer control at any time) without the need to launch an actual application—and without the performance hit that such a launch entails.

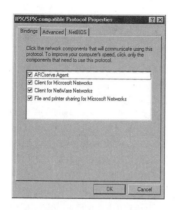

Here, the Bindings tab has been selected to reveal particular information that can help with troubleshooting.

For power-users, access to all of the workstation's configuration data is available through the Windows 95 Registry Editor (REGEDIT.EXE). This program provides an expandable tree view of all the settings that would have been included in INI files in the 16-bit Windows OSs and a great deal more. All the settings that are adjustable in Control Panel are also available here, albeit in a far more cryptic format. It is extremely important to know what you are doing before making any changes to Windows Registry settings. What you don't know here can hurt you a lot!

Unlike Windows 3.1, where you could always boot to DOS and tinker with INI file settings, there is no direct access to the Windows 95 Registry from the command line. If you make a change that prevents the Windows GUI from loading, then running REGEDIT.EXE from a DOS prompt allows a backup copy of the Registry to be imported, but no actual editing of the data is possible. It should also be known that the actual Registry data files, named USER.DAT and SYSTEM.DAT (and stored as hidden files in the \WINDOWS directory), are automatically backed up to files with the extension DA0, whenever changes are made to them. This provides a means of reverting to the most recent configuration at any time. Many of the hundreds of Registry settings are described in the Windows 95 Resource Kit, but changes should only be made in response to a particular problem or situation in which the precise effect of the change you're making has been fully researched; otherwise, extremely unpredictable behavior may result. In any case, it is recommended that the Export Registry feature be used to save a functional copy of the Registry files before you conduct any experiments.

Client Services for Microsoft

As with Windows NT, the native Windows 95 client for Microsoft networks is a 32-bit, protected-mode service that provides both peer-to-peer and client/server functionality, allowing connections to be established to Windows NT, Windows for Workgroups, and other Windows 95 machines, as well as to other SMB-based servers such as IBM LAN Server, LAN Manager for UNIX, DEC PATHWORKS, and AT&T StarLAN, as long as both machines are using a common protocol. When the File and Print Sharing for Microsoft

Networks feature has been added to the network client, Windows 95 workstation resources can be shared with other network users by means of individual passwords for each share (in the Windows for Workgroups model) or by user-level access, in which the user and group accounts defined on a Windows NT server that has been designated a primary domain controller provide security. The latter technique is also known as *pass-through validation.*

Access to all available shares on the network is provided through a unified file system in the form of the Windows Explorer, which in the Network Neighborhood provides seamless file management capabilities to all available shares without even the need for drive mapping. Early add-on products for Windows 95, such as Norton Navigator, even integrate FTP services into this metaphor (for workstations connected to the Internet through TCP/IP), allowing access to remote systems as easily as to local ones, without the need for an external application. The Windows protected-mode clients are able to use the same 32-bit caching (called VCACHE) as the rest of the Windows file system, improving network performance by storing the most recently used data in memory. Long file names of up to 256 characters—one of the most popular features to users of the Windows NT and Windows 95 OSs—are viewed, transferred, and manipulated easily between different machines on the Windows network.

Another new feature of Windows 95 is the capability for the storage of user profiles on the network. User profiles are collections of the drive mappings and desktop configuration settings for a particular user. In this way, the configuration of a Windows 95 machine can be varied according to the name of the user that logs on to it. A network administrator can, therefore, log on to any machine on the network and immediately receive access to all the tools and resources needed to perform the task at hand. Likewise, users of varying security levels or departments can switch Windows 95 machines for any reason and not have to completely re-create their individual preferences on the new workstation.

Various hardware profiles can also be created for instances when different sets of hardware are used with the same computer at different times. If a portable computer is sometimes used with a docking station, for example, then drivers and configuration settings for two different display options, keyboards, and network connections can be loaded, depending on whether or not the computer is docked.

Dialup network access is built into Windows 95, as it is with Windows NT. In Windows 95, however, it is configured just as any network adapter would be. Specific clients, protocols, and services can be bound to the dialup adapter so that the connection process is automatically initiated when access to certain network resources is requested. Windows 95 machines can also be configured as dialup servers, using additional software included in Windows 95 Plus! Thus, Windows 95 home or mobile users can easily dial into their office networks and be provided with the same network access that they would have if directly attached to the LAN (subject to the speed limitations of the connection).

NIC support is also excellent. 32-bit NDIS 3.1 drivers are included for a wide selection of adapters, including PC Card and parallel port products, but 16-bit real-mode NDIS or

ODI drivers can also be used, yielding a lower level of performance but providing almost universal compatibility. The auto-detection mechanism also functions quite well, successfully identifying many NICs with sufficient accuracy to allow a connection to the network. When hardware fully conforming to the Plug and Play standard becomes common, the process will become even easier.

In short, for Windows network users, there is no reason not to use the Windows 95 client. Its overall performance is excellent, whether connecting to a peer Windows 95 machine or an NT server. Security capabilities are extremely flexible, allowing the caching of passwords to be disabled, if desired, thus forcing users to log on to remote resources each time the machine is started. The full complement of Windows NT security mechanisms, as well as the NT Directory, can be used to provide detailed access control to a network of Windows 95 machines.

Fault tolerance for network performance is well-realized. If a connection to a shared network resource is interrupted for any reason—a file server goes down or a portable computer is detached from the network and carried across the room—both continue to perform as stand-alone machines without interruption. When network service is later restored, the client immediately reestablishes the connection, allowing the user to resume network access without any indication or delay. The addition of support for other networks, clients, protocols, or services is easily accomplished, with no apparent ill effect to the Microsoft client. There are limitations with respect to other network clients, as we shall see in the following sections, but as far as its native networking capabilities are concerned, there is little that Microsoft could have done to create a better client.

Connecting to NetWare Networks

Of course, the majority of Windows 95 users are not connecting only to Windows networks. The real test of the OS's networking comes in its ability to connect to NetWare servers, and with a few notable exceptions, Microsoft has done an excellent job here as well. Windows 95 ships with a 32-bit, protected-mode client for Novell NetWare that functions as a counterpart to the Windows network client. The two easily share the same NDIS 3.1 board driver that ships with the OS and can also share the services of the transport protocols installed on the machine. For example, the NetWare client requires the use of the IPX/SPX-compatible transport supplied with the OS, but this protocol can also be used by the Windows client to route NetBEUI traffic between network segments.

Microsoft Client for NetWare Networks. The Microsoft protected-mode NetWare client ships with the Windows 95 release and is installed in the same manner as the client for Microsoft Networks. It appears as one of the installable services in the Network tabbed dialog box of the Control Panel, and installation can often be as easy as selecting the service, specifying a preferred NetWare server, and rebooting the workstation. The protected-mode client is also, in most cases, installed by default when an existing NetWare workstation running one of the NetWare real-mode clients (NETX or VLM) is upgraded to Windows 95. The setup routine will rem out all the old network components from the workstation's AUTOEXEC.BAT file, modify the existing SYSTEM.INI file, migrate the settings found in the NET.CFG file to the Windows 95 Registry, and install and bind the appropriate protocols to the new NetWare client. Any existing networking component files (such as NETWARE.DRV) that are overwritten during the installation process are renamed with a tilde (~) in place of the last character in the extension, so a return to the original configuration is never hampered by the deletion of necessary files.

In most cases, it is preferable to utilize the protected-mode client whenever possible. It provides superior network performance without the memory utilization problems of the multiple TSRs needed for NETX and VLMs. NetWare API support is provided to Windows DOS sessions, allowing the use of nearly all NetWare command-line and menu-driven utilities (the exceptions being the NDS-related modules). The client supports the NCP Packet Burst mode as well as Large Internet Packets. Even the long file names that are native to Windows 95 machines can be stored on NetWare volumes, as long as they have been properly configured for the OS/2 name space.

Storing Long File Names on NetWare 3.11 Servers

Please note that the NetWare 3.11 release shipped with an OS/2 name space module that incorrectly stored long file names. A patch named OS2OPNFX.NLM must be applied before the OS/2 name space will function properly. This file is available from NetWire in an archive named 311PTD.EXE.

For this reason, Windows 95 will not by default write long file names to NetWare 3.11 server volumes. Standard DOS 8.3 file names are written instead. Once the patch has been applied, this default can be modified by adding the following section to the workstation's SYSTEM.INI file:

```
[NWREDIR]
SupportLFN=2
```

or by modifying the following Windows Registry setting:

```
Hkey_Local_Machine\System\CurrentControlSet\Services\VxD\Nwredir
```

The possible values for this Registry key are

0	This prevents all long file names from being written to NetWare servers.
1 (default)	This allows long file name support on NetWare servers version 3.12 and greater.
2	This allows long file name support on all NetWare servers that have OS/2 name space.

Unlike the Windows NT clients available from both Novell and Microsoft, the Windows 95 client for NetWare is capable of processing the bindery logon scripts associated with NetWare user accounts. Although this feature is not yet 100% accurate (problems with certain IF...THEN statements have been noted, for example), it is an excellent sign of the advancements being made by Microsoft in the area of client software design. The protected-mode client, at this time, also does not provide support for the NCP Packet Signature security options, NetWare IP, or IPX checksums, but these are relatively minor matters that do not significantly affect a large number of users.

As with the Windows network client, NetWare passwords can be cached by the Windows 95 operating system (if you desire), allowing for quick access to network drives in future logons. Network users are even provided with a choice of whether or not they want their network drives to be actually attached when the system is booted, or whether mappings should be performed, and attachment delayed until access to each device is individually requested. This provides a tradeoff between additional speed at boot time versus quicker initial access to network drives, depending on the user's preference. Microsoft even includes a protected-mode equivalent of the NetWare RPRINTER utility with Windows 95. NetWare print queues can be despooled to printers attached to a Windows 95 workstation.

Another excellent feature of the Microsoft client for NetWare is the *safe mode* that can be used in situations when a malfunction prevents the Windows GUI from loading properly. Safe mode can be selected from a list of startup choices that appear when the F8 key is pressed while the system is booting. When safe mode is selected, access to the network is granted using a real-mode client that does not support the advanced features of the Microsoft client such as long file names, packet burst mode, and auto-reconnection to servers but does provide emergency access to the network in situations that prevent the fully functional Windows interface from loading. Options like this are part of Microsoft's attempt to overcome the inherent limitations of the GUI. When an ancillary component such as a video display driver fails to function, the GUI might be inaccessible and an alternative means of accessing the operating system must be provided. The client's safe mode allows the additional benefit of network access, so that support personnel can access replacement drivers or diagnostic tools that can be used to remedy the problem.

File and Print Sharing for NetWare Networks. For a Windows 95 machine to operate in peer-to-peer mode with other workstations—that is, to share its drives and printers— a network service named *File and Print Sharing for Microsoft Networks* must be installed along with the Windows client. Also present in the pick lists of services that ship with the Windows 95 product is *File and Print Services for NetWare Networks*. In comparison with the features provided by its Microsoft counterpart, this may seem odd. A peer-to-peer function for NetWare? Actually, this service is a fully realized, fully integrated Windows 95 version of the FPNW add-on module for Windows NT.

Installing this service, which requires that File and Print Services for Microsoft Networks first be removed, allows any Windows 95 machine to appear on the network as a NetWare 3.12 file server. The installation process creates a subdirectory under \WINDOWS named \NWSYSVOL, which becomes the root of the "server's" SYS: volume. Any other shares that are created on the machine's drives become additional volumes. SAP packets can (optionally) be generated to advertise the machine's presence on the network, using the Windows machine name as the server name. Likewise, the share names become volume names.

Use of this feature requires a NetWare server to provide pass-though security validation. Just as a Windows 95 machine can access an NT domain server's account information, File and Print Services accesses the bindery of a NetWare 3.1x server to extract user and group information to provide access to the Windows 95 "server." There is no share-level password protection provided. Once a preferred NetWare server is specified, its bindery is accessed, and its user list presented on the Windows 95 machine. Users can then be selected and provided with read-only access to shared drives, full control of them, or customized access based on the standard set of NetWare file attributes.

Once this has been done, a user at a workstation running only a standard real-mode NetWare client can enter the SLIST command and see the Windows 95 machine on his list of servers (assuming that the creation of SAP packets has been enabled). The only indication of abnormality on the server list is the inclusion of the Windows 95 machine's full network and node addresses, as opposed to the listing of the internal IPX addresses for the real NetWare servers. The user can logon to the "server," watch his logon script run, and then manipulate files or print to printers just as though it actually was a NetWare server. In fact, except for subtle indications, such as the server listing cited above, it would be easy to mistake the Windows 95 machine for an actual NetWare server. The performance is that good. It is even possible to perform a backup of the Windows 95 machine using network backup software to address it as a server.

Of course, many of the NetWare server utilities are useless here. Users are created through the Windows 95 interface, not SYSCON, and PCONSOLE is not operational. It also cannot be forgotten that this feature provides file and print services only. There is no way to run NLMs on the Windows 95 machine. This spoils the ability to back up the "server," because a NetWare Target Service Agent cannot be loaded that would allow Windows 95 long file names to be successfully written to tape. Copy operations from the "server" to another Windows 95 or Windows NT machine—or an actual NetWare server (with OS/2 name space)—do preserve long file names properly.

While Microsoft is attempting to position the NT version of the FPNW feature as a transitional tool to aid in migration from NetWare to NT, the real power of its functionality is clear in the excellent performance of the Windows 95 version. Each Windows 95 machine running File and Print Services for NetWare appears to the network as a 250-user NetWare server, yet it utilizes only a single connection to an actual NetWare server. In this way, file and print services for an almost unlimited number of users can be provided for the price of the hardware plus a single NetWare server license. When it is made available on the Windows NT platform, then NT's own client/server application functionality, as well as file access and printing, will be available to the NetWare clients.

Other NetWare Clients. As with Windows NT, there has been a certain amount of confusion regarding whether Novell or Microsoft will be the primary supplier of NetWare client software for Windows 95. At this time, both companies are well into their individual client development projects. If nothing else, this should provide users with a range of choices to select from, as the development projects seem to be aimed in different directions, despite the basically similar tasks to be performed. This is an important point, because the Windows 95 NetWare client, while very well-realized for an initial release, is not yet complete. The protected-mode NetWare client supplied by Microsoft does not yet support NDS. This is a crucial element if Microsoft's plan to dominate the network desktop is to succeed. Both Microsoft and Novell are currently developing clients for Windows 95 that will be NDS-compliant, but in the interim, a significant number of users are compelled to utilize the standard Novell real-mode VLM client for NetWare on their Windows 95 machines.

Windows 95 and Real-Mode NetWare Clients. In its quest to create an OS as compatible with existing hardware and software as it could possibly be, Microsoft was wise to leave in the option to use a workstation's existing NetWare client software. While the lack of NDS support in its own client was no doubt a substantial factor in this decision, it also was a functional safety measure, in case Microsoft's NetWare client did not turn out to be as successful as it did. It must be remembered that, despite the massive beta testing program, Windows 95 was a tremendous gamble. Few software developers are able to anticipate the problems that will occur with their products once they are released to market.

NETX. Windows 95, therefore, runs with either the NETX or VLM real-mode Novell clients without any alteration to them. Because of the excellent performance of the Microsoft Client for NetWare, the only valid reason for anyone to be using NETX with Windows 95 would be to support a networking TSR that could function with no other client. If a network adapter was being used that did not have an NDIS 3.1 driver available, it would only be inertia on the part of network administrators that might prevent the use of at least VLMs. However, NETX can be installed and used, if you desire. The files needed to run NETX can be loaded manually through modification of the workstation's AUTOEXEC.BAT file, in the usual manner, but users must also install NETX support through Control Panel, just like the Microsoft network clients. To do this, you must remove the Microsoft NetWare client, if it is present, and in the Select Network Client dialog box, choose Novell in the left pane and Novell NetWare (Workstation Shell 3.x [NETX]) in the right. The files needed for the NETX installation, however, do not ship with Windows 95. It is necessary to provide the installer with a location where the proper files are located. NETX.EXE may be obtained from Novell's NetWire in an archive named NET33X.EXE.

It is also necessary to manually modify the LASTDRIVE= line in the workstation's CONFIG.SYS file. This is set to Z by both VLMs and Windows 95. When NETX is used, this value indicates the last drive letter that is to be considered as allocated for local workstation use. It is most often set to E, so that F will be the first available NetWare drive letter. It is also necessary to add NETX.EXE to the workstation's SETVER table. This should be done so that Windows 95 sees NETX as being designed for use with MS-DOS 7.0, which is how the DOS functionality in Windows 95 is labeled. This is particularly important if the %OS_VERSION variable appears in the user's logon script. The SETVER utility is no longer a separate executable in Windows 95. It is automatically loaded by the IO.SYS file during startup.

VLMs. It is more likely that users will run VLMs with Windows 95 than NETX. However, there are also some important concerns that should be addressed when this is done. The default Windows 95 installation process detects the presence of an existing NetWare client, and in some cases, removes it automatically, installing the Microsoft 32-bit client in its place and overwriting several of the VLM files with newer versions in the process. For this reason, it is recommended that the VLM client be completely reinstalled if the Microsoft Client for NetWare has ever been used on the system. This is because full Windows support for the VLMs must be activated, particularly if NDS access is required.

Many people assume that they need only to include the lines in the AUTOEXEC.BAT that execute the LSL, MLID driver, IPXODI, and VLM.EXE modules in order to provide full VLM client support, but this is not the case. The entire VLM client kit in its latest version (1.21, as of this writing, also available from NetWire) should be installed, using its own INSTALL.EXE program in Windows 95's MS-DOS mode, rather than through the Windows Control Panel. Be sure to specify that Windows support be installed for the client. MS-DOS mode in Windows 95 is achieved by pressing F8 while the machine boots and selecting Command prompt only or by choosing Shut Down from the Windows 95 Task Bar and then selecting to restart the computer in MS-DOS mode. The process should not be performed from a DOS session within Windows.

The original NET.CFG file from the NetWare real-mode client is not deleted or altered in any way by the Windows 95 setup routine, so any settings previously stored there by earlier VLM installations will be intact, and the file can be saved to another location—or renamed—and then returned to the \NWCLIENT directory after the VLM installation, if you desire. During the installation, the user may be prompted as to whether or not the NETWARE.DRV file should be overwritten. Always respond Yes to this question. NETWARE.DRV is a crucial part of the NetWare clients—NETX and VLMs, as well as Windows 95. Both the Novell and Microsoft client install programs overwrite this file, which normally resides in the \WINDOWS\SYSTEM directory, and full NetWare network functionality in Windows cannot be achieved if the incorrect version is used. Table 12.1 lists the sizes of the various versions of NETWARE.DRV. After restarting the computer, open the Network tabbed dialog box from Control Panel and install support for Novell NetWare (Workstation Shell 4.0 and Above[VLM]) through the normal Select Network Client dialog box.

Table 12.1 NETWARE.DRV Versions for NetWare Clients		
Name	**Version**	**Size**
NETWARE.DRV	Microsoft	1.6K
NETWARE.DRV	Novell NETX	125K
NETWARE.DRV	Novell VLM	160K

If the Microsoft Client for NetWare has never been installed on the system, and the VLM client is currently active, then it is only necessary to perform the Control Panel installation procedure. This ensures that the appropriate settings for Windows 95 are configured in the SYSTEM.INI file (such as the path, which is specified as \WINDOWS\SYSTEM by the VLM installation program but needs to be \WINDOWS\VMM32 in Windows 95).

There are some issues to be discussed concerning the actual use of the VLM client. Its compatibility with Windows 95 is not quite 100%. For example, due to improper routine calls made by Windows 95 to NETWARE.DRV, a user might see an attempt to restore drive connections occur before the workstation has connected with a NetWare server, causing an error message for each failed connection. The Restore Now option in NWUSER.EXE establishes connections after the errors have occurred, but they can be avoided entirely by logging on to the server from DOS before the Windows GUI has loaded. This is done by placing a LOGIN command in the workstation's AUTOEXEC.BAT file, or in a batch file named WINSTART.BAT in the Windows directory.

Loading TSRs Using WINSTART.BAT

WINSTART.BAT is a little-known convention in Windows 95 that has been carried over from Windows 3.1. A normal DOS batch file by this name, when stored in a workstation's \WINDOWS directory, is executed just before the Windows GUI loads. In Windows 3.1, one of the advantages of this file is that its contents are removed from memory when Windows is shut down. This obviously is not of any particular value in Windows 95, however, since shutting down the OS leads to a system reboot.

WINSTART.BAT is also useful for loading the DOS-based requesters for client/server systems such as Btrieve's BREQUEST.EXE. When Windows 95 is configured to use Microsoft's protected-mode clients, network support is not provided at the time that the AUTOEXEC.BAT file is processed, and an attempt to load Brequest fails since no IPX communication with the server is possible at that time. By the time that WINSTART.BAT executes, however, network support is active, and the requester can load properly.

As with Windows 3.1, it is necessary, when using VLMs, to create all the network search drives that will be needed for the session before the Windows GUI starts. Search drives created in a Windows DOS session are not carried over to other sessions or to the main Windows interface, so they should be specified in a logon script instead, for execution at system startup. As far as drive mappings are concerned, though, the opposite is true. The VLM feature that allows users to select whether drive mappings created in a DOS session should be global or private (that is, whether they should be carried over to the entire Windows environment or remain active only in that single DOS session), does not function under Windows 95. All drive mappings are global, and erratic behavior may result if the Global Drives and Paths option in NWUSER.EXE is not selected.

Finally, Windows 95 long file names cannot be written to NetWare servers using the Novell real-mode clients. The files themselves are written, but only the DOS 8.3 file name that is stored as part of every Windows 95 file gets written to the server volume, despite the presence of the appropriate name space. As a result, Windows 95 user profiles cannot be stored on a NetWare server with these clients.

What is less readily quantifiable is the reduced performance that the Novell real-mode clients provide, when compared with the Microsoft protected-mode client for NetWare. The real-mode ODI adapter drivers that NETX and the VLMs rely upon are inherently slower than their NDIS 3.1 counterparts used by the native Windows client. This can be proven easily since the ODI driver also can be used with the Microsoft Client for NetWare. The memory requirements of the real-mode TSR modules used by the Novell clients also place the user in virtually the same position as the one she sought to escape by switching to Windows 95. The DOS modules load in conventional memory—or they must be loaded into upper memory using EMM386.EXE or a third-party memory manager like QEMM, even in Windows 95. The price of loading them wholly in conventional memory is a reduction in the amount of available memory in each Windows 95 DOS session.

As is becoming increasingly plain to many users, the wishful thinking that has, for many months, fostered the claim that Windows 95 eliminates DOS and all its limitations is inherently untrue. The DOS base upon which Windows runs is still there. A simple change to the MSDOS.SYS configuration file allows a Windows 95 machine to boot to the DOS prompt, after which the user must type WIN to start the GUI. After all, how far could we really be from Windows 3.x and still remain backwards-compatible?

Such considerations are better left behind altogether, whenever possible, which means using 32-bit protected mode applications and services and abandoning the old ways as quickly as possible. The majority of people using VLMs with Windows 95 do so for NDS access alone. NWADMIN and the other NDS-related NetWare utilities do run well in Windows 95, when VLMs are used, although NDS print queues outside the current bindery context are inaccessible. Most network users in a well-designed NDS tree, however, should be capable of performing their normal daily tasks using the resources within their bindery contexts.

NDS Clients for Windows 95. In any case, it is no longer necessary for users to live without a 32-bit NDS client. What, at the time of the initial Windows 95 release, was a serious deficiency, is now rapidly becoming an embarrassment of riches. Both Microsoft and Novell have released NDS solutions for Windows 95. Microsoft's is an additional service that operates with the Client for NetWare Networks, and Novell's is a public beta of its forthcoming Client32 for Windows 95, which is a complete client in itself.

Novell is centering its 32-bit client development activities around an area of common code that it calls *Client32*, which will form the core of its collection of new 32-bit clients, to be developed simultaneously, including new packages for Windows 3.1, Macintosh, and OS/2. As evinced by the Windows 95 Client32 beta, the plan seems to be progressing well, when compared to the Novell Client for Windows NT discussed earlier in this chapter; the Windows 95 client is light years ahead, even in a beta release. While Microsoft has constructed a basic NDS-compatible client, providing access to all the necessary resources and capable of running logon scripts, Novell has set its sights much higher. It is, with these clients, beginning to demonstrate the true possibilities of NDS as a network management tool, as we shall see.

Nowhere in sight are the severe limitations imposed by the Novell NT client, like the proprietary DOS session and the lack of logon script support. This package installs easily from a local or network drive either by running a SETUP.EXE file from within Windows 95 or through Control Panel. Although the utility for making floppy install disks is again provided, its use is not required this time. The program detects a current installation of the Microsoft Client for NetWare (or either of the Novell real-mode clients) and removes them from the system configuration (although the files are left intact). Client32 can also be installed along with the Windows 95 OS, allowing administrators to custom script a *push installation* that will cause the client to be automatically installed from the network to every workstation as its user logs on. This type of installation is also possible with the Windows 95 operating system itself (as we shall see later in this chapter), and Client32 can be integrated into that installation, allowing for a one-stop upgrade of both OS and client.

The installation process allows the user to browse for a preferred server or tree name, a definite improvement over the earlier betas. The user's full context for an NDS logon must be entered manually, however. A successful logon causes bindery or NDS logon scripts to be executed, if desired, and while support for all the possible logon script commands is not yet complete, it is nearly so. Logging on under two different user names sequentially causes the two different environments to load smoothly. There are no complaints from Windows regarding changes in drive mappings or other settings. It is even possible, in the Login dialog box, to specify a different profile script to be executed during the logon or to provide values for up to four variables called by the logon script. Support for multiple users on a single machine is therefore quite good.

Once fully installed, the Novell client coexists very well with the Microsoft Windows client, allowing the Windows 95 machine to share its own drives and printers and to access the resources of others, with no interference. The Windows Explorer, under Entire Network, contains an expandable listing of all the servers on the network, as well as a representation of all the NDS trees present there. Users can navigate their way down the current NDS tree to select a particular resource, if desired, or they can expand the server tree all the way down to the file level. It is even possible for a user to log on to two separate NDS trees simultaneously!

Despite these features—or perhaps because of them—overall performance of this beta is not up to the level established by the Microsoft NetWare client. Noticeable delays occur when initially scanning directories on NetWare volumes, possibly due in part to the lack of the integrated network caching using VCACHE provided by the Microsoft client (although Client32 is supposed to provide its own caching). These delays were particularly noticeable when browsing with the NDS tree, but performance levels when actually accessing network files using an application were a good deal more acceptable.

Novell provides a wide array of configuration parameters for its client, accessible through the properties sheet in the Control Panel's Network tabbed dialog box. Many of these are counterparts to variables that can be set in a traditional Novell client's NET.CFG file, some of which can be used to optimize client performance. Their values are stored in the Windows Registry, as are those of the Microsoft client, but Client32 cannot yet parse an existing NET.CFG file and automatically add its settings to the Registry.

Support for the writing of long file names to NetWare servers is provided by the Novell client (except in the case of unpatched NetWare 3.11 servers, as noted earlier). However, it is not possible to create a directory with a name longer than 8.3 characters from the Windows Explorer, even though I can create such a directory from a DOS session. It also is not possible to delete files using DOS wild cards when the file name mask is greater than 8.3. Thus, **DEL FILE*.*** is accepted, but **DEL LONGFILENAM*.*** is not. As with the VLMs, all drive mappings are global, although Novell promises private mappings in

DOS sessions for a future release. Directory changes on mapped drives, however, remain local to the session where they are enacted. Thus, changing to a subdirectory while in a DOS session does not cause a Windows application to default to that directory on the NetWare drive.

Network fault tolerance in this client is no less than superb. Not only are broken network connections automatically and transparently restored, as with the Microsoft clients, but open files and locks are restored as well! A workstation left running NWADMIN.EXE displays as many as ten files open on the NetWare server console. This server, which not only contains the master replica of the NDS partition being edited, but the NWADMIN executable files themselves, can be brought down (using the DOWN command) and restarted with no interruption to other processes on the Windows 95 workstation. Once the server is completely activated again, operations in the NWADMIN window can be continued from the point at which they were abandoned, and the same open files are again displayed at the server console.

Printing to NetWare queues has changed little in the new client. It still is impossible to run the NetWare Rprinter or Nprinter utilities from Windows 95 (although a 32-bit Nprinter is promised), but NDS print queues are accessible from the Windows Explorer and the Network Neighborhood interfaces. Oddly, however, they are not displayed in the Printers/Add Printers dialog box within the My Computer window. Novell asserts that this is a limitation of that particular dialog box in Windows 95.

Aside from such minor difficulties, the NetWare Directory is completely supported by Client32. NWADMIN runs much the same as it does when VLMs are used, although the 32-bit version that ships with the Novell Windows NT client does not load. All the DOS-based NDS utilities are fully functional in the standard Windows 95 MS-DOS session. There is no need for a dedicated DOS shell to gain NetWare API functionality, as with the NT client. Not surprisingly, though, File and Print Services for NetWare will not be supported by the NetWare client.

Client32 provides many small improvements to the networking features of the Windows 95 GUI. Trustees to files and directories on NetWare drives can be assigned and modified directly through their properties sheets in the Network Neighborhood and Windows Explorer, with user and group account information drawn directly from the server. Additional NetWare-related information is also provided for network objects throughout the interface.

Finally, Novell with this beta has provided an inkling of the true potential of NDS as a centralized network management tool. A library file named APPSNAP.DLL, intended for use with NWADMIN, modifies the NetWare Directory schema so that a new type of NDS object can be created: an *application object*. Representing program files stored on network drives, application objects can be created for DOS, Windows 3.1, Windows 95, or Window NT executables. They are configured and modified through NWADMIN, like any other object, with properties that can provide the application with command-line parameters, working directories, drive mappings, search drives, starting and ending scripts, custom commentary and contact information for users, and other variables that can be used to control the environment in which the application runs. The modified schema also adds additional selections to the Detail displays of user, group, and container objects that allow access to the application objects to be granted, defined, and even imposed. It is even possible for the administrator to designate whether the environmental settings defined for the application should be applied only while it remains active or carried over permanently to the rest of the working system.

An executable program, called *NetWare Application Launcher* (NAL.EXE), also ships with the client and will eventually be available in versions for all the Client32 platforms. When executed at a workstation, all application objects to which the user has been granted access appear as icons in a window not unlike a Windows 3.1 program group. Alternatively, users (as well as groups and containers) can be configured so that some or all of the applications are immediately launched when NAL.EXE is executed. This concept allows network administrators to assign users access to customized suites of applications on a completely object-oriented level, from within the NWADMIN interface. There is no need to deal with individual application installations, the creation of program icons, custom logon scripts, or access to the proper application directories as separate tasks. Once application objects are properly configured, you can simply add new users to the appropriate groups or containers in the NDS to provide them with a ready-made Windows desktop, including access to all the applications they need—it's one simple operation.

Although not quite complete, either in its feature set or its performance levels, Novell's effort is considerably advanced for a beta release. Microsoft's own NDS-capable protected-mode client, on the other hand, was released to its online services for free distribution in October of 1995. Instead of reinventing the wheel, it chose to take advantage of Windows 95's networking architecture and provided a Service for NetWare Directory Services that works with the existing Client for NetWare Networks. Installing from Control Panel in the normal way, this client also allows the user to browse for a preferred server or tree, providing support for both NDS and bindery logons. Beyond this, however, Microsoft has opted for the no-frills approach. Its service provides the basic functionality required by the average NDS user and delivers better performance than Client32, all in a package that was released on time, while the actual release of Novell's client is again overdue.

Even without these clients, though, network access from both Windows NT and Windows 95 is far more advanced than that provided in earlier Windows versions. Those who remember the original Windows 3.0 and 3.1 releases should recall the way in which networking was tacked onto those products—almost as an afterthought—and how client installation, at that time, was a strictly manual process.

A great deal of progress has been made since then, and it is always with mixed feelings that veteran network administrators see some of the carefully honed skills that they have acquired over the years become obsolete with the advent of new and improved products. The manual tasks of configuring NICs and installing client software are going to all but disappear before long; it soon will be no more than a matter of inserting a card into a slot, powering up the machine, and watching the OS install the necessary client software. For MIS personnel responsible for hundreds of machines, this will be a miraculous improvement; however, there always will be other tasks to test their skills, as seen in the following sections.

Installing Windows 95 over the Network

The networking capabilities of Windows 95 are not limited to the various client packages that ship with the product. Microsoft has also devoted a good deal of attention to the installation process itself and particularly to the concerns of network administrators who may be responsible for the installation of the OS onto hundreds of machines. In a situation like that, it usually is impractical for network support staff to travel to each machine with a stack of floppy disks or a portable CD-ROM drive.

This may, however, be unavoidable, if a wide variety of system configurations are used on the network's workstations. The automated network installation capabilities of Windows 95 are based on the assumption that a large number of machines utilize the exact same system configuration. Networks in which users are responsible for configuring their own machines or selecting their own software probably will not benefit from these features, as they rely on careful scripting to provide responses to all the prompts requiring user input during a normal interactive Windows 95 installation.

Consideration also must be paid to the network users' level of expertise. Highly experienced computer users (who are also those most likely to have unique system configurations) are unlikely to need the simplification provided by the automated installation process, considering that the Windows 95 installation process is already quite user-friendly. It is the novice user—who remains blissfully unaware of underlying structures like networks and operating systems—for whom such a feature is needed. For users of this type, their normal daily logon procedure can be modified to automatically begin a pre-scripted Windows 95 installation process that requires absolutely no user interaction. In this push installation, the user is given no choice about when or how an upgrade is to be performed. The same sort of scripting can be used to create a procedure that a user can perform at her convenience by running a particular program, logging on to a special network account, or even clicking an object sent as an e-mail attachment.

Installation Scripts. The preparation and debugging of the script files needed for these installation processes can be a lengthy and time-consuming process. Although several different means have been provided to automate parts of the scripting process, there almost certainly will be sections or parameters that have to be manually modified and tested. It also is unlikely that a scripted installation will be entirely successful on 100% of the machines for which it is intended. As any network administrator will tell you, users have a way of thwarting any plan or device designed to make the administrator's life easier. There are bound to be a number of machines that have insufficient disk space, unexpected configurations, or some other factors that prevent a successful upgrade—this is another reason why these methods are recommended only when large numbers of installations must be performed. If a scripted installation is performed on 100 machines, and only 75 of them are entirely successful, the time and travel saved is well worth the effort. For less than 50 machines, though, it probably would be more efficient for an administrator to perform individual installations from a server-based copy of

Windows 95. When all the necessary components are assembled in one place, including any additional drivers or application files needed, the process can be streamlined to run very smoothly. In fact, trained personnel should be able to start the installation process on several nearby machines in succession and perform multiple installations simultaneously.

A network-based installation, however, is not simply a matter of storing a set of installation files on a server drive. It is important to note that, in most cases, the network client software itself is going to be upgraded during the Windows 95 installation process. This means that the software enabling the connection to the network that provides access to the installation files is going to be replaced in the process. In order not to figuratively saw through the tree limb that you are standing on, it is essential that the installation procedure be conducted using an entirely predictable and fully-tested routine, taking into account every workstation configuration that might be encountered on the network.

This routine is realized by the creation of a script file, which in Windows 95 is an ASCII text file with an extension of INF, that can be created by hand in any text editor or can be generated by a number of different utilities included with the OS. The function of the script file is to provide selections and responses to the various prompts and questions generated by the Windows 95 installation program. The questions range from the simple and mundane, such as into what directory Windows 95 should be installed, to the very complex, such as what networking protocols should be used. Selections can be made regarding every part of the installation, from what Windows 95 components to install, all the way down to what wallpaper should be used. In the process, the network administrator can configure the workstation to allow its user as much freedom, or as many restrictions, as the administrator deems fit. System policies can be established and stored on network servers that override the settings in the Registry of each Windows 95 workstation, and limit access to the OS resources that users may have insufficient training or authority to use. Server-based applications or third-party clients can even be installed at the same time as the OS, providing the user with a complete, ready-to-work system as soon as the scripted process is completed.

The simplest way to get an idea of what an installation script looks like is to examine the SETUPLOG.TXT file that is automatically created by Windows 95 during its installation. In fact, by performing such an installation on a representative machine, portions of a working script can be assembled from excerpted parts of this log. The script is structured in much the same way as the primitive INI files used in Windows versions of the past; headings in square brackets separating parameters with accompanying values associated by an equal sign (=). Aside from the setup log, two GUI-based utilities are provided that also have the capability of creating scripts.

The NETSETUP.EXE program is used to create a Windows 95 installation directory structure on a network drive. The operating system files are expanded from the *.CAB archives in which Windows 95 ships and are placed in a directory selected by the user, so that they can be used either to perform an installation to a workstation's local drive or as the server portion of a shared Windows 95 installation. Clicking the Make Script button in the Netsetup dialog box displays a selection of installation parameters in the familiar Windows 95 tree-style display (see fig. 12.8). Any item whose properties are modified is added to the script with the appropriate changes. All the parameters that remain unaltered are installed using their default values. Creating a script that completely automates the installation process is a matter of modifying every parameter that requires input from the user during installation to supply that input in advance and also making all the appropriate selections for the desired configuration.

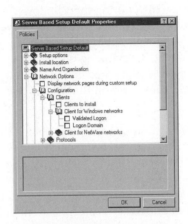

Figure 12.8

Installation scripts can be created with the Windows 95 NETSETUP.EXE utility.

The BATCH.EXE program is used only to create INF scripts, and provides a different interface with several screens, containing a wider, more detailed selection of installation parameters that can be modified to the administrator's specifications, as shown in figure 12.9. Its basic functionality, however, is the same as that of NETSETUP.EXE. Selections made in a point-and-click front-end are translated to the appropriate syntax for the installation script and saved as an ASCII file. Once a script file is created, it can be executed by specifying its name on the command line after the Windows 95 SETUP.EXE program (as installed to the server drive by the NETSETUP program), or it can be assimilated into the Windows 95 default installation script (named MSBATCH.INF) using the INFINST.EXE program. In this way, you can easily write a network logon script or batch file to initiate the installation process at some point during the user's normal daily activities. Usually, the only difficult part of this task is ensuring that the installation routine is not run repeatedly (every time the user tries to log on, for example). This can be done through script logic or by having users log on to a special network account created specifically for installations.

Network Client Upgrades. The Windows 95 setup routine, under certain conditions, automatically upgrades the network client software from a previous Windows installation, depending on the software that it finds already installed—these actions, too, can be modified to an administrator's specifications. By default, the network client for Microsoft is always installed if a NIC is present in the workstation. Whether or not the protected-mode NetWare client is installed, however, is dependent on what client software is currently installed, and how it is being used. For example, any workstation using the Novell NETX client or the VLM client to attach to a NetWare 3.x server is upgraded to the protected-mode client. However, a VLM client that is being used for an NDS logon is left intact since the protected mode client does not support NDS. Likewise, if any additional networking TSRs are detected whose functionality cannot be exactly duplicated by the protected-mode client, actions are taken to preserve them. These actions may consist of migrating the load line for the TSR from the AUTOEXEC.BAT file to the WINSTART.BAT, substituting a protected-mode equivalent for a required protocol or service (such as IPX or NetBIOS), or leaving the existing client software as it is. In this way, special real-mode implementations of network client software, such as those providing access to mainframes or specialized TCP/IP tools, remain functional after the installation.

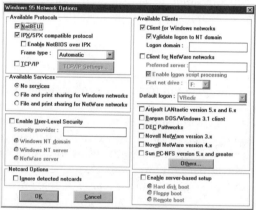

Figure 12.9

The Windows 95 BATCH.EXE program provides access to a more comprehensive array of script parameters.

The special considerations taken into account by the Windows 95 installation routine, as well as the actions to be taken upon detection of network client modules, are listed in a file named NETDET.INI, which is located in the \WINDOWS directory. This file can be modified by the network administrator to accommodate any networking software that is used on the network's workstations, so that the various network configurations found throughout a large enterprise can be individually treated in a wholly predictable manner.

Scripted Installations: Asset or Liability. There is, obviously, a great deal of middle ground between a normal interactive Windows 95 installation and the completely automated one described in the preceding section. It is up to the administrator to decide how much accurate input can be expected of the person at the machine when the upgrade is performed. Anticipating every nuance of the installation process can be a very difficult task, requiring a great deal of thought and experimentation, as well as careful debugging of the script. The BATCH and NETSETUP tools furnished by Microsoft are very basic in this respect. They provide no guidance for the creation of scripts to accommodate specific situations, and the graphical front-ends do not provide access to all the possible parameters that may be included in an installation script.

The truly indispensable tool for this job is the *Windows 95 Resource Kit*, which is included on the Windows 95 CD-ROM as a large WinHelp file and which can also be downloaded from Microsoft's various online services or purchased as a bound volume. The *Resource Kit* contains a complete account of the script file syntax as well as a comprehensive listing of all possible parameters. As stated earlier, the use of a script to perform a Windows 95 installation with no interaction from trained personnel is generally not recommended, unless a very large number of identical machines must be upgraded. Making modifications to the default script, however, can streamline the installation process very nicely, allowing junior network support staff—or even short-term consultants brought in for the task—to perform large numbers of system upgrades in a relatively short time.

Summary

At this point, there should be no doubt in anyone's mind that 32-bit desktop OSs like Windows NT and Windows 95 are here to stay. Once users get a taste of long file names and see what computing is like without the 640K DOS barrier hanging over them, there can be no going back. As far as networking is concerned, Microsoft has fashioned a better client platform than has ever before existed in the PC world. Although there is always room for improvement, the initial Windows 95 release is being assimilated into the network mainstream with far greater speed than many people outside of Redmond ever anticipated, and Windows NT is rapidly gaining wider acceptance in the ultra-conservative NOS market. Novell's decision to abandon its development of application server OSs has left a significant market share in that area wide open to Microsoft, and the rapid development of 32-bit, shrink-wrapped applications to feed the Windows software-buying audience will all but silence the objections that have been voiced by Microsoft critics in the past that there are no applications for these OSs. Of course, it has been said by many that the only predictable thing about the computer networking industry is its unpredictability, and no one can say what the outlook will be a year from now, but these OSs are a great leap forward, by any rational judgment, and all of us who have had just about all they can take of forced reboots and mysteriously dwindling system resources should now be able to endure a few more years.

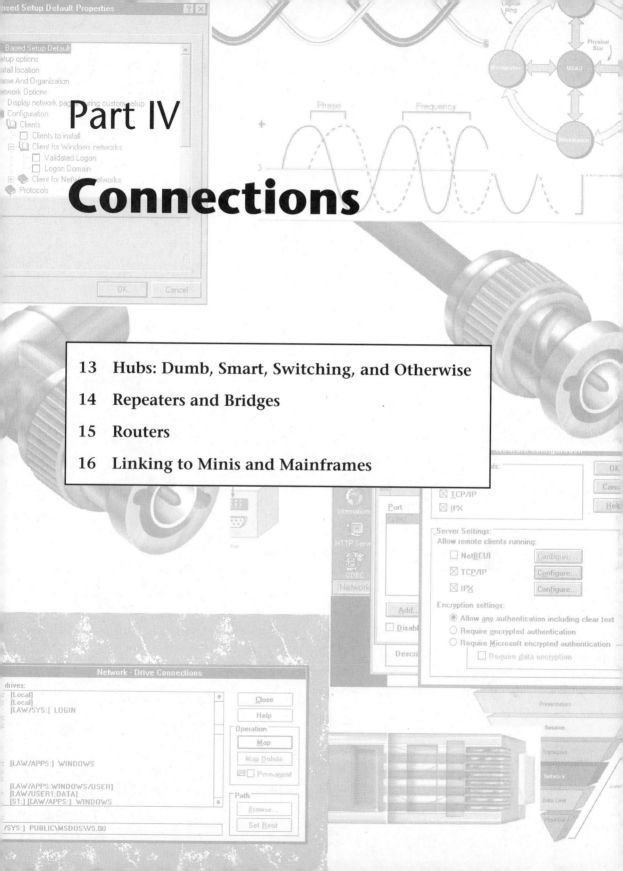

Part IV

Connections

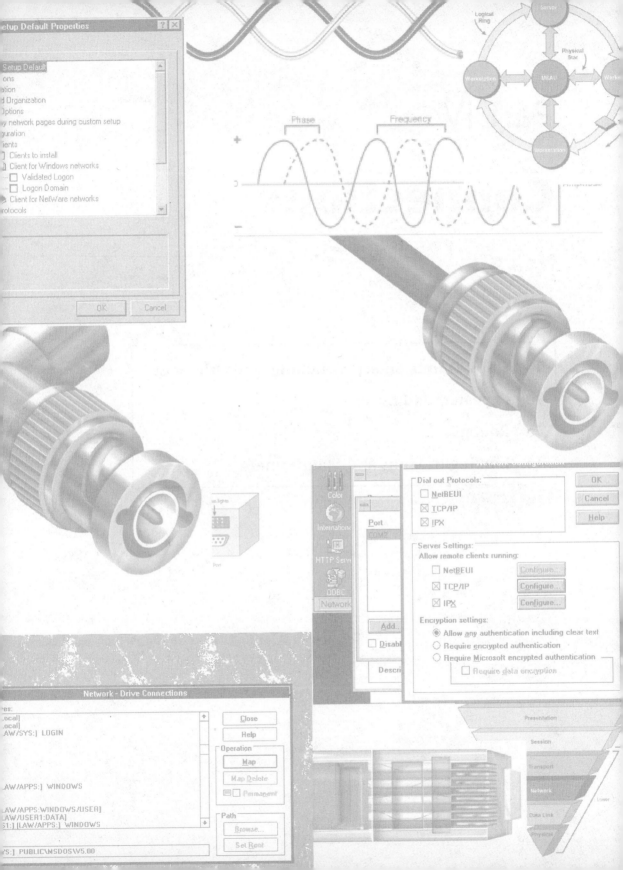

Chapter 13

Hubs: Dumb, Smart, Switching, and Otherwise

Earlier in this book, we discussed how a star topology can make cabling and maintaining your network easier. Rather than snaking a cable through the office and connecting everyone in a long row, you can run lines from a central location to each workstation—easier to cable, and easier to isolate and fix cable problems. To work, a star topology requires an extra piece of hardware that bus networks don't. The extra piece, which connects all the members of the network, is generically known as a *hub*.

"Hub" is sort of a catch-all phrase for a device that connects other networked devices to each other. Therefore, hubs can range in complexity from unpowered patch panels to complicated devices that can connect several kinds of local area networks and even connect them to wide-area networks. Clearly, you won't use the same device to connect a small LAN as you would to connect your site network to the network in the building next door. Therefore, in this chapter, we'll talk about the wide range of smartness and flexibility that the various kinds of hubs can represent.

Because prices and capabilities change, making specific recommendations is difficult, but this chapter will alert you to some of your options and help you figure out which are best for your particular situation.

> **Note**
>
> Although not all hubs are created equal, ranging from simple punchdown blocks to complex network administration tools, their basic purpose is the same: to act as a distribution point for the network. The logical topology of the network and the cable that it's strung with are irrelevant to this definition.

Hub Architecture

The essentials of a hub are the ports that network nodes can plug into to connect with each other. Beyond that, you can add management module ports that allow you to connect the hub to other hubs or connection devices, and so forth, but the essential component of a hub is its connecting function. Even a separate chassis is not essential; as we'll discuss, you can buy hub cards that allow you to turn your server into a hub.

Most often, however, a hub looks like a box with ports for LAN nodes to plug into. The type of connector will depend on the network type and cabling used, but the essentials look something like the example shown in figure 13.1.

Figure 13.1

Most 10BaseT network hubs share basic features.

The basics of the chassis are the same; it's the specifics that vary. For example, powered hubs have status lights. What those status lights mean and can tell you depends on how much network management the hub is capable of.

Compatible Ports

A hub port will only accommodate a particular kind of cable jack; RG-58 coaxial has different connections than RJ-45 UTP, and UTP uses connections different from the DB-9 connector used in token-ring networks. As with other network devices, you can't plug physical devices into ports with which they're incompatible. However, hubs are also like other network devices in that their ports are physically compatible with other like ports. In other words, if you have a 10BaseT network to hook up, it shouldn't matter whether you buy your hub from 3Com or Akbar and Jeff's House of Hubs; the physical interface is the same.

Caution

One caution on this point: token-ring hubs take a DB-9 connector, just like a video connector. Just as you shouldn't plug your token-ring cable into your monitor—it will at least turn your screen purple and at most smoke your monitor—be careful about *what* DB-9 connector you plug into a physically compatible connection on a hub. Although you may not smoke anything, you'll confuse a passive MAU because the device plugged into the port will *feel* like a token-ring connection, although it's not. It won't be able to remove the alien connection from the ring or ignore it, so the network won't work.

It's probably pretty easy to see why this kind of physical compatibility among cable types is important; if not, consider what it would be like having to buy all your cable and all your network cards and all your hubs from the same vendor. If hubs used proprietary cable interfaces, then you'd *have* to.

Hubs that can connect more than one kind of physical network will have a variety of port types to accommodate the various kinds of cables. AS/400 connections, for example, are available but relatively rare. ARCnet hubs, on the other hand, are quite easy to find even though few new networks use ARCnet.

Internal Connections for Ports

Ports in a hub won't do you any good unless they're connected in some way. Otherwise, the hub would work like a Roach Motel: data goes in, but it doesn't go out.

To let ports (and therefore, the nodes plugged into those ports) communicate with each other, you need some kind of bus system to transport the data between ports. One way for this to work is to build each port with a receiving connection and a sending connection. The receivers all connect to all the senders, so that the nodes can talk to each other.

The bus used will be the same speed as the network—if it's a fast token-ring hub, the bus will keep up with 16 Mbps; if Ethernet, 10 Mbps; and so forth.

External Connections

Not all of the ports on a hub are for local network connections. Some models have an additional port, called the attachment unit interface (AUI), for connecting to other hubs or other connection devices like bridges or routers. (Models with an AUI port usually list the total number of ports something like this: 12+1. This port number indicates that there are 12 network ports and one AUI port.) The cable connection between networking devices is called the *backbone*. Depending on the kind of hub, the backbone can be thin Ethernet (10Base2), thick Ethernet (10Base5), or fiber. Higher-end hubs generally have the fiber connections, and the top models will have an AUI port that you can double-cable for fault tolerance. If one cable breaks, then the other can take up the slack until you replace the broken one.

Some hubs will also have an RS-232 serial port to connect to a PC or modem for remote management capability that isn't affected by network crashes. Management that takes place via the serial connection is called "out of band," as it's independent of the network transmissions. We'll talk more about "out of band" management later in this chapter.

Management Capabilities

If you want to be able to manage your hub, you've got two choices: buy an upgradeable hub or buy one with the management module already in place.

A hub's management capabilities are tied up in a piece of smart hardware. (With on-board upgradeable ROMs, the line between hardware and software gets more and more squishy.) In most models, the hardware is another module like the ones used for the ports. Therefore, if you want a managed hub, you can fill the slot with a management module; if port connections are more important to you, you can use the slot for another connection module. A few models, such as 3Com's, include a proprietary port in the back into which you can plug a management module, a bridging module (to turn the hub into a bridge), or a combination of the two. The add-in module is about the size and shape of a deck of cards, so it doesn't add much to the size of your hub.

Whether your hub's management capabilities come from internal or external modules, you'll have to contact the hub's vendor for intelligence hardware. You can't take a module from one vendor and plug it into a hub from another vendor.

Hub Smarts: Some Are More Equal Than Others

Although the essential purpose of a hub remains the same no matter what kind of hub it is or what it can do, the fact remains that not all hubs are the same. Some can only provide a basic connection for the network, while others possess advanced troubleshooting capabilities. Some can amplify the signal to increase the span of the network, and others can only pass the signal along as it reaches them.

As we'll discuss, you can increase the intelligence of some hubs but not others. Some hubs will accept internal or external management hardware, and some of those have flash ROM that you can upgrade with software. (Software-upgradeable hubs are a really good thing to look for, as they extend the useful life of your hub by letting it take advantage of new information.) Upgradeability is a real issue if you expect your network to expand, so when you're buying, consider what your future needs will be, as well as your present needs.

Passive Hubs

A passive hub is only a contact point for the wires that make up the physical network. A punchdown block, one example of a passive hub, consists of a plastic, unpowered box that you can plug the cables of the network into, such as the RJ-45 cables used in a 10BaseT Ethernet network. When you plug in the cables, the wires inside the cable make positive contact with the punchdown block and, thereby, connect to the other cables used in the network.

Powered Passive Hubs. Not many networks use totally powerless passive hubs like punchdown blocks. More often, the center of each star will be a powered, but passive (non-repeating) hub, connected to any other hubs via a patch panel in a wiring closet.

In token-ring networks, a powered device called a *multistation access unit* (MAU) serves as the focal point of the network. MAUs are slightly smarter than punchdown blocks. *Bypass circuitry* is inherent in the design of these hubs, meaning that if a network node isn't communicating with the rest of the nodes plugged into the network—if the cable or its connection to the hub is dead—then the nonfunctioning member doesn't interfere with the rest of the nodes plugged into the hub. The dead node won't work, but the rest of the network will while you're figuring out what's wrong with that node.

Although brighter than punchdown blocks, ordinary MAUs don't have much intelligence built into them. They can distinguish between an active token-ring connection and a dead one, but they can't distinguish between an active 4 Mbps token-ring connection and the 16 Mbps one that should be there (for example), or between a token-ring connection and a video cable. Plug in a device that a passive MAU doesn't recognize, and the entire network may crash. The problem is that the MAU can't talk to a device that isn't using a signal that it recognizes, and a video cable or a token-ring connector set to the wrong speed doesn't communicate in any form that the MAU can recognize as a language. They don't have enough in common even to argue.

Applications for Passive Hubs. Like other network components, hubs are generally getting smarter as the price of computing intelligence drops, and performance and management standards get higher. Although passive hubs are still available on the market, they're not as common as they once were.

First of all, by definition, no Ethernet hub can be passive—every device connected to an Ethernet network (including the PCs) acts as a repeater for the signal. Repeating capability makes a hub active. Second, token-ring hubs are getting smarter. In the early 1990s IBM realized that they were going to lose market share to Ethernet if they didn't start making intelligent MAUs (like the intelligent hubs that the 10BaseT networks were using). Therefore, only older MAUs are passive hubs. We'll talk about the smart ones a little later in this chapter.

Passive hubs are a relatively inexpensive means of connecting your network, but they don't do anything in your network except provide a contact point for the network through which the nodes of the network can communicate with each other. With the growing importance of networks in the corporate world, that's rarely enough these days. If your network extends across a wide span and you're worried about signal degradation, or *attenuation*, you'll need a hub with repeating abilities to strengthen the signal—an active hub. For management capabilities, you'll need a hub with some smarts—an intelligent hub. Of course, a hub can be both. Although I haven't inventoried every commercially available hub, I can't imagine why someone would make an intelligent hub without repeating capabilities.

Active Hubs

Punchdown blocks and other passive hubs don't do anything except provide a contact point for the network cables. Hubs that are a little smarter than passive hubs have repeating capabilities. Rather than just passing the signal from node to node, an active hub can regenerate the signal so that it maintains its strength. As we discussed in the previous section, all Ethernet hubs are active, as repeating is inherent to the bus logical topology.

Active hubs are often called *concentrators* (either because they concentrate and thus strengthen the signal or because they concentrate the capabilities of an entire LAN into a box—I've heard both theories). Concentrators can accommodate more than one set of network connections; you can add modules to them to add more ports or (depending on the model) different kinds of ports. Thus, a concentrator could offer a connection for both your token-ring network and your 10BaseT network, if you had modules to support both kinds of ports. This can save you the cost of another hub.

You can also add a module to plug in a high-speed connection to another hub, which is useful when your network expands beyond the physical limitations of cable length or you run out of slots in the concentrator.

Intelligent Hubs

Intelligent, or smart, hubs include some kind of software management to detect and isolate network problems. Some intelligent hubs are smarter than others, but anything called an intelligent hub will have some kind of management and monitoring capabilities.

From the earlier discussions, you can see that management capability can be essential to keeping your network up and running. If it's a small network with one hub and a few nodes, cable and port testing is not that big a deal—if a problem in the hub is keeping the network from functioning, isolating the problem in a ten-node network is a pain, but not impossible. A larger network of ten connected hubs with twelve nodes each would not be as simple, however, and the time and effort required to manually troubleshoot a downed network would be more than most network or system administrators can supply. Therefore, if your star network extends beyond a few nodes, you'll need some kind of intelligence built into the system if you want to keep your sanity.

Intelligent hubs can offer both monitoring and managing capabilities—that is, they can keep track of how the network's doing and also take action to correct problems. How capable they are depends on the intelligence of the individual hub. Not all intelligent hubs are equally intelligent. As mentioned before, the intelligence comes from internal or external modules that you can add to the hub. The ones that have flash ROM that you can upgrade with software are best, because they allow your network management abilities to grow with the technology.

SNMP. The most popular management protocol that intelligent hubs use is called SNMP, or Simple Network Management Protocol. Almost any manageable device you buy will include SNMP in its management suite. SNMP acts as a sort of poll taker, going around to the devices that it's managing and asking them how they're feeling. Whatever the response, SNMP notes it down in a management information base, or MIB. In case of trouble, the network administrator can review the contents of the MIB to isolate the problem child.

SNMP is the main management protocol that you'll see for just about any manageable device, but like many other network standards this one came about by default rather than as the result of any planning. As networks developed, it became obvious that if network administrators were going to get any sleep at night, some kind of remote admin-istration was necessary. So a number of developers began working on high-powered management protocols (one of which was CMIP, discussed next). In the interim, how-ever, administrators clamored for *some* kind of managing ability, so the developers put together SNMP to hold off the demands for better control until their versions were complete.

Of course, the end of the story is predictable: SNMP became the standard because it was available when nothing else was, and the more powerful management protocols became proprietary.

Please note that not all SNMP implementations are equal. First, only those SNMP devices that are MIB-2 compliant will talk to each other so that you can get a complete picture of your network. Devices following older standards or those including proprietary exten-sions that increase the management capabilities may not talk to each other. Second, even those that follow the industry standards may include different features. Two devices from different vendors that are both MIB-2 compliant may have completely different capabilities. When shopping for SNMP-managed devices, be sure to check for MIB-2 compliance and get a copy of the MIB to see what the device can monitor.

Several companies offer management software that works with SNMP-managed devices to give you a graphical view of the network without leaving your desk. Although GUI management software can be nice, be sure to evaluate it (or at least demo it) before buy-ing. Some network management software is quite good; other products offer nothing more than pretty pictures that really don't tell you anything. If done right, network management software can save you time by putting the network in front of you without you having to leave your desk, but otherwise it's a waste of time and disk space. IBM's NetView and HP's OpenView are two examples of good SNMP management GUIs.

CMIP. The Common Management Information Protocol (CMIP) is a far less common network management tool than SNMP, but it has a small following. Using object-oriented descriptions, CMIP lets the network administrator define hundreds of param-eters for the system to monitor, including physical problems, security breaches, heavy network traffic, and so forth.

It works like this: rather than the network management software polling the pieces of the network, they volunteer information based on the parameters set by the network admin-istrator. A hub might tell CMIP that it's a 10BaseT hub hooked up to twelve normally functioning nodes, and that it's passing X number of packets per second.

The power of CMIP is that it provides the network administrator with the information that he or she needs. It has two major failings, however: it's a lot of work for the network administrator, and it requires many times more processing power than does SNMP.

How does CMIP represent more work for the network manager? Well, to get the network-specific information that the network manager needs to keep up with events, she has to define objects and parameters for each component of her network. If she replaces a component, then it needs a new object. For example, if you owned one CMIP-compliant hub and then replaced it with another model from the same manufacturer, you'd have to start from scratch to make the management system recognize it. You can't just tell CMIP, "Oh that? That's the new hub I bought. Treat it just like the old one."

The way that CMIP is customized for each network it manages means more work for the hardware, not just the humans. CMIP must be able to communicate specifically with each component, so generic responses from the network components are not possible. This means that CMIP-compliant devices need more on-board memory than SNMP-compliant devices, thus slowing down acceptance because of the larger costs involved.

Proprietary Management Protocols. It's hard to generalize about the way in which proprietary management works, as it's fine-tuned to the hardware it's meant to run on. Because the hardware and management are made for each other, they can sometimes do things that less specific management utilities can't. The details of what they do and how they do it depend on the vendor.

Proprietary protocols may be more efficient than general ones, but they've got the disadvantage of all proprietary components: they lock you into one vendor. This isn't necessarily a bad thing, as long as you're happy with your vendor and willing (and able) to buy all managed hardware from them, but it will limit your choices.

Can You Mix Managed Devices? Well, sort of. You can mix them, but whether or not you can manage them as a unit is another question entirely. (A question worth answering, if you're going to the expense of buying a managed hub.)

The problem is that the smarter a device gets, the more there is involved to make it compatible with like devices for management purposes. Fairly dumb devices, like network cards, can be mixed on the network because they function at a fairly low level on the OSI model. Smarter devices, like managed hubs and other network connectivity hardware, function at a much higher level—in some cases, at the application layer on top of the chart. To work together, the devices must only be able to communicate at the data link layer, but to be *managed* together requires the devices to be much more in sync.

As one 3Com representative pointed out, once the various vendors began creating their own management platforms, it was not to their advantage to make them compatible with devices from other manufacturers. The only person who would benefit from such cooperation is the user.

How Many Smarts Do You Need?

As always, the answer to this question depends on your situation and network requirements. A few thoughts, however:

- Passive hubs are cheap enough to be a "throwaway" solution for tentative or temporary networks. If you know that the network won't exist for long, or it's only in testing mode, then spending a lot of money on an expensive system may be unnecessary.

- You can buy an upgradeable hub so that you don't have to make the initial cash outlay for management, but retain the option of getting management ability later.

- Look either for hubs that can be managed using a common GUI (such as HP's OpenView for UNIX or IBM's NetView, which runs over OS/2), or choose a vendor with incompatible but really good management tools. Many consider Bay Network's Optivity system to be an example of a good, if proprietary, management system.

Improving Hub Reliability

Because of their place in the network, hubs have an inherent, serious failing: they present a single point of failure in the network. If the hub goes down, it drags the rest of the network with it, because no information can pass from node to node. Period.

Therefore, it's in your best interest to make sure that the hub keeps functioning. That means taking a few questions into account:

- How can I keep the hub powered?

- How can I prevent mechanical failures within the hub?

- How can I ensure that the hub is unaffected by network problems?

Power

As in every aspect of networking, one of the most important questions is how to keep power running to your system and how to ensure that it's the clean power that electronics prefer. This isn't just about blackouts, which are easy to see the effects of; it's about making sure that the hub isn't damaged by power surges or sags. Although a complete discussion on power is reserved for elsewhere in this book, it's worthwhile to make a couple of points about power here:

1. Power quality in the United States (and the rest of the world) is getting worse with the increasing demands placed upon the existing supply infrastructure. Barring drastic improvements in the power grid, this trend will continue.

2. Over a period of time, bad power can damage or destroy your network components.

So power quality is going to get worse before it gets better, and bad power kills network components. (This isn't limited to network devices, obviously; bad power is just as bad for stand-alone devices.) What can you do to keep good power running to your hub?

Isolate Hub Power. First of all, try to keep your hub on a circuit away from devices that dirty the power supply. That means no heating elements and no big motors, so coffee makers, refrigerators, and laser printers are no good. If you're not sure how the wiring in your building is arranged, check with the building manager or maintenance people and get the wiring blueprints. If you can't get the wiring blueprints, you can either guess or test the circuits some weekend when/if you can shut down parts of the power to the office and see what outlets are on the same circuits.

> **Caution**
>
> If you're not sure of what you're doing and don't have permission from the building management or your boss, do not flip circuit breakers to see what outlets are on the same lines. Shutting down some systems (servers, for one) without adequate preparations can be extremely bad for the devices you're shutting down. It can also be bad for your job security.

Checking the plugs to make sure that they're wired properly isn't a bad idea either. Sometimes, even three-prong plugs aren't grounded properly, or the polarities are reversed, or some such thing. Not all problems are bad enough to cause immediate problems on the order of explosions (in fact, if they're that bad, they generally get fixed fairly quickly), but you can find more minor problems that could turn out to be serious with the wrong set of circumstances. The testers don't cost much—I got mine for about $5. Plug it into an outlet, and the status lights will show you if the outlet is wired properly, or if not, what's wrong with it.

Regulating Hub Power. Sometimes, complete power protection in a star topology requires double protection: you need to protect both your hub and the data lines connecting the nodes to the hub. On the hub side, you can buy a UPS or SPS to plug into the serial port. You can determine the size of the device by the wattage that the hub uses. If the UPS or SPS includes a power conditioner, then your hub is protected from sags and surges as well.

The hub isn't the only vulnerable part of the network, however. The data lines can pick up electromagnetic pulses (EMPs) from nearby lightning strikes and conduct the pulses to the network nodes. This is odd but true. APC, for example, started developing data line protection after some of its customers who'd bought UPSs called to complain that they'd plugged everything in properly but a power surge had killed a network card anyway. On investigation, it turned out that the power surge had come from the air. Lightning in the area hadn't affected the power supply to the building, but the data line had picked up the EMP and conducted it to the network node.

This doesn't happen often, but it happens. Network cables extended more than about fifteen feet (which describes many networks designed in a star topology) make good antennae, and in locations with lots of electrical storms that can be dangerous. The damage could fry just the NIC, or it could fry the motherboard. To protect the data line, you can plug a small surge protector directly into the network card and then plug the line into the surge protector. To ground the surge protector, connect another cable to a properly grounded source, such as the computer chassis or (to be extra careful) the screw in the wall of a properly grounded outlet. APC only makes single data line protectors, but you can also buy protectors into which you can plug several nodes at once—the only difference is that those devices plug into the hub, rather than the NIC.

What kind of power protection should you get? It depends on your circumstances. If your network uses passive hubs, it might be cheaper to keep a replacement or two on hand than to buy a UPS for every hub. As for data line protection, it's not really necessary in most of the United States, but take the weather conditions into account when deciding whether you need it. The devices are very popular in Florida, due to the high number of electrical storms in the area.

You can read more about power protection in chapter 18, "Backup Technology: Uninterruptible Power Supplies."

Keeping Network Problems from Affecting Hubs

Simple problems, like disconnected nodes, shouldn't affect any hub. If nothing is connected to a port, or the connection isn't communicating with the hub, then the hub ignores that port and keeps the good ports connected.

Some problems aren't quite that cut and dried, however. For example, if a node on a token-ring network starts jabbering (sending streams of noise that tie up the network), then a passive hub or active hub without management capabilities can't shut up the offending node.

Remote Hub Administration. Some higher-end hubs are equipped with serial ports via which you can work with the hub even if the network is down. You can perform "out of band" management either from a PC connected to the hub with a serial cable or via a modem connected to the serial port. Using Telnet or (if supported) a GUI like OpenView, you can dial into the hub and operate it from across the telephone wire. The advantages to out-of-band management are twofold: first, you're not dependent upon a functioning network to access the hub, and second, you can manage hubs in another building without having to physically go to them.

Hub Redundancy

Network nodes plug into the hub via LAN modules. The number of modules in the hub depends on the hub design. Although it is possible (and cheaper) to plug a number of nodes into the same module, if that module fails, so does the hub. For better fault tolerance, the higher the ratio of modules to nodes, the better off you are. The fewer nodes that you have plugged into each module, the fewer nodes will be affected in case of a module failure.

For extra fault tolerance, you can provide important nodes with more than one LAN module. You'll need one link to each module, so it's a little more complicated than a normal network connection, but it's possible. A transceiver splits the links from the network node to the two modules, so that the redundancy doesn't cause any confusion on the network. This also works to connect a node to more than one hub to get the ultimate redundancy. That way, if one hub fails, the node will still be connected to the network via the other hub.

If your network includes more than one hub and these hubs are in a connected star topology, then you can build redundancy into your network with double cables. Only one of the cables is necessary for transmission, so if one cable breaks, the other cable can route the traffic between the hubs.

Server-Based Hubs

Although most hubs are stand-alone machines with their own chassis, they don't have to be—a few vendors sell hub cards that you can put in your file server (for small networks) or a dedicated hub machine (for larger networks) and thus lower the cost of a star topology. Unsurprisingly, card hubs are cheaper than stand-alones. Card hubs also have the advantage of instant intelligence, too. One model (now discontinued for reasons we'll get to in a minute) operated in cooperation with NetWare, so to make your dumb hub intelligent all you had to do was load an NLM (NetWare Loadable Module) for management capabilities.

A hub card fits into a slot on your motherboard like a network card. On the back, where a NIC would have one connector, the hub card has as many as twelve, sometimes with an AUI connection available for attachment to another hub. Like any other card, the RAM on the board itself makes a difference in speed, as does the speed of the hub server's CPU, but the biggest bottleneck in hub speed comes at the bus type. All other things being equal, the larger the data path, the better network throughput will be.

If you've made your file server do double duty before, perhaps as a print server, it's no surprise that placing the hub in a non-dedicated server (one not used *only* as a hub) does not do good things for either network performance or server accesses. The burden of handling all the network traffic in addition to dispensing information can really slow your server down. If you've got more than a few nodes on your network, it's better to dedicate a machine to being a hub. For that matter, that's probably the reason why stand-alone hubs are more common than hub modules that fit into a bus slot—once you've moved the hub capabilities to another machine, the cost savings realized from not buying the stand-alone disappear. For example, Intel discontinued their EtherExpress TPE 10BaseT card hubs two years after announcing them, because they couldn't compete with stand-alone models.

Essentially, card hubs are a good idea for a very specific set of conditions (a small network that wants the management ease of a star topology but can't afford a stand-alone hub), but beyond that set of circumstances a stand-alone hub probably will work better.

ATM Switches

To close this discussion of hubs, we'll discuss a relative newcomer to the hub market: the ATM switch. It's not a hub, but it can provide a high-speed backbone for hubs.

If you've worked with networks for any period, it's no surprise to you that the demands placed on networking are growing. E-mail isn't enough anymore—we want to transfer big documents, complex images, and real-time video with sound attached, and we don't want to have to wait for it. Asynchronous Transfer Mode (ATM) can make all this possible. Of course, ATM equipment is quite expensive at the moment (as is the equipment required to produce the kinds of complex files that need ATM to quickly get them from point A to point B), so don't look for ATM switches to be a part of Everyman's office for awhile. But the technology to connect LANs using ATM is available, and it's worth knowing about for the time when your data transfer needs expand to fit ATM, and the technology becomes a bit more affordable.

Although a detailed discussion of ATM is beyond the scope of this book (the topic hasn't been exhausted by the dozens of books written about it, so we're not going to cover it all in one portion of a chapter), we'll discuss some of the basic characteristics of ATM and ATM switches here.

ATM Basics

ATM is a connection-oriented networking technology, operating at the lowest layer of the OSI model (described in chapter 3, "The OSI Model: Bringing Order to Chaos"). The ATM switch converts the data transferred to it into 53-byte cells. To transmit those cells, the transmitting node must set up a connection with the receiving node. Once the connection is accepted, the cells are shoved along a high-speed cable (most often fiber, but sometimes Category 5 twisted pair) to the next ATM switch, where the cells are reassembled into their original form. The cells carry routing and data type information within themselves so that they can get to where they're going without help from other devices, and so the switch can sort them out into their various types once they arrive at their destination. This mode of data transfer is called *cell relay*. It's not entirely a physical standard—ATM is not locked into one kind of cable—but it's close.

> ### Note
>
> For purposes of describing how cell relay works, the lowest layer of the OSI model, the physical layer, is divided into two sub-layers: the transmission convergence (TC) layer and the physical medium dependent (PMD) layer. The TC layer is sort of the mail handler for the physical connection—it packages data into cells, sorts received cells into their appropriate categories, and performs flow control. The PMD carries the data.

Cell relay has two main advantages: it's very fast (ATM runs at 155 Mbps—more than fifteen times faster than Ethernet) and it can handle any kind of data that you throw at it: voice, data, or real-time video. Each of the cells includes a header that identifies the kind of data in the cell, so the switch on the other end can sort out the various kinds of data. The sorting-out part of the equation is where the money comes in: to avoid mixing up the various kinds of information, and to do this quickly, requires a lot of intelligence on the part of the switch doing the sorting. The intelligence and high-speed cables required to make ATM work are expensive, and that's held up the implementation of ATM on a wide-area basis. (Some vendors, such as AT&T, are offering it on a beta basis to a few customers, but that's about it as of early 1996.)

ATM Switches

ATM has been an "emerging" technology for quite a few years now, but its use currently and in the near future is mainly for providing high-speed backbones for hubs. You can insert ATM cards into high-powered workstations or servers and make them into ATM switches between hubs in a company's networking background.

A number of companies offer ATM cards that can provide speeds ranging from 155 Mbps to more than 2 Gbps. What characterizes these cards? Here are a few items:

- Most are designed to work with UNIX, although Plexcom cards support NetWare and NT.

- The transport protocol is TCP/IP.

- Most support fiber (especially multimode fiber), some support UTP, and none support coaxial.

- Most are managed by SNMP.

- They use a variety of buses; from the familiar EISA and PCI to Sbus and VME.

- The bit size in buses ranges from 16 to 64 (Sbus can support both 16-bit and 32-bit data transfer).

What drives these characteristics?

Operating Environment. Most ATM cards operate in UNIX boxes. Although as noted earlier, NetWare and NT Server are beginning to be supported, the problem with these operating systems has been that their "native" protocols aren't really compatible with ATM; NetBEUI isn't routable unless it's encapsulated in TCP/IP, and IPX was originally designed for connectionless networking, which doesn't work very well with a connection-oriented technology like ATM. The difference? In a nutshell, a connectionless communication doesn't require any call setup before the message begins. Connection-oriented communications require the node that wants to send data to arrange a link with the node that it wants to send data to. Without the previous arrangement, the nodes can't communicate. In other words, ATM requires a connection-oriented routable protocol, like TCP/IP.

Management Protocols. We've discussed in this chapter the reasons why SNMP can be an easier management protocol to implement within a LAN than CMIP is, and how proprietary management protocols can lock you into one vendor. Therefore, the fact that all the ATM cards listed in the 1994 *LAN Magazine Buyer's Guide* use SNMP as their primary management protocol shouldn't be much of a surprise. If you're going to use a switch with a proprietary management protocol, then buy from someone whom you're certain a) will be around in years to come, and b) has good support so you'll be happy with the product. Otherwise, you'll be left with the choice of keeping unsupported equipment or buying new switches when the first vendor jumps ship—not an attractive thought.

Although SNMP is becoming the de facto standard for LAN management, there's been some discussion of the possibility of CMIP being used for wide-area ATM management (when ATM WANs become a reality, that is). This could work well. As discussed earlier, CMIP can provide more information about a network's operation than SNMP because it's so tuned to the network that it's managing, and since the devices used in an ATM WAN are less likely to change than those used in a LAN, the housekeeping shouldn't be as much of a problem for the WAN administrators.

Cable Types. Most full-speed ATM runs over fiber (often multimode fiber); some runs over Category 5 UTP. None support coaxial, as it can't keep up with the transmission speeds required by ATM.

The bottom line here is that an ATM switch will use either fiber or high-speed UTP. Because of the distance limits inherent in UTP, you might be better off with fiber unless your hubs will be quite close together.

Bus Types. There's no real generalizations about bus type in ATM cards—they pretty much run the gamut of the high-speed buses. I expect to see more PCI buses used for PC ATM cards. Because there's little point in having a narrow data path for a high-throughput card, the 32-bit and 64-bit cards should squeeze out the few 16-bit cards on the market.

ATM's Place in the LAN

As of this writing, ATM's main role in networking is to provide a switching point on a high-speed backbone for a LAN. The switch doesn't replace the hub, it connects the hubs. Take a look at figure 13.2 to see how this works:

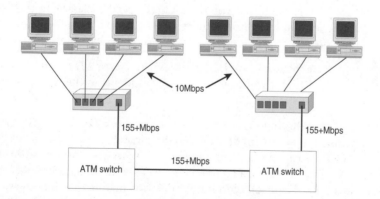

Figure 13.2

An ATM switch in an Ethernet network often provides a high-speed backbone connection.

For this to work, the ATM switches have to do something called "LAN emulation" in which the Ethernet packets are divided into cells and then reassembled for the hubs to route. More vendors support Ethernet than token ring, so ATM will be more useful for 10BaseT networks than token-passing ones.

What about ATM to the desktop? Well, in theory it's supposed to work like a token-ring network in which all stations think that they've got the token. Each workstation taps into an ATM switch via UTP (as low as Category 3) and can send data at any time because they're all fooled into thinking that they've got the token. (Token ring works, recall, by passing a token around the network that can be either free or busy. If a node has a free token and needs to send data, it can do so as long as it's got the token. If the token is busy when it passes the node, the node cannot transmit.) The ATM switch is in charge of filtering the cells sent to it from the various nodes, determining which are local traffic and which need to be sent to another switch. If traffic gets heavy, then the switch can get overwhelmed and drop packets, and due to the nature of ATM, there's no error-correcting ability—lost packets stay lost.

The biggest problem with ATM to the desktop, however, is that the benefits to be realized from using the existing cabling infrastructure, although significant in terms of cost, aren't enough for the increase in speed that you get. ATM to the desktop runs at 25 Mbps, not 155 Mbps, and it still requires a hardware investment in the form of an ATM switch and ATM cards for the workstations. If 16 Mbps isn't fast enough for you, how long will it take for 25 Mbps to not be fast enough?

The bottom line is that ATM in a LAN probably will be used to switch traffic quickly between connected hubs, not to bring ATM to each station.

Buying ATM Switches

You should buy ATM switches by the same rules as those you use to buy other connection hardware—think about what you're going to do with it a year or two down the line. The one thing all networks have in common is growth. This is especially true if your network needs are great enough that you need a high-speed backbone to the network. If you need ATM in your building now, you're surely going to want to expand ATM capability to other sites when ATM over the WAN becomes available.

First, make sure that the box has WAN capabilities. Wide-area ATM won't be around next year, but it's a good bet that it will be commercially available in the not-too-distant future.

Second, make sure that the vendor is going to be around in a few years. Ask for references. As a systems engineer friend of mine observes, companies should be glad to provide references, because that gives them an opportunity to show off how well they've been able to help someone else. If a company doesn't want you to talk to its other clients (with their permission, of course), then it might be worthwhile to wonder why. This is especially true because the standards for ATM are still in flux. As buying from a single vendor is currently the only way to really ensure interoperability between your ATM devices, you'd better be happy with the vendor.

Summary

Hubs provide a central connection point to a network. This connection can either be a purely physical relay for network signals, or it can incorporate management features to help you control and troubleshoot your network. Some hubs even offer "out of band" management, so the network does not have to be running to let you dial into the hub.

ATM switches can provide a high-speed backbone to connect a series of hubs. This is currently the most common use for ATM, as ATM to the desktop does not represent enough of a performance increase to justify the additional costs to most buyers, and wide-area ATM is not really commercially available.

Chapter 14

Repeaters and Bridges

If you want to extend or connect your LANs, then repeaters or bridges will likely be the tools that you use. Repeaters extend the reach of your network, and bridges connect like (or nearly like) networks to create one big network. Although it's difficult to generalize about the role of different connection hardware in a network, because the lines between connectivity hardware and internetworking hardware become blurrier by the hour, you could say that bridges and repeaters are both *intra*networking devices. They create larger networks, instead of connecting separate ones. Contrast them with routers, which are more *inter*networking devices that provide a meeting place for separate networks. (Routers are such a big topic that they get a chapter of their own; see chapter 15, "Routers," to read about what they are and how they work.)

This chapter discusses repeaters and bridges and includes the following topics:

- Function
- Operation
- Applications
- Limitations, including when it's time to stop using one or the other and use something else

Repeaters

Repeaters are devices that regenerate an electronic or photonic signal to extend the distance that the signal can travel. When repeaters receive a signal, they boost it to its original strength and condition, repairing any signal corruption that may have occurred due to noise along the way.

Repeaters are purely physical devices, operating at the lowest level of the OSI model. The only thing that repeaters do is strengthen the signal; filtering and routing are left to higher-level devices.

Repeaters' Place in the Network

Specifically, what purpose might a repeater serve in your network? Why is repeating the signal important?

Reduce the Effects of Attenuation. The reason for repeaters is simple: any kind of signal becomes weaker the farther it has to travel. The weaker the signal gets, the more vulnerable it is to interference and corruption, and eventually it becomes unintelligible. Think of throwing rocks in a lake. At the spot where the rock enters the water, the waves produced are strongest; other ripples at that point are unlikely to affect their path. The ripples spread out from that point and may travel quite a distance (depending on the size of the original splash) but become less and less pronounced the farther they travel. The smaller and weaker the ripple, the more likely that interference—perhaps another ripple—will disturb the pattern that the first creates or even stop it from traveling any farther. The way that the signal gets weaker as it travels is called *attenuation*.

Network signals work much the same way as the water ripples, although not all are equally affected by interference and distance. The kind of signal makes a difference (photonic signals are less affected by attenuation than electronic signals), and cable shielding can reduce the effects. However, no matter what kind of signal it is or what kind of cable it travels through, sooner or later the signal loses its strength to the point where the data it carries is no longer "intelligible" at its destination. Use a repeater to increase the distance by which the sender and receiver can be separated before attenuation becomes a problem.

Avoid Collisions. In bus Ethernet (10Base2) networks, repeaters can help avoid collisions. You'll recall from earlier in this book that one of the problems with Ethernet's broadcasting method of data transfer is the possibility of collisions when two or more nodes attempt to transmit data at the same time. (In fact, collisions are an inherent part of the Ethernet broadcast architecture.) As you remember, when an Ethernet node wants to transmit data, it first "listens" to see if the network is clear, rather like the old Westerns where the scout put an ear to the ground to hear if the cavalry was coming. If the network is not in use, then that node is free to transmit data. So far, so good. But a node's ears are only so good. If the cable segment is too long, then the node can't always hear network traffic, so it may attempt to send data when another node is already using the network. The result is increased collisions, which will ultimately reduce network performance. Repeaters can help solve this problem by shortening the cable segments required to fit all the nodes in the network.

Isolating Segments. Repeaters have yet another use: they can isolate segments of the network, while still permitting the LAN to operate as a unit. In a bus topology the biggest problem is that one break in the cable (whether an actual break or just being unplugged) keeps the network from functioning properly. A network divided into segments separated by hardware such as a repeater is less affected by cable breaks, as only the segment on which the break occurs is affected, rather than the entire network.

For example, consider the case of one computer training company. To give its students hands-on experience with PC troubleshooting and network maintenance, it wanted to develop a training area where the students could play with machines, cables, and network software without having to worry about using mission-critical parts of the network for training. After all, the last place that you want to put a person just learning about network operating systems is in front of the file server, right? So the idea was that some machines and a network could be set aside for training purposes, permitting the students to experiment without endangering operations.

The problem was that it was necessary for these machines to be networked *and* be able to get to the main office network, but the company didn't want the bus network to be broken when students forgot to terminate the network. Therefore, the company used a repeater to isolate the training segment. In the now isolated (but still connected to the office network) segment, the students could get hands-on experience with real and created problems without affecting the rest of the network.

Repeaters in the Wild

Repeaters are useful for those times when you need to segment your network without breaking it, but when you don't need any kind of routing or traffic-control capability.

The function of a repeater in the network is to regenerate the signal so that it can travel farther. Essentially, what happens is this: when data packets arrive at the repeater, the device takes them apart and reassembles them in the same form that they started out as. The repeater is not doing anything to the data—as physical devices, repeaters don't know data from a hole in the ground—it is revitalizing the packet so that it's ready to travel farther. Please note that there is *no* error-control inherent in this process: if the packets that arrive at the repeater are garbled due to line noise, that's what the repeater will send out.

Although repeaters operate on a physical level, they are not limited only to connecting the same kind of cable. Some modular repeaters can support twisted pair, coaxial, or fiber all in the same box—the exact configuration is determined by the modules you select. Repeaters cannot, however, connect two disparate network types, such as Token Ring to Ethernet, as they're not smart enough to perform any kind of packet conversion. As you'll see later in this chapter and in chapter 15, "Routers," this is a job left to the smarter bridges and to routers.

Repeaters versus Extenders. You'll notice that the name of repeaters is a little misleading. They don't just repeat the signal, they reassemble it to make it fresh. LAN *extenders*, which electronically boost the signal and don't repackage it, in some ways are the devices that might more properly be called repeaters. Extenders have much of the same function as repeaters, in that, by strengthening the signal, they permit you to place nodes farther apart than are normally permitted, but they don't work the same way and don't add to your repeater count. (What repeater count? As we'll discuss in a minute, you can only have as many as four repeaters in a network, and the number that you have is known as the repeater count.)

You can see the difference between repeaters and extenders illustrated in figure 14.1.

Repeating the Signal

Each repeater/hub repackages
the data before forwarding it to
the other repeater/hub.

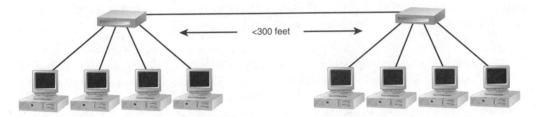

← <300 feet →

Extending the Signal

Each repeater repackages the data before
broadcasting it to the other repeater, but the
extender (in the middle) only amplifies the
signal. A repeater could perform the same function
but at the cost of increasing the repeater count.

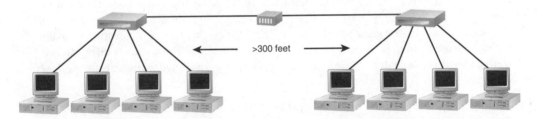

← >300 feet →

Figure 14.1

Repeaters regenerate the signal; extenders rebroadcast the existing signal.

Repeater Count, or Why You Might Need a Bridge. You can only have as many as
four repeaters in any given network, or else bad things (like network failures or delays)
may happen. There are two reasons for this. First, propagation delay may produce
collisions on the network. Every time a packet is disassembled and reassembled by the
repeater, there's an infinitesimal delay. This isn't a problem when the packet is only
reassembled once, but the more repeaters in the network, the more delays you have.
After a certain point, the delays accumulate to the point at which the sending node notices that it hasn't heard any acknowledgment of its transmission. "Looks like the packet
got lost on the way there," decides the sending node, "so I'd better resend it." Trouble is,
that packet is still on the network and in transit, so if the original sender retransmits the
data while the original packet is still out there, the two packets will collide. The result is
network delays because the sending node has to retransmit the data. As you'll remember
from chapter 7's discussion of the Ethernet logical topology, collisions don't seriously
slow down the network, but there's no reason to go looking for them.

The other problem that having too many repeaters can lead to is that of data corruption. Every time that a repeater disassembles and reassembles a packet, there's the chance that it may put the packet back together incorrectly, possibly substituting a 1 for a 0 and thus corrupting the data. It's rather like the joke about what happens if you take a computer apart and put it back together again—do it enough times, and you can build a new computer from all the spare parts. Take apart a packet and put it together enough times, and some parts may be missing or put back together incorrectly.

The four-repeater rule is not carved in stone—that is, this doesn't mean that your network will work perfectly with four repeaters and cease functioning altogether with five—but it's a good guideline to help you avoid problems. Networks fail enough without looking for problems. Therefore, if your network's span requires more than four repeaters to keep connected, you should consider a bridge.

Bridges

Bridges are a step up from repeaters in terms of complexity and capability. Instead of providing a purely physical connection between segments of a network, bridges have some intelligence to perform traffic control. They keep local traffic local and send traffic only to other segments on which it belongs. Bridges have the regenerating capabilities of repeaters, so you don't need to use them in tandem.

Place in the OSI model

Bridges operate in the data link layer of the OSI model, in the sublayers known as the media access control (MAC) layer and the logical link control (LLC) layer.

> **Note**
>
> These sublayers were not originally part of the OSI model developed by the International Standards Organization, but after the model was completed, the IEEE decided that the data link layer covered too broad an area to be useful for some definitions, such as explaining how bridging should work. Hence the sublayers—it's the same reason why the physical layer is subdivided; see chapter 3, "The OSI Model: Bringing Order to Chaos," for more information about the OSI model.

The MAC and LLC layers fit into the OSI model as shown in figure 14.2.

Media Access Control. Each of these sublayers plays a different role in the function of a bridge. The MAC sublayer, which is closest to the physical layer, specifies how a device transmits data and how that data travels over the physical medium, whether that be coaxial cable, fiber, or twisted pair. This layer is where the various kinds of networks (Ethernet, token ring, and FDDI) are defined.

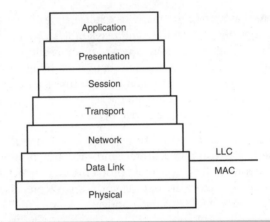

Figure 14.2

The MAC and LLC's layers are sublayers of the data link layer in the OSI model.

If you've heard of MAC addresses (and if you haven't, you will later in this chapter when we discuss filtering), then this is the layer at which they're applicable. MAC addresses are the network addressees burned into network cards at manufacture. Each MAC address is unique because the IEEE furnishes NIC vendors with available addresses from the three trillion or so available. Theoretically, duplication among MAC addresses is impossible. (In practice, this isn't always true, but we'll get to that a little later.)

Most bridges require compatibility at the MAC layer to link network segments—that is, Ethernet to Ethernet or token ring to token ring, but not (in most bridges) Ethernet to token ring. This compatibility means that the bridge can be insensitive to what's going on at higher levels, so the network operating system or network protocols used are irrelevant to a bridge.

Logical Link Control. The LLC's role is closer to the network layer and performs a function similar to routing. Because of its routing character, LLC type is defined in the IEEE standards, so that 802.3 (DIX) Ethernet uses LLC, but other Ethernet types may not. (In English, that means that other kinds of Ethernet may not be able to do the same kinds of bridge routing as the 802.3 standard.) This matters when you're bridging Ethernet to token ring (as we'll discuss later), so keep that in mind when choosing an Ethernet type for your network.

The LLC layer is responsible for how connections are established between sender and destination, how the data moves between them (flow control), and how the connections are broken when the data has been sent. It can define any one of three kinds of transmission methods:

- Datagram
- Acknowledged
- Logical

Each of these transmission methods works a little differently and is better used for a different purpose. The methods that include frame acknowledgment actually take over a task normally associated with higher-level protocols (such as TCP/IP). In providing this service at the data link layer these methods allow the connection to be made more quickly because the upper layers don't have to be concerned with whether the transmission was successful.

Datagram. The word *datagram* describes a data transfer method in which the sender transmits data to the recipient without first establishing any kind of connection and without expecting any kind of response. Delivery is in no way guaranteed, so if there's any problem in transmission, it's the responsibility of the recipient to notice it and request retransmission.

Datagram transmissions are similar to ordinary mail. Say you're sending a piece of mail to someone you're not on very good terms with, perhaps a former roommate or former spouse. You don't especially want to talk to him, but you want the mail to get to him in one piece—if nothing else, so he doesn't call you looking for it. Therefore, before sending him the mail you carefully check the contents and the addressing information, but you don't call the person to tell him that there's a package on the way, and once the package leaves your hands you don't call him to make sure that he got it. Unless the person calls you to say that the piece of mail never got there, you're going to assume that it arrived as sent. The onus of error-handling rests with the recipient, not the sender.

Acknowledged Connectionless. Datagrams are fast and efficient because there's no error-checking information required with the transmission, but you can see that they can be a little uncertain. If you're the sender, the only way that you get feedback about the transmission is if something goes wrong. For more certainty, the sender can require the recipient to acknowledge receipt of each packet of the transmission, increasing overhead but also increasing the likelihood of transmission integrity. If the sender doesn't receive acknowledgment of all frames, he assumes that something went wrong and resends the unacknowledged frames.

To continue the mail analogy, the difference between a datagram and an acknowledged connectionless transmission is the difference between sending a package regular mail and sending the package registered mail. As you may know from experience, you send things registered mail if you want to have proof that the recipient got them. If the recipient never signed for the package, you have to assume that she never received it. It's still connectionless, as you don't establish a connection before sending the data, but it's easier to establish successful delivery because of the required receipt. If the sender doesn't receive confirmation of receipt, the package gets re-sent.

Logical Connection. The surest way of transmitting data is to establish a connection before sending the data. Unlike the connectionless transmissions illustrated with the mail analogy, a logical connection is more like a telephone conversation. If you've got something to communicate to your friend across town, you don't just pick up the telephone and start talking—you dial her number, wait for her to pick up, and then give her the information. If she is not there (that is, if you can't establish the connection) then you don't transmit the data; instead, you make a mental note to try again later. But the important part is that you establish the connection *before* transmitting data.

So it is with a logical connection. Before the node that wants to send data begins transmitting, it first "calls" the recipient to make sure that it's available to receive data. If the proposed recipient doesn't answer, then the sender doesn't transmit the data. This pretty much ensures that the data reaches its destination in one piece because the "conversation" doesn't end until the sender and recipient are both satisfied with the state of the transmission. This is a good transmission method to use when bridging LANs, as it relieves the upper layers of the responsibility of making sure that the transmission was successful.

Bridges in the Network

So much for how bridges function in the theoretical world of the OSI model—what is their place in your network?

Bridges connect smaller networks to create one big one. This is different from repeaters (discussed earlier in this chapter), which extend the reach of your LAN by regenerating the signal, and different from routers (discussed in chapter 15, "Routers"), which connect individual networks but do not merge them. The difference lies in the OSI level at which bridges work: above the purely physical level but (mostly) below any routing capabilities found in the network layer. Essentially, the principal job of a bridge on a network is to connect network segments without burdening the entire network with traffic that only belongs on one segment; however, they can perform other functions as well. We'll look at the various possible roles of a bridge on a network now.

Traffic Control. Bridges keep records of the MAC addresses on each side of the segments they connect and can compare the source and destination address of a packet with the addresses in the table. If the destination is local, then the bridge filters out the broadcast and leaves it on the local segment. If the destination is on another segment, then the bridge passes the data along to that segment. Either way, the data is only passed to the segment(s) where it belongs, so the network isn't tied up with broadcasts that belong only to one segment.

Security. A bridge's filtering capability also makes it configurable for security purposes. You're probably quite familiar with the idea of limiting access to shared drives, directories, and files with user rights, file permissions, and passwords, but this kind of restriction goes one step further. Using the filtering capabilities of a bridge, you can forbid any physical connection between nodes, making it impossible for an engineer, for example, to access the accounting files from her local machine. You still need the logical security of passwords and user rights to protect against those times, but if you're feeling really hyper about security, address filtering can give you an added layer of protection.

Caution

Of course, if you've got users, you've got potential security breaches. If you're running NetWare, for example, you can substitute a node's physical MAC address for a logical one, thus bypassing any security relying on blocking a particular MAC address from accessing a particular segment.

Connecting Disparate Networks. As many networks are not the result of careful planning to produce an integrated system, the capability of some bridges to link more than one kind of network can be useful in making the corporate network more integrated. We're not talking about linking merely physically different networks here (for example, 10Base2 Ethernet and 10Base5 Ethernet)—a repeater can do that. This is about connecting networks that transmit data in entirely different ways and using different packet forms.

As you're no doubt aware, Ethernet and token ring (to use the two most common network types in today's LANs) don't work in the same way. Ethernet networks broadcast their data to every node within hearing (that is, on the segment before the bridge) but only the node for which the data is intended really pays attention. Token-ring networks seek to avoid the possibility of two nodes trying to "talk" over each other, which is inherent in broadcast networking. To do this, they pass around a null packet called a *token* that acts like a talking stick in a lodge meeting—only the node with the talking stick gets to transfer data at any given time. The packet forms for these two paradigms of networking vary as well, as you can see in figure 14.3.

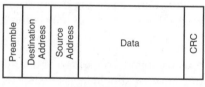

Ethernet frame

Token Ring frame

Figure 14.3

An Ethernet frame contains different information from a token-ring frame.

Therefore, it's a touchy proposition for these two network types to communicate. For a bridge to translate these network types, it must convert the frame headers and data fields of the packets to be translated.

> **Note**
>
> Protocol conversion only works with like hardware, such as micros to micros or PCs to PCs. If you need a gateway to help the machines talk to each other (such as a PC to mainframe connection), then you still need the gateway even with the protocol conversion. A bridge won't work, for example, to connect an Ethernet PC to a Token Ring VAX.

The packet's frame header and data field must be converted to transfer a token-ring packet on an Ethernet network or vice versa. Essentially, protocol conversion works like this: token-ring packets are stripped of the LLC protocol used for source routing, thus removing extraneous routing data that would only confuse the Ethernet network. Once on the Ethernet side, the packets are converted to Ethernet packets and sent on their way. Ethernet packets that must get to the token-ring network have routing information added because token-ring bridging requires the packets to carry routing information within them. The bridge adds the routing information from its own address database. No matter which way the packet travels, however, only the address changes; the data within the packet never gets touched.

Because protocol conversion connects a token-ring network to an Ethernet network, it requires a bridge that can speak to both. Spanning tree or source routing bridges won't work for this—you need a bridge that can perform translation functions.

Filter or Forward?

When playing traffic cop to keep network congestion to a minimum, a bridge's most important question is whether a packet should be filtered or forwarded. If the packet's destination is on the same network segment as the sender, then the packet is filtered out of the bridge and sent to its destination—the bridge doesn't have to do anything with it. If the packet's destination is on another segment, however, then it's forwarded to the bridge that connects to that segment. If the segment is not directly connected to the bridge forwarding the packet, then the bridge will send it to a bridge on the way to the proper segment. That bridge will then filter or forward the packet again, and so on until the packet gets forwarded to the proper segment and can be sent to its destination. The process is illustrated in figure 14.4.

In a nutshell, filtering works like this: the bridge checks the destination address in the packet header. If the destination address is on the same segment as the source address (as shown in the bridge's routing table), then the bridge filters the packet. If it is on a different segment, the bridge forwards the packet to the other active port. It's pretty much a no-brainer for the bridge, which is why bridges can keep up with network speeds.

The exact method by which the bridges determine how to route the packet depends on the routing method used, as discussed later in this chapter.

Forwarding Scenario

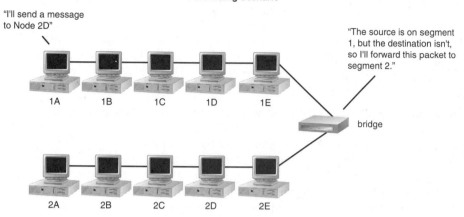

"I'll send a message to Node 2D"

"The source is on segment 1, but the destination isn't, so I'll forward this packet to segment 2."

1A   1B   1C   1D   1E

bridge

2A   2B   2C   2D   2E

Filtering Scenario

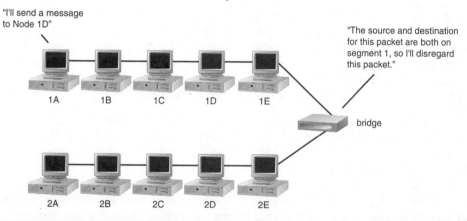

"I'll send a message to Node 1D"

"The source and destination for this packet are both on segment 1, so I'll disregard this packet."

1A   1B   1C   1D   1E

bridge

2A   2B   2C   2D   2E

Figure 14.4

Bridge filtering ensures that local traffic is combined to its home segment, rather than congesting the entire network.

You may see a similarity in the function of a bridge and a network redirector. We've discussed redirectors earlier in this book. They're the part of the network operating system that determines whether a command to the system hardware should be sent to the local hard disk (or a network-accessible hard disk). The redirector is necessary because most applications—word processors, spreadsheets, and games—don't know or care what networks are. They open files and save files, but whether those files are on a local disk or a disk across the room or state is not the application's concern. The network redirector monitors all disk accesses and determines the location of the hard disk that the application is asking for. If the disk access is local, then the redirector steps back and lets the operating system handle the transaction. If the disk access requires the network, the redirector puts on its operating system hat (this is transparent to the application and user) and redirects the command to the network.

This is essentially the same thing that a bridge is doing when it filters. The user (and node) shouldn't have to care whether the destination address is on the local segment or a bridged segment; the user accesses the network, and the bridge determines how the network access should be routed.

Where Does the Address Table Come From? Bridges forward packets from one segment of a network to another. Each bridge port is assigned an address for the segment to which that port is connected. When the bridge receives a packet, it looks at the packet's destination address and sends the packet to the port associated with that address. If the destination address isn't associated with any port (that is, if it's not in the bridge's *routing table*), then the bridge sends the packet to all of its ports. This is called *flooding*, and it's a perfectly normal thing for a bridge to do when attempting to discover the segment in which a particular destination address resides. (If a bridge is malfunctioning, it may flood the network unnecessarily, tying up traffic on the network with traffic that only belongs on one segment.)

Filter Types. Bridges aren't restricted to filtering based on addressing, however. Depending on the model of bridge, you can configure the bridge to filter based on the source address, destination address, bridge priority, port number, or any of several other variables. A few bridges (Computer System Products' StackUp Series Branch Office Relay and Presticom's BCX-6000 are two) even let you define custom filter types, although these bridges also make sure to have some default filter options as well.

Whatever the filter criteria used, all filters work pretty much the same. Almost all are based on the MAC addresses of the network devices. Bridges don't understand network destinations; they just understand MAC addresses, so they cache all MAC addresses that they receive to make a routing table. Once this table has been created, you can set the bridge to filter or forward packets to the addresses in the table, but you need the table first. As you'll see in chapter 15, "Routers," this differs from routing access lists. In routing access lists you have a wider latitude in how you can set router filtering than you have with bridges. Instead of being limited (mostly) to MAC addresses, you can set routers to grant or deny access permissions based on a MAC address, a node address (IP address), IPX number, network number, application call, or IP number.

Transparent Bridging versus Translation Bridging

The simplest method of bridging involves no previous route determination or intelligence in packet addressing. One bridge connects two segments and relays packets between them. This method, called *transparent bridging*, simply relays packets between network segments. Transparent bridging may use any of the routing types discussed here. The important part is that the bridge does not have to do anything to the packets it forwards to make them intelligible to the nodes on the other segment.

Translation bridging is used to connect networks that use different packets, such as Ethernet and token ring. The matter is a little trickier than just adjusting the contents of the packet header. Token-ring bridging requires some network traffic that isn't data, just so the nodes can get the routing information they need to address their packets properly. These null packets look like garbage to the Ethernet segment, which only passes data. Show a route discovery packet to an Ethernet segment, even with the routing information stripped off it, and the segment won't know what to do with it.

Therefore, the process of translating the packets from one network type to another requires the bridges to do a little disguise work. On the Ethernet side, the bridge pretends to be one more Ethernet node. When nodes send network traffic meant for a station on the token-ring side, the bridge claims the packets for its own, satisfying the sending node which only wants to know that the data it sent arrived safely. Once the bridge receives the packet, it puts on its token-ring hat, writes the routing information into the packet, and sends the data on its way. On the token-ring side, the bridge looks like just another bridge. When it receives data meant for the Ethernet segment, however, it puts on its Ethernet hat, strips the excess routing (but not addressing) information from the packet, and broadcasts the packet on the Ethernet segment. The node with the matching destination address collects the packet and acknowledges it.

Getting There from Here: Routing Methods

Discussing bridges leads to a lot of chicken-and-egg problems—it's hard to talk about how filtering works without mentioning how the bridges figure out how to route packets to their destinations. If you start with the routing discussion, then the reason for routing is difficult to discern. The following sections discuss how the packets get to their destinations once they've been forwarded.

Why Is Routing Necessary? After the explanation of transparent versus translational bridging, you may wonder where routing becomes necessary. Once the packet gets to the segment where its destination lies, it would seem to be a simple matter to get the packet home. In simple networks, this is true. If there's only one possible path between segments, then the bridge must only act as a relay center as shown in figure 14.5.

A bridge filters packets with a destination that's on the same segment as the sender and forwards packets on a different segment, so the data flows neatly in one port and out the other.

Most networks are more complicated than this, however. They may have an extra bridge for redundancy (in case the first fails) or to provide a connection to a different segment. Whatever the case, once you introduce a second bridge you introduce a second path for the data to travel (see fig. 14.6).

To see why this is a bad thing, remember the following:

- Bridges on Ethernet networks "hear" all network traffic, just like any other Ethernet node.

- Bridges forward everything they hear that has a destination address on a segment different from the one on which the segment originated.

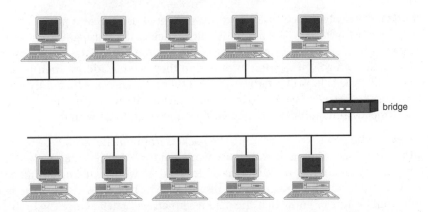

Figure 14.5

A simple bridged network requires no route discovery.

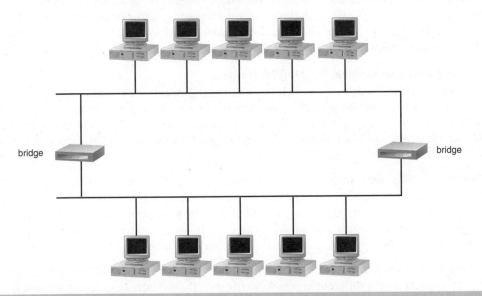

Figure 14.6

If more than one bridge connects the segments, only one path can be used.

In this scenario, illustrated in figure 14.7, a node on segment 1 has a message for a node on segment 2. Bridge 1 hears the message, notes that the address is not on segment 1, and so forwards it to segment 2. Bridge 2 hears the message broadcast to segment 2 and forwards it to segment 1. Bridge 1 hears the message, forwards it to segment 2... and so on. This is called *looping*, and it kills your network because it ties it up with unnecessary garbage that can never be cleared.

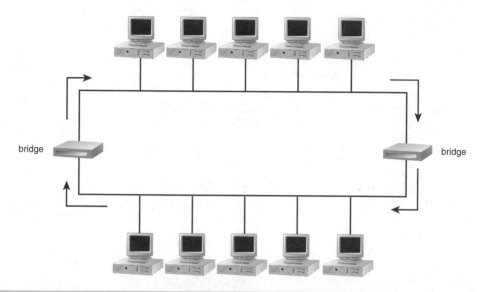

Figure 14.7

Bridge looping ties up your network with perpetual traffic and renders it inoperable.

To avoid looping, you'll need to purchase a bridge that uses one of the routing algorithms discussed in the sections that follow. Which one you choose depends on your network and specific needs. Once the packet is sent to the port connecting to the segment where its destination resides, its journey may not be over yet. Unless the network is a fairly simple one, with only one bridge, the packet might be sent first to one bridge on the way to its destination and then routed to another segment. The route that the packets must take depends on several variables: the physical layout and complexity of the network, the traffic patterns, and even the type of network being bridged. To describe the ways in which various bridges determine the best route to send packets along, several algorithms have been developed.

Spanning Tree Algorithm. DEC and Vitalink developed the first bridge routing standard, known as the *spanning tree algorithm (STA)*. This algorithm, adopted as a standard by the IEEE 802.1 committee, permits bridges to establish a "best route" to reach a given segment and then block off less desirable routes. This avoids the problem of looping described in the previous section.

Under STA, each bridge has an identifier with two parts: a priority level and an address. On power-up of the network, all the bridges in the network exchange information about their addresses and relative priority, until all recognize one bridge as having the highest priority. It's possible for more than one bridge to have the same priority level, so if this happens the bridge with the highest address outranks the others. The highest-ranking bridge is called the *root bridge*, and all other bridges define themselves in relation to that bridge. The process of determining a root bridge is illustrated in figure 14.8.

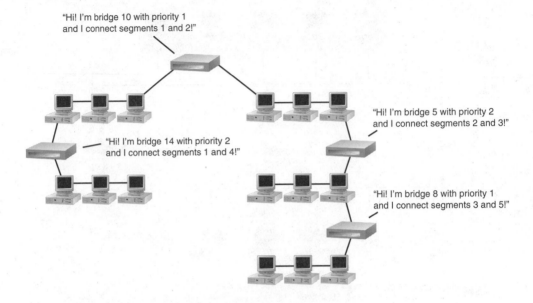

"Hi! I'm bridge 10 with priority 1 and I connect segments 1 and 2!"

"Hi! I'm bridge 5 with priority 2 and I connect segments 2 and 3!"

"Hi! I'm bridge 14 with priority 2 and I connect segments 1 and 4!"

"Hi! I'm bridge 8 with priority 1 and I connect segments 3 and 5!"

From the information that the bridges broadcast about their connections and priority, they choose a root bridge to route all traffic. Once the root bridge is chosen, all the other bridges will identify their connections in terms of their distance from the root bridge. In this case, the root bridge will be 10 because it has priority 1 and a higher address than the other priority 1 bridge.

Figure 14.8

The bridge with the highest network priority becomes the root bridge.

You (as the network administrator) can stack the deck to make a particular bridge the root—just give it a higher priority than any other bridge when you're setting it up.

After the root bridge has been determined, all the other bridges in the network determine which of their ports point to the root bridge (this part looks a little like the star logical topology, as all bridges are oriented toward a central point). That port becomes each bridge's *root port*, and it represents the direction from which that bridge will receive data. To send data, the bridge identifies one port leading *away* from the root port.

If a bridge doesn't have a direct connection to the root bridge, it must choose a path by way of an intervening peer bridge. The bridge it chooses is the one with the lowest transmission costs; that is, the fastest line, the least amount of traffic, and the greatest buffer capacity. If all costs are the same, the route to the root bridge will be determined by the fewest hops required to pass data from one LAN to another.

After all the negotiations as to what is the root bridge and which ports each bridge will use for incoming and outgoing data, the bridges set those ports for forwarding and block the others so that there's one pipe in and one pipe out. Any other ports are not disabled but they don't pass any packets. If one of the active ports stops working, a blocked port goes into learning mode—a sort of apprenticeship to becoming a forwarding port. During this apprenticeship, the blocked port examines the packets on the network, learns where all the bridges are in relation to each other, and then becomes a forwarding port. This should happen without any action being required on the part of the network administrator. Figure 14.9 shows a network using the spanning tree algorithm for packet routing.

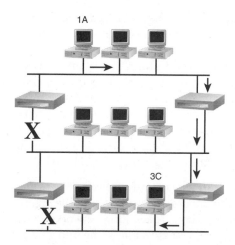

Data traveling from node 1A to node 3C (for example) must follow the path indicated by the arrows because the other path is blocked.

Figure 14.9

A spanning tree network blocks certain paths to avoid looping.

How static are these port configurations? Obviously, the best route at 9 AM might not be the best at 3:30 PM—perhaps a bridge may have gone down or there's a lot of traffic on one segment of the network. Thus, each bridge maintains a timer in the address database that it keeps. If the timer for a destination address on segment B runs out, the bridge checks to see if the route that it's been taking to get to segment B is still good or if a more efficient way has turned up since it last checked. If the network topology hasn't changed, then the bridge will select the same route and reset the timer; otherwise, it will search for a new route.

Although the spanning tree algorithm has the advantage of being protocol independent, it does not work for all networks—it is for Ethernet networks only. Although Ethernet is a more popular network type than Token Ring, IBM found it necessary to come up with a routing scheme of its own for networks too complicated to work with transparent bridging. This scheme, introduced in 1985, is called *source routing*.

Source Routing. Source routing is IBM's proprietary routing scheme—it's required to bridge Token Ring networks. In fact, if you're using one of IBM's operating systems (OS/2 or LAN Server) and you want to bridge the network, you must use source routing.

> **Note**
>
> Because it's really active above the data link layer of the OSI model, source routing depends on the network operating system to cooperate in route discovery. Therefore, not every NOS will support it. NetWare, Banyan VINES, OS/2, and LAN Manager are among those that do.

As it is not protocol independent (unlike STA) and relies on the network operating system to function, source routing has never caught on as well as the spanning tree algorithm (also due to the fact that Ethernet is more popular than Token Ring). However, source routing has got some design features that spanning tree lacks, so its existence is far from unnecessary. Spanning tree is static (until the timed intervals when it checks the paths that it's using to reach a particular segment); source routing checks the path every time that it sends data. There's more overhead involved because every time a packet crosses the network it's got to carry routing information with it, but in a network that changes frequently due to new members, breaks, or other circumstances, source routing would be able to pick up on the changes more quickly than spanning tree.

How Route Discovery Works. Logically speaking, there are three kinds of objects in a source routed network: the nodes, the bridges, and the segments (or in this case, *rings*, as by definition we're talking about Token Ring networks). Each of these objects has a unique address. The nodes get a 6-byte address, the bridges a 4-bit number, and the rings a 12-bit number.

Although the nodes in a source routed network do all the legwork in route discovery, each of the different object types plays a part in the process. To find the best route, the networked PCs need a road map of the network. Their first step is to broadcast a message to another node but without specifying any particular segment or route that the packets in the message should take. This message is called a *discovery packet* and contains buffer areas for the other network objects to fill in their numbers. As the discovery packet bounces around the network, attempting to find its destination, the bridges fill in the numbers for the rings that they connect and their own bridge numbers. When the packet reaches the destination node, it returns the packet to the sending node, thus giving the sender a road map of the path which the packet took. This process is illustrated in figure 14.10.

The Source Routing Process. After the sending node has figured out where all the pieces of the network are, it can send data. The sending part of the process looks like a normal Token Ring topology, except that the packets holding the data have the routing information embedded in the packet. The address field in a source routed packet has two main components: the I/G (individual/group) bit and the U/L (universal/local) bit. The I/G bit indicates whether the address is for an individual or a group, and the U/L bit indicates whether the address is a universal address supplied by the IEEE or a locally made address to override the IEEE address. Source routing takes the I/G bit in the source address (not the destination, but the address of the node sending the packet) and uses the information to set another bit, the routing information bit (RI), that indicates whether there's additional routing information required to get the packet to its destination. If the RI bit is set to 1, as many as 18 bytes of routing information are included in

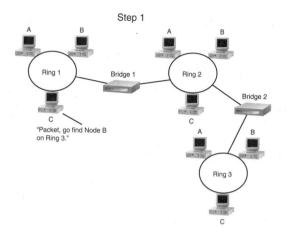

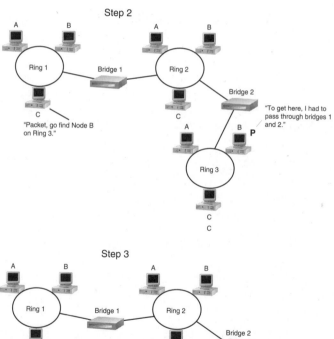

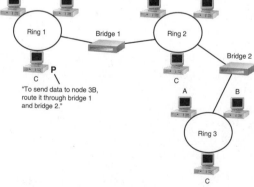

Figure 14.10

Route discovery explores the network topology and then reports the results to the sending node.

another field, thus providing an itinerary for that packet. That itinerary comes from the road map developed during the discovery phase. There's one limitation here: because the RI field is limited to 18 bytes, there's only room to define eight ring numbers (including the source ring), so the packet can only take as many as seven hops to get to its destination. The routing path uses the lowest number of hops possible. See figure 14.11 to see how the routing process works.

This sounds complicated, but the end result is straightforward: the packets have all the routing information embedded in them, so all that the bridges must do is look at the itinerary in the packet, note which ring the packet must get to and the route required to get it there, and send it on its merry way.

Making Source Routing Act Like Spanning Tree. You can make a source routed network act like a spanning tree network. In this case, the route discovery packet identifies only a single route between the source and destination (choosing the one with the lowest cost or fewest hops). The road map that the sending node gets back only shows one path to its destinations, so the routing information embedded in the packet only permits the bridge to send the packet using one path. This avoids any looping and dual packets. You can see how this works in figure 14.12.

Because source routing can keep up with network changes more easily than the spanning tree algorithm, why would you want to make source routing act like spanning tree? The answer is the one common to almost all networking questions: speed. Source routing requires more overhead than spanning tree because the fluid routes permit route discovery. If the network hasn't changed since the last time a node's road map was created, however, the route discovery is a waste of time. Therefore, if you create a rigid series of paths in the network, you remove some of the flexibility but decrease the overhead.

Source Routing Transparent Bridging. Remember the Reese's Peanut Butter Cups commercials that had two people walking around—one eating chocolate and the other eating peanut butter—until they ran into each other, mixed up the two, and discovered an entirely new taste treat? That's sort of how source routing transparent bridging works. Ethernet's spanning tree method is nice, but the routes are fairly static. Source routing is nice too, but it's NOS-dependent. Both of them have the drawback of only working with one kind of electrical topology: you can have Ethernet, or you can have Token Ring, but you can't have both.

Well, you can have both—if you use a translating bridge with a routing method called *source routing transparent* (*SRT*). SRT bridges can translate packets from one form to another, so that the two networks can be connected. In fact, SRT bridges are required for the purpose: if your network includes both Token Ring and Ethernet segments, then you'll need an SRT bridge to connect them and translate. The SRT bridge, however, is only necessary at the point at which the two network types connect; to connect Ethernet to Ethernet or Token Ring to Token Ring, you can use a spanning tree or source routing bridges, as necessary.

SRT bridging is not limited to networks with split personalities. You can also use SRT bridges in Token Ring networks to make the network protocol independent—if it runs on Token Ring, it will work with an SRT bridge.

Routing Packets on the Same Ring

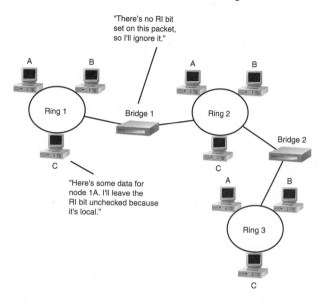

"There's no RI bit set on this packet, so I'll ignore it."

"Here's some data for node 1A. I'll leave the RI bit unchecked because it's local."

Routing Packets on a Different Ring

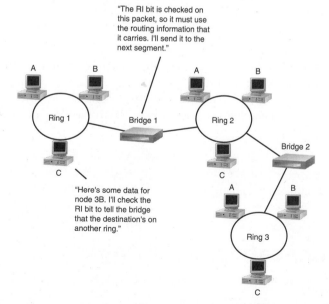

"The RI bit is checked on this packet, so it must use the routing information that it carries. I'll send it to the next segment."

"Here's some data for node 3B. I'll check the RI bit to tell the bridge that the destination's on another ring."

Figure 14.11

The presence or absence of the RI bit determines how packets are routed across the network.

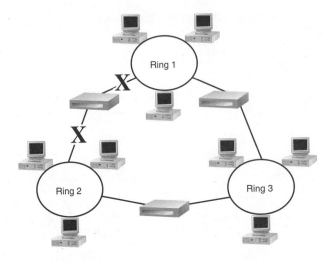

Even though this source routed network has redundant paths, source routed packets will only take the paths not Xed out, so as to reduce the overhead required for the routing process.

Figure 14.12

Source routing can be configured to work like the spanning tree algorithm.

Network Layer Routing. Sometimes when you're bridge shopping you'll notice bridges that support network layer routing. "Wait a minute," the alert shopper will say, "bridges are data link layer devices. How can a *bridge* be doing anything with the network layer?"

The answer, of course, is that it really isn't. The device that you're looking at is not exactly a bridge—it's a hybrid bridge/router sometimes called a *brouter*. Brouters are devices that perform the functions of both bridges and routers so that you can connect networks using protocols that can't be routed, such as NetBIOS/NetBEUI and SNA. Confusingly, they're often listed as bridges, but if the device does anything at the network layer, it's not a pure bridge.

Network layer routing (NLR) looks at the node's network layer address, such as an IP address, to decide how the packet should reach its destination. Because routing is covered in detail in the following chapter, we'll leave a complete discussion of how routing works for chapter 15, "Routers."

Buying Repeaters and Bridges

The key questions to consider when purchasing any network connection hardware are as follows:

- Can this hardware adapt to my network's changing needs?

- How much bang will I get for my buck?

- What kind of management does this model offer? How much do I need?

- What support does the vendor offer?

No matter what you're buying, these questions are the ones to answer before purchasing.

Adaptability

Networks aren't static and often they aren't simple. Vendors know that, so it's not hard to find repeaters that have a fighting chance of keeping up with you. The Black Box catalog, for example, sells both modular repeaters that you can design to exactly fit your cabling needs and a variety of media combinations if you want to buy an off-the-shelf model. If you're not sure about the direction in which your network will evolve, a modular repeater is an easy way of maintaining your flexibility for about the same price as a solid repeater. If one segment of your network changes media, you can swap out the old module for the new one without taking down the rest of the network.

Cost

The price of a repeater or bridge is based both on the number of ports in the device and the special features that it offers. For example, a transparent bridge costs less than a similarly capable translating bridge. Decide what you need, and then shop for a device that provides it. Once again, a modular bridge may give you a little more flexibility. Also, when comparing similar bridges, calculate how much you're paying per port.

Management Capability

If you want your repeated network to have management ability tied in with the rest of your network, look for a model with SNMP built in or attachable. Make sure that the SNMP implementation is MIB-II compliant and don't forget that the management capabilities of an SNMP-managed system vary, so ask for a listing of exactly what the management module can manage before you purchase.

Vendor Support

Notice how you're treated when shopping and collecting information. Although it's not a sure bet that a company that is helpful and supportive to potential customers will always be there for you after you've made the purchase, a vendor who's unwilling to help you collect information before purchasing probably won't improve when you need help with the unit. Notice things like how long you must wait for technical support (the best source of detailed information about a given unit), and whether they call back if you leave messages. I'd be a little wary of vendors who know very little about the products they sell.

Summary

In this chapter, we discussed two of the devices you can use to extend your network's reach: repeaters and bridges. The one you need depends on what you want to do. Repeaters are physical layer devices that extend the reach of a given network but don't restrict network traffic. Bridges are data link layer devices that both extend your network's reach and limit traffic to the node on which it belongs.

Bridges support a number of different filtering and routing methods to get your data to where it needs to go. The simpler the routing method, the less overhead is required but the less flexible the network is to changes in its topology. Although most bridges are limited to linking networks using the same logical topology, SRT bridges let token-ring and Ethernet networks communicate.

Chapter 15

Routers

The classic film *Casablanca* must surely be high on everyone's list of all-time favorites. So what does that have to do with your upgrade efforts, you ask? Think of it this way—those efforts do bear a resemblance to the film's plot. For instance, in both, several entities, whether LANs or individuals, must get together. If the LANs are of dissimilar types, there's a translation problem that rivals anything Rick's multilingual bartenders ever dealt with. And as if that isn't enough, there may even be a need to span the globe with your message—that is, talk to a WAN. You're definitely in the same boat (airplane?) as was Victor Laszlo.

There's one critical difference, of course. Instead of trading jewels or secrets for passports or plane tickets, you, as a network manager, must examine and decide between components whose job it is to connect networks or portions of networks. There are several such devices available. What distinguishes each from the other members of the group is the OSI level at which the particular mechanism can function.

Repeaters and Bridges—Network Glue

Repeaters and bridges, discussed in chapter 14, deal with the data link and network layers of the OSI model respectively. *Repeaters* offer the simplest means of interconnection. All they do is boost or regenerate a signal, thereby extending the physical distance that a network may traverse. *Bridges*, on the other hand, connect networks rather than simply extending them. Bridges, like repeaters, are hardware devices. But bridges also differ from repeaters. Bridges can link networks that have some differences at the physical or data link layers. Connecting a broadband network and a baseband network is one example of using a bridge.

Neither of these types of components needs to have sophisticated software or a great deal of memory. When all you're doing is, in effect, passing a signal with no concern for its format, your methods don't need to be fancy.

Routers

Routers, however, are a different animal altogether from repeaters and bridges. Routers make the connection between networks at the OSI transport layer. Recall from chapter 3, "The OSI Model: Bringing Order to Chaos," that the transport layer is where networks begin to operate in a more encompassing way. The transport layer handles tasks that are by definition critical to internetworking:

- Addressing
- Connect/disconnect protocols
- Packet management:
    - Error detection or correction
    - Routing

On top of everything else that the transport layer must deal with, it is at once concierge, traffic cop, and native guide of and between networks. That is why routers must be so much more sophisticated than their interconnectivity predecessors.

> **Note**
>
> Routers can connect networks that are dissimilar at the physical, data link, and network layers. However, routers cannot join networks that are dissimilar above the transport layer.

A router decides whether to forward a packet after it looks at that packet's protocol level (for example, TCP/IP or IPX/SPX) addresses; it ignores the MAC address. Routers, since they operate strictly at OSI level three, can also ignore differences in transport channels. Ethernet, FDDI, ISDN, and so on are all the same to these devices.

Each network interface on a router has its own unique IP address. The most important part of this address is what's properly called the *destination address*, which to most of us is the same thing as IP address—that set of four decimal numbers, separated by periods, which completely describes the interface as a node within the network. And because the router as a whole has its own IP address, it can and does exchange information with other routers. Such conversations concern the state of the network, which paths are free, which nodes (if any) are down, and so on.

You'll probably have gathered from the discussion to this point that you may not need a router. The topology of your network and its configuration (type and number of hosts and nodes) and characteristics (volume of traffic, peak traffic periods) might be better served by a repeater, bridge, or gateway.

For instance, some bridges can route between different media. Therefore, a network that has both thinnet and fiber-optic segments but doesn't need to go from TCP/IP to FDDI could use a bridge that conforms to the Translation Bridging Standard.

Bridges have the additional advantage of being much less expensive than routers. They're simpler devices in every way and therefore much easier to install and fine-tune. Many are self-configuring. A bridge's simpler technology also means that it's usually more reliable than more complex components like routers and gateways; there's simply less to go wrong.

Another factor that must be considered when choosing an appropriate interconnectivity device is the nature of the upper layers of the OSI model as those layers are implemented across your network(s). If the configurations you need to connect differ at the session layer (perhaps in having different algorithms for mapping device names to network addresses), neither bridges nor routers will suffice. Likewise, if your networks use different software to control the presentation or access layers, thereby having different schemes for access to or execution of applications, either a router or a bridge is moot. In cases like these, you'll have to use a gateway.

> ### Caution
>
> Even more touchy is the idea of running bridges and routers in tandem. Bridges, being less discriminating devices, may forward packets that a router may not have the ability to translate. Certain devices, like some older DECnet routers, also present a problem because they have the same MAC address on all ports, introducing the possibility of further confusion on the part of their peer routers and any bridges with which they must communicate. If you can, avoid running bridges and routers in parallel.

At this point, a few examples of the use of routers are in order. A router can connect

- A thinnet-based Novell LAN and a 10BaseT Banyan VINES network
- An Ethernet-UNIX environment to either a Novell LAN, 10BaseT Banyan VINES, or AppleTalk
- A thicknet backbone to several thinnet segments

Routers can ignore topologies and access protocols, unlike bridges. While bridges could handle the thinnet-to-10BaseT or thicknet-to-thinnet connections mentioned earlier, they could not translate the access protocols they found there. Bridges can be oblivious to access-level protocols, but the users in these two hypothetical configurations don't have that luxury.

On the other hand, routers need common ground at the upper layers of the OSI model, unlike gateways. That's why a connection like a Novell LAN to a mainframe will never appear in a list like the previous one. Such environments have nothing in common at any OSI layer. Therefore, they would have to be connected by a gateway rather than a router.

Routers in Pairs

A router is actually a pair of devices that can send, receive, and process network signals. A router's most frequent processing task is some form of protocol translation.

When a signal is forwarded to a router in preparation for being passed along to another network or segment, the signal is first stored and then translated so that its protocols are recognizable to the destination. Only then do the packets move to that other side.

Routers go beyond simple store/translate/forward devices, however. Most routers seek the optimum path to transmit data. They keep one ear glued to the networks or subnetworks that they connect, listening for bad segments or faulty nodes. They use such information in directing packets to avoid obstacles. Some of the more complex routers can even "hear" traffic jams on the nets or segments they service. Combining this input with their ability to reroute allows such devices to do *load balancing*. That is, these high-end routers can redirect network traffic so that gridlock is not only prevented, but precluded. With load balancing, packets are routed so that no network segment carries too heavy a traffic burden.

The Anatomy of a Router

Routers can operate over a variety of lines, including leased lines as well as the partially dialup ISDN lines that, because of their lower costs, are increasingly popular. Routers, regardless of the type of channel they must talk across, all do the following:

- Read a data packet
- Strip off the packet's protocols
- Replace the stripped-off information with the protocols the destination network or segment requires
- Add routing information
- Send the packet on its way to its recipient by the optimum path

In accomplishing this last point, routers use yet another type of specialized software called *routing protocols*. Beyond pushing packets out of a router's front door, routing protocols have another, very important responsibility. They handle the distribution, among routers on a given network, of the information regarding network conditions exchanged between those routers. That is, routing protocols decide the following:

- Which router needs to know about which routes and other routers
- How often to update this information

Under some of the older routing algorithms, every node on a network had complete knowledge about every other node and each path in that network. Such a scenario requires that each node, including every router, have a whale of a CPU as well as serious

RAM. Remember, we're talking about individual packets of data here—every time a single one is transmitted, a router using this methodology has to search a table containing every detail of network addressing and status.

More recently developed routing protocols distribute network status information among routers. Among these are the *Open Shortest Path First* (*OSPF*) routing protocol, developed out of a standard of the ISO, and the *Interior Gateway Routing Protocol* (*IGRP*), developed in the mid-1980s by Cisco Systems, one of the major manufacturers of interconnectivity hardware. Both OSPF and IGRP can handle larger and more complex networks than can some of the older routing protocols. IGRP, for example, had built into it from the earliest design stages the ability to handle a variety of bandwidth and delay characteristics.

Take a glance at the following table for a summary of the most widely used routing protocols. Then we'll discuss each in more detail.

Acronym	Full Name	Used with...
BGP	Border Gateway Protocol	TCP/IP
EGP	Exterior Gateway Protocol	TCP/IP
IGRP	Interior Gateway Routing Protocol	TCP/IP
IS–IS	Intermediate System to Intermediate System	TCP/IP
NLSP	NetWare Link Services Protocol	IPX/SPX
OSPF	Open Shortest Path First	TCP/IP
RIP	Routing Information Protocol	TCP/IP
RTMP	Routing Table Maintenance Protocol	AppleTalk

BGP. The *Border Gateway Protocol* (*BGP*) carries out interdomain routing. BGP can guarantee transmissions free of *loopbacks*—that is, when packets circle around and around within a closed path. With each trip through the loop, a counter is incremented. If that counter reaches the maximum allowed value for the protocol in use, a problem with the path or the message itself is assumed, further efforts to deliver the packet are dropped, and the packet itself is discarded.

BGP functions between *autonomous systems*. Autonomous systems are defined as a set of gateways under a single administrative control. Note that phrase "a set of gateways"; this isn't the same as a set of networks or network segments. For instance, a set of devices might connect the components of a campus network, while another set might connect that network to a regional network. Each of these sets of switches, not the networks with which it deals, comprises an autonomous system.

BGP works with the following information:

- Route numbers (actually, each route number is a network number)

- A list of autonomous systems through which transmissions have passed, called the *AS list*

- A list of other characteristics of each transmission path

BGP concerns itself primarily with the reachability of the networks that it seeks to connect to.

EGP. The *Exterior Gateway Protocol* (*EGP*) is used for communicating with routers in a number of governmental networks. In the *Defense Data Network* (*DDN*) of the Department of Defense, EGP talks to specific routers—those that have been designated as critical devices.

EGP has also been used to connect to other large backbone networks within the federal government, such as the *National Science Foundation Network* (*NSFnet*).

IGRP. IGRP allows the user to configure many of its operating characteristics, such as bandwidth, internetwork delays, and loads. It recognizes the following three types of routes:

- Interior (routes between subnets in a single network)

- Exterior (routes to networks outside the autonomous system that the router running IGRP belongs to)

- System routes (routes to networks serviced by members of the same autonomous system as that which the router running IGRP belongs to)

IS–IS. *IS–IS*, the *intermediate system to intermediate system protocol*, is actually a specification of ISO for a dynamic routing protocol—that is, one that can reroute on the fly to bypass obstacles or find optimum paths. A number of vendors have implemented IS–IS in such a way as to make it available as an IP routing protocol.

NLSP. The *Sequenced Packet Exchange Protocol* (*SPX*) makes diagnostic and management functions available to the station running it. SPX operates at the OSI network layer and has some of the abilities usually found in session layer protocols. But SPX cannot initiate a connection. That is why SPX needs the *Internetwork Packet Exchange Protocol* (*IPX*) to be up and running. IPX is a transport layer protocol that handles the addressing and routing every network conversation requires.

But neither IPX nor SPX can function outside a single network. To fill this need, the *NetWare Link Services Protocol* (*NLSP*) was developed by Novell to accomplish the interconnection of IPX/SPX LANs.

OSPF. OSPF is designed expressly for IP networks. It supports subnets, as well as the tracking of externally supplied routing information. OSPF uses IP multicasting as its transmission method. OSPF, one of the most widely used routing protocols, can

- Authenticate packets

- Talk to internal routers

- Talk to border routers (devices that connect to a number of subnets or segments)

- Talk to boundary routers (devices that comprise autonomous systems)

So you can see that any router running OSPF can send data within network segments or subnetworks, between such structures, and beyond to other such constructs, WANs, or other large networks.

OSPF can also be configured to operate without packet authentication and with connections only to specified environments. It even offers *virtual links*—a means by which breaks in a backbone (either physical or caused by routing problems) or backbones that have been segmented can be bypassed through the use of border routers.

RIP. *RIP*, the *Routing Information Protocol*, is one of the oldest routing schemes. It is based on an even older protocol, the *Xerox Network System* (*XNS*) but adapts that software for use in an IP environment. RIP is still widely used, however. Probably one reason for its continuing viability is that it was designed for small, homogenous environments.

RIP broadcasts packets every 30 seconds as a means of exchanging and keeping up-to-date routing information between routers. This process, common to all routing protocols, is called *advertising*.

If a router that relies on RIP doesn't receive an ad from one of its peer routers for a period of 180 seconds, it assumes that any routes served by its tardy coworker are no longer useable. Should the silence extend to 240 seconds or more, the router erases all routing table entries that pertain to its uncommunicative partner.

> **Note**
>
> A *routing table* is a file, maintained within a router and also on at least one of the hosts that it serves, which contains entries for all nodes on a network that packets must be directed to, and the router or gateway through which the data may pass. A line from a routing table might look like the following:
>
> ```
> 127.0.0.3     128.6.4.6
> ```
>
> The first of these IP addresses is that of a workstation; the second represents the router through which any packets requested by or intended for that station can travel.

In addition to being designed with the assumption that it will run in small to medium networks that contain little diversity of hardware or software, RIP has other constraints built into it. These include the following:

- RIP cannot connect networks in which any path goes through more than 15 switches.

- RIP cannot share traffic between parallel lines.

- RIP cannot adapt to changes in network load—that is, it cannot perform load balancing.

- RIP cannot easily reroute packets across lines of noticeably different speeds.

For these and other reasons, some vendors provide their own modifications to RIP to allow it, for example, to go beyond a path length of 15.

RTMP. AppleTalk has its own routing protocol, called the *Routing Table Maintenance Protocol* (*RTMP*). RTMP helps provide end-to-end connectivity between internetworked AppleTalk nodes. In other words, it does within an AppleTalk network or subnetwork the same thing that, for example, OSPF does in TCP/IP environments, keeping track of paths, addresses, and the best routes between and among those.

ICMP. There's one more piece of internal router software that you should know about. It's called the *Internet Control Message Protocol* (*ICMP*). It's ICMP's job to handle redirects—those instances when a router must, on the fly, send a packet along a different, faster route than that originally designated for it.

Identifying Physical Characteristics

Now that we've got a basic understanding of how routers do their jobs, let's turn to the physical characteristics that any router you consider should include.

Manageability. You should be able to control a router in a number of ways:

- Directly by means of the Simple Network Management Protocol

- Remotely through a Telnet session

- Remotely through a modem

A device that offers less flexibility than this in management probably won't stand up to the day-to-day variations in situations encountered by and problems posed to the average network administrator.

Modularity. Your router should be modular. If there is one constant in data processing, it's the rapidity with which things change. Both network software and network hardware can be expected to continue to evolve at rates as fast as or faster than we've become accustomed to. This being the case, a router's design, which is based on modules (for example, a CPU or NIC) that can be quickly and easily swapped in and out, can be a welcome island of stability in an ocean of seeming network chaos.

CPU and NIC. Any router worth its salt must have a processor powerful enough to deliver packets to a network at the highest speed that the network's cable is capable of. In today's terms, that means that any router you consider should run at a minimum of 14,400 Kbps. And as for NICs, a reputable router should offer connections to as many types of wire as possible. At the very least, Ethernet, FDDI, and token-ring connections should be available.

Memory. All the processing power in the world will do little good if a router's onboard memory isn't also up to the job. As was the case with the CPU, make sure that any router you consider has enough RAM to sling data at a minimum speed of 14,400 Kbps.

> **Note**
>
> Routers' RAM typically ranges from 2M in small models, such as a wire-speed segment router, to 8M in devices such as a high-speed wide area router. Memory requirements are also affected by upgrades to router software. While such upgrades don't necessarily require additional memory, failing to provide it (to device or host, or both) can cause degradation of performance.

Translation. Acting as an interpreter is one of a router's most important reasons for being. At a minimum, a good router should be able to handle AppleTalk, IPX/SPX, and TCP/IP. Adding DECnet, VINES, and X.25 as possibilities wouldn't hurt.

Routing Protocols. TCP/IP environments often include a number of routing protocols. For example, such an environment might include an older segment that uses RIP and a more recent one that employs OSPF. So don't think you're covered if the router you're considering speaks only one routing protocol. At a minimum, a truly flexible router should offer not only that routing protocol but also NLSP, RIP, and RTMP.

Prioritization

Some network software doesn't handle delays gracefully. NetBEUI is a prime example. NetBEUI is actually NETBEUI.COM, a *terminate-and-stay-resident* (*TSR*) utility that is the immediate predecesor of NetBIOS, IBM's transport layer protocol. Precisely because it is implemented as a TSR, NetBEUI, now largely obsolete, is prone to timeouts.

A router's ability, or lack thereof, to prioritize its handling of packets can have an enormous effect on the number of such errors a network produces, which you have to re-solve. As important as the protocols it translates and the ways in which it decides upon routes is a router's ability to prioritize tasks.

Comparing Performance

In evaluating the performance of routers, always keep in mind that different vendors use different measurements to describe the throughput of their products. While all are more than happy to talk about packets-per-second, vendors don't all mean the same thing when they use that phrase. Most count a packet only once as it goes through a router; some, however, count such packets twice, presumably operating under the premise that it is both leaving its source and going on its way to a destination. In any case, it's clear that routers described in these terms have a hidden, unfair advantage over some of their competitors.

Any comparison of routers should also determine what size of packet each router deals with. Fortunately, there is a formula so that such imbalanced presentations of router characteristics can be evened out.

$$\textbf{Throughput=Switching Time+(Packet Size}\times\textbf{Time per Byte)}$$

Look at this formula a little more closely. It says, for one thing, that the time normally needed to switch a packet is a constant, made up of factors like interrupt frequency, header processing, routing table lookup time needed, and so on. Also, the throughput formula claims that there is a component to throughput that is proportional to packet size and that represents the time needed to copy a packet before translating it.

Using this formula can be of some help in comparing routers whose vendors use differing yardsticks in measuring their products' performance. Another way of making sense of such comparisons is to obtain throughput statistics for different-size packets, perhaps of a minimum, middle, and maximum size. Or you could look for two different statistics—switching speed given in packets per second and throughput represented as bytes per second.

> **Note**
>
> As an additional check on how a router is doing, you might consider using one of the host-resident software modules, available for most of the popular routing protocols, that tap in on inter-router conversations. Such software maintains a complete picture of the up-to-the-nanosecond condition of your network—just like the data that routers share among themselves, except that it's accessible from the host.

Avoiding Pitfalls

Quite a few things shouldn't happen on a network, but you can wager that sooner or later they will. So any router you're considering should have mechanisms or algorithms for preventing or at least dealing with the following.

> **Note**
>
> These methods typically will be part of the job of the routing protocol. For instance, BGP maintains a table on the physical status of every segment that it deals with.
>
> Go over the documentation for your router candidates with a fine-tooth comb or simply ask the manufacturer or your retailer specific questions to determine how the routing protocols supported by any router you're considering handle these problems.

Electrical Faults. A short in a cable, a power surge, or drop-off can distort a signal on a line. Also, the way and frequency with which network cabling is maintained can affect its integrity.

Transceiver and Controller Problems. An ailing transceiver can generate signals that are healthy electronically but a bit peaked in other ways. For instance, a packet might refuse to relinquish the channel. Another might be infinitely long. Still another might cause or misinterpret collisions. While such problems aren't common, they can hobble communications at large and routers in particular.

Excessive Traffic Between Routers. Some routing software can sabotage itself by producing errors that in turn produce random, undue traffic on certain paths in a network. Be sure any router you consider can isolate and report such errors.

Traffic Overloads. An important subset of network planning and design is traffic planning. A properly planned network should never, in theory, experience overloads. But networks, like any other construct, can get out of hand or can be asked to do more than they were originally intended to do. A router that can perform load balancing as a means of optimizing transmission times can isolate overloads and work around them.

Router Planning

Just as you meticulously planned your network's configuration as a whole, you should give close scrutiny to what you want your routers to do and where you expect them to do it.

The discussion of routing protocols earlier in this chapter indicated an important fact of networking life. Few real standards exist for routers. This lack of a solid means of comparison of competing devices, added to the continually growing role routers play in allowing dissimilar networks to communicate, makes router modeling even more important. When you consider the cost of networking hardware and the investment of time that installing and fine-tuning it represents, having a reasonable idea up front of how routers can be expected to perform in your environment is practically critical.

By constructing scenarios and comparing router performances in such circumstances, you can be assured of buying the right routers and the right number of routers. And you can do more. You can design routing paths and allow for alternatives. You can estimate the effects that varying levels of traffic will have on router performance. You can evaluate throughput and translation time. You can even plan ahead for router failure. In short, simulations allow you to introduce just the right routers into your environment.

Network Role-Playing

In constructing the model against which you will evaluate the router candidates you're considering, be sure to include parameters that reflect the realities of your network. For instance, you might want to map out the network as it currently is configured, marking overall traffic volumes along paths. Include figures for acceptable end-to-end delays for applications. It is also helpful to indicate the nature of the packets that usually travel between specific nodes. That is, mark on your network map whether paths carry TCP/IP traffic, IPX/SPX, or AppleTalk. Mark packet sizes as well, and make sure to include a wide variety. One simulation recently published on the Internet suggests using packet lengths of 64, 80, 100, 120, 150, and 300 bytes. What's more, this same study recommends raising packet frequency figures in an inverse relation to packet size. In other words, your simulation should include the presumption that smaller packets are delivered at a higher rate than larger ones. This is not only the most common real-world case, but also reflects an important source of stress upon routers—the frequent arrival of small packets, each of which must be stored, translated, and forwarded.

Having constructed your scenario in this way, proceed to evaluate routers against it. Compare more factors than throughput. For one thing, be sure to look at the delays that different routers engender when faced with the following:

- Frequently sent large packets (those of 120 bytes or more)

- Infrequently sent large packets interspersed with smaller packets

- A steady, heavy stream of small packets

You'll probably find that some routers' behaviors are nearly indistinguishable under these conditions, while other performance characteristics vary widely. Of course, any factor that is particularly representative of your network should outweigh those that do not as clearly reflect it.

Tip

Keep in mind that in the real world, the bulk of network traffic consists of packets in the 60-, 80-, or 100-byte range. So whatever other traits your network has, the ability of a router to quickly process heavy streams of small packets is something to keep a sharp eye on.

Desktop Data

This section presents a scenario/simulation like that just described.

Desktop Data, a growing (but fictitious) desktop publishing firm, has a mixed-protocol networking environment. The MIS and Research departments run a Novell LAN. Art and Advertising (A/A), on the other hand, relies on a small network of Macs and PowerMacs. Technical Writing and Editing (TW/E) relies on a mixed bag of UNIX workstations and high-end PCs running xterm emulators, held together by TCP/IP.

The writers and editors frequently complain that the response times they encounter are

- Inadequate in general

- Lagging during periods of heavy network activity in particular

Artists, researchers, and administrators, on the other hand, are satisfied with the overall performance they encounter.

You, as network administrator, are faced with the task of reconciling these conflicting expectations. You have two goals in mind:

- Track down the causes of the delays that TW/E is experiencing and correct them in as cost-, time-, and labor-efficient a manner as possible.

- Do nothing, while making these corrections, to disturb the satisfactory performance that A/A and MIS have reported.

You start by drawing the layout of the network. You accurately represent the length of each of the thinnet segments that make up Desktop Data's network architecture. You place Desktop Data's two servers (MIS/Research and TW/E jointly use the same Sun SPARCStation as a server, while A/A's server is a SuperMac) at the points on your map that correspond to the actual locations of those machines. Next, you monitor traffic on each segment over the course of several days, noting not only volumes but also patterns in usage. For example, you realize that, despite the fact that each of the subnets in question has, on the average, five active users at any given point, TW/E places a heavier demand on its server than do the other departments. Its five users generate an average of 17 application requests per minute to the server, while A/A and MIS make 12 and 9 respectively. Since any single request to a server produces about 85 Kbps in network traffic, it appears that TW/E has a legitimate cause for complaint. At this point, you feel you have located the problem. Your current router cannot forward packets fast enough to handle the 17 requests per minute that are intended for the TCP/IP and Novell server. Its buffers fill up too quickly. Packet throughput on this segment starts to fall off when as few as four users are active. Your current router is not configured to prioritize requests; you reason that this inability might be contributing to the situation.

Your next step is to use the data you've compiled in a new equation—one into which you introduce statistics on routers that do offer job prioritization. You look at three such devices, plugging each of them into your scenario. In addition, you adjust the scenario to reflect the performance of your current router, with two enhancements:

- Priorities have been assigned to TCP/IP applications

- The router's memory has been reconfigured to work in tandem with this prioritization

Having made these adjustments, you discover that modifying your current router's setup in this way is sufficient to clear up the problems TW/E had been experiencing. As important, no significant degradation of response time for your Novell users is to be expected. Only if five writers and editors and four administrators simultaneously access the server they share will the latter group experience any appreciable drop in response time.

As a network administrator, you've hit a grand slam. You've cleared up a thorny problem without spending additional money or the time needed to install and configure a significant new network component.

Router Management. The Desktop Data scenario is an illustration of only a few of the issues involved in router management. Such administration also involves

- Initial configuration: defining the router's address, name, and so on

- Setting up time and date services—for example, time zone

- Configuring SNMP: access control, trap operation, server shutdown conditions, and so on

- Security: setting up passwords and access to certain commands and perhaps encrypting passwords, and setting up user name authentication

- Fault control: the ability to display system statistics such as memory and stack utilization and error messages, and to test connectivity, memory, and interfaces

- Performance management: Configuring switching, queueing, and scheduling priorities, and the ability to modify buffer size

Let's break some of the items in this task list down a little further.

Initial Router Configuration. First-time setup of a router is so extensive as to appear to deserve its own chapter in this book. Since *Upgrading and Repairing Networks* is already a hefty volume, we'll settle for looking at a synopsis of a real-world router configuration.

Cisco Systems specifies the following tasks as belonging to the initial setup of one of its devices:

- Acquiring the new router's IP address

- Resolving the address—that is, associating it with a device name in the host

- Loading the router's configuration file

- Modifying the boot field in the router's configuration register

- Specifying the system image the router loads during a restart

- Specifying the configuration file the router loads during a restart

- Specifying buffer size for loading configuration files

- Enabling compression of configuration files

- Enabling manual load of a system image

- Enabling loads of system images from the network

- Defining whether and how the new router acts as a TFTP or RARP server

Router Interfaces. To properly define all the connections to a router, you must take into account the following:

- The categories of interfaces

- Any special characteristics supported by any of those categories

The following table summarizes the most common interfaces, as well as factors that a router may need to know about them.

Interface	Characteristics
ISDN basic rate	Switch type Service profile Caller screening?
Ethernet	Tunneling?
FDDI	Timing parameters Duplicate address checking?
Asynchronous serial	PPP or SLIP?
Synchronous serial	Transmit delays Module timing Data compression rates
Token Ring	Token-ring speed Early release of tokens

Most of the router configuration parameters shown in this table are self-descriptive. One, however, may need some explanation.

Tunneling is a situation where a packet may travel through a router other than the default device that ordinarily handles it, to arrive at its destination (see fig. 15.1).

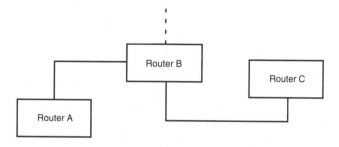

Figure 15.1

Packets traveling from Router A to Router B take a default path. The same applies to packets moving between Routers B and C, but traffic between A and C must tunnel.

Dialup Interfaces. If you anticipate remote access via modem to your network through the router you're configuring, you must, in addition to the interfaces described in the previous table, define the nature of the dialup interface to your router. (We didn't include dialup in the previous table only because this interface has enough parameters for a table of its own.)

In defining a dialup interface on a router, you have to specify quite a few parameters. For example, configuring a dialup connection to a Cisco router requires information on, among other things:

- Speed of transmission

- Start/stop bits

- Parity

- Automatic detection of the transmission speed in use

- Control flow

- Packet dispatch sequences

- Transport protocol

- Session time limits

- Automatic dialing

- Length of the wait before automatically redialing

- Number of redials

- Line timeout and automatic disconnect

- Terminal characteristics: screen length and width, escape character and other special key sequences, any terminal locking mechanism, line and connection information to be supplied after a successful logon, and any banner messages

- Telnet characteristics: echo, speed negotiation, end-of-line control, connection failure and success messages, recording of the location of the telnet client, and circumstances when a connection is refused

And that's not all. This information must be supplied for every dialup connection you are installing.

A Special Case. Whether to use an internal or external router is another question to be considered during router planning.

Novell is one networking environment in which there is a choice between a router that exists as a separate physical entity or a router that is internal to a file server. Internal routers are recommended only for small LANs to connect dissimilar cabling. For instance, the *NetWare 3.1.1 System Administrator's Guide* presents internal routers in the three configurations shown in figures 15.2, 15.3, and 15.4.

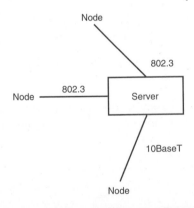

Figure 15.2

An internal router might be needed on an Ethernet Novell network.

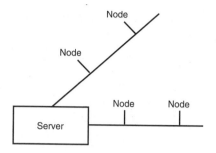

Figure 15.3

An internal router connecting Ethernet 802.3 and 10BaseT segments of a Novell network.

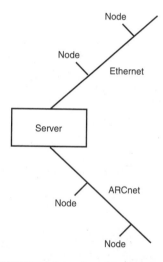

Figure 15.4

An internal router connecting ARCnet and Ethernet segments of a Novell network.

Keep in mind that all these scenarios involve connecting Novell LANs. None of the LANs in question are large. Since all are by definition IPX/SPX networks, no extensive protocol conversion is needed; at most, addressing structures must be translated from, for example, Ethernet to ARCnet.

In such a situation, an internal router is a feasible alternative. But in most environments that require a router in the first place, this kind of simplicity is only a dream. In the real world, protocols must be converted, network loads balanced, transmissions prioritized, and so on. Unless your environment is as streamlined as those in the previous figures, an internal router isn't an answer.

Router Configuration—Hints for the Real World

As the last stop on our cook's tour of router planning, configuration, and management, let's take a look at some points that can affect real-world router configuration.

> ### Tip
>
> In setting up your router to handle all the protocol types described in the following sections, the basic tasks you must carry out are
>
> - Enable routing
>
> - Establish security for access to the subnet in question
>
> - Enable monitoring of the subnet
>
> While only the first of these is actually required, all are strongly recommended.

AppleTalk. AppleTalk can run over Ethernet, token-ring, or FDDI channels, as well as on Apple's proprietary twisted-pair access system called *LocalTalk*.

The name AppleTalk is actually a catchall reference to a number of flavors of a protocol suite. Apple talks as summarized in the following table.

This "Talk"...	Talks Over...
EtherTalk	Ethernet
FDDITalk	FDDI
LocalTalk	Apple twisted pair
TokenTalk	Token Ring

Whatever dialect of AppleTalk you're dealing with, you'll find it contains a number of related protocols:

- AppleTalk Address Resolution Protocol (ARP)

- Datagram Delivery Protocol (DDP)

- Routing Table Maintenance Protocol (RTMP)

- Name Binding Protocol (NBP)

- Zone Information Protocol (ZIP)

- AppleTalk Echo Protocol (AEP)

- AppleTalk Transaction Protocol (ATP)

ARP, DDP, and RTMP accomplish end-to-end connectivity between internetworked nodes—that is, between nodes existing on separate AppleTalk networks. NBP and ZIP keep track of node name and location information. AEP is a reachability tester, analogous to the PING command. ATP is AppleTalk's transport protocol.

Banyan VINES. VINES is derived from the XNS protocol. It uses 48-bit addresses that are made up of a network number and a host number. The network number pertains to a VINES logical network, defined as a single server and a group of nodes. This first portion of a VINES address is 32 bits long. The host number takes up the remaining 16 bits of the address. For client nodes, it must be in the range 0x8001 through 0xFFFE.

VINES has a number of parameters that must be defined to your router. These include

- Means of displaying of host addresses
- Means of controlling of routing updates
- Enabling or disabling of fast switching
- Defining static routes
- Means of controlling of broadcast packets

DECnet. DECnet recognizes levels of routers. So, in addition to the three basic configuration tasks, setting up your router to talk to DECnet means identifying which levels it can occupy. In conjunction with setting up router levels, you will probably need to define areas of the DECnet that cannot be reached by a router at the level in question.

IP. IP configuration involves not only expected tasks like assigning addressing but also tasks such as defining alternative schemes for address resolution, enabling or disabling DNS, defining how broadcast packets are handled, enabling or disabling the receipt of protocol unreachable and similar administrative messages, setting up an audit trail, and so on. Of course, IP configuration on any router must begin with the big three. But it will extend to less common actions like those just described, and to configuring individual routing protocols. When one considers just how many of these there are in a TCP/IP environment, IP configuration can be seen for the weighty job it is.

Novell. The Internetwork Packet Exchange protocol, or IPX, is the communications tool through which Novell networks establish, monitor, and drop connections. IPX assigns addresses and routes to outgoing data messages and reads the addresses of incoming messages to direct them to the appropriate destination.

Because NetWare was intended from the start to act as a network operating system (rather than a suite of protocols interacting with a classic operating system), IPX is more closely linked to other portions of NetWare than, for example, TCP/IP is to UNIX. As an example, IPX does not handle the preparation of data packets for transmission. Before packets are handed off to it, they are assembled and formatted by the NetWare shell itself. Once in the hands of IPX, the data packet is forwarded partially through the services of a LAN driver that controls the NIC.

This closer relationship presents a few wrinkles of router configuration that are unique to Novell. You may, for example, need to distinguish between interfaces to Novell networks that can support a single LAN and those through which access to several LANs are possible. Or you might have to create filters to shield your router from some of NetWare's default broadcasts.

Router Profiles

More detail on router makeup, operation, and planning is out there, but when you move beyond the points we've discussed, you enter vendor-specific territory. So let's turn instead to some personality profiles for routers that would make excellent additions to any network. Each of the six routers outlined in the following sections also meet the more general criteria for router selection stated earlier in this chapter. Each is an external, dedicated router.

First, we'll look at specifications for four wide area routers, then we'll examine two local area devices. Also, be aware that each of these two groups contains routers that might serve as "upgrades" for some of the less powerful members of the same group. So if your current router isn't performing like it used to, the following sections may suggest alternatives.

An Ethernet-To-Internet IP Router

- Interfaces: dialup, leased/switched, or ISDN
- Connect protocols: PPP or Frame Relay
- Management: Windows, Macintosh, telnet, or SNMP
- Ethernet port: auto-switching between thicknet, thinnet, and 10BaseT Ethernet
- Number of WAN ports: one RS-232 operating at 128 Kbps in both synchronous and asynchronous modes
- Cost: $995.00

An Easy-To-Use Wide Area Router

- Interfaces: dialup, leased/switched, or ISDN; allows for isolation of low-usage links as dial-on-demand-only
- Connect protocols: PPP or Frame Relay
- Protocols routed: AppleTalk, DECnet, IPX, TCP/IP
- Management: Windows, Macintosh, telnet, or SNMP
- Ethernet port: auto-switching between thicknet, thinnet, and 10BaseT Ethernet
- Number of WAN ports: one RS-232 operating at 128 Kbps in both synchronous and asynchronous modes
- Cost: $1,295.00

A High-Speed, Multi-Port Ethernet-To-Intenet Router

- Interfaces: dialup, leased/switched, ISDN, or T1

- Connect protocols: PPP or Frame Relay

- Protocols routed: AppleTalk, DECnet, IPX, TCP/IP

- Management: Windows, Macintosh, telnet, or SNMP

- Ethernet port: auto-switching between thicknet, thinnet, and 10BaseT Ethernet

- Number of WAN ports: two T1/E1 rate synchronous V.35; two 128 Kbps synchronous/asynchronous RS-232

- Cost: $2,195.00

A High-Speed, Multi-Port Wide Area Router

- Interfaces: dialup, leased/switched, ISDN, or T1

- Connect protocols: PPP or Frame Relay

- Protocols routed: AppleTalk, DECnet, IPX, TCP/IP

- Management: Windows, Macintosh, telnet, or SNMP

- Ethernet port: auto-switching between thicknet, thinnet, and 10BaseT Ethernet

- Number of WAN ports: two T1/E1 rate synchronous V.35; two 128 Kbps synchronous/asynchronous RS-232

- Cost: $2,995.00

Wire-Speed Segment Router

- Segments managed: one Ethernet subnet

- Fault management: store-and-forward with error isolation

- Protocols routed: AppleTalk, DECnet, IPX, TCP/IP; ability to include other protocols (with upgrade/add-on)

- Management: Windows, Macintosh, telnet, or SNMP

- Ethernet ports: two; autoswitching between thicknet, thinnet, and 10BaseT Ethernet

- Cost: $2,995.00

Multi-Port Ethernet Switching Router

- Segments managed: multiple Ethernet segments

- Fault management: store-and-forward with error isolation

- Protocols routed: AppleTalk, DECnet, IPX, TCP/IP; ability to include other protocols (with upgrade/add-on)

- Management: Windows, Macintosh, telnet, or SNMP

- Ethernet ports: four; autoswitching between thicknet, thinnet, and 10BaseT Ethernet

- Cost: $3,495.00

Router Support

The perfect router should be accompanied, at no extra cost to you, by management software and a support agreement that make your job as network administrator at least a bit easier. This software and support are sketched out in the following sections.

Management Software

- X-Windows, Windows, and Macintosh versions of the management software should be available.

- Router parameters should be displayed in an easy-to-understand, needs-little-if-any-interpretation manner.

- You should have the option of viewing full or selected sets of router statistics.

- You should be able to manage both local and remote routers through the same software.

- You should be able to carry out downloads of software to the router from the management package.

Support Agreement

The availability of the following items is typical of data processing support agreements. One-year warranties are the norm; routers that offer extended warranties are usually high-end, high-cost devices. Software updates, telephone technical support, and replacement of defective components, on the other hand, are widely offered, particularly because no licensing questions apply here.

- Minimum one-year warranty; a three-year warranty is preferable

- Free software updates for the life of the router

- Free unlimited phone-in technical support

- Replacement of defective components (hardware or software) within 48 hours

A Real-World Router Monitoring Tool. As one example of router monitoring software, take a look at a product called RouterCheck.

RouterCheck is an AppleTalk router monitoring tool that profiles individual routers, reporting on router location and configuration. RouterCheck looks for inconsistencies in that configuration, and reports these as well, along with recommended corrective actions for each. RouterCheck can run from any version 6.0 or later Macintosh machine, within the network or across the Internet. Similarly, RouterCheck keeps tabs on any AppleTalk router, whether local or long-distance.

This management software package can report the following for every router that it is aware of:

- Router type

- Serial number

- Model number

- Software version

- Routing table contents

- Router statistics: packet receive and transmit counts, error counts, and collision counts

- Losses of connectivity

Information compiled by RouterCheck can be displayed in its entirety or in selected subsets.

Software Routers

If, after studiously reading everything in this chapter, you still haven't found the right answer to your routing problems, take heart! The last word on routers is this—you may not need one.

No, this isn't a return to the discussion of the difference between routers, bridges, and repeaters. It's a new topic altogether—routing accomplished strictly through software.

The most recent development in this area is the introduction by Microsoft Corporation of the MPR Service for Windows NT. The *Multi-Protocol Routing Service* (*MPR*) offers a low-cost LAN-LAN routing mechanism, eliminating the need for a dedicated router. It also facilitates migration from NetWare to Windows NT, by replacing NetWare-based LAN-LAN routers with Windows NT Server.

Windows NT Server, even before the addition of MPR, provided routing support for remote connection to a Windows NT LAN, as well as LAN-LAN routing support for connection to AppleTalk networks. With the addition of MPR, that LAN-LAN routing support has been enhanced to include TCP/IP and IPX/SPX networks. When used with appropriate additional NICs, MPR also enables the connection of Windows NT LANs to WANs.

Summary

Let's wrap up this chapter with a router quick reference in the form of a table summarizing the most important characteristics of routers, and the features that a good router should offer.

Trait	Needed or Just Nice?	Acceptable Minimum
Load-balancing	Nice	N/A
CPU	Needed	Powerful enough to transmit at 14,400 Kbps
RAM	Needed	Powerful enough to transmit at 14,400 Kbps
Protocols translated	Needed	AppleTalk, IPX/SPX, TCP/IP
Routing protocols	Needed	NLSP, OSPF, RIP, RTMP
Cabling supported	Needed	Ethernet, FDDI, ISDN, token ring
Ports	Needed	At least one Ethernet and one WAN port
Management software	Needed	At no extra charge and should provide the ability to view all or selected subsets of router information; that information should include packet counts and error counts
Support	Needed	At no extra charge, unlimited phone support

Chapter 16

Linking to Minis and Mainframes

There are a number of scenarios in which smaller computers or computing environments must interact with larger ones. Such interactions can take place within a single site or even a single room, or they can involve remote connections. We'll begin this chapter with a look at the history of smaller-to-larger hookups because contemporary solutions to the puzzle of linking to minis and mainframes must build upon what this history produced. Then we'll examine the means by which connections to minis or mainframes can be made; today's thoroughly distributed environments require such connections. Finally, we'll present scenarios that illustrate linking to minis and mainframes.

The Earliest Small-To-Large Computer Connections

There was a time when the term *network* meant "a big computer with a bunch of terminals hooked to it." But with the advent of PCs in the 1980s and the appearance of LANs soon thereafter, the lexicon of data processing was forced to expand. *Networking* became as much the province of the small computer as of the large.

The first inroads made by PCs into large machine/batch-processing environments came about because of the ability of a PC to wear two hats—that is, to act not only independently but also as a terminal to a mini or a mainframe. Such *emulation* was accomplished almost entirely by means of software. But as with all data entry or display devices smart or dumb, a cable had to connect the little guy to the big guy. Direct PC-to-mini/mainframe connections were usually cabled with coaxial cable and often required such extra hardware as multiplexers or communications controllers.

Figure 16.1 shows a PC-direct-to-large computer link of this sort.

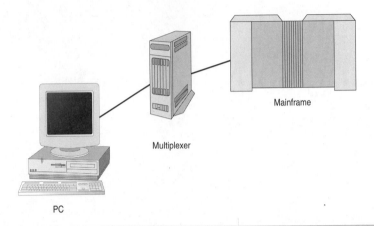

Mainframe

Multiplexer

PC

Figure 16.1

PCs were frequently connected to minis or mainframes with a coaxial link.

But simply laying down a length of cable wasn't enough to cut the mustard. The impersonation of a terminal by a PC was made possible by the development of software that allowed the PC to transmit to the mini or mainframe at the far end of the cable those signals expected from it and that identified its data entry and display devices. For instance, an early (and still widely used) terminal emulation package generated from the PC that ran it the control characters (*start of text* and so on) that identified it as a member of the 3270 family of IBM terminals.

In addition, the earliest PC-to-big machine hookups often were supported by the following two additional hardware devices:

- Multiplexers gathered together the relatively low-transfer-speed data streams originating at terminals, combined those streams into a single, multi-part transmission, and zinged them on to a mini or mainframe at speeds often over 2 Mbps.

- Communications controllers acted primarily to allow a single port on a minicomputer or a mainframe to service several devices, including a PC-as-terminal.

Note

One of the most widely used families of emulation software was and still is IBM 3270 emulation. *Families* is appropriate because many vendors produced such packages, which provide PCs with the ability to masquerade as any one of a number of the 3270 series terminals. These models are *intelligent terminals*. That is, they have the following characteristics:

- Transmit and receive in block mode, usually a screen at a time, rather than line by line

- Capable of full-screen operations and even windowing

- Offer text editing that includes block operations and automatic cursor movement

Similar combinations of communications controllers and emulation software have been and remain available for the DEC world. In fact, the VT100 terminal emulation is still one of the most widely used applications of this sort.

Caution

Even if some of your connectivity needs might be met by the controller/emulator combo, you must still evaluate the particular models you're considering. As might be expected, not all emulation software, whether 3270, VT, or other, is compatible with every IBM PC clone. In addition, you must be certain that the package you choose not only maps PC keystrokes to the signals that the large computer to which you're connecting expects, but also provides for transfer of data to and from the host. That is, the emulator must be compatible with whatever mini or mainframe operating system is involved.

Token Ring's Role in Small-To-Large Computer Connectivity

At the end of the 1980s and during the first couple of years of this decade, token-ring networks functioned not as autonomous LANs, but as the highest-tech solution to the PC-to-mini/mainframe puzzle. During this period, IBM made Token Ring a "strategic path"; however, there were reasons other than market forces that dictated its use.

- Token-ring networks or segments can operate at speeds up to 16 Mbps.

- In combination with appropriate communications controllers, token-ring networks can be a cost-effective means of connecting a group of PCs to a larger machine.

The use of token-ring as a means of linking to minis and mainframes foreshadowed many of the concerns that system and network managers would next have to grapple with, connecting LANs to larger computing environments.

A Small-To-Large Computer Connection's Similarities to Remote Access

When a LAN and a mini or mainframe are at the same site, their operating environments and circumstances still differ enough to make a direct connection of most of the types discussed to this point impractical. Even a token-ring LAN, if it is truly a LAN and not merely a physical segment of a larger computing environment that happens to consist of PCs, is functionally distinct enough from the machine that it must talk to that some provision must be made for its members to be able to continue to act as LAN workstations.

Only when an exchange of data with the mini or mainframe is needed should this role be exchanged for that of terminal. Therefore, establishing a LAN-to-large link is in effect, if not in fact, the same as establishing a *remote access* connection.

Applications That Lend Themselves to Small-To-Large Access

Some traditional and some more recent applications seem to be tailor-made for remote access and by extension for the PC-to-big-machine link. Chief among the first group are database-intensive tasks. If a station's primary reason for being is to input, access, or massage some portion of a database, there is little reason, given today's technology, to require that station to be close at hand to its host. The easy availability of software for the remote management of networks makes such neighborliness even less necessary. Of tasks that more recently have come to be popular with the "average" PC user, two—file transfer and electronic mail—also imply the processing and storage capacities of minis or mainframes, as well as the possibility of remote access.

Industries That Can Benefit from Small-To-Large Computer Connections

Because of their need for real-time or near-real-time access to data from a variety of locations, a number of types of organizations can benefit from connecting PCs to minis or mainframes, whether through in-house or remote access:

- Accounting
- Financial
- Insurance
- Medical
- Real Estate
- Telecommunications

Remote Access Methods as Models for Linking to Minis or Mainframes

There are three major types of remote access, each of which has its own methods and technologies—for more information on these and other remote access concepts, turn to chapter 27, "Adding Remote Network Access (Telecommuting)." These three, which can also serve as models for the small-to-large computer connection, are

- Application-specific, software-controlled access
- Remote control—that is, those situations where a remote machine accesses and logs on to or otherwise takes control of a networked station
- Remote node status, under which a machine interacts directly with a network and is as much a part of it as the PC next to the file server

Note

For a more detailed discussion on the technologies involved in accomplishing the three types of remote access, and in particular the remote control and remote node methods, turn to chapter 25, "Adding Network Modems."

The following table summarizes these remote access schemes.

Has These Strengths	And These Weaknesses
Application-Specific	
Consists of a single piece of software; therefore low-cost and easy to install at the client end; for example, remote software such as Carbon Copy.	Only allows access to a single application.
	May require separate host and client software.
	May require a dedicated gateway PC.
Remote Control	
Handles a large number of simultaneous sessions.	Can be expensive to set up and operate.
Compatible with most LANs and mini or mainframe hosts.	May not offer remote management.
Provides centralized management of remote stations.	Not easily upgraded or expanded.
	Support for Macintosh not readily available.
Remote Node	
Provides access to all network resources.	Requires more powerful machines as stations.
Can support the widest variety of PC platforms.	More applicable to mini-based LANs than to PC-to-mainframe connections.
Can support the widest variety of applications.	

Figure 16.2 traces the paths between the definition of your user's needs and the access methods that best meet those needs.

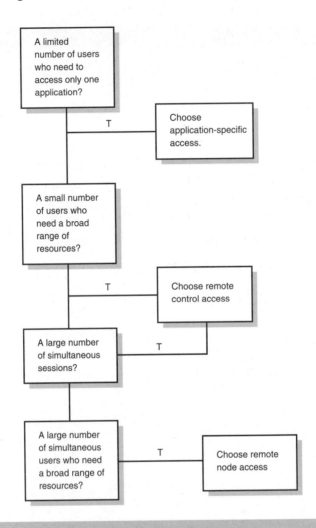

Figure 16.2
Clearly defining users needs facilitates choosing the right access method.

Details To Look for in an Access Method

Now that you've walked your way from "I only have seven users who need to talk to the corporate mainframe, and of those, no more than three need regular access" to "Looks like some form of remote control server is what's called for," let's take a look at the more detailed requirements your choice must meet:

- Support for as wide as possible a variety of PC/terminal hardware platforms. Ideally, IBM compatibles, Macintoshes, X-terminals, and workstations should all be under the remote access method's umbrella. At a minimum, be able to incorporate clones,

Macs, and workstations. In any case, the remote access scheme you implement must be able to handle all types of machines that will be dialing up or otherwise connecting to your mini or mainframe.

■ Support for as wide a variety as possible of operating systems. This requirement applies to both ends of the conversation; look for a remote access solution that can deal with the following:

- Macintosh

- MS/DOS

- MVS and VM

- UNIX

- VAX/VMS

- Windows (NT, for Workgroups, and 95)

■ Support for as many LAN operating systems as possible. Look for a technology that can handle

- AppleTalk

- NetWare

- Windows-based NOSs (for Workgroups, Microsoft Network)

■ Compatibility with a wide spectrum of protocols, both LAN- and host-supported

- AppleTalk

- IPX/SPX

- LAT (for VAX/VMS hosts)

- TCP/IP (for Macintosh, NetWare, OS/2, UNIX, and Windows in all its flavors)

- TN3270 (for IBM hosts)

■ Connectivity-specific features supported. Look for the following:

- Dial-in and dial-out capabilities

- Remote management by means of SNMP

- Remote terminal or remote node status available

- Routing management

- Security management, including but not limited to access restriction, activity logging, call tracking, and inactivity timeouts

- Support for a variety of modems and types of phone lines

  - Modems: V.32, V.Fast, and V.34

  - Wireless modems in addition to "traditional" models

  - Phone lines: analog, digital, ISDN, leased, and T1

Anticipating Your Network's Need To Link to Minis or Mainframes

As important as its ability to meet existing needs is the ability of a network to grow to meet needs as they change. In maintaining and enhancing access, for instance, you may have to add ports or support for PBX-type (that is, branch office) features, or enhance or change cabling. In addition, recent studies have found that while the number of network nodes and other means of remote access grows by about 40% annually, and the number of LANs and LAN segments increases by as much as 30% each year, budgets for system and network management grow by no more than an average of 12%.

Such conditions in the overall computing environment will undoubtedly affect the configuration of a link between PCs and larger computers. You can get a jump on needed future small-to-large computer connection (and on network management in general) by using some means of network modeling.

Do-It-Yourself Modeling or Software Tools?

As distributed processing grows and takes on new wrinkles, the number and rate of appearance of variables that system and network administrators must deal with grow proportionately. In such circumstances, paper-and-pencil analyses become unwieldy; there simply isn't enough time, money, or resources to study, model, and then recommend.

Unfortunately, only a few *computer-aided network design* (*CAN-D*) applications are available today, although the number is expected to increase steadily. However, the principles upon which such packages operate can be applied to a do-it-yourself analysis to make it as efficient as possible.

> **Note**
>
> Probably the best-known CAN-D package currently available is the Block-Oriented Network Simulator (BONeS) PlanNet from Systems and Networks.

Keep the following points in mind when conducting your analysis:

- Include elements that represent the entire spectrum of network or network segment types, not only those types that you're sure you'll be dealing with. Which is to say, allow for token-ring, Ethernet, 10BaseT, 10Base2, and optical-based nets or segments, as well as the WAN components mesh, serial link, and frame relay.

> **Note**
>
> Refer to chapter 4, "Upgrading to a WAN," if you need to review the characteristics of a WAN.

- Include a list of all possible interconnectivity devices. For instance, even if you don't currently use and don't think you'll ever need a translating bridge, include translating bridges in your set of possible connectors.

- Produce a list of all possible applications with which the distributed environment does or may have to deal.

- Have at hand a thorough and accurate outline of traffic patterns for individual applications, individual workstations, individual servers or hosts, and the environment at large.

With these outlines in hand, you can evaluate any remote access, or other anticipated, network enhancement, simply by measuring the effect of every candidate on each of the elements just presented.

Figure 16.3 sketches part of one possible checklist.

Technologies To Link to Minis or Mainframes

Let's review the definitions of user needs presented in figure 16.2, and use these as the basis for a discussion of specific technologies for linking to minis and mainframes.

Application-Specific Access

If your environment is one in which a handful of users, of individual PCs or networked ones, need to carry out a single application that involves interacting with a mini or mainframe host, a software solution, in combination with either a coaxial direct connection or a dialup link as appropriate, will suffice. Packages like the following are good candidates.

- Microcom's Carbon Copy
- Norton-Lambert's Close-Up
- Symantec's pcAnywhere

Access	Supports/Compatible With . . .

Coax/Mux

Segments
10BaseT ☑   10Base2 ☑   Thinnet ☑   Token Ring ☑   Optical ☑
WAN mesh ☐   WAN serial link ☐   WAN frame relay ☐

Connectivity
Xylogics Router ☑   U.S. Robotics PCMCIA modem ☐

Applications
x-terminal sessions ☑
Excel ☑
UNIX e-mail ☑
cc:Mail ☑

Figure 16.3

A checklist aids in modeling remote or small-to-large access.

Note

If the application in question is solely mini- or mainframe-resident—that is, if the PCs accessing it need no more than terminal emulation capabilities to do so—the Terminal utility available with Windows will fill the bill. And it's free!

An ingenious form of application-based access has been implemented at the University of California at Berkeley, running Carbon Copy on a dedicated LAN workstation. This configuration has proven faster than a true bridge for some applications. It doesn't pass the entire executable to the remote, but rather only displays and keystrokes, thereby achieving high performance while using very little bandwidth. While this imaginative, low-cost solution does not offer links to minis or mainframes, it could be modified to do so.

Combining Connectionless and Connection-Oriented Access: A Scenario

Consider the following:

A non-profit organization's headquarters in the Pittsburgh area must find a way for the PCs on its two LANs, one NetWare-based and the other TCP/IP-based, to download statistical data from a mainframe on a WAN operated by, let's say, the federal government's Department of Health and Human Services.

In researching the task, the network administrator identifies, as the potential source of her worst headaches, the fact that her LANs are *connectionless*, while the WAN through which they must communicate with the mainframe is *connection-oriented*.

But, ever intrepid, our network administrator comes up with a solution. She implements a *Switched Multimegabit Data Service (SMDS)*.

An SMDS is connectionless, but simulates a connection-oriented environment. SMDS access devices pass 53-byte packets to a switch. That switch determines the destination address and passes messages one at a time and in the correct order as do connection-oriented protocols to that destination *over any available path*.

Because SMDS is connectionless, it is readily compatible with LANs. SMDS can easily feed into WANs because it employs T1 and T3 circuits as its delivery system. SMDS also "bridges" other LAN/WAN gaps:

- SMDS can, like connection-oriented protocols, handle group addressing.

- SMDS uses a standard for addressing developed by the *Consultative Committee for International Telegraph and Telephone (CCITT)*. This addressing standard, E.164, is, like a better-known CCITT specification, X.25, connection-oriented. So much so, in fact, that E.164 addresses are structured like telephone numbers.

- SMDS offers SNMP-based management.

Tip

For more information on SMDS as a LAN-to-WAN solution, contact the *SMDS Interest Group (SIG)*, an industry association of service providers, equipment manufacturers, users, and others working to speed the proliferation and interoperability of SMDS services, products, and applications.

Phone: (415) 578-6979

Fax: (415) 525-0182

E-Mail: **sig@interop.com**

WWW: **http://www.zdexpos.com/zdexpos/associations/smds/home.html**

> **Tip**
>
> Another solution the network administrator in our example might have considered is the DIRECTROUTE family of products from Symplex Communications. These products use a combination of hardware and software features to present connection-oriented, switched internetworking that offers, in addition to the abilities commonly found in connection-oriented routers, bandwidth management, call and connection management, and data compression.

Strictly Hardware Driven Access: A Scenario

About two blocks away, another LAN manager in a multinational corporation's headquarters grapples with another variant on the small-to-large model. He must provide every PC on a departmental Novell LAN with the ability to access all the resources of the Ethernet LAN in another department and to carry out application-oriented access with a mini in that second department as well as a mainframe in MIS.

Like his peer down the street, this LAN manager is up-to-date on upgrading and repairing networks. His reading on this topic allows him to select a single communications controller that meets at least most of the criteria detailed in the "Details To Look for in an Access Method" section. The component in question offers the follwoing:

- Support for a wide variety of PC platforms
- Support for a similar variety of PC operating systems
- Support for all commonly used NOSs
- Support for all commonly used LAN and mini or mainframe host protocols
- Support for all commonly used modem and phone line types

Real-World Hardware-Driven Access Technologies

Such controllers include the Remote Annex line of products from Xylogics, the LANRover from Shiva Corporation, and components from U.S. Robotics and Microcom. However, some of these boxes have drawbacks. For instance, the relatively low speed of phone lines can be a problem that the LANRover cannot overcome.

Combinet manufactures a connection controller that combines an Ethernet bridge and an ISDN terminal adapter. This component can be hooked up to an ISDN line that has another Combinet component on the other end, yielding 56 Kbps–128 Kbps transmissions between LANS or between an individual user and a LAN. Actual bandwidth and line costs depend on whether true ISDN service is available between one Combinet controller and the other. The advantages of this solution are its speed and seamlessness; there is very little performance difference between a remote station using it and a local LAN station. However, this is not a low-cost connectivity option. Each of the pair of devices needed for a single ISDN hookup costs approximately $2,000.00.

Hardware-driven access to minis and mainframes can also be accomplished by a PC-based server that houses a modem, a multi-port serial card, or a switch that allows a number of sub-channels to access a single RS-232 circuit. Multi-port cards are available from companies such as DigiBoard. (For more detail on selecting and implementing access hardware, see chapter 25, "Adding Network Modems.")

Summary

Like all data processing technologies, the methods of linking PCs or LANs to minis, mainframes, or WANs have evolved at near-warp speed. The following checklist will help you make an informed evaluation of access methods for such connections:

- Number of users needing access

- Number of host resources that must be accessed simultaneously

- Volume of traffic such requests can be expected to generate

- Nature of host and client OSs, NOSs, and protocols

- Nature of communications media (for example, phone lines) that are available for the connection

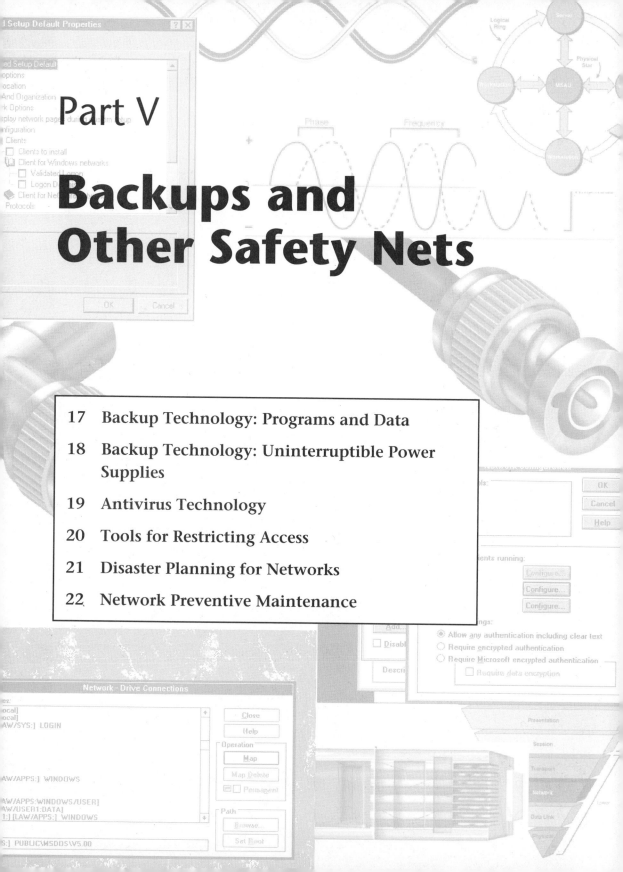

Part V

Backups and Other Safety Nets

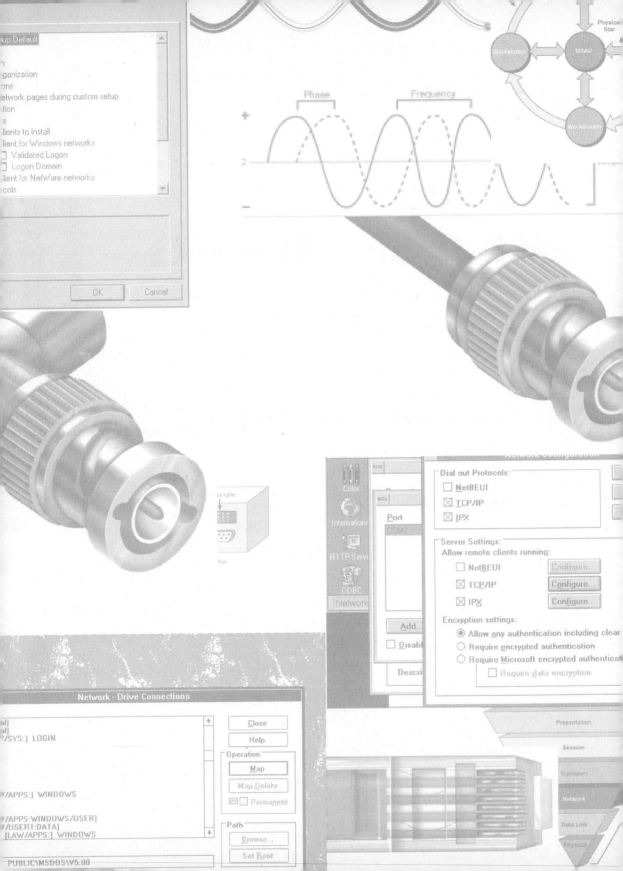

Chapter 17

Backup Technology: Programs and Data

"Make frequent backups" has become something of an oft-ignored litany in the world of computer publications. Countless authors have tried to emphasize the importance of frequent and reliable backups. When administering a network, however, backing up your systems becomes less a matter of convenience and more of an absolute requirement, if you intend to keep your job for any length of time.

Unfortunately, many erstwhile administrators learned this lesson in the same way that a student driver learns to drive a stick shift, that is to say, by stalling out in traffic. One day, you find yourself face-to-face with the boss, being told that the new guy in Accounting just deleted the master database file, and would you please restore it from yesterday's backup? No matter what the reason why not, if you don't have that file, you're about to learn a lesson that will remain with you for the rest of your brief career.

Backing up a stand-alone PC is more often a matter of preserving a carefully tuned environment, rather than protecting vital data, which can very likely be stored on a couple of floppies. The worst-case scenario would be having to reinstall and reconfigure all of the machine's applications. But, multiply this situation by dozens or hundreds of workstations, and add several servers full of vital company data, and the picture changes considerably.

There is no greater career pitfall than having to tell your supervisor that work needs to be redone because there is no backup. All of the computer jargon that you may have learned to throw at management up until now will be useless. They don't care why. At this point, they only see the dollar signs of lost production, as compared to the dollar signs of that expensive tape drive.

On a more serious note, it may not even be solely a matter of time or money. As more and more critical industries convert to client/server systems for their computing needs, the loss of data could lead to the interruption of vital services or, in a medical situation, even the loss of life. I can therefore safely add my voice to the chorus and say, with even greater emphasis, "Back up well, and back up often."

This chapter helps you toward that end by discussing the various criteria that should be considered before purchasing a network backup system. We will also discuss the general nature of network backup software, the configuration options available to help you devise a responsible long-term backup rotation scheme, some of the more common problems affecting network backups, and solutions that can help you troubleshoot any problems that may arise. The hardware used for backup systems is covered elsewhere in this book. SCSI and other peripheral interfaces are discussed in chapter 5, "The Server Platform."

Assessing Backup Needs

Unfortunately, making backups is not only more crucial on a local area network, it is also far more complex. It would obviously be impractical to furnish each workstation and file server on a network with its own means for backup. After all, sharing resources is what networking is all about, right? It is therefore a relatively simple matter to decide that there should be one or more backup drives located somewhere on the network, managed from a central interface. This is the last simple decision in the process.

The questions begin to come thick and fast at this point. "What kind of backup device should I buy?" "Where should the backup device be located?" "When should the backups be done?" "How can I make sure that they are done frequently enough?" And a dozen others. It is important to realize that most network backup systems utilize virtually every system that is part of the network, often stretching most of them to the limits of their capacity. There will be NLMs or services that run on the file server, a client program that runs on a workstation, and a level of data transfer between the two that greatly exceeds that of normal use. In short, there are a great many variables that must be considered in the process of backing up a LAN, and only you can determine which are the most important to the way that you, your department, and your company work.

In this chapter, we will first attempt to identify the right questions to ask in order to design and configure a centralized backup solution that is catered to your network's needs, and then discuss several possible network backup strategies in an attempt to answer them.

When To Plan a Backup Strategy?

The first question is the easiest. Whenever possible, the best time to plan a backup strategy is while the network is being designed or upgraded. Unlike many backup systems designed for use with single PCs, which can easily be retrofitted to an existing installation and moved to a different machine if necessary, network backup products are designed to be completely integrated into the network environment, particularly on the hardware level. SCSI has become the *de facto* standard for network storage subsystems, primarily because of its ability to effectively process simultaneous requests from different sources to multiple devices.

There was a time when tales of SCSI device incompatibility were rampant, and many administrators ended up with file servers containing several SCSI adapters, each addressing a single device, because of difficulties in getting the devices to work together on a single bus. The current generation of SCSI hardware, though, has come a long way in addressing these problems which, truth to tell, were probably caused as much by improper configuration as they were by badly designed hardware. There should be no problem in running today's tape drives on the same SCSI bus as hard drives, CD-ROMs, and other devices, as long as all of the devices are purchased with an eye towards interoperability.

Retrofitting a Backup Plan to an Existing Network

The majority of problems that arise in setting up backup systems come from attempts to add additional hardware to an existing system without fully researching the compatibility of the devices. It is essential that devices that are to reside on the same bus be compatible. Otherwise, a tape drive that has been band-aided onto an existing SCSI bus can cause problems with existing hard drive systems, leading to network interruptions and angry users.

This situation is particularly common when attempts are made to integrate the cutting edge of technology with older, legacy equipment. I encountered one case in which a person bought a brand new Pentium-based file server and a top of the line 4mm DAT tape drive, and then proceeded to stick his old ISA PIO-based SCSI card into the server. He then wondered why his hard drive volumes would frequently dismount and his backups would run so slowly, if at all. For the want of a new $300 SCSI adapter, his $15,000 investment was going to waste.

Therefore, when adding a backup system to an existing network or file server, the single most important factor is compatibility. Before you even begin to shop for products, you should have prepared a complete list of all of the hardware that you already possess, and everything about that hardware that might be significant. If you have a properly documented network, this process is already done. If, as in most shops, you do not, you will never regret spending a Saturday afternoon opening up your file servers and identifying everything inside. Gather the model numbers of all of the components and, where applicable, the firmwares being used as well. Hard drives, SCSI adapters, tape drives, and motherboards all have firmwares or chipset specifications that can be crucial in determining the compatibility of various devices. While you have the case open, take down the serial numbers of everything as well, in case of theft. If you have ever been in the position of taking over for a LAN administrator who has left a company without maintaining such a list, you will appreciate its value and, hopefully, be a little kinder to the next guy in your job, okay?

You may find, as a result of this process, that some of the hardware in the server from which you intend to back up your network is older or less powerful than you thought it was. In cases like this, it may actually be a wiser decision to add another SCSI card to a server for connecting to a tape drive rather than add to the burden of an existing SCSI bus that cannot readily be replaced at this time. It may even be time to think about purchasing an additional machine to augment or replace an aging one, rather than jeopardize the functionality of your existing systems.

The best possible way to create an effective backup system for a local area network, however, is to integrate the backup device into a fully realized storage subsystem that has been designed in consideration of the company's data storage needs. Answering a few vital questions at the outset of the project can save considerable time, money, and aggravation. As you decide how much disk space your network will need, you should also consider the type of data to be stored, how much there is of it, how volatile the data is (that is, how often does it change), and how much time is available to back it up. These are the kind of questions that should influence your purchasing decisions regarding backup media, hardware, and software.

Where Will Applications and Data Be Stored? Successfully organizing a network is a task that does not conclude with the signing of the purchase orders. One must also plan the way in which the network is going to be used, and creating a network backup strategy must be fully integrated into that process. Storage needs can be broken down into two basic categories: applications and data. Purchasing decisions concerning backups should be made after it has been decided where the applications will reside and where the data will be stored. Backing up one hundred copies of a word processing application installed to individual workstation hard drives is quite a different proposition from backing up one shared network copy of the application. The difference between the two should heavily influence the decision as to what the capacity and speed of the backup device(s) should be.

Remember also that restoring an application that has been lost due to drive failure is not simply a matter of the cost of the software itself. You must consider the amount of time and effort needed to restore the network to its previously functional state. Multiple copies of an application are likely to have been tweaked by their users to a state in which they are most useful to each individual. This may involve a significant amount of time and labor to re-create. Therefore, the nature of the applications (and their users) must also be considered when deciding whether or not to back them up. Devoting an extra hour or two of backup time each night to files that could take dozens of hours to restore manually is well worth the tradeoff.

In the same way, if data is to be stored on the workstation hard drives, as opposed to those of the file server, then the frequency of workstation backups is affected. This may influence the purchasing process towards a software package that has more extensive support for workstations running different operating systems or one whose cost includes a license to back up an unlimited number of workstations. Data is usually far more costly to replace than applications, so policies should be established and enforced that dictate where data files will be stored by users. Backup routines can then be customized to accommodate these policies. It is only by asking questions such as these and carefully planning your network that an intelligent determination can be made as to your backup hardware and software needs.

How Much Disk Space Is There? The next question to ask when considering backup needs is how much total disk space there will be on the network. Even this question, though, gives rise to many other questions. In most businesses, it will not be necessary to back up every byte on every drive throughout the network every day. There is, therefore, usually no need to purchase a tape backup system with the storage capacity to back up the entire network onto one tape. After arriving at a total quantity of disk space for the entire enterprise, an attempt should be made to prioritize the available storage space in order to determine what the daily backup requirements will be. These daily backups should be able to be conducted as one unattended operation. If there is too much data to fit onto one tape, then multiple tape drives or a tape autochanger may be called for.

Data files, of course, should be given first priority, and should be backed up at least once a day, depending on the type and amount of data. Priorities should also be established as to what quantity of data files change on a daily basis, as opposed to others that might be accessed often, but remain unchanged for long periods.

Applications, as a general rule, do not need to be backed up as often as data files, but while executables do not change, many applications maintain configuration files, properties, and definitions that can be as volatile as the data files themselves. These files should be backed up more often than the applications themselves.

Another consideration is the physical location of the hard drives on the network. The original concept behind the local area network was to have several file servers spread hard drive space throughout the enterprise, thus allowing for system redundancy. Many shops, however, are now adopting the "super-server" concept; setting up a single server with a huge amount of disk space in one storage array instead. Conditions such as these should be accounted for when attempting to estimate the length of the backup window, due to the variations in backup throughput of various devices on the network.

The *backup window* is the amount of low usage time that your company's operating schedule makes available for backup jobs to be conducted. As shown in figure 17.1, the fastest and most efficient backup operations will occur when file server hard drives are backed up to a tape device on the same SCSI bus. Next in overall throughput would be remote server drives being backed up over a high bandwidth backbone such as FDDI, then server drives being backed up over a standard Ethernet or Token Ring LAN connection, and then workstation drives over the LAN connection. Using a tape drive connected to a workstation reduces the backup rate of all targets (except the drives within that workstation) to the slowest of these figures. Obviously, the more data there is to back up and smaller the backup window, then the faster the backup throughput must be.

Another wrinkle to the equation is increasing use of WAN links to interconnect remotely located networks. Even a fully dedicated T1 link provides only a 1.55 Mbps maximum transfer rate, as opposed to the 10 Mbps rate of standard Ethernet. For this reason, it becomes increasingly difficult to back up significant amounts of data over a WAN link within the limitations of a given backup window. Although a backup of selected data files from a remote office can be more economically efficient than the purchase of another entire backup system, only actual testing will tell just how much throughput can be achieved over a given link. You should not, for example, count on a backup rate of 1.55 M/sec over a T1. Other network traffic must be considered, and the specifications of the equipment usually yield estimates that are optimistic, to say the least.

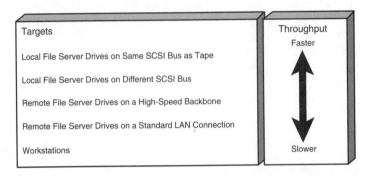

Figure 17.1

These are backup targets and their relative throughputs.

Where Will Users Store Their Data, Servers, or Workstations? One of the important factors in assessing a network's backup needs is whether or not workstations need to be backed up, and if so, how often. As a general rule, it is wise to have users store all of their data on file servers, rather than workstation drives. This helps to protect their files against the possibility of workstation crashes, accidental deletion, or theft. However, this does not necessarily mean that the workstations need not be backed up. In a case such as this, the frequency of workstation backups should depend on the company standards for the workstation environment.

If an organization has standardized on a particular workstation configuration and allows no individual software selection by users, then a master workstation replica can be stored on a server, and workstation backups can be omitted, except perhaps for Windows INI files and other unique configurational elements. Even a company that allows its users complete freedom of choice in software selection and configuration, however, should consider that backing up hundreds of identical DOS directories and useless Windows swap files is a waste of time, bandwidth, and media.

How Much Time Is There To Do It In? Whenever possible, system backups should occur at times when network usage is at its lowest. While, in some firms, this backup window may stretch from 5 p.m. until 9 a.m. the next morning, allowing plenty of time for backups, flextime hours, and multiple shifts, can in many cases drastically reduce the amount of time available to back up the network. This is a crucial factor influencing purchasing decisions of both hardware and software. A faster tape drive (or multiple tape drives) may be called for when there is a large amount of data to be backed up in a small amount of time, and the capabilities of a software package's scheduling features should be considered to ensure that backup jobs can be configured to automatically begin at the correct time, only on the days that you want them to.

Where Should the Backup Device Be Located? Once it has been determined how much data there is to be backed up, where that data is located, and when the backups should occur, the next decision concerns the location of the backup device and what system it is connected to. This is a crucial factor in terms of convenience, security, and especially cost. All of the repercussions of each option should be considered in relation to the way in which the network has been designed. Essentially, there are three possible solutions: a workstation-based tape drive, a drive attached to a production file server, and a dedicated backup server. The pros and cons of each method must be considered, as there is no definitive solution that will fit all cases. These methods are discussed in the following sections.

Workstation-Based Backups

There are several advantages to a workstation-based backup solution, the most prominent one being cost. There are several good workstation-based backup software packages available that are capable of backing up multiple file servers, and even other workstations, when they are made accessible through a peer networking protocol such as Windows for Workgroups' NetBEUI. In fact, these packages can usually back up any drive that can be mapped to a workstation drive letter. Software such as this is usually quite inexpensive, costing anywhere from $100 to $300, approximately 10% of the cost of an average server-based software package, which is usually priced according to the number or user-level of the servers being backed up.

While there are a great many backup software packages designed to be used for individual PCs with attached tape drives, comparatively few of these products address the needs of networks. In the networking context with which we are concerned, a software product should be able to back up a server volume, as well as protect its system files, such as the Windows NT Registry, the NetWare bindery, or the NDS database. Products like these are available from companies that are primarily devoted to developing backup software for the network environment, such as Cheyenne Software, Arcada, Legato, and Palindrome. All of these companies offer a wide array of solutions for different network types and operating systems.

Hardware, too, can be less expensive. While most of the same large capacity SCSI tape drives used on server-based systems can also be used with these lower-end software packages, there are also a large number of low-cost quarter-inch cartridge (QIC) tape drives on the market which are usually not recommended for server use, but which can be quite effective in this environment. Most of these, however, are obsolescing rapidly due to their limited capacity and the ever-increasing hard drive capacities being found on workstations and servers alike. When even an entry-level PC comes with a 500M hard drive, a 250M or even a 500M QIC tape drive does not appear to be a wise investment, especially for heavy use.

Another advantage of the workstation-based solution is the fact that, in a disaster recovery situation, a file server can be more easily restored from a remote system than from a drive that is attached to the file server itself. It would only be necessary to re-install enough of the network operating system to create the drive volumes and bind a network protocol. Everything else can be restored from the workstation. For this reason, many larger firms choose to assemble a redundant arrangement of backup hardware and software that can operate both on a workstation and a file server. Cheyenne Software, for example, markets software packages for both the workstation (ARCsolo) and the file server (ARCserve) that utilize the same interchangeable tape format. By purchasing external tape devices, the backup drive can swiftly be moved from file server to workstation in the event of a complete file server failure.

As you might expect, there are several major drawbacks to a workstation-based backup solution. The first and foremost is speed. Sending data from a file server to a workstation-based tape drive over a standard Ethernet or Token Ring IPX/SPX network connection will take far longer (roughly twice the time) than it would take to back it up to a tape drive installed on the file server itself, particularly when the hard drives and the tape drive are on the same SCSI bus. Another limitation is the fact that the workstation is limited to backing up only as many sources as can be mapped to its drives at any one time, which leads to the other major concern, which is security.

A workstation running software that schedules backups to occur during the night must be left logged in to all of the target servers with the appropriate rights to access all of their files. The memory resident application that is used to schedule the backups can also interfere with normal use of the workstation, so unless a computer is to be dedicated solely to backups and placed in a locked room, this sort of backup solution becomes less and less practical.

For a small business or workgroup consisting of a single server and a handful of workstations, however, this type of backup system is the most cost-efficient way of protecting the network against data loss. It is a mistake to let cost factors outweigh concerns for data integrity, but many small businesses allow themselves to be terrorized into the purchase of expensive, high-powered backup systems costing as much as their file servers, which are completely unnecessary for their current needs.

A good rule of thumb when making any purchasing decision in network computing is to base your purchase on what you need right now, and not on any future plans that extend more than two or three months ahead. Just about the only sure thing in the computer industry is that it continuously changes. No matter what you purchase today, there will be something available a few months from now that will be better, faster, and cheaper. There is nothing to be done about this except to try to keep current, and make the most intelligent decisions that you can *right now*.

File Server-Based Backups

The most common network backup configuration in use today is a NetWare NLM-based software package and one or more 4mm DAT tape drives attached to a file server's SCSI bus. When properly configured, this should allow approximately 15M to 20M of data to be backed up per minute onto tapes holding anywhere from 2G to 8G. This is usually sufficient protection for a medium-sized network, when the backup jobs are configured properly. Most of the major server-based backup software packages also allow multiple tape drives to run concurrently on the same SCSI bus, yielding cumulative backup rates of 100–150 M/min or more.

Depending on the number and current configuration of your file servers and your plans for future expansion, you may choose to add a backup system to an existing server or create a dedicated backup server. There are advantages and drawbacks to both alternatives. Adding a backup system to an existing server should only be done when that server has the resources available to support both the software and the hardware. Major NLM-based backup software packages may require up to 4M of memory to operate properly, in addition to what is already needed to support the operating system and the equipment already installed. Many packages, when actually processing a backup or restore job, spawn (or autoload) additional NLMs that are not resident when the software is loaded, but idle; so be sure to account for this when evaluating the additional load that such a system will add to your server. Another consideration may be processor utilization. Certain functions of backup software, especially database engines, can drastically increase the load on the server's CPU, at times. This can result in delayed access to users and even the temporary loss of the ability to communicate with the server.

In cases where it is felt that backup software places too much strain on an existing system, a file server dedicated to the performance of backups may be in order. A non-production server such as this, dedicated to network maintenance tasks (as opposed to servicing users), can also be the host for other network management products. As long as user access is restricted, then other network functions should not be disturbed by the backup process.

Another advantage to this concept is that, if it is absolutely necessary, backups can be scheduled to run during the workday. The problems caused by open files will still remain, as will a perceptible amount of network performance degradation, but in cases where there is no other choice, this method will minimize the impact of these problems.

The primary disadvantage to a dedicated backup server is the additional expense, not only for the hardware, but for the operating system as well. You must be sure that licensing considerations of the backup software allow you to back up all of your other servers. This may require you to purchase a network operating system license for a user level equivalent to that of your other servers, when there will actually be only a minimum number of users logged in to this server at any one time.

Another disadvantage may be that the speed of your backups will be negatively affected. A backup of a hard drive that is in the same machine as the backup hardware, or better yet, on the same SCSI bus, will always be faster than one that must travel over the network itself. If you have a high-speed network backbone, or if the length of the backup jobs is not critical, then this may not be an issue. In general, if you have a great deal of data to back up, or if you will be running multiple backup devices simultaneously, a dedicated backup server may be a solution that will end up causing fewer administration problems and being more economical in the long run.

Network Backup Software

The following sections examine the basic components of network backup software, and identify the areas in which the various products may differ. Some packages may be better suited to your network's needs for economic reasons while some may offer features that you require that others do not yet possess. It should be noted, however, that software of this type is continually developing as the rest of the industry develops. The basic goals of all network backup software packages are essentially identical—that is, to be capable of backing up and restoring all of the data types that may be found on today's heterogeneous networks as quickly and efficiently as possible. New developments in hardware and operating systems will inevitably be accommodated by backup software, and you may wish to choose a software vendor that most responsively and reliably updates its products to accommodate these innovations.

SBACKUP. Novell NetWare ships with a rudimentary file server utility called SBACKUP that will allow file servers and workstations to be backed up to a tape device. However, SBACKUP lacks nearly all of the advanced scheduling and convenience features found in any of the third-party products available. Consistency is everything in a reliable backup system, and SBACKUP, while it can effectively be used for a one-time job, leaves too many repetitive administration tasks to the operator to be a reliable everyday solution. Its use as a primary backup solution is therefore not recommended, but familiarity with its functions can be beneficial for two reasons.

First is the simple fact that every NetWare installation has it. In a situation when no other tools are available, such as that of a consultant visiting a remote site, the ability to perform a simple full backup of a server may be desirable, and SBACKUP can come in very handy at times. The other benefit of knowing SBACKUP is that it relies on the Novell Storage Management Services (SMS) system to perform its backups. Many third-party backup products use SMS for their own backups, to some degree, so familiarity with its modules and concepts can be useful in evaluating these packages.

SMS. Storage Management Services is an open specification developed by Novell for a standard set of Application Programming Interfaces (APIs) designed to provide a reliable interface between backup and storage management products and the various data types found in the modern heterogeneous network environment. When creating this specification, Novell clearly planned for its adoption by third-party developers. While SBACKUP utilizes the specification, it was no more intended to be a comprehensive backup solution than the Windows Terminal program was intended to be a full-featured communications package.

The specification consists of several basic components, each of which may or may not be used by a third-party backup package:

- The Storage Management Engine (SME) is the heart of any SMS compliant backup system and is the module most intended by Novell to be developed by other software vendors. It controls the communications with the backup hardware and provides the user interface by which backup jobs are created, scheduled, and administered. SBACKUP is Novell's implementation of an SME.

- The Target Service Agents (TSAs) are, on the other hand, the modules that are most likely to be utilized as is by third-party developers. These are the memory resident modules that perform the basic file system communications with the targets—that is, the parts of the network that are to be backed up. The TSAs, operating remotely throughout the network, are the only part of the SMS system that is in direct contact with the target data. They process the files on their designated targets and send the data to the SME via the Storage Management Data Requester (SMDR). Novell has made TSAs available for all of the basic data types found on most networks, including DOS, Macintosh, OS/2's HPFS, FTAM, NFS, and NetWare volumes, as well as for NetWare 4.x's Directory Services database, SQL database engines, and print servers. Other manufacturers have released TSAs of their own that conform with the Novell standard APIs and that can effectively be used with any SMS-compliant storage management engine.

■ The System Independent Data Format (SIDF) is a specification for the actual data format used to store files on tape. The TSAs send the target data to the SME using the encoding scheme specified in the SIDF specification. The developer of the SME can then choose whether to actually write the data to tape in this format or convert it to a proprietary one. This format, which has been adopted in theory by many of the major backup software manufacturers, should allow for tapes made with one software package supporting the format to be restored by another package. This interchangeability, however, has not been found to be as simple and reliable as some of the software manufacturers would lead you to believe. In most cases, transferring tapes between software packages should not be relied upon as a regular practice, unless careful testing is done beforehand. However, the continuing development of the standard bodes well for the backup industry in general, and lends a measure of assurance to the user that she will not find herself with a large library of tapes that has been abandoned by a manufacturer that has changed formats or gone out of business.

The interaction of the various modules is illustrated in figure 17.2

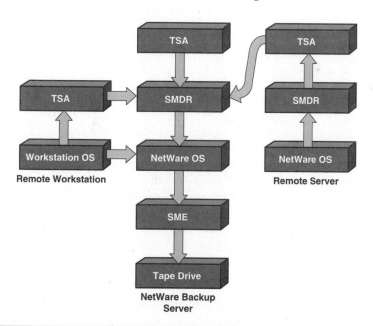

Figure 17.2

This is the Novell Storage Management Services Model.

The degree to which various backup software packages utilize SMS is highly variable. Novell has designated Level Two compliance to apply to any SME that fully utilizes the entire SMS specification. Some products, such as Palindrome's Network Archivist, offer such compliance. They are completely reliant on the SMS standards and are, in effect, guaranteeing the continued development of their product as long as Novell continues to support new data formats and operating systems with its TSAs. Palindrome has also written some of its own TSAs that are fully SMS compliant as well and can, therefore, be used with any other SMS-compliant software.

Level One compliance applies to software that can make use of the SMS TSAs to communicate with network targets. Many software developers use this as an optional feature for their products, or use the TSAs to enhance their range of services, employing proprietary communication methods for some file formats and using TSAs for others. It should be noted when evaluating products like these that any tape written using SMS can only be restored using SMS. Whether or not to choose a software package that is fully SMS compliant is a difficult question.

The main drawback to the specification is the greater amount of communications overhead involved than with most proprietary solutions, causing backup throughput speeds to be generally slower with SMS. I have not seen this difference in speed to be an overly dramatic one, however, and unless your installation requires the fastest possible backup speeds that you can achieve, this should not be a major factor influencing your purchasing decision. More attention should be paid to the present and future data types that you will be backing up, and whether or not the package that you choose can support them.

Some backup systems provide the option of not utilizing SMS at all, but care should be taken to note the instances when SMS is positively required to perform a proper backup job in today's networking environments. An interesting case in point is the need to back up the NDS databases that are the heart of the NetWare 4.x network operating system. The continued development of the NDS, since the original NetWare 4.0 release, has caused an ongoing problem for the developers of network backup software. At this time, there is no other backup agent available that can provide the full range of services to a NetWare 4.x server that Novell's own TSAs can, which includes complete backup of the NDS database as well as full support for NetWare 4.x's native compression features. This means that all files compressed by the NetWare 4.x operating system can be backed up and restored as compressed files, greatly reducing the amount of data traveling from the target to the backup hardware. However, even implementing the use of these TSAs has caused developers severe problems when modifying their existing products. While all of the major developers were in the process of readying native NDS implementations of their software, this process entailed major code revisions, in most cases, and a temporary solution was needed to accommodate the needs of their users.

The way in which various manufacturers worked to meet this need provides a good indication of their responsiveness to the market and the capabilities of their programmers to adapt their software to the changing needs of the industry. You may wish to ask how long it was before a particular manufacturer's product could be adapted to the backup of the NDS. You should also note the nature of the resulting product: was it a solution that was integrated into their existing software product, or an extra utility shipped to fill a temporary gap?

Backup Software Components

The average file server-based backup software package usually consists of a client application, a series of server modules, and a collection of agents. The "back end" or server portion will be packaged as NetWare NLMs or Windows NT services that perform three functions:

- Control communications with the backup hardware

- Manage a queue of backup jobs and the scheduling information to launch them at the appropriate times

- Maintain a database containing the details of all of the backup and restore activities that have occurred

The client or "front end" portion consists of a manager program through which backup and restore operations are created, controlled, and scheduled, and a series of agents that allow networked resources on various platforms to be backed up. Examining these in greater depth will allow you to intelligently compare the feature sets available in the various packages and thereby judge which of several admittedly similar products best suits the needs of your network.

The Tape Server. At the heart of any network backup program lie the device interface modules, or the means by which the target data is sent to the tape drive itself. It would seem to be a fairly simple proposition to feed the data that is gathered from the various target drives over the SCSI bus to the tape drive, but the process is actually quite complex. Tape drives are sequential access devices; that is, data is written in a contiguous stream onto the tape and must be accessed in the same manner. This is unlike a random access device such as a hard drive, in which files may be broken into separate sectors depending on the nature of the free space available on the device.

A hard drive's platters spin continuously, with the heads making contact with the appropriate sectors on the platters only when a read or write is requested. This is why a hard drive's access time is measured in milliseconds, because the head simply has to proceed to the proper position, and move a tiny distance to make contact with the platter. With a tape drive, however, the tape is only in motion during the processing of a request, and must be traveling at the correct speed across the heads for data to be read or written correctly.

Every time that a tape drive stops moving the tape across the heads during an operation, there is a period of lag time while the drive spins up to the proper speed for reliable access. Earlier incarnations of magnetic tape storage applications would simply wait for the tape drive to achieve the proper speed before actually performing the read or write operation, slowing down their operational throughput considerably. With modern tape backup systems, however, data is fed to the tape drive at the proper rate of speed to keep the drive *streaming,* that is, moving the tape across the drive heads at a uniform rate of speed with no starts or stops. In this way, data will be transferred at the best possible speed with the least likelihood of data corruption. Tape servers do this by storing small amounts of data that have been accessed from the backup target devices in memory pools created on the file server from which they can be smoothly fed to the tape drive.

Another factor to consider is the wide range of tape devices that are supported by the major network backup software packages. The various QIC formats, 4mm, 8mm, and DLT drives, all function in radically different ways, and the tape server must accommodate any of them. For example, QIC drives pass tape across stationary heads at rates of 25 or 50 inches per second or more. Helical scan devices such as 8mm and 4mm DAT drives use heads rotating at 2,000 rpm while tape is moved across them at approximately one inch every three seconds, allowing nearly 2,000 separate tracks to be written across a single inch of tape! The tape server must recognize the capabilities of the tape drive from an identifying signal sent across the SCSI bus, factor in the capabilities of the SCSI host adapter itself, recognize the resource constraints placed upon it by the configuration of the network operating system and file server hardware, and then come up with a solution that will feed the data arriving from the targets at the highest possible speed. Add to this the fact that most of these products can perform these functions for up to seven storage devices running seven separate jobs simultaneously, and their performance can be seen as no less than phenomenal.

It is important to consider that virtually no other operation stresses the limits of a network's communications, storage, and I/O systems more than backups do. Normal network usage makes regular but intermittent calls to a server's disk drives. Applications and data files may be loaded and unloaded at regular intervals on dozens of workstations, but rarely do applications call for a continuous stream of high-speed data transfer the way that a backup job does. When, for whatever reason, the data stream is slowed or interrupted, and the tape server has no data to feed to the drive, then the drive spins down to an idle state, and must spin up again before the data stream can be resumed. This condition is called *data starvation* and is one of the most common causes of unusually slow backup speeds and data corruption. For a smooth, continuous stream of data to be delivered to the tape drive at the correct speed, the interaction between the tape server module, the SCSI drivers, and the other devices on the SCSI bus must be consistent and predictable.

In addition to the transfer of data, a complex series of format conversions also takes place. Data is stored on NetWare volumes in blocks of a size specified during the creation of the volume. Workstation operating systems each have their own file systems that store data in different ways. All of this data, once it has arrived at the tape server, is written to the tape in blocks (of a different size and configuration) specified through negotiation between the tape server software and the tape drive itself. Some or all of the data may also be stored in a proprietary tape format that is specified by the software manufacturer.

Another major factor in this consideration is the existence of other devices on the SCSI bus. While it is perfectly practical to have a backup device on the same bus as hard drives, CD-ROMs, and other devices, the compatibility and configuration of these devices is vital for smooth concurrent operation. To mix devices such as these, a standard

SCSI protocol must be used, such as the Advanced SCSI Programming Interface (ASPI), which was developed by Adaptec and has since become the *de facto* standard in the integration of different manufacturers' SCSI devices on the same bus.

An ASPI driver is configured to directly address the host adapter and is loaded into memory. Then, all subsequent drivers for the various SCSI devices on the bus, including the tape server, address the ASPI layer instead of the adapter itself. The use of ASPI allows for virtually any modern SCSI device to be placed on a SCSI bus without interference from other devices, despite the overlapping requests that are generated by a network environment. While it is quite possible to attach a tape drive to its own dedicated SCSI adapter and eliminate possible interference with other devices and their drivers, this adds expense and driver overhead to the file server that may not be justified in some cases.

Thus, you can see that the operation of the tape server portion of any network backup software is far more complicated than it first appears. Software and hardware modules from three or more manufacturers must be made to interact without interfering in each other's processes. The most important factor in assembling a SCSI installation that will function to its fullest capacity is to gather components that are all designed to work together. This is why most vendors of network backup software conduct rigorous testing and certification procedures for both SCSI adapters and tape drives, most of them going so far as to certify not only specific devices, but specific firmware and driver revisions to be used with these devices.

Before making any backup hardware or software purchase, be sure that the adapter and the tape drive, their component firmwares, and any accompanying drivers have been certified for use with the software you are considering. Also, if you are going to run multiple devices on one SCSI bus, make sure that all of the hardware involved is ASPI compatible (as nearly all are these days). Avoid locking yourself into a proprietary hardware manufacturer or SCSI protocol, and be particularly skeptical of new trends in hardware development.

Caution

Remember, your backups are your safety net for any experimentation with new network products that you may care to conduct in the future. This is not the place to gamble on that slick new bus-mastering, error-correcting, self-caching SCSI wonderbus. Stick to the tried and true here, and you can be fearless anywhere else.

The Scheduler. While the tape server controls the actual transfer of data to and from the NOS and the tape drive, there must be another module responsible for seeing that the correct data is fed to the tape server at the correct time. This is the responsibility of the scheduler or backup manager. While a limited software solution like SBACKUP can initiate a single job at a specified time, all of the major third-party network backup packages can maintain and execute complete backup rotation schedules, allowing the administrator to create jobs that will launch at designated times and automatically reschedule themselves to repeat the next day, week, or month.

On a NetWare file server, this is usually accomplished using a job queue that is similar in nature to a network print queue. Jobs are created by a separate manager program and stored as encrypted files in coded directories located under the SYS:SYSTEM directory. The jobs are then executed at the appropriate time by a scheduling module that remains resident in file server memory. These same functions can be carried out by Windows NT services.

The most powerful of these products can maintain complete backup rotation schedules for up to seven different devices, running completely separate jobs at the same time. A virtually unlimited number of individual jobs can also be scheduled to run at any time, even months or years into the future. Many of these scheduling modules can also maintain a capability to perform scheduled copy jobs from one server volume to another. This would allow an administrator to schedule a regular "mirroring" job that would maintain an up-to-date replica of crucial files on another server at any interval desired.

When comparing the capabilities of the various software packages available, check on the different ways in which jobs can be stored and submitted to the queue in comparison with the layout of your network. While all should be able to submit jobs from a workstation-based manager program, others may also be able to submit them from a workstation's command line or from the file server console. This could be very useful if your servers are kept in a closet that doesn't contain a workstation. You should also be able to save a job configuration as a separate script file to be submitted at a later time. In this way, in a disaster recovery situation, complex backup rotations can easily be resubmitted to the queue.

The Database. All network backup products contain some means of tracking their activities. This is done to maintain a record of information such as when backup jobs were performed, what files were backed up onto which tape, and so on. Due to the sequential nature and slow seek times of magnetic tape devices, it is impractical to "browse" through a tape's contents in real time. It is therefore necessary to maintain a replica of each tape's contents in a database that will allow files to be chosen for restoration in the simplest and quickest possible manner. In addition to the file's existence on a tape, information as to its exact location will also be maintained. This will allow the tape server to utilize a high speed SCSI command to locate a particular file for restoration. An individual file can then be restored in seconds or minutes, rather than the several hours that may be required to read the entire tape, file by file, searching for the correct one.

Many products are also capable of maintaining database entries of other information concerning network backups, such as:

- Logs of all backup and restore activities

- Debugging logs of tape server activity, used to troubleshoot problems with tape drive performance

- Listings of the attributes of workstations being backed up, such as node addresses, login names, and so on

- Information about the tapes themselves, allowing users to be warned when a tape has been used too often or for too long a period of time

Care should be taken to examine what type of database is used by the various products being evaluated. Some vendors utilize commercial database engines such as Btrieve, while others have arrived at proprietary solutions. The use of a known database type has advantages in that there are likely to be third-party products available for database access and maintenance. Cheyenne Software's ARCserve, for example, ships with Crystal Reports, a reporting engine for Btrieve databases that provides extensive reporting and documentation capabilities as well as the ability to create customized reports. Their use of Btrieve also allows for the use of the maintenance utilities included with the Btrieve engine.

While Btrieve was originally developed by Novell and included as part of the NetWare package, it has since been sold by Novell and is now maintained by its own firm, Btrieve Technologies. This has had a positive effect on the overall product, and has resulted in the recent release of a solution to the primary drawback of the Btrieve client/server engine which is BREQUEST.EXE, the 75K DOS TSR requester that was required to be run at the workstation in order to access the server engine. A Windows DLL equivalent has recently been made available, which is quite effective and requires far less resources.

There are several other important factors to consider: What will the approximate size of database files be for the amount of data that you will be backing up? The database files will contain the name and location information for every file that is backed up during every job. These files can grow to be quite huge and steps may have to be taken to keep their size under control. A database engine should have the ability to be configured to purge database information when it has reached a certain age, shrinking the database files proportionately. Tools should also be available to repair databases that have become damaged or corrupted. Be aware that many database types will require a substantial amount of temporary drive space in order to perform such maintenance functions. Some products may allow these temporary files to be created on another volume, while others may not. Take these factors into account when planning an installation of these products.

In addition, there should be a means to restore files from a tape that does not exist in the databases. This may be done by addressing the tape directly, in order to perform a sequential search for the desired file, or to read the entire tape and assimilate its contents into the existing databases. A good database engine should have both of these capabilities, so that tapes made at an earlier time or at another installation can still be restored at will.

The use of a commercial database engine such as Btrieve provides extensive features and capabilities such as these to the application that utilizes it, but a trade-off must be expected in terms of both client and server resources as well as database size. If you are going to be backing up a relatively simple network and performing restores only in cases of the occasional mistakenly deleted file or disaster recovery situation, then such capabilities might fall into the realm of overkill. A product might therefore be called for that maintains a simple file and media index in which there is less possibility of corruption problems or system resource shortages.

Agents. Backup agents are software modules that run on the backup targets (that is, the devices to be backed up) that "package" the desired data and send it to the tape server where it is ultimately written to tape. Some backup software packages provide their own agents, while others utilize the TSAs provided by NetWare as part of the SMS specification. Some products may also use a combination of the two for coverage of various platforms or allow the user to choose between the two for a specific platform. Different agents are usually made available to address the various types of data to be backed up. These may include various workstation operating systems, server volumes supporting different file systems, and even special cases, such as live database files that must be backed up while in use. Obviously, you should ensure that the product you choose has agents available for all of the platforms that you wish to back up.

With today's heterogeneous networks, however, this may not be as simple as it sounds. Many of the packages have agents available for numerous flavors of UNIX workstations and OSs. With the growing popularity of 32-bit desktop operating systems such as OS/2, Windows NT, and Windows 95, you should carefully check whether your proposed backup software vendor has made agents available for all of the environments used on your network.

When evaluating agent coverage for your existing workstations, make sure that the product will function well with the way in which your users work. Remember, it is going to be the responsibility of the user to make sure that a workstation agent is loaded whenever a backup is scheduled. Whenever possible, it is a good idea to arrange your users' workstation configuration so that agent is loaded automatically. Most products will include both a DOS and a Windows agent, but the two are most likely to be exclusive. That is, the DOS agent will not function when Windows is loaded, and vice versa.

When conducting overnight backups, you must be conscious of the state in which your users leave their workstations at the end of the day. A DOS agent can be placed in the workstation's AUTOEXEC.BAT file or a Windows agent into the Windows Startup group, but neither will function if the workstation is turned off. Developing and enforcing a company policy in this respect will minimize the resource drain entailed by the loading of multiple agents and ensure that backups are performed reliably and on schedule.

Aside from coverage of all of the platforms on your network, there are also matters of price and performance to consider. Make sure of the agent's capabilities before you rely on them. For example, some Macintosh agent packages can back up and restore files to and from a Mac workstation, but cannot restore those files to a file server volume with MAC name space. Such limitations are obviously not well advertised by the manufacturers, but you should try to anticipate your backup and restore needs as completely as possible and determine if the products that you are considering can fulfill them.

Perhaps the most important consideration and the area in which you will find the most variance between vendors is in the price of agent coverage for your network. Most packages will ship with DOS, Windows, and OS/2 agents, but may not allow you to back up all of your workstations of those types with the base product license. Network backup products are usually priced either on a per server basis or in accordance with the

NetWare user license installed. With Cheyenne Software's ARCserve, for example, you must purchase the same user level as that of the NetWare server that you will be installing it on, regardless of whether you want to back up workstations at all. However, this license will allow you to back up an unlimited number of servers (of the same user level or less) or workstations. Legato Software's Networker is priced on a per server basis. The base package will run on any user level of NetWare, but it will only back up that one server and up to 50 workstations. Backing up additional servers and workstations requires the purchase of additional licenses.

Both of these policies effectively overcharge a substantial portion of their user base. An installation with one 250-user server that needs only to back up the server drives should not have to pay several thousand dollars more for a backup package that supports a 250-user license, nor should an installation with many smaller servers have to pay an equal amount of money for what amounts to nothing more than a piece of paper.

Another place in which additional charges for these products may accrue is in the purchase of additional agents. Most of the major packages ship with a small subset of their available agents and sell the others as add-on packages. Be sure to check the prices of these add-ons before committing to a particular product and also whether the additional cost includes a license for a single or an unlimited number of workstations.

In general, it would be a mistake to choose a particular software package on the basis of licensing issues alone, but being aware of these additional charges in advance can avoid severe budgeting problems later. It should also be noted that, with the release of NetWare version 4.1, Novell has altered its own pricing stratification system, allowing additional user licenses to be added to an existing server license. This will force the third-party backup software developers (particularly those who charge on a user level basis) to rethink and hopefully restructure their pricing plans so that users of all levels are paying a fair price.

Reporting. Another important aspect of any backup software package is its ability to inform you of its activities. When backup jobs are going to run unattended, it is important to check on whether the jobs are running successfully each night. All of the software packages available offer logs by which all of the activities of the software and hardware can be tracked or monitored. These logs can be the most valuable diagnostic tools available for hardware and job configuration debugging. Several can optionally track all SCSI activity on the bus, aiding in the resolution of hardware compatibility problems. Many packages also offer varying levels of notification options that can be particularly useful for the offsite administrator or consultant. These options can range from a daily report that is automatically sent to a network print queue after every job to fax and e-mail notifications to pager and SNMP (Simple Network Management Protocol) support (see also chapter 34, "Network Management and SNMP"). This is another way to ensure that backup tapes are being changed regularly. Some products, like Cheyenne's ARCserve, can also generate a wide assortment of reports containing information in varying degrees of detail concerning particular jobs, targets, or tapes.

The Manager. The manager is a client program that provides the actual user interface to the backup system. With this program, backup and restore jobs can be created, scheduled, and maintained, and real time tape manipulations, such as formatting and erasing, performed. All of the major packages support a client manager running on a DOS and/or Windows workstation. Some also have a manager interface on the file server console itself. This can be very convenient if your file server closet lacks a nearby workstation, but this interface should also be as simple as possible, or better yet, optional. Since NetWare file server memory that is devoted to the creation of popup screens on the file server console is taken from the operating system's Alloc Short Term Memory pool, it often cannot be returned to the main file cache buffer pool without restarting the server.

A good workstation-based manager program should be able to control all of the software's functions. There should be an interface that allows for direct manipulation of the tape drive, a means for monitoring the current activity of the backup system as well as the jobs that are currently queued for later execution, and the ability to view, utilize, and maintain the databases. This is in addition to a logical interface for the creation of backup and restore jobs.

Evaluation of the manager software, as with everything else about a backup system, should be performed with an eye towards the requirements that your needs will place upon it. A company that simply backs up its servers each night and only performs an occasional restore will be using the manager software far less often than a firm that archives large amounts of data to a tape library for regular access.

This could be an important consideration, as some of the manager programs available require significant amounts of workstation resources to function. As mentioned earlier, large TSRs may be required for database connectivity and the diverse nature of the manager's communications with the file server may require reconfiguration of existing network access protocol drivers. Users of workstations running other operating systems than that which the manager was designed for (such as OS/2, Windows NT, and Windows 95) should also be sure that the manager is compatible with their environment.

In the following sections, we will examine some of the various backup scheduling and tape rotation schemes advocated by the various software vendors. Since the manager program is the means by which these schemes are enacted, we will also be examining some of the ways in which user interfaces are designed to provide access to these features.

Backup Scheduling and Administration

When considering how to configure and schedule backup jobs to support a specific network installation, the amount of data to be protected should be compared to the capacity of the tape device being used and the amount of time available to actually perform the backup. The more data there is and the less time, then the greater the speed and capacity the tape drive should have.

The other major factor to consider is how often specific data types are to be backed up in order to provide the protection that the network needs. Most of the network software products have one or more preprogrammed backup rotation schedules that can be implemented with minimum user intervention, or you can create your own custom schedule. The alternative that you choose should depend on your perception and understanding of the concepts involved as well as the needs of your operation. By spending some time assessing the capabilities of your system and the ways in which they are implemented by the backup software, you should be able to decide on a backup schedule that will accommodate both your data protection and administrative needs.

Full or Partial Backups? In its simplest form, a backup rotation strategy consists of a full backup of all targets, every night of the week. Many shops follow this practice, and when implemented as a measure of additional security, it may be justified. But when it is done simply because it is the easiest way, then too much money has probably been spent on hardware and media. It is not necessary to have a tape drive that can store your entire network's data on one tape. As discussed earlier in this chapter, different data types make different demands on a backup system. Keeping dozens of copies of the same executable files serves no purpose other than to waste time and money.

Incremental and Differential Backups. Incremental and differential backups are the basic means by which data types may be distinguished. They also incorporate the simplest form of tape rotation into a backup solution. The idea behind both of these concepts is to make a full backup of a particular target on one day, and then back up only the files that have changed on each succeeding day. This may be through the use of the DOS archive bit, or by using the date-last-accessed attribute of the NetWare file system. The archive attribute is a single bit allocated by the DOS file system to keep track of a file's modified state. Whenever a file is altered, its archive bit is turned on during the file save process. If the bit is already on, then it is left on. When backup software is used to create a full backup of a target, it can be set to strip off the archive bits from all of the files as they are backed up. This leaves a drive with no bits set on any of its files. As specific files are altered throughout the next day, their archive bits are turned on. When an incremental or differential backup job is performed on that drive, then only the files that have an archive bit turned on are backed up. This will usually amount to a far smaller number of files than would comprise a full backup job.

The difference between an incremental and a differential job is whether the archive bits are turned off again or left intact during these secondary backup jobs. During an incremental job, the archive bits will again be stripped away, leaving no files with archive bits on the drive. The next day, the process is performed again in the same way.

Should the entire contents of that drive be lost, it will then be necessary to perform a restore operation of the original full backup tape, followed by additional restores of each successive incremental tape up to the day in which the data was lost. This is necessary because a file may have been written to tape during the full backup on Monday, then altered and therefore backed up on Tuesday, then left alone on Wednesday, and then altered again (and backed up again) on Thursday (see fig. 17.3). The most recent version of that file is therefore on the Thursday tape, and it won't be until restores are performed from all four days' tapes that the drive is returned to its original state.

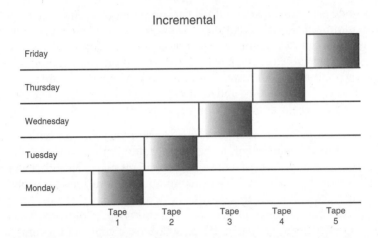

Figure 17.3

In an incremental job, each day's altered files are saved to individual tapes.

A differential backup job is the same as an incremental job, except that the archive bits are not reset during the secondary jobs. Thus, after a drive is backed up in full on Monday, Tuesday's job will only back up the files that have been changed since the full backup. However, since the archive bits have not been reset, Wednesday's job will back up all of the files that have been altered on both Tuesday and Monday, and Thursday's job will back up all of the files that have been changed on Wednesday, Tuesday, and Monday (see fig. 17.4). It is not until the next full backup that the archive bits will be reset and the process will start over again.

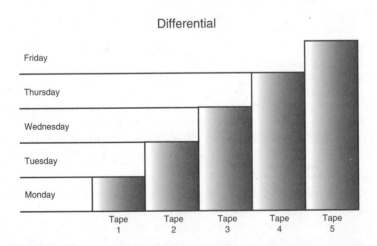

Figure 17.4

In a differential job, archive bits are not reset and all of the altered files since the last full backup are written to each tape.

Incremental backups, therefore, use the least amount of tape, because files are only backed up on the days that they have been modified. However, they are the most complex and lengthy to restore because each successive backup tape must be restored in the proper order to recreate a drive. Differentials utilize more tape because a file that is altered only once will be backed up in every successive differential job until the next full backup. When recreating a drive, however, it is only necessary to perform restores from the full backup tape and from the most recent differential tape, since all of the modified files for the week have been accumulated into that last backup job.

Since some file types (like Macintosh files) do not possess an archive bit, it may be preferable to utilize one of the NetWare file system's attributes, such as date-last-accessed or date-last-modified, if your backup software supports it. The date-last-modified attribute can be utilized in the same manner as the archive bit, but the date-last-accessed attribute may result in files being backed up that have not been altered, such as executables.

The use of these features does not mean that you must make a decision to use one or another of these methods for all of your data, however. You may decide that an incremental job is the best suited for your applications, while a differential is preferable for your data. There is no reason why you cannot split your network backups into multiple jobs addressing your different needs, as long as your backup software is capable of supporting it, your hardware is sufficient to the task, and your files are organized in such a way as to make the division convenient. This is why questions regarding the actual type of backup jobs needed are better considered before purchases have been made, software installed, and decisions made that may be difficult or impossible to change later.

Tape Rotation

Once you have determined which of these basic backup methods is most suitable to your network, the next task is to create a working process that accommodates both your administrative needs and those of your staff. Creating a tape rotation schedule is the process of setting up a system by which the greatest possible protection can be provided through the repeated use of the smallest number of tapes with the least amount of administrative overhead. In a system such as this, a predetermined number of tapes is used and reused according to a pattern of repetitive succession. This is to ensure that no tapes are being overused, and to make certain that an adequate "history" of your backup jobs is maintained at all times.

Remember that although it may be the most frequent, it is not always the case that you will need to restore a file that was backed up yesterday. Particularly when using incremental or differential backups, you may at some point have to retrieve a file from a backup made several days, a week, or several months ago. With the proper software, a proper tape rotation and a good administrative routine in place, you will be able to do so with no difficulty. If, however, when faced with this request, you must delve into that large box of unlabeled tapes in the back of the closet and try to determine which one contains the version of the file that you need, be prepared to work late that night (and probably the rest of the week).

At this point you must decide how many tapes are to be used, where they are to be stored, and who is going to be responsible for making sure that the tapes are changed regularly. The ideal network backup system is one in which the only regular mainte-nance necessary is to swap tapes in and out of the drive and to periodically clean it. When creating and scheduling backup jobs that are to run unattended, the one thing that you want to avoid is having a single job that requires more than one tape.

Some backup packages are able to track the patterns of your backup activities and make a reasonably accurate estimate as to whether or not you have enough tape available for the execution of a particular job; but prior planning is still the best way to ensure that your jobs execute properly and that an adequate backup history is maintained at all times. By examining some of the rotation schemes that are pre-configured into several of the backup software packages available, you should be able to judge whether or not they meet the needs of your network, and accumulate enough information to create a tape rotation scheme of your own, should you so desire.

Grandfather-Father-Son. The "Grandfather-Father-Son" tape rotation method is so named because three sets of media, usually corresponding to Daily, Weekly, and Monthly tapes, are used to represent the "generations" (see fig. 17.5). In this scheme, as with all tape rotation systems, a full backup of all targets is performed first. Subsequent jobs, which may be incremental or differential, are then run each day using the first media set. These are the "Son" tapes, so named because these tapes will be reused each week and will therefore remain the "youngest" in the rotation. After a full week's worth of backups, another full backup is performed. This is written to a tape from the second media set, that is, a "Weekly" or "Father" tape. The final weekly job of every month is then written to a "Monthly" or "Grandfather" tape from the third media set (see fig. 17.6).

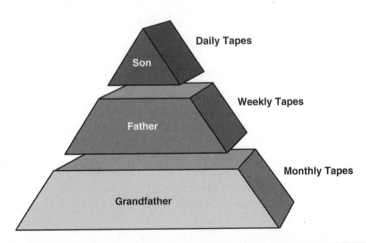

Figure 17.5

In a Grandfather-Father-Son rotation, three "generations" of tapes are used to ensure that an adequate backup history is maintained.

Sun	Mon	Tue	Wed	Thu	Fri	Sat
	D	D	D	D	W	
	D	D	D	D	W	
	D	D	D	D	W	
	D	D	D	D	M	
	D	D				

Figure 17.6

The scheduling of the daily, weekly, and monthly backup jobs in a typical Grandfather-Father-Son tape rotation.

Usually, one or more of these media sets will be designated for off-site storage. The number of tapes included in each media set will, of course, depend on how much data is actually being backed up. But working with a system in which one backup job is performed each day and the entire job fits on one tape, then 4 daily tapes, 5 weeklies, and 12 monthlies will account for a year's worth of backups. Some of the software packages that provide this rotation scheme allow a great deal of configurational leeway, and others offer none. However, most of the systems that automate the setup process for this sort of rotation will automatically name the tapes for you and tell you which tape is to be inserted for each day's job.

This, in itself, may cause problems. Some of these products assign rather cryptic names to the tapes. Usually, the name will be some combination of the date, the media set, and the type of job being run. This, in itself, is not too much of a problem, but the tape names will often change every time that a tape is reused. This means that every tape that is removed from the drive must be relabled with the new name in order to accurately maintain the rotation. For whatever reason, this relabeling is a task that often manages not to get done. One of the more brilliant ideas that deserves to be more widely implemented in the backup industry is to build an interface into the backup program that will print tape labels on one of those tiny desktop label printers.

In light of this problem, an important consideration for any rotation scheme of this type—especially when you are able to alter the parameters being used—is how the system will behave if the proper tape is not inserted into the drive on schedule. Some systems will not run the job at all, and others may mistakenly overwrite an important tape that is left in the drive. This is why it is important to consider who it is who is going to be responsible for changing the tapes. In most situations, this is a task that is best assigned to one specific person, rather than allowing it to be done on an *ad hoc* basis, by whoever happens to be nearby. Depending on the physical location of the tape drive (which should be under lock and key, if at all possible) and the skill levels of the personnel involved, modifications in tape labeling, and rotation methods may have to be made.

I heard of one site at which a large black Netframe file server was, for some unknown reason, installed in the waiting area of the office. Since Netframes are attractively sleek, black boxes with no attached monitor or keyboard, this one had been garnered into use as an endtable! Although she had no idea why she was doing it, part of the receptionist's daily routine was to water the plant sitting on the file server and change the tape in the backup drive.

While this is certainly not a recommended procedure, it serves to illustrate the fact that the person responsible for changing the tapes may not be (and need not be) fully versed in the intricacies of the tape rotation scheme, as long as a proper system is put into effect and the tapes labeled correctly. In extreme cases like this, it may indeed be preferable to create your own simple rotation rather than using a predesignated one. When you do this, you can give the tapes whatever names you choose and schedule the jobs according to your own backup and storage needs. You can also predetermine the way in which the system will react when an unattended backup job begins with the wrong tape left in the drive. If the job will continue regardless of the tape name, then a single tape could conceivably be left in the drive for months at a time by a lazy operator. The alternative, however, is for a backup job not to run because someone forgot to change the tape. The decision, as always, depends on your needs.

Tower of Hanoi. The Tower of Hanoi is another tape rotation system that (like Grandfather-Father-Son) was adapted from mainframe use. Use of this system is far less prevalent, however, because although it arguably provides more comprehensive protection utilizing fewer tapes, it is far more complex and difficult to understand. While the products that offer the Tower of Hanoi, most notably Palindrome's Network Archivist, leave very little for the administrator to do in order to set up and use it, most people prefer to have a stronger grasp of the concepts involved before they rely on it for their backups.

The Tower of Hanoi is based on an ancient mathematical puzzle in which there are three vertical posts, one of which has a number of round donut-like disks threaded over it, stacked in descending size order, the largest disk on the bottom ranging to the smallest on the top (see fig. 17.7). The object of the puzzle is to move the entire stack of disks to another of the three posts while moving only one disk at a time and never placing a larger disk atop a smaller one. In order to solve the puzzle, the smallest disk has to be moved with every other turn, while each successively larger disk is moved a proportionately fewer amount of times. The disks correspond to the media sets of the tape rotation scheme (which may or may not consist of one tape) and the moves to the backup jobs themselves.

In Palindrome's rotation scheme, therefore, the first media set will be used for every other backup job, while the second set will only be used half as often, that is, for one out of every four jobs. The third set will be used for one out of every eight jobs, the fourth for one out of every 16, and so on. The number of data sets can vary, usually from five to eight. This "binary exponential" rotation scheme will therefore retain several recent copies of any one particular file, and fewer, but regularly spaced older copies. Every additional media set that is added to the rotation also effectively doubles the period for which a full "history" of a target is maintained.

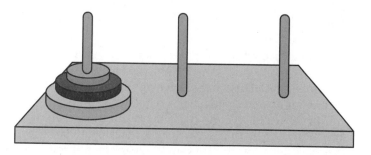

Figure 17.7

This is the Tower of Hanoi puzzle.

The basic theory by which this system works is difficult to grasp. An even more complex task would be to figure out exactly which tape contains a particular file. Fortunately, there is no real need for the backup administrator to understand these concepts. Virtually all of the major network backup products include a mode by which these schemes can be implemented with no considerations other than a dedication to following the instructions given by the software. Almost every case in which something goes wrong during the use of these systems is due to user error incurred by improper execution of the required tasks (such as labeling the tapes) or by attempting to alter the configuration of the pre-programmed scheme.

Custom Tape Rotation. Usually, the best course of action with these preconfigured tape rotation systems is to follow them to the letter or to abandon them completely. A great deal of time and effort can be spent on working out the nuances of these systems in order to alter the configuration, after which there are usually very little results to show for the effort other than an increased sense of confusion and a rotation that is ultimately less reliable.

The custom rotation scheme that I usually set up for the simplest possible administration consists of several complete weeks worth of tapes. Each week consists of a full backup and four or more incrementals or differentials. The tapes are simply labeled "Monday-1," "Tuesday-1," and so on for the first week and "Monday-2," and so on for the second week, and so forth. Each week's worth of tapes is kept in a separate box, and at the end of each week, the just-completed tapes are removed and stored off-site. You can create as many weeks' worth of tapes as you feel it necessary to preserve a history for, and optionally save the full backup tapes from each week or month for an archive.

In this way, the person assigned the task of changing media has only to put the tape named for the appropriate day of the week into the drive. A rotation of this sort can be made increasingly more complex, incorporating multiple incremental jobs on a single tape if desired, or archives of seldom used files that are never overwritten. The single most important consideration, though, when setting up your own rotation, is the skill level of the person who is actually going to be interacting with the system on a daily basis. A cryptic, complex system may be perfectly adequate, if you are the only person using it, but do you really want to get calls from the office on your day off just because someone needs a file restored?

Restores and Testing

Once a backup system has been installed and configured, it should be rigorously tested before the backups are deemed reliable. Just because no error messages are generated and the backup jobs are logged as having completed successfully doesn't necessarily mean that everything is running perfectly. I have seen many situations in which administrators have planned a server upgrade, purchased a new backup software package, installed it, and performed what appeared to be a successful backup. They then would blow away their server volumes, only to find themselves unable to restore them. The only way to positively ascertain the validity of your backups is to perform test restores from the tapes you have made. This is also the perfect time to familiarize yourself with the functionality of the software's restore capabilities. The wrong time to have to learn a new interface is when someone is looking over your shoulder waiting for a file to be restored.

When performing test restores, you should also examine the restoration capabilities of your system. A good software package should be able to restore any file or combination of files to any compatible target, with a number of options. It is generally recommended, when restoring selected files, that they be written to a scratch directory and then copied to their final resting place, but if you choose to restore files directly to their ultimate home, there are some factors to consider:

- The first item that should concern you is the method used by the software when it attempts to write to a file that already exists. Will you be prompted before files are overwritten? Will the dates of the files be considered? Most packages offer a range of options, allowing you to select whether you wish to be prompted before any overwrites are performed, or perhaps only when the file being overwritten is newer than the file on the tape. It is wise to be familiar with the settings that your software uses for its defaults, in this respect, so that you know when settings have to be changed.

- Another concern is the inclusion of directory information when files are restored. Some programs will, by default, re-create a file's entire pathname when performing a restore. Therefore, if you select a directory nested three levels deep as the file's destination, the software may append another three directory levels to your selection before actually writing the file. In a case like this, the proper thing to do would be to select the root of the drive that you wish to restore to and allow the software to follow the existing directory structure. A mistake like this is not a terrible tragedy, but when restoring an entire volume or a large portion of it, you could inadvertently make quite a mess that can quickly monopolize all available disk space on the destination drive. Again, most programs offer multiple options as to the creation of directories, and familiarity with the alternatives will allow a restore to be performed correctly the first time.

Traditional Backup Problems

The process of backing up local area networks has provided administrators with a number of unique problems not to be found when backing up stand-alone workstations.

These problems have been addressed by software developers in different ways and with varying degrees of success. Some of these situations may be of vital importance to your installation, causing them to weigh heavily on your choice of software depending on the solutions arrived at by the manufacturer, while others may not apply to your network at all.

Bindery/NDS/Registry

The first problem, one which applies to all networks, is the proper backup and restore of user accounts and trustee rights. In NetWare 3.1x, this information is found in the bindery. The bindery is composed of three hidden files that are located in the SYSTEM directory on the SYS: volume of a NetWare server. These files contain all of the information concerning user accounts and the properties assigned to those users, including trustee assignments and account restrictions. The protection of these files is not a terribly difficult problem to resolve, as the bindery is composed of files that, although hidden, are visible to the NetWare file system, and can be treated as such. During the restoration of an entire server, it is simply a matter of making sure that these files are restored to the SYS: volume first, so that trustee assignments and file owners can be properly registered when they are restored later. This is usually done automatically by the backup software.

With the introduction of NetWare 4.x, however, and the growing popularity of other network operating systems such as Windows NT, this problem has grown significantly. The NetWare Directory Services database, which is so integral a part of NetWare 4.x, is not visible to the NetWare file system. Also, the placement of the NDS as an enterprise-wide network resource, along with NetWare's capability to maintain replicas and distribute the database across various servers on the network, complicates the backup process and can make it necessary to restore specific parts of the NDS instead of always treating it as a whole. While virtually all of the major network backup products can successfully back up and restore the NDS database, several of them have not yet fully integrated themselves into the NetWare 4.x environment.

Most of the products are not yet fully NDS-compliant, requiring that a user log in to the network under bindery emulation to install and run the software. Most of the products also create users that allow the backup server access to remote targets, which are still being created as bindery accounts instead of fully qualified NDS objects. Various degrees of functionality are also available as far as the performance of partial restorations of the NDS database is concerned. Most of these perceived shortcomings are largely due to the continuing development of these NOSs themselves. Significant changes have been made to the NDS and to the tools used to maintain it in each successive revision of the NetWare 4.x operating system.

Software developers are inevitably forced to play "catch up" in situations such as this, when the environments that they are developing products for are changing as quickly as everything else does in this industry. The usual strategy for these developers is to provide a "Band-Aid" solution as quickly as possible and then integrate a fuller functionality into their next major revision. When exploring the capabilities of these backup products, I recommend that the software companies be contacted directly to ascertain the current condition of their software development cycle concerning these capabilities. When dealing with technical issues such as these, I also have found it advantageous to bypass the sales operations at these companies and talk instead to technical support personnel, who often have a better grasp of the software's current status.

Live Databases

Another extremely important problem to many administrators is the protection of database files while they are in use. Many organizations rely very heavily on their databases and wish to back them up while they are being accessed by users. This may be because they are in use 24 hours a day, or it may be that they want the added protection of several daily backups of these critical files. As a general rule, a file cannot be backed up when it is locked in an open state by user access. This does not apply to files like executables, which are accessed only for short periods while they are read into memory. If a file such as this is found to be in use during a backup operation, all software packages will repeatedly attempt to access the file, resulting in a successful backup in most cases. Many programs can also be configured to retry open files a specified number of times, and at specified intervals.

Database files, however, are usually far too large for any one machine to hold in memory. In addition there may be dozens, or even hundreds of users accessing and writing changes to these files at the same time. There is no way, under normal conditions, to back up a file that is perpetually opened to this kind of access. Many database systems, however, do have features integrated within them that allow a developer of backup software to create an agent that will, when it receives a request for access from the backup server, divert all of the changes destined for the database file to what is called a "delta" file. This is a temporary storage area for the modifications sent to the database manager, which is maintained while the agent closes the database file so that it can be backed up. When the file has been successfully copied, then the changes from the delta file are applied to the live database, and access continues as before.

Several backup software manufacturers, including Novell, have such database agents available, but they are always individually written for specific database systems, and are often specific revisions of such systems. These agents are usually sold as add-on products to the basic backup software package, and I strongly recommend that potential users of these products speak to the manufacturers of both the backup and database software packages. Attempt to ascertain whether or not the relationship between the companies is a strong one that will survive upgrades of both products in the future. Use of these products with live databases that contain mission-critical data, such as order entry and so on, should not be considered until extensive testing on off-line databases has been conducted. Remember, the entire object of this exercise is to protect your data. Be sure not to risk it unnecessarily on an untried product, especially when the result of a compatibility problem is not only a failed backup job, but may involve corruption of the original data as well.

Workstation OSs

In recent years, there has been a much greater tendency to run workstations with different operating systems on the same network. This may be done to accommodate a particular business application or the special needs of users but the quest for universal access to basic network services such as e-mail, printing, and Internet access has led to interoperability problems that were largely unheard of not long ago. For this reason, make sure that the backup products you purchase are capable of accessing all of the platforms that are in use on your network, as well as those that you are considering for the future. The move to 32-bit desktop operating systems that is currently being engineered by the industry has resulted in a lot of administrators doing testing on new OSs, such as OS/2, Windows NT, and Windows 95. It is a good idea to examine a software developer's plans for support of these platforms before a purchase is made.

This is particularly true for OSs that use proprietary file systems. When testing, make sure that a Mac file backed up from a Mac workstation or server volume can really be restored and used on a Mac. Very often, there are configuration settings to be adjusted for files like this, and failure to do so may cause the files to be incorrectly backed up as DOS files.

Security

Another highly significant issue with network backup systems is security. By definition, a backup system must be able to access all files on the network in order to protect them. This opens a number of avenues for security gaps that must be closed by the administrator. Very often, the backup software provides tools that help to do this, but it is up to the administrator to anticipate their need to make proper use of them. At the most fundamental level, users can be warned of the potential for danger, and instructed to use application-level password protection on their most sensitive files. But, action must also be taken by the administrator, as the most well-meaning users can become lax in their protective measures over time.

Fortunately, most workstation agents do not require that the workstation be logged in to the network in order to back them up. They function instead using the IPX connection that is established as soon as the network drivers are loaded. There is, therefore, no direct security hole at the site of the workstation itself. However, if your nightly backup job can access the workstation's files, then someone else's backup job can also. This problem can be remedied by a feature included in most major software packages, that is, the ability to password-protect the workstation agent. The user of the workstation specifies a password when loading the agent that must be duplicated by the administrator when creating the backup job. Otherwise, access to the workstation will not be granted.

Restrictions can also be set at several levels regarding access to the backup software's manager interface. This can be done by installing the client portion of the software to the local drive of a workstation that is kept in a secure environment, or by granting only specific network users the rights to access the software and create backup or restore jobs. Some software packages can also distinguish between backup users with full access to the system and those who are allowed to create and modify their own jobs, but cannot affect the status or properties of other jobs that have already been defined. In this way, users can be given the power to perform their own restores without the danger of other aspects of the system being affected.

Finally, the ultimate security hole is the backup tapes themselves. They should be able to be password-protected as well, and should be kept under lock and key or off-site, in any case. It may even be desirable to schedule backups of more sensitive material, such as accounting or personnel files, as separate jobs in order to allow other users access to their own files without endangering the security of the rest of the company's data.

Other, more complex, scenarios can also be developed in cases, for example, when it is desired that a person be given the ability to create a full backup job without giving him access to full supervisory privileges. In most cases, backup software can be configured to utilize a specified account and password (other than the one currently being used) when scheduling access to a server for backup. By creating a network user account on the target server with time and station restrictions that limit its access only to the midnight hours from a node address equivalent to that of the backup server, this account name and password can be supplied to a user without giving that user full supervisor access.

In many office environments, ignorance can be the best security tool available. By keeping backup software and equipment out of sight, and by keeping the details of your backup routines close to the vest, smart users will be less tempted to experiment on their own and not-so-smart users will remain blissfully ignorant of the payroll data coursing through the wires all around them.

Other Backup Options

We have, thus far, examined the components of a basic local area network backup system, as well as some of the options available. For the average network installation, this type of system should be able to provide sufficient protection. However, today's network requirements are growing at a phenomenal rate. New data types such as high-resolution graphics, sound, and video require ever-increasing amounts of bandwidth and storage capacity, and backup systems are growing in order to provide the protection that they need.

Autochangers

Most backup software developers provide support for tape autochangers usually as an add-on module to their products. An *autochanger* is a device that consists of one or more tape drives and a robotic mechanism that can swap tapes in and out of the drive(s). Changers can range from small models, containing one drive and slots for four tapes, to huge refrigerator-sized devices holding four tape drives or more, and upwards of 100 tapes. Some high-end models also have bar-code readers to facilitate the location and labeling of tapes. There exists another sort of device, called a stacker, which is no longer in general use. A *stacker* is capable of removing a tape from its tape drive and inserting the next one in a series, thus allowing a job to span more than one tape without operator intervention. An autochanger, however, can address any tape in the magazine at any time, allowing multiple jobs to be run on the same device.

A changer software module accomplishes this by causing each of the tapes in the magazine to be loaded into a tape drive for identification. This inventory is then maintained in memory, allowing a job to be configured to address any tape in any order. Depending on the capacity of the changer, this inventory process can take from several minutes to several hours, making it rather inconvenient to change tapes in the device frequently. It is important to know that a changer is composed of two or more SCSI devices that interact. Some changers will actually require two separate SCSI IDs to be set, while others utilize *logical unit numbers* (*LUN*), which is a means of multiplexing SCSI signals using only one ID.

In many cases, the tape drives within the changer are no different from the stand-alone drives made by that manufacturer. This allows for easy swapping of drives should replacement be required, but can also result in some peculiar design aspects to the device. Despite their high prices, some autochangers are remarkably ill-designed devices. The best and most reliable models are the ones that have been designed as an integrated unit. Others seem to be composed of disparate components that are slapped together as the need arises. I have even seen changers in which the tape is made to be ejected from the drive not through a software command sent to the tape drive itself, but through a command sent to the changer that sets a small robotic finger into motion which actually presses the tape eject button on the front of the drive. This sort of Rube Goldberg contraption is to be avoided. Never purchase an autochanger without actually seeing it run, and look for those in which the design is logically thought out, allowing the smallest possible amount of movement to change tapes.

These devices can vastly increase the capacity and convenience of a backup system, but considerable thought should be given to support and service of the unit by the dealer or manufacturer, as the hardware can be notoriously cranky. In fact, it is good to consider the subject of product replacement before any purchases of tape hardware are made.

If you make your purchases from a reputable source, you should be able to arrange a guarantee that you will never be without a drive for more than a day. Some manufacturers are extremely responsive in this respect, sending out replacement devices by overnight mail at the first hint of trouble, and others are less so, perhaps making a purchase through a VAR preferable. You should also check on whether the devices you purchase have firmwares that are upgradeable through software. You should no longer have to send a drive out for a firmware upgrade.

Hierarchical Storage Management

As data storage needs increased over time, many administrators realized that many of the files populating their network hard drives were only accessed occasionally, if at all. As a result, it was found to be economically more practical to archive the lesser used data to tape or another less expensive medium, rather than purchase additional hard drives. This process, while economical from a hardware standpoint, causes a significant increase in administrative costs. Companies with large amounts of archived data began to have trouble tracking the exact location of files as they were requested, resulting in delays to users and increased demands on MIS staff.

To address this need, a new class of data storage products has been created that is similar to, but not a replacement for, backup systems. Using storage devices with far lower per megabyte costs than hard disk drives, such as tape autochangers and optical jukeboxes, storage management systems now exist which can be configured to automatically track the ways in which files are accessed and alter their storage location accordingly. For example, a typical three-tier arrangement might be that when a file is not accessed for three months, it is moved from a hard drive to an optical disk. In its place on the hard drive, a tiny "key" file is left, which functions as a pointer to the file's actual location. The key also allows users to see the file in a directory listing as though it had never been removed from the hard drive.

If the file is still not accessed for three more months, then it is migrated to a tape in an autochanger and the key file updated. The next time that the file is requested by a user, the system automatically loads the proper optical disk or tape into the drive, accesses the file, and delivers it to the user in the normal manner. The only indication to the end user that a file migration has occurred is the delay caused by accessing the slower, less-expensive media.

Systems such as these are not designed to replace backup systems, and in fact complicate the task of performing a backup, but they do utilize much of the same hardware, and most, since they are made by backup software developers, work very well in conjunction with their manufacturer's backup products. They are also an indication of the direction in which the development of new backup systems is headed. Most of these storage management systems are designed to handle truly vast amounts of data, and in order to do so, they allow for hardware to be distributed throughout the network, thus helping to avoid system resource depletion and LAN traffic bottlenecks at any one particular point on the network. This is also the direction in which backup systems are headed, and in the future, I think that we will begin to see more completely integrated data storage, backup, and management systems that will allow the full measure of usefulness to be extracted from the hardware on the network.

Troubleshooting

Because backup systems interact with virtually every component of a network, they can be notoriously complicated to troubleshoot. Breakdowns or bottlenecks can occur at any of several key points between the targets and the tape, causing problems ranging from reduced throughput to corrupted data to complete dysfunction. When trying to resolve situations such as these, the first step is to identify the actual location of the problem. In most cases, backup problems can be traced either to the tape drive, the SCSI subsystem, the backup server, or the network itself. The best practice is usually to work your way back from the tape to the source of the data.

The most common cause of malfunctions when writing to tape is media errors and SCSI hardware configuration problems. These may be manifested as error messages generated by the backup software indicating write errors or controller problems, or as reduced throughput during backup jobs that is caused by the need for the drive to rewrite blocks. Most tape drives have some error-correcting capabilities, usually a means by which blocks are read after they are written, compared to the source, and then rewritten if incorrect. These drives will often report statistics concerning the frequency of these corrections to the backup software. This information may show up in the software logs as

Recovered Read or Write Errors. While a small number of such errors may be considered normal, a steadily increasing or very large number (for example, over 100) may be cause for alarm.

By asking a few simple questions, it can usually be determined whether media or hardware error is the cause of the problem, and which of the two is the most likely candidate.

Media Problem or Hardware Problem?

Has the tape drive ever functioned properly, or have there been problems from the outset?

If a tape drive has been functioning normally for some time and suddenly begins exhibiting problems, then media error becomes the most likely cause of the difficulty, and those steps should be performed first. If the tape drive is newly installed, or has been functioning properly in another environment and is now malfunctioning, check for hardware errors first.

Are there other devices on the same SCSI bus that are functioning properly?

If the answer to this question is yes, then the problem is likely to be situated in the device itself or in the connection of the device to the SCSI bus.

Media Error Troubleshooting Checklist. The term "media error" does not always mean that the problem lies within the tape cartridge itself. Rather, it indicates that a problem has been encountered during the process of reading or writing to the tape. The following steps should be taken when a media error is suspected. They will eliminate any transient causes as the source of the problem; if the problem persists, then the cause very likely resides in the tape drive or some other hardware component.

- Clean the tape drive heads. Most tape drive manufacturers recommend that heads be cleaned after every 20–25 hours of use. If it has been a long time since their last cleaning, or if the drive is located in a dusty environment, run the cleaning cartridge two or three times.

   Just because a drive is new doesn't mean that the heads can't be dirty. Factory testing and shipping may result in it being necessary to clean the heads of a brand-new drive.

- Make sure that the media being used is certified by the drive manufacturer.

   Use Data grade tapes only. Audio or Video grade tapes may damage the tape drive heads.

   Do not attempt to use tapes of a greater capacity than those recommended by the manufacturer.

- Try running the same job with a different tape, preferably a new one. It is not unheard of for more than one tape in a box or in a shipment to be defective. Environmental conditions during storage or shipping can result in an entire box of defective tapes. Take this into account when testing.

Make sure that the tapes being used have not been stored in conditions of excessive heat, dust, sunlight, or magnetism. Always store tapes in their protective boxes.

Hardware Error Troubleshooting Checklist. This section lists the items that should be checked first when a problem in the backup system concerning the SCSI or tape hardware is suspected.

■ Make sure that all devices on the SCSI bus have unique SCSI IDs.

Do not forget to take the SCSI host adapter itself into account, which is nearly always assigned SCSI ID 7 by default.

Many SCSI host adapters expect to find hard drives at SCSI IDs 0 and 1. Other types of devices may not function properly when assigned to these IDs.

If using a tape autochanger, remember that these consist of multiple devices within one box. Some changers utilize two (or more) SCSI IDs and others utilize LUNs, which allow several devices to utilize one SCSI ID.

SCSI IDs for different devices may be set in one of several ways. Some have a push-button selector, others use jumpers or DIP switches, and others are permanently set by the manufacturer.

■ Check that the SCSI bus is properly terminated.

A properly configured SCSI installation must have terminators at both ends of the bus. Most host adapters are terminated by default, so be sure that the last device in the chain is also terminated.

If there are both internal and external devices attached to one host adapter, it will be necessary to disable the termination on the adapter card if it is physically located in the middle of the bus.

Some SCSI devices are internally terminated (which may be disabled through a jumper or a DIP switch), while others utilize an external plug containing the terminating resistors.

■ Check the cables connecting the SCSI bus.

Use the best quality SCSI cables that you can find. It would be absurd to let the performance of devices costing thousands of dollars suffer for want of a $50 cable.

Make sure that all SCSI connections are tightly joined.

Examine all connectors for bent pins, foreign objects, or excessive amounts of dust.

If there is a cable available that is known to be functioning properly, then try swapping it with the one on the offending device.

■ Make sure that the SCSI host adapter card is firmly seated in the slot.

If there are problems with other devices on the SCSI bus as well, try moving the host adapter to another slot, if possible.

■ Check the configuration of the SCSI host adapter to see if the parameters set agree with those recommended by the backup software manufacturer.

Different host adapters set these parameters in different ways. Some utilize jumpers or DIP switches, while others use a software based configuration utility.

Not all host adapters may be capable of adjusting all of the recommended parameters. Those that can, however, should be set as recommended for optimum performance.

If a duplexed SCSI subsystem is being used, then both SCSI cards should be configured identically.

Make sure that the SCSI card is set to use Edge Triggering and not Level Triggering. Level Triggering involves the use of shared interrupts, which can cause problems in some systems.

If the manufacturer of your backup software does not recommend specific SCSI parameter settings, the following defaults may be used in the event of problems:

SCSI DISCONNECTION should be ENABLED.
SYNCHRONOUS NEGOTIATION should be DISABLED.
PARITY should be ENABLED.
SCSI TRANSFER RATE should be set for 5M/sec.

■ Check the offending device for any diagnostic readout capabilities.

Many tape drives have a means of indicating whether or not they are experiencing a problem. This may be a self-diagnostic mode or a particular display of blinking and/or colored lights. Consult the device documentation for more information.

■ Power cycle the offending device or the entire server.

Individual SCSI devices or even host adapters may, as the result of an error, "hang" or lock up. This will most often be manifested by an unending BUSY status. Usually the only way to proceed is to turn the device off and on again to force the device to reset itself.

External tape drives can usually be powered off and on without downing the entire server, but all drivers addressing the device should be unloaded first. This includes those supplied with your backup software as well as any prerequisite host adapter board or ASPI drivers.

Internal tape drives or an entire SCSI bus that is locked will require a power cycle of the entire server. This includes turning the power switch off, and not just a cold or warm boot.

Wait 30 seconds after powering any device off before powering it on again.

■ Check whether or not the hardware in use has been certified for use with your backup software.

Many software manufacturers certify host adapter cards as well as tape devices. Be sure to check both.

Be sure to check the firmware revision of the tape drive for certification, if your software manufacturer includes this information.

If a tape drive or host adapter is not certified for use with your software, this does not necessarily mean that it absolutely will not work, but if all other avenues have failed to resolve the problem, you may be faced with a fundamental incompatibility that cannot be remedied by anything less than a software or firmware revision.

File Server Problems

If backup malfunctions continue to occur after the media, the tape drive, and the SCSI bus hardware have been eliminated as possible causes, then it is time to begin to look at the file server where the backup software has been installed. Problems occurring here may manifest themselves as reduced backup throughput, a slowdown or stoppage in logins, file transfers, and general network performance, or server lockups and abends.

Backup Server Troubleshooting Checklist.

- Check to see that you have sufficient memory in your file server, taking the following factors into account.

  Backup software may utilize different amounts of memory while in different states of operation. Make sure that the server has adequate memory to support all of the NLMs and drivers that are loaded during a typical backup operation.

  Additional NLMs or drivers may be spawned (or autoloaded) at various points during the loading of the software or the processing of a backup job.

  The use of multiple tape devices to perform simultaneous backup operations may cause the loading of multiple copies of certain NLMs. Be sure to account for this in your memory calculations.

- Check the processor utilization of the file server for high levels that may interfere with other processes.

  Be sure to check the processor utilization levels both when the software is loaded, but idle, and when backup jobs are actually running.

  Many backup software packages will automatically run various background processes, even when backup and restore jobs are not running. These may include scheduling timers, database maintenance operations, and client tracking modules. These processes may often be optionally configured to occur at specified times. Scheduling these activities for non-peak usage hours may resolve the problem.

- Check for sufficient disk space on the volume where the backup software is installed.

  Backup software, particularly in its database operations, may require significant amounts of disk space to function properly, both when backup jobs are running and during background operations. Ensuring that sufficient disk space is available (and purging deleted files, in the case of a NetWare volume) can prevent slow-downs in backup job processing and in overall network performance.

■ Check the dates and revisions of all modules and drivers involved in the operation of the backup software and the tape drive.

Many backup software packages will require specific versions of particular modules depending on the hardware or network operating system version being used. Be sure to check all release notes and README files included with the software for the most recent driver information.

Remember that backup software may be highly dependent on drivers or NLMs that are manufactured by other parties. Check the revisions of ASPI and SCSI adapter drivers; it is a good idea to utilize the most current versions available from the hardware manufacturer, unless specifically told otherwise.

All third-party NLMs are reliant on the function calls and public symbols that are part of the network operating system's API. Check to see if the software manufacturer recommends the use of specific versions of CLIB.NLM or other modules crucial to the operation of the software.

■ Isolate the point where the error occurs.

If the problem is occasional, such as a network slowdown only at certain times, or immediate, such as an abend, try to ascertain exactly what circumstances led up to the error. Very often an exact sequence of events can lead to the cause of the problem.

Backup software will often spawn additional NLMs during the automatic processing of backup or restore jobs. The additional drain on system resources caused by this process may be the source of the difficulty.

In the case of a catastrophic error or abend, be sure to fully document any errors generated at the file server console. This may help to determine exactly what module caused the problem, and may also contain information that will be needed when requesting technical support from the manufacturer.

In cases of persistent errors or abends that cannot be resolved by any other means, it may be necessary to generate a core dump of the file server's memory or a debug listing of all communications occurring on the server's SCSI bus (usually a function of the backup software) for submission to the network operating system or backup software manufacturer's technical support department.

Network Communication Problems

As discussed earlier, it is important to be aware that performing a backup of a remote target (that is, a computer other than a server on which the backup software is installed) results in a far greater amount of traffic over the network medium than virtually any other process. It is quite possible for a workstation to function well under normal conditions, but to exhibit problems when being backed up, due to excessive traffic levels.

Problems of this type will usually manifest themselves as reduced throughput or failure to contact a target server or workstation for backup. It is usually fairly easy to isolate this as the cause of the difficulty, because operations internal to the backup server will proceed normally, and only those involving remote systems will cause problems.

Network Communications Troubleshooting Checklist.

■ Be sure that the agents on the remote systems are properly installed and operational.

While some of the basic agents for remote operating systems, such as DOS, consist of a single executable, others may require several files to operate properly. Be sure that all required elements for the proper operation of an agent are properly installed on the target system.

Some agents may not function in environments other than those for which they were specifically created. For example, a DOS agent may not function when Windows is running on the workstation, or if loaded in a DOS shell such as those provided by Windows or OS/2.

As farfetched as it may seem, a significant percentage of the workstation end user base seems to be unaware that a computer cannot be backed up when it is turned off. Be sure that workstations are being left in the proper state prior to the commencement of backup jobs.

■ Check the revisions of the network drivers running on both the target systems and the backup server.

Many target agents are designed to function only with NetWare's ODI drivers. Workstations running older, monolithic drivers such as IPX.COM may have to be upgraded. Check also if the agents are designed to run on workstations utilizing the NetWare VLM requesters or not.

File server LAN drivers are frequently neglected after installation. It may be necessary to acquire and install the latest drivers from the manufacturer of the server's network interface card. Whenever possible, the same NICs should be used in all servers on a network.

■ Check the revisions of all NLMs involved in network communications on all servers.

Modules such as TSAs, SMDR.NLM, TLI.NLM, and STREAMS.NLM are crucial elements in the communications between file servers on a network. It is advisable to keep the versions of these modules current, and to utilize the same versions on all servers throughout the network, whenever possible.

■ Check for problems with excess traffic and collisions or physical layer problems.

As dismal as the prospect may seem, problems occurring during backups may indicate a problem in the physical layer, or in the traffic patterns of your network's usage. It may be necessary to examine the network cabling itself for faults, or begin an analysis of traffic patterns through protocol analysis. Administrators that are unfamiliar with the maintenance of the physical layer or the proper use of analysis tools such as Lanalyzer may wish to obtain outside help for problems of this type.

Summary

As we have seen, backup systems are not "sexy," but they are necessary. The time spent in assembling and configuring a stable, reliable system can allow the LAN administrator the degree of freedom to experiment with new products in safety and without fear of damaging the network or interrupting users. This chapter has covered the software issues and theoretical background needed to develop a reliable network backup strategy. Clearly, an equally significant part of the system is the hardware involved. SCSI systems are covered at length in chapter 5, "The Server Platform." Both of these chapters should be studied before any firm decisions regarding software are made.

Chapter 18

Backup Technology: Uninterruptible Power Supplies

Overview

If LANs and PCs are the unsung heroes of modern business, then the *uninterruptible power supply (UPS)* is the "forgotten child" of most LANs—at least until there is a power problem! Unlike most other components of a LAN, the majority of UPSs spend 99% of their time *waiting* to do their job. Even tape backup units get at least some attention on a daily basis. When was the last time you did anything with your UPS?

UPSs used to be so undervalued that in the early days of LANs, many servers were installed without a UPS. It normally did not take very long before the value and importance of a good UPS system became very—sometimes painfully—clear. This chapter discusses why UPSs are essential to any LAN, and explains how to live with them.

Assessing the Need for a UPS System

All computers are electrical devices, which means that they need electrical power to operate. Fortunately there is plenty of electrical power available—AC outlets are everywhere—so this seems not to present a serious problem. While all electrical outlets look the same, however, the electrical power coming out of them is not the same, and a computer's power needs are different from most other electrical items' power needs. Computers are much more complicated than light bulbs, appliances, and even audio/visual equipment; therefore, the kind of electrical power that would be sufficient for those devices might not be appropriate for computers. While a brief power outage might cause only a barely perceptible flicker of a light bulb or radio, it could cause a catastrophic change *to the data* in a computer that's reindexing a database.

AC Power Is Not Always Constant

Unfortunately, the "AC" in "AC power" stands for "Alternating Current" and not for "Always Constant." What comes out of a typical AC outlet is supposed to be a *nominal 110 volts*. "Nominal" means "like" or "near" and this happens most of the time, which can cause problems for a computer that needs to be running all of the time. In a perfect world, every AC outlet would provide a constant 110 volts of AC power—what actually happens is quite different. A study by IBM has shown that a typical computer is subject to more than 120 power problems per month. Bell Laboratories has determined that the frequency of disturbances is as follows:

Disturbance Type	Frequency
Sags	87%
Spikes	7.4%
Blackouts	4.7%
Surges	0.7%

Deltec, another UPS vendor, states in its literature, "A recent power study showed that in a one-year period, the average data center incurred 36 spikes, 264 sags, 128 surges, and 15 blackouts."

The following sections explain what these unwanted electrical events are, what causes them, and what happens to a computer when they occur.

Sags. A *sag* or *brownout* is a temporary drop in the voltage reaching a computer. Sags are caused by a big motor (like an elevator, compressor, or large shop tool) starting up, or by the electrical company reducing the voltage supplied to particular locations during periods of high demand.

I had one LAN running happily in an office environment until it began having electrical problems every day from roughly 6:30 AM to 7:00 AM. It turned out that the space next door to the office had been vacated, and a work crew was starting a compressor every morning while refurbishing the space. All the workers had to do to solve our office's problem was to plug their compressor into a different circuit.

Another time, I moved a LAN into a new office and immediately noticed electrical problems each morning and afternoon. It turned out that the wiring for the LAN room was on the same circuit as the elevators, and when all the elevators were heavily used (mornings and afternoons) the power dropped on that circuit. Again, switching circuits solved the problem easily.

In both situations, the UPS alarm systems were the main indicator that something was wrong with the electrical system. At the same time, however, the incidence of system hangs, frozen keyboards, and other problems increased significantly. Without UPS alarms telling us about the electrical problems, who knows how long I might have spent checking out configurations, memory chips, keyboards, and the like before I figured out that it was a sag problem?

Spikes. A *spike* is an instantaneous high-voltage situation. These conditions typically occur when lightning strikes nearby or some kind of accident occurs at a power pole or power station. A car crashing into a power pole can cause headaches for others besides the driver!

One of the LANs I took care of was in the Atlanta area, an area of the country subject to frequent lightning storms. The UPSs on the file servers were protecting that equipment, but we were losing motherboards and monitors on the workstations at a horrific rate. We finally solved the problem by putting a UPS on each workstation. The $150 cost per workstation was more than offset by reduced maintenance costs and worker downtime.

Blackouts. A *blackout* is a total loss of power. It can last anywhere from a split second to many days. A blackout can be caused by nature (fire, earthquake, lightning, and so on), man (backhoe, auto accident involving power pole, and so on), or equipment failure (blown circuit breaker, power station failure, power grid overload, and so on).

Most PCs can handle a voltage loss of 1/20th of a second (50 milliseconds), but anything longer than that and they usually reboot themselves—no matter what they were doing at the time. Anyone who has watched the lights go out and then heard anguished cries of "My database!" will understand how heart-wrenching a blackout can be. Anyone who has been responsible for rebuilding a corporate database after the file server has irretrievably scrambled the data will *instantly* be a convert to the religion of reliable tape backups.

Surges. A *surge* or *overvoltage* is a high voltage situation that lasts for more than 1/120th of a second. These kinds of situations are typically caused when a large power-consuming device is turned off, spreading the excess voltage momentarily to other devices attached to the circuit. While not as instantly damaging as a spike, a surge eventually takes as much a toll on the equipment.

Noise. The "alternating" in "alternating current" means that the voltage alternates from one level to another. It does this in a smooth, sweeping motion called a sine wave. Computer equipment expects this nice, smooth transition and anything that disrupts the sine wave of the power can disrupt the operations of the computer. There are two primary kinds of *noise* that can alter the smooth sine wave, *electromagnetic interference* (*EMI*) and *radio frequency interference* (*RFI*). Since power cables travel long distances, they act like antennas and can pick up noise from a variety of sources: fluorescent lighting fixtures, generators, lightning, radio transmitters, and the like.

The results of noise on the line are varied and unpredictable, since the shape of the sine wave gets changed in unpredictable ways. Noise is comparable to having mini-spikes and mini-brownouts occurring at the same time.

Solutions for AC Power Problems

By now it should be apparent that depending solely upon consistent power from your common AC outlet is foolhardy. Even if you have a *dedicated circuit* (one with no other equipment on it), a car might crash into a pole outside your building and ruin everything for you. Wouldn't it be nice if you could avoid all these problems and have dependable AC power all the time—or at least enough time to shut down the system properly when there is a power problem, to avoid the catastrophic damage of a system crash? If you take the proper safety precautions, it's more possible than you think.

Inspect, Test, and Document

The first thing to do is to make sure you have proper wiring in your building. Then you need to determine how "clean" your power is. Perfectly clean power would be a constant 110 volts without ANY fluctuations. Since this is impossible in the real world, the question you need to answer is, "Just how 'dirty' is my power?" By doing this—and documenting everything you find out—you will have a known baseline from which to diagnose future problems.

Proper AC Wiring. Much goes into proper AC wiring, just as much goes into a good cable plant. Using the wrong type of wire and connectors or wiring up outlets improperly are just a couple of the things that can go wrong and cause power problems. (There are only three wires to a typical 120-volt AC circuit, but that means there are nine ways to wire it up, eight of which are wrong!) Since your goal is to maintain as trouble-free a LAN as possible, it makes sense to ensure that the site is wired properly *before* any computers are plugged in.

In a pinch you can look at the wiring yourself and use a pocket tester (obtained from a local hardware store) to test your circuits. The wiring is so important and fundamental to the operations of everything on the LAN, however, that I recommend hiring an electrical contractor to inspect and test your circuits. While doing this, they can also hook up an analyzer to tell you about the power you are getting from the power company.

Load Capacity. Just because a room has 14 outlets in it doesn't mean that you can plug in 28 power strips and start running 50 computers and 10 laser printers! You need to know which outlets are on which circuits, and what the rated load for each circuit is. Clearly documenting these on a floor plan is about the only way to keep track. I've found that using highlighters to color-code different circuits by load capacity and location works well.

For example, a typical circuit is rated for 20 amps. This means that there is a 20-amp circuit breaker for all the outlets on this wiring, and if you try to run more than 20 amps of load on it, the circuit breaker pops, turning everything off instantly. To calculate the number of computers you can plug into a 20-amp circuit, simply determine the amp rating for each piece of equipment and then add these values together. A computer with a local hard drive and monitor typically draws anywhere from 1.5 to 4 amps, so you could run 5–13 of these computers on a 20-amp circuit before it would pop. Don't forget, though, to allow for any lights, radios, heaters, fans, or other electrical devices on the circuit. Also, don't assume that two outlets in the same cubical or office are on the same circuit—this is where good documentation really pays off.

How Clean Is Your Power? Having proper wiring is half the battle. The other half depends on the quality of power your power company is providing you. Does it run at a constant voltage, or does it occasionally sag or surge? Does an analyzer detect any spikes in the circuit? How about blackouts? No power source is perfect, so don't be surprised if yours turns up some of these anomalies.

There are line voltage analyzers that can be attached to your incoming power circuits. They will report on the quality of the power being provided to you by your power company. You can rent these units but without proper training, they can be quite perplexing so I prefer to hire an electrician to provide a final report. Remember, the report will only tell you what happened while the unit was attached, so try to leave it attached for at least one week in order to get as complete a picture as possible.

Dedicated Circuits

A dedicated circuit, as mentioned earlier, simply means that the circuit is dedicated to a particular outlet. Therefore nothing else exists on the circuit to cause a problem with whatever is plugged into the dedicated circuit's outlet. I prefer to have several dedicated circuits available for my LAN room equipment because I like to prevent problems rather than fix them.

Use of a UPS System

Even after you have made sure that all your wiring is proper, and that the power company is providing you pretty clean power, you know that you are still going to be hit by sags, spikes, blackouts, and surges. The simplest way to prevent these electrical mishaps from disrupting your business and destroying your equipment is to install an uninterruptible power supply (UPS). This device is designed to eliminate sags, spikes, and surges while providing a temporary alternate source of power during a blackout. The following sections discuss several different ways that UPSs can be used.

Different UPS Topologies. A UPS does two different jobs: provides clean power (eliminates voltage sags, surges, and noise) whenever there is power from the outlet, and provides clean power for a while when the power goes off. There are a variety of topologies that aim for the same results—we will discuss each one so that you can determine which UPS system is best for you.

UPS versus SPS Terminology. There are some arguments about the differences between UPS systems and *SPS* systems; some people insist that only online systems should be called UPSs, while standby systems should be called SPSs (standby power supply). There are arguments made on both sides that make sense. The central issue is discovering what type of system will reliably and cost-effectively protect your equipment. The decision to buy a UPS system should be based on effectiveness and cost, not on what the system is called.

Online Topology. An *online UPS* runs everything off of a battery/inverter circuit at all times. A built-in battery charger keeps the batteries constantly charged. If the batteries ever fail, the equipment is switched over to a filtered AC circuit.

One advantage of an online system is that it never has to switch when there is a power outage. Since everything is already running off of the battery/inverter circuit, all the UPS has to do is to sound an alarm indicating an error on the input power side.

A disadvantage of an online system is that since everything is always running off of batteries, the built-in charger must be capable of providing as much charge to the batteries as the equipment is draining off—otherwise, the batteries run down quickly. The cost of keeping the batteries charged makes an online system more expensive than other topologies. This ongoing cost should be kept in mind when purchasing a unit.

Standby Topology. A *standby UPS* runs everything off of a filtered AC circuit until it detects a power outage. Then it switches over to a battery/inverter circuit.

Since a standby system only has to keep the batteries "topped off" for an emergency, it can get by with a much smaller battery charger. This also means that a standby system generates a lot less heat, since it is doing less charging.

One of the interesting arguments people use when evaluating online versus standby systems is that since there are virtually no standby systems for large minicomputers and mainframes, online systems must be better. The truth of the matter is that at the higher power levels required for these larger computers—typically 2000VA and above—the switches needed are too difficult and expensive to build, so standby systems are not feasible.

Another common concern about standby systems is that the time to transfer from AC to battery power might be too long. Current standby systems typically detect and switch over to battery power within 2–4ms, well under the 8.3ms standard for Computer Voltage Tolerance Envelope set by the Computer Business Equipment Manufacturers Association. Actual testing of IBM, Compaq, and other popular computers has shown that they continue to operate properly through transfer times of over 100ms.

Online without Bypass Topology. Take an online UPS and remove the filtered AC circuit side, and you get an *online without bypass UPS*. The problem with this type of UPS is that if the battery charger, batteries, or inverter ever fail, there is no provision for switching over to normal power, so the whole system fails.

Standby Online Hybrid Topology. A *standard online hybrid UPS* takes the input AC, rectifies it to DC, runs it through a combiner, and then inverts it back to AC for normal operations. If a power outage is sensed, the standby DC/DC converter on the batteries kicks in and sends power to the combiner, then out through the inverter to provide AC power. With this type of UPS system, power doesn't really run through the batteries in a true online sense. Also, if the inverter fails, the entire unit fails. This is called a *single point of failure situation* and is not desirable for a protection system of any kind.

Standby-Ferro Topology. Take a standby system, replace the filtered AC circuit side with a *ferro-resonant transformer*, and you get a *standby-ferro UPS*. One of the nice things about such a system is that the transformer truly isolates the output power from any glitches on the input side. Unfortunately, the transformer itself creates its own distortions and transients in the output power. Also, the transformer creates quite a bit of heat because of inherent inefficiencies.

Line-Interactive Topology. A *line-interactive system* looks too simple to work, yet when properly designed and engineered, can be very functional. The secret to this standby type of system is that all the power is always running through an inverter. The inverter provides protection from sags and also keeps the battery charged when input voltages are normal. When the input voltage drops, the power flow is from the battery back out through the inverter. Because *all* power is passing through the inverter always, it provides for additional filtering and reduced switching transients when compared to the basic standby topology. If the inverter is properly designed, it can fail but input AC power still gets routed to the output side. This is a very simple and efficient design that works well where there is very poor power.

Common Features of Modern UPSs. After you complete the daunting task of choosing the best topology, you also need to compare the various features and programs offered by different UPS manufacturers.

A UPS is no longer just a box with an On/Off switch, power cord, and some outlets. A modern UPS has lights, buzzers, software, and can do things such as page you when there is a problem! The following sections describe some of the more interesting and valuable features (by no means have we included all the features available on current systems), so that you are aware of some of your options when you decide to purchase, replace, or upgrade a UPS system.

Battery Status. Since batteries don't last forever, wouldn't it be nice if there were some way to tell if a battery is still good (without pulling the plug and seeing how long things continue to work)?

Some models don't have any battery-level indicators at all, and some have a light that comes on only when the battery needs replacing. I prefer models that have a series of LEDs that indicate present battery charge as a percentage of total battery capacity. Of course, nothing is a substitute for a real test. On a daily basis, however, it's nice to have some idea of how battery levels are changing before disaster strikes.

You can also find systems that provide software to monitor and log battery-level information so that you can keep in touch without looking at your UPS all day long.

Battery Replacement. This might not seem like much of a feature, but the method of battery replacement has a huge long-term impact. UPSs have batteries that wear out, so you expect to periodically replace the batteries. There isn't any way around this fact. Most UPSs require you to shut down the UPS, disconnect all devices, pull out the old batteries, insert the new batteries, reconnect all devices, and then restart the UPS. While this can be a real scheduling nightmare, it has long been an accepted inconvenience of LAN management. Someone has to come in at night or on the weekend and shut down the system while replacing the batteries.

Some manufacturers, however, have come out with *hot-swappable batteries*. You can swap out these batteries whenever you want, without having to bring down the system. This eases the burden of UPS management—and facilitates keeping good batteries in a UPS—so much that I consider hot-swappable batteries an essential feature of a UPS system. I'm also impressed with those companies which allow you to return old batteries to them for recycling.

Another point to look into about replacing batteries is how they are shipped. Some batteries require special shipping and handling, while others can be shipped by UPS or other major carriers.

Modular Batteries. As your system grows, your need for additional UPS power also grows. This could mean replacing your entire UPS system, or buying more UPSs. With some systems, you can simply plug in more battery modules when you need more UPS power. This means you don't have to purchase any more control modules—just batteries that plug into the control modules. Besides making things easier, this usually makes things cheaper.

AC Line Status. How's your input power looking? Are you getting a lot of sags, black-outs, spikes, or surges? The equipment attached to the UPS is protected, but what about all of your PCs and other devices that aren't on a UPS? Some systems provide software that allows you to track this important information.

Load Status. How hard are you pushing a UPS? Perhaps you have figured that it's only running at half capacity, but what does *it* think it's doing? Some systems provide soft-ware that allows you to track *load status information*, which is really handy when, let's say, your assistant decides to clean things up by rearranging all the power cables or by plugging something into an open UPS outlet.

Temperature. Battery life is directly related to temperature. Some manufacturers provide the ability to track the temperature of their UPS systems. I usually check the temperature to see if I should be worried about my file server or not. We ended up putting additional ventilation in one LAN room because the UPS temperature monitor showed that things became very warm in there on summer evenings after everyone went home and the air conditioning shut off.

Alarm Options. What happens if there is a problem? Is it enough that the UPS takes care of the problem, or do you want to know when there has been a sag, surge, blackout, or spike? If so, how do you want to be notified?

Audible. Just about every UPS has a very annoying buzzer alarm that sounds when an error condition occurs. You might not benefit from audible alarms, however, if you don't spend all your time in the LAN room.

Visual. For those of us who *do* live in the LAN room, frequent sags or spikes can keep a UPS buzzing all day long. Sometimes it's nice to be able to turn off the buzzer, and have LEDs flash to indicate alarms.

Send or E-Mail a Message. If your UPS detects a power error while you are in another room, wouldn't it be nice if it could e-mail you a message? Some manufacturers' software lets you do just that.

Pager. In the middle of the night at the end of the month, when an all-night database merge is being processed, you want to know if your UPS system detects a power loss—even though you're at home. Some manufacturers' software will dial your pager if alarms occur, giving you a chance to stop critical processes before the system shuts down.

Log Errors to a File. Of course, you want all the errors to be logged to a file so that you can monitor and track unfortunate trends and events. After all, good documentation is one of the keys to success in LAN management.

Self-Test Switch. How do you *know* that your UPS system will really work? You *think* the battery is still good, you *think* you haven't overloaded it, and you *think* your SHUT-DOWN TIMEOUT value is shorter than the expected battery time, but how do you know for sure? You have to test it!

A *pull-the-plug test* might not tell you if your UPS will really work during a power outage. This is because pulling the plug sends a "nobody else is on the circuit" type of signal to the UPS, while in a real power outage other devices in your building can still be connected to the circuit your UPS is on. When the power goes out, they can show up as a very large load to the UPS, confusing or slowing down the UPS's response.

Doing a pull-the-plug test tells you how long the batteries really last, but a *self-test switch* is also very important; pressing this type of switch tests exactly how the UPS will act when the power really goes out. Doing both of these tests gives you a sense of security that the UPS will not hiccup or die when the power goes out, and will keep running long enough for your shutdown routines to execute properly.

Link to a File Server. Probably the most important computer to be plugged into a UPS is the file server. There's no reason to spend time and money to set up a file server and load it with data, just to lose it all to a power failure. I feel so strongly about this that I will not work on a system that does not have a UPS for the file server. To me, running a file server without a UPS is like driving a car without a steering wheel. Sure, you might not run into anything today, but eventually you're going to crash. To paraphrase an old boater's saying: "There are two kinds of LANs—those experiencing a power failure and those that are going to experience a power failure."

If all the UPS does is postpone the power outage for a while, then what's the point? Of course, if you're nearby when the power outage occurs, you can run over and bring down the server properly before the UPS batteries are drained. What if, however, the power outage happens when no one is around, at night or on the weekend?

Almost all UPSs big enough to handle a file server include some kind of communications port so the UPS can talk to the file server. Whenever the UPS detects a power outage it notifies the file server and the server shuts itself down, preventing loss of data.

Some UPS systems require that a special card be installed in your file server for it to talk with the UPS. Other systems can talk directly to any free serial port on the file server. Depending upon your file server's configuration, this difference could be extremely important; operationally, though, the results are the same.

Monitoring. How do you stay in touch with the status of your UPS? One organization I worked with took the "If it ain't broke, don't fix it" logic to an extreme. They installed UPSs on every file server, then forgot about them. The only time any maintenance was done on the UPSs was when one failed. Sometimes they discovered that the only thing needing to be done was to reboot the server and replace the batteries. In some cases, data had been lost. In several cases, the batteries were so old that their cases had cracked, allowing fluids to leak out and destroy the UPS. One UPS's batteries had swollen so much that no one could open the unit to determine if anything was salvageable inside!

Obviously every piece of LAN equipment needs to be monitored. The more easily and completely you can monitor your equipment, the better off your LAN will be. Modern UPSs provide for monitoring in a multitude of ways. Choose the method that fits in best with your existing LAN monitoring policies and procedures.

Network Interface Port. Some UPS manufacturers provide their own software to expand on the services available through standard UPS-to-server communications links. Some functions available are: automatic battery testing, minimum and maximum power line voltages experienced, temperature, humidity, estimated battery runtime, incoming voltage, and current load on the UPS.

This software can be made accessible from any workstation on your network, so you do not even have to leave your desk to check every UPS on your system.

Network Interface Card/SNMP. Some UPSs allow you to install a network interface card—typically Ethernet—so you can monitor and manage your UPSs via Simple Network Management Protocol (SNMP). If you are using NMS, this allows you to integrate your UPSs into your system without loading or learning any new software.

Modem. If you can't hear, see, or access your UPS over your LAN, you might still be able to monitor it via a modem. If you have UPSs spread around the country that are all networked together, this can make keeping track of their status much easier. It also means that a system failure does not keep you from staying in touch with your UPSs.

Configuration Management. Not only do modern UPSs do more things, but you also can do more things to them. Because they include such a wide array of features—dialing in across the country to check your UPS system's status, configuring when alarms are triggered, choosing what will happen when an alarm is triggered, and more—modern UPSs are much more than dumb boxes sitting on the floor. Using the manufacturer's software, you can configure your UPS system to your specifications.

UPS ID. If you have several UPSs, you can assign unique ID codes to each one in order to keep track of your different units.

Low Transfer. The *low transfer* point is the voltage level at which your UPS begins to operate when there is insufficient voltage. You might want to raise this level if you have equipment that is particularly sensitive to low-voltage conditions. By raising the low transfer point, you tell the UPS to protect your equipment sooner than the UPS would if it were set at a lower low transfer point. On the other hand, you might want to lower the low transfer point a bit if your power company keeps hitting you with brownouts that are triggering alarms, but are not affecting the operation of your equipment. This might help extend the life of your UPS by not using its batteries as often.

High Transfer. The high transfer point is the voltage level at which your UPS begins to operate when there is too much voltage. If you have equipment that is sensitive to slight voltage overages, you might want to lower the high transfer point. On the other hand, if you are getting frequent overvoltage situations that you know your equipment can handle, you might want to raise the high transfer point in order to minimize wear and tear on your UPS system.

Sensitivity. Besides low and high voltage situations, UPSs can begin to operate if too much noise occurs on the incoming line. Fuel-powered generators typically create more line noise than your power company does, but not enough to damage your equipment. If your UPS is connected to a diesel generator, you might want to decrease the line noise sensitivity setting in order to minimize wear and tear on your UPS system.

Self-Test. Not only can modern UPSs test themselves, but also some of them do it automatically on a regular basis! Using the manufacturer's software, you might be able to set how often this testing occurs.

Alarms. If you have frequent power problems that your UPS system is handling properly, it can be quite annoying to hear alarms all the time. Some systems allow you to turn off the alarm, or have it sound only during long-lasting events.

Low Battery Capacity. If your system takes a long time to shut down, you might want to increase the low battery point to a higher level to give your server more time to finish its routines before the power is turned off by the UPS.

Minimum Battery Capacity. Unfortunately, power outages do not necessarily occur once and then wait a long time before occurring again. Imagine that your UPS system experiences a power outage. It runs as long as it can, but has to shut down the system sometime before the power comes back on. When the power is restored, the UPS tells the server to bring your system back up, then starts recharging its batteries. Suppose the power fails again. Since the batteries are completely drained, the UPS cannot provide backup power. Maybe you're lucky, and the system has stabilized with no activity in progress, so the crash doesn't damage any data. What if it happens, though, while your system is loading or when power has been on just long enough so that the system is up and some users have opened up files? Could be nasty.

To avoid such a situation, a good UPS system allows you to configure the UPS to not allow the system to come back up until the batteries have been recharged sufficiently to allow for a proper shutdown.

Return Delay. If you have several UPSs on the same circuit, it can cause a problem if they all turn on at once when the power resumes. By setting a different *return delay* for each UPS, you can avoid tripping a circuit breaker.

Error Notification. A UPS system can do more than just beep and notify the server to shut itself down when there is an alarm. Logging each incident to a disk file allows you to diagnose what went wrong—and when. Using special software on Novell systems, the servers can be configured to send messages to the system administrator or users in general to notify them that there is a power problem. Since some systems have more complex shutdown routines, the ability to run a custom command file can be particularly helpful. If you have proper equipment connected to your system, the server can even send e-mail messages or page you!

Special Programs. Some UPS manufacturers do more than just sell you a box. They appear to take into consideration all the possible issues surrounding your UPS system.

Battery Replacement. What do you do with those old batteries? Even if they are hot-swappable, old batteries have to be disposed of in some fashion; it isn't okay to just drop them in the trash. Some companies provide replacement batteries in a reusable container so that you can ship the old ones to a recycling center—or even back to the manufacturer! Convenient battery disposal might be a tempting factor when you are shopping for your UPS.

Operating System Certification. It's one thing to say that a UPS will work on your system. It's another thing if the UPS vendor has gone to the time and trouble to become certified by the vendor of the network operating system you are using. Look for such certification as an indicator that the UPS truly will work with whatever operating system you are running.

Warranty. How much confidence does the UPS manufacturer have in the product? 90 days worth? 1 year? 2 years? 10 years? Also, how does the manufacturer respond to a UPS failure? These are things best figured out before you have a failure.

Insurance Coverage. One company, American Power Conversion (APC), offers a $25,000 Lifetime Equipment Protection Policy with their units. This covers not only the UPS, but up to $25,000 worth of your computers and other equipment plugged into the UPS, should that equipment be damaged by a voltage surge—even lightning! This is such a valuable "plus" that I can't imagine other UPS manufacturers will not quickly follow suit.

Design

Once you have decided on a topology and a vendor, you still have to decide how many UPSs you need, and how big they should be. The following sections provide an overview of some common issues and questions you'll encounter. You'll want to refer to literature from various UPS manufacturers for full details.

What Needs a UPS and What Doesn't?

Obviously the file server, its monitor, and any attached external disk subsystems need to have UPS protection. This is the minimum acceptable level of UPS protection for a LAN. Then come the judgment calls—should you protect devices like the gateway to the mainframe, the routers and hubs, the communication servers, and the printers? A key determinant for this decision is whether or not your workstations have UPS protection.

The simplest, easiest, and cheapest solution is to just protect your file servers so they can shut down politely. As soon as you enter the arena of keeping one or more workstations plus the servers up and running during a power outage, things become complicated.

First, if you put a UPS on a workstation, then you have to provide UPS protection for any and all powered hubs between the workstation and the server. Next, there is the issue of maintaining a connection to the remote mainframe or other service while the local power has gone out. Not to mention printing and power requirements to drive a laser printer for even a few minutes. Or the inevitable demand by a user to be able to work for at least an hour.

Since most data only becomes corrupted if the server crashes, I argue that after the power has gone out, there is likely a very good reason to leave the building. Since the UPS cannot keep things running indefinitely, it is difficult to justify spending much money to keep things running for an additional 10 or 20 minutes.

Given my experience with local power fluctuations, however, I advocate including a small UPS with each workstation. The investment per PC (well under $200) is far outweighed by the benefits of less lost data, fewer user problems, and greater reliability from the PCs themselves.

Sizing for Your Needs

UPSs are rated in *volt-amps* (*VA*), from 200VA to greater than 5000VA. The bigger the number, the more powerful the UPS—and the bigger the price tag. While a 200VA UPS retailed for just over $100 in late 1995, a 2000VA costs around $2000 and a 5000VA unit goes for $5000 or more. The general interpretation of the rating is that the UPS can supply that many Volt-Amps for five minutes. Therefore, a UPS with a 600VA rating can provide 600 Volt-Amps for five minutes. Interestingly, if you only loaded a 600VA UPS with a 300VA load, it would last for 20 minutes. You need to decide how many Volt-Amps your equipment needs, and how long you need that power after the regular power supply has ended. While it would be nice to keep things running for hours on end, the cost can be prohibitive. The generally recommended runtime after a power outage is 15 minutes. This allows enough time to have your shutdown procedures execute completely, even leaving some room for additional equipment, batteries getting weak, and so on.

You can use the following calculation to determine approximately how long you have before your UPS is exhausted:

(Max. amp draw×120)+(Power supply (in watts)×1.4)=Total VA power requirements

(Max. amp draw×120) is the total amps of all the peripherals (such as the monitor) you have connected to the UPS, and (Power supply (in watts)×1.4) is the watts rating of your computer's power supply.

The general rule of thumb is

Full draw will give you approximately seven minutes of runtime.

Half draw will give you approximately 20 minutes of runtime.

So, for example, if your Total VA is 350 and the UPS you select is rated at 700VA, you should have at least 15 minutes of run time.

One Big Unit or Several Small Units?

What if you have several servers to protect? If you add up all the servers, disk subsystems, monitors, and other equipment, you could easily need 1500VA to 2000VA of power for 15 minutes. Should you purchase one big unit, then, or several smaller units? There are two primary factors in making this decision: price and redundancy. Let's use a three-server situation as an example, with each server and related equipment needing 500VA. The total VA requirement is 500+500+500=1500VA.

If we're willing to go with 14 minutes of runtime, we can get by with a 2000VA unit, but we'd probably be well advised to move up to a 3000VA unit in order to have 22 minutes of runtime. Retail price in late 1995 is roughly $2000 or $3000, respectively. If we use three 900VA units, we'll have 18 minutes of runtime at a retail cost of about $700 each, for a total of $2100.

The desire to avoid a single point of failure argues strongly for using three 900VA units instead of a single 2000VA or 3000VA unit. While the newest UPSs are miracles of modern technology and reliability, it's still preferable to have three chances at something staying running. On the other hand, if you had 15 or 20 servers in a room to protect, the logistics of managing a whole herd of small UPSs would start to argue for consolidating several servers onto a larger UPS.

Installing a UPS System

Unless you're purchasing huge (3000VA or bigger) UPSs, you should be able to install UPSs yourself. Even the 2000VA unit that weighs 100 pounds is actually two units of 40 and 60 pounds, respectively, so weight is not a concern. Since the batteries should be sealed units, there's no reason to worry about accidentally tipping a unit and spilling acid. That doesn't mean, however, that you can just turn on the unit, shove it into a corner, and forget it.

Access

While it is tempting to just tuck the UPS in an out-of-the-way spot, resist the temptation. You or someone else will have to change the batteries at some point, so don't wedge the unit into a corner, criss-crossed with power cables. You lose the benefit of hot-swappable batteries if you have to bring down most of your network in order to physically access the UPS.

Ventilation

Another problem with tucking the UPS into a corner is that doing so impedes ventilation. All UPSs create some heat as they charge their batteries, and put out about 10 times as much heat when running off of the batteries. Leave lots of air space around your UPSs.

Durability

UPSs seem big and heavy, but they are sensitive pieces of electronic equipment. Don't leave them out where they'll get kicked and banged around. You not only don't want to damage them, you want to make sure the ON/OFF switch doesn't get accidently tapped by someone's wing-tip!

Charging/Testing Batteries

Charging and testing the batteries should all be handled automatically by the system. There's no need with modern UPSs for you to unbox separate batteries, hook up the leads, and charge the system before bringing it online.

File Server Connection

Remember to hook up your server-monitoring cable! It's hard for you to overlook this cable during a new installation because the software usually has to be installed and tested at the same time. It is easy, however, to neglect to reconnect this cable after your UPS is moved. The problem often is that you become so concerned about getting all the power cables connected properly that the monitor cable is left out of the scenario—at least, until there is a problem that forces you to remember what that extra cable is for.

Software

Some network operating systems (NOS) are already UPS-aware, so you don't have to do much—if anything—to install the software. You're done after some very minor configuration. This software, however, is usually pretty rudimentary—the features you really want are only available if you purchase and install the vendor's software, and that's probably what you'll end up doing.

Documenting

Write everything down. It is shameful that most UPS systems are installed and forgotten without a lick of documentation. At least make a three-ring binder for your UPSs, where you can write down pertinent information. Much of the information you want to monitor will be recorded by the software, but things like the purchase date of the batteries or what gets plugged into what are not covered by the software.

Warranty Card and Battery Installation Date. Many people hate to do this, but it's important! Send in the warranty registration card for each new UPS. For your own reference I recommend you mark down when you installed the batteries and when you expect them to need replacing. It might not be for years, but the day eventually will arrive, and it's better to anticipate it than to be surprised by it.

What Plugs into What? You've gone to great lengths to figure out exactly what is supposed to be plugged into what, so write it down! If you're really cagey, make a chart that indicates what you've plugged in, how much it draws, and how much room you have left over. Then, when you need to change or add any equipment, you can easily determine how to protect it.

Labeling Cords and Cables. Labeling your cords and cables might seem like overkill, but unlike the different cables that plug into the back of a computer, all AC power cable ends look alike! The only things that plug into a UPS (aside from the monitor cable that you'll probably forget, anyway—see the earlier section "File Server Connection") are AC power cables. You can't tell the AC power cable end for a file server from the AC power cable end for a monitor. If you plug all your servers into one UPS and all your monitors into another, then when the power fails you have nothing but a handful of brightly illuminated monitors connected to dead servers.

Bundling and labeling all the cables that go to each UPS is a good way to ensure not only that the correct units are plugged into the correct UPSs, but also that the monitor cable doesn't get left in the bottom of a box!

Monitoring

Monitoring your system is not the same as responding to errors. The most important thing about monitoring is to be so in touch with your system that you see strange things going on before they turn into problems. In other words, you shouldn't be looking for errors, but rather indicators of future errors. If you plug everything in and it is running properly, then a failure cannot occur unless something changes. If you monitor enough factors about your system, you can see changes as they start to occur, and take necessary actions to avoid the changes escalating to a full-blown failure.

One of the essential aspects of monitoring is to compare the current status to a known, good status. This involves creating a baseline of values to compare against. Maybe your system runs on 117 volts most of the time with an occasional sag on Friday afternoons. If you know this, and then all of a sudden the voltage starts running at 114 volts with daily spikes, you have reason to investigate this situation. The situation is not abnormal yet, but something has changed and you need to know what it means before it becomes a real problem.

> **Caution**
>
> If you were monitoring only to make sure that operations fell within acceptable levels, you might never have noticed a shift from 117 volts to 114 volts, since both levels are normal. Monitoring for variations can give you early warnings about detrimental changes to your system.

Things To Look For

Always worry about the quality of the incoming power. The worse it is, the more work your UPS has to do, and therefore the sooner your UPS fails. Monitoring the incoming power condition for problems gives you some idea of how much work your UPS is doing. It also tells you when something has changed with the power going to your systems that do not have UPS protection. If everything has been running fine but your workstations start to lock up all the time, you should check the overall voltage level and incidence of sags to see if there's a problem with the power.

If your system has the ability to monitor temperature, you should check it regularly. Unlike mini- and mainframe data centers, LAN server rooms are not always air-conditioned, raised floor environments. You can use the temperature sensor in the UPS to monitor the conditions in your LAN room. Maybe everything is okay during business hours, but are you aware how hot that room gets over 4th of July weekend when the air-conditioning has been turned off for 3 days?

Battery level needs to be monitored carefully, because you want to replace batteries before they die, not after. All results of self-tests and pull-the-plug tests should be analyzed to make sure that you have full coverage at all times.

Frequency

With the advent of software to automatically log most of the important details, you no longer need to be checking things on a daily basis. There are not any hard and fast rules for how often to check things, but I usually get nervous if I'm more than a week out of touch with my systems. As important as how frequently you check is how regularly you check. By getting into a routine, you minimize your chances of forgetting to do it—moreover, if you always check at the same time, things should always look pretty much the same unless there's a problem.

Any time there is a significant error, increase your monitoring—trouble rarely travels alone.

Methods

Just about everything you need to monitor will be logged to a disk file by one program or another. Even a pull-the-plug test generates data points in the UPS's log file as well as the

SYSTEM ERROR log for most servers. Analyzing and making sense out of the information is up to you. You may prefer sheets of numbers to graphs with different colors. Whatever works best for you is what you should do, because you are the one who needs to understand what is changing and what is staying the same.

Documenting

There is little value to monitoring a system without writing down pertinent information and analyzing trends. If you're not watching for trends, then you are just looking for instantaneous errors, something the UPS is perfectly equipped to handle with its alarms and other capabilities.

Upgrading

Nothing stays the same forever, and UPS systems are no exception. At some point you'll be faced with upgrading your UPS system. The following sections present items to keep in mind when you consider upgrading.

How To Know When Upgrading Is Needed

Once you have your UPS system installed you had better start preparing to change it. The following sections discuss a few of the factors that could force you to change your system before the batteries have worn out.

Growth. Computer systems rarely get smaller, and with the advent of the Information Superhighway mentality, it stands to reason that computer systems are going to expand at an even more prolific rate. As your computer system grows, your UPS system needs to grow, also.

Features. Another occasion to upgrade is when your current system doesn't have all the features you want and need, but they are available on newer UPS systems. Perhaps some new monitoring feature, or the ability to hot-swap batteries, is all the justification you need to replace your current system.

Battery Replacement Cost. Some of the older batteries are so expensive that you can buy an entire new UPS for approximately the same cost as replacing the batteries in an old unit.

Adding More Capacity

Some newer units allow you to keep adding batteries (up to 100) to the main unit for rapid expansion of the capacity of your existing UPS.

Trade-Ins

Before you heave all your old UPSs out the door and buy new ones, check with the manufacturer for a trade-in policy. Not every manufacturer has such a policy, but it will save you a good deal of money if yours does.

Maintaining

UPSs are designed to be low maintenance; this unfortunately makes them easy to forget or take for granted. Unlike your PC that you boot up and use every day, your UPS might not actually do anything for months at a time. If you can remember to perform routine maintenance, however, you'll extend the life of your UPS.

Batteries Die! Plan for It

Everyone knows that batteries don't last forever. Yet most organizations have no plan, budget, or timeline for replacing UPS batteries. Think of these batteries as longer lasting—and slightly more expensive—printer toner cartridges. Put them in the budget and the schedule; the batteries shouldn't have to fail during a power outage to remind you to replace them.

Replacing Dead Batteries

If you don't have hot-swappable batteries, you have to schedule a time to bring down the system while you swap batteries. If you haven't been monitoring well, and you find all of a sudden that your batteries are completely dead—not just weak—you have to hope and pray that the new batteries get to you in time and that you can schedule replacement before you have a power outage. That's too nerve-wracking for me.

Being able to hot-swap dead or defective batteries is such a valuable feature that I won't purchase a system without this characteristic. Just make sure that you've left plenty of room to open the case without having to move any cables, and battery replacement will be a snap.

Terminal Connections

Some older UPS systems required you to open up the unit to tighten and clean the terminal connections to the batteries. Failure to do so resulted in improper charging and utilization of the batteries. Most newer systems do not require this often ignored bit of maintenance.

Testing

Just because the power LED is on doesn't mean that the unit is working. Even if the monitoring software says the unit is working, don't believe it is until you've tested it yourself. If the unit is continually handling sags, surges, and spikes, the question of what will happen when the power goes out still remains—you don't know how the unit will react, how long the batteries will run, and whether the shutdown software works properly.

Methods

Most units have a self-test that tests how well the unit would switch over during a power outage, and estimates how long the batteries would last. Pulling the plug is not a 100%

accurate way to test how the unit would switch over during a power failure, but a pull-the-plug test does let you know exactly how long the batteries will keep running, and whether or not the software is configured and operating properly.

Self-Test Simulation. I use the self-test only to test how the UPS switches over during an actual power failure. I would like to believe that if the UPS passes the self-test, my batteries are fine; however, I don't have that kind of faith. Of course, if the unit fails the self-test, I feel confident that I truly have problems. The first problem is whatever's wrong with the unit, but a more important problem is why I didn't get warnings that something was going on earlier—in time to check my monitoring policies and procedures.

One of the nicest things about the self-test is that it can be done anytime, since it does not affect the operations of the unit. In fact, some units actually self-test themselves periodically by default.

Pull-the-Plug. As mentioned earlier in this chapter, pull-the-plug tests don't create a true-to-life power failure. The power has failed, but since the UPS isn't plugged into the circuit along with everything else, the UPS gets different signals than it would during a real power failure. This is why I use the self-test to examine the system's switch-over capabilities.

A pull-the-plug test, however, does allow me to see exactly how long the batteries will run, and to make sure the software is configured and operating properly. It doesn't do much good to have the software configured to shut down the server after ten minutes if the batteries can only hold the server up for seven minutes! Moreover, if the monitoring cable is not connected, the software in the server never learns that the UPS is running on batteries, and is very surprised when the power goes out.

Even the best software in the world only works if it is loaded and running. If you don't add the correct software-loading commands to the automated start-up process, you could end up like I did once when I brought down a server to replace a defective NIC. After I brought the server back up, I noticed that the power protection software was not running because I had manually loaded the software when I had installed it. I immediately added the commands to my automated startup routine, and shuddered to think what could have happened because the software wasn't loaded had the system crashed during a power failure. The damage to the system would have been nothing compared to what my boss would have done to me.

The problem with pull-the-plug testing is that to do it right requires testing to make sure the shutdown procedures work. This means that you need to do it during a time when no one is on the system. In fact, since the system is going to be powered all the way off, be prepared for the possibility that it might not come back up right away. In the worst case scenario, one of your drives might die during the test, so make sure that you're aware of your tape backup situation. I like to do pull-the-plug tests on the weekend— often on Saturday morning—as soon as possible after the Friday backup has been completed.

By scheduling, notifying the users, and doing the test on Saturday morning, I minimize downtime for the users. This also gives me a chance to make sure that I have a good backup in case something goes tremendously wrong. Lastly, it gives me all weekend to get the system back up and running in case something goes catastrophically wrong. Starting a pull-the-plug test an hour before the users arrive on Monday morning is an invitation for disaster.

Frequency

Testing your system every month would be wonderful, but once per quarter is okay. You certainly should test it no less than twice per year.

Documenting

All the monitoring and software in the world is not as important as the actual trend in runtime numbers for the pull-the-plug tests. If you're losing a couple of minutes every six months on the pull-the-plug tests, it is easy to calculate when you should have to replace the batteries. If you don't measure and document the battery duration every time you do a pull-the-plug test, you won't have this information.

Repairing a UPS

What do you do when you know your UPS is defective? Maybe the batteries are dead, or maybe there is some kind of electronic malfunction. What can you—and should you—do? There isn't that much to do, but these are some of the things you can do.

Replace Batteries

Battery replacement should never be considered a repair to a UPS any more than replacing a toner cartridge should be considered a repair to a laser printer. Remember, though, that a battery or toner cartridge can be defective. Fortunately, replacing batteries in the new hot-swappable units is not much more complicated than replacing a toner cartridge.

Get a Loaner or Replacement

I believe the surest way to invite a massive power failure is to attempt to run a file server without a UPS for a few days. To make sure you don't invite such disaster after your regular UPS malfunctions, you should include your UPSs in a maintenance contract. Most service organizations provide an equal or better UPS replacement while your unit is being repaired. If you don't participate in this kind of loaner program, then you need to borrow or rent a replacement unit, or else temporarily move a UPS off of a less critical piece of equipment.

If you don't have a functioning UPS that you can move in this type of situation, you should consider purchasing a UPS for a marginally critical piece of equipment. In essence, you're buying yourself a hot spare, which you'll keep charged and ready at all times by using it on a device less important than the server. If your server UPS fails, you can start using a new unit immediately, get your system back up and running, and when the UPS comes back from repair, put it on something semi-important to prepare for the next disaster.

Moving the UPS

Appearances can be deceiving. UPSs are very heavy. But just because it looks like a brick doesn't mean you can or should treat it like a brick.

UPSs Are Heavy and Sensitive

Unlike PC cases, which are mostly air, a UPS case is mostly lead (from the battery), so be careful when you pick it up. They can weigh over 50 pounds—and usually sit on the floor—so watch your back and lift them carefully.

Remember that there is some very fancy electronic equipment in there along with the batteries! Don't drop, bang, or otherwise beat up the unit. If you treat it like a heavy computer, everything should be fine.

Leaking Batteries

If your UPS doesn't use sealed batteries, you need to be very careful that the unit doesn't tip over and leak battery acid. Battery acid is extremely corrosive. Please review the vendor's recommendations before you move the unit to be sure there's no chance of spillage.

Time To Replace the Batteries

As long as you're moving the UPS, this might be a good time to replace the batteries. You're already going to be doing 90% of the work required.

Replacing a UPS

If you've determined that your current UPS needs to be replaced, it really becomes a question of moving the old one out when the new one gets installed. You have to carefully plan what to do with the old one.

Surplus UPSs

Since UPSs are not machine-specific, just about anything that plugs into an AC outlet is a candidate for benefiting from a functioning UPS. Think about which devices deserve one of your older UPSs that otherwise would just sit around. Maybe there's a fax machine, critical workstation, emergency printer, or other device that doesn't justify a UPS purchase, but which would be valuable to have operating—even temporarily—during a power outage.

Keep in mind that most UPSs provide excellent noise, spike, surge, and sometimes sag protection, even when the batteries are shot and they can't provide backup power.

Don't forget the option of donating an old UPS to a school or college so that the next generation of engineers can learn about the technologies they will face when they enter the job market. The educational experience your old UPS provides might save *your* data someday. Or donate to institutions such as senior citizens' centers or homeless shelters, which have less critical equipment needs but whose need to keep operating is every bit as crucial.

Disaster Planning

It is critically important to include a properly configured UPS in any disaster-planning scenario because whatever causes the first disruption (earthquake after-shocks, flooding, riots, or whatever) might have multiple occurrences. You also have to take into account that the new site will not be as familiar to you as the original site, so mistakes can happen there. How embarrassing it would be to survive an earthquake, but then lose data due to a kicked-out plug or blown circuit breaker!

Security

Your UPSs need to be as secure as the power switches to your equipment. This usually is not a problem, since the UPS typically is in the immediate vicinity of the equipment it is protecting.

But unlike the power switches to your equipment, modern UPSs can be turned on and off by software. Controlling access to the programs actually running on the server is typically handled by limiting physical access to the server, as well as limiting who is allowed to remotely control the server.

A situation that is often overlooked is guarding the software run on a workstation that communicates with and controls the software running on the server. This software is meant to be used by the UPS administrator from his or her PC. The software runs on that PC, and has to find and communicate with software running on the server. If your software does not require a specialized installation routine that utilizes a key disk, password, serial number, or other security instrument, you might have a security problem.

If anyone can install the client software on their own workstation, and have it successfully find and communicate with software running on your server, then someone could deliberately or accidentally bring down your system by reconfiguring the controlling software.

Training

You might think that since the UPS just sits there, no training for using it is possible. There are many things, though, that you should train people to do properly: the hardware, the software, monitoring policies and procedures, and testing policies and procedures—just to name a few important things. Also, since documentation seems to be a lost art, if you don't train someone else to know what you know about the system, disaster could strike sometime when you are gone. Worse yet, disaster could strike sometime when *you* have forgotten how to reload the software, check the batteries, or calculate the capacity of the units.

Monitoring and testing are the two most overlooked yet important things to do with a UPS system. You need to have people trained to respond properly to alarms and error conditions, but it is equally important to make sure you train people on the policies and procedures for monitoring and testing the UPS system. Of course, this assumes you *have* policies and procedures for monitoring, testing, and responding to alarms.

All too often, a UPS is installed and someone configures it, but that's the last attention paid to the UPS. One day, the UPS starts beeping or sending out warning messages—the only person who knows what should be done is at home, on vacation, at class, at a different site, or not with the company anymore. Getting into a situation like this is like buying a gun to defend your fort, but having only one person trained to use it. It isn't much good if an attack comes when that person isn't available.

The following sections explain in more detail the types of UPS-related training you might want to do.

Hardware

There's not much to tell anyone about the hardware itself. The most important thing is to make sure that everyone who has access to the UPS system understands its importance, and knows that turning it off crashes the system. Another important point is to make it clear to all involved that just because there is an open outlet on the back of a UPS does not mean that you can plug anything at all into it. If you've labeled all the cables that are supposed to be connected, you reduce the chances of improper plugging.

Software

I've yet to find software that is so intuitive that no training is needed to know how to properly install, configure, and operate it. If there is a problem with the system while you are on vacation, who gets in trouble—the person you never trained to run the system, or you? It's easy to overlook the need for training, or even tempting to avoid training others because you want to feel indispensable. The mark of excellent managers, however, is that their systems run as well when they are gone as when they are there.

Responding to Alarms

Many decisions have to be made concerning all the possible error conditions a UPS can respond to. These decisions need to be formalized and proceduralized to prevent ignoring potentially catastrophic events, but also to eliminate overreacting to nuisance or expected errors.

I once had a conversation with a LAN administrator, during which his beeper went off. He glanced down at it, commented, "Oh, server *XYZ* switched over to battery power," and continued our discussion. My heart started racing a mile a minute, and I had to ask him why he wasn't doing anything about his apparent power problem. It turned out that he had been monitoring sags very closely, and had turned the low transfer point up very high so that the batteries would kick in at almost the slightest power sag. Since the batteries had kicked in, the system beeped him to let him know that a sag had occurred. It was a temporary situation he had created to closely monitor these events, and he knew that his system was in no danger. If you'd handed his beeper to me, however, I would have entered five-alarm fire mode. Training makes all the difference.

Monitoring

In order for monitoring to be effective, it needs to be constant and consistent. I can think of no way to do that without training people to do it. Train people to monitor regularly, and teach them what to look out for. The more eyes you have watching, the less chance there is that a surprise can sneak through and cause you trouble.

Testing

Testing, like monitoring, is only effective if is constant and consistent. Doing tests at different times and in different ways makes it much more difficult to detect any changes in the system. If everyone is trained to do tests the same way—and at the same time—there is not only consistency, but also less chance that the testing will be forgotten or postponed.

Future Trends

One of the most interesting developments in power protection is the creation of power protection devices for NICs, modems, and other communication devices. It is often overlooked that the electrical circuits of network wiring, phone wiring, printer wiring, and other similar items are subject to many of the same problems faced by AC wiring.

According to APC, the IEEE 802.3 Ethernet standard lists four electrical hazards to which networks are susceptible during use:

- Direct contact between local network components and power or lighting circuits

- Static charge buildup on local network cables and components

- High-energy transients coupled onto the local network cabling systems (those induced by other cables which are installed in the general proximity of network cables)

- Potential differences between safety grounds to which various network components are connected (such as the slight differences which may be found in safety ground from one building to another)

In other words, power problems not only occur over power lines but also over network cables, printer cables and modem cables due to static buildup, grounding potential differences and proximity to high voltage lines. For instance, a laptop traveler might be running off of internal batteries, but what happens when she plugs a modem into the data jack in her hotel room? A voltage spike could be created on her phone line by bad wiring or static buildup, and it could fry her modem and her computer. As computer components become smaller and more sensitive, we may find "data line surge suppressers" a requirement, not an option.

Troubleshooting

If you are having problems with your UPS system, you can use the following checklist to help pinpoint what is causing the trouble:

- How old are the batteries?

- Have there been any changes in the AC power source?

- When was the last time the UPS was monitored or checked? If there is a log file, what does it indicate? Are there any written records?

- When was the last time the UPS was pull-the-plug tested? How did that go?

Summary

UPSs are needed to provide constant power in an inconstant world. By providing constant power we not only get constant use from the equipment, we get longer and better use because the UPS also protects the equipment from damage that can be caused by "bad" or "dirty" power. Modern UPSs can test themselves, warn us when their batteries are getting worn out, and page us when they detect a power problem. But they still need to be checked from time to time and no battery lasts forever.

UPSs are used primarily on file servers and other critical devices. With the decrease in the cost of UPSs and the increase in the reliance upon our PCs, more and more PCs are getting their own UPSs.

Proper power protection has its costs, but so does equipment failure and loss of data and worker productivity.

Chapter 19

Antivirus Technology

Computer viruses represent a threat to the integrity of all computer systems but perhaps especially to networks where programs and data are shared to a greater extent than with stand-alone PCs. A network connection may make a computer more vulnerable to virus attack, but the same connection can also be used as part of an integrated system of defense against viruses.

This chapter describes the different types of computer viruses and the risk posed by each to networked PCs. It discusses antivirus strategies for networks and examines the features available on a range of workstation and server-based antivirus products.

Virus Basics

While the term "computer virus" has become common in the popular press over the last few years, it is quite often used inaccurately or out of context. This has given rise to many misapprehensions about what a virus is, how it works, and the harm that it can do.

The first step to protecting your network against viruses is a proper understanding of the nature of the adversary. This chapter, therefore, starts with a look at viruses in general.

What Is a Virus?

Viruses fall into the broad category of malicious program code. Most software is written to serve a useful purpose for the user, but programs have also been written that attempt to breach security, damage data, or display unwelcome messages.

Most of the code in this very wide category is designed to achieve its goal by being executed by an unwitting user. For example, a program for grabbing user passwords on a network might be called LOGIN.EXE; the user attempts to log on using this program, which behaves like the real LOGIN.EXE except that it also writes the user's ID and password to a file for later use by an intruder. Programs of this type are called trojan horses or "trojans" after the wooden horse of Troy—the classic example of getting your opponents to breach their own defenses for you by pretending to be something which you are not!

Viruses fall into the broad trojan horse category. What distinguishes viruses from other types of trojan horse is their ability to reproduce themselves. All viruses are trojan horses; they can propagate only if their code is executed by a person who is not aware of their existence. The converse is not true, of course—not all trojan horses are viruses. A password grabbing program is malicious and dangerous, but it cannot propagate itself.

> **Note**
>
> You will of course want to protect your system against all trojan horses, not just viruses. Many of the protective measures described later in this chapter will help to protect against all trojan horses, viruses and non-viruses alike, but for information more directly relevant to non-virus trojan horses, refer to chapter 20, "Tools for Restricting Access."

Virus code must execute to propagate. The most direct way to achieve this is for a virus to attach itself to a genuine executable program file in such a way that when the user runs the program, the virus code executes too. The virus can then attach itself to other executables, from which, in turn, it spreads to still more. Not all virus code needs to be attached to a file, however. Boot sector virus code copies itself from disk to disk as the workstation boots up but without attaching itself to any files. The various mechanisms used by viruses to propagate themselves are discussed in the "Virus Propagation" section later in this chapter.

Why Do Viruses Exist?

Every computer virus in circulation was written by someone who wanted it to infect other people's computer systems. In some cases, that was all they wanted: the knowledge that their code was passing from computer to computer, fanning out across the world over time. Many viruses have no direct effect on the computers that they affect other than the resources (disk space and memory) needed to propagate. These are not to be considered harmless though; virus code is complex and viruses can contain serious bugs that cause the virus to do things not intended by their author.

> **Note**
>
> Some viruses are designed to propagate without the explicit intent of causing harm. These should also be considered as malicious. Any code that executes on your system without your knowledge or consent represents, as a minimum, a breach of security and a potential risk to your data.

If viruses did no more than replicate, they would not represent a very serious problem. But the fact that they replicate means that they can in theory carry out any task that can be programmed on a large number of computers across the world. This is what seems to attract virus writers to the arcane art of low-level programming: The ability to gain temporary control of someone else's computer at a safe remove in time and space. This allows the virus writers to corrupt data, hang systems, display obscene or irritating messages on-screen, or whatever else they decide to program with little fear of having to account for their actions. As a social activity, virus writing fits in somewhere among the arts of mooning, graffiti, defacing banknotes, and the kind of actual vandalism that results in prosecution.

Such activity by a virus—actions other than propagation or avoiding detection—are referred to as the virus's "payload." Most viruses have a malicious "payload" of one kind or another. The payload is usually activated after the virus has been propagating for a time. If it were to activate every time the virus made a copy of itself, it would be noticed quickly and would not get beyond the first infection or two.

Types of Virus

Not only do viruses differ in the payloads they carry but also in the way that they propagate. Knowing how viruses spread and where they hide is vital to any effort to combat them.

There are two basic infection categories:

- File Infector Viruses
- Boot Sector Viruses

There are one or two viruses that fit into both categories, but that is because these viruses use both types of propagation mechanism. The mechanisms themselves are completely different, as the next two sections explain.

File Infector Viruses. Remember that virus code must execute before it can propagate. The easiest way to get an unwitting user to run virus code is to trick them into running it when they think they are running something else.

File infector viruses attach copies of their code to regular executable program files. When these programs are executed by the user, the virus code executes as well and it propagates itself to other program files. There are two basic types of file infector viruses:

- *Direct file infector viruses* attach themselves to the program in such a way that when the user executes the program, the virus code executes first. It copies itself to other programs and then passes execution to the original program. This means that the program appears to run normally, so the user suspects nothing until some time later when the virus delivers its payload.

- *Indirect file infector viruses* are also attached to a regular program. When the program executes, the virus loads into RAM before allowing the real program to execute. It remains in RAM without infecting other files until some time after the real program finishes. The virus only starts to infect other files at a later stage, as they are accessed for execution. Some indirect file infectors infect any executable file that is accessed, even if the file is not executing.

Boot Sector Viruses. Program files are not the only source of executable code on a computer. The boot drive has code in its boot sector that executes at boot time. Combine this with the fact that boot devices—floppy disks—move from one machine to another, and the virus writers have another opportunity to ply their trade.

A *boot sector virus* stores itself in the first sector of a disk, moving the original boot code to a different, unused sector. When an infected computer boots using that device, the virus code executes and the virus looks for other devices with boot sectors. If it finds one—usually when a workstation with a hard drive is booted from an infected floppy—it infects them, too. It also loads itself into RAM so that it can infect any other boot sectors that present themselves, such as when a file is copied to or from a floppy disk. Finally, it passes execution to the original boot code.

> **Note**
>
> All formatted floppy disks have a boot sector, not just "system" or bootable disks. Non-bootable disks have a minimal amount of boot code—just enough to give an error message if you try to boot a computer using one. This is enough for a boot sector virus, however, so even non-bootable disks can have a boot sector virus!

If this method of propagation seems less likely than the more straightforward file infection method, think again—the majority of actual virus infections are boot virus attacks, not file infectors!

Stealth Viruses. *Stealth viruses* cover their tracks in such a way as to make them difficult to detect. Typically, they watch out for attempts by antivirus programs to detect their presence in RAM or on disk and ensure that the antivirus programs get the "wrong" answers to any questions they ask the operating system.

An antivirus program, for example, may check for the existence of a boot sector virus by checking if the boot code is stored in the correct sector of the boot disk. A stealth virus that has moved the boot code to make room for itself intercepts the query from the antivirus program and returns the value that would have been returned had the disk not been infected. The antivirus program therefore reports that the disk has been checked and found not to have a boot sector virus.

Stealth viruses are no longer new, and antivirus packages attempt to detect their activity. This is not trivial, however, and the development of new stealth techniques with corresponding developments in antivirus software looks likely to continue for some time.

Many anti-stealth programs try to detect stealth activity by watching for suspicious activity on the DOS interrupts normally used for disk access or by comparing reported file contents with the actual contents of the specific disk sector on which the file is stored. These methods cannot detect stealth virus activity on networked drives, which are not accessed using the same interrupts and which are not, of course, read straight from a disk sector.

Companion Viruses. Not all file infector viruses attach themselves directly to a host program file. Some attach themselves logically; they create files that execute instead of the host program file.

Extension priority companions, for example, make use of DOS rules about program names. If a command (other than a DOS internal command) is issued and DOS finds two files in a directory with the same first name as the command but one having an extension of EXE and the other COM, the COM file executes. A companion virus may "infect" a file called PROGRAM.EXE, therefore, by creating a PROGRAM.COM in the same directory. This file contains the virus. When the user issues the PROGRAM command, the companion executes, runs its virus code, and then calls PROGRAM.EXE, making it look as if nothing out of the ordinary has happened.

Path companions are a little more indirect and can infect COM files too. They examine the DOS path and create a program of the same name in a directory with higher precedence in the DOS path than the program that they are infecting. So if PROGRAM.EXE is stored in C:\BIN and the DOS path is C:\DOS;C:\BIN, the companion is created in C:\DOS. Again, this companion program executes before the real program, does its virus thing, and then runs the real program.

The principle of these viruses is quite simple. While easily detected by a decent scanner, they can fool some integrity checkers that merely note the existence of a new executable file by calculating a checksum for the new file and storing it in their database.

Polymorphic Viruses. Early viruses replicated themselves precisely. When copying their code to a new host, whether a file or boot sector, they would copy the essential part bit for bit. This was necessary so that the vital part of the virus—the code that propagated it—was intact on the new host.

This made scanning for viruses relatively straightforward, if laborious. Once a virus had been isolated and identified, a distinguishing pattern of bits from its code could be extracted. A scanner program could simply check all executable files for a pattern of bytes that matched this pattern and report an infection when discovered.

Polymorphic viruses are different. They produce offspring with the same functionality as themselves but using a different sequence of bytes. This means that there is no guarantee that a sequence of bytes found in one infection by a specific virus exists in another infection by the same virus. Each type of polymorphic viruses uses a different method to produce this inter-generational variation.

The simplest polymorphic viruses store most of their code in encrypted form. The key used to encrypt the code varies at each infection, with the result that scanners cannot match any given string from the virus code from one instance of the virus to the next. However, the encryption and decryption code is the same in all copies of the virus. Scanners can simply search for the encryption/decryption code to spot such a virus.

Some antivirus scanners examine the sequences of instructions in executable files and try to detect when the code is capable of "virus-like" activity. Such scanners will not work with polymorphic viruses of this type because the virus-like instructions have been encrypted and are not visible to the scanner.

More complex polymorphic viruses store multiple encryption mechanisms and choose between them at random when they infect. This means that a scanner must check each file several times to be certain of detecting an instance of even one such virus.

Other polymorphic viruses intersperse their own code with random instructions that are not executed, making it impossible for a scanner to identify any consistent pattern of bytes that would reveal for certain that a file was infected with even one variant of a virus.

Polymorphic viruses are the most difficult to detect and as a result, they are fast becoming the most common. When choosing an antivirus solution, bear this fact in mind and make sure that the product you choose can reliably detect viruses of this kind.

Macro Viruses. Not all computer code is binary; many applications have built-in macro languages that let the user program a sequence of instructions to be executed by the application. The macro code is usually stored in its raw form—that is, without being compiled, as is the case with COM or EXE files—and is interpreted by the application at the time when the macro is executed.

While it has long been known that this type of code is capable of carrying a virus, it was not until late 1995 that the first such macro virus appeared "in the wild" on a significant scale. The Winword.Concept virus is attached to a Microsoft Word 6 document. When the infected document is opened, the virus installs itself in the global Word environment as a macro to be executed each time a document is loaded. From then on, any documents opened by that copy of Word are infected with the virus.

The Winword.Concept virus appears to have been written to illustrate the principle of macro viruses rather than to cause any particular damage. However, within a few weeks of its launch, a variant, Winword.Nuclear, was released that used the same basic mechanism as Winword.Concept but caused significant damage on many computers. At least two more Word macro viruses have been released since then. Now that the principle has been established, we can expect macro viruses to become as much a part of everyday life as the more conventional binary viruses.

By now, every major antivirus product can scan files on disk to locate infected Word documents and settings files and remove the virus. Live detection—while using Word in the normal way—is a little trickier and antivirus software vendors have tackled this problem in different ways. Refer to the "AVP" and "F-Prot" sections later in this chapter for information about how these two packages tackled this issue.

In the long run, however, there is a lot of scope for the application authors to tighten up their macro mechanisms. The fact that Word automatically executes a macro with a specific name, to take a case in point, is perhaps a little too trusting for the real world.

Virus Propagation

Viruses propagate from one host to another host of the same kind. Macintosh viruses, for example, do not spread to DOS machines; the machine code used by the two systems is quite different, so a virus written for one cannot execute on the other. Likewise, DOS viruses cannot infect Macintoshes, UNIX machines, or VAXs.

One apparent exception to this is when a DOS virus infects DOS executable files on an OS/2 machine. In this case, the virus executes and can propagate to other DOS files on the computer. It cannot successfully infect OS/2 executables, however, and the damage it causes if it tries is readily apparent and leads to early detection. In reality, this is not an example of cross-platform infection but of the infection of hosted files.

So viruses only move from one computer system to another of the same type. They don't move through thin air, of course. They require a vector of some sort to carry them, just as biological viruses do. In the case of computer viruses, the possible vectors are

- Floppy disks
- Hard disks
- Backups
- Other portable media
- The network
- BBSs
- The Internet

Strictly speaking, the vectors for the virus are executable files in the case of file infector viruses and boot sectors in the case of boot sector viruses. The viruses attach themselves to executable code, not to physical entities such as disks. The items in the preceding list, therefore, represent vectors for the vectors. However, it is more intuitive to refer to them as vectors, so a little linguistic license is applied in the sections that follow.

Floppy Disks. Viruses can be attached to a file on a floppy disk or stored in the boot sector. Floppy disks are the ideal vector for viruses: Portable, writable, and ubiquitous. That floppy disks are the primary vector for virus infections should come as no surprise.

Hard Disks. It may seem like a truism to say that if a hard disk from an infected computer is moved to another machine, the second computer will be infected. After all, it's the hard disk that was infected in the first place, so moving it to a different machine doesn't change much. However, the virus now has a new access point from which to spread, so it is a new threat, and as such it's something to be avoided.

Some service companies will replace a faulty hard drive with one that was already used ("We just tested it in one of our own machines...") without reformatting it. In fact, some will make a selling point of the fact that the disk is second-hand ("It has DOS and HyperBlip already installed!"). You may even transfer a virus yourself by borrowing a hard disk from a poorly protected machine. Although not nearly as common as delivery by floppy, this possibility should be eliminated by checking all replacement hard drives as soon as they have been installed. If in doubt, boot the machine with a "clean" floppy disk and scan the hard disk with a good antivirus scanner. Consider reformatting the hard disk completely in case any viruses are missed by the scanner.

Backups. Backing up an infected file to tape and restoring it later is another way to propagate a virus. The virus may be reintroduced to a system from which it had been cleared or introduced to a previously clean system. That much is simple common sense; the obvious corollary, scanning all files being restored from tape, is often overlooked.

Other Portable Media. Any medium that can store executable files can store a virus. CD-ROMs, WORM (Write Once, Read Many times) cartridges, magnetic tapes, and so on can all provide an exact replica of whatever was stored on them, possibly including infected files. As these media are passed from one system to another, they represent a risk of virus infection.

In the case of read-only media such as CD-ROMs, the risk is smaller: The CD-ROM cannot become infected as it is passed around. There is still a risk, however. If the original data is infected, the copy on the CD-ROM is, too. The CD-ROM is also immune from disinfection by any antivirus utility.

WORM drives can also represent a risk. An infected file stored on a WORM drive can be copied to a live system or executed from the WORM drive. Files on the WORM drive cannot be infected, however. The only way to alter a sequence of bits stored on a WORM cartridge is to turn on additional bits in the sequence—no bits can be turned off. This means that files on a WORM device can be obliterated but not changed constructively.

The Network. Networks are designed to be extremely efficient vectors of data in general, and infected files are no exception. An infected program on a file server, if executed by many users, can propagate much more quickly than by floppy disk transfers alone.

The network can transmit infected files but not (generally) boot sectors. This means that boot sector viruses cannot spread directly across the network. They may be encapsulated in a file in some way, of course, in which case they can be transmitted like any other data. However, they cannot spread by themselves by executing their fake bootup code. So using the network rather than floppy disks to transfer data may actually reduce the incidence of some viruses.

> **Note**
>
> The NetWare partition of a server cannot be infected by any virus known at time of writing. (Files on the DOS partition can be infected, as can the server's boot sector.) The NetWare partition can certainly store infected files and act as a dissemination point for the infected file and its viral passenger, but the server itself is not infected. The same is not true of machines on a peer-to-peer network, where one of the computers can certainly become infected by sharing a file with another computer.

BBSs. Bulletin Board Systems (BBSs) are commonly regarded as hot spots of virus activity. An infected file on a BBS may indeed propagate quite far, especially if the file itself is a popular utility or attractively named. In fact, some viruses have been "launched" on the world by being attached to fake versions of popular utilities (in one case, to a well-known antivirus package) and uploaded to a BBS for an unsuspecting public to copy.

Still, BBSs have had an unfair press. The fact is that you are much more likely to infect your PC using a disk borrowed from a colleague than by downloading a file from a BBS. This is largely due to the vigilance of individual BBS administrators, the majority of whom are well aware of the virus threat, know how to confront it, and adopt a strict policy of scanning all material for viruses before allowing it to go public.

The Internet. The same goes for the Internet, except that the loose organization and enormous scale of the network in this case make it impossible for anyone to monitor all uploads. This pushes the onus for checking for viruses back where it belongs, on the network user.

Individual archive sites may well scan for viruses, but don't rely on it; scan everything you download before unpacking it. Use an antivirus utility that can scan inside archives, as described in the "Workstation Utilities" section later in this chapter.

Vector Summary. Viruses are capable of moving across any pathway that can carry data. Examine the data paths in your organization and assess the vulnerability of each to virus infections. Remember, the media simply transport the data: When you receive programs from someone outside of your system, scan them for viruses before running them.

The Virus Threat

We have looked at how viruses work, why they are written, and how they propagate. Before moving on to discuss the details of how to combat them, it is worth taking time to consider the nature of the threat that they pose, particularly in network environments. This should help to inform the decisions you must take when formulating a detailed antivirus strategy for your network.

Effect of a Virus on One PC. As explained earlier, most viruses come with a payload that is harmful to one extent or another. It is this payload that is harmful, and as payloads vary from one virus to the next, so does the capacity for inflicting damage. The effect of a virus infection on a PC can range from no discernible effect to the complete loss of all data on the machine. The actions of viruses include

- Preventing the computer from booting
- Reformatting the hard disk
- Scrambling data on the hard disk
- Loss of partition table information
- Small scale (hence hard to notice) changes in data

- Displaying political slogans on-screen

- Displaying offensive or obscene messages on-screen

- Playing with the text on-screen, such as moving characters around

Some of these activities are irritating but not particularly damaging, while others represent a complete disaster. As long as the effects are confined to a single workstation, however, the infection is unlikely to be disastrous for the entire organization.

Effect of a Virus on a Network. A viral infection on a networked workstation is obviously a serious matter for the infected machine. The implications for other machines on the network vary.

- If the infected machine forms part of a peer-to-peer network, and if any files in its shared directories are infected, the virus may spread to other peer computers.

- If the infected computer is a client machine on a client/server network, the infection cannot spread to the server per se but may spread to files stored on the server. From there, it may infect other workstations on the network.

- The capacity for a virus to infect files on a server from a client machine depends on the access rights of the user who uses it to log on to the server. If they have minimal, read-only file access rights, the virus will not be able to infect files on the server.

- If the user has full rights, the virus may infect any files executed by the user (or in the case of some viruses, any executable files opened by the user). The most likely files to be infected on a NetWare server are those in SYS:PUBLIC that are shared by all users, so the virus infection could spread rapidly to a high proportion of the machines on the network.

- If the user stores files only in his own, personal area on the server, and if these files are not shared with any other users, the only machines that can be infected are those used by that user.

So on a client/server network, the threat from a virus infection on a workstation depends to a large extent on the privileges of the user of the workstation. This means that it is particularly important that any computer that may be used by a privileged user should be kept free from viruses.

Examples of danger points are

- Workstations in the offices of network administration staff, including supervisor equivalent users and workgroup managers.

- Workstations used for backups.

- End user workstations if used by a privileged user.

Although the seriousness of a viral infection can be more serious on a networked machine, as the virus uses the network to propagate more efficiently, the network can also be used to help to contain the spread of viruses. Sharing files using the network rather than floppy disk can reduce the circulation of floppy disks, the main vector for viruses in most organizations. Some antivirus products can refuse connections to workstations that are not running a particular antivirus scanner, ensuring that only "clean" machines connect to it.

So the network that accelerates the spread of an infection on the server can also help to prevent infections from happening in the first place.

The Likelihood of Contracting a Virus. Viruses still appear exotic to many people. The media hype, the crafty programming, and the constant battle between virus writers and antivirus software vendors, all contribute to a slightly unreal perception of the mundane reality of viruses. This can combine with a feeling of being remote from developments in computing to give a false sense of security. "We just do a little word processing," people say, "why would anyone infect our machines with a virus?"

The fact is that viruses have been with us for a long time now. Computer users all over the world share disks and programs, sometimes for software piracy, mostly for legitimate reasons. Viruses have spread to all corners of the world and are kept in circulation by a substantial percentage of computer users who do not take adequate precautions against them or who do not properly eradicate them once detected. The ongoing tussle for superiority between virus writers and the antivirus authors also ensures that new and more complex viruses emerge at a steady rate.

In a relatively recent development, some virus writers have released object code that allows virtually anyone with a little programming experience to produce complex polymorphic viruses. This brings virus writing within the reach of a much greater number of people than in the past. Although the antivirus software companies are dealing with the polymorphism problem, the precedent of encouraging large-scale, broadly based virus writing is worrisome.

In summary, viruses are ubiquitous and they are here to stay for the foreseeable future. Unless your network is hermetically sealed from the rest of the computing world—no floppy disks, no external network link, etc.—you are vulnerable to an attack. You don't even have to be a target. When the virus infection comes, it is much more likely to be from a computer game via a home computer than it is to be the result of a deliberate attempt to disrupt your organization. The best approach is to face the fact of the existence of viruses, minimize the risk of infection, and ensure that you are in a good position to recover should your defenses fail.

Antivirus Methods

Detection is the essence of any antivirus strategy. If a virus is found, appropriate action can be taken; the virus can be removed, the disk wiped clean, or the infected files replaced by clean backup copies. As a minimum, the infected machine can be taken out of use until the virus has been dealt with, thus protecting other computers. Adequate detection brings awareness of viruses, which is the first step in tackling them; poor or nonexistent detection leaves the user helpless.

False Positives and False Negatives. No virus detection method is perfect (contrary to some of the claims you may see in advertisements). There are two terms that are used to describe the accuracy of virus detection:

1. A *false positive* occurs when an antivirus program reports a virus infection where none really exists.

2. A *false negative* occurs when an antivirus program fails to detect the existence of an infection.

False Positives. False positives can occur when a clean program happens to contain a sequence of bits that resemble a virus signature (see "Scanning" later in this chapter for more information on virus signatures) or when a program contains instructions that are not malicious in any way but which an antivirus product regards as suspicious for some reason.

These reports are generally little more than an irritant. They can cause confusion, as they may be reported by one product and not by another; attempts to remove the "infection" will not, of course, be successful. By and large, however, false positives merely reflect the fact that an antivirus program is erring on the side of caution.

One situation when false positives are a serious problem is where an antivirus utility attempts to disinfect a file when, in fact, the file is not infected. The disinfection process involves rewriting some or all of the file; unneeded disinfection will scramble at least some of the file.

False positives are relatively uncommon. They typically arise in a new release of an antivirus product as a side effect of a change in the program and are quickly recognized once the product is released. The author of the antivirus product then usually releases a minor update that does not produce the false positive report.

False Negatives. A false negative is a failure by an antivirus product to detect the existence of a virus. This can happen for a variety of reasons: The virus may be new and hence unknown to the antivirus program, it may employ stealth techniques that evade detection, or it may be a type of virus for which the antivirus program does not search.

False negatives are obviously more serious than false positives, representing a failure by an antivirus product in their central function. They are also more common than false positives. This is because false positives are accidents, caused by the fact that virus code is program code and valid programs may sometimes resemble viruses in some chance way. Nobody tries to produce false positives, and antivirus software authors actively try to avoid them. False negatives, however, are the goal of virus authors who do not want their programs to be detected.

Barring the invention of a perfect virus detection mechanism, false negatives are a fact of life. Your goal, along with the antivirus software authors, should be to minimize them and to make sure you are well equipped to recover from a virus infection.

Detection Techniques

The most direct approach is to attempt to detect the existence of viruses before they activate. There are two ways to do this:

- Scanning
- Heuristic analysis

Viruses being what they are, however, the direct approach is not always the most effective. The indirect approach is used by two further methods:

- Behavior blocking
- Integrity checking

Let's take a look at each of these methods in turn.

Scanning. A scanner reads the contents of executable files, looking for virus code and notifying the user when any is found. Some scanners ask the users if they want to remove the virus from the infected file, while others leave that task to a separate utility from the same antivirus package. Every self-respecting antivirus package comes with a good scanner as its main element. Refer to the later sections of this chapter for a description of the criteria to apply when choosing a scanner and for a comparison of some of the available products.

A signature database is at the heart of all virus scanners. This is a collection of bit patterns found in files infected by a range of known viruses. The simplest scanners check each file for the existence of any of the virus signatures in the database. Using a single signature can lead to a high rate of false positives. There are only so many possible permutations of ones and zeros, after all, and whatever string of bits is selected as indicating the presence of a virus probably occurs in some genuine code sooner or later.

The best way to reduce the incidence of false positives is to use two or more signatures for each virus. If the first signature is found, the scanner checks for the existence of the second signature (and possibly more) before concluding that the virus is present. Most scanners now use multiple signatures, although some allow the user to trade speed for thoroughness by selecting the number of signatures used.

Advanced scanners also decrypt code that is encrypted, allowing them to detect polymorphic viruses with a high rate of success. The prevalence of polymorphic viruses means that this functionality is essential in a scanner these days.

There are two types of scanner utilities, on-demand and memory-resident.

On-Demand Scanners. *On-demand scanners* execute explicitly, either by the users issuing a command when they decide to check a disk or from a command line in a batch file. They perform a thorough scan of all executable files on a disk, searching for known viruses.

> **Tip**
>
> You can run a scanner with a command-line interface from the AUTOEXEC.BAT, but it's not really a good idea. Users will quickly get fed up with the long delay every time they start up and will disable the scanner. It's better to educate them in the need for regular scanning and encourage them to scan regularly on their own initiative.

Don't use any disks entering your organization unless they have first been scanned for viruses. It is often tempting not to wait the minute or so per floppy that a scan can take, but the cost in hours of missing an infected disk can be much higher. All users must be made aware of the importance of this step, as they all have the capability of introducing a virus to the organization.

Memory-Resident Scanners. Memory-resident scanners are loaded into memory when the computer starts up, and they remain there until the computer is shut down, scanning files as they are accessed. If a virus is detected, the scanner reports it and warns the user to disinfect the machine. Some memory-resident scanners lock the PC as soon as they display their warning message, preventing the virus, which is now in RAM and ready to infect, from inflicting any damage.

These scanners work in much the same way as their on-demand cousins, using a database of virus signatures and a scanning engine that attempts to match one or more signatures in each executable file. There are some differences though:

- Memory-resident scanners scan only those files and boot sectors that are accessed, unlike on-demand scanners which scan all files on a disk.

- Memory-resident scanners remain active at all times, unlike on-demand scanners which must be explicitly executed by the user.

- Memory-resident scanners generally use a less thorough scanning algorithm than their on-demand counterparts. This is to save memory and to minimize the performance impact.

- Many on-demand scanners can disinfect as well as detect. The memory-resident versions are alert-only utilities.

- On-demand scanners store their database in a file on disk. Memory-resident versions generally store a shorter database in memory, although some can save memory at the expense of performance by reading the signatures from disk every time a file is scanned.

Most nontechnical users are not willing to run an on-demand scanner on a regular basis. If you cannot persuade your users to do so, then installing a memory-resident scanner on all workstations is an acceptable compromise. This should of course be used in conjunction with other antivirus measures such as the footbath computers described in the "Sheepdips and Footbaths" section later in this chapter.

Whether the memory-resident scanner merely warns of the virus or locks the PC (a far safer option), it is important that users be briefed on how to respond; refer to the "Recovery" and "Education" sections later in this chapter for suggestions.

Scanners: On-Demand versus Memory-Resident. Most antivirus packages come with both on-demand and memory-resident utilities. These serve different purposes and the best approach is to use both:

- An on-demand scanner should be used on a regular basis to check all volumes on a workstation for virus infections since the last check. It examines all files, regardless of whether or not they are used. Scanners are very thorough, so this is the best way to ensure that viruses are caught.

- A memory-resident scanner should be loaded on each workstation at bootup time, always. This will catch most viruses as they load into RAM, preventing them from infecting the workstation or, if the workstation is already infected, preventing the infection from spreading to other files. While not quite as thorough as an interactive scanner, these TSRs can easily catch most viruses.

The best scanning policy, then, is to rely on a TSR as an early warning system and to sweep the system regularly with a good scanner for deep security. Scanning is at best only part of a proper antivirus strategy, however, as subsequent sections should make clear.

Heuristic Analysis. The principal drawback with scanners of the type previously described is that they can scan only for known viruses. A new virus, one without a signature in the scanners signature database, will not be detected.

Producing a program that can detect all viruses, even those not yet written, has been something of a holy grail to antivirus software authors for some time. Most viruses use one of the limited number of techniques described earlier in this chapter; a program that can detect patterns of behavior typical of such viruses should be able to detect all viruses of those types without the need for a signature string.

A program that scans files looking for such patterns is called a heuristic scanner, as it uses heuristic, or trial-and-error, methods to identify suspicious instruction patterns. Many scanners of the type described in the previous section use at least an element of heuristic analysis in tandem with signature scanning, while others use a separate heuristic analysis utility.

In reality, the task is more complex than what has just been stated. Many genuine programs use sequences of instructions that resemble those used by viruses. Programs that use low-level disk access methods, TSRs, encryption utilities, and even antivirus packages can at times all carry out tasks that are also performed by viruses. A heuristic analysis engine must attempt to distinguish between suspicious code that is malicious and that which is not.

There are other difficulties. As with all antivirus techniques, the existence of heuristic analysis engines has spurred virus authors to write viruses that can evade heuristic analysis. The difficulties are exemplified by those polymorphic viruses that intersperse their essential instructions with random "noise" instructions; how can a scanning utility properly distinguish between those instructions that form part of the virus's essential code and those that do nothing?

The net effect of these difficulties with heuristic analysis is that scanners which use the technique tend to produce a higher rate of false positives than signature-based scanners. This can have one of two undesirable side effects:

1. Users will get used to frequent messages warning about "possible virus activity" and will quickly learn to ignore them. When a genuine virus infection occurs, they may treat it like all the other (false) warnings they've seen and fail to react.

2. The irritation factor of lots of incorrect warnings means that many users will completely disable the scanner, possibly removing the entire antivirus package. This can leave them with an unacceptably low level of protection.

Nevertheless, heuristic analysis is a powerful technique. It can be particularly useful at detecting hitherto unknown viruses that have not yet become known to the antivirus authors or whose signatures are not in your current version of the signature database. The best approach is to use heuristic analysis on central checking machines (such as the footbath computers described in the "Sheepdips and Footbaths" section later in this chapter) and on the workstations of privileged users. These, after all, are the most critical in terms of preventing the spread of viruses across the network.

Behavior Blocking. Another approach to the idea of a generic antivirus utility is to monitor programs for "virus-like" activity while they execute. This is done using a behavior blocker, a TSR program that monitors activity by programs after they are loaded into the workstations memory and while they execute. If a suspicious sequence of instructions is carried out, the blocker warns the user and asks her if she wants to allow the program to continue.

The activities that can trigger a warning from this type of program are the same as those searched for in a different way by the heuristic scanners previously described: formatting commands, low-level disk accesses, strange file modifications, and so on. As with heuristic analysis, the tricky part of designing a behavior blocker is trying to distinguish between strange behavior that is malicious or that is legitimate.

The difficulties encountered are also similar. Behavior blockers generate a high rate of false positives and are liable to be rejected by users. They are perhaps best suited to particularly sensitive machines, such as footbath systems or workstations used by privileged users.

Integrity Checking. One of the simplest approaches to detecting virus activity is to note details about each executable file (and the boot sector, too, for good measure) and watch for changes. The virus may evade detection, the reasoning goes, but its effects certainly won't!

To this end, an integrity checker examines each executable file on the system. Checkers differ in their interpretation of what constitutes an executable file, with some including only COM, EXE, and SYS files while others embrace DLL, DRV, OBJ, LIB, OVL, and occasionally user-defined extensions as well. The checker calculates a checksum for each file examined and stores it in a database. It also calculates a checksum for the boot sector.

When one of these files is accessed, a TSR calculates the file's checksum and compares it with the checksum stored in the database. If the two values differ, foul play is suspected and the integrity checker warns the user.

On the face of it, this looks foolproof enough. Start out with a clean system, take a simplified snapshot of each file (the checksums) and watch for changes. Perhaps for this reason, the authors of some integrity checkers tout their packages as being the ultimate in protection, proof against all possible viruses, and so on.

In reality there are a number of practical difficulties with this approach.

- The system must be clean to start with. Any infected files will have their checksums calculated, virus and all, and will remain infected.

- The nuisance factor is quite high on any system where new executable code is created regularly—for example, in a programming environment. The integrity checker will spot new executable files or changed versions of existing files at each compile. It will request confirmation each time before allowing the new or changed file to remain on the system.

- Some integrity checkers—for example, those used by InVircible and ThunderByte—create a separate database file in each directory. Checksums for each directory are stored in the database file in that directory. This can be quite wasteful of space, as each file, no matter how small, will take up at least one disk cluster. The problem is exacerbated on network drives that use a larger blocking factor so that, for example, a file of a few dozen bytes in size can occupy a full 4K cluster. In a case like this, the checksums for a drive holding a few hundred directories could occupy a megabyte or more of disk space.

- Finally, the integrity database itself is often a favorite target of virus authors. Some viruses search out these database files and either delete or modify them to avoid detection. For this reason, it is vital that integrity checkers as a minimum warn users when their database file is lost; some checkers such as InVircible, however, will simply re-create a deleted database file, calculating new checksums for infected files and accepting them at face value.

In summary, integrity checkers are of limited use in programming environments or where new packages are regularly installed. They are also heavy on disk space and may be impractical to maintain on a network drive where there may be many thousand files occupying several gigabytes. Some viruses target the better known integrity checkers and in some cases are capable of evading detection.

They can, however, help to keep a clean, stable system clean. As such, they may be useful on a footbath machine or in a "cleanroom" environment where the integrity of files is accepted as being sufficiently vital to justify any potential nuisance value.

> **Note**
>
> All four detection methods listed above can run on any workstation, including a client machine. Behavior blocking utilities work only on a workstation at run time. This is because they need to sit in memory to watch other programs execute. The other methods can run either on a server or a client machine.

Antivirus Strategy

Having informed yourself of the threat posed by viruses, you should set about designing a strategy that will protect your installation from viruses. There is no perfect solution; some of the more effective antivirus measures are unacceptable to users because they are too intrusive or inconvenient, while others may be too expensive. You will need to weigh the cost of protection against the risk of infection and decide on an integrated strategy that is appropriate for you.

> **Note**
>
> This section should be read along with the chapters on restricting access, backups, and disaster recovery. These cover many topics of direct relevance to the formulation of an effective antivirus strategy.

Prevention. Prevention is certainly a good deal better than cure in the case of virus infections. It may not be possible to fully recover data damaged by a virus, and even if it is, the cost in time and computing resources may be high. In any case, prevention is relatively straightforward if appropriate measures are introduced and adhered to by all concerned.

Unsafe Practices. There are a number of computing practices that increase your exposure to viruses. While not directly related to virus activity, avoiding these practices can help to reduce the incidence of viruses:

- Make sure you have adequate backups at all times. These are essential for recovering from virus infections as well as from other disasters. Refer to the "Recovery" section later in this chapter for information about making a recovery disk.

- Don't use pirated software. There have been some cases of software distributors supplying infected disks, but these are given undue publicity and they are far outweighed by the enormous number of cases of infection by pirated software.

- Don't leave a disk in the floppy drive unless you are sure you want to boot from it. You may reboot the computer, or it may crash and reboot by itself (during a temporary power-outage, for example), giving any boot-sector virus on the disk all the opportunity it needs to infect the workstation.

- Don't use a privileged account on the server unless it is really necessary. You may inadvertently infect files on the server from an infected workstation.

- Don't log on to a privileged account from an end-user's workstation. They may not have the same high standards of virus protection as you, and the machine is more likely to be infected.

- If you must log on from a user's workstation or from any workstation with a dubious level of protection, boot from your own clean (check it yourself) boot disk and run your own network drivers from the floppy disk. Don't run any programs stored on their machine.

Detection. After an awareness of safe computing practices, the first active line of defense against viruses is a reliable detection mechanism. The different methods used were described earlier; specific products are covered later in this chapter.

Scanners and heuristic analysis utilities can help identify infected programs before they execute and behavior blockers can help to warn of impending virus activity. Integrity checkers can only tell you about virus activity after the fact, but they are a useful preventive measure nonetheless. By warning that a virus attack may have taken place, they alert the user to the need for action and can thus help to contain a virus outbreak.

Access Restrictions. A file infection on a file server can be disastrous, especially if the infected file is accessed by a large number of users. Such an infection can occur if the file is accessed by a user with write privileges from an infected workstation. You may not be able to guarantee that all workstations are free from viruses at all times, but you can go a long way towards reducing this type of risk by restricting the degree of access to the server for *all* users, including privileged users:

- Deny write access to all users to all areas except for their home area (refer to chapter 20, "Tools for Restricting Access," for details on how to do this effectively).

- Don't grant supervisor equivalence to anyone who doesn't absolutely need it.

- Warn all privileged users of the potential for accidental infection and remind them regularly of the need for vigilance.

- Don't log on using a privileged account unless it is really necessary. Warn other privileged users to take care.

- In extreme cases, it may be necessary to remove or disable the floppy drives in almost all workstations. Leave the floppy drives in one or two well-protected machines in a central location and insist that these machines alone be used for introducing data or programs from floppy disk.

> ### Tip
>
> The SUPER utility by Wolfgang Schreiber allows supervisor-equivalent users to toggle their supervisor-equivalence on and off. Use it in the logon script of all supervisor-equivalent users to turn their privileges off. They must then explicitly run the utility to turn their privileges on again.
>
> This means that privileged users will not normally have write access to public files on the server, significantly reducing the likelihood of infecting them with a virus.
>
> SUPER only works for users who start out with supervisor-equivalence, by the way, so it is not a security risk!

Sheepdips and Footbaths. A *sheepdip* or *footbath* machine is one that is used to check all disks coming into an organization. This machine is isolated from other machines and equipped with a high quality, up-to-date antivirus package (or two!). All incoming material should be scanned on this machine for viruses, and if a behavior-blocking utility has been installed, any incoming programs should be executed here first. The aim is to detect virus infections as they enter your system, rather than waiting until they manifest themselves on user workstations.

Systems of this type make little sense if material enters the organization by means other than floppy disk. If users have direct access to the Internet or to external BBSs, for example, they will download material directly to their workstation. They should then scan the material on their own machine before using it, and the footbath machine is not part of the process.

All users should be trained in how to use it and made aware of the importance of checking all disks before using them. Most importantly, the procedure to follow when an infection is discovered must be clearly explained.

Education. One of the most important steps in avoiding virus infections is to inform yourself and your users of the risks associated with viruses. While privileged users have a special responsibility for combating viruses in a network environment, all users can potentially introduce a virus into the organization. Except for the most extreme cases, it is not possible to prevent users from bringing data into the organization from outside.

It is therefore vital that all users be fully informed of the risks involved in transferring data, the precautions to take, and the steps to take should they see a warning about a virus. There are a number of steps:

1. Use seminars and newsletters to inform people about the reality of viruses, what they do, and how to combat them. Many people rely on the popular press for information of this kind and, as a result, have a poor idea of what viruses are all about.

2. Explain the reality of the virus threat to your enterprise. People are much more likely to cooperate in the antivirus effort if they perceive that it is in their interests and not just the hobbyhorse of the computer department.

3. Train users in the operation of whatever antivirus product is installed on their machines. Show them how to scan, tell them how often to do so, and make sure they understand what to do in the event of a virus alert.

4. Maintain an awareness of virus issues with regular newsletters, reminders, software updates, and so on.

Protecting Your Investment. Finally, an essential part of protecting against virus damage is to minimize the effects of losing any data on the workstation. Assume that a virus is going to get through sooner or later, and safeguard your data accordingly.

If you keep only a single copy of all essential data, with no backups and no way of retrieving data from a crashed disk, a virus infection that wipes the disk will be a disaster indeed. If you have recent copies of all essential material and back up disks that will allow you to reboot and re-install all applications, a virus attack won't be quite so serious.

A particularly useful measure is to prepare a recovery disk for each workstation. Make (and test!) a bootable disk with the following contents at least:

- Copies of the essential boot configuration files from the hard disk in case these become damaged or lost during infection or recovery.

- Copies of all driver files required to access all hard disks on the workstation. This applies particularly to machines with SCSI drives.

- Antivirus software. If you can squeeze the essential elements of two packages on here, do so. One may be able to fix what the other can't.

- Some DOS external command programs: FDISK.COM, FORMAT.COM, and SYS.COM.

- A text editor for editing configuration files. If you use EDIT.COM, remember to copy QBASIC.COM as well.

- Your favorite utilities to take the frustration out of the recovery exercise.

Examine the startup files on the disk and make sure that no programs are run from the hard disk. The aim is to be able to boot the workstation from the floppy only, without reading anything from the hard disk. The first time the hard disk is read following bootup will be when the scanner program kicks in.

Finally, write-protect the disk. This ensures that it remains uninfected. Floppy drives are built so that they will not write when the write-protect tab is open, and no virus has yet been written that can flip those little bits of plastic!

Recovery. No matter how good your protection strategy, viruses will occasionally infect machines on your network. For this reason, your antivirus strategy must look beyond the detection/protection stage and deal with failure—that is, infection.

When a virus infection occurs, the first thing you will want to do is remove the virus and get the machine working in a safe manner again. How you go about this depends on how the virus was detected and how much damage it did. In general, the sequence of events is

1. Deactivate the virus

2. Remove it from all disks

3. Recover any lost or damaged data

4. Prevent a recurrence

If the virus was detected by a memory-resident scanner, take note of the name of the virus that it reports. This information may be necessary at the disinfection stage if your antivirus package has separate scanning and disinfection utilities.

Deactivate the Virus. Not much can be done while the virus is active in memory. The first step must be to stop it from running. (This step obviously does not apply where a virus is inactive—that is, it was detected during a routine scan of a workstation—proceed to the next step in that case.)

First, turn off the computer as soon as the virus makes its presence known. This will halt any nefarious activity which it may be carrying out. Note that a warm reboot may not be completely safe, as some viruses intercept Ctrl+Alt+Del and simulate the effects of a reboot while remaining active.

Next, locate the recovery disk you prepared earlier. Make sure that the disk is truly clean by checking it from another workstation. If you can't locate the recovery disk, use a clean, write-protected boot disk.

Then reboot the computer using the recovery disk. The computer will now be running, with the hard drive accessible and the virus inactive. Only when you get to this stage can you proceed to the removal of the virus.

Caution

Do not access the hard disk now—not even to check if it is accessible.

Remove It from All Disks. With the virus inactive and the computer running, load the disinfection utility. Some antivirus programs use the same program for scanning and disinfecting, others have separate utilities.

Follow the instructions for the product you use, and attempt to remove the virus. This procedure may be straightforward or not, depending on the type of virus and the capabilities of your antivirus package. The details of how to go about it are different for each package.

Some boot sector viruses that infect the Master Boot Record (MBR) such as Michael-angelo and Stoned can be removed by rewriting the disk's Master Boot Record. Entering **FDISK /MBR** will create a new Master Boot Record. You can then make the disk bootable again using the DOS SYS command:

SYS C:

Caution

Depending on the type of virus present, this technique may render the data on the hard disk unusable! The One-Half virus, for example, encrypts the data on the disk and decrypts it as the user reads it back; as long as the virus remains active, the data appears normal. If the MBR is over-written, however, the decryption key will be lost along with the virus, rendering the encrypted data irretrievable. Use FDISK /MBR as a last resort or when you don't care about the data stored on the disk.

Recover Any Lost or Damaged Data. Once the virus has been disabled, the serious-ness of a debilitating viral infection depends largely on the state of the workstation's backups. Data recovery is not always possible, even with regular backups.

Many viruses are destructive; some will suddenly wipe the contents of a disk or overwrite the contents with garbage. Others are more insidious, changing a bit or two now and then. The latter type may slowly corrupt data over time before being detected, with the corrupt data perhaps being assiduously backed up at regular intervals.

It may not be obvious which files have been damaged, so you may need to examine each one separately. Consider whether the contents of these files are sufficiently important to justify this type of examination, let alone the effort repairing any damage. In the case of application directories, the simplest thing may be to restore the entire directory from backup or to reinstall it from scratch.

The best way to recover lost or damaged data is to restore an undamaged copy from backup. This may take a long time, especially if many files have been affected by the virus. It cannot be emphasized enough, though, that it is the only sure way of getting an undamaged file back.

Even restoration from backup may not be entirely safe. If an infected file was inadvert-ently backed up, you may reintroduce the virus to the workstation by restoring the file. For this reason, it is advisable to do a full scan of the workstation again after restoring any files from tape.

If your backups are inadequate you may need to rely on the disinfection features of your antivirus package. Such utilities can achieve wonders, but there are times, such as when two viruses infect the same file, that they are helpless. For this reason, it is best to use backups or reinstallations whenever possible.

Backups and Safety Nets

Prevent a Recurrence. The last thing you want is to deal with the same outbreak multiple times. Whenever you deal with a virus infection, stamp on it hard and make sure you have left no opening for the virus to reappear.

In all cases, following the disinfection of a machine, run a full scan (with the maximum level of "thoroughness" that the scanner is capable of) on all hard disks and on all floppy disks used on that machine since the last full scan. Notify all others in the vicinity (including those who do electronic business with the owner of the infected workstation) that a virus incident occurred, and encourage them to scan their own machines and floppy disks as a precaution.

The person who discovers the virus should always notify the designated contact person, even if she has managed to remove the virus from her own machine. Trying to figure out how the virus entered the system is important, and it will be necessary from time to time to make some adjustments to the antivirus strategy to take account of the real risks posed in your environment. There is no better way to identify those risks than to take proper note of each virus incident.

Finally, if you suspect that floppy disks used in the infected machine may have been sent outside the organization, don't hesitate to recall them; the potential embarrassment of doing so is less than the damage to your company if a virus spreads as a result of an oversight on your part.

Policy Issues. Viruses can disrupt your network and compromise your operation, so a coherent and well documented security policy for your network should cover antivirus procedures.

Start by evaluating the security of your network from the vantage point of a virus. Give your network a look over and identify all possible entry points for viruses. Examine your work practices and those of other users with a view to tightening up weak points. You will not be able to eliminate viruses completely, but there is no point in leaving unnecessary opportunities for them.

Next, try to figure out what the potential effect of a virus infection is. Estimate the cost of a serious virus outbreak in terms of human and financial resources, lost business, and tarnished image if the virus spreads beyond your company. This should help in establishing a budget for antivirus measures.

Then design a strategy to reduce the incidence of viruses and to minimize the effect of those infections that will eventually occur no matter what. The details of this strategy need to be particular to your environment, but the following points should be kept in mind:

- Install a quality antivirus package on each workstation in the organization. If you leave any machines unprotected you are presenting an opening to a virus. As a minimum, make sure each machine loads a memory-resident scanner that is regularly updated with new virus signatures.

- Insist that users run a memory-resident scanner at all times and perform a full scan of their hard disk at regular intervals. Opting out should not be tolerated.

- Give easy access to a footbath machine to all users. This machine should be bristling with antivirus measures and have lots of free disk space (cleared down regularly). Users should check all incoming disks on this machine. Make sure you explain to people what they should do if this machine detects a virus.

- Consider the possibility of taking disciplinary action against users who do not adhere to the antivirus policy. This should rarely if ever be necessary, but it is best to have it as an option in the policy from the beginning. If you try to introduce such measures only when they are needed, you may appear to be victimizing someone.

- Designate one person or a person in each section if appropriate as a contact point. They should be alerted to all virus incidents, even if the end user is able to deal with them effectively.

- All virus infections should be recorded by the contact people. In each case, they should take note of the virus, the suspected path followed by the virus and the cost in time and resources of dealing with it. This data will be invaluable for refining the antivirus strategy and for cost-benefit analyses of antivirus software.

- Define the criteria for deciding who gets supervisor equivalence. Too many privileged users, even in a highly trusted environment, hastens the day when a file in SYS:PUBLIC gets infected.

- Pay particular attention to the procedures to be followed by privileged users. This should cover items previously mentioned, such as booting from a clean floppy if using a user's workstation.

Once drafted, the policy should be discussed with all users before being formally adopted. Everyone has a role to play in the antivirus effort, and this phase can be used to heighten awareness of the issues as well as to ensure that users will not balk at unsuitable measures foisted on them without adequate consultation.

Finally, educate all concerned on the procedures to be followed. It is especially important that users and support personnel are aware of how to behave in the event of an outbreak to minimize damage and stop the spread of the infection to other machines in the organization.

The information gathering role is important. For example, if you find that a significant number of viruses are entering your organization on disks brought by staff from home computers, it may be in your company's best interests to purchase a comprehensive antivirus package for all such home PCs or to extend a corporate license to cover home PCs. If this seems like a lot of money to spend protecting privately owned computers, consider the alternatives: Tolerate an unnecessarily high incidence of virus outbreaks or try to prohibit users from bringing disks from home. The latter option is impossible to enforce in all but the highest security installations.

Antivirus Products

Viruses are not entirely bad news for everyone. Their success in spreading across the world and disrupting the work of computer users everywhere has led to the development of the antivirus software market.

A number of companies now make a living from producing antivirus programs. Their sales efforts are made easier for them by the fact that the popular media do a good job of raising awareness of the virus threat but a poor job of explaining what exactly it is. This means that everyone knows that they need antivirus software but few know what they need.

Some antivirus software houses have played on peoples fears and lack of information to sell substandard products. There is at least one antivirus package on the market that is so poorly written that it may represent a significant liability to the integrity of a user's data. (For obvious reasons, it cannot be named here.) The majority of producers are genuine in their efforts, but even among these, there are significant quality differences.

The difficulty faced by a system administrator trying to select a product is that so many claim to be the best and to use some new and particularly clever method to detect "all" viruses. In reality, some of the better results are obtained by products with little hype and using solid, established methods to achieve their ends.

Criteria

Short of building up a large collection of real viruses (an unsafe practice for sure, best left to the professionals) and testing each product on them, how do you choose between the different products on the market?

Number of Viruses. Many antivirus products invite you to choose them on the basis of the enormous number of viruses that they can detect. Figures of several thousand viruses are common enough in advertisements. The difficulty with figures of this kind is that companies count viruses in different ways. What is a virus to one is a variant to another. Unless the company adopts a formal set of naming conventions, such as those published by the Computer Antivirus Research Organization (CARO), comparisons of figures like this are meaningless.

The growth in polymorphic viruses also renders such figures increasingly meaningless. A scanner may be able to detect one instance of such a virus and miss others. What matters is its overall success rate, not whether it once managed to detect one case of the virus.

Percentage of Test Viruses. A more meaningful indication of the quality of a product is its score in an objective test where it is pitted against a large number of real viruses in a laboratory environment. The test data usually includes thousands of file and boot viruses, with polymorphic viruses making up a significant proportion. The results are usually quoted in terms of the percentage of each type of virus detected.

> **Tip**
>
> The *Virus Bulletin* is a good place to look for such results. This journal frequently provides objective comparisons of the performance of many of the main players in the antivirus market and can help greatly in assessing the merits of the various options available.
>
> Another place to check for review information is the Virus Test Center at the University of Hamburg. Its FTP server (**ftp.informatik.uni-hamburg.de/**) holds many product reviews in the pub/virus/texts/tests/vtc directory.

The top scoring packages generally catch 95%+ of the viruses in the test, with a success rate of less than 70% being considered very poor indeed. However, it is best not to get too hung up on these success rates. They depend in part on the test data used and, particularly with the polymorphic viruses, on an element of chance. A product with a 97% success rate may not really be any better than a product with a 95% rate. The difference becomes even less important if you consider that most users will come across a virus only rarely, especially if a proper antivirus policy is in place and adhered to in their workplace.

On the whole, comparative percentage success rates can help to separate out the very bad packages from the very good but should not be used by themselves as a means of deciding between the top scoring packages.

Other Criteria. Detection success rates are only part of the equation when selecting a product. Other factors include

- *Scanner speed*   Slow disk scans can be tedious to many users who may simply decide not to bother carrying them out.

- *Memory hit*   Memory-resident scanners and behavior blockers reduce the amount of available memory, in some cases by as much as 70K. Some can use extended or upper memory, others must stay in conventional memory. If available memory is tight, the difference could be important.

- *False positives*   A product with a high false positive rate will be considered objectionable by many users who may decide to disable it.

- *Regular updates*   New viruses appear all the time. Your antivirus solution should come with an option for purchasing or downloading regular updates. These updates may consist of new virus signature databases or of a revised version of the package as a whole.

- *Archive files*   Some products such as AVP can scan inside archive files. This feature is particularly useful if users download information from the Internet or from BBSs.

- *Two is better than one*   Use two products, even if one is only licensed on relatively few workstations. What is missed by one product may well be detected by the other.

- *Copy protection*   Don't buy an antivirus product if the distribution disks are copy-protected! It is essential that you be able to back up all software, including antivirus packages.

- *Modifications of executable files*   Beware of antivirus packages that "protect" executable files by modifying them. This can sometimes prevent files from running properly and may result in the corruption of your files. A program that cannot defend your data without mangling it is not worth buying.

- *Cost*   Cost is bound to be a very significant factor. Typical costs of $50 and up per workstation can add up quickly when applied to a network. Server-based scanners can work out cheaper at $500–$1,000 per server, but they offer only partial protection and are best used with workstation-based scanners as part of an integrated solution.

If you require a solid commercial package with good documentation and support, you will have to pay good money. If you are content with a package that is technically of a very high standard but comes without documentation or support, the shareware version of F-Prot is a good option. It costs just $1 per workstation (with up to 75% bulk discount!) and uses the same technology as F-Prot Professional.

Workstation Utilities

The essential components of a workstation-based product are a scanner and a disinfection utility. Most packages come with both on-demand and memory-resident scanners. Some also use heuristic analysis, and many come with other utilities not directly related to virus detection or disinfection.

The next sections outline the features of a number of the more common (and better quality) workstation-based packages. All of these packages score quite well in independent tests.

AVP. Produced in Russia by Eugene Kaspersky, AVP (Antiviral Toolkit Pro) is rich in features and particularly suitable for use by system administrators who like to get their teeth into a problem at a quite technical level. The menu interface is sufficiently simple to be used by most users, but the advanced features may intimidate some.

AVP has on-demand and memory-resident scanners, an integrity checker, and a host of utilities. The action of the scanning engine is highly configurable, with options for heuristic analysis, scanning of EXE headers or entire files, and so on. There are quick selection options for Fast versus Reliable scanning.

It also comes with a database editor that allows the user to add new virus signatures to the virus database. This is completely beyond the average user and tricky to do properly, even for the experienced. However, it may prove useful in the event of an infection by a new or unknown virus. The cynical network administrator may care to extract signatures from game programs and add them to the database.

Other utilities include a disassembler for examining active viruses, along with memory and interrupt probes. AVP can scan inside ZIP and ARJ archives on the fly, as well as properly interpreting the contents of packed EXE files.

The strategy used by AVP to block Word macro viruses is quite robust. It installs its own code as the macro to be executed when a new document is opened so that all documents subsequently opened are scanned for viruses. This is effective but the price may be too high for many users—the Word document wizard feature is disabled as an unfortunate side effect.

The AVP documentation gives an astonishing amount of information on the methods used by AVP to detect viruses and recover from infections. It is hoped that this Glasnost does not make AVP a target for the virus authors.

Dr. Solomon's Anti-Virus Toolkit. Dr. Solomon's Anti-Virus Toolkit, produced in England by S&S International, comes in separate DOS, 16- and 32-bit Windows, OS/2, and NetWare versions.

This is the pick of the corporate products, combining a smooth interface with a high detection rate. S&S and its various national agents have a good reputation for technical excellence. The price of $150–$200 or so per workstation reflects this, but bulk rates may be more attractive.

Dr. Solomon's comes with an integrity checker as well as the usual on-demand and memory-resident scanners. The on-demand scanner, FindVirus, is particularly strong on the detection of polymorphic viruses. It can scan inside ZIP and ARJ archives, as well as scanning packed EXE files correctly.

One noticeable drawback is that scanning an infected disk can take several minutes, a source of much anxiety for the inexperienced user who may already be in a state of panic at the time.

F-Prot. F-Prot is produced in Iceland by Frisk International. The founder, Fridrik Skulason, is an authority on viruses and his expertise makes this simple, non-fussy program a very solid performer.

F-Prot comes with a memory-resident scanner called VIRSTOP and an interactive, menu-driven program called F-Prot that both scans and disinfects. F-Prot performs signature-based scanning with an optional additional heuristic analysis. It can scan inside packed EXE files but not inside ZIP or ARJ archives. VIRSTOP is weaker than F-Prot on polymorphic viruses (by the author's own admission) but otherwise solid.

The strategy used by the F-Prot WVFIX utility to block Word macro viruses is different to that used by AVP. WVFIX also installs its macro code into a standard Winword macro name, but it is executed every time a document is saved rather than every time a document is opened. This means that it can protect against the macro viruses without interfering with the Word document wizard feature.

At $1 per workstation for commercial use (with discounts of up to 75% for bulk purchases) and no charge for personal use, F-Prot is a steal. It means that cost is no obstacle to dependable antivirus software.

McAffee's VirusScan. One of the longest established antivirus companies, McAffee Associates, produces VirusScan. This has two elements: Scan, an on-demand scanner, and VShield, a memory-resident scanner.

There are a plethora of command-line options that make customization by batch files simple. The main drawback with VirusScan is its low detection rate for polymorphic viruses. At $50+ per workstation, it is not particularly cheap, and the cost is not justified by its poor performance.

ThunderByte Anti-Virus. Written in the Netherlands by Frans Veldman, TBAV consists of a number of separate utilities: on-demand and memory-resident scanners, separate memory, disk and file access behavior blockers, an integrity checker, and a signature extractor.

The scanner is exceptionally fast and achieves one of the highest detection rates, particularly for polymorphic viruses. The virus signature extraction utility is not something for the average user, but as with AVP, it may be useful.

Disinfectant (Macintosh). Macintosh users have generally been spared the worst excesses of virus writers, perhaps in part due to the difference in cost of Macintosh and Intel-based hardware. Macintosh viruses certainly exist, however, and they are in wide circulation.

Without a doubt, the cream of the Macintosh antivirus programs is John Norstad's Disinfectant. It comes as a single application that consists primarily of an on-demand scanner along with a menu option for installing a memory-resident scanner. Disinfectant is a solid program with a very high success rate.

Disinfectant is free. It is available from **hyperarchive.lcs.mit.edu/info-mac/vir** and from many other locations as well. Updated versions appear regularly. All in all, there is no excuse for having a Macintosh without solid antivirus software.

Server Utilities

If the NetWare server is a PC, it can be infected by viruses like any client workstation. It has a boot sector and a DOS partition and runs DOS for at least part of its working life. Once NetWare starts to run, DOS is no longer active.

Despite the fact that the server is vulnerable to virus attack only for the brief time it takes to boot up and load SERVER.EXE, it makes sense to protect it from viruses. As a minimum, check for boot sector viruses and scan the DOS partition regularly.

Protecting Network Volumes. The real focus in server protection, however, is on the files on the network partition. As many of these files are accessed by a large number of users, it is particularly important that they be protected from infection.

These partitions are protected to some extent by features of the NOS. Access restrictions mean that only authorized users can access the server, and when they do so, they can only access designated files with predetermined rights. It is particularly important that these rights be limited to the minimum necessary.

Assuming that users have write access only to files in a designated home area, it may be sufficient to have each user run a regular scan of their home area as well as their workstation. Files on the server are still files, after all, and can be scanned like any others.

Server-Based Scanners. The fact that files are stored on the server opens up another possibility, however. A server-based program—an NLM, in the case of a NetWare server—can scan all files on any of its volumes at a time designated by the network administrator. It is not necessary for the user to initiate the scan or even to be aware of it. The NLM has full rights to all files.

This is not as comprehensive a solution as is offered by most workstation-based packages. An NLM does not run under DOS, and so it cannot perform any of the behavior-blocking functions employed to one extent or another by memory-resident utilities. Nor can it deal with boot sector viruses, the most prevalent type of infector in the real world.

It is also possible to make use of the fact that users log on to the server to verify that their workstation has the latest version of the antivirus software. This can be done using automatic distribution methods described or running a utility which verifies that the appropriate memory-resident scanner is active.

> **Caution**
>
> Don't load antivirus TSRs from the system logon script! Loading a TSR while LOGIN.EXE is in memory leaves a hole when LOGIN terminates, wasting a substantial chunk of RAM.

A number of antivirus software authors now provide NetWare server versions of their scanner product. This generally consists of the scanner engine incorporated in an NLM. The administrator can schedule the times when scanning should take place, the details to be contained in the report file, and any users to be excluded from checks by the NLM.

Some offer extra features. Dr. Solomon's Anti-Virus Toolkit for NetWare, for example, can deny logons to workstations not running VirusGuard, the memory-resident utility. It can also be used to distribute updates of VirusGuard to the workstations. Another novel feature is the ability of the NLM to take control of the scanner on the workstation, getting it to scan the workstation's memory or hard disk and report the results. McAffee's NetShield is much simpler and includes optional integrity checking measures.

In summary, server-based scanners can offer an extra level of protection against viruses in a network environment. Automated scans of network partitions can pick up infections missed by users who do not scan their own files. But these NLMs are not to be relied upon as the only antivirus measure for a network. Workstations are where viruses are active and where the thrust of antivirus activity should be.

Summary

Users of networked computers are potentially more vulnerable to computer viruses than are the users of stand-alone machines because infected files can be accessed so easily by many computers. The recent appearance of real macro viruses and their rapid spread across the world illustrates the potential for viruses to proliferate across a network if the necessary preventive measures are not in place.

The network can also be used to protect against viruses. Some of the best antivirus software can be downloaded from the Internet and file servers can be used to distribute antivirus programs within an organization. Using the network rather than floppy disks to share data helps to prevent the spread of boot sector viruses, the cause of most virus infections in the world today.

The existence of computer viruses is a reality for all computer users. Network managers must recognize this fact when considering the issues of access rights and security, while also being proactive in introducing antivirus strategies for their user community. The network can be viewed as a medium for the spread of viruses but also as a tool in the fight against them.

Chapter 20

Tools for Restricting Access

The continuing shift from centralized to distributed computing has brought a new vulnerability to computing systems. Users are given increasingly easier access to more data from more locations within both the LAN and the WAN. Modem access has the potential to extend the WAN to every point of the global telephone network. The potential for inadvertent or malicious loss of data and for unauthorized access to data has increased as the ease and scope of access has increased.

This chapter deals with the issue of controlling access to your network. It describes the forms that unauthorized access might take, how to protect the network and data in each case, and provisions for minimizing the impact of such unauthorized access. Finally, it describes the factors to consider when drafting a security policy and explains how you can use an auditing process to maintain the integrity of your network.

Security and Network Access

The security of a network can be considered as a number of objectives, including

- Securing the network hardware from theft or damage
- Securing the network from malicious disruption of service
- Preventing unauthorized viewing or copying of data stored on the server
- Preventing unauthorized modification or deletion of data stored on the server
- Preventing unauthorized viewing of data transmitted over the network
- Authenticating requests for access to data or to network services

These objectives can be met by implementing security procedures in the following areas: physical, electronic, and file.

The first item in the list should be self-evident—you obviously want to avoid the loss of network hardware. While this chapter will discuss those aspects of physical security that are directly relevant to the network, the more general issues involved in securing property against theft, fire, accidental damage, and so on are beyond the scope of this book.

The consequences of such loss or damage in terms of disruption of services should be considered when formulating a security policy.

The remaining items in this list cover the broad thrust of security concerns. In a nutshell, people should not be able to see what they are not supposed to see and should not be able to alter what they are not supposed to alter. They also should not be able to pretend to be somebody else in order to view or alter things they're not supposed to access.

Unauthorized access to data—viewing, modifying, and so on—refers to access either by a person who should not have access to the server or network or by a legitimate user of the server or network to some data that they should not be able to access.

Access to the network means different things in different contexts. It could mean the ability to change passwords on the server or the ability to divert network packets to an illicit connection. The various types of access can be divided into broad areas for convenience:

- Physical access
- Electronic access
- File access

A user ordinarily uses a number of different types of access to perform even the simplest of tasks, like viewing a file stored on a server:

1. Physical access to a workstation by the user
2. Physical access to the network by the workstation
3. Electronic access to the server when logging on
4. File access to the file when the user views it

The broad areas of network access are defined and described in the following sections. The security risks are outlined in each case, along with steps you can take to eliminate or reduce the risks.

Eliminating all risks is, of course, not always possible and practical. The purpose of your network may preclude some security measures, and the cost of certain security solutions may be prohibitive.

For example, you can prevent unauthorized access to the network from outside the LAN by providing absolutely no means of external access—no modems, WAN links, and so on. However, this might be completely unacceptable if you have users who require remote access to services for legitimate reasons or if you need remote access to the server console yourself.

As another example, suppose you wanted to eliminate the possibility of *sniffer devices* being attached to the network. These devices can collect network packets that are addressed to other locations on the network, allowing someone to read the data being transmitted on the network. You would have to physically secure all cables and devices, constantly monitor all cables and connections, supervise any repairs carried out by external maintenance personnel, and more. The cost in time and money for such operations would be prohibitive for most installations. It's far better to spend a lesser amount of time and money restricting the usefulness of any "sniffed" data.

Physical Access

A significant portion of the paths between users and their data is physical. This in itself is ample reason to carefully control physical access to the network. There is another reason: Unauthorized access to some of the physical components of the network could lead to a loss or disruption of service. Both of these aspects of physical access are covered in the following sections.

The types of physical access that need to be controlled are

- Access to workstations
- Access to the server
- Access to the network

Let's look at each of these in turn.

Access to Workstations

People need access to workstations to use the network, unless your network setup is very unusual. You can control the range of people who are allowed to use a workstation, the availability of workstations, the range of workstations that can connect to the server, the activities that can take place from a workstation, or a combination of these factors. The following sections describe how to implement this type of control.

Monitoring of Workstations. An unsupervised workstation is an easier place to carry out malicious deeds than a workstation that is watched over. Security cameras deter many unsavory activities—they even inhibit people from playing computer games, which in some circles is an unsavory activity. If cameras aren't an appealing solution, consider a live supervisor, who can be useful in deterring theft and attack, and also serve as a source of accurate information, protecting users from themselves.

Availability of Workstations. One of the simplest steps you can take toward securing the network is to lock up all workstations when they are not (or should not be) in use. If offices are locked when the people who belong there are out, and if PC rooms are locked when no supervisory staff are present, the risk of illicit access should decrease.

In extreme cases, access to workstations can be prohibited outside supervised hours. This is often impractical, of course, since workstations might be installed in offices that you have no jurisdiction over, or there may be a legitimate requirement for availability of workstations to access the server at any hour. If you can, though, lock away any workstations that can be accessed casually.

Bootup Passwords. The CMOS setup utility of most 486 and later PCs allows the specification of a password that must be typed in before the PC can boot up. This password can restrict access to specific workstations to people who know the correct password. A variety of third-party utilities exist that provide similar functionality for other PCs.

In practice, this feature is useful only in a very limited number of cases. Unless people use the same workstation every day, they need to know the password for each workstation. This inevitably means lists of written passwords, a disaster in security terms. If every workstation has the same bootup password, the password is an open secret and therefore of minimal use as a security measure.

The following are a few cases when a bootup password can be of use:

- Some responsible users may protect their own personal workstation using a bootup password. Their motivation for doing so is likely to be the protection of data stored on their own hard disk, rather than preventing the workstation from being used by others to access the network. Still, each user who does this reduces by one the number of workstations that might be used for illicit access.

- The supervisor account may be restricted to logging on from one network address or from a small range of designated addresses (see the later "Electronic Access" section). If so, using a CMOS password on the designated workstations provides an extra layer of security, albeit a thin one.

- Workstations sometimes are used to provide open access to information services— for example, in libraries. The service required is usually selected from a menu (see the later section "Restrictive Workstation Environments") that prevents the user from running software other than that listed on the menu. If such a workstation can be rebooted without running the menu program, it might be used for unauthorized network access.

  Setting a CMOS password can keep the user locked in to the menu, but it means that a staff member must key in the CMOS password every time the machine is rebooted. This is not such an onerous task, though, particularly if they simultaneously log on to the network with the appropriate restricted guest ID.

Restricted Workstation Environments. In some cases a restricted range of applications or network services are made available to users on a guest basis, with no user authentication. Examples include the provision of information services or Internet access in some libraries. These services often are provided by having a staff member log the workstation on to a guest account with very restricted access rights before use by members of the public.

The necessary access restrictions on the file server may be implemented by using trustee assignments, but this will not protect the workstation. The boot configuration (unless remote booted) and essential operating system files may be deleted or damaged unless protected. Unrestricted access to the workstation's hard disk may also give an intruder an opportunity to connect to the file server using an account other than the designated guest account. A restricted *workstation* environment is required to protect against such unauthorized access.

Such a restricted environment can be set up using third-party products such as IronClad from Silver Oak Systems, StopLight from Safetynet, or PC/DACS from Mergent International. These products allow the system administrator to control the type of access permitted to different users on a file-by-file and directory-by-directory basis. The workstation can be configured so that all applications and configuration information are write-protected, preventing modification for malicious purposes. The user can also be prevented from running software that is not explicitly designated as permitted. If you are concerned about users booting from a floppy disk to bypass this security mechanism, you can use the workstation's BIOS setup utility to prevent booting from the floppy drive.

Alternatively, the applications or services can be presented in menu form or within a Windows environment. The user is prevented from exiting the menu or Windows, ensuring that the range of software that they can run is carefully controlled.

If the user can exit from the menu (or from Windows) without logging out from the server, they retain a valid connection to the server. Assuming you have been successful in restricting the access rights of the guest account to the bare minimum, there won't be a lot they can do, but it's best not to leave this to chance.

In a DOS environment, use a menu program that prevents the user from exiting to the DOS prompt. Some menu utilities allow the user to exit only if they enter a password.

In Windows, remove all icons for non-required programs. That includes File Manager, which can be used to run other programs, and Write and Notepad, which can be used to read text files. In addition, prevent the user from running other applications that they might bring on a floppy disk. To do this in Windows 3.1x, add a [Restrictions] section to the workstation's PROGMAN.INI. Valid entries for the [Restrictions] section are listed in table 20.1.

Table 20.1 *[Restrictions]* **Settings for PROGMAN.INI**

Setting	Function
EditLevel=1	Disallow creating, deleting, and renaming program groups
EditLevel=2	Disallow creating and deleting program items
EditLevel=3	Disallow changing command lines for program items
EditLevel=4	Disallow changing any program item information
NoClose=1	Disallow exiting from Windows
NoFileMenu=1	Don't show the File menu
NoRun=1	Disable the Run command on the File menu
NoSaveSettings=1	Disable saving of settings

As an example, the following [Restrictions] section prevents the user from changing any program information, exiting Windows, or running programs not available as icons:

```
[Restrictions]
EditLevel=4
NoClose=1
NoRun=1
```

Windows 95 gives much greater control over the user environment. The System Policy Editor allows you to specify restrictions for the workstation as a network client or separately for individual users. The individual user options that may be restricted include access to the Properties sheets, the ability to run programs, set passwords and so on. The System Policy Editor is easy to use and it may be used to confine the user to a narrowly defined environment where only explicitly permitted programs may be executed.

These methods can provide a good deal of control over the range of activities that may be carried out from a workstation. If you install such a product on each workstation on the network, and if you make sure that no additional workstations can be connected to the network, you provide a layer of access security at the workstation level to supplement network and server security. From the point of view of restricting access to the network, however, the usefulness is significantly diminished if you do not have control over all client workstations.

Disabling Floppy Drives. An extreme method to secure data from being illegally copied from the network is to disable floppy drives on all client workstations. This also prevents users from introducing malicious or virus-infected software to the network.

In some cases, the floppy drives are removed completely. In others, a proprietary locking device is inserted in the floppy drive. This can be unlocked with a key and removed, allowing the floppy drive to be used by network administration staff when necessary. Another approach is to disable floppy drives using the workstation's CMOS setup utility. This is not a very robust measure, however, as any user with a copy of the CMOS setup utility will be able to bypass it.

The floppy drives on one or two designated workstations usually are left enabled. These are in a supervised area with anti-virus software installed; in many cases, they may be used only by network staff who will scan disks for viruses and malicious software or check that data is not being illicitly copied.

An alternative approach is found in StopLight, manufactured by Safetynet. Full disk access is allowed, but a data encryption mechanism prevents the data from being read on machines outside the StopLight domain where the data was written. The same system prevents protected workstations from reading data or programs from floppy disks brought in from outside the protected domain.

Disabling or removing floppy drives is of little use unless the network is hermetically sealed—that is, unless all workstations lack usable floppy drives and remote access via modem is completely disallowed. This is likely to be unpopular with users, who then have to go to a central location every time they want to copy a file to or from the network.

It might be appropriate, however, in networks where data is highly confidential or the network is mission-critical. It might also be appropriate in those cases where workstations are used to provide public access to information or network services, such as in libraries. In these cases, users can view information on-screen and perhaps print it, but they cannot copy data to disk and they have no way to introduce a virus or malicious program.

Tip

Disabling the floppy disk is of little use if the hard drive can be easily removed! Some PC cases snap open very easily, allowing the hard drive to be slipped out without difficulty. Someone stealing the hard disk can steal confidential data.

Moreover, if a troublemaker takes the hard drive to another workstation and introduces a malicious program to it, he can then reinstall it in the original workstation, circumventing the floppy disk lock.

The only solution is to lock the case securely—don't rely on the simple lock that comes with it—and keep a close eye on users of your supposedly secure workstations.

Trusted Workstations. Another way to prevent unwelcome access is to distinguish at the server between trusted and non-trusted clients. Mergent International's NET/DACS allows the system administrator to limit network access to trusted workstations only.

Minimizing the Impact of Workstation Intrusions. In most normal installations, there is a fair chance that someone, sooner or later, will gain access to a client workstation and try to do something you'd prefer they didn't do. This could be a malicious attack on data or applications, an attempt to steal valuable data, or perhaps a well-meaning attempt to "fix" a perceived software problem.

If you're protecting some highly prized data or a critical service, the more extreme measures previously listed may be appropriate. If not, however, it's generally better to focus on how to minimize the impact of this type of intrusion. The "File Access" section later in this chapter describes how to protect the integrity of the files on the server from accidental or deliberate alteration and how to contain the writeable area for each user.

Workstation Summary. Most of the methods previously described for restricting access at the workstation level are of limited use. Unless you can afford one of the third-party, high-security solutions (and are sure your users will tolerate the extra hassle involved), it's best just to assume that there are unsupervised workstations out there, and that these will be used at some point by someone who wants to get access to data they shouldn't. Workstation access is an area that you might have little control over. Server and network access, on the other hand, is where you call all the shots.

Access to the Server

The server is at the heart of the network. Unrestricted access to the server console brings with it complete access to user data, the ability to alter the server configuration, load or unload any server software, change any password, disrupt the service, and even to damage or steal some very expensive hardware.

Who Has Access? Start by deciding who should be allowed to physically access the server console. It is generally not desirable for all users to be able to freely access the server, but even in those rare cases when it is, you need to take steps to keep non-users away. If some users are to be excluded, is it even necessary for all network personnel to have free access to it? If not, which staff members truly require access?

If your server is mission-critical or is used to store sensitive data, you should also consider restricting the possibilities for access by third parties. Security and cleaning personnel generally have access to locations where many others do not; consider whether you need to exclude them from your server room.

Service personnel are often given free rein with the server without having their *bona fides* adequately verified. If you care about your data, have all service calls supervised by a trusted staff member. This is expensive in terms of staff time, but it is far more expensive to recover from industrial espionage.

Excluding users or staff members from a room in their own building, or looking over a technician's shoulder while they carry out maintenance work, can easily offend people because they feel that they are not trusted. Minimize the offense by explaining that strict adherence to security procedures is essential for your auditing process (see the later "Auditing Network Security" section). This helps remove any hint of personal bias in the act of exclusion. If the person still takes offense, review the criteria you applied when you decided to exclude them. If the criteria are sound and they still don't meet them, that's too bad—from your point of view, the integrity of your network matters a lot.

Server Location. No matter where you draw the line in deciding who should be able to access the server, it will be necessary to lock the server behind a door at some stage. It is not uncommon to see mission-critical servers located in open-plan office areas, as easily accessed as any workstation. This is acceptable only if access to the office itself is very carefully controlled (see the later "Physical Security Measures" section) and if all legitimate users of the office are also people who should have access to the server console.

In nearly all cases, the server should be located in a room dedicated to housing network equipment, rather than in somebody's office. The room should be walled off from office or open-access areas—don't rely on partitions—but still close enough so that there is enough human traffic going past to deter intrusion. A clear glass panel in the door, or a large internal window, also can help deter intrusion.

If the server contains data that might be the subject of aggressive attack—for example, where an intruder might attempt to erase data using strong magnetic fields—you need to take additional factors into account when choosing a location for your server. Those considerations are beyond the scope of this book; you need measures acceptable for protecting any precious commodity, a challenge best addressed by professional security consultants.

Physical Security Measures. Whether you place the server in an open office area to which access itself is very carefully controlled or behind triple-locked steel doors with armed guards, you must ensure that it is impossible for anyone to touch the server without some kind of verification of identity. This can consist of anything from possession of the appropriate door key to a retinal scan, depending on the level of security to which you aspire.

If the number of individuals with access is small—like five or less—a simple locked room is adequate protection. If the number of people with permission to enter is more than this, it can be hard to keep track of keys. Designate two or three keyholders and make them responsible for opening and locking the room. Combination locks save money on keys and eliminate the problem of keys being lost or stolen, but it is often easy for a would-be intruder to watch someone punching in the combination. There is the added risk that people often succumb to the temptation of writing down the combination or telling it to someone they shouldn't.

Motion detectors are relatively inexpensive and can be a sensible security measure for protecting servers. These are fitted to the server system box and can prevent theft as well as dismantling. They only make sense, however, if they are tied to a proper alarm system that can bring a prompt response from security personnel.

In some cases, a security guard at the machine room door is a worthwhile investment. If you can afford it, retinal scanning, voice recognition, or some other biological verification procedure may be appropriate. If you think you're ready for this type of security measure, consult security professionals.

> **Note**
>
> Remember, scale your investment to match the resource you are trying to protect. What would the impact on your company be if your data were stolen? A few days of downtime? Try to come up with a realistic estimate of the cost of dealing with a breach in security before you decide how much you are willing to pay for security measures.

Securing the Console. One of the simplest steps you can take toward securing the server is to password lock the console. On NetWare servers, load MONITOR.NLM, choose Lock File Server Console, and enter a password. The server accepts no further commands until either the same password or the supervisor password is entered. Windows NT machines may be locked at any time by pressing Ctrl+Alt+Del to invoke the Windows NT Security dialog box and selecting the Lock Workstation option.

Apply the normal password selection rules when choosing a password for locking the console. Refer to the later "Password Cracking" section for details.

> **Tip**
>
> Enter a random password (type one without even looking!) to ensure that only a person with the supervisor password can unlock the console. Of course, if the supervisor password is ever lost or forgotten, you will need to reboot the server to regain control.

NetWare has a server command that implements a few extra security measures. The SECURE CONSOLE command entered at the console prompt does four things:

1. Prevents NLMs from being loaded from any directory other than SYS:SYSTEM. This eliminates the possibility of, for example, one of the many password-setting NLM utilities being loaded from the floppy drive.

2. Removes DOS from server memory. If intruders manage to get to the server prompt, they cannot bring down the server without forcing it to reboot.

3. Prevents the server date and time from being changed. Doing this could disrupt some services that are time-synchronized, and certainly would upset user accounting.

4. Disables the server debugger, thus blocking one possible mode of access to data for technically minded intruders.

The second item is worth a closer look. It is a useful measure if, for example, the SECURE CONSOLE command is contained in the AUTOEXEC.NCF file. In that case, an intruder might try editing AUTOEXEC.NCF to remove the command, then bringing the server down and restarting it in an effort to get at an "insecure" console prompt. If DOS has been removed from memory, downing the server forces the machine to reboot.

Of course, this is quite satisfactory for the intruder, unless a bootup password has been set on the server. Disabling the bootup password would involve opening the machine to remove the battery, but that motion detector that you wisely fitted prevents them from doing that.

> **Caution**
>
> Despite its surface appeal, you should think twice before setting a bootup password on a server machine. If you set such a password, the server is never able to recover automatically after a power outage or a deliberate reboot carried out by the network administrator over a remote link.

Indirect Access to the Server. It may be possible to gain access to the server without physically touching it. Refer to the later "Electronic Access" section for a discussion of remote access to the server.

Minimizing the Effect of Server Intrusions. Assuming that an intruder manages to breach the physical security around the server and get past the console password, what damage can he or she do?

The answer depends on whether or not intruders can load their own NLMs. If you have not issued the SECURE CONSOLE command, they can load any of a number of utility NLMs that can alter passwords, including the supervisor password. This gives them free run of all data on the server. If you have secured the console, things are a little more difficult. If they can reboot the server, though, the SECURE CONSOLE command is easily bypassed.

In either case, your data can be compromised. If it is sensitive or confidential, you may not have any way to recover its value and the damage may be irreparable.

If you have secured the console, the intruder might not be able to access data on the server, introduce intrusive software, or alter passwords. In any event, with simple physical access to the server, a malicious intruder can damage your hardware and your data.

To minimize the effect of damage to the server or to your data, do the following:

- If the system is mission-critical, have a redundant server close at hand (but not in the same place!) so that you can get up and running again at short notice. Don't be put off by the cost of a redundant server. It doesn't have to be as efficient as your production server—remember that it is only intended as a stopgap solution.

- Ensure that the hardware is adequately insured and that you can secure replacement equipment promptly.

- Review your backup procedures and the state of your backups!

Server Summary. The ability to access the server represents the ability to read, modify, or destroy data as well as hardware. Evaluate the true value of your server and the data it stores, the possible impact on your enterprise of the theft of data, and the cost of replacing hardware or restoring data from backup. Then design and implement a firm strategy to limit access to the server only to those who need it and can be trusted.

Access to the Network

Unauthorized connections to the network can represent a significant security risk, so the network administrator should be aware of each and every network connection and the details of what is connected. This is possible only if there is some system to prevent the use of unauthorized connections.

Since it is usually impossible to police every meter of network cable in the network, the best approach is to configure the network to allow traffic from recognized network addresses and to bar traffic from unknown or unrecognized addresses.

This can be done using a structured cabling system that has intelligent hubs with port-level security features. Such a system can be configured so that ports must be explicitly enabled before use, and individual ports can be restricted to a single MAC address. This means that a new workstation isn't able to send or receive any traffic until the network administrator has explicitly enabled that port. Also, if a port is enabled for a particular workstation's MAC address, connecting a different workstation automatically disables that port, so it needs to be explicitly reenabled for use by the second workstation. In both cases, the network administrator is kept informed of changes in network connections.

> **Note**
>
> Refer to the "Firewalls" section later in this chapter for information on electronic access restrictions.

Electronic Access

The dangers of unauthorized physical access to the network are readily understood, even by those unfamiliar with how it works. The network is an expensive piece of equipment and a valuable resource, so it makes sense to protect it from physical intrusion. Electronic invasions often are harder to conceptualize, so it might be more difficult to explain the need for expensive security measures in this context.

This section deals with electronic access to the network or directly to the server and how to control such access.

> **Note**
>
> Not all networks are subject to electronic intrusion. If your network is purely local, with no links to the outside world by network router or modem, then this section does not apply in your case.

Electronic access to the network can mean a remote console session, a workstation connecting across a WAN, or other forms of traffic from outside networks. The different ways to access the network by electronic means can be grouped as follows:

- LAN access
- Remote console sessions
- WAN access
- Dial-up access

All these ways are discussed in the following sections.

LAN Access

Access to the server from within the LAN is normally limited to connections from workstations and from other servers. There might also be TCP/IP traffic from UNIX machines or AppleTalk traffic from networked Macintoshes. Each type of access carries its own risks.

In the normal course of events, a logon session from a workstation is what the network is all about. It becomes a problem when it is used to attempt to gain illegal access to data, as discussed in the following examples.

Masquerade Attacks. These occur when the password for a genuine user is discovered by an intruder and used in an attempt to log on. Protect against this type of attack by urging users to protect their passwords and by implementing regular password expiration using SYSCON (NetWare 3.x) or NETADMIN (NetWare 4.x). On Windows NT Server, use the User Manager to edit the Account Security Policy and set an appropriate value for the "Maximum Password Age."

Password Cracking. A password attack occurs when an intruder runs a program that generates a large number of random or dictionary-based passwords and tries to attach to the server using a particular user ID, and issuing each password in turn. An intruder may well be able to guess a correct password, particularly if users pick short or common words as passwords, but enabling intruder detection with a maximum number of logon attempts of three per fifteen minutes and a lockout time of an hour or more should easily defeat this type of attack. These values may be set using SYSCON under NetWare 3.x, NETADMIN under NetWare 4.x or User Manager under Windows NT (choose Policy, Account).

Of course, if your users have a lax approach to password security, an intruder may be able to access the server without needing an elaborate password cracking program. Passwords stuck to the monitor or written in diaries are a gift to such intruders. Advise your users of the importance of keeping their passwords confidential, and teach them how to choose a safe password. In general,

- Insist on passwords of at least eight or ten characters in length.

- Warn users not to use their name or any easily guessed personal information as part of their password.

- Tell users to use a mixture of alphabetic and nonalphabetic characters to make the password more difficult to guess.

- Reach a consensus with your users on the frequency with which passwords should be changed. You will probably want a shorter interval between changes than the users will.

- Idiosyncrasy is a useful trait when selecting a password! Encourage your users to give rein to their imagination when selecting a new password, and it won't seem like such a chore.

Packet Signature. A research team in Holland was able to demonstrate a potential security hole in NetWare, version 3.11 and earlier. They showed in a laboratory environment that it was possible for a workstation to fake network packets to look like they originated from a different workstation. If used while a supervisor-equivalent user was logged on, this method could be used to make requests to the server look as though they were made by the privileged user.

Novell released security patches for NetWare 3.11 that used a packet signature algorithm to prevent this type of security breach. If you use NetWare 3.11 or earlier, download the SEC*.ZIP files from NetWire and implement them. Versions of NetWare starting with 3.12 have incorporated this packet signature technique, but it must be explicitly enabled as explained later.

> **Note**
>
> This potential security risk apples only to NetWare. Windows NT Server uses a system of "access tokens" to authenticate user requests for access to system resources. These are broadly similar in principal to the system used by Novell to overcome their security threat—a unique signature is defined at log on time to enable the server to confirm that all requests really come from the user account which appears to send them.

The client and server negotiate over packet signature at logon time. Each has its own "signature level" as shown in table 20.2. The decision as to whether or not packets should be signed for the duration of the logon session is based on a combination of these signature levels.

Table 20.2 Client and Server Packet Signature Levels

Level	Meaning on Client	Meaning on Server
0	Don't sign packets	Don't sign packets
1	Sign if server requests it	Sign if client requests it
2	Sign if server can sign	Sign if client can sign
3	Insist on signed packets	Insist on signed packets

For example, if both the client and the server use signature level 1 (the default), no packet signature takes place. If the server is set to level 2, all packets to and from workstations with a signature level greater than 0 are signed. A server with signature level 3 refuses logons from a client with signature level 0. A workstation with signature level 3 cannot log on to a server with packet signature level 0.

Set client packet signature levels using the SIGNATURE LEVEL option in the workstation's NET.CFG file:

```
SIGNATURE LEVEL = 2
```

On the server, add the following line to the STARTUP.NCF file to override the default value:

```
SET NCP PACKET SIGNATURE OPTION = 3
```

There is a slight CPU performance overhead on the server as packet signatures are added and checksums are computed and compared. This overhead is usually very slight, however, as packets are normally sent in burst mode. Each "burst" of packets is signed, rather than each individual packet being signed.

Print Server Piracy. When print servers service a job in a print queue, they take on the access rights of the user who submitted the print job. A print server is thus supervisor-equivalent while servicing a print job submitted by the supervisor. If a print server is down, another workstation could be used to act as the downed print server, diverting print jobs and their associated access rights from the print queue.

To prevent this, set a password for each print server on the network. Also, use the workstation restrictions field under SYSCON to limit the print server account to logons from the designated print server workstation only.

Remote Console Sessions

Networking technology has made great strides in providing remote access to all types of systems—the server is no exception. RCONSOLE can bring all the power of the NetWare server console to any valid workstation. XCONSOLE can bring the server console to any X-Server on the Internet. ACONSOLE extends the realm of console access to the entire public telephone network. This vastly increased accessibility obviously brings greater risk of intrusion.

What might not be immediately apparent is the qualitative rather than quantitative increase in risk when remote access is provided. Bringing in additional physical server consoles leads to commensurate additional risk, assuming that each extra console had the same access restrictions as the first. An intruder still needs to gain access to a secure location and guess a console password before gaining access to data, but now they have multiple opportunities to do so. Providing remote access, on the other hand, overrides the physical security measures described above. An intruder can achieve a high level of server access without physically approaching the server.

Direct physical access has more dangers than remote access: Remote access obviously does not allow the intruder to steal or damage hardware, and if you have secured the console, they are not able to load their own NLMs. They are able, however, to destroy data, bring the server down, and so on. If you decide to implement remote access to the server, you should be aware of the risks and take appropriate counter-measures.

RCONSOLE. The RCONSOLE utility provides access to the server console from any point on the LAN. It is enabled by loading REMOTE.NLM and RSPX.NLM on the server and by entering a remote access password. To start a console session from a workstation, log on and run RCONSOLE. You will be asked to choose the remote server to connect to and then to enter the remote access password for that server.

Caution

The remote access password is all that keeps an intruder from gaining access to the console!

Any workstation on the network can be used for this purpose. It is not necessary to log on to the particular server that you want to access—in fact, it is not really necessary to log on to any server, as the required files can be executed from a local disk. All that is required is a copy of the files, a workstation on the network and—most critically—the remote access password.

It might seem like a truism, but the best way to prevent illegal remote server attacks is to avoid loading REMOTE.NLM on your server. Consider whether it is really necessary. If you use it to save a short walk every time you need to issue a console command, is what you save worth the added risk?

Remember, RCONSOLE gives access to the server console in all details. It does not bypass the console lock password if one has been set. If you must use RCONSOLE, at least set a console lock password to provide an extra barrier against intrusion.

ACONSOLE. The ACONSOLE utility provides over asynchronous connections what RCONSOLE provides over the IPX network. A workstation can be used to view and control the file server console, allowing console commands to be issued. It is every bit as powerful as RCONSOLE, and if used over a modem, it can provide console access to any point on the telephone network.

ACONSOLE with modems can be extremely useful for managing the server while off-site. As always, however, you should consider whether the benefits of greater accessibility outweigh the increased risk. If the server and the data it holds are critical, it might be better to resort to the technologically inelegant alternative of issuing verbal instructions to a staff member on-site.

ACONSOLE can be used over any serial connection, not just modems or phone lines. A cable from the serial port of a secure workstation to the server's serial port might be useful in those circumstances where it is inconvenient to walk from an office to the server room whenever access to the console is required—for example, where the office and the server are separated by a flight of stairs.

XCONSOLE. XCONSOLE allows the server console to be accessed from any X Windows server on a TCP/IP network. It is analogous to the RCONSOLE and ACONSOLE utilities, but if used on a server with an IP connection to the Internet, the scope for illegal access to the server is enormous. Bear in mind that the password is transmitted over the network in plain text, so a sniffer device can easily pick it up, compromising server security.

WAN Access

If your network is connected to other networks via a WAN link—for example, a router with a link to the Internet via a network service provider—your network might become a target for attacks from computers on the other network. If you have control over activities on the entire WAN, you may regard it as an extended LAN from the point of view of access restrictions.

If, however, a portion of the other network is carried over a public network—or another network over which you do not have jurisdiction—you need to take measures to control the ability of outsiders to access your network.

Firewalls. The basic requirement is to insert a control layer between your network and the outside. This layer, known as a *firewall*, allows some traffic through and prevents other traffic from passing through. The function of a firewall is illustrated in figure 20.1.

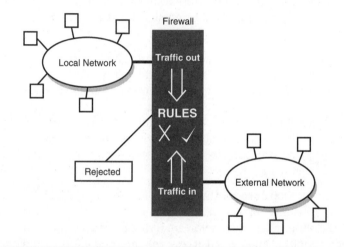

Figure 20.1

This is how a typical firewall operates.

The administrator of the local network configures the firewall based on the security policy of the local network. It's possible to block traffic of a particular kind, traffic from certain addresses, or traffic from all but a predetermined range of addresses.

Firewalls are rule-based entities. The network administrator decides on a series of rules that, when applied to a given network packet, decide whether or not the packet should be passed. The type of rule system varies depending on the form of the firewall. In general, more secure systems operate on the principal that no traffic is allowed unless the rules explicitly allow it—there are no permissive default rules.

Types of Firewalls. A firewall is a conceptual model for the protective layer between internal and external networks. In reality, it can be implemented in any number of ways. There are two classic types of firewalls:

- A *screening router* is a router connected between an internal and an external network, configured to permit only certain types of traffic. For example, it might permit packets of designated types or packets traveling between designated addresses.

■ A *proxy server* is a carefully secured UNIX machine that runs a range of proxy network applications such as FTP, WWW servers, and so on. External users connect to the proxy server, which decides, based on rules set by the system administrator, whether to allow them to access the system. If so, the proxy server passes traffic between the external user and the genuine application server—FTP, WWW, or whatever—that is on the local network. To the external user, it appears that they are connecting directly to the local machine.

Implementing a screening router using an existing router may be quite simple, depending on your security requirements. If you want to allow traffic only from designated addresses, simply screen out all others. More complex requirements need more time and thought to sort out, but it may well be possible to adequately protect the internal network without purchasing additional hardware or software.

A proxy server also can be developed at low cost using a range of public-domain software, but this is not an out-of-the-box solution and you should be prepared to invest a significant amount of time in setting up the system, recompiling applications, and testing the security of the system. If you can afford it, a third-party solution such as the Gauntlet Internet firewall from Mergent International is closer to the ideal of a plug-in solution. It still needs a certain amount of configuration, of course—a firewall is a mechanism for enforcing your security policy, so you need to formulate that policy and enter the rules that define it.

Firewall Costs. At $10,000 or so for the software alone, systems such as this represent a significant outlay. The only way to decide whether such a system is worthwhile in your situation is to assess the value of what you are trying to protect, the complexity of the balance between permitted and denied access, the time and effort required to roll out your own solution using router configuration tables, and the likely maintenance effort as your labor-intensive solutions must adapt to meet changing user requirements or an updated security policy.

Don't let the firewall brochures tempt you into throwing money at your security problems to make them go away. There is no such thing as a sure-fire firewall without a comprehensive and rigidly policed security system to accompany it. A firewall cannot do its job unless all external network traffic passes through it. Any machine-readable data can be taken outside a firewall; magnetic tapes and floppy disks may seem arcane in a world of high-speed internetworks, but they are quite efficient carriers of data in their own right.

The purpose of a firewall system is quite specific. It is meant to allow limited access between two networks. If you don't really need external network access from the entire network, don't connect it to the external network.

> **Note**
>
> Some products (such as Gauntlet) provide data encryption at the IP level. Two firewalls using this type of system can transmit data across a public network with a high degree of confidentiality.

Dial-Up Access

A modem link can provide access to the server console as described in the earlier "ACONSOLE" section. It also can be used to provide remote workstations with access to the network as clients. Chapter 25, "Adding Network Modems," has plenty of details on remote access implementations, but for the purposes of this section there are two broad categories of client dial-up access:

1. A workstation is set up with a network adapter connected to the LAN and a modem connected to an external telephone line. It runs a remote control package such as PC Anywhere or Carbon Copy. A user running the same software (or the client end of the same package) dials in over the telephone line, takes control of the workstation, and uses it as a network client in the normal way.

2. A dedicated remote access box such as 3Com's Access Builder is connected to the LAN. It incorporates several modems, into which a number of external users can dial at any time. The user's workstation is configured as a normal network client except that it runs a special driver that communicates with the remote access box over the modem link. The access box repackages network packets for transmission over the modem link and vice versa, giving a relatively transparent modem-to-network link.

In both cases, the external workstation should be considered in a similar light to an unverified workstation on the network. Refer to the earlier "Access to Workstations" section for information on the relevant issues. The significant difference is that you may have a degree of control over the workstations which connect to the LAN, but you have no say over modem connections to the public telephone network.

> **Caution**
>
> Configure remote control PCs to reboot automatically when the calling modem hangs up. This ensures that if a privileged user loses her connection or forgets to log off when finished, the next user does not inherit the privileged connection.

File Access

This chapter has focused until now on access to the server as an absolute; a given user either has access or does not, depending on the efficacy of your security measures. In reality, of course, no user should have complete access to all data on the server. This section looks at the NetWare tools for selectively controlling access to data on the server.

NetWare uses a combination of rights and attributes to determine the type of access allowed to a user for a particular file. Broadly speaking, *rights* are concerned with default access permissions, while *attributes* generally are used to explicitly override the defaults. Both are discussed in detail in the following sections.

Rights

When a user tries to access a file or directory on a Novell server, NetWare must determine whether the user has permission to do what she is trying to do. The access properties of files, the directories that contain the files, and the user accounts that might attempt to access the files all come into play in deciding the fate of a user's request for access.

It can be confusing trying to distinguish between these different factors. NetWare distinguishes between *trustee rights*, which pertain to specific user accounts and user groups (NetWare 3.x) or user objects (NetWare 4.x), and *inherited rights*, which pertain to files and directories. These are explained in the following sections.

Trustee Rights. The trustee rights of a user are the set of permissions which that user has to access specific files and directories. Trustee rights are associated with a user, not with files or directories.

Under NetWare 3.x, file and directory trustee rights are assigned to user accounts. Each trustee right granted to a user gives that user permission to perform a particular class of operation on the designated file or directory.

There are four types of trustee rights under NetWare 4.x. Object and property rights pertain to objects rather than to the file system:

- Object rights allow a user to browse, create, delete or rename an object. They do not confer any rights inside the object—to change individual properties, for example—unless the user also has the supervisor object right.

- Property rights refer to the contents of an object rather than to the object itself. Separate property rights can be given to any object—including a user—to allow it to read the property values of another object, change or delete them, or to compare them with specified values.

File and Directory rights behave in the same way as under NetWare 3.x as explained later.

User groups also have trustee rights, and users inherit the rights of any groups that they belong to. This means that individual users need not have any explicit trustee rights; they can inherit all they need from a group that they belong to. By default, NetWare gives Read access to SYS:PUBLIC to members of group EVERYONE. In practice, users generally also have explicit trustee rights to their home directory.

Tip

Use the access rights of user groups to assist in implementing your security policy. Create a number of groups with different access levels, and assign privileges to users by assigning them to the relevant group. This makes the administration of rights much simpler than assigning rights on an individual user basis.

The trustee rights which may be assigned are listed in table 20.3.

Table 20.3 NetWare 3.x File and Directory Trustee Rights	
Right	**Letter**
Supervisory	S
Read	R
Write	W
Create	C
Erase	E
Modify	M
File Scan	F
Access Control	A

The meanings of the various rights are as follows:

- Supervisory   The user has all rights to the file; in the case of a directory, the user has all rights to all files in the directory and its subdirectories. The Supervisory right includes the ability to grant the Supervisory right to others, unlike the Access Control right.

- Read   The user can read the file; in the case of a directory, the user can read files in the directory.

- Write   The user can open the file and write data to it; in the case of a directory, the user can open any existing files and write data to them.

- Create   The user can salvage the file if it is deleted; in the case of a directory, the user can create new files in the directory.

- Erase   The user can delete the file; in the case of a directory, the user can delete the directory, its files, and its subdirectories.

- Modify   The user can modify the file attributes, and rename the file; in the case of a directory, the user can do so for all files and subdirectories.

- File Scan   The user can list the file, as well as the path to the file from the drive root; in the case of a directory, the user can list the files in the directory.

- Access Control   The user can modify trustee assignments and the IRM for the file. With the Access Control right to a file or directory, a user can grant any right except Supervisory to other users for the same file or directory.

Inherited Rights. Trustee rights that apply to one directory automatically apply to any subdirectories of that directory. This makes sense; granting user SMITH full read and write access to HOME:SALES/SMITH means that she should have the same access in any subdirectories that she creates there.

It is often necessary to delimit the extent of this inheritance of trustee rights. You might want to grant access to a top-level directory but not to a particular subdirectory. That's where *inherited rights masks* (IRMs) and *inherited rights filters* (IRFs) come in—they act as selective filters on the trickling of rights from one directory level down to the next.

NetWare 3.x: Inherited Rights Mask. The IRM is usually represented as a list of the rights set out in table 20.3, in the sequence

    [SRWCEMFA]

with blanks representing rights that are not to filter through. The default IRM has no blanks and therefore has no effect on inherited rights.

Suppose SMITH grants Read, Write, and File Scan access for her directory to JONES. The directory HOME:SALES/SMITH/BACKUP has the default IRM, so JONES can read and list files there, too. If SMITH runs FILER and deletes W from the IRM for the BACKUP directory, so that it now appears as

    [SR CEMFA]

JONES will still have Read, Write, and File Scan access to HOME:SALES/SMITH but will no longer have write access to HOME:SALES/SMITH/BACKUP. If SMITH creates a new directory named SAVED below BACKUP, JONES will have Read and File Scan access there, also. This trickling and blocking of rights is illustrated in figure 20.2.

```
HOME:SALES/SMITH                    Jones' rights:    SRWCEMFA
                                    New IRM:          [SR CEMFA]
HOME:SALES/SMITH/BACKUP             Jones' rights:    SR CEMFA
                                    Default IRM:      [SRWCEMFA]
HOME:SALES/SMITH/BACKUP/SAVED  Jones' rights:    SR CEMFA
```

Figure 20.2

This is the flow of trustee rights through IRMs.

Note

IRMs are properties of files and directories, not of user accounts.

NetWare 4.x: Inherited Rights Filter. The IRF extends the idea of the IRM to NetWare 4's concept of objects and their properties. Rights filter by default from one directory level to the next, as under NetWare 3.x. They are selectively blocked by IRFs rather than by IRMs.

IRMs (NetWare 3.x) apply only to the file system. IRFs (NetWare 4.x) apply to either the file system or the NDS directory tree. When applied to the file system, IRFs are represented in the same way as IRMs, as a list of the rights set out in table 20.3 in the sequence

   [SRWCEMFA]

with blanks representing rights that are not to filter through. The default IRF has no blanks, and therefore has no effect on inherited rights.

Rights Summary. Rights accumulate as you move down the directory tree. IRMs block specific rights from a designated level in the directory tree, all the way down to the lowest level. Successive granting of rights and blocking of their progression through the directory tree can be used to exercise a high degree of control over file and directory access.

Attributes

NetWare extends the DOS file attributes with several specialized attributes to provide a greater degree of control over access permissions for network files and directories. The NetWare file and directory attributes are listed in table 20.4. Note that some of these apply to NetWare 4.x only, as they pertain to features of the NetWare 4.x file system not present under NetWare 3.x.

Table 20.4   NetWare File and Directory Attributes

Attribute	Symbol	File/Directory	NetWare 3/4
Archive	A	File	Both
Copy Inhibit	C	File	Both
Delete Inhibit	D	Both	Both
Don't Compress	DC	Both	NetWare 4 Only
Don't Migrate	DM	Both	NetWare 4 Only
Hidden	H	Both	Both
Immediate Compress	IC	Both	NetWare 4 Only
Indexed	I	File	Both
Purge	P	Both	Both
Rename Inhibit	R	Both	Both
Read-Audit	Ra	File	Both
Read-Only	Ro	File	Both
Read-Write	Rw	File	Both
Shareable	Sh	File	Both
System	Sy	Both	Both
Transactional	T	File	Both
Execute Only	X	File	Both

The following list explains these attributes:

- **Archive**   This is the same as the DOS Archive attribute, indicating that the file has been changed since it was last backed up.

- **Copy Inhibit**   The Copy Inhibit flag prevents users from making copies of Macintosh files.

- **Delete Inhibit**   This flag prevents the user from deleting or overwriting the file. If the user has write access to the file, she still may be able to alter its contents, even to the extent of removing everything in the file.

- **Don't Compress (NetWare 4.x)**   NetWare 4 can automatically compress files that have not been accessed within a certain period of time. This attribute prevents NetWare from doing so.

- **Don't Migrate (NetWare 4.x)**   NetWare 4.x can be configured to automatically migrate some files form the server hard disk to a slower storage medium after a designated period without being accessed. Files with the Don't Migrate attribute will not be migrated in this way.

- **Hidden**   This is the same as the DOS Hidden attribute. Files with this attribute do not show up in a directory listing. Hidden executable files can still run, but you must know the exact file name in order to run it.

- **Immediate Compress (NetWare 4.x)**   Files with this attribute are compressed as soon as they have been closed, without waiting for the usual period of file inactivity before doing so.

- **Indexed**   This attribute is used to increase access speed for large files. NetWare automatically builds an index for any randomly accessed file above a given size. This process takes time, but once the index is in place the server can jump directly to any requested record in the file rather than having to read through the contents of the file up to that point to reach it. This means that it can access the contents of the file much more quickly. It then retains the index in memory for a time so that subsequent accesses will also be faster. The Indexed attribute can be set manually, but it will have no effect unless set by NetWare.

- **Purge**   Files with the Purge attribute are purged automatically when deleted. They cannot be recovered thereafter using the SALVAGE utility.

- **Rename Inhibit**   Files with this attribute cannot be renamed.

- **Read-Only**   Read-Only files obviously cannot be modified or deleted. This is the same as the DOS attribute R.

- **Read-Write**   Files with this attribute can be written to as well as read from.

- **Shareable**   Shareable files can be opened for writing by multiple users at the same time.

- **System**   As in DOS, system files cannot be deleted, copied, or listed using DIR.

■ Transactional   Transactional files use NetWare's Transaction Tracking System to protect against corruption in the event of a crash.

■ Execute Only   The Execute Only attribute prevents EXE and COM files from being modified or copied. It was designed to protect against the illegal copying of binary files but has met with little success. Not all programs run if this attribute is set; those which do run are read from disk to memory and can be captured by devious means.

The Execute Only flag is a nuisance because it serves little purpose and has the infuriating property of rendering files undeletable, even by someone with Supervisor rights. The FLAG command cannot remove this attribute, either, so if you set it you might be stuck with it. (If you do get stuck with this problem, try the public-domain utility X-AWAY written by Wolfgang Schreiber. This may be found on NetWire in the NOVUSER/07 directory. Refer to appendix A, "NetWare Patches," for details on accessing NetWire and its Internet mirror sites.)

Combining Rights and Attributes

You've seen that there are three separate mechanisms for controlling access permissions on Novell servers:

■ Trustee rights

■ IRMs and IRFs

■ File/directory attributes

All of these serve different functions. Trustee rights are granted to individual users or groups to give them access permission for specific files and directories. IRMs and IRFs control the propagation of these rights to subdirectories. File attributes set particular properties of files and directories for all users.

A combination of these different features can be used to greatly fine-tune access rights on your network. Use a structured approach when determining the net result of the different layers of access control. For a given user and a given file, the following hold true:

■ By default—that is, unless you or NetWare explicitly grant rights—the user has no rights to the file. (Supervisor-equivalent users are an exception to this rule.)

■ Rights to a directory automatically confer rights to files within the directory, unless such rights are explicitly blocked using an IRM or IRF.

■ The user may have some trustee rights to the file or to the directory in which it is stored as a result of her membership in a group. For example, members of group EVERYONE have R and F access to SYS:PUBLIC by default.

■ The user may have trustee rights to a directory containing the file. Such rights might apply to the directory that the file is stored in or to a parent or higher-level directory that contains the file's directory as a subdirectory. These directory rights provide default access rights to the file.

Backups and Safety Nets

- An IRM or IRF—either to a higher-level directory or to the file's own directory—may be used to block such directory trustee rights from being inherited by the directory that contains the file.

- The user may have explicit trustee rights to the file, even if she does not have trustee rights for the directory that it is stored in.

- Directory attributes may affect the user's access permission to the specific file.

- The specific attributes for this file come into play for this user just as they would for any user.

In other words, file and directory rights are evaluated first using trustee rights and IRMs/IRFs. If the user is entitled to access the file on the basis of that evaluation, the relevant directory and file attributes are also evaluated.

So for example, since everyone has R and F access but not W access to the SYS:PUBLIC directory, everyone can read and execute MAP.EXE but not delete or overwrite it. This is true even if the file is flagged Rw rather then Ro—the trustee rights dictate that the user does not have write access, and file attributes cannot override this.

Appropriate Access Levels

Deciding what level of access certain users should have to network files and directories can be more complicated than implementing the necessary access restrictions. You need to evaluate the requirements of your users and the applications they use in light of your particular security policy.

The following set of rules is fairly typical:

- Deny all access unless it is truly required. Review the existing trustee rights for all users and groups, particularly for group EVERYONE.

- Remove C access to SYS:MAIL from group EVERYONE unless it's absolutely needed by your e-mail implementation. (NetWare grants Create access by default.)

- Apply a directory quota to each user's individual directory under SYS:MAIL to prevent them from using it as an unmonitored storage area. To do this, identify the user's bindery object ID using SYSCON and then run DSPACE to apply a directory quota to their MAIL directory. For example, if a user has a bindery object ID of 200001, use DSPACE to apply a directory quota to SYS:MAIL/200001. Note that this approach is preferable to setting a low quota on the SYS: volume, which may prevent users from queueing large print jobs.

- Grant R and F access and nothing more to shared application directories. Users need to run the applications, not delete or reconfigure them.

- Many applications assume that the user has full write access to the directories that program files are stored in. Try at all costs to find a workaround in such cases, rather than granting write or modify access to the application directory. If you absolutely must grant such access, use file attributes to restrict the extent of user access. Also, consider using DSPACE to place a limit on the amount that can be stored in the directory.

- Create a separate home directory for each user and grant him full access rights (everything except Supervisory) to the top level of his home area.

- Use workstation-based temporary areas rather then network directories. Apart from the network traffic inefficiency of storing temporary files on the server, it can be difficult to implement shared scratch areas without granting excessive access rights.

Remember that the effectiveness of this degree of access control depends on the security of user accounts and workstations. Don't use shared logon accounts or workstation-based accounts. Also emphasize to your users the importance of password secrecy, and monitor and review security on a regular basis.

Formulating a Policy

Now that we have covered the implementation details of access restrictions, we can look at the issues involved in formulating a coherent and appropriate security policy. Of course, in real life this stage must come before implementation. It's discussed at the end of this chapter only in the hope that certain issues were made clear through the discussions of implementation earlier in the chapter.

Responsibility

The first factor to consider is the responsibility for security provision. To what extent are you responsible for security on the network? Should you protect only the server and the data it holds, leaving the owners of workstations to fend for themselves? Do laptops, desktop machines, and other equipment also fall within your domain?

Insecure workstations do not make for a secure network. The issue here is to determine where the responsibility for security lies. The security policy should take this into account. For example, if workstation security is not under your control, then you may need to enforce strict criteria when allowing connections at the server.

Risk Assessment

The next stage is to assess the value of what you are trying to protect—your network hardware, user data, and possibly even the prestige of your organization. It might not be possible to evaluate everything in monetary terms. At the very least, make a list of the items at risk and quantify the following in each case:

- The monetary cost of replacement/repair

- The labor cost of replacement/repair

- The difficulty of recovering from exposure or loss

- The attractiveness of the item as a target

The last item in the list can be hard to quantify, but it must be considered. Is your data of commercial value? Is your enterprise likely to be the subject of hostile attack? Even the most benign enterprise with worthless data might be attacked by someone with nothing better to do, but if you are likely to attract more attention than an average installation, you should secure your system more strongly.

Try to evaluate the costs of loss or damage objectively. A break-in might be embarrassing, but will it harm your company's objectives? If so, to what extent? If you think it is possible that a break-in might put your company out of business for good, you might need to consider expensive security measures.

Authorized Access versus Unauthorized Access

The difference between "authorized" and "unauthorized" access is often a matter of interpretation. You must clearly define, in consultation with your users, what you mean by authorized access and what type of access constitutes a breach of security policy.

One important matter to be clarified is the ownership of accounts. People often regard their accounts as their personal property, to be shared with others if they choose. If this is indeed the case, you need to protect the server from the attentions of a wide range of potential users. If, on the other hand, the account is the property of the company—and the password merely represents permission to use it—the users should be made aware of this before you attempt to impose restrictions on their actions.

Users' Expectations

Heavy security can impose a burden on users. People are becoming accustomed to greater ease of access to computer systems from across the Internet or over dialup lines. If you impose restrictions on this type of access or completely disallow it, be prepared to explain why.

It helps if you can apply restricted access from the start. Introducing users to a secure system is much easier than imposing restrictions after users have become accustomed to a more relaxed approach. Strive to create a culture of security awareness, where users know the risks of unsafe practices. They might respond positively, policing the system themselves because they appreciate its value to them.

You might find that users are simply unwilling to accept the hassle of stringent security measures. If so, review the value of what it protects, as well as the issue of responsibility for security. If you find that it is both necessary and your responsibility, then users simply will have to accept it as part of the price of using a secure network. It is often possible, however, to implement security measures in a less intrusive way. This may involve paying more money for third-party security products with smooth user interfaces—another price your enterprise could have to pay for a secure network.

Finding an Appropriate Security Level

Taking all these factors into account, you need to find the level of security that is most appropriate for your needs. Consider the following factors:

- Value of resources protected

- Cost of implementation

- Limits on available funds

- Possible negative impact on user productivity

- Extensibility of the security solution

- Maintenance cost

The last factor is extremely important. You may be able to implement a set of measures that provide a good degree of security, using only your own time and expertise. The cost of maintaining this system, though, including future revisions to meet new external demands, may be quite high. Consider the cost of the manpower it takes to maintain the security system over time, and compare this with the cost of a purchased system.

Auditing Network Security

Finally, you need to know that your security solution is working. The best way to do this is to have someone carry out an extensive *security audit* at frequent (but not necessarily regular) intervals.

Security audits help to raise awareness of security issues among users and administrators alike. There is a need for procedures and standards to be seen being publicly enforced. Awareness of the possibility of an imminent security audit should help to focus the minds of all concerned on their respective roles in protecting the integrity of the network.

The person conducting the audit should be a trusted security professional who understands your work environment and your security policy. The auditor should look at your network from the point of view of a hostile outsider, trying to locate weaknesses in your defenses. She should also look at the security system from within, verifying that all users and administrators are adhering to the standards necessary to maintain a secure system.

Summary

This chapter explained some of the security problems associated with network use. In particular, the growing use of external access to networks raises new issues of user authentication and data security. These issues are in addition to the factors to be considered in the case of a strictly local network, where access rights and restrictions are also crucially important.

The time and money that you spend on security measures should reflect the value of what you are attempting to protect. If unauthorized access has a commercial impact rather than just a nuisance value, it makes sense to invest heavily in a comprehensive security system. In all cases, it is vital that a structured approach be taken to the issues raised and that a formal security policy be agreed upon with users and policed appropriately.

Chapter 21

Disaster Planning for Networks

Disaster planning is often one of those things that gets talked about, planned, and then never accomplished. Try questioning a group of network administrators about disaster planning. Ask them, "How many of you have disaster plans in place?" and you'll see some hands up. Ask, "How many of you have *written* disaster plans in place?" and many of those hands will go down. Ask, "How many of you have actually tested those plans and revised the parts that didn't work?" and most hands will go down. It's also a good bet that at least one of the people whose hand is still up is lying.

No one likes to think about the possibility of the network or the file server going down in flames, but it's better to dwell on this depressing possibility beforehand than to explain afterward to the boss why you weren't prepared for data loss. Therefore, in this chapter, we'll discuss the important elements of any disaster plan, who should be involved in its preparation, and how you can prepare for various disasters. This chapter can't write your plan for you, but your job should be easier.

The Nature of Disaster

"Disaster" is such a dramatic word that it might sound overdone. How likely is it that disaster could touch your company? If you think of disaster only in terms of natural disasters or massive hardware failures, then disaster might not seem very close at hand. If, however, you consider disaster in terms of anything that could stop the company from functioning for an undetermined length of time, then the notion of disaster is easier to accept.

Although this book is ostensibly about networking, the disasters that could slow or stop your company are not limited to network or data-related problems or even to events that happen at your site.

Broadly speaking, three categories of disaster could affect your organization:

- Natural disasters (events)

- Technical disasters (breakdowns)

- Human-related disasters (behavior)

These categories are not mutually exclusive. A disaster that apparently fits into one category could be slotted into another category because of its cause. For example, the slant on a power outage changes based on whether the cause is sabotage at the power company, an electrical storm, or a failed switch at your building. For the purpose of recovering from a problem, however, it really doesn't matter what caused it.

Events

Downed power lines, broken water mains, fire... Natural disasters don't have to be as dramatic as earthquakes swallowing your company headquarters. Hurricanes threaten coastal regions of the southeastern United States almost every year. If your office shares a building or office park with others, a fire starting in a neighboring company can threaten your operation. Even a broken water main can render your office unusable and possibly destroy data.

Natural disasters don't always directly touch your office, but their effects may be felt there. An area power outage can render your office unusable; a nuisance even if every server is equipped with a UPS and able to do an automated orderly shutdown. Even if you don't experience any data loss, how can your office work if a bolt of lightning blows the power out?

Breakdown

Technological failures are often the easiest disasters to anticipate and prepare for. The simplest plan usually is redundancy—backups, hot-start servers, and alternative office sites are fine examples of how redundancy can help you overcome some breakdowns.

Breakdowns aren't limited to network equipment. In a heat wave, you can't run computers without air conditioning. Breakdowns don't have to mean that the equipment's actually broken, either. If a virus renders your network server unusable because you're afraid of spreading the contamination, the server is effectively broken, even if it boots up fine.

Behavior

Human-related disasters are probably the hardest to prepare for. If you know your geographical region, you can prepare for weather. If you know your equipment, you can prepare for hardware failures. How do you prepare, though, for a bad outbreak of flu that keeps half the work force of your community—including temps—home for days on end?

Technological breakdowns can, directly or indirectly, be caused or exacerbated by humans. If the backup operator hasn't been doing his or her job, then a technological problem becomes a disaster when the server's hard disk fails and you need to reload the backups. Another behavior-caused technical disaster could be unlicensed software. If the Software Publishers Association catches your company with unlicensed software on company machines, they can temporarily incovenience your operation and levy very steep fines. It's odd to think, though it is illegal, that having too many copies of Microsoft Word 6 for Windows could destroy your company, but if a disgruntled employee calls the SPA on you (the SPA gets most of its information from tips like that), then it's a definite possibility.

Key Elements of a Plan

Five things are crucial to an effective disaster plan:

- Support from upper management
- A clear purpose
- Clearly defined responsibilities for all involved
- No single point of failure
- Flexibility

These are fine words, but what exactly do they mean?

Support of Upper Management

Before anything else, you must have the full knowledge and support of upper management. Disaster planning is not something that you can prepare as a surprise for the boss. It requires too much in the way of funding and the type of insights that the boss is privy to. She may like your initiative in coming to her with the need for disaster planning, but don't even think about starting without the go-ahead from upper management.

Clarity of Purpose

Before beginning to write your disaster recovery plan, you must determine what you're trying to accomplish so that you can define what you must do and how much it will cost.

Before considering these questions, some sort of *risk analysis* is in order. What kinds of disasters are likely to strike your organization? After all, there's no point in preparing for something that isn't likely to happen. If your company is in the Midwest, landslides probably aren't much of a problem, but tornadoes could be.

Don't eliminate potential disasters out of hand without some serious thought. Things change, and events that were unthinkable ten years ago could happen today. For example, in times past, ambitious thieves mostly went after banks or drug companies. High-tech centers, such as those manufacturing or distributing memory chips, are high among the new robbery targets. If you haven't considered how you'd manage a complete loss of your entire inventory, think about it.

> **Note**
>
> Disasters don't always occur at night or on weekends, and some of them can be hazardous to people as well as to businesses. If at all possible, maintain some emergency supplies on-site, ranging from food and water to first-aid kits and common tools. A flashlight (with extra batteries) is always a good thing to have around.

What Should This Plan Accomplish? What is the purpose of the plan? Is it to keep the network going under any circumstances or just to protect the company's informational assets from going up in smoke? This may seem to be a silly question, but the answer really drives the rest of the planning. If the goal of your disaster plan is to provide unlimited security for your company's operation, you should prepare yourself to spend unlimited funding. If the purpose of your disaster plan is only to maintain data integrity, the task becomes simpler and less expensive.

Think hard before settling on a definite purpose. A lot is involved in getting a company up and running, and reproducing it when the original plan doesn't work isn't an easy task. At best, a disaster plan ensures the continuity of your company's operations, but what exactly is involved?

Maintaining Continuity. The fundamental element of any disaster recovery plan is that it should be "business as usual" as soon after the disaster as possible. Continuity isn't just about doing backups or maintaining a spare server; it's about everything all the way up to a predetermined chain of command in case the CEO dies in a plane crash. Change is exciting, but unplanned change can be disastrous to a company's functioning.

All the information you need to keep the company going after disaster strikes should be part of your written disaster plan. This includes information like home telephone numbers for employees and contractors, vendor numbers in case you need to replace equipment, a chain of command, and so forth. At least one copy of this information should be maintained off-site, somewhere accessible.

Notification Procedures. If disaster strikes your office, who needs to know about it? Everybody. Those charged with solving the problem need to get the word and fix it. Those employees who don't already know of the disaster need to know what to do about coming to work: should they take the day off, report elsewhere, or work at home if possible? If your office has a customer base, you may need to inform them if the disaster impinges on your ability to deliver products or services. (Of course, you'd probably rather not tell customers this stuff, but sometimes it's unavoidable.)

The point is not just to tell people that a disaster has occurred, but to inform them what's being done about it or what they should do. It's not nearly as bad to tell your customers, "The office has flooded, but we've got your proofs ready for pickup at another location," as it is to tell them, "The office flooded last week, so we lost your order and the work already done on it. Can you resubmit the order?"

Communication is sometimes one of the first losses to disaster, just when it becomes most important. In a nutshell, the key people to notify are

- Those charged with solving the problem
- Employees affected by the problem
- Suppliers or vendors who can replace lost equipment
- Any customers who will be affected by changes brought about by the disaster

Preserving Data. Backups are probably the first thing you think of when it comes to preparing for disaster. Have you given any thought, however, to the data your office stores that can't be backed up? Not all the important data in your office is kept on the server. Much of it is probably not even electronic. Your company might have any or all of the following documents only in hard copy:

- Employee orders (handwritten)
- Signed contracts
- Accounting records (especially from previous years)
- Software licenses

How will you recover critical hard copy documents in case of disaster? It's better to make sure that you don't have to by using redundant off-site storage or a fireproof safe.

What's Critical? Not every function is equally essential to keeping the company rolling, and the definition of what's essential may change from enterprise to enterprise, or over time. Given that you can't do everything at once, you need to prioritize. What needs to be restored first, and how fast must it be brought up to keep the company going?

What Resources Are at My Disposal? Unfortunately, what you want the disaster plan to accomplish and the resources you have available might not always match. Although it would be nice to be able to maintain an entire network at a separate site so that, in case of fire, the entire company could just switch offices and life could go on as usual, the cost and complexity of such an arrangement render it no more than a dream for most enterprises. The U.S. government spent millions on a network (the Internet) that would stay running even if large portions of it got bombed, but most of us have business managers who hide the checkbook and snarl when they see us coming. Therefore, once you know what you want the disaster plan to do, you've got to talk to your business manager or CFO to find out how much you can spend to make it do that. Once you know what you want and know how much you've got available to spend, you can either revise the plan accordingly or negotiate for more funding.

No Finger Pointing. Disaster is bad enough; ambiguous responsibilities make it worse. When creating your plan, decide ahead of time who's responsible for each recovery task and exactly what that responsibility entails. For example, say that your plan makes the administrative assistant responsible for backups. Does that mean that the administrative assistant performs backups, stores backups, verifies backups, or all of these? Is he responsible for all the backups on the network or just one server? Who's responsible for any files that users store at their workstations?

As you can see, once you start asking questions, defining the scope of responsibility gets increasingly difficult. Do it now, so that when the server dies and it's discovered that the backups were cooked on a shelf in the sun and are totally useless, you know who's responsible. Better yet, if you define the scope of the task ahead of time, then you can make sure that whoever's got the responsibility knows how to do the job properly. If you know who's storing the backups, you can train them before the backups get fried.

Determining responsibility is important not only before disaster strikes but during the recovery stage as well. If the first person in the office on Monday discovers that the server died over the weekend, what procedure should they follow? To maximize your chances of recovering from disaster, everyone in the office, not just those who created the disaster plan, needs to know what to do and whom to call when something goes wrong. This means written instructions and prior training for everybody.

No Single Point of Failure

Well-defined responsibility is important, but ensure that the success or failure of the entire plan doesn't rest on one person's shoulders. Redundancy is a good idea for all elements of a disaster plan, not just the hardware. Make sure that the plan won't fail if one thing goes wrong. This means the following:

- A chain of command exists, describing who takes over for whom if an employee dies or becomes unable to do his or her job.

- Some recent backups are stored off-site to avoid fire or flooding that destroys the originals.

- The network uses hardware that can be replaced if necessary.

You can probably add to this list yourself. The bottom line is to make sure that your disaster plan won't fail because the business manager is on vacation with the key to the backups.

Flexibility

Finally, a good disaster plan is flexible and can adapt to change. This is important because, frankly, it will have to. Companies grow, personnel come and go, and hardware changes. If your disaster plan details an excellent recovery system that's too rigid, it won't remain useful for very long.

If you've paid attention to the other three key elements, this one shouldn't be difficult. Determine exactly what the plan is supposed to do, who's responsible for what (and what that responsibility entails), and make sure that you've got a fallback position if something goes wrong. Once you've done that, test the plan and update it annually or as needed. With this kind of preparation, very little can take you completely off-guard.

Creating the Disaster Planning Team

Thus far, we've been talking about a disaster plan as though it were the creation of one person. That's not accurate at all. For a plan to be really effective, it requires several sources of input:

- The people who need to use the network

- The people who know how to fix the network

- The people who control the resources available

- The person who's in charge so that he or she can contribute an overall perspective and approve funding

How many people crowd the table—and who they are—depends on the size of your enterprise. This list might mean the official CPO, CIO, CFO, and CEO, or it might mean the *de facto* holders of the same positions. One person in your organization might fill more than one of these jobs, but no matter how responsibilities are allocated in your enterprise you really can't create a useful plan without input from all these sources. Let's look at the role of each of these players in turn.

The Personnel Manager

The personnel manager, in this instance, means the person in charge of the staff. The disaster plan needs his perspective because he is the person who knows the most about what people are doing with the network. He should know what applications the staff uses most often, what time everyone comes in (and therefore the time that it would be nice to have everything fixed by), and in general, what everyone in the office uses the network for. This should help you prioritize if time is short and you have to figure out what to fix first.

The personnel manager can help prepare the staff for disaster, too. Training is key to surviving a problem, and the personnel manager is the most likely candidate for making sure that this training is accomplished. The personnel manager should make the following contributions to ensuring that the staff are prepared:

- Clear, complete, written job descriptions

- Regularly scheduled disaster-preparation training (including cross-training so that more than one person knows how to do each task)

The Network Administrator

The network administrator is the technical voice of the disaster planning staff. Of all the people creating the plan, she's the one most likely to know what recovery hardware and software are available, how much it all costs, and how to research other possibilities. Although the network administrator isn't likely to know everything about all company assets, she can help the business manager (whose role is described later) with details like preferred vendors and the computer needs for an alternative site.

Keeping tabs on the components of each machine on the network is another part of the network administrator's job, and this kind of information can prove valuable to the planning process. If, for example, the main server has an IDE controller, there's no point in buying a SCSI tape backup system for it unless you also purchase a host adapter. If this seems like an obvious point, think again. At one company I know of, the business manager purchased two new hard drives and controllers without first checking with the network administrator to see what slots were open in the servers those hard drives were for. When the day came to replace the hard drives, one of the servers had no VL-Bus slot available, rendering its new controller useless.

The network administrator must also work as the voice of reason. As the person who presumably has the most computing and networking knowledge, she has to explain to the others on the team why it's not practical to replicate all directories onto another server via a modem or what the current capacity limits for tape devices are. This kind of technical advice is vital to both the success of the plan and the network administrator's sanity. Much of the responsibility for developing and implementing the plan will likely rest on her shoulders.

The Business Manager

The business manager might have to act as another kind of voice of reason. As the person with the best idea of the company finances, the business manager has to take the pricing information that the network administrator provides and balance it against how much the company can spend on a disaster plan. Although it would be nice to believe that there's no limit to how much your company is prepared to spend on this worthy cause, that simply isn't practical. There's no point in the company running short on operating expenses in order to over-prepare for disaster—it's the job of the business manager to make sure that this doesn't happen. The personnel manager wants to make sure the staff is able to work and the network administrator wants to keep the network going, but the business manager is responsible for making sure that the company doesn't go broke fulfilling these goals.

Part of not going broke in the face of disaster lies in making sure that appropriate insurance covers the possibility. The business manager should bring all relevant insurance information to the meeting, including coverage data for the following :

- Casualty claims (from both employees and customers)
- Property damage claims
- Business interruption claims

The business manager can provide other information that's useful to the disaster plan. As the person in charge of purchasing, the business manager should have some kind of inventory of the company's hardware assets—even if the network administrator knows what's in each machine, she may not have a comprehensive list. Why does this matter to a disaster recovery plan? Two reasons, actually. First, a hardware inventory makes it easier to know how old all the hardware is and prepare accordingly. Second, a hardware inventory is useful for knowing what you've got around to fix the network or individual

PCs. To keep the list accessible in case of network disaster, don't keep it in a database on the server—an erasable whiteboard or chalkboard works better—and a copy of the complete list should be stored off-site and updated periodically.

The Boss

The boss, whether the company owner or just the general manager at your site, is ultimately responsible for what happens at your installation. He should have a good, broad view of the needs of network users, the money that's available for the project, and the capabilities of the network staff. The other members of the team can advise, but keep in mind that final decisions lie here, as this is the person who could go out of business or be first in line for firing if an unrecoverable disaster occurs at the site.

Enough about planning for disaster—what can you do about it?

Hot and Cold Sites

In a disaster, the biggest problem might not be how to fix the problem, but rather how to continue with business as usual while fixing the problem. Some organizations aren't dependent on a nine-to-five schedule, and if a network disaster keeps them closed on Monday it might be possible to make up for it with a double shift on Tuesday. For others, especially service-providers or those who work on daily deadlines, shutting down for a day can be more than an inconvenience and a late night to catch up—it can cripple company performance. After all, if you're providing a service like a newspaper or mail order, then as soon as you can't provide the service, your customers will go elsewhere. They'll start subscribing to the cross-town paper, or order their products from a different company, and you'll have lost them.

To avoid this kind of mishap, some enterprises that cannot afford to shut down for any reason maintain a second site to move into if the original office isn't working. These second sites (obviously demonstrating the precognitive talents of their network administrators) fall into one of two classes: cold sites and hot sites.

Cold Sites

There isn't really a hard-and-fast definition for a *cold site*, but it's generally acknowledged to be a site that can be a functioning office with a little work, but isn't ready to go at a moment's notice.

Cold Site Considerations. Cold sites are the compromise between the expense and maintenance requirements of a hot site and a closed office when the network's down. As such, they've got several tradeoffs to consider.

First, maintaining a separate office isn't cheap. To get the most effective use of your investment, consider leasing a site in another building from your main office. That way, if the disaster is something building-related, your cold site won't go down along with your main office. You might be able to reduce costs by subletting the site, but only if the persons leasing it understand that your office might kick them out at any time—you're not very likely to find tenants on these terms.

Second, perform regular maintenance checks on any site equipment. If you store extra machines there, make sure that they're still there and that environmental problems like leaks or fire haven't rendered your spare office useless.

Third, plan ahead. Think about what you'll need to bring with you if you must move the office operation to the new site. Most likely, you'll need more than computers. How about telephones? Paper files? Office supplies? Find out what people use every day and see if there's any way to take it along. (Of course, if the main office burns down, you won't be able to supply the second site from the first, but most disasters that could halt work for a day or two aren't quite that destructive.)

Cold Sites in a Branch Office. You might not have to rent another office for your cold site. If your company has a branch office in the area, you may be able to accommodate your people there, at least for a short while.

I know of one company with an arrangement like this. The main office and a smaller satellite office are in the same city, not too far from each other. The local power company once had a bad line day, and the three people in the satellite office were able to pick up their machines and move to the main office. When they arrived, they plugged into the network (a 10Base2 Ethernet, same as the one at the satellite office), restored the files that they needed to the local server from their own server backups, and were ready to go.

Of course, this only worked because of previous planning:

- Both networks used the same physical topology (10Base2 Ethernet).

- The main office network had room for more nodes (bus networks are by definition limited in the number of nodes they can support).

- They had recent backups and some room on the main office's server to put that data temporarily.

- The main office had some extra space to put people and workstations.

If you've got two offices in the same area, and enough space to squeeze in some people in a pinch, this kind of cold site might work for you. If nothing else, it keeps down the cost of an extra site. It might not be fun or convenient, but at least it keeps people on the job.

Hot Sites

Cold sites are good, but they take time to set up and get operational. If your organization must have nearly no downtime in case of an emergency, you probably need a *hot site*, which is one that's ready for your office to move in and begin working immediately.

At best, a hot site should have computers, loaded software, telephones, file cabinets, and so on. It needs all the things that your office uses every day but doesn't necessarily think about. If at all possible, this equipment should be set up in the form of an office, so that almost all you need to do in order to get the office working again is to bring in the staff.

Your network should be cabled, workstations arranged, backup tapes ready to restore to the server, and so on.

Hot sites are convenient, but for most of us the cost outweighs the advantages. First, the maintenance required on a hot site is more intense than that for a cold one, because you're replicating the entire network and therefore must make sure that each day's backups (if your organization requires a hot site, it's a pretty good bet that you're backing up every day) are ready to install on the server. This kind of preparation takes time.

Second, the costs of maintaining an entire additional office are high. Your best bet might be to share a hot site with another office with similar needs, and hope that you both don't need it at the same time.

Planning a Site

Whether a hot or cold site best fits your organization's needs, you'll need to figure out what your office staff requires to function every day and how you can get it to them. If your company maintains an alternative site, that site must be able to fulfill the following functions:

- Storing copies of your company's disaster plan

- Allowing your company to function as both an administrative unit and an operative one

- Storing data backups and the software library

For this to be possible, you need to make sure that the disaster recovery plan includes the following information about the site:

- How to get into it (directions and security information)

- Names and telephone numbers of the disaster recovery team

- Preparations made at the site (to avoid duplicating effort or forgetting anything)

Preparing for Viruses

Since they started getting a lot of press about ten years ago, computer viruses have been a major concern for businesses. In 1991, I saw one office shut down its computer operations entirely for a day, because it was Michelangelo's "attack date," and they weren't taking any chances. (None of their machines had tested positive for the virus, incidentally, and all were stand-alones except for one on a line to their main office.)

The trouble is that this kind of reaction is exactly the one that virus authors are looking for. Imagine, if you were addicted to that kind of power trip, how good it would feel to know that you'd shut down a large portion of corporate America for a day, just because of a *threat*. I admire the tenacity and talent of some virus authors, but I think that writing virus programs is a totally asinine way to spend this tenacity and talent. The best way I can think of to encourage them to find another outlet for their skills is to spoil their fun. To that end, let's talk about some ways in which you can avoid virus attacks, or recover from them without much difficulty.

Understanding Viruses

Computer viruses are not supernatural. They possess no intelligence and can't possibly do you any harm unless you let them.

How would you let them? By letting an infected floppy (the most common means of infection) into your computer. A virus can only get to your system in one of two ways: during bootup or if you run the virus's program file. Essentially, your computer must access the virus program in some way in order for it to take effect. Whether this happens by booting from the floppy—even an aborted boot usually infects your system—or by running the virus program is irrelevant. (By the way, an infected floppy doesn't have to be a boot disk to infect your machine by leaving it in drive A while rebooting. Any infected disk might do the trick.)

Copying noninfected files from or doing a DIR on an infected floppy does not spread the infection. Although the virus might show up in memory after you've done a DIR on an infected floppy, it's not written to disk until you put it there.

How Does a Machine Catch a Virus?

Not everyone understands how infection works, so it's worth explaining. Suppose, for example, that I go out to a client site to fix a network. While I'm there, I borrow a floppy disk to copy some code that I want to review at home. This floppy has a boot sector virus like B1 on it, but I don't know that. I bring the floppy home, and stick it in my floppy drive. I'm not infected yet. I do a DIR and pull off the files that I need, reading them on my machine. Still no infection. I write to the files on the floppy. Not a problem.

Then, I need to reboot for some reason. With the disk in drive A and the door closed, I press Ctrl+Alt+Del to restart the computer. When the computer halts during the reboot, I notice the familiar Non-system disk message on my screen. "You fool," I chastise myself and remove the disk to finish booting.

Now, I'm infected. I've made my computer access all the files on the floppy, looking for system files to boot from, so even though none of the files were bootable, the virus took hold.

The interesting thing is that, in most cases, I still don't know I'm infected. Not all viruses take the first opportunity to wipe out your MBR, format your drive, or display cutesy messages. Viruses can lie dormant for months or even years, waiting for their trigger: a particular date, a certain number of "copy" actions, a particular key sequence, or whatever. In this case, I might not find out that I had a virus until the next Friday the 13th arrived, or until I typed the word **Reagan**.

I think that this dormant stage of viruses is what makes them so scary to many people. You trust a computer with your data, and the idea that it might suddenly turn on you and format your hard disk at an inappropriate time is more than a little unsettling. Let's talk about how to avoid this unsettling behavior.

Preventing Virus Attacks

The comparison between biological viruses and cybernetic ones has been made so many times that I refuse to make it again, but it's pretty accurate. If you're living in a germ-free environment, you won't get sick; if you're computing in a germ-free environment, your computers won't get sick. A moderately strict quarantine system helps you avoid most viral infections, without having to institute Draconian measures that your users want to circumvent. Let's take a look at some of the measures that real-world enterprises are using to prevent virus attacks.

Quarantine Servers. Today, when more than a few people work at home at least part of the time, it's impractical to forbid people to bring floppies to work, but you can insist on a quarantine period. Create a company policy requiring people to drop disks off for checking when they first bring them in and before sticking them into a floppy drive.

Then it's up to you to virus-scan the floppies as quickly as possible. Do it early in the day if you can so that people don't start ducking the floppy bin because of delays in getting to use their data. If you've got an extra stand-alone machine that you can use as the virus-checker, do so. If not, just run the virus checks on any machine that you know is clean. If the scanner detects a virus, clean it.

If you follow this procedure for every floppy that comes in the door of your office, you should be able to prevent most virus attacks.

Educate Users. Educating your users about virus attacks goes a long way toward preventing virus attacks upon your network. Tell them what viruses are, where they can come from, what they can do, and how the measures you're instituting will prevent infections—but only with help from them. Instituting a mandatory disk-scanning program, for example, won't help at all if no one but you understands why you're doing it.

Users should know to do the following:

- Always open the disk drive before booting so that boot-sector floppies can't infect the hard disk MBR.

- Write-protect floppies that they don't need to write to, so the floppies can't get infected.

- Do not turn off terminate-and-stay-resident (TSR) scanners, even during floppy formats.

- Scan any programs that they download from BBSs before running them (especially game BBSs that cater to hackers).

With rare exceptions, the users on your network are not out there to ruin your day. If you tell them how to avoid infecting the network's machines and you explain why it's important, chances are they'll cooperate. If you act as though they should already know the reasons, you're more likely to meet resistance.

Running Effective Virus Scans

You can perform a real wall-to-wall search for viruses on a machine if you do it right. First, before scanning a machine's hard disk, format a floppy to be a system disk and then copy your favorite virus scanner onto the floppy. Next, *cold boot* (turn the machine off and then back on) from the floppy to restart the machine. Then run the virus scanner. Why cold boot the machine first? Some viruses can fake a reboot unless you've actually turned the machine off.

Second, make sure that you update your virus scanner regularly. Most makers of anti-virus software run BBSs of updated virus signatures. Download these on a regular basis. Remember, there's no generic "there's a virus here" signal; most scanners work by looking for signatures belonging to specific viruses. Even if it's a common virus, your scanner can't find it without knowing how to look for it.

Another reason to update your virus scanner's signatures regularly is to avoid false alarms. One government shop was preparing a number of black-and-white graphics for a presentation and had a virus checker running in the background. When the graphic artists began reading one file into memory, it set off the virus checker because the data pertaining to the large chunks of black contained long strings of 0s. The virus checker hadn't been updated for a while, and it identified the strings of 0s as a virus signature. The artists, a fairly computer-literate bunch themselves, had a heck of a time convincing the computer security types that the file itself might be setting off the virus scanner. It took several days to get the virus checker updated, but when the file was reread on the machine with the updated virus scanner, the alarm no longer went off.

Removing Viruses

This topic is covered in detail in chapter 19, but there are a couple of points worth reiterating:

- If you are running a virus scan under Windows 3.x, then always run the scan from DOS, not from a DOS prompt in Windows. If, however, you are working in Windows 95 or Windows NT, never use a 16-bit virus scanner; you should only use a 32-bit virus scanner.

- Boot sector viruses cannot infect program files; program viruses cannot infect the boot sector (the only viruses that can infect both are called *polymorphous viruses*). In the PC world, almost no viruses can infect a data file.

- If the virus scan detects a virus, stay calm. Do not immediately turn off your computer, as it may never boot again (this isn't a certainty, but it is a possibility). Before turning off your computer, make sure that you have a clean bootable floppy around and have backed up any vital files on the drive.

If you follow these rules, you'll detect more viruses and hurt yourself less trying to remove them.

Data Loss Planning

Preparing for data loss isn't very difficult and doesn't have to be expensive, but it's not always the top priority for either network administrators or their managers. There might be a feeling that, if the network is functioning properly, there's no reason to plan for data loss, but it doesn't take much imagination to think of plenty of situations in which you might need data backups even if the network is running fine:

- A disgruntled employee enters **c: erase *.*** from the command prompt before leaving, and blows away every file on the server.

- A virus wipes out the server's master boot record (MBR).

- Someone formats a disk and specifies the server's drive rather than their local floppy drive.

- Part of the building floods and destroys a server.

Malice, mistake, or mischance can destroy your company's data, and that's without even taking routine hardware failures or overwritten files into account.

You can prepare for data loss on your main server using either (or both) of two approaches: *dynamic data replication* of some sort (such as disk mirroring/duplexing or directory replication) or a *backup plan*.

Dynamic Data Replication

You have learned that there is not a lot of planning involved with duplicating your data as it's written: you decide how much protection you need, and then balance that against how much you can afford (although hard disks are getting cheaper all the time, any kind of redundancy requires an additional investment, and not all operating systems support RAID without additional software) and what kind of performance degradation you can live with. Once you've chosen the method that's right for you, that's pretty much the end of the story.

Backing Up

Even if you're dynamically replicating your data, a backup plan isn't dispensable. Although it's not as necessary for data integrity, a backup plan can be a useful archiving tool. Moreover, because many companies can't afford the hardware investment inherent in RAID, or the network degradation inherent in replication, backups are the only option for preventing data loss.

Chapter 17, "Backup Technology: Programs and Data," discussed the various kinds of backup hardware and software at your disposal. Armed with that information, you know what combination best suits your needs and your budget. At this point, we can tackle the question of how to put this backup hardware and software to best use in a backup plan.

Creating a Backup Plan. When thinking through the backup plan for your network's server or servers, ask yourself the following questions:

- Which data are most important?

- How much protection is too much?

- Who can perform the backups?

- Where is it safe to keep the backups?

- How will I test the backups?

- What kind of archiving is necessary?

- How can I make the backups easiest to do?

Your answers to these questions should help determine how stringent your backup plan needs to be, who's going to be involved, and how you're going to make sure the backups work down the line.

Which Data Matter Most? Backup plans are about data, but not all data is equally crucial. You've got limited time and money to spend protecting your company's data, so make sure you're protecting the right stuff.

Look at the distribution of data in your office and consult with the CEO and others who use the data. Which data are vital to the survival of the company? Protect that first. Which data are important but can be re-created without too much difficulty or expense? Which data are important more for historical purposes (like files containing old memos) than for immediate use? Which files are easily recovered if lost? This is not to say that you *shouldn't* back up all data whenever possible, but given a choice between backing up the application server holding only a few programs or the server holding all your accounting files, the latter should be backed up first.

Are You Protecting Too Much? If the concept of too much data protection sounds odd, think of this: what happens to network performance when the file server is busy doing something? It gets slower, right? Therefore, even knowing that if the server goes down at 3:00 PM you might lose all the data entered since yesterday's daily backup at 10:00 PM, you might not want to run continuous backups all day. For that matter, because a lot of backup software can't back up open files, you couldn't get a complete backup even if you ran backup after backup all day.

You can experience data loss even with the most complete backup system imaginable. The key here is to figure out how much you can afford to lose and then balance that against how much effort you're willing to put into data preservation. For most of us, a daily backup is good protection. If your enterprise's needs demand more frequent backups, consider another form of data protection, such as directory replication or disk mirroring.

Who Does the Backups? Backups are too important to say, "Some time during the day, somebody stick a tape in the drive and turn it on." Backups done under such circumstances are apt to be done haphazardly or not at all. To avoid data loss, you need to make sure that you allocate the responsibility ahead of time and teach whomever is responsible how to do the backup and make sure that it's complete.

The person doing the backups may determine to some extent when it gets done. Much backup software has a timing mechanism built into it so that you can delay backups to a time when network activity is at its lowest. If your package does not have such a mechanism or you're having trouble getting it to work properly, you may want to assign the task to someone who's there earlier or later than most people, so that backing up files doesn't slow down the network. In general, though, you should arrange for backups to be done when no one is accessing the server. As noted previously, most backup software can't copy a file and flip the file's archive bit when the file's in use.

Protecting the Protection: Storing and Verifying Backups. A damaged or corrupted backup is as bad as having no backup at all. Therefore, it's vital that you store the tapes, cartridges, or disks containing the archived files somewhere safe; also, test them periodically to make sure that you can restore them.

What's a good storage place? Well, the basics are simple: if you wouldn't like the temperature and humidity of the storage area, your backups probably won't, either. Electronic media do not like direct sunlight, extreme heat or cold (although cool temperatures are all right), or extreme dampness. If you keep your backups on-site, normal office conditions should be good for them, as long as you don't place them on sunny windowsills.

Your enterprise might have particular security needs relative to backups. If your data is particularly sensitive or liable to theft, then locking up the backups either on-site or at a secure location is a good idea. If you must lock up backups, keep the number of keys to a minimum, but make sure that a spare is available. The middle of a crisis is not the appropriate time to find out that a key fell off your keychain, so you have to bring in a locksmith on short notice.

Always label your backups with the date, source server (if you have more than one), and the type of backup. Further labeling is necessary if your server has more than one drive or if you're in transition between two types of backup software. For example, the backup made on July 15, 1995 from server ACCOUNTS might be labeled the following way:

07/15/95 Full Backup of ACCOUNTS (Backup Exec)

From this, you know how complete the information on the tape is, how recent it is, which server it belongs to, and which software must be installed to restore the backup.

Some organizations update the information on the backup label every time the media is rewritten, and some name media only once but keep a schedule of which tape is being used for a particular backup. Whichever method you use, make sure that you can quickly and accurately determine the tapes that you need to restore your data following a disaster.

Practice Restorations. It's a good idea to practice restoring data from the backups. Practice determines that you're sure of the restoration procedure and can do it with confidence when you really need to. More importantly, this practice confirms that the backup works. Although the "verify" feature that some backup software has is useful for telling you that what's on the tape after the backup matches what's on the hard disk, don't trust any verification totally until you've successfully restored files from the backup. After each backup is complete, choose a file that won't have changed in the interim, and see if you can restore it to the drive from the backup medium. If the test is successful, you can feel much more secure that the backup is good.

Archiving Old Backups. How many generations of backup tapes do you need? Depending on the kind of data that your enterprise produces and the likelihood that you'll need to restore old data, you may need to keep previous generations from as few as two previous backups or from as many as six months' worth of backups—even more than six months' worth for organizations using a backup system to archive seldom-accessed data for the purpose of saving hard disk space.

Keeping lots of archives has a few disadvantages:

- More generations of backups require more media and more storage space.
- Choosing the right tape for restoring can be trickier with more tapes to choose from.
- Tape rotation may be more complicated.

For some installations, however, the advantages are more important:

- You can restore files deleted several generations ago but only recently discovered to be missing.
- You have increased flexibility of restoration.

These advantages are more than hypothetical. Some information, like annual reports, might only be referred to once a year. If the file that these are in gets corrupted, will you be able to re-create the data? Or your art department might have created a series of drawings for a company publication; once the publication's out the door, everyone can forget about those drawings...until the next edition of the publication is due a year later and the art department finds that the drawings are gone. As you can see, archived backups can save your neck in some situations.

If you're going to keep many generations of backups, organization is crucial. You might consider keeping one series of tapes in the active backup file and another series in an archive file, so that you're not trying to manage tape rotation for fifty or a hundred tapes. If you've got more than one server's backups to maintain, organization and good labeling is even more important.

One final note on archiving: magnetic media doesn't keep its data forever. After a while, the data on the tapes or cartridges will fade. To keep your archives useful, cycle the tapes when the archives expire and format when recycling an old tape.

Making Backups Easy. No matter how good your backup plan is, it won't get done if you don't make it easy. That means plenty of easily accessible tapes, good training for each person doing backups, and backup software with a good interface. Whoever does backups should have a work area close to the server, if possible. If your server is in a separate room, try to give the backup person a work area not far from it.

Timing also plays a part in backup programs that are successful. The shorter the interval between backups, the more likely it is that the person doing them will remember, especially at first. (There are limits to this, of course—once a day is probably the shortest desirable interval between backups.)

Don't Skimp on the Software

You'd be surprised how much difference your choice of backup software can make. If your backup software has useful error messages and is easy to manipulate when something isn't working right, then the backups will get done even if there's a problem because the problem will be easy to fix.

I know a network administrator who recently purchased a good backup package with a very confusing interface—it wasn't a GUI, was arranged differently from the backup software on the other servers and was generally difficult to use and even more difficult to fix. One day, the person doing the backups noticed that the scheduling part of the program wasn't working right, and that it wouldn't accept the next tape on the schedule. She notified the network administrator, but a number of things kept him out of the office most of the time for several weeks, and he didn't have time to fix the problem. No one else in the office knew the software, so the problem remained. You can probably guess the ending. The hard disk on that server crashed one day, and the only reason that it wasn't a total loss was that some people working from that server noticed that the disk sounded funny and copied some working directories to their local drives fifteen minutes before the hard disk was silent forever. Some data was still lost, however. As you can see, there were two culprits here: a backup program with a lousy interface, and a single point of failure—only one person knew the software, and he didn't fix the backup problem in time.

Implementing and Following Up on the Plan

Once you've drawn up the basis of your backup plan, you get the ever-entertaining task of making sure that the plan is carried out. Whether you're the person doing backups and maintaining archives is irrelevant—you've got to keep an eye on the plan and make sure that it really protects your enterprise's data as well as you'd envisioned. Implementing and following up on your backup plan involves several different tasks.

Post a Schedule. Post a backup schedule—a written one, not a mental one. Every time that you (or whoever) performs a backup of the server, write down the date, the tape used, whether the backup verified successfully (aside from normal anomalies, of course), and your initials. Keep this schedule somewhere highly visible, like on the wall above the servers or a shelf above the desk of the person responsible. The purpose here is twofold: first, it encourages the person doing the backups to be extra-careful about making sure that they're done, and second, it means that you always know when the last backup was done (not just when it was supposed to be done), as well as what type of backup it was, and whether it was good. Thus, when the server crashes, you can tell at a glance exactly where you stand.

Take time to design your backup schedule well. Make sure that, just from looking at it, you get an overview of the backup scheme (this saves you from continually reminding people) and can see exactly where you are in the backup process. Each backup should have its own entry, with a place for the backup operator to sign off and verify that the backup is ready for restoration.

Test the System. Make sure to do trial runs periodically. Restore unchanging files from the backup, to make sure that you know how to do it and to check that the files restore properly.

Keep Backups Handy. Even if you keep some backups off-site for safekeeping, keep the most current one on-site (unless this is totally impossible for some reason, such as a security concern). Although you don't want every copy of your data to go up in smoke if the office burns down, you also don't want to make restoring backups any more difficult than necessary. Keep the most recent backup readily available, and the second-most-recent can stay in storage in case something destroys both the original data and the most recent backup.

Know Where Your Data Is. Keep aware of changes in the whereabouts of your organization's data. In January, the server by the printer might hold little important data, but by August, its data load could change enough to require daily backups. Admittedly, if you're the network administrator you aren't likely to be totally surprised by this kind of change, but you might not immediately think of it as a reason to change the backup plan. While you're thinking about which server's got the important data, don't forget to monitor disk size and adjust your backup system accordingly.

Keep Up with the Technology. Next, keep an eye on the available technology. Just because something works extremely well one year doesn't mean that a better solution couldn't come along later. For example, one company began its backup program in the late 1980s with a Bernoulli box. The box was marvelous in its day, but a couple of years later they had replaced their server's 325M (remember, this was a few years ago) hard drive with a 1.2G monster. 90M Bernoulli cartridges weren't going to be much help with something that big, and the cartridges were kind of unwieldy, so the company purchased a 2G tape drive. The new tape drive was the greatest thing since sliced bread for a couple of years, but recently the company replaced its 1.2G hard disk with a 4G disk. To keep backups on one tape, they've purchased a 4G DAT backup system.

The scariest part is that the 4G tape drive cost about as much as the original Bernoulli box, and the 4G DATs are much cheaper than the 90M cartridges were. As you can see, if you don't keep up with hardware and software trends, your system can suffer for it.

Summary: A Sample Disaster Scenario

The following scenario is based on a fictitious small company, but one that bears similarities to larger ones. First, this company has some disaster-planning mechanisms in place: a backup schedule and some redundant hardware. Other than that, however, they're not in a very good position to cope with problems. The situation and the problems facing the company are laid out in the following pages. Based on what you've read in this chapter, can you offer any suggestions on how Zippy's Gadget Training could survive a catastrophe with the business intact?

The owner of Zippy's, a well-known national marketer of training courses, realized one day that the company had no disaster plan prepared and that tragedy could strike at any time. Although staff members backed up their file server every day, the backups were stored on-site so that anything that damaged the office could damage the backups as well. Those backups comprised the entire disaster plan.

Zippy's is not a large company. Its staff consists of the owner, the business manager, a network administrator who also assists the business manager with purchasing, a coordinator who makes all the hotel arrangements for the classes, and a part-time receptionist. One day, the owner called a meeting of the business manager, network administrator, and coordinator. "Look," he said, "I know that everybody's busy, but we need to make sure that if I get sick, or the office gets hit by a bolt of lightning, or the server dies, that the company doesn't go up in smoke. Everybody take a week and come back with the information I'm asking for."

The owner asked the following people for various things:

- The coordinator to describe what she and the receptionist did each day, what equipment they used, and how much data they stored on the server each day

- The network administrator for a list of the hardware on the network, including printers, computers, cables, network cards, and so on; this list needed to be specific about interface types and what was inside each computer

- The business manager for a list of all software on the network and the license numbers for this software, an estimate of how much it would cost to get the office going again, and information about any equipment-related insurance already in place; if possible, the business manager was to look into the idea of an alternative site for the company

Everyone came back a week later with their information. The coordinator began, "I'm putting the bulk of the data on the server, as far as I can tell. All the hotel and travel information is there, as well as a complete list of our clients. I add to the hotel information just about every day, but the client list only changes every couple of months when we pick up a new client at a show. Also, I asked the business manager, and she says that all the accounts are stored on her local machine, which she backs up every night.

The owner nodded and turned to the network administrator, who said, "We've got one 486 workstation with 16M of RAM for each of us, and that spare 386 that we don't use since we upgraded the receptionist's machine. The hard drives on the workstations are not at capacity; most people have about 100M left because we got those big drives when the price had just dropped again. All the machines are two years old, the same age as the company, except for the 386, which you owned before and donated to the cause.

"The network is a 10Base2 bus topology, and everyone's using WunderLAN network cards. The main laser printer is connected to the file server. So far, our client/server Lightning LAN network operating system is holding up well for our needs, but I'd like to get another backup program. The tapes are fine, but no one knows how to back up the server except me, and the interface is horrible, so it'd really be hard to teach anyone."

"Not a bad idea," responded the boss. "What does the business manager have to report?"

"We've got enough licenses for the word processing program, but we need to get another one for the call-management program that the coordinator's using because the receptionist helps her organize calls and sometimes uses the program at the same time. The property insurance covers all the machines and office equipment (and it's all still under warranty for another three years), but we have no liability insurance in case anyone gets hurt on the job, and there is no insurance protecting us from losses incurred from having to shut down the office.

"Opening the office at an alternative site looks kind of tricky, but there are a couple of ways we might manage it. The cost of renting and equipping another office to move into if this one becomes unusable—floods or whatever—is far more than we can afford. There's another option, though. A company housed in an office building not far from here isn't using all of its suite, and we could rent the couple of rooms that aren't being used as our alternative site. We'd have to bring working computers and telephones (they'll let us use their printer if we chip in for paper and toner), but at least we'd have a place to run the office from. I can get a good price on the rooms as long as we're using them only as a temporary site, for a week or so."

The owner leaned back in his chair. "Okay," he said, "it looks like our situation is this: we've got a lot of data being updated every day and backed up every day. Our office equipment is new and still under warranty—that's good. We have a spare workstation if one of the PCs dies, but no spare server. The network is a type that, although prone to failures, is relatively easy to recable if we're all in one room or close to it. As far as I can tell, our biggest problems are these:

- The backups are stored in the office, so anything that ruins the office could ruin the tapes.

- We don't have an alternative site in place.

- We have no liability insurance.

- We have no spare hardware, except what we could cannibalize from the 386.

- Only one person knows how to do backups and restore them.

- There's no one officially in charge except me.

- We don't have any notification scheme in place to tell anybody in the office about a disaster or what they should do if there is one.

"Based on this information, what should we do to keep our office running if something happens?"

The rest of the meeting doesn't need to be recorded because only the end result is important. To solve the identified problems, the following actions were taken:

■ The two most recent backups were stored in the office; the others were stored at the office where the company decided to rent two rooms for a cold site.

■ The business manager consulted with their insurance company and purchased liability insurance.

■ The network administrator purchased a spare hard drive and spare network interface card (those being relatively inexpensive but crucial spare parts).

■ The network administrator researched and purchased backup software with a friendlier interface and taught the receptionist how to do backups. To keep her abilities sharp, the schedule was changed so that the receptionist did the backups.

■ The boss, if anything should happen to him, put the business manager in charge.

■ Everyone's telephone number, insurance information, and all backup and disaster recovery procedures were included in a disaster plan.

Zippy's disaster plan followed the template in figure 21.1.

DISASTER RECOVERY PLAN

Prepared by: Last Updated:

Corporate Contact Information:

Name	Position	Home/Alt Telephone Number	

Insurance Information:

Type of Policy	Policy #	Name of Agent	Telephone Number

Backup Information:

Name of backup administrator

Location of most recent and second-most recent backups:

Location of backup archives

Hardware Information:

Location of spare hardware inventory

Location of installed hardware inventory

Location of spare parts

Client Information:

Company Name	Contact Person	Telephone Number	

Vendor Information:

Company Name	Item	Contact Person	Telephone Number

Emergency Information

Location of first-aid kit

Hospital #

Fire Station #

Police Station #

Figure 21.1

This disaster plan template identifies some of the basic information that your plan should include. Based on your company's needs, you may change some entries or add others.

Chapter 22

Network Preventive Maintenance

A network is a collection of electrically-powered pieces of equipment, connected via cables, and running programs. In order for the network to work properly, every piece of the network must work properly. *Network preventive maintenance* (*NPM*) is concerned with anything that can be done to prevent any component of a network from failing.

A network is not just computers; therefore, NPM is not just concerned with blowing dust out of PCs. Each component of the network (cabling, servers, workstations, peripherals, and so on) has its own special usage and maintenance concerns that must be dealt with in order to provide maximum network reliability.

While proper preventive maintenance of any sort provides the opportunity to detect and correct problems before they become failures, it cannot prevent all failures. No amount of preventive maintenance would have saved the *Titanic*. Similarly, if you are driving down the road, then suddenly close your eyes and let go of the steering wheel, you will crash no matter when you changed the oil, washed the windshield, checked the brakes, or had a tune-up. I don't believe anyone thinks that proper maintenance makes an automobile last forever. All good automobile maintenance can do is provide maximum utilization with minimum downtime for the life of the car. Just as no car drives forever, no network runs forever. All a good NPM program can do for your network is detect and prevent more problems than if NPM were not done. No NPM program can possibly detect and prevent all failures, and eventually any network will have to be replaced.

The NPM program itself does not determine the reliability of the system—the quality of the system is the most significant factor. A low-quality system requires more preventive maintenance than a high-quality system, and since preventive maintenance cannot detect and prevent all failures, a low-quality system usually has more failures than a high-quality system no matter what preventive maintenance program is in place. You never get the same reliability from a used Yugo with 150,000 miles on it that you get from a new Mercedes, no matter what kind of preventive maintenance is done to the Yugo. Therefore, the results of any NPM program depend on the quality of the network itself. This means more than just hardware components—a network is a collection of hardware and software, all connected somehow. The quality of the software, connections, and how everything is assembled has to be taken into account when assessing the overall quality of a network. The best NPM program in the world is for naught if your cable plant is punched down with a pocketknife, your PCs are second-hand clones, you use only discount software or shareware, every time you install any software you do it differently, and your network documentation consists of a folder holding user's guides for *some* of your computers. The quality of the network is determined not only by the quality of the items you buy, but also by the quality of the effort made to install and keep track of these items.

There are three things that need to be done before you'll have a successful NPM program:

1. Do it right the first time.

2. Duplicate it the same way every time.

3. Document everything.

The following sections explain "The Three Ds" in detail.

Do It Right

This idea is so trite that it's almost useless. Even when it's stated as, "If you have enough time to make it right, you have enough time to do it right in the first place," most people hear the idea without really understanding or believing it. I have never heard of any study that has shown it is more effective and cost-efficient to fix a problem than to have done it right the first time. It is my experience that 99% of the things I do right continue to work, while 99% of the things I do wrong eventually fail. I have found that if I do something well today, I may have time tomorrow to do what needs to be done tomorrow. But if I do that thing poorly today, I have to not only do tomorrow's work tomorrow, but also redo today's work. It doesn't take long before the day arrives that I spend all my time redoing previous work.

(This means doing it and testing it myself. I won't say that something works until I've installed and tested it. I don't care if it is "supposed to work," "could work," or even "has worked" in the past. I've been burned too many times—by incompatible drivers, old DLL files, different versions of the hardware, defective equipment, and just plain old lies from the manufacturers—to make a commitment based on anyone else's word. Actually, no one who has worked with PCs for very long puts much faith in "The manufacturer says it will work" or "According to the spec sheet, we should be able to do this.")

The trick, of course, is knowing what "right" is. With all the new equipment and software that comes out, it is almost impossible to keep up with the various ways that new systems can be installed, set up, configured, and run, let alone the possible ways to make these systems interact. Add to this the fact that there is not necessarily just one way to do things right, and the mandate to "do it right" appears practically impossible.

Fortunately, there is a way to proceed even if you're not 100% sure that you're doing things exactly right—duplicate what you do.

Duplicate It

Do whatever you are doing the best way you know how, and then duplicate it whenever possible. This is one of the most powerful and least utilized tools available. Doing something the same way every time benefits you in two significant ways, even if you're not doing that thing right:

- Quicker and more thorough testing of your configuration

  By doing something the same way each time, each installation is testing the same configuration. If you do it differently each time, then you have single installations testing their own configurations. For example, if you install the same piece of software the same way on 20 workstations, you end up with one configuration being tested by 20 workstations. If you install the same software differently on the 20 workstations, you have 20 configurations being tested by one workstation each—this is not as beneficial. The more testing you do, the quicker problems should show up and the sooner you should be able to make things right.

- Easier fixes and upgrades

  If you find you need to fix something or upgrade it, it's far easier to figure out how to do it for one configuration than it is for multiple configurations. Fixes are inevitable because nothing is perfect, and upgrades are inevitable because technologies keep changing. Implementing a fix or upgrade on a unit is sometimes more difficult than installing something from scratch. Where you can decrease the difficulty is in subsequent implementations. If the second unit that needs a fix or upgrade is the same as the first, it's just a cookie cutter procedure. If, on the other hand, the second unit has a different configuration, it can be as hard as (or harder than) the first implementation.

By doing it as right as possible the first time, you make things work better for longer periods of time than if you implement quick-and-dirty shortcuts. Duplicating whatever you do allows you to test your configurations more quickly and thoroughly than doing custom configurations, and it makes fixes and upgrades much easier to implement. Even if you don't do it right or duplicate it, there is a tool at your disposal that will help you maintain your network and your sanity—document your work.

Document It

The partner to my "If I haven't tested it, it doesn't work" point of view is "If it isn't documented, it didn't happen." Not having its configuration documented obviously does not stop a computer from operating. Until it is documented, though, it cannot be maintained, upgraded, or fixed.

Unless you have access to a great deal of information about each and every component of a network, I submit that you cannot maintain it. If you don't know which directory an application is in, how can you upgrade it? If you don't know what the IRQ and address settings are for the NIC, how can you configure the new network driver? If you don't know which make and model of NIC the computer has, how can you know what driver to use, let alone how to configure it? If you don't know where the station jacks are and what their numbers are, how can you move or add equipment? This information has to be known in order for there to be any maintenance of the system. It can either be done on an ongoing, systematic basis, or else be done in a panic at the last minute. One way or the other, you have to write down the information before you can make any plans, purchase any equipment, or implement any fixes or changes. Having it in your head doesn't qualify.

It is important to keep in mind that documenting a system is not a one-time affair. Just like you don't balance your checkbook once and then forget it, you should not document your network once and then forget it. You keep updating your checkbook ledger because you keep making transactions and want to keep track of the current balance. In the same way, your network keeps changing and you need to keep track of its current status. Also, just as monitoring your checkbook might make you notice that you tend to always end up with the least amount of money near the end of the month, you can track your network's problem areas by writing down all relevant information and comparing today's information to previous information. Every time your network changes, write down exactly what changed. Periodically, sit down and reconcile your documentation to make sure that what you've written down agrees with what is really out there!

I don't know of a best way to document a network, or of any program that makes it a painless process. Every time I've investigated programs that have purported to do it all, I've found them lacking in some important feature, usually difficult to use, and expensive. In the meantime, I have found it works best for me to make changes on a piece of paper, since I don't always have access to a computer. But the changes have to be fed into a computer-based data file in order for the information to be analyzed and organized. Whether the data file is a spreadsheet, database, or even a word processing document depends more on how and why I am collecting the data, and how comfortable I am with the application. Since most projects and environments allow little or no time for documentation, I do the best I can with whatever time I can allocate for it.

If you do it right, duplicate it, and document it, I think you have every reason to expect a reasonably running and maintainable network. Even if you don't do it right or duplicate it, you've got a fighting chance as long as you document what you *are* doing. The more documenting you do, the more reliable and maintainable your network becomes. The less documenting you do, the less reliable and maintainable your network becomes.

In the following sections, we discuss these concepts as they pertain to the various components of a network, and examine NPM concerns for each component.

AC Power

Every piece of equipment on your LAN requires electrical power. Even the hubs and MAUs that do not plug into AC outlets get their power from something else that does plug into an AC outlet. There might not be much you can do about the power the utility company provides you, but that increases the importance of what you *can* do.

Do It Right

Until you know you have good, clean power, you always have to factor power problems into any troubleshooting situation. How can you make sure you have good, clean power? Base this information on actual tests of your power, not someone's casual assessment. Failures caused by power problems can cost you dozens of hours of troubleshooting, as well as thousands of dollars.

Duplicate It

Make sure all your wiring circuits are equivalent. Don't mix and match circuits of different load capacities, or put twice as many outlets on one leg as on another.

Document It

Make sure you have an up-to-date floor plan that includes the electrical wiring diagram. It should indicate where the circuit breaker panel and outlets are, and should clearly show which outlets are on which circuits.

Dos and Don'ts

Don't just assume that you have good power. Until it's been tested, assume you don't. Show your concern for your LAN server and associated equipment by having a special dedicated and isolated ground circuit installed just for them.

UPS System

Your UPS system is supposed to protect your critical equipment and provide enough battery-powered runtime to allow it to be shut down properly during a power failure. As such, it typically spends 99.99 percent of its time doing very little, but then suddenly needs to be doing its job exactly right to prevent a very serious problem. Proper preventive maintenance for your UPS system is essential if you want to be able to rely on it.

Do It Right

Make sure your UPS system is large enough to handle the load of all the equipment you have plugged into it. Also, while we usually think of UPSs as providing power during a power failure, they should also provide complete protection from sags, spikes, surges, EMI, and RFI—make sure that yours does.

Duplicate It

If you have more than one UPS, keep them the same. This means the installation and maintenance procedures are the same, reducing the chance for errors. It also means that you have 100-percent swappable units. If the UPS on your most important piece of equipment fails, you can replace it instantly with the UPS from another, less-critical piece of equipment without spending a full day reconfiguring it.

Document It

Keep copies of the original invoices, and register the units for warranty purposes. Document the expected battery life and make a note on your to-do list that informs you well in advance of this date. Document all test and monitoring results, and analyze them periodically for any trends or aberrations.

Dos and Don'ts

Do line up procedures and budget dollars to replace the batteries well in advance of their expected failure date. Test the unit regularly and document the results. Don't plug any additional equipment into an existing UPS without checking the load capacity of the UPS. Dispose of used batteries safely and properly. Higher temperatures decrease a battery's life, so don't place the UPS in an unventilated and crowded cabinet.

Cable Plant

Besides electricity, the other component of the LAN that every piece of equipment shares is the cable plant. No matter how varied or large your network, everything depends upon the connecting cabling to be working at 100-percent efficiency at all times. Cabling problems are among the most aggravating and frustrating problems to deal with, but a little preventive maintenance goes a long way in preventing cabling-related problems. Since the cabling literally just lies there, once you get it right it tends to stay right.

If you only have enough budget money to test either the AC power or the cabling, get the cabling tested first. There is less that can go wrong with AC power, and almost nothing you can do about AC power problems. On the other hand, there are many things that can go wrong with your cable plant, and there fortunately are many things you can do to fix these problems. Get your cable plant tested as soon as you can, and prepare to be surprised.

Do It Right

Make sure that your cabling has the capacity for, and is designed to work properly with, the kind of network you are running. Anything less than Category 3 (Cat 3) wiring is unacceptable for today's networks. Category 5 (Cat 5) wiring is typically installed today. Also, all the wiring needs to be the same—a common problem is mixing different grades of wiring in a network. Maybe the original network was Cat 3, but some stations have been pulled using Cat 5, and the patch cords are a mixture of Cat 3 and Cat 5. Or maybe some silver-satin phone cabling was thrown in, just to make things interesting! (The silver-satin cables used for phone wires are *never* acceptable as network wiring.) According to Frank Leeds of Seitel, Leeds, and Associates, a certified cabling expert, mixing different grades of cabling creates impedance mismatches that can cause problems for your network.

The wiring itself is not the only thing that needs to be category-certified. All the connectors, punch-down blocks, patch panels, hubs, and station jacks need to have the same rating as the wiring. If you scrimp on one link in the chain, you've crippled your entire cabling system.

Of course, using all the best components won't do you any good if the wiring is not installed properly. Crossing wires, untwisting the wires too far from the connectors, or not securing connections properly can kill any cabling system. A quick survey of your wiring closets and a couple of station jacks should give you a good idea of what your whole cabling plant is like. The best thing to do, however, is to get your cable plant tested by a certified cable installation company. Each and every run of wire needs to be tested to ensure that it meets the specifications of that category level. Since this test typically includes everything from station jacks to patch panels, it eliminates the need to test each component individually and also indicates the overall quality of the installation. If the numbers aren't up to specification, you'll have to start digging in to find out if you have substandard wall plates, poor installation, or possibly even the wrong cabling.

Duplicate It

Wire all the jacks the same way. Avoid having different station jack configurations as much as possible. This is likely to confuse you, and guaranteed to confuse your users. While it is an easy fix to make, unplugging a telephone from a data jack can be avoided.

Make sure that you have specifications and part numbers for all the components of your cable plant, so that when (not if) you have to add more pulls to your plant, they can exactly match your existing pulls.

Document It

Documenting the cable plant is a classic case of "pay me now or pay me later." It is so tempting to finally get everything working, and then just walk away from it. Once it is working, it shouldn't break, so why bother documenting it? Here's why—because there is no way that your computer system and phone system will not change in the next few years. Every minute spent documenting a cable plant upon installation would have to be multiplied by ten to do the same job down the road. Besides, what better time to straighten out any problems than right after the contractor has supposedly done the job right? Trying to get a cable plant documented and fixed before any changes to it are made almost never finds a place in the time and money budgets. Consequently, future changes are usually implemented based on assumptions that bear no relationship to reality.

Once, I was involved in installing a number of servers and workstations for a client. I was assured that the wiring was already handled. When it was time to plug everything in, we found that while all the wiring and components were indeed Cat 5, all the station jacks and patch panel ports had been wired for terminal communications, not for 10BaseT Ethernet. At the last minute, then, we had to purchase and install several hundred adapters to make the system work. As if that weren't bad enough, one site had previously reconfigured their wiring so many times that none of the labels were correct anymore, and we had to find and label each run ourselves. Proper documentation of the components and station pulls would have avoided the whole problem.

Documentation should include not only a marked floor plan, but each pull should be plainly, clearly, and unambiguously marked on each station jack and its terminating end in the wiring closet. Some people even label the patch panel to hub cables, but I personally find this to be of little use, as long as you use proper wire management accessories.

Dos and Don'ts

Do assume that any cable plant—new or existing—that has not been tested and documented is out of compliance with specifications. If you have an untested plant, get it tested and documented immediately.

If you are installing a new plant, make sure that the installation contract includes a test for each pull. All the results should be provided to you. Once the contractor is done, plug in a server and carry a laptop around to each port to verify that it can connect to the server before accepting the job.

Just because the contractor can pull a wire from one corner of your building to another doesn't mean it will work. Ethernet typically is limited to 100 meters (about 300 feet) from hub to workstation. Make sure you know and stay within the limits of your particular wiring and networking specifications (see chapter 7, "Major Network Types").

Hubs/MAUs

Keep hubs and MAUs dry and clean; also, make sure that you know what all the blinking lights and switches do. If you are having a system failure that you think is caused by something in the wiring, it helps to know if the light on your hub or MAU is supposed to be flashing green or solid red to indicate normal operation.

One time, I spent almost an entire day trying to upgrade an existing gateway on a LAN. We'd installed a new gateway and shut the old one down for a week while we waited to see if the new one was going to work. When it tested okay, I upgraded the software on the old gateway and tried to reconnect it to the LAN. It just wouldn't work. I redid the installation three or four times, then I downloaded and installed patches that the vendor had said could solve the problem. Finally, in exasperation, I walked over to the MAU rack and noticed that all the ports had switches. The switch for the port this troublesome gateway was on was switched differently than the others. It turned out that the switch isolated the gateway from the token-ring network. Someone at the company had flipped it because it was their standard procedure for unused ports. I flipped the switch and everything was just fine.

Don't forget to clearly mark all units, as well as the cables interconnecting the units, with descriptive identifiers.

A rule of thumb that has solved or prevented many problems for me has been to never mix different models of hubs or MAUs, let alone different vendors. I don't care how compatible a vendor claims their unit is with your installed devices. If you can't get any more of the old units, it's time to replace everything. Life is too short to spend it trying to track down incompatibilities between different makes and models of hubs and MAUs.

Backup/Archival System

While you might get by for quite awhile without doing any preventive maintenance for your AC power, UPS, or cable plant, almost no one can survive for long without a proper preventive maintenance program for the backup system. You might still have a job after a system crash that is caused by an equipment failure, but it's probably time to dust off your resume if you have a system crash and can't restore the backups (for any reason). There are so many ways for a restore to not work, that failure to implement a comprehensive preventive maintenance program for your backup system is tantamount to career suicide.

Do It Right

Install a backup/archival system that meets your needs. I prefer a system that can back up everything, every night, unattended, but sometimes the budget isn't there for this sort of "ultimate" backup system. Whatever system and rotation schedule you have, the most important preventive maintenance you can do for your system is to understand what it does and doesn't back up, and know how to get the data back! It's amazing how many backup systems are set up and then forgotten. I've seen more than one system where an unlucky assistant was popping tapes into a tape drive as regularly as clockwork— but the software wasn't configured to back up the appropriate files, or the tape drive had stopped functioning a long time ago. Since no one knew how to restore a file, they had never tested the success of their backups, until it was too late.

One time, I set up a system to back up everything in the single volume the user had. I did a test backup and restore, documented the procedures, trained the operator, and left. Some months later, they had a crash and couldn't find all their word processing files. After much research, it turned out they had upgraded their word processor to a newer version that created a different subdirectory in the root of the volume. Their backup software was backing up only those directories that existed at the time it was installed, and all new directories were ignored.

One of the first jobs I had as a LAN analyst for a Fortune 500 company was to straighten out a problem with their backup systems: they were using name-brand hardware with name-brand software, but not getting reliable backups. I discovered that they had turned VERIFY to OFF in order to have the backup completely done before the start of business each day. I turned VERIFY to ON at seven sites, and the next morning four of the seven units reported failures. It turned out that VERIFY not only meant to verify that what was written matched what was on the disk, but actually to verify that *anything* was written. Four of the seven tape drives were defective and hadn't been writing a thing to the tapes. With VERIFY turned OFF to save time, the system was never checking to see if anything had been written to the tape at all. We fixed the drives, kept VERIFY set to ON, and adjusted the backups to only back up and verify as much as they could each night. It meant changing from a full system backup each night to a differential backup, but at least we had some idea if the backup was failing or not.

Duplicate It

Most networks don't require multiple tape backup or archival systems. If yours does, however, then by all means duplicate whatever works. Backup systems have too many complexities, quirks, and idiosyncrasies for you to wrestle with more than one type of system at the same installation.

Document It

Write down which tapes rotate in and out, and when they are to be used. Note which tapes are stored off-site. Make a list of nightly backup procedures, post-disaster restore procedures, and at least three people who are trained and tested in restoring files. Finally, document procedures for determining which files have been backed up to which tapes.

Dos and Don'ts

Don't assume that because backup software gives you no errors, everything is okay. (I ran one program from a batch file that kept automatically clearing the screen of error messages before I could read them!) The only reliable and truly meaningful test of a backup system is to restore a file or set of files. Restore at least one random file from each backup set to be sure that the backup worked. This does two things for you: it tests to make sure the backup worked, and it keeps you practiced at restoring a file or set of files in case of emergency. There's nothing as stress-inducing as having the president of the company come barging into your room, demanding to know why the files haven't been restored, as you're flipping through the manual trying to figure out how to do it. Practice makes perfect, and helps you keep your cool—not to mention your job.

Clean the heads of your tape drives as the manufacturer says to do. Most drive manufacturers provide a head-cleaning cassette and recommend a certain cleaning schedule. Write down each cleaning on the cassette's label, including the date and initials of the person who did it; leave this cassette near the tape drive so that there is no excuse for ignoring it.

Maintain a book with the backup schedule in it, providing space for initialing by the person who starts the backup and the person who tests the backup.

Workstations

Every time I think I've found a great preventive maintenance for workstations, I discover I'm breaking about as many units doing the preventive maintenance as the number of units I am possibly saving from premature failure. I thought that cleaning floppy disk drives made a lot of sense until I read an article by a drive manufacturer that stated most of the cleaning solutions being used were more destructive than just letting gunk build up. I thought that blowing dust out of the insides of PCs with cans of air was a great (albeit messy) idea, until an engineer pointed out that there was a good chance of actually forcing dust and dirt into the cracks and crevices of the electrical connectors inside the computer. Heck, some monitors require special cleaning solutions even to clean the dirt off the glass! I'm almost afraid to crack a cover anymore for fear of the damage outdoing the good.

Do It Right

Buy the highest quality computers you can, because cheap ones take more support and cause more problems than more expensive ones—not every time, but far too often to bet against it.

Duplicate It

Whatever you're buying, try to buy only one make and model and always set them up the same. Or, if you have to buy more than one type, try to minimize the differences as much as possible. Always set them up the same way. I've found a very effective way to do this is to create a working model, then copy the image of the entire hard disk up to the network. Whenever I need to install a new computer, I simply wipe out its local hard disk and copy down the master image from the network after booting up from a floppy. Afterward, I need to make only the personality changes (TCP/IP addresses, LU assignments, user or computer name, and so on). Whenever I want to make a change to my workstations, I use the master image from the network as a model, and figure out the best way to make the changes to it. Of course, this only works as long as users aren't customizing their individual configurations too much.

Document It

In my opinion, the toughest thing to do on a network is to document and track the configurations of the workstations. There are so many things to track that the effort is overwhelming. These are some of the things that you might have to take into account when planning to fix or upgrade a group of workstations: boot-up configuration (contents and specifics of CONFIG.SYS and AUTOEXEC.BAT), DOS version (and REV level), Windows version and whether all are local or not, ROM BIOS version, NIC BIOS level, whether the NIC has a BNC or UTP port or both, NIC type, available card slots, available drive bays, video card type, number of serial or parallel ports, other equipment installed (sound cards, SCSI adapters, and so on), mouse type (PS/2 port, bus card, or serial port), free disk space, serial number, user name, user location, and station jack ID. No matter how sophisticated and complete the inventorying software is, I seem to always have to go out and document something by hand. The more you can collect automatically and electronically, though, the better off you'll be. Don't expect any package to do it all for you. I recommend using the best workstation inventorying package you can afford, but understand that you'll probably have to document something the next time you consider making wholesale changes to your workstations.

Dos and Don'ts

Don't crack a case unless you really have to. Try to keep workstations out of harm's way and never lay them flat on the floor (the dirtiest and dustiest computers are those placed flat on the floor). I prefer putting all workstations on the floor in a vertical position with just the keyboard and monitor on the desktop. Make sure the workstation will not fall over or be smacked by a foot or an opening drawer.

AC Power

Put a good quality surge suppresser on each workstation, or use a UPS if you are in an area subject to frequent power fluctuations. Make sure that there are no laser printers, fans, coffee pots, heaters, or other non-workstation related devices plugged into the workstation's surge suppresser. Laser printers create severe voltage sags every time they reheat the fusing roller—this happens every 40 seconds or so, and is hard on the workstation's circuitry. Everything else mentioned is just "noisy" and is exactly what you are trying to protect the workstation from. Here's a rule of thumb: the computer, monitor, and anything required by the computer can be together, but no printers at all. The printer, even if it isn't a laser printer, should have its own surge suppresser just to be safe. Double-check that the power cord is firmly plugged into the back of each unit. The surge suppresser must plug directly into an AC outlet, not into the end of a 15-foot extension cord. If you have to run an extension cord, make sure it is as thick as, or thicker than, the cord on the surge suppresser—plug *only* the surge suppresser into it.

LAN Connection

Make sure that the station jack is securely fastened to the wall or partition. Loose "biscuit jacks" on the floor are unacceptable; they get kicked around and eventually will cause problems. The station cable must be the same category level as the main wiring. Never, under any circumstances, use silver-satin phone cord for a station cable. Double-check that the station cable is plugged firmly into the NIC. If the station cable shows any signs of wear (loose connectors or cuts in the shielding), replace it immediately. Using a frayed or defective station cable is an invitation for workstation failure.

Hardware

Use the best equipment you can talk the financial folks into buying, and purchase as few different models as possible. Purchase everything from one manufacturer if you can. (That way, you only have to create a relationship with one tech support department!) Standardize as much as you can, but realize that you'll never be able to standardize everything.

Operating Systems

Keep everyone running the same version and revision number of the operating system, even if it means removing newer versions from recently purchased computers. Better to face the devil you know than the one you don't. New versions might solve some bugs you've had to work around on the older version—but they are almost guaranteed to create new problems for which you will have to figure out solutions.

Try to keep everyone using the same version; upgrade only after complete and thorough testing of the new version. Being the first one on your block to load the newest version of any program simply means you get to be first to crash and burn. You can always spot the pioneers—they're the ones with all the arrows in their backs. Here's a rule of thumb: If a version number ends in .0, skip it. Wait for the .01 or the .1—nine times out of ten, the wait is well worth the lost headaches and aggravation.

Applications

Everything that is true for operating systems is true for application programs. To make life simpler, more maintainable, and much more reliable, I advocate loading all applications on the network only. It's much easier to support and upgrade one configuration on the network, rather than a separate configuration on each workstation across the network. What might be lost in customizability and performance is certainly made up by reductions in support, maintenance costs, and downtime. Centralized applications should invalidate anyone's argument that the network is down too often to depend on.

Data

Users are notorious for expecting data they save on their local hard disks to be magically backed up by the network. While this functionality is available, it is neither common nor completely effortless to configure and implement. (And it never works if users turn off their computers at the end of the day!)

To prevent data loss, I try to set up all applications, whether loaded on the local drive or the network, to save by default to a user directory on the network. I let users know that this can be overridden if they want to save to a floppy or their local hard disk, but that by doing so they'll risk not having the data backed up in case of a drive problem.

Servers

I'm leery of cracking the case on a workstation, and therefore I'm practically terrified to crack the case on a file server. While dropping a screw or bending a connector on a workstation might inconvenience a user for a day or so while I get the PC repaired, the same simple error on the file server will inconvenience *me* until I get it back up and running. This is a reason to never make any changes to the file server an hour before everyone starts work. You'll end up starting your explanation of the prolonged server problem by saying, "All we had to do was…" or "It was supposed to be a five-minute job that…" Try working early on Saturday mornings instead. That gives you all day Saturday and Sunday to recover from a failure if one occurs. Other than that, the same admonitions and advice given for workstations also apply for servers.

Printers

Printers are arguably the most complex and maintenance-hungry components of a LAN. Just the fact that these devices can pick up only one piece of paper at a time, feed it through a series of rollers and guides without tearing it to shreds, and print something intelligible on it is amazing. Laser printers not only do that, but also bounce a beam of laser light off a rotating mirror, onto a drum that circulates through a cloud of carbon particles and creates text and graphics on a piece of paper. By definition, a laser printer actually prints using smoke and mirrors! Yet I find that most, if not all, printers are ignored and under-maintained. The only time they usually get any attention is when they finally fail.

Do It Right

Buy the best quality printers you can afford. Keep in mind that cheaper printers or off-brand printers can only claim to emulate the printer you know you ought to buy. "Emulate" means that an off-brand printer tries to work almost as well as the name-brand printer. I've discovered the hard way that the best way to find out what "almost" means is to have the president's assistant print out information for the president to present to a board meeting about fifteen minutes before the meeting starts. That's when you'll find out that it doesn't do landscape printing, the font spacing is erratic, the gray-shades don't work, or the graphs print only partway down the page.

Duplicate It

It's impossible, of course, to buy a new HP Series II printer these days to match your existing units. No one would be silly enough, I hope, to purchase an HP 4V and only use HP II drivers with it. So, what's a person to do? Just keep things as consistent as possible, and whenever you do install more than one of the same type of printer, configure them identically.

Document It

Never, under any circumstances, loan out the user's manual for a printer. Keep it in a safe if you have to. It is almost impossible to guess, remember, or figure out how to configure a printer. If your printer has lost its settings or someone has changed them, you'll need the manual in order to know how to reconfigure it. Knowing how to reconfigure the printer is only half the battle—if you haven't documented the working configuration, you'll have to start from scratch again. It's easy to waste half a day or more getting all the settings exactly right. Even then, invariably, someone will complain that their spreadsheets "just don't print the same anymore." In a pilfer-proof safe you should keep a user's manual and configuration listing for each printer. Woe to anyone who makes a change and doesn't document it! There's no feeling quite like having spent all morning to get a printer configured according to the latest documented configuration, then having users waltz in and say, "Yeah, now it's working like it was three months ago before Sally did something to make it work right. Please fix it that way again!"

Dos and Don'ts

How balanced is your printer sharing? Are all your printers being worked equally? Do you even have any idea how many pages each printer is printing per day/week/month? Is that old HP II still churning out all the end-of-month reports as well as the daily sales logs while the newer IIIsi idles along, producing an occasional memo or screen print? I once went to each of four laser printers and printed out the page count on Monday morning. After the fourth Monday I realized that one printer was printing over 50% of all pages printed for the company. By changing who printed to each printer, I was able to equalize the loading.

Remember that every printer has a recommended duty cycle (usually described as the maximum number of pages per month) and if your printers exceed this, you're more apt to have problems. If you have one printer doing more work than others, it makes sense to rotate them in and out of the "hot spot" so you don't have a premature failure. But to find potential problems like that, you have to know how much you are printing every month. If the configuration/monitoring software you install allows you to check a Pages Printed value, you can easily document this data. Otherwise, you need someone to do a test print and get it to you. A regular copy of the test print allows you to see if anyone is fooling with the printer's setup, too!

Keep it clean! Unlike PCs, printers really thrive and appreciate being cleaned out on a regular basis. Clean off the corona wires and get any excess paper gunk out of the feed assembly; always follow the manufacturer's recommendations.

Gateways and Routers

While it is easy to think of a LAN as just a server with some workstations and printers, it is rarely ever that simple. Most businesses require at least one connection to another system—a mainframe or mini, the Internet, or just another LAN. It is not uncommon to have a LAN connected to all three at the same time, which means that if the gateway or router device stops functioning, users are going to feel like the whole LAN is down. While most of us have had prior experience and knowledge of the server and workstations on a company's LAN, it is rare for individuals to have had formal training or education about gateways, routers, and other connective devices on any particular LAN. This situation is exacerbated by the fact that these devices are frequently installed and configured by "experts" with only cursory (if any) certification or training. Also, since these connective devices typically are plugged into something other than just another LAN, one needs to be somewhat conversant in the operations of the other system in order to really work with the device. In other words, if you don't know the difference between an LU and a CPU, you'll probably get pretty confused trying to reconfigure an SNA gateway that has just crashed.

It's not enough to have the mainframe staff tell you that the LU ID for a particular port needs to be changed from one value to another. If you don't know how to fire up the software to reconfigure the gateway, let alone how to run it, how can you possibly be expected to cope?

One time, when I was brought in to reconfigure a gateway, the controlling software required a password in order to change some simple, well-documented operating values. The gateway had been up and running for so long that the person who had last set the password was no longer with the company. What could have taken 15 minutes ended up taking several hours, since we had to completely reinstall the software with a new password. Fortunately, the system was still running and we could document all the configuration settings before we had to rebuild the gateway!

Do It Right

Realize that since the systems on each side of a connective device are changing all the time, it is unreasonable to expect one device to continue serving you perfectly over time. You usually will be notified of a need to change the gateway or router after you have made some minor change that renders the device inoperative. No matter how "right" your choice and installation of a gateway or router is the first time, the device is doing a tough job at a fundamental level of LAN operations. Pay these devices as much attention and treat them with as much respect as your file server, and you'll probably sprout gray hairs at a slower rate.

Duplicate It

By all means, use only one kind of device for each function. I use the same rule of thumb for gateways and routers that I use for hubs and MAUs: Try not to mix models, and don't ever mix vendors.

Document It

Just as with printers, you not only need to document the working configuration of gateways or routers, but have to keep documentation available that explains how to change the configuration. Trying to figure it out by loading various programs and searching Help files is a major waste of time and energy. Keep the user's manual, backup copies of programs, and a printout of the latest configuration parameters for each device in a safe place.

Dos and Don'ts

Don't take these devices for granted! They need care and feeding just as the file server does. Always follow the manufacturer's recommendations.

Summary

It's clear that a good NPM program requires much more than just following vendors' recommended cleaning and adjusting procedures. Unless your NPM program is built on a strong foundation of doing the job right the first time, duplicating systems and installations whenever possible, and documenting all configurations and procedures, it won't be effective. The three Ds can compensate for each other. If you can't get everything done exactly right, then by duplicating your work you can simplify debugging and upgrading. If you are unable to achieve duplication, then by documenting everything you do, you can understand the scope of what you're dealing with before you try to implement changes or repairs. Without documentation, you'll waste much effort during maintenance, upgrades, or disaster recovery.

Part VI

Adding Network Services

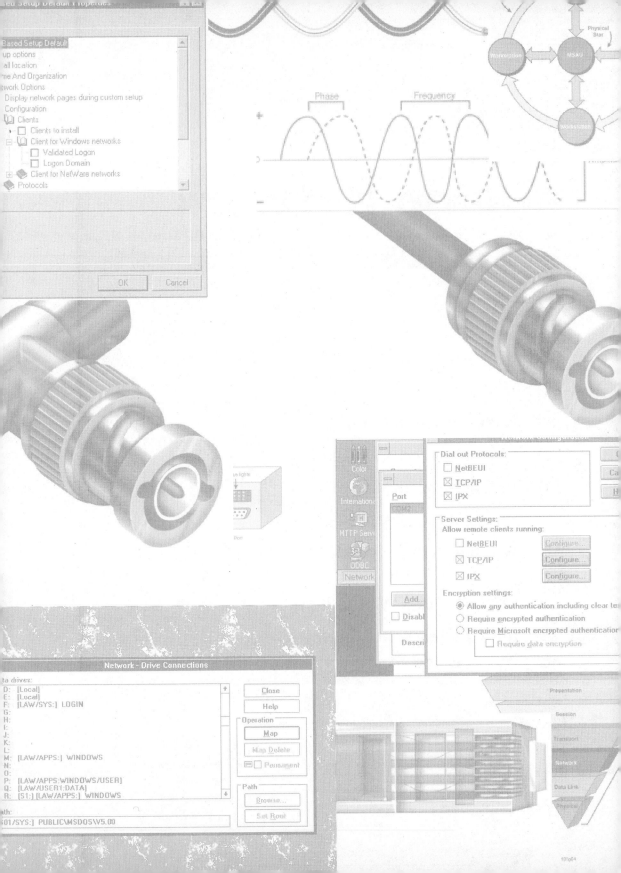

Chapter 23

Adding Network Printing

For many users, a network is little more than an elaborate device for producing print-outs. Time and effort invested in your network's printing capabilities can enhance the perception of the network, just as printing problems can tarnish the image of an otherwise perfect installation.

This chapter looks at the provision of print services on a network, covering the configuration, management, and maintenance of printers, print servers, and queues.

Networked versus Local Printing

Printers have traditionally been attached directly to stand-alone workstations. The path followed by data as it is printed is a straight one: The application running on the workstation sends data to a communications port; from there, the data travels directly to a printer that then processes the data.

As you might expect, networked printing is more complex. This is especially true in a client-server environment. The data must go from the application on the workstation, through the workstation's network interface to a server. From there it finds its way to one of an arbitrary number of printers, possibly a considerable time from when it was "printed" by the user and possibly following one of several viable paths. The data will then be processed by the printer as if the printer had been directly attached to the workstation.

Networked printing has some disadvantages. Users may not be willing to walk to a collection point that is any farther away than the end of their desk. They also may not trust the network to look after their printing needs—the rattle and hum of rollers and paper trays can be reassuring to many. Also, from the network manager's point of view, networking a printer is obviously more difficult than simply plugging a printer into the back of a PC.

You and your users need to decide before you start whether it's worth the effort. In fact, there are several compelling reasons why printing and networking go hand-in-hand.

These include the following:

- Shared printers

- More access points

- Print spooling

- Central management

- Access control

- Flexibility

These benefits are described briefly in the following sections.

Shared Printers

Perhaps the most obvious benefit of networked printing is the ability to share a single printer among many workstations. No workstation prints constantly, so why should a printer be permanently attached to it when there are other workstations around without printers?

This logic applies especially to expensive or specialized printers. A high-quality color printer, for example, may be an expensive purchase, but if it is set up on the network, it can be made available to many users at all times.

Greater Access

A printer that is not available from the network can be accessed from one point only— the workstation to which it is physically attached. Setting the printer up on the network makes it available from all network access points—that is, from all workstations.

Consider a nonnetworked printer that is connected to User A's workstation. Not only is the printer unavailable to users who do not have physical access to that workstation, but also it is unavailable to User A when she is not at her desk. Setting it up on the network is therefore of benefit to all users, including any person who may have had sole use of it in the past.

Print Spooling

An application that sends data directly to a printer must wait for the printer to finish processing the data before it can move on to its next task. To the user, this means an interruption in work—click the print button and then leave the workstation while the document is being printed. If the document is long or contains complex graphic material, the workstation may be unavailable to the user for other tasks for a considerable period of time.

The reason for the delay is generally not at the application end of things. The delay may be caused by a printer that is slow at processing the data or the communications link between, or a workstation may not be fast enough to transmit the data as quickly as the printer can process it.

Print spooling is the process of storing the data to be printed in an intermediate location. This location is rapidly accessible by the application so that the data can be written there quickly. The application (and the user!) can then move on to the next task. The data can be transmitted from the spool area to the printer at a later stage or slowly over time as the printer processes the data.

The DOS PRINT utility uses a RAM buffer as a spool area. Windows uses temporary files for the same purpose. In either case, control of the workstation is returned to the user shortly after the print request is made. The workstation may run more slowly than usual because it must now perform the additional background task of transmitting the data from the spool area to the printer.

Printing to a network printer makes even better use of spooling, in two ways:

1. The spool area is on a server rather than on the workstation. This means that it is the server's job to transmit it to the printer, so the user does not have to endure the performance degradation of workstation-based spooling.

2. The server's spool area will continue to hold the data until it has been processed. Even if the printer is unavailable or busy, the user can turn off the workstation without having to resend the data.

The printer will take the same amount of time to process the data with or without print spooling. But to the user, print spooling can mean much less time wasted on "printing."

Central Management

Putting printers on the network can mean having them in a central location, perhaps near you so that you can monitor and maintain them easily. It may also mean having them scattered across the network, close to the users who will want to collect them. In either case, the printing system that brings the data from the workstation to the printer can be managed centrally.

Access Control

You can make effective use of your network's security features to restrict access to printers to particular individuals or groups. This is possible because the spool area is on the server and access to it can be controlled in the same way as access to any other server-based service.

Flexibility

The combination of central management and print spooling can provide a considerable degree of flexibility in print management. You can add a second printer to service a busy queue, take a printer offline for upgrade or maintenance, switch a printer from a serial connection to the server to an Ethernet connection direct to the network—all without affecting users.

Printers and Interfaces

For all their differences in technology, type of mechanism, brand, and model, all printers on the market today use one of a small number of communications interfaces. The reason is simple: A printer must have an interface through which it can receive data, and this interface must be compatible with the communications interface on the computer that sends the data. There are three basic interface types at present:

- Parallel

- Serial (RS-232)

- Net-direct

The next few sections look at each interface type in turn.

Parallel

Parallel ports are designed mainly for transmitting data from computers to peripheral devices. The original IBM PC printer port was unidirectional, meaning that it was capable of transmitting but not of receiving data. That limitation didn't matter too much at first, as the aim when printing was to get the data *from* the PC *to* the printer. Some printers, however, need to talk back to the computer—PostScript printers, for example. The more recent bidirectional parallel ports allow two-way communication between the computer and the peripheral device. In addition to allowing PostScript printers and PCs to coordinate printing, the wide availability of these ports has facilitated the development of a range of peripheral devices. Ethernet adapters that plug into the PC's parallel port are one example.

Parallel ports get their name from the way in which they send a byte of data. All eight bits are transmitted at the same time, or "in parallel." Parallel ports have eight separate wires for this purpose, one per data bit. Bidirectional ports use 16 wires for transmitting data bits.

The PC's parallel port has a female connector with 25-pin sockets as illustrated in figure 23.1. The functions of the pins are listed in table 23.1.

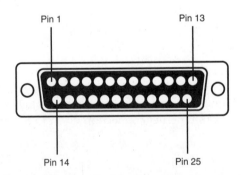

Figure 23.1

This is a typical PC parallel port.

Table 23.1	PC Parallel Port Pinouts	
Pin	**Signal**	**Direction**
1	Strobe	Out
2	Data Bit 0	Out
3	Data Bit 1	Out
4	Data Bit 2	Out
5	Data Bit 3	Out
6	Data Bit 4	Out
7	Data Bit 5	Out
8	Data Bit 6	Out
9	Data Bit 7	Out
10	Acknowledge	In
11	Busy	In
12	Paper End	In
13	Select	In
14	Auto Feed	Out
15	Error	In
16	Initialize Printer	Out
17	Select Input	Out
18	Data Bit 0 Return	In
19	Data Bit 1 Return	In
20	Data Bit 2 Return	In
21	Data Bit 3 Return	In
22	Data Bit 4 Return	In
23	Data Bit 5 Return	In
24	Data Bit 6 Return	In
25	Data Bit 7 Return	In

The parallel interface on the printer looks quite different, as can be seen from figure 23.2. It has a total of 36 contacts lined on the top and bottom of a wide slot. Pin connections vary a little from one printer to the next—consult the printer manual for specifics. A typical pinout for such an interface is listed in table 23.2. Note that unused connections are not listed.

Note

The printer parallel port was designed by a company called Centronics. Such printer ports are often referred to as "Centronics ports," while the cables which plug into them have "Centronics connectors."

> **Caution**
>
> Parallel printer cables should not be longer than two meters or so. The signal attenuation in longer cables may lead to the corruption or loss of data.

Figure 23.2

This is a typical printer parallel port.

Table 23.2	Typical Printer Parallel Port Pinouts		
Pin	**Signal**	**Direction**	**PC Port Pin**
1	Data Strobe	In	1
2	Data Bit 1	In	2
3	Data Bit 2	In	3
4	Data Bit 3	In	4
5	Data Bit 4	In	5
6	Data Bit 5	In	6
7	Data Bit 6	In	7
8	Data Bit 7	In	8
9	Data Bit 8	In	9
10	Acknowledge	Out	10
11	Busy	Out	11
12	Paper End	Out	12
13	Select	Out	13
14	Auto Feed	In	14
16	Ground		
19–30	Ground		
32	Fault	Out	15
33	Ground		
36	Select Input	—	17

DOS supports up to three parallel ports. Each uses an I/O port address to communicate with the system; an IRQ may or may not be used. The standard setups for systems with two and three parallel ports are respectively shown in tables 23.3 and 23.4.

Table 23.3	Parallel Port Configuration (Two Ports)	
Parallel Port	**I/O Port**	**IRQ**
LPT1	378h	None
LPT2	278h	5/None

Table 23.4	Parallel Port Configuration (Three Ports)	
Parallel Port	**I/O Port**	**IRQ**
LPT1	3BCh	7
LPT2	378h	5/None
LPT3	278h	None

Use a system analysis utility such as Microsoft's MSD to check the configuration of the ports in a PC. Some PCs allow these values to be set from the CMOS setup utility.

> **Note**
>
> A port that does not use an IRQ operates in *polled mode*, which means checking the port periodically, rather than allowing the port to interrupt the CPU when action is required. Interrupt-driven parallel ports—that is, those using an IRQ to communicate with the system—will give significantly better performance on NetWare print servers than those that operate in polled mode. Windows NT Server systems use interrupt mode only, so polled mode isn't an option in those cases.

Serial (RS-232)

The RS-232 (RS stands for "Reference Standard") port, also known as the asynchronous or serial port, is designed for two-way communication between a computer and a peripheral device. Figure 23.3 shows the original 25-pin form, and table 23.5 lists its pinouts. Figure 23.4 shows the newer 9-pin version, and table 23.6 lists its pinouts.

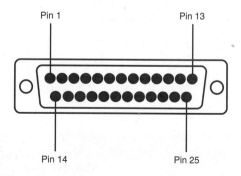

Pin 1   Pin 13

Pin 14   Pin 25

Figure 23.3

This is a 25-pin RS-232 port.

Table 23.5 25-Pin Serial Port Pinouts

Pin	Signal	Abbreviation	Direction
1	Chassis Ground		
2	Transmit Data	TD	Out
3	Receive Data	RD	In
4	Request To Send	RTS	Out
5	Clear To Send	CTS	In
6	Data Set Ready	DSR	In
7	Signal Ground	GND	
8	Data Carrier Detect	DCD	In
9	Transmit Current Loop Return	—	Out
10	(Not used)		
11	Transmit Current Loop Data	—	Out
12–17	(Not used)		
18	Receive Current Loop Data	—	In
19	(Not used)		
20	Data Terminal Ready	DTR	Out
21	(Not used)		
22	Ring Indicator	RI	In
23	(Not used)		
24	(Not used)		
25	Receive Current Loop Return	—	In

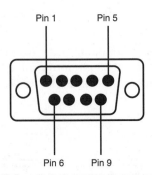

Pin 1   Pin 5

Pin 6   Pin 9

Figure 23.4

This is a 9-pin RS-232 port.

Table 23.6 9-Pin Serial Port Pinouts

Pin	Signal	Abbreviation	Direction
1	Data Carrier Detect	DCD	In
2	Receive Data	RD	In

Pin	Signal	Abbreviation	Direction
3	Transmit Data	TD	Out
4	Data Terminal Ready	DTR	Out
5	Signal Ground	GND	
6	Data Set Ready	DSR	In
7	Request To Send	RTS	Out
8	Clear To Send	CTS	In
9	Ring Indicator	RI	In

The serial interface on the printer generally uses a 25-pin connector. Table 23.7 lists the typical pinouts.

Table 23.7   Typical Printer Serial Port Pinouts

Pin	Signal	Abbreviation	Direction
1	Chassis Ground		
2	Transmit Data	TD	Out
3	Receive Data	RD	In
4	Request To Send	RTS	Out
5	Clear To Send	CTS	In
6	Data Set Ready	DSR	In
7	Signal Ground	GND	
8–19	(Not used)	—	
20	Data Terminal Ready	DTR	Out
21–25	(Not used)	—	

The PC sends data from its transmit pin to the printer's receive pin. Likewise, the printer can send data from its transmit pin to the PC's receive pin. The serial ports at both ends use the RTS, CTS, DSR, and DTR signals to coordinate signals. Tables 23.8 and 23.9 show typical cable arrangements for connecting a printer to 25-pin and 9-pin PC ports respectively.

Table 23.8   Typical 25-Pin Serial Printer Cable

PC Pin Connects To...	...Printer Pin
1	1
2	3
3	2
4	5
5	4
6,8	20
7	7
20	6,8

Table 23.9 Typical 9-Pin Serial Printer Cable	
PC Pin Connects To...	**...Printer Pin**
1	1
2	2
3	3
5	7
6,8	20

The data in the PC is in parallel form, in the sense that a byte moves around the bus eight or sixteen bits at a time. As you know from the previous section on parallel ports, transmitting data in parallel requires a complex cable that must be short. Serial communications links are often preferable to parallel links because they require fewer wires and can be transmitted over longer distances.

Serial ports convert the PC's data from parallel to serial form using a *universal asynchronous receiver/transmitter (UART)* chip. The UART also translates incoming serial data to parallel form. The 16550A UART is faster than the original 8250 version, which can still be found in many computers.

A serial port sends and receives characters one at a time at arbitrary intervals, either as they become available at the port or as the other device becomes ready to take the next one. Since the data can arrive at any time, the serial port needs to recognize when a character has started to arrive and when it has finished. This is done using a combination of mark, start, and stop bits that are sent in addition to the data bits.

Each byte is transmitted as a pattern of bits, with each bit having a value of either one or zero. The exact pattern of bits which is sent for a given byte depends on the mode settings for the serial port. The value of the byte can be transmitted using between five and eight *data* bits; another one or two *stop* bits are used to mark the end of transmission of the byte. The serial port at the receiving end of the transmission uses these stop bits to determine where the data for one byte ends and the next one begins.

An optional *parity* bit may also be sent for error-checking purposes. The serial port may be set to use *odd, even,* or *no parity.* If set to no parity, a parity bit is not sent. If parity is enabled, then for each byte transmitted, the data bits are added together. The serial port determines whether this sum is odd or even and compares it with the value of the parity bit:

- If the serial port is set to odd parity, then the parity bit should be 1 if the sum of the data bits is odd and 0 if the sum is even.

- If the serial port is set to even parity, then the parity bit should be 1 if the sum of the data bits is even and 0 if the sum is odd.

This is a little clearer if you think of the value of the parity bit as being either "true" (1) or "false" (0). If the sum of the data bits turns out to be odd, that's "true" for a port using odd parity or "false" for a port using even parity.

The following bits are transmitted for any given byte:

1. The mark bit is always 1 and is sent continuously when no data is being transmitted.

2. This stream of 1s is interrupted by a start bit, which has the value 0. When this 0 arrives, the serial port has been informed that a byte is about to be transmitted.

3. The next five to eight bits (almost always seven or eight) make up the actual byte being transmitted. The precise number of bits depends on the serial port mode.

4. A parity bit follows the data bits if parity has been enabled.

5. One or two stop bits of value 1 mark the end of the transmission of that byte.

The serial port needs an IRQ and an I/O address to communicate with the motherboard. The standard configurations are shown in table 23.10. Some systems have additional ports, but the BIOS only supports the first two. DOS can handle four at most. If your system has more than two serial ports, or if you are unsure about the first two, use a system information program such as Microsoft's MSD to check their configuration. Your PC's CMOS setup utility may also allow you to check this.

Table 23.10 Serial Port Configuration

Serial Port	I/O Port	IRQ
COM1	3F8h	4
COM2	2F8h	3

Serial ports are inherently slower than parallel ports. This is partly because of the overhead of all of those start and stop bits but mainly because of the need for the UART chip to translate data between parallel and serial form.

They have one significant advantage over parallel ports though: Serial data can be transmitted over significantly greater distances than parallel data. Serial cables can be over 15 meters long. Modems can connect arbitrarily distant serial interfaces over a telephone line.

From the print services perspective, printers tend to be near to their print servers, so distance is generally not an issue. If you can't locate a printer near the print server computer, or if no faster interfaces are available, a serial port will do at a pinch. Try to avoid using serial however—the throughput is very much slower than through a parallel connection. Unless use of the print service is extremely low, printing will be very slow and your users may be dissatisfied.

Net-Direct

Parallel and serial ports have their place in network printing. A workstation or file server can transmit data through a communications port to a printer, serving the printing needs of users at a different location on the network.

Apart from restrictions on transmission speed and cable length, such ports have one major limitation: They are designed to link the PC bus with a peripheral device, so the peripheral device can be used only by the PC to which it is physically connected. A more flexible arrangement in a network environment would allow all networked PCs to use the peripheral device.

Net-direct cards are network adapters for peripheral devices. They allow a device such as a printer to be connected directly to the network. No "host" computer is required. The net-direct adapter is in many ways more like a stripped-down workstation than a conventional communications interface. It has its own processor and RAM. It receives data from the network and passes it on to the peripheral in the "raw" format of the peripheral device itself. There is no need for the type of parallel-serial-parallel data transformation used by serial ports.

Net-direct adapters are available as options for many modern printers. Printer manufacturers produce adapters to suit their own range of devices, so there is no standard model or configuration. In general, they are available with a choice of network connectors (AUI, BNC, or RJ-45) and connect directly into a special socket on the printer. They are configured from a client PC on the network using proprietary software.

Definitions

Print queues and print servers are the nuts and bolts of networked printing. The next few sections define some essential terms. Others are defined in context as they arise throughout the chapter.

Print Queue

The server-based spool area described earlier is known as a *print queue*. It is a special directory, usually on the SYS volume.

Under NetWare 3.x, the print queue is registered in the bindery and the name of the queue directory is the queue's object ID with the extension QDR. So, for example, if you create a new print queue and it has an object ID of 27060024, the corresponding queue directory will be SYS:SYSTEM\27060024.QDR. NetWare 4.x print queue directories are assigned a number at random when they are created.

Note

Refer to chapter 8, "Novell NetWare," for more information about the bindery (NetWare 3.x) and NetWare Directory Services (NetWare 4.x).

Each NetWare queue directory contains two hidden configuration files with names based on the first four digits of the print queue ID. So if the print queue ID is 27060024, the hidden files are Q_0627.SYS and Q_0627.SRV.

> **Tip**
>
> NetWare saves deleted files on disk until the disk space that they used is required. This allows deleted files to be recovered using the SALVAGE utility. This is not necessary for files stored in print directories, so you can save some space by flagging the print queue directories on your file server to be purged automatically. Execute the following commands at the DOS prompt:
>
> ```
> map t:=sys:system
> flagdir t:*.qdr p
> ```

Print Job

When a user requests a printout, her workstation writes the print data into a single file in the server's spool area. The data in this file may constitute text or graphics; it may produce one page or many when printed; it may be a few bytes in size or a few megabytes. As far as the file server is concerned, it forms a single *print job*. The job is "submitted" when it is first written to the spool area and "serviced" when it leaves it.

Print job files have names related to the name of the print queue directory where they are submitted. The name is a combination of the first two pairs of digits of the print queue directory name in reverse order, followed by a four-digit sequence number and the extension Q. For example, the first file submitted to a print queue directory called 27060024.QDR will be called 06270001.Q. If a second job is submitted before the first has been serviced, the second job will be contained in 06270002.Q. The sequence numbers are recycled when the print jobs are serviced; if the first job in this example is serviced and a third job is then submitted, the third job will be written to 06270001.Q.

Print Server

A *print server* takes print jobs from a print queue and sends them to a printer for processing. The print server is registered in the bindery as a user (NetWare 3.x) or in the NDS tree as an object. It attaches to a file server like an ordinary user when servicing print queues.

The term "print server" can mean different things in different contexts. It is used to describe the software that handles the transfer of data, the physical device that transmits the data to the printer, and the bindery or NDS object that the print server software attaches to the file server.

The NetWare 3 print server can handle up to 16 printers, and the NetWare 4 print servers can handle up to 255 printers simultaneously.

Port Driver. The concept of a network port driver is new in NetWare 4. A port driver takes print jobs from print queues and passes them to a communications port. PSERVER.NLM and PSERVER.EXE performed this task in NetWare 3. In NetWare 4, the port driver functionality has been separated out into separate code. See the later "Types of Print Servers" section for details.

Printer. A printer, as far as NetWare is concerned, is a set of data related to communications port settings. In NetWare 3, a printer is a data structure owned by a print server.

In NetWare 4, a printer is an NDS database object in its own right. This is a useful development, as a user need only identify a printer by name to print to it—he doesn't have to know anything about print queues or print servers.

The Printing Infrastructure

This section describes the different types of print servers and looks at the issues involved in choosing one.

Types of Print Servers

The previous definition of a print server is quite broad: The software or device that takes print jobs from a queue on a server and passes them on to a physical printer. It can be implemented in a number of ways:

- File-server based
- Nondedicated workstation
- Dedicated workstation
- Print server in a box
- Net-direct

The following sections describe each setup, how it works, and the advantages and disadvantages of each. In all cases, print queues must be created and print server objects added to the bindery or to the NDS tree; these steps are described in detail later in this chapter.

File-Server Based. This is perhaps the simplest way to get print jobs from a file server to a printer. Just plug a printer into the file server's printer or serial port and load PSERVER.NLM on the server to handle the data. PSERVER.NLM can service up to 16 printers at a time under NetWare 3.x, with up to 5 of these attached directly to the file server. NetWare 4's PSERVER.NLM can service up to 255 printers, with up to seven of these attached directly to the file server.

PSERVER.NLM attaches to the server on which it is running, taking up a connection slot on the server just like its workstation-based cousin PSERVER.EXE.

In NetWare 4, PSERVER.NLM will autoload NPRINTER.NLM to provide port driver functionality to service the printer or serial port. This functionality was built into NetWare 3's PSERVER.NLM.

Using PSERVER.NLM requires no extra hardware. However, if it is used heavily there can be a performance degradation on the server. The printer must also be located beside the file server, so you'll have to deliver printouts to your users or else give them access to the file server—neither of which is desirable.

Workstation Based (Nondedicated). A workstation can process print jobs in the background while being used to perform other tasks. Load PSERVER.NLM on the file server. Then attach a printer to a serial or parallel port on the workstation, log on to the file server and run either RPRINTER.EXE (NetWare 3) or NPRINTER.EXE (NetWare 4). These files load into the workstation's memory and communicate with the file server in the background while the workstation is being used for some other purpose. They allow PSERVER.NLM to communicate with the printer as if it were attached directly to a port on the file server.

This is a useful option if resources are scarce and if the printer must be located away from the file server. But it can have a severe impact on the workstation where it is run in terms of both performance and memory. There may be an impact on the server too because PSERVER.NLM needs to process the data just as if the printer were directly attached to the file server.

Workstation Based (Dedicated). This solution is available only on NetWare 3. If you are using NetWare 4, set up a print server using the previous nondedicated procedure instead.

A dedicated print server workstation is fairly straightforward to set up. Attach a printer to a serial or parallel port on the workstation and run PSERVER.EXE.

The workstation attaches to the file server using the appropriate print server bindery ID. It is not possible to exit from PSERVER.EXE to the DOS prompt—the workstation must be rebooted. This restriction is aimed at eliminating the risk of illegal access to the file server using the print server account.

This program is a DOS version of PSERVER.NLM with the same interface and the same functionality. It can also service up to 16 printers.

This solution has no performance impact on the server or on any workstations other than the print server workstation itself. It is expensive in terms of hardware, however, as it permanently ties up a workstation that could otherwise be used as an extra client machine. If printing performance is not an issue, a 286 or XT machine can be used to carry out this function to keep the cost down.

Print Server in a Box. A dedicated workstation running PSERVER.EXE is in many ways a waste of hardware. The floppy drive, monitor, keyboard, etc., are not used except, perhaps, when booting up and starting PSERVER.EXE. You may even decide to remove the keyboard and monitor from such a print server to avoid interference if it is located in a public area.

Intel and other manufacturers now supply print server modules that have all of the essential components of a conventional workstation-based print server: a network interface, communications ports, and a processor. They boot from a file server and run proprietary software rather than PSERVER.EXE. It is possible to manage the unit's setup and even to upgrade its firmware—the software that controls the print server module and which is stored in the module itself—remotely, while logged on to a file server.

Physically, the units are not much bigger than a modem. They are generally available with a choice of serial and parallel ports. One of these systems can provide a network connection for four or five printers (parallel and serial) for less than $500. You should be able to find an old PC or XT that can service your printers for less than that price. However, it will be much bulkier and will not have the same life expectancy, and you won't be able to manage it over the network.

Net-Direct. Network interfaces are now available as an optional extra for many printer models. They run proprietary software that performs approximately the same function as PSERVER.EXE; in effect, the adapter acts like a stripped-down dedicated workstation. Unlike PSERVER.EXE, however, these adapters work with NetWare 4.x as well as NetWare 3.x.

These net-direct interfaces are proprietary—each interface model is designed to work with a particular printer make and model. Hewlett Packard, for example, manufactures a range of excellent network adapters for many of their printer models, but the LaserJet III model is completely different from the LaserJet 4 version. Digital, QMS, and other major printer manufacturers also make net-direct adapters for their own printer lines. If you decide to purchase a net-direct adapter for your printer, check first with your supplier that the adapter is appropriate for your printer make and model.

These adapters are generally quite simple to configure using the proprietary software that ships with them. They eliminate the potential bottleneck of slow serial or parallel interfaces while giving you the luxury of being able to configure the printer, check its status, and reset it from any client workstation. With prices starting at $400 or so per adapter, they are an excellent value in any printing environment where performance is an issue.

Remember when comparing the cost of this solution to the Print-Server-in-a-Box module that each net-direct card services only one printer; a print server module with multiple parallel and serial ports can handle four or more printers through a single network connection. However, the net-direct card will give higher data throughput.

Choosing a Configuration

Each of the previous types of print servers has its advantages. Consider these factors when choosing one for your network:

- Printer Performance   The two main bottlenecks when printing are usually the communications port and the printer itself in that order. A net-direct card will give a significant performance boost to all but the slowest of printers.

- Client/Server Performance   PSERVER.NLM will affect server performance if heavily used. RPRINTER.EXE and NPRINTER.EXE will use valuable memory on the host workstation as well as slow it down while printing. If at all possible, choose a dedicated print server. This can be a workstation running PSERVER.EXE (NetWare 3.x only), a print server box, or a net-direct card in the printer.

- Cost   You may want to avoid spending money on extra hardware when you can attach a printer to an existing port on a file server or workstation. But bear in mind the performance impact on the server or workstation—the real cost of diminished server or client performance may far outweigh the capital cost of a specialized network interface, print server module, or cheap workstation.

- Location   Attaching a printer to a file server is fine if you are providing a central printing service or if the file server is in a location accessible to users. Assuming that the file server is safely locked away, the printer will have to be somewhere else if users are to collect their own printouts.

Overall, the best bet is usually a fast printer with lots of RAM and a net-direct adapter. This gives excellent performance with no performance degradation on the server or on any workstations. It can also be managed over the network from a client, and many have the added advantage of being able to handle print jobs from NetWare, Macintosh, and UNIX clients at the same time.

> **Note**
>
> There are some good third-party print server software products on the market. An example is Pcounter, a shareware accounting print server produced by A.N.D. Technologies. Each user is given a balance, and Pcounter deducts a set amount for each page printed. Pcounter can be used with file-server-based, dedicated workstation, or net-direct printers.

Configuring Print Servers

Every networked printer requires a certain amount of setup work on the file server. This section focuses on NetWare print queues and print servers and the logical connections between them. By the end of this section, you should know how to create and manage both queues and server objects.

> **Caution**
>
> You might be able to get by without knowing how to do this; some print server modules and net-direct adapters come with proprietary menu-driven software that sets up queues and print server objects on the server for you. But it's always best when installing hardware or software to know what you're really doing and what the automatic installation software is doing behind the scenes on your behalf. It certainly helps when you're trying to diagnose problems at a later stage.

The logical relationship between queues, print servers, file servers, and printers can be confusing. Before digging into configuration details, it is worth pausing to consider the elements of networked printing.

- In the simplest case, there is a set of one-to-one relationships between the components. So to use your LaserJet 4 printer, you might create a queue called LJ4QUEUE. You need a print server to take the data from LJ4QUEUE and pass it on to the LaserJet printer; call it LJ4SERVER. The data goes to LJ4QUEUE from where LJ4SERVER takes it and passes it on to the LaserJet printer.

V

Adding Network Services

- If you want to use the same printer from multiple file servers you must create a queue on each file server. (You don't have to give it the same name on each server, although doing so can help you keep the logical connection clear in your mind.) All print queues can be serviced by a single print server. The queue to printer and queue to print server ratios are both many-to-one in this case.

- If you have more than one printer, the simplest thing is to create a separate queue for each one. There is no need to create multiple print servers, though—a single print server can handle up to 16 printers.

- It may be necessary to use more than one printer to print jobs from a single queue, for example when a queue is extremely busy and a single printer cannot handle the load. In this case, the additional printers can be regarded as a logical extension of the first. The print servers that service them, however, must be told about each printer individually. In cases like this, there are many printers to one queue and many printers to one print server.

Figure 23.5 shows a case with three file servers, two print servers, and four printers.

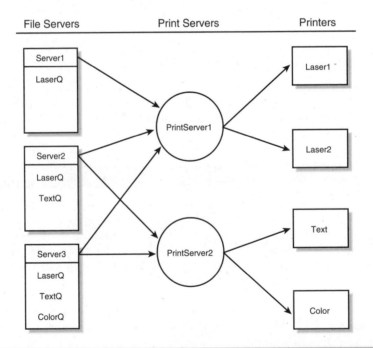

Figure 23.5

This is an example of printing entity relationships.

- Printers LASER1 and LASER2 act together, both taking jobs from the LASERQ queues. They are available to users on all three file servers.

- The TEXT printer is available to users on SERVER2 and SERVER3 via the TEXTQ queues.

- The COLOR printer is available to users of SERVER4 only via the COLORQ queue.

> **Note**
>
> Whether the print server machine is a file server or a workstation, you need to be certain that the printer and port are properly configured and that all components function correctly together. So attach the printer to the print server computer, configure its communications port, and test it thoroughly as a stand-alone printer. Make note of the port settings used: IRQ, I/O port address, and serial communications parameters for RS-232 ports.

PCONSOLE

PCONSOLE.EXE is usually copied into SYS:PUBLIC when NetWare is installed. It is a menu-driven program that can be used to perform most of the tasks associated with managing printing on a NetWare network.

PCONSOLE: NetWare 3.x. The main menu that appears when PCONSOLE is invoked under NetWare 3.x consists of the following three options:

Change Current File Server

Print Queue Information

Print Server Information

Each of these menu options is described briefly below. More detailed information on the relevant options follows later, under the "Managing Print Queues" and "Managing Print Servers" sections.

- Change Current File Server   The first option allows you to attach to additional file servers and to change your default server so that you can manage queues and print servers on more than one file server in a single PCONSOLE session.

- Print Queue Information   Selecting this option brings up a list of the currently defined print queues. The queues may be examined or deleted by a privileged user or new ones created.

- Print Server Information   Selecting this option brings up a list of the currently defined print servers. The servers may be examined or deleted by a privileged user or new ones created.

PCONSOLE: NetWare 4.x. PCONSOLE under NetWare 4.x has a different main menu:

Print Queues

Printers

Print Servers

Quick Setup

Change Context

Each of these menu options is described briefly below. More detailed information on the relevant options follows later, under the "Managing Print Queues" and "Managing Print Servers" sections.

■ Print Queues   Selecting this option brings up a list of the currently defined print queues. The queues may be examined or deleted by a privileged user or new ones created.

■ Printers   Selecting this option brings up a list of the currently defined printers. The printer objects may be examined or deleted by a privileged user or new ones created.

■ Print Servers   Selecting this option brings up a list of the currently defined print servers. The servers may be examined or deleted by a privileged user or new ones created.

■ Quick Setup   This option provides a convenient way to define new printers and print servers. A certain amount of customization will usually be necessary afterwards, however.

■ Change Context   Use this option to change your default NDS context. This allows you to manage queues and print servers in more than one NDS context during a single PCONSOLE session.

Using PCONSOLE. Whether using NetWare 3 or 4, most of the work is done using the Print Queue and Print Server options. Both are based on lists of objects. The objects are either print queues or print servers, depending on which option is chosen from the main menu. In either case, objects in the list are manipulated in the same way:

■ Create a new object by pressing the Insert key. Enter the name for the new object when prompted.

■ Delete an existing object by highlighting it and pressing the Delete key. Answer Yes when asked to confirm deletion or No to cancel deletion and leave the object as it is.

■ Select multiple objects for deletion by tagging them first and then pressing the Delete key. To tag an object, highlight its name and press the F5 key.

■ Rename an existing object by highlighting its name in the list and pressing the F3 key. Edit the name and press Enter.

■ Edit an existing object by highlighting its name in the list and pressing Enter. A configuration menu for the object will appear.

Creating and deleting works just the same for Print Queues and Print Servers. Editing is quite different for the two types of objects, as the following sections will show.

Managing Print Queues. This section takes you through the steps involved in configuring a print queue. If you're working on a new queue, create it first as previously described: Start PCONSOLE, select Print Queue Information if using NetWare 3.x or Print Queues if using NetWare 4.x, press Insert, and name the queue.

Note

NetWare doesn't care what names you give to your print queues, but your users might. When you create a queue, choose a name that signifies the printer which will eventually print the data. For example, names such as CENTRAL_LASER or DIV_INVOICE are preferable to QUEUE1 or LJQ2.

The default queue configuration under NetWare 3.x is as follows:

- All users (members of group EVERYONE) can place print jobs in the queue.

- Only SUPERVISOR can operate the queue—deleting print jobs, changing priorities, etc.

Under NetWare 4.x, the default queue configuration is quite similar:

- All users in the current NDS context can place print jobs in the queue.

- Only ADMIN is a print queue operator, with privileges to delete print jobs, change print job priorities, etc.

This default configuration is quite adequate in many cases. If so, you need only create the queue and assign a print server.

The following procedures explain how to adjust the configuration of an existing print queue. In all cases, start from the configuration menu for the queue that you want to configure: Start PCONSOLE, select Print Queue Information, (NetWare 3.x) or "Print Queues" (NetWare 4.x), highlight the name of the queue, and press Enter. The configuration options menu for the chosen print queue will then appear.

Restricting Access to Print Queues. All users can place jobs in the print queue by default. To restrict access, start by denying access to all users and then selectively granting access to the users and groups you want to use the queue.

To deny access to the queue—for example, to group EVERYONE—follow these steps:

1. Display the configuration options menu for the queue.

2. Select the Print Queue Users option. A list appears showing the users and groups currently allowed access.

V

Adding Network Services

3. Highlight the user or group to be denied access—for example, EVERYONE.

4. Press the Delete key and answer Yes when asked to confirm deletion.

To allow access to the queue—for example, to group ACCOUNTS—follow these steps:

1. Display the configuration options menu for the queue.

2. Select the Print Queue Users option. A list appears showing the users and groups currently allowed access.

3. Press the Insert key to add a user or group.

4. A list appears showing the currently defined users and groups on the server. This may take several seconds if the bindery is large.

5. Select the user or group to be granted access—for example, ACCOUNTS. You can select multiple users, multiple groups, or a combination of users and groups by tagging them with the F5 key.

6. Press Enter to grant access. The name or names of the chosen users or groups is added to the list of Print Queue Users.

Changing Print Queue Operators. Queue operator privileges are assigned on a queue-by-queue basis. You may want to allow a user or group to exercise control over one print queue—the queue which services their departmental printer, for example—but not over others.

Queue operators can perform the following tasks on the print jobs of any user in the queues which they operate:

■ Delete print jobs from the queue

■ Put individual print jobs on hold indefinitely

■ Defer printing of individual print jobs until a specified date and time

■ Change the priorities of individual print jobs

■ Edit the properties of individual print jobs, including banner pages, file content type, number of copies, etc.

By default, only SUPERVISOR (NetWare 3.x) or ADMIN (NetWare 4.x) or users with supervisor equivalence can perform queue operator tasks on a new queue. To add, for example, the MANAGERS group as print queue operators:

1. Display the configuration options menu for the queue.

2. Select the Print Queue Operators option. A list appears showing the current print queue operators.

3. Press the Insert key to add a user or group.

4. A list appears showing the currently defined users and groups on the server. This may take several seconds if the bindery is large.

5. Select the user or group to be granted operator rights for the queue—for example, MANAGERS. You can select multiple users, multiple groups, or a combination of users and groups by tagging them with the F5 key.

6. Press Enter to grant access. The name or names of the chosen users or groups is added to the list of Print Queue Operators.

Assigning Print Servers to Queues. Each queue must have at least one print server to service its print jobs. The print server must be defined before it can be assigned—refer to the following "Managing Print Servers" section for details.

> **Note**
>
> This step can also be carried out at the print server configuration stage. See the later "Assigning Queues to Printers" procedure for details.

There is no default print server, so the following procedure must be carried out in each case:

1. Display the configuration options menu for the queue.

2. Select the Queue Servers option. A list of the current print servers for this queue appears. The list is empty if the queue is new.

3. Press the Insert key. A list of currently defined print servers appears.

4. Highlight the name of the print server that is to service this queue.

5. Press Enter to assign the print server to this queue. Its name appears in the list of print servers for the queue.

Managing Print Servers. This section takes you through the steps involved in configuring a print server account. If you're working on a new server, create it first as described in the previous PCONSOLE section: Start PCONSOLE, select Print Server Information, (NetWare 3.x) or "Print Servers" (NetWare 4.x), press Insert, and name the server.

The minimum steps required to configure an existing print server account are defining a printer and assigning it to a queue. Remember that each print server can handle up to 16 printers, each attached to the print server using a separate communications port. The print server needs information on the configuration of each communications port if it is to pass the right data to each port in the correct form. The print server must also know where to print the jobs from each queue that it services.

The following procedures describe how to configure these items and a lot more besides. In all cases, start from the configuration menu for the print server that you want to

Adding Network Services

configure: Start PCONSOLE, select Print Server Information, (NetWare 3.x) or Print Servers (NetWare 4.x), highlight the name of the print server, and press Enter. The configuration options menu for the chosen print server then appears.

Defining Printers. Each of the print server's printers must be configured separately. Apart from the printer name, most of the information required is related to the print server's communciations ports.

The printer type describes the way that the printer is connected to the print server:

- *Local Parallel* printers are attached directly to a parallel port on the print server.

- *Local Serial* printers are attached directly to a serial port on the print server.

- *Remote Parallel* printers are attached to a parallel port on a workstation running RPRINTER or NPRINTER.

- *Remote Serial* printers are attached to a serial port on a workstation running RPRINTER or NPRINTER.

- *Remote Other* printers may be attached to either a parallel or serial port on a workstation running RPRINTER or NPRINTER. The print server is told the specific port that is being used when RPRINTER or NPRINTER starts.

- *Defined Elsewhere* printers have been configured on another file server. It is not necessary to enter the configuration details more than once if a print server is to service print queues on several file servers (using a separate print server account on each file server).

So a printer attached to the file server's parallel port is Local Parallel, a printer attached to the parallel port of a dedicated workstation running PSERVER.EXE is also Local Parallel, and a printer attached to a serial port on a nondedicated workstation running RPRINTER.EXE or NPRINTER.EXE is Remote Serial.

You should have the communications port information in hand before starting to configure printers. If you haven't already tested the printer and print server computer together, do so now and note which communications port settings were used.

Defining Printers: NetWare 3.x. The following PCONSOLE procedure defines a printer under NetWare 3.x:

1. Display the configuration options menu for the print server.

2. Select the Print Server Configuration option. You see a list of the 16 available printer slots on the print server. Any printers not already defined will be listed as Not Installed.

3. Select a printer slot by highlighting it and pressing Enter. Start with the first slot, printer 0. A Printer Configuration dialog box appears.

4. Enter a name for the printer.

5. Select the Type field and press Enter. A list of printer types appears.

6. Choose the appropriate printer type. Refer to the previous list for explanations of the different types. The remaining fields are filled in with default values depending on what printer type you specify.

7. Edit the Interrupts and IRQ fields to match the print server computer's port configuration. Refer to the notes you made when testing the printer and computer.

8. If the printer is attached to a serial port, enter the appropriate values in the Baud Rate, Data Bits, Stop Bits, and Parity fields. You should have noted these values when you tested the printer.

9. Press the Esc key to exit the Printer Configuration dialog box.

10. Enter Yes to save your changes.

Defining Printers: NetWare 4.x. NetWare 4.x treats printers as objects in their own right, rather than as properties of Print Servers as in NetWare 3.x. This is an advantage as it allows printers to be moved from one print server to another without the need to re-enter the printer data again. Communications-specific information may, of course change if the printer is moved to a different print server.

The basic procedure for defining a printer under NetWare 4.x is as follows:

1. Select PCONSOLE's Printers option.

2. Press the Insert key and enter the name of the new printer.

3. To edit the properties of the new printer, make sure its name is highlighted in the list of printers and then press the Enter key.

4. The Printer Configuration dialog box for that printer will appear.

5. Choose a print server from the list of defined print servers.

6. Select a printer type from the list of defined types: parallel, serial, etc.

7. Edit the Interrupts and IRQ fields to match the print server computer's port configuration. Refer to the notes you made when testing the printer and computer.

Printers can also be created under the Print Servers menu by pressing the Insert key while browsing the Printers list.

Assigning Queues to Printers. A print server may work with several printers and several print queues. You must configure the print server to associate each printer with the correct queue.

The following takes you through the necessary steps:

1. Display the configuration options menu for the print server.

2. Choose the Queues Serviced by Printer option.

3. Choose the printer from the list.

4. Press the Insert key. A list of queues appears.

5. Select the queue that this printer is to service.

6. You are prompted to change the print queue priority. Leave this at its default value, 1, unless you have a particular reason to change it. Refer to the following tip for more information on this.

7. Press Enter to save this printer assignment.

Tip

You may want to give some users higher printing priority than others. To do this for a single file server, create multiple print queues and restrict access to one (for example, LJ4HIPRI) to the high-priority users; then create another (for example, LJ4LOPRI) for the low-priority users. Finally, configure LJ4SERVER to handle LJ4HIPRI with a priority level of 1 and LJ4LOPRI with a priority level of 2 or more.

Setting Print Server Name and Password. You can optionally set a full name and a password for a print server. The full name is purely informational, while the password is a security feature.

The full name is the name displayed for the print server connection on the file server when you view a list of users using the USERLIST command. It is not the same as the print server name you used when you created the print server. For example, a print server called CENTRAL_SRV might have a full name of "Central Print Server, Accounts."

To set or change the full name of a print server, follow these steps:

1. Display the configuration options menu for the print server.

2. Select the Full Name option.

3. Type or edit the full name of the print server.

4. Press Enter to save the new name.

A print server account without a password is a security risk. If the real print server is not attached to the file server, another workstation with the same printer configuration can be used instead of it, acting as a print server and printing possibly sensitive data. Setting a password on the print server account can help prevent this kind of abuse because the person setting up the dummy print server has to know the print server account password.

There is a minor inconvenience of course, as the password must be typed every time the print server starts up. This can be more than a hindrance if the print server is in a remote location and there is a long delay in restarting printing every time the print server or file server is restarted.

Tip

You can secure your print server without a password by restricting the print server account to a specific workstation address. Start SYSCON, choose User Information, and select the print server account name. Choose Station Restrictions and press Insert to add the network number and workstation address of the print server machine.

To set or change a print server's password, follow these steps:

1. Display the configuration options menu for the print server.

2. Select the Change Password option.

3. Type the new password for the print server and press Enter. The password does not appear displayed on-screen.

4. Retype the new password and press Enter. This is a precaution in case you mistyped the password the first time.

Use the same print server password on all file servers serviced by the print server. Only one password is then needed when the print server attaches to the file servers.

Attaching Extra File Servers. A print server works by attaching to a file server using a special print server account, taking data from its queues, and passing it on to its printers. Attaching to several file servers is nearly as easy as attaching to just one, so with a little more work, you can get a single print server to service queues on more than one file server.

All of this happens automatically under NetWare 4.x as the NDS tree is distributed across servers. Refer to chapter 8, "Novell NetWare," for more information about NDS.

The procedure under NetWare 3.x is straightforward, but it can be confusing to perform multiple configuration tasks on more than one file server at a time, especially if the printers and queues have different names on each of the file servers. For simplicity, think of the task in terms of accurate advertising: One server knows about your print server, the queues it uses, and the printers it serves. All you need to do is tell the rest of the servers about the existing print server.

Note

The print server picks up its printer configuration details (printer ports, communications parameters, etc.) when it attaches to the first file server using the special print server account. There is no need to define these printer details on subsequent file servers.

The next procedure takes you through the steps needed to get an existing print server to work with an additional file server. It assumes that you have already set up and tested a print server using the preceding procedure. It refers to the preceding procedures for defining print queues and servers and for assigning printers and queues. Refer to those procedures as needed as you go through this procedure.

1. If you haven't already done so, log on to the first file server—that is, the one on which the print server is already defined.

2. Display the configuration options menu for the print server.

3. Take note of the exact spelling of the print server name, the names of each defined printer, and the names of the queues serviced by this print server.

4. Press Esc to return to PCONSOLE's main menu. Choose the Change Current File Server option. You see a list of the file servers that you are already attached to.

5. If you are already attached to the additional file server, skip to step 10.

6. If you are not attached to the additional file server—if it does not appear in the list—press the Insert key. You now see a list of the file servers that you are not attached to.

7. Select the additional file server from the list and press Enter.

8. Enter your user ID on the additional server. Note that you need to attach as SUPERVISOR or as a user with SUPERVISOR equivalence. Enter your password when prompted. The additional file server now appears in the list of servers that you are attached to.

9. Make sure the additional file server is highlighted and press Enter.

10. Press Esc to go back to the main menu; then choose the Print Queue Information option.

    Use the procedure described in the earlier "Print Queue" section to create any print queues that you need. In the simplest case, you will just be duplicating an existing print server so create queues that duplicate the relevant queues on the first file server. That means creating a set of queues with the same names and access rights as the queues you listed in step 3.

11. Press Esc to go back to the main menu; then choose the Print Server Information option.

    Use the procedure described in the earlier "Print Queue" section to create a print server with the same name as the print server account on the first file server. The spelling must be identical.

12. Select the Print Server Configuration option. For each printer in the list you made in step 3, define a printer for this print server. Use the procedure described in the earlier "Defining Printers" section.

13. In each case, define the printer type as Defined Elsewhere. The print server picks the port configuration information up from the first file server.

14. Use the procedure described in the earlier "Assigning Queues to Printers" section to assign each queue to the correct printer. Refer again to the list you made in step 3 to make sure you get the assignments right.

Managing Print Servers

Once a print server has been configured, it must be started and managed. The following sections describe how to start the various types of print servers and how to use the PSC utility to control them once started.

Starting a Print Server

The next sections show how to start and stop each of the various types of print server. You must complete print server configuration before starting the print server. The print server types are

- File-server based

- Dedicated workstation

- Nondedicated workstation

- Print server in a box

- Net-direct

File-Server Based. Load PSERVER.NLM at the file server console using the LOAD command. Specify the name of the print server account—for example, LOAD PSERVER ACCSERV.

If the print server account has a password, you are prompted to enter it before the print server attaches and starts working. If you enter the wrong password, PSERVER.NLM unloads, and you are returned to the console prompt.

If PSERVER.NLM loads successfully you will see eight boxes on-screen, each indicating a printer number, type, and name along with the current status of each. Press any key to see the other eight printers.

PSERVER.NLM can be unloaded from the console prompt using the UNLOAD command—for example, UNLOAD PSERVER ACCSERV.

Dedicated Workstation. Load PSERVER.EXE on the dedicated workstation and specify the name of the print server account:

```
PSERVER ACCSERV
```

If you log on to the file server before running PSERVER, all necessary files will be available in SYS:PUBLIC. PSERVER will then log you out from the server as soon as it loads. If you prefer to run PSERVER from a local disk without having to log on, copy the following files from SYS:PUBLIC to the local disk:

PSERVER.EXE

IBM$RUN.OVL

SYS$ERR.DAT

SYS$HELP.DAT

SYS$MSG.DAT

If the print server account has a password, you are prompted to enter it before the print server attaches and starts working. If you enter the wrong password, the workstation does not attach to the file server, you are logged off, PSERVER.EXE does not load, and you are returned to the DOS prompt.

If PSERVER.EXE loads successfully, you see a screen similar to the PSERVER.NLM screen. It is not possible to exit from PSERVER.EXE to the DOS prompt because that presents a security risk as the workstation is still attached to the file server using the print server account. The workstation must be rebooted to get back to the DOS prompt.

Nondedicated Workstation: NetWare 3.x. Start PSERVER.NLM on the file server first. Then load RPRINTER.EXE on the nondedicated workstation once for each printer that is attached.

You can specify the print server and printer number on the command line:

    RPRINTER ACCSERV 0

If you omit the parameters you are prompted to select values from a menu. If you defined the printer type as Remote/Other when configuring the print server, you are also prompted to specify port parameters at this stage.

It is not necessary to log on to the file server before loading RPRINTER. If you prefer to load RPRINTER from a local disk without necessarily logging on, copy the following files from SYS:PUBLIC to the local disk:

RPRINTER.EXE

RPRINTER.HLP

IBM$RUN.OVL

SYS$ERR.DAT

SYS$HELP.DAT

SYS$MSG.DAT

Disconnect a printer from the print server using the -R option:

    RPRINTER ACCSERV 0 -R

RPRINTER unloads from memory if no other printers are attached.

Nondedicated Workstation: NetWare 4.x. Start PSERVER.NLM on the file server first. Then load NPRINTER.EXE on the workstation once for each printer that is attached.

You can specify the print server and printer number on the command line:

```
NPRINTER ACCSERV 0
```

Alternatively, because printers are database objects in NetWare 4, you can specify the printer name on the NPRINTER command line:

```
NPRINTER CENTRAL_LASER
```

If you omit the parameters, you are prompted to select values from a menu. If you defined the printer type as Remote/Other when configuring the print server, you are also prompted to specify port parameters at this stage.

It is not necessary to log on to the file server before loading NPRINTER. If you prefer to load NPRINTER from a local disk without necessarily logging on, copy the necessary files from SYS:PUBLIC to the local disk. To find out which files are required by your version of NPRINTER.EXE, issue the command

```
NPRINTER /V
```

at the DOS prompt.

You can disconnect a printer from the print server by unloading its port driver using NPRINTER's /U option. If you have only loaded NPRINTER once, the command

```
NPRINTER /U
```

unloads the printer's port driver and disconnects it. If the print server has more than one printer and you have loaded multiple port drivers, you must unload each of the port drivers in reverse order until you have unloaded the port driver for the printer you want to disconnect.

Print Server in a Box. Connect the device to the network and power it on. It may look for a boot or configuration file on a file server. It should attach to the file server automatically, using whatever print server ID was specified for it during configuration. Refer to the documentation for your particular model for details.

Net-Direct. Reset the printer to force it to attach to a file server. Once it does so, it will begin to act as a print server. Refer to the documentation for your particular model for details.

The PSC Utility

PSC (Print Server Control) is a DOS command-line utility in SYS:PUBLIC. It can be used to control most aspects of the operation of a print server, including starting and stopping one. Most of the functionality of PSC is also available within PCONSOLE. PSC commands can be issued more quickly however.

The syntax of a PSC command is

```
PSC ps=PrintServer p=PrinterNumber command
```

PrintServer is the name of the print server to act on, *PrinterNumber* is the number of the printer on that print server to be controlled, and *command* is the action to be carried out. Some commands apply to all printers, in which case you can omit p=*PrinterNumber*.

The available PSC commands are explained in the following sections. Command abbreviations are indicated in parentheses.

Abort (*AB*). Cancels the current print job. The print server continues to run, moving on to the next job. Use the Keep (k) option to resubmit the job at the bottom of the queue.

Examples:

```
PSC ps=accserv p=0 ab

PSC ps=accserv p=1 ab k
```

Canceldown (*CD*). PCONSOLE can be used to schedule the print server to go down when the current print jobs have been serviced. This command cancels the downing of the print server.

Example:

```
PSC ps=accserv cd
```

Formfeed (*FF*). Force a printer to go to the start of the next page.

Example:

```
PSC ps=accserv p=0 ff
```

Mark (*M*). Print a line of asterisks at the current position on the page. This can be used to check whether the print head of a dot-matrix printer is correctly lined up with the top of the page.

Example:

```
PSC ps=accserv p=0 m
```

Mount Form (*MO F=*). Notify the print server that the form has been changed on one of its printers. Include the form number.

Example:

```
PSC ps=accserv p=0 mo f=2
```

Pause (*PAU*). Pause the printer temporarily—for example, while forms are changed.

Example:

```
PSC ps=accserv p=0 pau
```

Private (*PRI*). Disable sharing of a remote printer. The printer is then available only to the workstation to which it is attached.

Example:

```
PSC ps=accserv p=0 pri
```

Shared (*SH*). Enable sharing of a remote printer. The printer is then available to other network users.

Example:

```
PSC ps=accserv p=0 sh
```

Start (*STAR*). Restart a printer after it has been paused or stopped.

Example:

```
PSC ps=accserv p=0 star
```

Status (*STAT*). View the status of one or more printers. Omit the printer number to see the status of all printers on a print server.

Examples:

```
PSC ps=accserv p=0 stat

PSC ps=accserv stat
```

Stop (*STO*). Stop a printer. The current job will be deleted unless you specify the Keep (k) option, in which case it will be resubmitted at the top of the queue.

Examples:

```
PSC ps=accserv p=0 sto

PSC ps=accserv p=1 sto k
```

Print Service Upgrades

You can improve your print services in a number of ways. Buying a new printer is one way, improving an existing one is another. This section takes a look at some of the options available to you.

Upgrading Existing Printers

There are many ways to enhance a printer, just as there are many reasons for wanting to do so. Do you want your printer to print faster? On different media? From additional platforms? The broad areas that you can enhance are

- Performance
- Accessibility
- Functionality
- Media handling

The next few sections look at each of these areas in turn.

Performance. Printers can generally receive data faster than they can process it. If a printer is busy processing data, any additional incoming data is stored in a RAM buffer to be processed later. The printer's processor dips into this buffer when it is ready to process some more data. If the buffer is small, the processor will handle the data quickly and will then have to wait while more data is sent from the host computer. Ideally, the buffer will be so large that the processor only exhausts it when there is no more data to be printed. Adding more memory increases the buffer size and can significantly improve printer throughput.

> **Note**
>
> PostScript printers also need RAM to run the PostScript interpreter, the program that processes the PostScript code. The interpreter must be loaded into memory before it can run; it also grabs memory for stack space while it runs. All in all, several hundred K of printer RAM can be written off to the PostScript interpreter. If your printer comes with 2M of RAM the data buffer will be tiny. 6M is a more realistic starting point.

Memory upgrades come in a variety of forms depending on the printer model. Some printers have a slot into which a memory card or cartridge can be plugged. Others use SIMM slots like the ones on a PC motherboard. In either case, consult your printer manual for part numbers for memory options.

Examine each printer before you order a memory upgrade. If there is a single adapter slot, is it already in use? If so, you will have to remove the currently installed adapter. So if a printer has 2M consisting of 1M built-in and a 1M memory option, you will have to buy a 2M memory option to upgrade to 3M. Similarly, if the printer uses SIMMs, are there enough free slots to cope with additional SIMMs? If not, you may have to remove some of the current SIMMs and replace them with SIMMs of higher capacity. In either case, you will still have the old memory options and you may be able to reuse them in other printers.

Adding a network interface may also help performance, particularly in the case of a fast printer. A slow communications interface on a fast printer can mean that the printer spends a lot of time waiting for the data to arrive. Adding a network interface can remove the communications bottleneck and allow the processor to spend more time processing and less time waiting.

Finally, some PostScript printers can benefit from a change of PostScript interpreter. For example, Pacific Data Products manufactures a range of upgrades for HP III printers, including a PostScript interpreter cartridge with built-in RAM that outperforms the original HP III Postscript interpreter. Options such as this can be costly, however, with list prices of a few hundred dollars. Unless you can find them at a discount, the money is generally better spent on more memory.

Accessibility. Making an existing printer accessible to a greater range of clients can be an efficient way to enhance print services on a network. For example, installing NetWare for Macintosh on a file server can allow Macintosh clients to access network printers that you have already configured, without any need for changes to the printer. You will, of course, need to supply your users with an appropriate Macintosh printer driver for each particular printer model, just as you would for Windows users.

Net-direct interfaces can also be used to enhance the accessibility of a printer. They generally handle a range of protocols, including

- IPX   Novell clients

- TCP/IP   UNIX and other clients

- EtherTalk   Macintosh clients

You can configure the interface to use one of these protocols and ignore the rest, or you can configure it to switch automatically between protocols as different types of clients send data to be printed. A net-direct interface can allow a printer to be shared by a much wider range of users than any purely NetWare setup.

Functionality. It may be possible to upgrade an existing printer so that it handles more types of data.

Installing a PostScript cartridge in a non-PostScript laser printer is one such example. Many applications that cannot generate print data in proprietary print formats such as PCL can produce PostScript output. Users of such applications would benefit from a PostScript upgrade. However, many older applications cannot produce PostScript; you should check with your users first on whether the upgrade will be of benefit to them.

Caution

Adding a PostScript interpreter may mean a loss of functionality. For example, a HP LaserJet III can handle PCL data including plain text. Adding HP's PostScript cartridge switches the printer completely to PostScript mode, so when non-PostScript data such as PCL or text is sent to the printer it is discarded. If you want the printer to handle all types of data—PostScript *in addition to* PCL rather than *instead of* PCL—consider a third-party option such as Pacific Data Products' Page Express PE cartridge.

Adding additional font cartridges to non-PostScript printers is another functionality enhancement. A huge range of such cartridges exists: Discuss the issue with your users and identify their needs before you start searching for a product. In particular, make sure you don't swap out a cartridge that someone uses unless you are sure that the replacement cartridge will meet their requirements.

Media Handling. Additional print trays allow you to provide your users with a choice of print media. Store plain bond in the default tray and headed paper or transparencies in another, and the users can select the tray they need when they print (Windows printer drivers allow the user to override their default tray selection).

When you consider the possibility of making additional media available, remember that the printer may not be able to handle some types of media. Refer in particular to the "Print Media for Laser Printers" later in this chapter.

Adding Network Services

Duplexing units are available for some printers. These allow users to generate output printed on both sides of the page, saving paper and money and reducing waste. They will need a special printer driver to do this. Make sure that users have a choice as to whether their output is printed double- or single-sided. They may want to photocopy their hard copy, and not all photocopiers can handle double-sided sheets.

Other Enhancements. There are many other ways to enhance a printer. Special security cards that provide password protection for printer configuration, special sheet and envelope feeders, acoustic covers, and more are available for specific printers. Ask your supplier for information on the range of add-ons available for your printer model.

New Printers

Printers, like PCs, are becoming commodity items and prices are falling. This means that you can add an extra networked printer for a relatively small cost, providing a significant improvement in service to users.

Replacing an old printer may be a more attractive option than upgrading it. Adding a network interface, RAM, and PostScript cartridge to an existing printer may cost nearly as much as a new PostScript printer with the same amount of RAM. A new printer can be expected to keep working for considerably longer than an old one, and it will come with a warranty to cover the first year of service.

Your choice of printer model and its detailed specifications will depend on your budget and the requirements of your users. Some of the factors to consider when buying a new printer are:

- RAM   The more the better. 12M or 16M is recommended if you expect the printer to be busy. 6M should be seen as the bottom line, particularly for PostScript printers.

- Interface   A built-in network interface or net-direct card makes a lot of sense if you are buying a printer specifically for network use. If you don't buy a network interface for the printer, you will need to provide a connection to the network either via a workstation or directly from a file server. If a net-direct adapter seems expensive, consider the cost of a dedicated print server workstation or of the performance impact on a nondedicated or file-server based connection.

- Functionality   Check with your users before replacing an existing printer. If you decide to buy a PostScript printer, make sure it can auto-detect different types of data and that it can handle plain text as well as PostScript. If you are replacing a PCL printer, make sure the replacement can handle PCL data too. If it cannot, your users will have to reconfigure their applications to produce PostScript output.

- Color   Noncolor printers generally can't be upgraded to handle color. If color printing is likely to become a requirement during the life of the printer, consider buying a color printer now. There are a number of different color printing systems designed to meet different needs and budgets, so define your needs and price limit before you start shopping.

- **Media** You can't upgrade an existing letter-size or A4 printer to handle A3 paper. Decide what media are to be catered for and consider whether these requirements may change during the life of the printer. Also check the media specifications of any printers before buying them—they may not be able to handle some of the media you've been using in the past, for example transparencies or printed forms.

- **Warranty** Most printers come with a one-year warranty. Check what the warranty covers. Some warranties are void if you use refilled toner cartridges or adapters not manufactured by the printer manufacturer. Other warranties do not cover damage that, in the opinion of the printer manufacturer, was caused by third-party products, but they do not explicitly forbid the use of such products.

- **Service** Will the supplier service the printer on-site, or will you need to ship it back to the manufacturer for service?

Printer Cleaning and Maintenance

Printing can be a messy business, with ink and toner being scattered around at high pressures and temperatures. Printer mechanisms being so delicate, it's not surprising that they often fall foul of their own actions. Regular cleaning and maintenance can help extend your printer's life and maintain high print quality as well.

This section describes typical routine maintenance and cleaning procedures for a selection of printers. It is impossible to be exhaustive here, so refer to your printer manual for detailed instructions on the particular maintenance procedures most suitable for your printer model.

A section on print quality troubleshooting is also provided for each type of printer. Please note however that print quality problems are not network related, even on networked printers. You should consult your printer documentation for full details of how to rectify any print quality problems which you encounter.

Maintenance: Laser Printers

Laser printers use high pressures and temperatures to fuse toner to paper. This is an overview of the sequence of events involved in producing a printout:

1. A wire carrying an electric current (the primary corona wire) places a static electric charge on a photosensitive drum called the *electro-photostatic (EP-S)* drum.

2. A laser beam casts light on selected (image) areas of the EP-S drum. The electric charge on these areas changes as a result.

3. The EP-S drum is rotated so that the image areas pick up particles of toner.

4. A sheet of paper passes over another wire carrying an electric current (the transfer corona wire), which puts a static electric charge on the paper. The paper and the image area of the EP-S drum now have opposite charges.

5. The paper picks up the toner particles from the EP-S drum.

6. The paper is passed into the fusing unit, where a combination of high temperature and high pressure act to fuse the toner to the paper.

Figure 23.6 shows this process.

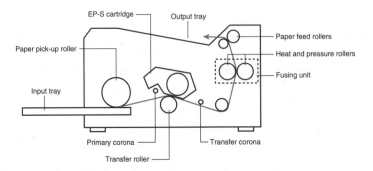

The components of a typical laser printer. The paper path is indicated by the dotted line.

Modern laser printers use combination EP-S cartridges that have a built-in primary corona wire, photosensitive drum, and toner hopper. Some older models require separate replacement of the primary corona wire, and they may use a separate receptacle for used toner.

Print Media for Laser Printers. The high temperature and high pressure of the fusing unit mean that many types of media cannot be used in laser printers. Check your printer documentation for details specific to your model. In general, print media for laser printers must be able to withstand temperatures of 200°C for 0.1 seconds. This means

- Do not use thermal printing paper

- Do not use carbon paper

- Do not use colorized paper where the color has been applied as a coating to the paper

- If using media with adhesive—for example, envelopes or sheets of labels—make sure the adhesive is acrylic-based

- If using media with adhesive, make sure no adhesive is exposed.

- Do not use envelopes with clasps, snaps, or transparent windows.

- Do not use envelopes that do not require moistening to seal. These use a pressure-activated adhesive that will be sealed by the fusion process.

- Preprinted paper such as letterheads, forms, etc., may not be appropriate. If in doubt, check on a small sample.

- Check the specification of any transparencies before trying to print on them. Your printer documentation should give acceptable ranges of weight, moisture, content, etc.

Store replacement EP-S cartridges in their sealed, foil wrappers to enhance shelf life. Store paper in its wrapper in a normal office environment.

Routine Maintenance for Laser Printers. Stray particles of toner or paper dust can adversely affect voltage levels on the corona wires, paper and EP-S drum. Regular, careful cleaning of the inside of the printer can help to keep print quality problems to a minimum. Check your printer documentation for detailed instructions on how to clean your particular model.

Caution

The fusing assembly of a laser printer can be extremely hot. There may be other hot or electrically live components. Always exercise extreme caution when working inside a laser printer: Disconnect main power, allow to cool, and do not use excessive amounts of water or solvent.

In general:

1. Clean the transfer corona wire with the special tool provided with your printer. If you can't find such a tool, use an unmoistened cotton swab. Slide the tool or swab gently from side to side along the length of the corona wire. Take care not to break any monofilament separation wires that may be arranged diagonally across the transfer corona wire.

2. The primary corona wire applies a charge to the whole area of the EP-S drum. It does not have such a critical effect on output quality as the transfer corona wire, so clean it only occasionally or when print quality deteriorates.

3. Brush out any dust from the antistatic teeth near the transfer corona wire. This can help to prevent paper jams.

4. Replace the fusing roller cleaning pad every time you replace the EP-S cartridge. Replace it between cartridge changes if necessary (see "Laser Printer Quality Problems"), but this is normally not necessary.

5. Wipe the exposed parts of the paper path inside the printer with a lint-free cloth, slightly dampened with water.

6. The fuser separation pawls are two little claws that peel the paper away from the fusing roller. Clean the tips of the pawls with a cloth lightly dampened with water. Do not touch the rest of the fusing assembly.

7. Replace the printer's ozone filter every 50,000 pages or so. This does not affect printer performance in any way, but excessive levels of ozone in the air may cause health problems.

Leave the printer open for a while after cleaning it to allow any moisture to dissipate.

Laser Printer Quality Problems. People have come to expect extremely high quality output from laser printers. When print quality deteriorates, as it will occasionally, take a few minutes to examine the problem and try to identify where in the printing process described above the problem occurred.

Some of the more common laser print quality problems and their solutions are as follows:

- Large amounts of vertical fading   Shake the toner cartridge to try to improve toner distribution. If that fails, replace the cartridge.

- Blurred vertical lines   Replace the fuser roller cleaning pad.

- Stray toner fused to paper   Replace the fuser roller cleaning pad.

- Vertical black streaks   Clean the primary corona wire. If the problem persists, there may be scratches on the photosensitive drum. Replace the EP-S cartridge.

- Small amounts of fading across the page   Clean the transfer corona wire.

- Light printouts   Clean the corona wires. Adjust the density setting if necessary.

- Faded-out blotches   Clean the transfer corona wire. If the problem persists, the paper may have an uneven moisture content. Try paper from a different batch.

- Streaks on leading edge of paper   Clean the fuser separation mechanism and all paper guides.

- Toner shadow in the background   The paper may be too heavy or the environment may be too dry. Try lighter paper and adjust the humidity. If the problem persists, replace the toner cartridge.

- Page completely black   The primary corona wire is broken or not making contact. Reseat the EP-S cartridge; if that doesn't fix it, replace the EP-S cartridge.

Maintenance: Dot-Matrix Printers

These are relatively simple machines with a purely mechanical mechanism.

Routine Maintenance for Dot-Matrix Printers. Preventive maintenance consists of little more than an occasional wipe around the outside and exposed inside parts of the printer with a slightly damp cloth to remove excess dust. Use a pair of tweezers to remove any small objects that may have fallen into the printer.

If there is an excessive build-up of paper dust inside the printer, you may want to try using a low-power vacuum to remove it. Be careful though—there are many delicate components and you may end up worse off after such an exercise. If you must vacuum, make sure you remove the printer ribbon first!

After prolonged use and if print quality problems persist, you may want to clean the print head. This is generally done by removing the print head from the printer and dipping the hammer end of it into rubbing alcohol. Consult your printer documentation to find out how best to do this for your printer model.

Dot-Matrix Printer Quality Problems. Some of the more common dot-matrix print quality problems and their solutions are as follows:

- Characters too light   Check if the printer ribbon is jammed. If not, check if the ribbon is out of ink. If not, move the print head closer to the paper. Consult your printer documentation to find out how to do this for your printer model.

- Characters smudged   Check if ribbon is twisted. If not, move the print head farther from the paper. Consult your printer documentation to find out how to do this for your printer model.

- Paper jams when using the tractor mechanism   Adjust the tractor units so that the paper is neither pulled tight nor sagging.

- Paper tears when using multipart paper   Move the tractor units closer together to reduce the tension in the paper. If the problem persists, move the print head farther from the paper. Consult your printer documentation to find out how to do this for your printer model.

- Lines of text overlap   Check if the paper is jamming.

- Lines of text are slanted   If printing cuts sheets, make sure the paper release lever is not in the tractor position.

- Missing dots, always in the same row   Replace the print head.

- Poor print clarity   Check that the printer has the correct type of ribbon and that you are printing on approved stock.

- Print carriage vibrates   The print head path may be blocked. Switch off the printer and check for obstructions.

Maintenance: InkJet Printers

InkJet or BubbleJet printers use a small nozzle with a heating element to squirt drops of ink onto the page. The nozzles are usually of quite simple construction, consisting of simple tubes with a heating element embedded along the side. The print head consists of an array of these nozzles, and the printer in other respects works quite like a dot-matrix printer—the print head moves across the page, the paper is fed through rollers, etc.

Routine Maintenance for InkJet Printers. The ink in the nozzle can dry out over time. The best way to prevent this from happening is to make sure you store the printer with a nonempty ink cartridge installed.

Many inkjet printers have built-in print head cleaning procedures that can be activated from their control panel. These procedures, which usually consist of a variation or two on the theme of squirting a lot of ink onto a test page, should be used in the event of print quality problems or after several months of storage.

Apart from the print head, maintenance is similar to a dot-matrix printer. Keep the outside reasonably dust-free and clean out the paper dust and debris from the inside occasionally.

InkJet Printer Quality Problems. The first answer to all InkJet printing problems is the same: Clean the print head using the built-in cleaning procedure. If that fails to improve matters, check that the paper and ink you are using are appropriate for this type of printer. Consult your printer documentation for details of acceptable paper stock and ink.

Summary

Printing is a core service in practically every computerized environment. This chapter explained how well-planned and implemented network printing can enhance print services and how poor network printing can make a good network look bad. Detailed instructions on print service implemetation were provided, as were upgrade options and troubleshooting procedures for a range of common printer types.

Network printing can take many forms. Consider the needs of your users and your management needs as network administrator before planning and implementing your network printing solution.

Chapter 24

Adding Network CD-ROMs

The past few years' evolution of data processing technologies can rival even science fiction in its ability to amaze. PCs have both fired and been the exemplars of quantum-speed growth and change. We've gone from machines with no hard drives at all, through ones where 20M was considered cutting edge, all the way to one-gigabyte drives becoming commonplace. Memory and processor speed have taken similar leaps forward. But perhaps the most radical recent development in data processing technology is the introduction of optical data storage and its corollary multimedia capabilities into the PC equation. Furthermore, the case could be made that CD-ROM storage has its greatest impact in networked environments.

The existence of a network implies great attention to the need to distribute information in a timely fashion. Another of a network's reasons for being is the business advantage it offers. (Knowledge is not only power, it's also efficiency and effectiveness.) Unfortunately, a network link is not the best method for handing out some kinds of data. Large volumes of information that are only periodically updated or massive amounts of data regardless of the update ratio are frequently found on networks but aren't well-suited to being distributed by traditional networking methods and media. CD-ROM drives, however, can pass this stuff along with one hand tied behind their backs because of their enormous data storage capacities and their admirable data transfer abilities.

It's for these same two reasons that CD-ROMs have become the distribution media of choice for more software than you can shake a stick at. There are over 10,000 software titles that offer no other distribution medium than a CD-ROM. The following table summarizes only a small percentage of the very significant PC software available on CD-ROM.

Software Available on CD-ROM

Operating Systems

IBM OS/2

Microsoft Windows NT

Novell NetWare

UNIX (several flavors, including SCO)

Windows 95

Office Suites

Lotus SmartSuite

Microsoft Office

Novell Perfect Office

Applications

Word

WordPerfect

1-2-3

CorelDRAW!

Access

You already know the basics about CD-ROM drives from chapter 6, "The Workstation Platform." Additional benefits of using CD-ROM drives include

- Saving the office space that is otherwise taken up by oceans of paper. The volume of data that CD-ROMs are able to store is particularly relevant in the financial, legal, and medical worlds, which are notorious for the amount of information they must retain and produce.

- Offering services as well as data online. Novell, for example, markets *NSEPRO*, a CD-ROM-based technical reference. Ziff-Davis offers *Computer Support on Site*, a CD-ROM that contains the kind of tech-support advice, from a number of leading vendors, that you'd ordinarily spend gobs of time on the phone to get.

The characteristic that most distinguishes CD-ROMs from all other storage media is the same quality that makes them particularly valuable in a network setting: their unique combination of storage capacity, data integrity, and easy accessibility. While there are some tape systems that can rival CD-ROMs in the volume of data they're able to store, no tape can protect data as well as a CD-ROM can or retrieve it as quickly.

Characteristics of CD-ROM Drives

Let's discuss some of the characteristics of CD-ROM drives that are particularly relevant to networks. Among these are speed of access to data, speed of transfer of data from storage medium to memory, the amount of preparation time a device must put in before it is ready to begin data retrieval (also known as access time), and the amount of buffer space a device holds within itself.

Note

A buffer, whether in memory and known there as a *cache* or on a storage device and referred to simply as a *buffer*, is a subset of storage held aside for some special purpose. In RAM, it's used for quicker access to frequently used data or program instructions. On a storage device such as a CD-ROM drive, a buffer does a similar job, holding data whose retrieval is otherwise deterred by unevenness or irregularities in the flow of data.

Speed

Quadruple, or *quad* (denoted by 4X), speed not only denotes the current top rate at which most CD-ROM drives in common use can transfer data, but also testifies to the rate of development of this particular technology. It's only within the past year or so that we've gone from double-speed to quad CD-ROMs as the standard. The "single-to-double" phase of CD-ROM evolution, on the other hand, lasted about two years.

4X CD-ROM drives move data at up to 600 kilobytes per second (K/sec). They outdistance 2X drives by a factor of—you've got it—two. Those storage stalwarts of last year pushed bits at only 300 K/sec.

Tip

Applications like animation or video, which not only take in but also create huge amounts of data, are best served by 4X CD-ROM drives. The higher data transfer rates of these devices helps ensure smooth, flowing movement of the images produced.

CD-ROM Drives—Continuing To Evolve at Quantum Speeds

As the song says, "You ain't seen nothin' yet." Many manufacturers are about to or already have released six-speed (6X) CD-ROM drives, which ship data down the line at 900 K/sec. The advantages of such throughput to data-intensive networked applications like graphics and databases is self-evident. But because 6X drives are very new and correspondingly expensive, you should consider them for your environment only if the volume of data you must transfer is so large as to make throughput your only concern. On the other hand, the price of a 4X drive has been cut in half, and easily in half again, during the species' brief lifespan; 4X drives that once cost $900 now retail for about $250. This factor alone might be the best reason to choose a 4X CD-ROM drive as a network storage subsystem.

(continues)

(continued)

Newer still are 8X CD-ROM drives. These shouldn't even be considered as a component for your network, at least for the immediate future. Their speeds of access and retrieval are fantastic, but these most recent CD-ROM devices have demonstrated a number of bugs, particularly in configuring, that rule them out of consideration for the next few months.

But while you shouldn't run out to purchase an 8X CD-ROM drive, you might, if your network must handle a large volume of archival data, consider purchasing a CD-ROM drive that can record as well as read. One such device is the Spresa 920 from Sony, which can function as a single- or double-speed internal CD-ROM reader and recorder. Other vendors such as Yamaha produce similar components. The Spresa is a SCSI-controlled component; other such devices may have proprietary controllers.

As previously mentioned, the unique combination of storage capacity, data integrity, and easy accessibility of these components makes them particularly well-matched with networks.

Access Time

Access time is that period needed by any data storage device to *prepare itself* to retrieve the information you've asked for. This includes locating the bag of bytes, as well as moving to its site. A good 4X CD-ROM drive should *find* (as opposed to display to you) the item you've requested in no more than 600 milliseconds, particularly since this level of access can even be found in some 2X drives. 4X devices with the best access times can find what you're looking for in as little as 300 or 450 milliseconds.

Consider this as a means of appreciating these intervals: human reaction time—that is, the time between, let's say, your eye recording the image of a tree and your saying to yourself "What a lovely fir!"—is about one-tenth of a second. An "average" 4X CD-ROM drive's access improves upon this rate by about 300 times.

Note

Access times have the greatest effect on overall application performance when dealing with very large databases.

The variation in access times arises out of the fact that CD-ROM drives, dealing as they do with different types of data, have a variety of access times. This, in turn, is due to the varying rates at which CD-ROM-stored data can be read. Audio input, for example, is normally read at 150 K/sec, while graphics are ingested at 300 K/sec, and "just data" data at rates as high as 600 K/sec. Since the drive has no way of knowing till it gets to it what type of data, and in what order, it must read, CD-ROM drives must slow down upon approaching audio, speed up when getting close to data, and so on. The variation in read speeds between categories of information is responsible for the variety of access rates that CD-ROM drives demonstrate.

Note

Remember that getting to data is a different function and is therefore measured in a different way than transferring that data. Access time represents the getting to and has a single, flat measurement in time, such as 450 milliseconds. Transfer, on the other hand, is expressed as a ratio of so much data per such-and-such an amount of time, as in 600 K/sec.

Note

Another factor affecting access time on CD-ROM drives is the layout of the CD-ROM itself. Data is imprinted on it in concentric circles. Therefore, finding and reading data at the outside edge of the CD-ROM takes longer than searching out data near its center.

Tip

Any drive with an *overall* access time larger than 300 milliseconds shouldn't be considered as a component for your network.

Plextor, a leading manufacturer of CD-ROM drives, recommends considering transfer rate (for example, 600 K/sec) as more important than access time in selecting a drive, if these two criteria turn out to be the deciding ones.

Buffering

Top-performing CD-ROM drives have a *data buffer* of 256K. Even lower-end models buffer their input in appreciable chunks, the most common being 64K.

The ability to send data to the CPU in more readily managed units, provided by buffering of any sort, speeds up overall throughput because it allows the CPU to take a break, lessening the likelihood of the processor's being bogged down by a large, lengthy stream of data.

Not only the presence of a buffer, but also something called the *buffer-full ratio* (*BFR*), influences a CD-ROM drive's transfer rate. The BFR is a measurement of how full a buffer must be, relative to the total size of the buffer, before the drive will actually transfer data to the CPU. Too large a BFR slows overall processing almost as much as a complete lack of buffering and for the same reasons. The CPU again bogs down under the weight of too much data sent to it too fast. A very small BFR, on the other hand, and its corollary more frequent transmissions to the processor, will tie up that engine in another way—too many individual requests that it must respond to.

> **Tip**
>
> Look for a BFR between 45% and 65%. For a CD-ROM drive with a 256K buffer, this works out to beginning data transfer when the buffer holds between 115K and 165K.

Interface to Controller

Recent tests by *PC Magazine* showed little if any difference in performance between *Enhanced Integrated Device Electronics (EIDE)* and *Small Computer Systems Interface (SCSI)* controlled drives.

When considering drives that employ these disparate controllers, keep the following sections in mind. They'll make factoring a CD-ROM drive into your network's equation much simpler.

EIDE Drives. EIDE drives, sometimes called ATAPI, are easier to install and configure than their SCSI counterparts. If yours is one of the many environments that still employs IDE controllers, incorporating an EIDE drive into your configuration is as easy as adding an adapter.

SCSI Drives. SCSI controllers can support larger, more powerful devices. They can also manage more components than IDE or EIDE interface boards. A SCSI controller allows you to daisy-chain up to seven components from itself. What's even better, these seven can communicate among themselves without having to route those conversations through a PC's CPU, which is to say that SCSI controllers are less likely to engender bottlenecks. In a network that demands ease of expandability coupled with a high degree of reliability, SCSI is the way to go.

> **Note**
>
> SCSI controllers, no matter what types of devices they manage, open up expansion slots in a PC. That's one reason they were developed, and it's still one of their most important contributions.

Another reason for considering a SCSI-based CD-ROM drive, particularly in a network setting, is that SCSI more readily supports multitasking and is the only controller that can unite Apples and PCs. Macintoshes don't have IDE capabilities but do have a SCSI port.

> **Tip**
>
> SCSI controllers come in 8- and 16-bit versions. The 8-bit SCSI cards are adequate for handling 2X CD-ROM drives. But the transfer rates common to 4X CD-ROM drives and the volume of data encountered in many CD-ROM-reliant applications such as graphics are such that a 16-bit board is necessary with these faster CD-ROM delivery systems.

Proprietary Controllers. Mitsumi, Panasonic, and Sony are among the many manufacturers of CD-ROM drives who offer proprietary interfaces for those drives. Such boards are usually quite inexpensive. However, they do tie you a little more tightly to the particular vendor. If ease of upgradability is a significant concern, proprietary interfaces aren't an option.

External or Internal

Chinon, Plextor, Sony, and other major CD-ROM drive manufacturers offer internal and external drives that are, functionally, mirror images of one another. The only difference in these components is where they sit.

External CD-ROM drives rest quietly beside your computer, occasionally and covertly blinking in red or green. However, external components do have drawbacks. For instance, external CD-ROM drives, like external modems or hard drives, are more expensive than their internal counterparts, by as much as $100 per model. On the other hand, they are light-years easier to install and configure. In addition, performance criteria such as access times and data transfer rates are identical within models between the external and internal members of that model.

> **Note**
>
> External drives offer the additional advantage of being portable—that is, easily transferred between servers.

External drives are predominantly SCSI devices. Only a few IDE external CD-ROM drives are available. Because connector cables for IDE and EIDE devices are about 18 inches long, any device they attach to must nestle side by side with its host computer. On the other hand, SCSI cables can be up to three meters long, thereby allowing some breathing room between drive and computer. Even this asset can have its problems, though. SCSI devices can sprawl out to take up too much desk or counterspace. If your workspace is limited, this "extension cord" capability of SCSI can become a drawback, particularly if you take advantage of the SCSI controller's ability to daisy-chain.

Ease of Installation. Anything more frustrating or stress-inducing than disassembling a network node, installing a new internally housed component, and reassembling and bringing back online the enhanced machine under a tight deadline is hard to imagine. Since most of us work under what might be called the "I need it yesterday" imperative, the much greater ease of installing an external CD-ROM drive is one of its most attractive characteristics, at least balancing out its cost.

> **Caution**
>
> Some external CD-ROM drives connect to their host by means of a parallel port. Since such a port sports a throughput rate worthy of a tortoise, as little as 30–40 K/sec, be sure to know the type of port any CD-ROM drive you're considering talks to.

VI

Adding Network Services

Audio Connectability. If you intend to make any use at all of the sound capabilities of a CD-ROM drive—for instance, in creating multimedia presentations—there are a number of points you must keep in mind.

Talking to Internal CD-ROM Drives. Internal CD-ROM drives should offer Red Book-compliant analog audio connectors and should be bundled with enough cable to hook up to the (similarly Red Book-compliant) audio connectors on the sound card through which they talk.

Talking to External CD-ROM Drives. External CD-ROM drives, on the other hand, must offer analog line-out RCA connectors if you're to use CD-ROMs to help build those dynamite presentations.

A Blueprint for a Networked, Audio-Capable CD-ROM Drive. If your network needs sound, the CD-ROM drive that provides it should, in addition to the traits already presented, have the following minimum characteristics:

- 10,000 hours Mean Time Between Failures (MTBF).

- Mode 1 capability (mode 2 and forms 1 and 2 optional); *mode* refers to the formatting used to produce the CD-ROM.

- Subchannel Q (subchannels P and R through W optional). If R through W subchannel support is provided, additional Application Programming Interfaces (APIs) must be implemented in the CD-ROM driver. Specifications for such APIs are available from Microsoft Corporation. (*Channels* and *subchannels* refer to the audio equivalents of ranges of bandwidths—that is, a single audio disc may carry music on one channel, voice on another, and voice in a second language on a third channel.)

- A driver that implements extended audio APIs.

- Consumption of no more than 40% of the CPU bandwidth, assuming a read block size of no less than 16K and access time no greater than that required to load one such block into the drive's buffer.

- Read-ahead buffering (a technique described in a specification available from Microsoft Corporation).

- Conformance to the APIs, functionality, and performance standards described in the *Microsoft Windows Software Development Kit* (Reference Volumes I and II) and in the *Microsoft Multimedia Development Kit Programmer's Reference*.

> **Tip**
>
> Microsoft's specifications for sound-related application program interfaces and drivers are recommended here largely because, as is the case with so many types of applications, software in this sub-genre was developed to adhere to the Microsoft standard. You can't go wrong by using these criteria.

> **Note**
>
> CD-ROM drives will often be used in a network setting as servers. Therefore, audio connectivity is probably the least important consideration in evaluating these subsystems for many people. But CD-ROM-driven audio is a topic of some complexity; pitfalls might await anyone trying to provide sound across a network. The information just provided should put the administrator who must provide sound on a network on firmer ground.

Loading. Some CD-ROM drives are more fastidious than others in protecting their media. Such devices use plastic caddies or cases into which a CD-ROM must be placed before it can be dropped into a drive. While caddies do minimize the potential for damage that any data storage medium is heir to, they also increase both cost and transfer speeds.

Another trait of caddy CD-ROM drives that can present problems is the nature of their loading and closing mechanisms. Automatic-loading drives begin to close and attempt to start spinning when a CD-ROM and its caddy are about halfway into the drive. This characteristic, intended to facilitate loading discs, can result instead in damaged drives when users mistakenly try to jam the caddied CD-ROM all the way into the device.

> **Note**
>
> Manual caddy drives are available and are considered virtually impervious to damage by even the impatient or inept.

In a "fast-food data" scenario, a caddyless, multi-disc drive might be your best option. Internal multi-disc CD-ROM drives most frequently offer a three-disc carousel. External multi-disc CD-ROM drives currently available can hold six or seven CD-ROMs at a time.

CD-ROM Changers. The next step up on the CD-ROM ladder is a CD-ROM changer. One such device, the DRM-1804X from Pioneer, houses three six-disc carousels. Such a storage device, while it does not provide simultaneous access to the media it houses, does greatly increase the overall capacity and decrease time needed to change those media.

To use any CD-ROM changer, you need specialized software to manage it. One such package is CD-View, from Ornetix. CD-View allows a dedicated PC housing a CD-ROM changer to emulate a NetWare server. Therefore, any Novell workstation can map and attach to this pseudo-server and access the CD-ROM drive it offers.

CD-View, unlike other similar packages, supports IDE-, EIDE-, and SCSI-based CD-ROM drives. But don't think that loading CD-View makes a machine into a real server. It doesn't; NetWare-specific configuration tasks like tailoring security must be done with SYSCON, from a true NetWare server.

Always-Available CD-ROMs. The mirror-image to a CD-ROM changer is what's known as an *always available* or *real-time* CD-ROM drive. Such devices can keep a number of discs loaded simultaneously. As their names imply, these drives are sophisticated mechanisms.

Personality Profile

To this point, we've covered a lot of ground. Table 24.1 traces our steps, presenting the most important characteristics to be considered in selecting a CD-ROM drive that will become part of a network. (The table even contains a few less central CD-ROM traits that haven't yet been presented. Those have been indicated with an asterisk.)

Table 24.1 A Summary of CD-ROM Drive Characteristics	
Characteristic	**Look for These Qualities**
Access Time	No more than 450 milliseconds overall.
Caddy?	Only if protection of discs is of prime importance. Even then, make sure the drive is a manual loader.
Data Transfer	600 K/sec (the rate demonstrated by a good 4X drive).
*Drive Door	Two doors—one door flush with the chassis, and the other door within the drive bay. This combination offers the maximum environmental protection to drive and discs.
*Driver Size	No more than 80K of conventional memory.
*Eject Mechanism	Motor-driven and easily accessible.
External or Internal?	The answer to this question is dependent upon several factors: Accessibility/availability of drive bays Nature of interface Volume of data to be stored In turn, the choice between an external or an internal CD-ROM drive affects the choice between a dedicated or a shared network CD-ROM server.
Loading Mechanism	Manual load if high volume and simultaneous access aren't important. CD-ROM changer if neither simultaneous access to media or a high volume of media in use at any given time is a factor in your environment.

Getting Your CD-ROM Drive on the Network

In a network, CD-ROM drives act very much as they do in stand-alone PCs, with a single very important exception. Such a drive's ability to simultaneously maximize storage and retrieval rates is even more important in a network than on an autonomous machine. As mentioned earlier, data-intensive applications like graphics will benefit from CD-ROMs in any setting. Factoring in the overhead that sharing such applications and their data across a network places on things like throughput makes choosing the right network CD-ROM drive even more critical.

CD-ROM drives intended specifically for the heavier loads and more frequent access of a busy network can be of two types: jukeboxes or towers.

> **Note**
>
> Jukeboxes and towers are actually the two major varieties of CD-ROM changers.

Each of these categories incorporates all the characteristics of CD-ROM drives discussed to this point. Each also goes beyond those basic CD-ROM traits by offering a scheme for rapid access to multiple media.

Jukeboxes

Like their audio alter-egos, jukeboxes operate by selecting a specific disc from an ordered group or stack. Jukeboxes are the simpler multi-CD-ROM mechanisms; some of the physically smaller of them can be incorporated into a PC. Assuming your server has a free bay of the appropriate size, installing a jukebox is feasible.

> **Note**
>
> The question of dedicated versus shared just peeked around the corner again. Even a jukebox, which is a pretty sophisticated way of delivering CD-ROM-based data to your users, cannot act as a dedicated server unless one of those old but still functioning PCs you noticed back in the storeroom can accept the jukebox.

CD-ROM Towers

CD-ROM towers house a number of individual CD-ROM drives. They allow your users access to several or as many as a dozen discs at once. The total number of discs available will of course be the product of the number of drives a tower contains and the number of discs each of those drives can handle.

> **Tip**
>
> Oddly enough, some jukeboxes can flip a larger total number of CD-ROMs than some towers. However, no jukebox can do what every CD-ROM tower can: offer simultaneous access to all loaded discs.

Most of the highest-performing CD-ROM towers are SCSI devices, many of which can be hooked to other, similar towers, or can house other SCSI devices such as tape drives in the same case that holds the CD-ROM drives. In addition, the component drives of some towers take a "multi-connectivity" approach. That is, these drives include an integral

Industry Standard Architecture (ISA) controller, the drive's 50-pin SCSI connector, and its power connector. This clustering of connections makes it easier to change an individual drive within a tower.

Management of CD-ROM towers can usually be accomplished through the NOS. The NOS deals with the tower as it does any file server. However, because of their muscle and complexity, CD-ROM towers benefit from third-party management software. The best of the big guys come with such software bundled.

Smart Towers. Some large jukeboxes and many of the latest towers have their own CPU and therefore can connect directly to a network. Smaller jukeboxes or older towers must be physically attached to a server, which brings up the quintessential networking question, "What if the server goes down?" If you're running most jukeboxes, your CD-ROM users, like all other users, have only one option—to take a break and get a cup of their choice beverage. If, on the other hand, you've implemented one of the new, smart CD-ROM towers, users accessing data or applications dished out by it just keep on trucking.

Tower Requirements

Even if your network is relatively small, you expect its extent, complexity, and heterogeneity to continue to grow. So don't consider a shared drive. Nor should you give a second glance to a dedicated internal CD-ROM server because it lacks the ability for simultaneous access to multiple discs, as do even the biggest and smartest jukeboxes.

Go straight to the CD-ROM towers of your favorite Value Added Reseller (VAR), a retailer. There, select a tower with the following characteristics:

- Nine component CD-ROM drives (the maximum currently available)

- A CPU running at a minimum of 60MHz

- Drives with integral controllers and connectors (fewer parts equals fewer opportunities for error in configuring or downtime)

- A minimum of 4M onboard memory on the tower's NIC

This tower could keep 27 CD-ROMs loaded and available to your users simultaneously. Assuming that each of those discs is actually holding about 50M, we're talking about 1.35G of data being online at any given moment.

Share and Share Alike

Much of the chapter to this point may seem to have had a slant toward dedicated CD-ROM servers. We've noted paradoxes like that of the much easier to deal with but also more expensive external CD-ROM drive, seemingly suggesting that internal-but-autonomous is the way to go. We've included volume of usage in discussions on everything from drive loading mechanisms to accessing multiple discs, possibly implying that dedicated servers, by virtue of having nothing else to deal with, are better suited to managing the problems that high volume can engender.

Dedicated devices aren't always feasible, though. If nothing else, the expense and effort involved in implementing a dedicated CD-ROM server on your network may mandate a CD-ROM drive that must contend with other subsystems for a server's resources. Therefore, to look more closely at just what's needed to make a shared network CD-ROM drive hum is wise.

How Do I Share?

There are a number of ways to share CD-ROM drives across a network. Choosing the right one depends on several things:

- The NOS you're running

- How many CD-ROM drives you need to share

- How often discs must be changed within an individual drive

CD-ROM versus NOS. Probably the most important factor in determining the mechanism by which you establish CD-ROM drive sharing is the NOS that ultimately controls that drive. Several of the most widely used NOSs, including LANtastic, NetWare, Windows NT, and Windows for Workgroups, provide software to accomplish CD-ROM sharing. Be aware, however, that this software carries some constraints. For example, the earlier versions of NetWare NLMs that permit sharing CD-ROMs don't support SCSI CD-ROM drives. So be sure to read the small print in your NOS's documentation in ferreting out whether your NOS can support the CD-ROM drive you're considering.

Tip

Under version 4.1, NetWare's CDROM.NLM supports these SCSI controllers.

Manufacturer	Model
ADIC	DCB-ISA, DCB-EISA
Always Technology	AI-6000
DPT	PM2012B, PM2011B/95
DTC	DTC3280, DTC3290, DTC3292
Hewlett-Packard	LM-SCSI

Detailed information on mounting a CD-ROM drive as a NetWare volume can be found on the Web at the following address:

http://www.zdnet.com/~coop/netware/9501/ntware1.home

A CD-ROM Drive on a Peer-To-Peer Network. Another, related factor is whether your network is peer-to-peer or client/server. In peer-to-peer networks, it is possible to share CD-ROM drives. However, this network algorithm adds a wrinkle or two to drive-sharing.

First, a shared CD-ROM drive on a peer-to-peer network must exist as a component of a dedicated workstation. So if you haven't gone back to the warehouse to look for that old 486, you'll have to do so now. You'll need it to house the CD-ROM drive that's to be shared across your peer-to-peer network. Once this dedicated station has been incorporated into the network, your users need only to map or attach to it to use the drive.

Second, your users have to load the Microsoft CD-ROM Extensions TSR utility, MSCDEX.EXE, at their station. It can't live on the dedicated station where the CD-ROM drive resides. In addition, all users must employ version 2.22 or higher of MSCDEX.EXE.

Hierarchical Sharing—the Novell Connection. NetWare's handling of shared CD-ROM drives is typical of how LAN operating systems manage these devices. When you combine this functional characteristic with NetWare's role as market leader among NOSs, we should take a closer look at administering shared CD-ROM drives under NetWare.

Caution

NetWare supports shared CD-ROM drives, with two important constraints. First, its default implementation doesn't support IDE- or EIDE-controlled CD-ROM drives. If you intend to use one of these, you'll need add-ons in the form of patches (see appendix A, "NetWare Patches") or of third-party software. Second, with versions of NetWare prior to 3.12, you cannot share CD-ROM drives of any kind.

If the CD-ROM drive you're going to be sharing isn't already present in or attached to an existing NetWare server, you of course must install it according to manufacturer's instructions. Then you must load the drivers for the drive itself and for any new interface board it may have brought with it. Only when these steps are complete can you load drivers that share access across your network to the new CD-ROM drive. This second category of drivers may be provided by Novell as NLMs or may be made up of third-party packages.

NetWare includes a file called ASPICD.DSK on its SYSTEM_2 disc. This file is its driver for shared CD-ROMs. However, ASPICD.DSK is not loaded during NetWare installation. So you'll have to manually copy ASPICD.DSK to an appropriate path on your server.

Another constraint that NetWare imposes on the management of shared CD-ROM drives is that it not only caches the volumes resident on these drives but indexes those volumes the first time they're mounted to provide faster access during subsequent mounts and dismounts. Given this scheme, you'd be well-advised to allocate additional server memory to handle CD-ROM drive volumes.

As is the case with all its security arrangements, NetWare controls access to shared CD-ROM drives by means of groups. The default is to give access to such drives to the EVERYONE group. Trouble is, EVERYONE is just that—this group most frequently includes all user accounts. If you need to narrow this generous focus, you'll have to do so from the command line prompt at the network console while the CD-ROM volume is being mounted.

This need to tailor access to a shared Novell CD-ROM drive emphasizes the only really weak point in NetWare's management of such drives. In any environment in which CD-ROM volumes must be mounted and unmounted regularly, the opportunity for unauthorized use of the server console increases. The corollary possibility of damage to network services by an inexperienced, inept, or simply curious user grows along with that.

To preclude such damage, there are a few things you can do. First, if their size doesn't preclude it, you could simply allow the CD-ROM volumes to remain mounted at all times. Second, you could remove the keyboard and even the monitor from the server that contains the shared drive and manage that server remotely by means of RCONSOLE. Third, you could limit access to the shared drive to users knowledgeable enough to mount or dismount it correctly.

If You Want To Be Really Sure. There are other, higher-tech and lower-likelihood-of-failure means of controlling access to network servers that include shared CD-ROM drives. One is a hardware device called Discport from Microtest.

Discport is analogous to a modem. In fact, it looks a lot like an external modem, being about the same size and shape. Discport has a network connector at one end of its cable and a SCSI connector at the other end. The network connector can be either Ethernet or token ring. At its SCSI end, Discport can talk to as many as seven CD-ROM drives.

Management of the drives Discport connects is done through its bundled, Windows-based application, Discview. Discview allows authorized users to mount and dismount CD-ROM volumes by clicking an appropriate icon; no chance for console command syntax errors here. Discview also can be used to access specific CD-ROMs that are already mounted.

Implementing the Discport/Discview combo doesn't preclude less flashy paths to NetWare CD-ROM drives. For instance, users can reach mounted CD-ROM volumes with the familiar MAP command. They'll never know that Discport and Discview are sitting between them and their NOS because MAP executes exactly as if it were being processed by NetWare itself.

Older NOSs. For NetWare releases predating 3.12, and for older versions of other NOSs, there is still a way to share CD-ROM drives across the network. In such cases, what's needed is the addition of third-party software to the configuration. Such packages supply drivers and management tools to the NOS that allow it to network CD-ROMs.

Two such products are systems from Meridian's CD Net and Online Products Corporation's OPTI-NET. Comparing these two accurately is difficult because each requires a different mix of hardware and software. The Meridian system, for example, handles inquiries from multiple workstations quite well but is not as quick as other packages in responding to requests from individual workstations.

Since the discussion of shared CD-ROM drives has, to this point, gone on largely in a Novell context, let's continue along that path, and take a look at one of these third-party applications in terms of how it can be used to augment an older Novell network. OPTI-NET is a LAN management program that supports networks fully implementing NetBIOS or IPX/SPX. OPTI-NET extends networking capabilities to CD-ROM drives, allowing users to share data housed there. The application connects CD-ROM drives to NetWare and allows those drives to be managed from NetWare.

> **Note**
>
> OPTI-NET is a software-only solution; therefore, existing network hardware need not be enhanced. OPTI-NET also runs under PS/1 and PS/2.

The OPTI-NET Value Added Process (VAP) version allows CD-ROM drives to be connected directly to a dedicated file server or to an external bridge. The VAP version of the package requires NetWare 286 Release 2.1 or later.

Software drivers for SCSI controllers are integrated into OPTI-NET VAP. Up to 28 drives per CD-ROM server are possible. OPTI-NET supports an unlimited number of CD-ROM servers per network. In addition, at each server that it supports, OPTI-NET can grant CD-ROM access to up to 100 simultaneous users, depending on the network type and the maximum number of sessions supported. Finally, OPTI-NET supports up to 64 CD-ROM drives per server and offers remote or centralized management tools because it does not require a dedicated server.

> **Tip**
>
> Even the simultaneous use from the same machine of a local CD-ROM and a CD-ROM shared across the network by means of OPTI-NET is possible. You simply use two different device names: one for the local driver and another for the OPTI-NET NETUSR device driver.

Disaster Planning for Networked CD-ROM Drives

Don't look now, but there's a networked CD-ROM drive disaster of some sort out there, and it's looking for you. You can elude it if you do the following.

Be meticulous in configuring access to your CD-ROM server, particularly if that "server" is actually a shared drive. Do nothing that might open a door for the inexperienced or the curious to experiment or interfere with the drive's operating parameters.

Keep duplicates of frequently used CD-ROMs immediately at hand, and copies of less-frequently accessed media not much farther away. Keep another set of copies of each of these in off-site storage that is as disaster-proof as possible: protected from fire, impact with heavy objects, and so on.

If your network is large enough or busy enough to justify a CD-ROM tower, it's also large and busy enough to need some of the drives in that tower to function as mirrored discs. Make use of this built-in opportunity for data redundancy.

Most failures of storage subsystems are electro-mechanical in origin. A cable or interface card, rather than data on the device it supports, will probably be the first to die. Protect these less glamorous network components. Adhere to the following rules:

- Never allow cable to be twisted or stretched tight.

- Never run cable through heavy traffic areas. (The duct-tape-over-the-cable technique is out.)

- Take great care in installing adapters to avoid bending the pins with which they snuggle into the motherboard.

- Never move a PC that has cables still connected to interface boards.

On the Horizon: Asynchronous Transfer Mode

This chapter began with a brief reflection on the quantum speed with which data processing technologies evolve. We conclude it with a look at one way in which that progression continues.

One of the newest sights on the connectivity horizon is Asynchronous Transfer Mode (ATM) networking technology. ATM was developed specifically to support the transmission of multiple, differing types of information, including audio, image, text, video, and voice, by a single switching interface. ATM is, for all intents and purposes, without any real transmission speed or throughput limitations. It can support a number of users from the relatively few that frequent a LAN to the many to be found on a WAN.

Perhaps most relevant to networked CD-ROM drives are two other characteristics of ATM. The new technology is *isochronous*. That is, it is transparent to the timing dependencies of data such as audio. Further, ATM interfaces are multimedia-ready and can increase or decrease bandwidth on demand.

Two examples of what ATM can offer are two NICs from Sun Microsystems. The ATM-155/MFiber adapter accomplishes 155 Mbps transmission over multimode FDDI channels. The ATM-155/UTPS card operates at 155 Mbps over Category five UTP cable. Both of these boards send not only text and graphics but also audio and video signals at the 155 Mbps rate. Both demonstrate low latency and high reliability.

Just approaching the networking horizon are the second generation of ATM cards. A number of vendors, among them Toshiba America Electronics Components, PMC-Sierra, and Siemens Components, brought to the 1995 Networld-Interop Conference their renderings of this second generation. While these latest ATM interfaces still operate at 155 Mbps, they offer improved formatting of data in preparation for transmission, as well as integration into a network at the physical layer. This latter is accomplished either through a multi-chip set with a PCI interface or by a single chip that integrates a PCI interface with a DMA controller. The single-chip card is clever enough to be able to access data without the help of other, off-chip memory on the card.

What's so exciting about ATM in the context of this chapter? ATM's inherent ability to simultaneously transmit several types of data. Most of our discussion of networked CD-ROM drives has involved making a number of choices: between internal and external, dedicated or shared, and mounted/dismounted or always-available servers. ATM, with its beefy bandwidth and throughput, may make such decision-making a thing of the past. Trading in even our idealized, nine-drive "super-tower" for a single ATM server would improve rather than reduce user access to CD-ROM-based data.

Summary

CD-ROM drives, because of their huge data storage capacities and their unsurpassed data transfer speeds, are particularly suited to networks. In addition, the collection of software titles that offer no other distribution medium than a CD-ROM could very well include some of your network's most important applications; such titles number more than 10,000. Finally, the ability of such sophisticated CD-ROM devices such as jukeboxes and towers to offer access, even simultaneous access, to multiple storage media and to multimedia data assures CD-ROM technology an ongoing role in distributed data processing environments.

One recent development that testifies to this role is the announcement in November 1995 by AT&T of a plan for a new multimedia communications server that it expects to be the cornerstone of its strategy for integrating voice and data transmissions over LANs. Called the *Multimedia Communications Exchange Server*, this combination of hardware and software will support real-time voice, video, and data applications. According to the October 30, 1995 issue of *Communications Week*, the Exchange Server will run under UNIX on an Intel 120 MHz Pentium processor, will interact with Hewlett-Packard and Sun Micro-systems workstations, will support up to 100 concurrent users, and will encompass client/server applications, protocol conversion, and even some network management functions. The Multimedia Communications Exchange Server will be tested in 1996, but general availability is not expected until 1997. (Other vendors, such as IBM and Microsoft, are considering a similar approach to networking multimedia.)

Chapter 25

Adding Network Modems

Modems are the most basic networking technology (other than cable itself), but in this era of Internet fever, modems challenge even "glamorous" components like memory and processors for "most favored" status. This chapter begins with a brief review of the theory behind modems. After that, it takes a look at current modem standards and technologies, and also at recent outgrowths such as communications servers and shared-access modems. Finally, a set of recommendations for choosing the best modem or comm server for your environment is presented.

Modulation and Demodulation

In case any of you still don't know its origin, the word *modem* is an acronym for what a modem does. A modem takes the digital or discrete signal that computers put out and changes it to an analog signal that can be sent across telephone lines. At its destination, the analog signal is retranslated to digital so that the receiving machine can understand it (see fig. 25.1). This conversion and reconversion is known as *modulation and demodulation,* hence *modem.*

> **Note**
>
> A digital signal is one that exists in either of two states and in only one of those states. Think of it in terms of numbers—no fractions here—just the values 0 or 1. An analog signal, on the other hand, can incorporate all possible fractional values.

The methods of signal alteration most frequently used by modems are

- Amplitude modulation
- Frequency modulation
- Phase modulation (a variant of frequency modulation)

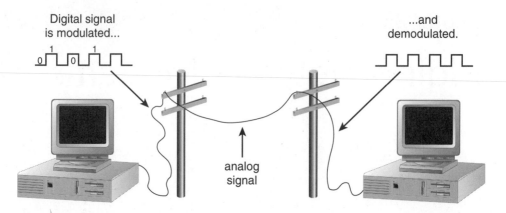

Figure 25.1

Modulation and demodulation give modems their name.

Note

If this sounds like detail more appropriate to a discussion of radio, that's because in converting digital to analog, modems produce *audible tones*. It's these tones that are sent across phone lines to a receiving system.

Some Basic Modem Characteristics

Modems, whatever their speed, however they check the data they transmit or receive, and wherever they're located in relation to the computer they serve, share certain basic qualities. Some of these qualities are

- Modems typically communicate with a host through a serial port.

- In the PC world, modems converse with the host through its bus by means of a special chip on the motherboard. That chip is called the *Universal Asynchronous Receiver/Transmitter (UAR/T)*.

Note

Regardless of the speed of your modem, data processed by it travels no faster than the top speed your UAR/T can handle.

- Modems can be configured to use either software or hardware flow control. Software flow control involves software-generated transmission on (XON) or transmission off (XOFF) signals. Hardware flow control uses the Clear To Send (CTS) and Ready To Send (RTS) channels (pins 5 and 4 respectively) of an RS-232 connector to signal that it's okay to transmit.

> **Note**
>
> *Flow control* is the regulation of the volume of data a modem sends or receives per unit of time.

- Other modem settings can also be customized. Such factors as number of redial attempts, intervals between redials, and what to do with a busy signal are all configurable by the user.

- Most modems take their internal commands from the de facto industry standard called the *AT command set.*

> **Note**
>
> The AT command set got its name because its developer, Hayes Microcomputer Products Inc., chose to use the string *AT*, literally meaning *Attention*, as the prefix to its modem commands and because Hayes modems using this command set became the standard against which so many later communications interfaces were developed.

- Modem initialization strings, those portions of the AT command set that get a modem ready to do its job, can, like so many other modem features, be tailored by the user.

Modem Standards

A decade ago, modems that met the Bell 103 standard, which operated at a blazing 1,200 baud, were considered top-of-the-line. At the beginning of the 1990s, the great majority of modems in regular use adhered to the 2,400-baud Bell 212 standard. Then, Microcom enhanced the performance of modems by introducing its *Microcom Network Protocol* (*MNP*). MNP made great strides in data communications error detection and correction. For the first time, modems could transmit over noisy lines without seriously degrading data integrity.

In 1990, Microcom defined MNP levels 6–9, which provided not only error correction and detection but also data compression, along with speeds of 9,600 baud. In 1991, U.S. Robotics came up with a then proprietary protocol, High Speed Technology (HST), whose default throughput was 14,400 bits per second (bps).

> **Note**
>
> What's the difference between baud and bits per second? The first, expressed in—just to make things even more confusing—bits per second, has been generally used as a measure of the rate at

(continues)

which data is transferred between any two devices. Baud rate may have been *expressed* in bits per second, but it did not take into account coding schemes like ASCII or EBCDIC, which use more bits per byte than did Baudot.

The word "baud" is derived from that of its inventor, J.M.E. Baudot, who developed the five-bit code used by teletypes to send and receive data and whose name was applied to that original five-bit code. Bits per second in an ASCII or EBCDIC context is the more current and correct measurement of modem data transfer because it takes into account the seven- and eight-bit byte sizes of the modern world. Bits per second also tacitly expresses a fact so often overlooked: contemporary data transfer involves two or three bits per byte which are not used for data as such but rather for control purposes. So if you want the "net" data transfer rate of a modem, multiply the vendor-stated bps rate by a rule-of-thumb 0.75.

Now, only five years after the groundbreaking MNP 6–9, 9,600 baud throughput is considered acceptable at best. As with every other data processing technology, modem standards have evolved not only faster than anyone expected but faster than we could have imagined.

Current Modem Standards

Table 25.1 summarizes and briefly explains today's standards for modem operations in four categories. The modem standards examined here came about because of the need, recognized by modem manufacturers at the beginning of this decade, to establish and adhere to a common set of communication protocols.

Table 25.1   Modem Standards

Standard Speed	Description
V.34	Ratified in September 1994; 28,800 bps
V.FC	"Fast Class"; an interim standard used before V.34 was generally approved by the modem industry. V.FC modems are capable of 28,800 bps but may not be able to connect with V.34/28,800 modems
V.32 bis	14,400 bps
V.32	9,600 baud
V.22 bis	2,400 baud
Error Detection and Correction Standard	
V.42	An effectively error-free transmission
Data Compression Standard	
V.34 bis	In theory, allows data compression and therefore an increase in net throughput, by a factor of four. Or, put another way, can (once again, in theory—there are a number of factors that affect actual modem performance from moment to moment) help your 28,800 bps modem transmit at 115,200 bps.
MNP Class 5	Compresses data by as much as a factor of two

Standard Speed	Description
Fax Speed Standard	
V.29	9,600 baud Fax transmission
V.17	14,400 bps Fax transmission

The sections that follow elaborate on some of the speed-related information shown in table 25.1.

A Closer Look at Standards for Modem Speed. What are the differences between V.34 and V.FC? First of all, the latter is a slightly earlier standard. It was developed by Rockwell International and is its proprietary modem technology based on the industry-wide "V.Fast" model.

Both V.34 and V.FC have a maximum modulation bandwidth of 3,429 Hertz (Hz); each requires a minimum of 3,200 Hz to support 28,000 bps communications. Each can have its speed lowered by a number of factors, the most common of which is the nature of the "local loop." The *local loop* is the copper-wire connection from a PC site to the telephone company. Factors like the length and loading ratio of the local loop can lower communications throughput rates.

The differences between V.34 and V.FC are

- The frequencies and intervals at which they sample the communications channel

- The means by which they deal with certain types of noise on a line

- Their internal coding algorithms

The major criticism of V.FC has been that it does not always connect to a V.34 modem, even if both devices are capable of the same speed. This a yes/no situation—it both is and isn't correct. If either end of the conversation is a V.34 modem that can fall back to the V.FC standard, the connection is made as a V.FC connection, at the highest speed available for that connection. If the V.34 member of the duo has no V.FC capability, the transmission falls back to the V.32 bis standard and is therefore not able to operate at speeds greater than 14,400 bps.

> **Note**
>
> Finding a roadrunner of a modem is simple. All major modem manufacturers have V.34 models available. The following companies all make a V.34 modem:
>
> AT&T Paradyne
>
> Hayes Microcomputer Products Inc.
>
> Motorola Information Systems Group
>
> Practical Peripherals Inc.
>
> U.S. Robotics Inc.

V

Adding Network Services

V.42 by Means of Software Alone. V.42 bis and MNP each increase the throughput of "host" modems by factors up to four or two times, respectively. Each delivers virtually error-free transmission. Unfortunately, V.42, the more capable data compressor, carries two types of overhead. It uses a text-based algorithm to accomplish both error correction and data compression. This text-based operation in turn forces other overhead by requiring larger Extended Programmable Read-Only Memory chips (EPROMs) and processors.

Rockwell International designed its Rockwell Protocol Interface (RPI) in an attempt to overcome these shortcomings. RPI is a modem protocol that allows a PC to carry out the error correction and data compression tasks that would otherwise be relegated to the modem it houses. This frees that modem to concentrate on signal processing alone. RPI operates between the PC and modem, using the same High Level Data Link Control (HDLC) methods employed by both V.42 bis and MNP5. In effect, it permits a V.42 bis conversation to go on between a remote V.42 modem and a less capable modem at the PC end.

Keep in mind that RPI is a Rockwell-proprietary product. However, you can find a number of communications packages that are RPI-compatible. These include

- ProComm Plus 1.0 and above for Windows from Datastorm

- COMit for Windows and DOS from Tradewinds Software

- Qmodem from Mustang Software

The PCMCIA Standard

It should be noted that the standards just described apply not only to both external and internal modems but also to modems that adhere to the Personal Computer Memory Card Association (PCMCIA) model. The PCMCIA standard defines, among other things, how wireless modems used to handle conversations involving at least one portable PC must be structured.

The most important characteristics of PCMCIA modems are

- PCMCIA modems can exist as wireless or "normal," cable-needed types.

- Either variety of PCMCIA modems operates without relying on the UAR/T chip on the motherboard.

- The "wired" type of PCMCIA modem can run at speeds up to 14,400 bps.

- Wireless modems in this group can run as full V.34 devices. Among the vendors who make such modems available are Apex Data and Motorola.

Internal versus External Modems. As is the case with so many other pieces of data processing or communication technology, two factors distinguish an internal modem from an external version of the same model.

- *Cost*   Internal modems tend to be about $15.00 cheaper than a comparable external modem.

- *Ease of installation*   External modems take this award hands down.

Communications Servers

The term *communications server*, like so many terms in the data processing industry, is not consistently applied. Some people use it to indicate any device which accomplishes multiple access to even one communications port. Others identify as communications servers only those devices capable of housing, within a single chassis, the equivalent of several PCs.

Furthermore, there are two types of remote access that can be accomplished by either of these broad definitions of a communications server.

Remote Control

Remote control, the variety of remote access in which a PC reaches software and data on a network indirectly by taking control of a station rather than by direct logon to a server, can be accomplished strictly through software. Hardware remote control solutions, on the other hand, can be more costly, depending on the number and special capabilities of the processors on which they rely. As "little" as $4,000 or as much as $20,000 can get you a remote hardware controller like those manufactured by Cubix and J & L. A remote communications server in this category looks like figure 25.2.

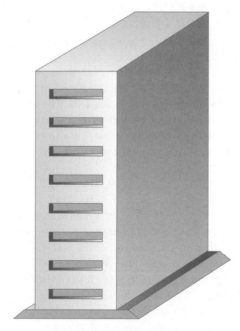

Eight slots, each of which houses
a high-powered modem

Figure 25.2

A remote control communications server.

Remote Access as a Workstation

A PC that acts as a remote workstation is, by means of its modem and the modem or communications server to which it connects, as much a part of the network, makes the same use of network resources, and accesses those resources in the same way as a machine that is just down the hall from the server. Remote access to a network requires both software and hardware.

Note

Access to a LAN as a remote workstation puts greater demands on the disk and processing capacities of a PC. This being the case, be sure to remember, if you're thinking of configuring your desktop PC at home as a remote client to your office network, to apply the workstation criteria set out in chapter 6, "The Workstation Platform."

Note

Both Microsoft Windows NT and Windows 95 include remote access server (RAS) and remote client utilities.

Many hardware vendors, such as Microcom and U.S. Robotics, offer remote-server hardware, and bundle appropriate server and client software with it.

Remote node hardware ranges from a controller for a single modem or fax line through multiple modems or fax management, to components that create, in effect, a *Private Branch Exchange* (*PBX*) running from a single network connection. Pricing for these units goes up in direct relationship to the complexity and variety of the functions they offer. For example, Global Village, Inc. listed on the World Wide Web in August 1995 its OneWorld FAX model 30-3600 at a price of $999. The 30-3600 is a one-line network FAX server for LocalTalk/PhoneNet networks. The 30-3750, listed at $2,099, from the same vendor offers a two-line network modem and fax server that runs on either Ethernet or LocalTalk networks. Even more complex, and more expensive, are the models CD-2, CD-4, and CD-8 Call Directors from Dataprobe. All the Call Directors act as de facto PBXs, switching calls coming in on a single line to two, four, or eight extensions (CD-2, CD-4, and CD-8 models, respectively). At the other end of those extensions, any one of a variety of devices may be installed. Modems, faxes, phones, answering machines, or dialup services can all be "end users" of the Call Director. Further, the Call Director carries out automatic polling, detection, and routing of incoming fax or modem connections and offers the ability to screen or restrict both incoming and outgoing calls.

Note

The remote server/client hardware/software bundles typically cost about $1,000 per incoming port. For example, the Shared Access LAN modem from U.S. Robotics is an external, two-port unit whose "network end" connects directly to an Ethernet network. Its July 1995 Web page listed it at $1,695. Their Shared Access Communications Server, also an external unit, priced out at about $2,000.

A remote control communications server such as the one in figure 25.2 can cost anywhere from $15,000 to $20,000.

Tip

Any means of remote access management worth considering should support at least TCP/IP and IPX/SPX connections; the addition of AppleTalk is also a plus. Also, look for the ability to manage V.34 modems and their 28,800/115,200 bps speeds.

Fax Modem/Server Standards. Fax servers were mentioned in the previous sections. These interfaces are backed up by a different and more extensive set of standards than modems. Table 25.2 summarizes fax modem/server standards.

Table 25.2   Fax Modem/Server Standards

Standard	Description
Group 3	Communications over ordinary phone lines
Group 4	Communications over digital telephone networks
T.30	International standard for establishing a connection, negotiating protocols, and controlling errors
T.4	International standard for fax image format, compression, and transmission
T.6	Advanced 2D coding; designed for Group 4 but usable by Group 3 with the addition of an API
Class 1	U.S. standard that adds fax API commands to the modem AT command set
Class 2	Evolving version of Class 1. Implements T.4 and T.30 on fax/modems
Class 2.0	Final draft of the Class 2 specification
CAS	High-level API for fax
T.611	Proposed international standard for high-level fax APIs

A Dedicated PC as a Remote Access Server

Another way of accomplishing remote access service is to configure a dedicated PC as a modem server. Such a machine typically houses a modem or a multiport serial card or is host to a similar device, a switch that allows a single RS-232 circuit to be selected by any one of four "sub-channels." In either of these scenarios, only one PC slot is required and as many as eight modem connections can be run from that slot.

Multiport Serial Cards. An example of a multiport serial card is the SS-554 four-port interface from Synergy Solutions, Inc. The SS-554 offers a number of features any network administrator would consider valuable. These features include

- The card is bundled with management software that makes the device transparent to the users who access a network through it

- Uses the 16C554 UAR/T chip, allowing data transfer at 28,800 bps and up with little or no error

- Requires only one interrupt for all channels

Note

Multiport cards that offer as many as eight serial connections are available from a number of companies, among them DigiBoard and StarGate.

Tip

Any PC you're considering as a server for as many as four modems/serial connections should be at least a 386. Use at least a 486 machine as a modem server for even more ports.

Third-Party Modem-Server Software. While most multiport serial cards come bundled with their own management software, buying third-party modem-server software is another, just-as-viable alternative. Any package of this sort that you consider must have the following characteristics:

- Supports NetWare (v3.11 and up), Windows NT, and Windows for Workgroups

- Supports IPX/SPX, NetBIOS, and TCP/IP

- Can manage either multiple modems or multiport serial cards

- DOS- or Windows-based versions

One such package is WINport from LANSource, Inc. This application allows you to locate a shared modem on a nondedicated Windows PC, a dedicated DOS PC (as old as a 286), or a Windows NT workstation or server running as an NT service. It can be configured to be completely "sharing-transparent," so that users sharing a modem or comm port are unaware of that shared status. WINport uses server and network resources effectively in that it has no TSRs under Windows and is capable of redirecting a call to the Windows COM port from communications software to the appropriate network device. The application also offers administrative and diagnostics utilities.

A more NOS-specific example of third-party modem server software is NMP2 from Network Products Corporation. NMP2 builds on Windows for Workgroups' capability to allow a network station to use a modem physically connected to another such station. Microsoft implemented this modem-sharing capability as a pooled faxing capability but made no provision for the full use of such a shared device as a "virtual" COM port accessible by any Windows-based communications software. NMP2 attempts to correct this problem.

> **Note**
>
> There are even shareware enhancements to the NMP2 product, available through FTP or the World Wide Web, from a company called Software Technology Service.

Port Switches. Unlike a multiport card, a port switch is an external component. One such device is the model 4P-CAS from Dataprobe. This switch allows a modem to be connected to a "master port" in the switch, which in turn selects from and connects to one of four DTE (Data Terminal) ports it houses. At the other end of those ports, a network component such as a workstation, server, or printer can be connected.

Port switches are simpler technologies than multiport cards and are correspondingly less expensive. The 4P-CAS lists at $325. However, these devices have a hidden cost, which you may have already guessed. Because of their means of operation—switching between users of what is, in reality, only one serial connection—these components are anything but user-transparent. In other words, if the accountant on PC #1 is "switched on" at the moment, neither the manager on PC #2 nor the secretary on PC #3 can send or receive anything.

Three Networked Modem Scenarios

This section contains examples of three environments whose needs have been met by using modem sharing or a communications server. These scenarios are used as the basis for compiling a single, concise "checklist" of what to look for in a network modem or communications server.

A Small LAN in a Public Library

In an effort to improve collection management, increase circulation through more efficient servicing of patron requests, and increase revenue through more efficient collection of fines, a small public library takes the plunge. It purchases and installs an Ethernet-based, NetWare-controlled LAN like the one in figure 25.3. While none of the library staff are data-communications literate, and many are downright PC-phobic, they quickly realize the potential benefit to the library and the community of offering "fee for service" features such as online research. Within months of the initial network implementation, the library's network is already experiencing a "turnpike effect," in which users' demands on a system or network increase as they become familiar and comfortable with the tools it offers them. How can this possible additional service be incorporated into their net? (They'd like every PC on the LAN to be Internet-capable.)

Order PC
which has been turned into
a "modern server"

Figure 25.3

A small library's LAN.

Two Departmental LANs

The seven-station, single-server Novell LAN in the Accounting department wants to exchange information and share all network resources with the five-station Windows NT network in Personnel. The trouble is, the two departments are at separate sites. Figure 25.4 illustrates this networking puzzle.

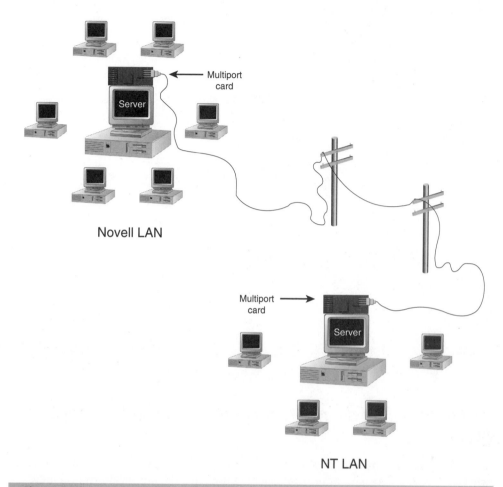

Novell LAN

Multiport card

Multiport card

Server

NT LAN

Figure 25.4

Two departmental LANs.

Linking to a WAN

The Anthropology Department of a university wants not only to become active as a Web server but also to link to the network of the National Foundation for the Sciences. The department has a five-station LAN made up of three Windows PCs capable of running xterm emulations and two UNIX workstations used primarily for graphics-based modeling applications, an adjunct to the department's research in the field. Figure 25.5 sketches what the department needs to accomplish.

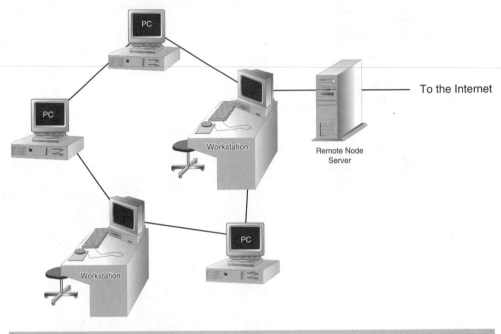

Figure 25.5

A LAN connecting to a WAN.

Network Modem/Communication Server Checklist

Table 25.3 contains data applicable to the three scenarios just presented. It can be used as a checklist for any network administrator who must add a communications or remote access server.

Table 25.3 Communications Service Checklist		
If You Have...	**And You Need To...**	**We Recommend...**
1 to 4 Users	Connect only to such services as online information, during normal business hours.	A shared-access V.34 modem. The sharing can be accomplished by any of the software packages mentioned in the section on "V.42 by Software Means Alone."
	Share a number of network resources.	A dedicated PC acting as a communications server, housing a multiport card; see the earlier section "Multiport Serial Cards."

If You Have...	And You Need To...	We Recommend...
	Share network resources, and connect to WANs.	Two communications servers: one a dedicated PC that handles remote access to network resources and the other a stand-alone device that carries out the link to the WAN. See the earlier sections "Remote Access as a Workstation," and "A Dedicated PCas a Remote Access Server," respectively.
More than 4 users	Connect only to such services as online information, during normal business hours.	A stand-alone communications server like that depicted in figure 25.2.
	Share a number of network resources.	A combination of hardware and software components to accomplish remote access as a workstation.
	Share network resources, and connect to WANs.	A combination of a "PBX emulator" like that described in the earlier section "Remote Access as a Work-station" and one of the hardware/ software combinations described in that same section.

Summary

In selecting a modem for any networking situation, take the following into consideration:

■ Standards for modem speed and modulation

■ Standards for data compression

■ Standards for error correction

If the modem in question must also handle faxing, you must also remember the fax-specific standards discussed in the section "Fax/Modem Server Standards."

If your task is to implement a communications server, be aware that

■ These devices can exist as software or hardware solutions.

■ Whether hardware or software, communications servers that must handle remote control differ from those that must accomplish remote node access.

■ The greater the number of users who require remote access and the greater variety of services they wish to use or share, the more powerful (and, unfortunately, expensive) your communications server will have to be.

Whatever the nature of the communications device you've chosen, adding it to your network requires you to attend to the following:

- Always verify that you are loading the driver(s) appropriate to the device and that you receive a message confirming that the board initialized successfully.

- If the drivers that you are using for your device seem old, contact the manufacturer to find out about and request any updated versions.

- A dedicated modem server requires that no other applications run on that machine. Make sure that such a server does not load any unnecessary software drivers or utilities (that is, mouse drivers or SMARTDRIVE).

- If you are using a memory manager, make sure it produces no conflicts with the memory the modem or communications server you've installed expects to use.

- During installation and configuring, make sure that you do not have any conflicts with other hardware such as a network card. Verify that the IRQ, base memory, and I/O address the modem or server will look for are not already in use.

- Problems typically encountered when installing and configuring a network modem or communications server include modems failing to initialize or initializing but appearing busy. In such cases, try standard troubleshooting techniques such as using a different port.

- When users can connect to a modem but do not get a response to specific commands or application requests, or when they connect but receive only garbage characters, check such configuration details as transmission speed.

Chapter 26

Adding Internet Access

The Internet has undergone remarkable growth over the last several years. That growth has been fueled both by individual users and by a rush of businesses, schools, and other groups connecting their internal LANs and WANs to the Internet. In this chapter you learn how to connect your own network to the Internet, how to configure your existing network servers and clients to use Internet services, how to publish information to the Internet from your servers, and how to secure your network to protect it from intrusions while doing all of the above.

Defining Internet

The Internet is just that: a large network which interconnects many smaller networks into a seamless whole. Originally developed by the U.S. Department of Defense, the Internet started by connecting internal networks at a few universities and think tanks, then gradually expanded. As other regional networks formed, like the New England Area Regional Network (NEARnet) and the Southeastern Universities Research Association Network (SURAnet), they joined the Internet. Commercial companies began to connect, drawn by the promise of easy access to information resources and the simplicity of joining LANs in different geographic regions.

Getting Internet Service

The metaphor of the Internet as an "information superhighway" has perhaps been overused, but it's accurate in some respects. If you build a house, you must make sure it's connected somehow to a street so that you can drive to and from your garage or carport. Likewise, the first step in connecting your network to the Internet is to find a way to move your packets between your LAN and the Internet itself.

Finding an Internet Service Provider

In all cases, you'll deal with an Internet service provider, or *ISP*, to get a connection. ISPs come in all shapes and sizes, from large national providers like UUnet, AT&T, and MCI, to regional providers like Mindspring (in the southeastern U.S.) and iQuest in the U.S.

Midwest, to local providers like AIRnet (serving small communities in northern Alabama) and Washington D.C.'s Digital Express.

Before you choose an ISP, it's important to think about your needs. Here are some factors to consider when selecting a provider:

■ How much bandwidth will I need? Most providers offer connections ranging from 14.4 Kbps to 1.544 Mbps; some larger services can even offer 45 Mbps service. Of course, the more bandwidth you want, the more it costs.

■ Are my bandwidth requirements constant, or do they vary? Some ISPs allow you to "reserve" a certain amount of bandwidth, then "borrow" additional capacity (at an increased cost) when needed. This option can be attractive if your average needs are relatively low, but you occasionally need more transmission capacity.

■ How important are reliability and availability? Not all providers have taken the extra expense of installing backup servers, uninterruptible power supplies, and other such equipment. Those that have can offer guaranteed availability, but it comes at a price. If you're depending on your Internet connection for critical communications, make sure to find out how your ISP plans to support you.

Choosing the Right Connection Method

After you've found an ISP to carry your traffic, you still need a physical data path to move that traffic back and forth. There is a variety of communications methods and speeds for connecting your network to the Internet; which one is right for you depends on your needs and your budget.

In this section, you'll learn about some different connection methods and gain an understanding of each method's benefits and drawbacks, as well as some sample costs.

> **Note**
>
> There are usually two separate costs involved in getting an Internet connection: the fee you pay to the ISP you choose, and the fee you pay your local phone company for the leased or dialup line that you use to reach the ISP.

Dialups. Dialup connections use an ordinary analog modem (usually at v.34 or v.32bis speeds) and an ordinary analog phone line to connect your network to your ISP. There are two types of dialup connections: *on-demand* and *dedicated*. As the names imply, an on-demand connection is only active when your network is generating or receiving Internet traffic, while a dedicated connection is always active.

Using dialup equipment offers some attractive benefits:

■ Dialup equipment is inexpensive, widely available, and useful for connecting to other services, like CompuServe or Lexis/Nexis. Ordinary phone lines are almost always less expensive than leased lines or ISDN.

- ISP charges for on-demand dialup connections are usually quite low—in many cities, as little as $15 per month.

- Dialup equipment is flexible; if you change ISPs, or if you want to send traffic to different destinations via different ISPs, modems are standardized enough that you'll have little trouble connecting.

Of course, dialup connections have some drawbacks, too:

- Dialup connections offer a maximum speed of 28.8 Kbps, and reaching that maximum depends on having "clean" phone connections. This speed limit is a problem if your bandwidth needs are high.

- If your office uses a private branch exchange (PBX) or private phone system, dialup lines may not work with it. If not, you'll have to get additional standard phone lines (that is, lines that don't go through the PBX) from your local phone company.

If you want more detailed information on connecting modems to your network, see chapter 25, "Adding Network Modems."

Connecting a Dialup Line to Your Network. There are two approaches to connecting your LAN to the Internet over a dialup connection. The first involves connecting one or more modems directly to your network. Just as some laser printers include an Ethernet port that allows them to be connected to the network, some modems or modem/router combinations can be connected directly to your network and shared. When a machine on your network requests a connection to an outside host, the modem connects to your ISP and begins routing packets.

The second, and very similar, approach is to mount a modem on one of your network servers and use the server itself to route IP packets destined for the Internet over the modem. This option is discussed in the section "Adding Internet Capability to Your Servers" later in the chapter.

Leased Lines. *Leased line* connections get their name from the fact that you lease an actual physical wire (or part of a larger-capacity channel, like an optical fiber) from the local telephone company to carry your traffic. This line is reserved for your use, and it carries your packets to your ISP.

Note

In the U.S. telephone system, a single pair of copper wires can carry 56 Kbps. 1.544 Mbps connections (often called a *T1* connection, after AT&T's internal code for a 1.544 Mbps line) are made up of 24 pairs of 56 Kbps lines. A *DS3* or *T3* line runs at a blistering 45 Mbps and is made up of multiple T1s.

Leased lines offer between 56 Kbps and 1.544 Mbps of bandwidth. *Fractional* leased lines offer smaller increments of bandwidth at a lower cost, but the leased line charges are usually the same. A hybrid line, like AT&T's Switched-56 service, offers the capacity of a leased line on an as-needed, dialup basis. However, these services are fairly expensive, especially when compared to ISDN.

Leased lines offer some unique benefits due to the nature of their physical setup:

- Leased lines offer much higher throughput than dialup connections; the lowest bandwidth leased line offers double the bandwidth of the fastest dialup connection.

- With the right switching and connection equipment and a fast enough connection, you can share leased lines between data, voice, and video streams. This *multiplexing* can reduce the overall number of lines you need, but it requires careful analysis of your average and peak usage requirements.

Of course, this speed and flexibility don't come without some additional difficulties:

- Leased lines are quite a bit more expensive than dialup lines, although the physical plant may be the same. Charges vary widely depending on your telephone service provider, although in many metropolitan areas competition between leased-line providers (including utility companies and even railroads!) is driving prices down.

- The connection equipment required to make use of leased lines also can be expensive. High-speed data communications equipment may require constant maintenance and handholding, and the skills required to maintain and troubleshoot it are relatively rare.

- Typical leased-line data rates are too high to directly connect to a PC's serial port, so you will probably need a router or brouter that can accept the analog leased-line signal and turn it into Ethernet or token-ring packets.

- When you lease a connection, the "wire" you're leasing only goes to one place. If you change ISPs or have to connect to multiple services, you'll need to plan ahead to make sure the new or added lines get in place.

Connecting a Leased Line to Your Network. The leased line requires special hardware, called a *channel service unit* (*CSU*) or *data service unit* (*DSU*) on each end to connect your existing network to your ISP's facilities. This hardware converts the digital signals from your LAN to analog signals suitable for transmission across the line. This hardware may be combined with a bridge or router to facilitate adding a connection to your existing network. Some manufacturers offer interface cards that fit standard EISA or PCI slots and put data directly onto the computer's bus; these cards can provide a simple way to get connected, especially if you're already doing IP routing on your server itself.

When your local phone company installs your leased line, you'll have a new jack, different from the familiar RJ-11 jack used with standard phones. The exact style of jack depends on the line type and the phone company. You'll use this jack to connect your CSU/DSU to the line.

If you're using a CSU/DSU built into a router, then you'll need to configure the router as part of your network; if you're using a card in your server, you'll need to configure the card using the manufacturer-supplied software, plus you'll need to tell the server how to route TCP/IP packets (see the section "Adding Internet Capability to Your Servers" later in this chapter).

If you need to know more about using bridges and routers in your network, see chapter 14, "Repeaters and Bridges," and chapter 15, "Routers."

ISDN. The Integrated Subscriber Digital Network, or ISDN, provides up to 128 Kbps over a single inexpensive copper pair. Each basic ISDN line (called a *BRI* line, for "basic rate interface") provides two 64 Kbps B channels (used for data or voice) and one 16 Kbps D channel (used for control and signaling). The B channels can be bonded to provide 128 Kbps of data bandwidth, or they can be used independently to carry voice or data.

If you need more bandwidth, you can get multiple ISDN lines and multiplex them together, all the way up to a *primary rate interface* (*PRI*) line—12 B channels and one D channel, for a total capacity of 768 Kbps.

> **Tip**
>
> To find out if ISDN is available in your area, call the National ISDN hotline at 1-800-992-ISDN. They'll ask for your address and phone number, then search your phone company's database to see whether service is available in your area.

The number of installed ISDN lines has been soaring in many regions. Here are some of the reasons why:

- ISDN call setup times are fast—around 0.5 seconds to go off-hook, "dial," and make a connection. With the right routing software, you can use a less-expensive on-demand ISDN connection from your ISP and only bring the connection up when incoming or outgoing traffic requires it.

- ISDN connections are more than twice as fast as dialups for less than twice the cost. For example, unmetered ISDN in BellSouth's service area costs about $70 per month, versus about $32 per month for a business phone line—but the ISDN line provides two channels that can be used as two 64 Kbps data channels, one 128 data channel, two voice channels, or one voice and one data channel.

As with leased lines and pure dialup connections, though, ISDN carries some negatives with it as well:

- Like leased line connections, ISDN requires special equipment. Although this equipment is dropping in price, a combination ISDN adapter and router can cost as much as $2,000.

- With ISDN, you can't mix ISDN and regular analog devices (like FAX machines or modems) unless your ISDN interface equipment provides standard analog jacks (some do and some don't).

- Not all ISPs or phone companies support ISDN yet (although most metropolitan areas have at least limited service), and many who do provide support don't have the needed expertise. Make sure you get in touch with your local phone company's ISDN office for service requests.

Connecting an ISDN Line to Your Network. ISDN connections require special hardware to link your network and the ISDN network. When the phone company installer brings your ISDN line to the point you specify, you'll have yet another kind of wall jack, called a *U interface*. Most ISDN devices, however, require a different kind of connection—an *S/T interface*. To bridge the gap between these interfaces, ISDN lines use a terminating device called an *NT-1*, which electrically terminates the ISDN line and converts the U interface into an S/T interface.

You have two options for actually connecting the ISDN line to your network:

- You can use an ISDN *terminal adapter* (*TA*), the ISDN equivalent of a modem, and attach it to your server just like a dialup modem. TAs, like modems, come in several forms—some are external boxes that feed data to your computer via an RS-232 port, some are ISA, EISA, or PCI cards, and some enterprising companies even sell PCMCIA ISDN TAs.

  This solution requires you to attach the TA to your server and use the server to route packets. When the server detects outgoing traffic, it will bring up the ISDN connection if necessary, then send the packets out.

- You can buy a combined ISDN TA-router, like the ones made by Combinet and Ascend. With this option, you get a separate hardware box that you connect to your Ethernet network. The router transfers packets over the ISDN link as needed.

Some ISDN TAs (usually the stand-alone, modem-style ones) include a built-in NT-1; that's a valuable feature because an NT-1 can cost as much as $200. Conversely, some "super" NT-1s (for example, Motorola's BitSurfr Pro) include not only the NT-1 but also standard phone jacks for connecting analog devices and even RS-232 ports! If you're connecting your server to your ISDN device, you may be able to use the RS-232 port on such an NT-1 and avoid a TA altogether.

> **Note**
>
> If you want to combine your two B channels into one 128 Kbps virtual channel (known as Bandwidth On Demand, or *BONDing*), be sure that your selected TA or TA-router supports this feature.

Frame Relay, SONET, and ATM. If you read industry publications like *Information Week* or *InfoWorld*, you'll see a lot of discussion of "supernetworks." These include Frame Relay, Synchronous Optical Network (SONET), and Asynchronous Transfer Mode (ATM) networks.

These three network types offer stunning bandwidth—ranging from a few Mbps all the way up to 1–2 Gbps. As you'd expect, they're quite expensive and are usually used to tie together corporate LANs into a wide-area corporate network *instead* of connecting to the Internet. However, as with most other technologies, increasing adoption is driving prices down, and some companies are starting to use these networks internally.

There are ISPs out there that can provide these types of exotic services, so if you need the bandwidth and don't mind spending the money, you can get connected!

Adding Internet Capability to Your Servers

After you have an ISP to carry your traffic and a physical connection between you and your ISP to do the actual work, the next step is to configure your network servers to speak the Internet's protocols.

The Internet's transmission protocol is, the *Transmisson Control Protocol/Internet Protocol* (*TCP/IP*). Although your internal network may be using NetBEUI or IPX/SPX, you'll have to make your servers and clients capable of speaking TCP/IP to exchange data with other Internet hosts.

Besides transmission protocols, there are several service protocols in common use; these protocols define how two computers can exchange mail, files, and Web pages over the Internet. Your clients and servers need to have the right software to make them compliant with these protocols as well; otherwise, they won't be able to communicate with the Internet.

Before You Get Started

Before you start making configuration changes to your servers, you need to ensure that all your Internet plumbing and wiring is in order. It's a good idea to set up a single client system, connected to your ISP via whatever connection method you've chosen, and test out your ISP's configuration with your clients. The sections that follow discuss some issues to be aware of.

Network Addressing. TCP/IP addresses are expressed as four numbers, each between 0 and 255 and separated by periods. For example, 129.135.1.1 is the address of Intergraph's corporate World Wide Web server. Network addresses are unique across the entire Internet; for example, only one machine can have the address 129.135.253.14.

If you're not already running TCP/IP on your internal network, then you face the task of assigning individual TCP/IP addresses to each machine that will be visible to the Internet. Your ISP helps you by assigning you a set of addresses for your network's use. These addresses are reserved for your use in the Internet Network Information Center

(InterNIC)'s database, so no one else can use them. However, you're responsible for assigning one address to each machine and making sure that there aren't any duplicates.

This can be a difficult job, especially if you have a lot of machines. Fortunately, there's an Internet protocol that can help: the *Dynamic Host Configuration Protocol (DHCP)*. DHCP provides a way for a not-yet-configured network node to ask a central server what its configuration parameters should be. MacTCP, Microsoft TCP/32 for Windows 3.11, Windows 95, Windows NT Workstation, and Windows NT Server all support DHCP, as do many UNIX versions.

Network Names. Each TCP/IP address also has a name associated with it; for Intergraph's WWW server, the name which matches the 129.135.1.1 address is **www.intergraph.com**. Your ISP will register a *domain name* for you with the InterNIC; this name is unique to your organization and identifies your machines and the type of organization they belong to. Table 26.1 shows some of the *top-level* domains on the Internet.

Table 26.1 Top-Level Domains Serve To Group Internet Hosts by the Organization That Owns Them	
Top-Level Domain	**Meaning**
.com	Commercial: companies and corporations
.net	Network: ISPs, network service providers, and so on.
.edu	Educational: colleges, universities, elementary schools, and so on.
.org	Organizational: nonprofit groups or organizations; non corporate entities
Country Code	Geographic: entries in this domain are grouped by country; for example, .ca for Canada and .uk for the United Kingdom

There are other top-level domains; for example, each country in the world has its own domain, like .uk or .fr. Each top-level domain is further subdivided, so that motorola.com, kraft.com, inria.fr (a French research institute), and mit.edu are all assigned blocks of TCP/IP addresses for their own use.

> **Note**
>
> .com is mostly used in the U.S. Because the Internet is global, the InterNIC is trying to encourage U.S. users to register by geographic domain instead of by organization, as Net sites in other countries have been doing for years. These U.S. sites fall into the .us domain. For example, the city of Austin, Texas, has a domain name of ci.austin.tx.us.

Mapping Names to Addresses. Computers don't care how they're addressed, but humans like easy-to-read names, like **www.intergraph.com**, not hard-to-remember numbers like 129.135.1.1. To simplify things for us humans, the *Domain Name Service*, or DNS, matches computer names to TCP/IP addresses. The Internet's DNS system provides a tree of DNS servers; each top-level domain has a master server, as does each second-level domain (like microsoft.com).

Your network's second-level domain will need access to a DNS server; your ISP will probably give you the address of one of its DNS servers for your use; however, if you're connecting more than a few machines, you may want to run your own local DNS server to allow name resolution within your network. You might also want to maintain your own master server for your domain so that you have easy control over host names and address-to-name mappings.

Microsoft offers a protocol called the Windows Internet Name Service, or WINS, which provides a DNS-like service for mapping NetBEUI names to TCP/IP addresses. When WINS is enabled, clients use broadcast name queries, plus the local LMHOSTS file, to map names to IP addresses. You may or may not run this on your network, depending on how many NetBEUI machines you have and whether you have to interoperate with other client types.

Gateways versus Routers. One distinction that we've glossed over so far has to do with how clients on your network reach the Internet. Before you see how to configure your server for TCP/IP, you should understand the distinction. There are two basic methods for providing Internet access to an existing network.

The first method is the easiest to understand: plunk down a router somewhere on your network, connect your Internet connection to it, and let it handle moving packets around. (Of course, the router might just be a routing process running on your server instead of a physical box.) This approach requires that every client that wants access to the service be configured to speak TCP/IP, so it can be quite labor-intensive. However, it doesn't impose any additional load on the server, and it may generate less network load than the second solution.

The second method involves using *gateways*. Gateways are programs (or hardware devices) that convert between different protocols on a network. For example, the Columbia AppleTalk Package (CAP) is a gateway that allows UNIX servers speaking TCP/IP to handle AppleTalk packets. By installing a TCP/IP gateway on your non-TCP/IP server, you move the workload away from the client and onto the server.

Most gateways depend on *tunneling* or *encapsulation* in some way or another. Both are schemes for wrapping a "foreign" packet, like TCP/IP, in a "native" network packet. As far as the client and server are concerned, a TCP/IP packet encapsulated in an IPX packet is just another IPX packet—until it gets to the gateway, which strips off the IPX header and framing data, decodes the TCP/IP packet, and sends it to the correct destination.

Which solution is right for you? Well, that depends on your network needs and wants. The add-a-router solution is easy to understand and easy to implement, and it scales well for handling heavy traffic loads. The downside: it can require a lot of work to configure each individual client. Using a gateway means more work for whoever maintains the gateway server, as well as more load on the server, but clients won't have to fiddle with their network configurations.

Adding TCP/IP Support to Your Server

Adding TCP/IP software (usually called a TCP/IP *stack*) to your server is relatively straightforward. In fact, TCP/IP connectivity has become so important in today's computing environment that, depending on the vendor, your operating system may have come to you with TCP/IP preconfigured and ready to run.

Adding TCP/IP to a NetWare Server. Novell NetWare servers speak Novell's IPX/SPX protocol. This is fine—until you want to connect to the Internet! The simplest solution to mixing TCP/IP and IPX is to run a gateway that converts between the two.

If the gateway's implemented as a NetWare Loadable Module (NLM), it can run on an existing server or a dedicated server; if it's a stand-alone system, similar in concept to a router, it will connect to the network at some other point.

In either case, each client machine will need Internet client software that can send out TCP/IP packets encapsulated in IPX packets. Most gateway vendors include a DLL that provides the Winsock interface for applications but emits encapsulated packets instead of pure TCP/IP. It's the gateway's job to take the encapsulated IPX packets, unencapsulate them, and send the resulting TCP/IP packet to the correct destination.

Firefox, Novell, Internet Junction, Internetware, and Performance Technology all offer suitable gateway packages.

Adding TCP/IP to Windows NT Server. Unlike Windows 3.x, Microsoft designed Windows NT to offer solid, fast TCP/IP support as part of the system's core networking tools. The NT Server installation process offers you a choice of whether to install TCP/IP as a supported protocol; if you said yes, you can skip over the rest of this section.

If you're still here, let's take a look at how you can install and configure TCP/IP on your Windows NT Server. Follow these steps:

> **Note**
>
> Most of these steps require that you have Administrator privileges on the machine you're configuring.

1. Open the Network control panel. To do so, go to the Program Manager, double-click the Control Panels icon, and double-click the Network control panel.

2. Scroll through the Installed <u>N</u>etwork Software list. If you see an entry for TCP/IP Protocol, then TCP/IP is installed, and you're done with this list. If you don't see TCP/IP Protocol listed, go to the next step.

3. Click Add <u>S</u>oftware, then pull down the <u>N</u>etwork Software combo list and choose TCP/IP Protocol and Related Components. Click OK.

4. The Windows NT TCP/IP Installation Options dialog appears (see fig. 26.1). If you're using DHCP on your network, make sure to check the Enable Automatic DHCP Configuration check box. Click Continue. Windows NT installs the software; it may prompt you for the floppy or CD-ROM with the Windows NT network drivers.

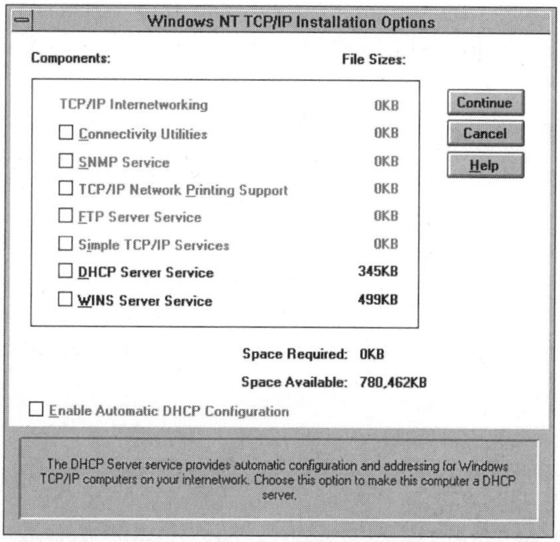

Figure 26.1

Use the Windows NT TCP/IP Installation Options dialog box to configure your TCP/IP installation.

If you want to, you can also host a DHCP server under Windows NT Server. To configure DHCP, use the DHCPADMN program, found in the Windows NT system directory. DHCPADMN allows you to set the TCP/IP configuration parameters for individual clients on your network, including the following:

- The IP address for an individual node.

- The subnet mask and default gateway.

- The DNS or Windows Internet Name Service (WINS) servers to use for resolving name-to-address queries.

- The time span during which these parameters are valid; the server will resend configuration parameters to its clients when this "lease time" is up.

When an individual machine is set to use DHCP, it can still override the settings from the DHCP server, but this isn't a very good idea. In general, networks that use DHCP should avoid mixing in manual configurations. Microsoft's TCP/IP stacks for its operating system usually prevent users from changing routing or gateway information when DHCP is in use.

UNIX Servers. UNIX servers are popular for Internet use because almost every UNIX variety includes a full range of TCP/IP capabilities, including packet routing, name resolution using DNS, and route tracing. Most manufacturers include software for all the major protocols, including DNS, FTP, SMTP mail, POP mail, and NNTP news, preinstalled on the system disk.

In addition, there's a huge number of third-party Internet packages for UNIX machines; many, like NCSA's Mosaic and HTTP software, are free with source code included or available.

Many UNIX manufacturers, including Sun and Silicon Graphics, offer specially configured Internet server bundles, made up of a UNIX workstation with preloaded software and authoring tools.

The chances are excellent that your UNIX servers already have TCP/IP installed and running; in fact, the whole reason why you have UNIX servers on your network may be because of their TCP/IP support! To configure a particular flavor of UNIX, please refer to your system documentation—a comprehensive guide for all the varieties is much too long to present here.

Adding Internet Capability to Your Clients

Adding the necessary capability to your servers is a critical first step; having done that, you'll want to configure your client machines so they can access the services you've made available via your servers.

This section explains how to configure your clients to use TCP/IP, how to add Internet client software for browsing Web pages, transferring files with FTP, and connecting to remote computers with telnet.

Adding a Client TCP/IP Stack

Before you can configure your network clients to access Internet services, you have to make sure that they speak the Internet's *lingua franca*—TCP/IP. This section shows you how to install and configure TCP/IP stacks on your network clients to prepare them for use on the Internet.

> **Tip**
>
> *Binding* connects a piece of hardware, like a modem or Ethernet card, to a protocol stack. Your network adapter understands how to speak TCP/IP after the adapter and stack are bound together.

Windows NT Workstation. Windows NT includes a fast 32-bit TCP/IP driver as part of the base OS; however, it may not be installed and configured during the default installation. These instructions are for Windows NT Workstation 3.51, but the procedure for Windows NT Server is almost identical.

> **Note**
>
> Most of the steps here require that you have Administrator privileges on the machine you're configuring.

How To Tell if TCP/IP Is Installed. Here's how to tell if TCP/IP is installed on your Windows NT client:

1. Open the Network control panel; to do so, go to the Program Manager, double-click the Control Panels icon, and double-click the Network control panel.

2. Scroll through the Installed <u>N</u>etwork Software list. If you see an entry for TCP/IP Protocol, then TCP/IP is installed.

Installing TCP/IP. To install or reinstall TCP/IP for Windows NT, follow these steps:

1. In the Network control panel, click Add <u>S</u>oftware, then open the <u>N</u>etwork Software combo list and choose TCP/IP Protocol and Related Components. Click OK.

2. The Windows NT TCP/IP Installation Options dialog box appears (see fig. 26.2). If you're using DHCP on your network, make sure to check the <u>E</u>nable Automatic DHCP Configuration check box. Click Continue. Windows NT installs the software; it may prompt you for the floppy or CD-ROM with the Windows NT network drivers.

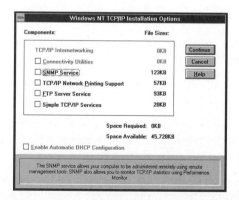

Figure 26.2

Use the Windows NT TCP/IP Installation Options dialog box to configure your TCP/IP installation.

Configuring TCP/IP. The Windows NT TCP/IP configuration dialog box is very similar to the dialog boxes for Windows 3.11 and Windows 95. If you're using DHCP on your network, you shouldn't manually configure the clients because any settings you change on the clients will override the settings from the DHCP server.

Now that the software is installed, you must tell your network adapter to support TCP/IP in addition to its other protocols and configure TCP/IP itself. Here's what to do:

1. Open the Network control panel and select TCP/IP Protocol from the Installed Network Software list. Select the network card you want to use with TCP/IP from the Network Adapter combo box. TCP/IP is now bound to the network adapter as a supported protocol.

2. Still in the Network control panel, click Configure. The TCP/IP Configuration dialog box, appears (see fig. 26.3).

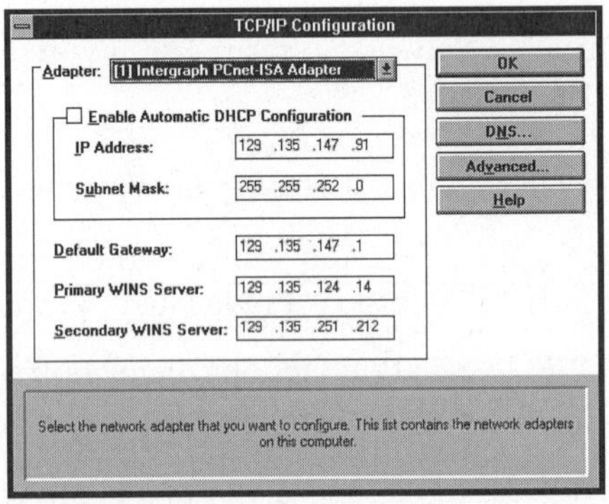

Figure 26.3

Use the TCP/IP Configuration dialog box to tell Windows NT about the gateways, routers, and addresses you want to use for communicating via TCP/IP.

3. If you're using DHCP on your network, check Enable Automatic DHCP Configuration and skip the rest of these steps.

   If not, enter the TCP/IP address and the subnet mask you want to use for this client machine into the IP Address and Subnet Mask text boxes.

4. Enter the IP address of the gateway for this machine in the Default Gateway text box. If you're using the Windows Internet Name Service (WINS), also fill in the Primary and Secondary WINS Server text boxes.

5. Click the DNS button. The DNS Configuration dialog box appears (see fig. 26.4). The Host Name text box reflects whatever the computer's NetBEUI name is; leave it alone. Put the domain name that this machine lives in into the Domain Name text box.

   For each DNS server you want Windows NT to use, type its address into the left text box in the Domain Name Service Search Order group, and then click Add to add it to the list on the right. Do this for each server you want to use.

You can also tell Windows NT to search the DNS servers for particular domains first; this helps you by letting you set the default domain to search for names with no domain specified. Add domains in the Domain Search Suffix Order group by typing the domain into the text box on the left, then click Add.

In both groups, you can reorder entries in the right list boxes by selecting the entry you want to move and using the Order buttons.

When you've entered all the DNS servers and search orders, click OK to save your changes.

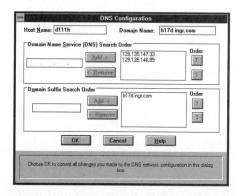

Figure 26.4

Use the DNS Configuration dialog box to tell Windows NT about the DNS servers you want to use for name resolution.

Depending on the changes you've made, Windows NT may require that you restart the machine before it can access TCP/IP services. If you need a restart, a dialog box appears asking your permission before restarting.

Windows 95. When Microsoft built Windows 95, it copied many of Windows NT's most successful features—including the 32-bit TCP/IP stack, which is built right into Windows 95. Depending on your machine's configuration, though, you may need to activate and configure the TCP/IP stack because it's not automatically installed by default.

How To Tell If TCP/IP Is Installed. Here's how to tell if Windows 95's TCP/IP is already installed and bound to one of your network adapters:

1. Open the Network tabbed dialog box by opening the Start menu, choosing Settings, Control Panel, and double-clicking the Network icon.

2. If you see TCP/IP listed in the list titled The Following Network Components Are Installed, it's installed. The entry shown indicates which network adapter the protocol's bound to. See figure 26.5 for an example.

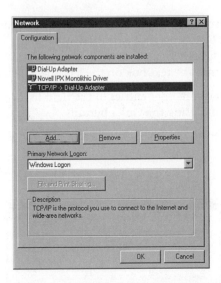

Figure 26.5

The Network tabbed dialog box shows whether TCP/IP is installed; in this case, it's bound to the Windows 95 Dialup Adapter, as it would be if you wanted to install TCP/IP for use over a modem.

Installing TCP/IP. If the steps shown previously indicate that TCP/IP isn't installed, you'll need to install it. To install TCP/IP, follow these instructions:

1. Open the Network tabbed dialog box. Click the Add button, select Protocol, and click Add. When the Select Network Protocol dialog box appears, select Microsoft from the Manufacturers list, select TCP/IP from the Network Protocols list, and click OK.

2. In the Network tabbed dialog box, look at The Following Network Components Are Installed list, which indicates which networking hardware and software you have installed. Your network adapter card should appear in the list; click its name and then click Properties.

3. Click the Bindings tab in the Network Adapter Properties sheet. A list appears that contains all the network protocols that your adapter can speak. Depending on your network, you may see entries for IPX/SPX, NetBEUI, or other network protocols; leave them alone. Make sure that the box next to TCP/IP in the list is checked, then click OK.

Configuring TCP/IP. Now that the TCP/IP stack is correctly installed and bound, you'll need to configure it so that it will work on your network. To configure Windows 95's TCP/IP stack follow these steps:

1. Open the Network tabbed dialog box, select your TCP/IP-to-network adapter binding, and then click Properties.

2. The TCP/IP Properties sheet appears (see fig. 26.6). Click the IP Address tab. If you're using DHCP on your network, mark the Obtain an IP Address Automatically check box and skip the rest of these steps.

If not, enter the TCP/IP address and subnet mask you want to use for this client machine into the IP Address and Subnet Mask text boxes.

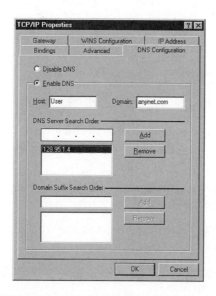

Figure 26.6

Use the TCP/IP Properties sheet to tell Windows 95 about the gateways, routers, and addresses you want to use for communicating via TCP/IP.

3. Click the Gateway tab. Enter the IP address of the gateway for this machine in the Default Gateway text box.

4. If you want this client to use the Windows Internet Name Service (WINS) for resolving the IP addresses of some machines, click the WINS Configuration tab and fill in the Primary and Secondary WINS Server text boxes with the addresses of your primary and secondary WINS servers.

5. Click the DNS Configuration tab. If you want this client to use DNS for name resolution, make sure the Enable DNS radio button is selected. The Host text box will reflect whatever the computer's NetBEUI name is; leave it alone. Put the domain name that this machine lives in into the Domain text box.

For each DNS server you want Windows 95 to use, type its address into the top text box in the DNS Server Search Order group, and then click Add to add it to the list below. Do this for each server you want to use.

6. You can also tell Windows 95 to search the DNS servers for particular domains first; this helps you by letting you set the default domain to search for names with no domain specified. Add domains in the Domain Search Suffix Order group by typing the domain into the top field and then clicking Add.

7. When you've entered all the DNS servers and search orders, click OK to save your changes.

Depending on the changes you've made here, Windows 95 may or may not require that you restart the machine before it can access TCP/IP services. If you need to reboot, a dialog box appears asking your permission before restarting.

Windows for Workgroups. Configuring TCP/IP services for Windows for Workgroups (WfW) is widely regarded as a black art. Until 1992, Microsoft didn't provide a standard for writing TCP/IP stacks for Windows, so every vendor wrote its own. The predictable result: applications from one vendor wouldn't run on another vendor's stack.

The Winsock standard, introduced in 1992, was an effort to create a standard set of features that all TCP/IP stacks could support. Today, it's quite rare to find any TCP/IP applications that don't support the Winsock specification.

How To Tell If TCP/IP Is Installed. To determine whether Microsoft TCP/32 is already installed on your client, follow these steps:

1. In the Windows Program Manager, open the Network program group and double-click the Network Setup icon.

2. In the Network Setup dialog box, choose the Drivers button to display the Network Drivers dialog box. When the Network Drivers dialog box appears, it will list the installed network adapters on your computer; each adapter will show the protocols bound to it. If Microsoft TCP/32 appears below your network adapter, then it has already been installed.

Installing TCP/IP. If the previous steps indicate that Microsoft TCP/32 isn't installed, don't panic; just use the following steps to install it.

Note

To complete the installation, you'll need the "Microsoft TCP/IP-32 for Windows for Workgroups 3.11" disk; Windows NT and Windows 95 provide the TCP/IP drivers as part of the installation, but WfW 3.11 doesn't.

1. Open the Network Setup dialog box by double-clicking the Network Setup icon in the Network program group.

2. Click Drivers, select your network adapter, and then click Add Protocol. In the Add Network Protocol dialog box, select Unlisted or Updated Protocol, (it should be the first item) and click OK.

> **Caution**
>
> If you've been using any other vendor's TCP/IP stack, Microsoft recommends that you uninstall it by using the Remove button in the Network Drivers dialog box *before* installing Microsoft TCP/32.

3. In the Install Driver dialog box, specify the drive and path to the Microsoft TCP/IP-32 for Windows for Workgroups 3.11 disk and then click OK. Windows shows another dialog box listing the protocols on the disk; select Microsoft TCP/IP 32 and click OK. Finally, Windows will install the TCP/IP files onto your disk. When installation finishes, the Network Drivers dialog box returns.

Configuring TCP/IP. Now that TCP/IP-32 is installed, it's time to configure it to work with your network. To do so, follow these steps:

1. Open the Network Setup dialog box by double-clicking the Network Setup icon in the Network program group; click Drivers, and then select Microsoft TCP/IP-32 3.11 from the driver list. Click the Setup button. The Microsoft TCP/IP Configuration dialog box appears (see fig. 26.7).

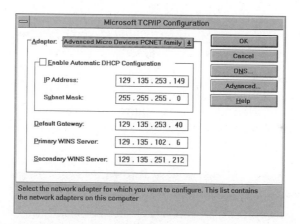

Figure 26.7

Use the Microsoft TCP/IP Configuration dialog box to tell Windows about the gateways, routers, and addresses you want to use for communicating via TCP/IP.

2. Select your network adapter from the Adapter drop-down list.

3. If you're using DHCP on your network, mark Enable Automatic DHCP Configuration and skip the rest of these steps.

If not, enter the TCP/IP address, subnet mask, and default gateway you want to use for this client machine in the IP Address, Subnet Mask, and Default Gateway text boxes.

4. If you're using the WINS, mark the Query WINS for Windows Name Resolution check box and fill in the Primary and Secondary WINS Server text boxes with the addresses of your network or subnet's WINS servers.

5. If you want WfW to use DNS for host name resolution, click the DNS button. The DNS Configuration dialog box appears. The Host Name text box reflects whatever the computer's NetBEUI name is; leave it alone. Put the domain name that this machine is part of in the Domain Name text box.

   For each DNS server you want WfW to use, type its address into the left text box in the Domain Name Service Search Order group, and then click Add to add it to the list on the right. Do this for each server you want to use.

   You can also tell WfW to search the DNS servers for particular domains first; this helps you by letting you set the default domain to search for names with no domain specified. Add domains in the Domain Search Suffix Order group by typing the domain into the left text box, and then click Add.

   In both groups, you can reorder entries in the right lists by selecting the entry you want to move and using the up and down arrow buttons.

   When you've entered all the DNS servers and search orders, click OK to save your changes.

After you've finished configuring Microsoft TCP/IP-32, you'll have to restart the computer for the changes to take effect.

Adding WWW Browsers

Many companies connect to the Internet just for access to the World Wide Web (WWW) and its wealth of information and reference sources. To access the WWW, you'll need a *browser*—the software tool that you use to view Web pages and communicate with Web servers.

> **Note**
>
> Netscape Navigator and NCSA Mosaic are both freely available on the Internet, but their use by companies is restricted. Please make sure that you comply with the provisions of their licenses and purchase copies as appropriate for your use.

Installing NCSA's Mosaic. The National Center for Supercomputing Applications (NCSA) invented the original Mosaic, the first graphical WWW browser. Although Spyglass now owns the commercial rights to both the Mosaic name and the code itself, NCSA has continued to develop new features and put them into public releases of its Windows version of Mosaic.

NCSA Mosaic for Windows 2.0, the latest version, is available via anonymous FTP to **ftp.ncsa.uiuc.edu** in the /MOSAIC/WINDOWS directory. There are separate subdirectories for Windows 3.1, Windows 95, and Windows NT. Note that there's no Win16 version; you must be running Win32s, Windows 95, or Windows NT to run Mosaic.

Windows Mosaic is packaged as a self-extracting EXE file; after you've retrieved the file, running the EXE file will produce a set of installation files. Run SETUP.EXE and Mosaic will be installed.

To facilitate installing Mosaic on all your client machines, you may want to create a central directory on one of your file servers so that users can connect to the server and install Mosaic themselves.

For more information on using Mosaic, see Que's *Special Edition Using the World Wide Web with Mosaic* (ISBN 0-7897-0250-9).

Installing Microsoft's Internet Explorer. Microsoft is among the companies that chose to license Spyglass Mosaic (the commercial version of NCSA's tool) rather than writing its own from scratch. To differentiate Internet Explorer from other Spyglass Mosaic versions, Microsoft has made it fully exploit the features of Windows 95, including support for long file names, shortcuts, and the Windows 95 user interface.

Internet Explorer is part of Microsoft's Plus! pack for Windows 95; to install it, all you have to do is insert the Plus! CD-ROM in your CD-ROM drive and click the Internet Jumpstart icon. The setup installer will place Internet Explorer onto your machine.

Note that Internet Explorer doesn't work with Windows 3.1, Windows for Workgroups, or Windows NT. For complete details on installing and using Internet Explorer, see Que's *10 Minute Guide to Microsoft Internet Explorer* (ISBN 0-7897-0628-8).

Installing Netscape's Navigator. Netscape, founded by several former NCSA programmers and the founder of Silicon Graphics, has one of the hottest software packages on the market right now: Netscape Navigator. Navigator offers a wealth of WWW, mail, news, and FTP features, all wrapped in a slick, multithreaded package that takes full advantage of Windows NT and Windows 95.

The latest version of Navigator 2.0, offers a host of new features—including a built-in scripting language, multiple "frames" on a single page, and a nicely integrated e-mail package.

Navigator is available via anonymous FTP from **ftp.netscape.com** in /NETSCAPE/WINDOWS. Unlike Internet Explorer and Mosaic, there is a 16-bit version of Navigator; the file names are N16E122.EXE for 16-bit versions and N32E122.EXE for 32-bit software.

Navigator's packaged as a self-extracting EXE file; after you've retrieved the file, running the EXE file produces a set of installation files. Run SETUP.EXE and Navigator is installed.

Adding Other Internet Applications

Of course, there's a lot more to the Internet than just the World Wide Web; Internet e-mail, file transfer (using the File Transfer Protocol, or FTP), and remote logon services (which use the telnet protocol) offer a lot more reasons to get wired. This section discusses installing and using telnet and FTP clients.

> **Tip**
>
> For Winsock users, The Consummate Winsock Applications List, available from **http://cwsapps.texas.net**, is an invaluable source of information. Mac users should visit the TidBITS page at **http://www.tidbits.com** for Mac-specific information.

OS/2, Windows 95, and Windows NT all include FTP and telnet clients, but they don't offer much beyond bare-bones functionality. For example, the Windows NT/Windows 95 FTP client is a command-line interface indistinguishable from its UNIX predecessors. Fortunately, because the Winsock standard defines how applications should access the network, it's very easy to change between clients. Let's see what else is out there!

FTP Clients. The basic purpose of an FTP client is to allow you to transfer files back and forth over the Internet. That may sound simple, but then so did the DOS command line.

If your FTP needs are occasional, you might be able to get by with the stock command-line FTP client—provided you don't mind learning FTP's command syntax. A better bet might be to use one of the excellent graphical FTP clients that exist for various platforms. Here are some features to look for when choosing an FTP client:

- The ability to store username, password, and directory settings for hosts you FTP to often; this eliminates the need for you to manually log on each time you connect.

- Long file name support. OS/2, the Macintosh, and most UNIX machines all support long file names, as do Windows 95 and Windows NT. Make sure that your FTP software does, too, or at least that it can gracefully deal with file names that are longer than the limit provided in the OS.

- The ability to retry connections when necessary. This can be a valuable feature when you're trying to connect to a busy site.

Telnet Clients. If you want to log on to other computers across the Internet, you'll be using the telnet protocol. Like FTP, telnet sounds simpler than it really is; although the built-in Windows telnet client offers a bare-bones solution, it lacks several essential features that you'll quickly come to miss.

Here are some features you should look for when choosing a telnet client:

- Good terminal emulation. If you're connecting to UNIX machines to run screen-based software like emacs or any curses-based package, you should make sure that your telnet program does a good job of emulating a VT-100, -200, or -220.

- Multiple windows. If you have to connect to more than one machine, the ability to have one window per session is a lifesaver.

- Configurations that can be stored and reloaded. Once you get the cursor style, font size, screen colors, and other settings adjusted the way you like, it's annoying to have to reset them each session. To avoid this hassle, make sure your chosen package offers the ability to store a configuration and reload it.

- Individual configurations for each host. Combined with the previous two features, individual configurations allow you to set all the emulation and display parameters for each host and store them by name, so that every session with a particular machine has the right settings.

Integrated Packages. Integrated packages that combine FTP, telnet, e-mail, and other functions (including WWW browsers, in some cases) have become increasingly popular. Why? They typically offer a consistent user interface, and the components work well together. For example, clicking a WWW URL in a mail message might launch an integrated suite's browser.

Some suites, like Apple's Internet Connection or Netscape's Personal Edition, are really bundles of individual programs, combined with dialup SLIP or PPP modules to provide dialup access.

Most suites depend on Winsock, which is fine if you're running on an OS that includes Winsock support. On Novell networks, you can use a product like Novell's LANWorks 5.0, which provides a Winsock-over-IPX layer that allows the suite to function normally.

Most integrated packages are commercial, like Wollongong's Emissary, InterCon's TCP/Connect II, or CompuServe/Spry's Internet in a Box package. However, there are a few shareware suites, like WinQVT.

Use the guidelines listed previously for choosing FTP and telnet clients to evaluate which integrated package is right for you. In addition, if you're buying a suite that includes e-mail or WWW browsing capability, make sure that what is included will suit your needs.

Publishing Information on the Internet

In many cases—perhaps yours—the driving force behind getting connected to the Internet isn't the desire to access information but the desire to publish it. Many traditional media outlets have discovered that the Internet offers a wealth of opportunity, and even small companies can maintain a visible, viable, and valuable presence on the Internet at a fraction of the cost of conventional advertising.

> **Note**
>
> Depending on how your network is configured, you may not be able to publish information to the entire Internet (for example, if your network is firewalled)—but you can still publish via FTP and WWW services for internal use!

HTTP Servers

HTTP is the HyperText Transfer Protocol—the engine behind the WWW. By running an HTTP server on one of your machines and making it visible on the Internet, you can open up a combination storefront, showroom, and technical support center to the 15-million-plus Internet users who can access the WWW.

In general, the current crop of WWW servers for Macintosh, UNIX, and Windows NT are all fairly similar: they serve WWW pages and can process interactive forms submitted by the client. Most offer address-level access controls and user/password authentication, so you can restrict access to material on your servers. Here's a short list of questions to ask to help find the right server package for your needs:

■ Do I want a single dedicated server or multiple, smaller servers? If you have multiple servers, will they be managed by individuals or by your network managers? If the latter, consider a package, like WebSTAR (Mac) or Netscape's servers, that can be remotely administered from a single point. Bear in mind that the very nature of the WWW argues in favor of having many small servers, all linked together.

■ Do I want to be able to process orders and other financial transactions? If so, you need a server that can accept encrypted transactions; choose a server which supports the Secure Socket Layer (SSL) or Secure HTTP (SHTTP) protocols, like Netscape's Commerce Server or Quarterdeck's WebSTAR.

■ Do I need technical support? If you're comfortable with the idea, there are a plethora of free or shareware servers for UNIX (Spinner, NCSA's HTTPD, CERN's HTTPD, and Apache, at least), Windows NT and Windows 95 (EMWAC's HTTPS, SAIC's HTTPD), and the Macintosh (MacHTTP). The low cost of these servers makes them very attractive in large companies where many individuals and departments want to have servers.

FTP Servers

Before there was a WWW, FTP provided a useful way to move files between computers on the Internet. The large FTP archives of Windows and Macintosh software at the University of Michigan, Washington University in St. Louis, and elsewhere remain among the leading Net sites, just because they're so useful.

You can easily set up an FTP server for internal or external use. FTP service is a nice complement to the WWW; sometimes, users just want to download a file, like a patch or a demo version of a program, and FTP does just fine for that.

You might wonder why you should bother with FTP when other file transfer tools, like UNIX NFS or Windows shared network drives, offer a standard interface that looks like the rest of the OS. Here's a one-word summary: interoperability. Clients using FTP can pull files from your site using anything from America Online to a Cray supercomputer, and everything in between. In addition, you can easily host an FTP server on anything from an old 386 running Linux to a fancy Silicon Graphics web server.

Most net archives, including those offered by major companies and universities, offer *anonymous* access—anyone can log on and fetch files (most sites prevent anonymous users from uploading files for obvious security reasons). Many sites also provide non-anonymous access; these sites require that you have a username and password to use them, just like logging on via telnet.

The considerations from the previous section apply here, too; you need to decide how many servers you need and whether you want to use one of the many excellent freeware or shareware servers (like Peter Lewis's FTPd for the Mac, or Alun Jones's program of the same name for Windows) or buy commercially supported servers.

A Word about Security

The Internet is large, international, and uncontrolled. These attributes have helped it blossom into the valuable resource that it is today, but they also introduce a degree of risk for organizations that connect their own networks to it.

Firewalls and Proxies

A *firewall* does just what its name implies: it separates "dangerous" things from things which need protection. For example, there's a firewall between the engine of your car and the passenger compartment. There may also be a firewall between your network and the Internet. Network firewalls serve two purposes: they keep unwanted traffic from reaching into your network, and they restrict the hosts and services that users on your network can connect to on the Internet.

Firewalls can be implemented in a number of ways. Many routers offer configuration options that allow you to force the router to ignore some routing requests, whether inbound or outbound; this blocking effectively prevents users from connecting to nonstandard ports or ports for services that you want to control access to. Several manufacturers make stand-alone firewalls which connect between your Internet connection and your network router. Finally, some software packages, like SurfWatch, allow you to restrict WWW browsing by users on your network.

Firewalls are typically not visible at the individual user level; the network administrators usually maintain them, and they can control which machines can "pierce" the firewall on an address-by-address basis.

If you already know what a proxy shareholder or a proxy holder is, then you understand *proxy servers*—all they do is accept client requests for services and forward them, if necessary, to a server that can answer them. In a typical proxy installation, all clients in a network point to one proxy server, which is the only machine permitted to make connections that pass through the firewall.

Almost all proxy servers, like those from Netscape and CERN, cache WWW pages. If multiple users request the same page, the page only has to be fetched over the Internet once, until it expires or changes.

Proxy servers are very useful for sites whose Internet connection is slow because proxy caching reduces the total number of requests sent out to the Net. Proxying can also provide useful anonymity for your users; some companies are very sensitive to competitive pressures and don't want to leave a clear trail of what pages their researchers or marketing employees have been visiting. If your ISP provides a proxy server, it's probably worth using it.

Security and Software

If you follow any of the major media, you've probably noticed a variety of reported security problems and vulnerabilities on the Internet. By design, the Internet is an open, collaborative network, with little security designed in. Many vendors have attempted—with varying degrees of success—to layer security on top of Internet standards.

> **Note**
>
> As of this writing, the Internet Engineering Task Force (IETF) has introduced a new version of TCP/IP, IPv6, that includes powerful features for verifying the authenticity of connections and protecting data from snoopers by encrypting it at the IP level. IPv6 can interoperate with "classic" TCP/IP, but if you're about to buy equipment or software, make sure to find out whether your vendor plans to support IPv6. The new features are well worth it!

Careful use of firewalling can greatly reduce the risk of an intruder breaking into your internal network from the Internet. Many corporations and universities have their firewalls set to disallow telnet connections to internal hosts from the outside world.

If you're running only machines whose operating systems don't support remote logons, like Windows and the Macintosh OS, don't assume that you have no worries; an attacker can still steal or damage files or data on these types of machines.

Most successful attacks that originate from the Internet are executed by hackers who steal, guess, or eavesdrop on passwords and access numbers—meaning that the best way to protect your machines is to carefully educate your users and administrators.

A complete discussion of security and the Internet could fill a book this size—and it has! The investment of time you make to learn about security risks on the Internet will be repaid many times over in both increased security and peace of mind.

Viruses

If you don't already have a policy for making sure that new software coming onto your computers is scanned for viruses and that all machines get regular scans, now is an excellent time to start!

Not many PC viruses have been widely spread by the Internet; most often, virus infections come from infected files passed directly from user to user. However, there's only one effective way to protect your machines and that's to *protect* them. Be sure that you obtain and use a good antivirus tool. Make it a habit—not just a policy—to use it on software you download from the Internet.

For more information on viruses, antivirus software, and protecting your computers from viral infection, see chapter 19, "Antivirus Technology."

Configuring for Security

Here are some recommendations for configuring your network and services for increased security and safety. This list is only a starting point; make sure to think carefully about your needs and liabilities when setting access and security policies.

- Use a firewall if at all possible. Many routers support firewall-type blocking and filtering.

- If you don't install a firewall, program your routers to reject incoming connections on nonstandard ports. You should also consider blocking telnet, FTP, and WWW connections to most machines on your network; instead, concentrate those facilities on one or two machines outside the main subnets.

- Depending on your network type, you may also want to configure blocking of non-TCP/IP services, like IPX and AppleTalk packets, which can be carried as encapsulated TCP/IP packets. For example, if you're on a Novell network you should ensure that your servers won't be visible to other Novell nets elsewhere on the Internet.

- Consider whether you can use a network gateway to connect your NetBEUI or IPX network to the Internet. By doing so, you avoid installing TCP/IP stacks on each individual client, which makes it much harder for an intruder to do any damage.

- If you offer an FTP server reachable from the outside Internet, consider turning off the ability for anonymous users to upload files. This protects you against having your site used as a drop-box for illegal or questionable material.

- Make sure to use whatever logging features are built into your operating system. Make a habit of scanning the logs (automatically or by eyeball) to look for suspicious activity.

Adding Network Services

Summary

As you've seen throughout this chapter, adding Internet access to your existing LAN or WAN isn't that hard. You do need to think ahead to decide what connection methods best suit your needs, and you'll find that extra time invested in security planning will pay off in peace of mind and increased security. Now that you understand what to do to bring Internet access to your network, you may find the following references helpful for providing more detail:

- For more information on bridges and routers, see chapters 14, 15, and 16 in part IV, "Connections."

- For more information on how to protect your networked computers from viruses, see chapter 19, "Antivirus Technology."

- Setting up your network for outgoing Internet access is similar in many ways to what you have to do to allow incoming access for remote and telecommuting users. See chapter 27, "Adding Remote Network Access (Telecommuting)," for additional details on adding and configuring remote access hardware and software.

- If you're looking for Internet client or server software for Windows 3.x, Windows 95, or Windows NT, drop by Forrest Stroud's Consummate Winsock Applications List at **http://cwsapps.texas.net**.

Adding Remote Network Access (Telecommuting)

You have probably noticed in the papers recently a lot of talk about the newest catalyst for change in employee work habits. Remote access or more popularly telecommuting has been heralded as *the* future of employee interaction with the workplace. As the word indicates, in tomorrow's world, employees will be able to sit at home and access resources at work—as if they were sitting in their offices—"commuting" over phone lines. They will be able to take calls from customers, access corporate databases, e-mail, and productivity applications without doing much of anything different on their PCs. While you may be skeptical of how seamless this would be—and rightly so—true telecommuting is closer than you think. Many companies either offer some kind of telecommuting services or are seriously looking at it right now.

Thanks to improvements in modem technology, growing acceptance of ISDN, and better application software in support of remote access, we now have the tools to provide quicker, easier access to all kinds of corporate data from almost anywhere. Of course, along with this ability comes a whole set of challenges for making such a system robust, fault-tolerant, secure, and flexible. You need to be able to provide it in such a way that it's supportable, manageable, and scaleable because you can be sure that once in place, more people than you expected will want to utilize remote access services.

In this chapter, we'll review some of the communications media available for remote access. We'll discuss the differences between the old way, remote control, and the new way, remote node, and where each has its place. Then we'll look at how to implement a telecommuting solution, including perhaps the biggest challenge—security. We'll also look at the various product-based software and hardware solutions to provide remote access as well as services that may be available from your local telephone company. Finally, we'll take a brief look at the organizational issues to be aware of when implementing a telecommuting solution. By the end of this chapter, you will be versed in the key concepts behind telecommuting and how best to implement it in your organization.

Introduction to the Communications Medium

Nowadays, there are many different media that we use to communicate. When we use that media, whether it be by making a voice phone call, sending a file across an Ethernet LAN, or dialing up a modem on our PC to access an internet provider, we enter a network using one topology, traverse either a public or private system of maybe a differing topology, and end up on some remote network of perhaps a third topology. The understanding of the different types of media, and their inherent characteristics, is key to developing an understanding of the issues around implementing remote access. This is due to the fact that as you develop a plan to implement a telecommuting solution in your environment, you may be forced to choose between one technology or the other based on cost, performance, or even availability, and it's imperative to know what each technology's advantages and disadvantages are.

The Different Types of Remote Access

While ISDN may be the next big technology for telecommuting solutions, the history of remote access has been defined by relatively slow-speed analog modems. As a result, this slow technology has very much affected the course of software development designed to facilitate telecommuting. In the days of DOS, 2,400, and even 9,600 bps analog modems, remote access had to be as efficient as possible, providing maximum functionality using limited bandwidth. This need prompted the development of so-called remote control applications.

Remote Control

Remote control software uses a simple concept to allow remote users access to corporate network resources. A host PC, connected to your corporate network, runs a piece of remote control software. It may then have a modem connected, or it may be connected only through the network. A remote user running the client piece of the remote control application dials up the host and takes over the host's screen and keyboard. That is, the remote user sees what a user sitting at the host PC would see. The application that the remote user launches is actually running on the host PC, not the remote one. This means that the speed of response for the remote user is dependent upon not only the modem speeds but also the horsepower of the host computer executing the application. When the remote user uses the keyboard or mouse, these commands are sent to the host as if the user were pressing keys or mouse buttons right at the host PC.

Software packages like PCAnywhere and Carbon Copy were some of the first using this remote control approach. As a result, only keystroke and mouse commands are sent across the wire, as are screen updates. Since this is a fairly low bandwidth type of transfer under an operating system like DOS, you could get fairly decent performance and had access, at least visually, to all the applications you normally would if you were sitting on the corporate network. If you want to actually transfer files to your remote PC from your network, you usually have to open an application under the remote control software that performs an asynchronous file transfer similar to your standard communications software using, for example, the Xmodem protocol.

When Windows hit the scene, remote control applications required some fine-tuning. Even sending only screen, mouse, and keyboard updates of a GUI-based environment like Windows required more bandwidth and, indeed, the first Windows-based remote control applications, used with the then current 9,600 bps modems, were painfully slow.

Uses of Remote Control. Because remote control applications pass only screen, keyboard, and mouse updates, they were useful for providing access to applications that would be too slow for users connected directly to the network via modem. This included applications like PC-based database systems or system administration tasks using GUI-based front-ends. Some LAN protocols didn't have the ability to provide dialup network attached connections. Interestingly, Novell's popular IPX network protocol was chief among those protocols that did not have available dialup software for quite a while. As a result, the only remote access solution was remote control.

Advantages. As indicated previously, remote control provided a means of providing remote access to your corporate network applications using relatively little bandwidth. Indeed, while remote control is quickly being replaced by remote node access today, there are still many advantages to using remote control in the LAN and WAN environments. Today's remote control applications have been optimized for GUI-based environments like Windows 95 and NT. Instead of passing screen and keyboard updates directly, today's programs allow the remote user to issue keyboard and mouse commands that get converted to direct device calls and are then sent to the host and delivered programmatically. In this case, for example, each pixel doesn't have to be sent to the remote user each time she scrolls a window; rather the Graphical Device Interface (GDI) commands are sent to the remote PC, where the screen responds accordingly. There are also some mechanisms that ensure that the screens on both ends are synchronized.

Remote control still has an important role to play as a troubleshooting and training tool in a LAN/WAN environment. For example, a system administrator might get a call from a user two states away who can't figure out how to access a macro in a word processing application. The administrator could take over the user's PC and guide the user through the process while the user watches and talks to the administrator on the phone. This kind of application relies on a higher-speed network infrastructure than analog modems but represents a good way to leverage existing remote control applications for use by LAN administrators and trainers.

Disadvantages. As mentioned earlier, remote control has played an important part in providing remote access to corporate network resources in the era of slow analog modems. But as we move into faster technology on both the analog and digital side, remote control has a number of costly disadvantages that make deploying it as a supportable remote access solution difficult to justify. Principally, remote control relies on the concept that for each remote user dialing in, a host has to be dedicated for that user to take over. This requires placing a dedicated PC resource on your network for each user who wishes to dial in. Not only is this costly, but it does not represent a very supportable solution.

There have been products that attempted to address this issue by providing turnkey plat-forms that utilize a single network-connected PC, running a multitasking operating sys-tem like OS/2, with specialized remote control host software. This PC would also contain some multi-port asynchronous serial card, supporting some number of modems (usually in 8-port increments). The product, called WinView from Citrix, was a good example of this. When a user logged on, he connected to the host and started a virtual Windows session under OS/2 (see fig. 27.1).

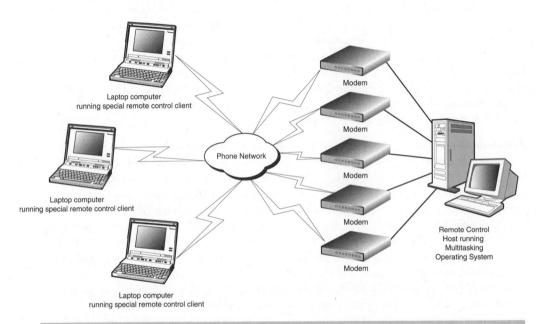

Figure 27.1

An example of a remote access configuration using a multitasking remote control server.

Depending on the resources of the host PC, you could accommodate several users at once, each remote controlling her own virtual Windows machine. This remote control approach, once stable, was a good solution for smaller remote access needs, but it simply didn't scale well. With anything more than 20 or 30 remote users at the most, imagine how difficult it would become to troubleshoot and manage a number of multitasking servers running numerous virtual remote control sessions over analog modems. Since remote control does not pass network protocols but does pass screen, keyboard, and mouse commands, it makes it very difficult to troubleshoot network problems. Any remote control solution, by definition, will require more host PC resources—either real or virtual—as you accommodate more users. This quickly becomes costly to implement and manage.

Since you are not actually connected to the network in a remote control environment, you cannot easily copy files between network resources and your machine. Generally, the remote control application requires you to start another file transfer application, which allows you to transfer files between your PC and remote resources, using some asynchronous transfer protocol like Xmodem. This is hardly easy to explain to a new user trying to do simple tasks remotely. While some remote control programs do provide some level of scripting to automate some of these tasks, it still represents a far more complex solution than simply being able to use a DOS copy command or the Windows 95 Explorer.

Finally, if you are still convinced that remote control is for you, consider that security should be one of your biggest requirements when providing access to your network. Given that, most remote control packages provide little serious security. Most come with a simple password scheme that may or may not synchronize with the network security you may already have in place. Many support *callback*, which means you can have a user dial up the host and then have the host disconnect the call and dial back the user at a predetermined phone number. This guarantees that the user is calling from a known location. Unfortunately, it does nothing to protect against someone using a remote user's PC without his or her knowledge at the given location.

> **Note**
>
> In general, unless you are building a very small remote access solution (fewer than 10–20 nodes), you should consider saving your remote control money and putting it into a remote node solution (discussed in the later "Remote Node" section).

Issues of Implementing Remote Control. Though we have discussed how remote control works in general, there are a number of points to consider if you decide to implement a telecommuting solution using remote control. First, make sure that you test modem compatibility end-to-end. Keep the list of accepted modems small, otherwise you will end up troubleshooting weird modem problems and learning more about the Hayes AT command set than you ever wanted. If you decide to use a version of remote control that uses the multitasking virtual machine method, make sure you err on the side of caution when specifying how much RAM and hard disk space you need. In this case, more is definitely better. Also, make sure the vendor provides a good way to manage the computer other than sitting at the console to check its condition. A good solution will provide some kind of remote management of the Remote Control Host, ideally using a standard management protocol like SNMP.

Remote Node

Since the advent of faster modems, the appearance of ISDN, and advances in software development, the remote node approach to telecommuting has become the preferred method to connect and manage remote users. Unlike remote control, where analog modems are used to pass only screen, keyboard, and mouse updates, remote node actually lets remote users act as if they are local to their home LAN. If a user normally sits in her office and connects to the corporate network via Ethernet, then remote node allows that user dialing in via modem or ISDN adapter to act as if she had extended that Ethernet across the phone lines to the remote computer.

Unlike remote control, which requires a specialized piece of client software running on the remote user's PC, remote node users actually run their network protocol stacks on their PCs, with a special driver to support either dialup analog modems or digital switched services like ISDN. That is, if you are accessing a Novell network remotely, you would run the IPX stack on your PC, and, instead of using a conventional Ethernet or token-ring MLID driver, you would have one that interfaced with your modem. Similarly, in the IP environment, your IP stack would interface with a Point-to-Point Protocol (PPP) or Serial Line Internet Protocol (SLIP) to access your modem.

Uses of Remote Node. Since remote node allows a remote PC to act as a real node on the network, extended through phone lines, it allows users to do things in generally the same way as they would at their office desks. That is, users log on as they normally do; access network drives and printers as always; run applications remotely like electronic mail, terminal emulation, host access; and, with some caveats, access word processing, spreadsheet, or other productivity applications' data.

Unlike with remote control, where applications run only on the host PC, all applications run over a remote node connection actually execute on the remote PC, just as normal network-connected clients do. As a result, it's important to recognize what effect launching an application may have across even a 28,800 bps modem line. This may be the single biggest limitation of remote node and requires user education to prevent undue angst on the telecommuter's part as he tries to launch a 6M application on a 14.4 or 28.8 modem. As more telecommuters move to ISDN, the effect of this will lessen, but there are definitely ways to optimize a remote node solution.

Advantages. The advantages of remote node are numerous, including better scalability, security, and manageability. For these reasons, most medium to large telecommuting solutions use a remote node type of access. This technology is more scaleable because it does not require any dedicated PC resources on the host side, as does remote control. Basically, any number of users may dial into the host, using either an asynchronous modem pool or leased lines utilizing any number of data services. Of course, the more users you have, the more modems you need to support. As an alternative, you can set up a leased line service at your host site, connected to a third-party network provider to provide higher bandwidth access to your users (more on this leased line method later). Remote node is also a more secure solution. Since your users are nodes on the network, they can utilize existing network password schemes to access resources, or with the help of third-party security tools, you can augment existing NOS security to provide additional protection. Finally, because remote node workstations run network protocol stacks just like normal LAN users, you can use the same network management infrastructure to manage remote user resources. This is very valuable when you need to control elements of remote access like user ID maintenance, resource access, capacity planning, and auditing of remote use.

Disadvantages. While remote node provides many features that make it the preferred telecommuting solution, it bears reminding that there are some limitations with the technology today. As alluded to earlier, certain kinds of operations should not be attempted across a remote node connection unless you have lots of bandwidth (for example, 2 'B' channel ISDN). Even then, the practice of launching Word for Windows across a remote node connection should only be performed in desperate circumstances!

Remember that since you are passing network protocols to and from a server, for example, you have the same overhead that you do locally. This includes protocols that require an acknowledgment for each packet sent out on the wire and requires education on the part of the end user since you may not be able to explicitly prevent a user from accidentally loading an application remotely. Because you are loading a network protocol stack on the end user workstation, there is some additional complexity required to support such a scheme, which varies depending upon which network protocol you're running. For example, if you're using TCP/IP, you need to decide if you want to give each remote user a fixed IP address or assign one at dial-in time. Despite these limitations, however, remote node represents the best option for remote access in today's high bandwidth network environments.

General Concepts When Configuring Remote Nodes. To set up a remote node system, you must first answer some questions about your configuration:

- How many users do you plan to support? A good rule is to double whatever you initially figure for; once some users get remote access, everyone will want it.

- What applications do you want to support and what platforms do they run on? You can greatly simplify your life by limiting the server and network protocol platforms you support.

- What kind of host-side access will you provide? Does the size of your installation warrant leased lines?

- Which modems and protocol stacks will your remote users be required to install? This may seem restrictive, but choosing a limited number and sticking to it will ease support issues in the long run.

- Will you have to accommodate digital (ISDN) users? This will require different resources on the host side. Does your host hardware/software support it? In your location?

- What kind of security do you require?

Once you answer some of these questions, you are ready to begin implementing a remote node solution. Depending upon your needs, there are a number of hardware- and software-based tools for configuring support for remote nodes. Some of these are discussed in the later "Product Solution" section, but in general, there are a number of issues common to all remote node platforms.

First, you will need to allocate at least one server, communications server, or router, depending on your implementation for use as a remote node host. You may want to have a redundant host available, either up and running for high demand periods or as a hot spare in case your primary hardware fails. This device will be attached to your network on one side and to some phone network on the other. Next, you will need to provide the hardware to connect to whatever access solution you decide upon. This is described later, but in general, if you are using an asynchronous modem solution, you will need some kind of support for multiple modem ports. This may be a multi-port serial card for a

Novell or NT server, or it could be a dedicated communications router that supports multiple modem ports on one side and standard network connections on the other.

After the host is in place, you will need either asynchronous or synchronous connections to the phone network. This may mean pulling a number of modem lines to your host or installing a leased line with DSU. If you decide to go with leased lines, make sure your particular remote node solution supports this kind of connection. Many low-end remote node solutions only support asynchronous connections. Next, you will need to configure your remote clients with a dialup protocol stack. Regardless of whether you're using Novell's IPX or TCP/IP, there are a number of access methods for each. For example, you can get a special MLID driver from some remote node solutions that runs just like a standard Novell IPXODI driver. A workstation with a driver such as this might load its network protocols as follows:

LSL

DIALER

IPXODI

VLM (or NETX)

In this case, the DIALER driver has an associated configuration that uses the modem installed in the PC as if it were a network interface card, specifying the number of your remote node host to call. Other IPX client stacks, such as those that come with Novell's Netware Connect product, Windows 95's dialup adapter, and Windows NT's RAS client, implement IPX (and TCP/IP) over standard PPP or SLIP interfaces, utilizing these standards-based protocols for dialup access. Regardless of the protocol, there always has to be some driver that interfaces between the protocol stack and the modem or terminal adapter.

Once the remote client's protocol stack is configured, you will need to set up security on the host side. Depending upon your solution, you may not have to do much. Regardless of whether you're using a server-based host, dedicated communications server or router, you have the option of setting up the host to provide pass-through authentication directly to your network. In that case, the user authenticates once using her normal network password. Or you can implement more involved security schemes, where the user has to authenticate to the public network when she initially dials, then authenticate with your remote node host, and then authenticate with your network operating system services. This latter combination provides maximum security but may also induce an undue and unwelcome burden on your users.

PPP versus SLIP. When you're looking at configuring the client's protocol stack using, for example, either IPX or IP, you'll probably need to decide whether to use PPP or SLIP as the underlying network protocol. SLIP was originally intended for IP dialup connections and provides no functionality beyond the framing of an IP datagram for serial communications. It does not provide any dynamic addressing functionality, as does PPP, nor does it have any authentication or reliability services. PPP, on the other hand, was designed to be a multi-protocol interface between the network protocol (for example, IP or IPX), and physical medium. It provides for dynamic host address (in the case of IP), authentication (PAP and CHAP), and reliability mechanisms. PPP is the preferred method for most dialup remote node solutions. Make sure any client stack and host software or hardware supports PPP, as opposed to some proprietary scheme for transporting network protocols.

Client Configuration Issues. When configuring remote node clients, it's much more important to think about where applications are executed. This includes applications like Word or Excel, as well as LOGIN.EXE or any other utilities that you normally access on a local LAN. This is because the time it takes to load and execute these applications over a remote node connection, especially an analog one, will literally take minutes and frustrate the user. While it may seem like an added burden maintaining multiple copies of an application, this will allow your remote node solution to do what it's best designed to do: allow easy transfer of data between host and client as if they were directly connected to their network. Indeed, remote node is ideally suited to true client/server applications. In this case, the front-end sits on the remote client, and the back-end does much of the processing and returns only the results to the client front-end application.

Tip

In general, a good rule is to keep all executables that you plan on running loaded on the remote machine's hard drive. Do not run them from the server across the remote node connection.

Using Dialup Analog Lines. Analog modems, both on the remote and host side are probably the simplest to set up. They don't require any specialized knowledge, as do leased-line solutions, and they don't require special services from a third-party network provider—you can access your host from the public telephone network. However, modems by nature are more difficult to manage remotely, and you need to add one modem for each additional remote user you want to accommodate at once. However, if you plan on using an analog solution, you have a number of configuration options.

Because you will need to accommodate multiple users, on the host side you need to set up a modem pool. A modem pool is a way of connecting multiple modems to your host, such that each one accesses your network independently when a user dials in. In the case of an asynchronous modem pool, you can set up a remote node server with a multi-port serial card, like the Digiboard, place modems on it as you need capacity, and provide remote node access to your network. If you have a PBX at your site that supports hunt groups, you can set up a group of these modems to accept calls to a single phone number so your users don't need to change their dialup number each time a call rings busy. As far as the remote node server is concerned, it thinks it has eight, sixteen, or however many modems your multi-port serial card supports.

> **Tip**
>
> If you choose to use a multi-port serial card, make sure your remote node server software explicitly supports it, with current drivers for your OS. Most problems with these solutions arise when you have unsupported hardware or out-of-date drivers.

Another option for analog modem support is to use a communication server to provide the access to your network. This is a hardware device that usually has eight to sixteen serial ports on one side and a network connection—like Ethernet or token ring—on the other. You can connect regular asynchronous modems to the communications ports, and configure it to provide authentication to the user just like a remote node server. Common examples of these types of boxes include Cisco's 500-CS or 3Com's Access-Builder. These boxes provide an easy means of setting up remote node services without the cost of server software and hardware. However, they are usually less feature-rich than a software-based solution. In fact, some vendors have used communications servers to provide the authentication mechanism and then pass the traffic to a server on the network that handles their remote user tasks. One solution allows the remote user to come into the network via communications server using a remote node connection that then passes the user to a remote control host. This hybrid solution has the effect of reducing the traffic the remote user has to pass across the phone line because they are only passing screen, mouse, and keyboard updates across their remote node connection. Of course, this requires them to run a special remote control client with support for remote node connections.

On the client side, your options are fairly straightforward. Whether you need a PCMCIA modem or an external one, make sure that you test whichever you specify with those on your host or server side. Just because a vendor says that a modem is Hayes-AT compatible doesn't mean that it will handshake correctly with its partner or maintain a connection at high speeds. While some people have strong convictions about which modem vendor they like, if you stick with the big names, like US Robotics and Hayes, you can't go wrong. It cannot be stressed enough that if you skimp on modems, you'll chase weird connection problems for most of your days.

Using Leased Lines and ISDN. If you are planning to accommodate more than 15–30 users at any one time, you should seriously look at a leased-line solution on your remote node server/host side. There are many technologies available to accommodate almost every level of need. For example, most good remote node server software, like Novell's NetWare Connect or Microsoft's Windows NT RAS server, supports X.25 connections right into the server. X.25, as you may know, is a packet-switching technology that has been around for quite some time. Its advantages are that it is available everywhere and allows you to multiplex multiple inbound calls into virtual ports on the server. To get X.25 access from a server-based remote node solution, you can buy an adapter card, like those from Eicon Technologies, that interfaces with your X.25 connection. Then your remote node software has drivers that work with the card to identify and control the virtual channels available across the network. Make sure you check with the X.25 card vendor to ensure that they provide drivers for your remote node software. Also, most hardware-based routers support X.25 connections.

In either the hardware router or software-based solution, once you decide you want to use X.25 (or any other transport mechanism for that matter), you will need to find a network provider that has an X.25 network you can use. There are many vendors who do, including most of the major long-distance phone companies and some of the large bulletin-board services like CompuServe. These vendors have Points-of-Presence (POPs) all over the country into their networks. This means that no matter where your remote user is, she can dial a local phone number to gain access into the X.25 cloud, where she is then routed to your remote node host and onto your network (see fig. 27.2).

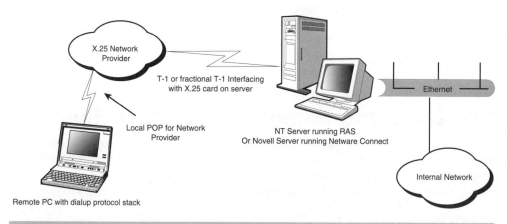

Figure 27.2

Example of a remote node configuration using X.25 to an NT or Novell server.

In addition to X.25, you have many other options for providing connections to your remote users using leased lines. For example, if you have ISDN users to accomodate, you might install a PRI at your host location. As you might remember from our earlier discussion of ISDN, a PRI gives you 23 'B' channel (64 Kbps) connections. To implement such a solution, you will need to find a third-party network provider that has built an ISDN network infrastructure. Many of the RBOCs and long-distance carriers have such an infrastructure. From them, you get a circuit, terminated at your server/router location, that provides PRI service. You then need an interface card on your server or router that supports PRI connections.

Once this is in place, your ISDN remote users dial a local POP for the network provider's ISDN network, and the call is switched to your host site and presented to your network. Remember, when planning for capacity, each ISDN remote user may have the capability of sending two 'B' channels worth of data. If you have 11 users doing this at once, your PRI is almost fully utilized. In some cases, this may not be a concern. Indeed, many ISDN network vendors don't yet support bonded 'B' channels, so even if the remote user tries to send two channels-worth of data, one of those will be dropped when it gets to the provider's POP. There are also limitations on the remote client side. Certain terminal adapter vendors don't yet support bonding of the 'B' channels, so the user will only ever get 64 Kbps of throughput. If 128 Kbps of throughput is required by your end-users, make sure you find out about this feature from both your TA vendor and network provider ahead of time. Remember, also, that installing a PRI is for ISDN end-users only. You generally won't be able to use it for your remote analog users unless your network provider can do some conversion within its network from analog to ISDN. You may need to build a separate leased-line service for your analog users.

If you find that you want to provide access to your ISDN users, but ISDN is not supported at the location where your remote node host or router is located, you may still be in luck. Many network vendors support ISDN into their network from your remote user, and then convert it to another switched digital service—like Switched 56 or Switched T1—outbound. In this solution, your ISDN users dial into the ISDN POP as always, but on your host side, you have a switched service that provides connection to your network. The same capacity rules apply.

Implementing Remote Access Solutions

Now that we have looked at the underpinning of remote access, you need to consider some implementation issues. Chief among these is security. While security is somewhat dependent upon whether you implement a remote node or remote control solution, there are some preferred ways of securing your network.

Security Issues

As you can imagine, the idea of opening up your sensitive corporate network to outside users presents several security challenges. The biggest of these is to protect your company's assets without making it difficult for the remote user to access your network. With this in mind, there are number of authentication and verification schemes you should consider.

Using Passwords and Callback. Most remote node and remote control server software supports simple passwording. That is, you can set up the software to prompt the remote user for a password just to get into the remote access server, and then the user still has to authenticate with the network operating system (for example, Novell NetWare or Windows NT). Of course, you then need to maintain two sets of passwords, which can be administratively taxing and add to the user's frustration. It also may not be very secure if the passwords are sent *in the clear*, meaning they are not encrypted at all. Anyone sniffing the wire can then get your password and hack into your network.

In addition to simple passwording, most software-based solutions like RAS or NetWare Connect provide a callback mechanism. This allows the system administrator to set up a list of users who are eligible to dial into the server and a fixed phone number where they are dialing from. When the remote user dials up, he enters his username. Then the server disconnects him and dials back to his predefined number. This option may not work if the remote user is mobile and requires administration if the remote user's number changes, but it provides an acceptable mechanism for basic security.

Using Authentication Services. Another security option is to require your users to authenticate to your remote access network protocol, prior to being granted access to the remote network services. Most PPP stacks supports one of two authentication options. These are Password Authentication Protocol (PAP) and Challenge-Handshake Authentication Protocol (CHAP). PAP provides basic password authentication to your network. That is, your remote user dials your host or router, is prompted for a password before being given access to your network, and then can use her normal NOS password to access network resources. PAP passwords are passed as clear text and are vulnerable to being tapped into. CHAP, on the other hand, uses a challenge-response mechanism to authenticate the user to the network. Each remote user has a secret that is known only by the host or router running CHAP. The user uses this secret to calculate a value using some algorithm, and that value is passed to the server. The server compares the value to its secret, spun against the algorithm and if they match, the user is allowed access to the network. This process continues periodically during the life of the connection to ensure that the connection remains valid. With CHAP, no passwords are sent across the wire, so the connection is harder to spoof.

There are many variations on CHAP that you can use. One common solution is to run an authentication server, which interacts with your remote access point, be it a router or a server, and employs some authentication scheme to permit the user access to the network. These authentication servers employ a number of different encryption algorithms to provide secure access, including well-known ones like the Data Encryption Standard (DES), RSA, Kerberos, and any number of proprietary schemes. This kind of configuration is illustrated in figure 27.3.

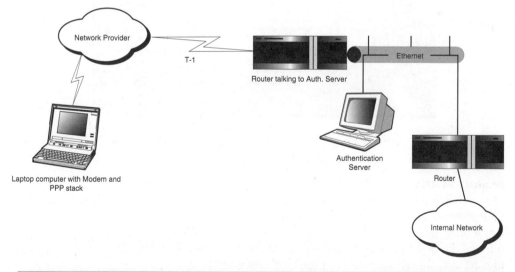

Figure 27.3

An example of a remote access solution using an encryption server.

In this scenario, the user carries a token when she is accessing the remote network. The token, which physically looks like a thick credit-card or calculator, is synchronized with the authentication server to provide a unique password that changes on a periodic basis (called a time-synchronous authentication scheme). This password is then used, sometimes accompanied by a user PIN, to authenticate the user to the network. There are also asynchronous authentication mechanisms available. These methods, also called challenge-response, present a challenge to the user, which requires a response; then she is prompted to provide a password, perhaps based on some token scheme. In this way, the user has to know the response to the challenge, as well as have a valid token-generated password.

All of these schemes address only authentication security and don't address payload security. That is, how is the data, carried on the line, protected? You will need to get additional software if you want to encrypt data sent back and forth. To do this, you will need more processing power on the server and client doing the encryption. Figure 27.4 shows a screen shot of some of the authentication and encryption options provided by Windows NT's RAS server.

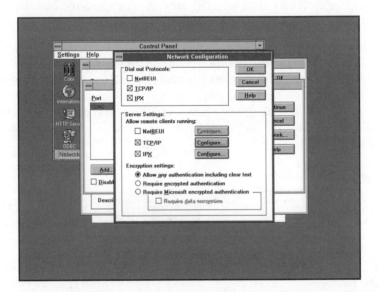

Figure 27.4

Windows NT RAS' authentication and encryption options.

Product Solutions

There are literally hundreds of vendors providing some basic remote control or remote node software and hardware. Rather than try to describe them all, we'll touch on just the major ones that are available with Novell NetWare and Windows NT, as well as discuss some of the available router-based solutions and some other unconventional options that are available either now or in the near future.

NetWare Connect. NetWare Connect 2.0 is Novell's newest offering in the remote access arena. It's a separate package designed to provide both dial-in and dial-out capabilities on a Novell network. It runs as a series of NLMs on your Novell 3.x, 4.x, or run-time server. It supports remote IPX, IP, and ARAP (AppleTalk Remote Access Protocol) clients, and provides (new to 2.0) PPP and SLIP drivers for IP and IPX clients. Each NetWare Connect server can support up to 128 simultaneous connections inbound and outbound. It can provide authentication using NDS or other more standards-based authentication schemes. NetWare Connect comes with its own Windows-based Management Console, called ConnectView. As a modem pool for outbound calls, it supports LAN redirectors like Int14 and NASI (Novell Asynchronous Service Interface). In this case, if a user on the LAN wanted to dial out to a bulletin-board service, he could use a communication package like Procomm Plus for Networks to access the NetWare Connect-attached modems using one of the LAN redirectors. NetWare Connect also supports inbound remote control connections, where a remote control host running, for example, PC Anywhere on your corporate LAN, can attach to a NetWare Connect port and wait for a remote control client dialing in. In this case, it is acting as a sort of remote control redirector.

NetWare Connect allows you to assign certain ports for either inbound or outbound usage and provides auditing and management of port usage. It can also be managed through an SNMP management platform. NetWare Connect supports asynchronous multi-port serial boards, as well as ISDN and X.25.

NT RAS. The Remote Access Service that comes with Windows NT was designed to provide both client and server remote node functionality. The RAS server service that comes with NT workstation only supports one inbound connection. The RAS server service that comes with NT server supports 256 simultaneous inbound connections. RAS does not have support for dial-out modem pooling, though there are third-party products available to do this. Both the RAS server and client software support IP, IPX, and NetBEUI. Additionally, it supports dynamic IP addressing using either a static IP address pool or Microsoft's Dynamic Host Configuration Protocol (DHCP). IP support includes both PPP and SLIP, and authentication can be done under PPP using PAP, Microsoft's own authentication or a third-party authentication service. Additionally, you can use either the Windows 95 dialup adapter or any third-party PPP stack to dial into a RAS server, using PAP authentication or even no authentication.

The RAS client comes with a crude scripting language for automating certain logon sequences. Setup of the RAS server is GUI-based and fairly straightforward. You can log user access to NT's event viewer, and there is an admin tool that allows you to define who in NT's domain database can log on to the RAS server.

Router-Based Solutions. There are any number of router-based solutions for setting up the host side of a remote access network. Most of them are remote node solutions, because they simply perform a routing function between some remote medium like ISDN-PRI or X.25 and the internal network. Some, like the 3Com Accessbuilder-Citrix solution, work with software products to allow hybrid remote node, remote control functionality. If you are building a fairly large remote access solution, a hardware-based router, in conjunction with some secure authentication service, is probably the most reliable, easy-to-maintain solution you will find. This is because routers as remote node providers fit easily into your existing network infrastructure, providing only slightly different functionality than they normally do.

Third-Party Network Providers. If you're looking to provide remote access to your mobile users utilizing the existing Internet and telephone networks, you have some interesting and innovative options. There is a service available on the Internet called Winserve (**http://www.winserve.com**) that provides Windows clients with a roving LAN resource. Winserve offers NT server file storage and client name registration using NT's TCP/IP-based WINS NetBIOS name resolution service, as well as Microsoft mail post office services for your Windows for Workgroups, Windows 95, and Windows NT clients. Basically, it's as if the Internet were your own giant NT LAN.

You dial your Internet provider, connect to the Internet, and register with WINS on Winserve's site; then you can browse NT server resources as well as other NetBIOS machines that have registered. From wherever you are, you can connect to an NT server where you have stored files and access them as if you were on your corporate LAN. Of course, you still have to deal with the security issues of Internet, but for non-sensitive files or mail, it's an innovative way of providing access to users from anywhere in the world.

On the Novell side, you also have an option. NetWare Connect Services, provided by Novell in conjunction with AT&T, provides you with a global IPX-based network. You can dial into AT&T's network and access pre-registered Novell services anywhere, including your own corporate NetWare Servers. There's also a gateway service to the Internet, providing a full-range of remote access possibilities in a mixed TCP/IP and IPX environment.

Options Provided by Your Local Telco. Your local telephone company may also have some resources that you might not have considered to facilitate your telecommuting solutions. Several RBOCs are proposing and have tested neighborhood telecommuting centers, where an employee can go with his laptop, plug into a desk that has an ISDN connection, and access his corporate network. In addition to just a desk and a plug, he also has general office services like faxing, voice and video conferencing, and printing. Companies can work with their RBOCs to provide access to these centers for their employees and save money by putting special connections in employees' homes, and they allow the employee to work close to home and still have all the resources they need to do their job. Expect to see these centers springing up more and more, especially as the phone companies push the "ISDN everywhere" concept.

Future Solutions. In the not too distant future, service providers that once were regulated out of the networking market will play a key role in the telecommuting world. Television cable companies are already planning how they will provide high-speed Internet connections to every person's home using the existing coaxial cable infrastructure, which is ideally suited to high-bandwidth network traffic. As the Internet becomes a more secure place to do business, more companies will be able to provide remote access over it, and more of today's Internet providers will become remote access providers as well. The key feature here is that higher bandwidth and greater accessibility to broadband high-bandwidth networks will make transfer of voice and data traffic much easier to implement within your organization. Once again, security is the key for this to happen.

Organizational Issues

While you may not think of it right away, providing a telecommuting solution to your end-users could fundamentally affect the way your company's employees interact. If you give the user the option to work at home, without restriction, chances are that they will. This may have an obvious effect on their productivity and accountability but also on the culture of your organization. It's definitely worth spending some time with management and a human resources specialist to define a very clear policy about telecommuting—including how often an employee can do it, which tasks are telecommutable and which must be done at home, how a manager can evaluate an employee if they are gone two days a week, and how to avoid bias against telecommuting employees, who may not be present when the good assignments are handed out, when the praises are heaped, or when something goes wrong.

Summary

We have looked at the many ways you can provide remote access to your employees via either remote control or remote node. Today, increasingly high bandwidth access methods like ISDN make remote node the most cost efficient, secure, and easy-to-manage function. Additionally, leased-line technology can allow you to accommodate many users at once, and third-party network providers can provide Points of Presence for your users, wherever they may be.

There are many vendors providing remote access solutions, from Novell's NetWare Connect product providing up to 128 simultaneous inbound and outbound IP, IPX, and Macintosh connections to Windows NT's RAS server with support for 256 simultaneous sessions of inbound IP, IPX, or NetBEUI clients. Along with these software products and hardware-based routers are the various security mechanisms for accessing your network, including the basic PAP protocol for PPP, the more feature-rich CHAP, and third-party authentication services that work in conjunction with hardware and software solutions.

Finally, as we move into the high-bandwidth days, your options for providing telecommuting to your employees will only expand, adding new players, like cable companies, and new challenges for your organization as you deal with employees who spend less time in the office and more time on the road or at home.

Adding Network Services

Chapter 28

Adding Diskless Workstations

This chapter explains how you can manage boot configurations centrally using *diskless workstations*. It explores the reasons why you might want to use diskless workstations, as well as looking at some of the drawbacks to their use. After some background on boot PROMs and how they work, it describes in detail how to set up diskless workstations in a single- or multi-server environment.

What Are Diskless Workstations?

Diskless workstations are client workstations that boot from a file server rather than from a local disk. The "disk" in "diskless" really refers to the boot disk. So-called diskless workstations frequently have floppy disk drives and sometimes have hard disks, but they don't boot from them. Instead, their boot configuration and startup files are stored on a server and accessed over the network. Diskless workstations generally boot up more quickly than workstations booted from floppies but not quite as quickly as workstations booted from a hard disk.

Remote Boot PROMs

This bootup behavior is achieved using a *boot PROM (programmable read only memory)*, an optional chip that plugs into a special socket on a network adapter. The boot PROM takes control of the workstation boot process and allows a special container file on the server (a *boot image*) to act like a phantom boot floppy disk. The effect is quite convincing—if the workstation has a floppy drive, its drive activity LED lights up and its spindle spins as it reads from a disk that does not exist! Once the bootup process has been completed, the boot PROM retires gracefully and the workstation behaves as if it had been booted from a floppy disk.

It is worth noting at this point that there are two basic types of boot PROM: the older Novell Remote Boot PROMs and the more recent (since 1992) Enhanced Remote Boot PROMs. The former type are variously referred to as IPX PROMs, traditional PROMs, or

Novell PROMs. The latter are referred to as RPL PROMs (RPL stands for remote program load), enhanced PROMs, IBM RPL PROMs, or FIND-FOUND PROMs. Both types carry out a similar function but in quite different ways. The differences in behavior are explained in context throughout relevant sections of this chapter.

The Remote Boot Process

This is an overview of the sequence of events which occurs when a diskless workstation boots from a file server:

1. The workstation's CPU executes the motherboard's ROM BIOS code.

2. The ROM BIOS searches the memory locations used by adapters and detects the boot PROM.

3. The boot PROM code starts to execute.

4. The boot PROM checks drive A for a boot disk. If it finds one, the boot PROM code terminates and the workstation starts to boot from the disk in drive A.

5. If no boot floppy is found in drive A, the boot PROM looks for a hard disk with a boot sector. If it finds one, a prompt appears on-screen asking whether the workstation should boot from the network using the boot PROM:

   ```
   Boot from Network (Y or N)?
   ```

   If the answer is no, the boot PROM code terminates and the workstation starts to boot from the hard disk. If the answer is yes, the boot PROM continues as described in the next step.

6. If no bootable disk is present in the workstation, or if there is a hard disk but the user has requested a network boot, the boot PROM locates a boot image file on the server and downloads its contents. A *boot image* is a special container file that encapsulates the entire contents of a boot floppy: boot sector, command interpreter, CONFIG.SYS, AUTOEXEC.BAT, and all the driver and configuration files needed to boot up and connect to a server. Finding the boot image file can be a complex matter. It is done in two completely different ways by the two different types of boot PROMs, as explained in the "Preparing the Server" section later in this chapter.

7. Whether it's an IPX or RPL PROM, the PROM downloads the contents of the boot image file from the server. The workstation processes the contents of the image file as if it were reading it from a boot floppy. It loads the DOS system files and COMMAND.COM, which parses CONFIG.SYS and AUTOEXEC.BAT in the usual way. Any drivers loaded before the workstation shell must be contained in the boot image file.

8. At the point when the workstation shell (NETX.EXE or VLM.EXE) is loaded—and the workstation connects to a server—the workstation switches from reading a batch file contained in the boot image file to reading a batch file with the same name but stored in the LOGIN area of the server to which it has just connected. The boot PROM's job is finished.

Why Use Diskless Workstations?

Boot PROMs can be a powerful management asset to many network managers, but they are not always appropriate. This section looks at the pros and cons.

Advantages to Going Diskless

Diskless workstations are particularly suited to environments where large numbers of similarly configured PCs are used or where users do not maintain the software on their own machine. Booting workstations from a file server has three major advantages over using floppy or local hard disks as boot media:

- Central management

- Sharing common files

- Write-protection of files

The next three sections examine these advantages.

Central Management. The simple task of upgrading a driver can be a logistical nightmare if that driver is used by a large number of client workstations. If the driver is stored on the hard disk of each client, you need to visit each workstation before making the change. If your users have their own boot floppy disks which they use to connect to the network, you are faced with the task of recalling and updating all boot floppy disks that are in circulation.

All startup files for diskless workstations are stored in a boot image file on the server, so you can manage them from any client that has access to that server. This gives you the luxury of being able to reconfigure the most remote workstation on the network without having to physically visit it.

Sharing Common Files. A number of workstations might have the same type of network adapter and load the same version of DOS, same network drivers, and same TSRs. Since all files required to boot a diskless workstation are stored on the file server, you can avoid maintaining duplicate sets of files by having all such workstations use the same boot image file. If the workstations need a new driver, you only need to update the boot image.

Write-Protection of Files. Using diskless workstations spares you the management overhead of all those local disks. Whether they're hard disk or floppy, conventional boot disks are prone to a range of disasters:

- Accidental reconfiguration

- Sabotage

- Virus infection

- Physical damage to the disk

- Loss (floppies)

- Theft (hard disks)

By storing the boot material in a safe, central place you can make good use of the security features of your network to protect your users from themselves and others.

> **Note**
>
> Diskless workstations are "read-only" in another sense: if a diskless workstation has no floppy drive, it cannot be used to download confidential data or to pirate software from your server. Likewise, it cannot be used to upload pirated software, viruses, or other undesirable material.

Drawbacks to Going Diskless

Diskless workstations are not for everyone. Some reasons for sticking with more conventional boot media are

- User-maintained boot configurations

- Cost of boot PROMs

- Dependence on the server

- Disk space overhead on the server

- Performance overhead on the server

- Performance overhead on the network

- Management overhead

User-Maintained Boot Configurations. Your users might prefer to manage the configuration of their own workstations. They might want the ability to experiment, or might not want to call you every time a minor amendment to CONFIG.SYS is required.

If so, you can consider installing both boot PROM and a hard disk. Users then would have the option at startup time of booting from the server (your configuration) or from the hard disk (their own). A choice of boot options can provide users the best of both worlds.

If you decide to go this route you should negotiate with users beforehand to ensure that you agree on where the responsibilities of each party begin and end. If you maintain the boot image but users consider you responsible when they mess up their own hard disk, you might find yourself with a doubled maintenance burden.

Cost of Boot PROMs. Boot PROMs cost money, but remember that the additional cost of a boot PROM in each workstation must be set against the cost of providing a hard disk or boot floppy disks to all users. You should also factor in the cost of the administrative overhead of updating local boot disks (either hard disk or floppy).

Dependence on the Server. If the server is down, diskless workstations will not boot. Of course, if applications are stored on the server, then users wouldn't be able to do anything even if they could boot up! In practice, with boot image files stored on multiple servers, this usually is not a problem.

Disk Space Overhead on the Server. If your client workstations use a wide variety of network adapters, then you may need to have several boot image files. Each can take up as much as 700K of disk space on the server. Besides reducing the amount of available free space on the server, a large number of boot image files can have implications for your backup system.

Adding an additional boot server does not affect the amount of disk space required on any one server, of course, as each server needs to hold its own copy of each boot image. Bear in mind, the total amount of disk space used by all servers for storing boot images increases proportionately with the number of boot servers.

Performance Overhead on the Server. Diskless workstations also have a performance hit on your server. The scale of the effect on performance depends on the number of diskless workstations, the number of servers supplying the boot images, and the frequency with which the workstations are booted. For example, in a student laboratory environment where a large number of workstations are booted regularly, the server has to send the boot image out on the network quite frequently. If the machines are all booted more or less on the hour, as is often the case, there may be intermittent but serious performance degradation on the server as dozens of machines clamor for boot images at the same time. In contrast, a small number of diskless workstations booted once or twice a day would have no noticeable impact on server performance.

Adding an additional boot server should give a proportionate decrease in the boot image load on each server. The total server resources given over to delivering boot images to the clients might increase slightly, however, as each server has to cache its own copy of the boot images.

Performance Overhead on the Network. There may also be a degradation in performance on the network between the server and the remote-booting clients. Those boot files need to travel to each client each time it boots, so frequent reboots can generate a lot of traffic that would not occur in the case of locally booted machines. The preceding comments about server performance overhead apply equally here: Large numbers of remote-booting clients rebooted simultaneously at regular intervals are likely to cause problems, while an occasional reboot will pass unnoticed.

Management Overhead. If you manage the boot configurations of a very small number of clients, or if your users are capable of configuring their own workstations, then it may be easier to deal with boot floppies or bootable hard disks than to set up boot image files.

In summary, you need to consider whether the advantages of central boot management are worth the overhead. Boot PROMs cost money and there is a disk space overhead on the file server. On the other hand, boot PROMs can save a lot of time and tedium in configuration maintenance for you and your users.

Preparing the Workstation

This section deals with planning and purchasing issues and describes how to set up a workstation to boot from a server.

> **Note**
>
> This process is closely linked to the workstation adapter installation and configuration. Refer to chapter 6, "The Workstation Platform," for detailed information on this topic.

Network Design Considerations

The smaller the number of boot images you have to manage, the better. Each boot image can support only one MLID (ODI network driver), so it makes sense to stick with the same network adapter model as much as possible when buying new machines or upgrading existing ones.

That's not always practical of course, but you should at least bear in mind, when buying adapters that every new model you install on your network means another boot image file to maintain. As a minimum concern, make sure your servers have sufficient disk space to store all the necessary boot images and that your backup system can cope with the volume.

Purchasing (Specification and Ordering)

Make sure when ordering that you specify which type of PROM you require, the older IPX or the newer RPL. Unless you have a particular reason for wanting IPX PROMs, specify RPL.

If you're ordering a set of adapters and PROMs that you intend to manage as a set, using a single boot image, your order should clearly specify the make and model of the adapter and PROM. Two different models might not work with the same drivers or settings. Watch out also for motherboard differences that may prevent you from using the same interrupt or RAM address on all machines in your set—the boot image can only hold one copy of NET.CFG.

Finally, beware of buying into discontinued lines. You might not be able to find matching adapters or PROMs in the future, and if you have to replace any hardware, you might be forced to set up a whole new boot image, possibly for a single workstation out of dozens.

If you are installing diskless workstations for use in an unattended environment, consider buying adapters with a hardware jumper that can be set to disable software setup. This prevents users from innocently or maliciously reconfiguring the adapter to prevent it from booting.

Installing the Boot PROM

Follow the manufacturer's instructions when installing a boot PROM. It is not uncommon, however, for PROMs to arrive without any documentation, so follow these general guidelines if you have nothing else to go on:

1. Remove the adapter from the workstation if it has already been installed.

2. Identify the PROM socket on the adapter. This should be obvious—if not, refer to the adapter documentation.

3. Line up the PROM with the socket, with the notched end of the PROM at the notched end of the socket.

4. Let the PROM sit on the socket with a pin in each hole. If any pins are slightly bent and don't fit, take the PROM aside and straighten the pins carefully.

5. When all the pins are straight and seem to fit, push the PROM into the socket gently and evenly. Don't push one end or side of the chip in ahead of the rest because the pins might bend.

6. After inserting the PROM, install the network adapter in the workstation according to the adapter manufacturer's instructions.

Configuring the Adapter

Once the boot PROM has been physically inserted, it must be configured for use. The boot PROM must be activated and configured to use a specific RAM area.

The procedure for enabling the boot PROM is different for every adapter model. Older adapter models such as the Novell NE1000 and NE2000 use physical jumper blocks. Remote reset jumper settings for Novell adapters are given in the *Novell Ethernet Supplement* shipped with all copies of NetWare.

More recent adapters that are partially or totally software configurable can be configured for remote boot by specifying a RAM address for the PROM using the adapter's setup utility. Even if you cannot obtain a copy of the adapter documentation, it is vital that you get a copy of the setup/configuration utility for the particular make and model of the adapter that you are using.

Don't rely too much on claims of compatibility: "NE2000 compatible" adapters may be fully software compatible with the NE2000 but may have a completely different physical layout, a different number of jumpers, or a software setup utility that was lost before the adapter reached you.

Gathering Information

Boot PROM installation time is a good time to record the information you will need to configure and manage the diskless workstation. That's because most of the information concerns the adapter you have in your hands while installing the boot PROM.

Whatever data you decide to gather, record the information systematically. Use a database package to keep track of the information if you're dealing with many diskless workstations.

The data required is

- Network number and adapter network address
- Adapter model and configuration
- Type of boot PROM (IPX or RPL)
- Workstation's physical location
- Workstation's model and serial number
- Contact name and number

Network Number and Adapter Network Address. The network number is required for creating the BOOTCONF.SYS file. You can find it on the BIND IPX line in the server's AUTOEXEC.NCF file.

The Ethernet address might be printed on the adapter, but if not, you should be able to determine it using the adapter's setup/diagnostic utility. Record the full, 12-digit Ethernet address in hexadecimal form. Separate pairs of digits with colons for clarity. 00:00:E8:C2:57:6E is easier to read than a string of digits (0000E8C2576E) and provides you less chance to accidentally drop a digit.

One way to find an RPL PROM's Ethernet address is to boot up the workstation that it is installed in, without connecting the workstation to the network. The Ethernet address will be displayed along with the adapter configuration details while the PROM waits in vain for an RPL server to respond.

Tip

If all other means fail, you can see the address of an adapter with an IPX boot PROM using the TRACK ON command at a server console. See details in the later instructions in the "Type of Boot PROM (IPX or RPL)" section.

Adapter Model and Configuration. The adapter model and configuration information should be at hand now since you've just used it to configure the adapter to use its boot PROM. Record the make, model, connector type, IRQ, I/O port, and RAM address.

Type of Boot PROM (IPX or RPL). Make sure you know which type of boot PROM you have just installed! This information is vital when preparing the boot image and the server. The RPL PROMs date from about 1992 onward and often are clearly labeled as RPL PROMs. Token-ring adapters always use RPL PROMs.

If you're still not sure whether the PROM is RPL or IPX, try the following:

1. Attach the workstation to a single-server network with no other workstations attached.

2. Issue the command TRACK ON at the server console.

3. Power up the workstation and allow it to try to boot using the boot PROM—this means no boot floppy in the floppy disk drive. If the workstation has a hard disk, answer yes when asked if it should boot from the network.

4. Watch the server console for GET NEAREST SERVER (GNS) frames from the boot PROM. These frames are sent only by IPX PROMs—RPL PROMs are not visible on the TRACK screen. If the server is configured to respond to GNS frames, you should see a GNS frame going out for each GNS frame received. Figure 28.1 shows the dialogue between a workstation with Ethernet address 00:00:E8:C2:57:6E and a file server named FLUFFY on network 20081014.

```
Router Tracking Screen
IN  [20081014:0000E8C2576E]   9:19:00am    Get Nearest Server
OUT [20081014:0000E8C2576E]   9:19:00am    Give Nearest Server LIFF
```

Figure 28.1

This is a typical server TRACK screen.

Workstation's Physical Location. Take the time to write down enough information to help someone else locate this particular workstation. If there are bad packets coming from 00:00:E8:C2:57:6E and your data only tells you that the workstation with that adapter is one of 20 workstations in room 120, you have quite a bit of work to do to find the faulty machine. It's much more useful if your data tells you that it is "third PC on left, back row, room 120."

Workstation Model and Serial Number. Even the most detailed descriptions of physical location are of limited use if someone moves the workstations around. Take note of the workstation model and serial number so you can be sure that you have a correct match of Ethernet address and workstation.

Contact Name and Number. The name and number of a contact person can save a lot of time, especially if the diskless workstation is very remote. If you just want to know if PC *X* is booting up as usual, you can call someone who is close to it and can check quickly, thereby saving yourself a long trip.

Preparing a DOS Boot Image

This section explains how to prepare a boot image file for a DOS workstation.

Before you begin, decide which version of DOS the diskless workstation is using. Note that all the DOS external commands have to be stored on the server for access by the diskless workstation. Since DOS versions don't mix very well (for example, DOS 6's XCOPY won't run on a machine booted using DOS 5), each server needs to keep a separate copy of each version of DOS used by any diskless workstations that may connect. It makes sense, therefore, to keep the number of DOS versions to a minimum.

> **Caution**
>
> Check that you have enough DOS licenses to cover all diskless workstations! If you intend to use more than one DOS version, check that you have enough licenses for each version. DOS upgrades are not free.

You need the following to prepare the boot image file:

- The information listed in the earlier "Gathering Information" section, particularly the adapter model and settings.

- Physical access to the diskless workstation. If you have all the information listed above, you can in theory prepare the boot image without going near the client. In practice, however, you need to test your work—this requires that you visit the PC.

- A workstation that you can log on to the server from. You can use the diskless workstation for this purpose if it has a floppy disk drive and if you can boot it from either a floppy or hard disk and then use it to connect to the file server which will store the boot image. Ideally, use a PC located close to the diskless workstation. This allows you to switch between working on the boot image and testing it, without having to travel too far from one machine to the other.

> **Tip**
>
> A laptop computer with PCMCIA network adapter, a range of transceivers, all the necessary network drivers, and your favorite diagnostic utilities is particularly useful when you're setting up and testing remote booting workstations.

- If the diskless workstation is going to use a different version of DOS than the workstation that you are using to log on to the server, you also need a boot floppy with the appropriate DOS version.

- Copies of all files to be used during bootup by the diskless workstation, including the MLID for its Ethernet adapter.

- An account on the server with full write access to the SYS:LOGIN directory.

- A blank floppy disk.

Finally, if the diskless workstation has an IPX boot PROM, you need a copy of RPLODI.COM. This is because IPX boot PROMs were designed to work with older, dedicated IPX drivers, rather than ODI drivers. They communicate with the server using dedicated IPX code, which is fine as long as the adapter loads a dedicated IPX driver from the boot image. If an ODI driver is loaded instead, the ODI code interferes with the boot PROM's IPX code, meaning that the PROM can read no more of the boot image. The error message

```
Error reading boot disk image file
```

appears on-screen and the workstation hangs. RPLODI.COM fixes this problem by looking after the hand-over from the PROM's IPX code to the boot image's MLID.

> **Note**
>
> RPLODI.COM is needed only for IPX boot PROMs, not for RPL boot PROMs.

> **Tip**
>
> You occasionally might have to replace an IPX PROM with an RPL PROM. If the workstation's boot image still loads RPLODI.COM, your users will see an error message and hear an irritating beep when RPLODI.COM discovers that the workstation on which it is being run has not been booted using an IPX PROM. If the boot image is not still used by IPX PROM workstations, simply remove the RPLODI.COM load line from the boot image's AUTOEXEC.BAT. If, however, there are still IPX
>
> (continues)

Adding Network Services

(continued)

workstations which use the boot image, you don't have to create a whole new boot image for this single workstation. Edit the AUTOEXEC.BAT to redirect RPLODI.COM's output to NUL, with

```
RPLODI > NUL
```

This stops RPLODI.COM from beeping and displaying its error message on-screen. RPLODI.COM continues to do its job for IPX PROMs but quietly ignores RPL PROMs.

Preparing the Master Boot Floppy

Use the following sections to prepare the master boot floppy that the boot image will be built from.

Boot a Master PC. Boot a PC that uses whatever version of DOS you want the diskless workstation to use.

Format the Master Boot Floppy. Format a floppy disk using the /S option (DOS) or choosing Disk, Make System Disk in Windows File Manager. The floppy disk then contains a boot sector, two hidden system files, and COMMAND.COM. This disk is to be your master boot disk, so be careful with it. Label it clearly with the identity of the diskless machine, the date created, the DOS version used, and the type of Ethernet adapter.

Copy Files to the Floppy. Copy all other required files to the master boot disk. Remember that you need to include all files used when booting, up to the point where the adapter's driver is loaded.

In particular, make sure you have the following:

■ CONFIG.SYS for the diskless workstation. Remember to include the line LASTDRIVE=Z if using VLM.EXE, but not if using NETX.EXE.

■ Any files referred to in CONFIG.SYS—for example, HIMEM.SYS or EMM386.EXE. Look for references to other files such as COUNTRY.SYS, and copy any such files to the master boot floppy. Remember to use the DOS version that was used to format the master boot disk—don't mix and match!

Tip

EMM386.EXE "remembers" the path with which it was loaded so that it can reload at a later stage. If it is loaded during a remote boot, the path is A:\. This can cause problems when, for example, a remote-booted workstation tries to load Windows—it looks for EMM386.EXE on drive A but the file is not there any more. To avoid errors, use the /Y switch to specify the full path to a copy of EMM386.EXE after logon. For example, you might use

```
DEVICE=EMM386.EXE /NOEMS /Y=F:\WINDOWS\EMM386.EXE /X=D000-D800
```

■ AUTOEXEC.BAT for the diskless workstation

- Any files referred to in AUTOEXEC.BAT, such as DOSKEY.COM. Remember that some programs may look for other files when they load—for example, the MODE command may need to read EGA.CPI. Copy any such files to the master boot floppy. Again, don't mix and match DOS versions!

- LSL.COM

- NET.CFG—make sure it accurately reflects the adapter's hardware settings as recorded earlier. Refer to chapters 11 and 12 for NET.CFG details.

- RPLODI.COM if the diskless workstation has an IPX boot PROM. Edit AUTOEXEC.BAT to load this after the LSL but just before the MLID:

  ```
  lsl
  rplodi
  ne2000
  ipxodi
  vlm
  ```

- The MLID (ODI driver) for the Ethernet adapter

- IPXODI.COM

- NETX.EXE or VLM.EXE

- *.VLM if using VLM.EXE

- An antivirus TSR (load one at this stage because some do not work correctly if loaded before the workstation shell)

Note

If your copy of DOSGEN is version 1.2 or later, then you can store some of these files in subdirectories. If it's older, leave everything in the root directory of drive A because older versions of DOSGEN don't support subdirectories.

Copy Files to the Server. If this is the only boot image you will have on the server, copy AUTOEXEC.BAT to the SYS:LOGIN directory. See the later "Multiple Boot Images" section if you expect to have more than one boot image.

Any programs run from AUTOEXEC.BAT after the point where the workstation shell is loaded should also be copied to SYS:LOGIN. This might include mouse drivers, menu programs, and so on.

Switching to the Server. The boot PROM shuts down once the workstation shell is loaded during remote boot. Its job is done—the PC has found a boot device, loaded an operating system and network drivers, and connected to a server. At this point—when NETX.EXE or VLM.EXE loads—the diskless workstation switches from reading a batch file in the boot image to reading a batch file of the same name in the SYS:LOGIN directory of the file server.

It does this by keeping track of its position in the batch file as it processes the boot image. This position is recorded as a byte offset amount from the start of the batch file. When control is handed over to the SYS:LOGIN batch file, processing begins at the byte offset position.

As long as the contents of the two batch files are identical, the use of the byte offset ensures a smooth transition from boot image to logon area. If the copies are not identical, the byte offset might point to the wrong location in the second batch file and strange results might occur. Consider these two batch files:

Boot image copy of AUTOEXEC.BAT

```
lsl
smc8000
ipxodi
netx
mouse
```

SYS:LOGIN copy of AUTOEXEC.BAT:

```
lsl
ne2000
ipxodi
netx
mouse
```

The only difference is that the first contains smc8000 where the second contains ne2000—the latter is one character shorter. The byte offset calculated for the first file is therefore too great for the second file, which will start processing after the m in mouse; the first command executed will be ouse, probably resulting in an error.

That's what can happen with a one-character offset difference. If one file contains entire lines that the other file does not contain, the likelihood of error is much greater. The second batch file might try to load network drivers that are already in memory or that clash with software already in memory. That the workstation might hang is a possibility.

Multiple Boot Images. The byte offset mechanism can give rise to difficulties with multiple boot images. Each boot image insists on using its own byte offset when passing control to SYS:LOGIN. If the workstation shell has been loaded from AUTOEXEC.BAT, this can mean different byte offsets being used on the same AUTOEXEC.BAT file—after all, there can only be one copy of this in any one directory.

There are various tricks that allow you to work around this to some extent, such as renaming all MLIDs so that they are exactly the same length. These tricks are based on the fact that, strictly speaking, the files need not have identical content as long as the byte offset after loading the workstation shell ends up at the correct value. Trying to maintain files this way, though, is bound to cause problems.

There is an easier approach—don't load the workstation shell from AUTOEXEC.BAT. Instead, rename the AUTOEXEC.BAT for each workstation using a name matching the boot image name. Then create a dummy AUTOEXEC.BAT that calls this surrogate AUTOEXEC.BAT. As long as each surrogate is uniquely named, you can maintain a copy of each in SYS:LOGIN. Then you just need to make sure that the surrogate batch file in SYS:LOGIN is an exact copy of the surrogate in the corresponding boot image.

For example, given two batch files named NE2$DOS.SYS and SMC$DOS.SYS:

1. Rename AUTOEXEC.BAT on the NE2000 master boot floppy to NE2AUTO.BAT.

2. Create a new AUTOEXEC.BAT on the NE2000 master boot floppy consisting of one line:

   ```
   NE2AUTO
   ```

3. Copy NE2AUTO.BAT to SYS:LOGIN.

4. Rename AUTOEXEC.BAT on the SMC master boot floppy to SMCAUTO.BAT.

5. Create a new AUTOEXEC.BAT on the SMC master boot floppy consisting of one line:

   ```
   SMCAUTO
   ```

6. Copy SMCAUTO.BAT to SYS:LOGIN.

You then can maintain the two boot images and their surrogate AUTOEXEC files independently from one another. The AUTOEXEC.BAT files in the boot images remain there—no AUTOEXEC.BAT is required in SYS:LOGIN unless it is used by another boot image.

> **Tip**
>
> Adopt this procedure even if you are creating only one boot image. It takes little or no effort, and greatly simplifies the process of adding more boot images later if that becomes necessary.

Test the Master Boot Floppy

Test the boot disk now by using it to boot the target workstation. Don't skip this step! You need to test the exact set of files on the disk—that CONFIG.SYS, those particular NET.CFG entries, the versions of the network drivers—on the workstation or workstations that will actually use the boot image. Don't assume that because a boot floppy disk works properly on one machine, it will work on another. Even if both have the same type of Ethernet adapter, you might have difficulties with differences between model revisions or clashes with other adapters that were not present in the first workstation.

If you have loaded RPLODI.COM, expect an error message when you boot the diskless workstation using the master boot floppy. RPLODI.COM looks for a stamp left in memory by the boot PROM's IPX code. As you're booting from a floppy disk, the boot PROM code is not present, so RPLODI.COM beeps and displays an error message:

```
FATAL: BootROM Stamp not found.
```

This message should appear only when the workstation boots from the master boot disk, not when it boots from the file server.

Making the Boot Image File

This procedure copies the contents of the master boot disk to a boot image file on the server.

The default name for a DOS boot image file is NET$DOS.SYS. You need a separate boot image for each boot configuration—generally speaking, one boot image for each adapter model—so choose an appropriate name for each boot image. Names such as ACC$DOS.SYS, SMC$DOS.SYS are better than NET1$DOS.SYS and NET2$DOS.SYS. (The *xxx*$DOS.SYS naming convention is not essential but it makes the function of these files obvious.) The section later named "BOOTCONF.SYS" explains how to make each workstation pick up the correct boot image.

DOSGEN. DOSGEN is a NetWare utility that reads the contents of your master boot floppy and transfers them to the special container file which is a boot image. It reads the floppy's boot sector and File Allocation Table, as well as the files you copied onto the floppy.

The syntax for DOSGEN is

```
[path]DOSGEN drive: [imagefile]
```

where *path* specifies the directory path to DOSGEN, *drive* is the drive with the master boot floppy, and *imagefile* specifies the image file to be created.

The default drive is A: and the default image file name is NET$DOS.SYS.

You usually need to map a drive letter to SYS:SYSTEM to pick up DOSGEN and another to SYS:LOGIN so that you can specify the destination for the boot image. Figure 28.2 illustrates a typical sequence of commands issued when using DOSGEN.

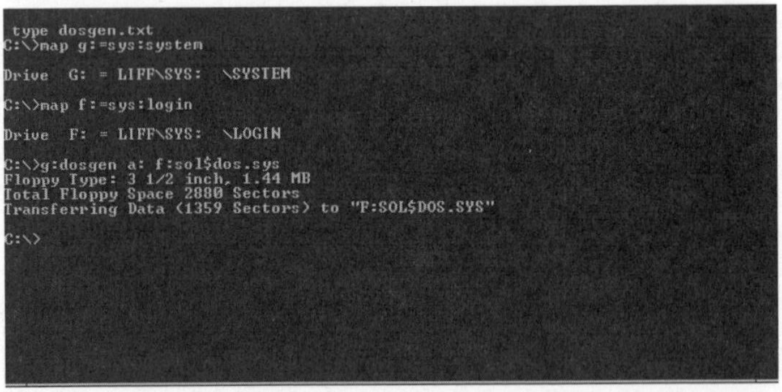

```
type dosgen.txt
C:\>map g:=sys:system

Drive  G:  = LIFF\SYS:  \SYSTEM

C:\>map f:=sys:login

Drive  F:  = LIFF\SYS:  \LOGIN

C:\>g:dosgen a: f:sol$dos.sys
Floppy Type: 3 1/2 inch, 1.44 MB
Total Floppy Space 2880 Sectors
Transferring Data (1359 Sectors) to "F:SOL$DOS.SYS"

C:\>
```

Figure 28.2

This is a typical use of DOSGEN.

> **Note**
>
> If you have version 1.2 or later of DOSGEN, the directory structure of your master boot floppy is copied to the boot image along with any files in subdirectories. Earlier versions of DOSGEN complain about subdirectories on the master boot disk by beeping and displaying an error message (...Not supported) beside the name of the subdirectory.

RPLFIX.COM

IPX boot PROMs need a little help to work with DOS version 5 or later. This is because DOS 5's COMMAND.COM is much bigger than COMMAND.COM in earlier versions of DOS. Here's the sequence of events without RPLFIX:

- The diskless workstation loads the boot PROM code into memory and executes it.

- The workstation locates its boot image and loads DOS from it.

- DOS parses CONFIG.SYS and then loads the command interpreter, COMMAND.COM. At this stage, the workstation is still relying on the boot PROM code in memory to download the boot image file for processing.

- COMMAND.COM overwrites the boot PROM code in memory.

- The rest of the boot image is not downloaded.

- The workstation fails to complete booting up and hangs indefinitely.

RPLFIX modifies the boot image file so that COMMAND.COM does not overwrite the boot PROM code while it is still active in memory.

The syntax for RPLFIX.COM is

```
RPLFIX imagefile
```

where *imagefile* is the name of the boot image file to be patched, including the path if the file is not in the current directory.

RPLFIX should report that the image file has been successfully modified. For example,

```
C:\> G:RPLFIX F:SMC$DOS.SYS
NetWare Boot Disk Image Patch Program  v1.03 (930630)
(c) Copyright 1991, 1993 by Novell, Inc. All rights reserved.
This program fixes Boot disk image files for:
    MS-DOS 5.xx, 6.xx, and DR-DOS 6.xx
Boot disk image file has been modified
```

RPLFIX needs to be run only once on a given boot image file. If you run RPLFIX on an image that has already been RPLFIXed, RPLFIX tells you so and won't modify the image again.

If you run DOSGEN again to regenerate the boot image file for any reason, you should run RPLFIX on the new image.

Adding Network Services

> **Note**
>
> RPLFIX.COM is only for DOS version 5.0 or later, and only for IPX boot PROMs. RPL PROM code is not overwritten by COMMAND.COM as it loads, so RPL PROMs do not require this fix.

Putting the Boot Image in Its Place

Finally, make sure the boot image file is properly accessible by the diskless workstations. It must be

- Located in SYS:LOGIN—that's the only place from which a NOT-LOGGED-IN workstation can read.

- Located on each server where a diskless workstation might look for it—see the later "Considerations with Multiple Servers" section for more detail.

- Flagged as *shareable* so that more than one workstation at a time can boot from it. If a workstation hangs while it is booting or is turned off before it has finished booting, the boot image file will still be held open by the workstation's connection, and no other workstations will be able to boot until the connection has been dropped. The NetWare FLAG command can make it shareable:

  ```
  FLAG F:SMC$DOS.SYS S
  ```

> **Note**
>
> For the same reason, you should flag as shareable any of these files which are in SYS:LOGIN: BOOTCONF.SYS, AUTOEXEC.BAT and any batch files called by the boot image's AUTOEXEC.BAT in a situation with multiple boot images.

Preparing the Server

A server must be correctly configured if it is to deliver boot images to diskless clients. This section looks at configuration issues for both types of boot PROMs.

> **Note**
>
> Many different types of computers can act as an RPL server: NetWare file servers, UNIX machines, Windows NT Servers, even Personal NetWare clients. Because NetWare servers are by far the most common, this section will cover NetWare server RPL configuration issues only.

The Logon Area

All boot files must be stored in the logon area, SYS:LOGIN. This is the only area on the server accessible by NOT-LOGGED-IN connections.

The following files should be in SYS:LOGIN:

- All boot image files.

- BOOTCONF.SYS if you have multiple boot images.

- The bootstrap program for your network—for example, RBOOT.RPL if using enhanced RPL boot PROMs. See table 28.1 for a full list. If in doubt, copy them all to SYS:LOGIN.

Table 28.1   Bootstrap Files

Network Adapter Type	File
IBM MCA Ethernet	ETHER.RPL
IBM Model 25SX Ethernet	F1ETHER.RPL
IBM PC Baseband Network	PCN2L.RPL
Adapters using Enhanced Boot PROMs	RBOOT.RPL
IBM Shared RAM Token Ring	TOKEN.RPL

- Exact copies of the AUTOEXEC.BAT or its surrogates from the boot images. See the earlier "Multiple Boot Images" section.

- Any programs run from the AUTOEXEC.BAT or its surrogates after the point when the MLID is loaded. This might include mouse drivers, menu programs, and so on.

Flag each of these files as shareable (the process is described in the earlier "Putting the Boot Image in Its Place" section). This allows more than one remote booting workstation at a time to use them.

Do not flag these files as read-only because that would make it awkward to update them. (A read-only flag is of no real benefit as a security measure unless your logged on users have write access to SYS:LOGIN.)

BOOTCONF.SYS

The default file name for DOS boot images is NET$DOS.SYS. If all diskless workstations on your network have the same boot configuration (in practice, the same network adapter model and settings), only one boot image is required and you do not need to create a BOOTCONF.SYS file.

If you have more than one boot image, the diskless workstations need to determine which one they should use when booting. That's what BOOTCONF.SYS is for. It is a text file with a one-line entry for each diskless workstation, indicating which boot image it should use.

The basic syntax for a BOOTCONF.SYS entry is

```
0xnetwork,address=bootimage
```

where *network* is the server's IPX external network number in eight-digit hexadecimal form, *address* is the 12-digit address of the workstation's Ethernet adapter, and *bootimage* is the name of the boot image to be used by that workstation.

Create BOOTCONF.SYS with a text editor. Use the notes you took when installing the boot PROMs to ensure a full list of Ethernet addresses and to match each address with the correct boot image. Meaningful boot image names are particularly useful at this point.

For example, assume that network 8C87 has three diskless workstations. The boot images are SMC$DOS.SYS for SMC8000 adapters and NE2$DOS.SYS for NE2000 adapters. The adapters are

1. SMC8000 card, address 08:00:67:37:e8:f4

2. Novell NE2000 card, address 00:00:e8:c2:57:6e

3. SMC8000 card, address 08:00:67:37:e8:a2

BOOTCONF.SYS:

```
0x00008c87,08006737e8f4=smc$dos.sys
0x00008c87,0000e8c2576e=ne2$dos.sys
0x00008c87,08006737e8a2=smc$dos.sys
```

Here's some further explanation of the BOOTCONF.SYS entries:

■ Entries in BOOTCONF.SYS are case-insensitive. Enter Ethernet addresses in lower-case for greater clarity—8BB8 and 8B88 can look similar, but 8bb8 and 8b88 are more distinct.

■ The network number should be eight characters long and preceded by the string 0x, as shown in the example previous BOOTCONF.SYS file.

■ Whole comment lines may be inserted anywhere in BOOTCONF.SYS. When the file is scanned for a workstation address, lines not containing the address are not parsed any further. No special comment delimiter is necessary. For example, the following entries are valid:

```
Gerry's PC:
0x00008c87,08006737e8f4=smc$dos.sys
Print servers:
0x00008c87,0000e8c2576e=ne2$dos.sys
0x00008c87,08006737e8a2=smc$dos.sys
```

> **Note**
>
> Bear in mind when adding comment lines that they make BOOTCONF.SYS longer. This means slower parsing and, in the case of IPX PROMs, more network traffic. This is unlikely to be notice-able, however, especially if the number of diskless workstations is on the order of dozens rather than hundreds.

This section covered the basic syntax for BOOTCONF.SYS. Everything mentioned previously applies to both IPX and RPL PROMs. See the "BOOTCONF.SYS RPL Enhancements" section later for details of some extra features available when using RPL PROMs.

IPX PROM Specifics

IPX PROMs look for their boot image file in the LOGIN area of the server that they first attach to:

1. The boot PROM sends an IPX protocol GNS frame on the network.

2. A server responds with a GNS frame identifying itself.

3. The workstation enters the server's logon area (SYS:LOGIN).

4. The remote booting workstation looks for a text file named BOOTCONF.SYS. This file is a map that matches boot images to client Ethernet addresses.

5. If the workstation finds BOOTCONF.SYS, it searches this file for a line containing the workstation's Ethernet address. If such a line is found, it is parsed for the name of the boot image file to use.

6. If no such line is found, or if BOOTCONF.SYS does not exist, the workstation assumes that the boot image file is named NET$DOS.SYS.

7. The workstation downloads the appropriate boot image, and the workstation boots from it.

Make sure that all servers with the boot images are configured to respond to GNS requests. This is the default behavior, but you can turn it on explicitly using the SET command at the server console:

```
SET REPLY TO GET NEAREST SERVER = ON
```

Servers without boot images should not respond to GNS requests. If they do, workstations will attempt to download boot images from them and will hang, resulting in an error message. You can use the console to explicitly turn off a server's ability to reply to GNS requests. Enter the following in the AUTOEXEC.NCF of all non-boot servers on the network:

```
SET REPLY TO GET NEAREST SERVER = OFF
```

RPL PROM Specifics

RPL PROMs need an RPL server on the network. This is either a NetWare server running RPL.NLM or, in the case of Personal NetWare, a client workstation running RPL.COM. It may or may not have copies of the boot image files.

The following sequence of events illustrates how an RPL PROM finds its boot image. It is a typical rather than a definitive description because the default behavior of an RPL server may be overridden in many ways. The features of an RPL server and the enhanced syntax of BOOTCONF.SYS for RPL PROMs are explained in detail in the "BOOTCONF.SYS RPL Enhancements" section later in this chapter.

Adding Network Services

An RPL PROM typically finds its boot image file in the LOGIN area of a file server as follows:

1. The boot PROM sends an 802.2 protocol FIND frame on the network.

2. An RPL server receives the frame and identifies itself with a FOUND frame.

3. The PROM sends an 802.2 protocol SEND.FILE.REQUEST frame to the RPL server.

4. The RPL server scans its BOOTCONF.SYS for an entry for the workstation's Ethernet address. If such a line is found, it is parsed for the name of the boot image file to use.

5. If the workstation's Ethernet address is not found or the RPL server has no BOOTCONF.SYS file, the workstation assumes that the boot image file is named NET$DOS.SYS.

6. The RPL server sends the workstation a *bootstrap program* that contains all the information needed by the workstation to locate its boot image file: the server where the boot image is located, the name of the boot image to download, and any parameter overrides to be used by the workstation when booting.

7. The bootstrap program enters the logon area of the server indicated by the RPL server.

8. The bootstrap program downloads the appropriate boot image; the workstation boots from it.

The behavior of RPL servers may be configured in two ways:

■ The RPL server software has several optional parameters that modify its default behavior.

■ RPL PROMs can make use of optional enhancements to the format of BOOTCONF.SYS, modifying the default action for individual diskless workstations or groups of workstations.

Together, these options give system administrators the ability to customize remote boot activity for the whole network—or for individual machines—in a variety of ways not possible with IPX PROMs. The following sections look at each in turn.

RPL.NLM. An RPL server is usually a NetWare server running RPL.NLM. RPL.NLM provides diskless workstations on the network with the information they require to locate their boot images. It may also instruct them to download the boot image in a non-default way. A NetWare server running RPL.NLM may also provide boot images to clients or may direct clients to look for boot images on other servers.

Load RPL.NLM on the server using the LOAD console command, bind it to any network adapter in the server that is using the Ethernet 802.2 frame type. For example,

```
LOAD NE3200 SLOT=3 NAME=ipx_drv FRAME=ETHERNET_802.3
BIND IPX TO ipx_drv NET=8C87
LOAD NE3200 SLOT=3 NAME=rpl_drv FRAME=ETHERNET_802.2
BIND IPX TO rpl_drv NET=8C8B
LOAD RPL
BIND RPL TO RPL_DRV
```

That is enough to provide the default behavior. Set up the boot image or images as described earlier with a BOOTCONF.SYS if there is more than one boot image.

RPL BIND Parameters. The flexibility of RPL.NLM is achieved through a range of optional parameters used at BIND time. These parameters are summarized in table 28.2.

Table 28.2   RPL BIND Optional Parameters

Parameter	Values	Default
ACK		No
FRAME	Ethernet_802.2 Ethernet_II Ethernet_SNAP	Ethernet_802.2
GNS		No
NODEFAULT		No
PROTECT		No
PS	Server	Boot Server
WAIT TIME	0–65535	0

These parameters are explained further in the following sections.

ACK. The RPL server normally sends the FILE.DATA.RESPONSE in packet burst mode. If this causes problems for your boot PROM—if the PROM cannot keep pace with the server—use the ACK parameter to slow things down. The RPL server waits for the boot PROM to acknowledge receipt of each FILE.DATA.RESPONSE frame as it is sent. Use this parameter only if you suspect communications difficulties with RPL PROMs.

FRAME. The bootstrap program will use the Ethernet 802.2 frame type unless instructed otherwise. If either EII or SNAP is specified, the bootstrap program sends a GNS frame on the network to find a server to search for a boot image.

GNS. Forces the workstation to use a GNS request to find a server to search for a boot image. You might want to use this to provide boot server redundancy—see the "Considerations with Multiple Servers" section later for more information. The default is to search the server specified in the bootstrap program.

NODEFAULT. By default, the RPL server responds to any FIND frame that comes its way. If the NODEFAULT parameter is used, the server only sends a FOUND frame if the workstation's Ethernet address is found in BOOTCONF.SYS. This means that the workstation won't even start to boot unless an entry for it is added to BOOTCONF.SYS.

PROTECT. If you suspect that the bootstrap program is being overwritten in memory by another program during the boot process, use this parameter to make the bootstrap program "claim" the memory it occupies.

> **Caution**
>
> Use this parameter only as a last resort. The memory thus claimed is not freed up after the workstation finishes booting, so the amount of conventional memory available might be reduced by as much as 60K.

PS. The bootstrap program will look for the boot image on the server which is running RPL.NLM unless instructed otherwise using this parameter. Use this parameter if you want to have separate RPL and boot image servers.

WAIT TIME. The RPL enhancements to BOOTCONF.SYS (see "BOOTCONF.SYS RPL Enhancements" later for details) allow you to specify multiple boot images for a single workstation, giving users the choice at boot time of which image file to use. As explained in the later "Multiple Boot Images" section, they are presented with a list of boot image names and invited to select one. The default behavior is for the workstation to wait indefinitely for the user to choose an image.

The WAIT TIME option can be used to force the automatic selection of an image if the user has not selected one after a given length of time. The value is expressed in seconds. The default value is 0, meaning that no automatic selection will take place.

Here's an example of how to use this parameter:

```
BIND RPL TO RPL_DRV WAIT TIME=5
```

RPL BIND Parameter Overrides. Many of RPL.NLM's optional BIND parameters can be overridden for specific workstations or groups of workstations by additions to the relevant workstation lines in BOOTCONF.SYS. This gives finer control over remote booting than setting parameters either for all workstations or for none. The parameters that can be overridden are listed in table 28.3 and are explained in the sections that follow.

Use these overrides if you have used an RPL BIND parameter that you do not want to apply to all diskless workstations or if you want to experiment with RPL BIND parameters on some workstations without affecting others.

Table 28.3 RPL BIND Parameter Overrides in BOOTCONF.SYS

Override	Default
NOACK	ACK
NOGNS	GNS

Override	Default
NOPROTECT	PROTECT
REP *string1|string2*	None

NOACK. Turns off the ACK BIND time parameter for the specified workstation. The RPL server will not wait for this workstation to acknowledge each FILE.DATA.RESPONSE frame.

NOGNS. Turns off the GNS BIND time parameter for the specified workstation. This workstation will not send a GNS frame to locate a server from which to download its boot image.

NOPROTECT. Turns off the PROTECT BIND time parameter for the specified workstation. The bootstrap program will not protect itself in the workstation's memory, and available conventional memory will not be reduced.

REP. This is a global replace function for an entire boot image. The text strings must be ASCII text, separated by a vertical bar (¦). The replacement string cannot be longer than the original. If it is shorter, it is filled out with space characters to the length of the string being replaced.

This replacement function is case-sensitive. For example, the effect of `REP horse¦cow` on

    A HORSE is a Horse is a horse

is to change it to

    A HORSE is a Horse is a cow

REP is a powerful feature. It can be used, for example, to set an environment variable to different values on different workstations:

```
0x00008c87,0000e8c2576e=ne2$dos.sys REP GO32VAR¦C:\TMP
```
and
```
0x00008c87,0000e8c248f5=ne2$dos.sys REP GO32VAR¦D:\
```

If the AUTOEXEC.BAT for NE2$DOS.SYS contains the line

```
SET GO32=GO32VAR
```

GO32 is set to C:\TMP on the first workstation and D:\ on the second.

Watch out for the padding spaces if you replace existing strings with a shorter string. Suppose that you want AUTOEXEC.BAT to run a program MYPROG using the line

```
PROGDIR\MYPROG
```

where the directory path PROGDIR varies from one workstation to another. REP can cause problems here because

```
REP PROGDIR¦C:\BIN
```

will replace the line in AUTOEXEC.BAT with

```
C:\BIN \MYPROG
```

resulting in an error.

In cases like this, you can replace the entire string. In AUTOEXEC.BAT, include the line

```
MYPROGFULLPATH
```

and at the end of the workstation line in BOOTCONF.SYS, use

```
REP MYPROGFULLPATH¦C:\BIN\MYPROG
```

Tip

The REP parameter is particularly useful when used with the BOOTCONF.SYS extensions that allow for the use of wild cards in Ethernet addresses. For example, REP can be used to replace strings with different values for different makes of card.

The RPL Server and BOOTCONF.SYS. The RPL server usually caches the contents of BOOTCONF.SYS in memory so that it, and not the boot PROM, can parse it. This saves the PROM from having to download all of BOOTCONF.SYS, which might be quite large, to find a few bytes of information. However, if BOOTCONF.SYS is too large for the RPL server to hold in memory, the RPL server does not store it—the PROM must download it and parse it itself. Every 100 entries in BOOTCONF.SYS takes only 5K or so of RAM, so this is unlikely to be a problem on a NetWare server.

BOOTCONF.SYS RPL Enhancements. RPL behavior can be customized for specific workstations or groups of workstations using extensions to the BOOTCONF.SYS syntax.

Note

Do not use the enhancements in this section for IPX PROMs—they are valid only for RPL PROMs. The effect on IPX PROMs would be the same as having a corrupt BOOTCONF.SYS file. The most likely result is that they will either attempt to boot from a non-existent file or, if they fail to find their address in the file, try to boot using the default boot image file name, NET$DOS.SYS. If the former happens or the latter in cases where NET$DOS.SYS does not exist, the workstation will hang with an `Error opening boot disk image file` message.

RPL PROMs can take advantage of three major improvements to the BOOTCONF.SYS syntax:

- Wild-card characters
- Multiple boot images for one workstation

■ Multiple lines for each address

Wild Cards. Most BOOTCONF.SYS files contain a lot of repeated information. A batch of NE2000 adapters, for example, will have Ethernet addresses with the first several digits in common. If they all use the same RPL BIND override parameters—or no parameters— then you can save a lot of typing by using wild cards.

The valid wild-card characters are the asterisk and the question mark. The asterisk masks a range of characters, and the question mark masks a single character.

For example, a group of entries like

```
0x00008c87,0000e8c2576e=ne2$dos.sys
0x00008c87,0000e8c25602=ne2$dos.sys
0x00008c87,0000e8c2570b=ne2$dos.sys
0x00008c87,0000e8c257f4=ne2$dos.sys
0x00008c87,0000e8c24e71=ne2$dos.sys
```

can be replaced with either

```
0x00008c87,0000e8c2*=ne2$dos.sys
```

or

```
0x00008c87,0000e8c2????=ne2$dos.sys
```

> **Note**
>
> BOOTCONF.SYS is only scanned for a given Ethernet address until a match is found. This means that lines specific to one adapter should be placed near the top of the file, lines for groups of adapters later in the file, and any line intended to apply to adapters not matched by those lines should go at the end of BOOTCONF.SYS.

Multiple Boot Images. One of the disadvantages of boot images is that they encapsulate a single, fixed boot configuration. This cannot be optimal for all users and all applications. For example, one application might require that EMM386.EXE be loaded at boot time, but another application might not run at all if EMM386.EXE has been loaded.

The ability to specify more than one boot image file per workstation offers a solution to some of these difficulties, while maintaining all the benefits of centrally-managed boot configurations. One boot image has a CONFIG.SYS that loads EMM386.EXE, and the second does not; the user chooses between the boot images at boot time, and the workstation loads EMM386.EXE or not, as appropriate.

Multiple boot images are specified in BOOTCONF.SYS by listing after an equal sign the names of all boot images for a given workstation, separated by spaces. For example,

```
0x00008c87,0000e8c2576e=ne2$dos.sys ne2noemm.sys
```

gives the user at address `00:00:e8:c2:57:6e` a choice between two boot images at boot time (see fig. 28.3).

Adding Network Services

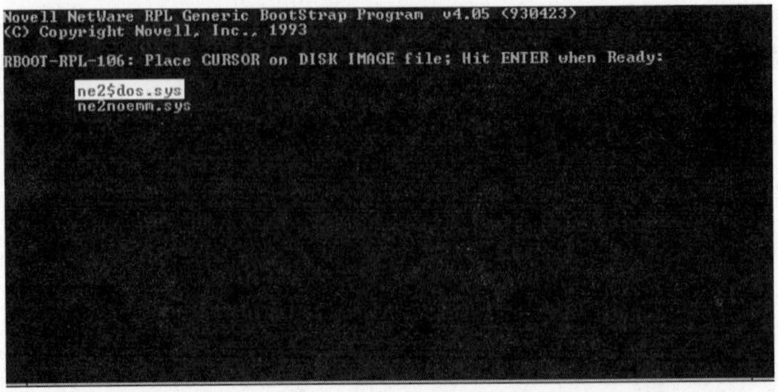

Figure 28.3

This is the workstation screen with a choice of boot images.

The first file name is highlighted. The user can select the other file name by using the cursor keys. When the user presses Enter, the bootstrap program downloads the selected boot image.

You can use this feature with a wild card to offer a choice of boot images as the default. If the last line in BOOTCONF.SYS is

```
0x*=ne1$dos.sys ne2$dos.sys smc$dos.sys 3com$dos.sys
```

any workstation that does not have an entry earlier in the file will present the user with the names of the four images listed on this line and allow them to choose which one the workstation boots with.

Multiple Lines. Finally, the ability to override RPL BIND parameters and to specify multiple boot images can lead to very long lines that are difficult to edit. The introduction of the continuation character was therefore necessary.

Place a space and a colon at the end of a line in BOOTCONF.SYS to force RPL.NLM to treat the next line as a continuation of the current line. For example,

```
0x00008c87,0000e8c2576e=ne2$dos.sys ne2noemm.sys :
PROTECT ACK REP TMPDIR¦C:\
```

DOS on the Server

DOS is more than a boot sector and command interpreter. There is also the matter of dozens of so-called external commands such as XCOPY and MODE that are not built into COMMAND.COM but live as independent programs in a directory of their own. This section describes how to make such commands available to users of diskless workstations.

DOS Directories. A DOS workstation with a hard disk generally stores the programs in C:\DOS and has this directory in its DOS search path. A remote booting workstation with a local hard disk can also do this, of course—just make sure that the programs stored in the local DOS directory are from the same version of DOS that the workstation uses to boot.

A workstation with no local disk must rely on the server to store the DOS program files. If all workstations use the same version of DOS, this is very simple to organize:

1. Create a directory on the server that all users have read and file scan access to. At the C:\ prompt, enter the following commands:

> **MAP G:=SYS:PUBLIC**

> **MD G:DOS**

2. Copy all of the DOS program files to the new directory with the following command (be careful to copy the correct version):

> **COPY C:\DOS*.* G:DOS**

3. Give all diskless workstation users a search mapping to this directory by adding a MAP command to their logon script:

> **MAP INS S1:=SYS:PUBLIC\DOS**

The users then have access to all DOS commands, just as if the DOS program files were stored on a local hard disk.

The process is rarely that simple, though. It might not be possible to insist that all diskless workstations use the same DOS version—for example, old applications might not work under newer DOS versions. New applications might require a more recent version of DOS than the one currently installed on the server, but you might not want to upgrade DOS on all the workstations for other reasons. In short, you probably should bank on having multiple DOS versions on the server at the same time.

Creating several DOS directories is simple, but how can you guarantee that each workstation gets a search mapping to the correct DOS version? Remember that mappings are created at or after logon time, so you cannot configure them in the boot image.

The answer lies in some obscure logon script variables provided by Novell. As long as you name the DOS directories according to Novell's conventions, these variables allow you to use a single MAP statement in the system logon script to map to the correct DOS directory, no matter which version of DOS the workstation is running. Table 28.4 lists the relevant variables.

Table 28.4 Logon Script Variables for DOS Search Mapping

Variable	Meaning
MACHINE	Workstation Type
OS	Type of DOS on the Workstation
OS_VERSION	Version of DOS on the Workstation

In most cases the only variables needed are OS_VERSION and OS. If all your diskless workstations are using MS-DOS, then only the OS_VERSION variable is required. The MACHINE variable should be needed only if one or more diskless workstations are not 100% IBM-compatible.

A typical system logon script entry for mapping the DOS directory appears as follows:

```
MAP INS S1:=SYS:PUBLIC/%OS/%OS_VERSION
```

On a workstation booted using version 5.00 of MS-DOS, this line is interpreted as

```
MAP INS S1:=SYS:PUBLIC/MSDOS/5.00
```

Plan your DOS directory structure accordingly. The simplest system is to create a SYS:PUBLIC/MSDOS directory with subdirectories named 3.30, 5.00, 6.00, 6.20, and so on, as necessary.

Setting COMSPEC. DOS sometimes needs to reload its command interpreter; for this reason, it stores the command interpreter's location in an environment variable named COMSPEC. When a diskless workstation boots up, COMSPEC is set to A:\COMMAND.COM. You must change this value to point to a copy of COMMAND.COM (of the correct DOS version) as a user logs on because A:\COMMAND.COM will cease to exist.

There should be a copy of COMMAND.COM in the relevant DOS directory in SYS:PUBLIC, but you have no way of telling which drive letter will be mapped to that directory for a given logon. The drive letter used will be decided only when the MAP INS command is executed.

COMSPEC is best set in the system logon script immediately after the DOS directory search mapping is created. At that point, you can be certain that the first search mapping is S1, regardless of its DOS drive letter. If you get LOGIN.EXE to resolve S1, then the problem is solved. For example,

```
MAP INS S1:=SYS:PUBLIC/%OS/%OS_VERSION
COMSPEC=S1:COMMAND.COM
```

> **Note**
>
> Many programs overwrite the transient portion of COMMAND.COM when they execute, forcing the PC to reload it from disk when the program terminates. It is essential that COMSPEC is set before this situation arises, so apply the previous solution as early as possible in the system logon script.

Restricting to Diskless Workstations. Adding a search mapping to the DOS directory and resetting COMSPEC are necessary for diskless workstations to function but might interfere with normal operation on workstations with a local copy of DOS. You might find that you need to restrict these logon script entries to diskless workstations only.

One way to do this is to set an environment variable to any value in the AUTOEXEC.BAT file of any remote booting workstations, for example,

```
SET REMOTEBOOT=Y
```

The system logon script can then check this variable and pick up DOS from the server or not depending on whether it has been set:

```
; Pick up DOS for remote booting clients only:
if not %<REMOTEBOOT>.=. then begin
  map ins s1:=sys:public\%os\%os_version
  comspec=s1:command.com
end
```

Considerations with Multiple Servers

If you have a single server on your network, it must act as an RPL server (if using RPL PROMs) and as a source for boot images for all diskless workstations. This section discusses issues that might arise if you have more than one server and details some extra configuration steps that might be necessary.

Choosing the Number of RPL and Boot Servers. RPL.NLM does not place an appreciable load on a server, so in the normal course of events, one RPL server should be sufficient for any network. If the server running RPL.NLM happens to crash, however, no diskless workstations with RPL PROMs can boot. It is therefore desirable to have at least one additional RPL server on the network as a backup.

The same redundancy argument holds for servers carrying the boot images. If one server goes down, the diskless workstations still will be able to boot up. Unlike with RPL servers, there might be a performance payoff in replicating boot image servers; on the other hand, there will be a cost in server disk space. Weigh the pros and cons carefully before deciding on the number of boot servers to use.

It's important to remember to keep the configuration of multiple RPL and boot servers properly synchronized. If you change the BIND RPL line on one server but not on the other or a boot image on some servers but not on others, remote-booting clients may experience erratic behavior or intermittent faults.

It is worth spending some time developing automatic or semi-automatic procedures for synchronizing BOOTCONF.SYS, boot image files, and the surrogate AUTOEXEC.BAT files across servers. The simplest approach is to write a series of custom batch files that use the NCOPY command to copy updated files from one server to the others. More elaborate approaches involve mirroring the relevant files from server to server. Once such procedures are developed, the administrative overhead of adding another boot image server is minimal.

GET NEAREST SERVER Requests. Make sure that servers without boot images do not respond to GNS requests from boot PROMs. If they do, the PROMs will look for BOOTCONF.SYS and boot image files where they don't exist, and workstations will hang when they try to boot. Turn off the server's capability to respond to GNS requests at the console.

The following command should be entered in the server's AUTOEXEC.NCF to ensure that the setting is still in place after the server reboots:

```
SET REPLY TO GET NEAREST SERVER = OFF
```

This is a trivial matter if you have management authority over all servers on your network. If not, though, it is essential that you secure the cooperation of the managers of the other servers in setting this parameter on your behalf. If they are reluctant to do this, point out to them that each diskless workstation that gets a response to a GNS frame from their server will take up a connection on that server.

Making the Connection: Troubleshooting

Don't be put off from boot PROMs if the instructions so far seem hopelessly convoluted. In normal use, boot PROMs operate quietly, efficiently, and reliably. The work required to configure them is more than repaid by years of trouble-free booting and by the ability to reconfigure any number of workstations across the network without leaving your seat.

You might run into difficulties in the early stages, of course, and again from time to time as network or hardware trouble arises. This section covers some pitfalls to avoid and some error messages that you might see.

Normal Sequence of Events

Knowing what to expect in a working setup can help when you're trying to diagnose initial problems.

IPX PROMs generally just display a copyright message and version number on-screen before DOS starts to load. This PROM information may or may not remain on-screen until scrolled off the top as DOS loads—some brands clear the information from the screen as soon as contact is made with the server. Some IPX PROM brands are quite informative, displaying information messages as they contact a server, open BOOTCONF.SYS, search for the boot image, and so on.

RPL PROMs are quite verbose by comparison. A typical PROM startup screen displays the adapter Ethernet address, adapter settings, and the number of FIND frames sent. Figure 28.4 shows a typical example.

This screen is usually visible for only an instant. Once the RPL server responds, the screen is cleared and the RPL bootstrap program displays its version and copyright information at the top of the screen. This remains visible while DOS starts, until it is scrolled off the top of the screen.

Preliminaries

First of all, make sure that the diskless workstation can boot properly from the master boot floppy. The problem may be as simple as a typographical error in a batch file or a missing driver file. If the workstation has no floppy drive, you have to assume that the master boot floppy is valid for the workstation until you discover otherwise.

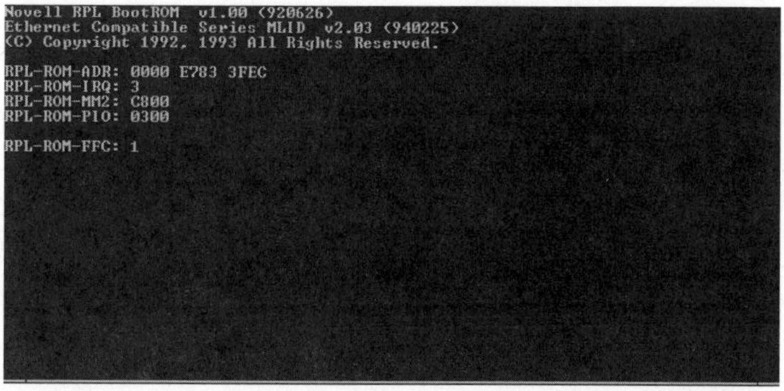

```
Novell RPL BootROM  v1.00 (920626)
Ethernet Compatible Series MLID  v2.03 (940225)
(C) Copyright 1992, 1993 All Rights Reserved.

RPL-ROM-ADR: 0000 E703 3FEC
RPL-ROM-IRQ: 3
RPL-ROM-MM2: C800
RPL-ROM-PIO: 0300

RPL-ROM-FFC: 1
```

Figure 28.4

This is the workstation screen during RPL PROM startup.

Testing with the boot floppy can also reveal network or cabling problems. If the workstation can't connect to the server when booted from a floppy, it certainly won't be able to do so using a boot PROM.

Check also that the boot PROM version information is displayed on-screen when the workstation is powered on. If not, the PROM has not been properly installed and you need to repeat the installation process before you try again.

In short, make sure that the problem is related to the remote boot process before proceeding with this section.

Bear in mind the following when debugging remote boot problems:

- Be consistent across servers. If you update a boot image on one server, copy the updated image to all other boot servers.

- If you are working with IPX PROMs, remember to rerun RPLFIX every time you rerun DOSGEN.

The next sections cover errors that may arise during three separate stages:

- While locating the boot image
- While loading the boot image
- After booting

Errors While Locating the Boot Image

Errors covered in this category occur after the PROM code starts to execute but before the workstation starts to download its boot image.

RPL PROMs Only. The following sections deal with aspects of this class of problems specific to RPL PROMs.

No RPL Server Response. If no RPL server responds to an RPL PROM, the PROM's startup information as illustrated above remains on-screen as the PROM continues to send FIND frames. The FIND frame count at the bottom increases by one every couple of seconds until an RPL server responds with a FOUND frame:

```
RPL-ROM-FFC: 2
```

Determine why the RPL server is not responding:

- Check that RPL.NLM has been correctly loaded and that RPL has been bound on the server to an adapter using the 802.2 frame type.

- If RPL.NLM has been bound using the NODEFAULT parameter, check that this workstation's Ethernet address has been entered correctly in BOOTCONF.SYS.

RPL: No Boot Server. The RPL PROM startup information is cleared from the screen as soon as the RPL bootstrap program starts. The bootstrap program attempts to connect to the file server where the boot image is stored. If it fails to do so within a few seconds, it hangs and offers you this message:

```
RBOOT-RPL-100: Unable to CONNECT to File Server; RPL HALTED
```

Establish why the boot server is not responding:

- If the RPL server and boot image server are not the same, check that the boot image server is running.

- Check that IPX has been bound to the same network number on the boot image and RPL servers.

RPL: No Boot Image. If the bootstrap program connects to a file server but cannot locate the designated boot image—NET$DOS.SYS or the file specified in BOOTCONF.SYS—it reports an error:

```
RBOOT-RPL-104: Unable to OPEN NET$DOS.SYS; RPL HALTED
```

If multiple boot images are specified in BOOTCONF.SYS, and if the selected file cannot be opened, the error message is slightly different. RPL does not halt but instead asks the user to select a boot image again:

```
RBOOT-RPL-104: Unable to OPEN NET$DOS.SYS
RBOOT-RPL-106: Place CURSOR on DISK IMAGE file: Hit ENTER when Ready:
```

In either case, determine why the boot server cannot locate this workstation's boot image:

- Check the name of the file reported on the RBOOT-RPL-104 error line. If it is not the file that should be used by this workstation, check BOOTCONF.SYS for syntax and accuracy. Make sure that you have recorded and entered this workstation's Ethernet address and the network address correctly.

- Check that the relevant boot image file is in SYS:LOGIN on all boot image servers.

- Make sure that it is flagged as shareable on all servers.

■ If RPL has been bound on the server using the GNS parameter, or if the GNS override appears on this workstation's BOOTCONF.SYS entry, check that all servers without boot images have had REPLY TO GET NEAREST SERVER set to OFF. Remember that this should be done in the AUTOEXEC.NCF.

IPX PROMs Only. The following sections deal with aspects of this class of problems specific to IPX PROMs.

IPX: No Boot Server. If no server responds to the GNS request within a few seconds, an IPX PROM displays an error message: `Error finding server`.

Establish why the workstation is not able to get a response from the server:

■ Check that the server with the boot images is configured to respond to GNS frames. At the server console, issue the SET command. Enter **1** for Communications; then verify that REPLY TO GET NEAREST SERVER is ON.

■ Recheck the cable and network connections by booting from the master boot floppy.

IPX: No Boot Image. If the PROM gets a FOUND GET NEAREST SERVER frame from a server but cannot find its boot image on that server, it hangs and gives you the following message: `Error opening boot disk image file`.

Determine why the boot server cannot provide the workstation with its boot image:

■ Check BOOTCONF.SYS for syntax and accuracy. Make sure that you have recorded and entered this workstation's Ethernet address and the network address correctly.

■ Check that the relevant boot image file is in SYS:LOGIN on all boot image servers.

■ Make sure that it is flagged as shareable on all servers.

■ Check that all servers without boot images have had REPLY TO GET NEAREST SERVER set to OFF. Remember that this should be done in the AUTOEXEC.NCF.

■ Some older IPX PROMs have the name of their boot image file hard-coded. Check the manufacturer's documentation to see if you must use a particular boot image file name.

Errors While Loading the Boot Image

Errors covered in this category occur while the boot image file is being downloaded.

RPL PROMs Only. The next section deals with aspects of this class of problems specific to RPL PROMs.

RPL: HIMEM.SYS Error. Some versions of HIMEM.SYS perform a comprehensive memory test as they load. Among other things, the test writes to memory areas and then reads back from the same areas to see if the write was successful. The bootstrap program can cause this test to fail, resulting in this message:

Adding Network Services

```
ERROR: HIMEM.SYS has detected unreliable XMS memory at address 00800000h.
XMS Driver not installed.
```

Extended memory will not be enabled.

Instruct DOS not to carry out this test at boot time. Turn off HIMEM testing in the CONFIG.SYS with the following:

```
DEVICE=HIMEM.SYS /TESTMEM:OFF
```

IPX PROMs Only. The following sections deal with aspects of this class of problems specific to IPX PROMs.

IPX: Boot Image Not RPLFIXed. As explained earlier in this chapter, a problem with DOS 5 and IPX PROMs occurs when the command interpreter is loaded and overwrites the IPX code in memory. The command interpreter is loaded immediately after CONFIG.SYS is processed, its first job being to run AUTOEXEC.BAT.

Therefore, if all CONFIG.SYS statements are executed but no AUTOEXEC.BAT commands are, a boot image is out there that has not been RPLFIXed. Examine the messages displayed by device drivers and so on as they load to ascertain if this has happened.

Make sure that all copies of the boot image are RPLFIXed:

- Run RPLFIX on the boot image again. You might have neglected to do this after the last time you ran DOSGEN.

- Check the time stamp of the boot image file on all servers. It should be the same on all. If not, make sure that the most recent version is RPLFIXed, and copy it to all boot servers.

Remember that running RPLFIX on a boot image that has already been RPLFIXed has no effect (but does no harm either).

IPX: RPLODI.COM Not Loaded. RPLODI.COM deals with the hand-over from the PROM's IPX code to the MLID's ODI code. If RPLODI.COM has not been loaded, the MLID loads but the workstation hangs with the error message:

```
Error reading boot disk image file
```

Make sure RPLODI.COM is loaded correctly:

- Check the boot image's AUTOEXEC.BAT or surrogate batch file to make sure that RPLODI.COM is loaded after the LSL but before the MLID.

- Make sure that the boot image contains a copy of RPLODI.COM.

Errors in Loading the Workstation Shell. The batch file that NETX.EXE or VLM.EXE is loaded from must be the same within the boot image and in SYS:LOGIN. If not, the byte offset might be wrong, and a variety of errors are possible, like Batch file missing or Bad command or file name.

Synchronize the relevant batch files:

- Check on all boot servers that the boot image for this workstation contains the correct version of AUTOEXEC.BAT or the surrogate batch file.

- Check SYS:LOGIN on all boot servers for the correct version of AUTOEXEC.BAT or the surrogate batch file.

Errors after Bootup

Errors covered in this category occur after the workstation boots or starts to download its boot image but are related to the fact that the workstation was booted remotely rather than from a local floppy disk.

COMSPEC. The COMSPEC environment variable must be set during logon to point to a valid copy of COMMAND.COM for this version of DOS. If not, the following error message can appear when DOS tries to reload part of its command interpreter, typically after you exit an application:

```
Invalid COMMAND.COM
Cannot load COMMAND, system halted
```

- Reboot the machine, log on, and check the value of the COMSPEC variable before running any application. Make sure that the value of COMSPEC is a valid path to COMMAND.COM for the version of DOS that you are running.

- Refer to the earlier "Setting COMSPEC" section.

EMM386.EXE. If EMM386.EXE was loaded in CONFIG.SYS without the /Y switch, it assumes that it can reload from drive A. This results in an error when, for example, Windows is started:

```
EMM386: Unable to start Enhanced Mode Windows due to invalid path
specification for EMM386.
```

- Edit CONFIG.SYS to use the /Y switch with a valid path for EMM386.EXE after logon. For example,

```
DEVICE=EMM386.EXE /NOEMS /Y=F:\WINDOWS\EMM386.EXE /X=D000-D800
```

Tricks and Tools

The nature of remote booting can lead to peculiar difficulties not normally encountered with ordinary workstations. For example, an error in the boot image can stop your workstation from booting, and you cannot log on to fix the error without going to a non-diskless workstation. The following sections discuss ways to get around some of these problems.

Grabbing the Phantom Floppy. During the remote boot process, the workstation "believes" that it is really booting from its floppy drive although no boot floppy disk is really present. The files contained in the boot image appear to the workstation as if they really are on drive A until the workstation shell loads, so it is possible to get hold of the files in the boot image by getting access to this phantom floppy disk.

Press Ctrl+Break (repeatedly if necessary) after the workstation starts to execute the commands in AUTOEXEC.BAT but before the workstation shell is loaded. Enter **Y** when you are asked

```
Terminate batch job (Y/N)?
```

You then should find yourself at the A:> prompt with access to all the files. You can use any of DOS's internal commands—DIR, COPY, and so on—to look at or manipulate files (watch the drive spinning when you enter DIR). Of course, external commands such as FORMAT and EDIT are not available.

Unpacking the Boot Image. Your master boot floppy might get lost or become corrupt. If the boot image is intact, you can unpack the files in it onto a disk using the /U option of DOSGEN, version 1.2 or later with the following command:

```
DOSGEN /U NE2$DOS.SYS A:
```

The disk must be of the same density and capacity as the original master boot floppy used to generate the boot image.

Maintaining Boot Images on the Fly. Making a minor change to a file in a boot image can be a lot of work. You need to find the master boot floppy, make the change, run DOSGEN again, RPLFIX the boot image if necessary, copy it to all the boot servers, and check the flags.

Alasdair Grant of the University of Cambridge, England has written an excellent utility named NETBOOT that allows you to manipulate the contents of an existing boot image *in situ*. It can be used to extract, replace, or delete files without the need to regenerate the boot image after doing so. Even an RPLFIXed boot image remains RPLFIXed after you change something using NETBOOT.

NETBOOT is command-line oriented rather than menu-driven. This means that multiple NETBOOT commands can be contained in a single batch file, making it possible to update the same boot image file on all servers at once. This reduces the possibility that an essential change will be missed on one or more servers.

In short, NETBOOT is an invaluable tool to anyone working with boot images.

Summary

Setting up a diskless workstation can be a complex business when compared to the ease with which a local boot machine can be prepared. There are extra layers of complexity in the preparation of the boot image file and in configuring the server to deliver the boot image. The payback for this extra work comes with the use of multiple similarly configured workstations. A single boot image can serve multiple workstations, so you can manage the boot configurations of an arbitrary number of workstations as if they were one.

This chapter explained how to configure and manage diskless workstations. It detailed the steps involved in preparing the workstation, boot image file, and file server and gave detailed troubleshooting procedures for the most common types of fault that arise when using diskless workstations. For more information on troubleshooting procedures and fault solving, refer to chapters 31, "Locating the Problem: Server versus Workstation versus Links," and 32, "Repairing Common Types of Problems."

Chapter 29

Adding Wireless Networking

What is *wireless networking*? Although at first you might think of wireless networks in terms of simple LANs and desktop machines, in reality a wireless network can consist of almost any kind of computing machine and can extend over any area. Essentially, a wireless network transmits data along a certain frequency through the air rather than through a cable. Wireless networks include

- LANs without fixed workstation locations

- Mobile networks, such as fleets of trucks connected via satellite

- Telecommuters who dial into their offices using wireless modems

These are just examples—after reading this chapter, you'll probably start recognizing wireless networks in other places as well.

The size of the network and the transmission medium are irrelevant to the definition of a wireless network. The main thing that most wireless networks have in common is a need for mobility. Few wireless networks evolve from traditional wired LANs—more often, they stem from a unique need for networking components that are difficult or impossible to connect in any other way.

Much current wireless networking technology uses *radio frequency* (*RF*) signals to transmit data, but microwaves and infrared signals are also part of wireless technology. In this chapter, we'll talk about various kinds of wireless technologies and topologies that are most common among commercial systems, potential applications, and some policy and technical issues that affect the development of wireless networks.

Pros and Cons of Wireless Networking

Like networking in general, wireless networking has things to recommend it, as well as definite detriments. Whether the pros outweigh the cons depends on your particular needs.

Pros

Most of the positive things about wireless networking stem directly from the lack of cabling to deal with. No cables potentially means the following:

- Networks in areas that are difficult or impossible to cable (for example, in less-developed countries or in buildings that are expensive or dangerous to cable)

- An easier network setup

- Printer sharing without a network

- Interoffice networking with no cabling "right-of-way" required

- Network access for those who can never be cabled (such as people with "virtual offices" in their cars)

- Modem use is possible without an outside telephone jack (a problem, for example, in hotels using switchboards)

Networks in Inaccessible Areas. In parts of the world where there either is little cable infrastructure or it has been damaged by war or environmental disaster, wireless communications can keep remote sites in touch with each other. How do you connect a remote mining site to the city office to discuss equipment needs? Or coordinate rescue efforts after an earthquake? In these cases, a cable infrastructure either never existed or no longer works. The only way to expeditiously share information in such circumstances might be a wireless network.

Easier Network Setup. If a network's components (PCs and peripheral devices) are fluid, then a wireless configuration can make setting up the network much easier. This can work even if the network is a hybrid of wired and wireless connections. For example, if you have data on your notebook computer that you need to print out, a wired network provides you with a couple of options for getting that data from the notebook to the printer. You could sever the printer's usual connection and plug it into the notebook— or if the notebook had a docking station and NIC, you could plug the notebook into the network and thereby connect to the printer. If neither of those options were possible, you could copy the files to be printed to a PC that did have access to the printer—assuming that the application software used for the files was on the wired PC as well as the notebook. No matter which method you use, though, it's something of a hassle and requires a bit of setup time.

An easier solution would be a wireless connection between the two (assuming that both the notebook and printer were equipped for it). That way, you could send a job to the printer with no cable swapping, and without shoving components aside to make room. Just make sure that the printer and notebook are fairly close to each other with no obstructions and that the two components can be connected via a *virtual cable*.

This example illustrates the next point, as well—printer sharing without a network. If the printer is wireless-equipped (such as HP's 5P) and the notebook also is (such as IBM's ThinkPad), then one computer can connect to the printer via the parallel port and another via the infrared port. The PC connecting to the printer via the parallel port doesn't have to be wireless equipped at all, unless the two computers need to be able to share files. (We'll talk about *hybrid networks*, or networks with both wired and wireless components, later in this chapter).

Networking Mobile Clients. Two trends of the 1990s—increasing worker mobility and increasing dependence on up-to-the-minute information—drive mobile computing and make it vital for mobile computing clients to have network connections:

- Drivers for delivery services need addresses to pick up packages

- Insurance salespeople need estimates based on actuary tables located in the office database (and sometimes they need this information before they get to the client's site)

- Fishing boats need market information to tell them which port will get them the best price for their fish. The fishermen might even manage to sell the catch before they get to shore by contacting a client over a wireless link

In all these situations, the clients need information that they can't get using a wired connection. (It's ridiculous to consider connecting fishing boats with cables.) If these mobile computing clients are to have access to networked information, their connection must be wireless.

Wireless Modem Connections. The advantages of a wireless modem connection are a little different from those of a wireless printer. With a wireless modem, you can potentially carry your office anywhere that you and your laptop go—a much more likely scenario than lugging a wireless printer around.

Wireless dialup capabilities offer great advantages for people who work a lot on the road and must rely on hotels to act as their office. For one thing, some hotels route all calls through a switchboard, so using a traditional modem isn't possible—you can't just unplug the telephone and plug your modem into the wall to get to an outside line. For another, printing on the road is often a major hassle and expense. Even if the hotel in which you're staying has a computer center (and many do not), printing charges in hotels range from fairly pricey to downright exorbitant. Via the modem, you can fax your document to the hotel's fax number and address it to yourself. The final product may be on thermal paper, but if all you need is hard copy and quality is not the main concern, then that's an easy and inexpensive way to get a printout.

Essentially, the advantages of wireless networking are mobility and flexibility. Wireless networking makes it possible to share information when the infrastructure or circumstances seem to make networking impossible. Wireless modems come either as PC-Card (PCMCIA) devices that fit into a slot on your PC, or as a separate device with an antenna, which can plug into any RS-232-compatible serial port.

> ### Tip
>
> If you're not sure that your serial port is RS-232 compatible, don't worry too much—most are.

Cons

Mobility and flexibility aren't everything in a network. Wireless networks have some inherent disadvantages, although some are more perceived than actual. Generally speaking, the following hold true:

- Wireless networks are either slower or shorter-range than wired networks

- Wireless networks tend to be more expensive than wired networks

- The limited number of frequencies available for wireless communications means that fewer transmission paths are available, unless some method of conserving frequencies is used

- Environmental conditions have more of an effect on wireless networks than on wired networks

- Many people are concerned that wireless transmissions are less secure than wired transmissions

Even if some of these considerations (such as the security concerns) are more perceived than actual, perceived detriments often do as much damage to a product's acceptance as real ones, so they're worth considering.

Limits of Speed and Distance. Wireless communications are inherently limited by their lack of cabling. If the wireless medium is a radio-frequency signal, then it can travel for a long way, but it's slow (and often uncertain) compared to a wired connection. Slow, in this context, means that a high-speed wireless link is about 1.6 Mbps for a LAN and 64 Kbps for a WAN. Considering that most wired LANs run upward of 10 Mbps, and many WAN technologies (as discussed in chapter 4, "Upgrading to a WAN") start at more than 1 Mbps, wireless speeds don't compare very well.

If the medium is an infrared signal, then it's faster (as fast as a wired network), but it's limited in the distance that it can extend without regenerating the signal and is also dependent on line-of-sight between the device sending the signal and the one receiving it. Even trees can disrupt an infrared signal. We'll talk about why this is so a little later in this chapter, when we discuss how frequencies work.

Higher Cost. Wireless technology is relatively new and complex, so like other new computing technology it tends to be expensive. Wireless LAN network cards, for example, run about $400 for an Ethernet connection, while wired ones are available for $50 to around $100. Connection time for dialup wireless connections costs, too (but then so do some wired dialup connections). (This applies to wireless solutions that let you dial into your company's network.) Of course, wireless networks don't carry the cost of pulling cable, which is not inconsiderable (the exact amounts depend on your installation, requirements, and the part of the country you're in), and gets quite expensive for complex installations.

Environmental Constraints. Because of their physical structure, wireless networks are vulnerable to environmental factors that under normal circumstances don't affect wired networks, such as

- Physical obstructions (like walls)
- Other wireless transmissions on the same local frequency
- Rain or other precipitation

Of course, not all these circumstances affect all wireless communications the same way, and newer technology has improved the situation. Environmental factors, however, are still a consideration.

For example, properly shielded wired connections aren't sensitive to other wired connections in the same area. You can have a jumble of cables in the same space, and as long as you're using properly shielded cables the signals won't interfere with each other under normal circumstances. (If your cable installation uses UTP, don't worry—the twists in the wires contained in the cable help protect against interference.)

Wireless networks are different. Because the medium of transmission is a naked electronic signal using a certain frequency, two transmissions on the same frequencies in the same area will interfere with each other unless some sort of spectrum-sharing technology is used. This is really no different from the interference problem that you encounter with poorly shielded cables, such as the ribbon cables used to connect printers to PCs.

One of the challenges facing wireless networking is that the higher the frequency used (and thus the bandwidth), the more vulnerable the signal is to interference. There's a direct tradeoff between carrying capacity and stamina, which is discussed more in the following section.

Bandwidth Constraints. Increased use of higher frequencies and digital "messaging" techniques that permit greater throughput on the same bandwidth mean that there's no reason for wireless transmissions to be slower than wired ones, but current cost and policy issues—combined with the fragility of the signal at higher frequencies—mean that for all practical purposes they are slower. Although you can get equivalent bandwidths from wired and wireless networks, it costs you far more to get the wireless speed because of the following:

- The more sensitive equipment required to receive higher frequency transmissions
- In some cases, the cost of purchasing rights to a particular frequency (an indirect cost to the consumer, but one that you'll see nonetheless)
- The cost of installing sufficient transmitters to get the signal to its destination (because the unprotected signals of wireless transmissions suffer more from attenuation than do the protected signals of wired networks)

How Secure Are Wireless Transmissions? Anyone who's ever accidentally overheard a neighbor's conversation on his cordless telephone is aware that data traveling through the ether is pretty open to tapping. Anyone who is equipped with the proper equipment can intercept the signal. However, this is not a problem unique to wireless networks—it's just easier to intercept a wireless signal accidentally.

Before you decide that wireless communications (especially data) are more vulnerable to tapping than wired ones, consider the following points:

- To tap any transmission, you need to have the receiving device in the area where the signal is—this means that cables, which show the signal's path precisely, are in some ways easier to tap.

- No cable, even fiber-optic cable, is completely safe from illicit access.

- *Digital encoding* can scramble the information transmitted from the sender to the receiver, making any tapped information useless without the decoder.

- Although older RF transmissions used a transmission method called *direct sequencing*, which was vulnerable to tapping because it sent the data all on the same frequency, newer transmission methods call for *frequency hopping*, in which the transmission uses more than one frequency during a transmittal, making the signal more difficult to intercept. Combined with encoding, frequency-hopped transmissions are relatively secure.

- The narrow beam of some wireless transmissions (such as infrared signals) makes them almost impossible to tap unless you are at one end of the transmission and can determine the exact path.

Health Concerns. The possibility of health risks posed by wireless transmissions are not yet fully known, but some dangers definitely exist. Unshielded microwave transmissions such as those used in some military communications can be dangerous (the reason that microwaves in public places don't carry warning signs anymore has more to do with improved shielding than with safer microwave signals). Therefore, it's possible that some people may be affected by RF signals since microwaves are just another part of the electromagnetic spectrum. For the moment, however, this doesn't seem to be a major problem for anyone except those who look directly into an infrared transmitter's LED.

A Brief Introduction to Wireless Technology

Before jumping into a discussion of wireless technology, it's helpful to understand the basic structure of this technology. In this section, we'll discuss the basics of what a frequency is, what affects its speed, and what the differences are between the various frequencies.

The basic thing to understand about wireless signals is that every signal operates at a certain frequency—that is, the number of oscillations per time unit that the signal makes. More oscillations means higher frequency, as you can see in figure 29.1.

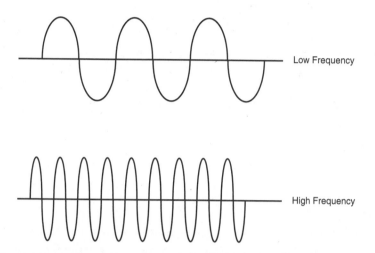

Figure 29.1

A low frequency has fewer oscillations per minute than a high frequency.

The number of cycles per second is measured in *hertz* (abbreviated *Hz*). Most measurements we care about when discussing wireless communications involve *megahertz* (*MHz*) or *gigahertz* (*GHz*). A signal with a frequency of 30MHz, for instance, oscillates 30 million times per second. A higher hertz rate means that the signal has a greater bandwidth because more information (1s and 0s, represented by the waves) is included in the signal each second.

Frequencies are divided into discrete groups, called *bands*, based on their hertz rate—thus, based on their carrying capacity. Table 29.1 shows some of these bands.

Table 29.1 Important Radio Frequency Wireless Bands	
Band	**Hertz**
High Frequency (HF)	3–30MHz
Very High Frequency (VHF)	30–300MHz
Ultra High Frequency (UHF)	300MHz–3GHz
Super High Frequency (SHF)	3–30GHz
Extremely High Frequency (EHF)	30–300GHz

The radio-frequency bands currently used most often are HF, VHF, and UHF, with the higher-frequency bands coming into greater use as the lower-capacity bands are either saturated or unable to carry the data loads that newer wireless transmissions demand. For instance, a frequency that can easily handle textual dispatching information might have problems carrying real-time video. Infrared (IR) transmissions use frequencies high above the levels listed in table 29.1—at the high end of the visible spectrum. Because of their higher frequency, IR transmissions have greater carrying capacity than RF transmissions but have a much shorter range. Generally speaking, the higher the frequency, the greater the bandwidth and the shorter the distance it will travel.

> **Note**
>
> Because of their limited bandwidth, bands below HF, low frequency (LF) and medium frequency (MF), are not suited to wireless data transmissions.

Band Frequency Characteristics

How does a signal's frequency affect its ability to transmit data? We've already discussed one effect of higher frequency: more bandwidth. Another effect, however, is increased vulnerability to interference and attenuation. This is a direct result of the shorter wavelengths that you saw in figure 29.1. Shorter wavelengths make the signal less flexible, and therefore less able to "bend" around blockages and more prone to interference from other signals. This is just like the difference between a loosely twisted rope and a tightly wound rope. You can bend the looser rope around obstacles without much problem, but the tighter one won't bend as easily.

> **Note**
>
> Although interference and attenuation have similar effects on data transmission—they distort it—they're not the same thing. *Interference* is a stray electronic signal that distorts the signal being transmitted, possibly corrupting the data that it's carrying. *Attentuation* is the increasing weakness of a signal as it travels a longer distance than it's meant to; the fading signal can distort the data. Interference affects data transmission in the same way that too many people talking at once can make it difficult for you to understand one person. Attenuation adversely affects transmission in the same way as it's hard to understand a person across a room and speaking at face-to-face volume.

As you can see in figure 29.2, increased bandwidth means less signal staying power.

This is not an exact charting, as the effects of distortion on a signal are impossible to measure exactly—even if you deliberately distorted a signal and measured the result, how would you know that nothing else had affected the signal?—but should give you the general idea.

> **Note**
>
> Wireless transmission signals occupy part of a band, not the whole band. If a signaling technology uses frequencies in the VHF band, it is limited to only a few of those frequencies, not the entire run from 30MHz through 300MHz.

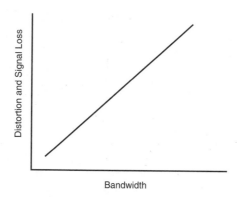

Figure 29.2

The greater a frequency's bandwidth, the more quickly its signal degrades.

How Frequencies Transmit Data

That's the basic story of what frequencies are, but how does the data get from your PC to the frequency and from there to its destination? To begin with, the data is a series of electrical impulses at certain intervals, usually represented with 1s (impulse) and 0s (no impulse)—in this instance, let's say that it's an e-mail message. When you click the Send button (or equivalent thereof), you send the collection of 1s and 0s that make up your e-mail message and addressing information to a transmitter. Depending on what kind of transmitter it is, the transmitter converts the 1s and 0s to a related pattern of electrical signals that can be sent on a particular frequency band. For example, if your PC is equipped with a radio-frequency (RF) transmitter, then it will send the signals via either the HF or VHF bands shown in table 29.1. A reciever of the same type in the area can then pick up on the signal that you transmitted if it's tuned to the same frequency.

That's the easy part. The complex part comes when you try to limit the number of receivers (you'll note that, in this scenario, anyone who has a receiver tuned to the same frequency and is within range gets your message) or when you've got a number of devices that want to use the same bandwidth.

Conserving Bandwidth

You now know in general terms what frequency is, and how bands with different frequencies respond to environmental conditions and carry data. You might be wondering how, since there are a finite number of bands, wireless services can expect to expand. For that matter, how have they expanded as far as they have without using up all the available bandwidth?

This question is crucial to wireless networking. Like any other resource, radio frequencies are limited but the uses for them are not. When wireless transmissions were only for television signals and CB radios, this was less of a concern. (For the record, however, the CB craze in the 1970s caused a real bandwidth saturation problem—the more crowded a frequency gets, the harder it gets to use it.) Today, though, wireless communications are increasingly important to many business applications. Where will the bandwidth needed to sustain growth in these services come from?

Isolating Frequencies. Part of the answer stems from the fact that RF signals don't extend forever. A particular frequency can be in use in more than one place at a time, as long as the usages are separated enough not to interfere with each other. For example, you can use the frequency 33MHz in Melbourne and Seattle at the same time, attenuation would prevent signals that originate at points so far apart from interfering with each other. By the time the Seattle signal gets to Australia, it is so weak as to be practically nonexistent.

The fact that you can use a frequency in more than one place at a time naturally has led to the creation of frequency "cells" that electrically isolate geographic areas from each other. These cells are hexagonal in shape and have a transmitter located at their center to handle transmissions. The closer a subscriber is to the transmitter, the stronger the signal is, but it won't cut off until the subscriber moves to a different cell. Within cell A, for example, a frequency can only be used by one signal at a time (that's for starters—there's more to this story that we'll get to in a minute), but that frequency also exists in cell B, cell C, and so on. Electronic barriers between the cells keep the signals from extending beyond their cell. Adjoining cells can't use the same frequencies at the same time—in cellular communications, they must be separated by at least six cells—but the cells allow some level of frequency reuse. The smaller the cells are, the greater the possible frequency reuse.

There is a tradeoff, however. Since it's obviously not acceptable to chop off signaling when a person making a cellular transmission crosses a cell's border, some kind of switching mechanism is in order. The switching mechanism is the problem. Switching the signal from cell A's transmitter to cell B's transmitter takes time and can result in a lost connection if something goes wrong. Thus, although smaller cells (like those used in personal communications services, discussed later in this chapter) mean greater frequency reuse, they also mean more switching.

Data Compression. To get more use out of available bandwidth, you can make sure that the data takes less time to travel to its destination, thus freeing the bandwidth sooner for other transmissions. Since the mid-80s, the algorithms for compression have dramatically improved due to better design and better processing hardware.

Channeling Methods. Another means of conserving bandwidth is to channel the frequencies so that more than one subscriber can use them at once. There are a number of different methods of doing this, but here we'll restrict the discussion to two that you're likely to encounter: *time-division multiple access* (*TDMA*) and *code-division multiple access* (*CDMA*). Although these channeling technologies function differently from each other, they have the same purpose: to let more than one signal use the same frequency in the same place at the same time.

TDMA uses the same multiplexing techniques that *time-division multiplexing* does. Bandwidth is split into a number of logical channels, and each signal gets one of the channels. For example, six devices can transmit data at 330MHz in the same place at the same time. The process actually involves extraordinarily rapid switching of the channel among its various "simultaneous" users so that each of them has the apparent sole use of the channel but is in fact sharing that channel with all its other users, occupying it for specific segments of time. Think of it as shuffling the users in and out of the channel at predefined intervals but doing the shuffling so quickly that it is transparent to them.

CDMA, also called *spread-spectrum technology*, works a little differently. Rather than dividing the frequency into perhaps six channels, as TDMA would, it mixes the six transmissions and sends them all as a heap. Each transmission has a unique digital code assigned to it that permits the recipient to sort out its own data from the other transmissions. CDMA works like a *packet-switching network*, the characteristics of which are discussed in chapter 4, "Upgrading to a WAN." This sounds confusing, but it's not that complicated. Think of a mailbox in an office building. If each office in the building has its own mailbox and must pay rent on it, that can get expensive and is unnecessary for those who don't constantly send mail—much more efficient to have one big mailbox in the office building that everyone shares rent on. To keep everyone's mail from getting mixed up, each office color-codes its envelopes: Rutger's Insurance uses blue envelopes, Wilson Industries pink, and so forth. Thus, all of the offices can share transmission bandwidth (the mailbox) and jumble their signals together to get the most use out of the available bandwidth, but the data (that is, the mail) doesn't get confused because each piece is coded for the recipient).

The differences between the two modulation techniques are visible in figure 29.3.

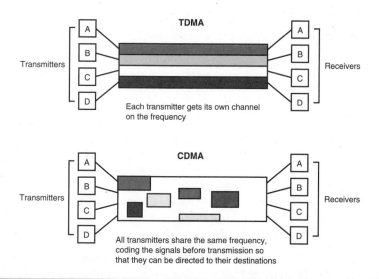

Figure 29.3

TDMA allocates bandwith by time slot; CDMA allocates bandwidth by packet.

Using cells, digital compression, some kind of logical bandwidth division, or a combination of the three, you can squeeze enough space out of existing bandwidth to hopefully fulfill the needs of wireless communications. If that doesn't work, there's always pressure from new services that require bandwidth insisting that "less crucial" users give up their bandwidth to others.

> **Note**
>
> Frequency reallocation questions lead to highly charged political wrangles. Bandwidth users with big audiences but less serious topics (like Saturday morning cartoons) must wrestle over frequencies with users who have more serious topics but much smaller audiences. Look for increasing numbers of slugfests as the competition for bandwidth increases.

Keeping Communications Secure

You'll recall that when you transmit a signal, any receiver in the area that's tuned into the same frequency can pick up the signal. This is great for radio stations but less desirable for your company's budget projection for next year. One method for getting around this is called *frequency hopping*. This is exactly what it sounds like: instead of using a single frequency for the duration of the transmission, the transmitter will first send an encoded key to the receiver, telling it what frequencies that it's going to use for the transmission. Then the transmitter will begin the transmission, jumping around in the spectrum to keep any receivers in the area from inadvertently picking up on the signal for more than a flash.

Ten years ago, frequency-hopping was largely limited to secure government and military wireless transmissions, and even today it's not required for all situations. Other security methods include encoding transmissions and password-protecting files. The high-end wireless carriers (like those providing microwave services) have government-approved measures that can keep your data secure.

RF Links

Historically, the majority of wireless technologies have relied upon RF signals to transmit data. There are several reasons for this. First, RF signaling was the earliest electronic form of wireless communications. Although original usage was restricted to lower frequencies, it was natural as needs changed to keep moving up to higher levels of RF signaling, rather than abandoning RF technology to explore new media. Related to this point, RF signaling was a medium with which most developers were familiar through radio and television, and presumably were more comfortable.

RF technology works for a number of different networking applications in both LANs and WANs. Inside, antennae in serial ports or transceivers in PC-Card slots can connect the portable computers to each other or, via a gateway machine, to a wired network. The speeds involved are not great (ranging from a couple of hundred Kbps to 1.6 Mbps). For transferring relatively simple files such as text-only messages, however, they're perfectly acceptable. Desktop machines also can connect to a wireless network, via an ISA (or PC-Card) wireless transceiver, or an external antenna.

Applications

Who might benefit from wireless networking? The next few sections introduce you to typical beneficiaries of wireless technology.

Companies That Maintain Inventory. Which would you rather do: perform inventory with a clipboard in your hand and then enter your tallies in the computer when you get back to your desk, or enter the tallies directly into the inventory database? The first method might work if you have a standard inventory form and don't have to try to decipher your abbreviations or do the math five times to make sure your numbers are right, but it's twice the work for the same result and takes longer to get an accurate count. You could take a stand-alone notebook computer to do inventory, but the updates would not be automatic. Sooner or later you'd have to copy the files from the notebook's hard disk to merge them with the main inventory database. Even having a network connection and docking station in the storage room might not work, because you can't carry the notebook with you when it's in a docking station.

If, however, your notebook had a wireless connection to the inventory database server, you could do inventory and update the database at the same time. You would just type in the entries as you went.

Companies with a Mobile On-Site Workforce. I bought a car not too long ago, and one of the major hassles about the purchase process was that every time the salesperson wanted to run some numbers through the auto dealership's database, he had to walk to a terminal at the other end of the room and do the work there. This was irritating not only because he kept disappearing for extended periods of time, but because a couple of times he forgot the numbers that he wanted to input and had to come back to get them. It was annoying for me, and probably frustrating for him as well. Since only a few salespeople had their own desks, it wasn't practical for them to have wired computers on the desktops, since on a busy day they'd be stuck waiting for a desk with a computer, or hovering unprofessionally over each other, waiting for a crack at a computer.

If all the salespeople had a portable PC, on the other hand, they could access the information they need, and make their comparisons without having to leave the desk. This could expedite the entire process, and it certainly would make customers happier—if you must wait, it's easier to wait when you know what's going on, not just that the salesperson has disappeared again.

Companies with a Mobile Off-Site Workforce. Many salespeople spend most of their time either at the client's site or traveling to it. A wireless WAN that permits these salespeople access to the office network might make a sale. The principle is the same as that of the on-site salesperson: information available at your fingertips, so that the customer doesn't have to make another appointment to get readily available facts, results in happier customers and a more likely sale.

For that matter, when those mobile salespeople come back on-site, wireless technology can make it easier for them to connect to the network and even print. A wired/wireless bridge or gateway machine can let a laptop—as long as it's equipped with a transceiver and client software—plug into the network without having to find a docking station.

Equipment Used in RF Wireless Networking

The components of a wireless network are not very different from those used in a wired network. At a minimum, you need a device to connect the PC to the network, and a slot on the PC into which you'll plug the device. With those items, you can create a network of wireless computers. If you'd like to connect the wireless network to a wired network, you use either a gateway machine (containing one wired card and one wireless card) or a local bridge that includes both a transceiver and a connection to the wired network. You can see some of the wireless LAN possibilities in figure 29.4.

All-wireless network

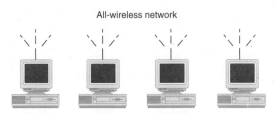

All the wireless PCs can see each other.

Hybrid wired and wireless network

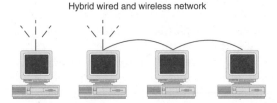

The wireless PC can see all the wired PCs via the gateway.

Figure 29.4

Wireless LAN configurations can appear in many different forms.

To connect dial-in wireless clients to the network, you'll need a wireless modem (many fit into a PC-Card slot) and some kind of cellular or packet-switching wireless network service. You can't start running a private wide-area wireless network any more than you can get a bulldozer and start installing cable across the county; to provide WAN service you need right-of-way, whether it's to run cable or to utilize a given frequency. Public wireless networks are available in most urban areas in the United States.

Wide-Area RF Protocols

Over distances longer than a few hundred yards, some kind of protocol for setting up the connection and transmitting the data is necessary. Wireless communications can pass over either analog or digital signals, so we'll discuss the more common protocols that pertain to each.

Cellular Protocols. In the beginning, there was cellular.

Unless you've been living under a rock for the past decade or so, you're familiar with the concept of cellular telephones: small, wireless telephones with which the user can place calls within a certain area. Many urban areas are divided into hexagonal *cells* that contain a centrally located transceiver to route calls to their destinations. You can see the arrangement in figure 29.5.

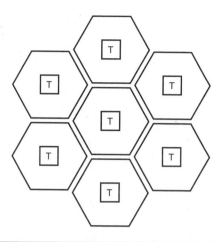

Figure 29.5

A cellular network can connect you to other cellular users, permit you to dial into your office, or pick up Internet e-mail on the fly.

Cellular communications work all right for voice (although there is a certain level of distortion), but isn't really suited for data transmittal, because it's slow (often limited to less than 1200 bps actual throughput) and because the noise and activity on a cellular connection are not good for data integrity or connection stability. It's got one big advantage over digital, however: the infrastructure is already in place. It may not be great, but it's there, and it works.

The lack of data support might not seem extremely important since cellular systems still carry mostly voice traffic, but data traffic is increasing in proportion to voice traffic in cellular systems. Voice usage of cellular systems isn't going away, but it's going to be coexisting more often with data usage. Thus, improving cellular's data handling is important.

MNP10. To alleviate the problems with cellular data transmissions, some developers began working on a protocol that could handle conditions unique to cellular transmissions, instead of trying to treat the connection like a faulty wire. In 1992, Microcom came up with a protocol named *MNP10* that was based on the wired modem protocol *MNP4*. MNP10 had some error-checking capabilities and allowed for significantly increased throughput, but also had some problems. First, it was proprietary: to gain any benefit from the new protocol, the hardware at both ends of the connection had to support MNP10. Second, MNP10 perceived cellular events as noise, so the modems had to be resynchronized after every bleep on the connection. Cellular connections have a lot of bleeps, so this meant that MNP10 did not provide as significant an increase in speed as you'd expect. Modems spent a lot of time recovering from events, rather than transmitting data.

ETC. In 1993, AT&T/Paradyne developed a protocol named *Enhanced Throughput Cellular* (*ETC*). This protocol, based on the wired modem protocols *V.42* and *V.32bis*, allows for speeds of up to 14.4 Kbps (before compression) and requires a modem supporting ETC on only one side of the connection (although AT&T recommended that ETC be present on both ends for best performance). Like MNP10, ETC sees cellular events as noise, requiring resynching time, but it has the advantage of being required only on one side of the connection.

CDPD. In 1994, IBM and others released a new way of sending data over an analog cellular system. This method, *Cellular Digital Packet Data (CDPD)* is a packet-switching overlay on top of the existing cellular system. In the overlay, data to be transmitted is placed in packets and then sent in the open bandwidth. It works much like wired packet-switching access protocols like *frame relay* and *X.25*, which are described in chapter 4, "Upgrading to a WAN." Like frame relay, CDPD is best suited for *bursty transmissions* rather than long, time-sensitive files. (Bursty transmissions are those in which the data comes in bursts, rather than in streams. If you're sending a graphic here and a text file there, those are bursty transmissions because they come and go quickly, and it doesn't matter what order the data arrive in so long as the ending file is in one piece. Time-sensitive transmissions, like voice and real-time video, are less suited to packet switching because they don't look or sound right unless the data in them arrives in a certain order and at a set pace.)

> **Note**
>
> CDPD's similarity to frame relay is more than coincidental. In at least one CDPD network, frame relay is the access protocol used to transmit the messages. Recall from chapter 4, "Upgrading to a WAN," that frame relay is not a network type—it's an access protocol to a network, either wired or wireless.

CDPD has a number of advantages:

- It's faster than other cellular protocols: 19.2 Kbps, with a real throughput of about 9,600 bps under optimal conditions. (It has a lot of overhead attached, which reduces the amount of user data that gets transmitted.)

- It uses bandwidth already in use by other transmissions, filling in the holes that the others aren't using. This conserves bandwidth.

- It's not proprietary at all, but fully compatible with V.42 (a protocol supported by all major modem models).

- It's compatible with voice transmission and is full duplex in design, meaning that users can send data and talk at the same time.

CDPD won't replace older cellular designs completely, at least not yet. First, it's really meant for short, bursty traffic like e-mail and short text files. Longer files are more expensive to transmit via CDPD than traditional cellular transmissions, because it's billed on a per packet or per byte basis. Second, it's not widely available yet (as of late 1995) and it's not nationwide. To send data from one cellular region to another using CDPD, you must set up an address in the other region or send the data to a gateway mailbox to which the message's recipient has access. Third, if you leave your subscription area and enter another one, you may not be able to send data—and the areas are pretty small because CDPD is designed to be very efficient with its bandwidth.

Even with its current limitations, CDPD might be the protocol that keeps cellular data communications from becoming obsolete. It certainly has the speed edge on the others, and the other bugs might get worked out with time. However, it has a long way to go before gaining real market credibility.

Enhanced Specialized Mobile Radio. Motorola and others offer a competitor to cellular services called *enhanced specialized mobile radio* (*ESMR*). This wide-area data service, built from underutilized fleet-management frequencies, is offered throughout many urban areas in the United States, and has the potential to become a unified national service. It was formally approved as a wide-area transmission protocol by the FCC in 1991.

ESMR takes low-bandwidth frequencies, digitizes them and uses TDMA to create as many as six channels in each frequency. Digitizing data makes it possible to reduce its bandwidth use, and time-slot channels should allow more than one subscriber to simultaneously use the same frequency without noticing any degradation in service. The equipment required is a ESMR-compatible transmitter and receiver, available from the vendor.

Although its frequencies have lower bandwidth than those used by cellular communications, ESMR can compete because of its significantly lower startup costs, and effective use of the bandwidth it has. If ESMR makes it as a national service, and is marketed well, it could offer stiff competition to the entrenched cellular services.

PCS. Although it's not out at the time of this writing (late 1995), *personal communications services* (*PCS*) promises a great deal to wireless networkers. It's going to take some time (the service isn't scheduled to be offered until 1996 or 1997) to see if it can live up to those promises.

Similar in structure to cellular services because of its physical organization, PCS has the following characteristics that distinguish it from analog cellular systems:

- It uses digital, rather than analog, signaling.
- It operates at higher frequencies (near the 2GHz band as opposed to the 900MHz band).
- It is organized in smaller cells.

In February 1995, the FCC allocated 50MHz of noncontiguous spectrum to private sector use. Three of the bands within this 50MHz were destined for PCS. The idea is that the PCS frequencies will be isolated in very small cells, and the frequencies used for transmission will be used as efficiently as possible.

High-Speed WAN Connections

Although signals sent in the HF and VHF bands aren't high-intensity enough to make good inter-building transmitters, those in the SHF band (3–30GHz), or microwaves, are sufficiently high-intensity to provide a reasonable level of bandwidth. On a more-or-less line-of-sight basis (that is, the transmitter and receiver must be visible to each other), you can transmit data at high speeds between buildings or facilities, without having to install a cable.

Because microwave must be line-of-sight, the transmitters and receivers are often not on the buildings that need to be connected but are instead on towers on mountainsides or high hills and then connected via a high-speed cable to the main network. The higher the tower is off the ground, the wider its range.

Microwave is limited in a few ways. First, the microwaves are bad for humans (the reason why you don't see many warning signs about microwave ovens and pacemakers any-more is because the ovens are better shielded than they used to be, not because the waves are less dangerous). Second, you must apply to the FCC for a license to transmit along a certain SHF frequency, and the license requires both time and money. Third, the equipment is expensive. However, if you really need a long-range secure wireless connec-tion, then microwave is a good bet.

Limitations of RF Wireless Networks

RF networks have some limitations, of course. First, they frankly don't offer the perfor-mance of a wired connection. Unless there's a physical reason why you can't run cable in your office building, desktop machines benefit from a wired connection. Wired networks generally are faster, cheaper (not surprisingly, a transceiver is much more expensive than a network card), and since desktop machines aren't often moved, the lack of mobility inherent in wired communications isn't any drawback. Most of the time, if you must move a desktop PC, you disconnect it from the network, lug it to its new location, and plug it back into the network without any major hassle. The minute it takes to reconnect a computer to the network hardly justifies the slower speeds and greater expense of a wireless connection. In general, if you don't have portable PCs (notebooks and laptops) that require network access, wireless technology really is not for you.

Second, even office networks composed mainly of portable PCs can have wireless prob-lems. RF signals can be stopped by obstacles such as thick concrete walls or iron girders. Even without physical barriers, distance plays a part in wireless office networking. About 300 to 500 feet is the distance limit within most offices, extending to around 800 to 1,000 feet outdoors or in very open office environments. Wireless networks work best in open areas without a lot of walls to block the signal. The more walls you have in the way, the shorter distance the signal will travel.

Third, too much wireless traffic can cause congestion on the network. RF technology uses a limited band for transmission, and if more clients attempt to use that band than there's capacity for, the signals can interfere with each other. Signals from other sources on the same frequencies can also interfere with wireless network transmissions. Band-width-sharing technology like TDMA and CDMA can somewhat alleviate the traffic situ-ation, but it's still a point worth considering. For this reason, many transmissions used in urban areas and within offices use lower wattage than the FCC says they can, to reduce the amount of crosstalk between transmissions.

Infrared Wireless Networks

Infrared (IR) technology is not new (it's part of your television's remote control device, for example) but it's relatively new to wireless computing. This section discusses what infrared signals are and how they're coming to be used in wireless networking.

What Are Infrared Signals?

Infrared frequencies are those found at the extreme upper end of the visible electromagnetic spectrum. They have extremely high bandwidth and a correspondingly short range, as discussed earlier in this chapter. For the most part, infrared signals are limited to applications where the receiver and transmitter are directly in sight of each other, as IR signals can't pass through walls or most other fairly solid obstructions. Brief interruptions, like people walking in front of the signal, won't break an IR connection, but protracted interruptions will.

> **Note**
>
> The short range of infrared signals means that IR, as a technology, is currently more generic than RF. For the most part, an infrared signal is an infrared signal; they're kept from interfering with each other by their low diffusion and short range.

IR Applications

The use of IR signals in networking is still in its infancy, but here are a few of the current applications:

- Laptop networking within enclosed areas
- Cableless printing
- Wide-area connections between buildings located close together

The following sections explore these applications in detail.

Laptop Networking. Although infrared transmissions don't mix well with the rabbit-warren layout of many offices, mobile computing is used in more places than the office. For example, a college computer class can use laptop computers networked with infrared transceivers, allowing students in the open area of the classroom to network, but keeping the signals from leaving the room. Thus, the members of the class can interact with each other and the professor. In addition, with the right software in place, students can get help from the professor if they run into problems—the professor can bring up their screens on her computer and see what the problem is.

Wireless Printing. Hewlett-Packard recently released the LaserJet 5P, the first printer with a built-in infrared port. A PC with an infrared transceiver can send print jobs to the printer via this port without being cabled to the printer. The printer and PC must be located fairly close together (about three feet according to HP, but about six feet in real-world testing) and the signal path unobstructed. The PC and printer must be on stable platforms to maintain the connection. Other than that, the connection works like a wired connection, even matching the speed of a printer cable.

If you don't have an HP 5P, you still can make your printer wireless with a device named JetEye, offered by Extended Systems. Via a six-foot cord, the receiving device plugs into the parallel port (meaning that only IR devices can access the printer when you've got it set up for wireless networking). The device works up to four feet from a notebook under optimal conditions.

Connecting Buildings. Although IR is not currently supported for most wide-area networking, one device, SilCom's FreeSpace, permits buildings close to each other (up to about 1,000 feet apart) to be connected at native LAN speeds. Ethernet, full duplex Ethernet (20 Mbps), and both token-ring LANs are supported currently, with ATM and Fast Ethernet support planned for the near future.

Why not use a fiber to connect the sites? Well, it's not always feasible or cost-effective to do so. First, if there's a road between the buildings to be connected, you can't run a cable across the road or dig up the road surface to run it beneath. Second, the telephone company might not run the fiber for you: in the United States, at any rate, most WAN vendors have stopped offering dark fiber since the FCC told them that they no longer have to do so. Third, if you need something that can be set up fairly quickly, a solution that doesn't involve running cables is faster to install than one that does.

Why not microwave? Cost and convenience. The IR device has a shorter range, but it's cheaper than microwave and doesn't require an FCC permit to use a certain signal.

A wireless building connection works this way: three devices, one on each building and another between the buildings, handle the IR transmission. The device between the buildings sends signals to, and picks up signals from, the transceivers on the sides of the buildings. Within each building, a fiber cable connects the transceivers to a bridging device that connects the fiber to the network. As long as the bridging device can support both fiber on the transceiver side, and Ethernet or Token Ring (as appropriate) on the LAN side, it doesn't matter what kind you use. The whole setup resembles the one shown in figure 29.6.

If you want to connect two buildings within sight of each other that are not very far away, and a fiber connection is either too expensive or impossible, an IR solution might suit your needs.

Consider the following advantages of using an IR connection between buildings:

- Fast setup (a couple of hours)
- Provides native LAN speed between buildings
- In North America, no government regulations—and thus, no paperwork hurdles
- Relatively secure from tapping, because the beam is so narrow it would take special effort (and equipment) to pick up the signal

- Fairly inexpensive (a one-time charge of about $15,000 for the infrared hardware, not including the bridging mechanism)

- Not disturbed by inclement weather or birds flying through the signal (although coatings of snow or ice on the lens will impede transmissions)

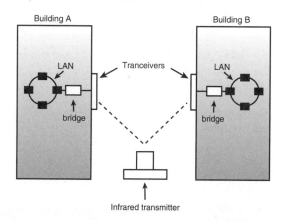

Figure 29.6

The components of an inter-building IR connection are not complex.

Although infrared has limited applications, it looks capable of performing well within its sphere.

Disadvantages of IR

The biggest problem with IR wireless networking is a lack of support from the PC end. As of late 1995, not very many PCs—portable or not—have infrared ports (IBM's ThinkPad is one example of a notebook that does). Additionally, if you have an IR port, you need software supporting it so that connected devices can use the wireless connection. Moreover, no infrared bridges seem to be on the market, so you must take the short range of IR connections into consideration when determining whether it works for your needs.

There are other considerations as well, including the environmental restrictions of walls and the possibility of interference from other light sources—but neither of these concerns is insurmountable. If an IR device can't pass signals through walls, then you can use fiber to connect it to a device that can. In fact, for some applications, the physical restrictions that walls impose are more an asset than a liability, since that isolation increases security and potential frequency reuse. Once there is more support for the technology, you can expect infrared transmissions to be increasingly prevalent in wireless networking applications, within the boundaries of their usefulness.

A Comparison of RF and IR Signaling

Because RF and IR signals are dissimilar enough to compete significantly with each other, it's worthwhile to recap their relative advantages so that you can decide which one might best suit your needs.

RF Signaling

RF's main advantage is that the technology is well entrenched. Because the first forms of wireless networking used RF signals, a good deal of development work has gone into extending the capabilities of RF transmissions. It's not difficult to find RF-compatible networking solutions, in the form of either wireless modems or transceivers for PCs.

Second, RF signals are comparatively durable. Despite the fact that higher frequencies are more affected by interference and blocking than lower ones, any RF signal deals with interference better than a microwave or infrared signal. Infrared transmissions require line-of-sight between the transmitter and the receiver. RF signals do not, although they do perform better with fewer obstacles.

Safety is also an issue. RF transmissions can be used both indoors and outdoors, since at this point no harmful effects are associated with them. If high-powered enough, IR signals can be dangerous indoors (or anywhere that they're easily accessible). The transmitting beam of a powerful infrared device—or even a laser pointer—can damage your retina if you look directly into it.

> **Note**
>
> Of course, not all infrared light is dangerous; for instance, biometric security devices that scan your retina use infrared light. The rays are not dangerous at that intensity (the devices are not especially reliable, either).

IR Signaling

For all of RF's entrenched position, IR could offer it some competition if the industry supports IR. First, it's high-speed—able to keep up with wired LANs and more. This isn't very important in places where wired LANs are possible, but when you want to connect LANs in a situation where you can't just tack another segment on the network (such as connecting a LAN to another LAN in a neighboring building), IR can make the connection with no loss of speed.

Second, IR doesn't have the bleed-over problem of RF signals, which can interfere with each other if the frequencies used are too close together. IR signals are tight beams with a short reach, so they tend to keep to themselves.

Third, because of the concentrated beam they use, IR signals are more secure than some other types of wireless transmissions (especially non-encoded ones that use the same frequency for the life of the connection). They're not totally secure—nothing is—but tapping them would require getting very close to a short signal, which is hard to do unobtrusively.

The Future of Wireless

Don't expect wireless networking to replace wired networking; it will work in tandem with it. If you've got a wired LAN, then there's no impetus for you to run out and replace the cabling and network cards you've already got with transceivers. You'd be spending a lot of money to reduce the reliability and performance of your network.

As you've seen in this chapter, however, there are real applications for combining wired and wireless networks. You can connect two wired LANs in adjoining buildings using an infrared transmitter, or permit a mobile employee to dial into your office network without having to search for a telephone jack. These capabilities, and many others, have the potential to extend computer networking to areas where it would have been impossible in previous years.

Summary

Wireless technology is not a monolith; it varies in form and application from sending files to a printer to connecting buildings miles apart. Wireless takes two main forms: radio-frequency signals, which use radio bands, and infrared, which uses light to transmit data. Although when wireless first appeared on the scene, some envisioned that it would replace wired technologies, it now appears more likely that wired and wireless networks will become more common, allowing networks to benefit from both technologies.

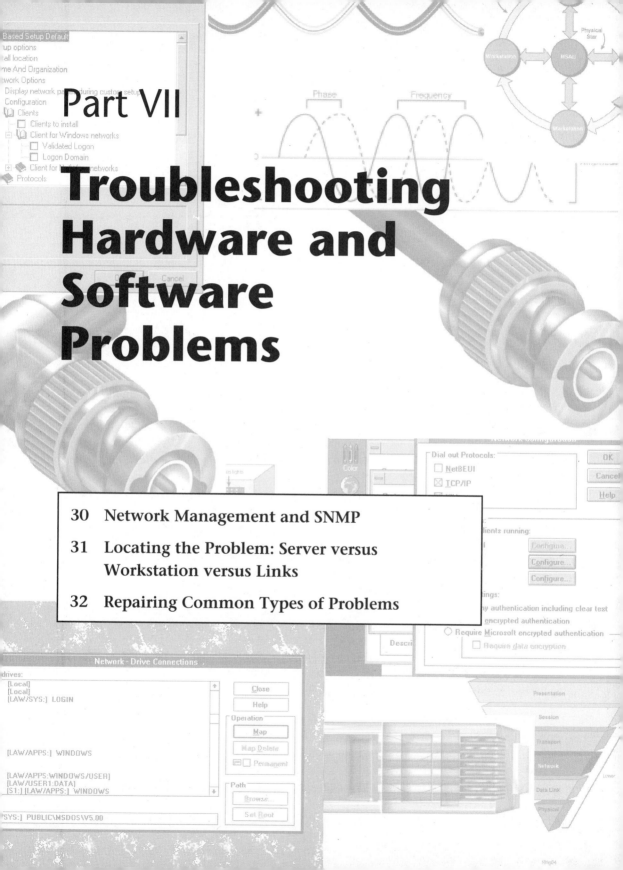

Part VII

Troubleshooting Hardware and Software Problems

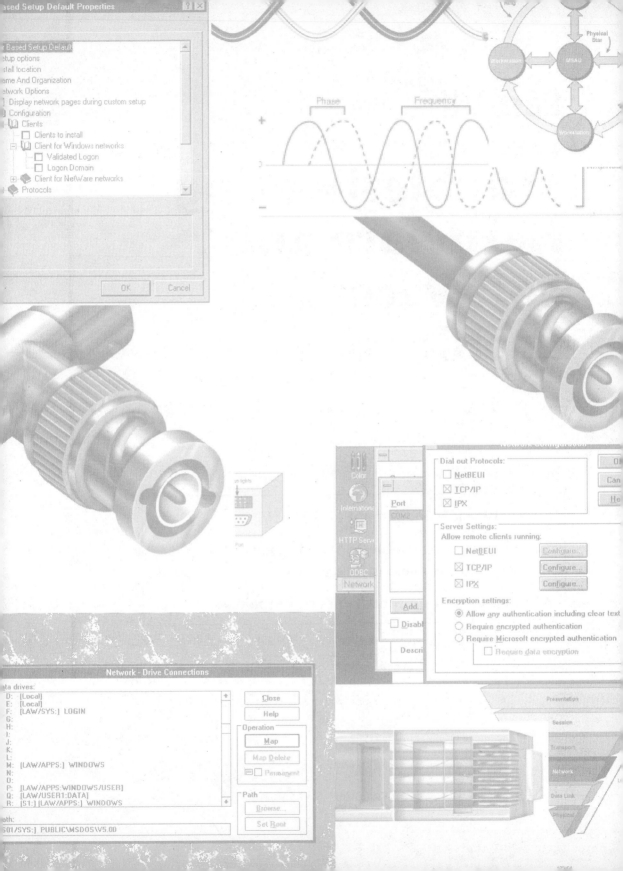

Chapter 30

Network Management and SNMP

By now, you have had a chance to learn about the many different parts and pieces that go into creating a networked environment. Management of that network is vital regardless of whether you're supporting 20 LAN users or 50 offices connected via a WAN. Good network management can save you time and help prevent the problems that occur if you currently react to network support issues in "fire-fighter" mode—killing the fire after it has started.

Networks are by nature difficult beasts to get a hold of. In the old days, when a PC or Macintosh was an island, problems could only go so far. Nowadays, we connect PCs, Macintoshes, UNIX boxes, and even mainframes together over Ethernet, token-ring, FDDI, T1s, Frame-Relay, ATM, ISDN, dial-up lines, and even wireless networks, using multiple vendors' hubs, routers, gateways, NICs, DSU/CSUs (digital service unit/channel service unit), and modems. You get the picture: a dazzling array of hardware and software that can quickly become difficult to manage. When computers were isolated, it was easy to determine why an application wasn't printing correctly. But in a networked environment, you may need to look at not only the application but also how it's loading from the file server, whether the token-ring segment it's on is beaconing, or even whether the printer's network adapter is failing. All this may be happening 20 miles from where you're located and where you may not be able to access the faulty device directly.

Indeed, you would be surprised how many companies build vast, complicated multivendor networks with little or no network management in place, under the thought that "We'll build that in later." If you think that you can't afford the infrastructure costs of building in network management up front, just remember that the biggest cost of a network infrastructure is not the initial hardware or software installation, but the maintenance once everything is in place. Without good network management and, as you'll see later, systems management in place, those maintenance costs can quickly devour an entire IS budget.

By the end of this chapter, you'll learn what a network-management platform should provide, some features common to all good network-management systems, and the difference between network-management and systems management. You'll also learn about how the Simple Network-Management Protocol (SNMP) works, and how to use it in TCP/IP and Novell IPX/SPX environments. We'll also talk about how to plan, choose, and set up a network-management system (NMS), including some of the challenges of multivendor, multiprotocol networks. Finally, we'll look at some of the issues surrounding the emerging switching technologies and how best to manage them.

Network-Management Functions

When you begin to consider implementing a network-management strategy (NMS), it's very helpful to know what functionality you will have at your disposal. You may be asking, "Can I configure all my 'Brand X' routers from a central console?" or "Can I have all my Novell servers send a message when they are experiencing excessive errors on the Ethernet that they are connected to?" In this section, we'll go into detail about what sorts of things most network-management platforms can and should provide. One thing to keep in mind throughout this discussion is that despite what you can get from a given platform, you should always keep in mind what you need for your environment. Implementing an overly complex network-management solution because it has lots of neat features is going to cost you proportionally more time than the management problem you're trying to solve is worth. A management platform should give you the basic features you need now, with the capability of being easily upgraded with additional functionality as you need it. Keep this in mind while planning a network-management strategy, and you'll always add value without adding unnecessary complexity.

NMSs typically provide functionality to a certain class of devices. If we follow the OSI seven-layer reference model described in chapter 3, "The OSI Model: Bringing Order to Chaos," then most traditional NMSs provide management up to layer three, the network layer, and sometimes four, the transport layer. If we follow this model, then network management should encompass at least the following devices:

- Layer One—Physical NICs, modems, DSU/CSUs, multiplexors, or any other device that provides physical access to a network medium

- Layer Two—Data Link Bridges, hubs, repeaters, switches, or any other device that defines the signaling of data onto the physical medium

- Layer Three—Network Routers, translational gateways, switches that implement layer three routing, or any other device that makes decisions about where data will go based on some network-addressing scheme

- Layer Four—Transport (optional) Including TCP and UDP, IPX/NCP, SPX, or any other protocol that provides connection-oriented or connectionless services between end-nodes

You will notice that the first three layers specify hardware devices, whereas layer four is expressed purely in software. Layer four information, while protocol-dependent, can provide useful information for managing a network. You may find it helpful, for example, to know whether a UNIX server running TCP/IP has a TCP connection with another host and on what port or how many UDP broadcasts that host has generated. Support for all of these layers is usually provided by some network-management protocol, which either has built-in support for these devices or provides extensibility for a vendor to add the required functionality. For example, as we'll discuss later in the chapter, the Simple Network-Management Protocol (SNMP), implemented over TCP/IP or even IPX/SPX, can provide management for many of these devices in a generic way without any additional software.

What a Network-Management System Should Provide

When you sit down and start planning an NMS, you should think conceptually about what you want to accomplish—that is, what is your strategy for network management? Are you hoping to become more proactive in support of your systems? Are you trying to provide more centralized control? Whatever the goal, the importance of deciding this ahead of time will affect what features you look for, what devices you decide to manage, and how you implement your management system. These last two points will be discussed at length in the later section "How To Plan for a Network-Management System." Whatever the purpose, all NMS implementations should provide some basic things.

Over the past 10 years, a lot of research and development has been put into the idea of network management. The International Organization for Standardization (ISO), the same group that helped develop the OSI Model, also put together a network-management framework to support its *Common Management Information Protocol (CMIP)*. CMIP is the OSI-standard protocol for network management. The OSI framework consists of five points that are considered imperative to a good network-management implementation. These are as follows:

- Fault Detection   The ability to detect and report on faults in the network. It's also desirable if the management platform can act in some predefined way in response to a fault. For example, it could shut down a hub port that is sending excessive bad packets.

- Configuration Management   The ability to remotely affect the configuration of a managed physical or logical device.

- Performance Analysis   The ability to look at performance statistics on the network for the purposes of trend analysis and capacity planning.

- Security Control   The ability to control access to devices on the network from the network-management platform. This would include, for instance, controlling authentication policies to routers, hubs, or other network devices to prevent unauthorized configuration.

- Accounting   The ability to collect data on who's using the network, how much, and for what purpose.

What you will find is that most NMSs provide a generic set of tools that give you the ability to perform a number of key functions on elements of your network. You should always look for a core set of functionality that addresses most, if not all, of the five points.

Functionally, what you usually get when you buy an NMS is software that allows you to set up a *network-management console*—or simply the *Network Manager.* The Network Manager is the master control panel. With the Network Manager, software runs as agents on each device that you want to manage. The agents communicate with the Network Manager to provide all the information you need to manage a device. Some agents are proprietary in nature and some follow standards, but generally both serve the same purpose: to interact with the managed device to find out its status and then report back to the Network Manager. While agent software varies from vendor to vendor, most provide the following basic functionality:

- Status information about the managed device.

- Statistics about the managed device's network interface(s).

- An interface to the managed device's configuration.

- The ability to detect faults in the managed device and report on them to the Network Manager. This reporting mechanism is often referred to as a *trap.*

- The ability to provide authentication and security to the agent such that only a Network Manager with the correct security may access the above functions on the agent.

You'll notice that these agent features are similar to the five OSI-mandated functions for network-management systems. Indeed, it is primarily the agent's responsibility to carry out these key functions as they are implemented on the managed device.

Now that we have looked at what layers of the OSI model are involved in network management and what functions an NMS should provide, we can define what network management really is. If you take all the devices that encompass layers one through three (and optionally four) of the OSI model—for example hubs, routers, bridges, NICs and gateways—and provide the agent software on each of them that performs the above five functions—fault detection, configuration management, performance analysis, security control and accounting—you have network-management in a nutshell. The combination of managed devices, agents that run on them, and the Network Manager are common to almost every NMS, proprietary or not.

In addition to the earlier five points, there are some other important elements that a good NMS should provide and that you should seriously consider when looking at functionality:

- A graphical user interface, with the ability to visually map elements of the network

- Support for third-party plug-ins

- Operating system independence—that is, you should have the choice of which OS you run your NMS on

- Support (if possible) of industry-standard protocols and management information (for example, SNMP and MIB-I or MIB-II)

An NMS can serve many other functions; however, as previously mentioned, it's important to keep the goal of your system in mind before being wooed by some vendor proclaiming absolute control over every aspect of your environment. Make a checklist that includes the preceding five points of network management, add to it the previous four important elements and then add any needs specific to your environment. Submit that to each vendor for response, and you'll be able to compare apples to apples when making your NMS decision. The "Criteria for Choosing a Network-Management System" section later in this chapter is devoted entirely to the decision-making process.

Network Management versus Systems Management

We have talked about network management in the context of layers one through four of the OSI model. Now consider the situation where you not only want to provide configuration, fault detection, performance analysis, security control, and accounting to network devices but you also want to be able to add users to a Novell NetWare 4.x directory tree or check on the progress of a software distribution job from Microsoft's Systems Management Server to your 200 Windows 3.1 workstations across a nationwide WAN. Suddenly the lines of functionality between normal network-management functions as earlier described and what we'll call systems-management functions become less clear. For example, if in the previous example, your SMS distribution job fails, you may need to look to the network—your hubs and routers—to determine why. As we'll see, this blurring of functionality is a difficult challenge to meet, and one that all network administrators must deal with.

What Is Systems Management? If you talk to four different NMS vendors, they will each give you a different definition of what network management is and what systems management is. What we'll call traditional *network management* usually includes managing only those devices that make up the network-infrastructure—those devices in layers one through three (and sometimes layer four). *Systems management*, however, is huge, nebulous, and at best can be defined as the management of hosts, workstations, service providers, and the protocols and services that they use to communicate with each other. What this translates to in reality can best be described with an example. Imagine you had an NMS that provided a view of the routers in your Novell network. You can view the configurations on the routers, and even change them. This would be a classic network-management function.

Now suppose you had a button on the Network Manager that allowed you to run Syscon, Novell's utility for server and user configuration. Maybe you would click an icon of the Novell server you want to manage, and then click on the Syscon button. You are authenticated to that server and provided with an option to add users to that server's bindery. This is systems management, albeit a simple example. More likely, you may want to manage a more complicated task, like inventorying all the PCs on your network and using that information to create a database from which you can build a network map, a graphical picture of what and how devices like PCs and servers are laid out on your network. There are a number of functions that are traditionally deemed systems management, and as such, are usually not included in traditional network-management software. Some of these are

- Inventory and Asset Management   Usually a database of all the devices on your network, with information about what hardware they have, what their configuration files contain, and what software is loaded on them.

- Operating System Configuration and Tuning   This may include functions like the Syscon example; modifying Novell Server set variables; or loading, stopping, or starting new services on a Windows NT server.

- Software Distribution   This includes functions like copying a new application to a group of workstations or servers, such as that provided by Microsoft SMS software, and the mechanisms to verify delivery and version.

- Remote Control/Administration   This includes the ability to take over a user's desktop for purposes of support, or just the ability to "touch" a remote workstation or server to restart a service, reload a NetWare Loadable Module (NLM), or kill a rogue process.

While you will find many of these systems-management functions in stand-alone software packages, you may find it useful to implement some of them as an integrated part of your network-management platform, especially if you are in a small organization, where the same group provides both network and systems support. In that case, make sure the network-management platform supports some of these stand-alone packages as plug-ins. Most network-management software provides an Application Programming Interface (API) that allows software vendors to take their stand-alone systems-management application and make it an integrated part of the Network Manager. For example, Intel's LANDESK software is a plug-in for Novell's ManageWise. Landesk's functionality is fully integrated with ManageWise's such that Landesk tools can interface directly with devices managed by ManageWise. This is an example of a fully integrated plug-in. On the other hand, some vendors may say they plug into an NMS but may only provide an icon that allows you to launch it from the Network Manager. So it is desirable to find an NMS that supports as many plug-in applications as possible if you see the need to do both network and systems management from the same Network Manager.

Deciding What To Manage. If you are faced with deciding how much systems management you will implement on your network-management platform, the best thing to do is look at how you support your network and systems now. If you work in a small shop, administering a few Novell or Windows NT servers, your needs for complex network management will probably be small in comparison to system-management needs, and you are likely responsible for both. In that case, look for a management platform with strong systems support, and the ability to plug in better network-management tools as your network grows. The reason for this is that when your network infrastructure is small, maybe two or three segments in one or two buildings, it's probably just as efficient to physically visit each site as it is to set up a complex network-management platform. However, as your network infrastructure grows, you will need to be in more geographically diverse places at the same time, and that's where good network management really helps.

If you're working for a large organization and planning for a network- or systems-management platform, the task becomes more difficult. Chances are that there are different groups doing systems management and network management. You may have one group that troubleshoots workstations, file servers, and printers. Another group may be responsible for hubs and routers, and another still for software distribution. In this case, the roles of systems and network management are less clear. This is especially true because the higher-end platforms for systems and network management tend to be more complex and therefore more difficult to integrate with each other. Many people will be tempted to try and integrate all of their network and systems management needs under one "super-console," with all functionality available on a single screen.

The advantages of integrating all these systems is that information from a system inventory database, for example, could be used to populate a network map or identify who is using a machine that is generating large amounts of network traffic. You can also use systems-management information in conjunction with network alerting and reporting to automate your trouble-ticketing system. But, be warned, such an integration task is by no means trivial. Trying to get one vendor's inventory database to feed information to another's network-management map or trouble-ticketing system will take a lot of development resources. It really only makes sense for very large organizations. And, even then, this sort of project is not for the faint of heart. More importantly, integrating all systems may not make sense organizationally if you have decentralized support staff that each support different areas. To create a synergistic management platform should be the goal of any IS organization. But don't lose sight of the real goal, which is to provide a useful management platform for the support staff doing the actual work.

Common Network-Management System Features

In this section, we'll look at some features that most NMSs support. Generally, each of these features is implemented using either industry-standard protocols, such as SNMP, or proprietary methods. Regardless of implementation, they serve the same purpose, which is to allow a network-management console to collect data about the devices it is managing and generate information from that data.

Polling

Polling is a key feature of all NMSs. It is also where you need to do a lot of planning before implementing your system. A Network Manager periodically queries all devices that it manages to determine their status, which is called *polling*. There are a couple of ways to implement polling. Usually, you configure how often a Network Manager polls. This is important because on larger networks, where a Network Manager has to keep track of thousands of devices, the traffic generated by this polling function can be quite significant and can adversely affect network performance. The challenge is to configure the polling interval to be long enough so that it doesn't generate a large amount of traffic, but not be so long that, if a device fails, you don't find out about it in a timely manner.

An alternative to this is a process called *trap-based polling*. In this scenario, when, for example, an interface on a router fails, a message or *trap* is sent to the Network Manager indicating a problem. The Network Manager can then poll the device in question to determine the extent of the problem. This is a more desirable approach than periodic polling because it is event-driven and only generates traffic as needed. Of course, some NMSs may not support this. In that case, the best way to tune polling is simply to start with a fairly infrequent polling interval, maybe 15 minutes or 1/2 hour, and then adjust it downward as you find your response time requires it. In a fairly stable network, where your response to a problem is not measured in seconds or even minutes, this should be sufficient.

Auto Discovery

Auto discovery is one of those functions that sounds good on paper, and most NMS software will boast but in practice has been problematic to implement. Basically, the idea behind auto discovery is that you can install a Network Manager package, plug it into the network, choose an icon that says Discover and it will send out a query packet to all devices on your network and build a graphical map or database of all your devices based on the responses. The mechanisms to accomplish this vary, depending on your networking protocol, but what you will usually find is that many NMS packages' auto-discovery functions don't work flawlessly or even at all. Especially on the low-end PC-based packages, this functionality seems to have been given less attention by the developers. It's a feature most vendors include because everyone expects it, but they put varying levels of attention into getting it right.

In most cases, you should expect to provide at least some information to the Network Manager regarding what devices to look for. For example, in a TCP/IP environment, some Network Managers will ask that you build a "seed" file of subnets to send a query. In a Novell environment, you may be asked to enter a range of IPX network addresses or even server names. Then the Network Manager will query an attached server's bindery to find out how to get to the other devices. In any case, don't depend on an auto-discovery process to correctly discover all devices in your network. It's best to use it as a starting point, with a list in hand of all the devices you want to manage to fill in the blanks.

Device Configuration

Device configuration is a feature that all network-management and many system-management platforms should support. Some implement it using industry-standard protocols like SNMP, and some will use proprietary agents and protocols, but regardless of the mechanism, you should have some way of affecting the configuration of large numbers of devices from your management console. This may be anything from shutting down the number one token-ring interface on your router in another state to setting up a SAP filter on your Novell router next door. The important thing is that regardless of location, you can modify configurations as if you were at the device. What you will find is that due to the multi-vendor nature of most networks, a given NMS will provide generic configuration control, using a protocol like SNMP, and then a vendor will often plug in a module specific to their devices. For instance, you can do some rudimentary configuration of a Cisco router using any number of network-management platforms, but if you plug in CiscoWorks, you get many more features specific to these routers like advanced configuration control of many devices or the ability to script and track configuration changes.

Graphical Mapping

As mentioned earlier in the chapter, a GUI is one of those "nice-to-have" features. In this day of GUI-based everything, suffice it to say that an NMS system without a GUI is not long for this world. Not only is it easier to visualize network problems when they are displayed graphically, but you can use features like color-coding and blinking to visually alert you to different levels of problems on your network. There are some Network Managers that even let you build physical maps of your environment and then let you overlay managed devices. For instance, you could draw a layout of your computer room and place all managed routers, hubs, and servers where they actually sit. This makes troubleshooting for someone not familiar with all your systems very easy and provides excellent documentation of your network as well. Novell's ManageWise product is a good example of an NMS that provides this feature.

Trapping Events

As alluded to earlier, traps are an important way an agent, running on a managed device, can let a Network Manager know about unusual events. Traps are, in fact, exception reports. They let a Network Manager know that an interface is down or has come back up or that someone has tried to access a device without the correct authorization. Traps, like polling can quickly generate large amounts of traffic if not managed correctly. Because traps are implemented on the agent software running on the managed device, they can take up valuable resources on that device if they happen frequently. This is especially true if a trap is configured against a given threshold. In this case, the agent has to do some work every time the device does to determine if the threshold was exceeded. In a busy network, where all devices are doing a lot of work, this may take up valuable CPU cycles. So it is just as important to tune trap generation on an agent as it is to tune polling on a Network Manager. Ideally, an agent should generate a single packet of data when a trap event occurs. Then as previously mentioned, a Network Manager can poll that agent for more information as required. A good rule when considering trapping and polling is that you should let the Network Manager do as much of the work as possible and the agent as little as possible.

Event Logging

Event logging is a Network Manager function where all the results of polling and trapping are collected in logs, which can be viewed then or saved for later analysis. You can also log events like who used the Network Manager last, what configuration changes were made to a given device, or any number of other auditing functions. Your NMS should give a lot of options for events that can be captured. Since a large network is likely to generate a lot of events, make sure that your event logs are configured, which prevents them from growing to epic proportions in a short period of time. Many logging facilities give you the ability to save logs up to a certain size or time and then will roll over the events in the log. If you plan to use the logs for future analysis, make sure that if you roll over the log file, you have a way to archive the log information you need, preferably in an automated fashion.

Protocol Analysis

Protocol analysis may be the single most powerful tool an NMS can provide. What this amounts to is having a Protocol Analyzer, offering functionality like the Network General Sniffer or Novell's LANalyzer, available to you from a Network Manager console on each segment of interest throughout your network. If you support a geographically diverse environment, you can quickly benefit from the power of this tool. Imagine getting a call from a user two states away who is experiencing slow response on their PC. After checking your Network Manager for unusual activity, you might want to install a protocol analyzer on the wire to get more detailed information about the problem. Instead of catching a plane to the remote site, it's much easier to click the segment in question on your NMS console, select a menu item for *protocol analysis*, and see all the packets that were going across the wire at that remote site. This feature is implemented by various vendors in many different ways. Some vendors provide special software agents that run on a device attached to a given segment. You can then access the agent using a special network monitoring package and can capture packets at varying levels of detail. Some provide a high-level view of who is talking to whom, what protocols they're using, and a breakdown of the class of packets. Others provide full packet decoding.

Examples of these agents are Novell's LANalyzer agent for ManageWise, which is an NLM that runs on a NetWare server and provides packet decoding for all the segments connected to that server. Also available is Microsoft's Network Monitor Agent, which is part of Systems Management Server (SMS) and runs as a service on a Windows NT server or workstation. Then there are hardware devices dedicated to packet capture and decoding, which connect to multiple segments and provide information back to a central network monitor. Examples of this are Network General's Distributed Sniffer or any of the various RMON probes that are available. (We'll take a look at RMON later.)

There are two things to be aware of when implementing remote protocol analyzers. First, remember that if you are capturing network data in real time from a remote segment, then you are generating extra traffic on the network between your remote agent and the Network Manager. This may or may not actually affect the data you're capturing, depending on the severity of your problem. The second issue is related to the software agents. All of these agents rely on capturing data through the NIC on the device that they're installed in. All of these agents require the NIC to support something called *promiscuous mode*, which means that the NIC has the ability to collect and open packets that aren't specifically addressed to it. Not all NICs support this. For example, IBM's original 16/4 Token Ring NICs don't, nor do many older Ethernet NICs. Make sure you check with your NIC vendor before deciding to use the software agent approach. It's also important to realize that the software agent will impose some resource requirements on the server and NIC that may not be acceptable on a very busy system. Finally, any solution, agent or dedicated hardware, will quickly become costly if you try and monitor every segment in your network. Pick the most heavily utilized segments first and then add as needed.

Network-Management Protocols

Depending on your platform, you may be able to implement any number of network-management protocols to support your network. The *network-management protocol* is the method by which your agents and network managers exchange information. The protocol will define what transport mechanisms can be used, what information exists on an agent, and in what format that information is arranged. By far, the most popular protocol for managing networks is the *Simple Network-Management Protocol* (*SNMP*). Originally designed for the TCP/IP-based Internet, it has been implemented on other protocols, including Novell's IPX/SPX, Digital's DECNet, and AppleTalk. Since it is based on widely accepted Internet standards, it has a great many advantages and is supported by most, if not all, serious network-management vendors. Because of this role, it is highly recommended that if you are planning a network-management strategy, you focus on SNMP as your protocol of choice. In the long run, it will give you the most flexibility, extensibility, and vendor and end-user support.

Understanding SNMP History

SNMP was actually not the first management protocol defined for use on the Internet. Back in 1987, the *Simple Gateway Monitoring Protocol* (*SGMP*) was defined by a Request for Comment (RFC) to manage the ever-expanding router network on the Internet.

How the RFC Process Works

The group that requests and defines the standards for the Internet, called the Internet Engineering Task Force (IETF), established a "working group" to develop a Request for Comment (RFC). RFC's are, in effect, the written specifications for a given Internet standard. As a working group begins to work on a standard, it is given a number and is given *Draft* status, indicating it is still a work in progress. When a standard has been agreed upon by all parties involved, it is given *Recommended* status and becomes the official specification for that standard.

In 1989, the first RFC on SNMP received Recommended status, having been built on the experience learned from the short life of SGMP, and the need to manage devices other than just routers. Currently, RFC 1157, written in 1990, is the most recent update to SNMP version 1. Related to the SNMP standards are the associated *Management Information Base-I* and *-II* (MIB-I and MIB-II, respectively) standards, which define the contents of the agent software. If we refer back to our discussions of agents, then the MIB is a specification for what items are managed by the agent software. The MIB attempts to provide a generic list of functions that many network devices have in common. For vendor-specific features, the MIB provides a way for vendors to add on their own.

To better understand the relationship between the MIB standards and SNMP, think of the MIB as the agent software, running on the managed device, and SNMP as the vehicle by which information is shuttled between the MIB and the Network Manager. Both the MIB and SNMP in concert provide an Internet standards-based way to manage your network. This vehicle is described in more detail later in this section.

There has been a lot of work in the last couple of years on SNMP version 2, which among other things, seeks to enhance how SNMP implements security. Unfortunately, as of this writing, there hasn't been a consensus among the involved parties, and some parts of this standard have yet to be solidified.

How SNMP Works. SNMP got its name from its goal to provide simple network management. To do this, its creators decided to take as much intelligence out of the agent as possible, and place it squarely on the shoulders of the Network Manager, assuming that while the Network Manager was destined only to manage, MIB agent software would run on devices that were responsible for other tasks like bridging, routing, or repeating. As a result, SNMP performs only four basic functions on the MIB agent. These are

- Getting a specific value in an agent (get)

- Getting the next value in an agent (get-next)

- Setting a specific value in an agent (set)

- Allowing an agent to send a trap to the Network Manager (trap)

When we speak of values above, we are referring to elements in the MIB that provide information about a specific function on the managed device. For instance, the value of "percent bandwidth utilization on router interface one." These four functions, working in conjunction with the MIB agents, provide all the functionality most NMSs need. This elegant solution allows a manager to query an MIB agent for its current status or configuration (get), traverse or "walk" the MIB from element to element (get-next), make configuration changes on an agent (set), and receive exception reports from an agent in trouble (trap).

A trap is generated by an MIB agent as a result of a predefined set of occurrences in that device. When a trap is sent, it is accompanied by the network address of the sending device, the type of trap, a trap code, the time the device has been up, and any other "interesting" information. The possible types of traps are

- ColdStart   Indicates that the device is reinitializing itself and that the device's configuration may change as a result. For example, this trap might be sent by a router that has just been reconfigured and requires a restart for the changes to take effect.

- WarmStart   Indicates that the device is reinitializing but that no configuration change will occur as a result.

- **LinkDown**   Indicates that the device has encountered a failure in one of its interfaces. This may include, for example, a router interface that has gone down or a file server with a failed NIC.

- **LinkUp**   Indicates that one of the interfaces on a device has just started. This may be an initial startup, as in the case of a newly defined interface, or a restarted interface that had previously registered a LinkDown.

- **AuthenticationFailure**   Indicates that someone tried to access the SNMP information on the device without the proper security authority (described later in the "Security and Communities" section).

- **EGPNeighborLoss**   This trap is used when a router utilizing an exterior gateway protocol experiences a peer that has gone down.

- **EnterpriseSpecific**   Identifies that the agent has encountered an enterprise-specific event. This would result from a vendor who has made custom additions to the MIB in the enterprise-specific area. The trap code field will be used to detail what the exact nature of the trap is.

Because network-management information was viewed as a necessary but not critical piece of network traffic, SNMP is implemented in TCP/IP over the User Datagram Protocol (UDP), which is the connectionless protocol for use in IP networks. Because it is connectionless, there are no guarantees of delivery as in TCP. SNMP uses UDP port number 161 for requests and port number 162 for SNMP traps. Ports are the service points that an IP-based device uses to uniquely identify the protocol being sent or received. Because UDP is connectionless, if an SNMP packet fails to reach a Network Manager or agent due to a bad link or congested network, the intended party will not try to retransmit but will simply resubmit the request at the next interval. This is desirable because you don't want network-management traffic to take away bandwidth from "production" applications doing important work, by retrying the request until the packet has been delivered, as it would do using TCP.

Since its initial development, SNMP has been defined over a number of different transport protocols in addition to TCP/IP. In 1993, RFCs 1419 and 1420 defined SNMP over both AppleTalk and Novell's IPX protocols, respectively. Particularly in the Novell environment, this has been useful in providing standards-based network-management services to IPX-based services.

MIBs and Agents. MIBs (versions I and II) define the objects that are contained within agent software. When the standards for SNMP were written, it was determined that there needed to be a standard format for information within an agent that interfaced with the network-management protocol. This standard format was defined as the *Structure of Management Information (SMI)*. If you think about an MIB as a database of items to be managed, then the SMI is the structure, or schema, of that database. The MIB is a hierarchical tree that contains definitions for a standard list of functions or characteristics to be managed on the device. These functions or characteristics are referred to as objects. If we follow the database example, they can also be thought of as fields in the database. Each object, or field can then take a value, depending on the state of that object in the managed device. For example, the "IP address of router Ethernet interface number one" would be an object that would have a given value depending on how it is configured on the managed device.

Each object in the MIB has a number of characteristics that allow it to work with SNMP to provide its four basic functions (get, get-next, set, and trap). Characteristics that are common to every object are

- ACCESS, which defines the access rights to the MIB object.

- DESCRIPTION, which describes what this object provides—for example, an object that lists a managed device's name might have a description that says "Host Name of Managed Device."

- STATUS, which indicates whether this object must be implemented in this MIB agent. This is primarily used by the IETF to let vendors who write MIBs know whether a given object is absolutely required, perhaps optional, or no longer relevant.

- SYNTAX, which describes what the proper format for the value of this object should be. For instance, if the object defines how long this router has been up, the syntax may say that "how long" should be defined in seconds.

ACCESS, for instance, can take one of four possible values:

- read-only   That object can only be read

- read-write   That object can be read or set

- write-only   That object can be set but not read

- not-accessible   That object cannot be set or read

Keep the ACCESS item in mind as we talk about security and communities in the upcoming section.

As mentioned above, STATUS indicates whether this object must be implemented by the MIB agent—that is, whether or not an agent must track a particular item on the device it's monitoring. This item takes the following values:

- mandatory   The agent must implement the object

- optional   The agent can implement the object

- obsolete   The object is no longer required

Each object in the MIB is uniquely identified by a kind of addressing, called the *Object Identifier (OID)*. The OID is a convenient notation for locating a MIB object, and you will often see it referred to on Network Managers when you query a device's configuration or status. When the IETF defined the MIB, they attempted to build a "tree" that includes not just information on the MIB standard, but information about other kinds of information, including definitions for other organizations besides the IETF, and other types of information other than network management. While this may seem like a lot of information, the MIB-II standard represents just one "branch" on the tree. In figure 30.1, you see the whole tree, starting at the root of the tree and presenting all of the relevant "leaf objects" that lead to where the MIB-II definitions are. The reason we need to follow the tree from the root to the MIB-II part is that the OID refers to the MIB starting from the root. Within the MIB-II tree, each standard object that defines an element on a managed device is referred to by a unique OID.

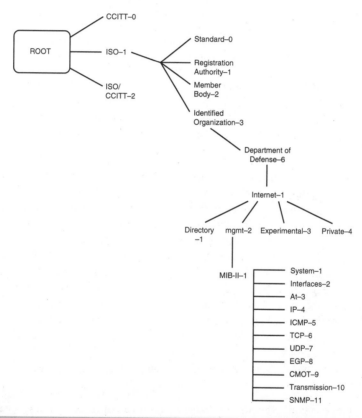

Figure 30.1

This is a look at the path to the MIB-II "branch" of the IETF Object Tree.

To define the OID for the start of MIB-II, for example, you use the notation 1.3.6.1.2.1, which refers to the numeric value of each branch leading to the MIB-II branch. In fact, every OID for elements within the MIB starts with this same dotted decimal notation (1.3.6.1.2.1). You might also see the OID represented in terms of the *branch names*, instead of the decimal notation. In this case, the OID for MIB-II starts at iso.org.dod.internet.mgmt.mib-II. Each element within the MIB can be identified in this way. When using the get-next SNMP command, you have the ability to move from

OID to OID, retrieving the value of each object. This is especially useful when you are trying to obtain values in MIB tables.

Tables are basically a set of OIDs that represent the columns and rows of a table. For example, a router's routing table is in an MIB table—where each row/column element of the table has its own OID—and benefits from the use of the get-next command to collect all the routing entries available. Additionally, there is a place in the MIB tree for vendors to put MIBs specific to their products, allowing their management software to address them. This place in the MIB is designated by the OID 1.3.6.1.4.1 or iso.org.dod.internet.private.enterprises. Under this OID, vendors can implement additional objects that are specific to their product line.

You may be wondering if you have to memorize the OIDs for every object you want to manage! Don't worry, most Network Managers shield you from ever having to look at OIDs. They translate that long dotted notation OID into plain old English like "router at interface one, number of Ethernet collisions since the router has been up." The only time you need to know about OIDs is if there is a value in an MIB object that your Network Manager doesn't know about. In this instance, you have to manually adjust it. Most Network Managers provide this kind of manual interface with the MIB for this purpose.

Security and Communities. The creators of SNMP sought to provide some rudimentary level of security, such that any user with an SNMP manager could not issue, for example, a set command to change a router's interface IP address. To support this security need, the concept of *communities* was developed. You can very easily think of communities as user IDs of a sort. When an SNMP agent is configured on a device, you can assign access-levels based on a *community name*. As mentioned above, each MIB object can have four ACCESS types: read-only, read-write, write-only, and not-accessible. Generally, when you configure an agent, you provide it with a community name for read-only and read-write access. In effect, this is your password to attain that level of access. When configuring a Network Manager, you provide a community name for each device you want to manage. When the Network Manager sends, for instance, a get packet to a given OID on a device, it sends along the configured community name. The device's agent receives the community name and, based on its community name configuration and the access-level for the OID, provides a *community profile*. The profile indicates your effective rights to the requested object.

For instance, suppose your Network Manager provides a community name to an agent. The agent has been configured to allow that community name, read-only access to the MIB. If the Network Manager is trying to issue a set command on an MIB object with an access type of read-write, the set command is disallowed because the only operations that the Network Manager can perform are get and get-next (read operations only). In this way, the community profile provides a restricted view of the MIB to the Network Manager.

It's important to be aware that community security is only a rudimentary form of authentication. Community names are sent in the "clear," or unencrypted, as part of an SNMP packet and are therefore easy to discover. And any community name implementation is also only going to be as secure as the security on the Network Manager console, which generally hard-codes community access into its configuration.

Implementing SNMP in IP and Novell Environments. Most major NOSs today come with support for SNMP. What this means is that they provide agent software running on both client and server. In the TCP/IP environment, this may come in the form of the snmpd daemon on a UNIX system or the SNMP Service on a Windows NT workstation or server. In the Novell environment, you can implement the SNMP NLM over either IP or IPX. Figure 30.2 shows the SNMP configuration options for Windows NT.

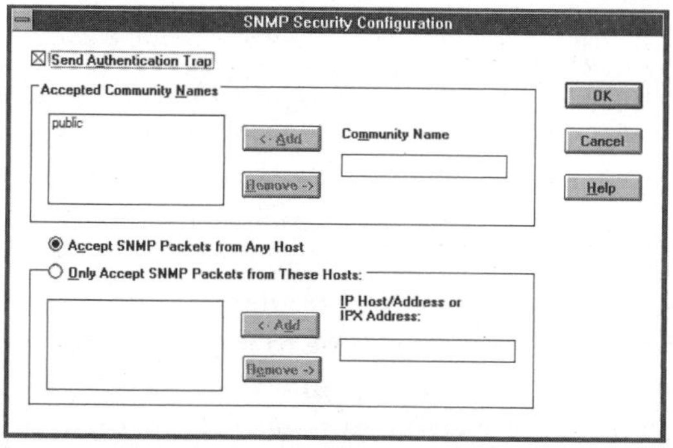

Figure 30.2

Configuring Windows NT's SNMP service installation options.

If you have TCP/IP configured on your Novell server, you can also configure it with SNMP support. Novell provides an SNMP NLM that provides an MIB agent for your server. You can configure the NLM with community-based security and specify the network address of your Network Manager for purposes of sending traps.

Generally, each vendor will implement some relevant subset of the MIB specification as part of their SNMP agent. For example, Novell's SNMP NLM allows you to configure all the elements of the Systems group, indicating Name of Server, Location, Contact Name , UpTime, and so on. From any SNMP Manager, you can then add the server as an object on your map and get this basic information. You can also color-code the map so that you know if the server goes down or maybe even have it page you when an outage occurs, depending on the features available to the Network Manager. As an example, I used Cabletron's Remote LanView product, primarily for managing its hubs via SNMP, to map a large number of Novell servers in order to find out about outages in a timely manner. This same basic functionality is available for accessing Windows NT's SNMP service.

If you are interested in managing workstations as well as servers, you have a number of options. In the Novell client environment, Novell's VLM architecture includes an SNMP module, implemented as a software driver, that allows you to manage a workstation to get system information as well as packet data flowing through the NIC. Additionally, many NIC vendors implement SNMP agents on the hardware. For example, 3Com

Corporation's Ethernet NICs let you configure an SNMP agent implemented in hardware on the NIC. Using the NIC's configuration utility, you can enter in the System Name, Location or Contact Name, and manage the NIC from a central SNMP Manager.

RMON

RMON stands for *Remote Network Monitoring.* The RMON MIB extension was first defined in RFC 1271 in 1991 and recently updated in RFC 1757. The purpose of RMON is to extend the MIB-II standard so that it could provide a mechanism for the unattended capture of more detailed data than that provided by the standard MIB-II groups. You can retrieve that data later and use it to determine characteristics like utilization, error rates, and so on.

The RMON MIB fits in the MIB tree, shown in figure 30.1, at the same level as the other MIB-II objects, like System, and Interfaces. The RMON objects begin at OIDs 1.3.6.1.2.1.16, which if you refer to «B_Ref343929807», is under the MIB-II branch. Within the RMON MIB are nine groups of statistics that can be implemented. If a vendor chooses to provide support for a given RMON group within an agent, then the standard requires them to support all objects within that group. However, not all groups need to be implemented. Indeed, many vendors choose to implement only a subset of the groups to conserve valuable resources on the device running the RMON agent. Because the nature of RMON is to capture and hold data until needed, the more groups that an agent supports, the more memory and processor resources are required to maintain it.

How RMON Works. When implementing RMON, hardware-based "probes" or software-based agents are placed at various points of interest on the network. These probes or agents' sole function is to capture data of a number of types or "groups" into the RMON tables. At a later time, one or more management stations can then access the probes or agents to get a variety of statistics, generate graphs, and do trend analysis. The probes and agents also prove useful when trying to troubleshoot problems. Since they can run all the time, they can capture events leading up to network trouble and allow you to go back and determine where and why the problems occurred.

Hardware-based RMON probes are usually small boxes, which contain nothing more than an NIC and a lot of memory to store data. Depending on the configuration, sample intervals, and number of statistics collected, some probes can capture one or more month's worth of data. This can be very valuable if you are trying to baseline a network for future capacity planning. There are a number of vendors that either build RMON probes or install software-based RMON capabilities into their network devices. For example, HP's LAN Probe can work in conjunction with an application called Netmetrix to configure and analyze remote probe data. Many hub vendors also include at least some of the nine RMON groups in software on their management modules to provide more complete data about the packets going through the hub.

The Nine Groups of RMON. As previously mentioned, the RMON specification provides nine different categories or groups of data that can be captured. It's broken down this way so that the RMON vendor has the option of providing only the most vital groups necessary or all the functionality available. These groups are implemented on the RMON probe or software agent. The following lists the nine RMON groups, their Object Identifier to indicate their place in the MIB hierarchy, and a description of their function:

- Statistics (OID: 1.3.6.1.2.1.16.1) This group provides basic statistics for the given network interface type on the probe. For example, it will collect a breakdown of packet sizes on the segment over time.

- History (OID: 1.3.6.1.2.1.16.2) The history group is responsible for storing periodic samples of the segment for later analysis. The size and sample interval of the history group can be configured on the probe.

- Alarm (OID: 1.3.6.1.2.1.16.3) Using preconfigured thresholds on the probe, this group can generate alarm events when a parameter surpasses a threshold. This group requires implementation of the Event group to generate alarm events.

- Hosts (OID: 1.3.6.1.2.1.16.4) This group keeps track of the MAC addresses of the devices that are communicating on this segment. It keeps track of both source and destination addresses to determine who is talking to whom.

- HostTopN (OID: 1.3.6.1.2.1.16.5) This group is used to store data regarding the top "talkers" based on some criteria provided by the management station. Basically, this group forms a holding area when a management station requests a report of the most active devices.

- Matrix (OID: 1.3.6.1.2.1.16.6) This group holds a table that defines pairs of devices who are talking to one another. While it is similar to the Hosts group, the Matrix group is really only concerned with providing a table of "conversations."

- Filter (OID: 1.3.6.1.2.1.16.7) This group allows a Network Manager to define one or more filters, based on a value and offset, for packets that want to be captured. The definition of that filter(s) exists in this group. This group depends on the Capture group to actually do something with the filtered packets.

- Capture Packets (OID: 1.3.6.1.2.1.16.8) This group requires the presence of the Filter group and provides a means of capturing packet flowing through the network interface for later review. This group actually stores the contents of each packet flowing into the interface and meeting the filter criteria. This data can then be utilized by an application similar to a protocol analyzer to view the contents of the packets.

- Event (OID: 1.3.6.1.2.1.16.9) This group provides the mechanism for the device to generate events and alarms. It is basically the holding table for any events that occur on the device, either through configuration or exception.

Once you have installed RMON probes or software agents onto your network, you can use the data they collect to perform many functions. Depending on which groups the probe or agents implement, you can configure them to collect, for example, collision and utilization statistics on a given network segment. You could have the probe capture this data for a month; then utilizing software like Netmetrix, you could graph this information over the month to determine peak utilization and peak collisions and make decisions about whether you should further segment your network or even provide more bandwidth.

Using the Alarm group, you could set thresholds on these two statistics, and each time the thresholds are reached, the probe or agent would report it to the Event group's table to be viewed later. Finally, if you had Packet Capture and Filter capabilities, you could store the packets during times of heavy utilization and view them later to determine which devices were doing the most talking. The biggest advantage that RMON provides over the standard MIB-II object set is the ability to capture and store historical data for later review. The values contained in standard MIB-II objects represent only what is going on at any given moment, providing an instantaneous view of the managed device.

Advantages and Limitations. As mentioned earlier, RMON devices can be a great tool for gathering network statistics without having to constantly monitor a given segment via a Network Manager. They are basically designed to plug in and be forgotten. However, there are several issues to consider before running out to buy probes for every segment in your network.

First, if you are considering implementing RMON in an existing hub, router, or other network device whose primary function is not RMON, then remember that this kind of remote monitoring is resource-intensive. Don't go out and implement a RMON agent that supports all nine groups on all your hubs if you don't need all nine groups. Similarly, if you are considering implementing stand-alone RMON probes, you will find that they are pricy little investments, costing as much as $1,500 to $2,000 each. Sit down with a map of your network and decide what segments really need probes. Consider starting out by putting them on busy server and user segments or remote segments that are geographically difficult to access. And make sure that you purchase them with enough memory to store a sufficient amount of data in case you don't get to check them for a few days.

Planning, Choosing, and Setting Up a Network-Management System

Now that we've discussed the various mechanisms available to you for managing networks and systems, we'll go over the process of building a network-management infrastructure in your organization. This process involves planning a strategy for your NMS, choosing a vendor or vendors to provide the hardware and software, and setting these systems up in your environment in a way that provides robust, easily accessible network-management resources.

Just as a warning, implementing network management is an evolutionary process, especially in today's growing distributed environment. Don't expect instant results. Most network administrators are "brought up" as fire fighters, responding to problems as they arise. Installing network-management promises to make them proactive, but it will take education and time before a network-management tool can enable your network administrators to provide the kind of support needed to grow with your organization and its networking needs.

How To Plan for a Network-Management System

Installing an NMS differs from other types of software installations you may have performed. Unlike basic applications such as word processors or spreadsheets, NMS software requires some forethought, some planning, and some real analysis of what you are trying to accomplish. As mentioned at the beginning of this chapter, it's easy to build a very complex NMS that doesn't address what you really need to manage. Following are some steps you can take to ensure that before you actually choose a software vendor, you have thought about what you want to do with your NMS.

Defining Needs. The first step in planning an NMS is to determine what it is you need to manage. We covered in an earlier section the differences between network and systems management. The first decision you need to make is: Are you going to do some elements of both? If so, do you plan on integrating both on the same platform from the very start? If so, then this may guide your decision from the very beginning.

When you define your needs, think about what devices you want to manage first. Start small, choosing only those network devices in OSI layers one through three. This means hubs, routers, bridges, and maybe NICs in servers. I say maybe on NICs because in a large environment this may mean making software changes on a large number of servers to accommodate SNMP, or whatever network-management protocol you choose. Most hubs and routers have SNMP support built-in, and it's simply a matter of defining community names and setting up your NMS console, and away you go.

Also, think about which of the functions you want to have right off the bat. To start with, you may want to consider sticking to the basics like fault detection, configuration management, and performance analysis. This can be implemented without a lot of changes in your infrastructure. If you decide you need to have protocol analysis, historical reporting, or even systems management, then this will likely have a greater impact on your infrastructure, require more time and money to implement, and introduce greater complexity. There may also be significant time and resources required if you are planning on building your NMS based on an OS you don't have experience with. For instance, if you support Novell and Windows on Intel platforms and are considering implementing NMS on UNIX (a common NMS platform), you may require additional time to get up to speed on administering the OS before you can get up to speed on the NMS.

Infrastructure Costs To Consider. Speaking of money, you will need to consider what costs, both hidden and obvious, you will incur when building your NMS. The obvious ones are hardware and software. You will need at least the following:

■ Some kind of workstation to serve as the NMS console (you may want to buy several for different locations). These workstations will need to be quite powerful, including lots of RAM and disk space to manipulate and store the management database.

■ Depending on the vendor, you may need to add a management module to each of your hubs, routers, or bridges to support network management.

■ You will need software for each management console you build. Depending on the company, they may license you based on how many network devices you are going to manage. Additionally, you may incur separate costs for agent software if you are using a proprietary-management protocol.

■ If you are implementing some kind of remote protocol analysis solution like RMON or software agents, you will need to purchase hardware or software for every segment you want to analyze. Then you may need to purchase separate console software to read the data from the agents.

■ Finally, don't forget the soft costs of setting up the console, building your network map, and setting up any event reporting, alarms, and so on. Also, you may have to make some network protocol changes to accommodate the NMS. For instance, in a TCP/IP environment, you may find it useful to use a service like DNS to refer to all your hubs, routers, and other IP devices that are being managed. This may require building such an infrastructure if it's not already in place. If you estimate man-hours to complete this phase, double it to be on the safe side. This is by far the most challenging portion of the process.

Defining the Scope of Implementation. When you define the scope of your NMS implementation, make sure you plan to install critical elements in phases. For example, start small by deciding that in the first phase, you will install the NMS software and populate the network map with all the hubs and routers in your local location. Then maybe the next phase includes adding devices across one or more WAN connections to the picture. A third phase may include integrating one part of a systems-management solution. Don't try to do everything at once, and do take time between phases to work out the bugs of the previous phase.

Defining the Method of Implementation. How you implement your NMS solution is mostly a function of your organization's environment. But there are a few things to be aware of before you dive right in. Count on any changes you make to managed devices, like hubs, routers, and so on to be disruptive. That is, even if a vendor says adding SNMP support is Plug and Play, plan for it not to be and schedule work accordingly. Also, any new software agents you install on any systems, especially file servers, should be tested thoroughly before installing them in production environments. This includes looking for memory leaks that may slowly cripple a server or other obvious anomalies. The best advice is to test, test, test any new hardware and software before implementing it. While this may seem obvious, you'd be surprised how many organizations don't do this, only to discover that the seemingly benign NMS software cripples their network.

Criteria for Choosing a Network-Management System

In an earlier section, we talked about the features and functions of a good NMS. Depending on your environment, however, you may be constricted in your choice of available systems. If that is the case, the best advice is to build in extra time to implement any nonstandard solution. Otherwise, the choices for standards-based NMSs are quite complete, and you should have no problem choosing a vendor solution that meets your needs.

Industry Standards Compliance. In some situations, adhering to industry standards can sign the death knell for a piece of software or hardware. In the case of network management, however, SNMP has become the standard for managing a variety of network types. This is evidenced by the majority of vendors that provide SNMP solutions. Suffice it to say that unless you have a very small environment with very specialized needs, your best bet is to implement a management system based on SNMP. By doing so, you will give yourself the flexibility of having the widest choice of vendors and products, and the protocol with which most network administrators are experienced. This recommendation applies not just to TCP/IP environments, but also to Novell, Apple, and any other platforms that support SNMP.

Availability of Third-Party Add-Ons. No matter which network-management vendor's software you buy, it is unlikely that it will have everything you need. So it is important that the vendor supports add-ins of other companies' products. This generally comes in the form of an API that they provide to allow developers to write additional modules. Examples of products that support this are HP's Openview platform and Novell's ManageWise software.

> **Note**
>
> No matter what other features a given NMS touts, make sure it supports plug-in modules for other nonstandard network components, and make sure there are vendors who actually write these plug-ins. This cannot be emphasized enough. Make sure that the modules you need actually exist, and that there are at least some well-known vendors supporting and writing software for the platform.

Distributed Database Support. Most NMS platforms keep all the information they have learned about your network in some kind of database. Some use industry-standard database engines from Sybase, Oracle, or Microsoft's SQL Server. Other systems use a proprietary format. There are arguments to be made for choosing an NMS that supports one of these popular engines because it makes any future development utilizing the database engine simpler. Perhaps more importantly, however, is that the platform supports a distributed database model. In reality, very few do support this model. The reason this is useful is that, if you have support staff located in different locations, who need access to resources on the NMS, it would be useful to provide them with their own NMS console without having them build their own map and corresponding database. Without distributed database support, each NMS console you build requires you to build the network map and corresponding database from scratch each time. This process is time-consuming enough without having to do it for each console.

Unfortunately, many NMS vendors don't yet provide this support, so you have to weigh the costs of having this feature against other features a particular vendor may have. If you don't mind having to do a little extra work up front and on an ongoing basis and have good backups, you may not need this feature.

Some Well-Known Management Platforms. While there is no one vendor's platform that meets all needs, there are a number of companies who have large percentages of market share because their applications are "open," standards-based applications that many vendors write add-ins for. Generally, most high-end NMS software runs on some flavor of UNIX. This is generally due to the inherent robustness of UNIX as a 32-bit multitasking OS. What you will also find, is that recently, many vendors have been announcing ports of their NMS applications to Windows NT because they have the same 32-bit features as UNIX. If you are more familiar and comfortable with setting up and administering Windows-based systems, this may be a good alternative. For these same reasons, Windows 3.1 makes a poor network-management OS platform for any but the most basic types of management. The following are some examples of the more popular NMS systems, with their attendant OSs:

- Hewlett Packard's Openview platform (UNIX, Windows 3.1 version also available)

- Cabletron's Spectrum (UNIX)

- IBM's Netview and Netview-6000 (SNA & UNIX)

- SunSoft's Sun NetManager (UNIX)

- Novell's ManageWise (Windows 3.1)

This is by no means a complete list but gives you an idea of the "big" players in the network-management world.

Setting Up and Maintaining a Network-Management System

Once you have planned your NMS and chosen a vendor, you will then need to set it up in your network environment. This involves not just populating your network map and configuring alarms and thresholds, but also finding a place for the console to sit and providing the most reliable path to the rest of the network.

Where To Put It? You might think that deciding where to put your NMS system is a trivial issue, but realize that its connection to the network is the only way it can keep track of devices going up or down and gather statistics. If something happens on this local segment, the rest of your network may be fine, but your NMS console will never know about it. It will light up like a Christmas tree and you'll think the whole network has failed. So when you're placing your system, make sure that you have redundant paths to the rest of your network. As an example, you could connect two routers to the segment such that you have two paths to the other segments in your environment. This is illustrated in figure 30.3.

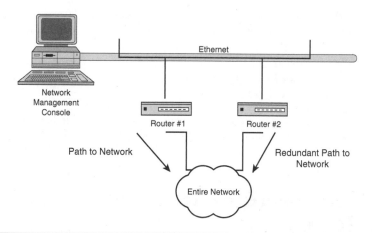

Figure 30.3

How to place a Network Manager Console on your network for fault-tolerance.

Baselining and Setting Thresholds. After you have installed the system, installed the software, and populated your network map through either a manual or auto-discovery process, you will want to start capturing statistics on your network for purposes of providing a baseline for network activity. The baseline is the level at which your network is normally operating. This relates to utilization on the various segments, response times to various parts of the network, and levels of resource utilization on your network devices. You should capture statistics for a good representative period of time to allow your network to reach an equilibrium point. This may be one day or one week, depending upon the stability of your network.

Once this baselining process is complete, take a look at your data to figure out where your network is normally operating. You can look at things like utilization, collisions, and errors on various key segments. Now you can begin to set thresholds. Thresholds are "high-water" marks that you can set on various network attributes. When statistics exceed these marks, an alert is generated and sent to your console. If you are using RMON, these alarms can be set on the RMON agent and picked up by your RMON Manager. If you don't have an RMON-like mechanism, most network-management platforms themselves support alarms based on thresholds you configure. Once the thresholds are set, go back every so often and rebenchmark your network to determine if your baselines have changed.

Setting Up Event Notification. Many systems support various mechanisms for notifying you in the case of a network problem. Visual alarms are the simplest way. These are usually pop-up windows that appear on your screen when alarms are reported. Since you may not always be sitting in front of the NMS console, it's useful (but perhaps not desirable!) to have mechanism to notify you wherever you are. Many NMS packages and third-party add-ins support mechanisms to page you, send you e-mail, or even flash a message on the screen of any system you're logged on to! If your required response times to a problem are quick, you may want to consider one of these technologies.

Backups. Methods for backing up your networked systems were discussed at length in chapter 17, "Backup Technology: Programs and Data." However, backups of your NMS are very important, especially if you don't have distributed database support, and each NMS console's database exists as a stand-alone. Losing a stand-alone database could take days to rebuild, not to mention the lost baseline data, threshold, and alarm configurations.

When backing up most SQL-based database engines, you usually need to take the database offline, do a dump of the data, back up the dump, and bring the database back online. Refer to chapter 17 for more information on backup strategies.

Managing Emerging Networking Technologies

Most networks today consist of Ethernet, Token Ring, FDDI, and maybe some Local-Talk segments. These segments contain any number of workstations and servers, on a "shared-media." That is, whatever their network topology, they must share resources on their wire with other devices, limiting their access to the full bandwidth available for that technology. Many of these segments are connected together by routers, which provide network-layer packet forwarding to shuttle traffic from one segment to the other. Additionally, routers keep certain types of traffic from leaving the local segment, such as broadcasts, and topology-specific problems, like collisions. However, they also introduce latency into the network, as a packet traveling from one segment to another has to undergo some routing calculation to determine its destination at the router. As a result of these and other issues, *switching* has emerged in the last couple of years as the next generation network technology. Perhaps spurred on by the increasing popularity of Asynchronous Transfer Mode (ATM) technology, which is inherently switch-based, Ethernet, Token Ring and FDDI switching is fast becoming the preferred method of networking technology.

Basically, switches do what bridges used to do before routers became fashionable. That is, a switch gets a packet in and, based on its data link layer source and destination addresses, makes a decision to forward it to the port of its destination device. Since no network layer decisions are made, switches move packets very quickly, on the order of up to a million packets per second for the faster switches. In contrast, most routers don't forward packets at rates much higher than a couple hundred thousand packets per second. Additionally, a single device, such as a server, plugged into a switch port, effectively has the full data transfer rate available to it during each packet transmission. So a server attached to a 10 M/sec Ethernet switch has a full 10 M/sec available all the time. In contrast, depending on the number of devices connected to a share media 10BaseT hub, each device may get only about 10–30 percent of the 10 M/sec rate, due to collisions and contention. So you can see the lure of switching technology. However, what this means is that, as switched networks grow, networks become flatter, or less segmented. Additionally, broadcasts that were originally blocked by routers suddenly get forwarded to all devices within a switched environment. Therefore, the need to effectively manage traffic in a switched environment becomes very important.

Managing a Switched Network

Management of the switched environment definitely presents new challenges. Most vendors today have network-management software to cope with these changes, but it's important to recognize how switching changes the way you think about troubleshooting your network. What you will find is that most switch vendors implement the same kind of support that they had for their shared-media hubs, including a management module containing SNMP support and even some number of RMON groups. But they will also include support for the new switched paradigm, including ATM support, virtual LANs, and new ways to monitor switched traffic.

What Changes? Most importantly, moving your network to a switched environment presents the opportunity, as mentioned earlier, to build a flatter, less segmented network. As great as this may sound, it has several implications. First, if your environment is primarily TCP/IP, you may have a fixed IP address space that you have chosen to subnet to provide maximum segmentation for the routed environment. Now you install some switches, flatten out your user segments, and suddenly, instead of having 50 IP hosts per subnet, you have 200. You either have to re-address all your workstations to support the flatter network or do some magic on the routers you have left to accommodate multiple IP subnets on one segment. Management of either solution is challenging to say the least.

More importantly perhaps, is what implementing a switched network does to your ability to troubleshoot problems. If we remember the discussion of the different tools available to most NMSs, protocol analysis, and especially remote protocol analysis through distributed RMON agents, presented a powerful way to capture packets on the network remotely and decode them to determine where a problem lies. With switches, things get tricky. If you have a switch with 12 ports, and five of the ports have, for example, a Windows NT server plugged into them, where do you plug in your RMON probe, or even your network-monitoring agent software? If you plug them into any old switch port, they will never see the packets going from one device to another because the switch receives a packet from server A, destined for server B, and forwards it right to server B's port!

Protocol Analysis Options. Now faced with the above problem, how do we do effective protocol capture and analysis in a switched environment. Different vendors have different solutions, depending upon the switch. On some switches, the vendor has implemented, usually in a combination of hardware and software, all nine RMON groups on each port in the switch. This allows the RMON agent to capture packets, alarms, events, and so on from each port and store them in some area of memory to be analyzed later by a Network Manager.

The limitation of this solution, of course, is related to the inherent performance advantages of switches. Switches forward so many packets at a time, that a large switch would spend all its processor and memory resources trying to keep up with populating the RMON tables with statistics. For larger switching solutions, most vendors implement some kind of special port on the switch, where you can install either a protocol analyzer or dedicated RMON probe. Through the switch's management software, you can then configure the switch to take all packets that come into it from any of its ports, and copy them also to the port connected to the analyzer or probe. In some cases, the probe or analyzer will be on the same switch that it's gathering data from. In other cases, you can actually configure the switch to copy all its packets to some remote port, maybe on another switch, where the probe/analyzer is connected. In this latter case, be aware that you will then be sending additional traffic, in the form of copied packets, along whatever path leads to the probe.

Virtual LANs

Virtual LANs (VLAN) were developed in conjunction with today's switching technology to aid managing switched networks. What VLANs do, in the simplest case, is provide some functionality to segment devices within or between switches—similar to what a router did. This is done through the management software supporting the switch. Essentially, you can assign one or more ports on a switch or across switches to form a VLAN. All packets from devices in the VLAN will only be forwarded by the switch to other members of the VLAN. This includes broadcasts and has the effect of providing a means of controlling who gets broadcast traffic in a switched environment. Depending on the vendor solution, you can either assign VLANs based on a given set of switch ports or by a given MAC address on a device connected to the switch. Currently there is no one standards-based way to implement VLANs. Therefore, one vendor's VLAN may not talk to another's. Additionally, each vendor implements management of VLANs slightly different. Some allow you to graphically drag and drop ports from one VLAN to the other. Some allow you to define complex rules for the flow of traffic among VLAN members and to other VLANs. Regardless of the implementation, switching in general and VLANs in particular, will add additional challenges, require quite a bit more planning, and demand a new set of skills to manage them properly.

Summary

In this chapter, we've discussed what kinds of features and functions you should expect to find in today's NMSs. A good NMS should have features like fault detection, configuration management, performance analysis, security control, and accounting. Systems management features like asset management, remote control, and software distribution were discussed as optional elements to your network-management strategy but ones that add complexity to your management strategy. Additionally, we talked about the industry standard SNMP protocol, and its attendant MIBs, for keeping information about network devices. SNMP is the protocol of choice for network management in today's networks. We also discussed the RMON portion of the MIB. RMON provides a mechanism to capture historical statistics, errors, and packets remotely for more complete management of distant sites. Next, we talked about the issues of planning, installing and setting up an NMS, including the idea of starting with a simple plan to manage a base set of network devices, building on that as the system stabilizes. Once the NMS is built, we talked about the need to baseline the system in order to set thresholds for notifying the network support staff of problems. Finally, we talked about how network management, and especially protocol analysis, change in the new switched environments, and how VLANs add complexity to the network-management picture.

Regardless of your environment, it's important to realize the need for good network management. The underlying goal is to build a management system that enables you to see problems before they become epidemic and to better plan for growth in your network. If you're able to accomplish either of these goals, you're on the way to building a better network. If you accomplish both, congratulations, you have done something that most organizations can only dream of!

Chapter 31

Locating the Problem: Server versus Workstation versus Links

Modern computer networks are complex, high-speed marvels of technology with advanced server, client, and network hardware and software working in close cooperation. They are so fast and complex, in fact, that it can sometimes be difficult to trace the source of problems that arise.

This chapter deals with methodology for identifying underlying causes of faults in a client/server network environment. It examines the complexity that can make problem identification so difficult and includes recommendations for precautionary measures that can help you get a handle on the complexity of your particular network. This chapter then provides a roadmap for identifying the underlying cause of a network problem.

Note

This chapter focuses on fault identification methodology. It does not describe network troubleshooting tools and how to use them. This chapter also does not describe how to correct a problem once it is identified—chapter 32, "Repairing Common Types of Problems," does that for the most common network problems. The information required to fix other problems can be found elsewhere in this book in the relevant chapters.

Note

While this chapter focuses on client/server network faults, the methods described are generic and can be applied equally to peer-to-peer networks.

Methodology

An initial *fault report*, also known as a *problem report*, is generally a description of one or more symptoms rather than of the underlying problem itself. The problem can be regarded as successfully *located* when it has been redefined in a specific hardware or software context where it can be dealt with directly.

For example, a problem might be reported initially as "Can't connect to server." After investigation, you might be able to restate the problem as "The server has a faulty network adapter" or "The client is using the incorrect frame type." In the first case, the server's network adapter needs to be replaced; in the second, the client software needs to be reconfigured. In both cases, the problem has been located (though not yet resolved).

How do you get from the initial statement of the problem, phrased in the user's terms, to a statement in your own terms of the specific locus of the underlying problem? The following sections look at a few possible approaches.

Trial and Error

The *trial-and-error approach* is one way to find causes of problems—try changing a component here or a driver there and see if it all starts working again. This is a bad approach, but let's think about why it is bad.

First, there is an underlying assumption that you don't really understand the way your network works. If you did understand how the network works, then you'd make use of your insight—rather than trial and error—to approach the problem in a logical way.

Second, there is no guarantee that you'll ever locate the problem. It might be caused by a combination of factors, and unless you happen to eliminate both factors at the same time, the problem will persist.

This doesn't mean, however, that there isn't a useful element of trial and error in properly planned troubleshooting. You need to experiment with the network to some extent to find answers to your questions about the problem (for example, "Does the problem persist if I use a different connection?"), but such tests should be used as part of a methodological approach to identifying the source of the problem—they should not constitute the entire methodology.

Expert System

Another approach, more commonly used in real life, is the *expert system approach*, where you use your expert knowledge of the network to short-circuit the troubleshooting process. For example, two users complain that they can no longer connect to the server. You can see the server from your workstation, so you immediately suspect the repeater, which you know sits between them and the server.

You can thus use your insight into your network to pounce quickly on the obscure cause of a problem that might be difficult to solve in a step-by-step way. Combined with the trial-and-error approach, troubleshooting like this can be very successful.

The trouble with this approach is that it not only *uses* your insight into the network but *relies* on that insight. If you don't have all the information, you might arrive at the wrong answer. Consider the previous example—suppose one of the two users had moved temporarily out of his office, because it was being painted, and into a colleague's office, where he brought his own workstation and connected it to the second user's thinnet strand. Given that information, you would make a very different first guess about the nature of the problem.

Generally it is best to use your expert knowledge of the network (along with trial and error) as part of a methodological approach rather than as the entire basis for the troubleshooting effort.

Problem Space

A more abstract approach, the *problem space approach*, is to regard the underlying problem as a point (or possibly a series of points) in *n*-dimensional space. Each of the *n* dimensions represents a possible parameterization of the problem in a specific hardware or software context. For example, you might have the following dimensions:

- Workstations affected

- Servers affected

- Bridges affected

- Routers affected

- Repeaters affected

- Frame types

- Duration of problem

- Frequency of problem

The extent of the problem can then be clearly identified by investigating the problem in the context of each of these dimensions.

The usefulness of this way of looking at the problem lies in its comprehensiveness. Define each possible dimension of your network this way before a problem arises. Whenever a problem comes up, you can check it on each dimension in turn. This means that you are unlikely to overlook some aspect of the problem or to be misled by apparently "obvious" causes.

Of course, this approach is not realistic. It is impossible to define all the possible dimensions that apply to any network. Even if you did, this approach would simply allow you to accurately identify the *extent* of the problem, not its underlying *cause*—pinpointing the cause would require a logical leap of some sort. The underlying idea, however— trying to comprehensively identify all possible problem dimensions—can be usefully incorporated into a structured troubleshooting methodology.

A Structured Approach

The three approaches previously described can be combined in a structured way into a useful system. Avoid adopting an ad hoc approach to combining them—simply mixing the ingredients of trial and error, insight, and a long list of things to look into will not get you very far. Combine them using the following steps:

1. Before any problems arise, collate information about your network with a view to troubleshooting. Start by trying to identify as many problem dimensions as possible; then ensure that you have all the relevant data for each dimension.

2. When a problem arises, get as complete a statement of the nature of the problem as possible. Your fault report form should aim at gathering information on each of the dimensions you defined in step 1. The sample fault report form in figure 35.1 shows the type of approach to take. If you take verbal fault reports, be prepared to ask the user a series of questions to obtain the same information.

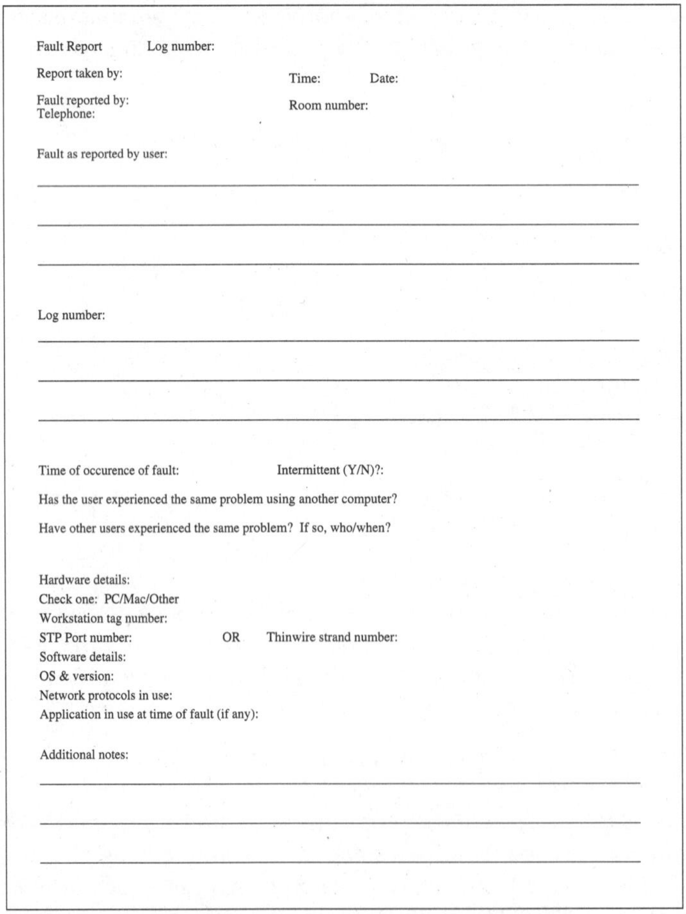

```
Fault Report        Log number:

Report taken by:                      Time:        Date:

Fault reported by:                    Room number:
Telephone:

Fault as reported by user:

_____

_____

_____


Log number:

_____

_____

_____


Time of occurence of fault:              Intermittent (Y/N)?:

Has the user experienced the same problem using another computer?

Have other users experienced the same problem?  If so, who/when?


Hardware details:
Check one:  PC/Mac/Other
Workstation tag number:
STP Port number:              OR      Thinwire strand number:
Software details:
OS & version:
Network protocols in use:
Application in use at time of fault (if any):

Additional notes:

_____

_____

_____
```

Figure 35.1

This is a sample fault report form.

3. Perform whatever tests are necessary to determine the real extent of the problem. The initial fault report most likely will be from one user's point of view. Redefine the problem statement in light of your findings.

4. Based on your knowledge of the network, form a working hypothesis about the underlying cause. Frame your hypothesis in a form that can be definitively confirmed or rejected. For example, "It's the workstation's connection to the network" is not as useful as "The workstation can't receive packets from the network."

> **Note**
>
> A definitively refuted hypothesis can be as useful as a definitively confirmed hypothesis. What matters is that you use a hypothesis that you can test and each of the possible outcomes eliminates a range of possible problem causes from consideration.

5. Perform an experiment that will either confirm or refute your hypothesis. Be absolutely clear what your hypothesis is before you test it. This will help you choose the most appropriate test and will also make it easier to interpret the results of the test without getting confused. An experiment in this context can be as simple as running SLIST or as complex as using a sniffer to analyze traffic patterns. Make sure you keep full notes on all configuration changes that you make so that you can revert to the original configuration after the experiment.

6. Revise the problem statement based upon the results of your experiment.

7. If you have not yet located the problem, go to step 4 and form another hypothesis. Choose a hypothesis that narrows the search for the problem.

This sequence is illustrated in figure 35.2. In many cases, of course, the experimentation loop will not be quite so tight as illustrated; a test may produce unexpected results which means that the extent of the problem is not quite what you originally thought. If that happens, you will have to redefine the scope of the fault and proceed again to the formulation of a new hypothesis.

This method uses elements of each approach described earlier:

- The trial-and-error approach is used, but the trials are carefully designed to advance the resolution of the problem, rather than work ad hoc; the errors are used to differentiate between clearly defined areas of problem space.

- The expert system approach is also incorporated. You design the hypotheses and experiments based on your knowledge of the network and your expectation of the most likely fault sources. If you are mistaken in your expectations, this method lets you know fairly quickly.

- The problem space approach is also used but only as a means of ensuring that you have all the relevant data at hand when a problem arises and that you have a complete statement of the problem before you start to trace it.

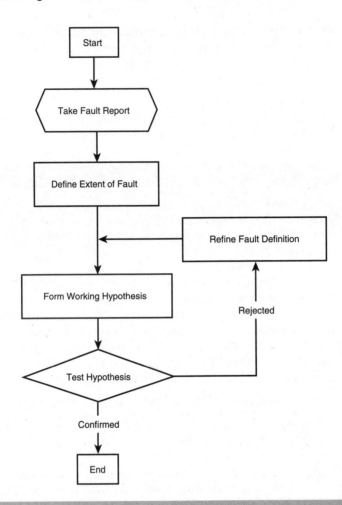

Figure 35.2

This is the suggested troubleshooting process.

The underlying method here is to continuously restate the problem in a context more amenable to direct action. The problem originally is stated by the user in his or her terms. You then investigate the problem, restating it in your terms and in light of your findings.

The following is an example to illustrate the method:

1. John calls and says that he can't log on.

Problem: **John can't log on.**

2. You determine that the only place that he's tried logging on is from his office.

Problem: **John can't log on from his workstation.**

3. You ask what happens when he tries. He says he gets a `Server SAL not found` message.

Problem: **John's workstation can't see server SAL.**

4. Since John's workstation can run the LOGIN command, it must be connecting to a server. You run SLIST on another workstation and server SAL is not listed.

Problem: **Multiple workstations can't see server SAL.**

5. A quick look at SAL's console tells you that it has crashed.

Problem: **Server SAL is down.**

Now that the problem has been localized to the server, it can be dealt with on a direct basis—you need to establish why the server crashed, bring it back up, and so on.

Notice that the initial fault report was refined in the first three steps. John said that he couldn't log on, but it was necessary to establish whether he had tried from one or more workstations (step 2) and what had happened when he tried (step 3). At that stage, it was clear that the problem as far as John's workstation was concerned was that it couldn't see the server.

The focus then shifted to determining the extent of the problem. If any other machines could see server SAL (step 4), then the focus could shift to John's workstation and his part of the network. Since a second machine could not see the server, though, there was a good chance that the server was the source of the problem.

Step 5 confirmed this, though of course this might not have been the case—the server might have been fine, with the two workstations both affected by another network problem of some sort. The decision to check the server rather than the network in step 5 was based on the expectation that the network was unlikely to act in such a way as to prevent two clients from seeing a working server—the possibility that server SAL was down seemed more likely.

Here's another example:

1. John calls and says that he can't log on.

Problem: **John can't log on.**

2. You determine that the only place that he's tried logging on is from his office.

Problem: **John can't log on from his workstation.**

3. You ask what happens when he tries. He says he gets `Invalid drive letter` when he tries to switch to drive F.

Problem: **John's workstation is not loading the NetWare shell.**

4. You go to his workstation and watch it booting up. NETX reports that it cannot connect to a server and fails to load.

Problem: **John's workstation can't see a server.**

5. You run SLIST on your workstation and SAL is listed (along with other servers).

Problem: **John's workstation can't see servers that are visible to other workstations.**

6. You run the diagnostic utility for John's network adapter. It passes all internal tests.

Problem: **John's network adapter works, but his workstation can't see servers that are visible to other workstations.**

7. You use the diagnostic utility to watch for packets. It can send and receive packets successfully.

Problem: **John's network adapter and network connection both work, but his workstation can't see servers that are visible to other workstations.**

8. Suspecting a configuration error, you check John's NET.CFG file. It is set up to use the wrong frame type.

Problem: **John's workstation is not using the correct frame type.**

In this case, steps 1–4 refined the problem. Again, John said that he couldn't log on, but it was necessary to establish whether he had tried from one or more workstations (step 2) and what happened when he tried (step 3). It then was apparent that NETX had not loaded, but it was not apparent why—it might have been, for example, that IPXODI or the MLID was not loaded. Step 4 determined that NETX did not load because it could not see any server.

At that point, the focus shifted to determining the extent of the problem. Since other machines could see server SAL (step 5), the focus became John's workstation and his part of the network. Steps 6 and 7 were aimed at determining whether the problem was internal or related to John's network connection. The diagnostics confirmed that the hardware and the network connection were fine.

Since the server, network (up to and including the workstation connection), and workstation hardware looked fine, the only thing left was the workstation software. The NET.CFG file (as the locus for much configuration information) was the first place to look (step 8).

This guess proved successful in the example, but it might not have in reality. A routing problem on the network might have prevented John's workstation from seeing SAL, even though both SAL and the workstation were functioning properly. If that had been the case, then correcting the frame type error would not have resolved the difficulty, and additional steps would have been necessary:

9. You connect a laptop (one that you know works!) to John's network connection. It also can send and receive on the network but cannot see SAL.

Problem: **Valid connections at John's connection point cannot see servers with valid network connections.**

10. The network itself is suspect, so you start to trace the problem back toward the server. John's thinnet connection goes via a bridge to the servers. You find that the laptop can see the servers when connected on the server side of the bridge but not when connected on John's side.

Problem: **Valid connections on John's side of the bridge cannot see servers with valid network connections.**

After step 10, you know that the problem is with the bridge, and you can debug it.

In both of these examples, a more specific problem statement generated by a thorough fault report would have been preferable to the initial problem statement "John can't log on."

If, in the first case, it was "John gets a `Server SAL not found` message when he tries to log on from his workstation," you would have known right away that NETX was loading (so that his workstation could see at least one server) and that the workstation simply couldn't see SAL.

If, in the second case, it was "NETX on John's workstation gives a `Cannot connect to server SAL` error message," you would have known that the situation was worse, in the sense that the workstation could see no servers. Whether this is actually worse or not is unimportant here—what matters is that you get enough information at an early stage to distinguish between different symptoms.

Information Gathering

The process of redefining the problem into a manageable context requires knowledge about various facets of the particular network that you are dealing with:

- Network topology
- Network hardware
- Frames and protocols
- Server configuration
- Client configuration
- Applications
- User profile

Collect information about each of these areas when the network is up and running normally. This allows you to investigate fault reports on the basis of firm information, categorized according to the contexts into which you need to resolve the problems. The following sections look at each of these areas in turn.

Network Topology

You need to understand the topology of a particular network if you hope to troubleshoot network problems on it. Review the structure of the network and draw two maps of it:

- A *logical map* showing rings, segments, and so on, as well as the logical relationships between various components.

- A *physical map* indicating clearly how the network relates to the buildings where it runs. Show buildings and individual floors (if necessary), and include room numbers where active equipment is stored.

In both cases, show all bridges, repeaters, routers, hubs, and segments. Indicate where all servers and clients are connected (grouping large numbers of clients together for convenience).

> **Tip**
>
> Remember to keep both maps updated as your network grows.

Network Hardware

A detailed inventory of all active network equipment will accelerate the troubleshooting process. You might need to check model numbers or firmware revision levels when tracing a fault, especially if you need to discuss things with the vendor. Everything proceeds with more speed and less panic if all the relevant information has been collected at an earlier, calmer stage.

Gather at least the following information for each piece of equipment:

- Make and model
- Location
- Firmware revision
- Settings: hardware switches, jumpers, and software settings
- Connections: which ports and to what

Server Configuration

A detailed hardware and software inventory for your servers is essential. Gather at least the following information for each server:

- System make and model
- Physical location
- Manager (if it's someone other than you)
- OS/NOS version

- Hard copy of all configuration files
- Amount of RAM
- Frame types used
- Protocols used
- Internal network address
- UPS make and model if any

Gather at least the following information for each network adapter:

- Adapter make and model
- Network address
- Driver version number
- Jumper and DIP switch settings
- Slot number (PCI/EISA/MCA systems)
- IRQ, I/O port, and shared RAM area
- Transceiver type if any
- Connections: connector type, connected to what
- IPX cable number of network to which connected
- Protocols bound to adapter
- Keep a copy of the AUTOEXEC.NCF and STARTUP.NCF for each server as well

Gather at least the following information for each SCSI controller:

- Adapter make and model
- Firmware revision level
- Jumper and DIP switch settings
- Slot number (PCI/EISA/MCA systems)
- IRQ, I/O port, and shared RAM area
- SCSI ID
- Whether terminated
- List of connected devices, with SCSI IDs

Gather at least the following information for each hard drive:

- Make and model

- Formatted capacity
- Partition information (names and sizes)
- Size of hot fix area
- SCSI disks: SCSI ID number
- SCSI disks: which SCSI controller if more than one
- SCSI disks: whether terminated

Gather at least the following information for each adapter (besides SCSI and network):

- Make and model
- Jumper and DIP switch settings
- Slot number (PCI/EISA/MCA systems)
- IRQ, I/O port, and shared RAM area

Make the compilation of this information an integral part of the installation procedure for new servers. Remember that an installation isn't worth much unless it's stable. That means that you must be able to respond quickly to the problems that will inevitably arise. Proper documentation of this sort should be regarded as an investment in the stability of the service. Keep this list up-to-date as the server configuration changes.

Client Configuration

It might not be practical for you to keep a detailed inventory of all clients on the network. There might be too many of them, or they might be managed by someone else, meaning that the information does not normally come your way. If you are expected to provide support for these workstations, however—even if you only support their use of the network—you must have a certain amount of information about each workstation.

Gather at least the following information (if the workstations are managed by other people, insist that those people provide this information for each workstation they connect):

- System make and model
- Physical location
- Person responsible: name and number
- OS/NOS version

Gather at least the following information for each network adapter:

- Adapter make and model
- Network address

- Connections: connector type, connected to what
- Protocols bound to adapter

Applications

Information about the range of applications in use on the network will help to inform your troubleshooting efforts, but it's more difficult to define and collect than the information about hardware elements discussed in preceding sections.

A knowledge of the patterns of network use can also be helpful. You should be aware if the network is likely to be sporadically or continuously heavy; intermittent problems, for example, might arise only when network traffic is unusually heavy.

User Profile

Similarly, it is vital that you make yourself aware of the background of network users. In particular, talk to them about their expectations of the network, as well as their likely uses of it. You may find that their perception of the extent and purpose of the network is at odds with your own or that the level of service that they anticipate is unrealistic.

Understanding the vantage point of the user when you discuss a problem helps you get beyond their description—possibly inaccurate—of the problem. For instance, a fault report of "I can't log on" requires one response if the person reporting the problem is an experienced user but requires a different response if the user is unclear on the distinction between logging on and starting an application.

The Information Database

What do you do with all this information after you gather it? You must store it somewhere accessible in a format that suits your needs. Where you store it and which format you choose depends on your particular environment and preferences.

If you store the data electronically, you might find it useful to keep it on a file server so that it can be accessed from a range of locations. Remember, though, that this data will be required when the network is acting up, so storing it on a local hard drive might be more sensible. A compromise is to store the data on a server, but maintain a local copy for backup; if you do this, you must institute a procedure for making sure that the local copy is updated on a regular basis.

Deciding on a storage format is largely a matter of taste. Remember that the information is there for use in a crisis—it doesn't have to look pretty, but it has to be there! A small, uncomplicated network can be documented on a few sheets of paper in a folder. A large WAN might require a specialized database application to keep tabs on developments. In many cases, flat text files are adequate. They can be searched using a range of utilities, they are not application-specific, and there is little or no overhead to setting them up (unlike setting up a relational database).

Finally, it is essential that you keep the information up-to-date. Most networks are dynamic entities, with changes occurring on a regular basis. Keeping the database up-to-date must become an integral part of the culture of the people who manage the network if the database is to serve its purpose and assist you in tracking down network faults.

The Fault Report

Every network problem that comes to your attention appears first as a *fault report*. It may be very informal—"Hey, why can't I print?"—or may be a formal report that is part of a well-defined fault reporting system. Even faults that you discover yourself can be regarded as fault reports in this sense. They are of the informal type, but the difference is that you immediately switch into troubleshooting mode and define the problem more succinctly.

The quality of the initial fault report can have a major bearing on the time and effort required for you to identify the underlying cause of the problem. Sketchy or incorrect information can be a major hindrance to resolving the fault.

Spend some time defining the fault reporting procedure. It can be formal or informal, but it must be structured. If you support the network alone and deal with a small number of users, it might be adequate for you to ask a list of questions whenever a problem is reported. If you work as part of a team or deal with a large number of users, a more formal fault reporting procedure is probably appropriate—a formal procedure might include fault log numbers and a signoff system. In any case, record at least the following information for each fault:

- Time of fault
- Client or clients who were affected
- Duration: short-lived or continuous?
- Frequency: once, occasional, frequent, or constant?
- Context (booting up, logging on, running an application, printing, sending e-mail, etc.)
- Full text of any error messages
- Person reporting the fault: name and phone number

The most useful item in terms of resolving the problem is the context. When someone reports a problem, spend some time talking to them about it and find out exactly what they were doing when the error occurred. Ask as many questions as are necessary to define the problem in your terms, rather than theirs. Users unfamiliar with the system might report inaccurately—for instance, believing that they were logged on when they were not—and even experienced users might not think of mentioning some vital facts.

Discussing the problem at some length often sheds unexpected light on the problem. Facts that to users might seem completely irrelevant ("Well, everything was fine before that little cable broke...") can have significant bearing on the problem. In particular, ask users about recent changes in their hardware and software setup and whether or not they fiddled with any cables.

Verifying the Fault Report

One of the first decisions you must make when you receive a fault report is whether or not you trust its accuracy. This is where a good working relationship with your users is invaluable. If a user says that his workstation can see server X but not server Y, should you accept that as a fact?

The user's level of understanding of the network is obviously a factor. A naive user could mistakenly think that server X is accessible when in fact it is not, or she could be doing something wrong when she attempts to attach to server Y. If you know that the user is experienced with the procedures for attaching to servers, you might decide to accept that part of the fault report as being as factual as if you had observed it yourself.

A lot also depends on the particular user's understanding of the fault diagnosis process. Even a technically advanced user might neglect to provide information that would be useful to you in tracing the problem. A user who is familiar with the type of information you require and the way in which you use it is likely to provide most of the relevant information from the start: when the error happened, what they were doing at the time, the full text of any error message, and so on.

Users unfamiliar with your procedures, however, might provide incomplete information. Inexperienced users might not notice or understand some aspect of the problem. Experienced users might selectively omit details that they decide are not relevant to the problem at hand. In fact, inexperienced users are more likely to write down the full text of an error message that appears. More confident users are likely to interpret the message when they see it and then report their own interpretation of the message to you.

There is no hard-and-fast rule about the veracity of the fault report. Bear in mind that it could be inaccurate and, depending on your estimation of the user's understanding of the network and the fault diagnosis process, either verify each detail yourself or take it as fact. If you accept it as fact, however, make a mental note that the facts are unconfirmed and realize that you might need to backtrack to establish their accuracy at some later stage in the investigation.

Intermittent Problems

One of the more intractable problem types is the *intermittent fault*. A user might report that his connection to the server is dropped at arbitrary intervals or that he occasionally needs to boot up twice before establishing a connection. If the problem cannot be reproduced at will, debugging it is very difficult.

The most common cause of such errors is a loose connector or a faulty cable. If an intermittent error occurs on a particular machine, replace the network adapter, cable, and connector. Check the power supply for output quality. If the problem still occurs intermittently, you can adopt a few different approaches.

One approach is to pretend that the problem happens constantly rather than intermittently, and then try to imagine what sort of underlying cause it might have. This is little more than idle speculation. It can be useful if the problem proves intractable, in that it might prompt you to consider some factor which you have neglected up to that point; however, it is not much of a practical step toward solving the problem.

A more positive method is to review the configuration of all affected machines. There might be, for example, some old, unstable drivers that execute sometimes, along with newer, stable drivers that execute more often.

Another useful approach is to watch the user while she goes through her normal daily startup procedure. Sit with her while she powers on the computer, logs on, and starts her usual applications. The problem might arise when you are present, giving you a chance to do some on-the-spot investigation. Or you may notice some aspect of her work patterns that you were not perviously aware of, perhaps inspiring you to look at the fault from a new angle.

If you have no success with these methods, get the user to start logging the error so that you can see if any pattern emerges. There could be a correlation between the incidence of the error and some other event—perhaps it always occurs when the server is being backed up or when some extra demand is placed on the electrical power supply.

Finally, don't discount the possibility of inappropriate practices by the user. They might be logging off while in a DOS window under a networked Windows session, for example, or disconnecting and reconnecting cables at unsuitable times.

Tracking Specific Problems

Given a network, a fault report, and a proper methodology, it should now be possible to locate the underlying problem. You also need some data, insight, time, and occasionally a bit of good luck.

The remainder of this chapter is devoted to a series of instruction sets that offer some guidance on how to find the underlying cause of some common faults. This list cannot be comprehensive, given the endless variety of computer networks and the rate at which they change. However, it should serve as an adjunct to a sound problem-solving methodology by providing pointers for many real-life situations that commonly arise. Chapter 32, "Repairing Common Types of Problems," explains how to fix the most common problems.

The following pointers are divided into client and server sections, reflecting the usual starting points of fault reports. It is assumed that vague fault reports such as "I can't log on" have been clarified to the level of "I get an `Access Denied` error message from the server when I try to log on."

> **Note**
>
> Remember that you can enhance the initial fault report by asking additional questions until you are confident that all relevant details have been obtained. Then you can decide whether to verify the facts stated by the user.

Client Fault Reports

The majority of fault reports that are difficult to localize arise in the context of problems experienced by users of client workstations. There are a number of broad categories of fault:

- Remote booting workstation will not boot.

- Workstation does not load NETX or VLM.

- Workstation can see some but not all servers.

- Workstation can connect to server but the user can't log on.

The following sections discuss these broad categories in turn.

Remote Booting Workstation Will Not Boot. If a remote booting workstation will not boot, try booting the workstation from a copy of the master boot floppy. If it doesn't boot, make sure that the boot sector of the floppy disk is valid; if so, either the motherboard or floppy drive is faulty.

> **Note**
>
> Chapter 28, "Adding Diskless Workstations," contains detailed information on remote booting workstations.

If it boots from a copy of the master boot floppy, can it connect to a server? If not, treat the problem as if it's on a local booting workstation. Proceed to the "Workstation Can See Some but Not All Servers" section or later section as appropriate.

The remainder of this section applies only to remote booting workstations that will not remote boot but will connect to a server when booted from a copy of the master boot floppy.

Establish how far the workstation gets when remote booting. Do this by watching the monitor as the workstation attempts to remote boot.

For workstations using IPX boot PROMs, do the following should you receive an Error finding server message:

1. Check that at least one server is replying to GET NEAREST SERVER requests.

2. If so, watch the router tracking screen on the server (type **TRACK ON** at the console prompt) while the workstation boots.

3. Look for a GET NEAREST SERVER request from the faulty workstation's network address.

4. If you see it, the problem is at the server end.

5. If you don't see it, the GET NEAREST SERVER request might not be getting through to the server. Check that the server's network adapter is bound to the Ethernet 802.3 frame type. Also check that any bridges or routers between the workstation and the server are passing 802.3 packets.

6. Alternatively, the boot PROM might be faulty. Try replacing it with one that definitely works.

For workstations using RPL boot PROMs: If the workstation gets no response from an RPL server, the Find Frame Count (FFC) at the bottom of the screen, which looks like

RPL-ROM-FFC: 1

will be incremented by one every second or so.

If this happens, use the following procedure to identify the fault:

1. Check that RPL.NLM has been loaded on at least one server and that RPL has been bound on the server to an adapter using the 802.2 frame type.

2. If RPL.NLM has been bound using NODEFAULT, has the workstation's Ethernet address been entered in BOOTCONF.SYS? Has it been entered in the correct format?

3. Check that any bridges or routers between the workstation and the server are passing 802.2 packets.

Workstation Does Not Load NETX or VLM. Check the error message displayed by NETX or VLM when it refuses to load. If it complains about the MLID, IPIXODI, and the like not being loaded or about the DOS version, then the problem obviously is linked to client configuration.

If NETX or VLM pauses at load time, and then says it can't connect to a server, check that there is at least one server running with REPLY TO GET NEAREST SERVER turned on. If not, get a server running this way before you try connecting again.

Run the network adapter's diagnostic utility to confirm that the adapter can send and receive packets. If the adapter can send and receive packets, then the problem might be due to client misconfiguration (incorrect INT, PORT, and MEM settings or incorrect frame and protocol type definitions in NET.CFG) or routing/bridging problems on the network.

Use this procedure to distinguish between client configuration and network difficulties as the source of the fault:

1. Connect a laptop (one that works!) to the same connection point and see if it can connect to a server.

2. If so, the workstation's configuration is at fault.

3. Otherwise, IPX packets might be unable to get past a router between the workstation and the server.

If the adapter is unable to send and receive packets (using the adapter's diagnostic utility), then the problem might be due to a faulty adapter or faulty network connection.

A procedure similar to the preceding one should help establish whether the fault is related to the client's network adapter or to the network:

1. Connect a laptop (one that works!) to the same connection point and see if it can connect to a server.

2. If so, the workstation's network adapter is at fault.

3. Otherwise, the link from that connection point to the server is at fault.

Notice that a working laptop was used to decide between workstation configuration and network routing in the first case and to decide between the network adapter and the network link in the second case. Simply attaching a laptop right away to see if it worked would not have resolved the issue as clearly as the approach taken here.

Workstation Can See Some but Not All Servers. If the workstation can see at least one server, then the workstation's adapter and network connection can be assumed to work. If there are some servers that it cannot see, do the following:

1. Verify that the missing servers are actually running and that they can be accessed from other points on the network.

2. If the missing servers are running but cannot be accessed from any workstation, refer to the later "Server Fault Reports" section.

3. If the missing servers can be accessed from some points but not from others, check the frame types used by the servers and by those clients that cannot access the servers.

4. If they use different frame types, reconfigure the clients.

5. If the frame types match, the network is likely at fault. Check that packets from the problem workstations have a path to the server.

Workstation Can Connect to Server but the User Cannot Log On. If a workstation can connect to a server, but the user cannot log on, you need to first eliminate the most obvious possibility—improper logging on. Check that the user is attempting to log on to the correct server with the correct user ID and password. If the user can log on successfully from another workstation, then do the following:

1. Check the NCP packet signature level on the server.

2. If it is level 3, the server insists on signed packets. Check the packet signature level on the problem workstation.

3. If the workstation's signature level is 0, the server will refuse logons. Increase the level and try again.

4. If the workstation's signature level is the default value of 1 or higher, then check the version of LOGIN.EXE used by the workstation. It might be an old version of LOGIN.EXE that does not support packet signature.

Server Fault Reports

Fault reports starting at the server that are difficult to localize are less common with servers than with clients. It is generally apparent if, for example, the server has crashed! There are only two categories of fault here:

- Server is running but no workstations can access it
- Server is running but only some workstations can access it

It is sometimes desirable to take the network out of consideration when trying to identify the source of a fault affecting a server. In these circumstances, it is useful to connect a single workstation—perhaps a laptop—to a strand of thinnet and then connect the server to the other end. Remember to terminate both ends.

This takes the usual network out of the loop and makes the debugging process more straightforward. If the laptop can connect to the server using this setup, then the network is the likely cause of the problem; if it cannot connect, then the problem is with the server. This type of setup is referred to in the following sections as *single-strand setup*.

> **Note**
>
> It is important to use the usual network connector on the server's adapter. If the server has a thinnet connector but does not normally use it, then don't use it while testing! You need the test setup to accurately reflect the setup you are trying to debug, so instead use a thinnet transceiver attached to the server's usual network connector.

Server Is Running but No Workstations Can Access It. If you know the server is running but no workstations can access it, load MONITOR.NLM on the server (if it is not already loaded) and look at the network statistics.

If the incoming and outgoing packet counts are static, or if the outgoing packet count increases very slowly and the incoming packet count remains static, then the server is not communicating with the network. Try the following steps:

1. Check that IPX has been bound to the adapter. IPX should be listed under the network statistics for the adapter. If it is not, bind IPX to the adapter and try again.

2. Check the status LEDs on the server's network adapter. If they indicate an error or no link integrity, bring down the server and run the adapter's diagnostic utility.

3. If the adapter's diagnostic utility can send and receive packets on the network, then the problem is with the particular packets being sent by the server in NetWare mode. Use the single-strand setup previously described to determine whether the problem in this case is with the server configuration or the network.

4. If the adapter's diagnostic utility cannot send and receive packets on the network, then the problem is with either the adapter itself or the server's network connection. Try a different network adapter in the server to determine which is at fault.

> **Tip**
>
> When changing the adapter in an EISA server to determine whether the server's original adapter is faulty, use an ordinary ISA card. This is likely to be easier to find than a spare EISA card, and it will be quicker to set up since there is no EISA configuration procedure. The poorer performance of this card won't matter because the exercise is designed to give a simple yes or no answer.

If the incoming and outgoing packet counts are increasing, then the server is able to communicate with the network. Use the single-strand setup described above to confirm that the network is at fault.

Server Is Running but Only Some Workstations Can Access It. Check whether the workstations that cannot attach are able to attach to any other servers. If not, refer to the "Workstation Does Not Load NETX or VLM" section earlier in this chapter.

If the workstations are able to attach to another server, the problem lies in either the network or the frame types being used.

Check whether frame type mismatches are responsible by doing the following:

1. Check whether the workstations that cannot attach to the server are using the correct frame type. If not, correct the frame type and try again.

2. If the frame types match, the problem lies with the network configuration.

Summary

Depending on the conclusions that you reached during the troubleshooting process, the fault is by now localized to one or more clients, one or more servers, or the network infrastructure. You may, perhaps, have completely identified the problem along the way, in which case it is just about resolved.

It is more likely that a substantial amount of investigative work remains to be done at this stage. The time spent defining the problem as explained in this chapter will help you to avoid wasting precious time looking in the wrong places.

For further information, refer to chapter 32, "Repairing Common Types of Problems." This chapter describes how to resolve some of the many problems that you will have to contend with.

Chapter 32

Repairing Common Types of Problems

The increasing complexity of modern networks—and the growing diversity of network hardware and software—is reflected in the range of faults and glitches that today's network administrators must face. This chapter deals with some of the most common faults.

It would be impossible to cover the symptoms and fixes for all such problems here. For faults not explicitly dealt with in this chapter, the troubleshooting procedures outlined in the previous chapter—and, to a lesser extent, in this chapter—may be used to identify the approximate cause of any fault. You would do well at that stage to refer to the chapter dealing specifically with that element of the network.

This chapter describes typical symptoms and troubleshooting procedures for problems in the following broad classes:

- Server
- Links
- Workstation
- Applications

You may need to refer to other chapters when attempting to solve a specific problem. For example, chapter 31, "Locating the Problem: Server versus Workstation versus Links," deals with problem-solving methodologies. Information related to a particular hardware or software component can be found in the relevant chapter of this book.

Server Problems

Because of the central role file servers play in their networks, server faults can cause serious disruption to a large number of users. In small networks, a crashed server can mean no service at all—if the server is down, the network is of no use. As a result, server troubleshooting is generally more urgent than workstation troubleshooting.

Hassle from users and the need for haste can get in the way of a clear-minded, methodical approach to solving server problems. Therefore, unless the source of the problem is immediately obvious, the first step is to create some space for yourself. Get someone to act as a buffer between you and the users so that your investigation of the problem is not constantly interrupted by people asking when the server will be back up. Announce the problem to your users so that they are aware that you are working on it.

In some cases, it is impossible to down a server or even to experiment much with it to examine a noncritical fault. If you fail to diagnose the problem while the server is "live," schedule some downtime when you can tackle the problem, and announce the downtime to your users well in advance.

Troubleshooting

Debugging the server startup process can be a tricky business. Text messages might flash by on-screen too rapidly for you to read, or the server might load an NLM at startup that causes the server to hang immediately. The following tips explain how to control the startup process and how to watch what happens at each step.

ECHO ON. The server normally shows the output resulting from commands in a script file without showing the commands themselves. It can be useful to see the commands while debugging, so add the line

```
ECHO ON
```

at the start of the AUTOEXEC.NCF file on each server. Each command in AUTOEXEC.NCF is then echoed on-screen as it is executed, prefaced by a ">" sign, as in the following example:

```
>load tcpip
Loading module TCPIP.NLM
  TCP/IP  v1.00 (910219)
  Auto-loading module SNMP.NLM
  SNMP Agent  v1.00 (910208)
>load 3C503 DIX int=3 mem=c8000 port=300
Loading module 3C503.LAN
  Previously loaded module was used re-entrantly
>bind IP to 3C503 address=111.222.333.444
IP: Bound to board 2.  IP address 111.222.333.444, net mask FF.FF.0.0
IP LAN protocol bound to 3Com EtherLink II 3C503  v3.11 (910121)
```

This makes it easy for you to match messages on-screen with the commands that generated them.

CONLOG. The blur of text that whizzes past when the server starts is usually of little or no interest, as long as the server is working properly. When you are trying to track down a fault, however, you might want to examine each message in detail. This can be difficult, because there is no way to pause the screen (or SERVER.EXE) so that you can read messages before they scroll off.

CONLOG.NLM can help with this. This utility writes a copy of all text that appears on the console to a file on the server's NetWare partition: SYS:ETC/CONSOLE.LOG. To start logging console messages, just add the line

```
LOAD CONLOG
```

near the top of AUTOEXEC.NCF, immediately after the FILE SERVER NAME and IPX INTERNAL NET lines. If you try to start the log before these lines, SERVER.EXE has to prompt you for the file server name and IPX address before it can load CONLOG.

CONLOG starts a new CONSOLE.LOG file each time it loads, erasing the previous copy. This helps to keep the size of CONSOLE.LOG within reasonable limits; if CONLOG always appended data to the existing file, CONSOLE.LOG would grow rapidly. However, this start-from-scratch aspect can be a nuisance if the server crashes and you want to examine the log file since restarting the server overwrites the log file!

If you want to see CONSOLE.LOG after a server crash, you can manually restart the server without executing the AUTOEXEC.NCF file (see the discussion on the -NA option below) so that CONLOG is not loaded, and the file is not erased.

Alternatively, use a utility such as Pierre Blanco's NCL.NLM to automatically make a copy of the previous CONSOLE.LOG before loading CONLOG. Something like the following in the AUTOEXEC.NCF file should do it:

```
LOAD NCL
NNCOPY SYS:ETC/CONSOLE.LOG SYS:ETC/CONSOLE.OLD
LOAD CONLOG
```

You may want to add the line

```
UNLOAD CONLOG
```

at the end of AUTOEXEC.NCF, to stop logging at the end of the startup process. This is not necessary, but it helps to prevent the CONSOLE.LOG file from becoming too large.

CONLOG can also be useful when debugging problems that arise during normal operation. Leave it running to gather messages over a period of time when dealing with an intermittent fault or any fault that is not readily reproducible.

Tip

The file appears to be zero bytes in length to a user at a client workstation as long as CONLOG is running. That doesn't mean that the file is empty—it just means that the file has not been released by CONLOG.

The main limitation of CONLOG when trying to track down serious faults is that it may not always manage to write the message text to the file before the system crashes. Even if CONLOG does its job successfully, the crash may cause the SYS volume to dismount, preventing the output that CONLOG traps from being saved to the file.

CONLOG does attempt to write each message to the file as it appears on the console, however, without any intermediate buffering. This means that, in general, CONLOG catches enough information to be of great use in post-crash debugging.

Server Startup Options. SERVER.EXE has some optional command-line parameters that can be used to control how STARTUP.NCF and AUTOEXEC.NCF are treated at startup time. The following sections describe these parameters.

-NS. Use the -NS option to prevent the server from reading both STARTUP.NCF and AUTOEXEC.NCF. This is particularly useful when debugging faults that arise during the startup process. After starting the server in this way, you can manually enter the commands in the usual startup script one at a time, while watching for errors.

This also is a sensible approach to take when tracing other difficult faults, as it reduces the unknown quantities to a minimum.

-NA. The -NA option is somewhat similar to -NS. It prevents the server from reading AUTOEXEC.NCF, but the commands in STARTUP.NCF are executed. If STARTUP.NCF does no more than load a disk driver, as is often the case, then you may want to run it before you begin debugging. In this case, use SERVER -NA and not -NS to begin your debugging session.

> **Tip**
>
> Create a special, stripped-down AUTOEXEC script for debugging sessions, and save it on the server's DOS partition as, for example, MYDEBUG.NCF. It should contain no more than the bare minimum to get the server started:
>
> ```
> ECHO ON
> LOAD NCL
> NNCOPY SYS:ETC/CONSOLE.LOG SYS:ETC/CONSOLE.OLD
> LOAD CONLOG
> ```
>
> You then can use SERVER -NA to start the server without loading the usual AUTOEXEC.NCF; supply the file server name and number when prompted, and then enter **MYDEBUG** to get into fault finding mode.

-S (Alternate Script). Use the -S option to specify an alternate startup script file. The specified file is parsed instead of STARTUP.NCF. For example, consider the following line:

```
C:\NETWARE.312> server -s C:\UTIL\STARTDBG.NCF
```

This line tells SERVER.EXE to use C:\UTIL\STARTDBG.NCF instead of the usual STARTUP.NCF. The AUTOEXEC.NCF file is parsed in the usual way, unless you use the -NA option as well.

Either a DOS path or NetWare path may be specified. The full path must be given, including the DOS drive letter or NetWare volume name.

Disk Drives

The need to provide more and faster storage space on servers encourages the use of relatively new, complex, or innovative technologies. This can apply to the hard disks themselves, the disk controllers, or the type of bus slot used. File server disks are likely to be quite busy, as they are used by a number of people simultaneously; they also are likely to be in use for longer periods of sustained activity than a workstation hard disk. It is hardly surprising, then, that disk problems are relatively common on file servers.

The impact of disk problems can be quite severe. Aside from the obvious danger of losing precious data, the operation of the server as a whole may be affected. After all, the bindery/NDS database is stored on disk and so are the files that comprise the NOS itself. Corruption of these files can mean server faults of many kinds. Complete disk failure can mean total loss of service.

> **Caution**
>
> There is no substitute for proper backups. Data is sometimes irretrievably lost from disk; even if a disk fault is completely rectified, some damage may have been done that cannot be undone. If you're reading this while trying to solve a server disk problem, and you don't have adequate backups, it may be too late—you'd better hope that the fault did no damage.

Disk Troubleshooting. Start by determining the extent of the problem. You need to establish answers to the following questions:

- Is the fault really disk-related?
- Are all volumes on the disk affected or just some volumes?
- Is the problem with the disk or the controller?

There is little point in wasting precious time trying to resolve faults that don't exist; it's better to take a while getting an overview of the nature and extent of the fault before launching into a repair procedure. Determining the answers to the above questions can bring you a long way toward full identification of the fault and can save you a lot of time in wasted trial-and-error troubleshooting.

Is It a Disk-Related Fault? Many problems appear to be disk-related when their causes actually lie elsewhere. For example, an inability to write a file to a volume might be due to access rights or quotas or corruption of data might be caused by network errors.

Real evidence of a disk-related problem includes the following:

- One or more volumes dismounted
- `Drive deactivated` messages on the console
- VREPAIR reports errors

Checking the Volumes. The first thing to check is whether all volumes are mounted. If you know which volumes should be there, you can check this quite easily by entering the `volumes` command at the file server console. All mounted volumes are listed, along with the name spaces used by each:

```
Mounted Volumes          Name Spaces
   SYS                      DOS
   APP1                     DOS
   APP2                     DOS
   HOME                     DOS
```

This output is useful, but only if you know which volumes to expect. If you're not familiar with the server, then the only volume you can expect to see for certain is SYS; other than that, if you don't know what's supposed to be there, you can't tell what's missing.

Use MONITOR.NLM and INSTALL.NLM for a more thorough check. Load the NLMs on the server with the following command if they are not already loaded:

```
LOAD MONITOR
LOAD INSTALL
```

If you can't do so, there may be a problem with the SYS volume. In that case, load the NLMs from the server's DOS partition:

```
LOAD C:\NETWARE.312\MONITOR
LOAD C:\NETWARE.312\INSTALL
```

If you do not have a copy of the NLMs on the hard disk, or if the server's DOS partition is inaccessible for some reason, get copies on floppy disk and load them.

Now, check that all disks are physically functioning:

1. Choose Disk Information from the main menu of MONITOR. MONITOR lists each hard disk.

2. If any disk is missing, check that the driver for that disk's controller is loaded by using the `modules` command at the console prompt.

3. If the driver is not loaded, load it manually and check the disk again.

4. If the driver is loaded but the disk is not listed, suspect physical failure of the disk or its controller—refer to the "Disk or Controller?" section that follows.

5. Select the first disk in the list. MONITOR displays information about the disk.

6. Check that the Hot Fix Status field reads Normal. If it says Not Active, then it is likely that there are an unacceptably high number of bad blocks on the disk. Consider the disk faulty and replace it.

7. Look at the Redirection Blocks and Redirected Blocks fields. If the number of redirected blocks is more than 50% or so of the total number of available redirection blocks, then the disk is likely to fail in the near future. Even if the number of redirected blocks is small but rising, the disk is deteriorating and should be replaced.

If all disks appear to be responding, check the partition tables:

1. Choose Volume Options from the main menu of INSTALL.

2. Press Enter to view information for the first volume in the list.

3. Look at the Status field—it says either Mounted or Dismounted.

4. If the volume is dismounted, try mounting it by using the mount command at the console prompt, as in the following example:

   ```
   mount home2
   ```

   If the volume fails to mount, note the error message.

5. Repeat steps 2 through 4 for each volume in the list.

At the end of these checks, you should know which disks are responding and which volumes are available. Use this information to determine your next course of action:

- If one or more disks are not responding, see the "Disk or Controller?" section that follows.

- If all disks are responding, but one or more volumes cannot be mounted, see the "Using VREPAIR To Solve Volume Errors" section that follows.

Eliminating Simple Causes. A quick check of some of the more common causes of disk faults might save you a lot of time. If you suspect physical failure of the disk or controller, then check the following before launching into any elaborate, time-consuming, or expensive troubleshooting and repair procedures:

- The connecting cable between the controller and the drive should be securely connected at both ends. First, make sure that each connector is sound—not split and no pins missing or bent—then push it into place carefully but firmly.

- The connecting cable should not be stretched or pinched. If it seems tight, either rearrange it so that it has a shorter path to follow or replace it with a longer cable. Make sure the computer case does not pinch it when you reassemble the box.

- Check the cable orientation. Pin 1 on the controller should go to pin 1 on the drive. Most SCSI cables have a colored wire on one side to indicate pin 1.

- Check the connector orientation. Most connectors are shaped in such a way that they can be inserted only one way, but there are some that can be inserted backwards by accident.

- The bus slot connectors on some inferior motherboards are prone to slight oxidization. Over time, this can decrease the conductivity at the connection between adapter and slot connector to the extent that the adapter ceases to function. Removing the adapter board, cleaning the contacts, and reseating it can sometimes work wonders.

- Controller boards should be properly seated in their slots. Press each board firmly into place.

- Check that the power connectors for each drive are securely in place. If the controller requires a power source, make sure that it has one.

- If investigating a SCSI device, check that the SCSI chain is properly terminated; that is, make sure that the last device in the chain is terminated, and that no other device is terminated. Consult the documentation for each SCSI device for termination details—they vary considerably from one device to the next.

- Make sure that all SCSI devices have unique SCSI IDs. Don't forget that the controller also needs a unique SCSI ID! The IDs generally are set using DIP switches on the drive or controller, but refer to the documentation for each device for details.

- Check all relevant settings for the controller, paying particular attention to EISA or MCA configuration details. For example, some older SCSI drives do not identify themselves to the controller until they have completed "spinning up"—that is, until they have reached the necessary rotation rate. If the SCSI controller scans for devices at power-up time, it might not see such disks. (Typically, the disk is usable after a warm boot because it is already spinning at full speed but not after a cold boot.) In this case, the controller's EISA configuration must be told to wait for each device to spin up.

- Many inexplicable problems are due to buggy or inadequate drivers. You might have a new disk, for example, that uses some hot new technology, and this new technology might not be supported by the controller without a driver upgrade. It generally is a good idea to check for a more recent driver. Read any notes that come with the upgraded driver to see if any changes have been implemented since your current version that may be relevant to the problems you are experiencing. Even if the notes don't give you any clues, it still might be worth trying the new driver—quite often, one bug fix also cures a number of seemingly unrelated problems.

Obviously, some of these situations are not going to spontaneously occur on a working server; for example, SCSI cables cannot switch orientation by themselves. Many disk problems arise, however, pretty soon after other work has been carried out on the server—it is possible that a disk fault could have arisen due to oversight or an accident during some previous work.

Disk or Controller? It isn't always obvious whether a fault is due to a disk or a controller failure. If a controller services multiple disks, you might be able to infer something; if all the disks are affected, it's likely to be the fault of the controller. If just one of the disks is affected, it's more likely to be the fault of the disk than the controller. These conclusions aren't definite, though, and in many cases, there is just one disk per controller.

The situation is easiest to diagnose when the suspect disk is the home of the server's DOS partition. If the server boots successfully from this disk, then physical problems are unlikely; run a DOS-based disk-checking utility such as Norton's Disk Doctor or Microsoft's Scandisk for a quick check. There's no guarantee that the disk is trouble-free if such a utility fails to turn up any errors, but you can at least eliminate total physical failure from the list of possibilities. If the volumes on the NetWare partition of such a disk cannot be mounted, then refer to "Using VREPAIR To Solve Volume Errors" later in this chapter.

Quite often, the only way to determine whether the disk or controller is at fault is to *swap in* a working replacement. If you can read a different disk using the original controller or read the original disk using a different controller, then you know which to replace. But should you replace the controller or the disk?

You do not always have a choice. Many IDE disk controllers are built into the motherboard, in which case you need to find a working IDE disk with which to test the controller. You might have a spare disk on hand, but no spare controller; or you might have a spare controller, but no spare disk.

If a replacement controller is available, it makes sense to try that first. Installing it is not too big of a job—just insert it, load the driver, and configure the board. If the original controller was faulty, and the disk is not, the server should be up and running immediately with the new controller. You have, in effect, combined fault-tracing with repair work.

If you replace the disk instead of the controller, and find that the problem persists—implying that the controller is faulty—then you have to replace the controller, anyway. Of course, you might reach the conclusion that the disk is faulty in either case. If so, restoring service is a big job; the replacement disk might need to be formatted, and certainly does need to be partitioned. You then need to re-create the original volumes, and perform a full restore from tape.

> **Caution**
>
> When replacing a controller for diagnostic purposes, make sure that it can properly support any drives that are attached to it. Some older controllers cannot support drives larger than a gigabyte, for example. These may actually destroy data stored on a disk that is beyond their storage capacity.

If you decide that either the disk or the controller is physically faulty, replace it. There generally isn't anything you can do to repair physical faults in either case, and your priority must be to restore the server to production mode as quickly as possible.

Using VREPAIR To Solve Volume Errors. VREPAIR.NLM is designed to check the integrity of information on server disks at the volume, directory, and file levels. It cannot directly detect physical disk errors, but quite often you can make deductions about such problems based on error reports from VREPAIR.

Use VREPAIR to examine and fix problems on volumes that are visible under INSTALL.NLM (see "Checking the Volumes," earlier in this chapter) but that will not mount. If all volumes are mounted and you still suspect disk errors, dismount each volume in turn and run VREPAIR on it using the following steps:

1. If you haven't already done so, disable logins and get all users to log off the system. This helps to avoid confusion and possible loss of data by users while volumes are being dismounted and remounted.

2. If you haven't already done so, load VREPAIR. It's best to keep a copy on the server's DOS partition and load it from there—such a copy is always accessible, even when SYS is not:

   ```
   load c:\netware.312\vrepair
   ```

3. Choose Repair a Volume—if only one volume is dismounted, VREPAIR immediately starts to diagnose it.

4. If more than one volume is dismounted, VREPAIR offers you a choice of volumes to repair. Go through the list one at a time, running VREPAIR on each in turn.

5. If VREPAIR finds an error on a volume, it reports the error on-screen. Take note of the type of error—for example, directory entry mismatch. The file names don't matter in this context, although they might be of interest to a user whose data has possibly been lost.

6. Keep going until VREPAIR has completed its sweep of the volume. If there are very many errors, you can speed up the process by pressing F1 when an error report is on-screen and turning off the Report Errors to Screen option.

7. If VREPAIR found errors on the volume, run VREPAIR on the same volume again. Repeat as necessary until VREPAIR reports no errors for the volume. If the errors persist—if VREPAIR reports the same errors during subsequent sweeps, indicating that it could not repair them, or if the total number of errors refuses to fall over a number of sweeps—then there probably is a physical fault.

8. Repeat this process for any other volumes that might be having problems. In particular, if VREPAIR detects errors on one volume of a physical disk, use VREPAIR to scan all other volume segments on the same disk.

9. Mount any volumes that were dismounted, using the mount command, as follows:

   ```
   mount sys
   ```

   If the volume fails to mount, check the available cache buffers. If this value is less than approximately 40%, then it is possible that the server could refuse to mount a perfectly good volume.

10. Reenable logins when you are satisfied that the problem has been resolved.

Network Adapters

Network adapters are less likely to fail than hard disks, perhaps because they have no moving parts. They can and do fail physically, but this is relatively rare, and the majority of problems with server network adapters can be traced to software or configuration issues. When a network error is traced to a server, therefore, it is advisable to check the server's network configuration before examining the network hardware in detail.

> **Tip**
>
> Make sure that the server's SYS volume is mounted and functioning—if it is not, then the server will not respond, no matter how well the network adapter operates.

Traffic Statistics. Begin with a quick check of traffic statistics for the server's network adapter:

1. Load MONITOR if it is not already loaded.

2. Choose LAN Information from the main menu in MONITOR. MONITOR displays a list of the network drivers that are loaded. Drivers are listed once for each time they were loaded, so if the same driver has been used for two identical network adapters—or for two different frame types on the same adapter—it is listed twice. The traffic statistics for both instances are the same, however, so it doesn't matter which you choose.

3. Scroll down through the LAN Information screen to the General Statistics section. The Total Packets Sent and Total Packets Received values refer to all protocols used by the adapter, not just the protocol shown on this screen. For a properly functioning adapter on a typical network, both values should climb steadily, with increments every second or so. If this is the case, then you may assume that the adapter and its network connection are functional and that any problems you observe are due to frame or protocol misconfiguration.

4. Even on a network with no other traffic, the Total Packets Sent value should increase by one every couple of seconds as the server sends SAP packets to advertise its presence. (Realize that this might be spurious; the adapter has no way of telling how far any of its packets get after it sends them, so these packets might not really be transmitted.) If the Total Packets Sent value is static—or just increasing by a packet every second or two—and the Total Packets Received value is static, then you should treat the adapter as if it were passing no traffic at all.

5. Check the NO ECB Available Count value just below the traffic counts. This value reflects the number of times that a packet arrived at the server and the server had to allocate memory for an Event Control Block from its memory pool. This should never happen; if it does, the server is in need of tuning or the adapter driver is faulty.

Frame Type and Protocols. If the adapter appears to be handling at least some incoming and outgoing traffic, take a look at the protocols and frame types in use on the server. Use the `protocol` command at the server console:

```
protocol
The following protocols are registered:
    Protocol: IPX  Frame type: VIRTUAL_LAN    Protocol ID: 0
    Protocol: IPX  Frame type: ETHERNET_802.3 Protocol ID: 0
    Protocol: ARP  Frame type: ETHERNET_II    Protocol ID: 806
    Protocol: IP   Frame type: ETHERNET_II    Protocol ID: 800
    Protocol: IPX  Frame type: ETHERNET_II    Protocol ID: 8137
```

This lists all protocols the server knows about. It does not differentiate between different adapters or drivers or between different instances of the same driver. It is useful as a first step, however. If you don't see IPX loaded, for example, or if the server isn't using the frame type used by your workstations, then something obviously is amiss.

Use MONITOR.NLM for a closer look:

1. Choose LAN Information from the main menu in MONITOR. MONITOR displays a list of each instance of every network driver that is loaded. Unlike when you checked the traffic statistics using MONITOR earlier, it now matters which instance you choose—check each one in turn unless you know in advance which one is for the particular protocol you want to investigate.

2. Select the adapter driver instance that you want to inspect. MONITOR displays a screenful of statistics for the adapter.

3. Look for the Protocols heading near the top of this window. Any protocols bound to this instance of the adapter are listed there, along with information relevant to the particular protocol. If IPX is bound, for instance, then the network address used on the `bind IPX` line is displayed here. Remember that separate instances of the adapter are displayed separately by MONITOR—if you don't see a protocol that you expected, it may be because it's listed under a separate instance of the same adapter.

4. Check the other information for each listed protocol. In the case of IPX, the network cable address should be listed; in the case of IP, the server's IP address should be listed. Verify the details of what MONITOR displays here.

By now, you should be able to place the problem in one of the following categories:

- Adapter driver not loaded
- Adapter functioning for some protocols/frame types but not for all
- Adapter functioning, but server communications parameters need tuning
- Adapter sending and receiving no packets

If the problem falls into one of the first two categories, load the correct adapter driver with the correct frame type. Load the appropriate protocol stack, if necessary, and then bind it to the adapter.

Problems in the third category generally can be resolved by reviewing the server's communications parameters—for example, MIN PACKET RECEIVE BUFFERS—and adjusting them appropriately.

The remainder of the server network adapter coverage in this chapter deals with problems in the last category—where the adapter shows no life whatsoever or at most just an occasional outgoing packet.

No Adapter Throughput. Such symptoms can be caused by either a malfunctioning adapter or a faulty network connection. Chapter 31, "Locating the Problem: Server versus Workstation versus Links," describes how to distinguish between these two classes of fault; the description of a simple, single-strand thinwire network is particularly relevant in this case. Follow the instructions in that chapter to determine whether the adapter or its network connection is at fault.

If the adapter is still totally lifeless at this stage, check the following:

■ If the adapter came with a diagnostic utility, boot the server (or down and restart it, if it's up), and run the diagnostic software from the DOS prompt. If the adapter passes the diagnostics, recheck the network connection and the server's network configuration.

■ Is the adapter properly seated in its slot?

■ Try removing the adapter and reinserting it—the conductivity of the contact points might have been impaired by slight oxidization.

■ If the adapter has not been in regular use, check that you have loaded the latest available version of the adapter driver.

■ Is the adapter configured to use the correct connection/transceiver type? Some adapters have jumpers that must be changed to switch between different interfaces. Check the EISA/MCA configuration for the adapter, if relevant. Note that the language used may be confusing; a reference to a transceiver may apply to an on-board transceiver on the adapter, rather than to an external transceiver. Read the documentation carefully and check the settings.

■ If the server is an ISA bus machine, check for interrupt clashes. Is the IRQ used by the adapter already in use? Don't forget any printers that are attached to the server—what interrupts do their communications ports use?

After checking all of that, only the crudest of debugging methods remains: Replace the adapter with one that you know to be functional. Ideally, use an identical adapter model.

If the replacement adapter doesn't work either, then the server system probably is faulty. Double-check this by installing the original adapter in another computer and testing it. If it works in the second system, then the first system needs attention. Of course, if the original adapter doesn't work in either system, it is possible that both the adapter and motherboard in the original server are faulty, perhaps as a result of a power surge.

If the replacement adapter works in the original server, then the original adapter is either faulty or misconfigured. Check the configuration of the original adapter.

Links—Connectivity Problems

Communications problems are often much more difficult to identify than server faults. The server is relatively finite, with a small number of components located at a single point in space; the network usually is more amorphous, comprising many active and passive components and possibly extending over a number of buildings. It is particularly important, therefore, that a logical investigative procedure be adopted when checking out communications faults.

Overview of the Fault

Start by determining the extent and general nature of the problem. A report from a single user of an inability to connect using the network could have many causes; workstation misconfiguration, user error, a server down, or perhaps a genuine network fault. If you have not already done so, use the procedures outlined in chapter 31, "Locating the Problem: Server versus Workstation versus Links," to determine whether the fault is definitely network-related.

The next step is to try to identify the extent of the problem in terms of the network. The details of how you go about this, and the questions you need to answer, depend on your particular network configuration; for starters, at least, consider the following:

- How many workstations are affected—all, some, or only one?

- How many servers are affected—all, some, or only one?

- How many subnets are affected—all, some, or only one?

It should be possible to zero in on the affected part of the network using this type of logic, with a certain amount of testing along the way. Apart from attempting to establish connections between a workstation and server, you may want to test individual cable runs with a cable tester.

> **Tip**
>
> Discard any faulty cable sections, connectors, or terminators as soon as you discover them. If they are left lying around, they might be reused by mistake, and you could find yourself debugging the same problem a second time.

Structural Limitations

Network problems sometimes arise as a result of the expansion of the network. The maximum number of nodes, maximum cable length, and other parameters are defined in the standards for each type of network; breaching these limits can mean overloading the active equipment or expecting too much of a network adapter or cable run. The following sections contain guidelines for each subnetwork.

Thinwire Networks. The relevant limits for thinwire or coaxial cable networks are the following:

- The maximum number of nodes per segment is 30. This limit is the most likely to be breached in the normal course of events, as workstations often are added to an existing infrastructure without careful checking.

- When counting nodes for the preceding rule, terminators, transceivers, and repeaters each count as a single node. T-pieces and barrel connectors each count as two nodes.

- The maximum number of nodes per network is 1,024.

- The minimum distance between T-connectors is 0.5 meters. Shorter connections invite unacceptable levels of interference.

- The maximum permissible length of a cable trunk segment is 185 meters.

- At most, five cable segments may be used to form the trunk segment, of which only three can have network stations connected. The other two must be simple connecting lengths of cable with no stations attached.

- The maximum trunk cable length is 925 meters (185×5).

- Each segment may have at most 60 junctions.

- The maximum number of repeaters on the signal path from one node to the next is four.

- Terminators should have an impedance of 50 ohms to within plus or minus four percent. If in doubt, check with a multimeter.

- A terminator should be connected to each end of the trunk segment. One end must be grounded.

Thinwire cable is more prone to damage and poor connections than other types. This is, in part, because it is physically lighter than thickwire cable, yet less flexible than twisted pair. It also is the most likely to have incorrectly installed connectors.

As a matter of policy, use the smallest possible number of cable segments in any given run. This minimizes the amount of cable splicing and reduces the risk of a faulty connection. It's also important to avoid crimping the cable or bending it in such a way as to cause kinks, which can damage the insulation. Try to secure the cable to fixed points rather than letting it run loosely across the floor (where you might pinch it by, for example, moving furniture).

When performing diagnostic tests on a network adapter with a thinwire (BNC) connector, attach a T-piece to the adapter and connect a 50-ohm terminator to each end of the T-piece.

> **Tip**
>
> Individual thinwire cable segments may be tested using an ordinary digital multimeter. Terminate one end of the cable segment using a 50-ohm terminator and attach the multimeter to the other end. The resistance should be 50 ohms. Now shake the cable a bit, in particular jiggling the ends near any connectors. Watch for any sudden changes in the resistance displayed by the multimeter—these indicate a poor quality connection that might lead to intermittent faults.

Thickwire Networks. The relevant limitations for thickwire Ethernet networks are the following:

- The maximum number of nodes per segment is 100. A repeater counts as a single node. This limit is the most likely to be breached in the normal course of events, as workstations often are added to an existing infrastructure without careful checking.

- When counting nodes for the preceding rule, terminators, transceivers, and repeaters each count as a single node.

- The maximum permissible length of a cable trunk segment is 500 meters.

- At most, five cable segments may be used to form the trunk of the network, of which only three can have network stations connected. The other two must be simple connecting lengths of cable with no stations attached.

- The maximum trunk cable length is 2,500 meters (500×5).

- If the trunk segment is a combination of thickwire and thinwire and is of length *S* meters, then the maximum length of thinwire cable that may be used is

    1,640–(*S*÷3.28 meters)

- The minimum distance between transceivers is 2.5 meters. Shorter connections invite unacceptable levels of interference.

- Terminators should have an impedance of 50 ohms to within plus or minus four percent. If in doubt, check using a multimeter.

- A terminator should be connected to each end of the trunk segment. One end must be grounded.

Twisted-Pair Networks. The relevant limitations for twisted-pair networks are the following:

- The maximum cable length from the adapter to the concentrator is 100 meters, including patch cables.

- The maximum number of nodes per network is 1,024.

A twisted-pair adapter must be connected to a properly functioning concentrator before full diagnostics can be carried out.

Workstation Problems

Client workstations often are the least stable part of a network. This is partly because they are not dedicated network devices in the same way as file servers or active network equipment and also because these are the pieces of the network to which users have direct access.

Private, office desktop PCs are often prone to reconfiguration. The owner may decide to upgrade the operating system or hardware without consulting you or might try out some completely inappropriate network software. When the computer can no longer access the network, the problem suddenly becomes yours.

Public access computers, such as those used in student laboratories or shared facilities, fall victim to another set of problems. These machines often are in use for several straight hours per day, far more than the typical office or home computer. They also are used by a number of different people in the course of a typical day, making the machines much more prone to physical wear and tear, virus infection, or someone's burning need to delete all that messy operating system stuff to make room for a really neat game.

The volatility of the average network client can be multiplied by the total number of client machines to estimate the magnitude of this particular maintenance headache for the network administrator. Most networks have far more client workstations than the combined total of servers, routers, concentrators, and computer support staff.

All in all, client faults should be expected to form a significant portion of the problems arising on any network. The remainder of this chapter deals with the most common problems, and suggests some possible solutions.

Caution

You must establish at an early stage where your responsibility toward a user's workstation starts and ends. If you are responsible only for the user's network connection and not for the configuration of the machine for optimal performance, make this clear at the outset; if your responsibilities extend to network software optimization but not to application tuning, let the user know. This can help you avoid being sucked into support issues far beyond the call of duty. If it is completely up to you to configure the machine in all details—system and network software, applications, and hardware—then this is not an issue.

Troubleshooting Procedures

Start by trying to replicate the reported problem. Remember that, unlike server and network equipment fault reports, workstation faults are likely to be reported by users without the technical expertise to tell a network fault from a typographical error. Normal network behavior is sometimes viewed as aberrant by new users. Discuss the circumstances of the problem with the reporting user, and establish whether what he saw was actually a network-related fault.

Once you have satisfied yourself that there is a reproducible error or reasonable cause to suspect one, then you can begin to look for the underlying cause. How you go about this depends on the nature of the problem's symptoms.

Bootup Trouble. First, make sure that the workstation functions correctly as a stand-alone machine. At a minimum, this means that the machine should boot up normally without connecting to the network. The following guidelines should facilitate your ssessment:

- Boot the machine and start DOS or Windows as appropriate.

- If the machine does not boot properly, try booting it without network drivers; comment out all relevant lines in CONFIG.SYS, AUTOEXEC.BAT, and any batch files called by AUTOEXEC.BAT. (A quick way to achieve the same result is to re-name the CONFIG.SYS and AUTOEXEC.BAT files. Be careful with this, though; some hard disks need special drivers loaded from the CONFIG.SYS file. If you re-name CONFIG.SYS, the hard disk might become inaccessible.)

- If the machine still does not boot, try removing the network adapter and booting. There might be a hardware resource conflict between the adapter and some other component. If it boots without the adapter, then refer to chapter 6, "The Workstation Platform," for information on adapter configuration and the resolution of resource conflicts.

- If the computer does not boot with the network adapter removed and no network drivers loaded, then the problem is not network-specific and, therefore, is beyond the scope of this book.

Errors Loading Drivers. Watch out for error messages while the workstation loads the network drivers. These are relatively uncommon, but occasionally you might see an error message from IPXODI.COM or the adapter's MLID if the version of LSL installed on the workstation is particularly old.

Verify that LSL.COM, IPXODI.COM, and the MLID are all loading successfully. If not, check the NET.CFG file for possible errors. Make sure that the workstation is using the latest available version of LSL.COM and IPXODI.COM; try to update the adapter's MLID if possible.

The most common error that occurs at this stage is generated when the shell or redirector cannot attach to a server. The shell reports `A File Server could not be found`, but the redirector is more verbose:

```
A file server could not be found. Check the network
cabling and the server's status before continuing.
```

Both cases are dealt with in the following section.

Workstation Can't Connect to Server. Establishing the initial connection between the workstation and the server is often problematic. It is fairly easy to get to this point with an improper configuration or a faulty network adapter; the network drivers generally load without complaint. But that final step, where the workstation and server recognize each other, can't happen unless the adapter and its network connection are functioning, and the workstation's network configuration is at least mostly correct.

Start by checking whether the adapter is functioning properly. The base criteria for deciding this is checking whether the adapter can send and receive packets to and from the network:

- If there are any status or activity LEDs on the adapter, watch them to see if the adapter transmits any packets when the shell/redirector tries to load. If it does, then the adapter is likely to be physically sound and you should concentrate on configuration issues.

- If there are no LEDs, or if they show no activity, run the diagnostic utility that came with the adapter. If the adapter passes its internal tests and manages to transmit and receive on the network, you should suspect configuration problems.

- If the adapter fails to pass its internal tests, review the adapter configuration. Look in particular for resource conflicts. If the adapter cannot be made to pass its internal diagnostic tests, replace it.

- If the adapter passes all internal tests but fails to communicate on the network—remember, reports that the adapter is transmitting successfully sometimes turn out to be spurious—check that the network connection is valid. If you have a properly configured and working laptop computer with the same type of network connector, attach it to the network at the workstation's access point. If the laptop cannot transmit and receive on the network, then there is a network fault.

- If the laptop can send and receive packets from the workstation's access point, but the workstation cannot, and if you have eliminated all resource conflicts, then the adapter's transceiver is likely to be faulty. This may be either built into the adapter—in which case, the adapter should be replaced—or external, in which case the transceiver should be replaced.

If the adapter can transmit and receive packets on the network but still cannot connect to a server, then the problem is most likely due to misconfiguration of the workstation's network client software. There are a few other simple possibilities that must be eliminated first, though:

1. Has a preferred server been specified for the workstation's shell or requester? If not, and if no servers on the network are set to reply to GET NEAREST SERVER requests, the workstation will not get any response from a file server. Try loading the NetWare shell with the /ps=<server> option (if using NETX), or add a preferred server=<server> line to the NetWare DOS Requestor section of the workstation's NET.CFG file (if using VLM).

2. Is the server working? Check that you can attach to it from another workstation. If this is impossible, then refer to chapter 31, "Locating the Problem: Server versus Workstation versus Links," for broad troubleshooting instructions.

3. Does the server have the right protocol loaded? If so, is it bound to the correct adapter using the correct frame type? If in doubt, refer to the "Server Problems" section earlier in this chapter.

4. Are there any available connection slots on the file server? Examine the number of connections in use (shown on the main screen of MONITOR under the heading Connections in Use). If none are available, clear some connections and try again.

At this stage you have established that the adapter is functioning, the network connection is valid, and a working server with a free connection slot is available on the network. The only remaining reason why the workstation would be unable to connect is a mismatch of frame or protocol types.

Review the workstation's NET.CFG file:

■ Check that there is a LINK DRIVER section for this workstation's adapter. Check the adapter documentation to see if the name given on the LINK DRIVER line matches the internal name of the MLID—MLIDs occasionally are shipped with one name but programmed to look for their LINK DRIVER section using a different name. For example, an MLID named NP500 might have been renamed ODINP500 before being shipped. It still looks for a LINK DRIVER NP500 section, not LINK DRIVER ODINP500.

■ Check the hardware settings listed for this MLID in its LINK DRIVER section. They should match the physical configuration of the adapter.

■ Make sure that the protocol and frame type used by the server are defined in the adapter's LINK DRIVER section.

■ Check the protocol ID value for each protocol. Remember that this value varies with frame type; for example, IPX over Ethernet 802.3 has an ID of 0, while IPX over Ethernet II has a hexadecimal ID of 8137. Refer to the client configuration information in chapter 11, "Network Client Software," for more information on this aspect of client network configuration.

If any changes are made to the NET.CFG file, you need to unload IPXODI.COM and LSL.COM and then reload them before attempting to reconnect. Here's an example:

```
ne2000 /u
ipxodi /u
lsl /u
lsl
ipxodi
ne2000
vlm
```

Some MLIDs are a little buggy, so you might need to reboot the workstation after making such changes.

User Can't Log in to Server. With the basic connection established between server and workstation, most of the work is done. There still are some things that can go wrong, though. One of the more frustrating problems from a user's point of view is the inability to log in, in spite of being able to get to the server's login prompt. When you are faced with such a situation, proceed in the following manner:

■ Has the user connected to the correct server? Her workstation might specify a preferred server, but what if that server is down—is she inadvertently attempting to log in to the wrong server? Check this by getting her to specify the server name on the login command line, as in the following example:

```
login server1/jdean
```

■ Verify that the user is entering a valid user ID and password. See if he can log in from another, functioning workstation; alternatively, see if another user with a user ID and password that definitely work can log in from the problematic workstation.

■ Does the server require signed packets? If so, is the server configured to sign packets when requested to do so by the server? Look for a `Packet Signature Level` entry in the workstation's NET.CFG file, and refer to chapter 11, "Network Client Software," for information on client packet signing.

■ If packet signature is enabled on the client, and if the server accepts signed packets, does the workstation's client software support signing? Update an old version of the client software, and try again.

■ Similarly, check that the version of LOGIN.COM in the server's login area supports packet signature.

■ Finally, make sure that the user doesn't have any old copies of LOGIN.COM lying around on the workstation. The user inadvertently might be running a version that does not support packet signature.

Workstation Hanging. Intermittent hanging of the workstation is another frustrating problem. This almost always is caused by a memory or hardware interrupt configuration clash. Refer to chapters 6, "The Workstation Platform," and 11, "Network Client Software," for detailed information on the relevant configuration issues, and how to check for and resolve resource conflicts of this type.

The workstation's power supply is another possible cause of such glitches. A digital multimeter may be used for a simple check of the output voltage, but it won't necessarily catch periodic or occasional fluctuations. If you suspect the power source rather than the workstation's power supply, consider investing in a low-end UPS for the workstation. Refer to chapter 18, "Backup Technology: Uninterruptible Power Supplies," for details.

Windows Problems. Some workstation faults appear under Windows but not under DOS. These most often are due to configuration issues, in particular shared RAM.

If the workstation uses EMM386 for memory management, make sure that the adapter's shared RAM has been excluded using the X= option on the EMM386 load line in the workstation's CONFIG.SYS file. Check the EmmExclude= line in the Windows SYSTEM.INI file, too.

If these lines appear correct, check whether the adapter uses 16K or just 8K of shared RAM—some cards use as little as 2K. What matters is that EMM386 and Windows know which area to exclude, and that means specifying the precise memory range, not just the starting point.

Another common cause of Windows problems is having mismatched network driver files. NETWARE.DRV and its associated files should always be upgraded as a set; refer to chapters 11, "Network Client Software," and 12, "Network Client Software for 32-Bit Windows," for details.

Application Problems. Many problems that appear to be the fault of the workstation are in fact due to unusual behavior by application software. The application might attempt to write a temporary file to a location where the user does not have write access, for example. A well-written application informs the user what it has tried to do and what error has occurred, but many programs simply ignore such errors or even hang the workstation.

On investigation, you should be able to determine what the application was trying to do and where. Some applications write to the location specified by the TMP or TEMP environment variables. Others write to the current default directory, while some insist on trying to write to the directory where the application itself is stored. Be careful not to grant write access too liberally as a quick fix—refer to chapter 20, "Tools for Restricting Access," for advice on access restriction as related to application setup.

Some application-specific problems can be resolved by adjusting the client configuration. Many applications—Windows applications in particular—need to hold a large number of files open simultaneously. Increasing the FILES= setting in the workstation's CONFIG.SYS can solve problems in such cases.

Other applications are sensitive to the combination of the read only compatibility= setting in NET.CFG and the user's write access on the server. In such cases, refer to the documentation for the particular application that is causing difficulty—there is no single correct way to resolve these issues.

Summary

Tackling faults on a live network can be a stressful business. Make it easier on you and your users by announcing that you are aware of the problem and working on it. If possible, announce downtime in advance. This should give you the space required to tackle the problem in a cool, logical way. Take care when making preliminary assessments of the type of problem; a mistake at this stage can cost a lot of precious time. And once you locate the source of the problem, draw freely on all the information available—including the relevant chapters of this book—before launching into a solution.

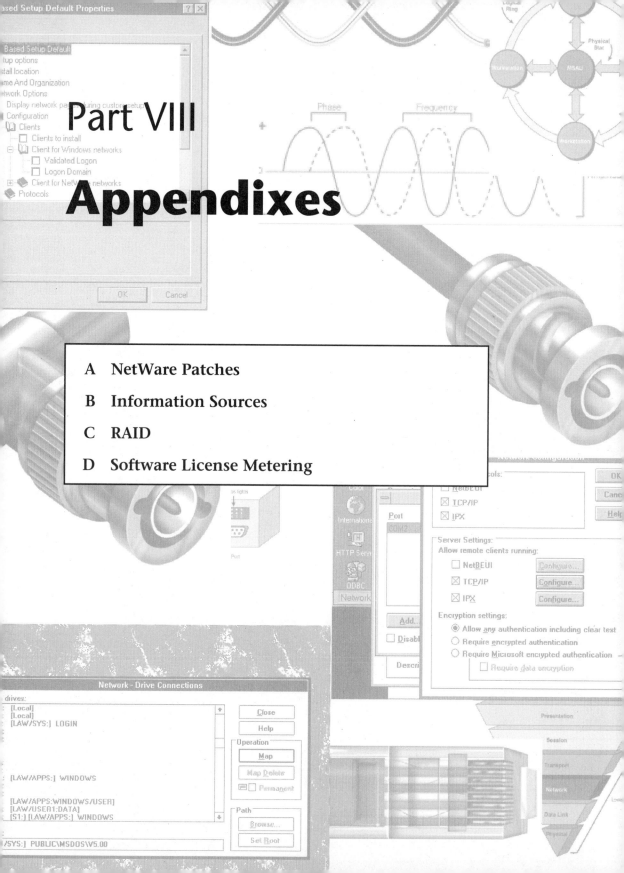

Part VIII

Appendixes

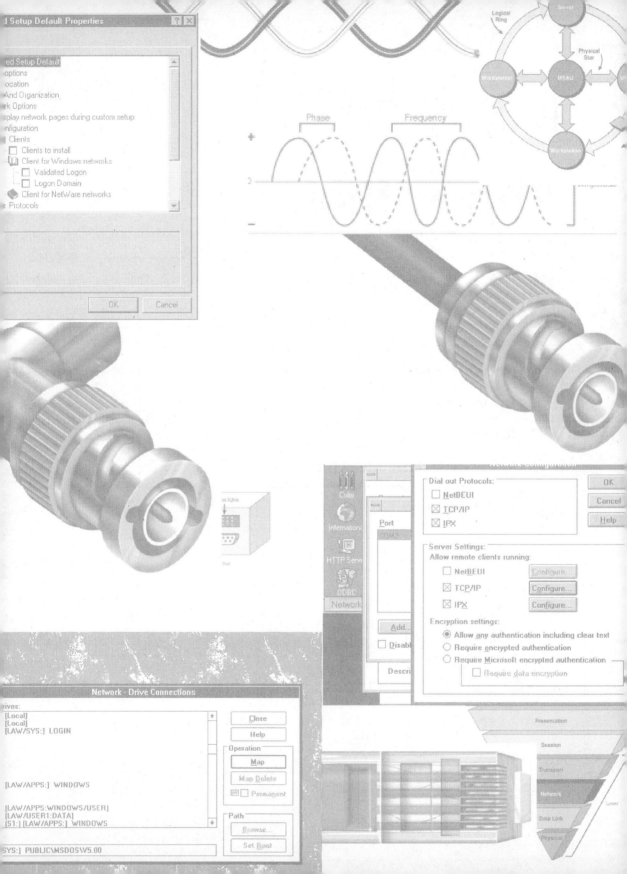

Appendix A

NetWare Patches

Novell periodically release patches and fixes for all its various products. Novell distinguishes between patches and updates; a *patch* is usually a small fix for a specific problem and works with an existing part of the NOS, while an *update* completely replaces one or more components of the NOS. There are different types of network operating system patches as well. *Static patches* are DOS executable programs that are applied once and modify the executable code of a module as it is stored on disk; the only way to "undo" such a patch is to restore a backup of the original file. A *semi-static patch* is loaded after the module it affects, modifying the memory image of the code, and then usually unloads. These patches can be undone by unloading the modified module from memory and reloading the original, which remains unmodified on disk. *Dynamic patches* are the most common for NetWare itself. These are small programs supplied as NetWare Loadable Modules (NLMs) that modify the executable code for a module in memory. The original version of the module can be restored simply by unloading the patch. The currently loaded dynamic patches can be listed with the server's MODULES command.

Being able to undo a patch once it is applied is important. All too often, a patch meant to solve one problem causes another, possibly more serious problem with a different function of the system. Many problems with patches can be avoided by thoroughly reading the documentation files that come with the patches. Unless you have experienced a particular problem addressed by a newly released patch, you may want to wait a week or two after the patch is released before using it. Sometimes, Novell withdraws or modifies a patch soon after it is released to address some problem not found in internal testing.

Table A.1 indicates the major current (as of February 12, 1996) patches available from Novell's NetWire libraries for its major OS and client products. By the time you read this, there may be many more. Not listed are patches for compatibility with rarely used hardware, documentation updates, and some utilities for installation, upgrade, and migration. Patch files with "!" after the name are strongly recommended for all sites running the applicable version of NetWare. Other patches should only be applied in certain circumstances. If in doubt, review the documentation files. Following the tables are some tips and suggestions for several of the various collections of patches.

Note

Type **GO NWOSFILES** on CompuServe to access the Novell operating system file libraries.

Novell seldom modifies the shipping versions of its NOS products. The NetWare 3.12 that you could buy when it was first released will probably be unchanged until NetWare 3.13 is released or the 3.x product line is dropped. The patch files, bug fixes, and interim updates periodically released on Novell's online services and through the NetWare Support Encyclopedia CD-ROM are the only way to keep your NetWare installation up to date. Unfortunately, Novell usually does not automatically notify registered customers that an update is available, even if it fixes a critical bug.

Table A.1   NetWare OS Patches and Updates

NetWare Operating System Patches and Updates	NW 2.2	NW 3.11	NWSFT 3.11	NW 3.12	NW 4.0x	NW 4.10
22DOS5.EXE 19,951 10-17-95 Lets 2.2 run with DOS 5.0 on server	X					
286DWN.EXE 61,891 8-21-95 Fixes some abends when downing server	X					
311PTD.EXE! * 132,224 9-1-95 OS patch collection		X	X			
312DU1.EXE! 188,415 8-21-95 Updates FCONSOLE.EXE and SESSION.EXE				X		
312PT6.EXE! * 74,614 9-25-95 OS patch collection				X		
401PT6.EXE! * 79,295 10-24-95 OS patch collection 4.01 only					X	
402PA1.EXE! 42,873 8-21-95 Provides PAUDIT.EXE 4.02 only					X	
402PT1.EXE! * 50,737 10-6-95 OS patch collection 4.02 only					X	
410PT3.EXE! * 376,602 2/5/96 OS patch collection						X
41NDS5.EXE 720,873 2/1/96 NW 4.10 DS.NLM 4.89c						X
41RTR1.EXE! 853,424 8-21-95 OS Protocol Update						X

NetWare Operating System Patches and Updates	NW 2.2	NW 3.11	NWSFT 3.11	NW 3.12	NW 4.0x	NW 4.10
41NWAD.EXE 1552513 8-21-95 4.10.2 of NWADMIN						X
4X241.EXE 466,968 3-20-95 DS REPAIR needed to upgrade from 4.0x to 4.1					X	
BNDFX3.EXE! 54,221 8-21-95 Updates BINDFIX.EXE		X				
CDROM3.EXE! 117,609 11-27-95 Updates CDROM.NLM				X	X	
CDUP2.EXE 135011 11/27/95 Updates CDROM.NLM; provides IDE CD-ROM support for NW 4.1 & 3.12				X		X
CHK375.EXE! 30,799 10-24-95 Updates CHKDIR.EXE		X				
CONLOG.EXE 27,438 8-21-95 Provides CONLOG.NLM		X				
DFS108.EXE 27,018 10-11-95 Updates DIRECTFS.NLM		X	X	X		
DRV2X.EXE! 259,966 8-21-95 Updates LAN Drivers	X					
DS310.EXE! 242,836 10-6-95 Updates Directory Services					X	
DNSENH.EXE 713,313 11-27-95 Contains DS.NLM 4.89 - addresses all known issues						X
DSMNT2.EXE 82819 11-7-95 updated version of DSMAINT.NLM (version 4.90)					X	X
DSREPS.EXE! 74,020 8-21-95 Updates DSREPAIR.NLM					X	

(continues)

Table A.1 Continued

NetWare Operating System Patches and Updates	NW 2.2	NW 3.11	NWSFT 3.11	NW 3.12	NW 4.0x	NW 4.10
DSVIEW.EXE 33,596 8-21-95 Provides DSVIEW.NLM					X	
EXTRTR.EXE 411,640 10-11-95 Provides External Router software				X	X	X
FIL376.EXE! 158,446 10-12-95 Updates FILER.EXE		X		X		
FLGDIR.EXE! 38,027 8-21-95 Updates FLAGDIR.EXE	X	X				
IDE.EXE 36,043 11-29-95 Updates IDE.DSK		X		X	X	
IDE286.EXE 24,552 8-21-95 Updates IDE Driver	X					
IDE386.EXE 27300 8-21-95 IDE disk driver		X				
INTCFG.EXE! 81,892 8-21-95 Updates INETCFG.NLM 4.01 only					X	
INTRUD.EXE 35,521 8-21-95 Fixes Intruder Detection	X					
IPXRT3.EXE 1,207,210 11-27-95 IPX Upgrade for NetWare servers, enhanced enterprise connectivity with NLSP routing		X		X	X	
ISA311.EXE 31,546 8-21-95 Updates ISADISK.DSK		X				
ISAREM.EXE 24,391 8-21-95 Updates ISADISK Driver	X					

NetWare Operating System Patches and Updates	NW 2.2	NW 3.11	NWSFT 3.11	NW 3.12	NW 4.0x	NW 4.10
LANDR4.EXE! * 238,838 11-10-95 Server LAN Drivers for NExxx.* boards, plus TOKEN, TRXNET, and PCN2L		X	X	X	X	X
LG4084.EXE! 180,540 8-21-95 Updates LOGIN.EXE 4.01 only					X	
LIBUP6.EXE! * 578,389 1/18/96 Updates Server Library NLMs		X	X	X	X	X
LOG376.EXE! 74,768 11-29-95 Updates LOGIN.EXE				X		
LOG412.EXE! 168,063 10-9-95 Updates LOGIN.EXE						X
MAP312.EXE! 48,964 11-15-95 Updates MAP.EXE		X		X		
MAP412.EXE 144,680 9/28/95 Updates MAP.EXE					X	
MENU34.EXE! 87,520 8-21-95 Updates MENU.EXE	X	X				
MKUSER.EXE! 96,673 8-21-95 Updates MAKEUSER. EXE	X	X				
MON176.EXE! 68,504 11-27-95 Updates MONITOR.NLM		X				
MONSFT.EXE! 66,024 5-18-95 Updates MONITOR.NLM			X			
NDR345.EXE! 59,495 8-21-95 Updates NDIR.EXE	X	X				
NDR425.EXE! 173,243 5-4-95 Updates NDIR.EXE					X	X
NDSPX.EXE 41,652 8-21-95 Allows more than 15 SPX sessions	X					

(continues)

Table A.1 Continued						
NetWare Operating System Patches and Updates	**NW 2.2**	**NW 3.11**	**NWSFT 3.11**	**NW 3.12**	**NW 4.0x**	**NW 4.10**
NDSTAC.EXE 20,023 8-21-95 Prevents abends on non-ded. server due to hardware int.	X					
NFOLI.EXE 284,117 11-9-95 Updates NFOLIO.COM	X	X				
NOVADF.EXE 24,900 8-21-95 ADF files to install Novell cards in PS/2 computers	X	X				
NWPSLB.EXE 80,771 5-18-95 Updates PSERVLIB.NLM				X		
PAT311.EXE 29863 8-21-95 patch FOR CLIB v3.11		X				
PATMAN.EXE 30322 8-21-95 contains PATCHMAN.NLM	X	X				
PBURST.EXE 63,237 11-27-95		X		X	X	
P2SCSI.EXE 33,893 5-12-95 Updates PS2SCSI.DSK					X	X
PS3X02.EXE! 162,367 10-17-95 Updates Print Server	X	X		X		
PS4X03.EXE 85,566 1/29/96 Updates Print Server					X	X
PU3X01.EXE! 453,054 10-31-95 Updates Print util.	X	X		X		
PU4X03.EXE! 553,603 11-14-95 Updates Print util.					X	X
RCONSL.EXE! 68,819 11-27-95 Updates RCONSOLE.EXE		X		X		

NetWare Operating System Patches and Updates	NW 2.2	NW 3.11	NWSFT 3.11	NW 3.12	NW 4.0x	NW 4.10
RENDR.EXE! 29,797 8-21-95 Updates RENDIR.EXE	X	X				
RPLKT2.EXE 140,471 4-10-95 Updates RPL files	X	X		X	X	X
SBACK3.EXE 281,386 11-30-95 Updates SBACKUP.NLM		X		X	X	X
SECDOC.EXE! 29,661 8-21-95 SECDOS.EXE! 310,609 8-21-95 SECNNS.EXE! 632,669 8-21-95 SECPRN.EXE! 449,590 8-21-95 SECSYS.EXE! 322,007 8-21-95 SECUT1.EXE! 510,733 8-21-95 SECUT2.EXE! 556,873 8-21-95 SECUT3.EXE! 431,691 8-21-95 Security updates for 3.11.	X	X				
SECLOG.EXE! 167,904 8-21-95 Updates LOGIN.EXE 4.02 only					X	
SFTUTL.EXE! 67,817 8-21-95 Updates for SFT-III			X			
SMSUP4.EXE 567,727 11-30-95 Updates server backup drivers		X	X	X	X	X
SPXSTR.EXE 73,117 12/22/95 Updates Streams and SPXS.NLM						X
SROUT2.EXE 37,293 10-11-95 Updates Source Routing	X	X		X	X	
SRTFX.EXE 22,555 8-21-95 Updates Source Routing		X		X	X	

(continues)

Table A.1 Continued						
NetWare Operating System Patches and Updates	**NW 2.2**	**NW 3.11**	**NWSFT 3.11**	**NW 3.12**	**NW 4.0x**	**NW 4.10**
STRTL4.EXE! * 177,911 1/12/96 Fixes and patches for all SPX, TLI, and STREAMS communication and server problems		X	X	X	X	
SYS368.EXE! (also in UPD311) 159,178 8-21-95 Updates SYSCON.EXE	X	X				
SYS376.EXE! 161,608 11-20-95 Updates SYSCON.EXE				X		
TIM286.EXE 33,888 8-21-95 Keeps accurate time	X					
TLIWS3.EXE 382,513 1/8/96 contains TLI 4.x files and fixes.					X	X
TSAOS2.EXE 23,024 10-24-95 Updates TSA_OS2.NLM				X	X	
UDF355.EXE! 103,354 8-21-95 Updates USERDEF.EXE	X	X				
UIM413.EXE! 187,812 8-21-95 Updates UIMPORT.EXE					X	
UPD311.EXE! * 509,794 10-17-95 Containd several important updates of 3.11 utilities.		X				
VRP31X.EXE! (also in UPD311 and 311PTD) 60,269 8-21-95 Updates VREPAIR.NLM		X				
VRPUP1.EXE 192945 11/27/95 Updated VREPAIR.NLM (except 4.10)		X	X	X	X	

NetWare Operating System Patches and Updates	NW 2.2	NW 3.11	NWSFT 3.11	NW 3.12	NW 4.0x	NW 4.10
XLD386.EXE! 49,801 8-21-95 Updates SERVER.EXE		X				

* See notes later in this appendix on 311PTD.EXE, 312PT6.EXE, 401PT6.EXE, 402PT1.EXE, 410PT3.EXE, LIBUP6.EXE, STRTL4.EXE, and UPD311.EXE.

311PTD.EXE is the fourteenth and last in a series of patch sets released for 3.11. It contains a total of 50 patches, mostly dynamic in the form of small NLMs. All the patches can be used with the 5–250 user-level versions of 3.11, but some cannot be used with either the 1 or 1,000 user versions. Many of the patches are clearly identified in the documentation as only needing to be used if there are Macintosh, OS/2, or UNIX clients or with certain types of hardware; these should not be loaded on 3.11 servers that don't meet these criteria. Novell's advice on the rest of the patches varies. At times in the past, it has recommended loading only those patches which address specific problems that you have encountered with your servers. More recent documents suggest loading all the patches in the PT-series patch collections, particularly before calling Novell technical support! In addition, UPD311.EXE is a special collection of updates that should be used on all 3.11 servers.

The order in which these patches are loaded is very important in some cases. Some can only be loaded in the STARTUP.NCF (and need to be located on the server's DOS partition) and some need to be loaded near the beginning of the AUTOEXEC.NCF. If it is not specified, I suggest loading the patches at the end of the AUTOEXEC.NCF. There are special instructions for some of the patches, including procedures that must be done before a few of the patches are loaded for the first time.

Similarly, 312PT6.EXE is sixth in a series of patch sets released for 3.12. It contains about 25 patches, all of which can be used with any user-level version of 3.12. Again, read the documentation carefully before applying these patches. New with 312PT6.EXE are some different instructions for loading the patches. Novell has divided the patches in the archive between those that need to be loaded in STARTUP.NCF and those in AUTOEXEC.NCF. In addition, Novell has included NCF files giving examples of the order the patches should be loaded in. The example AUTO.NCF can be used as is; all that is needed is a reference to the NCF file in the AUTOEXEC.NCF. NetWare can call nested NCFs simply by naming them. When the called NCF is done executing, control returns to the calling NCF at the correct point. Calling external NCFs is not supported from STARTUP.NCF, however. The commands to load these patches will have to be included in the actual STARTUP.NCF.

401PT6.EXE and 402PT1.EXE are similar collections for NetWare 4.01 and 4.02. Rather than spend a lot of time patching NetWare versions 4.0, 4.01, or 4.02, it is better to upgrade to NetWare 4.10, which includes all the fixes released for previous versions of 4.0x and provides many new features. Patches for the 4.10 OS are included in 410PT3.EXE.

LIBUP6.EXE is a collection of updated library files for several versions of NetWare. These libraries contain functions and code used by many different NLMs. LIBUP6.EXE has a special installation program that will copy the appropriate updates to all servers you are attached to, making a backup of the old files at the same time. STRTL4.EXE also contains updates for several versions of NetWare but does not include a nice installation utility like LIBUP6.EXE, so the files have to be manually copied to all servers. For the LIBUP6 or STRTL4 updates to take effect, the server has to be downed and restarted.

Appendix B

Information Sources

If there is one inviolable law of computer networking that has been repeatedly mentioned in this book, it is the law of mutability. Nothing is more certain in this business than the fact that networking technology is continuously advancing, and it is crucial for a network administrator to keep current with the latest developments.

Of course, the problem is usually that there is no shortage of information to be had, and few network support personnel have time to read half of the material that comes their way. To be familiar with the resources at your disposal is important, however, so that when information is needed, whether for making a purchasing decision or resolving a technical support problem, it can be located quickly and easily.

Many parts of this book have tried to help the LAN administrator to make purchasing decisions by telling them what features to look for in a particular product or what class of product they should most profitably investigate. Locating that information is left up to them, however, and getting beyond the marketing hype for a product and find the really useful information can often be difficult.

Technical support has also become more of a "do-it-yourself" activity than it has ever been. Free live technical support is largely a thing of the past. It is a great financial drain on a manufacturer and is subject to the repeated abuse of customers unwilling to read the fine manual. As a result, many companies have begun to make a great deal of technical support information available to the user, often free for the taking, to make him the first line of support. Before spending money on a technical support call, exploring the alternative support avenues that a product manufacturer may supply is a good idea.

This appendix lists some of the different informational resources available to the networking professional and outlines the various media used by technology companies to disseminate information to their users. Familiarity with these media can often free the network manager from the need to engage high-priced consultants or run up technical support fees as well as minimize his exposure to the high-pressure salespeople that can often be a source of incomplete or incorrect product information.

Print Media

Of course, the most traditional medium for networking information is print. In its many forms, the print media provide pre-sales and technical information in enormous quantity. Placing a single phone call to a vendor or manufacturer of networking products can result in a flood of printed material, if desired. Much of this material can be highly subjective and misleading, however. Care in selecting the right documents and in assigning the right priorities in reading them is paramount here.

You are aware, if you are reading this, that the book publishing industry provides a wealth of information on computers. However, the number of titles devoted to networking is far smaller than those aimed at the home computer user. The most important factor to consider when considering books as information sources is the date of publication. Unfortunately, the bargain book bin is rarely a source of current information. A book published even a year ago may be concerned with software versions that have been superseded or hardware that is no longer in production. Many of the more successful titles are revised regularly, however, to keep them up to date. Call a publisher to find out when a revision is expected to avoid buying a book that is replaced soon afterwards.

Of course, the books that you are most likely to own are frequently those that you are least likely to read. I'm speaking of the product manuals that accompany virtually all networking hardware and software products. Naturally, the quality (and quantity) of the documentation furnished with computing products can vary widely. I've encountered many manuals that are unintentionally hilarious because of inept language translation. On the other hand, a great many computer books are also sold that are little more than rehashed versions of product manuals. Familiarity with the materials that you already possess can save time and expense in the future. Another element that must be included as part of any product's documentation are the README files that are often included on the floppy disks or CD-ROMs of software products. These provide the manufacturer's most recent information, which could not be included in the printed manuals.

Quite possibly the most consistently up-to-date and informative material available to the network administrator comes in the form of the many magazines and newspapers devoted to computing. My advice to anyone seeking an introduction to personal computing is always to begin by reading the monthly magazines—that is, the glossy newsstand magazines aimed at the individual PC user, such as *PC Magazine* or *PC World*. Reading publications like these from cover to cover are an excellent way to begin a computing education. You are bound to pick up facts that may not be pertinent to you now but that could well become valuable later.

For the more experienced networking professional, however, these magazines quickly become elementary. Of greater use are the weekly tabloid newspapers that are aimed more at the corporate network administrator, such as *InfoWorld*, *PCWeek*, and *LAN Times*. These are limited circulation publications that are distributed free to qualified networking professionals, usually upon completion of periodic questionnaires regarding the reader's participation in his company's purchasing practices. All of the revenue from these publications is derived from their advertisers, on the assumption that they will be reaching a more focused audience than a commercial magazine would. Since most are weeklies, the information presented is more recent, and the emphasis is more on business computing, both in editorial and advertising content.

While the networking content in monthly magazines such as *PC World* and *PC Magazine* is usually rather slim, the problem with the trade weeklies is often the opposite. It's easy to find yourself with five or six of these papers on your desk each week, and not many LAN administrators have the luxury of doing this much reading during business hours. To keep abreast of the latest technological developments, though, it is a good idea to at least scan a few of these papers on a regular basis. Having the subscriptions delivered to your home instead of to the office can sometimes be a good way of making the time for reading. For successful network administrators, work is seldom limited to nine to five.

CD-ROM Resources

While the print media are good for late-breaking news and fairly objective product information, technical support and reference materials are more readily available today on mass storage media such as CD-ROM. The primary advantage of a CD-ROM is the huge amount of data packaged into a small space and the ability to search for the information required, usually by a variety of criteria.

Because they are inexpensive to produce, CD-ROMs can be updated frequently. Many of the major technical reference products must be purchased on a subscription basis, either quarterly or monthly. Usually the amount of new information on the disk with each successive revision is relatively small, sometimes five percent or less, but you are assured of having the latest data available.

The *Novell Support Encyclopedia* (or NSEPRO) is probably the most well-known networking support CD-ROM. Produced monthly, this product (which has recently expanded to a two-disc format), contains a huge amount of material, including the full text of the *Novell Application Notes* publication going back several years, complete product documentation, all of the currently available software patches and updates, demonstration versions of Novell software, and an enormous amount of technical support material going back many years.

NSEPRO is designed as a mass compendium of virtually all of the technical material produced by Novell. Some of it is well-edited for publication, while other parts seem rather unprocessed. A good deal of it also ranges back several years and is, therefore, of limited value to most users. The text retrieval engine is based on Folio Corporation's Bound VIEWS product, which provides excellent text searching and indexing capabilities using a well-designed GUI interface. The disc ships with readers for the Windows, DOS, and Macintosh platforms. For people supporting a large number of Novell product installations, NSEPRO is an invaluable resource.

In roughly the same type of format, Microsoft publishes a monthly CD-ROM set called TechNet, which contains a similar array of information to NSEPRO. Of particular value are the resource kits for all of the Windows products, as well as all available software updates, most of which are packaged in what Microsoft calls Service Packs. Unlike Novell, which tends towards large numbers of small patch releases, these Service Packs usually contain a large number of code changes and can be very large in size. Having them on CD-ROM eliminates the need to perform multi-megabyte downloads from online services whenever a Microsoft OS software is upgraded.

Many other manufacturers of networking and computing products also release technical CD-ROMs, including Intel, Banyan, Sun, Cheyenne, and others. Prices vary widely, from free handouts to expensive subscriptions, and so does the usefulness of the products. I've seen CD-ROMs that are little more than a company's technical support call tracking database dumped onto disk, unedited and unfiltered. Others tend to concern themselves more with selling products than supporting them.

The other general category of technical CD-ROM is that produced by a more impartial body, allowing the content of various manufacturers to be included. One of the best examples of this type is the Support-on-Site CD-ROM, produced by Ziff-Davis. Available quarterly in editions devoted to either networking or stand-alone PC products, Support-on-Site contains book excepts and magazine compendiums, as well as technical material of various types provided by manufacturers themselves. The front end and search engine are of proprietary design and are simple to use and quite powerful. In covering a much wider range of products, a certain amount of depth is obviously sacrificed, but Support-on-Site is an excellent general technical support resource for network support personnel of any level of expertise.

CD-ROMs are rapidly becoming the simplest and most inexpensive method for companies to publish both documentary and binary materials. A great deal of technical material is free for the asking with demo CD-ROMs having all but replaced the floppy-based demonstration programs of the past. The only drawback to the CD-ROM is that you can't reuse them as you could with floppies.

Online Services

The popularity of online services of all types has exploded in recent years, with millions of home and business users accessing information of all types. Users like the 24-hour access and particularly the ability to download document files and software whenever they are needed. Online services is a catchall phrase for many different types of technologies, with varying capabilities.

Fax-On-Demand

Although a computer is not directly used to access its resources, the fax-on-demand system can be considered to be an online service like any other. Fax-on-demand takes the form of an interactive voice response system in which a user dials a phone number and responds to prerecorded inquiries regarding the information that she would like to obtain. Typically, a table of contents is available on the first call, and individual documents selected from this can be requested during later calls. The user is prompted to enter the phone number of his fax machine, and usually within a few minutes, the documents are automatically faxed to that number.

Obviously, the greatest advantage of this system is that a computer is not needed nor is there any cost beyond a phone call and some fax paper. For these reasons, fax-on-demand systems exist for many types of products aside from computers and networking. Virtually every hardware and software manufacturing company has such a system, and the document libraries of the larger corporations can contain thousands of documents.

Bulletin Board Systems

The oldest dialup computer service still in use today is the Bulletin Board Service (BBS). These are private networks of computers and modems that users can call into with a standard communications package. BBSs are usually of two types, company resources that specialize in software downloads or technical support for the company's products, or private affairs that often cater to the special interests of certain groups of computer users. Many commercial BBSs exist that, for a subscription fee, provide numerous types of technical and entertainment services.

Again, most manufacturers of computer products have a BBS. The primary limitation of most of them is that the screen display is limited to ASCII only. There are usually no elaborate graphical displays involved. The primary advantage is low cost. Company BBSs almost never carry a charge, and their services can be had for the price of a phone call (although this may often be a long-distance toll call).

CompuServe

The oldest of the subscription-based dialup services, CompuServe is a venerable institution that boasts some 15 million members worldwide. Its resources are vast, and information on almost any subject can be had, usually from experts in the field. For computers and networking, the most valuable areas are the forums. These are individual messaging and download areas maintained by individual companies or user groups.

Many companies have technical support employees dedicated to answering user questions online, but on CompuServe, even those that don't can be very helpful. Due to the huge user base and high traffic, technical questions are nearly always answered by someone, usually with a surprisingly high quality response. Often the reason for this is that the true computing professionals are more likely to use CompuServe than any other service. Sometimes you can even find yourself asking questions about a product of the person who designed it.

CompuServe also has an enormous library of files available for downloading, as well as other services that will let you do everything from booking airline flight reservations to stock trading. Traditionally, the downside to CompuServe has been its relatively high cost, but increased competition in the world of online services has seen the hourly rate for CompuServe use drop from approximately $20 per hour five years ago to $2.95 per hour today. There are also subscription packages that provide unlimited access to some services for a flat monthly fee.

NetWire

CompuServe is also notable for being the host of NetWire, the original online resource for Novell products. NetWire is accessible through a separate subscription arrangement or is included as part of a standard CompuServe subscription package. As on most CompuServe areas, NetWire offers all of the latest Novell patch files, as well as product and technical support information. It is also the best source of inexpensive NetWare support available. The sysops of the various Novell forums are not Novell employees, but they are generally a highly knowledgeable group of experienced users, and the help they provide can be invaluable.

Other Subscription Services

Quite a few other subscription-based online services are available, with more being created all of the time. Many of these are geared primarily to the home or entertainment audience and offer little in the way of real technical information. Others cater to more specialized audiences, like investors and business-people, and are likewise less valuable to the average networker. Many of the newer services, like The Microsoft Network, are only just getting off of the ground. Time is often a major factor in building a good online service. You don't assemble a great library in a matter of months. Before the technical content of any of the newer services can rival that of the old guard, years of collecting and time to attract an audience need to occur.

The Internet

Clearly, the most rapidly growing online resource in the world today is the computing phenomenon known as the Internet. The amount of information available here is staggering and is still growing at an astonishing rate.

The Internet consists primarily of different types of files stored on computers all over the world, all opened to public access. By dialing into the network of an Internet Service Provider (for a monthly fee) or accessing the network through a LAN connection, access is granted to this entire network, all at one time. The original problem with the Internet was that, unless you knew where to go, there was no way to get there. There was no browsing capability.

The World Wide Web

All that changed about two years ago with the advent of the World Wide Web. Using a piece of client software called a browser, Internet users are provided with a GUI interface to the files stored on sites everywhere. Not only does every major computing company now have a Web site, but virtually every trade publication, as well as many nonprofit, governmental, and educational organizations will have one. An incredible wealth of reference material on networking is available, much of it furnished by impartial parties that are not concerned with steering the user towards any particular product.

Newsgroups

Newsgroups are another feature of the Internet that are a tremendous source of technical information. These are essentially messaging conferences divided by subject—over 10,000 of them on every topic under the sun, from artificial intelligence to brewing your own beer. There are hundreds of computing and networking related groups on which people leave messages asking questions and making comments and other people respond to the earlier messages. Again, a great deal of information is available here, but it is often not of as high a quality as that of CompuServe and other more moderated forums. Most newsgroups are not moderated or censored in any way, and behavior can be a little rambunctious at times.

FTP

FTP is the primary file transfer protocol used over the Internet. While the Web and new servers deliver documents usually designed to be viewed online, FTP is for file transfers only. Due to the high download speeds available using dedicated network Internet connections, many professionals utilize FTP to download files whenever possible. Depending on the available bandwidth, a file that could take an hour to download over the highest speed modem can be transferred in seconds using FTP.

Listservers

A listserver is a computer set up to do messaging over the Internet on a specific topic, but it uses standard Internet e-mail instead of a dedicated newsreader. A user sends a mail message to an automated server, stating that she wants to subscribe to a particular list. The server then begins to send her all of the mail addressed to that list. Responses to other users' e-mails are likewise posted to the list, creating the effect of an e-mail party line that can often manage to flood your inbox with mail.

Summary

Although the traditional print media are still a viable resource, the online world has become the most up-to-date and voluminous source of reference material available today. A small amount of time spent in learning the techniques through which material on specific topics can be located will save you time and expense and will be an environmentally positive act as well.

Appendix C

RAID

Redundant Arrays of Inexpensive Disks (RAID) is a setup that uses multiple disk drives, special disk controllers, and software to increase the safety of your data and the performance of your disk subsystem.

RAID protects your data by spreading it among multiple disk drives, and then calculating and storing parity information. This redundancy allows any drive to fail without causing the array itself to lose data. When a failed drive is replaced, its contents can be reconstructed from the information on the remaining drives in the array.

RAID increases disk subsystem performance by distributing read tasks among several drives, allowing the same data to be retrieved from different locations, depending on which happens to be closest at hand when the data is requested.

Different levels of RAID exist, each of which is optimized for certain types of data and storage requirements. RAID can be implemented in hardware or as add-on software. Modern NOSs like Novell NetWare and Microsoft Windows NT Server provide native support for one or more RAID levels.

The various component parts of RAID technology were developed originally for mainframes and minicomputers, and were until recently limited by high cost to those environments. In the past few years, though, RAID has become widely available in the PC LAN environment. The cost of disk drives has plummeted. RAID controllers have become, if not mass market items, at least reasonably priced. Cost-based objections to RAID have just about disappeared. Your server deserves to have RAID, and you shouldn't consider building a server that doesn't.

In this chapter, you learn the following:

- How to use RAID to increase the security of your data and the performance of your server

- How to understand the benefits and drawbacks of the various RAID levels, and how to choose a RAID level to match your specific data storage requirements

- How to decide between hardware-based RAID implementations, third-party software-based RAID implementations, and the RAID implementation native to your NOS software

RAID Levels

Although various component parts of RAID have been used in the mainframe and mini-computer arenas for years, the RAID model was properly defined in a white paper published in 1987 by the University of California at Berkeley. This paper sets the theoretical framework upon which subsequent RAID implementations have been built. It defines five levels of RAID, numbered 1 through 5. These *RAID levels* are not indicative of the degree of data safety or increased performance; they simply define how the data is divided and stored on the disk drives comprising the array, and how and where parity information is calculated and stored. A higher level number is not necessarily better.

Disk drives really do only two things—they write data and they read it. Depending upon the application, the disk subsystem might be called upon to do frequent small reads and writes, or it might need to do less frequent but longer reads and writes. An application server running a client/server database, for example, tends toward frequent small reads and writes, while a server providing access to stored images tends toward infrequent large reads and writes. The various RAID levels differ in their optimization for small reads, large reads, small writes, and large writes. Although most servers have a mix of these, choosing the RAID level optimized for the predominant computing tasks in your environment should maximize the performance of your disk subsystem.

The various RAID levels are optimized for varying data storage requirements, in terms of redundancy levels and performance issues. Different RAID levels store data bit-wise, byte-wise, or sector-wise over the array of disks. Similarly, parity information may be distributed across the array, or may be contained on just one physical disk drive. RAID levels 1 and 5 are very common in PC LAN environments—all hardware and software RAID implementations provide at least these two levels. RAID level 3 is used occasionally in specialized applications, and is supported by most hardware—and some software—RAID implementations. RAID levels 2 and 4 are seldom, if ever, used in PC LAN environments, but some hardware RAID implementations offer these levels.

Although RAID actually has only levels 1 through 5 defined, you commonly see references to RAID 0, RAID 0/1, RAID 6, RAID 7, and RAID 10, all of which are *de facto* extensions of the original RAID specification. These usages have become so common that they now are universally accepted. Because RAID is a model or theoretical framework, rather than a defined protocol or implementation, manufacturers continue to market improved RAID technology with arbitrarily assigned RAID levels.

The RAID Advisory Board (RAB)

The *RAID Advisory Board* (*RAB*) is a consortium of manufacturers of RAID equipment, as well as some other interested parties. RAB is responsible for developing and maintaining RAID standards, and has formal programs covering education, standardization, and certification. Supporting these programs are six committees, including Functional Test, Performance Test, RAID-Ready Drive, Host Interface, RAID Enclosure, and Education. RAB sells several documents, the most popular of which is *RAIDbook*, first published in 1993. This publication covers the fundamentals of RAID and defines each RAID level; it is a worthwhile acquisition for those who want to learn more about RAID.

The *RAB Certification Program* awards logos to equipment that passes its compatibility and performance testing suites. The *RAB Conformance Logo* certifies that the component bearing the logo complies with the named RAID level designation, as published by RAB. The *RAB Gold Certificate Logo* certifies that a product meets both the functional and performance specifications published by RAB.

For further information about RAB and its programs, you can contact Joe Molina, RAB Chairman, in one of the following ways:

RAID Advisory Board
Technology Forums LTD
13 Marie Lane
St. Peter, MN 56082-9423
Phone: (507) 931-0967
Fax: (507) 931-0976
E-mail: **0004706032@mcimail.com**
Web: **http://www.andataco.com/rab/**

RAID 0

RAID 0, illustrated in figure C.1, is a high-performance, zero-redundancy array option. RAID 0 is not technically RAID at all. It stripes blocks of data across multiple disk drives to increase the throughput of the disk subsystem, but offers no redundancy. If one drive fails in a RAID 0 array, then the data on all drives on the array is inaccessible. RAID 0 is a sports car with a powerful engine, but bald tires and no brakes—some would say there's no steering wheel, either.

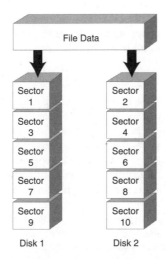

Figure C.1

RAID 0 uses sector striping to increase performance.

Nevertheless, there is a place for RAID 0. Understanding RAID 0 is important because the same mechanism used in RAID 0 is used to increase performance in other RAID levels. RAID 0 is inexpensive to implement, for two reasons. First, no disk space is used to store parity information, eliminating the need to buy larger disk drives—or more disk drives—for a given amount of storage. Second, the algorithms used by RAID 0 are simple ones that do not add much overhead or require a dedicated processor. RAID 0 offers high performance on reads and writes of both short and long data elements. If your application requires large amounts of fast disk storage, and if you have made other provisions for backing up this data to your satisfaction, then RAID 0 is worth considering.

RAID 0 uses *striping* to store data. This means that data blocks are written in turn to the various different physical disk drives that make up the logical volume represented by the array. For instance, your RAID 0 array might comprise three physical disk drives, which are visible to the operating system as one logical volume. Let's say that your block size is 8K and that a 32K file is to be written to disk. With RAID 0, the first 8K block might be written to physical drive 1, the second block to drive 2, the third to drive 3, and the fourth 8K block to drive 1. Your single 32K file is thus stored as four separate blocks residing on three separate physical hard disk drives.

This introduces two parameters used to quantify a RAID 0 array. The size of the block used—8K in our example—is referred to as the *chunk size*. The chunk size determines how much data is written to a disk drive in each operation. The number of physical hard disk drives comprising the array determines the *stripe width*. Both chunk size and stripe width impact the performance of a RAID 0 array.

When a logical read request is made to the RAID 0 array, and fulfillment requires an amount of data larger than the chunk size to be retrieved, this request is broken down into multiple smaller physical read requests, each of which is directed to and serviced by the individual physical drives upon which the multiple blocks are stored. Although these multiple read requests are generated serially, doing so takes very little time. The bulk of the time needed to fulfill the read request is used to transfer the data itself. With sequential reads, which involve less drive head seeking, bottlenecks can occur due to the internal transfer rate of the drives themselves. With striping, the transfer activity occurs in parallel on the individual disk drives that make up the array, so the elapsed time until the read request is completely fulfilled is greatly reduced.

Striping does not come without some cost in processing overhead, and this is where chunk size impacts performance. Against the benefit of having multiple spindles at work to service a single logical read request, you must weigh the overhead processing cost required to write and then read this data from many disks rather than from just one. Each SCSI disk access requires numerous SCSI commands to be generated and then executed, and striping the data across several physical drives multiplies the effort required. Reducing the block size too far can cause the performance benefits of using multiple spindles to be swamped by the increased time needed to generate and execute additional SCSI commands. You can, by using too small a block size, actually decrease performance. The break-even point is determined by your SCSI host adapter and the characteristics of the SCSI hard disk drives themselves; generally speaking, a block size smaller than 8K risks performance degradation. Using block sizes of 16K, 32K, or larger offers correspondingly greater performance benefits.

Sequential reads and writes make up a small percentage of total disk activity on a typical server disk subsystem. Most disk accesses are random, and by definition this means that the heads probably need to move to retrieve a particular block of data. Since head positioning is a physical process, it is, relatively speaking, very slow. The benefit of striping in allowing parallel data transfer from multiple spindles is much less significant in random-access situations, since everything is awaiting relatively slow head positioning to occur. Therefore, striping does little to benefit any particular random-access disk transaction. Strangely, however, it does benefit random-access disk throughput as a whole.

Here's why. Imagine a scene at your local hardware store. There is only one checkout line, and the owner is considering opening more. The single existing checkout line works well when the store is not busy, but at peak times customers have to stand in line too long. Some customers pay cash, and others use credit cards. The owner opens four additional checkout lines, but he decides to dedicate particular lines to particular items—one line for garden supplies, one for paint, one for tools, and so on. He notices that although this scheme does reduce the average wait, there are times when one checkout line has people backed up while other lines are free. His next step is to allow any of the five lines to process any type of item. He immediately notices a big drop in average wait time, and is satisfied with this arrangement until he notices that the backup hasn't completely disappeared. Because some individual transactions take longer than others, any given line can unpredictably move more slowly than others, leaving customers standing in line while other checkout lines are free. His final modification is to install a serpentine queue prior to the checkout lines, thereby allowing each customer in turn to use whichever checkout line becomes free first.

In this example, the checkout lines are analogous to the physical hard drives in the array, and the customers represent disk transactions—cash payments are like disk reads, and credit card payments are like disk writes. Just as a checkout clerk can ring up only so many items in a given amount of time, even a very fast hard drive is limited in the number of disk transactions per second it can execute. Just as many people can suddenly show up at a checkout line almost simultaneously, a server can generate many more disk requests in a short period of time than the disk can process. Because server requests tend to be *bursty*—many requests occurring nearly simultaneously, followed by a period with few or no requests—the disk subsystem must buffer or queue outstanding requests at times of peak demand, and then process these requests as demand slackens.

Because striping distributes the single logical volume's data across several physical drives, each of which can process disk transactions independently of the other drives, it provides the equivalent of additional checkout lines dedicated to particular products. Requests are routed to the physical drive that contains the data needed, thereby dividing a single long queue into two or more shorter queues, depending on the number of drives in the array (stripe width). Because each drive has its own spindle and head mechanism, these requests are processed in parallel, shortening the average time required to fulfill a disk request.

In most servers with a disk subsystem bottleneck, the problem is an unequal distribution of workload among the physical disk drives. It is not uncommon to see servers with several physical drives in which 90 percent or more of the total disk activity is confined to just one of the drives. RAID 0 addresses this problem through striping by distributing the workload evenly and eliminating any single drive as a bottleneck. RAID 0 improves both read and write performance for random, small-block I/O as well as sequential, large-block I/O.

What RAID 0 doesn't do is protect your data. There is no redundancy, and the loss of any single drive in a RAID 0 array renders the contents of the remaining partitions, which comprise the RAID 0 array, inaccessible for all practical purposes. Because both Windows NT Server native software RAID 0 and every hardware RAID 0 implementation that I am familiar with refuse to allow you to access the remaining partitions directly, the only alternative method available to access the data on the remaining partitions is to use a low-level sector editor similar to the Norton Utilities DiskEdit. Because each file's data is distributed in chunks across two or more physical disk drives, the chances of salvaging usable files with this method are very small.

RAID 1

What do you do to make sure you don't lose something? The obvious answer is to make a copy of it. *RAID 1*, illustrated in figure C.2, works this way, making two complete copies of everything to *mirrored,* or *duplexed,* pairs of disk drives. This 100-percent redundancy means that if you lose a drive in a RAID 1 array, you have another drive that contains an exact duplicate of the failed drive's contents. This offers the greatest level of redundancy, but requires the highest expenditure on drives.

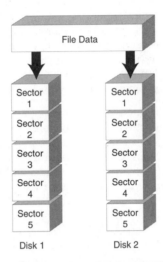

RAID 1 uses mirroring or duplexing to increase data safety.

Mirroring means that each disk drive has a twin. Anything written to one drive is written to the second drive simultaneously. Mirroring is 100-percent duplication of your drives. If one drive fails, its twin can replace it without loss of data. Mirroring has two disadvantages. First and most obvious is that you must purchase twice as many disk drives to yield a given amount of storage. Second is that the process of writing to both drives, and maintaining coherency of their contents, introduces overhead that slows writes. The two advantages of mirroring are that your data is safely duplicated on two physical devices, making catastrophic data loss much less likely, and that read performance is greatly increased because reads can be made by the drive that has a head closest to the requested data.

Duplexing is similar to mirroring, but adds a second host adapter to control the second drive or set of drives. The only disadvantage of duplexing relative to mirroring is the cost of the second host adapter. Duplexing eliminates the host adapter being a single point of failure.

RAID 1 is the most common level used in mainframes, where cost has always been a low priority relative to data safety. The rapidly dropping cost of disk storage has made RAID 1 a popular choice in PC LAN servers, also. Conventional wisdom says that RAID 1 is the most expensive RAID implementation due to the requirement for purchasing twice as many disk drives. In reality, RAID 1 might be the most expensive way to implement RAID, but it also might be the least expensive, depending on your environment.

In a large server environment, the cost of duplicating every disk drive quickly adds up, making RAID 1 very expensive. With smaller servers, though, the economics can be very different. If your server has only one SCSI hard disk drive installed, you might find that you can implement RAID 1 for the relatively small cost of buying another similar disk drive.

RAID 1 is provided as a standard software feature with most NOSs. Even if your NOS doesn't offer RAID 1, you might find that your SCSI host adapter does—although it might be called something else. If the host adapter manual doesn't mention RAID 1, check for references to hardware support for mirroring or duplexing. If you find that your SCSI adapter does support hardware mirroring, you have what you need to implement RAID 1 in hardware. Simply install another drive similar to the existing one (or identical, depending on the host adapter requirements), reconfigure according to the directions in the manual, and you're running RAID 1. If you have a choice between using either the NOS native RAID 1 support or the support provided by your SCSi host adapter, choose the hardware solution every time. It should offer better performance and not put any additional load on the server. Now, let's look at RAID 1 in more detail.

RAID 1 reads usually are faster than those of a stand-alone drive. Returning to the hardware store analogy, we now have multiple checkout lines, each of which can handle any customer. With RAID 1 reads, any given block of data can be read from either drive, thereby shortening queues, lowering drive utilization, and increasing read performance. This increase occurs only with multi-threaded reads. Single-threaded reads show no performance difference, just as no gain is realized in the hardware store when all but one of the checkout lines are closed.

Most RAID 1 implementations offer two alternative methods for optimizing read performance. The first is referred to as *circular queue* or *round-robin scheduling*. Using this method, read requests are simply alternated between the two physical drives, with each drive serving every other read request. This method equalizes the read workload between the drives, and is particularly appropriate for random-access environments where small amounts of data— record- or block-sized—are being accessed frequently. It is less appropriate for sequential-access environments where large amounts of data are being retrieved. Most disk drives have buffers used to provide read-ahead optimization, where the drive hardware itself reads and stores whatever data immediately follows a requested block, on the assumption that this data is most likely to be requested next. Alternating small-block requests between two physical drives can eliminate the benefit of such read-ahead buffering.

The second method used in RAID 1 to increase read performance is called *geometric, regional,* or *assigned cylinder scheduling*. This method depends on the fact that head positioning is by far the slowest activity a disk drive does. By giving each of the two drives comprising the RAID 1 array responsibility for covering only half of the physical drive, this head positioning time can be minimized. For example, using mirrored drives where each has 1,024 cylinders, the first drive might be assigned responsibility for fulfilling all requests for data that is stored on cylinders 0 through 511, with the second drive covering cylinders 512 through 1,023.

Although this method is superficially attractive, it seldom works in practice. First, few drives have their data distributed in such a way that any specific cylinder is equally likely to be accessed. Operating system files, swap files, user applications, and other frequently read files are likely to reside near the front of the disk. In this situation, your first disk may be assigned 90 percent or more of the read requests. Second, even if the data were distributed to equalize access across the portion of the disk occupied by data, few people run their drives at full capacity, so the second drive would have correspondingly less to do. This problem could be addressed by allowing a user-defined split ratio, perhaps assigning disk 1 to cover the first 10 to 20 percent of the physical drive area, and disk 2 to cover the remainder. In practice, I've never seen a RAID 1 array that allows user tuning to this extent.

RAID 1 writes are more problematic. Because all data has to be written to both drives, it appears that we have a situation where the customer has to go through one checkout line and complete his transaction. He then has to go to the end of the other checkout line, wait in line again, and complete the same transaction at the other register. RAID 1 therefore provides a high level of data safety by replicating all data, and an increase in read performance by allowing either physical drive to fulfill the read request, but a low level of write performance due to the necessity of writing the same information to both drives.

It might seem that RAID 1 should have little overall impact on performance since the increase in read performance might be balanced by the decrease in write performance. In reality, this is seldom the case.

First, in most server environments, reads greatly outnumber writes. In a database, for example, any given record might be read as many as 100 times for every single time it is written. Similarly, operating system executables, application program files, and overlays are essentially read-only. Any factor that benefits read performance at the expense of write performance does greatly increase the overall performance for most servers, most of the time.

Second, although it seems reasonable to assume that writing to two separate drives would cut write performance in half, in reality the performance hit for mirrored writes is usually only 10 to 20 percent. Although both physical writes must be executed before the logical write to the array can be considered complete, and although the two write requests are generated serially, the actual physical writes to the two drives occur in parallel. Since it is the head positioning and subsequent writing that occupy the bulk of the time required for the entire transaction, the extra time needed to generate a second write request has only a small impact on the total time required to complete the dual write.

RAID 2

RAID 2, a proprietary RAID architecture patented by Thinking Machines, Inc., distributes data across multiple drives at the bit level, using Hamming code error detection and correction. RAID 2 uses multiple dedicated disks to store parity information, and therefore requires that an array contain a relatively large number of individual disk drives. For example, a RAID 2 array with four data drives requires three dedicated parity drives. Consequently, RAID 2 has the highest redundancy of any of the parity-oriented RAID schemes.

The bit-wise orientation of RAID 2 means that every disk access occurs in parallel. RAID 2 is optimized for applications like imaging that require transfer of large amounts of contiguous data. RAID 2 is not a good choice for random-access applications that require frequent small reads and writes. The amount of processing overhead needed to fragment and reassemble data makes RAID 2 slow relative to other RAID levels. The large number of dedicated parity drives required makes it expensive. Because nearly all PC LAN environments have heavy random disk access, RAID 2 has no place in a PC LAN.

RAID 3

RAID 3, illustrated in figure C.3, stripes data across drives, usually at the byte level, although bit-level implementations are possible. RAID 3 dedicates one drive in the array to storing parity information. Like RAID 2, RAID 3 is optimized for long sequential disk accesses in applications like imaging, and is inappropriate for random-access environments like PC LANs. Any single drive in a RAID 3 array can fail without causing data loss, since the data can be reconstructed from the remaining drives. RAID 3 sometimes is offered as an option on PC-based RAID controllers, but seldom is used.

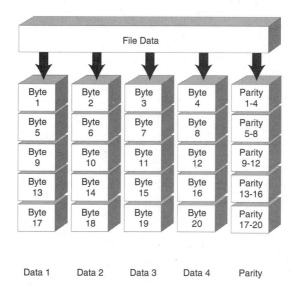

Data 1   Data 2   Data 3   Data 4   Parity

Figure C.3

RAID 3 uses byte striping with a dedicated parity disk.

RAID 3 can be considered an extension of RAID 0 because RAID 3 stripes small chunks of data across multiple physical drives. For example, in a RAID 3 array that comprises four physical drives, the first block is written to the first physical drive, the second block to the second drive, and the third block to the third drive. The fourth block, however, is not written to the fourth drive; instead the round-robin moves to the first drive again, and writes the fourth block there. Instead of storing user data, the fourth drive stores the results of parity calculations performed on the data written to the first three drives. This small chunk striping provides good performance on large amounts of data since all three data drives are operating in parallel. The fourth drive, the *parity drive*, provides redundancy to ensure that the loss of any one drive does not cause the array to lose data.

For sequential data transfers, RAID 3 offers high performance due to striping, and low cost due to its reliance on a single parity drive. It is this single parity drive, however, that is the downfall of RAID 3 for most PC LAN applications. By definition, no read to a RAID 3 array requires that the parity drive be accessed, unless data corruption has occurred on one or more of the data drives. Reads therefore proceed quickly. However, every write to a RAID 3 array requires that the single parity drive be accessed and written to in order to store the parity information for the data write that just occurred. The random access typical of a PC LAN environment means that the parity drive in a RAID 3 array is over-utilized, with long queues for pending writes, while the data drives are underutilized since they cannot proceed until parity information is written to the dedicated parity drive.

Returning to the hardware store analogy, RAID 3 allows multiple checkout lines, all but one of which accept only cash. The sole remaining checkout line accepts only credit cards. As long as most customers pay cash, this scheme works well. If, instead, many customers decide to pay by credit card, the queue for the single checkout line that accepts credit cards grows longer and longer while the checkout clerks in the cash lines have nothing to do.

Thus, RAID 3 works well in read-intensive environments, but breaks down in the random-access read/write environments typical of a PC LAN.

RAID 3 is a common option on hardware RAID implementations. In practical terms, RAID 5 is a universally available option and is usually used in preference to RAID 3, since it offers most of the advantages of RAID 3 and has none of the drawbacks. Consider using RAID 3 only in very specialized applications where large sequential reads predominate; for example, in a dedicated imaging server.

RAID 4

RAID 4 is similar to RAID 3, but stripes data at the block or sector level rather than at the byte level, thereby providing better read performance than RAID 3 for small random reads. The small chunk size of RAID 3 means that every read requires participation from every disk in the array. The disks in a RAID 3 array are therefore referred to as *synchronized* or *coupled*. The larger chunk size used in RAID 4 means that small random reads can be completed by accessing a single disk drive instead of multiple data drives. RAID 4 drives are therefore referred to as *unsynchronized* or *decoupled*.

Like RAID 3, RAID 4 suffers from having a single dedicated parity drive that must be accessed for every write. RAID 4 has all the drawbacks of RAID 3, and does not have the performance advantage of RAID 3 on large read transactions. About the only environment in which RAID 4 makes any sense at all is one in which nearly 100 percent of disk activity is small random reads. Since this situation is not seen in real-world server environments, do not consider using RAID 4 for your PC LAN.

RAID 5

RAID 5, illustrated in figure C.4, is the most common RAID level used in PC LAN environments. RAID 5 stripes both user and parity data across all the drives in the array, consuming the equivalent of one drive for parity information. With RAID 5, all drives are the same size, and one drive is unavailable to the operating system. For example, in a RAID 5 array with three 1G drives, the equivalent of one of those drives is used for parity, leaving 2G visible to the operating system. If you add a fourth 1G drive to the array, the equivalent of one drive is still used for parity, leaving 3G visible to the operating system. RAID 5 is optimized for transaction-processing activity, in which users frequently read and write relatively small amounts of data. It is the best RAID level for nearly any PC LAN environment.

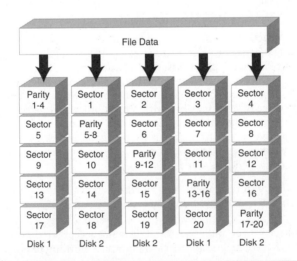

Figure C.4

RAID 5 uses sector striping with distributed parity.

The most important weakness of RAID levels 2 through 4 is that they dedicate a single physical disk drive to parity information. Reads do not require accessing the parity drive, so they are not degraded, but each write to the array must access this parity drive, so RAID levels 2 through 4 do not allow parallel writes. RAID 5 eliminates this bottleneck by striping the parity data onto all physical drives in the array, thereby allowing parallel writes as well as parallel reads.

RAID 5 reads, like reads with RAID levels 2 through 4, do not require access to parity information unless one or more of the data stripes is unreadable. Because both are optimized for sequential read performance where the block size of the requested data is a multiple of the stripe width, RAID 5 offers sequential read performance similar to that of RAID 3. Because, unlike RAID 3, RAID 5 allows parallel reads, RAID 5 offers substantially better performance on random reads. RAID 5 matches or exceeds RAID 0's performance on sequential reads because RAID 5 stripes the data across one more physical drive than RAID 0 does. RAID 5 performance on random reads at least equals the performance of RAID 0, and usually is better.

RAID 5 writes are more problematic. A RAID 0 single-block write requires only one access to one physical disk to complete the write. With RAID 5, the situation is considerably more complex. In the simplest case, two reads are required, one for the existing data block, and the other for the existing parity block. Parity is recalculated for the stripe set based on these reads and the contents of the pending write. Two writes are then required, one for the data block itself, and the other for the revised parity block. Completing a single write therefore requires a minimum of four disk operations, compared with the single operation required by RAID 0.

The situation worsens when you consider what must be done to maintain data integrity. Because the modified data block is written to disk before the modified parity block is written, the possibility exists that a system failure could result in the data block being written successfully to disk, but the newly calculated parity block being lost, thereby leaving new data with old parity—and corrupting the disk. Such a situation must be avoided at all costs.

RAID 5 addresses this problem by borrowing a concept from database transaction processing. *Transaction processing* is so named because it treats multiple component parts of a related whole as a single transaction. Either the whole transaction is completed successfully, or none of it is. For example, when you transfer money from your checking account to your savings account, your savings account is increased by the amount of the transfer, and your checking account is reduced by the same amount. This transaction obviously involves updates to at least two separate records, and possibly more. It wouldn't be acceptable to have one of these record updates succeed, but the other one fail (either you or the bank would be upset, depending on which one fails).

The way around this problem is a process called *two-phase commit*. Rather than writing the altered records individually, two-phase commit first creates a snapshot image of the entire transaction, and stores this image. It then updates the affected records, and verifies that all components of the transaction have been completed successfully. As soon as this is verified, the snapshot image is deleted. If the transaction fails somewhere in the middle, the snapshot image is used to *roll back* the status of whatever portion had been updated, returning the system to an essentially unmodified state.

RAID 5 uses a two-phase commit process to ensure data integrity, further increasing write overhead. It first does a parallel read of every data block belonging to the affected stripe set, calculating a new parity block based on this read and the contents of the new data block to be written. The changed data and newly calculated parity information are written to a log area, along with pointers to the correct locations. After successfully writing the log information, the changed data and parity information are written in parallel to the stripe set. After verification that the entire transaction has been completed successfully, the log information is deleted.

This process obviously introduces considerable overhead to the write process, and in theory slows RAID 5 writes by 50 percent or more, relative to RAID 0 writes. In practice, the situation is not as bad as you might expect. Examining the process shows that the vast majority of the extra time involved in these overhead operations is consumed by physical positioning of drive heads, which brings up the question of caching.

At first glance, caching might appear to be of little use for drive arrays. Drive arrays range in size from a few gigabytes to a terabyte or more. Most arrays mainly service small random read requests—even frequent large sequential reads can be considered random in this context, relative to the overall size of the array. Providing enough RAM to realistically do read caching on this amount of disk space would be prohibitive simply due to cost. Even if you were willing to buy this much RAM, the overhead involved in doing cache searches and maintaining cache coherency would swamp any benefits you might otherwise gain.

Write caching, however, is a different story. Existing RAID 5 implementations, to avoid most of the lost time described earlier, relocate operations whenever possible from physical disk to non-volatile or battery-backed RAM. This caching, in conjunction with deferred writes to frequently updated data, reduces overhead by an order of magnitude (or more), and allows real-world RAID 5 write performance that approaches that of less capable RAID versions.

Returning to the hardware store analogy, RAID 5 allows multiple checkout lines, all of which accept both cash (disk reads) and credit cards (disk writes). Because each checkout line is equipped with a scanner, it doesn't take much longer to process many items (large, sequential disk access) than it does to process only a few items (small, random disk access). As long as most customers pay cash, this scheme works well. The lines are short, transactions are completed quickly, and nobody has to wait long. Even though some customers pay by credit card, the lines remain relatively short because most transactions in any given line are cash. If, instead, many customers decide to pay by credit card, each checkout line grows longer because checkout clerks take much longer to process credit card transactions than they do to process cash. In the same way, RAID 5 works well in any environment—like a typical PC LAN's—that involves mostly reads, with less frequent writes.

Proprietary and Non-Standard RAID Levels

RAID is the hottest topic in mass storage right now. Only a year or two ago, articles on RAID were seen only in magazines intended for LAN managers. Today you see RAID discussed in mass-market computer magazines like *PC Computing*. Inevitably, suggestions of using RAID in workstations rather than just servers have begun to appear.

As is usually the case with a hot product category, manufacturers push the envelope, developing their own proprietary extensions to the standards-based architectures. Also in keeping with tradition, some of these extensions originate with the engineering folks and represent real improvements to the field, while others come from the marketing department and represent nothing but an attempt to gain a marketplace advantage.

RAID 6. The term *RAID 6* is now being used in at least three different ways. Some manufacturers simply take a RAID 5 array, add redundant power supplies and perhaps a hot spare disk, and refer to this configuration as RAID 6. Others add an additional disk to the array to increase redundancy, allowing the array to suffer simultaneous failure of two disks without causing data loss. Still others modify the striping method used by RAID 5 and refer to the result as RAID 6. Any of these modifications might yield worthwhile improvements. Be aware, though, that when you see RAID 6, you need to question the vendor carefully to determine exactly what it means.

RAID 7. *RAID 7* is patented by Storage Computer Corporation. From published documents, it appears that, architecturally, RAID 7 most resembles RAID 4 with the addition of caching. RAID 7 uses a dedicated microprocessor-driven controller running an embedded propriety real-time operating system named *SOS.* Storage Computers equips its arrays with dual Fast SCSI-2 multi-channel adapters, allowing one array to be simultaneously connected to more than one host, including mainframes, minicomputers, and PC LAN servers.

Storage Computer Corporation claims that RAID 7 provides performance equal to or better than RAID 3 on large sequential reads, while at the same time equaling or bettering RAID 5 on small random reads and writes. Anecdotal reports have claimed performance increases of between three and nine times, when compared with traditional RAID 3 and RAID 5 arrays. The claimed benefits of RAID 7 have been hotly debated on the Internet since the product was introduced. Some posted comments have reported significant increases in performance, while others have questioned the benefits, and even the safety, of RAID 7, particularly in a UNIX environment. The jury is still out on RAID 7.

Stacked RAID

One characteristic of all RAID implementations is that the array is seen as a single logical disk drive by the host operating system. This means that it is possible to *stack* arrays, with the host using one RAID level to control an array of arrays, in which individual disk drives are replaced with second-level arrays operating at the same or a different RAID level. Using stacked arrays allows you to gain the individual benefits of more than one RAID level, while offsetting the drawbacks of each. In essence, stacking makes the high-performance RAID element visible to the host while concealing the low-performance RAID element used to provide data redundancy.

One common stacked RAID implementation is referred to as *RAID 0/1* or *RAID 0+1*, which also is marketed as a proprietary implementation named *RAID 10.* RAID 0/1 is illustrated in figure C.5. This method combines the performance of RAID 0 striping with the redundancy of RAID 1 mirroring. RAID 0/1 simply replaces each of the individual disk drives used in a RAID 0 array with a RAID 1 array. Since the host computer sees the array as RAID 0, performance is enhanced to RAID 0 levels. Since each drive component of the RAID 0 array is actually a RAID 1 mirrored set, data safety is at the same level you expect from a full mirror. Other stacked RAID implementations are possible. For example, replacing the individual drives in a RAID 5 array with subsidiary RAID 3 arrays results in a *RAID 53* configuration.

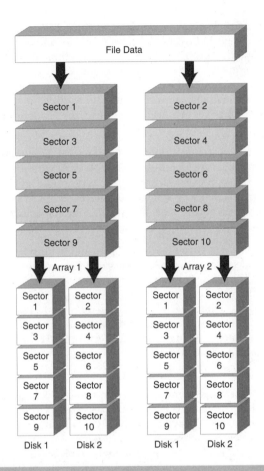

Figure C.5

RAID 0+1 uses sector striping to mirrored target arrays.

Another benefit of stacking is that it can build arrays with extremely large capacity. For the reasons described earlier, RAID 5 is the most popular choice for PC LAN arrays. However, for technical reasons described later, a RAID 5 array normally should be limited to five or six disk drives. The largest disk drives currently available for PC LANs hold about 9G, placing the upper limit on a simple RAID 5 array at about 50G. Replacing the individual disk drives in a simple RAID 5 array with subsidiary RAID 5 arrays allows you to extend this maximum to 250G or more. In theory, it is possible to use three tiers of RAID—an array of arrays of arrays—to extend the capacity to the terabyte range.

Sizing the Array

Although we've talked a great deal about redundancy, we haven't examined in detail what happens when a drive fails. In the case of RAID 0, the answer is obvious. If your RAID 0 array comprised partitions on two physical disk drives, the data remaining on the good drive is unusable. You could, of course, spend hours, days, or weeks attempting to piece together file fragments remaining on the good drive. If your RAID 0 array comprised partitions on more than two physical disk drives, the situation is even more complex because you have file fragments distributed over additional drives. The only realistic alternative when one drive in a

RAID 0 array fails is to replace the failed drive and rebuild the RAID 0 array from a backup set. With RAID 1, the answer is equally obvious. The failed drive was an exact duplicate of the remaining good drive, all your data is still available, and all your redundancy is gone until you replace the failed drive. With RAID 3 and RAID 5, the issue becomes much more complex.

Because RAID 3 and RAID 5 use parity to provide data redundancy, rather than physically replicating the data as RAID 1 does, the implications of a drive failure are not as obvious. In RAID 3, the failure of the parity drive has no effect on reads, since the parity drive is never accessed for reads. In terms of RAID 3 writes, failure of the parity drive removes all redundancy until the drive is replaced, since all parity information is stored on that drive alone. When a data drive fails in a RAID 3 array, the situation becomes more complicated. Reads of data formerly stored on the failed drive must be reconstructed using the contents of the other data drives and the parity drive. This results in a greatly increased number of read accesses, and correspondingly lowered performance.

With RAID 5, any failed drive is similar to RAID 3 with a failed data drive. Because every drive in a RAID 5 array contains both data and parity information, the failure of any drive results in the loss of both data and parity. An attempt to read data formerly resident on the failed drive requires that every remaining drive in the array be read, and parity used, to recalculate the missing data. For example, in a RAID 5 array containing 15 drives, a read and reconstruction of lost data requires 14 separate read operations and a recalculation before the data can be returned to the host. Writes to a RAID 5 array with a failed drive also require numerous disk accesses.

To make matters worse, when the failed drive is replaced, its contents must be reconstructed and stored on the replacement drive. This process, usually referred to as *automatic rebuild*, normally occurs in the background while the array continues to fulfill user requests. Because the automatic rebuild process requires heavy disk access to all other drives in an already crippled array, performance of the array can be degraded unacceptably. The best way to limit this degradation is to use a reasonably small stripe width, limiting the number of physical drives in the array to five or six at most.

Choosing a RAID Implementation

Choosing the best RAID implementation for your needs means making two decisions. First, you must determine which RAID level or which combination of RAID levels provides the optimum mix of speed and safety for the type of data that you need to store. Second, you must decide whether to implement that RAID level by using Windows NT Server native RAID software or by purchasing a dedicated RAID hardware solution.

Picking the Best RAID Level for Your Needs

In theory, there are two important considerations in selecting the best RAID implementation for your particular needs. The first consideration is the type of data to be stored on the array. The various RAID levels are optimized for different storage requirements. The relative importance in your environment of small, random reads versus large, sequential reads—and of small, random writes versus large, sequential writes—as well as the overall percentage of reads versus writes can determine, at least in theory, the best RAID level to use. The second consideration is the relative importance to you of performance versus the safety of your data. If data safety is paramount, then you should choose a lower-performing alternative that offers greater redundancy. Conversely, if sheer performance is the primary goal, then you should choose a higher-performing alternative that offers little or no redundancy, and instead use backups and other means to ensure the safety of your data. Also lurking in the background, of course, is the real-world issue of cost.

Here are some specific guidelines that might help your decision:

- RAID 0 striping offers high performance, but its complete lack of redundancy—and concomitant high risk of data loss—makes pure RAID 0 an unrealistic choice for nearly all environments. It does make sense, though, in applications that generate large transitory temp files. RAID 0 is inexpensive, because it is supported by many standard SCSI host adapters, and it requires no additional disk drives.

- RAID 1 mirroring provides 100-percent redundancy for excellent data safety, and at the same time offers reasonably good performance. RAID 1 is an excellent choice for small LANs, offering decent performance and a high level of safety at a reasonable cost. Because RAID 1 is supported by most standard host adapters, and requires that each data drive be duplicated, it is inexpensive to implement in small arrays, but very expensive for large arrays.

- RAID 3 byte striping with dedicated parity offers good data safety and high performance on large sequential reads, but its performance on random reads and writes makes it a poor choice for most LANs. The growth of imaging applications is revitalizing RAID 3 to some extent, since these applications fit well with RAID 3's strengths. If you are doing imaging, consider implementing RAID 3 on the logical volume used to store images. RAID 3 is moderately expensive to implement. Although it requires only one additional disk drive to store parity information, RAID 3 is not commonly available on standard disk adapters, or as a software implementation, and therefore requires a special and moderately expensive host adapter.

- RAID 5 sector striping with distributed parity offers good data safety, good read performance (for both small, random reads and large, sequential reads), and reasonable write performance. RAID 5 usually turns out to be the best match for the disk access patterns of small and mid-sized LANs. RAID 5 can be implemented inexpensively, since it requires only a single additional disk drive, and can be implemented in software. Various RAID 5 hardware implementations are available also; these offer better performance than software implementations, but at a higher price. If your server is getting only one array, RAID 5 is almost certainly the way to go.

- Stacked RAID is useful when both performance and data safety are high priorities relative to cost. In particular, RAID 0+1 when properly implemented can combine the high performance of RAID 0 with the complete redundancy of RAID 1, while eliminating the drawbacks of both—except, of course, the cost. Stacked RAID is also useful if your total array capacity must exceed 50G or so.

- Multiple arrays are worth considering if your data storage requirements are large and diverse. Rather than trying to shoehorn all your data into a single array running a compromise level of RAID, consider installing multiple arrays, each of which runs the RAID level most appropriate for the type of data being stored (and the patterns of access to that data).

Understanding RAID Product Features

RAID can be implemented in a variety of ways. The SCSI host adapter in your current server might provide simple RAID functionality; if so, you can replace it with a host adapter that offers full RAID support. Software RAID support is provided natively by most NOSs; if the RAID functionality provided by your NOS is inadequate, you can find what you need in third-party RAID software. If you are purchasing a new server, chances are that hardware RAID support is standard, or at least available as an option. If you need to upgrade your existing server, you can select among various external RAID arrays that provide features, functionality, and performance similar to that provided by internal server RAID arrays.

Each of these methods has advantages and drawbacks in terms of cost, performance, features, and convenience. Only you can decide which method best suits your needs. Let's look first at some of the features of various RAID implementations, and then at some of the tradeoffs involved with each.

Disks for Hot Swapping and Hot Sparing. Most external RAID subsystems—and many servers with internal RAID subsystems—allow hard disk drives to be removed and replaced without ever turning off the server. This feature, known as *hot swapping*, allows a failed disk drive to be replaced without interrupting ongoing server operations.

A similar method, known as *hot sparing*, goes one step further by providing a spare drive that is installed and powered up at all times. This drive automatically—and on a moment's notice—can take the place of a failed drive. Most systems that provide hot sparing also support hot swapping to allow the failed drive to be replaced at your leisure.

Obviously, both the drive itself and the system case must be designed to allow hot swapping or hot sparing. Most internal server RAID arrays, and nearly all external RAID arrays, are designed with front external access to hard drives for just this reason.

Automatic Rebuild. With either hot swapping or hot sparing, the integrity of the array itself is restored by doing a *rebuild* to reconstruct the data formerly contained on the failed drive, and re-create it on the replacement drive. Because rebuilding is a resource-intensive process, a well-designed RAID subsystem gives you the choice of taking down the array and doing a *static rebuild*, or allowing an *automatic rebuild* to occur dynamically in the background while the array continues to service user requests. Ideally, the array should also let you specify a priority level for an automatic rebuild, allowing you to balance your users' need for performance against the time needed to reestablish redundancy.

In practice, performance on an array with a failed drive—particularly a RAID 5 array—might already be degraded to the extent that attempting any sort of rebuild while users continue to access the array is unrealistic. The best solution in this case is to allow the users to continue to use the array as is for the remainder of the day, and then do the rebuild that night. In this situation, you choose a static rebuild, which is far faster than a background rebuild.

Disk Drive Issues. In the scramble to choose the best RAID level, fastest RAID controller, and so on, one issue that frequently is overlooked is that of the disk drives themselves. The RAID implementation you select determines how much flexibility you have in choosing the drives to go with it.

External RAID arrays and internal server RAID arrays typically offer the least flexibility in choice of drives. Although they use industry-standard disk drives, these drives are repackaged into different physical form factors to accommodate custom drive bay designs as well as the proprietary power and data connections needed to allow hot swapping. Because these proprietary designs fit only one manufacturer's servers—or sometimes even fit just one particular model—they are made and sold in relatively small numbers. This combination of low volume and a single source makes these drives quite expensive. Another related issue is that of continuing availability of compatible drives. Consider what will happen a year or two from now when you want to upgrade or replace drives. The best designs simply enclose industry-standard drives in a custom chassis that provides the mechanical and electrical connections needed to fit the array. These designs allow the user to upgrade or replace drives by merely installing a new standard drive in the custom chassis. Beware of other designs that make the chassis an integral part of the drive assembly—you will pay a high price for replacement drives, if you can find them at all.

Third-party RAID controllers offer more flexibility in choosing drives, at the expense of not providing hot swapping. These controllers simply replace your existing standard SCSI host adapter, and are designed to support standard SCSI disk drives. The situation is not as simple as it seems, however. You might reasonably expect these controllers to be able to use any otherwise suitable SCSI drive. The reality is different—most of these controllers support only a very limited number of models of disk drive, and often specify the exact ROM revision level required on the drive. Before you buy such a controller, make sure that the drives you intend to use appear on this compatibility list. Make sure also that the controller's drive tables can be easily updated via flash ROM or similar means, and that the manufacturer has a history of providing such updates. Don't assume any of this—ask.

Software-based RAID offers the most flexibility in selecting drives. Because most software-based RAID implementations—those native to NOSs and those provided by third parties—are further isolated from the disk drives than hardware-based RAID implementations are, they care little about the specifics of your disk drives. Software-based RAID depends on the host adapter to communicate with the disk drives themselves. As long as your host adapter is supported by your RAID software, and your drives in turn are supported by the host adapter, you should have few compatibility problems with software-based RAID. Typical software-based mirroring, for example, does not even require that the second drive in a mirror set be identical to the first— only that it be at least as large.

Power Supplies. Most external RAID arrays—and some internal server RAID arrays—use dedicated redundant power supplies for the disk drives. The arrangement of these power supplies has a significant impact on the reliability of the array as a whole. Some systems provide a dedicated power supply for each individual disk drive. Although this superficially seems to increase redundancy, in fact it simply adds more points of failure to the drive component. Failure of a power supply means failure of the drive which it powers. Whether the failure is the result of a dead drive or a dead power supply, the result is the same.

A better solution is to use dual load-sharing power supplies. In this arrangement, each power supply is capable of powering the entire array on its own. The dual power supplies are linked in a harness that allows each to provide half the power needed by the array. If one power supply fails, the other provides all the power needed by the array until the failed unit is replaced. Another benefit of this arrangement is that because the power supplies normally run well below their full capacity, their lives are extended and their reliability enhanced, when compared with a single power supply running at or near capacity. Power supplies also can be hot swappable, although this feature more commonly is called *hot pluggable* when referring to power supplies.

Stacked and Multiple-Level Independent RAID Support. Some environments require a stacked array for performance, redundancy, or sizing reasons. Others require multiple independent arrays, each running a different RAID level or mixture of RAID levels. If you find yourself in either of these situations, the best solution is probably either an external RAID array or a high-end internal server RAID array. The obvious issue is whether or not a given RAID implementation offers the functionality needed to provide stacks and multiple independent arrays. The not-so-obvious issue is the sheer number of drives that must be supported. External RAID arrays support many disk drives in their base chassis, and usually allow expansion chassis daisy-chaining, to extend even further the maximum number of disks supported. High-end servers support as many as 28 disk drives internally, and again often make provision for extending this number via external chassis addition. Mid-range servers are typically more limited, in the number of drives they physically support, and in their provisions for stacking and multiple independent arrays. A typical mid-range server RAID array does not support multiple independent arrays, but might offer simple RAID 0+1 stacking.

Manageability. Look for a RAID implementation that provides good management software. In addition to providing automatic static and dynamic rebuild options, a good management package will monitor your array for loading, error rates, read and write statistics by type, and so on. Better packages will even help you decide how to configure your RAID array.

Hardware RAID Implementations

Hardware RAID is available in many forms. If you are purchasing a new server, chances are that the manufacturer offers one or more hardware RAID options for that server. If instead you plan to install hardware RAID on an existing server, you have even more choices available. You might decide to mirror or duplex drives using your existing SCSI adapter or you might install a dedicated RAID controller. Whether you are adding RAID to a new or existing server, buying an external RAID enclosure might make more sense than the alternatives. The available choices vary widely in both features and flexibility and may vary even more widely in cost. Let's look at these choices in more detail and see why one might be much better for your environment than another.

RAID as a Server Option. If you are purchasing a new server, then by all means consider the RAID options offered by the server manufacturer. Any system seriously positioned for use as a server will have RAID as an option (most low-end servers), or as standard equipment (mid-range and high-end servers). Servers that come standard with RAID often offer optional external enclosures to expand your disk storage beyond that available in the server chassis alone.

Purchasing RAID as part of your server has several advantages, most of which are related to the single-source aspect:

- Because one manufacturer supplies both the server and the RAID hardware, the RAID hardware can be tweaked to optimize performance.

- Internal server RAID offers the best chance to avoid nasty compatibility problems, ROM revision-level issues, and so on. If you do have a problem, you can complain to one source and not have to worry about finger-pointing by different vendors.

- Driver updates are available from a single source, relieving you of having to play systems integrator the next time you want to upgrade your NOS or replace a disk drive.

■ You can enjoy the single-source warranty and maintenance. If you buy a combination server and RAID array from a major manufacturer, you need to place only one phone call when your server breaks. Large server manufacturers probably have trained service personnel located somewhere near you, and they often provide service around the clock, seven days a week.

■ You can expect greater availability of known-compatible disks at upgrade time. Server manufacturers realize that you aren't likely to buy their server unless you are certain that parts for it will continue to be available for some time.

■ There usually is full or partial support for the convenience and extended-reliability features listed above (hot swappable drives, power supplies, and so on).

Upgrading an Existing Server to Hardware RAID. If your current server is otherwise suitable, upgrading it to hardware RAID is a viable alternative. This upgrade can range from something as simple and inexpensive as adding another disk drive and enabling mirroring on your SCSI host adapter, to something as complex and potentially expensive as adding an external RAID array cabinet. A happy medium in both cost and complexity is replacing your existing SCSI host adapter with a dedicated RAID controller. Each of these solutions provides the basic reliability and performance benefits of hardware RAID, and each varies in the level of features, convenience, and extended RAID functionality it provides.

Mirroring with Your Current SCSI Host Adapter. The SCSI host adapter in your current server might support RAID 0, RAID 1, or both. If it supports none of those, then replacing the host adapter with one that offers simple RAID support is an inexpensive alternative. If your server has only one or two SCSI hard drives, this method allows you to implement mirroring at the cost of simply buying a matching drive for each of your existing drives.

This method buys you 100-percent redundancy and decent performance, and does so inexpensively. What it does not provide are other features of more expensive hardware RAID implementations—hot swappable drives, redundant power supplies, and so on. Still, for smaller servers, this is a set-and-forget choice. You can do it, walk away from it, and stop worrying about it. If your server is small enough that buying the extra disk drives is feasible, and if you don't care that you have to take down the server to replace a failed drive, this method might be the best choice. It gives you the overwhelming majority of the benefits of a full-blown RAID implementation, for a fraction of the cost.

Adding a Dedicated RAID Controller Card. The next step up in hardware RAID, in terms of both cost and performance, is the dedicated *RAID controller card*. This card replaces your existing SCSI host adapter, and includes a dedicated microprocessor to handle RAID processing. Such a card can range in price from less than $1,000 to perhaps $2,500, depending on the levels of RAID it supports, its feature set, the number of SCSI channels provided, the amount and type of on-board cache supplied, and so on. All cards support at least RAID 1 and RAID 5, and the newest ones offer a full range of RAID levels, often including various enhanced non-standard RAIDs.

The prices of dedicated RAID controller cards have been dropping rapidly, due to increasing sales volume and to competition from RAID software alternatives. The best cards offer RAID functionality and performance comparable to internal server RAID arrays and external RAID array enclosures. In terms of convenience features, however, the cards are obviously at an inherent disadvantage—they can do nothing to provide hot swap capabilities, redundant power supplies, and so on.

Most RAID controller cards are sold through OEM arrangements with server manufacturers. For example, the Mylex DAC960—one of the better examples of this type of card—is used by Hewlett-Packard to provide RAID support in its NetServer line of servers. HP modifies the BIOS and makes other changes to optimize the DAC960 for use in its servers.

Think long and hard before you decide to buy one of these cards as an individual item rather than as part of a packaged solution. Although the card itself seems inexpensive relative to the quoted price for an external RAID enclosure, you usually will find that after adding up other costs—including disk drives, cabling, and possibly an external enclosure—you have met or exceeded the price of the turnkey solution. To add insult to injury, it's then still up to you to do the systems integration, locate and install the appropriate disks and drivers, and maintain the subsystem. If you decide to use one of these cards, budget for two of them. Few organizations tolerate having their LAN down for an extended period because the RAID controller has failed. On-site maintenance is the exception rather than the rule for these cards, and even using overnight delivery, a swap requires that your LAN be down for at least a day or two.

Using an External RAID Enclosure. *External RAID enclosures* are the high end of hardware RAID products. They offer everything that internal server arrays do, and then some. Hot pluggable, load-sharing dual power supplies are a common feature, as are hot swappable drives, extensive management capabilities, a full range of RAID options, and provision for stacked RAID. Most of these units support multiple independent RAID arrays, and some allow connection of more than one host. Most units allow you to add additional slave enclosures to expand your disk capacity. As you might expect, all this functionality doesn't come cheaply.

These units are of two types. The first is based on one of the dedicated RAID controller cards described in the preceding section. In this type of unit, a *dumb external array*, all the RAID intelligence is contained on the card installed in the host, and the external enclosure simply serves to provide space and power for the disk drives. The enclosure makes provision for hot swapping, redundant power supplies, and so on, but the actual RAID functionality remains with the host server. RAID configuration and management is done at the host server. Although they physically resemble more sophisticated external arrays, in concept these units are just simple extensions of the dedicated RAID controller card method, and are accordingly relatively inexpensive. They are in the $3,000 to $5,000 range for the enclosure and controller, without disk drives.

Dumb external arrays often are created from their component parts by mail-order to allow second- and third-tier computer companies to offer a RAID solution for their servers. These arrays suffer from most of the same drawbacks as the dedicated RAID controller cards do— limited drive type support, infrequent driver updates, lack of on-site maintenance, and so on. Think twice before choosing one of these units—then think some more.

The second type of unit, a *smart external array*, relocates RAID processing to the enclosure itself, and provides one or more SCSI connectors by which the host server or servers are connected to the array. The host server sees a smart external array as just another standard SCSI disk drive or drives.

With this type of array, RAID configuration and management is done at the array itself. Because these arrays are intended for use in diverse environments—including NetWare, Windows NT Server, and UNIX—they usually offer a variety of methods for setup and programming. A typical unit might be programmable in a UNIX environment by connecting a dumb terminal to a serial port on the external array, or by using Telnet. In a NetWare or NT Server environment you instead might use provided client software for that NOS. These arrays have full software support—drivers, management utilities, and so on—available for several operating systems, although they usually come standard with support for only one operating system of your choice. Support for additional operating systems, or for extended functionality with your chosen operating system, is often an extra cost option. Smart external arrays start at around $8,000 without drives and go up rapidly from there.

Smart external arrays offer everything you might want in a RAID unit, including support for stacked RAID, multiple independent arrays, and support for multiple hosts. Because manufacturers realize that these are mission-critical components, on-site maintenance is available, provided either by the manufacturer itself or by a reputable third-party organization. In construction, these units resemble minicomputer and mainframe components more than typical PC components.

There are, as always, a few things to look out for when shopping. Make no assumptions about compatibility, cost, or support. Ask, and even if you like the answers, get them in writing.

The first major concern is drive support. Some units allow you to add or replace drives with any SCSI drive of the appropriate type that is at least as large as the old drive. Other units require that you use only drives that exactly match the existing drives in make, model, and sometimes even ROM revision level. Still other units can only use drives supplied by the array manufacturer, because the drives have had their firmware altered somehow. These manufacturers usually tell you they make such alterations for performance and compatibility reasons, which could be true. The net effect, though, is that you are chained to that manufacturer for new and replacement drives, and will have to pay their price for the drives.

The second major concern is software support. With smart external arrays, you are at the mercy of the array manufacturer for NOS support, drivers, management utilities, and so on. Make absolutely certain before purchasing one of these arrays that it has software support available—not only for your current NOS environment, but for other environments that you might reasonably expect to need in the future. Examine in detail which NOSs are supported, and at what version levels. It does you no good to accept a vendor's assurance that the array supports UNIX, only to find later that the array supports SCO UNIX when what you needed was support for BSDI UNIX. Similarly, support for BSDI 1.x doesn't help if you're running BSDI 2.0.1.

Check the array manufacturer's history of providing support for NOS upgrades soon after the upgrade's release. Although this is not a perfect means of prediction—companies can change for the better or worse—a history of frequent updates for many NOS environments is a reasonable indicator that the company is committed to providing continuing support for its users. On the other hand, a supported driver list that includes older versions of NOSs but fails to include later versions might indicate that the array vendor tends to drop support for environments that do not sell in large volumes. This might not be a major concern if you use a mainstream product like NetWare or Windows NT Server, but is cause for great concern if your NOS is less popular.

The third major concern is understanding the pricing structure of the array manufacturer. Since these units do not sell in high volume, development costs for drivers and so on have to be distributed over a relatively small number of users. This can make updates, enhanced optional features, and support for additional NOSs very expensive. If you might want to add, for example, SNMP management to your array in the future, do not assume that it will be inexpensive or free. Ask lots of questions before you buy.

External RAID enclosures can be your best choice, particularly if you require large amounts of disk storage, have multiple servers, or use more than one NOS. Don't rule out external RAID enclosures simply on the basis of sticker shock. Examine the true cost involved in acquiring, maintaining, and managing one of these units, versus the cost involved—including increased staff time—in providing similar functionality using other means.

One final item—some external RAID enclosures exist that use no RAID processor at all, depending instead on the server processor to perform RAID operations. These units run only with NetWare, using an NLM to provide RAID processing. Because these units support only NetWare—and for other reasons covered fully in the upcoming "Novell NetWare Software RAID" section—they are best avoided.

Software RAID Implementations

All the RAID implementations we have examined so far have their basis in specialized hardware. It is possible, however, to use the server CPU to perform RAID processing, and thereby avoid buying additional hardware. NetWare and Windows NT Server, which between them dominate the PC LAN NOS market, provide native RAID support. Although there are obvious cost advantages to using software-based RAID, there are also subtle drawbacks to doing so, both in performance and reliability.

In theory, at least, there are some scalability performance advantages to using software RAID. Because software RAID depends upon the server processor, upgrading the server processor simultaneously upgrades the RAID processor. In practice, however, this potential advantage turns out to be illusory. Benchmark tests nearly always show software RAID bringing up the rear of the pack, and hardware RAID out in front.

Microsoft Windows NT Server Software RAID. RAID 1 mirroring is supported directly by Microsoft Windows NT Server for any hardware configuration with at least two disk drives of similar size. NT Server does not require that the mirrored drive be identical to the original drive—only that it be at least as large. This considerably simplifies replacing failed drives if the original model is no longer available. Similarly, RAID 1 duplexing is supported directly for any hardware configuration with at least two disk drives of similar size, and two disk controllers. As with any duplex arrangement, this removes the disk controller as a single point of failure. As with mirrored drives, NT Server does not require duplexed drives to be identical.

RAID 5 also is supported natively by NT Server for any hardware configuration with at least three disk drives, and one or more disk controllers. NT Server allows as many as 32 drives in a stripe set, although for the reasons mentioned above it is a better idea to limit this number to five or six drives. Microsoft refers to this RAID 5 support as *Disk Striping with Parity*.

Since NT Server itself provides these disk redundancy options, you might wonder why anyone would purchase expensive additional hardware to accomplish the same thing. The first issue is performance. Although Microsoft has done a good job of incorporating RAID functionality into NT Server, a well-designed hardware RAID solution offers better performance, particularly on larger arrays. Also, although using the server CPU to perform RAID processing can be acceptable on a small (or lightly loaded) server, doing so on a heavily loaded server—particularly one running as an application server—steals CPU time from user applications, and therefore might degrade overall server performance.

The second issue that speaks against using NT Server software RAID is that of flexibility and convenience. Unless you are running NT Server on a system equipped with hot swappable drives and other RAID amenities—which usually would be equipped with a hardware RAID controller, anyway—you lose the ability to hot swap drives or otherwise maintain the array without taking down the server.

If yours is a small array on a server supporting a limited number of users, then the drawbacks of NT Server software RAID might be an acceptable tradeoff for reduced costs. For larger arrays and mission-critical environments, however, do it right and buy the appropriate RAID hardware solution.

Novell NetWare Software RAID. Like Microsoft Windows NT Server, Novell NetWare provides native software RAID support. Unlike NT Server, which provides both RAID 1 and RAID 5, NetWare offers only RAID 1 mirroring and duplexing. As a result of user demand for RAID support beyond that provided natively by NetWare, various third-party vendors supply software to add enhanced RAID functionality to NetWare.

NetWare software RAID solutions—both those native to NetWare and those supplied by third-party vendors—suffer the same performance and flexibility drawbacks as do the solutions for NT Server. In addition, NetWare products have problems all their own. To understand why, it is necessary to understand a little bit about the way Intel processors work, and some of the architectural differences between NT Server and NetWare.

Intel processors allow processes to run at different *privilege levels*. The highest privilege level, referred to as Ring 0, is the fastest and most dangerous level. Processes at Ring 0 have complete access to the processor, and a rogue process running at Ring 0 can crash the whole system. Processes running at higher levels are more restricted in how much damage they can do, but they in turn run more slowly because of the extra overhead involved in moving between rings.

NT Server does not run any user processes at Ring 0, including low-level processes represented by vendor-supplied drivers. Windows NT is therefore inherently more stable than NetWare is, but at the same time is inevitably slower. NetWare uses *NetWare Loadable Modules* (NLMs) as plug-ins to enhance and extend the capabilities of the base operating system. Because NLMs run at Ring 0, any NLM, no matter how poorly written, has full access to the CPU—and therefore has the potential to crash the entire server. NLM technology is speedy but dangerous. With later versions of NetWare, Novell has made provision for testing NLMs at higher ring levels to determine their stability, but a functioning NLM in a production server still runs at Ring 0.

Consider, then, what might happen to the NLM you use to provide RAID services. Even if the RAID NLM itself is well-written and stable, running another NLM can cause a server crash. If this occurs, the possibility exists that the contents of your RAID array are corrupted beyond salvage. You can minimize this risk by using only Novell-certified NLMs, but even then the possibility of data corruption remains. NetWare integral mirroring has been available for years, and has been used on thousands of servers with few problems. Reports of problems with NetWare duplexing are less uncommon, but still rare. Attempting to extend NetWare RAID functionality with third-party products is more problematic.

If, for some reason, you must use one of these products, at least understand the differences between the two Novell levels of approval. The less rigorous level is indicated by a symbol incorporating the Novell logo with the word Yes superimposed, and the phrase It runs with NetWare appearing below the logo. This symbol means little more than that the manufacturer has tested the product with NetWare, and represents that the product is NetWare-compatible. The second, more rigorous level also uses the Novell logo with the word Yes superimposed, but has the words NetWare Tested and Approved below the logo. This symbol indicates that the product has undergone testing by Novell Labs and has been certified by them as NetWare-compatible. Give strong preference to the latter symbol.

Recommendations

Given the wide diversity of RAID products available, and the equally broad range of needs and budgets, it is difficult to make hard and fast recommendations for the most appropriate means of implementing RAID. However, the following observations should serve as useful guidelines:

- If your disk storage requirements are small, consider using your existing SCSI host adapter to implement mirroring. If your host adapter does not support hardware mirroring, consider replacing it with one that does. Purchase an additional disk drive to mirror each existing drive. The result is greatly increased data safety, and better performance, at minimal cost. Choose this hardware method in preference to the RAID 1 software functions of NT Server or NetWare on the basis of performance and minimizing load on the server.

- If your disk storage requirements are moderate, and in particular if you need RAID 5, begin looking at hardware alternatives. Do not consider attempting to implement RAID 5 on a NetWare server using software RAID. NT Server RAID 5 support appears to be rock-solid, and performs well, particularly on smaller arrays. It is worth considering if the tradeoffs in flexibility and ease of maintenance do not concern you.

- If you are purchasing a new server, buy one with built-in hardware RAID support. In addition to the performance benefits of hardware RAID, the presence of hot swappable drives and similar components will contribute to increased uptime for your server.

- If your storage requirements are large—or if you need stacked RAID, multiple independent arrays, or support for multiple hosts—a good external RAID enclosure is the only way to go. Give preference to units that use industry-standard components over those that use proprietary hardware modifications.

Appendix D

Software License Metering

Unless you've been living in a cave for the past couple of years, it's not news to you that you need to own a license for all the software you use for home or business. Over the past few years, it has become steadily less acceptable to pirate software, and more dangerous to do so.

First, there's an ethics question: the software companies survive by making software good enough for people to buy it. No matter how much you enjoy programming, there's a limit to how much you're willing—or can afford—to do for free. Pirating software is not a statement against big software companies; it's stealing someone else's work.

Second, pirated software is an excellent source of viruses. This is less of an issue (but not unheard of) if you're pirating by passing a single copy of an application around your organization without buying licenses for everyone; however, if you download illegally copied software from a bulletin board service (BBS) catering to self-proclaimed "hackers," you're really risking your hard disk. Face it: the type of person who thinks it's okay to copy someone else's work, and distribute it to anyone who wants it, may also be the type of person who'd infect that work with a virus before posting it on the bulletin board. Of course, if you pick up an illegally copied program and it's virus-infected, you've got little recourse with the original product manufacturer.

Third, an organization named the Software Publishers' Association can impose fines or temporarily shut down your organization for even a single software license violation. We'll discuss this organization and its role and powers later in this chapter, but at the outset you should be aware that this organization exists, and that they can go after you even for unlicensed *shareware*.

For these reasons, it's best to be conscientious when it comes to software licensing. This chapter covers the following topics that should make keeping track of your organization's licenses a bit simpler:

- What a license is
- Different types of licenses
- Available methods for tracking licenses
- What the SPA is and does

What Is a License?

In its simplest form, a *license* is a proof of purchase. This proof can take a variety of forms, such as the following:

- The envelope that the disks (or other component of the product) came in that says something along the lines of, "When you break this seal you are agreeing to the terms of the license agreement."

- The disks themselves

- The page in the manual titled "Licensing Information" or other wording to that effect

- A paid receipt for the software (not a purchase order, which is simply a proof of intent to purchase)

Not all licenses give you the same powers and privileges: they can authorize the use of software by a machine, person, network, site, or company. The following sections provide a general overview of the various license types, but please note that licenses vary by manufacturer, and the specific license for each product is the one to which you must adhere. Also, keep in mind that not all software is available with all the following license types. Check with specific vendors to see what's available.

User Licenses

A *single-user license* gives the person to whom the software is licensed the right to use it on any machine, as long as he or she is the only person to use that software. In other words, if your word processing program carries a user license, then you can use that program on your home machine, work machine, and a laptop you take on business trips—as long as you're the *only* person using the software. A user license does not give your friend the right to use your word processor on your home machine while you're at work, or give one of your co-workers the right to use the word processor on your machine while you're on the road.

Many licenses for common applications are user licenses, but be sure to read the fine print on each license (discussed later in this chapter) and check each manufacturer's policy before you start installing your software on all your personal machines.

User licenses often are available as a *block license* in increments of 25 or 50 users, particularly for network software such as an operating system.

Usage Licenses

A *usage license*, also known as a *workstation license*, authorizes anyone to use the software, as long as it is used on only one machine at a time. On a network, a usage license usually authorizes a certain number of concurrent users. Once you install software licensed to a workstation on your work machine, for example, you cannot legally copy that software onto your home machine, even to work at home with the same files and for the same company as when you're at the office.

> **Note**
>
> Usage licenses are increasingly popular, touted as a way to reduce costs by paying for usage rather than for each person using the software. Some packages on the market today let you choose between user licensing and usage licensing.

Usage licenses are good for situations like shift work, where three people might do the exact same job, but do it at different times of the day. Usage licenses also are good for users who only use packages sporadically during the day, because you can get double- or triple-duty out of one license. For roving users who constantly use the same package throughout the day, however, a usage license might not be very practical. Likewise, a usage license is not a good idea for anyone who may use one machine one day, but a different machine the next.

Network Licenses

Not surprisingly, a *network license* gives anyone on the same network the right to use the software. The definition of a network in this context is less flexible than some of the networks discussed elsewhere in this book: in terms of software licensing, a network usually refers to the machines connected to a single file server—almost certainly it's limited to a LAN rather than a WAN (see chapter 4, "Upgrading to a WAN," if you need a refresher on the difference).

> **Note**
>
> Unless you have only one network in your workplace, a network license is not the same thing as a site license (described in the next section).

A network license is broader-reaching than a block license that is used on a network (refer to the "User Licenses" section), because a network license is not limited to a particular number of users; however, a network license usually is more expensive.

Site Licenses

A *site license* is the next step up from a network license. Rather than limiting you to using the software on a single network, a site license permits anyone at your office's physical location to use the software. This permission is limited to those in that building, however; users at a branch office connected across a wide-area link are not included, and you should check with the specific manufacturer to see if telecommuting employees have rights to the software on the days when they dial into the office from home. It's possible that you'll have to buy extra licenses for them to use the same software on their home machines.

Enterprise Licenses

The broadest permission to use software is an *enterprise license*, by which any member of your organization has the right to use the software. (*Enterprise*, in this case, means the corporate enterprise rather than a network connecting more than one kind of NOS.) The rights granted by an enterprise license generally extend to dialup users, users across WAN links, and so on. As you might expect, this type of license is quite expensive—it's only cost-effective for very large organizations in which many employees use the same software packages.

Hybrid Licenses

A license from a particular vendor might not always fit neatly into one of these categories, and might even overlap more than one category. For example, the license for MicroGrafx's Windows Draw! provides instructions for setting up the software both on a single-user basis and on a network (see fig. D.1).

MICROGRAFX SOFTWARE LICENSE AGREEMENT

This is a legal agreement between you (an individual or an entity), the end user, and Micrografx, Inc. If you do not agree to the terms of this Agreement, promptly return the disk package and accompanying items (including written materials and binders or other containers) to the place you obtained them for a full refund.

1. *GRANT OF LICENSE.* This Micrografx Software License Agreement ("License") permits you to use one copy of the Micrografx software product ("SOFTWARE") on any single computer, provided the SOFTWARE is in use on only one computer at any time. If you have multiple Licenses for the SOFTWARE, then at any time you may have as many copies of the SOFTWARE in use as you have Licenses. The SOFTWARE is "in use" in a computer when it is loaded into the temporary memory (i.e., RAM) or is installed into the permanent memory (e.g., hard disk, CD-ROM, or other storage device) of that computer; however, a copy installed on a network server for the sole purpose of distribution to other computers is not "in use." If the anticipated number of users of the SOFTWARE will exceed the number of applicable Licenses, you must have a reasonable mechanism or process in place to assure that the number of persons using the SOFTWARE concurrently does not exceed the number of Licenses. If the SOFTWARE is permanently installed on the hard disk or other storage device of a computer (other than a network server), then the person authorized to use such computer also may use the SOFTWARE on a portable computer, laptop and home computer. If such person's authorization to use such computer ceases for any reason (e.g. termination of employment), then such person's authority to use the software on a portable computer, laptop and home computer shall cease.

2. *COPYRIGHT.* The SOFTWARE is owned by Micrografx or its suppliers and is protected by United States copyright laws and international treaty provisions. Therefore, you must treat the SOFTWARE like any other copyrighted material (e.g., a book or musical recording), except that you may either (a) make one copy of the SOFTWARE solely for backup or archival purposes, or (b) transfer the SOFTWARE to a single hard disk provided you keep the original solely for backup or archival purposes. You may not copy written materials accompanying the SOFTWARE.

3. *OTHER RESTRICTIONS.* This License is your proof of license to exercise the rights granted herein and must be retained by you. You may not rent or lease the SOFTWARE, but you may transfer your rights under this License on a permanent basis provided that you transfer this License, the SOFTWARE and all accompanying written materials, you retain no copies, and the recipient agrees to the terms of this License. You may not decompile, or disassemble the SOFTWARE. If the SOFTWARE is an update, any transfer must include the update and all prior versions.

4. *MULTIPLE MEDIA SOFTWARE.* If the SOFTWARE package contains both 3.5" and 5.25" disks, or other media, then you may use only the media appropriate for your single designated computer or network server. You may not use the other media on another computer or computer network, or loan, rent, lease, or transfer them to another user except as part of a transfer or other use expressly permitted by this License.

Figure D.1

A license agreement can encompass more than one kind of license.

License Tracking

Now that you've got a basic idea of the various kinds of licenses, how can you make sure you're doing the right thing when it comes to licensing? Well, if you've got more than a couple nodes on your network, you need an organized system for tracking licenses—this can be either paper-based or computer-based.

Manual Tracking

All right, you're a network administrator, and you're used to handling computer software. Why would you manually track licenses when there are automated systems that can do it for you?

One reason is that complexity might be brought about by a particular network design. For example, if users store their applications locally, but you have peer-to-peer connections in your network, then software metering needs to be local as well. There's a flaw in the design of some metering programs that won't release a license if the user doesn't exit an application normally (for example, if there's a sudden power outage and the user's computer shuts down). More metering programs are being designed to avoid this problem, but the time required to meter all the applications on a system still can be considerable. It might be easier to set up a less proactive—but less time-consuming—manual tracking procedure, like those described in the following sections.

Tip

Manual tracking works best for small networks—when you get bigger, it's often easier to automate.

Physical Tracking. For networks in which each workstation has a fair amount of storage space nearby, you can just assign each software package a number, and then give each employee using that package a numbered copy. When the employee receives the software, the business manager gets a signed receipt. The business manager also needs a signed inventory form from each employee, listing the software loaded on his or her machine. The inventory form should look something like the one shown in figure D.2.

Tip

Assigning the software by number rather than by name prevents the confusion that can arise when two people with the same name are on the network, or when Bob leaves and the new employee, Janet, inherits software named something like "Bob's SmartSuite."

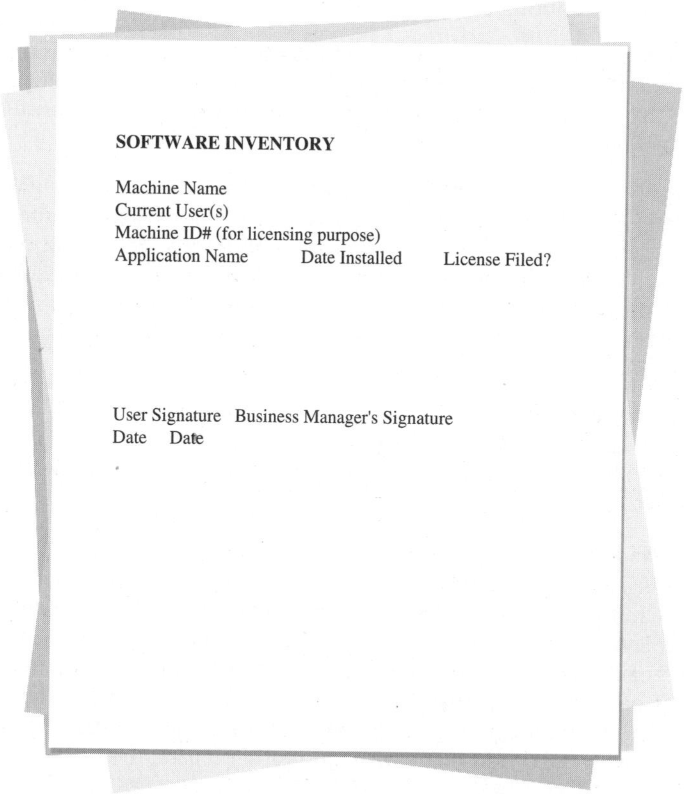

SOFTWARE INVENTORY

Machine Name
Current User(s)
Machine ID# (for licensing purpose)
Application Name   Date Installed   License Filed?

User Signature   Business Manager's Signature
Date   Date

Figure D.2

A software inventory for each machine makes it easier to track licenses and keep unauthorized software off the network.

Thereafter, each employee is responsible for keeping track of his or her work software and licenses—if something happens to the software, then it's up to that employee to replace it or at least to request a replacement through the appropriate channels.

Although the physical method has real advantages for a small network with a relatively stable population, it has some pretty serious disadvantages as well. First, you might not want everyone on the network to have direct access to disks. If you've installed a limited version of the software on their system (for example, you've installed Windows without games), then you certainly do not want them to circumvent your planning. Giving people direct access to disks is also potentially dangerous in terms of licensing and viruses. If an employee decides that he needs that software on his home machine, he might violate the license agreement, and worse yet, might infect the disks if there's a virus on the home system.

Second, many workstations don't really have the space to keep a bunch of software boxes around. If they *do* have sufficient storage space, is it secured with a lock? If another user does not have their own software anymore (for whatever reason), he might be tempted to "borrow" the software assigned to another person if that software is easily accessible.

In short, having everyone on the network keep track of their own software is only a good idea if you have a small network with a highly computer-literate, responsible staff, as well as plenty of storage space that can be locked. If you can't meet these requirements, consider a more centralized form of license control.

Paper Tracking. For those who want to keep track of their software licensing without installing an automated system to do so, it may be practical to put one person (perhaps the business manager, in cooperation with the network administrator or software support types) in charge of license tracking. The network administrator gets the software, the business manager gets the licenses, and the user provides a statement of the software installed on the machine. If the user brings in any outside utilities (such as shareware), he or she must account for them and provide licensing information.

It's true that this method still relies to an extent on the honesty and record-keeping abilities of the users on the network, but it has the advantage of centralizing control and licensing accountability. It's also a system capable of maintaining records of the software on each system without metering each system.

Automatic Methods

For larger networks, where the bookkeeping involved is too much for the business manager to track licensing manually, there's no shortage of metering and monitoring programs on the market. McAfee, Frye, and 3Com are just three of the big-name makers of such utilities, and there are dozens of shareware metering programs available through the Internet or online services such as CompuServe. The shareware metering programs usually are cheaper and less powerful than off-the-shelf programs, but are just right for some networks. Some NOSs (such as Microsoft's NT Server 3.51) now come with monitoring capabilities.

> **Note**
>
> Don't forget that shareware metering programs are subject to the same licensing rules as software that you buy in a store. If it says "unregistered copy" and you've had it on your system longer than the evaluation period listed in the accompanying licensing information file (usually a 30-day period), then you're in violation of the license.

Metering versus Monitoring. In automatic license tracking, there are basically two approaches: *metering* and *monitoring*. The essential difference is that metering prevents violations, and monitoring, well, monitors them—that is, rather than ever preventing use, monitoring software just watches and keeps track of the number of users accessing a piece of software at any given time. Although this isn't easy to diagram literally, figure D.3 illustrates the conceptual difference between metering and monitoring, using a fictional software package named DrawRight.

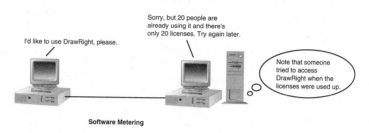

Software Metering

Software Monitoring

Figure D.3

Metering prevents extra users from accessing licensed software; monitoring keeps track of the software's usage.

How Metering Works. Properly executed, software metering only permits a certain number of people to access a program. If the meter is set up for 20 simultaneous users, then when the 21st person attempts to start the program, he or she sees a message saying that the licenses for that program have been used up, and that he or she should try again later.

Although the exact procedure varies from product to product, you set up a meter in the following fashion:

1. Install the software on the machine where the program to be metered resides. The software probably has to be in the same directory as the program.

2. Run the meter in administrative mode, and select the program or programs to be metered.

3. Specify the number of instances of that program that are allowed to run simultaneously. This number should be equal to or less than the number of licenses you have purchased for the program.

4. Enable the logging feature (if available) so that you can see how many times people try to access the file. This can help you determine if and when you need more licenses.

5. Save and exit.

Again, the specifics vary by program, but that's the basic idea. What you're doing is making the meter intervene between the user and the application, so that the meter can regulate usage. The log keeps track of those accessing the program, and also those attempting unsuccessfully to do so. If you don't choose to have the access activity logged, the metering itself can still occur—you just don't get any record of access activity.

How Monitoring Works. Software monitoring is more useful for seeing just how many licenses you need before you buy them. Assume, for example, that you have a copy of Word on the server, and you think that ten people are using it. You've got ten licenses, so you're in the clear. When another user develops a need for Word (perhaps when someone who has always had an assistant type their letters begins typing their own, for some reason), that's an eleventh person who needs the software. Unfortunately, the network administrator and business manager might not think to add this person to the list of people needing licenses for the software because the change in business practice seems to only affect who's typing a letter. Monitoring software enables you to track the number of Word users versus the number of valid licenses and to obtain another license for the eleventh person.

Making Automated Tracking Useful. With anything automated, there's a serious temptation to buy it, install it, and let it take care of itself. Automated license tracking systems don't work that way. Although they represent an easier means of tracking a large number of licenses than doing it by hand, the automated systems do still require some effort from you. They can't tell you anything if you don't help a little.

Here are some tips to help you improve your software metering or monitoring practices:

- *Set it up as soon as possible.* It's easy to get bogged down with network updates and other distractions, but metering or monitoring software won't do you any good if it sits on the shelf. Make time to set it up as soon as possible for all the applications that are to be tracked.

- *Make updates on a regular basis.* This follows naturally from the previous tip. It's tempting to say that you'll make all necessary licensing changes as soon as they are required, but most people are too busy to be sure that they'll have the time. It's easier to schedule updates—users to be added, licenses to be added, or new applications to be monitored— if you plan to do them at a regular interval, like once a week.

- *Back it up.* The information garnered by your tracking system is important. Make sure that it's part of your regular backup program, so that if something happens to the hard disk that's being metered, you don't lose all the data you've gathered.

- *Don't keep the results to yourself.* This information might do you, the network administrator, some direct good, but often, you're not the only one concerned about the results of the metering and monitoring logs. You set up the tracking to accumulate certain information: making sure that the information goes where it's supposed to.

Who Enforces Licensing?

This chapter has talked a lot about what a license is, and how to keep up with your licensing obligations. You may be wondering, however, who will care if you don't live up to these obligations. How will a manufacturer ever find out?

Actually, the manufacturer does not have to find out. A non-profit organization named the *Software Publishers' Association (SPA)* can take action on behalf of the software manufacturer. Let's learn more about the SPA.

What Is the SPA?

The SPA is a non-profit private organization based in Washington, D.C. (they're not an arm of the federal government—they just have offices in the city). It was created in 1984, with 25 member companies, in order to provide a voice to represent and protect the software publishing industry. The SPA's anti-piracy campaign began in 1989. As of late 1995, its membership numbered over 1200 companies. Member companies pay dues and authorize the SPA to audit businesses on their behalf.

How Does the SPA Investigate a Violation? Most of the SPA's actions begin with a tip on its hotline (currently the hotline receives about 30 calls per day). The SPA evaluates the tip in terms of its factual basis, the extent of the violation (unsurprisingly, one extra copy of a shareware game, for example, is of less concern than 2,500 unlicensed copies of Lotus 1-2-3), and the perceived motivations of the person calling—that is, is the person calling out of genuine concern about the violation, or is the call motivated by revenge? If the latter, does the call seem legitimate? Much of this sort of evaluation is done by instinct, rather than established criteria.

Once the SPA decides that a tip is worth looking into, it conducts its own investigation to verify the alleged violation. If it cannot substantiate the violation, the process ends there.

If the SPA collects enough information to file a lawsuit (the group does not act unless it does collect enough), it contacts the company to notify it of the identified violation, and informs the offending company of the action it intends to take. In most cases, this action takes the form of an *audit*, in which the SPA's auditors physically check the software on each computer in the company against the proof of purchase that the company provides. The best proof of purchase is an invoice or paid purchase order because that's probably the easiest thing for most companies to lay hands on, but disks or manuals sometimes are accepted. On average, the audit takes about four months (the exact time depends on the size of the company and how cooperative it is), during which time the company can operate normally except that its employees occasionally might have to deal with auditors bumping them off a machine to audit its contents. If the violation is confirmed, then the company must pay a fine to the SPA in the value of the unlicensed software, and the illegal copies are destroyed.

In serious cases, the SPA does not perform an audit but instead files civil or criminal charges against the offending company. The SPA has permission from all its members to audit companies on their behalf, but if a lawsuit is necessary, the member company must grant permission to the SPA to file the lawsuit at that time. The fines can be up to $100,000 per civil violation, and up to $250,000 (as well as up to five years in prison) per criminal violation. Once again, the pirated software is destroyed so that the offender has to buy legitimate copies as well as paying any fine that is levied.

In the most drastic scenario, the SPA can get a judge to issue a warrant to perform a *raid* on a company (audits, remember, are announced by letter before the auditors show up). In such a case, a federal marshal accompanies the auditors to protect them (in case the offending company has a bad reaction to the auditors' appearance) and to explain that they are authorized to be there. This sounds dramatic, but once the initial few exciting minutes are over, the raid proceeds like a normal audit.

Who Will the SPA Act For? The SPA is not an organization of crusaders; it looks out for the interests of its members. This means that if a tip reports a license violation concerning software published by a company that is not a member of the SPA, then the SPA will not take action *on the basis of that particular violation*. If the violation is large enough to pursue, however, chances are good that the offender is violating the license of a member company as well, so the SPA may investigate anyway. If this turns out to be the case, then the SPA conducts an audit on behalf of the non-member company as well as the member company. Since all fines go to the SPA rather than to the company, this doesn't change anything as far as fines are concerned.

What Else Does the SPA Do? The SPA's function goes beyond punishing software licensing violations. They also provide training, educational software, and videos (including a rap video titled, "Don't Copy that Floppy") to explain why you should keep up licensing, and to help you do it right. To fund these activities, the SPA relies on the fines from licensing violators as well as the dues paid by its member organizations.

Why Is Licensing a Problem?

Why is an organization like the SPA necessary in the first place? The answer has to do with the peculiar nature of software as *intellectual property*. Copying has been around as long as originals have been around. Books, cassettes, compact discs, and videotapes are common targets. However, the market for the originals of these products (where originals are available and relatively inexpensive) is less easily affected because of two characteristics of the copies:

- They take some effort to make.

- Their quality normally is lower than that of the original, and gets worse if subsequent generations of copies are made.

In other words, a printed work usually is more readable as a bound book than as a sheaf of photocopies, and music or video usually sounds or looks better on the original than on copies. Where they violate copyright laws, illegally-made copies of books or videos are also hard to distribute on a large scale without getting caught.

Software is a kettle of fish of a different color. No matter how many generations you make of a binary file, it's still the same file. If you load Microsoft Word on 50 machines, the application works as well on every machine as it did on the first. That's true even without the original disks—if you copy the disks over and over, the quality of the copy does not deteriorate with each generation.

Understandably, this creates some worry for software manufacturers. It's no good to sell the world's best software if one person can buy it and give it to all of his or her friends. This was less of a problem several years ago, when hard disk space was still rare and expensive. People had to keep program disks around if they wanted to use complex programs, since the hard disk didn't have enough space to store lots of applications. As disk space has become more affordable, the scope of the problem has increased.

For a time, some software vendors tried using *key disks* (you needed a "startup" disk to run an application), and special codes in the manual that were needed to start an application, but these protection means were cumbersome, so consumer demand has sent them the way of the dodo. Software vendors now are dependent on the ethics of consumers who buy their software, and on organizations like the SPA, to make sure that they are paid for their product.

Summary

This chapter described various types of software licenses, provided information to help you identify your present licensing situation, and explained some ways that you can make sure you're fulfilling your responsibilities to software manufacturers. You also learned about the SPA, how it polices software licensing, and what penalties exist for certain violations.

Armed with this knowledge, you should be prepared to keep track of your network's licenses, and make compliance adjustments as necessary.

Index

Symbols

U

Z